CW01509067

THE BUILDINGS OF ENGLAND

FOUNDING EDITOR: NIKOLAUS PEVSNER

OXFORDSHIRE: OXFORD AND THE SOUTH-EAST

SIMON BRADLEY
NIKOLAUS PEVSNER
AND
JENNIFER SHERWOOD

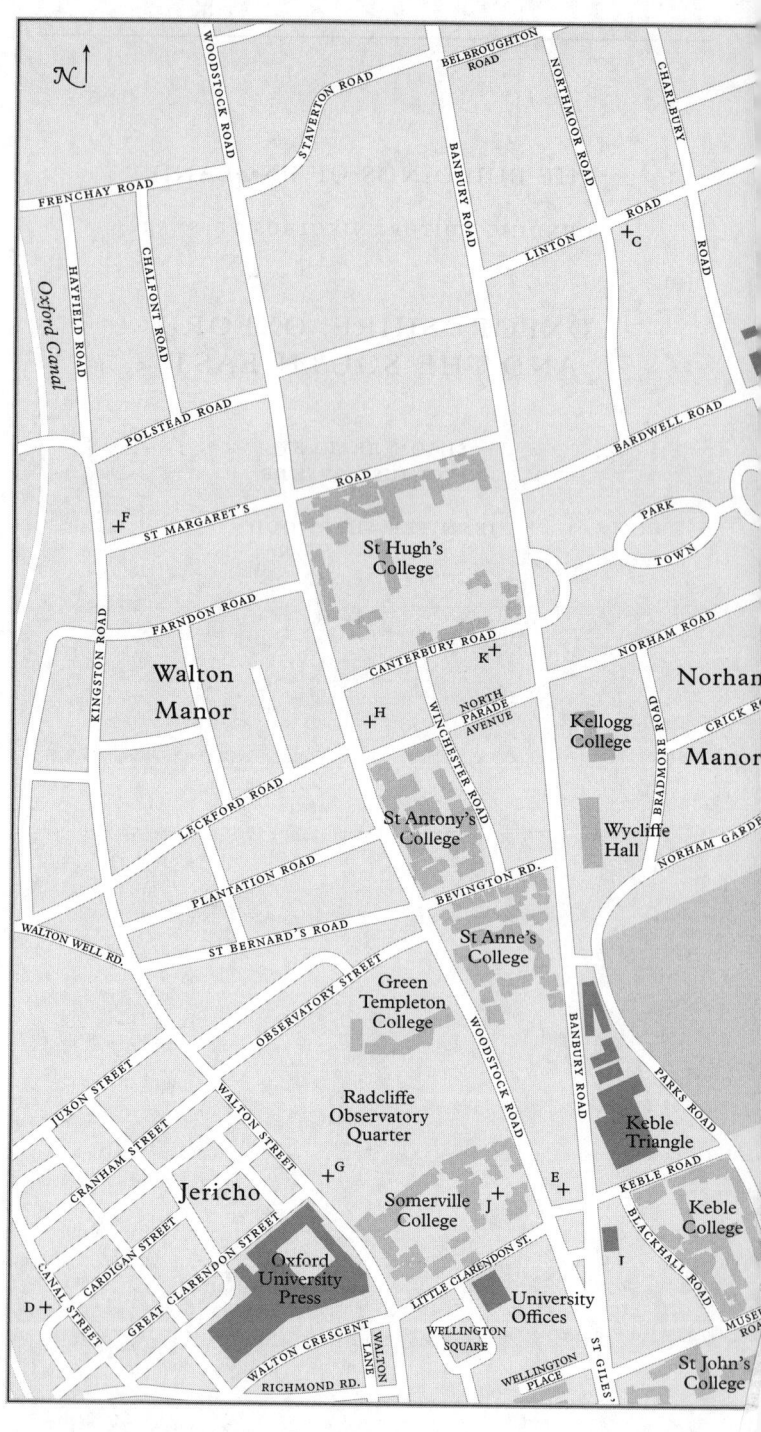

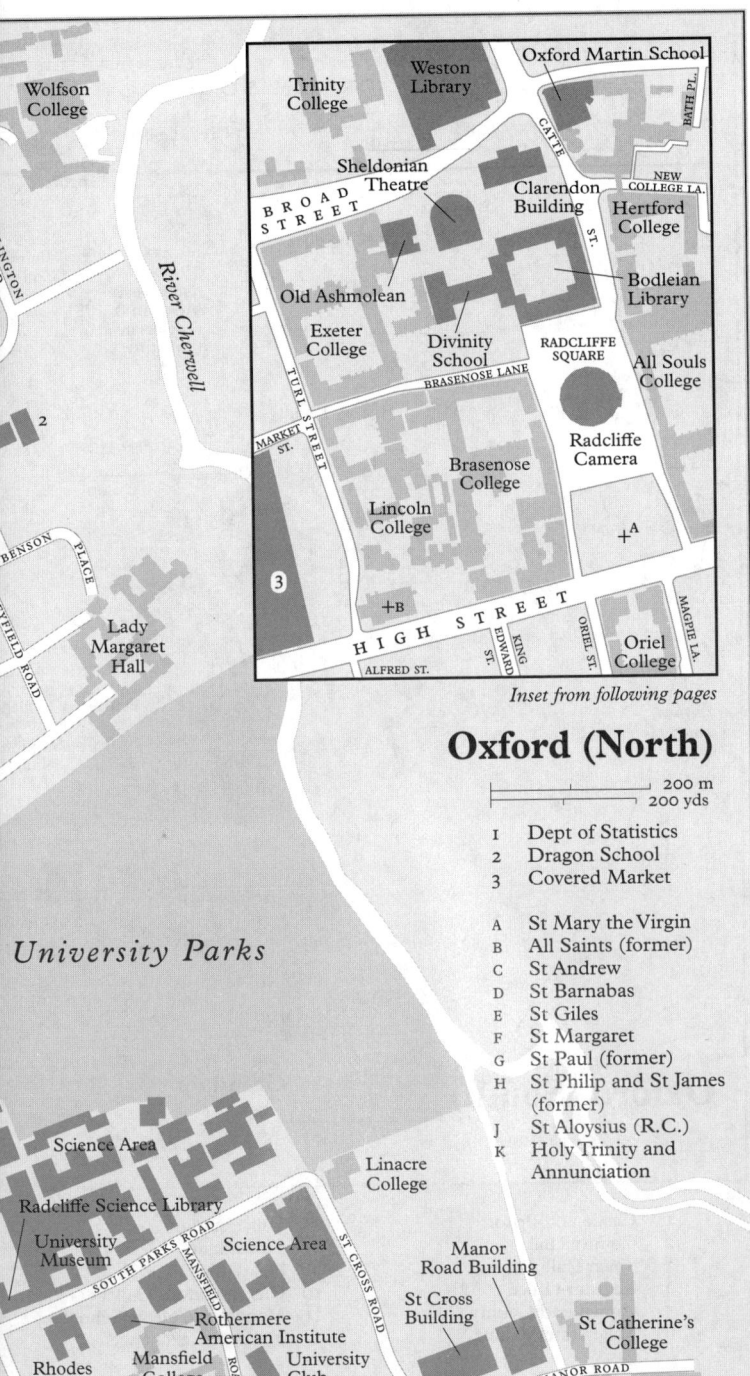

Inset from following pages

Oxford (North)

|⊢———————|——————⊣ 200 m
|⊢———————|——————⊣ 200 yds

1　Dept of Statistics
2　Dragon School
3　Covered Market

A　St Mary the Virgin
B　All Saints (former)
C　St Andrew
D　St Barnabas
E　St Giles
F　St Margaret
G　St Paul (former)
H　St Philip and St James (former)
J　St Aloysius (R.C.)
K　Holy Trinity and Annunciation

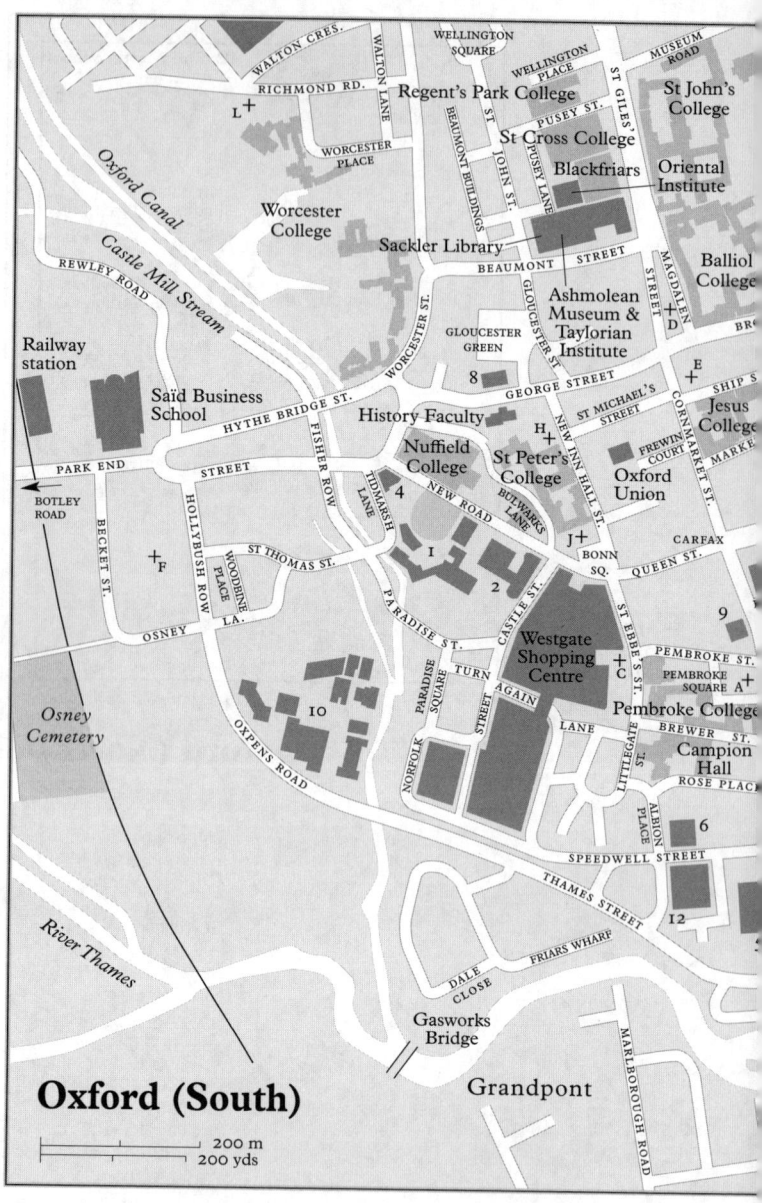

Oxford (South)

|⊢———⊣ 200 m
|⊢———⊣ 200 yds

1   Castle and Prison
2   County Hall
3   Town Hall
4   Register Office
5   Crown and County Court
6   Magistrates' Court

7   Police station
8   Fire station
9   Post Office
10 City of Oxford College
11 Magdalen College School
12 Telephone exchange

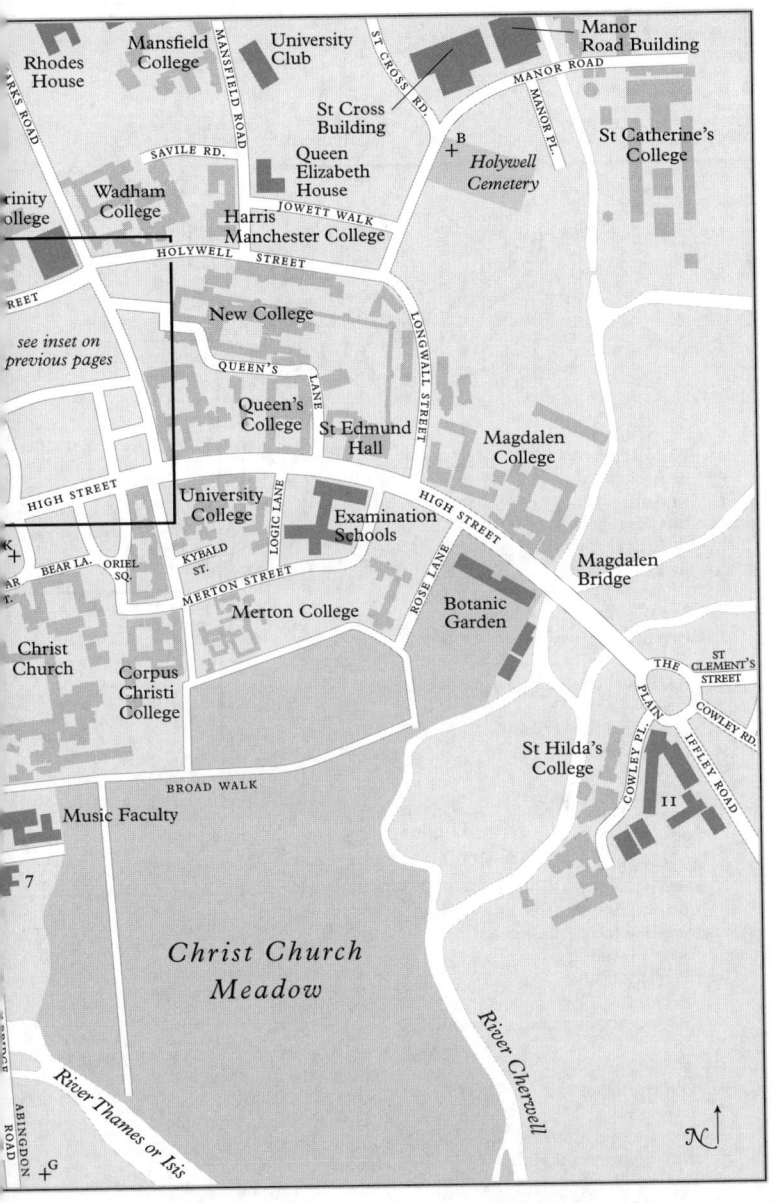

A   St Aldate
B   St Cross (former)
C   St Ebbe
D   St Mary Magdalen
E   St Michael at the
    North Gate
F   St Thomas

G   Holy Rood (R.C.)
H   Wesley Memorial Church
J   New Road Baptist Church
K   St Columba
    (United Reformed)
L   Synagogue

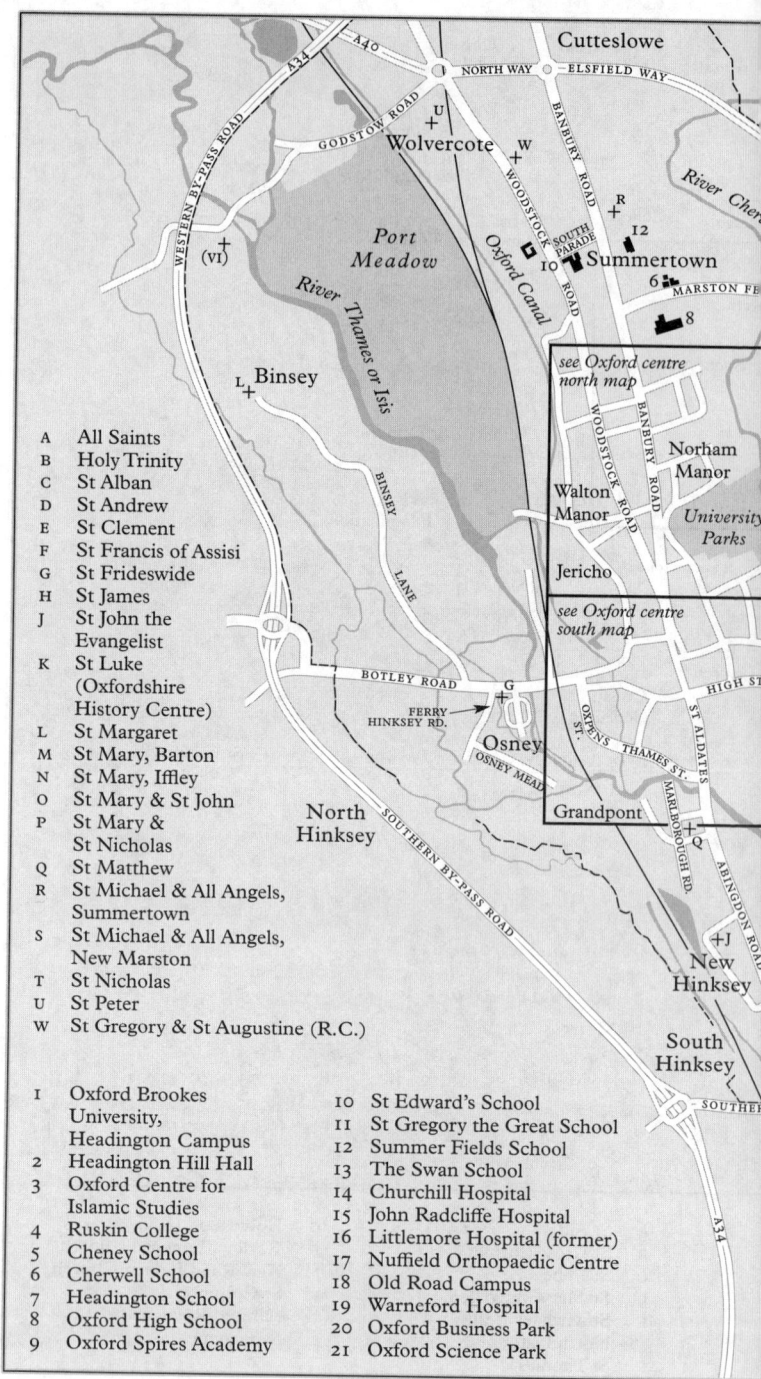

A All Saints
B Holy Trinity
C St Alban
D St Andrew
E St Clement
F St Francis of Assisi
G St Frideswide
H St James
J St John the
   Evangelist
K St Luke
   (Oxfordshire
   History Centre)
L St Margaret
M St Mary, Barton
N St Mary, Iffley
O St Mary & St John
P St Mary &
   St Nicholas
Q St Matthew
R St Michael & All Angels,
   Summertown
S St Michael & All Angels,
   New Marston
T St Nicholas
U St Peter
W St Gregory & St Augustine (R.C.)

1   Oxford Brookes
    University,
    Headington Campus
2   Headington Hill Hall
3   Oxford Centre for
    Islamic Studies
4   Ruskin College
5   Cheney School
6   Cherwell School
7   Headington School
8   Oxford High School
9   Oxford Spires Academy
10 St Edward's School
11 St Gregory the Great School
12 Summer Fields School
13 The Swan School
14 Churchill Hospital
15 John Radcliffe Hospital
16 Littlemore Hospital (former)
17 Nuffield Orthopaedic Centre
18 Old Road Campus
19 Warneford Hospital
20 Oxford Business Park
21 Oxford Science Park

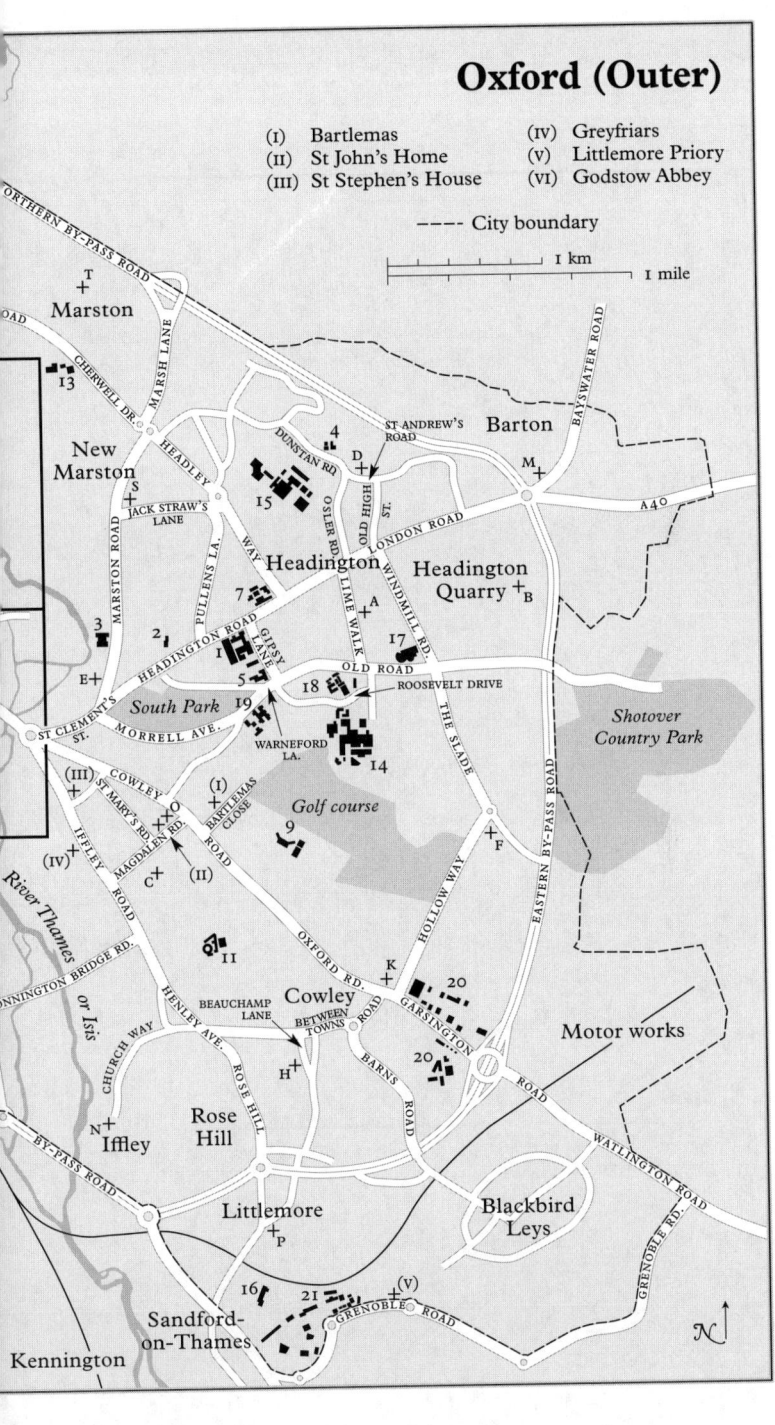

Oxford (Outer)

(I) Bartlemas
(II) St John's Home
(III) St Stephen's House

(IV) Greyfriars
(V) Littlemore Priory
(VI) Godstow Abbey

----- City boundary

I km   I mile

Oxford & South-east Oxfordshire

Oxfordshire: Oxford and the South-East

BY

SIMON BRADLEY

NIKOLAUS PEVSNER

AND

JENNIFER SHERWOOD

THE BUILDINGS OF ENGLAND

YALE UNIVERSITY PRESS
NEW HAVEN AND LONDON

YALE UNIVERSITY PRESS
NEW HAVEN AND LONDON

302 Temple Street, New Haven CT 06511
47 Bedford Square, London WC1B 3DP
www.yalebooks.co.uk/pevsner
www.yalebooks.com

Published by Yale University Press 2023
2 4 6 8 10 9 7 5 3 1

ISBN 978 0 300 20929 7

Originally published in 1974,
© Nikolaus Pevsner and Jennifer Sherwood
Revised in 2023, new material © Simon Bradley

Printed in China
through World Print
Set in Monotype Plantin

MIX
Paper | Supporting
responsible forestry
FSC® C014688

The first edition of Oxfordshire
was dedicated as follows

OXFORD
FOR
DOROTHY DORN
for whom my writing had no terrors
[N.P.]

OXFORDSHIRE
FOR
MY MOTHER
[J.S.]

★

2023 dedication

FOR

AB   AF   AF   AT   AV
CC   CH   COB   CP   CW
DWL†   EH†   FK   GMcC   GT
JN†   JO   JS   KM
MF   MH   MH†   MR
RH   RP   RS

*fellow authors with whom I have worked
as editor with the* Buildings *series
over three decades*

[S.B.]

CONTENTS

LIST OF TEXT FIGURES AND MAPS

Every effort has been made to trace or contact all copyright holders. The publishers will be glad to make good any errors or omissions brought to our attention in future editions.

OXFORD

MAPS

PHOTOGRAPHIC ACKNOWLEDGEMENTS

The photographs are by James O. Davies. All but a handful were specially taken for this book. We are grateful to all building owners and custodians for allowing access and granting permission for photography. Additional acknowledgements are as follows:

Courtesy of the Warden and Fellows of Merton College, Oxford: 12, 13, 15, 41, 42

Courtesy of the Warden and Fellows of All Souls College, Oxford: 62

Courtesy of Colin Dunn (Scriptura)/The Warden and Fellows of All Souls College, Oxford: 89

Courtesy of the President and Fellows of Kellogg College, Oxford: 92

Reproduced by kind permission of the copyright holders and the Master and Fellows of Balliol College: 108

MAP AND ILLUSTRATION REFERENCES

The numbers printed in italic type in the margin against the place names in the South-East Oxfordshire gazetteer of the book indicate the position of the place in question on the INDEX MAP (p. ix), which are divided into sections by the 10-kilometre reference lines of the National Grid. The reference given here omits the two initial letters which in a full grid reference refer to the 100-kilometre squares into which the county is divided. The first two numbers indicate the *western* boundary, and the last two the *southern* boundary, of the 10-kilometre square in which the place in question is situated. For example, Henley-on-Thames (reference 7080) will be found in the 10-kilometre square bounded by grid lines 70 (on the *west*) and 80, and 80 (on the *south*) and 90; Sandford-on-Thames (reference 5000) in the square bounded by the grid lines 50 (on the *west*) and 60, and 00 (on the *south*) and 10.

The map contains all those places, whether towns, villages or isolated buildings, which are the subject of separate entries in the text.

ILLUSTRATION REFERENCES are given as marginal numbers for photographs, and as marginal *italic* cross-references for images on other pages of the text.

FOREWORD AND ACKNOWLEDGEMENTS

Oxfordshire was the penultimate book in the first *Buildings of England* series, appearing on the same day as Nikolaus Pevsner's *Staffordshire* – officially the final volume – in June 1974. Pevsner's share of the book, covering Oxford only, had been completed as far back as 1969; the rest of Oxfordshire was surveyed by Jennifer Sherwood, who also undertook the preparatory research for city and county together. As well as being the most protracted in terms of writing, the book was also the stoutest in the original sequence, at 948 pages. In order to do justice to the territory in the revised series, the county therefore had to be split in two. Alan Brooks's *Oxfordshire: North and West* duly came out in 2017. Now the revised *Buildings of England* series is itself approaching completion, and the present companion volume again places Oxford within the penultimate instalment; the last book of all will once again be the new *Staffordshire*, scheduled for 2024.

That symmetry may look like design rather than accident, but in truth *Oxford and the South-East* was first scheduled to appear somewhat earlier. Two things chiefly account for this delay. First, Oxford proved to be a more complex and challenging project than I had expected, coming fresh from the revision of *Cambridgeshire* and its smaller and more comprehensively published university city. Second, the pandemic made visiting difficult or impossible for much of 2020–1, and severely restricted access to libraries and archives. So the first drafts of the Oxford perambulations had to be written at the home desk under lockdown, drawing on memory and the magic carpet of Google Streetview, before they could be checked on the ground. Once the city was covered in full, the county area was surveyed in 2022, in thirty-two day trips spaced over nine months.

In his acknowledgements Pevsner confessed to a lack of familiarity with Oxford by comparison with Cambridge, where he had been Slade Professor for seven years and a college fellow for a quarter of a century. His first thanks were therefore to St John's College, for making available a flat in St Giles' House as a base for visiting and working. For the revised volume these thanks are repeated and redoubled, especially to the Rev. Professor William Whyte and the then President Professor Maggie Snowling; for I was made a Research Associate of St John's over the five years in which the bulk of the Oxford text was researched and written, with the use of a study in St Giles' House and the option of staying in a guest room for overnight visits. Many of the Oxford entries draw on discussions and helpful leads from other members of the college's Senior Common Room, where I was made very welcome. Earlier explorations of the buildings of St John's were conducted by the late Sir Howard Colvin, with whose final year of undergraduate teaching I was lucky to coincide in 1986. Such things go deep.

Also in Oxford, valuable help was supplied by Oriel College, where I was made a member of the SCR in 2020–1 when the outer Oxford visiting was under way; my grateful thanks to Lord Mendoza as President and to his assistant Rebecca Bricklebank. Transport in this period was by bike, kindly lent by my colleague Mark Eastment of Yale University Press. For the county, what could not be reached easily by bike, public transport or on foot was visited with friends and colleagues who generously gave up their time to drive me from place to place. As with the Cambridgeshire visiting, Alan Hollinghurst provided impeccable driving over multiple days, and brought an acute eye to the architectural puzzles encountered. Donald Rice was an expert guide to his former home territory of the Miltons and the Haseleys, and opened the way to some rewarding house visits. Other motorised days were spent with my colleagues Charles O'Brien and Linda McQueen, accompanied by our picture researcher Lydia Smith; with James Davies, also the distinguished photographer for this volume; with Rebecca Lane of Historic England; and with Cathy Kneafsey. In addition, Geoffrey Tyack (previously my senior co-author for the Berkshire volume) gave an expert tour of Nuneham Courtenay, Malcolm Airs showed the architectural riches of Dorchester – additional thanks to both for their hospitality – and Leigh Bartlett whisked me *impromptu* between the churches at Shiplake, Harpsden and Dunsden. Special thanks are due to Jackie Brookes and the late Alan Brookes at Goring, who provided a safe berth for my bike between trips into the hills over the summer of 2022. Ahead of the start of work, Simon Wartnaby prepared a digital version of the old text and gathered some useful research material, bolstered once again by Michael Breen's very helpful harvest from historic periodicals in the RIBA library.

The text of the present book is based wherever possible on the 1974 edition, allowing for the goals of expansion, correction and updating. To start from scratch would have been daunting, and the original entries by Pevsner and by Jennifer Sherwood always provided a stimulating place to start, even in entries where little of the old wording has been kept. This time round, there has also been space to include much more on church furnishings and stained glass, on vernacular buildings, commercial architecture and houses of all periods, and on much else that will be familiar to aficionados of the revised *Buildings* books. By convention, anything that was not seen at first hand is indicated by brackets within the gazetteer entries. Public access should certainly not be presumed for houses or other private properties included in the book.

Expert contributors have always had an essential share in the revised *Buildings* series, and this volume is no exception. Alan Brooks's *Oxfordshire: North and West* included introductory chapters by Philip Powell on geology and building materials and by Gill Hey and Paul Booth, respectively on prehistoric and on Roman and Anglo-Saxon archaeology. Those chapters, slightly adjusted and updated, appear again here, with renewed thanks to their authors. The Introductions also contain entirely new chapters by David Clark on domestic and vernacular buildings, counterparts to his chapter in *North and West*, and the gazetteers have benefited too from his close reading and suggested improvements. I am also very grateful to Peter Howell and to Malcolm Graham, who likewise read much of the text in draft, and whose feedback saved me from many errors and omissions; remarkably, both were also thanked by Pevsner for their help with the 1974 edition. More, the present gazetteers incorporate some of the many entries and insertions on Victorian and C20 subjects supplied by Peter Howell and Andrew Saint for the first edition. Much of the draft text was also read by Julian Munby, another close observer and scholar of Oxford's buildings over half a century, and by Geoffrey Tyack, to whom further thanks are due for adjustments and improvements. To conclude the list of contributors, the descriptions of medieval stained glass are based on those provided by the late Peter Newton for the 1974 volume.

So to the colleges and halls of the University, and here a simple list must suffice of those who helped with access, information and queries, with apologies for many omissions of titles and roles. At All Souls, Norma Aubertin-Potter, Richard Davenport-Hines, the Very Rev. Dr John Drury and Anthony Geraghty; at Balliol, Bethany Hambleden, John Jones and Naomi Tiley; at Blackfriars, Fr David Goodill; at Brasenose, Georgina Edwards and Simon Smith; at Campion Hall, Peter Davidson, Fr Gerald MacLoughlin and Fr Ken Vance; at Christ Church, Judith Curthoys, Jim Godfrey, Graham Keevil and William Thomas; at Corpus Christi, Julian Reid, Andy Rolfe, Luke O'Byrne and the late Mark Whittow; at Exeter, John Maddicott and Hannah Parham; at Green Templeton, Michael Pirie and Sue Wilson; at Harris Manchester, Sue Killoran; at Hertford, Roy Foster, Lucy Rutherford and Christopher Tyerman; at Jesus, Robin Darwall-Smith and Caroline Stanford; at Keble, Nicholas French and Eleanor Ward; at Kellogg, Malcolm Airs and Geoffrey Tyack; at Lady Margaret Hall, Oliver Mahony; at Linacre, Simon Bailey; at Lincoln, Carmella Elan-Gaston, Lindsay McCormack, Peter McCullough and Julian Mitchell; at Magdalen, the Rev. Dr Jonathan Arnold, Charlotte Berry, Mark Blandford-Baker, Laurence Brockliss, Anne Cheshier, Robin Darwall-Smith, Robert Langley and Ben Taylor; at Mansfield, Sally Jones; at Merton, Alan Bott, Julian Reid, Emma Sillett and Julia Walworth; at New College, Michael Burden, Roland Harris, Jacqui Julier, the Rev. Dr Erica Longfellow and Rhian Samuel; at Nuffield, Richard Mayou and Elena Sorochina; at Oriel, Rebecca Bricklebank, the late Jeremy Catto, Ian Forrest and Rob Petre; at Pembroke, Amanda Ingram and Tim Brindley; at Regent's Park, the Rev. Emma Walsh; at Queen's, John Davis, David Prout and Michael Riordan; at St Antony's, Gareth Tebbutt; at St Catherine's, Barbara Costa; at St Cross and Pusey House, Suzy Hodge, Anna James and Sir Diarmaid MacCulloch; at St Edmund Hall, Nicholas Davidson, Blanca Martin and Jayne Taylor; at St Hilda's, Oliver Mahony; at St

Hugh's, David Hodges and Amanda Ingram; at St John's, the late Peter Day, Georgy Kantor, Michael Riordan, Geoffrey Tyack and William Whyte; at St Peter's, Richard Allen, Geoffrey Fouquet and Matthew Walker; at Somerville, Oren Margolis; at Trinity, Clare Hopkins and Bryan Ward-Perkins; at University College, Robin Darwall-Smith; at Wadham, Jane Garnett and Marco Zhang; at Wolfson, Alan Berman and Dame Hermione Lee; at Worcester, Mark Bainbridge, Emma Goodrum, the Rev. Dr Peter Groves, Jo Parker and Mike Waters.

To that long list can be added those who assisted at the University's buildings, especially Alice Millea at the Bodleian, James Tibbert at the Examination Schools, and Ruth Langley and Martin Maw at Oxford University Press. Liz Cull helped to clarify the history of the Oriental Institute, and Timothy Baker generously shared his knowledge of Oxford's science buildings. More generally, the conservation plans prepared by Patrick Maguire were an immensely valuable source.

Oxford's churches and religious houses were unfailingly welcoming. Particular thanks are due to help received from the late Mark Barrington-Ward at St Giles, from Colin Dobson, Philip Lockley and Helen Ward at St Clement, from the Rev. Dr Peter Groves at St Mary Magdalen; in the outer areas, from the Rev. Margreet Armitstead at Littlemore; from the Rev. Canon Geoff Bayliss and Sally Hemsworth at Cowley; from Michael Daniell and Wendy Sobie at Wolvercote; from James Larminie at All Saints, New Headington; from Paul Spencer-Longhurst at St Frideswide, Botley Road; from the Rev. Canon Dr Robin Ward and Fr Andreas Wenzel at St Stephen's House; from Wilbur Wright at St John, New Hinksey; and from Fr Giles Zakowicz at St John's Home.

A great debt is also owed to the many scholars and friends of the *Buildings* series who supplied information and answered queries. Users of more recent volumes will recognize the initials of Geoffrey Fisher, who once again provided details and attributions for post-Reformation church monuments, and those of Peter Cormack and Martin Harrison (the latter of whom also helped with *Oxfordshire*'s first edition), who shared their expertise in C19 and C20 stained glass via emails which were a reliable source of delight. The coverage of Elizabethan and Jacobean plasterwork in city and county draws on Claire Gapper's expertise, Paul Tindall supplied useful details of Oxford's organs, Philip Ward-Jackson resolved puzzles among the C19 and early C20 church monuments and sculpture, and John Goodall and Paul Binski both shared thoughts and insights on medieval churches and chapels. The late Fr Jerome Bertram, Patrick Hollins, and the Rev. David Meara all assisted with entries on brasses, Christine Casey with C18 plasterwork, Jane Geddes with medieval ironwork, Tim Ayers and the late Michael Kerney with stained glass, and Emily Cole, Luke Jacob and Mike Slaughter with C20 pubs. Two great and much-missed scholars, Mark Girouard and Elain Harwood, helped respectively with Oxonian questions from the late C16–early C17 and from the post-war decades.

On the works of particular architects and artists, I am grateful for assistance received from Megan Aldrich (Rickman), Gillian Argyle and Jim Girling (T. Lawrence Dale), Nicholas Arnold (Clough Williams-Ellis), Will Aslet (Gibbs), Sandra Beresford (Bazzanti), Hilary Calvert (Compton pottery), Ian Dungavell (Aston Webb), Julia Gatley (Jock and Elizabeth Shepherd), Anthony Geraghty (Wren and Hawksmoor), Martin Jones (T.G. Jackson), Elizabeth McKellar (Peter Boston), Joshua Mardell (the Bucklers), Ken Powell and Tim Sturgis (Arups), John Martin Robinson (James Wyatt), Otto Saumarez Smith (Leslie Martin), Andrew Tierney (the O'Sheas) and Adam White (Nicholas Stone). Architects who helped with coverage of their own work include Oliver Caroe, Mark Hines, Peter Jamieson, Robbie Kerr, Colen Lumley and Lyall Thow. On individual buildings in Oxford, Nick Wright clarified the original form of St Giles' House, and Laurence Dardenne helped with the details of Summer Fields School. Other individual entries benefited from help from Steven Brindle (Grandpont), Mark Chatfield (Medley Manor House), Roger Crisp (Cromwell's House, Marston), the Rev. Martin Henig (Binsey church), Colin Thom (Littlewoods) and Jonathan Ungar (No. 84 St Aldate's).

Useful information came from past and present authors of other Pevsner guides: Bruce Bailey, James Bettley, Alan Brooks, Andy Foster, Clare Hartwell, Mike Hill, Peter Leach, Julian Orbach, Chris Pickford, Richard Pollard and Chris Wakeling. Other insights and suggestions were supplied by a wide cast of friends and supporters, including David Boswell, Roger Bowdler, the late Geoff Brandwood, Alex Bremner, James Campbell, Catherine Croft, Laura Cumming, William Filmer-Sankey, Michael Hall, Susie Harries, James Jago, Richard Hewlings, Chris Holland, Emily Lane, David Lermon, Jeremy Musson, Alan Powers, Pete Smith, the late Gavin Stamp, Robert Thorne and Lucy Worsley. In Oxford, Debbie Dance, Emily Gee, Clare Hills-Nova, Liz Kitch, the Rev. David Meara, John Steane, Nick Thomas and John Whitehead all assisted with the project in sundry ways.

Coming to the county section, I was lucky to coincide with a golden age in Oxfordshire for the Victoria County History, whose latest instalment, the exemplary vol. xx (*Caversham, Goring and Area*), appeared in 2022. Simon Townley of the VCH kindly allowed access to the finished text ahead of the book's launch at Shiplake Court, where the co-authors Simon Draper, Stephen Mileson and Mark Page joined the celebrations.

Church visiting was eased by the help and guidance freely offered by clergy and churchwardens across the territory, of whom my particular thanks to the Rev. Mark Ainsworth at Bix, Fr Paul Fitzpatrick at the Sacred Heart, Henley, Toby Garfitt at Great Haseley, Rodney Mann at Wheatfield, Gillian Ovey at Rotherfield Greys, Linda Parker at Crowmarsh Gifford, Charles Peers at Chiselhampton, Nick Room at Kidmore End, and the Rev. Robert Thewsey at Harpsden and Shiplake. It is good to report that a high proportion of parish churches in the area are kept open for visiting.

Nearly all of the houses which had opened their doors for the first edition of *Oxfordshire* generously did so again, and very few explicitly refused a visit. Particular thanks go to Robin Abraham at Eyot House, Sonning Eye, Cecilia Akerman Kressner at Britwell House, Lady Alvingham at Bix Hall (also to Kathy Webster), Jeff Banks at Crowsley Park, Dr Francis and Christine Brown at Fifield Manor, the Didcocks at East End House in Watlington, Lord Esher at Beauforest House, Newington, John Joseph Eyston and Lady Anne Eyston at Mapledurham (also to Kate White), Mike Fensome at Wyfold Court, Ulrich and Susie Gerhartz at Past Field, Henley, Olivia Harrison at Friar Park, Henley, Rachel Jacques at Chalgrove Manor, John and Waveney Luke at Denton House, Cuddesdon, Dr Paul and Mina Matthews at Thame Park, Aidan Meller and Lucy Seal at Hardwick House (also to Sir Julian Rose), James and Alexandra Nettleton at Newington House, Susan Robinson and Jonathan Darby at Garsington Manor, Veronica Sandilands at Baldon House (also to Natasha Eliot, and Lachlan), John and Nicola Simonson at Culham Manor, Sam Swire at Haseley Court, Bernard and Sarah Taylor at Rycote Park, Ian and Gigi Wason at Harpsden Court, Janet Williamson at Kingston Blount, Nicholas and Philippa Wills at the Great House, Great Milton, and George and Angela Yannaghas at The Monkery in the same village. Among the schools, colleges and other institutions, my thanks to Canon Mark Chapman and Jacqui Gunn at Ripon College Cuddesdon, to Dave Gavin and Nigel Spencer at Blount's Court, Rotherfield Peppard, to José Gomez at Flint House, Goring Heath, to Doug Stephenson at Nuneham Park, to Nicky Tarrant at the Oratory School (Woodcote House), to Dom Walker at the Aston Martin Heritage Trust, Drayton St Leonard, to Lynn Wood and Sophie Huyghues Despointes at the Europa School, Culham College, and to the team at Braziers Park, Ipsden.

These plain lists must stand for a great deal of help and hospitality, freely offered and gratefully received, including at places where my visit came unannounced. Many owners and custodians also allowed photography, including Philip and Rhuann Kaye at Incurvo, Goring, where a tight itinerary had kept me from ringing the doorbell as I cycled on to Ipsden. Additional help with arranging visits came from Martin Gibson, Alexandra Harris, James Joll, Charles Kingsley-Evans, Adam Menuge, Sir Tim Rice, Olivia Stockdale and Enid Worsley.

Local knowledge was kindly supplied by Ruth Gibson and Michael Redley, whose reading of the Henley draft resulted in many upgrades, and by Nick Rogers, who read the draft text for Thame. Dan Miles provided valuable details of dendrochronology, and useful leads came also from Edward Diestelkamp on Chiselhampton, Lynn Holmes on Greys Court, Charles Saumarez Smith on Cuddesdon, and Liz Shatford on Sandford-on-Thames. The library staff at Henley, Thame and Goring were helpful, as in Oxford were those of the Bodleian and City libraries, the libraries of St John's College and the Oxford Union, and the Oxfordshire History Centre. At the London end, my thanks once again to the staff of the London Library, the British Library, the Institute of Historical Research, and the libraries of the Society of Antiquaries and the RIBA.

Suggested improvements and corrections were sent in over the years by John Ashdown, William Fawcett, Amis Goldingham, Mr D.A.A. Holloway, Christopher Jordan, the late David W. Lloyd, George McHardy, Donald Rice, the late Ian Sutton, and Roger White. Any remaining errors or omissions are my own. They may be set right when this book is reprinted, and any notifications from readers will be welcomed by the publishers.

That brings the roll-call to well over three hundred names – a measure of how much the *Buildings of England* series has always depended on help freely and willingly given. Turning the results into a book requires collaboration of a different kind. Here my thanks go especially to my colleagues Linda McQueen, our calm, committed and assured production editor, and Lydia Smith, our diligent picture researcher. Hester Higton was a sympathetic copy-editor, Katy Carter and Charley Chapman observant proof-readers, and Nicola King a model indexer. Martin Brown once again brought order and clarity to my optimistic roughs for the maps and plans, and James Davies captured the territory in his radiant photographs, often returning several times over to secure the master shot.

The revision project would not have been possible without the secure foundations for the ongoing Pevsner series established in Penguin days by our predecessors Bridget Cherry and Elizabeth Williamson, ably assisted by Gavin Watson of the Pevsner Books Trust, and carried forward splendidly at Yale University Press by Sally Salvesen after 2002. The research and writing of the book were funded by our long-term supporters the Paul Mellon Centre for Studies in British Art, the photography by a generous donation from James Joll. Throughout, my fellow editor and friend Charles O'Brien was an invaluable support in everything to do with the progress of the series.

To have worked on the Pevsner guides for nearly thirty years, and in such company, has been an extraordinary privilege. Research, visiting and writing for my own revised volumes supplied many of the highlights, but the editorial role has been no less rewarding. Hence the dedication of this book, with additional thanks to all those authors who have joined in the great project of revising the *Buildings of England*, or have bravely broken fresh ground in the other nations of these islands.

Simon Bradley
July 2023

OXFORD

INTRODUCTION

Pevsner closed his Introduction to *The Buildings of England: Oxford-shire* (1974) with some general observations on the University city:

The best I can think of in an endeavour to characterize Inner Oxford is to compare it with Cambridge. At first sight the skeleton of the two centres appears similar, the Trinity Street–King's Parade–Trumpington Street axis corresponding to the High, the Regent Street–St Andrew's Street axis to the Broad. But there the similarity ends; the colleges from Magdalene to Queens' and even to Peterhouse turn more to the Backs than to the street, whereas the hub of Oxford is between the High and the Broad; it is in fact precisely the Radcliffe Camera. Christ Church Meadow and Merton Fields no-one would dare to rank as high as the Backs, but Cambridge has no such hub as Oxford. So Cambridge colleges, at least a whole string of them, turn outward, Oxford colleges, many of them, turn inward. Round the Camera it takes some sorting out to be sure what building belongs to what college. There is a density of monuments of architecture here which has not the like in Europe. The Cambridge image is buildings in a landscape, *riant,* if you are lucky, the Oxford image is a landscape made of stone, sombre at its best.

And there are other contrasts. Oxford is stone – brick is a recent addition displayed as something in its own right for the first time at Keble; Cambridge is traditionally brick, though stone could be and was got from not too far away. And it was good, durable stone, not the friable Oxford stone which has caused the recent wholesale refacing and cleaning[...]

Then Cambridge has no skyline, Oxford has the most telling skyline of England, though dreaming spires is nonsense in every respect. Surely, in spite of St Mary, All Saints, and the cathedral, and now Nuffield, Oxford is remembered less for them than for Tom Tower, the Camera, and Magdalen tower. It is the variety of the shapes which makes the skyline. And as for 'dreaming'? Stupor say the enemies, inertia say even some of the friends, serious search

Oxford from Headington Hill.
Engraving by J. Basire after J.M.W. Turner, 1848

for truth among the undergraduates, search for knowledge among the dons, less serious search for publicity – single out what you will, dreaming is not a figurative Oxford quality, by criteria either of the mind or the eye.

Pevsner would have had the other place freshly in mind: the second edition of his *Cambridgeshire* appeared in 1970, and he had been a college fellow and lecturer at Cambridge since the mid 1950s. His biographer even detects 'a whiff of lingering prejudice' in this comparison of the ancient University cities.* Either way, Pevsner's summing up skips over a great many Oxford essentials. There is the city's distinctively patchy layout, with settlement weighted to the E and N of the historic centre, and remarkably much low-lying, flood-prone land left open and green right up to the city's heart. The rivers themselves have a great part to play, the Thames or Isis and its tributary the Cherwell, with all their branches and back channels, urban or sylvan, as well as Oxford's own canal: an intricate system compared with the straightforward arc of the Cam. North Oxford can also boast one of England's most celebrated Victorian suburbs, fiercely Gothic in its pioneering phases, more eclectic in the later districts, but remarkably intact and well kept.

*Susie Harries, *Nikolaus Pevsner: The Life* (2011).

But it is of course the University which has made Oxford famous, and the ancient college system which has fostered so much distinctive and rewarding architecture, just as at Cambridge. In numerical terms at least, Oxford's colleges have the edge: thirty-nine as of 2023, with Kellogg (1994) and Reuben (2019) as the newest arrivals, as against thirty-one at Cambridge. Visitors from that city should also watch for some shibboleths of architectural terminology: Oxford's colleges have quads and not courts, with common rooms rather than combination rooms for socializing, and lodgings, not lodges, for the variously titled college heads. Such differences apart, at both Oxford and Cambridge the earliest college buildings are older than anything put up by the University, and it is with the endlessly varied colleges that the gazetteer of this book begins.

MEDIEVAL OXFORD

The Anglo-Saxon town*

The settlement at Oxford became the county's only formally laid-out town in the ANGLO-SAXON period.[†] The *burh* was established on the Mercian side of the Thames (which marked the boundary between Mercia and Wessex), probably in the late C9, on a site with fairly limited indication of preceding early and middle Anglo-Saxon occupation. Oxford is first mentioned in the *Anglo-Saxon Chronicle* in 912, and there were meetings of the Great Council there in 1015, 1018, 1035 and 1065.

Despite an increasing body of evidence, many aspects of the layout and organization of the *burh* are closely debated. It incorporated within its area the minster of St Frideswide, probably in existence by the early C8, which was most likely sited beneath present-day Christ Church overlooking a crossing of the Thames from the S. The river was much wider than it is today, and comprised a complex arrangement of channels and small islands; a crossing, roughly on the line of the modern street of St Aldate's, was probably achieved with a combination of fords and bridges, an example of the latter being dated to the middle Saxon period. The primary approach and the eponymous 'Oxenford', however, was on the SW side of the town, perhaps leading to the area later occupied by the Castle.

The *burh* had earthwork defences augmented by a stone wall in the later Saxon period, on a line broadly similar to that of the medieval town walls. In its initial form it may have been roughly rectangular, but it is now known that defences extended west-wards to incorporate the area of the Castle and these probably

---

* By Paul Booth.
[†] Important foci of earlier prehistoric ritual activity and Roman settlement just N of the modern centre of Oxford may have influenced the layout of subsequent development.

also belong to the primary *burh*, the eastern side of which may have lain approximately on the line of Catte Street and a southward projection from it. A secondary extension of the circuit to the E may have followed the original foundation relatively swiftly, perhaps in the early C10, but this is much less certain, and a bank on its N side has an earlier date.

The core of the primary *burh* enclosed a more or less regular layout of streets, of which the principal ones were surfaced many times, but the eastern extension included a road running diagonally from its NW corner towards the E gate. Internal buildings were mainly of timber, but are relatively poorly known except for the cellar pits of various sizes which were characteristic of many of them, particularly in the later Saxon period. Burials are recorded from the area of St Frideswide's minster and St Aldate's, but little is known of the stone-built churches of this period until the C11, when the tower of St Michael at the North Gate was built (*see* below). St George's Tower, on the W side (later incorporated into the Castle), although different in form from St Michael's tower, may also have served to guard a gateway into the town. St Mary the Virgin and St Aldate were also probably associated with gates in the *burh* circuit, though they do not have surviving pre-Conquest fabric. In total as many as seventeen parochial churches in Oxford (including extra-mural ones such as St Mary Magdalen) may have been pre-Conquest foundations. These were mostly concentrated within the primary *burh*, while the eastern extension mostly lay within the single parish of St Peter-in-the-East, the site of an important minster perhaps of C10 date, though again no pre-Conquest fabric survives.

Early medieval buildings

Enough survives in Oxford to illustrate the main lines of development of English architecture from the C11 onwards. From before that date there is a fragment of a C10 cross-shaft, found in 1999 in the wall of St Aldate's church. The story really begins with the tower of St Michael at the North Gate, of *c.*1010–60, with its long-and-short quoins, and baluster columns in the superimposed twin bell-openings, both characteristic ANGLO-SAXON motifs. There is also the near-featureless but visually powerful tower near the site of the old West Gate, which may well have been of secular rather than religious status when first built. In the 1070s it became the W tower of the collegiate church of St George, established to serve the castle built by Robert d'Oilly on behalf of William the Conqueror, which was placed across the line of Oxford's defensive wall. The foundation date is reflected in the style of the church's reconstructed crypt, the earliest datable NORMAN architecture in Oxford. This has crude capitals with typical late C11 ornamental forms like large ribbed leaves. No other masonry at the Castle is so early, but the original motte survives. D'Oilly also made a substantial causeway called Grandpont on the road into Oxford from the S, and parts of its stone arches survive under the present roadway.

It is instructive to compare the carvings in St George's crypt with those at the mid-C12 church of St Peter-in-the-East (now St Edmund Hall's library). This highly sophisticated building also has a vaulted crypt, with internal passages that suggest the former presence of a shrine or reliquary. The crypt still has some heavy scalloped capitals of Early Norman type, but also foliage capitals and one with figures, monsters and so on, reminiscent of the capitals of the Canterbury Cathedral crypt. St Peter's crypt has plain groin-vaulting, but the chancel vault is ribbed and decorated with chevron and a distinctive chain motif, and the s doorway has beakhead ornament. Beakhead and chevron also occur at the reconstructed mid-C12 doorway at St Ebbe's church. Similarities in motifs and treatment suggest that the St Ebbe's doorway and the chapter house doorway at St Frideswide's Priory (*see* below) are by the same workshop, as also the carving of the doorways at the lavishly treated Iffley church, the one Norman parish church that may be compared with St Peter-in-the-East as an architectural conception.

Several other parish churches retain Norman features. St Cross has a plain chancel arch of *c.*1100; St Andrew, Headington has a mid-C12 chancel arch with continuous orders of chevron; St James, Cowley has elements of a chancel arch of the same date with the original scheme of painted decoration, and two re-set doorways; St Aldate has a re-set length of C12 wall arcading; St Giles some blocked openings and two re-set shafts with capitals. At St Frideswide's, now the Cathedral, two shafts and capitals in the s transept triforium have early C12 detail that is inconsistent with the rest of the church. These appear to be *spolia*, probably from the cloister: evidence that the foundation of *c.*1120–2 provided quarters for the monastic community first, before the new church was started.

On the SECULAR side, the only building to rival the Castle was Henry I's foundation of Beaumont Palace just N of the city wall, the royal residence where Richard I was born. Its last remnants were destroyed when Beaumont Street was made in the 1820s. Other early houses in the town are discussed on pp.18–21.

Work on the cathedral church began probably in the 1160s, and was completed around 1200. It remains substantially as then designed, with a straight E end (which is unusual for the date), transepts with aisles (the s transept W aisle later absorbed into the cloister), a crossing tower and an aisled nave. The piers are round and have very flat foliage capitals, waterleaf details in the earlier parts making way increasingly for crockets and more intricate acanthus-like leaf patterns in the later parts to the W. There is a triforium, but it is tucked under the arcade arches, so that a lower arch has to spring to support it from some way up the piers. The same system was adopted earlier at Romsey in Hants and Jedburgh in Scotland. The aisles are rib-vaulted, and provision was made for rib-vaults in the main vessels too. Pointed arches begin to appear in the upper parts and at the crossing.

The church was built for the Augustinian order, for whom the ancient priory of St Frideswide was re-founded by Henry I. The other MONASTIC FOUNDATIONS of Oxford are as follows. The greatest, also Augustinian, was Osney Priory (soon elevated to Osney Abbey), established in 1129 on a site W of the walled town. Only one small early C15 outbuilding survives, but the plan of the church is known: it was half as long again as that of St Frideswide, even before the latter was cut short in the C16. A few years before the Augustinian houses, around 1115, Godstow Abbey was established for Benedictine nuns at Wolvercote, and here we have one late medieval chapel building and little more. Rewley Abbey, on what is now the site of the Saïd Business School by the railway station, was Cistercian, founded in 1281. All that can now be seen is part of the precinct wall and one C15 doorway.

There is more to show from Oxford's two medieval HOSPITALS, both of which later passed into the hands of colleges of the University. St John's Hospital, extant by the late C12, was given new buildings by Henry III in the C13. The shell of its two-storey former chapel survives within the early C16 street range of Magdalen College, and the shell of a hall building was retained for the college's kitchens. St Bartholomew's Hospital (Bartlemas), for lepers, was founded by Henry I in the 1120s, well to the E of the town. Oriel College took it over in 1329 and provided a small chapel, which survives.

By that date the FRIARS were well established in Oxford. The Dominicans or Blackfriars came in 1221, moving in 1245 to a new site S of the walled town. Theirs was the first Dominican house in Britain, and the largest outside London. The Franciscans or Greyfriars arrived in 1225, also moving in 1245 to a new site, close to the Dominicans. Both establishments had impressive buildings, Blackfriars especially, with its double cloister and its church over 240 ft (73 metres) long. Excavations have revealed much about the arrangements, which included some striking divergences from the standard mendicant plan-forms. Above ground, however, there is not much to see: part of a re-set tiled pavement from the Greyfriars cloister walk at the Westgate Centre, and elements of a C13 gateway to Blackfriars within a C17 house in Albion Place. Other friars settled at Oxford too: the Carmelites who came in 1256 and in 1318 were given a site by the king which formed part of Beaumont Palace, the Austin Friars who in 1268 moved to where Wadham College now is, the Trinitarians who were granted a house in 1293, the short-lived Friars of the Sack who came in 1262, and the even shorter-lived Crutched Friars who came in the 1340s.

Returning to the architectural story, the GOTHIC style had generally prevailed by c. 1200, and before approaching the emergence of the University it is worth surveying the first, EARLY ENGLISH phase of the new style in Oxford. The most accomplished designs are at the Cathedral. The crossing tower and stone spire date perhaps from c. 1220–30, the oldest steeple on the Oxford skyline, with a conspicuous display of plate tracery in the bell-openings. The elegant rebuilding of the chapter house is of the same period, with its rib-vault, its paintings in roundels on the vault, its lancet windows with detached shafts, its stiff-leaf decoration and its excellent bosses and figured corbels. In the same years the church acquired a Lady Chapel, unusually placed parallel to the chancel N aisle, and this space retains its painted rib-vault on clustered shafts with crocket capitals. A little later, probably from the mid C13, is the much-altered shell of the refectory on the S side of the cloister. Among the parish churches there is distinctive C13 work at St Peter-in-the-East, where the N chapel arcade has quatrefoil piers and stiff-leaf capitals; at St Giles, including the richly treated N aisle with its cross-gables and internal shafting; at St Michael at the North Gate, a restored chancel with lancets; and at St Mary the Virgin, where the big N tower has Geometrical tracery motifs of *c*.1270. In the outlying parishes, St Andrew, Headington has a mid-C13 S tower and short S aisle; St James, Cowley a C13 chancel. The earliest ROOFS so far identified appear to be early replacements, at the Cathedral chapter house (1260/1) and St Giles chancel (1288).

SECULAR BUILDINGS from the C13 include the WALLS of Oxford, which were rebuilt in 1226–40. Much of the circuit survives, including quite a number of bastions, i.e. semicircular projections not closed at the neck. The most impressive section is in the grounds of New College, part of the NE quadrant of the walls. In this sector the defences were formerly supplemented with a lower, outer wall apparently added later in the C13: a unique feature among English medieval town defences. The base of a mid-C13 tower survives at the Castle, and a rib-vaulted well chamber within the motte. By that time the town already

11,
p. 212

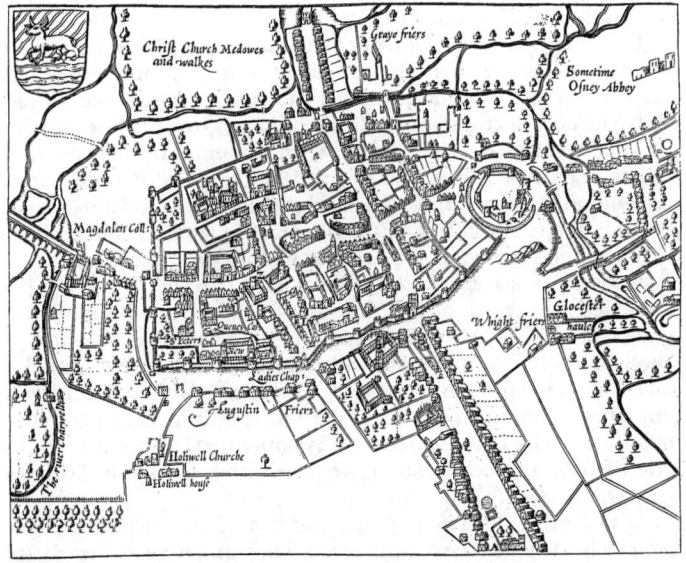

Pictorial map of Oxford, from the north.
Engraving by John Speed, 1605

had a charter, granted by Henry II around 1155, and in the
C13 a stone-built town hall was acquired, which lasted until the
mid C18. Merton Street has Oxford's earliest surviving HOUSE,
of c.1200 (see p.18).

The medieval University and its colleges

That so many friars' houses were established at Oxford is due
largely to the presence of the UNIVERSITY, the first in England.
The word is the translation of *universitas* and at first simply
meant the totality of the masters (*magistri*) who were licensed to
teach. The more usual medieval term was *studium generale*, the
term which the Dominicans also applied to their Oxford house
to designate it as the order's place of study in England.

Before there were universities, the lower as well as the higher
grades of teaching were confined to the schools attached to
cathedrals and monasteries. The first universities belong to
Italy. Bologna, established in 1088, is considered the earliest. It
specialized in civil as well as canon law. The university at Salerno
was famous for medicine. It was for such practical subjects that
the ecclesiastical schools seemed inadequate. Closer to hand was
Paris, which in the course of the C12 developed into the intellectual
centre of Europe. Its university was formally recognized in 1200.
There were four faculties: arts, medicine, law and theology. The
Faculty of Arts comprised the founding *Trivium* of grammar,
rhetoric and logic, and the higher *Quadrivium* of arithmetic,
geometry, music and astronomy. This was the model that came
to be adopted at Oxford.

The first references to higher teaching at Oxford are somewhat
sketchy. Theobald of Etampes, active from the late 1090s into
the early 1120s, is reputed to have had sixty or a hundred pupils.
Robert Pullen lectured on Scripture in the 1130s, and later rose to
be chancellor at Rome. Continuity of teaching through the mid
C12 is less certain, but in 1187 or 1188 Gerald of Wales went to
read aloud his *Topography of Ireland* at Oxford, the town in which,
he said, 'the clergy of England are in greatest strength and repute'.
From other sources it is clear that Oxford was also a centre of
instruction in law by the late C12. The expansion of teaching is
indicated by the life of St Edmund of Abingdon, who is said to
have lectured on Aristotle around 1200. The papal interdict of
1208–14 and a local dispute with the town authorities caused a
hiatus in teaching – the migration of students to Cambridge was
one of the consequences – but the settlement in 1214 allowed a
fresh start. The first chancellor was appointed, with authority to
grant licences to teach, and to represent the *magistri* in dealings
with the town.

At Oxford we also hear by the mid C13 of the existence of *hospitia* or hostels where students lived. They might be any premises
used for the purpose, typically by a *magister* who rented the building from its owner. Of these HALLS, as they were called, Oxford

had far more than there were colleges throughout the medieval period. Similar provision was made at Cambridge, where 'hostel' was the preferred term. By the early C14 there were probably over a hundred of them in Oxford, mostly in the eastern parts of the town. At the middle of the C15 the number stood at around seventy. By that date all undergraduates had to belong to a hall or college. Tackley's Inn and Beam Hall survive to show the essentially domestic character of these academic halls (*see* pp. 19–20). Hart Hall, now part of Hertford College, is a mid-C16 example, much altered.

p. 19

COLLEGES differed from halls in that they were endowed and self-governing bodies. The corporate character of a college is, as the name implies, like that of other medieval communities, with separate living quarters but a common hall and chapel, such as the vicars choral of a cathedral, or even warden and pensioners in almshouses such as Sackville College at East Grinstead or the College of Matrons at Salisbury. Hence the varied titles of the heads of the older colleges, which recur in other establishments: wardens at Merton, New College, All Souls and Wadham; masters at University, Balliol and Pembroke; rectors at Exeter and Lincoln; provosts at Oriel, Queen's and Worcester; presidents at Magdalen, Corpus Christi, Trinity and St John's; principals at St Edmund Hall, Brasenose, Jesus and Hertford; dean at Christ Church.

Colleges were established in part to satisfy the need for educated administrators, in part to secure intercessory prayers for their founders, as monasteries and chantries were also founded. These founders included not only kings, queens, archbishops and bishops, but also a nobleman (John de Balliol) and a lawyer and courtier (Sir Richard Sutton, co-founder of Brasenose). The earliest colleges catered for graduates exclusively, as did the colleges already established at Paris, until the system of graduates and undergraduates living together was created by William of Wykeham's foundation of New College in the late C14. The medieval colleges also included several houses founded by monastic orders, to make it possible for monks to be taught at the University: Gloucester College (1283), later Gloucester Hall, then Worcester College; Durham College (1286), later Trinity; Canterbury College (1362), later incorporated in Christ Church; St Mary's College, later the house known as Frewin Hall (1435); and St Bernard's College (1437), later St John's. The last was Cistercian, in succession to Rewley Abbey; St Mary's was Augustinian; the others were Benedictine; and – once again – there were the houses of the friars.

The first three colleges all date from the mid C13. University College began with a bequest of 1249, Balliol College with a subsidy to house some students in the 1260s. Both foundations took longer to acquire permanent buildings and a charter of incorporation. The first to achieve these was Merton College, founded in 1262 by Walter de Merton, clergyman, newly appointed Chancellor to the King, and in the end Bishop of Rochester. Merton's first buildings were conceived on an accordingly grand scale. First came a substantial hall on a raised basement, completed by 1277. Some of its masonry survives, as does the original door with wonderful ironwork scrolls. Next to the hall is the stone-roofed Exchequer Building, and the chancel of the college

12 chapel of the 1290s, high and long and yet meant to be only a choir to which a crossing, transepts and an aisled parochial nave were to be added. The idea of a nave was eventually abandoned and the crossing and transepts were somewhat delayed, but the chancel was rapidly completed, and stands as a lavish exemplar of early DECORATED Gothic. The tracery of its windows is nationally important as a dated example of how at the end of the C13 the severe discipline of Geometrical tracery was loosened, with spherical or rather convex-sided triangles as a favourite motif. The fourth C13 component is the original Warden's Hall of 1299–1300, which may incorporate part of an earlier house. It is altered and drastically restored but it retains windows with a spherical triangle in the heads, and an original roof (*see* p.18). The sacristy added to the chapel in 1310 also deserves mention as an early appearance of reticulated tracery, a characteristic form of the later (flowing) Decorated style.

The early buildings at Merton are grouped informally around a quadrangle that took until the C15 to complete. The irregular grouping of functionally separate elements is also characteristic of great secular houses of the period. But in the C14 the college

13 also undertook a second quadrangle, Mob Quad, on the same axis as the chapel, though visually separate from it. Begun in 1304 with an extension to the Exchequer Building, it took over seventy years to complete, and it is unlikely that the quadrangular form was intended at the outset. Yet Mob Quad established two enduring features of collegiate architecture at Oxford. First, the residential parts were organized as a series of chambers opening off shared staircases. Second, the quad includes a library built in 1371–8, placed on the first floor, and with those closely and regularly set windows from which one can recognize libraries in later colleges.

The C14 brought new college foundations, including Exeter (1314), Oriel (1326) and Queen's (1341). All three were built piecemeal and informally, and in each case the C14 buildings have been replaced, as have the earliest buildings at University College and Balliol. To balance these losses there is the two-storey, partly vaulted Congregation House added to St Mary's church in 1320. This provided the UNIVERSITY with its own meeting place and library, although the latter took until the early C15 to complete.

23,   NEW COLLEGE begins a fresh chapter. It was founded in 1379
p.212 by William of Wykeham, courtier and Bishop of Winchester, with *William Wynford* as master mason. The site chosen was in the NE quarter of the walled area, much of which had been left vacant by the Black Death and by a general downturn in Oxford's trade and prosperity since the C13. By 1386 the main parts of the quad were complete, the other buildings not long after. Nearly everything was new about the college, including the concurrent founding of

a grammar school at Winchester, the present Winchester College, to be the preceding part of a single educational progression. Another innovation was that at New College undergraduates were to live side by side with graduates, and under their charge. That combination set the pattern for future colleges (except All Souls), and made them more fully educational establishments rather than sodalities of Fellows. Architecturally, too, the college was like nothing previously seen at Oxford, though the 1360s works at the Upper Ward of Windsor Castle provide several precedents. It was built on a grand scale and to a clear, logical, easily comprehended plan, with the chapel and hall in line on the N side of a quad and very much part of it, the hall placed on the upper floor – *in modum solarii* (in the manner of a solar), says Wykeham in the Statutes – with a vaulted gate tower at the W entrance to the quad, the Warden's Lodging in the gate tower and extending towards the chapel, the library with its closely set windows in the E range of the quad, and to the W of the chapel a cloister with a bell-tower on its N side. The sets of rooms in the quadrangle are of a type which became standard, as expressed in the alternation of two- or three-light with one-light windows, the former standing for the shared sleeping room, the latter for study cubicles – for teaching graduate and taught undergraduate were intended to live together. The chapel has an antechapel with transepts across the W end, i.e. a T-shaped plan, and this was also imitated at several later colleges. The style of Wynford's architecture, moreover, is PERPENDICULAR. It is the earliest surviving Perp in Oxford – not an early date, if one remembers Gloucester Cathedral in the 1330s; but then it was not the earliest in Oxford originally, for Canterbury College of *c.* 1370 onwards (demolished) had Perp tracery.

23

Nothing as grandiose as New College was done in Oxford for nearly a century. The first new foundations of the FIFTEENTH CENTURY were smaller in scale, Lincoln founded by a Bishop of Lincoln in 1427, All Souls by Archbishop Chichele of Canterbury in 1438. Magdalen, the only one to emulate New College, was founded in 1458 by Bishop Waynflete, another Bishop of Winchester, on a spacious site outside the walls; its buildings were not started until 1474, under the Oxford master mason *William Orchard*. Of these C15 colleges a good deal more is preserved: at Lincoln the Front Quad, two-storeyed, though as usual in Oxford with walls refaced and windows re-managed one way or another, and the ground-floor hall and kitchen, both with their original roofs, and at All Souls the Front Quad too, including the chapel. This repeats the New College type, including the arrays of pinnacles and the extremely slender piers which subdivide the antechapel into two aisles from W to E. The hammerbeam roof is original, the first of its kind in Oxford. Also medieval, at least in most of its architectural parts, is the full-height reredos – necessary because the E wall again abutted the hall, now demolished, which here stood N–S. The reredos is also derived from New College, where however what we see now is almost entirely C19. The type is one of tiers of ornate canopied niches for images, as

26

p. 12

25

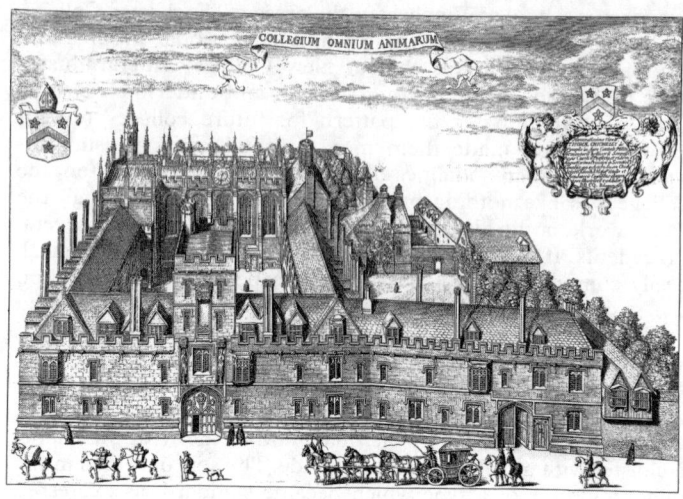

All Souls College.
Engraving by David Loggan, 1675

close a piece of all-over decoration as Spanish *retablos*. All Souls'
chapel entry and the entry to the former hall have fan-vaults,
again the earliest in Oxford. There was a cloister too, placed to
the N and since rebuilt, and a bell-tower was intended.

Magdalen followed New College in scale and in the integration
of the plan. But whereas at New College and All Souls the cloister
was placed inconspicuously to one side, at Magdalen the cloister
is integrated within the main quad, as Waynflete had already
done at Eton in his time as Provost there. T-shaped chapel and
first-floor hall are again in line at Magdalen, here on the S side.
To the S of the quad a bell-tower was provided (begun 1492),
that handsome tower with its elaborate battlements and pinnacles
which greets those entering Oxford from the E, together with a
low attached range along the High Street. There are two more
towers, the ornate Founder's Tower on the W side of the quad
which was meant as its main entrance, and the plainer Muniment Tower between it and the antechapel. Immediately SW of
the antechapel is that Oxford curiosity, an external pulpit. The
whole is probably the most impressive ensemble from medieval
Oxford, particularly for variety of spaces.

There are other C15 college buildings at Oxford, including at
those which retain parts of the monastic colleges which were their
predecessors, as already mentioned. At Gloucester College (now
Worcester), of which much of a small quad and one long range
remain, the accommodation was uniquely divided into houses,
each built by a different monastery from within the Province of
Canterbury. Of Durham College one side of the quad remains as
the Durham Quad of Trinity, of 1417–21, including the library; of
St Bernard's College there is the Front Quad of St John's, of 1438

etc., of which the least altered parts include the gate tower and the rib-vaulted buttery cellar. St Mary's College of 1435 etc. was not re-founded, but parts of the late medieval buildings remain at Frewin Hall, as well as the Norman undercroft from an older house which the college had taken over. St Mary's should not be confused with St Mary Hall, one of the more durable academic halls; this eventually became part of Oriel, where a little of its medieval fabric survives. Another academic hall bequeathed its name to Brasenose College, which retains the late C15 kitchen of its predecessor. Part of Urban Hall may survive at Corpus Christi, and Pembroke College preserves the hall of Broadgates Hall.

Older colleges were also busy bringing their buildings up to date. At Merton, the gate tower from the street was built in 1416–18, with later enhancements. Its Warden's Lodgings were also augmented late in the C15, of which the surviving parts include a large gateway of 1497 adjoining the hall, with a complex lierne vault and delightful Zodiac bosses. The spacious transepts of the chapel were completed in the C15 – the space doubled as a parish church – and in 1448–52 a richly handled crossing tower 12 was provided, with *Robert Janyns Sen.* as master mason, earlier the deputy mason at All Souls. At Balliol the N range of Front Quad is C15, with the big library with its blunt-headed windows, as also is the W range with the former hall. Exeter College has Palmer's Tower of 1432 and a few adjacent rooms, now curiously situated within the college, but originally serving as its main entrance from the N.

The C15 also brought new buildings for the UNIVERSITY. Classrooms ('schools') were required for teaching purposes, and at first these were provided *ad hoc*, often in properties rented from local monasteries. Cambridge took the first step beyond, making a start on what became its Old Schools court around 1370–80. At Oxford the story begins with the Divinity School, *p.329* the first fully detached University building. It was begun by 1423, with *Richard Winchcombe* as the first master mason named, and finally completed in the 1480s. As at the C14 Congregation House the upper storey housed a library, augmented by generous gifts of books by Humphrey, Duke of Gloucester, and heightened by means of a reconstructed roof in 1485–6. The Divinity School itself occupies the ground floor, with six-light Perp windows and 27 the most ingenious vault, installed in 1478–82. The mason's name is not documented, but the initials w.o. appear five times on the vault, which points to *William Orchard* as executant. Given the long gestation of the building, Orchard may perhaps have been carrying out a design inherited from a predecessor. As the work progressed, an earlier master mason had been instructed to adopt simpler mouldings, a change visible on the window jambs. The vault signals a return to complex display. It has strong, four-centred transverse arches with twin pendants halfway up, and is constructed to look as if the lierne vaults (almost fan-vaults) issued from the pendants, which of course they can't. It is a feat of make-believe as cunning as any of the Italian and German Baroque. The combination of arches and pendants appears to

10 derive from the high lierne vault of the choir of the Cathedral, an undocumented work frequently ascribed to Orchard, but which has detailed motifs that place it firmly in the late C14.

So to the SIXTEENTH CENTURY. Two more colleges, both on the small side, appeared in the first two decades: Brasenose, founded in 1509 by a bishop and a lawyer in the service of the Lady Margaret, mother of Henry VII, and Corpus Christi, begun in 1512 by Richard Fox, yet another Bishop of Winchester. The Old Quad at Brasenose still has its small hall with bay window. Its gate tower is elaborated in the manner of the Founder's Tower at Magdalen, but the windows round the quad have uncusped lights, a C16 sign. Front Quad at Corpus includes the hall, with another hammerbeam roof, and the chapel, which here projects from the E side. It had a small cloistered quad alongside, replaced in the C18. Fox initially intended the college to provide for monks from Winchester, but changed his mind in favour of teaching secular clergy, who were to be instructed in Greek as well as Latin: a sign of growing Humanist influence at Oxford.

The master builders employed at Brasenose are known to have been local, but at Corpus the work was directed by men from the king's service, the master mason *William Vertue* (active otherwise at St George's Chapel Windsor, Henry VII's Chapel at Westminster Abbey, Eton College, the Palace of Westminster etc.) and the master carpenter *Humphrey Coke*, with assistance from *William East* and *Robert Carow* of Oxford. A similar pattern appears at Christ Church, or rather Cardinal Wolsey's Cardinal College, Oxford's third early C16 foundation. Established in 1525 on the site of the suppressed monastery of St Frideswide, it was at first built very fast, with *Henry Redman*, *John Lubyns* and *William Johnson* as masons. Redman had already worked for Wolsey at York Place in Whitehall and at Hampton Court, projects of quasi-royal grandeur which Henry VIII was quick to acquire when the opportunity occurred. Wolsey took from New College and from King's College, Cambridge the idea of a new grammar school as a feeder, though the foundation in his home town of Ipswich did not flourish as Eton and Winchester have done. He also included an almshouse foundation, of which some buildings survive as part of Pembroke College, across St Aldate's. From his own college of Magdalen he took the concept of a main quad with cloister walks, although here the cloister was never built. Still, the quad, Tom Quad, was larger than any yet, its ranges deeper in plan and its windows taller than at any previous college, just as the bay-windowed hall was larger and placed higher than

33 any yet. As at Corpus, its hammerbeam roof was designed by *Humphrey Coke* and made by *Robert Carow*. Altogether new was the location of the intended chapel, not in line with the hall but on the opposite side across the quad, which would have allowed it to have a great E window as at King's College Chapel in

32 Cambridge. Similarly, the gate tower as begun is not of the rectangular type of New College etc. but more like those of King's or St John's at Cambridge, i.e. with polygonal angle turrets. The form of these turrets is very interesting and also very typical of

the most sophisticated works of the early C16 (cf. e.g. Henry VII's Chapel). Each is square in plan, with a triangular projection from the middle of each side, i.e. one square set into the other diagonally. The s end of the frontage finishes with a projection with simpler octagonal turrets, and on the coving of the oriel between the turrets is a little carved Renaissance decoration, the first in Oxford, as the classical motifs at Hampton Court had been among the first in England. The answering N end was not built until the C17, and belongs with the story of Christ Church after Wolsey's fall.

Later medieval churches

Oxford has only one CHURCH with outstanding work of the C14 and C15, and that is St Mary's. The splendid spire, more crocketed and with more ballflower than any other – dreaming is the most inappropriate word for this exuberant display – is an addition of about 1310–30, distinctive especially for its placing of the corner pinnacles in two rising tiers. Close in date is the Brome Chapel at the same church, still with its arcade of continuous hollow chamfers, although the original windows have gone. Elsewhere, the Cathedral is the best place to see the later development of the DECORATED style. The N transept was extended around 1330–40 with a new chapel, the Latin Chapel, placed parallel to the C13 Lady Chapel and equal to it in length. Its N windows have inventive patterns of flowing tracery, and the vaults and arcades of the two chapels help to create a space of great visual richness. A little later is the E window of St Lucy's Chapel in the s transept, where the tracery design appears uncomfortably stretched.* Then there is the extraordinary choir vault, already mentioned. Among the smaller parish churches, St Peter-in-the-East has a C14 N aisle with flowing tracery, and St Mary Magdalen and St Michael at the North Gate both have s chapels with reticulated tracery, suggesting a date c. 1320–40.

For the PERPENDICULAR style St Mary the Virgin is the exemplar, made still more impressive by the panel-traceried re-windowing of the C14 parts to correspond. The rest was almost entirely rebuilt on a large scale – six-bay nave, five-bay chancel – from c. 1462 to c. 1500. The piers have a characteristic profile, more elaborate than those of the antechapel piers of New, All Souls and Magdalen colleges. The result can stand comparison with great C15 town churches elsewhere, but the rebuilding was essentially an academic project, reflecting the use of the church for University gatherings. The civic church of the town was St Martin at Carfax, of which only the late medieval tower survives, heavily altered and restored. St Thomas also has a Perp W tower. At the Cathedral, the cloister was rebuilt in the 1490s, and partially demolished shortly afterwards for Wolsey's

22

10

22,
p. 385

*The original chapel of Queen's College also had an E window with elongated flowing tracery, a late example, as it was started only in 1373.

new college works, as the w end of St Frideswide's church was also demolished. It remains the only vaulted cloister to survive from medieval Oxford. From the very end of the period there is the octagonal two-storey chapel of *c.*1520 by the long-lost Smith Gate, which survives, drastically reconstructed in 1931 as part of Hertford College.

Monuments, sculpture and church furnishings

The Cathedral is naturally the best place for medieval CHURCH MONUMENTS. The earliest is also the most important, the beautiful shrine of St Frideswide, almost certainly of 1289, with its riches of naturalistic leaves. What remains is a scholarly reconstruction, remade in 2001–2 with additional fragments inserted. From the C14 there are the monuments to Prior Sutton †1316(?) with its effigy under a canopy powdered with ballflower, and to Lady Montague †1354, which lacks a canopy but has much original colouring, and little figures of *pleureurs* against the tomb-chest. The early C15 monument of Sir George Nowers(?) has an alabaster effigy. Also of the C15 is the ornate but mysterious sepulchral monument with a wooden upper storey which may have served as a watching loft for the saint's shrine. Finally there is one of the familiar recessed Purbeck wall monuments with a tomb-chest and a flat-topped canopy. This is to Robert King †1537, last abbot of Osney and first Bishop of Oxford, whose interiors at Thame Abbey (p.755) include copious classical motifs, yet the tomb has not one inch of Renaissance decoration. Elsewhere, Magdalen chapel has a tomb-chest with an alabaster effigy, the father of the founder, brought from Lincolnshire and of mid-C15 date, and there is another at St Aldate (†1522).

In college chapels, BRASSES were the normal means of commemoration. The best collections are at Magdalen, Merton and New College. Merton has the earliest, a bust in the head of the indent of a cross (†1322), and also a similar design of the mid C14 with a small figure in the cross-head, and a double brass of *c.*1420 with little figures on a bracket under a canopy. On a grander scale are the canopied brasses to Thomas Cranley, Archbishop of Dublin †1417 at New College and to Merton's Warden Sever †1471.

There is much medieval SCULPTURE, though many external figures have been replaced by copies. The gate tower of New College for instance has original late C14 statues in niches on the outer face, the Virgin, the founder and an angel, but in the equivalent group towards the quad the founder's figure is an early C21 substitution. The trio of figures appears again on the Muniment Tower. Also at New College, in the cloisters, are the weathered early C14 statues saved from the spire of St Mary. All Souls has moved the two fine statues probably by *John Massingham* from its gate tower to the antechapel, but at St John's gate tower the C15 figure of St Bernard remains, as do the C15 figures of the Virgin and St John in their niches on the N transept of Merton chapel. The most beguiling exterior sculpture is on the gate tower alongside, the scene of Walter de Merton and John the Baptist in a garden of animal allegories, carved in 1463–4 by *R. Janyns Sen. & Janyns Jun.* Also intriguing, though much restored, are the 'hieroglyphics' or figure groups of 1508–9 on the cloister buttresses at Magdalen. On a lesser scale, the vault and end walls in the Divinity School are thickly populated with statuettes and statuary groups of the late C15. 26 27

The most interesting CHURCH FURNISHINGS are generally in college chapels. CHOIR STALLS include the restored late C14 sequence at New College with their famous misericords, where the arm-rests are carved too. All Souls and Magdalen have also retained their original stalls and misericords, though these are not as accomplished as the New College series. Simpler stalls without misericord carvings are at St Mary the Virgin and the Cathedral. The chapels of Balliol and Corpus have the first of Oxford's eagle LECTERNS of brass, of c.1500 or not long after. They were a standard production, and examples exist as far away as Urbino. Merton chapel has an uncommonly fine brass lectern of c.1503, of the gabled type, as at Eton and King's, Cambridge. A secular metalwork item of interest is the Romanesque bronze door knocker in the hall at Brasenose, introduced in the late C19. College chapels generally lack FONTS, but in the parish churches there is a C13 one at St Giles with vertically applied dogtooth, highly decorated C14 ones at St Mary Magdalen and St Michael at the North Gate, and a Perp one with lions and angels at St Aldate. St Mary Magdalen also boasts a distinctive early C14 CHEST.

Oxford also has an outstanding sequence of medieval STAINED GLASS, much of it produced by local glass-stainers. The late C13 is represented by some small but exquisite figures in St Michael's church. These have been re-set, but the side windows at Merton chapel have kept their glazing of 1310/11 by *William* of Thame, band-type compositions with figures of saints and little suppliant scholars; and glass of different medieval dates is collected in the E window. Slightly later is the glass of the Latin Chapel and the Chapel of St Lucy in the Cathedral, large single figures under canopies in the first, small-scale scenes and figures in the ogee tracery of the other. The stained glass of the 1380s in New College chapel, attributed to *Thomas*, glazier of Oxford, is excellent by any standards. All Souls has a series of large figures of the 1440s in the chapel, as well as C15 glass displaced from the college library, and a smaller assembly of re-set early C15 figures is in Trinity's library. Re-set early C16 glass appears in the chapels at Queen's (1518) and Balliol (1529–30). The latter, which shows strong Renaissance influence, may have been made for Wolsey's Cardinal College (Christ Church), where the hall and chapter house retain heraldic glass by the German- or Dutch-born *James Nicholson*. In the parish churches only some incomplete C15 figures at St Peter-in-the-East deserve mention here. 15

DOMESTIC BUILDING IN OXFORD
UP TO THE C18
BY DAVID CLARK

Medieval houses

Most of the domestic evidence for NORMAN Oxford lies underground. One cellar with an arch of *c.* 1080 under the former Clarendon Hotel in Cornmarket Street was recorded during demolition in the 1950s. The most significant survival is the sub-vault at Frewin Hall, the undercroft of a Norman town house dating to 1090–1150. Possibly built by Geoffrey de Clinton I, a chamberlain of Henry I, or by Henry of Oxford, a leading citizen of the town, it seems to have been part of a large urban estate.

Perhaps the earliest STANDING BUILDING is in Merton Street, which seems to have been a stone hall house built *c.* 1200. An engraving of 1750 shows two Late Norman or Early Gothic windows, which suggests the transitional date. The house was clearly a 'cellar and solar' type, of which there were many examples in Oxford. A house on this site belonging to Matilda Edrich is documented in 1228. The Edriches were a prosperous family, and the house had, unusually, an inside toilet. Acquired by Merton College in 1272–3, it was converted into stabling at an early stage.

Another early house in Merton Street, the old Warden's Hall at Merton, was built in 1299–1300. Although Pantin used it as an example of a hall with a right-angled (perhaps chamber) wing, as a college building it is something of a special case: there was no door to the street, and there is some doubt as to how the building was used.* It apparently had a cellar, in which there may have been services, with a chamber on the upper level. The roof structure, however, makes it a very special building. This consists of one central and two terminal tie-beams, arch-braced to wall-posts supported by wooden corbels. The tie-beams sit on wall-plates, but the feet of the rafters are fixed on to a raised wall-plate supported by ashlar pieces. On these tie-beams are pairs of queenposts supporting flat-laid plates (acting as purlins) and collars, again with arch braces. The queenposts have moulded capitals and bases, and on the collars are crown-posts, also moulded, with four-way bracing to upper collars and a crown-plate. There are dragon ties at the corners between the purlins and the collars, rather than in the usual, lower position between wall-plate and tie-beam. The queenposts have horizontal stub ties to the principal rafters, one of which has a distinctive triangular 'snap' from trestle-sawing. A traite-de-Jupiter scarf joint in the plate near the central truss is also a late C13 feature. One puzzle is whether this house was completely new in 1299 or an alteration to an earlier house acquired in 1268. The walls of the hall are

---

* W. A. Pantin, 'The Development of Domestic Architecture in Oxford', *Antiquaries' Journal* 28 (1947).

all of different thicknesses, which may indicate different phases, and some elements of the stonework cannot be explained by the likely configuration of the 1299 building.

There are several survivals from the later Middle Ages, of which the C15 Littlemore Hall (Nos. 82–83 St Aldate's) is one of the few purely domestic examples. Another is Holywell Manor (1516), though this was at the time in a suburban village. Owners in the main commercial streets needed to make maximum use of their land by building multi-purpose structures. There were shops on the frontage, often cellars below, while living accommodation was above and behind. The growth of the University also encouraged owners to include space for an ACADEMIC HALL – the prototype college. A good example is Tackley's Inn at Nos. 106–107 High Street, where shortly before 1300 the parson of Tackley, Roger le Mareschal, built a row of shops above a five-bay undercroft with quadripartite vaulting. Behind was the academic hall, its roof dating from c. 1512–14, but with a tall C14 window in its rear wall. In 1324 the building was occupied by Adam de Brome as part of the foundation that became Oriel College. Beam Hall in Merton Street was also an academic hall, taking its name from Gilbert de Biham, Chancellor of the University in the C13. Its present E

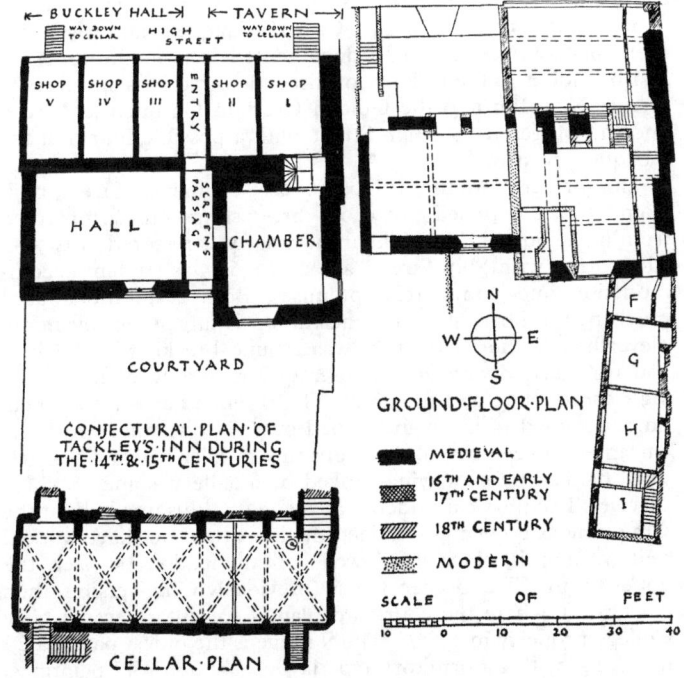

Tackley's Inn, High Street.
Conjectural plan by W. A. Pantin, 1947

part seems to be a late C15 hall house, parallel to the street and entered from it via a screens passage. A solar extended over the screens passage and one of the three bays of the hall, which has arch-braced collar-beam trusses: an ingenious solution to the problem of fitting accommodation into a tight urban space. A considerable w extension in 1586 seems to have obliterated the former service end.

The undercroft at Tackley's Inn was let as a tavern by 1363. TAVERNS – wine-bars for the better-off – are documented in Oxford from before 1313, when University scholars were banned from drinking in them. Documentary and fabric evidence strongly suggests that all the vaulted medieval undercrofts accessible from the street were at some time used as taverns. Other well-known Oxford examples were the Swindlestock Tavern formerly on the sw corner of Carfax, the Oldyeldhall next door, and across the road the Falcon in Knap Hall, now the Town Hall's Plate Room. The Swan was beneath Ducklington's Inn, where the St Aldate's Post Office now stands.

INNS offered accommodation, food and drink for travellers. They were also meeting places and where entertainments such as plays were put on – especially in the courtyard inns, where the galleries would have been useful as viewing platforms. The records in 1300 name none of the inns in Oxford; by the 1350s they appear with their owners' names; by 1400 they have the usual names such as George, Crown, Chequers and Swan. By then there were twenty-one documented inns in the town, or just outside it to the N. Parts of three medieval inns survive: the former New Inn and the Golden Cross in Cornmarket Street, and the Mitre on the High Street, with a possible fourth at the Chequers nearby.

1,
p. 423

The former New Inn at Nos. 26–28 Cornmarket Street, built from 1386, comprised five (now three) shops on Cornmarket, fronting a courtyard inn. The front range was restored in 1950–2 (the corner with Ship Street) and in 1986–7, as student accommodation and commercial premises. Both restorations used much new timber, and the fenestration is largely an invention. Nevertheless, the 1980s work was ground-breaking for Oxford, and was carried out with a surer understanding of the building's earlier state and functions. The N range had an open hall, timber-framed to the s and jettied over a stone wall. From the entrance between two of the shops the traveller reached a courtyard, flanked by E–W wings linked by a gallery, some of which survives. The physical evidence suggests that this was built at the same time as the wings – indeed the inn would not have worked well without it, since it allowed communication between the upper rooms. The Golden Cross (previously Gingiversinn, then the Cross), where the courtyard plan is still intact, was a New College property in 1387/8. The N range is the oldest part, dated to 1534/5, with a dormitory-type layout (see also wall paintings, p. 23). Early fabric also survives at the Mitre, documented as Bicester's Inn from the C14, which became part of the original endowment of Lincoln College in 1429. It has a medieval cellar.

The Chequers, s of the High Street, could do with further invest-igation. Its C15 features include a stone panel with three highly decorated quatrefoils and a headless figure. This does not seem to be an overmantel, and may not be *in situ*.

Salter's survey sets out the intensity of SHOPPING in the Cornmarket and High Street: in 1279 there were 147 shops, concentrated around Carfax.* Most of these were in Northgate Street (now Cornmarket) and the High Street, probably because Great Bailey (Queen Street, where the butchers' stalls were) and Fish Street (St Aldate's) were not places conducive to other trades. The spicery, selling exotic goods, was between St Mary's and All Saints churches on the High Street, and there were goldsmiths w of All Saints. Bookbinders and parchment makers could be found near the University, in Catte Street.

Some of these shops were like market stalls – though they could be locked up at night – and these were sometimes grouped in properties called 'selds'. The frontage shops became, over time, part of the property behind, and today's pattern of shops with alleys beside on the s side of the High Street is a relic of the need for access to the rear property. No structural evidence survives in Oxford for the characteristic wide-arched windows and narrow doorways of medieval shops, though parts of the timber frames of those at Nos. 26–28 Cornmarket can be seen inside. This arrangement of shop with living accommodation above is found throughout the C13 to C15. Heating was an issue, and perhaps a fire downstairs may have served for heating and cooking, as well as for the workshop process, if required. Coroners' records of fires in Oxford show that some tradesmen slept in their shops, which probably doubled as a family room.

C17 and early C18 town houses

Comparing Agas's map of 1578 and Loggan's in 1675 shows a considerable increase in the density of housing in the centre of Oxford, owed in part to the need to expand college accom-modation (*see* pp. 25ff). This expansion brought with it a more general growth in the economy of the city, where evidence of new building survives, particularly in the High Street, in Pembroke Street (including after the fire of 1644) and in St Aldate's. The city walls were also falling into disrepair, and in Ship Street and to an extent in St Michael's Street, mural landowners appropri-ated walls and bastions and built new houses against them. There was also new building outside the walls. On the N side of Broad Street, Kettell Hall was built in stone *c.* 1620 by the President of Trinity College, as a property to rent to college members. Holy-well Street was developed about the same time, while later C17 development extended up St Giles' to the N.

*H.E. Salter, *Mediaeval Oxford*, Oxford Historical Society (1936).

TIMBER FRAMING is very much in evidence in this period; the prohibitions applied in London did not extend to the provinces. There are surviving timber houses dated 1588 and 1613 in Magpie Lane on the S side of the High Street, and at Nos. 42–43 on the N. Nearer Carfax, Kemp Hall at No. 130 was built in 1637 at right angles to the street on the rear of a burgage plot. Thomas Smith, mayor and M.P., built his timber-framed town house

p. 447

('The Old Palace') S of Carfax in 1622–8, placed gable-end to the street to use the length of the plot. His near neighbour Thomas Seymour, Manciple of Corpus Christi College, built in 1637 a multi-purpose timber-framed wing – partly domestic, partly business premises – to the rear of his earlier three-storey house at No. 84 St Aldate's. Many of the Pembroke Street and Holywell Street houses of the period are also timber-framed. Nos. 38 and 39 Pembroke Street were built as a pair in the late C17, though Nos. 17–18 of c. 1600 opposite are of stone, while Nos. 13 and 14 have stone and timber. After the fire of 1644, Pembroke Street also shows the development of the standard post-medieval TOWN-HOUSE PLAN, as at Nos. 38 and 39: one bay wide, with a passage from the front door to the rear and the staircase to one side, perhaps wrapped around the chimneystack. This was very suitable for properties which combined business and domestic uses, and has been interpreted as a rural lobby-entry plan turned through 90 degrees. It was also suitable for rear access when the streets were still unpaved, keeping inside and outside separate. The hall-and-staircase plan seems to be later, and in Oxford probably goes with the paved streets after 1771 and a desire for a more polite 'meeting and greeting' area inside, separate from the living rooms.

The development of Holywell Street began after 1613, when houses were needed to replace those removed when the Schools Quad was rebuilt. With less pressure on space, there are often two rooms to the street frontage (e.g. Nos. 13 and 35), though some developers built a pair of houses on a single plot (e.g. Nos. 15 and 16). Timber-framed survivals include No. 20 (1635) and No. 35 (1626), the latter dated on its oriel brackets. Where it was necessary to build a timber-framed house between existing buildings, 'platform construction' was used: the ground floor is built in the normal way, then used as a platform on which to build the upper storey. It can be identified where the pegs for the upper floor are hammered in from the inside – cheaper than erecting scaffolding, but with the downside of water ingress via the peg-hole. The rear building at No. 84 St Aldate's was built this way, as was part of the C17 houses at Nos. 7–8 Brewer Street.

EXTERNAL DECORATION is an enduring feature of C17 houses in Oxford. Gables abound, and the oriel window provided a canvas to display the date and the owner's initials. The fleur-de-lys decoration on the doorway of No. 17 Holywell Street is by *Thomas Holt*, the Yorkshire carpenter, who lived there in the early C17. A similar design also appears on a doorway at Kemp

p. 447

Hall (1637). Pargeting features at the Old Palace, and historic images show it on other timber-framed houses. The refronting of medieval houses was also an opportunity to make a fashion statement: No. 126 High Street was given a spectacular new façade with Ipswich windows in the late C17,* and the enlarged Mitre Inn bears the date 1631 on the bracket of an oriel at the rear.

INTERIOR DECORATION of the period included wall paintings and ceiling plasterwork. One of the most accessible C17 domestic interiors is that of Kemp Hall, which retains an original staircase, fireplace and overmantel. For Renaissance PLASTERWORK, St Philip's bookshop at No. 82 St Aldate's is a fine example, equivalent in status to the magnificent work nearby at the Old Palace, and elsewhere in Oxford such as at No. 90 High Street, No. 20 Holywell Street, Frewin Hall and in the colleges (*see* p. 30). The Golden Cross has a remarkable set of C16 WALL PAINTINGS, conserved and on public view. Those from *c.* 1570–80 have a red and black geometric pattern partly painted in cloth, a rare survival of great importance. In the westernmost room are grotesques, pillars and arabesques with foliage and heads, in white on a black ground, dating from *c.* 1550–60. Some thirty years later the room was panelled, but a frieze was left above on which another design was painted, datable between 1595 and 1604. Often open to public view are the wall paintings of *c.* 1570–80 in the upper room at No. 3 Cornmarket Street. The survival of these – and some others in college buildings – is largely due to the change in fashion around 1600, when they were covered by panelling.

Comparing Loggan's map of 1675 with Isaac Taylor's survey of 1750 shows that the built-up area hardly increased, reflecting the decline in Oxford's population during the C18. The essentially C17 aspect of the city thus survived into the C19, as seen in views such as those of Malchair and Buckler. However, there was a widespread movement to refront the C17 houses, while largely retaining the internal layouts and features, as for example at No. 20 Holywell Street. Nos. 7–8 Brewer Street was smoothed and rendered in the C18, when sash windows replaced the former casements. Close examination showed that these sashes did not fit properly into the rebated casement frame. The later phases here also show the introduction of softwood from the Baltic and new forms of roof truss with suspended kingposts, derived ultimately from the Italian Renaissance. Baltic timber is often recognizable by its port-of-origin markings (some are visible in the rebuilt roof of the Sheldonian Theatre), and was most popular in the late C18 and early C19. In an early C19 extension to the Brewer Street house was a short-lived phase in which cast-iron nails were used in conjunction with softwood laths.

In the early C18 the wholesale demolition of houses to form Radcliffe Square forced their inhabitants out of the central area. New houses were built for rent elsewhere, often still

*Named after Sparrowe's House of *c.* 1660–70 at Ipswich; the type has an arched middle light, sometimes reaching higher than the others in the manner of a Venetian window.

timber-framed and in pairs, such as Nos. 9–14 Longwall Street, with mirror-image plans about central stacks, and Nos. 16 and 17 in stone, brick and timber, which all seem to be speculative housing. In Holywell Street there are also early C18 houses such as Nos. 61–62 with flat hoods supported by scrolled brackets above the front doors. But there is a conservatism in house design – the classically inspired terraced house came late to Oxford – that was probably due to the ownership pattern in the central area. Most of the land here belonged to the colleges, and short leases encouraged leaseholders to let them run out rather than to undertake repairs.

REFORMATION TO INTERREGNUM

The sixteenth century

The REFORMATION had drastic effects on Oxford and its University. By Henry VIII's Dissolution of the religious houses, large areas of the city effectively became derelict, especially in the SW quarter with the friars' houses. The monastic colleges were also abolished, and the future of the remaining colleges briefly hung in the balance. Under Edward VI (1547–53) even the University's library was stripped of its books and furnishings. By that time Oxford had at least been made the seat of a bishop, subdividing the huge medieval diocese of Lincoln. Henry VIII first directed that Osney Abbey should serve as Oxford's cathedral, but in 1546 the truncated church of St Frideswide was adopted instead, as part of the dual foundation of Christ Church, successor to Wolsey's stalled Cardinal College (*see* p.14). Thus Osney Abbey too fell into ruin.

The early 1550s found the University at its lowest point, with members numbering barely three-fifths of the late C15 total. Under Queen Mary there was a modest revival, and two new COLLEGES were founded, St John's by Sir Thomas White, merchant taylor of London, 'to strengthen the orthodox faith', and the College of the Holy and Undivided Trinity by Sir Thomas Pope, a civil servant and fervent Catholic, both in 1555 – the same year in which two of Oxford's three Protestant martyrs, Latimer, Ridley and Cranmer, were burnt at the stake in Broad Street. Both establishments, as we have seen, took over the premises of monastic colleges, and both have little left of their own early years. In 1571 Jesus College followed, the Protestant foundation of Dr Hugh Price, Prebendary of Rochester Cathedral and Treasurer of St David's Cathedral. Two sides of its First Quad are of the 1570s, with some original windows, and these are of the Elizabethan type, i.e. mullioned windows no longer with arched lights. There was no gate tower, but the main entrance was originally stressed by superimposed half-columns, apparently the earliest explicit display of CLASSICISM in Oxford – though sadly unsophisticated by the standards of Cambridge, where the

first of the elaborate gateways at Dr Caius's college had appeared
in the 1560s.

C16 instances of the Renaissance style at Oxford otherwise fall
chiefly under the heading of INTERIORS. The first datable examples come from the panelling of college halls, an improvement
that the C16 increasingly favoured: a frieze on the linenfold panelling of 1533–5 at New College hall, and the figured relief panels
dated 1541 placed amid the linenfold in the hall at Magdalen.
Also of the 1540s is the thin-ribbed ceiling in the Warden's Lodgings at New College, to a design derived from Serlio, and there is
a renewed thin-ribbed ceiling of early C16 pattern in Brasenose's
Old Library. Under Protestantism it was possible for the heads
of houses to marry, and at many colleges their lodgings were
expanded and enhanced in the C16 and early C17. The best such
interior is in the President's room at Corpus Christi gate tower,   34
with arcaded panelling of Elizabethan type and an ornamented
plaster ceiling with pendants, of a design that recurs elsewhere in
Oxford and the county. Panelling brought into the colleges from
town houses includes an iconographically interesting interior
with reliefs dated 1575, now at University College.

The ELIZABETHAN period saw numbers at the University
rising again, especially of commoners, i.e. students not supported by the foundation, who often paid fees and expected good
accommodation in return. One result was a steady upgrading of
older ranges, and their enlargement by making an extra storey in
the roof space ('cockloft' is the Oxford term) by means of attic
gables and dormers. Even All Souls, which has never admitted   p. 12
undergraduates, acquired dormers in the C16–C17, since replaced
in stone. The last C16 decades also brought new building, or
rebuilding, to the colleges. At Merton, for example, part of the
street range was rebuilt in 1589–91. Just to its E is the retained
frontage of St Alban Hall, built in 1599 for one of the few
academic halls then still extant, but now part of Merton. This
features a classical doorway with paired half-columns and the
motif of continuous or running hoodmoulds which step up and
down over the window heads. The windows have mullions and
arch-headed lights of late medieval type. So this somewhat overlooked design appears to be Oxford's earliest surviving instance
of a Gothic elevation with a classical portal, characteristic of the
first half of the C17. Mention should also be made of St Edmund
Hall, which has a range of c. 1596. At the same time, in 1596–8,
St John's College acquired a library building (*see also* below),
placed behind the old monastic quad and originally linked to
it by a cloister. Otherwise the arrangement was conventional, a
first-floor library room with chambers below.

The colleges and the University in the early seventeenth century

A new chapter for COLLEGE ARCHITECTURE begins with the
Fellows' Quad at Merton, built in 1609–10 under Sir Henry
Savile. Warden Savile assembled a team of builders from his

native Yorkshire to do the work, led by the masons *John Akroyd the elder* of Halifax and *John Bentley*. The first new quadrangle to be added to any of the existing colleges, it was also the first to have three full storeys – well behind Cambridge, where the Old Court of King's College adopted the form in 1441. A fourth storey is provided in the attics, with gable windows all round the outer sides, alternating with chimneys – fireplaces in the best rooms being expected by this date. The windows have arched lights and running hoodmoulds, the doorways have pointed heads, but the frontispiece on the inner S side is classical, with pairs of classical columns and entablatures arranged in four tiers, according to the sequence laid down by Serlio. The frontispiece motif of superimposed orders is of Italo-French descent, appearing first in England at Somerset House in London around 1550. Later iterations include those at Burghley House (Peterborough) in the 1580s, at Stonyhurst (Lancs.) in the 1590s, and at Hatfield House (Herts.) in 1608–12. Jacobean Oxford took this aristocratic motif to heart.

The influence of Fellows' Quad appears strongly at the first C17 newcomer, Wadham College, founded by the Somerset landowners Nicholas and Dorothy Wadham and built in one go in 1610–13. They too brought in builders from their native county, headed by the experienced master mason *William Arnold*. As at Merton, the work is extremely well preserved. The quad is large and nearly square, again of three full storeys plus an outward-facing gable storey, and exactingly symmetrical on the frontage and the inner faces, as Renaissance principles required. On its far side there is the hammerbeam-roofed hall on the r., the chapel on the l. The chapel continues the T-plan of New College, so it is actually the antechapel which matches the hall, while a wing housing kitchen and library projects at right angles behind the hall to balance the chapel proper. The central focus of the quad is a grand composition of a frontispiece with coupled columns in four orders, and the doorways on each side are classical too, with open pediments. But the hall and antechapel windows are Gothic, if only in an allusive way, and the chapel has windows that are orthodox Perp. Parallels for the latter may be found at all three of the Turl Street colleges: Jesus, where the hall of 1616–18 has cusped Gothic lights, albeit in flat-headed windows, and the chapel of *c.*1619–1636 has windows again almost indistinguishable from C15 Perp; Exeter, for the Perp-windowed hall of 1618 with a bay window just like that at Jesus; and Lincoln, for the chapel given by Bishop Williams of Lincoln in 1629–31 as part of the new quad there. At Trinity the hall of 1618–20 also presents a late medieval appearance, except for the storey of chambers placed on top. Gothic too are the hall and chapel of St Mary Hall, now part of Oriel, as rebuilt in double-decked form in 1639–40.

The juxtaposition of STYLES, classical and Late Gothic, requires explanation. There is a story referring to St John's College, Cambridge which sheds light on the problem. In 1623–5 a new library was built there, with money given by the same Bishop Williams of Lincoln. Williams was shown the plans, and at first objected to the proposed Gothic windows, but relented when told that 'men of judgment like the best the old fashion of church windows, holding it the most meet for such a building'. Yet above the windows of the building as constructed are cornices, and these are firmly of classical inspiration. Such mixtures at both universities are quite distinct from the more familiar versions of the Elizabethan and Jacobean styles, seen e.g. at the great houses of Robert Smythson, in which late medieval silhouettes of towers and pinnacles are dressed in classical forms derived from Italy or the Low Countries, strapwork and fretwork and obelisks, as well as the classical orders. For, in an academic context, buildings were expected to stress institutional continuity and a commitment to the religious imperatives inherited from the Middle Ages. An architectural vocabulary derived from the late medieval colleges – crenellations, pinnacles and traceried or arch-headed windows externally, fan-vaults and hammerbeam roofs inside – made this explicit, without ruling out localized displays of more up-to-date classical forms. The latter were typically combined with heraldry and in grander cases also sculpture, as was done at the Wadham frontispiece. This stylistic hybridity flourished at Oxford, even more than at Cambridge.

Only one early C17 project at Oxford shows the consistency of Wadham and indeed a yet greater, an almost ruthless, consistency: the Schools Quadrangle of the UNIVERSITY. Properly p.329 speaking, only the lower floors were for the schools or lecture rooms, whereas the third floor was a library extension. In this enterprise Sir Thomas Bodley was greatly involved. It was not the first library extension. Just before the Schools Quadrangle was begun, in 1610–12, Bodley added a spacious lateral vestibule to the Divinity School, the Proscholium, and a room above as an extension to the renovated Duke Humfrey's Library – what is now called Arts End. Afterwards, in 1634–7, a second addition 44 was made at the other end of Duke Humfrey corresponding in shape to Arts End: Selden End. The ground floor of this holds the Convocation House and the Chancellor's Court. With these 48 two ends the building thus became H-shaped. The Proscholium is externally panelled with long, lean Gothic blank panelling, an exaggeration of that on the C15 E wall of the Divinity School; its vault is an elaborate lierne vault; and the greater windows of both cross-ranges are firmly Gothic too.

The Schools Quadrangle was begun in 1613 and completed c.1620, replacing the old Schools of 1440. The master masons were *Akroyd* and *Bentley*, as at the Proscholium and at Merton before that: for Bodley was a former Fellow of Merton and a friend of Warden Savile, who helped to see the project through after Bodley's death in 1613. The quadrangle is exactly square, with the Proscholium as its W range and square staircase enclosures in the angles. Its walls are subdivided by moulded strings and have absolutely regular fenestration, the main windows all being of the same size and shape, of four tall lights with cinquefoiled heads. Other Gothic motifs include the crenellated parapet with crocketed pinnacles, like those of the Divinity School but no longer placed on top of buttresses in the medieval way, and the lierne vault under the gate tower. The gate tower as such of course is also a standard Oxford motif. But here the inner side has a classical frontispiece prouder than any in England, with a full five orders of coupled columns. The gateway itself also has the most impressive C17 door of Oxford, of twenty-eight panels with painted shields (the door to Oriel College is similar).

One more COLLEGE, Pembroke, was founded before the Civil War, in 1624. Like Jesus College it took over an existing academic hall, and its first quad was completed slowly. The C17 buildings are modest and have been drastically gone over. At other colleges there is much more. The most complete ensemble is at Oriel, which was entirely rebuilt in 1620–42. Here the name of the mason or designer is lost. The new quad introduced a fresh motif to Oxford, that of the Jacobean shaped gable. But whereas in country houses shaped gables usually appear a few at a time, in Oxford colleges they are small and go right round the quad. The windows still have arched heads linked by running hoodmoulds, but for the first time at a college quad they are of uniform type (two lights), rather than alternating between single and double lights for the studies and chambers. The arrangement of hall and antechapel towards the quad is like that at Wadham, the antechapel only by some ingenious manipulating, here with a bay window for each. Their window tracery is again allusively Gothic, and between them is a canted porch (not a full frontispiece) with openwork lettering in the balustrade, a motif of French C16 origin. Next to rebuild was University College, beginning in 1634 under the master mason *Richard Maude*, and completed in the 1670s. Its mid-C17 classical frontispiece has gone, but the hall and chapel windows to left and right have quasi-Gothic tracery like that of Oriel, and little shaped gables run round the other sides.

The shaped gable motif can be followed to Second Quad of Jesus College, begun by *Maude* around 1639 and not finished until *c.* 1712, and to St John's, where the little Cook's Building of 1642–3 etc. has an even more fanciful version. By then St John's had completed its own second quad, Canterbury Quad, given by Archbishop Laud and built in 1631–5. It is at once a milestone and a dead end in the course of Oxford architecture. Its E and W sides have cloisters or rather loggias of classical columns, like the arcades in Jacobean mansions or those at Nevile's Court at Trinity College, Cambridge (completed in 1612), here with rich classical details and a sequence of busts in the spandrels. Each side also has a frontispiece more fully classical and indeed Baroque than any yet seen at Oxford, with a giant broken segmental pediment on paired columns, and a broken pediment on single columns to frame the central statue. Yet even here the rest of the upper storeys and the whole N and S sides (with the 1590s library incorporated) are handled according to the Gothic Oxford tradition, and in the passages behind the frontispieces there are fan-vaults. The masons of the work are known – they included *Richard Maude*, who provided the shaped gables on the outer N side – but the designer or designers cannot be pinned

43
45
p. 276

down with certainty, not least because it took three successive masons or teams of masons to finish the quad.

A similar commitment to a bolder and more fully understood classicism – though not the pure Neo-Palladian manner of Inigo Jones – prevailed in 1632–3, when *Nicholas Stone* built gateways for the University's new Botanic Garden next to Magdalen Bridge. Stone was a sculptor as well as an architect-mason, and was also the son-in-law of the Dutch architect Hendrick de Keyser. The latter's designs may have supplied the motifs of the main gateway with its intricate play of pediments, one in front of another or one inside another, and its intermittent vermiculated rustication. It is Oxford's first entirely classical building. Only slightly later was the classical gateway of 1633–5 at Magdalen by *John Christmas*, a London mason and sculptor, of which only fragments survive. Then there is the s porch at St Mary's church, added under the aegis of Archbishop Laud as Chancellor of the University in 1637. Often attributed to Nicholas Stone, it was built by *John Jackson*, the mason who completed Laud's Canterbury Quad. The top has another fantastic interaction of pediments, placed on detached twisted columns of Italian derivation, but as at St John's there is a fan-vault inside. 50

This great period of building reflected a dramatic growth in numbers at the University, in the 1630s especially. Admissions in that decade have been calculated at 5,300, up from just under 3,600 in the 1590s. It has been claimed that a larger proportion of the population of England received a higher education in the 1630s than in any decade until the interwar years of the C20.

The CIVIL WAR put an end to architectural investment, as Oxford became the headquarters of Charles I and his queen from 1642, then the object of a siege by Parliamentary forces in 1645. Earthwork defences were built by the Royalists outside the city walls, of which a few features remain in the gardens of Wadham College and along Mansfield Road. The siege led to great destruction in the suburb of St Clement's E of Magdalen Bridge, and the incoming Parliamentarians demolished most of the Castle as a precaution, but the city itself was spared much damage and there was no wholesale iconoclasm.

In the calmer 1650s building work resumed at some colleges, and it was even possible for one to initiate its second quad by means of a new chapel and library. This was at Brasenose under *John Jackson*, and the dates are 1656–64. The work remains the most telling example of the transitional state of Oxford's architecture and decoration before the age of Wren. Thus the side windows of the chapel are of the allusive Gothic of Oriel, Wadham and University colleges, but the traceries of the E and W windows and the antechapel windows – this being Oxford's final T-plan chapel – are much further removed from medieval forms. Moreover, the windows are framed by overlapping pilasters and richly treated classical friezes. A cloister is attached and continues at right angles under the library (now enclosed), and the forms of this, including oculi and upright oval windows, are completely free from Gothic, while the portal is of Nicholas Stone character, with columns and a wide-open pediment. The skyline is of pediments alternating with battlements on the library, elongated urns instead of pinnacles on the chapel, where the E wall finishes as a crocketed gable with concave sides. It is the climax of C17 hybridity at Oxford, and the last innovative example before Hawksmoor revived the concept at All Souls in the early C18.

College and University interiors

Little has so far been said of the INTERIORS of these buildings. Here it is useful to make a distinction between masons' and carpenters' or joiners' work, which proved much less beholden to medieval forms. On the masons' side, Gothic FAN-VAULTS remained current, as we have seen, with further examples of the 1620s–30s in the gate towers of Oriel and University College. The culmination is the spectacular fan-vault over the hall staircase at Christ Church, built c.1632–40 and carried on a single slender pier. It was reportedly built by one *Smith* of London, whose precise identity cannot be established. At the Convocation House of 1634–7 there was a fan-vault of plaster, the earliest recorded plaster vault in Oxford, but this was replaced in stone in the C18. The glorious plaster fan-vault of Brasenose chapel is a special case, based as it is on the reused early C16 chapel roof taken from St Mary's College.

49

Other PLASTERWORK at the colleges belongs to a wider group with examples also in the best houses of the town (*see* p.23). Thin ribs in interlaced geometrical patterns with single floral and similar motifs in the panels, sparse or abundant, are for instance in the room over the gate tower at Corpus, the ribs more substantial than most, and in the tunnel-vaulted Old Library of 1598 of All Souls. Broad bands instead of thin ribs, a later form, occur in Merton library in 1623 and, with closely interlaced flower trails, in the Tower Room at Oriel, i.e. c.1622. The same room has Oxford's only C17 plasterwork overmantel. Most plasterwork of the period was made by itinerants or by London-based workshops, but at the library of Corpus Christi the splendid stuccowork of 1604–5 is recorded as the work of an Oxford man, *William Pearson*. A ceiling of the 1630s at the President's Lodgings at St John's reverts to one of the early C16 designs from Serlio.

34

For the larger spaces of halls, chapels and libraries, timber ROOFS were still preferred over plaster ceilings. For halls especially the late medieval hammerbeam type remained current, if now of leaner form, as may be seen at Wadham and Oriel, and as survives above an inserted ceiling at Jesus. University College had a hammerbeam roof too, as late as 1656–7, of which a few timbers remain in the early C20 replacement. Exeter's hall is the exception, a design of thin arched braces, much embellished in the early C19. In early C17 college chapels a canted and panelled roof treatment was more common, but these have survived less well; the type is represented by the 1680s example at Lincoln.

47

Libraries also have some canted roofs or ceilings, a form that can be traced back to the remodelling of Merton's library in 1502–3. But at the Bodleian, to give it that name, both the Arts End and the renovated medieval roof of Duke Humfrey's Library are instead divided into compartments with PAINTINGS of cartouches with the University arms. There is comparable heraldic painting of 1612 in the roof of the Old Library at Christ Church, converted from part of the old refectory. Later, in 1618–19, the second floor of the Schools Quadrangle was painted with an interminable frieze of authors' heads.

Nothing has so far been said of the furnishings of LIBRARIES. There is no counterpart at Oxford to the Elizabethan library of Cambridge's Trinity Hall, a late instance of the medieval lectern-type arrangement. The earliest intact library is at Merton, as remodelled by Warden Savile in 1588–9 and extended in 1623, and this may be the very first example anywhere of a stall-system library, i.e. one subdivided by full-height bookcases, typically with reading benches or desks between. Other colleges rapidly took up this more efficient system: at the new St John's library of 1596–8, at Corpus in 1604–5 and at Trinity in 1625, all of which have since had their bookcases heightened. Duke Humfrey's Library was given the same arrangement when Bodley revived it in 1602. But when it came to furnishing the Arts End and Selden End a different system was adopted, with shelving placed against the walls, and balconies or galleries for access to the upper level. This too is the earliest English example of such an arrangement. Examples of Elizabethan or early C17 library furnishings and woodwork also remain at All Souls, Balliol, Jesus (of c. 1628, and especially good) and St John's (from Laud's library extension of the 1630s).

The furnishings at Merton library include little arched screens of 1623, smaller cousins of the major SCREENS provided at the entries to college halls and chapels in the period. Strikingly, these are in character not Gothic at all, even of the hybrid form, but purely Jacobean or Carolean classical. At Exeter's hall the screen has large pierced-strapwork crestings, which appear also on the chapel and hall screens at Wadham, all three of the 1610s and all apparently by the joiner *John Bolton*, who also worked at the Bodleian and probably at Corpus library. The later screen at Jesus hall is similar, but has lost its cresting, as has the Corinthian-columned screen at Magdalen's hall. At Lincoln's chapel the screen of 1636 shows a decided advance to a more fully classical manner.

Most chapel screens belong to ensembles of furnishings, including the STALLS which are generally integral to their construction. The ornamental forms used on these screens and stalls are common to other classes of superior JOINERY, of which Oxford has an *embarras de richesse*. Not all of this work is dated or datable, but the progression of motifs may be noted. Stumpy blank arches were current from the late C16, seen e.g. on the stall backs at Wadham chapel, as were overmantels with caryatids, atlantes or herms, as e.g. at the relocated panelled interior at University

Convocation House, panelling.
Elevation drawing by S.J. May, 1886

College. The early C17 introduced the type of panelling with four
L-shapes round a centre. Early examples are at Merton library
and the Jesus and Wadham hall screens, i.e. 1610s–20s. A slightly
later type has instead of the stubby Elizabethan blank arches a
sort of perspective effect, as at the pulpit of the 1630s at Balliol. In
Thomas Richardson's superb panelling in the Convocation House
of 1634–7 and the stall backs at Oriel chapel the perspective-
arched form is elaborated as a sequence of pedimented aedicules.
Lincoln chapel has aedicules without the perspective arches, and
Brasenose chapel (*c.*1660) has perspective arches without the
aedicules. In the Convocation House and at Oriel, Brasenose,
Corpus and University incidentally the stalls have plain balls
on the ends, 'pummels on the toppe like globes', as they were
described at New College in 1638. Yet another new motif is
ovals, mostly vertically placed. The Principal's Lodgings at Jesus
include a dignified and splendid room panelled with them *c.*1623.
Ovals also appear in the chapel screens at Oriel and at Lincoln,
and these ovals are open, not blind, according to the importance
given to openwork carving through the C17 generally.

Finally STAIRCASES, which in this period come to include
some open-well examples at the colleges, typically with turned or

shaped flat balusters. The type appears first at Oriel in the 1620s. There are more ornate examples at Merton Warden's Lodgings, where the newels have square finials and pendants, and from the 1630s at the President's Lodgings at St John's.

Church furnishings, monuments and sculpture

The screens and stalls of the college chapels were of course supplemented with other FURNISHINGS. The best individual survivals from the period are LECTERNS, for which the eagle type remained in favour, as at Exeter and Magdalen, both of the 1630s, and at Oriel, dated 1654. The type remained current into the C18. The finest PULPIT is at the Cathedral, made in 1608–9 by *William Bennett*, complete with sounding-board and ogee-ribbed crown. College pulpits of the C17 are chiefly of a distinctive type raised on slim legs. Most chapels also acquired black and white marble PAVING.

The Cathedral and the college chapels have a near-monopoly of early C17 STAINED GLASS, of which Oxford has the best collection in England. There is no better illustration of the Church of England's rapprochement with religious art under Laudian influence. The sequence begins at Wadham chapel in the 1610s with the side windows of Prophets and Apostles, done respectively by a local maker, *Robert Rudland*, and a Frenchman, *Louis Dauphin*. In 1622 an E window with pictorial scenes was provided by the Dutchman *Bernard van Linge*, whose brother *Abraham* shortly became the chief provider of glass to Oxford up to the 1640s. His fullest sequences are at in the chapels at Lincoln (1629–30) and University College (1641–2), including vividly imagined if somewhat clumsy scenes, in the manner of late C16 Netherlandish Mannerism. Just one bold window survives entire from his sequence of 1638 at the Cathedral. Re-set glass by Abraham from the same decade is preserved in the chapels of Balliol and Queen's. The other big scheme is at Magdalen chapel: large grisaille figures of 1637–*c.*1640 by *Richard Greenbury*, who also supplied a huge Last Judgment *à la* Michelangelo for the W window, replaced with a new version in the C18. 46

Oxford's CHURCH MONUMENTS of the period are also distinctive, on account of the preponderance of portrait busts, the accepted form for scholars and divines. The most interesting examples are both at Merton. Here Sir Thomas Bodley himself appears frontally, in an oval recess – an early example – flanked by piles of books instead of columns, with allegorical figures in relief as well as free-standing statuettes.* The monument is of 1615 by *Nicholas Stone*, his first Oxford work. It is in the N transept. In the S transept Warden Savile †1622 corresponds to 42

---

*Books arranged architecturally are an enduring motif of C17 Oxford monuments: Wadham chapel †1614, St John's chapel †1634, St Mary Magdalen †1635, All Souls' chapel †1665, Cathedral †1670; also the doorcase to the library of 1680–6 at St Edmund Hall.

Bodley, and he appears, with figures of great scholars of the past around, as a frontal demi-figure, one hand on a book. The earliest of these bust monuments at Oxford is at Magdalen, †1589. Among the many successors, that to President Langton †1626 at Magdalen has a canopy with small figures holding back curtains, a type associated with *Maximilian Colt* (another is at Jesus, †1630); that to Robert Burton †1639 at the Cathedral has a modest but interesting oval recess of Mannerist forms; that to Sir William Paddy †1634 at St John's is an ambitious architectural composition attributed to *John Jackson*, with a split pediment. *Nicholas Stone* did one at New College (1632), but is much more individual at his Lyttleton Monument at Magdalen of 1635, where two draped youths inspired by classical sculpture frame the inscription. At the Viscount and Viscountess Brouncker monument at the Cathedral (†1645 and †1649) the couple appear in everyday dress sitting at a table, within an architectural frame.

Of other schemes, that of kneeling figures, so frequent all over the country, is rare in Oxford. There are two at St John's (†1600, †1603), one at Jesus (†1630) and others elsewhere. Recumbent effigies still go on, but after the early C17 these were on the way out. Of these Oxford has Sir Thomas Pope and wife of *c.*1567 at Trinity and William Levins †1616 at All Saints' church (now Lincoln College library). By that time the reclining effigy, alive and relaxed, was on the way in. An early example is Sir John Portman †1624 at Wadham, with an architectural backing and allegorical statuettes. At the other extreme, small memorial BRASSES were still produced, of which the intricate designs by *Dr Richard Haydock* at Merton and Queen's have a special interest.

Other SCULPTURE includes the figures of founders and patrons on frontispieces at Wadham, the Schools Quad, St Mary's porch and elsewhere, of which very little original stonework survives, and which seems generally to have been of markedly lower artistic standard than monumental sculpture. But there is also an accomplished group of works in bronze, which in the 1630s briefly became the courtly material. The leading maker nationally was a Frenchman, *Hubert Le Sueur*, responsible for the statues of Charles I and Henrietta Maria at St John's Canterbury Quad, for the bust of the same king at the Bodleian, and almost certainly for the Earl of Pembroke's statue now in the Schools Quad.

Buildings of the town

Oxford prospered with its expanding University, the population growing from *c.*3,000 in the mid C16 to over 10,000 in the 1660s. HOUSES of the period are discussed on pp.21–4. The tentative application of classical details to the timber-framed domestic tradition in the C17 also appeared at Nixon's Free Grammar School, built in 1659 on part of the present Town Hall site. The town's pre-eminent display of Jacobean classical ornament was close by, in the form of the lavishly ornamented Carfax Conduit of 1617, which survives as a Georgian reconstruction in the park at Nuneham Courtenay (p. 708).*

LATE C17 AND C18 OXFORD

The University and the colleges, c.1660–c.1700

Academic Oxford, a Royalist and Anglican stronghold, greeted the Restoration of 1660 as a signal to resume unfinished business. The UNIVERSITY's first building project was the Sheldonian Theatre of 1664–9, which realized the executed Archbishop Laud's aspiration to provide a secular setting for academic ceremonies that had long been held at St Mary's church. Its architect was *Christopher Wren*, then Oxford's Professor of Astronomy, who was aged thirty-one when he designed it. Wren was already a mathematician and geometer of repute, as well as a skilful experimental scientist; the great sundial at All Souls is very probably his design, having been made in 1658–9 when he was bursar of the college. He was also one of the founding circle of the Royal Society, which he served as President from 1681 to 1683, though by then he was chiefly engaged on architecture as Surveyor to the King. English architecture of the final third of the C17 altogether stands under the sign of Wren.

The theatre was named after its donor, Archbishop Sheldon, a former Warden of All Souls. In the same year 1663 Wren designed the chapel at Pembroke College at Cambridge, also to oblige its donor, who in that case was his uncle. The chapel is a straightforward classical box without Gothic or Jacobean reminiscences, and the Sheldonian is wholly classical too, but with a much wider range of references: Palladio's reconstruction of the C4 Basilica of Maxentius for the admittedly awkward s façade, with its halfpediments rising against the pedimented centre; recent French architecture (Vaux-le-Vicomte) for the arcaded elevations of the flanks and the D-shaped N end; Antiquity again for the outer enclosure of herms or sculpted heads on piers; a memory of the *velarium* of Roman amphitheatres for the interior, with its network of gilded wooden 'ropes' across the painted ceiling. That ceiling was made possible by an innovative kingpost roof structure using scarfed beams (since replaced), which presented a flat surface of unprecedented breadth for England. *Robert Streeter*'s allegorical painting of the ceiling may be no masterpiece by Continental Baroque standards, but its ambitions and its didactic programme are clearly aligned with Wren's architecture.

2

p.12

p.338

---

*Properly Oxford after 1542 should be called a city not a town, but the usage was never strict.

A second University building followed, again of wholly classical inspiration, and placed like the Sheldonian to the N of the Schools building. This is the Old Ashmolean, built in 1678–83 as a three-storey combination of museum, lecture room and laboratory. The design is credited to its builder, the Oxford mason *Thomas Wood*, but the concept probably derives from a lost scheme by *Wren* from the 1660s. Its details are homelier than those of Wren, but the main portal is another grand classical accent and the carving (much renewed) is of a high order.

At the COLLEGES the picture is less clear. This was due in part to the need to complete older projects with a degree of consistency. At Christ Church for example Tom Quad was finished in the 1660s with elevations to the C16 design, and Jesus College perpetuated Maude's shaped gables of 1630s when finishing its Second Quad. But when the time came to build a wholly separate block at Christ Church (Killcanon, 1671–4) it was still given a pointed archway, combined with classical details of mid-C17 character. The main quads at Exeter and Pembroke *p.148* were completed in subdued versions of Jacobean collegiate with hoodmoulds etc., but their gate towers were exercises in artisans' classicism, neither of which survived early C19 remodelling (although Exeter's domed gateway vault of 1701–3 survives).

Wholly classical collegiate architecture again begins with *Wren*. He designed for Trinity a free-standing block, built in 1665–8. In its original form it had the standard cross-windows of the later C17 (as at the Old Ashmolean), a three-bay pediment and a mansard roof of French derivation. It also appears to have introduced the double-pile plan to Oxford, i.e. the block is two rooms deep – just a few years ahead of Cambridge (St John's, Third Court, 1669–73). Also reconstructed in its upper parts is *Wren*'s more substantial Williamson Building of 1671–4 at Queen's, where some of the cross-windows survive. They remain too on the chapel and library range in the main quad at St Edmund Hall, built in 1680–6 by the Oxford mason-architect *William Byrd*. This has window pediments in addition, and a somewhat squeezed-in motif of giant columns flanking the middle bay and carrying a steepish pediment. Byrd's other major work is at New College, 56 where in 1682–4 Wykeham's E range was made part of an open-sided quad by means of castellated wings added at right angles. The windows at both of Byrd's designs are vertically linked, as too are those at the Old Ashmolean. Another open-sided, garden-facing quad was made at Trinity in 1682, when a right-angled range was added to link Wren's building to the old quad.

Wren's final college project was the completion of Tom Tower 32 at Christ Church. His letter to Dr Fell tells much about his attitude to the Gothic style. Wren wrote: 'I resolved it ought to be Gothick to agree with the Founders worke', though this means that it 'will necessarily fall short of the other way'. So Gothic is not as good as classical, but conformity with the visible past must be preserved. But Wren also wrote that he would not be 'soe busy as he [the Founder] began'. Indeed Wren's work is less elaborate. He discontinued the angle turrets and the close panelling and made an octagonal tower instead, with Gothic bell-openings, a characteristic ogee cap, and a fan-vault below. Some of the mouldings betray the late C17 date, but the whole may fairly be called Oxford's first major episode of the Gothic Revival, its form unmistakably different from those of medieval collegiate traditions.*

Wren's responsibility for the design of Tom Tower is clear, but the two most important college projects of the 1690s, Queen's library and Trinity chapel, introduce more complex questions of authorship. The library of 1692–5 at Queen's marks the step into grand classical clarity. Its open arcaded ground floor and arched upper windows recall Wren's Trinity Library of 1676–91 at Cambridge, but the three-bay pediment on pilasters gives it a different character altogether. The master mason was *John Townesend I*, but the best claim to the design is that of the versatile architectural amateur *Henry Aldrich*, Dean of Christ Church (of whom more later), although it is likely that collaboration and consultation played a considerable part in the process. The interior is of the stall system with grandly enriched bookcases, gorgeous plasterwork and carved stone ornament, and the exterior displays the new fashion at Oxford for full-size statues on parapets as well as in niches. Trinity chapel, of 1691–4, has no clear candidate for architect, though it is known that *Aldrich* was one of the three 'able judges in architecture' consulted by the college President Dr Bathurst, and that adjustments were made to the resulting design following a correspondence with *Wren*. Here again is a fully classical building, with alternating pilasters and arched windows along the sides, a balustrade with flaming urns, and the added emphasis of a statue-crowned gate tower that doubles visually as a W tower. The interior has prodigious work in wood, of a quality not surpassed as an ensemble by anything in Britain. The limewood carving of the reredos is almost certainly by *Grinling Gibbons* himself. Names recorded for the rest – communion rails, stalls, screen etc. – are *Jonathan Maine* of London, who also worked for Wren in St Paul's and the City churches in the 1680s–90s, and the Oxford joiner *Arthur Frogley*. The naturalistic plasterwork is not inferior, and there is a painted ceiling by *Pierre Berchet*. Both these splendid buildings, library and chapel, point forward to the achievements of the early C18 at Oxford.

Late C17 college interiors

The Restoration encouraged a renewed emphasis on dignified worship, and other college CHAPELS have much to show from the period. This encompassed the completion of some existing schemes, as at Brasenose in the 1660s, or their enhancement, as at Lincoln in the 1680s (openwork communion rails, statues on the stalls, reredos carvings etc.). At University College the

---

*The Gothic doorway dated 1669 added to the Sheldonian side of the Divinity School is probably also by *Wren*.

chapel was rebuilt in the 1660s and given furnishings by *Arthur Frogley*, followed in 1694 by an especially fine Corinthian screen by a maker from London, *Robert Barker*, with carving from another hand. More modest ensembles are at Corpus (screen and stalls surviving) with work by *Richard Frogley*, 1676–7, and at St Edmund Hall by *Arthur Frogley*, 1682. The first correctly classical chapel SCREENS to appear at Oxford were designed by *Wren* in the 1660s–70s for All Souls, Merton and St John's, of which All Souls' was reworked in the early C18 and Merton's was reconstructed in 1960. All Souls and Magdalen were also given huge, coarsely painted REREDOSES by *Isaac Fuller*, who did the ceiling at All Souls as well, of which some fragments survive. The Cathedral has the oldest ORGAN CASE at Oxford in something like its original form, made by *Bernard Smith* in the 1680s, and a superbly ornamented marble FONT of 1693, made for Ely Cathedral. Lingering older traditions are represented by the fan-vaulted Baylie Chapel added to St John's chapel in 1662, and by the continuing series of eagle LECTERNS: Queen's 1662, Wadham 1691, and so on to Brasenose 1731 (a gift) and University College perhaps yet later.

College chapels also have plenty of MONUMENTS of the period, typically architectural tablets or cartouches, some rustically naïve, others highly accomplished. A rare larger monument is that made *c.*1675 for the Baylie Chapel at St John's. It has a reclining effigy attributed to *Jasper Latham*, placed on an enriched tomb-chest and with an architectural backdrop in the characteristic C17 combination of black and white marble. Otherwise the best monuments of these years are the architectural ones without effigies in the Cathedral, such as Viscount Grandison, *c.*1670 by *Latham*; Lord Mounslowe of 1683, attributed to *Edward Pearce*; and Bishop Fell †1686.

So to SECULAR INTERIORS. There is no other LIBRARY from the period of comparable ambition to that at Queen's. Jesus College made a good job of reconstructing its 1620s installation in its new building of 1676–9, squeezing in a gallery shortly after. At St Edmund Hall the little library in the 1680s building retains its wall shelving, the earliest in an Oxford college library, and some decades ahead of Cambridge (Clare College, 1729). No new halls were built, but colleges began to provide COMMON ROOMS for the Fellows, and in time these acquired panelling and carved overmantels of a quality approaching those in the lodgings of college heads. Merton's is one of the earliest, designated in 1661, with panelling and overmantel of 1680 by *Arthur Frogley*. At Lincoln the corresponding dates are 1662 and 1699, at Trinity 1665 and 1681, both also done by *Frogley*. At St John's the Senior Common Room took the form of a small extension built in 1671–3, and was panelled from the outset.* New College exceptionally also has a Junior Common Room, located within one of

---

*The colleges proved curiously less receptive than those of Cambridge to grand displays of architectural joinery at the dais end of their halls. The best examples are at St John's and Trinity, both C18.

Byrd's 1680s wings, which were built after the decision to admit fee-paying gentlemen commoners to the college. The grander scale and better facilities of post-Restoration additions to the colleges generally – fewer shared sets and unheated rooms – is explained by the expectations of students of this class, whose growing presence also helps to account for the declining academic standards at Oxford into the C18.

The University and the colleges, c.1700–c.1760

The EARLY EIGHTEENTH CENTURY was a period of great architecture at Oxford, and English architecture in its Baroque aspects cannot be fully understood without the city's contribution. At the same time, the problems of attribution already encountered at Queen's library and Trinity chapel only intensify after 1700. Of the great names, Wren had little do at Oxford after the 1680s, and of the younger generation neither William Talman nor Sir John Vanbrugh secured work at either university, though Vanbrugh was of course working a few miles away at Blenheim Palace during these very years (*see Oxfordshire: North and West*). But at Blenheim he had as his second-in-command and co-designer *Nicholas Hawksmoor*, and Hawksmoor, independently, designed much for Oxford. The two completed projects safely to be considered wholly his are the Clarendon Building of 1712–15 and the Great Quad of All Souls of 1710–35. Then there were two Oxford scholars who were amateur architects, *Henry Aldrich*, Dean of Christ Church (1648–1710), already encountered at Queen's library, and his friend *Dr George Clarke* (1661–1736), M.P., Fellow of All Souls, and benefactor of Worcester College, i.e. the re-foundation of Gloucester Hall by Sir Thomas Cookes, a Worcestershire landowner, in 1714. *Aldrich* was certainly responsible for Peckwater Quad at Christ Church, built in 1706–14, and the design of All Saints' church of 1706–10 was attributed to him as early as 1756. After Aldrich's death, *Clarke* was closely involved with the rebuilding of Queen's, begun 1710, and the incomplete rebuilding of Worcester, begun 1720, both in collaboration with *Hawksmoor*, as well as designing the detached library that completes Peckwater Quad, begun in 1717. Finally there is the immensely successful Oxford master builder *William Townesend* (1676–1739), son of the John Townesend who built Trinity chapel. William worked on all the above projects and more, sometimes with the other leading Oxford mason of the period, *Bartholomew Peisley III*. He also worked for Vanbrugh at Blenheim, and for Gibbs at the Radcliffe Camera (*see* p.42). At Queen's he is called 'architectus' in accounts, and he was certainly capable of designing buildings as well as erecting them. But to attribute such buildings to Townesend in cases where no other name is documented is not good enough.

Now for the buildings in more detail. The college projects begin in 1706 with *Aldrich*'s Peckwater Quad at Christ Church, the largest unified scheme to date. This is of fifteen by fifteen by

2, 59
60

58

65

58

fifteen bays, three sides of a quad, and has a five-bay pediment on giant columns in the middle of each side, and giant pilasters otherwise. The conception of a giant order on a rusticated basement storey is taken from Palladio via his English followers of the time of Inigo Jones. But All Saints' church, also begun in 1706 to *Aldrich*'s designs, belongs somewhere between Wren's City churches and the Baroque heroics of the new London churches built after the Act of 1710. The exterior has paired Corinthian pilasters, changing to columns for the tall N and S porches on the westernmost bay, and overlapping pilasters in the ashlared interior, which has a clerestoried attic and a rich compartmented ceiling. The W tower is a posthumous addition of 1718–20, with a steeple encircled by a rotunda of attached columns. *Aldrich* and *Hawksmoor* both made designs for a tower for the church but none of these matches the anonymous built version, although the lovely reredos of *c*.1717 is probably Hawksmoor's. A strong case can also be made for *Aldrich* as designer of the Fellows' Quad at Corpus (1706–12), another project undertaken by *Townesend*. This has as its main façade a simplified version of Peckwater, with other details such the keystoned ground-floor windows that also occur at All Saints.

So to the 1710s, the entry of HAWKSMOOR and the zenith of the Baroque. A prolific designer, *Hawksmoor* made sweeping plans for the centre of Oxford *c*.1713, plans and a model in the 1710s for the project that became the Radcliffe Camera, and plans in the 1720s–30s for rebuilding Brasenose and for a near-total rebuilding of Magdalen. At Cambridge too he made grandiose ideal designs, for a replanned town centre and for a rebuilt King's College, but nothing was done. At Oxford his genius found a warmer reception.

For the University there is Hawksmoor's Clarendon Building (University Press) of 1712–15, placed N of the Schools Quad and extending the academic quarter's presence on Broad Street. The building is monumental beyond its size, of a sombre majesty with its Doric portico to the N (Oxford's first free-standing portico), its pedimented ends, and its windows surrounded by broad flat raised bands instead of mouldings. Also the whole vertical area surrounding the windows of every other bay is slightly sunk behind the front surface of the wall. The tunnel-vaulted passage from the portico aligns with the cross-axis of the Schools. Of Hawksmoor's works for the colleges, the Great Quad at All Souls (1710–35) is the most extensive, though falling short of the intended full rebuilding. His early proposals were Baroque classical, but the gift of money from Christopher Codrington to build a great new library along the N side prompted a change to Gothic, apparently so that the library would complement the retained C15 chapel on the S side. Here is a new aspect of the Gothic Revival. Hawksmoor nowhere tried, or wished, to imitate. The 'Venetian' windows of the library range are fancy Gothic to echo the genuine Perp chapel W window, and the two tall display towers of the centre of the middle range are fancy Gothic too – a Baroque Gothic anticipated to a certain extent by

2, 59

60

Brasenose chapel. The forms at the tops of the towers are very similar to those Hawksmoor used in two of his London churches, St George-in-the-East and St Anne Limehouse. The ends of the N and S ranges are linked by an arcaded cloister with a gate pavilion, and in this design Hawksmoor allowed himself yet more freedom. The library has a very long, very noble, entirely classical interior, where the externally Gothic end windows are treated as orthodox Venetian windows, and is placed on the ground floor, a first for Oxford. The work includes a new hall, begun in 1730. The grandeur of the exposed stone of its inner walls, and the motifs of the walls and especially the dramatized plaster vault, are all typical Hawksmoor. The attached buttery is an oval room – a rare thing in England – again with an ingenious vault pattern. 62

The picture at Queen's is more involved. Put simply, it appears that *Hawksmoor* supplied designs from which *Clarke* made selections and adaptations, followed by further modifications by *Townesend* once work started in 1710. *Hawksmoor*'s authorship is easily traced in many motifs. For instance, the way the wall surface is recessed around the first- and second-floor windows on the residential sides of Front Quad is very like the wall treatment at the Clarendon Building, and the vaulting of the passage between the Doric-pilastered hall and chapel with a saucer-dome flanked by two sail-vaults is like that in the equivalent passage at All Souls. The window aprons, very cubic and entirely unmoulded, are also typical of Hawksmoor, as are the French-inspired segmental pediments lifted up in the middle of the side ranges. The front screen is characteristic of his style too, and the domed rotunda of columns above the gate pavilion is known to have been designed by him, though altered by *Townesend* in execution. No equivalent drawings by Hawksmoor survive for the hall or chapel interiors, but the hall and hall vault especially have a clear affinity to All Souls' hall. Together with All Souls' Great Quad, the completed quad gave Oxford a fresh type of composition, of three full-height ranges linked by a low screen and gateway on the model of the French *hôtel*: a lineage explicitly acknowledged by the Provost of Queen's. p. 242 61

Worcester College also acquired a new hall and chapel, though the other medieval buildings inherited from Gloucester Hall were not replaced entirely. Numerous variant drawings survive, but they do not make it easy to distinguish the specific contributions of *Clarke* and *Hawksmoor* to the work begun in 1720. Here the elements of hall, chapel and library are composed in a new and original way, hall and chapel projecting to make an entrance forecourt, and library placed on the first floor behind, with a loggia below. Progress was slow, and the entrance side has some motifs that clearly go with the later C18 completion, but the garden side is detailed in Hawksmoor's style, with unmoulded impost blocks on the vaulted and arcaded loggia and the central window arrangement derived from a Roman triumphal arch. 24

The chief work of *Dr George Clarke* without Hawksmoor is the library of Christ Church, begun in 1717. The mason was again *William Townesend*. This is also Baroque, but in a less specifically

English way. It has really gigantic giant columns rising right from the ground all along its seven bays, and an originally open ground floor like that at Queen's, here with a secondary order to the arcading. The Hawksmoorian façade of the buttery of Christ Church, done in 1722 and mixing classical and Gothic, is another *Townesend* job and may be to his own design. A wholly different project of *Clarke* and *Townesend* was Radcliffe Quad at University College, built in 1716–19 entirely as a continuation of the quad of 1634, little shaped gables and all. Its gate tower even has a fan-vault, though now with certain frankly C18 motifs. The name incidentally commemorates Oxford's greatest C18 benefactor Dr John Radcliffe, physician to Queen Anne.*

63

Other COLLEGES were busy through these decades too. The most interesting projects are as follows. Back Quad of Queen's was completed in 1706–21, *John Townesend I* acting as mason for the first phase. The quad has old-fashioned elevations *à la* Byrd, i.e. with vertically linked windows. Byrd's own Garden Quad at New College was extended by two offset blocks of 1700 and 1707 in matching style, notable as the first known instance of domestic sash windows at Oxford. Hart Hall – Hertford College after 1740 – acquired new buildings including a little arch-windowed chapel of 1716, and in 1728–32 Pembroke built a chapel too, a rusticated and pilastered box which may have been designed by its builder, *William Townesend*.† Corpus acquired a Gentleman Commoners' Building in 1737, again with *Townesend* as mason, though the uncomfortable proportions may indicate that he was not the designer. Magdalen's gentlemen commoners were provided for in the New Building of 1733–9 by another Oxford amateur, the former Fellow *Edward Holdsworth*. Meant as the first instalment of something much larger, it is strikingly plain and would be barrack-like save for the loggia all along the ground floor. Conscious conformity with older work is represented by the Robinson and Carter buildings at Oriel of 1719–20 and 1729 (the former another *Townesend* project), both with shaped gables, and by the W half of the N range at St Edmund Hall, copied in 1746–7 from the Elizabethan E half.

56

p.189

One great Baroque building, a University commission, remains to be described: the RADCLIFFE CAMERA of 1737–49, England's most accomplished domed building and the masterpiece of *James Gibbs*. The idea of a rotunda for the new library came from *Hawksmoor*, who made several designs for the long-delayed project but did not live to see the start of work. Gibbs originally supplied a rectangular design but soon reverted to a domed rotunda, placed on a new site which required the clearance of all the houses between St Mary's and the Schools Quad – an objective left over from Laud's time. Gibbs's design is much more

65

---

* He left £5,000 for this project and £40,000 for the Radcliffe Camera, and his trustees subsequently paid for the Radcliffe Infirmary (£5,692) and the Radcliffe Observatory (£31,661). The Dr Radcliffe who is commemorated in Peckwater Quad is a different man.

† Up to that time the college used an aisle of the adjacent St Aldate's church for worship, an arrangement common at Cambridge but exceptional at Oxford.

urbane and supple than Hawksmoor would have been, and the building encapsulates his style, an amalgam of Wren with the Rome of about 1700, when Gibbs had studied there. The interior with its circular arcade and balcony is as perfectly managed as the exterior. Elsewhere in Oxford, *Gibbs* designed the stone screen of 1742–3 in St John's hall, and in 1750–1, shortly before his death, he completed Hawksmoor's library at All Souls.

Before saying more about interiors of the period, the fashion for STATUES is worth comment. It began properly in the 1690s at Queen's library and Trinity chapel, as noted, and reached an early peak with the lead statues designed by *Sir James Thornhill* for the parapets of the Clarendon Building. In a niche of the same building is Clarendon's statue by *Francis Bird*, again of lead. Front Quad at Queen's has statues on the skyline too, as well as reliefs on the pediments, all heavily renewed. Queen Caroline in the rotunda of the gate pavilion there is by *Sir Henry Cheere*, 1733. The tradition of statues in the niches of gate towers also carried on. In 1719 *Bird* did one of Wolsey now on Tom Tower and one of Dr Radcliffe for University College, which also has statues of the last reigning Stuarts: James II in Roman dress (1687), Anne (1709) and Mary (1719, by *John Nost II*). The three grandest libraries of the period all have statues inside: Codrington in the library funded by him at All Souls, of 1732–4 by *Cheere*, in Roman garb; Locke at Christ Church library by *Rysbrack*, 1755–8, in Antique robes; and Dr Radcliffe inside the Radcliffe Camera, 1745–7, by the same. BUSTS are mentioned only here and there in the gazetteer, including the plaster series of famous Fellows by *John Cheere* in Codrington's library.

Interiors and furnishings, to c.1760

Many of the most important new INTERIORS of the period have already been mentioned. Some of them have PLASTERWORK by *Thomas Roberts* of Oxford, equal to the best displays of stucco-work in England from the middle third of the C18. The climax is his contribution to the Upper Library at Christ Church when this was furnished in 1756–62, where the rich ceiling is complemented by naturalistic trophies on the walls and by finely executed wall shelving with a gallery, an arrangement also adopted at All Souls and at Worcester not long before. Other work by Roberts includes his Senior Common Room ceiling of 1742 at St John's and the Rococo enhancements of 1756 to the library ceiling at Queen's. At the Radcliffe Camera Roberts worked under two plasterers from the Continent, *Joseph Artari* and the Danish-born *Charles Stanley*, after Gibbs abandoned his plan for a stone dome in favour of one of lead, timber and plaster. *Roberts* also worked in 1742 on the hall ceiling and walls of Jesus College, one of several colleges where open hall roofs were ceiled during the C18. Brasenose and St John's have likewise kept their C18 hall CEILINGS, but others were removed in the C19 or early C20, including *Henry Keene*'s Gothic installation of 1766 at University College.

More modest detailing in the Georgian Gothic mode survives in the Old Library at All Souls, designed by *Sanderson Miller* in 1750. Where lesser COLLEGE ROOMS are concerned, the style of woodcarving and chimneypieces did not change much from the late C17 to the early C18. An especially good example not from the colleges is *Hawksmoor*'s Delegates' Room of *c.*1715 in the Clarendon Building, with its noble pilasters.

The FURNISHINGS of college chapels also show continuity with the later C17, here and there with heightened architectural emphasis. That applies to *Thornhill*'s elaborate reconstruction in 1716 of Wren's screen at All Souls, and the somewhat similar screen provided slightly later at Queen's. *Thornhill* also provided the PAINTING of the ceiling at Queen's, and a new altarpiece at All Souls (removed). Generally, however, paintings at the altar end took longer to come back into favour, and it is telling that the reredos at Pembroke's new chapel in its original form and

49   that of 1738–48 at Brasenose's chapel were or are purely architectural affairs of grey marble. The custom of bringing in religious paintings for altarpieces began in 1745 at Magdalen, with a C17 picture from Spain. The revival of STAINED GLASS after the van Linge decades had begun in 1687 with *Henry Giles*'s E window at University College chapel, followed in 1696 by *William Price*'s new E window at the Cathedral. Both have been destroyed, but Price also did a new E window for Merton chapel in 1702, of which some surviving parts are now displayed again. His brother *Joshua Price* provided the new glass at Queen's chapel in 1717, and *William Price Jun.* was employed in 1736–40 for figures at New College chapel. From later in the C18 there is *William Peckitt*'s poorly surviving glass of 1767 at Oriel, and of the 1770s at New College; *James Pearson*'s glass of 1776 after *J. H. Mortimer* at Brasenose; and *Thomas Jervais*'s famous windows of 1778–85 after *Reynolds*, the pictorial apogee of Georgian painted glass, again at New College. Brass CHANDELIERS also arrived in the

49   C18; Queen's chapel has two given in 1721, Brasenose two of 1749.[*]

Major FUNERARY MONUMENTS are surprisingly rare. Busts on top of tablets were popular: see one in New College chapel (†1703), and a livelier one by *Sir Robert Taylor* at Brasenose chapel (†1745), and among the parish churches two at St Mary (†1703 and †1708, the latter by *William Townesend*). Also in St Mary is a very Italian bust in relief with a Baroque surround to Elizabeth Cary †1723, and in the Cathedral Aldrich's monu-

66   ment by *Sir Henry Cheere*, set up in 1732 to a design attributed to *George Clarke*, which has a tondo with the dean's profile. The strictly architectural type already pointed out for the later C17 is represented e.g. by the anonymous Bishop Berkeley monument (†1753), also in the Cathedral. One of the finest, again anonymous, is in the chapel of St John's: a black urn in a recess set into the wall. This is for Bishop Rawlinson, who died in 1755.

[*]The earliest dated one in Oxford is at St Thomas's church, of 1705.

A speciality of these years not yet mentioned is WROUGHT IRON. It replaced carved openwork as the favourite material for college communion rails, as at Queen's and Brasenose. Fine secular examples include the gates of All Souls' Great Quad, the gates and grilles in the hall at Queen's, the gates of the hall screen at St John's, and the balustrades of the staircase of Christ Church library and of the spiral staircase at the Radcliffe Camera. The last of these buildings also has screens and gates to the ground-floor openings made by *Robert Bakewell*, the most famous of the C18 ironsmiths. The gate to the Clarendon Building is good too, and – moving outdoors to finish – there are elaborate gates or screens by *Thomas Robinson* at the gardens of New College 56 (renewed) and Trinity, of 1711 and 1713.

C18 domestic and urban building

Most PRIVATE HOUSES of the first half of the C18 in Oxford are timber-framed (*see* pp. 22–4). By *c.*1700 a growing number of stone-built examples had also begun to appear. The largest and best of these early houses is St Giles' House of 1702, built prob-ably by *Bartholomew Peisley II*. It is seven bays wide, with quoins, a later three-bay pediment, and a superb shell-hood at the back, and has an exceptionally spacious stair hall. The staircase has twisted balusters, the usual late C17 and early C18 form; most of these at Oxford are of course in the colleges. Another shell-hood is at the house formerly called Greyfriars in Paradise Street, more probably late C17 than early C18. This has in addition an ornate portal to the entrance court, and some of Oxford's limited stock of domestic C18 plasterwork. The Baroque style is represented by the front added around 1721 to *Bartholomew Peisley III*'s house 64 in St Michael's Street, overloaded with motifs from Blenheim, where Peisley and his father both worked, and understandably called Vanbrugh House. Its five bays boast two broad giant pilas-ters, a piece of entablature above them projecting like a hood, and cubic aprons to some of the windows. Later in the C18 some houses adopted red brick, barely seen at Oxford before. Of these, No. 8 New College Lane remains; the finer Nos. 69–70 High Street was stuccoed over in the 1930s.

Some CHARITABLE BUILDINGS survive from the early C18. *Peisley II* built Stone's Court Almshouses in St Clement's, dated 1700. The little John Combes's School of 1702 at St Thomas's church shares with the more formal almshouses the motif of raised bands round the windows and the same sort of band running as a string course along the front.

The first PUBLIC BUILDINGS of the C18 have mostly not survived. Carfax acquired a building called the Butter Market, built in 1709–13 broadly in the Townesend manner and comprising a market colonnade and an assembly room for the municipal body. A new Town Hall followed in 1751–2, to a Palladian design by *Isaac Ware*. Also demolished is the rebuilding of St Peter-le-Bailey's church from 1728–40. In the eastern part of the city, the little Music Room of 1742–8 survives in Holywell Street (now with Wadham College). A simple pedimented building like an early Nonconformist chapel, it was designed by the amateur *John Camplin*, Vice-Principal of St Edmund Hall.

From around 1760 the pace begins to quicken. The Radcliffe Infirmary of 1759–67, now used by the University, gave the town its largest secular building since the Castle was demolished. Designed by *Stiff Leadbetter*, it was a near-copy of the recent infirmary at Gloucester, with a long frontage in a neutral Palladian style. A new Workhouse followed (*John Gwynn*, 1772–5), then a City Gaol (*William Blackburn*, 1786–9), both in the w part of the town. These have been demolished, but at the Castle some parts of *Blackburn*'s county prison of c.1785 remain, not much altered from their original state. They are of national importance as examples of the reformed penal architecture of the late c18.

With the University's support, the Corporation also addressed the shortcomings of Oxford's disorderly STREETS. In 1769–70 a new route (New Road, with Park End Street) was cut through the Castle enclosure, to make an easier approach to the centre from the w. The Oxford Improvement Act followed in 1771, under which a body of Paving Commissioners was set up to drive things forward, with *John Gwynn* as Surveyor. Gwynn, who had already designed bridges elsewhere, replaced the old Magdalen Bridge with his splendid rusticated structure of 1772–8. He also took down the remaining town gates, and moved the main market from the roadway to a compound N of the High Street, fronted by a grand pedimented composition of shop-houses. Other ashlar-faced HOUSES were built in widened stretches of the High Street, culminating in 1802 with the very large Magdalen Gate House on the s side. Away from the improved thoroughfares, St Giles' was also favoured for superior stone-faced houses, and outside the built-up area a few pioneering villas appeared. These include Professor Sibthorp's house of c.1780, now much altered and incorporated in St Hilda's College, the rendered Grandpont House of c.1785 s of Folly Bridge, and a group on the heights at Headington, including a charming example of 1773–4 by *Henry Keene* that now belongs to the John Radcliffe Hospital. A rarer building type is represented by the real tennis court of c.1798 in Merton Street (the shell of another, of 1637, survives s of the High Street).

Back in the town centre, the arrival in 1790 of the OXFORD CANAL effectively created a new industrial quarter N of New Road. The canal's basin and wharves have gone – Nuffield College occupies much of the site now – but the company's first offices of 1797 by *Daniel Harris* survive in modified form as the entrance building of St Peter's College.

The University and colleges in the late c18

Building at the COLLEGES slackened markedly in the later c18. The chief explanation is the steady reduction in membership. A few figures make the pattern clear. The total number of entrants to twelve representative colleges throughout the 1710s amounted to 1,825.* By the 1750s this had slumped to 992. A modest but uneven recovery followed: 1,162 in the 1760s, 1,338 in the 1770s, 1,415 in the 1780s, 1,350 in the 1790s. Architecturally this encouraged a concentration on upgrading the colleges' facilities, rather than the bold expansion of the early C18.

Another change was the eclipse of both the amateur architect and the master builder as designers of new projects. Instead, college work after c.1760 was dominated by two London-based architects in succession, *Henry Keene* (†1776), then *James Wyatt*. As Surveyor to Westminster Abbey, *Keene* was familiar with Gothic, and by the 1760s he was an accomplished practitioner in the thin and decorative mid-C18 phase of its revival. His only work of this type at Oxford was the remodelling of the hall at University College, already mentioned. Everything else is classical. The Anatomy School (now Senior Common Rooms) of 1766–7 at Christ Church is just like a very plain private house. More demonstrative are his Fisher Buildings of 1769–70 at Balliol, with a nine-bay pedimented front to Broad Street, no longer in its original state. His best work is the Provost's Lodgings of 1773–6 at Worcester. This continues the N range built in 1753–9 to the plans by *Clarke* and *Hawksmoor* from thirty years before, but its W face is a fresh and lively design which combines Palladian and Neoclassical motifs. The external details of the completed hall and chapel at Worcester may also owe something to *Keene*. Another project was the enclosure of the ground floor of the library at Christ Church in 1769–72, where the internal details are again decidedly Adamish.

Wyatt's first Oxford commission was also his largest, Canterbury Quad at Christ Church, begun in 1773, when he was only twenty-seven, to replace the old buildings of Canterbury College. It is largely plain except for the entrance, which is treated as a *p.138* triumphal arch with Doric half-columns without bases, the first large-scale use of this Greek convention in British architecture. The only other complete college building by him is the library at Oriel, of 1788–96. This is a very elegant classical design of 73 seven bays with unfluted Ionic upper columns and an apse with a screen of columns inside. The shelving is of the wall type, as also adopted at Christ Church library.

Elsewhere, Wyatt was chiefly in demand for the completion or remodelling of major college INTERIORS. At Worcester he designed accomplished Neoclassical schemes in 1783 to finish the hall and chapel, both of which were overlaid or replaced in the 1860s–70s by *Burges*'s redecoration, only for the hall to be restored to a version of Wyatt in the 1960s. The library interiors at New College (1778–9) and Brasenose (1779–80, with another apsed end and column screen) have survived better. For the projects after 1780 his style switched to Gothic, with which

*Balliol, Brasenose, Christ Church, Corpus, Lincoln, Magdalen, Oriel, Pembroke, St John's, Trinity, University College, Wadham.

Wyatt was quite as much at home as with classical. These have lasted less well, most having been weighed in the balance of Victorian medievalism and found wanting. So there is now little or nothing to see of Wyatt's plaster vaulting and other introductions at the chapel and hall at New College (1786–94), the hall at Merton (1790–2), and the hall and chapel at Magdalen (1790–3), although at Magdalen chapel his vaulting was used as the basis for *Cottingham*'s renovation in 1830–3 (*see* p.50). That leaves chiefly the old hall and the library at Balliol (1792–4), where the crenellations, plaster vaults and Gothic bookcases survive, and the hall at Christ Church (1801–4), where Wyatt provided Tudor-style panelling and fireplaces, and placed the beautifully judged grand staircase under the C17 fan-vault of the entrance hall. Wyatt's builder and right-hand man at Oxford was *James Pears*, who also did a few jobs independently, e.g. the crenellated Holmes Building of 1794–5 at St John's.

The most original building by *Wyatt* at Oxford is the RADCLIFFE OBSERVATORY, which is also the only important commission for the University in these decades. Built in 1773–8, supplanting a proposal by *Keene*, it is an observatory like no other: a large and high tower with tripartite windows, its form an octagon or more strictly a canted square, interpenetrating a two-storey block with low wings and a splendid big bustle at the back, i.e. a semicircular extension. For the tower Wyatt took as his point of departure the Tower of the Winds at Athens, as lately published by Stuart and Revett: another early episode of the Greek Revival. The interiors as completed *c.*1790 are as fascinating, with the rib-like bands of the vaults and the lightweight staircase to the upper balcony.

The Observatory tower is notable, too, for its Neoclassical SCULPTURE, including the reliefs of the Winds carved by *Bacon the elder*, who also modelled the top figures, and the Signs of the Zodiac by *Rossi*, which are made of *Coade* stone. Again by *Bacon* is the seated figure of Blackstone, the great lawyer, now in All Souls' library (1784). A tour of the college chapels in these years can show monuments by some other leading sculptors, notably the diverse group by *Flaxman* (†1794–1818) at University College, and *Westmacott the elder*'s figure reliefs from the Wyatt reredos at New College, retained in its successor. The dainty wooden eagle lectern of 1773 by *Leonard Snetzler* at St John's is also worth seeking out.

THE EARLY C19

Oxford grew rapidly in the first four decades of the C19. In 1801 the population numbered 11,921; by 1841 it had more than doubled to 24,458, including some 2,000 in the lately incorporated parish of St Clement's. Numbers at the University increased too, annual matriculations rising from *c.*230 in the 1800s to *c.*400 in 1820s, after which the figure remained roughly constant until the 1860s. By Early Victorian times the University was therefore a less dominant presence in proportion to the rest of Oxford.

The simple figures disguise a more complicated story of growth and change. Academic standards had declined during the C18. Adam Smith, who came as a graduate scholar in 1740, later wrote of Oxford that 'the greater part of the public professors have...given up altogether even the pretence of teaching'. The colleges were comfortable homes for sons of the nobility and gentry, many just waiting for a living to fall vacant. Entry depended largely on patronage. The University continued to resist external demands for reform well into the C19, but some changes were made internally. Separate examinations for different subjects, Mathematics and *Literae humaniores* (Classics), were established in 1807. Residence was also more strictly enforced, and a few colleges became centres of serious intellectual endeavour in the early C19 – Oriel especially, where fellowships were now awarded entirely on academic merit. And there was the increase in numbers.

Some of the fresh demand for Oxford places was taken up by the remaining ACADEMIC HALLS, which depended on fees for their income. The largest project was the partial rebuilding of the failed Hertford College in 1820–2 for Magdalen Hall, the successor to the school which Bishop Waynflete had established alongside his new college, which was seeking a new home. The buildings were designed by *William Garbett* of Oxford, two thoroughly conventional Palladian blocks with an entrance screen between, the latter replaced after the hall was re-founded as Hertford College. The revived New Inn Hall acquired a two-storey hall block by *Thomas Greenshields* in 1832, also classical, and now part of St Peter's College. At St Mary Hall (now with Oriel College) the London architect *Daniel Robertson* designed the new range of *c.*1826, in a lively Gothic style quite distinct from the more archaeological versions already in favour elsewhere.

Several of the COLLEGES also made additions in the period, but something must first be said of the various campaigns of REFACING. This was done in many cases to make good the decay of old Headington stone, worsened by the effects of coal smoke, and sometimes also to expunge mixed-classical features of C17 origin, in line with the age's general turn to medievalism. At the Cambridge colleges most of the refacing had already been done in the C18. Hence the results look Georgian at Cambridge, scrubbed medieval at Oxford. The ashlaring of Corpus in 1804 is an early and conservative example. At Lincoln in 1815–19 *Thomas Knowles I* went further, enlarging windows and generally enhancing the C15 details. All Souls' High Street front received similar treatment from *Robertson* in 1826–7, and he also applied a new Palladian façade to the early C18 Warden's Lodgings by *George Clarke*. In 1837–8 the front range of Merton was reworked in an unconvincing Dec style by *Edward Blore*, who also imposed a lifeless Neo-Perp ceiling at Wadham chapel in 1830–1.

81

At Pembroke the refacing dates are 1829–30 (*Daniel Evans*), at Exeter 1834–5 (*H.J. Underwood*).

Exeter is also among the colleges with NEW BUILDINGS from the period, a short range of 1833–4 in C15 style, again by *Underwood*, the local architect who took over Robertson's Oxford practice after he was arrested for debt. Earlier, in 1822–7, the buildings on two sides of the cloister at Magdalen were reconstructed to a conservative design by *Joseph Parkinson*, in a divisive episode in which the antiquarian architect and topographer *J.C. Buckler* agitated in defence of the old buildings (the scholarly restoration of the chapel interior by *L.N. Cottingham* in 1830–3 was another antiquarian victory). Oriel went for hoodmoulds and crenellations in *Henry Hakewill*'s additions of 1815–17, but at Balliol in 1826–7 *George Basevi* extended Bristol Buildings in a classical style, to go with the C18 work.

p.189

Of all these architects only Basevi and Blore had a wide and diverse national practice, and generally Oxford in these decades made little use of the leading designers of the age. Of the triumvirate who succeeded Wyatt as the official architects to H.M. Office of Works, *Soane* provided some unexecuted designs for Brasenose in 1807, *Nash* made changes to Jesus's First Quad and Exeter's hall in the 1810s, *Smirke* did some new interiors at the Bodleian and the Clarendon Building in 1830–1, and that is all.

Among non-architectural college projects in this period, Worcester acquired landscaped GROUNDS with a lake in the 1810s, and The Grove at Magdalen was also informally landscaped. Early C19 SCULPTURE includes a relief of *c.*1835 for Magdalen chapel reredos and the seated statue of Dean Jackson of 1820–5 now in Christ Church hall, both by *Sir Francis Chantrey*, the pre-eminent sculptor of his generation.

p.360

The one major building of the UNIVERSITY in these years was the new home for the University Press, the chief work at Oxford by *Daniel Robertson*, built in 1826–32 in the new quarter of Jericho (*see* below). It is a large quadrangle in plan, the sides as bare as mills or barracks, but with a dynamically composed front range centred on a columned Roman triumphal arch that outdoes even Wyatt's gateway to Canterbury Quad at Christ Church. The wider rediscovery of Roman classicism in these years ran parallel with the latter end of the Greek Revival, represented by *Underwood*'s professorial house of 1834–5 at the Botanic Garden. The 1840s would bring a fusion of Greek and Roman to Oxford in the form of the new Ashmolean Museum, but that is for the next chapter.

The growth of the CITY in these years was concentrated in three areas, St Clement's E of Magdalen Bridge, St Ebbe's to the SW, and Jericho to the NW. Much of the small-scale terraced HOUSING of the period has been cleared, but Jericho retains enough to give a sense of its original character. Another active area or suburb was Summertown, N of St Giles'. Its houses were generally of a higher standard, including a scatter of villas of the 1820s–30s. Closer to the centre, the final development of Oxford's timber-framed housing can be seen at St Giles'

Terrace, built around 1800 at the s end of Woodstock Road, with proportions and detailing in line with those of brick-built terraces elsewhere in the city. But the most ambitious residential project of the period is Beaumont Street and its connections, laid out from 1822 between the s end of St Giles' and the frontage of Worcester College. With its standardized types of three-storey houses, and the consistent use of newly available Bath stone for the main frontages, the development has more in common with contemporary Bath or Cheltenham than with the rest of Oxford. Of individual houses or pairs elsewhere, the N end of St Giles' has the best collection, including *Daniel Evans*'s own Nos. 34–36 of 1828–9.

By that time the High Street was dominated more than ever by commerce, and Oxford's best SHOPFRONTS are here. Especially good are *John Plowman Sen.*'s Greek Doric colonnade of the early 1830s at Nos. 86–87 and its Corinthian neighbour at No. 84, the former coffee room of the old Angel Inn, where the columned interior of *c.* 1815–20 also survives. Other commercial or INDUSTRIAL activities of the period have left little trace. The gas works established in 1818 in the s part of St Ebbe's is recalled by Wharf House of *c.* 1830 by Thames Street, and the Oxford Canal company's headquarters of 1827–8 by *Richard Tawney* – another C20 acquisition by St Peter's College – makes a smart Greek Doric display. Nearby is the former maltings of 1823 in Tidmarsh Lane. The best remaining industrial group is by Folly Bridge, the boat-builder's house and workshop of 1827 now used as the Head of the River pub, and another boat warehouse on the s bank, of 1835–6 by *Thomas Greenshields*. It is significant that all of these businesses were placed alongside active waterways.

Folly Bridge itself is among the notable PUBLIC BUILDINGS of the period, as rebuilt by *Ebenezer Perry* in 1825–7. Oxford also acquired the Warneford Hospital, one of the earliest mental hospitals on the reformed model, built as a private venture at Headington in 1821–6 to an austere design by the Nottinghamshire architect *Richard Ingleman*. The extreme stylistic pluralism of the 1830s is illustrated by the County Hall on the N side of the Castle, an operatic Neo-Norman affair of 1839–41 by *John Plowman Jun.*

CHURCHES of the period show a similar stylistic variety, despite the general rise of the Gothic tide. Thus *Daniel Robertson*'s St Clement of 1825–8 is Neo-Norman, otherwise little used for churches until the 1840s, and *Underwood*'s St Paul of 1835–6 is Greek, with a portico of fluted Ionic columns, to complement the University Press on the opposite side of Walton Street. Underwood also designed an Early English Gothic church for Summertown (St John, 1831–3, dem.) and a similar one for Littlemore (1835–6), then still beyond the city boundary. The most conspicuous Gothic project was the rebuilding of all but the tower of St Martin, Carfax in 1820–2 by *Daniel Harris & John Plowman Sen.*, demolished in 1896. Some other medieval churches in Oxford were partly rebuilt in the 1810s–30s, including St Ebbe and St Cross, the latter in the charge of *Plowman Sen.* or *Jun.* The younger Plowman's short-lived brother *Thomas* designed the most notable FURNISHINGS of the period, when St Mary the Virgin was equipped in 1827–8 with a w gallery, chancel screen and other pieces all in a well-observed Perp style. The most interesting stained glass of these decades is the C16-style work by *J.A. Edwards* at St Peter-in-the-East, 1837. Of the NON-ANGLICAN denominations, the earliest surviving buildings date from a little before the period: the heavily altered former Catholic chapel of 1793 at St Clement's, and the New Road Baptist Church of 1798, enlarged and classically refronted in 1819 by *John Hudson*.

VICTORIAN AND EDWARDIAN OXFORD

Oxford in 1840 was not fundamentally different from what it had been seventy years before. Seven decades later, both University and city had been transformed in multiple ways. The University was no longer an exclusively male and Anglican body, nor was it quite so dominated by the colleges.* A Royal Commission appointed in 1850 had exposed much at Oxford that was lax or moribund, and by the resulting Act of 1854 the University was given a new constitution, and more college fellowships were opened to laymen. Other landmarks from the 1850s included honours degrees in Natural Science and jointly in Law and Modern History, which were followed by a widening range of humanities and science subjects into the C20. Degrees were opened to non-Anglicans in 1854, and after 1871 those entering the University at senior level were likewise no longer required to be members of the Church of England. From 1869 the age-old restrictions on Fellows marrying were lifted incrementally. A second Royal Commission led to a further Act in 1877, by which money was diverted from the richer colleges to more equitable uses, and provision for the sciences was boosted. Numbers also increased markedly, from around 400 matriculations a year at mid-century to some 1,000 on the eve of the First World War – of men only, for women could not matriculate as members of the University until 1920, long after the first women's colleges were founded.

The city expanded as the University grew, and also developed a more vigorous economy of its own. The Great Western Railway arrived in 1844, reaching the present station site in 1850, where it was joined by an adjacent station for the London & North Western Railway. Oxford's coaching inns dwindled accordingly, and much of its river traffic fell away. The professional and commercial classes increasingly moved out of the centre to new residential districts, especially to the N and E, where sub-centres developed at Summertown and Cowley, and along the Abingdon Road to the S. Boundary extensions in 1889 took account of this

---

* Over 49 per cent of the men who matriculated at Oxford in 1848/9 were subsequently ordained; for 1897/8 the figure was 18 per cent.

expansion, and in 1890 Oxford was made a County Borough. By the early C20 the city also had the beginnings of its most important C20 industry, in the form of the first Morris motor works.

All of these changes had consequences for the architecture of Oxford. Its development over the period is rich and complex, and falls roughly into two parts, with the 1870s as a time of transition.

The University and the colleges, c.1840–c.1875

The 1840s began with the century's one great classical commission by the UNIVERSITY, the Ashmolean Museum and Taylorian Institution by *C.R. Cockerell*, 1841–5. Composed with exceptional assurance, it achieves a scholarly fusion of motifs from Greek, Roman and Italian Renaissance sources, with jutting entablatures to the wings and Oxford's last external parade of classical statuary. The early 1840s also overlapped with the High Church revival known as the Oxford Movement – alias Tractarianism, after the *Tracts for the Times* published from 1833 – and it was taken as a riposte to the Tractarians when the Martyrs' Memorial was erected in 1841–3, across St Giles' from the Ashmolean and Taylorian, to a design by the young *George Gilbert Scott*. This is one of the first exemplars in the country of a new conception of Gothic, no longer Rococo or Romantic, but attempting archaeological accuracy. 'Middle Pointed' Gothic, i.e. that of the late C13 and early C14, was to this new generation the best style England had ever had. A.W.N. Pugin pleaded its case with the passion of the Catholic convert; the Cambridge Camden Society was pleading for it in *The Ecclesiologist* with evangelical passion from 1839; and similar sentiments were voiced by the Oxford Society for Promoting the Study of Gothic Architecture (later the Oxford Architectural and Historical Society), also founded in 1839, in which the Tractarians' publisher, the architectural scholar J.H. Parker, was a leading light.

So the archaeological GOTHIC REVIVAL began. *Scott*, whose earliest Gothic efforts fall well short archaeologically, was now convinced by Pugin's arguments. His Martyrs' Memorial is a bigger Eleanor Cross, and *Scott & Moffatt*'s contemporary Martyrs' Aisle at St Mary Magdalen alongside is likewise made up consistently from motifs of the latest C13. There would have been more Neo-Gothic architecture close at hand if *Pugin*'s scheme of 1843 to rebuild the Broad Street front of Balliol had come about. In the event, all that Pugin did at Oxford architecturally was a gateway of 1844 for Magdalen which does not survive. Elsewhere, the 1840s–50s brought several additions at the COLLEGES that carry forward the 1830s Neo-Perp or Neo-Tudor manner with sharper attention to accurate detail. (In Cambridge the rush had come earlier, and Wilkins's courts and ranges there are pre-archaeological.) There is a range by *Sir Charles Barry* at University College, 1841–2, a grand bay-windowed hall and adjacent residential range by Barry's son-in-law *John Hayward* at Pembroke, 1845–8, and

83, p.353

84

a range with a gate tower and oriels at Balliol by *Salvin*, 1852–3. In the same Perp spirit is the former Magdalen College School building within that college by *J.C. & C.A. Buckler*, 1849–51, and the Bucklers also reworked and extended the main fronts of Jesus College in 1854–5.

By that time *Scott* was busy with his first college commission, across the road at Exeter. His buildings of 1854–9 there are instructive for what they show of the development of the Gothic Revival beyond Anglocentric archaeology. The new Broad Street range has the traditional Oxford gate tower but otherwise uses late C13 motifs in wholly original ways, as Pugin had hoped to do at Balliol. For the soaring chapel Scott adopted French Gothic, with echoes of the Sainte-Chapelle in Paris, and a stone tierceron-vault inside. The library is more English in character, but also creative in its deployment of C13 forms (there were of course no C13 collegiate examples to follow). Scott won many other commissions at the colleges, as he got hundreds in the country. He did the library at University College in 1859–61, and the looming range at New College towards Holywell Street, a late work of 1872–7. Otherwise his engagements of the 1860s–70s at Oxford were largely restoration projects, in which he was the acknowledged expert: the chapels of All Souls, New College and University College, the halls of Merton and New College, much at the Cathedral, and some work at St Mary's church.

Other architects advanced further beyond period imitation, and with Middle Pointed materials designed in unmistakably contemporary ways. This more radical High Victorian attack on large-scale building was first seen in Oxford at the UNI-VERSITY MUSEUM by *Sir Thomas Deane, Son & Woodward* of Dublin, chiefly *Benjamin Woodward* with his younger partner *Thomas Newenham Deane*. Built in 1855–9, the museum presents a symmetrical façade with a steep-roofed middle tower, much Geometrical tracery and a didactic programme of naturalistic carving, both animal and vegetable, by the *O'Shea Bros* and their nephew *Edward Whelan*. Geographically its sources range from the Low Countries to Italy, the inspiration for the use of banded stone (structural polychromy). Internally, the materials were augmented by specimens of British and Irish stones in the polished colonnettes of the central courtyard. Ruskin was interested in the building and supported the carving project, but his growing opposition to the use of iron-and-glass construction set him at odds with the one feature of international importance, the five-naved exhibition hall, with its steep glass roofs carried on iron piers and sharply pointed arches enriched for the eye by the most daring foliage yet attempted in wrought iron. *Skidmore* of Coventry were the makers.

Woodward's Union Society chamber of 1856–7 (now library) is less iconoclastic, though the sawtooth cutting of its red bricks is a characteristically bold motif, and the interior will always be celebrated for the – alas hardly recognizable – wall paintings high up, done in 1857 by *Rossetti, Burne-Jones, William Morris, Hungerford Pollen* and others. *Deane*'s Meadow Building for

87

p.212

p.366

89

Christ Church of 1862–6, designed after Woodward's death in 1861, is stone, long, asymmetrical and polychromatic, with a tower with steep stepped gables, some naturalistic carving, and certain decidedly Venetian arches and balconies. Ruskin's *Stones of Venice* had come out in 1851–3, and Deane & Woodward were admirers of his. They did a few lesser jobs at Christ Church and elsewhere, and *Deane* also designed some of the later science buildings alongside the Museum.

The greatest exponent of polychromy was *William Butterfield*, the favourite of the Ecclesiologists but after *c.* 1850 not an imitator at all. His first building at Oxford was the new chapel of 1856–7 at Balliol, which shows his characteristic polychromy. Butterfield also designed the Grove Building at Merton of 1863–4, a less interesting design, cut down and reworked in 1929–30. But his *magnum opus* is of course Keble College, the new foundation begun in 1868 with the aim of bolstering theological education at the University. It has all his qualities and all his foibles, his forceful and even ugly forms, unexpected rhythms and violent skylines, and besides it is very sensitively planned with two quads not entirely enclosed so that space can flow into space, and the high chapel is spatially very moving. Keble incidentally is also notable for having corridor instead of staircase access to the living quarters, an arrangement later adopted by the women's colleges. 88

Of other national figures in the Gothic Revival, *G. E. Street* did no more for the University or the colleges than a restoration of Jesus College chapel in 1863–4, and *J. L. Pearson* no more than some embellishments to the restored reredos at New College chapel in 1888–91. *William Burges*, a wilder talent, was called in to transform the interior of *Wyatt*'s chapel at Worcester from 1864, unexpectedly in a Neo-Renaissance style; his remodelling of Worcester's hall in 1876–9 has been largely expunged. There is rather more of *Alfred Waterhouse*, perhaps an unexpected choice given his Nonconformist allegiances, though these proved no hindrance to a large collegiate practice at Cambridge. In 1867–8 he provided the new Broad Street range to Balliol's Front Quad, p. 97 one of the most resourceful pieces of collegiate Gothic at Oxford, characteristically High Victorian in its jerky, rugged asymmetry. His hall of 1876–7 for the college is smoother, and his Debating Hall of 1878–9 for the Oxford Union is smoother still.

The city, c. 1840–c. 1875

The population of Oxford in 1841 was 24,258, in 1871 31,404, with thousands more in the outer areas that were annexed in 1889. By 1891 the figure was 45,742, by 1911 52,979.

The expanding city required new CHURCHES, and for the rest of the C19 these were overwhelmingly Gothic. Holy Trinity, Headington Quarry is routine *Scott* of 1848–9. The High Victorian moment arrived with *Street*'s St Philip and St James p. 455 of 1860–6, a large church for the affluent new North Oxford, with a French-inspired steeple over the crossing, polychromatic

stonework and lancet windows or plate tracery. A still more
radical design is St Barnabas by *Arthur Blomfield*, 1868–72, for
the poor district of Jericho. It was to be built big and with barely
any ornament other than surface decoration. For the church
Blomfield chose Italian Romanesque; for the campanile, one of
the signs of Oxford for the railway traveller, Italian Gothic. He
had intended to use mass concrete for the walls to achieve the
largest spaces most cheaply. In the end he used concrete only in
minor ways and otherwise rendered rubble laced with brick, and
he succeeded by gilded surface decoration in achieving richness
all the same. It is probably the most interesting building by an
architect not always very interesting, though his chapel of 1863–5
at the Radcliffe Infirmary is a good and original design. The one
other violently High Victorian church is St Frideswide, Osney, by
Teulon, 1870–2, with its unfinished octagonal crossing tower and
Teulon's characteristic French plate tracery. France is also the
chief inspiration for the most ambitious NON-ANGLICAN church
of these years, St Aloysius (R.C.) by *J. A. & J. S. Hansom*, 1873–5,
which has one of the elder Hansom's typical very wide naves and
apses. The intended steeple was never built. The Nonconformists did better on that score, staking their claim on the Oxford
skyline with the spire of *Charles Bell*'s Dec-style Wesley Memorial
Church of 1877–8 in New Inn Hall Street. Its near neighbour is
the rebuilt St Peter-le-Bailey of 1872–4 (now St Peter's College
chapel), an early work by *Basil Champneys*, of whom Oxford
would see much more. This exemplifies the more nuanced revival
of English Gothic forms that took hold in the later C19. Finally
there are the continuing RESTORATIONS and enlargements of
Anglican medieval churches. The most thoroughgoing was *J. T.
Christopher*'s near-replacement of St Aldate in 1862–73. Among
the rest, St James, Cowley and St Ebbe both have blunt C13-
style work from the 1860s by *Street*, Oxford's Diocesan Architect
from 1850.

Oxford's churches were joined from the 1860s by sundry RELI-
GIOUS HOUSES, following the Anglican revival of religious orders
for both sexes. The earliest was the Clewer Sisterhood's 'Female
Penitentiary' at Holywell Manor, of which one wall from the
chapel of 1862 is all that survives. The Society of the Holy and
Undivided Trinity then built a tough Gothic convent on the
Woodstock Road in 1866–8, by *Charles Buckeridge* of Oxford, a
pupil of Scott. Buckeridge designed a vaulted chapel too, executed
posthumously in 1891–4 by *Pearson* with only a little modification.
Both buildings now serve St Antony's College. Another foundation designed by *Buckeridge* and taken forward by *Pearson* (from
1873) was St John's Home in Cowley, a nursing home which
continues in use, although here Buckeridge's vision was markedly
scaled back. Its co-founder was Father Richard Meux Benson,
who also established the male order of the Society of St John
the Evangelist, alias the Cowley Fathers. Their original building
of 1868 (now St Stephen's House) is austere in the extreme, of
ordinary brick, its top storey housing a small chapel with a rose

window and a bell-turret. Only after Benson's retirement was there a serious investment in architecture (*see* p. 62).

All these buildings are, or were, Gothic. Oxford's PUBLIC BUILDINGS of the period were likewise marked by medievalism. The County Hall of 1839–41, already mentioned, was joined at the Castle gaol site by substantial crenellated blocks of the 1840s–50s, now in hotel use. There is little municipal architecture as such, though the Corporation did modernize the water supply, with a pumping station of 1856 off the Abingdon Road. The need for public PARKS, a major concern of many Victorian municipalities, was addressed by the University's own spacious Parks, laid out from 1864 to the N of the University Museum. The most notable SCHOOLS of the period are Gothic, *Street*'s St Barnabas (originally St Paul's) of 1855–6 in Jericho, and St Edward's School in North Oxford, a public school with a big chapel and other buildings by *William Wilkinson* of Oxford, 1872–81.

COMMERCIAL ARCHITECTURE came within the Gothic orbit too. The most conspicuous example is also by *Wilkinson*, the Randolph Hotel of 1864–6, which snaps its fingers at the beautiful smoothness of the ashlar façades of Beaumont Street. Also Gothic is the former London & County Bank of 1867–8 in the High Street by *F. & H. Francis*, a non-identical twin to their bank at Cambridge.

Both these buildings are of yellow brick, a material then newly prominent at Oxford, including for HOUSES. It was used extensively in the Norham Manor Estate in North Oxford, laid out from 1860 with *Wilkinson* as surveyor. Shortly before, in 1853–*c*.1860, the more compact estate known as Park Town had been built off the Banbury Road, with *S. L. Seckham* as surveyor and chief designer. Its crescent-shaped Late Classical terraces and the use of stucco for some of its villas raised no echoes at Norham Manor, and very few among the first developments at the Walton Manor Estate to the W, where *Wilkinson* succeeded *Seckham* as surveyor in 1860. The best groups of early villas are in Norham Gardens and on the E side of Banbury Road, all high, all gabled, all brick, red or yellow in loose alternation, with mostly Gothic motifs from stop-chamfers to colonnettes with foliage capitals and occasional Geometrical tracery. Architects represented besides Wilkinson include *Buckeridge*, *E. G. Bruton*, *Frederick Codd* and the less prolific *John Gibbs*, who ventured into Neo-Romanesque at Nos. 54 and 58 Banbury Road. Other houses of North Oxford Gothic character were built further S, along Parks Road, South Parks Road and Keble Road especially, but a great many of these have made way for the University's science buildings. Casualties include *Woodward*'s house of 1857–8 for the curator of the University Museum, effectively the first of the type. Further N, the Walton Manor Estate has some lively one-and-a-half-storey Gothic terraces of 1870–3 by the young *C. C. Rolfe*. Building continued on both estates into the early C20 (*see* pp. 62–3).

Elsewhere, there is a less talked-about sequence of Gothic brick terraces of the 1860s on the Iffley Road and in Stanley Road, one of the many side streets around the Iffley and Cowley roads with respectable terraces of the later C19. W of the railway, Osney Town is an intact enclave of small Jericho-type houses of 1851 onwards. Much of Oxford's worst housing was in the old SW quarter, where in 1866–8 Christ Church provided the city's earliest social housing in the modern sense, a group of 'improved' dwellings (flats) on the London model, by *Bruton*. In the city centre, King Edward Street was cut through from the S side of the High Street, with unlovely yellow brick houses chiefly by *Codd* and of 1873–4. They mostly served the new demand for digs for students, who were permitted to live out of college after 1868. Wellington Square, developed from 1869 on the old workhouse site off Walton Street, has larger houses of similar character. Oxford's greatest mid-C19 private house is Headington Hill Hall by *John Thomas*, 1856–8, for the brewer James Morrell Jun., still in the undisciplined Italianate-cum-French of the Early Victorian years.

86

The Late Victorian and Edwardian University

The dominant figure in the academic architecture of late C19 and early C20 Oxford is SIR THOMAS GRAHAM JACKSON (1835–1924). A graduate and Prize Fellow (i.e. non-resident) of Wadham College, *Jackson* aligned himself very successfully with the party of reform at the University, and his architecture too expressed novelty, innovation and a more secular outlook after the high medievalist decades. An early calling card was his late C17-style organ case of 1876–7 at the Sheldonian. Also in 1876, Jackson won the competition for the Examination Schools on the High Street (1877–82), the University's greatest building project of the C19 and the best manifesto of its commitment to the authority of written examinations and public lectures. More than any other building, it shows Jackson's ready licence in mixing motifs from anywhere between the Italian Quattrocento and the Georgian, with a special gusto for Elizabethan and for the impure classicism of the English mid C17. Jackson was a scholar as well – he wrote books on the Balkans and on Byzantine, English, French and Italian architecture, besides monographs on St Mary at Oxford and on Wadham – and he knew exactly where he was going for motifs and what he was doing with them. Nearly always his arsenal is English. 'Anglo-Jackson' the impudent results have been called. Yet there was a tremendous panache in the way he handled big jobs, no fear of over-ornateness, no fear of noise.

98

And after the decades of Gothicism, Oxford must have loved it. For here is the list of Jackson's major works after the 1870s. For the University, the Examination Schools complex was extended by buildings for non-collegiate students, 1886–7 (now the Ruskin School of Art), and for the Local Examination Delegacy, 1895–7. In the fast-developing area around the University Museum he designed the Radcliffe Science Library, 1898–1900, and the Electrical Laboratory, 1908–10, in the Wren style. For the colleges, Lincoln, Grove Building, 1881–3; Somerville, the addition to

Walton House (not very big nor very good), 1881–2; Brasenose, New Quad, 1881–1909; Trinity, Front Quad and President's Lodgings, 1883–7; Corpus, Jackson Building across Merton Street, 1884–5; Hertford, much work, 1887–1926. p.297

Not all of this is as exuberant as the Examination Schools; the front of Brasenose to the High Street for instance is relatively orthodox Neo-Perp, except for the very pretty free carving. The most adventurous commissions are the rich Jacobethan ranges for Trinity, and the very various and protracted works at the p.297 re-founded Hertford College. Here Jackson created a Renaissance centrepiece to link the two plain early C19 ranges, with a first-floor hall placed broadside over the gateway, reached by an enclosed spiral staircase *à la* Blois on the inner side. The main 99 quad also has his Italian Renaissance-style chapel of 1907–8. To Holywell Street he carried on a version of the early C19 design, but switched to Jacksonian-Elizabethan for the New Buildings opposite, then in 1913–14 he linked them by means of the familiar Bridge of Sighs, which has details of mid-C17 inspiration – but there is altogether no end to wonderment when one studies Jackson's details. That he left Oxford a grosser place than it had been, nobody should deny, but he left it as a place with potential for architectural adventure, and for that one should be grateful.

The architect who came closest to Jackson's range and manner in academic Oxford was *Basil Champneys*, already mentioned for St Peter-le-Bailey. In the 1870s his Newnham College brought the freshly minted Queen Anne style of Norman Shaw *et al.* very prettily to Cambridge, but his Divinity School for the University there is Gothic. Likewise, at Oxford he used attractively detailed C14 Gothic to extend Scott's Holywell Street building for New College (1884–5, 1896–7), and for the new Mansfield College (1887–9), but Queen Anne for the new Lady Margaret Hall (1880–3), one of the first women's colleges. His best building at Oxford is the former Indian Institute of 1882–96 at the E end of Broad Street, a Jacksonian mixture of mid-C17 and Elizabethan. From the early C20 there are the library for Somerville College (1903–4) with sparing mid-C17 detail; the St Alban's Quad at Merton, Free Tudor (1904–7); and two markedly Jackson-C17 compositions, the Warden's Lodging of Merton (1907–8) and the gargantuan Rhodes Building for Oriel (1909–11).

Other practitioners of Gothic in the late C19 show a general quietening after the excitements of Butterfield and Waterhouse. The most distinctive work is *George Gilbert Scott Jun.*'s range for St John's North Quad, of 1880–2. He was a more sensitive designer than his father, and his façade is subtler than it first seems. Similarly *Bodley & Garner* appear self-effacing at Oxford. Their work fits in, even where they built in famous, much visited places. This is true of the Fell Tower and Wolsey Tower in Tom Quad at Christ Church (1876–9) and of the St Swithun's Buildings and the President's Lodgings at Magdalen (1880–8). For the Master's Lodgings at University College (1878–9) they went Jacobean, an instance of the stylistic latitude in Bodley's secular work after *c.*1870.

Major changes at the University in these years included the arrival of new COLLEGES, some already mentioned. The period of wholly new colleges begins with Keble in 1868. Mansfield and Manchester colleges were Nonconformist foundations which later joined the University; the first buildings at Manchester (1890–3; now Harris Manchester) are unyielding Gothic, by the Manchester architect *Thomas Worthington*. By the end of the C19 there were also five WOMEN'S COLLEGES or their forerunners. Cambridge preceded Oxford as a centre of university education for women, Girton College and Newnham College both having opened in the first half of the 1870s. At Oxford women first sat University examinations in 1878. Hostels for those working for the exams were a necessity, and so Lady Margaret Hall (Anglican) started in the same year, Somerville Hall (non-denominational) followed in 1879, St Hugh's Hall in 1886 and St Hilda's Hall in 1893. The fifth body was the Society of Oxford Home Students, later St Anne's, the last to adopt the title of 'college' (1952). Hugh's, Hilda's and Anne's made their homes in existing buildings at first, but the two pioneering colleges built extensively, and with the sense that Gothic had finally run its course. Besides its buildings by *Jackson* and *Champneys*, Somerville commissioned *H.W. Moore*, Oxford's busiest Late Victorian architect and the former partner of William Wilkinson, as well as *Walter Cave* and Champneys's pupil *Edmund Fisher*, whose Neo-Wren hall dates from 1910–13. At Lady Margaret Hall the young *Reginald Blomfield* was commissioned for the Wordsworth

104 building of 1896 and retained for its successors up to 1926, a more attractive and festive display of the Neo-Wren or William-and-Mary style, red brick with ample stone dressings in the Hampton Court manner. A plainer version of that style was adopted when St Hugh's began building in 1914–16, by *H.T. Buckland* of Birmingham. When the older colleges took up the William-and-Mary manner, as at Lincoln (*Read & MacDonald*, 1906) and Balliol (*E.P. Warren*, 1906–7), ashlar was preferred.

Meanwhile the number of SCIENCE BUILDINGS was growing markedly. *Jackson*'s contributions have already been mentioned. *p. 371* Others in the main Science Area E of the University Museum include *Paul Waterhouse*'s Dyson Perrins Laboratory of 1913–16, another Neo-Wren brick job. A fresh enclave to the NW, the so-called Keble Triangle, was opened up by means of *W.C. Marshall*'s Engineering Building of 1914, a late instance of Neo-Jacobean.

Before bidding farewell to the Victorians and Edwardians a few lines should be given to buildings for SPORT. The oldest from the C19 is a private venture, the gymnasium of 1858–9 by *Wilkinson* in Alfred Street. The University Parks have *Jackson*'s cricket pavilion of 1880–1, an early instance of tile-hanging and half-timbering at Oxford. The University's boathouse of 1880–1 by *J. Oldrid Scott*, also timbered Old English, burnt down in 1999. Cambridge built boathouses for the colleges as well, but at Oxford until the mid C20 the college clubs had ornate barges instead, some designed by architects; the survivors are no longer at their original moorings. The colleges acquired playing fields too, with pavilions; the most interesting is *Clough Williams-Ellis*'s for University College off the Abingdon Road (1914).

The city, c.1875–c.1914

By far the greatest PUBLIC BUILDING of the late C19 in Oxford is the new Town Hall by *Henry T. Hare*, won in competition in 1892. Hare intended to out-Jackson Jackson, and did. The building is also deftly planned, a skill which Jackson never mastered. A new Corn Exchange and Fire Station were built in George Street (1894–5), one of *H.W. Moore*'s more hurried designs. The same goes for his Christ Church Cathedral School (1892–4), one of the many SCHOOLS that proliferated across the Late Victorian city. The finest is by *T.G. Jackson*, the splendidly enriched former High School for Boys of 1880–1 in George Street. He also designed the contemporary High School for Girls in the Banbury Road with its pretty Cinquecento terracotta embellishments, and used similar motifs at his buildings for the short-lived Military College at Cowley (1877–81). The next episode of high interest is the group of three schools of 1900–1 by the reliably original *Leonard Stokes*. The best preserved are the former Central Girls' School (now part of St Peter's College), a Free Style design with a flat roof, and the artfully planned former Central Boys' School at Gloucester Green, with its Cotswold echoes. *Blomfield*'s buildings of 1893–4 for Magdalen College School are a dull take on English C17. Early adult education is represented by the former Ruskin College building in Walton Street, routine Neo-Wren of 1912–13 by *Joseph & Smithem*, now an outstation of Exeter College.

The expanding suburbs required new CHURCHES, many of which achieved an impressive spaciousness within the conventions of Gothic. Anglican examples include *A. Mardon Mowbray*'s St Mary and St John at Cowley (1875–93, another of Father Benson's foundations) and St Michael, Summertown (1908–9, unfinished), *H.G.W. Drinkwater*'s St Margaret in North Oxford (1883–91), and *Arthur Blomfield & Sons*' All Saints, New Headington (1909–10). A Neo-Norman curiosity from North Oxford is St Andrew by *A.R.G. Fenning*, 1906–7, for a Low Church congregation. *Bucknall & Comper*'s St John the Evangelist at New Hinksey of 1899–1900, of red brick but otherwise of East Anglian inspiration, progressed no further than the nave. Its vicarage of 1887–8 shows how good *H.W. Moore* could be when he tried, and *Moore*'s Headington cemetery chapel of 1884 displays a nice facility with Free Gothic. Of buildings for non-Anglican denominations, *Stephen Salter*'s Methodist church on the Cowley Road (1903–4) is another Free Gothic essay, *Ernest Newton*'s little St Gregory and St Augustine (R.C.) of 1911–12 on the Woodstock Road is Oxford's closest thing to a pure Arts and Crafts church, and *Williamson & Beart Foss*'s St Edmund and St Frideswide, Iffley Road (R.C.) of 1910–11 is another Neo-Norman essay, here with flint facing.

This was the greatest age for building at Oxford's RELIGIOUS HOUSES. In Cowley, St John's Home raised a tall and magnificent

106 chapel in 1905–7 by *J. Ninian Comper*, another design of East Anglian Perp character, with a richly carved stone rood screen. The Cowley Fathers added a large but plain mission house in 1900–1, designed by *Brother Maynard* under the eye of *G.F. Bodley*, who was busy with his greatest work at Oxford, the Fathers' adjacent church of St John the Evangelist (1894–1907). This is especially memorable for its broad, vigorous W tower and for the long line of Bodley's nave and chancel roof. Of the Roman Catholic houses, the Convent of the Society of the Holy Child Jesus took over a big 1880s house in St Cross Road (now Linacre College), to which *Champneys* added a chapel etc. in 1907–9. Other RELIGIOUS FOUNDATIONS include two from opposite ends of the Anglican spectrum. Wycliffe Hall, an Evangelical college and a Permanent Private Hall of the University, was founded in 1877 in a house in Banbury Road, with additions including *William Wallace*'s Gothic chapel of 1896. Pusey House, a High Church stronghold founded in 1884 and now shared with
p.257 St Cross College, built a quasi-monastic home on St Giles' in 1913–18. This is a self-assured design by *Temple Moore*, with a capacious chapel in the Early Perp manner popularized by Bodley.

The best equivalent to the Town Hall among COMMERCIAL ARCHITECTURE of the period is *Stephen Salter*'s Lloyds Bank at the widened Carfax, a Jacksonian design of 1901–4. From the later C19, Cornmarket Street and Magdalen Street acquired a distinctive character as Oxford's prime commercial axis, with showy buildings of up to five storeys. PUBS, a more widespread building type, acquired a distinct architectural character in these years without falling under the sway of any single style. The centre alone can show e.g. free C17-style terracotta at The Grapes in George Street by the prolific *H.G.W. Drinkwater* (1894), proto-Neo-Georgian by *Moore* at the St Aldates Tavern (1897), and half-rendered Arts and Crafts at *J.R. Wilkins*'s Red Lion in Gloucester Street (1905). At *H.T. Hare*'s former Elm Tree on Cowley Road (1899–1901) the debt to Arts and Crafts conventions is still more explicit. CINEMAS arrived shortly after, and next to the Elm Tree is a well-preserved early survivor of 1910–11, another design by *J.R. Wilkins*.

There is less to show of INDUSTRY. Late C19 buildings from the Lion and City breweries survive in new uses, and the façades of the late C19 power station in Osney are being retained in a new building for the Saïd Business School. *Herbert Quinton*'s jam
103 factory for Frank Cooper in Park End Street (1903) is Free Style in jolly mood. *Tollit & Lee*'s Morris motor garage (1910) is Neo-Wren, no doubt to suit the sensitive location of Longwall Street.

The advent of Late Victorian modes in North Oxford was
93 signalled in 1880–1 by the arrival of two red brick HOUSES by *J.J. Stevenson* among the Gothic villas in the Banbury Road. Stevenson was one of the pioneers of the misleadingly named Queen Anne style, and the houses' rubbed brick and white-painted woodwork are characteristic of the revived interest in mid-C17 motifs. The retreat from Gothic now opened the way to a rich variety of materials and styles in the later streets of North Oxford.

These contain a great deal by *H.W. Moore*, Wilkinson's successor as surveyor to the Norham Manor Estate after 1881, and some strikingly individual houses of the 1900s by scarcer contributors such as *E.W. Allfrey* and *A.H. Moberly*. Arts and Crafts principles and motifs also spread widely in the period, exemplified by *C.C. Rolfe*'s own Holywell Ford (1888), since annexed by Magdalen College. Of other houses close to the centre, *T.G. Jackson* designed King's Mound (1892–3), a giant among the group of dons' houses in Savile Road. Other grand residences of the period were built on the heights of Headington, e.g. *Walter Cave*'s High Wall in Pullen's Lane (1910), and on Boars Hill on the Berkshire side, SW of the city.

Sculpture, stained glass and church furnishings

Oxford is a happy hunting ground for lovers of Victorian art in every medium. That the city has so many portrait STATUES of the period is owed chiefly to the University Museum, with its effigies of notable scientists by sculptors such as *Joseph Durham, Alexander Munro* and *Thomas Woolner*. There is also the earlier seated group of Lord Eldon and Lord Stowell at University College by the Cumbrian sculptor *Musgrave Lewthwaite Watson*, 1842–8. Later SCULPTURE includes the spectacular white marble figure of the drowned Shelley by *Onslow Ford* (1892–3) at the same college, in its domed setting by *Champneys*. Ford also provided the little sculpted bronze tablet to Benjamin Jowett at Balliol chapel (1897), one of several examples of late C19 miniaturism among CHURCH MONUMENTS.

Of the Museum sculptors, Munro and Woolner were members of the PRE-RAPHAELITE BROTHERHOOD. Their fellows *Morris* and *Burne-Jones* had of course been undergraduates at Exeter College together in the 1850s, and shortly returned with their friends to try their hands at wall paintings in the Oxford Union's debating hall, as already noted. More enduring was their work in STAINED GLASS, which began with *Burne-Jones*'s remarkable Cathedral window of 1860, i.e. before the Morris firm existed. It is not at all like their later work, which can be seen at its finest in the window of St Edmund Hall chapel of 1865. *Morris* in the 1860s had found a perfect balance such as no other designer for glass at that time could achieve in any country. The Morris–Burne-Jones windows of the 1870s in the Cathedral are a little smoother, just a little languid, though again no-one else in England or abroad could work so entirely in the spirit of the material and the technique. Of the firm's later work, the set of windows in Harris Manchester College chapel of 1895–9, largely to designs by *Burne-Jones*, is a pure joy.

Any account of the Pre-Raphaelites at Oxford must also include *Holman Hunt*'s painting *The Light of the World* (1845–53), installed at Keble chapel. The mural mosaics and stained glass there are by Butterfield's favourite practitioner, *Alexander Gibbs*, whose work in glass is closer to English norms, but has a distinctive

100

90

readability and clarity of light colours. Most of the other important makers of the period are represented by superior works at Oxford, too many to list or describe here. They include the Pre-Raphaelite follower *Henry Holiday*, who worked for Burges at Worcester chapel, and the influential *Charles Eamer Kempe*, who provided the set of chapel windows of 1884–93 at Pembroke, his old college. Kempe also thoroughly remodelled the chapel in an unusual Raphaelesque style, which with Worcester chapel is one of the best instances of ECCLESIASTICAL DECORATION from the period. Among the variously enriched parish churches, the
91   most distinctive work is at St Barnabas, with its gilded apse and baldacchino and its partially completed mosaics of saints and martyrs by *Powells* (1905–11). Of individual CHURCH FURNISHINGS, the gorgeous silvered lectern at the Cathedral may be singled out, made in 1874 by *Skidmore* to designs by *Scott*.

BETWEEN THE WARS

More than half of the COLLEGES added substantially to their buildings in the 1920s–30s. Some pressed on with plans formulated before 1914, under tried and tested architects: *Jackson* at Hertford, *Blomfield* at Lady Margaret Hall, *Buckland* at St Hugh's. These new works are mostly simpler and plainer than what came before. By contrast, Lincoln called back *Herbert Read* to add the Rector's Lodgings (1929–30), still in an entirely Edwardian-Georgian manner. Other variants of late C17 or C18 English were embraced at the new St Peter's Hall (*R. Fielding Dodd*, 1929–31), at St Hilda's (*Sir Edwin Cooper*, 1933–4) and at Worcester (*W.G. Newton*, 1938–9), while St Edmund Hall's additions simply defer to the C16 and early C17 setting. The influence of Beaux Arts classicism may be felt at Trinity's partially completed library
111   (*J. Osborne Smith*, 1925–8), and more subtly in some of the works of *T.H. Hughes* of Glasgow, especially his Regent's Park College of 1938–40, later a Permanent Private Hall (PPH) of the University. Another foundation that has become a PPH is Blackfriars in St Giles', where *E. Doran Webb*'s buildings of 1921–9 combine a late C17-style front range with a Neo-Perp chapel. An altogether
110   more original project is the Jesuits' Campion Hall, *Lutyens*'s only substantial commission at Oxford (1934–6): a stylistically subtle work on an awkward site, with episodes of characteristic brilliance among its interiors. Lutyens's late works are the chief influence on *R. Courtenay Theobald*'s chapel block at Somerville, with its conspicuous set-backs (1933–4): a companion for *Morley Horder*'s rustic neo-1700 Darbishire Quad for the same college.

    The Oxford colleges brought out the stylistic responsiveness of *Sir Giles Gilbert Scott*, Lutyens's nearest rival in terms of range and attainment in these decades. He extended the Bodley & Garner buildings at Magdalen in a simplified version of the same style in 1928–30, then provided Lady Margaret Hall with

a Neo-Georgian hall and a cruciform quasi-Byzantine chapel 107
in 1931–2. Also by Scott are the first buildings of St Anne's, of
1937–8, where the idiom is the attempted fusion of traditional and
Modern which he also employed at his New Bodleian (*see* below).
The chief practitioner of this squared-rubble Oxford manner was
Sir Hubert Worthington, son of the Mancunian Thomas Worthington. He did the new New College library (1938–9) and the
Rose Lane Buildings at Merton (1939–40), and also the original
buildings of St Catherine's Society in St Aldate's, later the Music
Faculty (1935–6). As well as their squared-up outlines and gen-
erally Georgian proportions, all these works have in common a
kind of ornament of a non-period character, inspired probably by
Østberg's Stockholm City Hall and the Paris Exhibition of 1925.

Continued expansion at the colleges also led to the first off-
site ANNEXE, when Balliol took over Holywell Manor as a home
for its postgraduates. The house was extended by *Kennedy &*
Nightingale (1931–2), and enhanced by some ambitious murals by 108
Gilbert Spencer. Later 1930s outstations are more house-like, as at
J.E. Thorpe's Longwall Annexe for Magdalen and *T.H. Hughes*'s
tutors' flats for Merton in Holywell Street, or they adopt the
Cambridge expedient of residential storeys over ground-floor
shops, as at Lincoln's Lincoln House in Turl Street, by *Worthing-*
ton and *G.T.F. Gardner*.

Buildings for the UNIVERSITY show a similar range of styles,
even extending to belated Neo-Jacobean at *E.P. Warren*'s Engineering extension of 1927. A larger work by Warren is the Pathology Building of 1926–7, which is Neo-Wren. *T.H. Hughes*, always
interesting, achieved a successful Cockerellesque manner at the
Taylorian extension of 1931–8. Meanwhile *Sir Herbert Baker*'s
Rhodes House of 1926–8 first introduced the combination of
squared rubble in small blocks with ashlar dressings that proved
so attractive to academic patrons in Oxford into the 1950s. As
a composition Rhodes House is a strange one-off, like a large
Cotswold mansion of the late C17 with balustrade, hipped roof,
and two front wings embracing a small classical rotunda with
portico. Ahead of his college jobs, squared rubble was taken up
by *Worthington* for the Radcliffe Science Library extension in
1933–4, and also by *Sir Giles Gilbert Scott* for the New Bodleian of 1936–40, both with doorways etc. in the quasi-modern
manner of their college equivalents. For the less costly buildings in the Science Area, *Lanchester & Lodge* supplied a sort of
neutral stripped-brick style, beginning with Physical Chemistry
(1938–41).

Unlike at Cambridge, neither the colleges nor the University
can show a MODERN MOVEMENT building from these years.
In the late 1930s iconoclastic designs were made for the partial
rebuilding of All Souls by *Maxwell Fry* and of Balliol by *Samuel*
& Harding, but these remained on paper.

The CITY continued to grow, and in 1929 took over sup-
plementary outer areas including Headington, Cowley and Wolvercote. Additional civic offices were provided on the Carfax side
of the Town Hall in 1930–2, to a design by *Ashley & Newman*

that was mirrored by a new bank on the corner opposite. Further down St Aldate's, the old houses on the E side were cleared for street widening and the displaced population moved to new COUNCIL HOUSING on the Abingdon Road. Before its absorption Headington RDC was also busy building council houses, and the cumulative results across the city are unusually varied. Among Oxford Council's projects is Morrell Avenue, a boulevard-type road of 1929–31 which includes a few private houses. PRIVATE HOUSES from these years include Oxford's oldest surviving Modernist building, *Stanley Hamp*'s Osler House of 1932 at Headington, now part of the John Radcliffe Hospital complex.* Headington village also has some attractive cottages of 1938 by *Fielding Dodd*, in a late Arts and Crafts manner. North Oxford continued to be the favourite suburb of the better-off, with Neo-Georgian designs taking a growing share of the market. *Christopher Wright*'s houses of 1924 onwards in Belbroughton Road are among the livelier examples. A few blocks of MANSION FLATS appeared in the area not long after, *Fielding Dodd*'s Woodstock Court (1933–5), and *E. R. Barrow*'s Belsyre Court (1934–6), conspicuous on the Woodstock Road.

Among other public buildings, two expansive SCHOOLS were built in Headington: *G.T.F. Gardner* and *Thomas Rayson*'s Headington School, Neo-Georgian of 1928–30, and the porticoed Milham Ford School, completed in 1939 and now part of Oxford Brookes University. COMMERCIAL ARCHITECTURE proved more receptive to the Art Deco version of Modern, most notably at the cinemas of 1936–7 by *Robert Cromie* in George Street and Cowley Road, and at *T. P. Bennett & Son*'s bold interior at the New Theatre of 1933–4. Oxford's other new theatre, among the 1820s terraces of Beaumont Street, was The Playhouse, with a respectful Neo-Georgian façade by *Edward Maufe* (1937–8). It has beautiful lettering by *Eric Gill*, one of over two dozen commissions in Oxford, including the pillar at South Park (1935). *Harry W. Smith & Son*'s Morris Garages of 1932–3 in St Aldate's have the air of a classical public building, and the retained elevation now serves as a suitable frontage for the Crown and County courts.

CHURCHES of the period are classical or Gothic in about equal measure. Gothic appears at *H. S. Rogers*'s St Luke at Temple Cowley (1937–8; now Oxfordshire History Centre), built with funds from Lord Nuffield of Morris Motors. Other churches were intended to expand, but never grew beyond a hall-like first phase; *T. Lawrence Dale*'s St Alban, Cowley (1928–33) and St Francis, Headington (1930–1) are examples. The religious houses continued to embellish their chapels, and in the 1930s Pusey House and St Stephen's House both acquired baldacchinos by *Comper*, the former lavishly gilded, the latter a component of an unearthly all-white chancel extension. The Roman Catholic orders were busy too. In 1930–1 the Franciscans added a friary by *G.T.F. Gardner* to the Edwardian church of St Edmund and St

---

* *Hamp*'s Maternity Wing (1931) and nurses' home at the Radcliffe Infirmary have been demolished.

Frideswide, using the same strange flint-and-sandstone mixture. Less conspicuous is *Paul Waterhouse*'s Convent of the Incarnation of 1922–3 nearby, with its Spanish Baroque-inspired chapel.

FROM 1945 TO THE C21

Oxford escaped air-raid damage in the Second World War. With no urgent reconstruction in play, the architecture of the first years after 1945 is marked by strong continuities with the interwar period. PLANNING was likewise steered initially by slum clearance and road improvement projects that drew on proposals from before 1939. The policies that had swept away old St Aldate's now turned westward, beginning the clearance of the quarter of St Ebbe's. Long-standing questions of traffic circulation around and across the city were ultimately resolved by means of an outer

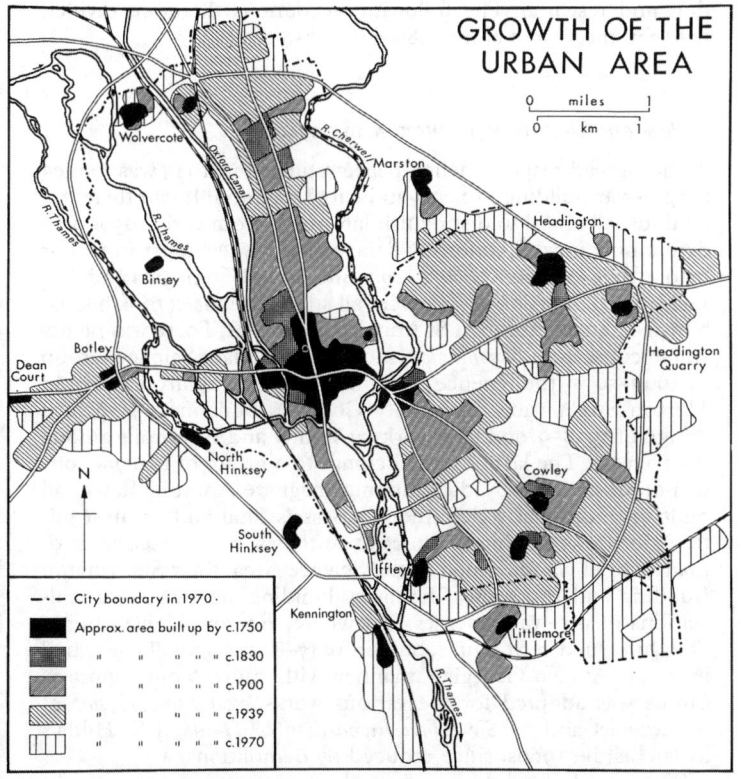

Oxford, growth of the urban area to 1970.
Map, 1979

ring road and two inner links, Donnington Bridge Road to the s and Marston Ferry Road to the N and NE. A more contentious proposal to drive a boulevard across Christ Church Meadow in order to relieve the High Street was finally abandoned in 1968. Another pressing issue was the treatment of Cowley, which continued to expand, along with its motor works. The planned outer suburb of Blackbird Leys was designated in 1953 with this growing industrial population in mind. A large shopping precinct was also provided at Cowley, but more radical proposals to establish a new civic centre there came to nothing. (The plan was echoed half-jokingly by Pevsner in the 1974 edition of *The Buildings of England*: 'The ideal firmly to be envisaged ought to be Oxford as the Latin Quarter of Cowley' – though he accepted that this would never happen.) Further outward growth was constrained by the designation of a green belt around Oxford in 1956, the first outside London.

The later 1970s brought retrenchment to the motor industry, and a low point in the graph of new building for the University and the colleges. Thereafter, Oxford would be less of an industrial city, and increasingly dominated instead by the needs of education and research. The following account is therefore divided between the years before 1980 and those after.

College and University architecture to c.1980

A widespread response when peace returned in 1945 was to pick up pre-war building projects and carry them on. It can therefore be unusually hard to distinguish late 1930s from early 1950s academic buildings at Oxford. Of the ARCHITECTS most in favour before 1939, *Sir Giles Gilbert Scott*, *Sir Hubert Worthington* and *T.A. Lodge* of *Lanchester & Lodge* were all still active. *Scott* took his last bow with an extension at St Anne's, of 1949–51. There was plenty still to come from *Worthington*, including the Plant Sciences group of 1947–50 in the Science Area, the History Faculty Library in Merton Street (now University College), built in 1954–6 to a design of 1938–9, and new works at Trinity and Pembroke among the colleges. The last of these belongs to a group of benefactions to poorer colleges by the shipping magnate Antonin Besse, all built in traditional styles (though Besse's final and greatest gift to Oxford was anything but: *see* St Antony's, p. 70). *Lanchester & Lodge*'s brief was confined to the Science Area; their Sherrington Building and Inorganic Chemistry building are two more realizations of pre-war schemes. Elsewhere, *Edward Maufe*'s pretty Dolphin Quad at St John's, built in 1947–8, was actually designed in 1942. A Neo-Georgian manner with more 'contemporary' motifs was adopted for the various works by *Geddes Hyslop* at Somerville, and by *Sir Albert Richardson & Houfe* at St Hilda's as late as the 1960s, since reduced by demolitions.

Three traditional designs from these years stand out as works of compelling originality. By far the largest is the new graduate foundation of Nuffield College, built in 1949–58 with funds

from Lord Nuffield. *Harrison, Barnes & Hubbard*'s stripped-   112
Cotswold design represents a reworking of the stylistically
unclassifiable proposals of 1939 by *Austen Harrison*, which had
not found favour with the patron. The most memorable feature
is the book-stack tower and slim spire, which Pevsner judged to
have 'something of Lutyens's felicitous manipulation of period
details into a non-period whole'. At Queen's College, *Raymond
Erith* adopted Mannerist rustication at his villa-like Provost's
Lodgings of 1958–60. Erith also designed a new quad for Lady
Margaret Hall, built in 1959–66, of red brick with sparing but
powerful classical details, again at some distance from stock
Neo-Georgian formulas.

In material terms, all these buildings can claim only a small share
of the traditional architectural forms from the post-war decades
that now meet the eye in Oxford, owing to the city's gigantic
programme of REFACING. The process was not new – early C19
episodes have already been mentioned, and Christ Church redid
the inner faces of Peckwater in 1924–30 – but it now expanded   58
into a rolling project, funded by public appeal and applied to
selected churches as well as to University buildings and colleges.
The peak years were 1957–69, though much remained to do
even after that. Clipsham stone from Rutland, first introduced
to Oxford by Jackson in the late C19, was the most common substitute for the blackened and blistering stone from Headington,
and wholesale replacement was usually preferred to patching or
scouring. So the city centre which present-day visitors see, at
least as far as older stone-faced buildings are concerned, is to a
large extent a C20 artefact.

Here and there the opportunity was taken during the work
to re-create lost features, as at *W. Godfrey Allen*'s overhaul of
the Old Ashmolean and the Sheldonian (1957–8 and 1958–61).   2
At the Bodleian, the external works overlapped with internal
reconstruction for reading rooms with steel and concrete floors,
which concluded with *Robert Potter*'s discreet renewal of much
of the Selden End interior in 1960–3. Even the Emperors' heads
around the Sheldonian made way for new ones, replacing not
the C17 originals but their Victorian successors. In an extreme
case of renewal, Trinity College replaced the rubble-walled cottages on the other side of Broad Street with deceptive replicas
in 1969. These are incidentally among the relatively few college
buildings to have resumed a green cladding of creepers, Oxford's
favoured adornment for crumbling old walls in Victorian and
Edwardian times.

Meanwhile the architectural expectations of academia were
starting to shift. An early sign was the replacement in 1955
of Lanchester & Lodge by the Modernists *Ramsey, Murray,
White & Ward* for new buildings in the Science Area and Keble
Triangle. Another University project, the Oriental Institute of
1958–60, went to *Easton & Robertson, Cusdin, Preston & Smith*,
an established Modernist firm who had already done much
at Cambridge. The late 1950s were the turning point for the
COLLEGES too, as the old guard made way for younger architects

and a general mood of innovation and experiment. The following decade and a half proved to be one of the great ages for architecture at Oxford.*

The largest single project was another entirely NEW COLLEGE, St Catherine's (successor to the non-residential St Catherine's Society), built on a fresh site in 1960–4. The college is also one of Oxford's few works from the period by a non-British architect, here *Arne Jacobsen* of Denmark. Sharp, exacting, and strictly rectilinear in plan and elevation, it re-composes the traditional collegiate components – *sans* chapel – as a symmetrical com-
116 pound of low-rise blocks, with full-height glazing between concrete cross-walls on the twin residential ranges. Another new foundation, *Powell & Moya*'s Wolfson College, followed in
120 1968–74, for graduates only. Placed on a slope overlooking a punt dock by the River Cherwell way up in North Oxford, it is expansive where St Catherine's is introverted, but otherwise the two colleges show a comparably consistent approach to materials and structural expression – here of concrete framing with pre-cast aggregate panels. An earlier graduate college was St Antony's, established in 1950 in the former Trinity convent on Woodstock Road. Additional funds from Antonin Besse made
119 possible a new college centre by *Howell, Killick, Partridge & Amis* (*HKPA*; 1968–70), a rigorous construction of pre-cast concrete framing, meant as the first instalment of something larger. St Antony's was incidentally the first male college to admit women, in 1962 (Nuffield was mixed from the outset), and the older men's colleges followed from 1974 onwards. The tally of colleges increased further by the promotion of St Anne's, St Peter's and St Edmund Hall to full status (1952, 1957, 1961), and by the inauguration in the 1960s of two more graduate colleges, Linacre and St Cross, neither of which was yet ready to build.

Most additions at the OLDER COLLEGES in these years were constrained by the sites available, and many are tucked away in odd corners. *Powell & Moya*'s pioneering project at Brasenose (1959–60), for instance, is invisible from the older quads there. Its vertical articulation of the residential staircases and its combination of concrete and Portland roach stone facing recur at the same architects' much larger Blue Boar Quad of 1964–8 at Christ Church, where they also designed a beautifully lucid, part-sunken picture gallery, both likewise discreetly placed behind older buildings. By contrast, the aggregated hexagons of
114 the *Architects' Co-Partnership*'s Beehives at St John's (1958–60) completed an existing historic quad – admittedly a very miscellaneous one – with great panache.† Balliol and Exeter went further, sacrificing some Victorian fabric to make way for new

---

* In Pevsner's words from 1974: 'it has been a bumper harvest in these last few years, just as it has been at Cambridge, even if the quality taking it all in all has been higher at Cambridge'.

† Already present as a rear appendage to the quad was the first Modernist addition at any of the colleges, the Senior Common Room extension of 1953–5: an indifferent design by *David Booth* of *Booth & Ledeboer* (demolished).

Modernist works. Exeter's addition (1961–4) is by *Lionel Brett* of *Brett & Pollen*, with a sheer ashlar façade and cut-out windows of various shapes that look ill at ease on Broad Street. At Balliol, *Geoffrey Beard* of the *Oxford Architects Partnership* book-ended Waterhouse's hall with new blocks of 1964–8, which attempt a complementary richness of articulation. The impatience with plain and simple functionalism among many younger architects also marks the tucked-away addition of 1969–71 at Jesus College by *John Fryman* of the *Architects Design Partnership*, an extreme instance of the fashion for canted edges, and the contemporary Middle Common Room building at the back of University College, by the same.

A more compelling rejection of flush walling was achieved by *Sir Philip Dowson* of *Arup Associates* at his blocks for Somerville (1958–66 and 1964–7), which feature an exoskeleton of concrete framing within which the rooms are recessed or protruded. These belong with a larger family of Dowson/Arup buildings (at Cambridge too) which culminate grandly with the Sir Thomas White building of 1972–5 at St John's, another project in which the ground floor is given over to communal functions. Its nearest equivalent at Oxford in terms of redefining the college perimeter is *Ahrends, Burton & Koralek*'s brilliantly original complex of 1970–7 at Keble. This long range of yellow brick starts as a high enclosure around a tiny quad, unfolds and continues northward, stepping down as it goes. The outside is all towering square projections and tall window slots, but the inner side is altogether different, with continuous mirrored glazing that slopes forward below, over a sunken concourse.

A calmer way with yellow brick is represented by the insistently horizontal library and accommodation block from the 1970s at Pembroke, both by *Sir Leslie Martin*. Neutral horizontals also prevail at *David Roberts*'s Sacher Building of 1961–2 for graduate students at New College. Later, at the Kenyon Building of 1964–6 at St Hugh's, Roberts was free to design in the round, adopting a wedge shape of fiery red brick, rooms with corner windows or chunky concrete balconies, and an unexpectedly grand internal staircase. Another Cambridge-based practice, *Lyster, Grillet & Harding*, designed two mini-towers of comparably varied outline at Lady Margaret Hall (1970–2), also of red brick. Of the other women's colleges, St Anne's moved beyond the Giles Scott era with *Gerald Banks*'s hall of 1958–9, Oxford's first Modernist college hall. In the 1960s *HKPA* took over, for two convex-sided residential towers – six were intended – with the same cantingout of all four sides of the windows as those used at St Antony's, and a gatehouse building that has since been demolished. At St Hilda's, *Alison & Peter Smithson* designed the curiously wilful Garden Building (1968–70) with its apparatus of timber beams applied to the concrete framing. For vertical accents there is *Casson, Conder & Partners*' garden block at Worcester (1959–61), with its grouped or slit windows and steep mansard roof.

The traditional mansard motif is a reminder of the constraints imposed by CONSERVATION in so much of Oxford. Similarly,

St Edmund's Hall's Back Quad (*Kenneth Stevens & Associates*, 1968–70), a grab-bag of Modernist motifs below, is topped with a row of little gables to lessen the impact on more distant views. At the contemporary Carrodus Quad of Queen's College next door, *Marshall Sisson* hid his new buildings behind pastiche fronts and retained house façades on the High Street and Queen's Lane. *Maguire & Murray* adopted a similar policy at the Cumberbatch Buildings for Trinity (1964–8), a complicated project which includes a facsimile house on Broad Street and a huge basement extension for Blackwell's bookshop, hidden below the new quadrangle behind (since partly replaced). *Gillespie, Kidd & Coia*'s works for Wadham began with another joint development with Blackwell's (1969–71), whose new music shop was tactfully interlocked with adapted houses in Holywell Street; a new college library followed (1973–7), at which the late Brutalist forms are already softened by historical references. A second project using adapted houses in Holywell Street is *Shepheard, Epstein & Hunter*'s Holywell Quad for Hertford College (1974–81), where the new parts adopt the pitched roofs of the Neo-vernacular manner. Examples of this self-effacing formula of new buildings tucked behind adapted or imitated houses continue into the 1980s and beyond, e.g. the auxiliary St Aldate's site of Christ Church and the Dorothy Hodgkin Quad of Somerville. Annexations of a different kind in the 1960s–70s turned the redundant churches of All Saints and St Peter-in-the-East into the libraries of Lincoln College and St Edmund Hall.

p. 260

OUTSTATIONS also began to proliferate in this period, as the colleges endeavoured to house more of their own students. Magdalen crossed the bridge to build its Waynflete Building (*Booth, Ledeboer & Pinckheard*, 1960–1), a big, stodgy disappointment. Other colonies followed along the same branch of the Cherwell, most notably *James Stirling*'s wildly original and profoundly problematic Florey Building of 1968–70 for Queen's. An incomplete polygon clad in flaming red tiles, it features staggered floors raised on raking concrete trusses and mostly sloped glazing on the inner faces, and has never worked well as a place to live. In North Oxford, even further from the main college sites, University College has some disappointingly blunt satellite buildings by *Sir Philip Dowson* (*Arup Associates*) of 1970–3, while *John Fryman*'s Stevens Close for Jesus College (1973–5) combines partial polygons with an attempted rapprochement with historical forms.

p. 451

As the numbers of postgraduates boomed – reaching 3,125 by 1971, of a total student body of 11,071 – the UNIVERSITY also moved to provide some accommodation. The first instalment comprised family flats in northern North Oxford, of 1962–6 by *HKPA* (altered). Closer to the centre, the N side of Wellington Square was rebuilt in 1973–5 by *Sir Leslie Martin* with *David Owers*, an underwhelming strip-windowed slab (though with more appeal than the same architects' glum University Offices alongside). *Martin*'s best project for Oxford remains his first, the St Cross Building of 1961–4, designed in partnership with

118

Colin St John Wilson. Three faculty libraries were provided here, each different in size but of similar plan. All three are adroitly interlinked around a grand external staircase, in a severely cubic brick-walled composition with long sweeping window bands. Another major work by *Martin* was the Tinbergen Building (Zoology and Pharmacology) of 1965–70 to the S of the main Science Area, a concrete structure with more pronounced Brutalist echoes, co-designed with *Colen Lumley* (demolished). It was built after the rejection of *Chamberlin, Powell & Bon*'s prodigious scheme for a Zoology building with a 240-ft (73-metre) tower, an episode which helped to draw an enduring line against high-rise design for central Oxford. Similarly, *Pier Luigi Nervi* and *Powell & Moya*'s unbuilt project of 1966 for a new Pitt Rivers Museum on Banbury Road tested the limits of permissible redevelopment in the North Oxford suburb.

So it fell to *Sir Philip Dowson* of *Arup* to design the most declamatory addition to the sciences group in the period. His Denys Wilkinson Building (Nuclear Physics) of 1963–71 in the Keble Triangle is a deck-access complex, notable for its prominent Brutalist accelerator tower. *Arup*'s Holder Building of 1973–6 in the same cluster is no less tough-minded. But when the time came to expand the Radcliffe Science Library in 1971–5, the solution adopted on this sensitive site was simply to hide the new rooms underground. The designer was the University Surveyor *Jack Lankester*, a busy jack of all trades from the late 1950s into the 1990s. His other works include additions to the former convent house on St Cross Road that became the home of Linacre College, and some modest Neo-Georgian buildings for the graduate foundation of Green College (now Green Templeton), established in 1979 with the Radcliffe Observatory as its centrepiece.

The Modernist ascendancy also found expression in WORKS OF ART. Even at Nuffield, the traditional architecture is offset by an abstract sculpture by *Hubert Dalwood*, a lush semi-abstract mural by *Derrick Greaves* and *Edward Middleditch*, and abstract stained glass in the tucked-away chapel by *John Piper* and *Patrick Reyntiens*, all of the 1950s–60s. St Catherine's and the Sacher Building of New College are each prominently accompanied by one of *Barbara Hepworth*'s non-figurative sculptures, and St Catherine's also displays a bust by *Epstein*, whose major work at Oxford is the Lazarus statue in the antechapel of New College (1949–51). Other college chapels can show stained glass by *John Hayward* (St Peter's, 1964) and a reredos by *Ceri Richards* (St Edmund Hall, 1957–8), both from the Romantic-Expressionist end of the Modernist spectrum. 113

Buildings of the city to c.1980

The city took longer than the University to resume building after 1945. Even the early 1950s can show very little. The national policy of attracting foreign tourists no doubt explains why the

Randolph Hotel was allowed to extend in 1951–2, in a version of the 1860s design. Modernism arrived in Cornmarket Street with *Lord Holford*'s carefully judged frontage of 1956–7 for Woolworth's, the first major work of COMMERCIAL ARCHITECTURE from the period. By the 1960s any city of Oxford's size was expected to provide a dedicated shopping centre with multi-storey car parks, and these duly appeared at Cowley (1960–5 and later) and in central Oxford at Queen Street (Westgate Centre, 1969–72). Designed by successive City Architects, *E. G. Chandler* and *Douglas Murray*, neither complex is (or was) a superior work of architecture. The same goes for the OFFICIAL BUILDINGS of the period, whether by City, County, or Government architects. Even prestige jobs such as the new College of Technology on Headington Hill (*Chandler*, then *Murray*, since drastically remodelled for Oxford Brookes University) and *A. E. Smith*'s New County Hall of 1973–6 fail to rise to the occasion. In HOUSING too the city was content to follow rather than lead. Some of the displaced inhabitants of St Ebbe's were rehoused on the old gas works site, where the quadrangular slabs of *Chandler*'s Friars Wharf were built in 1959–62. The new low-rise housing at e.g. Blackbird Leys and at the far N end of the city is no less generic, and the four tower blocks provided by the council in the outer eastern suburbs even include two system-built contractor's jobs. Only in the 1970s did things improve, with some well-handled infillings in St Ebbe's and especially in Jericho, where the remaining older terraces were largely spared.

Despite these disappointments, the city still has much of interest from the period. New CHURCHES include a little-known late work by the versatile traditionalist *Thomas Rayson*, the well-crafted Friends' Meeting House (1951–5), behind the houses of St Giles'. *Lawrence Dale*'s St Michael and All Angels in New Marston (1954–6) retains a traditional outline but shows concrete arches inside, and is notable too for its works of religious art. *N. F. Cachemaille-Day*'s St Mary, Barton (1956–8) is more explicitly Modernist, though still of a traditional aisled plan. Meanwhile the Liturgical Movement challenged the historic division between nave and chancel, and encouraged new adventures in church planning. Especially radical is *Colin Shewring*'s Anglican parish church for Blackbird Leys (1964–5), now condemned by the structural failure of its hyperbolic paraboloid roof. Of new Catholic churches, *Gilbert Flavel*'s Holy Rood, Abingdon Road (1959–61) places a square lantern over an octagonal interior equipped with some interesting furnishings, and *Peter Reynolds & Partners*' church at Littlemore (1965–9) has a showier roof composed of glass pyramids. Also by *Reynolds* is the wedge-shaped John Bunyan Baptist Church at Cowley (1963–4), the decade's most compelling Nonconformist design. Of other buildings with a religious connection, *Ahrends, Burton & Koralek*'s deliberately contrasting extension of the University's Catholic Chaplaincy at the Old Palace in St Aldate's (1970–2) includes a multi-purpose chapel space within its varied yellow brick outlines.

By far the greatest PUBLIC BUILDING of the period is the giant John Radcliffe Hospital of 1968–79 at Headington by *Yorke, Rosenberg & Mardall*, a monumental example of their use of white-tiled facing. Among SCHOOLS, the most interesting jobs are from the private sector: boarders' houses for St Edward's School by *Sir Robert Matthew, Johnson-Marshall & Partners* (1963–5) with boxed-out bays and oriels; the elongated hexagonal hall for Magdalen College School by *Pinckheard & Partners* (1964–6); and one neo-Neoclassical work, the headmaster's house at Summer Fields School by *Francis Johnson*, 1971–2. An independent educational foundation within the University's orbit is the Maison Française in North Oxford, which has calm and rational buildings of 1965–7 by *Jacques Laurent* with *Brian Ring/ Howard & Partners*. By way of contrast, the small British Council offices off Beaumont Street are another of *John Fryman*'s lively distillations of 1960s motifs.

COMMERCIAL AND INDUSTRIAL buildings from these decades on a grander scale include *Harry Weedon & Partners'* enormous office slab of 1965–6 at the motor works, still a landmark on the eastern edge of Oxford; the tightly integrated Oxford Mail and Times building by *Arup Associates* at Osney Mead (1968–71, demolition pending); and the former headquarters of Blackwell's by the *Oxford Architects Partnership* (1970–2), largely of curtain walling, but with an angle tower of reeded concrete towards Hythe Bridge Street.

There is no roll-call of Modernist PRIVATE HOUSES to rival those of Cambridge, though *Ernö Goldfinger*'s No. 16 Bedford Street off the Iffley Road (1963–4) is a worthy contender, and *Sir Howard Colvin*'s self-designed No. 50 Plantation Road (1969–70) deserves an honourable mention. The 1960s did better at Oxford in terms of small groups of houses, notably the flat-roofed trio next to Keble in Blackhall Road by *Michael Powers* of the *Architects' Co-Partnership*, the interlocking terraces of *Brett & Pollen*'s Benson Place in North Oxford, and especially *Ahrends, Burton & Koralek*'s cluster in Dunstan Road, Headington, all angles and rather fortress-like to the street. Another good work in Headington is Emden House, informal sheltered flats of 1979–81 by *Philip del Nevo* of *Oxford Architects Partnership*. The same firm contributed some of the better designs among the numerous blocks of private flats of the 1960s–70s in North Oxford, e.g. Martin Court off South Parade.

It may be useful to conclude with some details of notable LOCAL ARCHITECTS. The *Oxford Architects Partnership* was founded in 1962, with *Geoffrey Beard* as leading designer in the early years, joined in the 1970s–80s by *del Nevo*. The firm continues as *Oxford Architects*. Also busy at Oxford from the 1960s, the *Architects Design Partnership* had *John Fryman* as its foremost designer into the 1980s. In the early C21 the name changed to *ADP*. More complex is the history of the practice founded in 1939 by *David Booth & Judith Ledeboer*, which became *Booth, Ledeboer & Pinckheard* in 1956, *Pinckheard & Partners* in 1962, then (through *R.B. Gray*) *Gray & Baynes*, and so in 1980 to *Gray Baynes & Shew*.

College and University architecture after c.1980

After a lull in the first half of the 1980s, building by the COL-LEGES resumed at a steady rate and has barely slackened since. Besides the need to accommodate a higher proportion of their students, colleges have sought to provide new facilities such as large-scale lecture halls, invaluable for the conference trade. Part-nerships with outside bodies based on shared use of new build-ings have also proved fruitful (Harris Manchester, Mansfield, St Antony's, St Hugh's), and college outstations have grown in number and ambition.

The first project of the 1980s belongs with perhaps the most impressive body of work at Oxford (and Cambridge too) by a single post-war practice, that of *MacCormac, Jamieson & Prich-ard*. Their Sainsbury Building of 1980–3 at Worcester takes the pitched roofs of the Neo-vernacular as one element of a spatially rich and diverting composition, beautifully placed by the col-lege's lake. At the Bowra Building of 1988–92 for Wadham, the accommodation is grouped in a sequence of offset towers linked by a concourse above communal ground-floor facilities. Here the vocabulary comes closer to the revival of historical forms asso-ciated with Postmodernism. Balliol's Jowett Buildings (1992–6 onwards) are similarly evocative, but the boldest Postmodern adventure is St John's Garden Quad of 1991–4, especially in the podium deck with its references to Soane. The sequence concludes with Kendrew Quad of 2007–10, an outstation also for St John's. Here historicist details have disappeared, as have separately expressed residential staircases, in favour of a corridor plan served by cylindrical enclosures for the stairs and lifts – for Oxford's ancient staircase system has been overtaken by the need to provide equal access for the less able-bodied.

Other widely employed practices include *Maguire & Murray*, latterly *Maguire & Co.* Their chief projects are the complex but self-effacing new kitchens for Magdalen (1986–9), the Sir Geoffrey Arthur outstation for Pembroke, on the s bank of the Thames (1986–90, damaged by partial rebuilding), a towered complex in the gardens for Worcester (1988–90), and two outstations in East Oxford, for Christ Church and Corpus (1989–92) and for Jesus College (2000–1). All of these feature gables or pitched roofs, and are evocative of tradition without deploying historical details. The same goes for most of the various college projects by the *Architects Design Partnership* in the period, including the blocks at the same Jesus College site (1989–90 etc.). The levels of Postmodern historical detailing are higher on the *Alec French Partnership*'s range of 1991–2 at St Anne's and *van Heyningen & Hayward*'s Jacqueline du Pré building of 1992–5 at St Hilda's.

The Postmodern turn in the late C20 went hand in hand with a full-blooded revival of TRADITIONAL ARCHITECTURE.

122

p.418

The first appearance at the colleges was some rather skimpy Neo-Georgian blocks at Harris Manchester of 1990–2 by the *Peter Yiangou* practice, since joined by a rather overdone Neo-Jackson building by the same designers. Magdalen has the Grove Buildings of 1991–8 by *Demetri Porphyrios*, juxtaposing stripped Perp and stripped classical. At Lady Margaret Hall, *John Simpson* has picked up Raymond Erith's baton with his explicitly Neoclassical buildings of 2008–17. The latest example is at Trinity, where *ADAM Architecture* have replaced much of *Maguire & Murray*'s 1960s work with a large building of interwar Neo-Georgian character.

C21 Oxford also has a strong showing by *Niall McLaughlin Architects*, whose works are distinguished by their sharp profiles, vertical proportions and well-crafted finishes within a Modernist idiom (St Cross, Somerville, Balliol Master's Field site, and the Nazrin Shah Building for Worcester). The local firm of *Berman Guedes Stretton* has been similarly busy, including some well-judged additions to Wolfson College (2004–16) and a big new quad for Pembroke, linked by bridge to the main site and provided with a complex series of decks and terraces (2010–13). 126

The rest of the college story is likewise a Modernist one, but any tour will show how diverse that category has become. Many of the differences arise from the choice of materials and textures. At the gentler and more tactile end are such recent projects as *Gort Scott*'s Boundary Building of 2018–21 that forms the new centrepiece at St Hilda's, and *Allies & Morrison*'s outstation of 2017–19 for Wadham on the Iffley Road, both of pale brick. Somewhere near them on the scale are *Rick Mather*'s red brick additions to Keble (1993–5 and 2000–2). Ashlar facing is used in rectilinear Modernist compositions by *Stanton Williams* for Lincoln (2012–15), by *John McAslan & Partners* for New College in Mansfield Road (2016–19), and by *MICA Architects* for Jesus College's Fourth Quad (2018–22). *Alison Brooks*'s Cohen Quad for Exeter (2013–17), incorporating façades from the old Ruskin College building in Walton Street, combines ashlar facing with a hefty tiled mansard and some complicated internal sections. The machine aesthetic of glass, steel and spare framing prevails at the new buildings for St Peter's (*Chamberlin, Powell, Bon & Woods*, 1987–9, and *Design Engine*, 2016 onwards), St Catherine's (*Hodder Associates*, 1993–5 and 2003–5), St Hugh's (*David Morley Architects*, 1998–2000 and 2011–14, with much terracotta facing), and St Anne's (*Kohn Pedersen Fox*, 2002–5). The shiny and swooping addition to St Antony's by *Zaha Hadid*, 2013–15, and the calmer but equally shimmering blocks by *AL_A Architects* at Wadham, 2017–20, push the possibilities of metal cladding to extremes. *p.251*

College halls and chapels largely remain as they were in the 1970s, but several colleges have recently sought to enhance or extend their LIBRARIES. At Magdalen in 2014–16, *Wright & Wright* were required to insert a larger storey below the existing C19 building, a near-impossible challenge in aesthetic terms. Much better is the architects' Study Centre of 2014–19 at St John's, a complex assembly of stone-faced volumes in a garden 130 setting. *Fletcher Priest*'s library for St Anne's of 2010–16, also stone-faced, is straightforwardly cubic. Colleges on constricted sites have more limited options: at Queen's, *Rick Mather Architects*' new library is placed alongside the old, almost entirely underground. A noteworthy building in a class of its own is University College's BOATHOUSE of 2005–7, a brooding affair of black brick with a hovering roof slab, by *Belsize Architects*.

124

The UNIVERSITY in this period undertook little until the late 1990s, when additions began to appear in and around the science quarter. *Foster & Partners*' Manor Road Building for Social Sciences (1998–2004) shows the fashion for random fenestration within an upright grid of cladding, whereas *RMJM*'s Chemistry Research Laboratory on South Parks Road (1999–2003) is more studiedly neutral. The adjacent Rothermere American Institute by *Kohn Pedersen Fox* (1998–2001) does more to express its internal spaces and circulation. *Maguire & Co.*'s University Club in Mansfield Road (2000–4) falls into arbitrary shape-making. Elsewhere in the city, *Dixon Jones*'s Saïd Business School by the railway station (1997–2001) is a calm and well-judged quadrangular compound of yellow brick, with a touch of fantasy in its ziggurat-like spire. The University's one venture into Classical Revival, the Sackler Library of 1997–2001 (Classics and History of Art) by *Robert Adam Architects*, was squeezed on to back land by the Ashmolean; its big drum promises more excitements than the interior delivers. The same cannot be said for *Abdel-Wahed El-Wakil*'s Centre for Islamic Studies (2001–5) on Marston Road – properly not part of the University, but built in close association – with its lavish detailing in traditional Islamic styles inside and out.

123

Further from the historic heart of the University, things have been stirring at the Old Road Campus (Medical Sciences) in East Oxford. The first instalment, *Anshen/Dyer*'s Wellcome Institute for Human Genetics, was completed in 2000. Bold and strongly contrasting buildings have followed, designed by *Nicholas Hare*, *Make* and *SRA*. Non-medical sciences have been catered for by selective demolition and rebuilding within the congested main Science Area: a contrast with Cambridge, where expansion can be directed to the huge West Cambridge Site. Good buildings have followed from *Wilkinson Eyre* (Earth Sciences, 2008–10) and *Hawkins/Brown* (Biochemistry, 2004–21). The latter's spatially exciting interior has an intricate counterpart at the same architects' Beecroft Building of 2015–18 (Physics).

129

Hawkins/Brown are also represented by the more modest New Radcliffe House (2011–12) at the RADCLIFFE OBSERVATORY QUARTER, i.e. the former Radcliffe Infirmary site, which the University bought in 2003. The converted older buildings there have been joined by *Rafael Viñoly Architects*' angular Mathematical Institute of 2010–13 and *Herzog & de Meuron*'s unearthly Blavatnik School of Government of 2013–15, composed as a glinting stack of glass drums. The next instalment will be *Hopkins Architects*' Humanities Building, a surprisingly conservative design externally, due for completion in 2025.

125

So to the University projects which ordinary visitors to Oxford are most likely to encounter: the Ashmolean and Pitt Rivers museums and the New Bodleian, all remodelled or extended since 2000. The Ashmolean replaced most of its jumble of rear extensions with varied new galleries by *Rick Mather Architects* (2006–9), organized around a full-height void. The Pitt Rivers appears little changed as far as *T.N. Deane & Son*'s galleried 1880s interior is concerned, the new facilities being concentrated in *Pringle Richards Sharratt*'s addition, also of 2006–9. Emptied of its book stacks, the New Bodleian has become the Weston Library at the hands of *Wilkinson Eyre* (2010–15), with a new entrance from Broad Street and a popular atrium-type interior that is accessible to all.

The city since c.1980

The late C20 and early C21 have brought relatively little change to the CITY CENTRE. *Kendrick Associates*' enclosure of Gloucester Green with fancy red brick ranges in 1987–9 is Oxford's best Postmodern commercial project, bringing life to what was a bleak and neglected space. Another success has been the transformation of the redundant prison buildings in 2004–6 into a hotel and historic attraction, with a fair amount of new construction. The one really big project since then has been the remodelling and enormous extension of the Westgate Centre in 2014–17 to a masterplan by *BDP*, with better results than most buildings of the type. A little further s, the ice rink of 1982–4 by *Nicholas Grimshaw & Partners* remains as an early monument of the High Tech school.

Viewed from further out, rather more has been going on. Buildings for EDUCATION continue to appear in quantity, led by the former College of Education (later Oxford Polytechnic) in its post-1992 guise as Oxford Brookes University. The remodelling and extension of the Headington complex in the 2010s by *Design Engine* and *Berman Guedes Stretton* is commendably ambitious and good to explore. The best new school buildings continue to come from the affluent fee-paying sector, led by St Edward's School: *Haworth Tompkins*'s characteristically thoughtful North Wall Arts Centre, converted from older buildings in 2003–6, and the big Christie Centre of 2016–20 by *TSH Architects*, which includes an auditorium for public performances. Noteworthy buildings for HEALTH include *Wilkinson Eyre*'s informal, timber-built Maggie's Centre of 2009–14 at the Churchill Hospital, close to the Old Road Campus. Oxford has also acquired a SCIENCE PARK on its southern edge, developed by Magdalen College from 1989 and still being filled, and an architecturally less interesting BUSINESS PARK on land vacated by the motor works at Cowley.

Then there is the insatiable demand for new RESIDENTIAL architecture. The results are rarely of special interest, though the overall standard tends to be higher than average. The *City Architect's Department* continued to do good work into the mid 1980s,

even venturing into Postmodernism at Mill Street, Botley. Of
the scanty amount of SOCIAL HOUSING built since then, *Allford
Hall Monaghan Morris*'s two projects of the 2010s at Cowley
are confidently planned and cheerful in their use of colour, and
more recently *Levitt Bernstein* have also done good work. Private
STUDENT HOSTELS are proliferating in the C21, as in many other
cities, but have yet to produce any architecture of distinction.
Worse, the University's own Castle Mill student accommodation
of 2011–13 interrupted a treasured view at Port Meadow with
bland and unworthy buildings, to widespread disgust. PRIVATE
HOUSES of note remain surprisingly few. Some of the best are
by *Adrian James*, combining formal inventiveness with a satisfy-
ing use of materials; Botley, Jericho and Cowley have examples.

Most of Oxford's new housing is being provided not by such
small-scale projects, but in large new EXTENSIONS to the N, NE
and S. Of these, only Barton Park has made much progress at
the time of writing. Begun in 2015, its houses include some five-
storey brick-faced blocks by *Alison Brooks Architects*: a startlingly
urban form in these outskirts, conceived in response to the
demand for homes in a city that must find new ways to grow
while somehow also staying recognizably the same.

FURTHER READING

The *Victoria County History* heads the list, with essential volumes
on the University (*Oxfordshire*, vol. 3, 1954) and the city (vol. 4,
1979). Also valuable on many subjects is C. Hibbert (ed.), *The
Encyclopaedia of Oxford*, 1988. Many buildings and related topics
are covered in depth by articles in *Oxoniensia*, the journal of the
Oxford Architectural and Historical Society (https://oxoniensia.
org/oxo_toc.php).

The best single account of the ARCHITECTURE is Geoffrey
Tyack's *Oxford: An Architectural Guide*, 1998, a lively, well-
illustrated and scholarly narrative history which includes a
detailed bibliography. Otherwise the most detailed architectural
description remains the *City of Oxford* survey by the Royal
Commission on Historical Monuments (England), 1939, though
this is limited to buildings up to 1714. The greater medieval
colleges are analysed in A. Emery, *Greater Medieval Houses of
England and Wales*, vol. 3, 2006. D. Reed and P. Opher, *New
Architecture in Oxford*, 1977, is useful on early post-war buildings,
and J. Simmie, *Power, Property and Corporatism*, 1981, covers
post-war planning. Good detailed studies of C20 buildings are in
E. Harwood, A. Powers and O. Saumarez Smith (eds), *Twentieth
Century Architecture 11: Oxford and Cambridge* (Twentieth Century
Society), 2013. A. F. Kersting and J. Ashdown, *The Buildings of
Oxford*, 1980, is an attractive pictorial survey. Thomas Sharp,
Oxford Replanned, 1948, and Howard Colvin's *Unbuilt Oxford*,
1983, show in different ways what might have been.

For the buildings of the UNIVERSITY, colleges included, there are relevant chapters in the eight volumes of *The History of the University of Oxford* (1984–2000), including excellent coverage of the C16 and C17 by John Newman, and Peter Howell's survey of the C19 and early C20, with a tabulated list. The best single-volume history of the University is that by L. Brockliss, 2016, especially for the science story. The central cluster of buildings has been well covered recently by G. Tyack, *The Historic Heart of Oxford University*, 2022. Individual studies include S. Gillam, *The Divinity School and Duke Humfrey's Library*, 1998; M. Clapinson, *A Brief History of the Bodleian Library*, 2015; E. Craster, *History of the Bodleian Library 1845–1945*, 1952; A. Geraghty, *The Sheldonian Theatre*, 2013; J.A. Bennett, S.A. Johnson and A.V. Simcock, *Solomon's House in Oxford*, 2000 (Old Ashmolean); S. Hebron, *Dr Radcliffe's Library*, 2014 (Radcliffe Camera); S.A. Harris, *Oxford Botanic Garden and Arboretum*, 2017; H.A. Morrah, *The Oxford Union*, 1923; R.F. Ovenell, *The Ashmolean Museum*, 1986; P. Sutcliffe, *The Oxford University Press*, 1978; and J. Selby-Green, *The History of the Radcliffe Infirmary*, 1990. G. Barber, *Arks for Learning*, 1995, is an illustrated survey of Oxford's libraries. J. Morrell, *Science at Oxford 1914–1939*, 1997, is helpful for the Science Area. The University's conservation management plans, available at https://estates.admin.ox.ac.uk/conservation-plans, can also be illuminating.

Most of the COLLEGES have their own histories and guides, and a few have specialist architectural accounts in addition. For All Souls, see H. Colvin and J.S.G. Simmons, *All Souls: An Oxford College and Its Buildings*, 1989; for Balliol, J. Jones, 1988; for Brasenose, J. Mordaunt Crook, 2008; for Christ Church, W.G. Hiscock, 1946, J. Blair (ed.), *St Frideswide's Monastery*, 1990 (taken from *Oxoniensia* 53, 1988), S.J. Gunn and Philip Lindley (eds), *Cardinal Wolsey: Church, State and Art*, 1991, C. Butler (ed.), 2006, and J. Curthoys, *The Stones of Christ Church*, 2017, and *The King's Cathedral*, 2019; for Corpus Christi, T. Charles-Edwards and J. Reid, 2017; for Exeter, F. Cairncross (ed.), 2013; for Green Templeton, J. Burley and K. Plenderleith (eds), *The History of the Radcliffe Observatory*, 2005; for Jesus, F. Heal (ed.), 2021; for Lincoln, V.H.H. Green, 1977; for Magdalen, R. White with R. Darwall-Smith, *The Architectural Drawings of Magdalen College Oxford*, 2001, L.W.B. Brockliss (ed.), 2008, D. Roberts, *Hidden Magdalen*, 2008, and C. Ferdinand, *An Accidental Masterpiece* (on the New Building), 2010; for Mansfield, E. Kaye, 1996; for Merton, G.H. Martin and J.R.C. Highfield, 1997, and A. Bott, *Merton College: A Longer History of the Buildings and Furnishings*, 2015; for New College, A.H. Smith, 1952, and J. Buxton and P. Williams (eds), 1979; for Oriel, J. Catto (ed.), 2013; for Pembroke, D. Macleane, 1900, and the college's *Gentle Histories* of the chapel and Master's Lodgings, 2014 and 2017; for Queen's, R.H. Hodgkin, 1949; for St Anne's, R.F. Butler and M.H. Prichard (2 vols), 1930 and 1957; for St Antony's, C.S. Nicholls, 2000; for St Catherine's, R. Ainsworth and C. Howell (eds), 2012; for St Cross, J.-G. Deutsch, D. MacCulloch and

T. Pound, 2014; for St Edmund Hall, J.N.D. Kelly, 1989; for St Hilda's, M.E. Rayner, 1993; for St Hugh's, P. Griffin, 1986; for St John's, W.C. Costin, 1958, H. Colvin, *The Canterbury Quadrangle*, 2008, G. Tyack, 2000, and G. Tyack, *Modern Architecture in an Oxford College*, 2005; for St Peter's, E.H.F. Smith, 1978; for Somerville, P. Adams, 1996, and A. Manuel (ed.), *Breaking New Ground*, 2013; for Trinity, C. Hopkins, 2005, and Martin Kemp's study of the chapel, 2013; for University College, R. Darwall-Smith, 2008; for Wadham, C.S.L. Davies and J. Garnett, 1994; for Worcester, J. Bate and J. Goodman, 2014. In addition, M.B. Vickery, *Buildings for Bluestockings*, 1999, includes coverage of the early years of the women's colleges.

Medieval BUILDING ACCOUNTS have been published for All Souls, ed. S. Walker with J. Munby, 2010, and for Corpus, ed. B. Collett, A. Smith and J. Reid (*Oxford Historical Society* 48), 2019, as have those of the C18 library at Christ Church, ed. J. Cook and J.F.A. Mason, 1988. Other detailed surveys cover All Souls' stained glass, by G.M. Rushforth with F.E. Hutchinson, 1949, and its chapel reredos, by P. Horden (ed.), 2021; the stained glass of Merton chapel, by T. Ayres (*Corpus Vitrearum Medii Aevi*, 2 vols), 2013; and the glass of New College, by C. Woodforde, 1951. COLLEGE GARDENS are the subject of books by Mavis Batey, 1982, and T. Richardson, 2018.

Studies of ARCHITECTS active in Oxford include Kenneth Powell on Ahrends, Burton & Koralek, 2012, and on Arup Associates, 2018; Richard Fellows on Sir Reginald Blomfield, 1985; Michael Hall on G.F. Bodley, 2014; Paul Thompson on William Butterfield, 1971, also the Victorian Society's *Butterfield Revisited* (*Studies in Victorian Architecture and Design* 6), 2017; Elain Harwood on Chamberlin, Powell & Bon, 2011; D. Watkin on C.R. Cockerell, 1984; S. Symondson and S. Bucknall on J.N. Comper, 2006; J. Myles on L.N. Cottingham, 1996; Lucy Archer on Raymond Erith, 1985; T. Friedman on James Gibbs, 1984; J. Rodger (ed.) on Gillespie, Kidd & Coia, 2007; K. Downes and V. Hart on Hawksmoor, 1959 and 2002, also R. White, *Nicholas Hawksmoor and the Replanning of Oxford*, 1997; S. Cantacuzino and G. Franklin both on Howell, Killick, Partridge & Amis, 1981 and 2017; William Whyte on Sir T.G. Jackson, 2006 (also for the academic context), plus Jackson's own *Recollections*, ed. N. Jackson, 2003; G. Adler on Maguire & Murray, 2012; P. Carolin and T. Dannatt (eds) on Sir Leslie Martin, 1996, also the architect's own *Buildings and Ideas 1933–1983*, 1983; Janet Dunmur on Edward Maufe, 2019; K. Powell on Powell & Moya, 2009; G. Tyack on George Gilbert Scott, in the collection on the architect edited by P. Barnwell, G. Tyack and W. White, 2014; A. Berman, 2010, M. Crinson, 2012, and A.R. Lawrence, 2013, all on James Stirling; C. Cunningham and P. Waterhouse on Alfred Waterhouse, 1992; K. Downes, 1988, on Wren; and J.M. Robinson on James Wyatt, 2012. Local architects covered by articles in *Oxoniensia* include W. Wilkinson, H.W. Moore and C.C. Rolfe, all by Andrew Saint (vol.35, 1970) and S.L. Seckham, by Peter Howell (vol.41, 1976). Also useful is S. Huxley, *Eric Gill in Oxford*, 2011. Three books on long-lived Oxford BUILDING FIRMS are D. Sturdy, *A History of Knowles & Son*, 1997; B.R. Law, *Building Oxford's Heritage: Symm & Company from 1815*, 1998; and Liz Woolley and Siân Smith, *Kingerlee: Craftsmanship in Construction*, 2018.

The chief ANTIQUARIAN ACCOUNTS are those of Anthony Wood (1632–95), edited by J. Peshall, 1773, and J. Gutch, 1786–96; and of Thomas Hearne (1678–1735), edited by the Oxford Historical Society (11 vols, 1885–1915). The most important ILLUSTRATIONS of Oxford published before the C19 are in Loggan's *Oxonia Illustrata*, 1675; W. Williams, *Oxonia Depicta*, 1733; and the engravings collected in H.M. Petter, *The Oxford Almanacs*, 1974. J.B. Skelton, *Oxonia Antiqua Restaurata*, 1823, is another good topographical source.

GENERAL BOOKS about Oxford fill many shelves. Some rewarding C20 examples are John Betjeman, *An Oxford University Chest*, 1938; Jan Morris, *Oxford*, 1965; F. Markham, *Oxford*, 1967; and the anthology *The Oxford Book of Oxford*, ed. Jan Morris, 1978. J. Ingram, *Memorials of Oxford*, 1837 (3 vols), stands out among C19 accounts. THEMATIC STUDIES of special interest include W.J. Arkell, *Oxford Stone*, 1947, a first-rate account of the building materials, and W.F. Oakeshott, *Oxford Stone Restored*, 1975, on the post-war refacing campaign. J.S. Curl, *The Erosion of Oxford*, 1977, puts the case for conservation. Recent surveys of Oxford's ARCHAEOLOGY and early history include A. Dodd, S. Mileson and L. Webley, *The Archaeology of Oxford in the 21st Century*, 2020; D. Griffiths *et al.* (eds), *The Archaeology of East Oxford*, 2021; and Anne Dodd (ed.), *Oxford before the University*, Thames Valley Landscapes Monograph 17, 2003. Also of great value is A. Crossley (ed.), *British Historic Towns Atlas vol. VII, Oxford*, 2021. D. O'Connell, *Oxford: Mapping the City*, 2016, is a wide-ranging exploration of MAPS through the ages.

The buildings of the CITY can be explored with Malcolm Graham's six excellent *Oxford Heritage Walks* booklets, published by Oxford Preservation Trust, 2013–20. On the PARISH CHURCHES, there are books by T.G. Jackson on St Mary the Virgin, 1897; by Alan Palmer on St Mary Magdalen, 2001; by R.R. Martin on St Michael, 1967; by J. Whitehead on St Thomas, 2002; and good guidebooks on St Barnabas, St Frideswide, St Giles and Iffley church, among others. Memorial brasses are covered by J. Bertram, 2019. Catholic church buildings are surveyed at https://taking-stock.org.uk. Two good accounts of RELIGIOUS HOUSES are S. James, *The Cowley Fathers*, 2019; and A. May, *An Oxford Parish: The Church of SS Edmund and Frideswide*, 2012. Several SCHOOLS have their own histories: Magdalen College School, by R.S. Stanier, 1958, D.L.L. Clarke, 1980, and L. Brockliss, 2016; New College School, by M. Jenkinson, 2016; St Edward's School, by R.D. Hill, 1962; Summer Fields School, by R. Usborne (ed.), 1964. The origins of Oxford Brookes are covered by B. Brown, *John Henry Brookes: The Man Who Inspired a University*, 2015. Among other going concerns, there are histories of the Warneford Hospital by B. Parry-Jones, 1976, and of the Oxford Playhouse by

D. Chapman, 2008. For CINEMAS see P. J. Marriott, *Early Oxford Picture Palaces*, 1978. On COUNCIL HOUSING and its precursors up to 1939 there is M. Graham, *Wholesome Dwellings*, 2020. On the archaeological side, the CASTLE is covered by J. Munby, A. Norton, D. Poore and A. Dodd, *Excavations at Oxford Castle, 1999–2009*, Thames Valley Landscapes Monograph 44, 2019.

AREA STUDIES include Tanis Hinchcliffe's essential *North Oxford*, 1992; Ruth Fasnacht, *Summertown since 1820*, 1977; J. Badcock, *The Making of a Regency Village*, 1832 (1983 edn), also on Summertown; Mary Prior, *Fisher Row*, 1982; R.C. Whiting, *The View from Cowley*, 1983; J. Cook and L. Taylor (eds), *A Village Within a City: The Story of Old Headington*, 1987; L. Carr, R. Dewhurst and M. Henig (eds), *Binsey: Oxford's Holy Place*, 2014; and online at https://southoxfordhistory.org.uk.

ARTICLES of enduring interest include W.A. Pantin, 'The Development of Domestic Architecture in Oxford', *Antiquaries Journal* 27, 1947; R.H.C. Davis, 'The Chronology of Perpendicular Architecture in Oxford', *Oxoniensia* 12–13, 1946–7; H.S. Goodhart-Rendel, 'Oxford Buildings Criticised', *Oxoniensia* 17–18, 1952–3; E.A. Gee, 'Oxford Masons 1370–1530', *Archaeological Journal* 109, 1953; Liz Woolley, 'Industrial Architecture in Oxford, 1870 to 1914', *Oxoniensia* 75, 2010.

The best holdings of LOCAL MATERIAL are at the Oxfordshire History Centre in Cowley. Oxford City Library retains a good collection of publications. Many WEBSITES also have good material. Up-to-date coverage of recent buildings may be found at https://newoxfordarchitecture.com. For the period up to the early C20 there is a great deal at the British Newspaper Archive, www.britishnewspaperarchive.co.uk (subscription). The County Council's collections, including images, are accessible at https://heritagesearch.oxfordshire.gov.uk. For detailed coverage of some central streets and outer areas, see www.oxfordhistory. org.uk/. Many of the heritage assessments that accompany C21 planning applications include good research, accessible through the City Council's website.

Finally, publications and resources of county-wide or national scope with material relevant to Oxford are included in the Further Reading for South-East Oxfordshire, pp. 578–81.

OXFORD

COLLEGES OF THE UNIVERSITY

ALL SOULS COLLEGE
High Street

All Souls was founded by Archbishop Chichele in 1438, with Henry
VI as co-founder. That was three years before Henry founded
King's College at Cambridge, and one year after Chichele's own
foundation of St Bernard's (*see* St John's College). All Souls was
for a Warden and forty Fellows. There were to be no undergraduates, nor are there any today. Front Quad was built in 1438–43
and is still essentially in its original state. *Richard Chevynton* of
Abingdon was master mason, with *Robert Janyns Sen.* as deputy
at a lower wage. (Yet only a few years later Janyns was master
mason at Merton and at Eton.) Chichele was a graduate of New
College, which served as his model for the buildings, including
the grouping of chapel and hall – except that the hall projected
N–S at All Souls, and the chapel was placed commandingly across
the N side of the quad, rather than laterally. Also as at New
College a cloister was built. It lay N of the chapel, was three-
quarters complete by 1491, finished *c.*1510 (minus an intended
bell-tower), and demolished in 1703. On the site in 1710–35 arose
Great Quad, *Hawksmoor*'s astonishing Neo-Gothic monument,
with a new library N, replacement hall S, and a replacement
cloister along the W side, towards Radcliffe Square.

Front Quad and Warden's Lodgings

p.12 The FRONT of All Souls to the High Street is two-storeyed with
dormers, long and asymmetrical. Gate tower of four storeys,

All Souls College

1   Warden's Lodgings
2   Chapel
3   Library
4   Hall
5   Visiting Fellows' Studies

C15   C19
C16   C20
C18

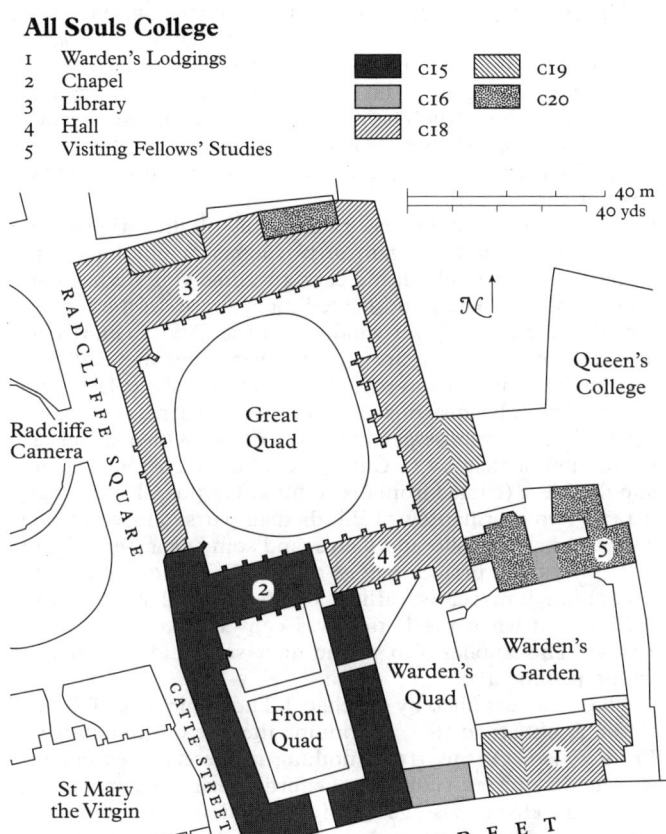

with a four-centred gateway arch and a (rebuilt) stair-turret to the NW. Three big and ornate niches, and in them two statues of the founders and a relief of Christ in Judgment: replacements by *W.C.H. King*, 1939–40, the relief in the Gill style. The whole C15 front was refaced in 1826–7 by *Daniel Robertson*, who souped it up with bigger oriels, high polygonal chimneystacks and stone gables large and small, in place chiefly of dormers added in the C16–C17. A few of the one-light windows correspond to the C15 arrangement. Battlements added *c.*1510. The E part with the second gateway was finished in 1553, and provided larger lodgings for the Warden. It keeps to the C15 model. The main gateway has two bays of lierne vaulting with bosses, the liernes forming an octagon. The basic pattern is repeated in the E gateway vault, but this must be early C19. A third doorway, on the w front to Catte Street, is of 1908 by *H. Quinton*, to serve an electricity substation.

The present WARDEN'S LODGINGS, further E, date from 1704–6 and were designed and built by *Dr George Clarke*, architectural amateur and Fellow of All Souls, for use in his own lifetime. Originally the lodgings were embattled, and the entry was in the E bay. The present six-bay Palladian façade is *Robertson*'s, done in 1825. It has a rusticated ground floor and a first floor whose first and last windows are distinguished by straight entablatures.

FRONT QUAD internally has ranges still of the original two storeys, with windows again of two lights or one light – the pattern of New College, indicating rooms with studies part-itioned off the shared and heated main space. In the E range, first floor, the closely set windows of the OLD LIBRARY are at once noticed. There are eight of them, and they still have cusping. The interior was remodelled in 1598 with a plaster tun-nel-vault with beams showing and open pendants. The panels have thin ribs in loose geometrical patterns. Other details are restoration of 1884 by *G. Curtis*, including the heraldic shields and the frieze (copied from the soffits at Corpus Christi library, p. 143). Two overmantels of Elizabethan parts, one with panels with figures of Apollo and Ceres, and some ornamented ends of the old book presses reused as panelling. Most of the wall decoration however is earliest Gothic Revival by *Sanderson Miller*, from when the library was converted to chambers in 1750–1. This applies also to the door surround (Gothic, yet with a pediment!).

The N range is filled by the chapel. The original hall followed to the E, but stood N–S, continuing the line of the E range of Front Quad. Of this HALL nothing is preserved except one passage bay of fan-vaulting – Oxford's earliest example, with that of the chapel passage – and a small doorway with quatre-foiled spandrels, in the NE corner. Also the buttery CELLAR of three by two bays, under the chapel E end. Its vault has octagonal piers and ribs with a sharp chamfer. The chapel is approached similarly by a passage of fan-vaulting, comprising four bays. The outer doorway is small, with quatrefoiled spandrels.

The CHAPEL itself has to the quad five bays with buttresses, bat-tlements and pinnacles. The windows large, of three lights, with panel tracery under four-centred arches. All this was renewed by *Henry Clutton* in 1871–2. The antechapel projects into the W range with two closely set three-light transomed windows. The chapel W front has a seven-light window flanked by three-light ones, all transomed like the others, but with two tiers of panel tracery in the central window. The upper tier of panels have cusped arches at both top and bottom. To Radcliffe Square a stair-turret at the NW corner, and a finely detailed doorway to the entrance passage, S, now blocked.

The CHAPEL INTERIOR reveals at once the T-form, repeated from New College, though here partly skewed in plan. As at New College the antechapel is two bays deep from W to E, with a slender pier for each arm. Their profile is the usual one of four shafts and four hollows. Two-centred arches. Beneath the W window high blank panelling. Similar panelling by the SEDILIA and PISCINA, but here nearly everything belongs to *Sir George Gilbert Scott*'s internal restoration of 1872–7. The roof however is original, Oxford's earliest of hammerbeam type; the carpenter was another Abingdon man, *John Branche*. It is of shallow pitch, with angels on the beams carved by *Richard Tyllok*. Original also, and marvellous, is the REREDOS, or at least much of the architectural framework. Documentary references and stylistic details (e.g. the use of small-scale curvilinear tracery) both suggest that it must be an early replacement or reworking of the 1440s reredos, as argued by Christopher Wilson.* He proposes the date *c.*1493–1511 and identifies *John Fusting* as the carver. It was restored by *Scott*. The figures, large and small, are (all but one) by *E. E. Geflowski*, 1873–5, the architectural elements mostly by *Henry Terry*. The framework is as thoroughly covered with decoration as are the *retablos* of Spain, but it has the dry, repetitive logic of the English Perpendicular, the very opposite of the wild exuberance of Spanish Late Gothic. Spun-over with ornament are the uprights, the figure bases or brackets, and the big canopies; the panelled backs of the niches are pierced; much original paint and metal leaf remains. RETABLE of coloured relief sculpture by *Kempe*, 1889. Six additional altars stood in the antechapel before the Reformation.

OTHER FURNISHINGS. The STALLS are of the mid C15, though the top parts are *Scott*'s, reportedly after fragments found. The original desk-ends have poppyheads (including the figure of a bishop), the stalls a set of forty-two excellent MISERICORDS. *Tyllok* may well have carved these too. Their motifs are simpler than those of the New College misericords, mostly heads or single animals; but also a mermaid and a man playing the bagpipes, N side W, and two royal subjects, S side: the Prince of Wales's feathers and a splendid swan with crowned neck. – LECTERN and standing CANDELABRA of brass, 1870s. – TILES. Some original ones in front of the stall fronts, re-set in *Scott*'s FLOOR, which becomes wonderfully rich towards the altar; *Farmer & Brindley* made it. – The SCREEN is a reworking of 1716 by *Sir James Thornhill* of one designed by *Wren* in 1664. The changes include the broad arched centre crowned by a broken pediment. Parapet with openwork foliage; Corinthian columns. Thornhill also painted a mural at the E end, replacing an altar-wall Last Judgment of *c.*1660–3 by *Isaac Fuller*.† – PAINTINGS from the accompanying roof panels by *Fuller*, large Michelangelesque figure fragments, are in the antechapel. The quality is low. – COMMUNION TABLE, *c.*1600, antechapel. – Two original STATUES of Henry VI and Chichele, once on

*In P. Horden (ed.), *The Reredos of All Souls College Oxford* (2021).
†Fragments of Thornhill's painting, which depicted the Apotheosis of Archbishop Chichele, are displayed in the library's W staircase. A later ALTARPIECE, a Noli me tangere by *Mengs*, 1771, is on loan to the National Gallery.

the gate tower. Though somewhat restored they are obviously of the time of the foundation, and of the highest quality. Probably by the master carver *John Massingham*, and with affinities to his effigy of Thomas Beauchamp at St Mary, Warwick. – SCULPTURE. In the passage, slab with the Resurrection of the Dead, once on the gate tower. Fragmentary, but recognizable as fitting a date *c.*1440.

STAINED GLASS. The accounts record two payments in 1441 to *John Glasier* of Oxford, towards windows in both the antechapel and the inner chapel. The first antechapel w window was paid for in 1447. What remains in the antechapel is of extremely good quality in design and technique. The restorations by *Clayton & Bell* in 1870–9 are very difficult to detect. E windows, each with traceries of four figures of Seraphim and two scrolls with the name Emanuel in the traceries, Apostles in the upper lights, Holy Women below. From N to S: first window, upper lights St Peter, St Andrew, St James; lower lights St Anne and the Virgin, the Virgin and Child, St Mary Cleopas. Second window, upper lights St John the Evangelist, St Thomas, St Matthew; lower lights St Mary Salome, St Mary Magdalene, St Anastasia (actually St Agatha).[*] Third window (S of the screen): upper lights St James the Less, St Philip, St Bartholomew; lower lights St Elizabeth with the infant John the Baptist, St Helena, St Agatha (actually St Anastasia). Fourth window: upper lights St Jude (actually St Simon), St Simon (ditto St Jude), St Mathias; lower lights St Etheldreda, St Katherine, St Sidwell or Sativola.

Antechapel w and N windows. The C15 glass in the two smaller windows in the w wall and in the half-window above the N door was originally in the Old Library. It appears to be from a different workshop from the chapel glass proper. The present ordering is *Clayton & Bell*'s of 1876–9; likewise the canopy-work, several heads, other figures as dated below, and some of the identifications of ecclesiastics. w window S, kings: top tier King Constantine, St Ethelbert, St Oswald; second tier kings Alfred, Athelstan, Edgar; third tier St Edward Martyr, Canute, St Edward the Confessor; bottom tier Edward II, John of Gaunt, Henry V. Tracery lights (1876) with half-length figures of saints and royal saints connected with England. – w window N, ecclesiastics: top tier St Cyprian, St Augustine of Canterbury, St John of Beverley; second tier St Dunstan, St Oswald, St Alphege; third tier St Ambrose, Archbishop Stratford (1876), St Jerome; bottom tier St Augustine, Archbishop Chichele (1876), St Gregory. Tracery lights, half-length saints (1876). – Window over the N door. Upper tier St Dunstan, St Edmund, Archbishop Odo of Canterbury; lower tier Henry VI, Archbishop Chichele, King Arthur. Tracery lights (1879), half-length angels holding scrolls inscribed Alleluia.

---

[*] On the restorers' misidentifications, *see* G.M. Rushforth with F.E. Hutchinson, *Medieval Glass at All Souls College* (1949).

Victorian glass: main chapel all *Clayton & Bell*, 1877–9; antechapel W window characteristic *Hardman*, 1861–2.

MONUMENTS. N arm of the antechapel. Brass of Richard Spekynton †1490, 12-in. (30-cm.) figure. – Christopher Perry †1610, split-pedimented tablet. – John Meredith †1665, big architecture with apron of book-ends. – Marow Knightley 'alias Wightwick' †1721, architectural, with a weak portrait bust. – Dodington Grevile †1737, standing monument with an urn on a sarcophagus. Attributed to *Sir Henry Cheere*.

Antechapel S arm. Brass demi-figures of David Lloyd and Thomas Baker †1510, 12-in. (30-cm.) half-figures. – Brass to Philip Polton †1461, kneeling figure of 11 in. (28 cm.). Partly lost. – Robert Hovenden, Warden, †1614. Frontal demi-figure with book and skull. Columns, a little strapwork and a wide open segmental pediment. – Edward Man †1673. Extremely gristly cartouche. – John Isham †1716. Good tablet with pilasters, foliage and flowers. By *Thomas Cartwright III*. – Dr George Clarke, Fellow and gentleman-architect (*see* below), †1736. Standing monument with an urn on a sarcophagus. Drapery beautifully around the urn, and an architectural background of rather Hawksmoorian brusqueness. Attributed to *Cheere*. – Elizabeth and Stephen Niblett †1766 and 1765, by *Nicholas Read*. With a trophy of books and an engulfing cloth. Strange. – John, 7th Viscount Tracy †1793; Henry Denison †1858. Roman altars; the latter by *W. Theed*. – Montagu Bernard †1882, designed by *Sir T. G. Jackson*, with small portrait. – B. H. Sumner †1951. Lead relief made in 1954 by *David Wynne*, in an elliptical recess.

Facing the sedilia, Sir William Anson, Warden, †1914. White marble recumbent effigy by *John Tweed*, setting by *Sir R. Blomfield*, 1918.

Great Quad and Warden's Quad

The passage to the E of the chapel leads to GREAT QUAD. The first bay is the fan-vaulted one to the former hall; the next bays however – groin-vault, saucer-dome, groin-vault, all on unfluted Ionic half-columns – at once spell out *Hawksmoor*. For Hawksmoor is the architect of Great Quad. Its genesis was in 1703, its progenitor *Dr George Clarke* of All Souls. Clarke first offered to build a house for himself somewhere on the old cloister site, which would revert to the Warden on Clarke's death. The cloister was then mostly demolished, and a short-lived colonnade made along its old W wall, from which the half-columns in the passage were later reused (more in the present W cloister and hall screen).

Designs for a new quad on the site were made *c.*1708–9, including proposals by *Clarke*, by *Dean Aldrich* of Christ Church, by *William Townesend* and by the connoisseur-collector *John Talman* (partly north Italian Baroque, partly wild Italo-Gothic). *Hawksmoor* seems to have been called in in 1709.

Many drawings of his exist for the quad, both classical and Gothic. At this early stage a grand residential range was intended across the N side, with cloister walks to E and W and the rebuilt or part-rebuilt old college to the S. But in 1710 the Barbadian plantation-owner Christopher Codrington bequeathed £6,000 to build a lavish new library. A new plan was then adopted, by which the residential part would be on the E side, the library on the N and the retained chapel and a new hall on the S. All this was to be Gothic, and firmly symmetrical, with a cross-axis from a new gateway in the cloister, W, to the centrepiece of doubled towers in the E range. Hawksmoor's designs were adopted in 1716, and work on the library began in that year. The E range was built in 1722–35, the cloister and gateway in 1728–34, the new hall with kitchen and buttery in 1730–3. The chief masons were *William Townesend* and *Bartholomew Peisley III*, and *Clarke* was closely involved throughout – although it is Hawksmoor's spirit that presides.

Thus Hawksmoor allowed the C15 chapel to determine his design – one of the 'antient durable publick buildings', whose virtues he had pleaded in a letter to Clarke in 1715. His SOUTH RANGE takes in antechapel and chapel and continues the new hall with the same tall windows, though without tracery and with Georgian glazing. There are six bays of passage and hall. The passage comes out in a portal with an ogee gable ending in an over-sized finial. But the raised, square band instead of capitals betrays Hawksmoor. The NORTH RANGE, the side of the library, repeats the same fenestration, and even the antechapel-like two-bay projection at the W end. In the middle, however, above the finely carved door, is a big SUNDIAL on a segment-headed panel with a putto head. Designed almost certainly by the young *Christopher Wren*, who was then the bursar, and made in 1658–9 by *William Byrd*. Moved in 1877 from the S parapet of the chapel.

60 The EAST RANGE of the quad is the show side, with its two Hawksmoor-Gothic towers. This side is fifteen bays long, with the TOWERS marking bays six and ten. They are square, with thin square buttressing, changing at parapet level. The square upper parts end in Gothic arched and cusped friezes. Then follow two recessed and canted stages starting behind angle pinnacles. These top stages are telescoped and again thinly buttressed.* With strict archaeology all this has nothing to do (though Hawksmoor's project to repair the twin towers of Beverley Minster may have presented him with a model). The fenestration is likewise very personal. Between the towers is first a large ogee-hooded Venetian window, then three with four-centred arches, and then three more, with ogee hoods. The top cresting has a giant Gothic middle pinnacle but a blunt, entirely un-Gothic parapet. The parts of the front on either side of the towers are of three storeys too, but considerably

---

*Octagonal stages renewed in 1836, and again in 1961–2 by *P. Faulkner* and *R.W. Wardill* of the *Ministry of Works*, during the general refacing.

lower. The first- and second-floor windows are set together in giant recesses, and their tops are again four-centred.

Great Quad is closed to the w by a SCREEN and a GATEHOUSE, as Hawksmoor, Clarke and Townesend also did at Queen's. In this fourth side of his quad Hawksmoor somehow felt much freer. He no more than alluded here and there to the Gothic. His arcade has round arches, and in the s half are groin-vaults on Doric demi-columns (with more reused shafts). The parapet is again of the blunt un-Gothic pattern. The centre gatehouse is a domed octagon, the lantern pierced by small quatrefoiled openings. The outline of the dome is ogee, and its heavy ribs have quasi-crockets, but the crowning motif is a fantastic Composite capital carrying an urn. That is Hawksmoor's finial. From Radcliffe Square the appearance is this: the screen is closed, with thin semicircular shafts and battlements. The entry is flanked by two buttresses with pinnacles and has a round arch and blank Perp panelling over. The RELIEF of Chichele on the turret was renewed by *David Kindersley*, 1991. Beautiful GATES made by *Thomas Goff*, of Swedish iron. *Hawksmoor* received payment for their design in 1734. But the boldest Baroque-Gothic is the w front of the library. Here Hawksmoor repeated the composition of the C15 antechapel completely, but his side windows have no tracery and the centre window is an ingenious variation on the fabric of the Venetian window which backs it. The side parts have cusped lancet arches, the middle a round arch with unprecedented panel tracery over. The pattern is very similar in the E window, where it is seen (from Queen's Lane) next to the E window of Hertford College chapel.

INTERIORS. Codrington's LIBRARY is as wholly classical inside 62 as it is Gothic outside. The interior is a single room just under 200 ft (61 metres) long, with a broad recess in the middle of the N side. It is also Oxford's first ground-floor library, secured against damp by means of extensive cellars below. The final cost was £12,100. Large and splendid Venetian windows in the E and W walls, the externally Gothic features already commented on. Hawksmoor stipulated deep coffering, but the executed ceiling is flat and chastely compartmented, the original plasterwork infill and friezes (by *Thomas Roberts* of Oxford, 1750–1) having been almost completely stripped in 1804. All four walls are shelved. A gallery which stops short of the windows in the end walls serves the upper shelving. The bays of shelving are divided by pilasters, and a band of metopes and triglyphs runs beneath the gallery. Hawksmoor had intended two gallery storeys; the upper one was omitted on the advice of *James Gibbs* (1740). Gibbs also recommended the existing upper cornice, which carries BUSTS of distinguished fellows (including Wren), alternating with urns. They are of painted plaster, all but one by *John Cheere*, 1749–50. Originally the entrance was in the centre, but the W vestibule now serves instead (with an external doorway for visiting readers, made 1876). The library was last restored in 2000–1, by *Donald Insall*

Associates. – STATUES: Christopher Codrington, by *Sir Henry Cheere*, 1732–4. He stands in Roman dress, a commanding figure on a high pedestal. Sir William Blackstone, 1784 by *Bacon the elder*; originally in the hall. Seated on a throne, holding a roll (Magna Carta) in his l. hand with his r. arm resting on a volume of his *Commentaries*. An excellent, uncommonly masculine work. Also an imperious BUST of Chichele by *Roubiliac*, vestibule.

The SUB-LIBRARIAN'S ROOM, NW, was adapted in 1838 with three upper galleries all round, spectacularly reached by a timber spiral stair in the central void. By *Wyatt*, apparently one of the several Oxford builders of that name rather than a member of the architectural dynasty. Inserted to its E, the ANSON READING ROOM, 1867 by *Bruton*; gallery added 1885. E of the library transept a BOOK STORE, 1908 by *H. Quinton*.

On the E side the COMMON ROOM is placed centrally. An imposing space, not cosy in the late C17 fashion. Near-square plan, under a shallow rib-vault, i.e. a quasi-Gothic treatment. Plain panelling; an arched recess on each side. Marble fireplace of 1790, and over it a copy of *Pearce*'s bust of the young Wren. Behind is the COFFEE ROOM, *H.W. Moore*'s rebuilding of 1896 of one added in 1823 by *Samuel Benham*. Moore also remodelled the SMOKING ROOM of 1881 to the S, making a bay window.

The HALL is very high in proportion to its width. The stone walls are exposed above the panelling. At the E end is a stone SCREEN with shell-headed niches and a raised centre arch carried on engaged unfluted Ionic columns, with a corniced feature with three urns over. A little foliage carving on the doorway woodwork, but the heraldry above merely painted on. At the other, high-table end are two shell niches high up. But the vault is the really amazing thing, a shallow tunnel-vault with penetrations which also coves down on the short sides and has penetrations there as well. There are transverse arches with guilloche decoration on corbels, not pilasters, and the panels of the vault have ovals along the apex. E of the hall is the BUTTERY. It is an oval room – an Italian Baroque, not an English motif – and is stone-vaulted. The coffering is most ingenious as it expands to the crown of the vault and contracts again. Borromini is the source. Hawksmoor could have studied him in engravings. Narrow Venetian window in the E wall. The lead BUST of Hawksmoor – the only known likeness – is by *Sir H. Cheere*, 1736, possibly after a lost original by Roubiliac. Also some pieces of C15 STAINED GLASS.

WARDEN'S QUAD lies S of the hall, E of Front Quad and N of the old Lodgings. Hawksmoor's hall architecture is to the N, with a return façade for the kitchen. To the S are the old Warden's Lodgings of 1553, already described. In the HOVENDEN ROOM here, ground floor, a late C17 overmantel with herm pilasters and arched panels, above a Baroque fire surround of *c.*1700. (Upper room with accomplished panelling of *c.*1600 with a Doric frieze, and another overmantel with blank arches.)

To the E the WARDEN'S GARDEN, with the plain back of the C18 Lodgings to the S. These have additions to the W, 1858, Gothic, and to the E, 1885 by *W.C. Marshall*. On the N side a plain, rambling building of stone gables and sash windows, chiefly comprising the VISITING FELLOWS' STUDIES of 1966–7. By *I.W. Beese* of *Oxford Architects Partnership*. The W part incorporates the MANCIPLE'S HOUSE, remnant of a building of 1594. Earlier proposals for this range included a radical, ribbon-windowed Modernist project of 1937–8 by *Maxwell Fry*.

BALLIOL COLLEGE
Broad Street and Magdalen Street

According to legend, John de Balliol of Barnard Castle kidnapped the Bishop of Durham, his local rival, sometime in the later 1250s. As a penance John rented a house at Oxford and paid to maintain some scholars there, an arrangement in place by 1266. His widow, Dervorguilla, gave the foundation a charter in 1282. The scholars were to study up to the M.A. but not to the higher, i.e. the theology, degree. That was amended in 1340, when the scholars were increased in number from sixteen to twenty-two. By then the college also had a stone-built chapel, but a proper quad was not built until the C15. This is the century of the few surviving medieval parts. Even of these, not much is in the original form. Balliol indeed, in spite of some quite substantial Georgian ranges, is essentially a C19 college. Its rise during the mastership of Richard Jenkyns (1819–54) to the climax under Jowett (1870–93) is familiar as part of the intellectual history of Oxford. Architecturally it means *Basevi, Salvin, Butterfield* and *Waterhouse* – architects of character and competence. Yet Balliol has been unlucky with them. None of the four is at his best here, and the shape of the two quads is such as to have offered little opportunity for consistent compositions. The C20 filled the remaining gap in Garden Quad, and replaced some lesser ranges with blocks by *Geoffrey Beard* of *Oxford Architects Partnership* in 1964–8.

Facing Broad Street and Magdalen Street

Balliol has the longest FRONTAGE of any Oxford college. It stretches for some 800 ft (245 metres), along Broad Street then northward along Magdalen Street and into St Giles'. From the E the first item on Broad Street is *Waterhouse*, 1867–8, his first Oxford commission. His range, immediately adjoining the gates of Trinity, is Gothic, of late C13 French motifs, approximately symmetrical, but only at first glance. In fact the interest of the composition is the off-centre placing of the gate tower, *p.97*

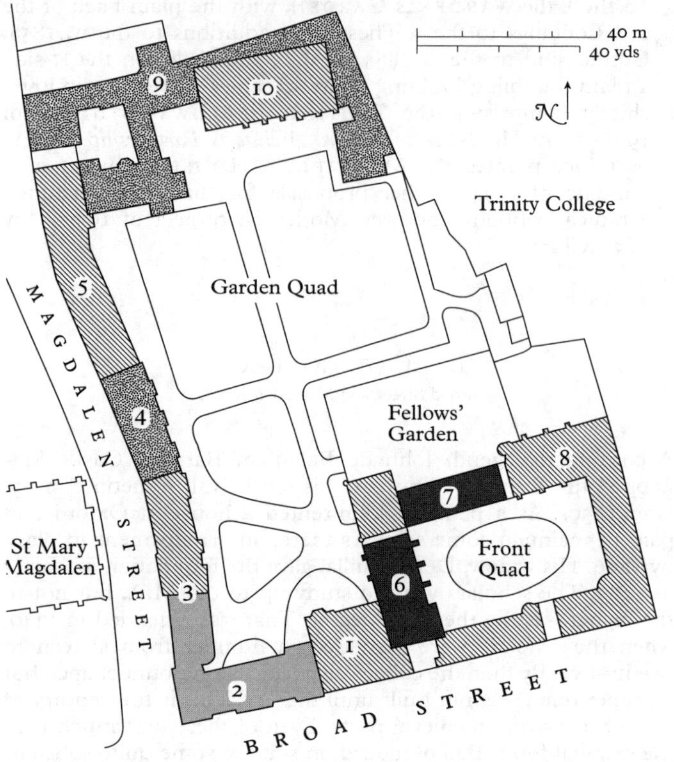

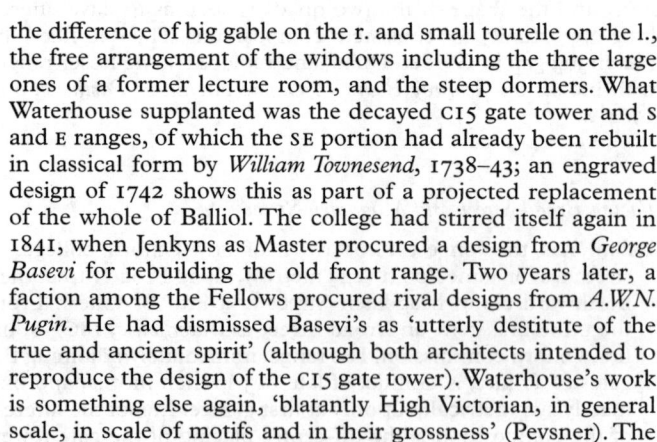

Balliol College

■	C15	▨	C19
▨	C18	░	C20

1	Master's Lodgings	6	Old hall
2	Fisher Buildings	7	Library
3	Bristol Buildings	8	Chapel
4	Warren's Buildings	9	New Building
5	Salvin's Buildings	10	Hall

the difference of big gable on the r. and small tourelle on the l.,
the free arrangement of the windows including the three large
ones of a former lecture room, and the steep dormers. What
Waterhouse supplanted was the decayed C15 gate tower and S
and E ranges, of which the SE portion had already been rebuilt
in classical form by *William Townesend*, 1738–43; an engraved
design of 1742 shows this as part of a projected replacement
of the whole of Balliol. The college had stirred itself again in
1841, when Jenkyns as Master procured a design from *George
Basevi* for rebuilding the old front range. Two years later, a
faction among the Fellows procured rival designs from *A.W.N.
Pugin.* He had dismissed Basevi's as 'utterly destitute of the
true and ancient spirit' (although both architects intended to
reproduce the design of the C15 gate tower). Waterhouse's work
is something else again, 'blatantly High Victorian, in general
scale, in scale of motifs and in their grossness' (Pevsner). The

black pointing of the Bath stone especially is difficult to love. The gate tower was to have had in addition a pyramid roof, but the college demurred.

Waterhouse's MASTER'S LODGINGS, which follow as a visually separate building, are in the same style and share many motifs. They too date from 1867–8. After that we reach FISHER BUILDINGS, of 1769–70 by *Henry Keene*, named after a former Fellow who gave £3,000. Nine major bays to the Broad, four to the w. The centre has a pediment, the two end bays tripartite first-floor windows with columns. In detail however the design is now not all Keene, because *Waterhouse* did some gratuitous tinkering when he refaced it in 1870. Originally the tripartite windows were of the Venetian type, i.e. with an arched head at the centre instead of the present little pediment there. Waterhouse also added the bracketed pediment over the middle window, erased the carved garlands in the main pediment, etc. That accounts for the slightly Victorian-municipal look.

BRISTOL BUILDINGS towards Magdalen Street follows immediately. It is earlier – of 1716–20 – but was at first only six bays long. To reface it and extend it into a unified façade of fifteen with a three-bay central pediment but lacking in other decorative elements was *Basevi*'s job. The enlargement made in 1826–7 is called BASEVI BUILDINGS, and the whole now sports an ungainly mansard added in 1926 by *E. P. Warren*. Next are WARREN'S BUILDINGS of 1912–13, all *Warren*'s own, and one of the most successful buildings of Balliol. The window rhythm is 1:2:1:1:1:2:1. The pairs and the central window are placed in projections and end in pediments. It is neither Palladian nor Grecian, though in its motifs classical. *Salvin*'s SALVIN'S BUILDINGS, which follow, are plain collegiate Perp, asymmetrical, with gables and oriels. The dates are

Balliol College, Broad Street frontage.
Lithograph by E. Wimbridge, 1869

1852–3, and 1873–4 for *Waterhouse*'s short matching addition N
of the gate tower. Finally another building by *Warren*, 1906–7,
of yellow Doulting stone, also asymmetrical, but in the style of
*c.*1675. Cross-windows and a three-bay pediment, handsome
and certainly not run of the mill.*

Front Quad

FRONT QUAD is not large. It consists of *Waterhouse*'s E and S
ranges, *Butterfield*'s chapel on the N side from the decade before,
and in addition the W half of the N range and the W range, the
only medieval remains of Balliol. These have been so much
restored that they don't spell C15 any longer. In fact the quad
leaves one with a feeling of lopsidedness, due to Waterhouse's
scale and the grossness of his details already commented on.†
Butterfield also is never a convenient neighbour, though he is
quieter here than at Keble.

The W range has as its principal feature the former HALL,
part of the library since 1878. It must have been complete
by 1430, when glass was given. The present high, transomed
two-light windows with minimum Perp tracery are apparently
reliable, but the battlements and the plaster vault within belong
to *James Wyatt*'s remodelling of 1792–4. He also changed the
screens end from S to N. One of the doorways of the old screens
passage is exposed inside the present College Office corridor.
Its arch has two broad continuous hollow chamfers and a
deeper moulding between. The stained glass includes re-set
C15 and C16 shields in the E windows. In 1960–1 the room was
floored across by *Geoffrey Beard*, in tandem with refacing of
the college's medieval parts. S of the hall were the C15 offices,
with part of the Master's Lodgings above and facing Front
Quad. Of these the large and wide oriel window bears witness,
though heavily renewed. It is canted and transomed, with four
lights to the front. Pretty tracery below the transom. The arms
on the corbels refer to Bishop Gray of Ely (†1478). The N end
of the former hall range is an addition by *Salvin* in 1853–4,
before the college outgrew its old hall altogether. New kitchens
were included, and a new cross-passage entry to the hall (and
through to Garden Quad) in succession to the passage which
Wyatt had made within the old hall space. The original doors
from the C15 gate were placed here in 1926. Salvin's addition
ends in a tower with higher stair-turret.

The N range has the LIBRARY, built in two phases: the
W part probably by 1431 (date in stained glass), the E part
*c.*1475–83. Its close-set windows are unmistakable. They are
original, of two lights, with plain transoms and very depressed
pointed arches. Another C15 feature is the renewed ogee-gabled

*The staircase is mid-C18, reused from the previous house here (also panelling etc.).
†In Staircase II room 5, lively MURALS of the college's foundation legend, 1933 by
Christopher Fremantle, then a recent graduate.

doorway to the chapel passage, E, relocated from the hall entrance when *Wyatt* remodelled the library in 1792–4. The battlements are again his, and the pretty plaster rib-vault. By Wyatt also the bookcases, quite simple, but with fancy-Gothic tops to the ends. The library is altogether the best survivor of his medievalizing Oxford interiors. The scrolly woodwork round the entry and the sculptures at the far end (St Catherine and angels) are however from the refurnishing of the old chapel, c. 1635–40. Very rustic figure-work. Above the entrance a handsome late C17 cartouche in the Gibbons style.

The library's STAINED GLASS is fragmentary but original, and seems to have followed a consistent scheme. An important feature was a series of shields of arms of benefactors, originally surrounded by elaborate garlands and intertwined with inscribed scrolls. Also on the shields the Arma Christi (Instruments of the Passion) and the Trinity, S side, W. In the vestibule C15 figures of the prophet Sophonias and St Jerome, probably also from the original glazing.

Butterfield's CHAPEL, replacing that of 1522–9, was built in 1856–7 and cost £8,000. The architect used his favourite horizontal stripes of Italian derivation, here of white and red stone irregularly spaced. The voussoirs are also irregularly banded. The style is late C13, the tracery is Geometrical and there is a thin polygonal NW turret in succession to that of the C16 chapel. After years of post-Victorian denigration, Butterfield's interior was neutered in *Sir Walter Tapper*'s renovations of 1925–37: the elaborate alabaster polychromy has mostly been painted or plastered over, and the Victorian fittings removed. (*T. G. Jackson* had already made designs in 1911 to rebuild the chapel, but the donation offered for the purpose was not taken up.) *Tapper*'s replacements are broadly Neo-Wren. The best are the 1920s pieces at the E end, especially the rich PANELLING carved by *Laurence Turner*, and the silvery ALTAR FRONTAL. This looks Continental Baroque but is a war memorial of 1927–8, designed with the architect's son *Michael Tapper* and executed by *Bainbridge Reynolds*.* – ALTAR RAILS by *Maufe*, 1960. – PULPIT. 1630s. It has the familiar perspective arches. – LECTERN. A splendid crowned eagle of brass, c. 1500. The inscription dates from the 1630s refurnishing. – ORGAN CASE. 1937, by *Michael Tapper*.

STAINED GLASS. The C16 chapel contained an important series of contemporary windows, now partly re-set, if somewhat dislocated. They may have some link with work for Wolsey's Cardinal College (Christ Church), which stalled in 1529. At least, an inscription identifies the E window as given in that year by Lawrence Stubbs, one of Wolsey's chaplains, and brother to Richard Stubbs, Master of Balliol in 1518–25. A stylistic connection has been suggested with *James Nicholson*, a glass-stainer of German or Netherlandish origins who

---

* *Butterfield*'s altar is now at Litton Cheney church, Dorset.

worked for Wolsey at Oxford, and for the king at King's College Chapel, Cambridge.

E window. Passion and Ascension scenes, reassembled by *Hugh Arnold* in 1912. In at least two cases – Agony in the Garden and Ecce Homo – the glass-painter used designs from Dürer's engraved Passion of 1512. From l. to r., starting at the bottom row: Angel with the arms of Stubbs, with fragmentary inscription giving the date 1529; kneeling figure of Lawrence Stubbs; fragments; kneeling figure of Richard Stubbs; angel with the arms of Balliol. Second row: St Lawrence with the arms of Stubbs; Christ at the Column; Pilate washing his hands; Pietà; St Richard with the Stubbs rebus. Third row: Agony in the Garden; Crowning with Thorns; Crucifixion (the upper part *O'Connor*'s restoration of 1857); Ecce Homo; Resurrection. Fourth row: Betrayal of Christ (upper part much disturbed); Christ carrying the Cross; Arrest of Christ; Ascension. Tracery: fragments and the Stubbs initials.

S side, first window from E. Six scenes from the legend of St Catherine, dated 1529. Also given by the Stubbs brothers. From l. to r., lower row: St Catherine converting the Empress; St Catherine enthroned (very worn and disturbed); St Catherine buried by three angels on Mount Sinai. Upper row: the Breaking of the Wheel; St Catherine bound to a column and scourged; her decapitation. Second from E, C16 panels, incomplete and partly composite, with C17 insertions: St Edward the Confessor; the Virgin (from a Crucifixion); St Frideswide; St Lawrence (head and shoulders lost); St Hugh of Lincoln; part of a St Mary Magdalene; fragments.

N side, first two from E, and antechapel windows. These contain glass by *Abraham van Linge* from two windows of 1637. On the N side are the Sickness and Recovery of Hezekiah; in the antechapel St Philip and the Eunuch. Third window from E, mostly 1529–30. Fragmentary and dislocated inscriptions below, two dated 1530, the other recording Richard Atkins's benefaction, all in the same fine classical lettering. Second row, from l. to r.: John Hygden, President of Magdalen College; Sir William Compton and two sons (incomplete); Thomas Knolles, Sub-Dean of York. Third row: Virgin adoring the Child, with two inserted C16 heads; Thomas Chase, Master in the 1410s, and eight Fellows, from a C15 window formerly in the library W wall; C17 panel, van Linge style (identification uncertain). Fourth row: shields, including two from the Compton window.

MONUMENTS. Antechapel. Bishop Parsons †1819. By the younger *Bacon*. No figures. – John Seymour, full-length brass of 1844 by *Hardman*, designed by *Pugin*. – James Riddell †1866. Another brass in the medieval tradition. – Chapel. Benjamin Jowett †1893. By *E. Onslow Ford*, 1897. Miniature of a large conception, in green marble, bronze, and gold mosaic. Recumbent effigy on a sarcophagus. Two putti l. and r. – Sundry tablets, e.g. Sir John Conroy †1901 and Richard Nettleship †1892, with floral surrounds. Of the many minor bronze panels, two are by *Eric Gill*: E. Caird, 1911 and H.H. Asquith, 1929 (antechapel).

– By *Gill* and his brother *Macdonald Gill* the WAR MEMORIAL of 1922 in the chapel passage, also of bronze panels. *F. Etchells* designed the Second World War panels, 1950–1.

Garden Quad

GARDEN QUAD is a garden, not a quad (part of it was formerly known as The Grove). One must of course not be pedantic about quads being quadrangular, but what is essential for a quad is the feeling of enclosure. This does not arise here. The size is too large, the form too irregular, the buildings too discrepant, the trees, especially the group of chestnuts, too big. The s and the long w ranges are continuous and largely confirm what their outer façades have shown, though the Lodgings are quieter here, and Basevi less orderly. Between these, *Keene*'s Fisher Buildings shows a nice symmetry in the staircase arrangements.

N of the chapel is the FELLOWS' GARDEN, enclosed by *Butterfield*'s wall. In the garden an assembly of FRAGMENTS from the C15 gate tower. They include a doorhead with quatrefoils and vault bosses from the passage. Also a wooden SEAT designed by *Comper*, 1936.

At the N end of Garden Quad is the NEW BUILDING of 1966–8, by *Oxford Architects Partnership* (*Geoffrey Beard*): two parallel ranges connected by a bridge at second-floor level. The boldly chamfered sills and the way in which some of the windows are broken round the angles date the building unmistakably. The most characteristic motif is pairs of thin concrete posts, quite high, to support projections and e.g. the bridge. The materials are ashlar and pre-cast concrete. The building replaced some lesser ranges by *Waterhouse*, and has also obstructed Salvin's gateway to St Giles'. Its counterpart is the SENIOR COMMON ROOMS of 1964–6 (with lecture room, teaching rooms etc.), built on to the SE angle of *Waterhouse*'s HALL of 1876–7, again with the sacrifice of lesser buildings by that architect. True, the hall is second-class Waterhouse, but, as it is now placed, it is in a deadly embrace. The overemphasized verticals of the E attachment, no doubt meant to harmonize with Waterhouse's buttresses, do not really do that. They are multiplied on the upper floor, and the asymmetry at the top clashes with Waterhouse's endeavour in the late C13 style. Waterhouse's best features are the spacious outer staircase up to the porch and the mighty but intricate framing inside the roof, below the flèche (this now unbalanced visually to the outside, because the chimneys have been lopped short). The dais end has a big window with odd personal details about the gable. This and the porch detail alone might make one guess Waterhouse. In the hall the two fireplaces are in the long sides, but not opposite one another. The Neo-Elizabethan panelling and screen are by *Paul Waterhouse*, 1910. He blocked up the lower parts of the windows. Organ case of 1911 above the screen. The lower storey contained the usual services, but also teaching rooms and a chemistry laboratory.*

For HOLYWELL MANOR, MASTER'S FIELD and JOWETT WALK *see* Perambulation 2, pp. 417–20; for the HISTORIC COLLECTIONS CENTRE *see* St Cross church, p. 392.

BRASENOSE COLLEGE
Radcliffe Square and High Street

The college dates its foundation to 1509, jointly by William Smith, Bishop of Lincoln and Chancellor of the University, and Sir Richard Sutton, a lawyer and courtier. There was provision for a Principal, six senior Fellows and four or five probationary ones, eleven graduate students, and additionally six sons of noblemen who were to pay their own way – 'gentlemen commoners', after the fashion of those at Magdalen. But this is to neglect the prehistory, for by the 1500s there was already a Brasenose Hall on part of the site (the name is thought to come from a brass door knocker at this hall). First recorded in 1244, this proto-Brasenose was bought by the University in 1262 but then leased independently from 1381. By the early C16 Brasenose Hall had taken over no fewer than ten other halls, most notably Little University Hall on the corner of Brasenose Lane, where University College had its first home (*see* p. 299). Of all these early halls the former kitchen of Brasenose Hall is the only remaining part, s of the Old Quad of the C16 foundation.

The C17 added a very demonstrative chapel and library to the s of Old Quad, completing the little quad known as Deer Park. New Quad followed to the w and s in the late C19 and early C20, taking the college down to the High. Its architect was *Sir T. G. Jackson*, who also incorporated a few older buildings by St Mary's church. The counterpart to these, hidden behind the w side of New Quad, is *Powell & Moya*'s inspired infill of 1959–60.

Old Quad and Deer Park

OLD QUAD has a renewed foundation stone of 1509 (overdoor, SW corner), and a likely completion date in or just after 1518, when payment was made for lead for the gate-tower roof. It shows one characteristic of a C16 origin at once: the typical college windows, mostly of two lights or one, have uncusped,

---

*The hall would have been doomed altogether under *Godfrey Samuel & Valentine Harding*'s Modernist proposal of 1936 for a replacement hall on the site of the Master's Lodgings, but this was only ever the pet scheme of one Fellow. In 1961–2 the college again mooted demolition along Broad Street, this time of Waterhouse's gate-tower range, for a building by *R. D. Russell & Partners*.

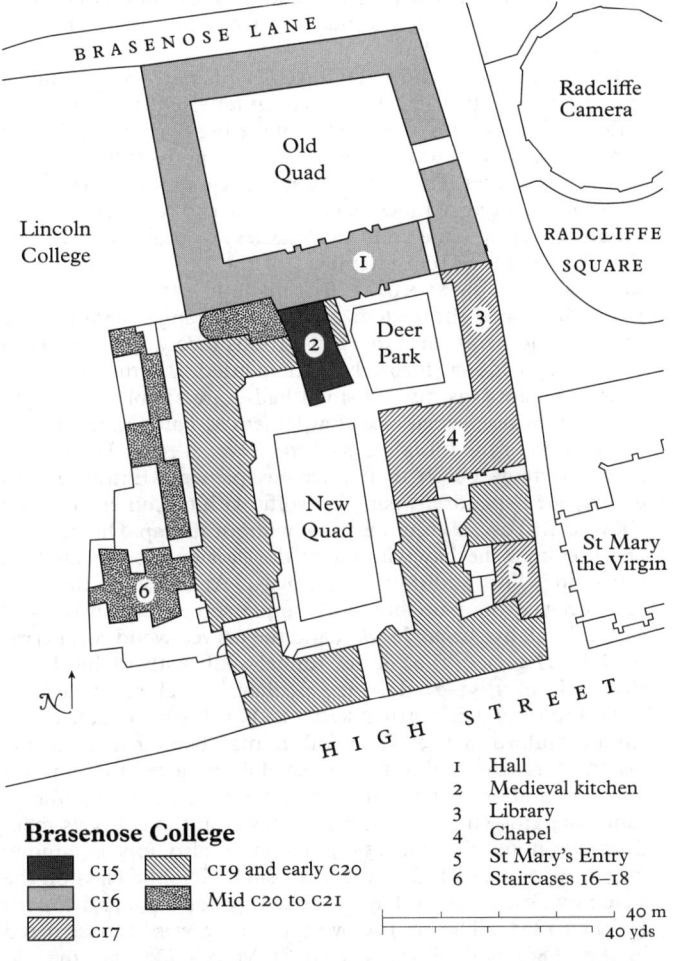

Radcliffe
Camera

Old
Quad

Lincoln
College

RADCLIFFE
SQUARE

Deer
Park

New
Quad

St Mary
the Virgin

N

HIGH STREET

1   Hall
2   Medieval kitchen
3   Library
4   Chapel
5   St Mary's Entry
6   Staircases 16–18

Brasenose College

■ C15 ▨ C19 and early C20
▨ C16 ▨ Mid C20 to C21
▨ C17

40 m
40 yds

round-arched heads. The gate tower is a rich and sophisticated
design, owing much to the Founder's Tower at Magdalen. Entry
is through the original doors, within a broad, flattened four-
centred archway with quatrefoiled spandrels. All-over panelling
above, up to the beginning of the two topmost stages. Here the
frontage steps back, and a shallow-sided oriel appears between
twin statue niches and twin half-octagonal buttresses. A third
niche is placed centrally on the topmost floor. The windows
below, fitting neatly into the panelling system, are reinstatements of the C16 form by *J.C. Buckler*, 1863. The statues too
are his, and the rib-vault of the gate passage. Externally the
tower is now crowded by the quad's battlemented third storey,
begun in 1605 and extended all round in 1635 (mason *Richard
Maude*). The four pretty oriels distributed across the E front are

also 1630s; by 1733 the far l. one had been extended to ground level. Next to this bay the mid-C17 work begins, library and chapel, described below.

Inside the quad the gate tower is plainer, with a higher stair-turret rising in its NW corner. Otherwise the quad is very different from all others by virtue of the big dormers of the C17 top storey, which contrast with its continuous-wall treatment on the outer faces. The lower storeys have a variety of windows: some original (e.g. E range, N part), some C17 (e.g. oriels on the N and W sides), some early C18 (sashes, W and S sides), some Victorian (sundry reinstatements of the C16 pattern). The N side also has a big SUNDIAL first made in 1719.

On the S side the system of the other ranges continues W and E of the HALL, and this also groups nicely. It has a broad canted bay window, formerly battlemented. But the other two windows – for it is quite a small hall – are simple three-light windows of no special size. Battlemented parapet, inset with naïve busts of the founders by *Hugh Davies*, 1636. Then a bay with a shallow porch to the screens passage. Entrance with quatrefoiled spandrels, panelled soffit within. Lantern of 1782 above with Tuscan columns, now without its cap. On entering one sees that the bay window at the dais end is repeated on the S side. This addition is of 1683–4. At the same time the hall received the panelling and simple screen with its carved garlands, all by *Arthur Frogley*, and the carved wood royal arms by *John Hugeloot*. The plaster tunnel-vault with its big lobed shapes is of 1751–2, the nice pedimented chimneypiece of 1748. Over the dais a DOOR KNOCKER, probably C12, brought from Stamford in 1890. The college maintains that it was the original 'brazen nose' of Brasenose Hall, removed to Stamford in the migration of 1333. It may rather have been a handle or sanctuary ring (the present brazen nose on the college's main door was noted there in 1534). The nose also appears among minor 1630s stained-glass pieces, N side. Heraldic glass on the S side by *Powells*, 1889 (bay; designed by *Jackson*), and *Francis Eginton*, 1821. (The roof above the ceiling was reconstructed in the 1680s with timbers from St Mary's College, the old Austin Canons' establishment in New Inn Hall Street, later Frewin Hall (cf. the chapel roof, below). It has cambered collar-beam trusses and wind-braces. Below the hall a vaulted UNDERCROFT of 1680, now partitioned. Three of the columns remain; cf. Lincoln College undercroft.)

The present KITCHENS and other rooms W of the hall were renovated in 2009–12 by *Berman Guedes Stretton*. A domed cylindrical lobby was created within the SW angle, improving the circulation between rooms and floors. The first floor W of the hall was originally occupied by the chapel, with the original library in a corresponding position on the N side; the chapel at least may have been conceived as a temporary arrangement. The SENIOR COMMON ROOM, panelled in 1708–11 (Corinthian pilasters), now occupies its space. In the W range alongside is the SMOKING ROOM, made in 1899 by *Jackson* and extended by *Guy Dawber* in 1936. The former LIBRARY has also been panelled, by *Arthur Frogley* in 1678. Its ceiling is a renewal of 1886 by *Curtis* of the ribbed early C16 design. (In other rooms an unusual frequency of worthwhile chimney-pieces of different C17 dates, one with an overmantel landscape painting. Also in the Eckersley Room, SW, a concealed section of early C16 boarded wall painted with yellow stars.)

The PRINCIPAL'S LODGINGS are now confined to the room over the gateway and the rooms to the N. The TOWER BURSARY (over the gateway room) has a ceiling of *c.*1635 with nice rib panels, all four identical, and central pendant. Panelling of 1699, with fat garlands and arms over the fireplace. DRAWING ROOM (over the porter's lodge) with entirely mid-1630s panelling, figured frieze and columned overmantel. The MUNIMENT ROOM within the tower has cupboards and a stone groin-vault all of 1816–17. In the HULME LIBRARY, S of the tower, two elaborate brick chimneystacks are exposed in the wall. They date from the early C16, i.e. before the C17 top storey engulfed them, and have no known parallel at Oxford.

The DEER PARK, alias CHAPEL QUAD, represents mid-C17 Oxford at its most distinctive. The W side however is the MEDI-EVAL KITCHEN, i.e. the retained late C15 kitchen of old Brase-nose Hall, attached askew to the hall and used since 2012 as an additional dining room. The big collar-beam roof with two tiers of arch braces is original, the brick Tudor-style chimney is an enhancement of 1912. For the rest, the S side is the chapel, the E side the cloister and the library above it. They date as a group from 1656–64, and were originally complemented by an ornamented wall to screen the kitchen to the W. *John Jackson*, chief mason for Canterbury Quad at St John's back in the 1630s, was in charge (master joiner *John Wild* of London, master carver *Simon White* of Oxford). Funds for a new chapel had been accumulating since 1613, and it is likely that the outlines of the design at least were established well before breaking ground. However, much of the classical vocabulary that is intermingled so potently with its Gothic detail is bang up-to-date for the 1650s. We know also that Jackson was paid £20 in 1659 for his 'model' (design) for the chapel roof, 'and his paynes taken about it'. So it seems likely that the other details of this complex and sophisticated project also belong to the 1650s, which would make it a rare showpiece indeed from those lean years, and not just in Oxford.

The CLOISTER details are intensely surprising: instead of buttresses there are short, broad, attached pillars, and between them, instead of normal openings, two vertically placed oval openings per bay. Frieze of fat garlands; doorcase at the N end with interpenetrating pediments. Yet the plinth is Gothic in outline, and the LIBRARY above has closely set transomed two-light windows with Perp tracery but a classical apron below each. Towards Radcliffe Square there are nine such library windows, then an untraceried Venetian oriel window with thick garlands and other decorative motifs accompanying those of the chapel E end. By contrast the cloister windows here are insertions of 1807, of standard Perp type, after more ambitious proposals by *Soane* were abandoned. On both sides the parapet alternates between castellation and taller sections topped with broad triangular pediments, stressing again the alternation between classical and Gothic.

The CHAPEL takes this hybridity to still greater heights. Towards the quad the cloister runs W along the side until the antechapel is reached; for Brasenose chapel still continues the T-plan, the final example of this Oxford convention. The windows are separated by deep pilasters, effectively half-square Corinthian columns, with a cornice above. The window tracery is of the simplified, post-Perpendicular kind typical of the mid C17. To the sides the main motif is a plain circle. High parapet with urns looking much like Wren's or Vanbrugh's. The antechapel N portal has Baroque Ionic columns and a wide open segmental pediment and nothing Gothic. In the spandrels little leather faces, like those Jackson used at St John's. The big window above is oblong, i.e. not arched at all. However it operates again with the circles – two this time – and above it is a pediment, but the top parapet curves up to another urn, and the curves have crockets. It could be Hawksmoor nearly. The E and W windows are elaborately Gothic too, and incorrect in outline only in so far as the rose in the top of the tracery is not a circle but a horizontally placed oval. The W front otherwise was given an orthodox Perp parapet and pinnacles in *J.C. Buckler's* refacing of 1869, but the E front preserves the C17 design, without which Radcliffe Square would be much the poorer.* Here the angles are pilasters, and above the window is a big, wilfully incurved open pediment, and above that again an upswept and crocketed parapet with urns – the mixture as before.

The CHAPEL INTERIOR is unforgettable because of its intricate plaster vault. This glorious climax of C17 Gothic has strong affinities with the Perp vault of the cathedral choir, itself a playful evocation in stone of the lower stages of a timber hammerbeam roof. But the relationship here is the other way round, for the plasterwork hides a timber roof reused from the early C16 chapel of St Mary's College (*see* Frewin Hall, p. 436). The design is close enough to that of Corpus Christi hall, finished in 1516, to suggest the same master carpenter, *Humphrey Coke*, or perhaps his assistant *Robert Carow*. As transformed for Brasenose, the central section between the lateral arches that connect the posts is fan-vaulted, with a central row of pendants. (Above are the upper collar-beams, and tiered windbraces.) Window jambs from St Mary's chapel were also taken for reuse. As finished in 1659 the vaulting plaster was simply whitened; present decoration of 1895, designed by *Kempe*, executed by *Charles Powell*.

*The window tracery here was first replaced in 1845, by *Philip Hardwick*; some C17 remains are built into garden walls at Denton House, Cuddesdon (q.v.).

FURNISHINGS. REREDOS, 1738–48. Of various marbles and imitation marbles; heavily renewed in 1902. The centre has a pediment on two grey Composite columns. – COMMUNION RAIL. Mid-C18, of fine wrought iron. Now turned sideways l. and r. of the altar. – STALLS, *c.*1660. Backs with simple perspective motifs, extremely projecting cornice. – PULPIT. Square, on legs. Also with these perspective motifs. – LECTERN. Given in 1731. The traditional brass eagle, but bigger than usual. – CHANDELIERS. Of brass, Baroque shape. 1749. – SCREEN. Largely of 1892 by *T.G. Jackson*, to carry his ORGAN, but with late C17 parts. – PAINTINGS (antechapel). The Child of Hale, a giant who visited the college in 1617. Copy of 1842 of the original at Hale Hall, Lancs. Also two paintings of the Child's handprint. – STAINED GLASS. Patchy E window by *Kempe*, 1894–6. Displaced to the W window, figures by *James Pearson*, 1776, to designs by *J.H. Mortimer.* The present surround of 1897 is also *Kempe*'s. Choir side windows by *Wailes*, 1844 (SE) to 1860s. Antechapel: S, 1887 by *Powells*, designed by *Jackson* (Mark Jones); N, *Clayton & Bell*, 1894. – SCULPTURE. Bust of the 1st Baron Grenville by *Nollekens*, given 1811. – MONUMENTS. Robert Shippen, Principal, †1745. By *Sir Robert Taylor.* With a bust on top, the head turning sideways. Originally a standing monument. – Hugh Cholmondeley, by *Chantrey*, 1817–18. No figure. – Frodsham Hodson †1822. By *Samuel Manning I.* Gown and cap draped over the sarcophagus. – James Smith †1838. By *R. Westmacott Jun.* A seated and a standing youth, both in profile. Very still. – Walter Pater †1894, Fellow of Brasenose. Bronze plaque in an alabaster frame. Medallions of Pater, Plato, Dante, Leonardo and Michelangelo, and a spreading willow about them. Designed by *Sir W. Blake Richmond.* – Albert Watson, by *Eric Gill*, 1905, i.e. very early. This is recognizable by the stubby columns l. and r., of Webb–Lethaby descent, and by the lettering not being yet of Gill's later purity. – First World War memorial by *Laurence Turner*, 1921. – Cloister. Second World War memorial, 1951. Designed by *Maufe*, carved by *Barry Hart.* – Cartouches, including John Myddelton †1671, by *Thomas Wood* of Oxford.

The LIBRARY INTERIOR is by *Wyatt*, 1779–82, with *James Pears* as executant. Wyatt gave the room a tripartite arrangement with screens at each end of two Corinthian columns with figured capitals. The S end is apsed. Segmental vault with discreet painted plasterwork in two registers of shallow sunk panels. Projecting bookcases of 1891. Wyatt's arrangement blocked the W windows with shelving, removed in 1954. In 2015–17 the cloister below was converted for library use by *Lee/Fitzgerald Architects.*

New Quad

NEW QUAD opens out from the SW corner of Deer Park. The architect is *Jackson*, the dates 1881–6, W side, and 1887–9 and

1907–9 (W of the tower), S and E sides. Jackson's job was a big
one: S to the High Street, a long W side, and a short lower N
link with the old kitchen which, most praiseworthily, it was
decided to keep. Thus Brasenose, which had grown greatly in
numbers through the C19, achieved a façade to the High. In this
façade Jackson surpassed himself. It fits in with the Victorian
tradition of Gothic gate-tower façades, with motifs taken over
from C15 and C16 Oxford but significantly modified. The gate
tower has big carved heraldry – a borrowing from Cambridge
– and is of course asymmetrically placed. Three gables W, four
and an angle tourelle E, where new Principal's Lodgings were
provided. Each bay has an oriel, which again was a novelty (but
cf. G. G. Scott Jun. at St John's, 1880). Also new for Victorian
college work was the embrace of rubble stone rather than
ashlar for the ordinary walling. Otherwise the frontage best
establishes its post-Scott, post-Waterhouse date by the exquisite close foliage decoration of the oriel parapets (chief carver,
R. H. Maples of *Farmer & Brindley*). This is Arts and Crafts at
a very early moment. The quad likewise is handled with conscious regard to picturesqueness, here with more of Jacobean
than of Tudor inspiration. The liveliest motif is the stair-turret
with ogee cupola, behind the gate tower – for the tower as built
does not extend right through the S range. Also broad and less
broad canted bays, bigger canted projections for some of the
staircases, and a couple of oriels. The one on the N side by the
kitchen was for the undergraduates' library; now the SHACK-
LETON ROOM, with access via the new circulation drum.

The E side of New Quad now also takes in two substantial
houses S of the chapel, formerly rental properties of the college.
ST MARY'S ENTRY, S, is timber-framed and C17 towards St
Mary's church. Underbuilt and renovated in 1884 by *H.W.
Moore* for Canon Wordsworth, including the ornate door hood
on satyr brackets, carrying the jetty above. Also by *Moore* is
STAMFORD HOUSE, N, 1894–5; stone in front, brick behind,
turning timber-framed at the top.

The making of New Quad fulfilled an enduring ambition
at Brasenose. *Hawksmoor* had produced at least five designs
for the site in the 1720s–30s, all grand and classical, some of
which also encompassed the replacement of Old Quad. *Soane*
supplied classical designs in 1804 and 1807, the teenaged *Philip
Hardwick* a Gothic one in 1810. A modest residential range was
added instead, and this was demolished by Jackson.

STAIRCASES 16–18. After the Second World War the college
needed more accommodation. The only vacant space was the
desolate back bit behind Jackson's W range and N of some
annexed High Street houses, and here *Powell & Moya* managed
to make something delightful. Preliminary designs were made
in 1956, construction followed in 1959–60. The job architect
was *Richard Burton*, later of Ahrends, Burton & Koralek. This
was Powell & Moya's first university project. Blue Boar at
Christ Church (p. 139) and Cripps Building at St John's, Cambridge would not have happened without it, and the executed

version shares motifs with both. It is a most ingenious infill, at once powerful and intimate. Two four-storey staircases, slightly deflected in plan, and more strongly modelled than the practice's earlier work. Sheer walls, with Portland stone facing (to establish dignity while keeping a distance from Oxford tradition), but also sills and transoms of pre-cast concrete with quartzite aggregate. Lead cladding for other panelled faces, including the shallower bridge-like rooms that link the stone-faced bastions. Behind, along a turfed strip, an unexpected one-storey extension. On one wall here an abstract MOSAIC by *Hans Unger*, 1972.

For FREWIN HALL, New Inn Hall Street, *see* Perambulation 5, p. 436; for the ST CROSS ANNEXE, St Cross Road, *see* Perambulation 2, p. 419; for HOLLYBUSH LODGE, Hollybush Row, *see* Perambulation 5, p. 442.

CHRIST CHURCH
St Aldate's and Oriel Square

Everything is spacious at Christ Church, the largest quad in Oxford, the largest single C18 building, the largest Gothic Revival range. Even its 1960s infill job is on a different scale from such infillings in other colleges. And that is as it should be; for Cardinal Wolsey, when he founded Cardinal College in 1525, had certainly intended to outdo all others, just as he had unwisely intended to outdo all others, including his master, when he built Hampton Court. At the time of his fall, in 1529, the s side of the quad was complete, with the hall, about three-quarters of the w side, with the lower parts of the gate tower, and at least as much of the E side. It had been Wolsey's intention to demolish the C12 church of the priory of St Frideswide, which he had suppressed in connection (along with twenty other monastic houses), and to place his college chapel on the N side. The chapel roof that was being made at Sonning in 1528 can only have been for this projected building. Henry VIII scrapped the idea, and so St Frideswide became the college chapel.

Not until 1546 was the orphaned college fully embraced by the king. His re-foundation thriftily doubled as a cathedral, thus transferring the new see of Oxford from Osney Abbey. The newly renamed Christ Church was to have a dean, eight canons (who could marry), three Regius Professors to give public lectures, and a hundred students of varying rank, comprising both graduates and undergraduates. There were also chaplains, clerks, choristers, almsmen (in an establishment across St Aldate's, now part of Pembroke College, p. 236) and fee-paying undergraduates or commoners. These arrangements have of course changed a great deal; but with its dean, canons and Cathedral, Christ Church remains *sui generis* among the colleges of Oxford and beyond.

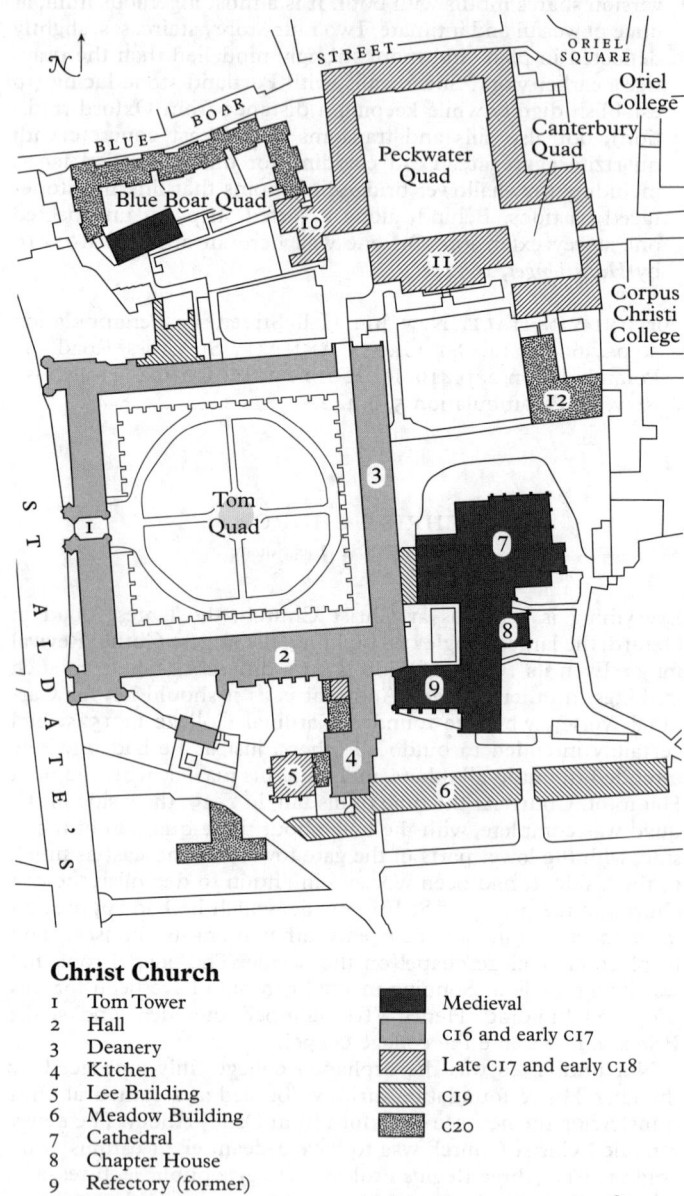

Christe Church

1   Tom Tower
2   Hall
3   Deanery
4   Kitchen
5   Lee Building
6   Meadow Building
7   Cathedral
8   Chapter House
9   Refectory (former)
10 Killcanon
11 Library
12 Picture Gallery

Medieval
C16 and early C17
Late C17 and early C18
C19
C20

80 m
80 yds

Henry also annexed two older establishments, Peckwater Inn to the NE, and Canterbury College just beyond it. Thus the college could boast three widely spaced quads from the start, even before the Great Quadrangle, familiarly Tom Quad, was finished in the 1660s. Peckwater was grandly rebuilt in 1706–14 by *Dean Aldrich*, and completed as a quad with *Dr George Clarke*'s library on its S side from 1717. Canterbury Quad was rebuilt next, by *James Wyatt* in 1773–83. Both reflect the C18 heyday of the gentleman commoner, when Christ Church was Oxford's most fashionable college. The next big project was *Thomas Newenham Deane*'s Meadow Building S of the Cathedral cloister, in the 1860s. The 1960s brought *Powell & Moya*'s Blue Boar Quad to the NW, and their discreetly handled Picture Gallery off Canterbury Quad. All these buildings are on an expansive scale, and display both high originality and clarity of purpose. So in architectural terms Christ Church is altogether the most exciting, if not quite the most lovable, of the colleges of Oxford.

A strictly chronological exploration would make little sense. The description below puts Tom Quad first, then the buildings and gardens to the S, the Cathedral and old priory after that, and finally the later quads to the N.

TOM QUAD

Wolsey's master masons for TOM QUAD were *Henry Redman* or *Redmayne*, *John Lubyns* or *Lebons*, and *William Johnson*. Redman and Lubyns had worked for him before, at York Place in London or at Hampton Court. Redman was in addition the king's chief mason, and Lubyns had served as a royal mason too. All three masons visited the site in February 1525, 'devysyng the beyldyng'. It is likely that *Redman* took the lead, as the most experienced designer, allowing always for the undoubted personal interest of Wolsey himself. Detailed comparisons are not always easy, for Hampton Court is of brick, Wolsey's college lavishly of ashlar throughout.

Exterior

Christ Church has a long formal FRONT to St Aldate's, the first true display front among the colleges. That it is essentially symmetrical may be due rather to the C17 than the C16, for we do not know how far Wolsey's intended chapel would have showed its W front here. The separation of chapel from hall across the quad is, incidentally, a clear break from the Oxford tradition embodied by New College and by Magdalen, Wolsey's own former college, in which chapel and hall are lined up side by side. The front is built on falling ground, so that the plinth at the S end stands high. That end corresponds to the southernmost bastion of the city walls. It projects boldly, and has two bold octagonal turrets. Between them is a large oriel window, and the coving supporting this has the shield, emblems and motto of Wolsey, and all this is of playful Italian Renaissance forms with native versions of putti. It is true that Wolsey had introduced some stray Renaissance motifs already at Hampton Court about 1520, but this small and unrenewed panel is the clearest touch of the Renaissance in the original work at Christ Church, and also the earliest such instance at Oxford. Another turret (for the stairs) at the SE angle. The whole projection was called a 'great tower' in 1526, and it should indeed be understood as only the start of something meant to have been much taller. At the N end the turreted projection is repeated, but this belongs with the mid-C17 completion of the quad. The top balustrade all along is of this period too. The Bereblock engraving of 1566 shows instead elaborate battlements, and pinnacles with little figures on top, in the Hampton Court spirit. The rest of the front excepting Tom Tower has windows of two lights and one light, in the college tradition, but here taller than before, transomed and straight-headed, with cinquefoiled heads.* This great display of fenestration was made possible by putting the chimneys on the quadrangle side – another innovation. The rather good paving in front, designed by *Playne & Lacey*, goes with the refacing of 1963–6.

32   In the centre is TOM TOWER, its lower part Wolsey's, its upper part *Wren*'s work for Dean John Fell. He did it in 1681–2. *Christopher Kempster* of Burford was chief mason, working with *Thomas Robinson*. Wren was anxious that it should be done in the Gothic style, as indeed it was, to the extent that innocent visitors never notice the difference. This is what he wrote to Dr Fell on 26 May 1681: 'I resolved it ought to be Gothick to agree with the Founders worke, yet I have not continued soe busy as he began.' Nor is it. There are in fact plenty of differences, and not only in the matter of plainness. The lowest stage was started with two turrets flanking the archway, as was the late medieval and Tudor tradition (e.g. Hampton Court and St James's Palace), and also the mode of the C15 royal foundations at Cambridge (King's Hall (now Trinity), Queens', King's). The turrets have a very singular plan: square below, with, projecting from the middle of three sides, panelled triangular spurs. It is really two squares set across one another. This breaking up of surfaces was a fashion of the latest Perp. The nearest parallel is the E end of Henry VII's Chapel at Westminster Abbey, completed c. 1510, both externally and in the screens inside. The gateway entrance between is a wide four-centred arch with quatrefoil spandrels, with the original doors. The next stage of Wolsey's turrets is simply octagonal with ogee caps. But on the cap is an ogee with a Gothic finial, and on the outer shafts acorns, so we have reached *Wren*.

---

*The change in cusping from a thinly curving to a straight tip was suggested by W. D. Caröe as marking the junction between C16 and C17 parts ('*Tom Tower*', *Christ Church, Oxford* (1923)), although the crucial cross-wall inside comes some way N of this. *Caröe* himself refaced most of Tom Tower in 1909–10.

Wren did not continue the Tudor scheme but built one tower without turrets instead. His lower stage is a chamfered square, then follows an octagonal bell-stage with two-light openings, Perp indubitably, and then the big ogee cap, perhaps the most telling element in the skyline of Oxford, though few would praise this big ogee shape for its beauty. Wren's also is the band of rich reticulation over the archway. Above, in place of the Tudor oriel of which Loggan's engraving shows the abandoned beginnings, is a large five-light window with an ogee gable. In the middle light, in an ogee-capped niche, is a statue of Wolsey by *Francis Bird*, made in 1719 and moved from the SE corner of the quad in 1876. The tower houses Great Tom, a mighty BELL saved from Osney Abbey; last recast in 1683. Also original are the extraordinary mast-type SPIRAL STAIR inside with its thin turned balusters (*Richard Frogley*, carpenter), and the shapely weathervane.

The gate passage has a fan-vault with a lozenge motif, but its centre is a wreath around the bell-hole. That must be *Wren*, and so must therefore be the fan-vault, which in itself would be convincing for the C16 except for the serried shields of arms in cartouches. Inside the bell-hole is a wooden panel carved like a rose window. Also Wren's are the panelled arches to E and W that prepare Wolsey's oblong space for the square-plan vault and tower above. The arch to the quad is wider and deeper, and the façade there instead of full turrets has lesser polygonal projections. The statue in the niche is of Queen Anne, 1706, sculptor unknown.

Interiors

TOM QUAD measures 276 by 271 ft (84.1 by 82.6 metres). The distance would be less if Wolsey's intended cloister had been built. Unlike the one at Magdalen, this was to have been single-storeyed. It was therefore easily omitted when the C16 work stopped, leaving only the outlines of the intended vaulting. The corner bays are distinguished by broader, panelled wall-shafts, of a standard design seen throughout the college. It also appears in contemporary works by other royal masons, notably St Stephen's Cloister at the Palace of Westminster (1526–9). These vaulting outlines however are largely reinstatement or enhancement from *Bodley & Garner*'s restoration of 1873–9, when it was still hoped to make the cloister a reality; likewise the buttress bases projecting from the raised walks. The battlements are 1870s too, replacing the mid-C17 balustrades, as are the fancy tops to the side projections of Tom Tower, the hall pinnacles and the other two towers – giving Tom Quad what variety of skyline it has.

As to the ranges themselves, they are all two-storeyed with small doorways with decorated spandrels, and windows like those of the W façade. The chief difference between Wolsey's work and the mid-C17 completion on the N side is the more

regular alternation there between two-light and one-light windows.* Some good, deeply undercut carving of the doorway
spandrels, e.g. Staircases 3 and 4, W side. Some other doorways
are Victorian, e.g. Staircase 7. Also non-original are the little
windows inserted above some doorways, and the twin opening
in the E range. This is *G.G. Scott*'s doing of 1872–3, and it
leads into a spacious entrance lobby to the Cathedral, previously accessible only from the cloister. In fact one foretaste
of the Cathedral is experienced already as one stands in Tom
Quad – the tower and spire. Of the details of Wolsey's intended
chapel we have John Aubrey's tantalizing drawing of a moulded
and decorated plinth, cleared away in 1671. If an antechapel
in the Oxford manner was also intended, the whole may have
filled the entire N side.

In the middle of the quad is the FOUNTAIN with a copy
of Giovanni da Bologna's Mercury. It was given in 1928,
and *Lutyens* added the pedestal in 1934. (An earlier Mercury
statue lasted from 1695 to 1819.) Its BASIN dates from 1670,
after the centre of the quad was lowered. The present WALKS
with their big salient buttress bases are of the 1870s, as already
noted. By Tom Tower, well-handled access ramps and railings of 2013 by *Montgomery Architects*, who also renovated the
porter's lodge.

Now to the *Bodley & Garner* towers, and the hall. FELL
TOWER (1876–8), in the NE corner, is slim, with a higher
stair-turret. Statues of deans Fell, S, and Liddell, N. The eared
arch surround and the vault within, typical transition from
posthumous Gothic to classical, show that the gateway is of
Fell's time, i.e. 1660s. Much more prominent and sumptuous
is the WOLSEY TOWER in the SE corner (1876–9). It was built
after a competition in which *Scott, Jackson* and *Champneys* also
contended. The upper walls are really just screens to hide the
timber housing which Scott provided for the displaced cathedral
bells in 1872. Two smallish, widely spaced Perp openings on
each side, highly ornamental corner turrets with statue niches,
bigger statues in niches over the entrance (Wolsey between two
angels; by *Farmer & Brindley*). The intended openwork lantern
of leaded timber was alas never built.

The HALL is on the first floor, as at New College and Magdalen.
So it rises dramatically towards the quad, with its four-light
windows and *Bodley & Garner*'s battlements and pinnacles. All
eight windows of four-centred arches. The big eighth window
marks the dais. It starts lower and ends lower than the others,
and has two transoms. The principal bay window is in fact to
the S – one bay further E, i.e. not tallying with the dais. This
has a six-light (3:3) window with three transoms. The ornate
C16 louvre has gone from the roof, destroyed by fire in 1720.

---

*Anthony Wood recorded that Dean Samuel Fell raised the walls of the two canon-
ries here in 1638–41, and that his son Dean John Fell finished the job externally
in 1662.

Under Wolsey Tower is the HALL STAIRCASE, that spectacular piece of C17 Gothic. It dates from *c.* 1632–40, years for
which no accounts survive. It has an exceptionally slim centre
pier and a fan-vault of oblong plan, carried on odd corbels
whose detailing is the only obviously C17 touch. According
to Anthony Wood, the mason was '*Smith*, an artificer from
London'. One contender is the *William Smith* who was Warden
of the London Masons' Company in 1640. Mark Girouard
made the case for the Oxford mason *Robert Smith*, whose
partner Hugh Davies had provided designs for the intended
Bodleian staircase. Robert died in 1635, just one year after
fund-raising began to complete Tom Quad, so if the vault
is indeed his design it was probably built posthumously.
The present staircase itself is of course entirely un-medieval,
running up in two flights of unequal width to a spacious intermediate landing, and returning at 180 degrees in a wide single
flight to a spacious upper landing. All this, with renewal of the
vault pier, is *James Wyatt*'s work, *c.* 1801. His Gothic balustrade
is non-period, but his details below the stair are fully Wolsey-
Perp, as is his doorway to the ante-hall at the top. To its r. is
the C16 doorway, of matching design but visibly older fabric;
converted to a window now, with an inserted Wyatt balustrade
and 1860s glazing. Tall two-light 1520s windows in the S and
E walls, on the latter side originally extending further down.
Splendid cast-iron lamps of *c.* 1862 on the newels.

What sort of staircase Wolsey had in mind is unclear. The
expected early C16 arrangement would be a single straight
flight between enclosing walls, as at Henry VIII's Hampton
Court. This big space and the position of the original upper
doorway imply more than one flight, placed at right angles.
The earlier history of the tower itself is mysterious too. Agas
and Bereblock both show something big and tall, perhaps
the result of a bequest of 1559 towards building work. Joist
holes in the walls just below the present vault must be from
a floor within this tower. By Loggan's time its parapet was no
higher than that of the hall, and a screen wall ran between
them, with a balustrade of C17 type. Williams's plan of 1733
and Rowlandson's Dr Syntax drawing indicate a staircase of
similar plan to Wyatt's but of different proportions, built of
stone integrally with the 1630s pier and vault, and already with
classical balustrade and ball finials.

The large ANTE-HALL replaces the traditional screens
passage. To the S is a simple arch framing a stone doorway
and hatch to the buttery. What the C16 provided beyond is
unclear, as the doorway now opens to *William Townesend*'s
replacement BUTTERY of 1722 (dated and inscribed wooden
cartouche inside). Next to the arch is a Wolsey-style doorway,
probably from *Thomas Newenham Deane*'s kitchen alterations
of 1866, but replacing an earlier doorway to a staircase within
the C18 buttery block (for which *see also* p. 117). Opposite is
the STATUE of the reforming Dean Jackson, seated and robed,
brought from the Cathedral. By *Chantrey*, 1820–5. Wolsey's N

windows have radial decoration in the tympanum, a minor Renaissance detail. The doorway to the hall is *Wyatt*'s.

The HALL is the largest pre-Victorian one in either university – 115 by 40 ft, and 50 ft high (35.1, 12.2 and 15.2 metres). It has a superb hammerbeam roof, designed by *Humphrey Coke*, the king's master carpenter, with *Robert Carow* of Oxford as executant. Braces of broad four-centred profile, and also broad four-centred arches longitudinally from hammerbeam to hammerbeam. Rich lantern-type pendants on the hammerposts. In the bay window a delicate fan-vaultlet also with pendants. Panelling and cornices all *Wyatt*'s, 1801–4. Also the dark grey marble fireplaces, made by the elder *Westmacott*. Until the fire of 1720 there was a central open hearth. STAINED GLASS mostly of 1979–82 by *Patrick Reyntiens*, in a fine Late Victorian spirit, with diagonal lettered bands of C15 derivation, portrait medallions, and in one window a few 'Alice' details. The easternmost pair survive from *Horwood Bros'* sequence of 1872. Bay and dais N windows, lower lights, historical figures by *Burlison & Grylls*, 1878, 1883. Upper lights, re-set roundels and heraldry from the original series by *James Nicholson*, 1529 (*see also* Balliol chapel, p. 99). More in the W window. Wolsey's badge of crossed pillars and cross-staff recurs.

OTHER INTERIORS. The LAW LIBRARY below the hall, converted 1975–6, preserves much of the plain groin-vaulting inserted by *William Townesend* after the fire of 1720. Further W, the SENIOR COMMON ROOM conceals a later fireproofing system of iron girders and concrete arches. Done by *E. G. Bruton*, 1870. Also *Caröe*'s spiral STAIRCASE up to the hall dais, inserted 1909. Wolsey appears to have intended the rest of the S side for the Deanery, i.e. off the high end of the hall, incidentally the preferred location at Cambridge for the lodgings of heads of houses. Burnt out in 1809, this part was reconstructed by *Wyatt*, with severe iron-balustered STAIRCASES of stone. On the W side, doorways 3 and 4 still show the C16 straight STAIRCASES between timbered partitions. The N side is mostly three-storeyed behind, where it has multiple additions, 1848, 1933 etc., for individual canons' houses.

Finally the E side, with the DEANERY at the N end. Dean Liddell reworked the big open-well 'LEXICON STAIRCASE' in 1855–6 to designs by *John Billing*, supposedly paid for from the proceeds of Liddell and Scott's Greek lexicon. Stylistically uncertain, with thin Gothic balustrade but naturalistic friezes in the wall timbers, carved by *Messrs Baker* of Lambeth. Other embellishments of the interiors for Liddell were stripped in the mid C20. The STUDY, N, has two big Neoclassical niches and a tripartite French window with Gothic hoodmould to the outside. The combination is suggestive of *Wyatt* and the tenure of Dean Bagot (1777–83). Miscellaneous early C16 panelling is assembled in the S room on the first floor. An original fireplace here. In the Cathedral vestibule the college WAR MEMORIALS, lettered panels of 1921, N, and 1951, S (carver *Darsie Rawlins*).

BUILDINGS TO THE SOUTH

Kitchen, Meadow Building and south-east outliers

A passage through the S side, not normally visitable, leads to SCHOOL YARD (also reached from a passage off the hall staircase), with Wolsey's KITCHEN placed on the E side and some way S. Originally it presented a symmetrical front with a very broad chimney-breast between transomed windows, three-light above, two-light below. The chimneystacks are cut down now, and the elaborate louvre has also gone. A crenellated false gable remains, the kitchen being roofed N–S. Big chimneys also in the W and S sides. The steep-gabled SCULLERY adjoins to the S, also 1520s. It was reconstructed by *Deane* in 1865 with residential rooms on top, hence the dormer gables on the S side next to Deane's Meadow Building (*see* p. 118). Low service additions of 1909 by *Caröe* to the S. The kitchen is a daunting 40-ft (12-metre) cube inside, with three-bay kingpost roof and three vast fireplaces. Original N and S doorways, and scullery passage S doorway, on a single axis. Outside, to the l. and facing School Yard is the SERVERY, by *C.C. Handisyde*, a clever deception of 1949. Really it is a shallow addition against older buildings, with some replication of their buried façades. That applies to the part next to the hall, a facsimile of *Townesend*'s BUTTERY of 1722. Something of the Hawksmoor character here: three moulded arches with blocks instead of capitals and three moulded round windows above, but then a change to Perp two-light windows on the top storey. A drawing of 1722 confirms that this incongruity is original, no doubt to make a better match internally and on the E side, where the buttery originally showed above the C16 kitchen passage. The lower, classical parts house (or housed) a staircase from kitchen lobby to ante-hall, wine vaults etc. The rest of the 1949 front has a continuous mullioned strip window above, tall cross-windows below. Behind this part is the C16 kitchen lobby, and, superimposed above it, the MCKENNA ROOM, a lecture room built in 1829, with access from the ante-hall landing via a corridor raised over the kitchen passage. The 1829 windows, now visible only on the E side, follow C16 models. Mezzanine windows below the McKenna ones belong to the KITCHEN OFFICES inserted by *Deane* in 1866. The stone access gallery inside, and the lower parts of the staircase to the ante-hall, are Deane's too.

The LEE BUILDING on the S side of School Yard – particularly incongruous here – appears as a perfectly normal three-bay Georgian house with a porch of paired Tuscan columns and pediment. This was built by *Henry Keene* in 1766–7 as the Anatomy School. Before then, the Old Ashmolean served as the place for public dissections. The basement is vaulted. The building later served as chemistry labs (a gabled top storey came and went, 1904–29). In 1969–71 converted for extra Senior Common Rooms by *Playne & Lacey*, with service additions E and S.

Free-standing to the w is AUDEN COTTAGE, actually a converted brewhouse of the mid C17 or earlier, named from the poet's residence here in 1972–3. Across the lane to the s, GARAGE of 1927 by *John Coleridge*, deceptively rustic-looking towards the War Memorial Garden with which it belongs (*see* below).

MEADOW BUILDING, that big, heavy Gothic Chinese wall shutting off the meadow, completes the southern sequence around the cloister. The major work at Christ Church by *Thomas Newenham Deane* of Dublin, it was built in 1862–6 to replace Fell's Buildings, a bulky but strangely featureless residential range of 1669–79. The cost was £22,000. On the college side especially it is a joyless building, though it would perhaps have been less grim if all the foliage carving had been done (the carver, incidentally, was *Edward Whelan*, nephew of the O'Sheas of the University Museum). From the N, as one approaches from the college, it has two-light windows, a gate tower with very steeply crowstepped gables and a handsomely carved portal to the archway, and a loosely symmetrical composition, except on the w return, next to the kitchen, where an extra staircase appears (actually an insertion within the refaced scullery behind). There is plate tracery here. The s façade on the other hand is asymmetrical and creeper-grown, of three storeys, plus a top storey which here is wholly of dormers rather than gables as behind. The tower is further E than the centre, and has a through-storey oriel. Another such oriel to the E. Staircase windows at half-height, grouped in shallow recesses. These have plate tracery of Early French type, but also long bands of red and grey stone in the Bath stone walls, and plate-traceried Venetian balconies with Venetian Gothic arches over the windows opening on to them – a reminder that Deane was an admirer of Ruskin.

Gardens and Meadow

To the s of the w front of Christ Church is the WAR MEMO-RIAL GARDEN, made in 1925–6 when much of St Aldate's was cleared and widened. Layout and piers by *John Coleridge*, iron gates designed by *R.M.Y. Gleadowe* of Winchester College. In the round enclosure to the SE is the little SERPENT FOUNTAIN which was in the basin of Tom Quad from 1670 to 1695. The E–W axis continues as BROAD WALK, of C16 origin, formerly with a famous avenue of elms. The avenue walk going s from the gate of Meadow Building dates from 1868–72. On its w side is the college's VISITOR CENTRE, 2015–19 by *Purcell*. Barn-like; mostly traditional materials including squared rubble and thatch, thoughtfully handled. The cues came from a real thatched BARN of 1851 to the s, duly adapted and incorporated.

E of Meadow Building is the MASTERS' GARDEN, made 1926–7. Big wrought-iron gates here too, designed by *Coleridge*.

CATHEDRAL CHURCH OF CHRIST

The present Cathedral started life as an Anglo-Saxon nunnery which claimed the c8 St Frideswide as its foundress. No sure remains of early buildings have been found, but it is likely that the church stood within the footprint of the present, largely c12 one. St Frideswide's church was burnt in the anti-Danish pogroms of 1002, then rebuilt ('renovata') by the king. By that time the nuns had gone, replaced by secular canons. They in turn made way for Augustinian Canons in Henry I's re-foundation of c. 1120–2. The cathedral of today is the priory church of this c12 monastery, spared from demolition – as we have seen – only because Wolsey fell from power before there was time to build the grand chapel intended for his new college. It then became the chapel of Henry VIII's re-foundation, and in 1546 also the cathedral of Henry's new diocese of Oxford. Three or more western bays of the nave had then already been cut off, to make Tom Quad possible. What is there now is small for a cathedral: only about 175 ft (53 metres) long internally, as against the 305 ft (93 metres) of Rochester, an unusually small cathedral, or indeed the 289 ft (88 metres) of King's College Chapel at Cambridge.

No documents or chronicles tell us when the church was begun or when it was completed. On grounds of style, the story begins c. 1140–50 with the chapter house entrance in the cloister E range. A start on the church must have followed not long after. There is evidence above and below ground here that smaller transepts,

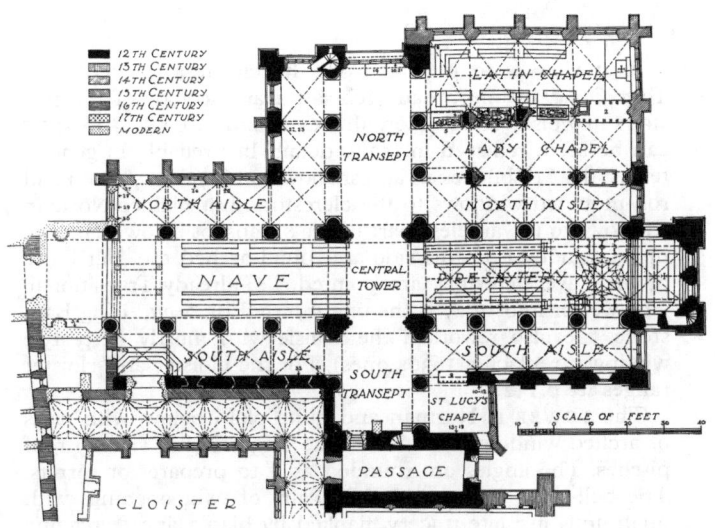

Christ Church, Oxford Cathedral.
Plan, 1939

without aisles, were at first intended.* Their unusual aisled form
must therefore have been adopted while work was still at an early
stage (unlike e.g. the Cistercians, the Augustinian order had no
standard church plan-type). A date *c.*1160–70 seems likely for the
E arm. Frideswide's remains were translated in 1180, so the transepts, saint's chapel and crossing were surely ready by then. That
would leave *c.*1180–1200 for the nave, or what we still have of it.
A fire recorded in 1190 may have occasioned some changes to
the parts already built. The bell-stage and spire over the crossing
followed in the first decades of the C13, during which the chapter
house was also rebuilt. There followed a sequence of eastward
extension and replacement of the N transept chapels up to *c.*1340,
partly to enhance the setting for Frideswide's shrine. Nothing was
added after that, but some parts were rebuilt: notably much of
the cloister in the late C15, and the nave N aisle in the early C16.
Much of the present cloister belongs however with the campaign
of 1870–8 by *Sir George Gilbert Scott* under Dean Liddell, when
£24,000 was spent: by far the most important phase of the Victorian restorations.

All that remains to add is that the ordinary visitor cannot see
the exterior at all well, and even less at close range. The cloister
allows near views of the nave S side and S transept, while quad
and meadow between them offer more distant views of the spire
and E end. As to the W front, this effectively ceased to exist when
Scott added a bay between the truncated nave and the E range of
Tom Quad, to join up with his new entrance there (*see* p.114).

Cathedral exterior

The best view is to be had from the cloister, reached from
Tom Quad by the broad archway near the foot of the hall
stairs in Wolsey Tower. Here the NAVE and SOUTH TRANSEPT
can be seen, renewed in many details but reliable in general
terms: flat C12 buttresses and shallow corbel table, shafted and
roll-moulded windows to the clerestory, but plainer Norman
windows to the aisleless part of the S transept below that. The
upper windows on this side are round-arched too, but those
of the nave clerestory are pointed, i.e. already Transitional.
The westernmost bay is the one inserted by *Scott*, using Bath
stone. He also reworked the S aisle with mostly Perp-style
windows (replacing 1630s ones). For the cloister and cloister
ranges *see* p.132.

The TOWER is Norman and quite plain below, with pairs
of arched windows set wide of the original (still visible) roof
pitches. The angles are rounded as if to prepare for turrets.
The bell-stage is C13 and E.E. Pairs of twin openings with
quatrefoils in plate tracery, flanked by blank lancet arcading
that follows, but sits back from, the rounded C12 corners. A
pointed-arched frieze on corbels ends the tower part. On the

---

* See the partially differing interpretations of David Sturdy, Richard Halsey and
John Blair, articles in *Oxoniensia* 53 (1988).

four corners are shafted pinnacles, and between them rises the spire, of stone, octagonal and comparatively short, without broaches. Large gabled lucarnes rise direct from the parapet at the cardinal points. They also have twin lights and a quatrefoil in plate tracery. Belfry and spire must therefore be of one phase, perhaps *c.*1220–30. The type is that of the W towers of St Etienne, Caen (cf. also Witney, North Oxon).

Back now to the S transept. Its S window, high up and hard to see because of the cloister E range, is of five lights and has cusped intersecting tracery with ogee heads below, i.e. of *c.*1300. After that the only close views are from the cathedral garden. The E clerestory windows here are like the western ones. Below, the CHAPEL OF ST LUCY appears, i.e. the rebuilt S transept E bay, datable to about 1340–50 by the strangely elongated tracery of the E window: two tiers of reticulation and then freer flowing shapes (cf. Dorchester E window, p. 626).

The CHOIR has a S aisle with shafted Norman windows, again much renewed, and a Norman S doorway below. The flowing Dec window which ends the aisle, E, is 1870s. Clerestory above with three-light Perp windows that must be of *c.*1390–1400 (*see* interior, p. 123). Very flattened four-centred arches at their tops. Grotesque carvings on the string course of the parapet. The choir EAST WALL is as much 1870–1 and *Scott* as it is C12. On the strength of traces found in the fabric he removed a large three-light E window, apparently an unusual C17 instance of the imitation of late C13-type tracery, and installed a Norman rose window under blind arcading. The details of the rose are all his. The same applies to the pair of big round-arched windows below. Original are the square angle turrets with their blank arcading, round-arched and intersecting below, simple round-arched and then pointed-arched above. The keeled shafts of the arcading imply a late C12 date for this easternmost bay, though it is hard to explain why the E end of *c.*1160–70 might have needed reworking so soon, even allowing for the 1190 fire. Also C12, though renewed, are the one S and the one N window of this E bay, projecting beyond the choir aisles. The choir clerestory on the N side is as on the other.

The choir N aisle appears next, in line with two separately gabled CHAPELS to the N. The aisle wall is indeed Norman, though its Dec-style window tracery is all 1870s. Next to it one genuine Norman buttress, shallow, as they were. Then follows the window of the Lady Chapel with another display of 1870s flowing tracery, and then the Frideswide window in the Latin Chapel, a one-off insertion of 1860 by *Benjamin Woodward* (of *Deane & Woodward*), and indeed evidently pre-Scott, heavier and cruder with its plate tracery. Carving by one of the *O'Shea* brothers, left incomplete. Of this LATIN CHAPEL of *c.*1330–40 there remain to the N four Dec windows with resourceful flowing tracery, all different, in bays of uneven width. Gabled buttresses between, strong plinth below.

The NORTH TRANSEPT is almost flush with the Latin Chapel. It has Norman angle turrets with pointed blank arcading in two tiers below, round arcading at the top stage, and recessed circular pinnacles, also with shafting, as the top motif. The large Perp N window of five lights is by *Scott*, his biggest reversal of the 1630s refenestration, and a credible one in terms of the early C16 work on this part (*see also* interior, p. 124). The Perp windows of the W aisle to both N and W are likewise *Scott*'s. At the NW corner between them a Norman clasping buttress, and on it a pinnacle of late C14 type with a perished statue of St Frideswide in a niche. The clerestory here has its northernmost W window Perp (and so is the opposite window facing E, i.e. above the Latin Chapel, visible from within). Unlike those of the choir, these Perp clerestory windows have straight sides to the arch, after the mid-C15 type of the Divinity School (p. 328). The other transept windows are Norman and shafted with a roll in the arch, as in the S transept. Perp carving along the string course of the parapet.

The NAVE continues with Perp-style aisle windows by *Scott*, and shafted, pointed-arched late C12 clerestory windows above. The aisle wall here was rebuilt *c.* 1500. Finally the far W bay provided by Scott, with an awkward junction to the back of Tom Quad.

Cathedral interior

We begin in the CHOIR, a choir of four main bays in length. Here the system is at once established which was not to be changed to the end of the building operations. Tall round piers carry arches, and there is a triforium of twin openings, but this is not above the arches, as say at Gloucester and Tewkesbury, but below them, tucked into them. The aisles therefore are not as high as the piers, and so second arches are needed below the triforium. It is a highly unusual, though not a unique system; Romsey in Hampshire is an earlier example (and the choir of Jedburgh Abbey in Scotland). The origin may have been Reading Abbey, another foundation of Henry I.

Description must indeed be more detailed. The piers have interesting, again unusual, capitals. They are narrow and have loosely intertwined trails, or (at least five times) crockets, or a combination of both. The super-arches have strong roll mouldings. But the sub-arches are unmoulded, and there is no visual or structural logic in the way they join the round piers. Instead, strange half-capitals intercept the sub-arches and provide the springing for the transverse arches across the aisles. The system is best seen in the S aisle: rib-vaulted with wall-shafts and head corbels against the outer wall, simple hollow-chamfered transverse arches, and ribs of a thick roll moulding. Also one tiny boss. The Norman-type S windows here are *Scott*'s doing, as is the Dec-type E window, though its ballflower enrichment is vouched for by the similarly decorated early C14 splays and adjacent vault-ribs. Also in this bay a pretty C14 PISCINA.

The E wall inside is mostly *Scott*'s reconstruction of 1870–1, with carving by *Farmer & Brindley*. Below the rose window however is a row of intersecting arcading which reportedly contains bits from a C12 predecessor. The C12 side walls of this extreme E bay relate puzzlingly badly to the aisled sections further W.

The Norman choir was meant to be rib-vaulted too, or perhaps was rib-vaulted. In any case there are Norman vaulting shafts, rising from heads just above the main capitals. Above them, all was changed when the choir finally was vaulted, or re-vaulted. The vaulting bays had to be oblong. The designer wanted to make them square. So he started from N and S by big and strong arches treated exactly as if a timber hammerbeam roof was intended. Even the pendants are as in such roofs. The areas between the hammerbeams towards the windows are panelled. The windows have a wall passage and their heads are panelled too. That left the designer his sequence of square bays in the middle, and they have complicated lierne-star vaults with many bosses. The thick arches seem to disappear behind that vault, a motif also taken up in Henry VII's Chapel at Westminster Abbey, started in 1503. The square bays left a narrow strip across the vault just E of the crossing arch. Here are four statues under canopies, and little attentive figures leaning out below. This strip is bounded by more ornate wall-shafts. Their capitals are polygonal, with concave sides. The shafts start from corbels carved as busts, also with convex-polygonal tops.

A date c. 1480–1500 has often been suggested for this vault, and a parallel drawn with the Divinity School vault as executed by William Orchard in the 1480s (*see* p. 331). It also happens that Orchard (†1504) was buried at St Frideswide's Priory, to which he made a bequest. But the details are quite wrong for so late a date, and much closer instead to the last years of the C14. The small, blobby vegetal ornament in such places as the wall-passage openings with their sub-cusping, and the style of the statues and their canopies in the western strip, are especially telling. Beyond the basic motif of cross-arches there are also no direct reminiscences of the vault at the Divinity School, as one would expect if the same master mason had done both. These problems disappear if one accepts the choir vault as the forerunner, not the successor, of the Divinity School system.*

The CROSSING has tall piers with many shafts. Crocket capitals appear, but also waterleaf. The arches are round to E and W, but pointed to N and S, a clue that the tower plan is rectangular, not square (cf. St Mary, Devizes, Wilts., another church under the aegis of Bishop Roger of Salisbury). Bases now of waterholding type, as also in the transepts and nave. Inside the tower is first a wall passage with low arcading of seven bays each side. Short columns. Then, where the Norman windows are, there is thin and large blank arcading. The C13

---

*The late C14 date has been proposed by Christopher Wilson. Another early example is the Lady Chapel vault of c. 1400 at Christchurch Priory, Hants. I am grateful to John Goodall for his thoughts on these vaults.

stage is hidden by a ceiling, probably early C16. *Scott* moved this up from just above the crossing arches.

The TRANSEPTS have aisles: E and W on the N side, only E on the S, because of the cloister. The main wall system is the same as in the choir. The major capitals continue with exceptional variety, and few are run of the mill. Crockets appear everywhere, waterleaf more rarely. The N transept also has some with two rows of five-lobed early stiff-leaf, a little like Bourbon lilies. The clerestories have the usual Anglo-Norman tripartite arrangement with low arches flanking the high window arches. Short columns, and in the middle short thinner nook columns on them. The original vaulting shafts carry half-capitals. In the SOUTH TRANSEPT there is even the start of the springing of a vault, indicating transverse and diagonal members, all slim. The S wall of this transept has a VESTRY in mid-C13 Gothic. This belongs to *Scott*'s work, who justified it from having found traces of a vaulted chamber here. Its lower storey encompasses the slype of the C12 cloister range (p. 132). Middle storey cross-vaulted, top left open as a gallery. Above, l. and r. of the window of *c.*1300, the outer parts of the C12 clerestory arrangement remain.

In the S transept two details need pointing out. First, the triforium bay closest to the vestry has colonnettes which are the earliest architectural evidence we have yet seen. They have steeper bases than the rest, and two-scallop capitals. One would call that *c.*1100, but it may be *retardataire* and as late as *c.*1140. Slots cut in the shafts indicate reuse from some other context, of which the C12 cloister is the most plausible. We know that this was rebuilt in the late C15, and this would also explain the second detail, namely the way in which the pier at the corner with the nave S aisle has been built against on the nave side (compare the plain angle at the junction of N transept and nave aisle). In other words, the chapel to the E must originally have been balanced by a single-bay W aisle to the S transept, swallowed up when the cloister was rebuilt. The variant triforium window was probably inserted in connection.

The shallow-pitched ROOFS of the transepts with their plain moulded timbers are early C16. The beginnings of a new or replacement vault for the N transept were certainly made, shown by the stone panelling around the two northernmost clerestory windows, which were altered in connection with straight-sided arches of mid-C15 Perp type. That points to a substantial interval between the choir vault and the aborted vault here. Large blank Perp panelling below the main N window. This window now has *Scott* tracery, but was described in the will of James Zouch †1503 as having been built by him (*see* monument, p. 130). Zouch also left £30 for vaulting, but the tree-ring date of 1506 for the N transept roof indicates that a cheaper solution was adopted. Vaulting – for the nave too – was on the Victorian wish list, but funds were not forthcoming; the plain ceiling over Scott's vestry, filling the gap left when an inserted verger's house was removed, was

meant as a makeshift. By contrast, the s transept E aisle (St
Lucy's Chapel) has a rich roof with close-set arched braces
that must also be *Scott*'s.

The bays of the transept AISLES are separated by unmoulded
transverse arches. In the N transept E aisle only the southernmost vault bay has original cross-ribs. Its irregular overall
shape, incidentally, is one pointer to there having been originally no intended aisle arcade to the N transept here. The other
vaults were changed when additions were made in the C13 and
C14, of which more below. In the corresponding W aisle the
transverse arches are slimmer and hollow-chamfered, and the
ribs too are thinner, with three slim rolls.

The NAVE modified but did not alter the main system.
There are now alternating round and octagonal piers, after
the Canterbury Cathedral choir of 1175–9 (the source too for
the fleshy acanthus capital of the easternmost pier, N side).
Keeled roll mouldings on the main arches, clerestory with
the pointed windows seen outside. The wall-shafts have been
given concave-sided Perp capitals, like those of the choir. The
roof is also late medieval, partly renewed in 1816. Semicircular
arched braces, the unexpected profile apparently generated by
following the crossing arch. Traceried panels with ogee heads
in the spandrels. Also ogee heads to the openings above the
tie-beam. Aisle vaults like those of the N transept W aisle, but
with pointed cross-arches. The N aisle has no wall-shafts, only
corbels. Aisle windows mostly Perp work by *Scott*; also the S
doorway. The one Neo-Norman S window was made for new
stained glass, given not long before Scott was appointed. The W
wall and doorway of this S aisle survive from the W front made
across the shortened nave in 1578–82. The main W bay beyond
is *Scott*'s, and was designed to allow expansion with aisles and a
new W end if required. Plain Y-tracery in the N aisle W window.
Its special interest (also for its contemporary glass) is as the
only one left from Dean Duppa's 1630s renovation, which took
Dean Liddell so much trouble to reverse.*

Now the CHAPELS to the NE, or more properly the choir N
aisle, Lady Chapel and Latin Chapel, going from S to N. The
starting point in the late C12 was an unusual square chapel on
this side, almost certainly built for Frideswide's shrine. It was
of two bays by two with a central pier. The W bays of this square
chapel are effectively subsumed into the transept E aisle. Next,
around 1220–30, a LADY CHAPEL was added alongside the
choir N aisle, i.e. in line with the central bay of the transept.
It thus annexed the SE bay of the C12 chapel, adding two
new bays beyond. The old aisle N wall was replaced by piers

*Other work of the 1630s included remarkable openwork Gothic SCREENS to the
choir aisles, of stone, with curving tops that made circular apertures by mirroring
the C12 arches above. They also included classical doorways. *Nicholas Stone* was the
joint mason and likely designer. A start was made on purging the C17 installations
in 1856–7 by *J. Billing*, followed by *Bruton* in 1861. After Scott's death in 1878,
Bodley & Garner took over for the chapter house restoration and remaining
cathedral furnishings.

with clusters of shafts, partly with fillets, keeping just enough of the C12 on the S face to carry the aisle vault. Small and pretty crocket capitals, finely moulded arches also with fillets. Vaulting of a rib section not much different from that of the W aisle ribs. Richard K. Morriss attributed the work to masons previously employed on the choir of Pershore Abbey, Worcs., which has multiple similarities.* Trefoil-headed PISCINA in the E wall. The small blocked arch in the E wall, and that in the choir aisle adjacent, are explained as temporary access points for the workmen.

The N wall of the Lady Chapel disappeared around 1289, when an extension was made here to house a new shrine for the saint (see p. 130). This extension, which lasted only a few decades, took the form of a narrow two-bay addition to the NE bay of the square C12 chapel. The chief visible evidence for it is the remaining shafts and bases of the piers between the Lady Chapel and the chapel to the N, which show various small differences from the early C13 type.

Finally the LATIN CHAPEL to the N. This represents an enlarged rebuilding around 1330–40 of the two C12 bays and two added late C13 bays (dedication 1338/9). Morriss attributed the chapel to *Richard Wy*, from similarities to his work of 1323 onwards at St Albans. The new capitals are all moulded, with new arches above and octagonal bases below, and the vault has bosses and decorated ridge ribs. To fit the inherited bay spacing, the two E bays are longer. Flowing tracery in the four N windows. Yet the fabric of the square C12 chapel was not wholly erased even then, for the first pier going E from the transept preserves part of its former E respond, complete with NW nook-shaft. The chapel E window is of 1860 by *Woodward*, the carving (as outside) by *O'Shea*, as a setting for the glorious *Burne-Jones* window (p. 127).

Furnishings, from east to west

CHOIR. RETABLE of 1880–1 by *Bodley*. Of red sandstone and red marble, not originally coloured. Figure carving by *Farmer & Brindley*. Lowered in 1960, when some of the steps were removed. – The STALLS and fine iron SCREENS are *Scott*'s, 1870–4, since 2006 somewhat depleted. *Messrs Skidmore* of Coventry made the screens, *John Chapman* of Oxford carved the stalls' New Testament scenes and mythical bestiary finials.† – BISHOP'S THRONE and iron canopy by *Sebastian Comper*, 1955, feeble by comparison with *Scott*'s sumptuous predecessor. – Also *Scott*'s is the PAVEMENT of 1871, made by *Clayton & Bell*, with roundels of seated Virtues executed by 'an Italian or

---

* In *Oxoniensia* 53 (1988).
† Displaced 1630s stalls are at Cassington (*see Oxfordshire: North and West*) and at Easthampton (Bracknell, Berks.).

Maltese artist' (*Jackson's Oxford Journal*, 12 November 1881).
– STAINED GLASS. E windows also by *Clayton & Bell*, 1875.

CHOIR SOUTH AISLE. MILITARY CHAPEL furnished by
H. S. Rogers, 1931: retable, communion rails, screen etc. The
style similar to *Comper*, represented here by the WAR MEMO-
RIAL BOOKCASE on the NW pier, 1920. – STAINED GLASS. E
window of 1877–8 by *Morris & Co*. One of four windows in
the Cathedral that epitomize *Burne-Jones*'s assimilation of the
Italian Renaissance in the 1870s. Three white figures, St Lucy
flanked by angels with blue wings. Demi-figures of angels in
the tracery, stories below. S aisle, two by *Clayton & Bell*, †1871.
Next W, Bishop Robert King, 1638, attributed to *Abraham van
Linge*. With achievement of arms, impaled by shields of arms of
the See and Osney Abbey. The ruinous abbey is the backdrop.

CHOIR NORTH AISLE. ALTAR and CROSS, 2000. Made by
Jim Partridge. Of blackened rough timber. – SCULPTURE.
Virgin and Child statue, 2015 by *Peter Ball*. – STAINED GLASS.
E window by *Morris* and *Burne-Jones*, 1874–5. Like its S aisle
counterpart, with three white-clad figures (St Cecilia central),
angels in the tracery, stories below.

LADY CHAPEL. ALTAR and CORONA designed by *Martin Stan-
cliffe*, 1989. – PAINTING. One vaulting bay has eight censing
angels, probably of *c*.1354 (*see* Montague tomb, p.129), but
ruinous. – STAINED GLASS. Vyner memorial window. Again
Morris and *Burne-Jones*, but four lights this time, and of 1872–3.
All white figures: Samuel, David, St John the Evangelist,
Timothy. The tracery is mostly foliage. Narratives below. The
glass-painter was *Charles Fairfax Murray* (initialled, bottom r.).

LATIN CHAPEL. For the shrine *see* Monuments, p.130. – STALLS
and BENCHES. Displaced from the choir in the 1630s, and
altogether much interfered with. No backs or canopies, just
seats. Very good poppyheads, the best in Oxford. One has a
cardinal's hat, which points to Wolsey and a 1520s date. (Four
plain MISERICORDS.) – CANDELABRUM by Frideswide's
shrine. Made by *Michael Jacques*, 2013. Standing ironwork,
like a burning bush. – SCULPTURE. Another *Peter Ball* figure:
St Frideswide, 2015.

STAINED GLASS. E window, the life of Frideswide, glazed 90
in 1860 by *Powells* to designs by *Burne-Jones*. The setting is
the window designed in 1858 by *Benjamin Woodward*, architect
of the University Museum and a friend of Ruskin and the
Pre-Raphaelites. Morris started his firm only in 1861, so this
is Burne-Jones pre-Morris, and one of his earliest works. It
is much bolder and more forceful than Morris ever was. The
whole is scenes crowded with many figures. Nothing statuesque,
as his late designs in the Cathedral are. Nor does it depend,
like them, on backgrounds designed by others. The colours
are violent, the types straight from Rossetti. The flaming red
Ship of Souls in the top roundel is the most easily remembered
piece. Trees of Life and Knowledge in the sexfoils. The scenes
below are so close-cropped only because Woodward supplied
the artist with incorrect measurements.

N windows. Three here retain much of the original mid-C14 glass. The canopy designs show developments in the use of perspective which are paralleled in contemporary manuscript painting, and which anticipate the late C14 glass at New College (p. 214). The trellises of white quarries painted with trails of roses or oak, the border designs (except for the centre lights) and the tracery glass are mostly restoration by *Powells*, 1862–3. Second window from E, St Margaret, St Frideswide, St Katherine; original Holy Dove in the apex. Third from E, the Archangel Gabriel, an archbishop saint, the Virgin Annunciate (arrangement not original). The borders of the centre light contain interesting grotesques: beasts, monkeys and birds. Traceries with two original lower lights, each containing a human head, set against foliage. Fourth from E, St Katherine, the Virgin and Child, St Hilda(?). Original heads of a king and a bishop in the main traceries. In the apex light a shield of arms of Courtenay with a label. Easternmost window of matching type by *Clayton & Bell*, 1880.

NORTH TRANSEPT. STAINED GLASS. N window, the War in Heaven, 1875 by *Clayton & Bell*. They are less happy on such a scale than in the smaller rose window, E. W aisle windows, mutilated fragments in the traceries from *Abraham van Linge*'s sequence of 1638.

CROSSING. PULPIT, S side. Made by *William Bennett*, 1608–9. Large, with a tester with hanging arches and open-ribbed ogee crown. The motifs small and intricate, not yet the broader forms of the Laudian 1630s. Pelican finial also of 1608, but made by *John Bolton* to ornament a former organ. Stair railing in early C18 style, but post-1872 and probably a *Bodley* job. – VICE-CHANCELLOR'S THRONE, N side. Of 1614, also made by *Bennett*. The canopy stands on thin shafts. – STAINED GLASS. Below the tower ceiling, installed by *S. E. Dykes Bower*, 1961. Made from broken-up bits of *A. & H. Gerente*'s long-displaced E window of 1847.

SOUTH TRANSEPT. COMMUNION TABLE of cedar by *Scott*, 1872, from the choir. – LECTERN also by *Scott*, 1874. Eagle type, unusually fine, of parcel-silvered brass. Made by *Skidmore*. – FONT, installed 2017. Made for Ely Cathedral in 1693, but displaced from there (by Scott, as it happens) in 1850; latterly in Prickwillow church, Cambs. An exquisite white marble piece. The bowl is decorated with large shells and strings of pearls emanating from them and wound round the pretty necks of cherubs. On the base and the rim spreading acanthus leaves. According to its inscription it was given by Dean Spencer. Who might have designed it? No doubt one of the leading London craftsmen; there is, however, no similar font in any of the City churches. Geoffrey Fisher suggests *Caius Gabriel Cibber*.

STAINED GLASS. In St Lucy's Chapel the E window tracery still has all the original glass, a gorgeous display of *c*. 1340–50. The design is very striking, with unusual background patterns and deep-coloured glass throughout. Beginning at the lower l., the subjects are: head of a queen, St Blaise, St Cuthbert holding the head of St Oswald, head of a king. Next row, St Augustine preaching, Martyrdom of St Thomas Becket, St Martin dividing his cloak. Next two rows, small grotesque animals and dragons, also grotesque naked woman and man, harpy, youth, bird of prey, centaur, lion. Next row, kneeling donor canon, two shields of arms, kneeling donor monk. Apex, two censing angels, with Christ in Majesty above. The Becket scene, a rare survival, is justly celebrated. Main lights, collage of 1980 including a C14 donor and a C14 head of a monk. – S window, *Clayton & Bell*, 1891.

NAVE AND AISLES. ORGAN. Main case of the 1680s by *Bernard Smith*, but the lower part with carved screens goes with the new *Rieger* instrument (1978–9). Chair case of 1871 to *Scott*'s design, respectful to Smith. The ORGAN GALLERY includes fabric from the 1630s, when it stood E of the crossing. The rest of 1888 by *H.W. Moore*, and later. – STAINED GLASS. N aisle W by *Abraham van Linge*, dated 163-. Jonah seated under a fabulous gourd, surveying the city of Nineveh to the r., a fabulously big town climbing up. N windows, two by *Clayton & Bell*, †1873 and 1875. S aisle W by *Morris* and *Burne-Jones*, 1871–2. Three Virtues in turquoise, red and blue. Slim upright angels in the drapery. S wall, W to E: *Wailes*, 1858; *James E. Rogers* of Dublin, made by *Powells*, 1864, a single light (Life of St Peter, bold and unconventional); *Clayton & Bell*, 1872 and 1873. – WEST DOORS. Outer doors of glass, 2007. Designed by *Jane McDonald*.

Monuments, from east to west

CHOIR SOUTH AISLE. S wall, far E, brass to Stephen Lence †1587, with two-thirds figure. – Leopold, Duke of Albany, youngest son of Queen Victoria. By *F.J. Williamson* of Esher, 1884. Williamson was much patronized by the royal family. White marble with bust in oval recess; Salon type. – Bishop Mackarness, 1891, with low-relief bronze portrait. Sculptor *George Frampton*, designer *Leonard Stokes*. – Bust of Pusey, a cast after George Richmond's portrait of 1883. – Sarah Acland (†1878), Sir Henry Acland's wife. Exquisite profile in oval. By *Alexander Munro*, 1854.

(CHOIR NORTH AISLE. Brass to Canon Courthorpe †1557. 32-in. (81-cm.) figure. Covered.)

LADY CHAPEL. For the double-decked monument on the N side, E end, *see* the Latin Chapel, below. – Elizabeth Mountfort, Lady Montague †1354. The effigy has the typical coiffure of the time. Much original colour, as also on the (reassembled) tomb-chest. Cinquefoiled arches in its sides with sculpted mourners, including senior clerics of both sexes. They may represent her children individually. The most rewarding (though headless) are on the N side. To W and E a large quatrefoil with a standing figure between the symbols of the Evangelists, hard to see against the arcade piers. Originally the tomb stood further S.

The painted decoration of the vault probably went with it.
– Prior Alexander Sutton †1316(?). Recumbent effigy in prayer.
Canopy over his head (horizontally speaking). Vaulted tomb
canopy of three arched and cusped bays with much ballflower.
It has statue niches at the angles, set diagonally, and rests on
Purbeck marble shafts. Extra detached shafts survive to the s,
pinnacles too, but on the N side both are lost. – Sir George
Nowers(?). Early C15 recumbent effigy. Alabaster and wood
repairs. His head on a big helmet with an ox crest. Tomb-chest
with big plain quatrefoils. – Brasses to John Fitzalan †1452 and
Edward Courtenay, mid-C15. 14-in. (36-cm.) figures. – Two
small scholar brasses on a N pier (†1588, †1613). – Also some
specially good C18 ledger slabs.

LATIN CHAPEL. ST FRIDESWIDE'S SHRINE, probably of 1289,
the date of the second translation of the body of the saint.
Reconstructed from fragments, first in 1889 in the Lady
Chapel by *James Park Harrison*, then again here in 2001–2 by
Prof. John Blair of Queen's College, after more pieces turned
up. Of this time most of the Purbeck marble parts (slabs
and colonnettes). The whole comprises a low tomb-chest with
unencircled quatrefoils with faces or foliage. The canopy is two
bays long, with arches all cusped. Foliage in the spandrels, and
it is naturalistic foliage: hawthorn, vine, ivy etc. That fits a date
*c.*1290 perfectly. Some little faces looking out of it. The likeliest original position is in the bay to the w. The shrine proper
would have rested on top.

WATCHING LOFT or MONUMENT, suggested as that of Sir
Robert Danvers †1467 and wife.* An uncommon combination
of a canopied tomb-chest of stone with an enclosed upper
storey of wood. Enriched quatrefoil panels on the chest sides.
Canopy with a tight frieze-like array of small pendant arches. A
fan-vault inside. The slab has a matrix for brasses of a civilian
and wife. On the shrine side a doorway with stone stairs up,
and recessed sedilia. The upper part, also of two stages, is open
along three sides. Pinnacled canopies all along, partly post-war
renewal, and pinnacles on top, rising higher in the middle. A
timber vault within. Both parts, stone and wood, include a
vine-scroll frieze. No evidence for an altar has been found,
and the top deck has been interpreted instead as a watching
loft or singing loft.

BRASSES. Frederick Barnes †1859, with effigy in the medieval style. Also three with crosses only, †1866–†1877, all made
by *Hardman*.

NORTH TRANSEPT AND AISLES. James Zouch †1503, against
the N wall. Short tomb-chest with quatrefoils. For Zouch's
architectural contribution here *see* p.124. – Brass, to the l.
Henry Dowe †1578. Palimpsest. On the backs a large C14 head,
and canopy-work of *c.*1500. – Thomas Morrey †1584. Brass
with kneeling figure, similar to Dowe's. – E aisle, fragment of
the coffin-lid of Ela, Countess of Warwick †1297/8. From a

---

* *See* Jerome Bertram in *Oxoniensia* 53 (1998).

viscera burial in Osney Abbey. Two lines of lettering and a border of thin vine scroll. – William Goodwin †1620. Demi-figure with book; l. and r. all manner of memento mori, strung along ribbons. – Robert Burton †1639. 'Democritus junior' appears duly as a bust in oval recess, horribly repainted in 1965. Emblems l. and r. The inscription refers to his *Anatomy of Melancholy*. – w aisle, N wall. J.T. James, Bishop of Calcutta, †1828. By *R. Westmacott Jun*. Profile in roundel. Poor. – Lord Charles Somerset †1713, canon of Christ Church, by *William Townesend*. A superior double cartouche against drapery. – w wall. Dr Leonard Hutten †1632, brass in the unusual form of eight separate scrolls, one above the other. – John Torksey †1702. One of many more cartouches in the Cathedral, some good, some quaint and some downright funny.

SOUTH TRANSEPT AND AISLE. Bishop King †1557, last abbot of Osney and of Thame, and first Bishop of Oxford. Purbeck marble tomb, still entirely without Renaissance motifs, despite King's embrace of the style in his work at Thame (p. 755). Very richly panel-traceried tomb-chest. Canopy on a flat arch and with a straight cresting. To the s seven lights. Panelled E wall and traceried vault. No effigy. – The rest comprise an exceptionally interesting mid- to late C17 group. s wall, E to w. Richard Gardiner †1670. Oval inscription in a complex frame partly of piled-up books. – 2nd Viscount Grandison †1643. A rare signed work by *Jasper Latham*, made probably *c*. 1670. High plinth, wreathed urn, sumptuous trophy of arms behind. Quite splendid altogether. – Peter Wycher †1643. Gristly cartouche with four chunky putti. It looks later than the 1640s. – John Banks †1644, below. By *John Stone*, son of Nicolas Stone, 1654. Cartouche with cherub heads and drapery. – Viscount and Viscountess Brouncker †1645 and †1649. A variant of the distinctive composition used for Lady Crewe's monument in Westminster Abbey (GF). Small, white marble tablet. Pilasters and an open pediment with putti holding up drapery. Below, the two sit by a table l. and r., with a skull between them. The background includes a lightly indicated pointed arch. – w wall. Edward Littleton, Lord Mounslowe †1645; erected 1683. High pedestal. Urn and piled-up armour on top of it. Framing this are two detached Ionic columns and a big broken segmental pediment. Attributed to *Edward Pearce* (GF).

NAVE. Crossing s side, Dean Aldrich †1710. Made in 1732, the 66 design attributed to *George Clarke*, the bust by *Sir Henry Cheere*. Roundel with an excellent profile. A winged and crowned skull below. – George Berkeley, Bishop of Cloyne, the philosopher, †1753. Sarcophagus with straight tapering sides. A black obelisk behind, with crozier, torch and palm fronds. – Thomas Tanner, Bishop of St Asaph, †1735. Opposite. Architectural tablet, convex in plan. – John Walrond †1602, w of Berkeley. Small brass with original painted surround. Quite a rarity. – Minor monuments designed by *Comper* (Canon Scott Holland †1918) and *Dykes Bower* on the piers further w. – Dr Pusey †1882, tomb-slab designed by *Bodley*. – Dr John Fell, Dean of

Christ Church and Bishop of Oxford, †1686. w of the screen, moved from the Latin Chapel. Standing monument; extremely unenriched. Two urns l. and r. on the base, achievement on top. Attributed to the *Townesend* workshop (GF). – Opposite four Grecian tablets, two with profile heads: Alexander Nicoll †1828, Edward Burton †1836. – Lettered floor slabs to Ruskin and Locke by the *Cardozo Kindersley Workshop*, 1996.

NAVE NORTH AISLE, E to W. Alexander Gerard †1601, an undergraduate, aged nineteen. Pitiful painted inscription with amateurish picture. – Philip Barton †1765. With a small reclining putto below an urn. Attributed to *P. Scheemakers*. – John Wall †1666. Cartouche incorporating a fat laurel wreath. – William Levett †1694. Cartouche with two putti drawing drapery down over a skull.

NAVE SOUTH AISLE, E to W. Edward Pocock †1691. Bust on top with mortar board. – John Corbet †1688. Cartouche with two putti. – Bishop Wilberforce. Bust in a quatrefoil, of wood. Salvaged from *Scott*'s bishop's throne of 1876. Carved by *Farmer & Brindley*. – James Narbrough †1707, by *William Townesend* (W wall). Specially good cartouche, with seashells.

Cloister and monastic buildings

The CLOISTER is recorded in 1499 as the gift of Robert Sherborne, Dean of St Paul's and a Fellow of New College. It may well be a work of the Oxford master mason *William Orchard*, whose will requested burial in the priory church in 1504. Only the S part of the E walk and the S walk are original, and the W side is lost entirely to the hall staircase. The walks have conventional three-light Perp openings and tierceron-vaulting with many bosses, including women's heads in C15 dress. The parts reinstated by *Scott* in 1871–2 begin with the central section of the E side. Here he made a timber vault that imitates the stone one, but is pushed higher. In the stone-vaulted parts to the N the carving was mostly done later, 1885–99. The old N side had been reworked with Gothick windows by *Henry Keene* in 1772, for a muniment room. On this side MONUMENTS to Lord Charles Scott †1747, carved hanging drapery, and Osborne Gordon †1883, with near-caricature bust in relief signed *Conrad Dressler*, best known for his ceramic work. The low, plain UPPER STOREYS date from 1604 (E side) and 1610–11 (S side). The E walk of the cloister has to the N an opening to the tunnel-vaulted SLYPE or through passage of the C12 priory, as noted inside the S transept. The wrought-iron GATE looks C18.

Then follows the CHAPTER HOUSE. The entrance of this is Norman and of *c.*1140, i.e. twenty or more years older than the main features of the church. The doorway has two inner orders of continuous doubled chevron and two outer orders with columns, carrying on the r. scallop capitals, on the l. more complex ones with small beast-heads swallowing stems of foliage. These are one of several motifs here deriving from

Reading Abbey and the 1120s–30s. An outer band of shallow demi-lune motifs. Much of the stonework is blackened, but not the lowest parts, and these are plainer than the rest. The explanation is that the ground level has been lowered, which must have happened after the fire of 1190. The side openings have restored details but original jambs, evidenced by the faint outline PAINTING of a gesturing male figure on the far l. jamb.

The INTERIOR has on the N side half-chopped-off Norman blind arcading with chevron. Two full bays are preserved, and part of a third. So the walls thus far are Norman. The rest of what is seen belongs to the second quarter of the C13 and is of classic perfection. It has its E wall filled with five stepped lancets, and to the side walls groups of three lancets with the side-lights blind, two such to the S, one to the N. These windows all have boldly detached shafts inside, the E window also dainty dogtooth on the detached shafts, and in the spandrels spreading stiff-leaf. The W half of the room has only one small three-lighter in the gable, also with stiff-leaf around. Vaulting shafts against the walls, standing on excellent busts, some in 'listening' postures. Capitals stiff-leaf throughout. Quadripartite rib-vaults with fillets and bosses. The bosses show the Virgin and Child (the finest of them), Christ seated, St Frideswide, and four lions with one head. All have stiff-leaf lapping around. Above the vault a roof of coupled rafters with two collars, tree-ring dated to 1260–1, which seems too late. It probably represents the replacement of a failed earlier roof. The Perp S doorway and chequered floor are from *Bodley & Garner*'s restoration of 1879–80.

In the E wall is the re-set DEDICATION STONE of 1528 from Cardinal Wolsey's college at Ipswich, given 1789. This was projected to be the chief grammar school for his college, on the Winchester–New College pattern. – PAINTING. In the vault of the E bay four exquisite medallions with figures: St Peter, a male and female each with book, and a male with sword. One more in the next bay. Background of restored stoning outlines. – STAINED GLASS. E window, painted glass symmetrically arranged, mostly early C17 heraldry (1602, 1607, 1609 dates). N and S windows, miscellaneous late C15–C16 items. The most important panels are the Virgin and Child, the Assumption, Wolsey's badge from *James Nicholson*'s 1520s series for the hall (*see* p. 116), and Pilate washing his hands. The last is Flemish work. Staircase window, assembly with three large and most unusual roundels of the late C15. Below, a 'Maria' monogram with the Assumption depicted on the initial letter; next the IHC monogram with the Crucifixion depicted on the letters; the top very like the first. This class of design suggests knowledge of Continental woodcuts and engravings.

PRIORY HOUSE continues S from the chapter house. This mostly represents the worked-over shell of the monks' DORMITORY. The doorway with trefoiled spandrels and two long-haired headstops for the dripmoulding goes with the late C15 cloister work. A small quatrefoil to the N, where the C12 doorway was.

9

The dormitory floor was raised on a vault (fragments remaining at the s end). To the E a rubble-stone front with an unevenly spaced row of sashes to the first floor, casements to the floor above, all with big plain surrounds that look C18, and five pretty tile-hung gables no later than the mid C17. Roof including reused C13 members. The narrower s continuation of the range, originally part of the C15 Prior's House, was demolished when Meadow Building (p. 118) went up. Its present s wall is a shapeless makeshift. On the w side here two gabled bays remain, with standard straight-headed Perp two-light windows. The fancier ground-floor windows (renewed) are a puzzle, for views up to 1865 show a doorway in the N bay here. They may go with the ceiling and other ornate details in the passage, with the carved date 1891.

The s range of the cloister comprised, as usual, the REFEC-TORY. Externally this appears late C15, but the structure is mid-C13, as indicated by the exposure in 2021 of clustered shafts in all four internal corners. The refectory was on the upper floor, where there are first of all four large Perp three-light windows to the N. The five-light E window is hidden by Priory House; the answering, even taller w window has been blocked. The s side looks curious. It is now a tall, well-buttressed range of college rooms on four quite low floors. The broad twin windows with depressed-arched lights, hood-moulds and pointed-arched glazing bars are clearly Georgian, as is confirmed on the cloister side, where the ground-floor windows have four oval openings above. What happened was that *Wyatt* came in 1776 to split up the range for Westminster students, keeping the big N windows to light the corridors. But the evenness of the s front is still interrupted by a weird projection on two figure corbels, evidently the reading pulpit customary in refectories. Before Wyatt the pulpit had slim two-light windows on each face. Charming C15 lierne vault inside, with original red and starred blue colouring. The tall thin sw turret remains, offset at a curious angle. Blind Perp arcading on the main N wall within, both original and restored. Before Meadow Building went up there was a parallel s range also inherited from the monastery buildings (the infirmary?), thus comprising a quadrangle known as Chaplain's Quad.

Until the C18 the refectory interior served as the OLD LIBRARY, with a porch at the w end. The present Art Room at the w end of the range has a pitched roof and CEILING with thirty-two panels painted with shields in strapwork car-touches, and scroll-painted tie-beams in addition. This is in fact a restored composite of surviving elements rediscovered in 1954. The panels can be dated from a renovation of 1612 largely paid for by Otho Nicholson, who also gave Oxford the Carfax Conduit (*see* Nuneham Courtenay, p. 708). Other reassembled panels were re-set in the Selden End of the Bodleian, where they are an almost exact match in treatment for the Arts End ceiling of *c.* 1612. The C17 library furnishings, also modelled on Sir Thomas Bodley's, are lost. There remains the ALLESTREE

LIBRARY over the s cloister walk, installed in 1680 and still complete with its shelving and books. Floor of reused TILES, chiefly C13 and C14; probably introduced in the early C17 (cf. Merton library, p. 200). Access is via the w bay, which goes with Wolsey Tower and is entered from the spiral stair in the tower's SE turret.

The GARDEN in the cloister garth is of 2008, with a lead FOUNTAIN designed by *Gary Breeze*.*

QUADS TO THE NORTH

Peckwater Quad

We leave Tom Quad by Fell Tower. On the l. ahead is KILLCANON, built in 1671–4 to replace a burnt canonical lodging in Chaplain's Quad. The N bay of its originally three-bay façade has been cut across by Peckwater. It had two projections and a recessed centre. In the l. projection a big filled-in archway with a pointed arch but also ears and a big open segmental pediment – all in the spirit of Brasenose chapel. The balustrade too may belong. But the windows have been changed to sashes, and given alternating pediments. The garden side has windows with hoodmoulds, as depicted by Loggan in 1675. There is here one wing projecting much further than on the front, and a late C18 addition where the arched passage formerly went through. Elegant half-round staircase inside. The C17 staircase has curious split-level oblong newels with ball finials.

PECKWATER QUAD represents the college's replacement of the much-renovated Peckwater Inn. The greater part was designed by *Henry Aldrich*, Dean of Christ Church, and built with the help of £2,833 given by Canon Anthony Radcliffe, whose name is prominently recorded. The dates are 1706–14, the builder *William Townesend*. It is amazingly classical, not only in contrast to C17 continuations in such places as Oriel and University colleges, but also in contrast to the Baroque of Hawksmoor. The building, impeccably uniform, occupies three sides of the quad. Each side has fifteen bays. There are two and a half storeys, with channelled rustication and hefty key blocks on the ground floor, and giant Ionic pilasters over. But the central five bays of all three ranges project with attached giant columns and a pediment. Balustrading to the rest. The short sides are of five bays in the W, of three bays in the E range. On the angles here the pilasters are offset, and a half-pilaster appears between. The inner angles manage just a single Ionic volute. Neither motif would be acceptable under the coming Anglo-Palladian orthodoxy, but the overall treatment of an applied order over a rusticated basement storey is Palladian indeed, and Aldrich's discriminating interest in Palladio and his C17

58

*Until 1985 exposed foundations made of reused medieval stone survived here, plausibly identified as the remains of a temporary belfry made *c.* 1528–9, in anticipation of Wolsey's intended new bell-tower.

English followers is well attested. In 1924–30 the façades were renewed in Clipsham stone.

Peckwater is planned mostly with sets of one large front room and two small back rooms, opening off staircases with twisted balusters. In the inner corners and SW angle the arrangements are necessarily more complex. The grander rooms were meant for gentleman commoners of the wealthier sort, hence the provision of wine cellars.

The LIBRARY followed immediately after, and that all but closed the quad. All but – for it is a building detached on both short sides. It was begun in 1717 to replace the library in the former refectory (p. 134), roofed only in 1742, and not completed internally until 1772, at a total cost of £15,517. The design is much stronger than that of Peckwater, but it is worth recording that *Aldrich* had likewise designed a block with a full-height Baroque order to stand on this site.* This was meant to be three-storeyed and residential, however, and so for the library a new design was needed. Aldrich having died in 1710, the project passed to his friend *Dr George Clarke* of All Souls. *Townesend* was again the builder. Clarke's façade – seven broad bays, in place of Aldrich's intended nine – has giant unfluted Corinthian columns starting right off the ground. John Webb had done that in the King Charles Building at Greenwich, the earliest example of the English Baroque, Wren likewise in the late designs for Whitehall Palace. But nowhere is it done as consistently and sweepingly. The upper windows have pediments alternately triangular and segmental. The ground floor introduces a subsidiary order, one of several reminiscences here of Michelangelo's Capitoline palace in Rome. It has Doric pilasters, a Doric cornice all across, and big arched windows with their own imposts between. These were originally left open. On the short sides the paired giant pilasters are repeated, with a large, Corinthian-pilastered Venetian window on the upper floor, echoed in Doric form below. An upper Venetian window intended for the central bay towards the quad was reversed during construction. The top is a truly monumental cornice and a balustrade. The contrast of white Portland and buff Clipsham stone dates from *Playne & Lacey's* renewal of the N, E and W sides in 1960–2, and is bolder than the original combination of Headington and Burford stones.

On the seldom-seen S side the treatment is plainer. Simple modillion cornice. The centre projects, pedimented over the staircase part. The bays to r. and l., matching those of Clarke's range at Worcester College (p. 319), house library offices, with orangeries for the Deanery garden below.

The INTERIOR is a surprise, as the furnishing and decoration is all post-1750. The entrance is in the middle, and a hall here leads to the STAIRCASE, in a long apse-ended room placed parallel to the main library. Splendid wrought-iron balustrade by *Nathan Cooper*, 1762. In niches high up a statue of

* *See* James Weeks in *Architectural History* 48 (2005).

John Locke by *Rysbrack*, 1755–8, and a bust of Dean Aldrich, unsigned and undocumented – which is a pity, as it is surprisingly dramatic with the sideward fling of the head. Stucco ceiling by *Thomas Roberts*, with fine garlands of flowers around a diapered centre panel. The entrance to the upper room is by a wooden doorway with Ionic columns and a pediment.

The UPPER LIBRARY itself is superb, long and not very high, with bookcases only along the long sides. Their arrangement derives in outline from a proposal from the 1740s by *James Gibbs*, who had also steered the library at All Souls to completion. The cases were made in 1756–62 by the versatile London joiners and builder-developers *George Shakespear* and *John Phillips*. On the back wall a balustraded balcony on Ionic columns, coming forward in the middle above the entrance. On the front wall the cases have two frontispieces, as it were: raised centrepieces with broken pediments above arches. The outer pairs of windows are thus blind. Above the cases is more glorious stuccowork by *Thomas Roberts*, large, bold wall panels and intricate trophies of musical and scientific instruments. His ceiling stucco is simpler, divided into three main parts, with the larger middle one coved. Among the motifs here, incidentally, are large ogee arches. Much renewal of the lesser mouldings in 1892–5; decoration by *John Fowler*, 1965, 'Neapolitan pink', after the original c18 shade. The back wall includes doorways at both levels to the smaller rooms.

The GROUND FLOOR is in two sections, l. and r. of the entrance. They were enclosed by *Henry Keene* in 1769–72, to provide space for the paintings given to the college by General John Guise and now accommodated in the Picture Gallery (*see* p. 139). Details no longer Rococo but of the Adam stage of development. Each room is tripartite, with broad Venetian-pattern openings with coupled unfluted Ionic columns with Grecian capitals, and sparing stucco. On the E side an unfinished renovation of 1869 by *T.N. Deane* and *Bruton*, who filled one bay and part of the next with clashing galleries etc.

In the entrance hall is a display of BUSTS: *Bacon Sen.*'s Archbishop Robinson and Bishop Trevor (both 1770), *Bacon Jun.*'s Archbishop Markham (formerly Dean; 1804), *Chantrey*'s Bishop Bagot (1830; another former Dean), *Roubiliac*'s singular Dr Richard Frewen or Frewin (1757), Dr Busby by *Rysbrack* (attributed), and, of the c20, Dean Lowe by *Epstein* (1957), the only one in bronze.

Canterbury Quad

CANTERBURY QUAD opens off the SE corner of Peckwater. It was built chiefly at the expense of Richard Robinson, Archbishop of Armagh (*c.* £4,000), and this is also recorded. The buildings are by *Wyatt* and, as they date from 1773–83, they are an early job of his; in 1773 he was twenty-seven years of age. *James Pears* was the executant, Wyatt's usual man for

Oxford projects. Canterbury is a small quad, but being of the
CI8 it does not discard monumentality. Two tall storeys only,
except that Wyatt repeated the three-storey three-bay end of
Peckwater opposite to the s as a fitting end to his quad. The
difference between the grandeur of 1705 and the reticence of
1773 is telling here. Otherwise only the centre of the E side is
emphasized, with a broad, pedimented triumphal-arch motif
for the gateway. Niches in the side parts. Pendentives and a
stone dome within the passage, and GATES of 1926, in CI8
style. Frieze inscription cut by *David Kindersley* for the refacing of 1965. The view from Oriel Square is more monumental.
The centre is a noble triumphal arch fully expressed, with
four engaged Doric columns, shallow blank niches and upper
panels l. and r., and a plain attic. The columns are fluted, and
they lack bases, in the Greek way – the first external British
example of this on a grand scale. To l. and r. are three bays also
with no openings at all, only blank recesses or niches and upper
panels again, with a delicate fluted frieze between. Formerly
these side bays had balustrades on top. Very plain windowed
bays beyond. The triumphal-arch motif appears a third time,
in wholly blind form and with Peckwater-type pilasters, where
the w end faces the Deanery Garden.

Canterbury Quad is the replacement for CANTERBURY
COLLEGE, founded by Archbishop Islip in 1362 for Benedictines from Canterbury Cathedral. Unlike Peckwater Inn this
was a college in full: hall, chapel and library arranged around
a single quadrangle. Built *c.* 1370–*c.* 1450, it was the first in an
Oxford college to employ the Perpendicular style.

As a coda to this side, the PIERS and WALL where Peckwater
faces Oriel Square are of 1877–9 by *Bodley & Garner*, well-
observed mid-CI7 classical style.

Christ Church, Canterbury Quad, east front.
Engraving by J. Cole after Michael Angelo Rooker, 1781

C20 buildings

Finally to the C20, which at Christ Church means *Powell & Moya*. Theirs is the masterly PICTURE GALLERY of 1964–8 behind the S range of Canterbury, very discreetly announced there. It is built at basement level, taking up the E part of the Deanery Garden, and appears there low and non-committal, faced with coursed rubble and having a flat roof reached by gentle ramps. The interior is all. It is ingeniously planned, but the ingenuity is never made a display of. The entrance is down stairs within the Wyatt range. The direction continues as a passage with unbroken glazing to an entirely enclosed lawn on the l., and roof rising gradually towards the print gallery and curator's office, placed up steps at the far end. To the r. of the passage are the two main galleries, originally finished in white plaster, and these are day-lit from above. In the larger space there is a clerestory arrangement around the solid centre on its four round piers. Throughout one feels enclosed, in a world apart, and segregated from the college.

BLUE BOAR QUAD is *Powell & Moya*'s other project, exactly contemporary with the Picture Gallery, and likewise tucked away from the rest of the college. Access is now made round the back of Killcanon. As one approaches from the S the building appears chiefly as a number of identical units, in a long arrangement with shorter returns to E and W, but they are strung up so intelligently that no uniformity appears. It is done exactly as on the much larger scale of the architects' Cripps Building, St John's College, Cambridge (1963–7), and shares with that building an ancestry in their pioneering infill project at Brasenose (p. 108). Each unit is two large horizontal windows wide and three high, with broadly chamfered mod-elled concrete sills, and square buttresses faced in shelly Portland roach stone placed between and to l. and r. A penthouse storey, originally comprising larger sets for Fellows, sits on top. The two-bay units are paired across narrow recessed bays for the staircases, and separated by single bays stepped back not quite so far, most visibly where the E–W range is bent at a slight angle. The W end of this range is now deceptive, the rooms having been knocked through in *Purcell Miller Tritton*'s renova-tion of 2007–9 to create a double-height lecture theatre. The hard landscaping at this end was altered too, and the top storey rebuilt all along in thicker forms and with extra rooms fitted in, to the detriment of Powell & Moya's carefully calculated skyline. The same applies to the view along Blue Boar Street, in the intervals between the original staircase enclosures with their lead-faced water tanks, appearing here above a sturdy retained wall.

The S side of Blue Boar includes the rubble-walled BREW-HOUSE, a substantial building of rubble stone with a dormer storey in its steep-pitched roof. In 2007–9 a new home was made here for the college archives, and the unusual roof with upper and lower collars opened up. Its tree rings have been dated 1404/5.

Originally the entrance to the quad was via the open passage in the E side, and a handsome DOORWAY with a pediment on brackets in the back wall of Peckwater, to the r. This was salvaged from the palace at Cuddesdon (q.v.), rebuilt by Dean Fell as Bishop of Oxford in 1679 and pulled down after a fire in 1958. By *Thomas Wood* of Oxford, and similar to the portal of his Old Ashmolean building (p. 339).

For CHRIST CHURCH CATHEDRAL SCHOOL and ST ALDATE'S QUAD *see* Perambulation 6, p. 446; for the LIDDELL BUILDING *see* Iffley Road, p. 502.

CORPUS CHRISTI COLLEGE
Merton Street

At Corpus everything is on the small side; that is what makes it so lovable. Front Quad, the quad begun by Bishop Fox of Winchester even before the college received its charter in 1517, is nice and intimate, and the ranges are not high, and Fellows' Quad is just a cloistered strip in front of a new C18 building. Other additions, C18 and later, are in proportion. Even in the C19, when the college had to go across Merton Street to develop at all, nothing big was built.

At first Fox intended the college to house eight monks from his cathedral at Winchester, as well as eight secular scholars. That would have given Oxford another monastic foundation on the model of St Bernard's (now St John's) or Durham College (now Trinity). But soon after construction started he decided it should educate secular clergy instead, with an up-to-date emphasis on Greek as well as Latin. The completed college had twenty Fellows and three public lecturers under a President, all of whom were accommodated in Front Quad.

Front Quad

FRONT QUAD was built in one go, in 1512–18. The chief craftsmen came from the royal service: *William Vertue*, master mason, and *Humphrey Coke*, master carpenter, assisted respectively by two Oxford men, *William East* and *Robert Carow*. The hall is on the E side, library on the S side, chapel also on the S side but projecting E, and thus invisible from the quad. The other accommodation was in pairs of rooms, reflecting the original arrangement by which each Fellow had a junior student or *discipulus*. The little C16 cloister, S of the chapel, was rebuilt in the C18.

The NORTH FRONT to Merton Street is of three storeys, but the third with its crenellations is a heightening of *c.* 1740 (continued on the W side), and so the gate tower seems small

Corpus Christi College

1   Hall
2   Library
3   Chapel
4   Fellows' Building

5   Gentlemen Commoners' Building
6   Old Lodgings
7   MBI Al Jaber Auditorium
8   Jackson and Oldham buildings

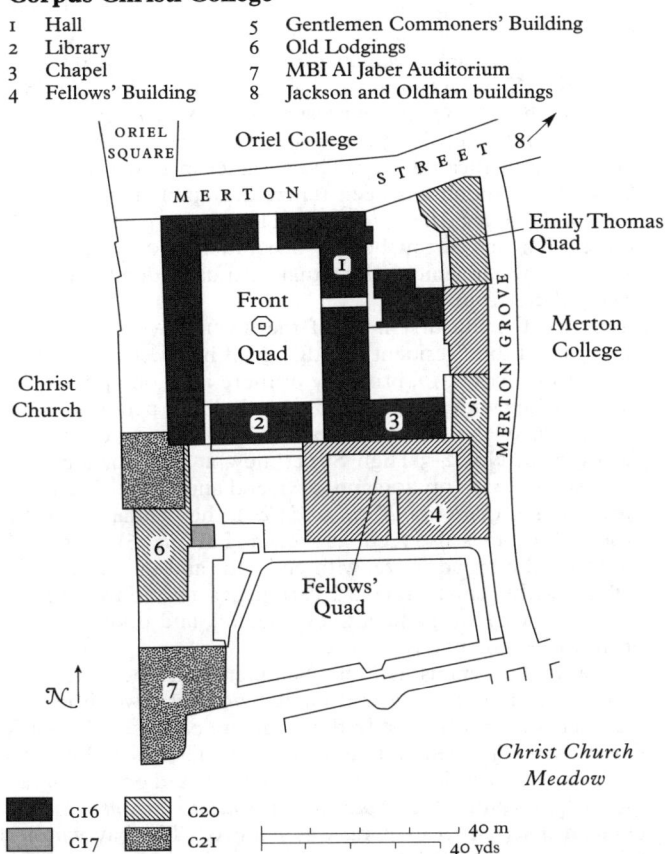

C16
C17
C18
C20
C21

40 m
40 yds

again. Archway with heraldic roundels in the spandrels. Original door, quite plain. Embellished oriel with two niches l. and r., mid-niche on the second floor. The niche details are sophisticated: complex diagonal shafts, intricate miniature vaults. The rest of the frontage has the usual rhythm of two-light and one-light windows. However, one window, l., is much bigger. It looks ecclesiastical but belongs to the hall. Fan-vault in the gateway, much renewed, as indeed is all the external stonework. Unusually for a C16 college the walls were originally of rubble and render, but all are ashlared now. The builder of the C18 top storey was *John Townesend II*. Its pie-crust cornice must derive from Hawksmoor's tower range at All Souls, where Townesend's father was mason.

Front Quad inside is of two storeys plus a dormer storey. Square stair-turret to the gate tower. The stepped-up mid-piece facing the gateway displays a statue of the founder inserted in

1817. Earlier, in 1804, the quad walls were ashlared.* The uniform two-light windows on the first floor of the S side indicate the library, the traceried windows of the E side the hall – but the latter are speculative restoration of 1853, reversing C18 losses. The hall doorway has roundels in the spandrels. Likewise that to the chapel passage in the SE corner.

In the middle of the quad is the celebrated SUNDIAL, with the college's pelican on top. The designer in 1581 was *Charles Turnbull*, but much has been renewed, notably between 1967 and 1981 (carver *Michael Black*). The square part at the top of the pillar has cartouches for decoration, a C17 motif. Also of the C17 the ingenious perpetual calendar, added 1605. The paving dates from 1973.

INTERIORS. On the first floor of the GATE TOWER is a room once part of the President's Lodgings. It has decoration of the later C16 or early C17, probably of more than one phase. The stucco ceiling with thin ribs and many bulbous pendants is one of the best of the period in Oxford. The design matches the ceiling from Nos. 2–3 High Street, now at The Shrubbery in Woodstock Road (pp. 409 and 468), and another at Chastleton House (*see Oxfordshire: North and West*); the pendants and the little acorn sprays also recur at Frewin Hall (p. 436). Outstanding too is the broad frieze, with emblems and the arms of the colleges within close strapwork cartouches derived from Vredeman de Vries. Also panelling, overmantel, and doorways with primitive pediments.

The HALL retains its fine hammerbeam roof, designed almost certainly by *Coke* and made by *Carow*. Two differentiated tiers of wind-braces. In the frieze are badges and a shield dated 1516. The pendants and other details lower down are likely to be restoration of 1853, apparently based on the engraving in James Smith's *A Specimen of Antient Carpentry* (1736), after an inserted C18 ceiling was removed. The bay window, E side, has a panelled stone vault. Tracery of 1853 here. Fine centrepiece below the big N window with a segmental pediment. The WOODWORK is of 1701–5, to the designs of the prominent London surveyor *John Oliver* (*c.* 1615–1701).† The carpenter was Oxford's *Arthur Frogley*, the ornamental carver another Londoner, *Jonathan Maine*. The screen is richer than some, though flat. Segmental pediments over the entrances. Pedimented top achievement with side scrolls, oddly proportioned but sumptuously carved. Fireplace inserted 1741, restored 1979 after a design by *Gibbs*.

The LIBRARY is approached by a staircase of *c.* 1700 in the E range. Bookcases of 1604–5, heightened *c.* 1700, with benches attached and bench seating between. Some wood appears to have been discreetly reused from the lecterns made by *Cornell Clark* in 1517. Of *c.* 1700 the hardware for chaining the books and locking the shelves. The date 1604 is in the

---

* Battlements added in 1625 were removed in 1935.
† Also co-designer of the woodwork of Emmanuel College chapel, Cambridge.

overmantel of the doorway to the chapel W gallery and on the E doorway itself. The carving was by *Thomas Key* and one *Bolton*, almost certainly the *John Bolton* who later worked at Wadham etc. Also of 1604–5 the splendid stucco achievement above, and the delicate work in the window soffits (matching those in the gate tower), by *Pereson*, identifiable as the Oxford plasterer *William Pearson*. To the W a room annexed from the President's Lodgings in 1872, and so to the intended 2020s library extension (*see* p. 145).

The CHAPEL has three-light windows, not very large. In 1676 it was lengthened a little to the W, the space being taken off the library, and the black and white PAVING was laid. At the same time a vestry on the N side was demolished. The easternmost window there now is an insertion (old window outline visible outside). In the S wall an ornamented SEDILIA recess with arched head, behind a hinged panel. The panelled roof is of 1843, but old materials were reused. Among these are the bosses, carved in 1517 by *Thomas Russell* of Westminster. The STALLS are of 1676–7. Big balls on the ends, backs with a late appearance of simple perspective motifs (cf. Oriel chapel). – SCREEN also of 1676–7. Relatively modest, but of cedarwood rather than oak, with detached Corinthian columns and a big segmental pediment. The doorway spandrels in openwork. Two return stalls with the perspective motif, under canopies on thin shafts. *Richard Frogley* provided at least some of this 1670s woodwork. – REREDOS and side panelling of 1938, designed by *Goodhart-Rendel* in Neo-Baroque mood. ALTAR PAINTING, an Adoration of the Magi from the *Rubens* studio, given 1804. – LECTERN, an eagle of brass. Given by the first President (†1537) or in his memory. Exactly the same type as at Cropredy (*see Oxfordshire: North and West*), at Chipping Campden in Gloucestershire, at Cavendish and Woolpit in Suffolk, etc. – ORGAN CASE, W of the screen. By *Jackson*, c. 1881. – STAINED GLASS. E window by *Henry A. Payne*, 1931. St Christopher, against a sea crowded with galleons. – MONUMENTS. John Claymond, the first President, †1537 (antechapel floor). Brass. A shrouded skeleton, 31½ in. (80 cm.) long. – John Reynolds or Rainolds, President, †1607. Demi-figure in a niche. – Dr John Spenser †1614. Demi-figure, remarkably relaxed. Columns and strapwork. – Thomas Turner, President, †1714. Large tablet with semicircular top. In this a profile bust between two cherubs. Made in 1729 by *William Townesend*, from a draft by '*Mr J. Tinney*'.

Fellows' Quad, with the rest of the main site

FELLOWS' QUAD is reached by the chapel passage. This is the smallest of Oxford quads, a narrow rectangle with the cloister to the N and Fellows' Building to the S. Both were built in 1706–12, replacing Fox's cloister and chambers of 1517–18. The CLOISTER has a very squared exterior, English Baroque in mood, formerly with urns all along the parapet. Plaster vault with occasional stucco decoration. It turns s at both ends to connect with FELLOWS' BUILDING. This is a serious building, nine bays long and three storeys high. Three doorways on the N side, and on the s side, facing towards Christ Church Meadow, a more conventional eleven-bay composition with a three-bay pediment on giant Ionic pilasters and straight entablatures for the first-floor windows. On the w side four bays, all blank, including arched niches on the first floor. All the ground-floor windows segment-headed, with big keystones. Apart from this storey the Neo-Palladian main elevation is very close to Peckwater Quad at Christ Church by *Dean Aldrich* (*see* p.135), and the ground-floor windows are like those of the basement of his All Saints' church, also begun in 1706 (*see* p.388). So he is the best candidate for architect. The contracting mason was *William Townesend*, who may have had a share in the design. Roof storey rebuilt for accommodation, with refacing and renewal of the cloister arcades, 1954–62. Among the monuments a draped tablet to Christopher Wase †1711, and a memorial of 2004 to John Ruskin, honorary Fellow at Corpus from 1871.

The E side of the cloister was rebuilt behind the arcade in 1928–9 by *T.H. Hughes*, with an upper storey including the barrel-vaulted SENIOR COMMON ROOM. The present MIDDLE COMMON ROOM is on the ground floor here, behind the chapel. In it a re-set chimneypiece with pilasters and the simplest of perspective arches – Jacobean or a little later. The outside of this part (seen from the footpath between Corpus and Merton) is seven bays wide, with the middle window pedimented on brackets, not at all the mood of the cloister.

From Fellows' Quad the choice is N to the lesser quads, or s and w to the gardens.

A passage by the chapel E end leads N to GENTLEMAN COMMONERS' QUAD. Named from the GENTLEMEN COMMONERS' BUILDING, E side. Rebuilt in 1737, and decidedly conservative for its date. Five bays, three storeys, tall and narrow proportions. Bays one and five project and have quoins of even length. The windows are framed, and all the openings on the lower floors have big key blocks. *William Townesend* was again the builder; the design is unlikely to be his, lacking the assurance of his independent projects. The E front is a utilitarian affair – smooth, of seven bays, with two projecting chimney-breasts – and extends further N, behind the kitchen. This KITCHEN is part of the original buildings, though heavily altered now.* Its w part was floored across in 1982 to form the FOUNDER'S ROOM, architect *Geoffrey Beard*, and in this upper room the collar-beam roof is exposed. The w side of the quad was raised to three full storeys by *Hughes*, 1938.

---

*It may represent a surviving part of the former Urban Hall: roof and wall timbers have yielded felling dates between 1498 and 1508.

EMILY THOMAS QUAD lies N of the kitchen, with access via the hall screens passage. The N side is mostly open to Merton Street, the E side is the THOMAS BUILDING, again by *T.H. Hughes*. It is of 1927–9 and looks 1900. Tudor-collegiate style. The entrance is in the re-entrant angle of the L-shape. Obtrusive roof storey by *Berman Guedes Stretton*, c.2001.

Now SW, to the OLD LODGINGS. The building is T-shaped, with a central projection to the E. This part represents a wing added c.1690 to lodgings of 1607, now lost. It has sash windows and an originally open ground floor with Tuscan half-columns, and has been stuccoed. The N and S parts are of 1905–6 by *Thomas Case*, President, for himself. His S wing is of stone, with engaged columns and rustication to the dining room below, cross-windows throughout, occasional ovals, and a hipped roof. The N wing however is Gothic, and matches the C16 library adjacent. Everything behind this Gothic façade was rebuilt in 1957–9 by *Michael Powers* of the *Architects' Co-Partnership*, with a new N entrance range facing the cul de sac off Merton Street, i.e. between Corpus and Christ Church. Notable as an early Modernist addition to an Oxford college, it was disappointing as architecture; 'a pretty, but decidedly mannered job' (Pevsner). Being replaced by *Wright & Wright*'s LIBRARY EXTENSION, begun 2022.

S of the Old Lodgings, contrived within a bastion of the CITY WALL and replacing an older music room there, is the MBI AL JABER AUDITORIUM. By *Rick Mather Architects*, 2006–9. Externally the structure has a plate-glass entrance wall, a set-back upper level with partly stone walling and external steps up, then more steps to a top platform with railings, much too prominent on the skyline. The stonework of the BASTION is exposed inside, with two casements. It is the only known British bastion to be thus placed within an angle in a defensive wall. Alongside, E, part of the MOUND or mount made in 1596–7, then a stretch in which the wall has been lowered and railings installed, probably in 1782.

w of the Fellows' Building a charmingly minimal GREENHOUSE by *Mather*, 2009, just frameless glazing on a rubble base.

North of Merton Street

At the corner of Merton Street and Magpie Lane, Corpus put up a four-bay building in 1884–5, now the JACKSON BUILDING. Architect indeed *T.G. Jackson*, as the overcrowding of decoration, the bay windows, the two superimposed aedicules all show, i.e. the apparatus as well as the handling. Doulting stone. It was meant as the beginning of a new quad. The next instalment had to wait for the OLDHAM BUILDING of 1966–9, by *Powell & Moya*. It extends N along Magpie Lane. Walls faced in coursed Bladon rubble, with concrete floor bands. Broad but shallow concrete-framed window projections with spandrel panels of lead. Renovated in 2015–16 by *Berman Guedes Stretton*, and the courtyard remodelled. *Jackson* also adapted the w part of the adjacent BEAM HALL for the college (No.3 Merton Street), hence its red brick rear additions; now the PRESIDENT'S LODGINGS. Built in 1586. Two rendered storeys plus four gables, mullioned windows. Ground-floor windows under a running hoodmould, which if original would be the earliest dated occurrence in Oxford. On the ground floor is an excellently panelled mid-C17 room with a chimney-piece to match. The panelling is of the type with four L-shaped parts and has a blank arch in the centre. The overmantel has short paired columns and head corbels above them. (On the upper floor an overmantel with just two big blank arches.) Beam Hall's E part is late C15, much lower, of exposed stone. C17 dormers, two big, one small; also one C17 ovolo-mullioned upper window, from when a floor was inserted. (A moulded beam to the w marks where the hall screen stood. Original arch-braced collar-beam roof.) The name is from Gilbert de Biham, a mid-C13 Chancellor of the University; it lasted as an academic hall until 1553.

For Kybald Twychen in Kybald Street *see* p.413; for the LAMPL BUILDING, Park End Street, *see* Perambulation 5, p.442; for the LIDDELL BUILDING, Iffley Road, *see* p.502.

EXETER COLLEGE
Turl Street and Broad Street

Founded by Bishop Stapeldon of Exeter in 1314, to promote clerical education in his own diocese. Stapeldon Hall, as it was first known, had twelve Fellows under a Rector. The name Exeter College was current by *c.*1470, but the crucial transformation followed the re-endowment of 1566 by Sir William Petre.* Only after that did the college achieve a full quadrangle. Nothing remains of the C14 cluster of buildings, and of the C15 only Palmer's Tower and some masonry to its E. The principal impression now from Turl and Broad streets is C19 and C20, in the quad C17 and C19, with *Scott*'s chapel predominant – a reminder that mid-Victorian Exeter was among the most populous colleges at Oxford.

FRONT QUAD has in its NE corner PALMER'S TOWER, built from a gift by William Palmer, Rector, in 1432. It is of moderate size and has no spectacular features. Attractive two-bay vault inside with diagonal and ridge ribs on angel corbels. Also bosses. W wall with buttresses and refacing of 1856 by *George Gilbert Scott*, who infilled the gateway to serve as a porch to his new Rector's Lodgings alongside (*see* below, p.150). Scott's lancets

---

* Father, incidentally, of Dorothy Wadham, co-founder of Wadham College.

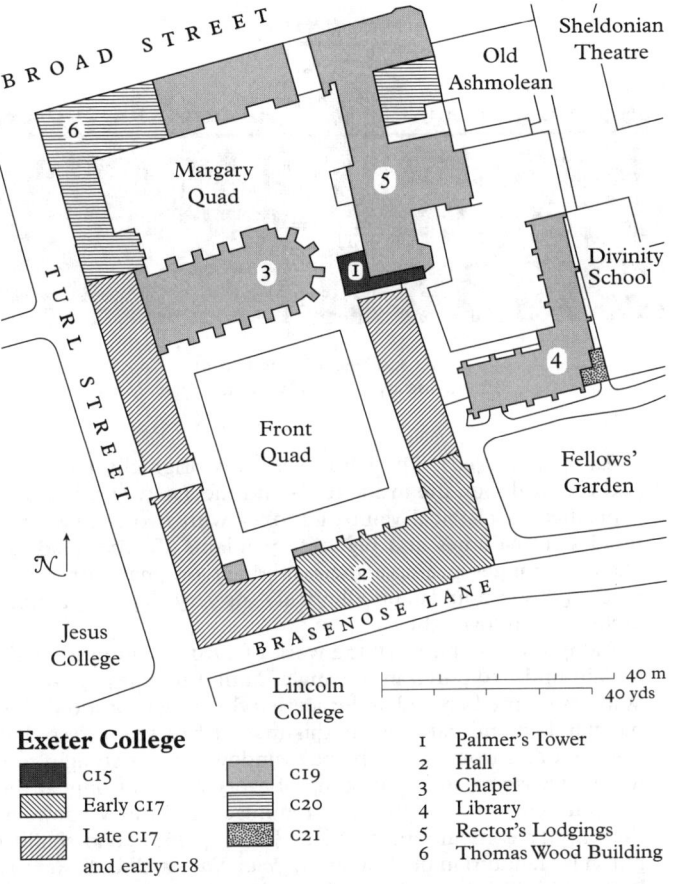

Exeter College

CI5
Early CI7
Late CI7 and early CI8
CI9
C20
C2I

1 Palmer's Tower
2 Hall
3 Chapel
4 Library
5 Rector's Lodgings
6 Thomas Wood Building

now have pale stained glass of 1949 by *Margaret Chilton*, part of a war memorial. Walling from a chamber range of *c.* 1432 continues to the E, now incorporated into the Lodgings, but the windows here are much later. The tower stands where it does because the original approach to the college was from a lane that ran just within the city wall, to the N. That must be why the N archway is more richly treated, with a big hollow moulding.

Front Quad is now entered from Turl Street. The WEST RANGE has towards that street a long smooth Gothic façade of 1834–5 by *H.J. Underwood*, of Bath ashlar stone, with a near-central gate tower and balancing oriels near the ends. The windows straight-headed, with depressed pointed lights. *Sir Reginald Blomfield* – an old member – added gables over the oriels in 1907. But Underwood's Gothic is only skin-deep, for the range itself was built in 1672 (N part, or most of it) and 1701–3 (gate tower and s part, by *John Townesend I* and

Exeter College, old west front.
Engraving by William Williams, 1733

William Townesend). The gate tower was originally pilastered and classical – on the inside too – and the gateway still has its sophisticated classical vault of 1701–3 with two shallow coffered saucer-domes and big leafy pendants. To the quad the chamber ranges preserve their subdued original form, with running hoodmoulds and elliptical – or very slightly pointed-arched – window lights.

Along the SOUTH SIDE the work of 1701–3 continues, with a plain mid-C19 porch in the angle, until it touches the HALL. With its pointed-arched and traceried three-light windows, big bay window and battlements this may at first seem Perp, but the hall dates from 1618. The bay window with its straight top, its two transoms and its cusping of every light not only at the top but below every transom is reminiscent of the windows of the exactly contemporary hall at Jesus (p. 161). The shallow porch is an addition of 1818–20 by *John Nash* with *G. S. Repton*, harsh and ill-informed Gothic replacing Jacobean classical. Also apparently by Nash the screens-passage vault. The hall roof must also be regarded with caution: the thin members, pendants and general outlines are of the early C17, but the cusped uprights and the horizontal grid-like quatrefoil tracery above the collars are Nash and Repton's doing.* In C17 terms the surprise is the use of arched braces, rather than hammerbeams as at Wadham, Jesus and elsewhere. The braces rest on head corbels. The screen with its columns decorated with strapwork is original, as are the openwork strap achievements at the top. The maker was probably *John Bolton*, known to have worked in Exeter's old chapel of 1623–4, which had a similar screen (cf. Bolton's Wadham screens; also the Jesus hall screen). The two fireplaces with their vine-columns, garlands and obelisks are however of 1904 by *Sir R. Blomfield*. Originally the hall had a central hearth and roof louvre. Heraldic stained

---

*As observed by Julian Munby. The C17 form is depicted in James Smith's *Specimens of Ancient Carpentry* (1787).

glass of 1906–14 by *Powells*. The hall stands on a BASEMENT (now student bar) with short pillars and brick vaults.

The EAST RANGE starts by the hall with PERYAM'S BUILDING, also of 1618, and continues N with ARMAGH BUILDING of 1708–10. The side of Peryam's towards the quad is refaced and now has the up-and-over hoodmoulds and straight parapet of the later ranges on the W side. But the original straight string courses survive on the garden side, where Peryam's also has two canted bay windows.

The NORTH SIDE of the quad is *G. G. Scott*'s prodigious CHAPEL,   87 built in 1856–9 in place of the old, double-naved chapel of 1623–4 and the Rector's Lodgings to its E. It cost £15,000. Proposals for a new chapel were canvassed in 1847 from *Scott*, *Salvin* and *J. P. Harrison*, whose designs all adopted English Middle Pointed.* When Scott was called back in 1853 he steered his course towards French Gothic instead, with soaring proportions, a polygonal apse and a flèche all reminiscent of the Sainte-Chapelle in Paris or of lesser-known C13 chapels such as that at Chaalis. Tall three-light windows with Geometrical tracery, buttresses with statuary niches and gablets. Ornate S portal, also with figure-work. The tympanum is by *J. Birnie Philip*, who did most of the other carving inside and out, assisted by *John Lockwood Kipling*, father of the writer. Statues on the buttresses followed in 1872–9, by *Farmer & Brindley* (one renewed). Roof of Westmorland slate, 1884, replacing Scott's Stonesfield slates.

An earlier design by Scott (1853) was intended to be let into the centre of the E range, with its entrance on axis with the Turl Street gateway. Its high W end would thus have matched the gate tower, and its bulk (covering roughly the area of the present library) would have been seen chiefly from the Fellows' Garden in conjunction with the tall structures of Radcliffe Square – instead of overpowering the quad.

The INTERIOR reaps the benefit of the great height. It is vaulted with diagonal and ridge ribs and one pair of tiercerons in each N and S cell. Bands of brown stone in the vault cells, wall-shafts of coloured Devonshire and Cornish granites. The effect is intensely rich, accentuated by the stone SCREEN with naturalistic leaf capitals etc., the lushly decorated arch into the small vestry, formerly Rector's pew, N, and the stone ORGAN GALLERY, again with naturalistic leafage. Its wrought-iron BALCONY comes from the destroyed organ case of *c.*1880 by *J. Oldrid Scott* at New College. – GATES of iron and brass in the screen by *Messrs Skidmore*. – STALLS of wood, with canopies etc. added by *Bodley*, 1884.† – PAINTINGS. Four, from C14 Sienese altarpieces. The larger two, single saints,

---

* *See* Geoffrey Tyack in *Architectural History* 50 (2007).
† Jacobean stalls were sent to Merton church (*see* *Oxfordshire: North and West*) and to Long Wittenham church, Berks., with parts from the screen. Other parts from the chapel are at the Museum of Oxford and at Weston Manor, Weston on the Green, North Oxon.

attributed to *Luca di Tommè*, *c.*1370. – MOSAIC by *Salviati*, 1868–9, in the arcading round the apse. – CREDENCE SHELF in the apse carved by one of the *O'Shea* brothers. – TILES by *Minton*. – TAPESTRY of the Adoration of the Magi given by the *Morris* firm, designed by *Burne-Jones* and made in 1886–90. It has the Late Victorian sombre colours, but goes well in the setting. Morris and Burne-Jones met while undergraduates at the college in the 1850s. – Brass eagle LECTERN, the chief pre-Victorian piece, presented in 1637. It may well be by the same craftsman as that of 1638 at St Mary Redcliffe in Bristol. – STAINED GLASS by *Clayton & Bell* in nearly all the windows, with their characteristic colours and borders. The earliest in the three central apse windows, 1859–61. Already by 1862 (S side, first E from apse) these vibrant colours are muted. Other windows up to 1890, with one of 1919 over the door. – WAR MEMORIAL by *Sir R. Blomfield*, 1921. – MONUMENTS. Mutilated kneeling effigy of John Crocker †1629 (apse). – Bust of J.R.R. Tolkien by *Faith Tolkien*, 1977.

The FELLOWS' GARDEN is reached through the E range. Here is the LIBRARY, built as a detached structure in the garden in 1856–7 by *Scott*, on the site of *John Townesend III*'s classical library of 1779. Also in the late C13 style, but more personal in the handling. The upper floor keeps up the medieval tradition of closely spaced library windows by closely spaced blank arcading, though not allowing more than four lancets to the front. Fine timber-vaulted interior on this upper floor. Dormers with Geometrical tracery, ground-floor windows just turning ogee-headed. In one of these windows two exquisite stained-glass roundels have been introduced, early work by the *Morris* firm: heads after cartoons of 1862–3 by *Burne-Jones*, quarry pattern by *William Morris*. At the back a one-storey reading room running N from the E end, and in the angle a stout polygonal stair-turret with spire. The library and indeed the E wall of the main range all but touch the buildings of the Bodleian (the Selden End). The library is being renovated by *Nex Architecture* (2023).

The garden is bounded by a WALL of 1573, against which is a raised terrace walk. This originated as a MOUNT in 1605–6; extended *c.*1618. The garden's present naturalistic planting dates probably from the 1790s.

MARGARY QUAD lies N of the chapel. On the E side are first the RECTOR'S LODGINGS, of 1856–7 by *Scott*. Sheer three-storey Gothic front, two-light windows with a little carving. Scott's porch joining on to Palmer's Tower was removed in *T.H. Hughes*'s remodelling of 1943–9, when the back parts were given windows of neo-1700 type. Next to the Lodgings a still plainer façade, also by *Scott*, of 1854–6 (extended behind in 1988), and this plain treatment continues along the N side. Scott however did not build the whole BROAD STREET RANGE. When he was called in, *H.J. Underwood* had already, in 1833–4, put up a short range between the site of Scott's gate tower and the Old Ashmolean. This is archaeological C15 Gothic, without any fancies – in fact quite up-to-date in this respect (compare e.g. St Mary Hall at Oriel in the 1820s, p. 231). Four bays, regularly distributed windows with straight heads and cusped lights, four identical dormers, and an extra E bay an oriel, later enlarged to a through-storey bay window. Scott succeeded in making one forget this existing building, and certainly not by imitating it, but by being frankly different and accepting asymmetry. Scott is High Victorian also in his higher relief, his composition with two tall staircase windows with bar tracery, and the prominent chimneystack between the steep dormers. The back towards the chapel is smoother and, though Gothic and asymmetrical, utilitarian. But the W part here is refaced, after Scott's cross-range of 1858 was demolished to make room for the THOMAS WOOD BUILDING in the NW angle. By *Lionel Brett* (*Lord Esher*) of *Brett & Pollen*, 1961–4. Its fine, smooth ashlar and sparing fenestration make it a better neighbour for Scott on the inner side than towards the street, where the effect is painfully bald. At the SW end a six-storey tower, awkwardly close alongside the chapel. On Broad Street there are windows of many sizes and shapes and a split-level shop, originally Parker's bookshop. SCULPTURE of 2009 on top, one of *Antony Gormley*'s vigilant figures, and another SCULPTURE in the quad: Alma Mater, a blackened Travertine abstract by *Joxe Alberdi*, 1968.

For COHEN QUAD, Walton Street, *see* Perambulation 4, p. 432; for EXETER HOUSE, Iffley Road, *see* p. 503.

GREEN TEMPLETON COLLEGE
Woodstock Road

Green College was founded in 1979, primarily for postgraduate medical students. The name is from its benefactors, Dr and Mrs Cecil Green of Texas Instruments. Templeton College began life in 1965 as the Oxford Centre for Management Studies, with a campus at Kennington (*see The Buildings of England: Berkshire*). The colleges merged in 2008, and the Kennington site passed to the Saïd Business School (p. 358). Architecturally, however, the Woodstock Road site means first and foremost the Radcliffe Observatory.

RADCLIFFE OBSERVATORY. Built for the University by the Radcliffe Trustees, who gave Oxford the finest observatory Europe had yet seen. The spot was characterized at the time as 'a calm and refined locality'. Designs, now lost, were commissioned from *Henry Keene* in 1772, but in the following year he was hustled off in favour of *James Wyatt*. The builder was *James Pears*, and Keene and then his son *Theodosius Keene* were kept on to supervise the work. Structurally

Wyatt's observatory was complete in 1778, but its decoration and furnishing took until the mid 1790s to finish. The total cost was £31,661. Between 1935 and 1976 the building was used by various University medical departments, in conjunction with the Radcliffe Infirmary to the s (p. 362).

C18 observatories required much space for large fixed apparatus. That helps to explain why Wyatt's building is not at all what one expects an observatory to look like. It is a broad spreading structure with a broad and high tower, and has no dome for a movable telescope. N and s sides are differently treated, but equally impressive. The whole s front is of fifteen bays, but ten of them are in single-storey attachments. These have minimal entablatures, just a simple guilloche band, to reduce visual disruption caused by the slots for instruments that were originally cut through the upper walls. The wings each have at their ends an overarched Venetian window and paterae l. and r. The centre is of five bays, with a canted middle part, and a porch with fluted columns, fluted frieze and pediment. The wings have arched niches alternating with windows, and arched niches are employed in many other places, outside and inside. The first floor is treated as a *piano nobile*. It has pilasters, Ionic, unfluted, paired at the angles; reliefs of the Signs of the Zodiac above the windows (by *Rossi*, made of *Coade* stone, one with a date 1796); and a top balustrade. But then Wyatt by a stroke of genius decided to put on top a Wyatt version of the Tower of the Winds, adapted from the engravings which Stuart and Revett had published not long before. Wyatt continued the canting, which, as is usual with canted bays, has a long front side and short diagonal sides. So his Tower of the Winds is not a regular octagon, but a strongly canted square, as it were. The main sides have large tripartite windows with columns and a pediment, the short sides less tall windows, and high up are the eight reliefs of the Winds with their Greek names. They are by *Bacon the elder*, carved *in situ* in 1792–4.* Bacon also did the lead group on top of Hercules and Atlas supporting the copper-sheathed globe, *c.* 1794, all now stone-coloured to match.

The N elevation of the Observatory itself is a new surprise. Here the two-storey part below the octagon is much larger, and semicircular in plan. The ground floor is plain, with a modest doorcase, and above is the same order of pilasters as on the s side, but between them are large tripartite windows with columns alternating with simple niches. Above these niches the Signs of the Zodiac, as on the other sides, but on plaques changing from square to round for the convex part. Between them and above the tripartite windows are bigger oblong reliefs representing Morning, Noon and Evening, modelled by *Rossi* after drawings by *John Smirke the elder*.

---

*The s and sw winds are copies done during the refacing of 1960–9 under *Marshall Sisson*.

The INTERIOR is a delight too, especially since the recent   74
restoration. There is an oval stone staircase placed laterally on
the N side, and three major rooms on the S, one on top of the
other. They all have the shape of the exterior, i.e. the octagon
with short diagonal sides, and that leads to some interesting
patterns in the ceiling plasterwork. The ground-floor room
(now DINING ROOM) has stumpy Tuscan half-columns. The
vault has much thicker ribs than the Georgian norm, decorated with guilloche. Apse-ended rooms to either side. In the
COMMON ROOM on the first floor there are no columns,
and the guilloche ceiling bands are thinner. In the centre a
big square with its own sparse decoration. Two high arched
openings lead off diagonally to barrel-vaulted lesser rooms at
the NE and NW. In the OBSERVATORY TOWER the Corinthian
columns of the tripartite upper windows repeat inside. The
angles then narrow by squinches to support a circular gallery
running around more than halfway up. The ceiling ribs and
other elements are the most elaborate here. The gallery railing
and the amazingly light iron stair up to it were made in 1796
by *John Mackell*, smith. In the E wing, N side, a room preserves
the diminutive balcony and stair where the ZENITH SECTOR
instrument was housed.

OTHER BUILDINGS. The E wing is continued by a quadrant link
to connect with the OBSERVER'S HOUSE, a three-bay-by-
three-bay, quite plain ashlar house that antedates the main
building by a year, and so must be *Keene*'s. He probably also
designed the simple STABLES to the E, with its basic pediment
and lunettes. The college has also inherited the domed and
octagonal TELESCOPE HOUSE of 1848, S of the Observatory.
By *George Gutch*, architect to the Radcliffe Trustees. – STATUE
of Dr John Radcliffe to the W by *Martin Jennings*, 2018.

NEW ACCOMMODATION for the college was provided by
Jack Lankester, University Surveyor. In deference to context
it is ashlared and Late Georgian in style, and is placed well
clear of the Observatory. LANKESTER QUAD (1977–9), at the
entrance from Woodstock Road, includes a little clock turret.
The sturdy GATEPIERS with fluted caps went with a now
demolished lodge by *Sir Hubert Worthington*, 1935. MCALP-
INE QUAD to the S has a building of 1989 by *Michael Harrison*, matching Lankester. Across the main garden to the W,
the DOLL BUILDING, residential, 1981. Proposals of 2022 by
Feilden Fowles would replace the Doll Building and the lodge
section of the Woodstock Road group.

HARRIS MANCHESTER COLLEGE
Mansfield Road

The college began as a theological training college chiefly for Uni-
tarians, founded at Manchester in 1786, several times relocated,

and transferred finally to Oxford in 1889. The name was changed in 1996, and full collegiate status achieved, following an endowment by Lord Harris of Peckham.

The C19 buildings, now TATE QUAD, were erected in 1890–3 by the Manchester architect *Thomas Worthington* of *Worthington & Elgood*, father of Percy Scott Worthington and of Sir Hubert Worthington. It is conventional architecture he provided, neither as forceful as that of Keble nor as sophisticated as that of Mansfield. There is the four-stage gate tower, the gabled range to its r. ending with the big oriel and gable of the library, and one bay to the l. and then the big chapel window. The quad is open in the SW corner. On the S side the chapel with its side windows, on the W side only the service range (for the college was not originally residential), on the N the long side of the library with its big chimney for the inglenook. The other long side faces Savile Road, and that view with the adjoining archway and the middle oriel of the library is the best. A flavour more northern than Oxonian prevails throughout the quad, owing partly to Worthington's rather Waterhousey style, partly to the use of durable grey Darley Dale stone. The chief donors were indeed from the great northern Unitarian families, e.g. Sir Henry Tate of Liverpool, who gave the library.

The CHAPEL is a straightforward volume with a hammerbeam roof ceiled with panelling between the trusses. It is most memorable for its STAINED GLASS by *Morris & Co*. This was installed in 1895–9 by *Henry Dearle* of the Morris company, and is colourful, with more ruby areas and more green foliage grounds than in earlier Morris glass. The foliage is somewhat routine. Lighter quarries as the background of the figures in the ritual E window. The figures of Joseph and Mary Magdalene here (upper row) use designs by *William Morris* himself; all the others are from *Burne-Jones* originals. Of these, Religion, Liberty and Truth in the ritual W window were specially designed for the chapel in 1896. The iconography overall is interesting. The three two-light N windows have the Six Days of Creation, six times with the motto Elargissez Dieu ('magnify the Lord', from Diderot), a favourite motto of James Losh, grandfather of the donor. The figures here were blown up from cartoons for smaller figures supplied in 1870 to Middleton Cheney church, Northants. – ORGAN with pipes painted by *Dearle*, 1897. – STALLS, SCREEN etc. finely carved by *Earp, Son & Hobbs*; PEWS with ends carved by *Pearson & Brown* of Eccles.

The LIBRARY now has galleries as anticipated by Worthington; inserted 2011. Stained glass by *Heaton, Butler & Bayne*, 1897–8, iconographically interesting too. In the E bay also the seated statue of James Martineau by *H. R. Hope-Pinker*, 1898. In the VESTIBULE another, smoother window, by *Henry Holiday*, 1903. The LOWER CORRIDOR has two portrait reliefs also by *Hope-Pinker*: Frances Power Cobbe, 1908, with lettering by *Eric Gill*, and the Rev. John James Tayler, 1897.

s of Tate Quad is ARLOSH HALL, added in 1913–14 by *Percy Scott Worthington*. With its minor gate tower against the vestry-like projection of the chapel it composes well here, although the plain doorway end hints at incompletion. Fine, well-made interior with timber tracery above the tie-beams.

Originally for assemblies only, the hall now has a KITCHEN behind, added 1993, and MAEVADI HALL, infill of 2017–18 (lecture rooms etc.), both by the *Peter Yiangou* practice. Their other NEW BUILDINGS, all in traditional styles, make strange company both for the Worthingtons and for one another. First, in 1990–2, three identical ACCOMMODATION BLOCKS along the back wall with Wadham, w. The early C18 style with thick quoins and platbands is reportedly a homage to the Warrington Academy building of 1757, the Cheshire precursor of the first Manchester College. But each unit is centred on its own pedimented entrance bay, which looks quite wrong when multiplied three times over, and the red brick cladding is laid as a stretcher-bond skin under a skinny cornice, both of which look wrong too. To the N and making a garden quadrangle is FARMINGTON HOUSE, 1996, grander and more plausibly villa-like, though the cornice is still skimped. Its rooms are split between new lodgings for the Principal and an institute for promoting religious education, and this duality within such a monumental form feels wrong as well. In front, STATUES of Lord Harris (2018) and his father, Charles Harris M.C. (1995), by *Etienne Millner*.

The SIEW-SNGIEM CLOCK TOWER and SUKUM NAVAPAN GATE are the latest arrivals, 2013–14, on the s side in front of Arlosh Hall. By *Ross Sharpe* of the Yiangou office. The gateway is Italian Mannerist, the tower a sort of Neo-Jackson. Both are of cast stone and suitably solid, but the proportions don't quite come off, nor would Jackson have married an irregular octagonal base to a regular octagonal lantern so laboriously. Inside the tower are student bedrooms, on top is a cutesy weathervane. The traditional-style part s of the tower belongs with it; for the annexed houses on Holywell Street *see* p. 417. – STATUES of two benefactors, again by *E. Millner*, 2018.

HERTFORD COLLEGE
Catte Street and Holywell Street

Sir Thomas G. Jackson designed most of Hertford College, and anybody who wants to study his style will not find a better place than Hertford. However complex its prehistory, in the end it became Jackson.

The forerunner of the present college originated around 1280 as one of the innumerable small halls where students lived. By 1301 it was known as Hart Hall after its founder, Elias de Hertford. Not long afterwards the hall was acquired by Walter de

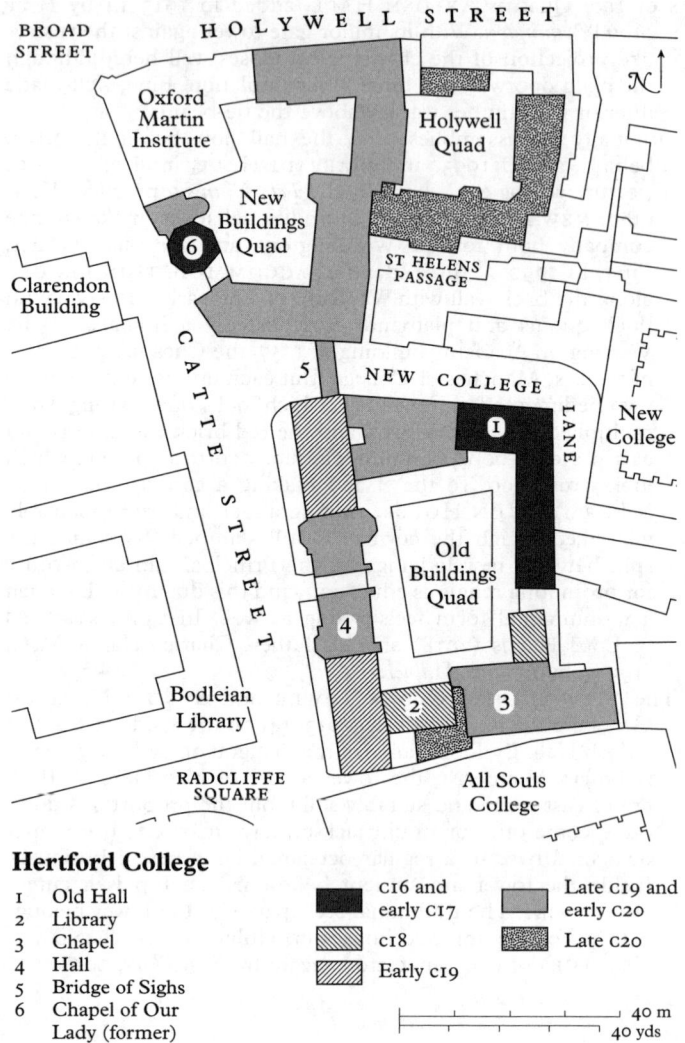

Hertford College

1 Old Hall
2 Library
3 Chapel
4 Hall
5 Bridge of Sighs
6 Chapel of Our
Lady (former)

c16 and early c17

c18

Early c19

Late c19 and early c20

Late c20

40 m
40 yds

Stapeldon as a stopgap while he founded his own college, Exeter College, which thereafter kept the hall as a rental property. The buildings were of the usual L-plan, and these survive in their mid-c16 and early c17 incarnation.

Early c18 additions were made by the ambitious Dr Newton, the Principal who in 1740 obtained a charter to change the name to Hertford College. In 1805, however, the near-empty college was dissolved. It happened that the President of Magdalen then wanted to get rid of Magdalen Hall (*see* p. 190) as an inconvenient occupant of part of his college's land. He therefore obtained authority in 1818 to repair and extend the Hertford buildings and transfer Magdalen Hall. The transfer was expedited by the fact that the old Catte Street frontage of Hertford collapsed suddenly with a great crash in 1820, and that in the same year Magdalen Hall was badly damaged by fire. But in 1874 the college was re-founded, largely thanks to a benefaction from the banker Thomas Baring, and the name Hertford College was reassumed. Baring was a conservative who wanted the college to resurrect Anglican privileges that were everywhere dwindling in Oxford. However, the next Principal, Henry Boyd, was of the reform party, among whom *T. G. Jackson* was the favourite architect. Jackson started at Hertford in 1887, and was kept busy into the 1920s as the college expanded N of New College Lane. The results are described by William Whyte as 'the high point for Jackson in his role as arbiter of the university style'.

Old Buildings Quad

The main FAÇADE, set well back from the pre-C19 frontage line, looks W across Catte Street towards the Bodleian. It is long, and consists of two plain Palladian side pieces of six bays each and an ornate centre of nine. These three-storey side pieces are of 1820–2 by *William Garbett*, built for Magdalen Hall. The original screen wall and low archway between were replaced by *Jackson* in 1887–8 with a new centrepiece, making the wings serve the glory of the newly reinstated Hertford. An archway framed with Tuscan columns and a pediment, four upper attached Corinthian columns and three Venetian windows, a frieze carved with running harts, an assertive balustrade and – to connect with 1820 – two canted bay windows (with by the way some minimum Elizabethan decoration). A festive display, no doubt about it, and in its mixed quasi-Palladian style one that fits this demanding part of Oxford perfectly. The main DOORS are of *c.*1690, from the pre-1820s gateway. Scrolly flowers in the tympanum. *Jackson* also inserted the Venetian-pattern doorway in the S wing, for the Principal's Lodgings.

The QUAD is entered by a gateway which to that side has another pedimented portal. Here you find an extra Venetian window to the S but to the N a stair-tower, bastard child of Blois, provided with a Jacobean doorway cresting and an upswept Baroque parapet. Also big pilaster-buttresses, and a chimney that cuts across two Venetian windows. Jackson knew no fear in using elements from different styles in the same façade. He knew his history – he was himself to write in old age a three-volume history of Renaissance architecture in Italy, England and France – and it was a game to mix motifs, as long as the total would be lavish display. 99

The NORTH RANGE is largely *Jackson* again, 1888–9, though here for some reason in pale Hanborough stone. Three more Venetian or Palladian windows, and more pilaster-buttresses. But humble next to it is OLD HALL, the oldest remaining part of Hart Hall, as rebuilt *c.*1550. Top storey late C17 or early C18;

the old gable outline of the buttery end, E, still visible to New College Lane. Interior with panelling of *c.*1710 (restored 2015), plain coved ceiling of *c.*1890. The two N windows each of three arched lights are not original.

The EAST RANGE is Hart Hall too, but of the early C17. To the S it has an original canted bay window. Additional top floor of 1849. Next to this a plain four-bay section of after 1710, when Dr Newton began his campaign to elevate Hart Hall to Hertford College. To the same end an engraving was produced in 1740 showing a proposed regular rebuilding with similar ranges in all four angles, and larger blocks for hall, library, chapel and Principal's Lodgings on the main axes. By that time a chapel, now LIBRARY, already stood on the S side, as consecrated in 1716. Three bays (the engraving, puzzlingly, has four), arched windows, plain key blocks and a big parapet. S extension by *R.B. Gray* (*Pinckheard & Partners*), 1966–7, concealed behind. A matching C18 block on the N side was swept away by Jackson.

Likewise, the rest of the C18 S range was demolished for *Jackson*'s CHAPEL of 1907–8. It is six bays long and has, to respond to the Blois tower, a NW tower, polygonal from the ground and topped by an order of eight detached Tuscan columns and a round bellcote with a copper dome. Along the N side between tower and E range are two bays of cloister, treated once more as Venetian or Palladian openings. The chapel windows are Jackson at his most enterprising. They are very tall, of two lights, and have attached columns between the lights but decorated Quattrocento pilasters l. and r. Moreover at the bottom each light has a kind of transom with arches under. It really was an irresponsible thing to do, and inside one finds that the last windows to the E go almost as low, below the transoms, as the backs of the stalls. The E window, undeniably, is a splendid sight from New College Lane: five lights with only the centre light arched, i.e. the Venetian window conception, and with columns and garlands. Columns also inside, and a fine Cosmati-style inlaid PAVEMENT, but only part of Jackson's intended pilasters and carving across the altar wall. The SEDILIA are Venetian Quattrocento, with a semicircular pediment. – REREDOS with a marble Crucifixion in high relief, by *Sir George Frampton*; 1919. – STALLS with shallow backs with detached columns and a frieze with pendants, and plenty of foliage decoration up there. Reportedly they are free copies of those made *c.*1590 for the cathedral at Ypres, destroyed in 1914. – WAR MEMORIAL designed by *Jackson*, *c.*1921. – STAINED GLASS. William Tyndale, in a light-box. Made 1911 by *Powells* for the British and Foreign Bible Society's London headquarters, brought here 1994. – BRASS. John Meeke †1665. Small, with a half-figure in an oval between two broad garlanded pilasters, like the frontispiece to a book.

The monumentality of the W range finds its justification in that Jackson, very ingeniously, placed his HALL there, above, behind the Venetian windows and with one of his two canted bays as the high-table bay (which incidentally absorbs two levels of outer windows, and it is decidedly odd that inside Jackson gave pediments to the lower set). The fireplace overmantel has Jackson columns on Jackson brackets, but the screen is chaste, with two entrances and thin pediments on columns with leaf trails around.

The quad, to sum up – and this is the remarkable thing – does not strike one as disjointed.

Plans by *MICA Architects* for a new subterranean library beneath the quad and the C18 chapel, with rebuilding of its 1960s S extension, were approved in 2021.

New Buildings Quad and Holywell Quad

In 1897 Hertford bought the corner site N of New College Lane, and asked *Jackson* to develop there. He began with the S and E ranges of NEW BUILDINGS QUAD, in 1901–7. This is Jackson much more as one knows him elsewhere. Tudor gables with canted bay windows, but also cross-windows, places with attached columns in two tiers, and striped brick chimneys, i.e. C17 inspiration, mostly English – Anglo-Jackson, it has been called – but an amalgam of the motifs of several phases. *Jackson*'s also was the brilliant idea of the BRIDGE OF SIGHS across the lane, with its ornate centre with columns on decorated brackets and open scrolly pediment. First proposed 1899, with a choice of Gothic or classical designs, but not built until 1913–14. Incorporated on the Broad Street side is the former CHAPEL OF OUR LADY, an exceptional two-storey octagonal building of *c.*1520. Originally it stood alongside the long-vanished Smith Gate in the city wall. It had survived in mutilated form as part of a house and shop. Restored in 1931 to designs left by *Jackson*, with a new parapet, window tracery and pyramidal leaden roof. The small S doorway survives, with its lintel block on which an Annunciation is carved in small figures. Original also some of the upper window surrounds (depressed four-centred arches), blocked lower windows, and polygonal angle buttresses on the E and NE sides. To the N is more from *Jackson*, of 1923–4. At first he wanted to build storeys on top of the chapel and arching over the gateway approach, which is why a patch of red brick was left on the flank facing the chapel doorway.

Inside the quad, Jackson's buildings envelop three of the irregular sides. The fourth side, i.e. the NORTH RANGE, is what anybody at first sight might mistake for a big Late Georgian house. Stucco, five bays, with a sixth on the l., with two doorways and a centre window which is tripartite with a segmental tympanum over all three lights decorated fan-wise. Nine bays to Holywell Street. It is by *T.H. Hughes*, 1929–30, *Jackson*'s designs of the 1910s having been set aside. In the NW corner is the ugly brick back of the Martin Institute (*see* p.343), and this hobbles the quad as a coherent space.

The college did better with HOLYWELL QUAD to the E, of 1974–81. By *Shepheard, Epstein & Hunter*, project architect *Peter Lyon*. Three plain brick blocks, informally designed and discontinuous; the N side joining on to adapted Holywell Street houses (*see* p. 416). Pitched roofs, generally Neo-vernacular, save for two polygonal slit-windowed stair-turrets. Between S and E ranges a single-storey lecture room, allowing a view of the New College bell-tower.

For WARNOCK HOUSE, St Aldate's, *see* Perambulation 6, p. 448; for the Winchester Road site *see* North Oxford, p. 463; for the GRADUATE CENTRE at Folly Bridge and ABINGDON HOUSE, Abingdon Road, *see* South Oxford, p. 515.

JESUS COLLEGE
Turl Street

Jesus College was founded in 1571 by Dr Hugh Price, son of a butcher, Prebendary of Rochester Cathedral and Treasurer of St David's Cathedral. The official founder was actually Queen Elizabeth, having been petitioned by Price. There were to be eight Fellows and eight Scholars under a Principal, increased to sixteen of each when statutes were obtained in 1622. Until the mid C19 the membership was almost entirely Welsh. There are now four quads, the first Elizabethan and C17, the second mostly C17, the third created by C20 additions along Ship Street to the N, and the fourth of 2018–22 by *MICA Architects*, with a W front to Cornmarket.

FIRST QUAD is of 1571–4 in its E side and part of the S side, and otherwise C17, partly on the site of the annexed White Hall. However, the E range was entirely refaced towards Turl Street by *J.C. & C.A. Buckler* in 1855. The *Gentleman's Magazine* commented that 'Messrs Buckler are entitled to credit for their courage in resisting the stream, and following the style of the fifteenth century'. The stream of course is Second Pointed, i.e. the style of *c.*1300, and the later English Gothic was decried as decadent by Pugin, the Ecclesiologists and the rest. The frontage is of three storeys, with the Bucklers' regular three- and four-light windows, corbelled-out chimneys and added gate tower. (Loggan shows that the C16 gateway was towerless, with two scanty superimposed orders – probably Oxford's first display of classical architecture – but *John Townesend III* had made the whole front fully classical in 1756.) At the N end of the frontage is the end of the chapel, part of a lengthening of 1636. Its E window, of seven lights, is of that date, though almost every detail comes from the C15 Perp repertoire. In the 1850s it was faithfully renewed. N of the quad is the Principal's Garden, with a classical GATEWAY to Turl Street by *Thomas*

Jesus College

1 Principal's Lodgings
2 Chapel
3 Hall
4 Library
5 Old Members' Building
6 Habakkuk Room

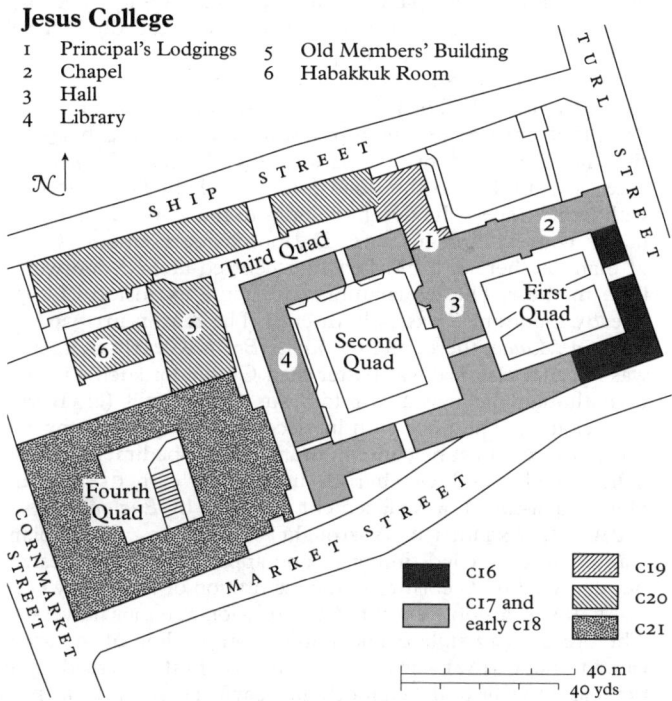

Knowles I, 1826. The s range is the *Bucklers'*, of 1854, in its aspect towards Market Street. Here the joint between Elizabethan and Jacobean is visible as a change of alignment.

The quad is small and pretty from inside, especially because of the variety of its ranges. The E side is the *Bucklers'*, except for the archway, but the SOUTH RANGE at least is essentially original. Mullioned windows arranged symmetrically (first floor: 2–4–3–4–2–4–3–4–2) and with lights no longer arched. The hoodmoulds are horizontally linked: probably an alteration, as Loggan shows the windows unhooded. The top storey is certainly later. It began in the 1730s on the N side, when the cockloft dormers there were made into a full storey, and concluded with *John Nash*'s regularizing and battlementing all round in 1815–18.* The WEST RANGE is two-thirds the HALL, built in 1616–18, with kitchen, buttery and the two adjacent staircases of the s range. Its windows are straight-headed with two transoms, and all lights – also below the transoms – are cusped. They are different from all other C17 Gothic windows in Oxford except those of the exactly contemporary hall bay window of Exeter (p. 148). Clock in the parapet, of 1831. The

---

*Nash later asked that his PORTRAIT by *Sir Thomas Lawrence* should hang in the hall, where it remains.

oriel l. of the screens passage was added in 1913–14 by *Reuben England*, the college's surveyor. To Second Quad the hall has a broad bay window with Perp details, rebuilt 1878.

The NORTH RANGE contains the chapel and the PRINCIPAL'S LODGINGS. The three bays of the lodgings are of *c.* 1625, except of course for the top storey, and also the beautiful shell-hood of the doorway, made in 1698 by *John Townesend I.* The CHAPEL has to the quad four three-light Perp windows with panel tracery. Its design belongs to the work which ended in the consecration in 1621. The porch represents a change of plan, as there is a blocked four-centred-arched doorway a little to the r. The explanation is that the extension of 1636 already mentioned was at both ends. The mason in 1636 was *Richard Maude*, the carpenter *James Booth*. Clearly by then it was felt that classical was better than Gothic for such a portal, even though the new E window was Gothic still (cf. Brasenose chapel). The door with its decorated tympanum and the doorway arch must be contemporary, but the pediment with its palm branches and two cherubs' heads looks early C18. Square Gothic bell-turret, a replacement of *c.* 1915 by *England*.

CHAPEL INTERIOR. A straight oblong, i.e. not T-plan. Canted and panelled timber ceiling apparently of C17 design, but deprived of its cornice in the restoration of 1863–4 by *G.E. Street*. It was his only executed commission at either university. The present C13-style chancel arch – on the line of the abolished E wall of 1621 – is his. Also the Gothic stone arcading in the N and S walls of the chancel, the heavily gorgeous REREDOS carved by *Earp*, the alabaster PANELLING to its l. and r., and the STALLS.* The floor has TILES by *Minton*, and reused slabs from black and white paving of 1648. – PULPIT. Jacobean, square. – PAINTING. Big copy of Guido Reni's St Michael. Given *c.* 1800 as an altarpiece. – LECTERN. Brass. Given 1721(?). – SCREEN. Probably of 1693. Tripartite, with detached columns and a segmental pediment over the centre and wide open horizontally placed ovals in the side pieces. Openwork spandrels and openwork panels. The cartouche with shield over the door comes from the screen, displaced in 1899 for an organ. Present ORGAN by *William Drake*, 1994. – STAINED GLASS. E window, 1856 by *Hedgeland*, 'under direction of' *Charles Winston*. A busy, somewhat gloomy piece with many small scenes. One N window by *Kempe*, 1898; one S window by *Kempe & Co.*, 1908, weaker. Also one N by *Lavers & Westlake*, 1894, and one S, †1873, by *Clayton & Bell*. – MONUMENTS. Sir Eubule Thelwall †1630. Of the not uncommon formula with kneeling figure under a semicircular projecting canopy, from which two female figures draw a drapery open. Obelisks and raised pediment. Attributed to *Maximilian Colt* (GF). – Tall late C17 and C18 architectural wall monuments, several to college Principals.

The HALL now has a shallow tunnel-vault of 1741–2 with just one stuccoed centrepiece, by *Thomas Roberts*. On the end

---

*Some C17 panelling was reused at Forest School, Epping, East London.

wall much big plasterwork by the same, including a large rich cartouche with shield. Fire surround also of 1741–2, but made to fit an existing chimney, the C17 hall having been built already without the traditional open hearth. Bronze bust of Elizabeth I over it, probably of 1838 and by *Thomas Cooper*. The panelling however is of *c.* 1620, the screen of 1634. The latter in its lower parts is close enough to the Wadham screen to suggest the hand of *John Bolton* (cf. also Exeter's hall). Elaborately decorated columns, mostly arabesque work; panels of four L-shapes; dragons along the frieze. Top balustrade and gallery of 1913–14 by *England*. Above the hall, incorporated within inserted rooms, the C17 hammerbeam roof structure remains. Turned balusters over the hammerbeams.

The PRINCIPAL'S LODGINGS have a staircase with twisted balusters, probably contemporary with the doorcase of *c.* 1698, although the plan with a triangular well points to a rearrangement. Drawing room with splendid panelling assigned to 1623. Three tiers of panels, every one with a vertically placed oval. Similar overmantel, with tapering pilasters. The lodgings were built by Principal Thelwall (†1630) and the panelling is most likely to be his doing. The Jacobean-style plaster ceiling however is part of the major works at the lodgings by *Bodley & Garner*, 1884. They added the w oriel to Second Quad, and a substantial NORTH WING. The study (ground floor) has nice Neoclassical detail of the early C19.* *Bodley & Garner* also reconstructed several STAIRCASES within the s range, 1883.

SECOND QUAD is reached through the hall screens passage. It was carried out from *c.* 1639 to *c.* 1712 as a uniform composition, beginning with the nearer parts of the N and s sides and finishing with the NW corner. For the first phase *Richard Maude* was again the mason, and the details of the small top gablets with their ogee sides and semicircular tops match his work at University College. Three storeys, regular fenestration by windows with round-arched lights, their hoodmoulds forming a continuous frieze. Doorways still with four-centred arches. One, to the passage through the N range, is bigger. In the w range is the LIBRARY, and the access to this is by a portal with a classical segmental pediment. But then the library section was built only in 1676–9. Within the portal is a twisted-baluster staircase of unequal dog-leg plan, late C17 in its motifs. *Bodley & Garner* 'restored and improved' the staircase in 1884; how much is theirs? The library s window is Gothic, of four lights under a single gable, all to a design of 1875. An engraving of 1740 shows a C17 Gothic window and triple shaped gables above. There was an earlier library of *c.* 1628, built out by Thelwall from the w side of the Lodgings, with a cloister below it; but this was taken down *c.* 1639. From it come most of the bookcases with strapwork cornices and the openwork cresting over the entrance (the two s pairs apparently matching work

---

* *Nash* advised on alterations to the lodgings in 1802, but his plans do not match what is there now.

of *c*. 1680). The gallery with openwork foliage panels along the
E wall is an early addition, perhaps of 1685. More than this,
there is evidence that the library was originally lower, but was
raised at an early date to match the three storeys of the rest.*
Staircase to the gallery within a timber cage in the Bodleian
manner, here with twisted uprights. The SENIOR COMMON
ROOM below has wainscoting of 1736.

THIRD QUAD, too long and narrow to be a true quad, is reached
through the bigger entrance in the N range of Second Quad.
The N side is a long range of 1906–8 facing Ship Street,
another contribution by *Reuben England*. To the street it is
entirely of the medieval and Buckler tradition, of Doulting
stone, with gate tower and oriel (and, originally, laboratories).
To the W of this range another, with shops below and four
symmetrically grouped gables at the top. Four oriels, mullioned windows with arched lights, carvings below the parapet.
This is by *England* too, 1908–12, at the cost of the back parts
of the C14 New Inn (*see* Cornmarket, p. 423). At the far W end
is the OLD MEMBERS' BUILDING, by *John Fryman* of the
Architects Design Partnership, 1969–71. Concrete-framed, it is
faced in Clipsham stone, with brick behind. It holds twenty-
four study-bedrooms and has at the top a music room. Access
is from a staircase rising from a deck on the first floor, as most
of the lower floors are taken up by an electricity substation and
a back extension to W. H. Smith's in Cornmarket. The deck is
reached by staircases set diagonally. Pevsner in 1974 disapproved of 'the canting fashion... canted back, canted exposed
supports on the entrance floor, canted base to the two upper
floors. The windows go one step further. They are tripartite,
and the broader centre light is pushed out to form a triangle
plan. It is a mannered and modish design.' A diagonal bridge
connects it with the Ship Street range. The deck continues W
to the HABAKKUK ROOM for conferences, 1989 by *Architects
Design Partnership*. Rather lumpy, with a leaded mansard.

The college's FOURTH or NORTHGATE QUAD is immediately S
of these C20 additions, fronting Cornmarket as well as Market
Street, and standing free of the back of Third Quad; also
called the CHENG YU TUNG BUILDING. It swept away some
dull 1960s commercial buildings on the Cornmarket side,
and *MICA Architects* were duly required to incorporate two
retail storeys in their ashlar-faced replacement of 2018–22.
The result is a quad like no other at Oxford, in that its heart
is at second-floor level. So the approach from the college side
is dramatic, through a broad ground-floor passage to an open
staircase climbing ahead, then a second flight at right angles
to the S. Accommodation on all four sides, facing the quad for
the most part with an orderly rhythm of dark main windows
vertically linked and thin upright windows alongside. The S
side includes a café, and a tower-like feature to the E with a
function room on top, linked inside by a pure white staircase

---

* Carved woodwork in a very similar style is now in Bodedern church on Anglesey,
reportedly given by the college.

to the storeys below. So far, so good; but along Market Street there is altogether too much going on: multiple rectangular shapes piled up and pushed together, set about with windows of many shapes and types, flush, recessed or projecting. To Cornmarket the frontage is stronger, the residential windows and bronze-clad dormers appearing above boxed-out windows to the first floor of the shop section, but the flat, non-matching ends are too weak to carry the composition.

For the SHIP STREET CENTRE *see* Perambulation 3, p.424; for HERBERT CLOSE, off Cowley Road, *see* South-east Oxford, p.499; for STEVENS CLOSE, Woodstock Road, *see* North Oxford, p.467.

KEBLE COLLEGE
Parks Road

When the Oxford Movement luminary John Keble died in 1866, a public appeal was launched for a college to be built in his memory. It was to be firmly theological in emphasis, and was meant for students of moderate means. The complex was built in 1868–83: Oxford's first entirely new college since Wadham in the early C17. The chapel was given by William Gibbs of Tyntesfield (it cost some £40,000, over a quarter of the total spent), the hall and library by his sons. They were all fervent Tractarians. Keble College is indeed the final triumph of the Oxford Movement, a solid symbol of what it had achieved and of how it wished to appear: Anglican, not Roman as Newman liked his architecture. Keble is earnest and exacting, it shuns all levity and it is overwhelmingly what the age called 'real'.

The college was designed – need one say? – by *William Butterfield*. He had already in the early 1840s been a favourite of the Cambridge Camden Society and its journal *The Ecclesiologist*, and had established his style in essence at All Saints, Margaret Street, London, in 1849. Butterfield was fifty-four when he began to design Keble, and it can be called a summing-up of his ideals as well as his motifs. The motifs are familiar enough: red brick (in a limestone city – but the college was not being built for the rich), with polychrome patterns: bands, chequers and trellises in buff stone and, on a smaller scale, in yellow brick and blackish-blue brick. No symmetry ever, broken skylines by different heights, here mostly three storeys, but also two and accents of four, and accents by sudden large windows at surprising heights. At Butterfield's Rugby School one can see them all, but the job was smaller. At Keble he could operate with very large ranges.

What is less familiar and perhaps more remarkable is Butterfield's spatial composition. There are two quads, but they are not quads in the full sense. Butterfield avoids total enclosure. Wide gaps allow spaces to look into spaces.

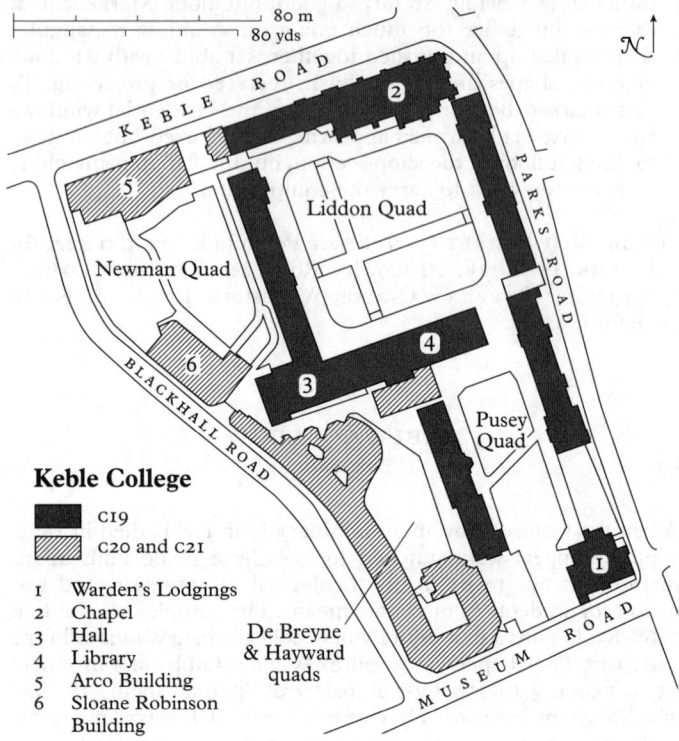

80 m
80 yds

KEBLE ROAD

PARKS ROAD

Liddon Quad

Newman Quad

BLACKHALL ROAD

Pusey Quad

MUSEUM ROAD

Keble College

■ C19

▨ C20 and C21

1   Warden's Lodgings
2   Chapel
3   Hall
4   Library
5   Arco Building
6   Sloane Robinson
    Building

De Breyne
& Hayward
quads

The FAÇADE towards Parks Road reveals at once all the motifs
enumerated. At the S end are the WARDEN'S LODGINGS,
built in 1876–7. They stand wholly detached, as the rest of the
W range was never completed to join up with them. Notice
the three gables at once, at different heights and at different
distances from the frontage. The style is Gothic of course,
and still the High Victorian Middle Pointed, though by 1870
Bodley and a few others had begun to return to Perp for
inspiration. The range which follows is very long indeed, and
it needed Butterfield's ingenuity to divide it up. For example,
the entrance doorway and the window above it are set in one
giant arch, and the end blocks are heightened by an extra floor.
The chimneystacks are grouped in bold blocks, and there are
the patterns. They get more violent, and the skyline gets more
jagged, when the corner to Keble Road is reached; for here is
the CHAPEL, very high, with windows only very high up. The
E window is of five lights. Blind arcading below on the Keble
Road side. Here in addition there is a broad transeptal bay,
which however is kept very shallow. The W bay has chimneys
too. Then another long residential range, with a return of the
two-light window type in the college tradition. But the patterning remains the same. Among lesser motifs is an insistent use

of little stone gablet pieces to step up the party walls, towards the bases of the chimneystacks.

Keble's architecture has always divided viewers. For Pevsner in 1974 it was 'actively ugly' – though he allowed that a younger generation of Brutalists might find in it a shared ideal. He also quoted the hedged-around admiration from Eastlake's *Gothic Revival* of 1872: 'Posterity may find something to smile at as eccentric, something to deplore as ill-judged, and much that will astonish as daring, but they will find nothing to despise as commonplace or mean.' But for many, Keble will always represent Victorian Oxford at its most courageous and inspired, and the C21 cleaning of its defiant red brick walls will be an additional cause for celebration.

Admiration in fact grows, as one enters – by the archway which has a pointed tunnel-vault with many transverse ribs. For this archway does not lead into either quad. It leads into both. The dividing range of hall and library stops short of the archway. Turn r. if you like, or turn l.

Right is LIDDON QUAD, the principal quad, with its surprising sunken lawn. It has the back of the front range on the E, and the chapel and N range round the corner, but then a gap to get by a wide gate into the garden. The W range then is detached here, but its S end is linked to the hall range, whose enormous patterned slab of a chimneystack rises above. The hall itself extends both E and W, and the four identical transomed two-light windows belong with it. Then a gabled centrepiece with a big canted oriel to light the hall stairs (and at the back a balancing projection with a four-light window), and another five windows of slightly different pattern to light the library, set under relieving arches. On the W side towards the garden the hall ends in a large five-light window, and with balancing projections to N and S, each with a large four-lighter under a cross-gable.

The CHAPEL went up in 1873–6. It measures 124 ft (38 metres) long, and thanks to the Gibbs benefaction is even higher than first intended. It has a S entry in a very high gabled recess, but it is usually entered from the W, where in the residential range three bays of a kind of cloister are incorporated. The exterior to the quad is again as discrepant as it could be made. Tall narrow gable above the entrance recess, crowned by a statue, two nave windows, a transept with a wider gable (it in fact includes the organ chamber), and two narrower chancel windows – and of course pinnacles. As on the street side there is blind arcading below and a concentration of patterning on the upper parts. The roof however has plain slopes of lead rather than coloured tiles. The builders (and for hall and library too, in 1875–8) were *Parnell & Son* of Rugby. The statues, incidentally, are a rare external instance in Butterfield's work; that now on the gable is a 1960s copy.

The CHAPEL INTERIOR is moving indeed, owing to sheer height, increased in effect by the high placing of all windows, by the quadripartite rib-vaulting and by the deliberately low

88

stature of the furnishings. The vault includes a longitudinal ridge rib and a narrow extra w bay. The walls have high blank arcading, a motif carried through from outside, and an upper blind arcade with a sequence of religious pictures in white-ground mosaic. All the windows are filled with bright figures in STAINED GLASS by *Alexander Gibbs* (Butterfield's favourite, and no relation to the donor). The MOSAICS are by the same; Gibbs was sent to Venice to study the technique. They include big scenes of the Sacrifice of Isaac, Moses and the Brazen Serpent, Nativity, Crucifixion (N wall, w to E), Noah giving thanks, Joseph sold into slavery, Resurrection (S wall, w to E), Last Judgment (w wall) and Revelation (E wall, with Christ in a quatrefoil above the altar). Much richness of carving in the string courses, and richness too in the change from stone to alabaster for the arcading of the choir and REREDOS. *Butterfield* also designed the PULPIT with its openwork iron and brass body, and the brass LECTERN and CANDLESTICKS. Exceptionally for a college chapel, the SEATS face the altar, church-fashion.

The chapel in the s transept was created in 1891–4 by *J.T. Micklethwaite* to house *Holman Hunt*'s famous PAINTING of 1845–53, The Light of the World. Martha Combe, widow of Thomas Combe (*see* St Barnabas, p.391) gave this to the college after her husband's death in 1873. – Also a PAINTING of the Lamentation by *Willem Key* (*c.*1520–1568) and studio, and more STAINED GLASS: a small s window by *Kempe*, 1896. – WAR MEMORIAL, in the cloister entrance. Of 1922 by *F.C. Eden*, an old member of Keble. Contrived within an internal arcade, like a little chantry chapel.

The short w extension of the chapel range was built in 1955–6 by *A.B. Knapp-Fisher* and *Thomas Rayson*, with money from Antonin Besse (*see* St Antony's College, p.248). Commendably close to Butterfield on this side, but Rayson's ashlar bay window round the corner spoils the effect. Originally this range was meant to continue all along the garden N side. Instead, there are big GATES of 1959 to finish.

Of other INTERIORS, library and hall share a monumental STAIR-CASE, very broad and with brickwork all exposed and patterned under a patterned tunnel-vault. To the w is the HALL, at 127 ft (38.7 metres) longer than that of Christ Church, though not quite as wide. Striped stone-faced lower walls, exposed and patterned brick upper walls, arch-braced roof ceiled with canted and painted panelling. Opposite the big sturdy fireplace is the serving entrance. Iron columns support a balcony or singing gallery above it. Stained glass again by *Gibbs*. E of the staircase landing is the LIBRARY. It has the brickwork exposed too, and a similar ceiling, and the wooden screens to the cubicles with the shelves and tables are also by *Butterfield*. In the floor the opening of a spiral staircase inserted by *Ahrends, Burton & Koralek* in 1980, when the rooms below were annexed. Also on the ground floor the SENIOR COMMON ROOM, a large room with a green damask-like wallpaper. This, it has been claimed, was chosen by Butterfield, and yet it has nothing of the manliness of his architecture. Mostly the other rooms are reached by corridors, the first example of this plan-type in Oxford, rather than opening straight off separate staircases in the traditional collegiate way.

PUSEY QUAD is less eventful. Again the W range was separate from the hall range, though the original screen wall has been replaced with a single-storey Butterfieldian insertion (by *Alan Stubbs*, 1967). The long W range is of two phases, 1872–3, N (servants' rooms), and 1881–2, S (bursary and students' rooms). The N part has the square little clock turret of the college, the S part illustrates the turn to shallower roof pitches in Butterfield's late work. The S end is left undecided. There is now only, in the SE corner, the detached Warden's Lodgings.

DE BREYNE QUAD and HAYWARD QUAD to the SW represent Keble's first substantial enlargement, in 1970–7. The college chose *Ahrends, Burton & Koralek* (with *Ove Arup & Partners* as structural engineers), and did well with them. First of all the new buildings were placed to the SW, along Blackhall Road and Museum Road, where Butterfield did not dominate. They were thus able to avoid compromise. To drive that point home, the architects chose yellow, not red brick. They also chose full-height glazing to the inside. The range stretches along Blackhall Road, rising from N to S and at the S end finishing with an angular coil that turns back on itself, making a tight enclosure around a big tree. A towering eminence for a spiral staircase makes an end-stop here. To the road the brick has oblong projections with showers and lavatories – garderobe towers, almost – and a canted angle where the coil proper starts. The service rooms get light from vertical slits in the angles between wall and projections. The wall between has a few window slits too, in singles and pairs, in which the floor slabs appear like recessed transoms. The base of the wall is canted outwards. The inner side is totally different – all reflective smoked glass in big upright panels, starting with a half-sunk walkway with a lean-to glass roof. Above, the first-floor glazing is slightly raked (cf. the architects' slightly earlier Centre for Management Studies at Kennington, Berks.). The other three floors have uniform vertical glass to the rooms, with nothing to give away the staircase arrangement. The effect is somewhat like a bowl, and in this strikingly similar to James Stirling's Florey Building for Queen's (*see* p. 450). Stirling came first, but the motifs are all transformed. The serpentine walkway with its rising and slanting courses inside is also an original element. At the N end it splits in two, and one route swerves outwards to reach a bar and student common rooms, under their own flat roof. A single-storey outlier further N was demolished to build the Sloane Robinson Building (*see* below).

NEWMAN QUAD is the name for the sunken garden to the NW. Here are two detached buildings by *Rick Mather Architects*, of different composition but similar handling. Each is pushed into the surrounding slope. The ARCO BUILDING of 1993–5,

N, mostly residential, combines a flat-roofed front range with taller, pitched-roofed sections behind. Entry is by lateral walkways to the first floor, or via the ground floor with its pilotis and glass-fronted function rooms etc. behind. Arco was the first UK building to feature a ground-source heat exchange system. Communal spaces predominate in the SLOANE ROBINSON BUILDING of 2000–2, W, where the residential part is restricted to two top storeys. Below these a floor of seminar rooms (six widely spaced windows), then a dark-glazed void with double-height columns. A lecture theatre lies behind, with dining room and recital room above it. Both buildings feature grey-painted welded-steel staircases that climb as free structures inside white-walled voids. Externally they share a facing of very thin stack-bonded brick, used mostly vertically, but also horizontally. The combination may seem arbitrary, especially so close to Butterfield's forthright stratifications.

For the H.B. ALLEN CENTRE on Banbury Road *see* North Oxford, p. 430.

KELLOGG COLLEGE
Banbury Road
see North Oxford, p. 463

LADY MARGARET HALL
Norham Gardens

Lady Margaret Hall was founded for women students in 1878. It was named after the Lady Margaret, Henry VII's mother, 'a gentlewoman, a scholar and a saint', and was strictly Anglican. Full college status was granted in 1959. Nearly all the buildings are Neo-William-and-Mary to Neo-Georgian or classical revival, and nearly all are of red or brown brick. The architects with the biggest presence are *Sir Reginald Blomfield*, followed by *Sir Giles Gilbert Scott*, late 1890s to 1930s, then *Raymond Erith*, 1950s–60s, and *John Simpson*, 2000s–10s. The site, at the far end of Norham Gardens, also includes a generous allowance of gardens, and the final result is of quite a majestic size.

To Norham Gardens the college is mostly *Simpson* in front of *Erith*, but the chronological story can be picked up here too. On the S side of the forecourt is the college's first home, OLD OLD HALL, a sad Norham Gardens off-white-brick house of 1879. It has a Gothic portal with stubby columns. In 1880–3 *Basil Champneys*, fresh from his first work at Newnham College, Cambridge, built an extension to the E, NEW OLD HALL. It is noteworthy in that its style is what was then vaguely called Queen Anne. This is what Champneys had used at Newnham,

Lady Margaret Hall

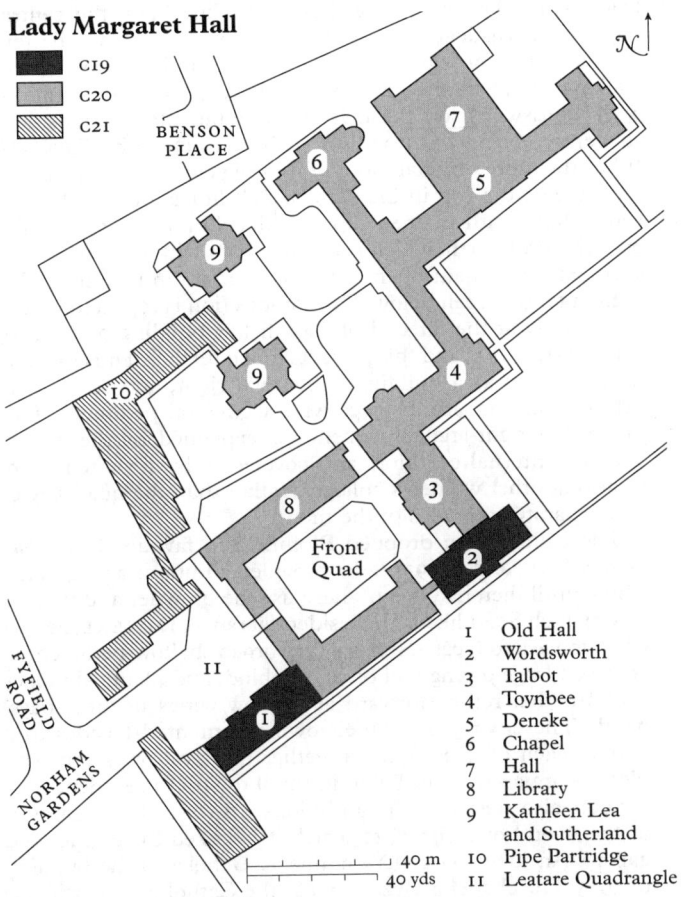

■ C19
▨ C20
▨ C21

BENSON PLACE

Front Quad

FYFIELD ROAD

NORHAM GARDENS

	1	Old Hall
	2	Wordsworth
	3	Talbot
	4	Toynbee
	5	Deneke
	6	Chapel
	7	Hall
	8	Library
	9	Kathleen Lea and Sutherland
40 m	10	Pipe Partridge
40 yds	11	Leatare Quadrangle

and Queen Anne for the ladies seemed a more convincing battle-cry than the Gothic of Waterhouse's Girton College, Cambridge. The display front was on the w side, but this was lost to what appears to be *Giles Gilbert Scott* infill of *c.* 1930 (visible from the garden). On the forecourt side just four bays of red brick, with a little cut-brick and red terracotta decoration. The linking bay with Old Old Hall was designed to be removable in case the college failed or departed, to allow for separation into individual houses.

The first big buildings were by *Sir Reginald Blomfield*, and these comprise the E and s sides of FRONT QUAD. The best view however is from the gardens, to the s and SE. First up was WORDSWORTH, in 1896. This however does not join on to Champneys; there is a long *Blomfield* range between called ELEANOR LODGE, which is of 1926 but simply repeats Wordsworth. Wordsworth is William-and-Mary. It is of orange-red

104

brick with Clipsham stone dressings. Nine bays, the central
bay with a rusticated ground floor, a pair of giant pilasters
above, and a big segmental pediment. Round the corner, still
walking along in the garden, you have a new composition,
with Wordsworth on the l. It is a monumental composition.
Its centre, called TALBOT, was built in 1909–10 by *Blomfield*.
It has the more original motif of four big closely set buttresses,
receding at the top in big scrolls. Ball finials on top; hipped
roof behind, with an open cupola with columns. On the l. is the
end of Wordsworth, which is of three bays with a portal with a
segmental pediment open at the top and a top pediment also
segmental but open below. The composition is repeated on the
r., but only at the far end of Blomfield's building of 1914–15
called TOYNBEE, and this projects much further. Thus the new
wing appears as a building in its own right, and so its long
side has another frontispiece with segmental pediment. This
protracted right-angled sequence is explained by the preference for internal corridors and covered walks for circulation,
as also at other women's colleges, rather than the quadrangles
and separate staircases of the men.

The college then dropped Blomfield in favour of *Sir Giles
Gilbert Scott*, and in 1931–2 he provided additions as big as the
whole until then had been. These use the browner and thinner
brick which Scott liked. His residential range, DENEKE, lies NE
of Toynbee and faces S. It has a very broad shallow-pedimented
centre, a large dining hall on axis behind, and identical ranges
l. and r. that return forward as shallow wings of three bays'
width. These wings have their own pedimented façades to E
and W, each of five bays. Altogether the style owes much to
Neo-Georgian without being in thrall to strict precedent.

Scott also designed the ambitious CHAPEL. This stands N
of the W end of Deneke, to which it is linked by an enclosed
gallery. An identical gallery connects Deneke to the building
of 1915. The chapel is Byzantine, as the Catholics in particular
liked it in the 1930s. It is oblong with shallow transepts, and has
a dome over the centre, appearing outside as a pointed-roofed
dodecahedron. White walls inside, with a patterned pavement
of tawny shades. The detail altogether is a discreet mixture of
styles, from *W. D. Gough*'s Italo-Romanesque carving of the
W portal towards Benson Place, to the decorative fashions
which came from Østberg and the Paris Exhibition of 1925,
e.g. in the ORGAN CASE (1934) and the CHANDELIERS, to
English Arts and Crafts, e.g. the ALTAR with its inlaid Tree
of Life. – BALDACCHINO over the altar, and as the ALTAR
PAINTING a smallish Flagellation of Christ, Italian Cinquecento. – Other PAINTINGS include a beautiful small triptych
by *Burne-Jones*, 1862: Annunciation, Nativity, Flight into
Egypt. – MONUMENTS. Stone effigy of Lady Margaret, signed
G. Scott and *E. Pascoe*, 1977–8. – Good lettered tablets in the
linking gallery.

The HALL shows itself E of the chapel. Placed N–S, with
round-arched clerestory windows set close, and a big beamed

ceiling within: echoes of the main reading room at Scott's contemporary University Library in Cambridge. Balustraded gallery at the end opposite the dais.

The advent of *Raymond Erith* also marked the college's embrace of full quadrangular planning. Specifically, Erith designed the N and W sides of FRONT QUAD, begun in 1959–61 and finished in 1963–6. Erith was a wholly convinced Neo-Georgian, but his buildings are far too original to be mistaken for C18 or early C19 work. The main entrance from Norham Gardens is especially impressive: an almost blank high brick wall, and against it a very solid pedimented portal of Portland stone. In further contrast the top feature is a dainty square clock turret like something from a stable. The S part was never built: a reprieve for Champneys. Inside the quad, the N side also plays on classical themes with considerable licence – see the flushness of the simple two-plus-two-light windows; the very close arcading below, of Hawksmoorian details; and the LIBRARY with its seven lunette windows along the top of the W part. The library is reached by a memorable barrel-vaulted stair that rises in one slow flight from the cross-passage near the E end. Inside, it is determined by the long row of white wooden Tuscan columns carrying the upper shelving and running along all four sides of the long, rather narrow room. Shelving is of the cubicle type on both levels. The lunettes are placed above the upper level of cubicles. A little 1820-style plasterwork on the ceiling.

The other sides of Front Quad are of course *Blomfield*: 1896 and 1926 on the S side, 1909–10 on the E. The latter was formerly the main gate of the college. The road then came right up to the semicircular columned porch under the big pediment, with its carved tympanum by *W. Aumonier & Son*. Within was the college's first shared dining hall, and on the top floor above it the OLD LIBRARY, a fine apsed-ended space with a barrel-vault that is intersected by tunnel-vaults carried cross-wise on plain Doric columns. The niches in the 1926 building with busts of Roman emperors were inserted by *Erith*.

Modernism finally appeared at LMH in 1970–2, in the form of two squat residential towers by *Christophe Grillet* of *Lyster, Grillet & Harding*, KATHLEEN LEA and SUTHERLAND, N of Front Quad. Red brick, with open-well stairs behind a glazed wall, N side, and balconies, S side. The swept brick corners evoke Berlin *c.* 1930, e.g. Fahrenkamp's Shellhaus.

A third tower was intended, but instead the gap between the existing two is now filled by the E end of *John Simpson*'s PIPE PARTRIDGE, 2008–9. As an inventive, committed and craftsmanlike classicist, Simpson is a true heir of Erith, but his references are more eclectic and archaeological, and his freedoms more extreme. So here we have two residential storeys above two big archways placed defiantly off-centre. These open to the cloister that runs round the inner side of the long L-shaped building. Elsewhere are sunburst voussoirs, Lutyens-fashion, and window guards with acroteria. In the W arm are the MONSON ROOM for functions and the saucer-domed SIMPKINS LEE THEATRE, both firmly in the manner of Soane. Timber cloister along the outer side.

The new LEATARE QUADRANGLE by *Simpson* – more fore-court than quad – was completed in 2017. It is an eventful assembly, including substantial three-storey ranges: the DONALD FOTHERGILL BUILDING, N side and aligned E–W, and CLORE GRADUATE CENTRE, S side and aligned N–S. Further variations on themes from both Pipe Partridge and Erith's quad, here offset by a primitivist Doric pavilion where the cloister meets Fothergill, and a non-primitivist Doric colonnade (paired columns) on the garden side of Clore. But it is the two Doric LODGES that are the naughtiest and most memorable component. Their porticoes are of two bays rather than the canonical three, the columns changing from round to square where the railings join on. In the pediments are six big round holes, derived from the plebeian Baker's Tomb at Rome, of the CI B.C.: an educated quotation certainly, but curiously irrelevant here.

LINACRE COLLEGE
St Cross Road

Linacre College started in 1962 as a society for male and female graduate students coming from outside Oxford. It became a full college in 1986. The former St Catherine's Society buildings in St Aldate's were its first home (later the Music Faculty; *see* p. 350). In 1977 the college moved to CHERWELL EDGE, a big Queen Anne house by *J. W. Messenger* at the NE corner with South Parks Road. The dwelling of 1886–7 had already been greatly enlarged in 1907–9 by *Basil Champneys* for the Convent of the Society of the Holy Child Jesus: one block, S, with Gothic-traceried chapel (now library) on the top floor; another, E, with rounded oriels high up.*

Linacre's own new buildings are mostly Neo-Queen Anne, tall and slab-like. The cumulative effect is more institutional-conventual than domestic. The older parts (now the O.C. TANNER BUILDING) have been extended to the N by *Jack Lankester*, University Surveyor: a new entrance wing, 1992–3, and low dining hall behind, 1975–7. Also the BAMBOROUGH BUILDING, 1983–5, detached to the S. E of the 1970s hall is the ABRAHAM BUILDING of 1992–5 by the *ECD Partnership*: externally like Bamborough, but with an inventive interior designed for energy efficiency. The GRIFFITHS BUILDING, 2006–8 by *Hall Needham Associates*, is placed N–S to form a small quad with the Abraham and O.C. Tanner buildings.

*The convent also provided lodgings for women undergraduates, mainly from the Society of Oxford Home Students: *see* St Anne's College.

LINCOLN COLLEGE
Turl Street

Lincoln College was founded in 1427 by Richard Fleming, Bishop of Lincoln, who sought to combat the heresies of the Wycliffites. Initially it had a Warden and seven scholars or Fellows, plus two chaplains. Fleming died in 1431, not having had time to build much. The chief benefactor soon after him was John Forest, Dean of Wells and a Prebendary of Lincoln, of whom it was said in 1437 that he 'Collegium in integrum aedificavit' ('built it into a complete college'), with chapel, library, hall, kitchen, and upper and lower chambers. Two more campaigns finished the quad later in the C15; the second of these was the gift of Thomas Rotherham, Bishop of Lincoln and later Archbishop of York, who reconstituted the college in 1478. The C17 brought a S quadrangle with a new chapel; the Victorians and their successors added buildings to the E and S – all within a modest compass. In the 1970s the college also took over the nearby All Saints' church as its library, but this is treated separately (p. 388).

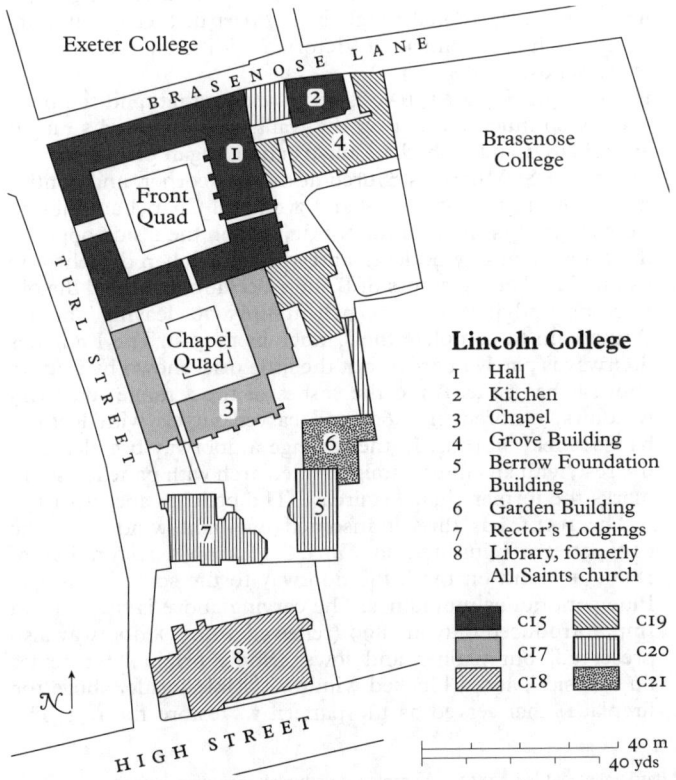

Lincoln College

1 Hall
2 Kitchen
3 Chapel
4 Grove Building
5 Berrow Foundation Building
6 Garden Building
7 Rector's Lodgings
8 Library, formerly All Saints church

C15   C19
C17   C20
C18   C21

40 m
40 yds

Front Quad and Chapel Quad

Lincoln has preserved more of the character of a C15 college than any other at Oxford. This is due primarily to the fact that its FAÇADE and its Front Quad have remained two-storeyed. For otherwise the appearance of the ranges has been allowed to change radically. The two quads stand side by side along Turl Street, with a three-storey gate tower with higher stair-turret leading into Front Quad, and a second gateway to Chapel Quad, S. The single consistent façade is owed to the fact that both parts were refaced and embattled evenly by *Thomas Knowles I* in 1815–19 (not to mention various renewals since). That erased the differences between the C15 and C17 parts, and provided an anachronistically generous display of windows, albeit all in C15 style. Even the quatrefoiled spandrels over the tower archway are an early C19 improvement. But the little niches and window of the top stage are reliable (the STATUES are by *Stephen Cox*, 2009), as is the two-bay entrance vault with its slim hollow-chamfered ribs. Likewise the one single-light window l. of the archway, cusped and without hoodmould, restored in 1958 during *Kenneth Stevens*'s refacing campaign. Along the narrow Brasenose Lane the C15 walling survives better, including one two-light window on the ground floor. The steep-roofed, single-storey part further E is the C15 kitchen. Then a glimpse of Victorian additions, and the start of Brasenose College (q.v.).

The charm of FRONT QUAD is in its scale – that, and the presence of so much creeper on the walls. The W, N and S ranges are ashlared and sashed.* Construction began on the W side, sacrificing St Mildred's church at the NW corner, and continued in the 1430s with the N and E ranges. Chapel and library were on the first floor of the N side, hall on the E side opposite the gateway, at ground level, and with the kitchen detached on its far side. The executors of Bishop Beckington added the old Rector's Lodgings S of the hall in 1465–70, leaving Thomas Rotherham to complete the S range in 1475–9. The Lodgings doorway is partly in order, but the little oriel shown by Loggan above it has gone. Amid the sashes of the S range some C15 windows, restored in 1960, and carved angels with Rotherham's shield of arms. In the N range a doorway broader than the rest, with an almost straight-sided arch with panelled soffit, marks the former chapel staircase. The bellcote above is C19.

The HALL has three transomed two-light windows – the C15 pattern, reinstated in *Sir T.G. Jackson*'s restoration of 1889–91 – and on the l. the doorway to the screens passage. Fine continuous mouldings. The carving above is the Lincoln Imp, introduced only in 1899 (renewed 2001). E doorway also preserved, but plainer and lower. Some original buttresses on this side, and a blocked window (visible inside, above the fireplace) that served as the pattern to restore the rest. The

---

*Battlements added *c.*1852 were replaced with plain parapets in 1959.

hall roof is original, with collar-beams, arched braces, three tiers of wind-braces, and louvre. Until 1889 it was hidden by a ceiling, part of renovations of 1697–1701, of which the screen and panelling remain. The screen has a narrow middle bay of fluted Ionic columns and segmental pediment. The ornate Gothic fireplace is *Jackson*'s. In 1640–1 the hall floor was raised when a CELLAR was made below. This became 'Deep Hall' – the students' bar, one of the first such in a college – in 1938. Three of its row of mid-columns are preserved. N of the hall is the BUTTERY, reconstructed and extended E in 1999–2000 by *Rodney Melville & Partners*.* It joins up with the square KITCHEN, with an original wind-braced roof. The middle trusses are of an unusual pattern, having curved ashlar posts and also a yoke at the top, a detail more common in cruck construction. Large fireplaces, and an inserted bread oven, N wall.

OTHER INTERIORS. On the N side upstairs the former library, now with early C17 panelling and chimneypiece. To its E, the former chapel is now the BURGIS ROOM (Senior Common Room), extended and fitted up with two reused Tuscan columns *c.*1969. Below are two more common rooms: the eastern with a Jacobean overmantel, the western (the original SENIOR COMMON ROOM, since 1662) with close panelling and a garlanded overmantel framed with swags. This is work of 1699, by *Arthur Frogley*. On the E side in the Old Rector's Lodgings, the BECKINGTON ROOM has panelling and a garlanded overmantel done for Fitzherbert Adams, Rector 1685–1715, now painted and gilt. The garlands are superb, in a naturalistic Gibbons style unlike that of the SCR overmantel, though not necessarily by a different hand (cf. the chapel reredos). Also lesser decoration round the doorcases and on the ceiling beams. (Similar decoration in the first-floor room above.) In the S range behind the eponymous bronze bust is the WESLEY ROOM, a pastiche of 1928 with linenfold panelling 'understood to have come from a western district of the country'.

Through the S range one enters CHAPEL QUAD. This dates from 1607–31. The W range came first. This and the E range have windows no longer with arched lights, but still of course mullioned. Incidentally they retain the medieval rhythm of several lights then one light, indicating rooms and study cubicles. The Gothic bay window high on the S wall of the W range, conspicuous from Turl Street, probably belongs with the 1810s refacing. (One room in Staircase 7 with fragments of an early C17 panoramic wall painting.)

On the S side the CHAPEL, built in 1629–31 with money from Bishop Williams of Lincoln. The windows are of three lights and essentially Perp, but the broad ogee arches within the tracery give away the C17 date. E window of six lights

*The buttery ceiling was dated by its tree rings to 1436/7. Experts identify it as Oxford's earliest-known use of a soffit tenon with diminished haunch.

(three plus three), without ogees. The battlements are original. Simple doorway with three-centred arch. Panelled, canted roof with shields and pretty motifs in the panels: a type already current by 1630, but here of *c.*1685. Buttresses on the s side remade in 1886 by *Wilkinson & Moore*. Further restorations in 1958 (ceiling) and 1994–6.

The rich C17 FURNISHINGS are of special interest. Of *c.*1630–40 (the early phase) are the stained glass, the black and white PAVING, the cedarwood PANELLING with its typically post-Jacobean pedimented motifs, and most of the STALLS. These still have misericords, of simple ogee shapes with elementary leaf carving. Complicated scrolly desk-ends. The FRONT STALLS however are a late C17 addition. Inlay fronts, and on the ends a series of interesting statuettes. The carved swags and vine applied to the REREDOS are 1680s, by *Frogley*. The PULPIT is 1630s, square and with motifs to match the panelling; but the COMMUNION RAIL is late C17, with openwork foliage. Finally the SCREEN. Because this cuts across the panelling, and because its architectural elements are advanced – thin Corinthian columns (pilasters on the chapel side), broken segmental pediment in the centre – this has usually been taken as a 1680s enhancement too. But an 'excellent fayre Skreene all of Cedar' was noted here in 1636, and a closer look shows indeed that the pierced side pieces are still reminiscent of strapwork, in the pre-Restoration way. They frame vertically placed ovals, with pediments above. – Two C17 wooden STATUES (antechapel), from an organ case(?). – ORGAN. Instrument of 2010, sympathetically encased by *Laurent Robert*. It rests on two fluted late C17 COLUMNS (brought in). – DOORS in the screen, engraved glass by *David Peace & Mary Scott*, 1992.

STAINED GLASS. An important series dated 1629–30 (s side), apparently all by *Abraham van Linge*, whose initials have been found on one s window. In the E window a series of types and anti-types from the Old (below) and New Testaments. From l. to r.: the Creation of Adam and Eve and the Nativity; the Crossing of the Red Sea and the Baptism of Christ; the Feast of the Passover and the Last Supper; the Brazen Serpent and the Crucifixion; Jonah and the Whale and the Resurrection; the Ascent of Elijah in the Chariot of Fire and the Ascension. In the tracery lights simple architectural designs. The N and s windows have three large figures each, Prophets on the N and Apostles on the s, as already deployed at Wadham chapel (p.309). Each stands under an elaborate canopy, with a panel below bearing the names and appropriate text.[*] N side: David, Daniel, Elijah; Isaiah, Jeremiah, Ezekiel; Amos, Zachariah, Malachi; Elisha, Jonah, Obadiah. s side: St Peter, St Andrew, St James the Great; St John, St Philip, St Bartholomew; St Matthew, St Thomas, St James the Less; St Jude, St Simon, St Mathias. In the traceries a repeated design of angels holding various shields of arms of Bishop Williams.

---

[*] On the s side, the part of the Creed ascribed to each Apostle.

Additions, C19 to C21

Round the periphery E and S of the two quads the later buildings had to be fitted in. First GROVE BUILDING to the NE, 1881–3 by *Sir T.G. Jackson*, placed just S of the kitchen and facing S. Essentially asymmetrical Free Jacobean, with a few self-willed motifs such as the pedimented top windows and segmental doorheads. Jackson's high-pitched and tiled roof made way for a mansard storey in 1950. Of 1884–5 is the gabled EXTENSION to the former Rector's Lodgings, facing Grove Building. It is by *Wilkinson & Moore* and not worth further descriptive effort. At the S end it joins on by means of a covered corridor to the former LIBRARY of 1906 by *Herbert Read & R.F. MacDonald* (now the Berrow Foundation Building). A delightful classical design, not large, by the churchyard of All Saints. Five main bays, the middle one a big bow. The ground-floor windows have pediments. The upper ones are of the late C17 cross-type and separated by full columns. Other decorative motifs free William-and-Mary, sparingly used. But that is not all, for the former staircase bay, l., is now subsumed in *Stanton Williams*'s GARDEN BUILDING of 2012–15. It is a bold step – too bold for some, as it introduces the first Modernist accent to this end of Turl Street. But the design is both intelligent and refined: a two-storey box of ashlar and glass, the lower windows recessed, the upper ones larger, set flush, and making a glazed NW corner. Lecture rooms and performance spaces within, all the spaces calm and impeccably detailed. Finally the present RECTOR'S LODGINGS, across the garden and facing the Turl. 1929–30 by *Herbert Read*, well-meant Neo-Early Georgian and no harm done.*

For the present LIBRARY *see* All Saints' church, p.388; for LINCOLN HOUSE in Turl Street and the BEAR LANE SITE *see* Perambulation 1, pp.411 and 412; for the EPA SCIENCE CENTRE in Museum Road *see* Perambulation 3, p.428; for the GRADUATE BUILDING in Little Clarendon Street *see* Perambulation 4, p.433.

MAGDALEN COLLEGE
High Street

Visually Magdalen is the ideal college, with a firm centre and around it in all directions quads, or rather areas of all sizes and odd shapes, with buildings large and small, seemingly scattered over a spacious site and yet, fortuitously or consciously, forming attractive groups, and moreover groups merging – at least on the

26

---

* *Read*'s proposed quad on the W side, linked by a covered bridge across the Turl (*The Builder*, 20 May 1927), would have been a different story.

E and N sides – into gardens and a planted grove. Architecturally also there is plenty to enjoy, and the medieval core happens to be enjoyable throughout as well.

Magdalen was founded by William Waynflete, Bishop of Winchester and Chancellor of England, in 1458. Building did not start at once. The site finally chosen included St John's Hospital, at the E end of Oxford outside the city walls, which covered quite a large area and ran down to the river. The hospital had been rebuilt under Henry III's patronage, and some of these C13 buildings were retained and survive within the present college. Waynflete had previously been headmaster of Winchester College and then Provost of Eton, and his Oxford establishment

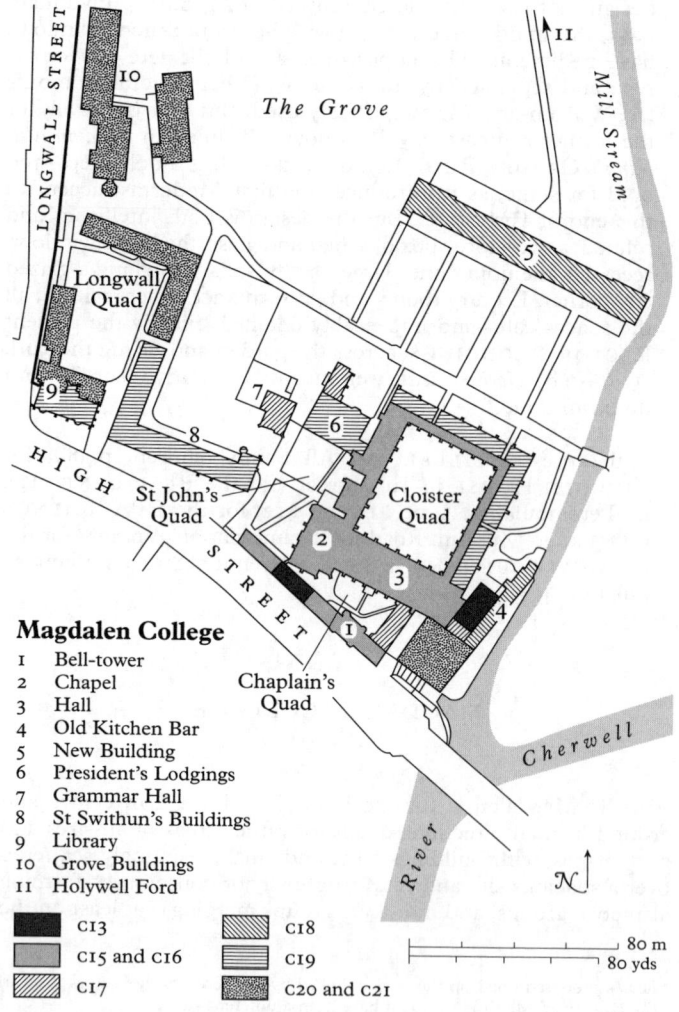

Magdalen College

1   Bell-tower
2   Chapel
3   Hall
4   Old Kitchen Bar
5   New Building
6   President's Lodgings
7   Grammar Hall
8   St Swithun's Buildings
9   Library
10 Grove Buildings
11 Holywell Ford

C13
C15 and C16
C17
C18
C19
C20 and C21

80 m
80 yds

included a grammar school too, placed to the W. Even without the school, Waynflete's foundation was large indeed: a President and forty Fellows, thirty scholars (called demies), three readers (to provide public lectures), eight clerks, sixteen choristers and twenty places for 'gentlemen commoners', who paid for residence and instruction.

The battlemented precinct wall around college and school was started in 1467, building proper not until 1474. By 1480–1 the college chapel, hall, Muniment Tower, Founder's Tower and most of the cloister were standing. Architecturally New College was the model, with some telling differences. The New College cloister was for burials, but Magdalen's cloister is incorporated within the main quad, as Waynflete had already done at Eton. The quad itself is set back from the High Street behind a separate range incorporating part of the hospital buildings. Also in this range stands the mighty bell-tower, begun in 1492. Another novelty was use of crenellation throughout. *William Orchard* of Oxford was the master mason from 1468 ('principalis lathomus dicti operis'), and supplied much of the stone as well. Orchard is known at Eton too, and the primary buildings at Magdalen must be assigned to him. *John Bowden* of Burford served as master carpenter and woodwork contractor in 1474–9, the peak years of construction. By *c.*1510 the main buildings were complete.

The post-medieval story is complicated by the college's tendency to commission or attract unbuilt schemes – enough to fill a book, indeed.*What was built on the main site comprises chiefly the classical New Building, early C18, to the N, extensive Victorian and early C20 Neo-Perp ranges to the W, and late C20 outliers in traditional styles, placed further NW and N. But strict chronology must be forsaken at Magdalen, where topography takes over.

MEDIEVAL MAGDALEN

Bell-tower and front range

Magdalen's BELL-TOWER dominates the High Street range, so the description starts here. It was begun in 1492, possibly as an afterthought – the college had inherited a bell-tower of some kind from the hospital buildings – but still within *William Orchard*'s time as master mason. Another mason, *William Reynold I*, was paid £70 for work on it up to completion, *c.*1505/6. *Robert Carow* was the master carpenter. There are four main stages, rising sheer and without set-backs, to a height of 144 ft 6 in. (44.3 metres). Big polygonal angle buttresses, paired three-light bell-openings, a rich parapet partly pierced, and eight panelled pinnacles. A splendid anomaly among the colleges, it really belongs with the widespread later C15 type of turreted church tower in which ornament is concentrated at the top. Here the details of the parapet especially owe much to

26

Merton chapel tower (q.v.). Another parallel is with the tower proposed for King's College at Cambridge, known from a C15 drawing. Heavily renewed in 1977–81 by *Richard Biscoe-Taylor*. New carving by *Michael Groser, Pat Conoley* and *Percy Quick*.

The tower stands near the E end of the FRONT RANGE, likewise refaced, but less reliable as to the original form. E of the tower a short section built from c.1508 (*Richard Hays*, mason), with steep, steeply gabled dormers of 1855 by *J.C. Buckler*. The short wing running N from here is C17. Four bigger gables along this front. The hall with its big angle turret appears behind, and to its E the kitchen. W of the tower a long two-storey battlemented range also of early C16 fabric, with an ornamented string course. The running hoodmould linking the first-floor windows – not an early C16 motif – again seems to be an intervention of 1855 by *Buckler*, who was commissioned to make the windows taller. Chimneystacks and oaken dormers from restoration in 1892 by *E.P. Warren*, whose brother was then President. The W gable in its present form is C19, the oriel below it a C16 feature. But the external uniformity is doubly deceptive, for the middle third of the range incorporates the shell of the two-storey late C13 CHAPEL from St John's Hospital. Its exterior was altered to match in 1665–6, and the clearest traces now are in the CELLAR – fragments of a rib-vault, NE corner, and a blocked S doorway of C16 type.

The GATEWAY from the street, immediately W, is an ornate Waynflete Gothic piece of 1885 by *Bodley & Garner*. Before then the college was approached from the W, via a now lost gateway on Longwall Street. Also of 1885 the entrance doorway inserted in the front range. To the W from here all is Victorian, and is described below (p. 190).

St John's Quad

Passing through the entrance one is at once in ST JOHN'S QUAD, a paved space with a variety of buildings all separated from each other. On the N too they are chiefly Victorian, and for these we must return later. But on the E is the W front of the chapel, with the Muniment Tower and Founder's Tower l., and a slipway into a yard r. In the corner where there is access to that yard is an external PULPIT with a decorated stone canopy. The CHAPEL was built in 1474–80, on the T-plan of New College chapel. To the W it has a large doorway, allowing access without entering the main quad. It has spandrels with flying ribs, and battlements decorated exuberantly with statuettes under canopies and ornamented quatrefoils. Three windows over, the simplified tracery of the middle one of c.1640, and battlements above. The side windows are of three lights, as are the two of the antechapel to the S and the two-plus-two to the E. The chapel side windows, five to the N, five to the S, are also of three lights. All have the characteristic mid-C15 panel tracery. CHAPLAIN'S QUAD, to give the yard to the S its proper name, is a *Restraum*, as the Germans say – leftover space – and reveals the side view of the chapel and of the hall in line on the N side. It also reveals the inner side of the street range, with rougher masonry for the hospital part, and the unfeelingly refaced back of the C17 E range already mentioned, with added C19 gables. The SCULPTURE is Noli me tangere by *David Wynne*, 1963. A small attached chapel on the N side was demolished *c.*1730. Heating chamber in the NW angle, added when *L.N. Cottingham* restored the whole chapel in 1830–3.

Back to St John's Quad, with its two towers on the E side. The MUNIMENT TOWER, begun in 1474, adjoins the front of the chapel immediately N and, though called a tower, is barely higher than the chapel. It has three storeys, and a doorway with a straight-sided arch and decorated spandrels – but this is of 1901, *Bodley*'s replacement for a classical doorway applied in the 1630s. Tierceron-vault inside, with three tiercerons in each cell. Rich and varied bosses. (MUNIMENT ROOM, top floor, with the original document cupboards.) The chapel doorway opens off S, with carved angels in the spandrels, carrying inscribed ribbons. Ahead, the space narrows to a passage to the cloister with close-set transverse ribs. WAR MEMORIAL on the walls here: inscribed stone panels of 1921, designed by *Alfred B. Yeates* (of *Sir Ernest George & Yeates*).*

The FOUNDER'S TOWER, four storeys high, also connects St   26
John's Quad with the cloister. As the original main entrance to the college, and as the chief part of the President's original lodgings, it received special treatment. Two-storey panelled oriels to W and E, richer than the previous Oxford model. Nice frilly details on the W front: two tiers of statue niches on each side, blind panelling in a band below the oriel. The doorway again with flying-ribbed spandrels. Original panelled DOORS. Lierne vault inside, of two bays, with the liernes forming squares. The tower is deep enough to run right through to the cloister garth. Here it has on the SE corner a higher stair-turret with crocketed spirelet. *Orchard* contracted for this part in 1479. Study of the timbering has shown that the W range was first constructed with a first-floor hall (cf. Merton), which was rapidly subdivided for state rooms, then again modified to insert an additional upper storey. (Panelled arches to the oriel windows inside. In the first-floor STATE ROOM an original fireplace with foliage spandrels. Linenfold panelling of 1898. Lost, the interior work designed by *G.G. Scott* and executed by *Crace* in 1856.)

Chapel interior

The CHAPEL INTERIOR is covered by plaster vaulting from *Cottingham*'s precociously scholarly restoration of 1830–3. Cottingham in turn reworked *Wyatt*'s false vault of 1790–3, introducing archaeologically correct ribs, wall-shafts etc. *Scott*

---

*A memorial CROSS also by *Yeates* stood in St John's Quad until 1940. Now in Wheatley old burial ground (*see Oxfordshire: North and West*).

provided an unused design for decorating it (1866–7). The antechapel is, like that of New College, two bays deep from W to E. The slender piers have the usual section of four shafts and four hollows, but taller bases than at New College. Unorthodox little sprigs on the capitals. *Cottingham* was responsible also – and very creditable they are – for the SCREEN of Painswick stone, very Perp indeed, the REREDOS with its tiered stone niches (based in part on C15 fragments) on the windowless E wall, the stone PANELLING l. and r. of this wall, and the main STALLS. On the N side the panelling is pierced to reveal the CHANTRY CHAPEL built for the founder's tomb, but never so used. The chapel retains its fan-vault with dainty details. Original stonework from the chapel front, and from the two vestry doorways in the E wall, survives reassembled at Theale church in Berkshire, which was built in 1820–2 by the sister of the President, Dr Routh.

OTHER FURNISHINGS.* In the chapel: ALTARPIECE. Painting of Christ carrying the Cross. Spanish, assigned to *Valdés Leal* (1622–90). Set up here in 1745, the first 'Old Master' altarpiece in an Oxford chapel. The C17 treatment was a large Resurrection painted by *Isaac Fuller*, 1663/4, above a grisaille hanging of the Last Supper by *Richard Greenbury*, 1630s. – SCULPTURE. High up in the reredos, Noli me tangere, by *Chantrey*, c.1835. In the reredos niches, STATUES of prophets, saints and angels by *Earp*, 1864–5, after designs by *Clayton & Bell*. – CANDELABRA. A standing pair, of bronze. Apparently of c.1834 and by *Cottingham*. – LECTERN. A brass eagle; 1633. Very similar to those of Exeter College and St Mary Redcliffe at Bristol. – CHEST. Early C14. With a net-traceried and painted front. Heavily restored. – PAVING. Black and white, c.1635, re-laid by *Cottingham*. – ORGAN. The instrument of 1985–6 with its case by *Julian Bicknell* is due to be replaced with one by *Hermann Eule*, in a case designed by *Stephen Oliver*.

Antechapel: around the walls thirty-two original STALLS, displaced there in the 1830s. All but three have MISERICORDS, including a monkey, an owl, fox and geese, a horse on its back, and several grotesques. In addition three separate STALLS also with misericords, reportedly brought from Hampshire in the 1960s; in the antechapel (two) and chantry chapel. – CHANDELIER with concentric rings of lights. Designed by *John Brandon-Jones*, c.1980. – Two late C19 STATUES of female saints, brought in. – Standing CANDELABRUM by *Hardman*, 1863, of brass. – SHRINE with twisted columns and small Flemish C17 paintings. – MODEL in coloured wax of Waynflete's tomb at Winchester Cathedral, in a glass case. 1840s. Made by the sculptor *Richard Cockle Lucas*. – PAINTING. Under the organ a panel with a male saint, given 2013. Identified as part of a cycle of saints painted in the 1630s on the former stall backs.

---

*Late C17 woodwork from the chapel is reused in the churches at Ducklington and Cokethorpe (*see Oxfordshire: North and West*), and parts of *Robert Dallam*'s organ of 1631 survive at Tewkesbury Abbey.

STAINED GLASS. All the antechapel glass is grisaille. W window, a huge Last Judgment, a repainting or replacement by *Francis Eginton*, 1793–4, of the original window of *c.*1640 by *Richard Greenbury*. Michelangelo is the source. Reinstated in 1996, with further repainting by *Peter Archer*, very well done. – The seven smaller windows have six large saints in each, all by *Greenbury*, 1637–*c.*1640. They are grouped in trios, the outer figures turning towards the middle one. Described clockwise. N antechapel E wall: N window, St Barnabas, St Titus, St Crispus above; St Epimachus, St Dionysus, St Cleophas below. S window, St Christina, St Catherine, St Clare; St Helena, St Brigid, St Ursula. – S antechapel E wall: N window, St Cornelius, St Clement of Alexandria, St Cyprian; St Basil, St Gregory, St Cyril. S window, St Julius, St Polycarp, St Ignatius; St Clement, St Timothy, St Irenaeus. – S antechapel S wall: E window, St Mary Magdalene, St Anne, St Martha; St Agnes, St Theodosia, St Eulalia. W window, St Gregory of Nyssa, St George, St Cyriacus; St Hippolytus, St Nicholas, St Lawrence. – S antechapel W wall, St Euphemia, 'Maria dei pub', St Salome; St Burchardus, St Aristarchus, St Patricia. – N antechapel W wall: St Anselm, St Nemesius, St Huldrucus; St Wenceslaus, St Agathon, St Januarius. – Back-lit panel by *John Piper*, installed 2001. A duplicate of his Nativity window at Iffley (*see* p.508). – In the main chapel ten windows with large figures by *Hardman*, 1857–60, not in his mature style.

BRASSES. Chancel floor, Dr Martin Routh, President, †1854 in his hundredth year ('aetatis suae C'). Designed by *Buckler* (probably *C.A.*), made by *Hardman*. – William Tybard, the first President, †1480, 3 ft (91 cm.). Restored 1911. – Arthur Cole †1558, President, 3 ft 1½ in. (96 cm.). A palimpsest of several brasses, one (†1431) identified as from the Greyfriars church in London. – S antechapel. E wall, two demi-figures of clerics: Roger Bulkeley †1465, 14½ in. (37 cm.); Ralph Vawdrey †1478, 18 in. (46 cm.). – Eight more clerical brasses within *Julian Bicknell*'s timber VESTRY ENCLOSURE of 1999: anonymous figure (George Epworth †1489?), 24 in. (61 cm.); Thomas Freer †1490, 27 in. (68 cm.); Richard Barnes †1499, 26½ in. (67 cm.); George Lassy, *c.*1500, demi-figure, 12 in. (30 cm.); Thomas Mason †1501/2, 18 in. (46 cm.); Walter Charyls †1502, headless, 6 in. (15 cm.); William Goberd †1515, 19½ in. (50 cm.); Nicholas Goldwell †1523, 16 in. (40 cm.). – S antechapel floor. Thomas Sondes †1478, 3 ft 1 in. (96 cm.). – John Hygden, President, †1533, 30 in. (76 cm.), mutilated.

MONUMENTS, all in the antechapel. N arm, Richard Patten, the founder's father, *c.*1450. Removed in 1819 from Wainfleet, Lincs., when the church there was replaced. At first placed in the chantry chapel, but since 1980 in the recess which *Cottingham* designed for it. Recumbent civilian effigy of alabaster. Figures by the pillow, identifiable as the founder and his brother John, Dean of Chichester. Tomb-chest with vertically panelled front. Angels bearing shields at the head end. – Above this John and Thomas Lyttleton, both drowned while one was trying to save the other. 1635 by *Nicholas Stone*, the great innovator in English monuments at that period. Here two heavily draped classical youths, with full faces, stand on big brackets l. and r. of the inscription. – William Langton, President, †1626. Demi-figure with book and skull under a moving-forward entablature. Two allegorical figures hold drapery open. Three more allegorical figures on top. Attributed to *Maximilian Colt* (GF). – Walter Wallwyn †1640. A big, pedimented Artisan Mannerist piece. – Tablet to Frederick Bulley, President, 1886. Designed by *G. F. Bodley*. – Also by *Bodley* are Prince Christian Victor etc., 1901, N wall, and Sir John Stainer's tablet, 1905, w. – Sir Herbert Warren, President, †1930. Tablet, no doubt designed by his brother *E. P. Warren*.

Antechapel s arm. Laurence Humphrey, President, †1589. Another demi-figure with book. He seems to be preaching. – Thomas Cradocke †1678. Gristly cartouche. – Edward Butler, President, †1745. Excellently detailed wall monument without figures. – Thomas Stafford (†1722), erected 1753. Clearly by the same hand. – Maria Butler †1730, superior cartouche.

Cloister Quadrangle

The CLOISTER QUADRANGLE dates from 1474–*c.*1490. The side ranges are of two storeys, fully embattled. The CLOISTER runs round the inside, placed within the lower storey, as at Eton and at Queens' College, Cambridge. Uniform three-light openings here, with broad flattened arches, and flat roofs of timber. On the N, E and W sides the cloister buttresses support the 'hieroglyphics': mysterious statues of emblematic or moralizing character, carved mostly by *Robert Buce*, set up in 1508–9 (renewed). Straight-headed windows of one or two lights on the upper floor, i.e. the familiar collegiate pattern. On the W side towards the N however a uniform sequence of ten double lights, marking the Old Library. The statues here include Moses (with horns) and two figures clasping each other, perhaps Jacob and the Angel. But much of the cloister is deceptive, for the ranges behind the N and E walls were controversially torn down and rebuilt in 1822–7. The old structures were much less regular, especially to the N, having had the usual sashes, cocklofts etc. added; evidence also exists that the E side was at first meant to have had three storeys. The replacement ranges were designed by *Joseph Parkinson*, subject to adjustments urged by the architect and antiquary *J. C. Buckler*, a stern critic of the project. In 1990 a dormer storey was reintroduced on the outer N side by *Brandon-Jones & Partners*. The large oriel at the W end of this range is of 1822 and belongs to the OLD LIBRARY, the largest medieval library remaining at any Oxford college. Access from the cloister is through a large doorway N of the Founder's Tower, originally also serving the President's Lodgings. The staircase with plaster vault, the Gothic bookcases within, and the flattened Gothic surround to the N oriel are all *Parkinson*'s. Simply panelled pointed-arched ceiling by *Booth & Ledeboer*, 1954.

All this is to neglect the S side. Here the cloister is treated as a single-storey enclosure, so that the chapel appears above, making one composition with the HALL, E. As at New College this is on the first floor. Begun like the chapel in 1474, it has tall, transomed two-light windows along the sides, a three-light window to the E, and a canted bay window to the cloister in its westernmost bay. Entry is via a prominent doorway in the cloister SE corner. It is wide and has straight shanks. The staircase starts immediately below, rising under a complicatedly moulded arch which dies into the imposts. On the landing is a wooden doorway with the Prince of Wales feathers, suggestive of the royal visit in 1605, and then one is in the screens passage. On the l. four openings, including two serving doors and a large hatch between. The arches again straight-shanked. The hall INTERIOR was restored by *Bodley* in 1902–3. By him the Gothic fireplace, the restoration of the E window, and the low-pitched roof, based on traces of the original roof. That meant sweeping away *Wyatt*'s roof and plaster vault of 1790–2. SCREEN probably of *c.*1625–30, with fluted Corinthian columns and a parapet with the familiar blank arcading. Linenfold PANELLING on the other walls. At the dais end, set into this panelling, are seventeen deeply carved Early Renaissance panels, one dated 1541, another with the figure of Henry VIII. Five are from the legend of St Mary Magdalene. The date 1541 is a good match for the frieze of putti etc. and for the widely spaced pilasters, and there are indeed payments for carving in the hall then. Yet a job lot of panelling was bought in London just before, apparently second-hand.* This may account for the linenfold work, i.e. an older (but still current) form, to which more fashionable and specific carvings were added. Transversely ribbed vaulting in the bay window. The older STAINED GLASS is gathered here, including heads of Charles I and Henrietta Maria by *Richard Greenbury*, 1632. In other windows heraldic glass by *Burlison & Grylls*, 1903.

Below the hall is the SENIOR COMMON ROOM, established in 1661. Originally the vestry, with access from the doorways in the chapel E wall. Now lined with late C17 panelling, and entered from the N and E. Ceiling of 1962, when the hall floor had to be replaced. Service rooms to the E, largely reconstructed at the same time.

A final thing to note in the cloister. Set into the walls in the SW corner are two deceptively medieval-looking PANELS carved with shields and angels. They come from the former W gateway of 1844 by *Pugin*, his only architectural work in Oxford. Until 1883 it stood on axis with the Founder's Tower in St John's Quad, having in turn replaced a classical gateway of 1633–5 there by the London mason and sculptor *John Christmas*. Some

---

*Information from Robin Darwall-Smith.

SCULPTURE from this older gateway survives inside the bell-tower, with other Pugin statues and fragments.

Kitchens

E of the cloister at the hall end are the KITCHENS. The largest room, now the OLD KITCHEN BAR, stands at a slight angle to the hall, which is suggestive. It is indeed another C13 survival of St John's Hospital, understood as a hall formerly attached at right angles to the N side of the infirmary proper. The hall probably served as part of the residence of the King's Almoner. For its new role the college gave it a big but utilitarian new roof with straight tie-beams and collar-beams, and two tiers of wind-braces. Converted to a bar by *Maguire & Murray*, with the riverside terrace and the admirably discreet new KITCHEN, all of 1986–9. The last is placed in a former service yard to the S, with the main space on the upper floor. From the High Street this kitchen appears as a stone-slated double roof with glazed gablets, behind a castellated wall retained from the Victorian bathhouse. The small but obtrusive glazed box W of the kitchen is from a renovation of 2019–20 by *Robinson Thorne Architects*. The wall continues N along the river terrace too. But between this part and the Old Kitchen is a tall block of chambers facing S, added in 1635. Its blunt E oriel however is obviously mid-Victorian, though undocumented. The low castellated range attached to the E of the Old Kitchen and continuing N is WEST'S BUILDING, built by *John Burrough & Stephen Townesend*, 1782. The N part is the lavatory block. Small windows for the separate stalls towards the river. A few mid-Georgian Gothic details, simple and flat, on the landward side. Three blocked lancets on the refaced Old Kitchen N wall here look 'Gothick' too, but are interpreted as C13.

NEW BUILDING

NEW BUILDING stands N of the N range of the cloister, at a distance which becomes its size and stateliness. Of 1733–9, it is the only known work by *Edward Holdsworth*, who had resigned his Fellowship in 1715 rather than swear loyalty to George I. His designs were realized by the masons *William King & Richard Piddington*. In addition, the builder *William Townesend*, the architect *James Gibbs* and the amateur *William, 5th Lord Digby* were all consulted at different times. No intricacy here, no variety, no elaborate decoration, none of the tradition of collegiate quads. An absolutely even range, twenty-seven bays long, just with a five-bay pediment. First and second floors of equal heights, indicating the grand sets of rooms within. The ground floor is arcaded to the S, and in the arcade is modest plasterwork by *Thomas Roberts*, his earliest-known work. To the N Gibbs surrounds to the ground-floor windows.

Magdalen College, Cloister Quad and New Building.
Engraving by J. Le Keux after F. Mackenzie, 1834

That is all. But the intention was to continue S with right-angled ranges as far as the cloister, which was to be rebuilt too. Thus the field was left open for others to stake their claims. *Hawksmoor* and *Holdsworth* both worked on designs in the 1730s–40s.* At various times in the 1790s–1820s *James Wyatt*, *Humphry Repton*, *John Nash* and *John Buckler* all made plans for side wings connecting to or projecting towards the cloister, with or without replacing the cloister ranges, and with or without gothicizing the C18 building. Instead, as we have seen, the cloisters were partly rebuilt along the old lines, and in 1824 the unfinished ends of New Building were tidied up to match the C18 design. The job was given to *Thomas Harrison* of Chester, yet another who had submitted unused designs, with *Parkinson* as executant architect. The different colours of stone have been perpetuated in refacing. Attic storey formed in 1937, C18 rooms modernized 1984–94.

The STONE SEATS in front of New Building are of 1934, designed by *W.G. Newton*. On the E side of the lawn is an C18 iron GATE with rather Baroque spur walls, and a C17 BRIDGE. It leads across the mill stream to Addison's Walk (*see* p. 191).

THE PRESIDENT'S LODGINGS, ST SWITHIN'S QUAD AND LONGWALL QUAD ETC.

Now we return to ST JOHN'S QUAD. On the N side here are the PRESIDENT'S LODGINGS, a considerable extension NW

Hawksmoor also drew up his own proposals for the new building around 1725, as did *Dr George Clarke*, c. 1730.

of where they originally were. They are largely of 1886–8 by *Bodley & Garner*, replacing lodgings composed of work from the late C15 to C18. The s façade is quiet, though asymmetrical, with Perp mouldings etc. based on what was found when the old lodgings were taken down. The back is livelier and includes a wing partly of *c.* 1530–1, NW. Gothic windows and gables. (Interiors in historic styles, including a large open-well staircase of early C18 type. Drawing room on the first floor, with a big N bay and a re-set C15 fireplace. Four Flemish early C16 tapestries, original to the college, hang in the hall.)

Next to the Lodgings on the W is the old GRAMMAR HALL, the only fragment of MAGDALEN HALL to escape demolition in 1844. It began as the grammar school founded by Wykeham next to his college, from which it was originally separate. In the C16 the school buildings came to accommodate an academic hall, and in the early C19 this body moved to what remained of Hart Hall (*see* Hertford College). The surviving bit comprises the NE corner of what had grown into an irregular quadrangle with the medieval hall along its E side. The square bell-turret now picturesquely placed at the SE corner formerly belonged to the N end of this hall, and its refaced gable-end wall must be represented by the present s wall. The rest (dated 1614 on the W gable) served as lodgings for the Principal of Magdalen Hall. Gutted for undergraduate sets in 1885, converted to offices by *J. Brandon-Jones & Partners*, 1985–6.

Part of the site is now taken by the end of ST SWITHUN'S BUILDINGS, a little way to the s. The architects were again *Bodley & Garner*, and building took from 1880 to 1884, after a competition in which *Wilkinson, Champneys* and *Street* all contended. The style here too is Magdalen Gothic, in Burford stone. The quality is high.* Even William Morris liked it. The start is another four-stage gate tower, answering Founder's Tower to the E. The building runs E–W and turns N. No battlements, but gables on both sides. To the High Street it has a series of very ornate oriels. Original carving throughout by *John McCulloch*. But the N continuation of the N range, and the continuation to the W from its N end (instead of returning E, as the 1880s plan had it), are much later – 1928–30, by *Sir Giles Gilbert Scott*. He carried on with few changes, e.g. single-storey oriels rather than two-storey, and only the slightly Spanish-Gothic doorways show a personal touch.

W of this range is LONGWALL QUAD, bounded on the W by the battlemented precinct WALL. Closing the s side is the LIBRARY by *J.C. & C.A. Buckler*, built in 1849–51 for Magdalen College School, i.e. the continuing grammar school. A very attractive, compact job. The style is again C15 Perp, the obvious choice for a Waynflete foundation even at this high tide of Middle

---

*Also of the interiors, which were designed with close attention to undergraduate needs as the 1880s understood them. The staircases for instance incorporate 'light and airy' arches, so that 'a man on the top landing may make the scout in his room in the basement hear without straining his lungs': *Oxford Times*, 13 October 1883.

Pointed. Five bays to the s; tall straight-headed transomed windows with panel tracery to the single big hall. In the middle of the N side the porch with a perky stair-turret with spire. Also battlements, as on the s side too. *Scott* converted the big main schoolroom for the college library in 1931–2, but his inserted floor made way for a free-standing two-tiered structure in *Wright & Wright*'s renovation of 2014–16. Externally the new work shows as an excavated basement floor of ashlared walls, coming forward from the old building into the quad, and extending also as a top-lit reading room along the w side. But what hits the eye ahead of all this is the enormous terrace composed of stone steps, sloped paving and plant beds that takes the ground level down to the new entrance. Could a simpler ramp not have done the job?

GROVE BUILDINGS stand N of Longwall Quad, on a different alignment close against the wall. By *Demetri Porphyrios*, designed 1991, built 1994–8, after *Ian Ritchie*'s High Tech proposals of 1990 were set aside. The style is mostly a sort of pared-down Cotswold-collegiate – complete with purely ornamental chimneys – as if picking up from where Giles Gilbert Scott left off in 1930. The exception is the auditorium on the w side, an instance of the architect's stripped Neoclassical-cum-Tuscan mode, with its own little octagonal entrance pavilion, s. A Gothic screen wall links the auditorium to a battlemented gate tower against the w range. Load-bearing walls and good Ketton stone ashlar throughout. As a composition the quad suffers from the lack of the intended N range, leaving the NW angle unresolved. Two STATUES from *Pugin*'s gateway of 1844, one (Waynflete) in the w loggia, the other (St Mary Magdalene) in a niche, facing N.

THE GARDENS AND HOLYWELL FORD

The GARDENS of Magdalen are bewilderingly large. They include THE GROVE or DEER PARK N and w of New Building, which took on its present informal character in the C19, and the water meadow between the mill stream and the Cherwell, which is bounded by the raised path now known as ADDISON'S WALK. Between water meadow and grove, just N of the college wall and not normally accessible to visitors, are the buildings of HOLYWELL FORD. The stone house of this name was built for himself by *C. C. Rolfe* in 1888, replacing an old mill. L-plan, placed cleverly round and over the mill stream. Interesting Arts and Crafts work, especially the w end with its blunt bow window set askew. HOLYWELL FORD QUAD, for graduates, extends N and E from the house. Three buildings of 1994–5 by the *RH Partnership* of Cambridge, pitched somewhere between Neo-vernacular and Postmodern. Yellow-brown brick with cast-stone dressings. The smallest of the buildings is treated as a gate tower to a bridge across the stream. Gables and cross-gables on the others. w of this group are SQUASH COURTS by *Porphyrios Associates*, 1994–6. Surprisingly monumental, without embracing a particular historical style. Three courts, with changing rooms etc. and a viewing gallery. To the front a round-arched loggia with a timber loggia above. Big staircase drum to the l. The material is reused red brick.

A few things to note in the gardens further E. By the NE angle of Addison's Walk, GATES of wrought iron, C18. Brought in 1955 from Joseph Addison's Bilton Hall, near Rugby. Across the Cherwell footbridge from here, in Bat Willow Meadow, a quizzical steel SCULPTURE by *Mark Wallinger*, 2008. Called 'Y'. The shaft or trunk splits in two, each arm bifurcating on the fractal principle to make a flat schematic tree.

For the LONGWALL ANNEXE, High Street, *see* Perambulation 1, p. 415; for the DAUBENY BUILDING *see* the Botanic Garden, p. 349; for the WAYNFLETE BUILDING, St Clement's Street, *see* Perambulation 7, p. 450.

MANSFIELD COLLEGE
Mansfield Road

Mansfield College started in 1838 as Spring Hill College at Birmingham, a theological training college chiefly for Congregationalists. It was transferred to Oxford in 1886 (cf. Harris Manchester), and the buildings were erected in 1887–9 at a cost of £40,000. The designer was *Basil Champneys*, with furnishings by the Cheshire architect *George Faulkner Armitage*; the unsuccessful competitor was *Waterhouse*, who offered something along French Renaissance lines. Mansfield became a Permanent Private Hall in 1955, a full college in 1995. The name commemorates the family who founded the college at Birmingham.

The C19 BUILDINGS are Gothic, of the later C14 period when mature Dec was making way for Early Perp. On Mansfield Road they don't make much of a show, as one comes in on the E side not through any gateway or lodge. Seen from the spacious quad, however, they are remarkably lavish. The principal elements are clearly indicated on the three sides: the chapel placed N–S along the street to the E, high and with high windows above narrow aisle passages with lean-to roofs, and a high attachment housing the organ; the hall on the first floor of the N range with its generous bow window, and the gate tower next to it; the library in the W range, again on the upper floor, with five broad canted oriels and another to the S. Below the library are lecture rooms; behind and to the W are the Principal's Lodgings, and then the garden. Throughout Champneys's Gothic there is an enjoyable freedom of handling, especially in the size, type and placing of openings in his Taynton stone-faced walls. The gate tower incidentally lacks an answering gateway to the N, as there is no access from that side.

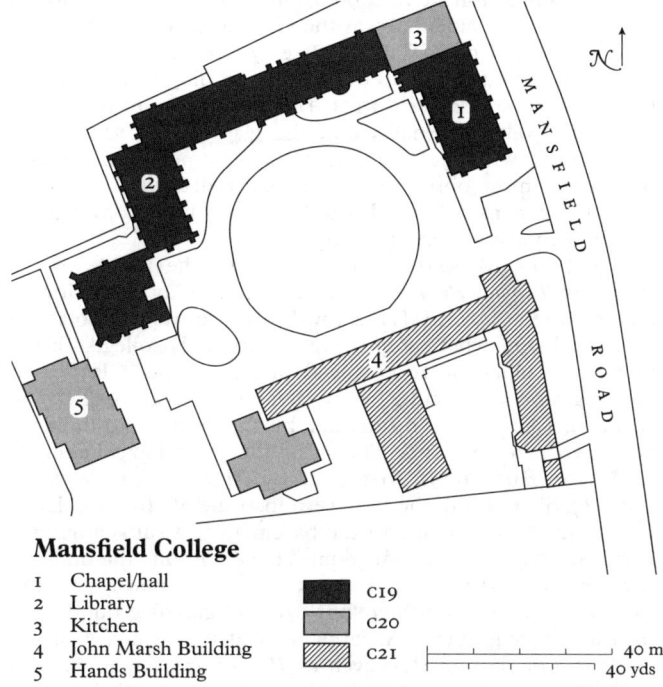

Mansfield College

1   Chapel/hall
2   Library
3   Kitchen
4   John Marsh Building
5   Hands Building

	C19
	C20
	C21

40 m
40 yds

The CHAPEL was made so large because it was meant as a place of worship for all the University's Nonconformist students. The inside is lined with Bath stone. The aisle passages are divided into two bays for each window bay, and an oversized statuary niche is corbelled out above each of the subdividing piers. STATUES inside and out by *Robert Bridgeman* of Lichfield. Half-tunnel vaults to the aisles, thin diaphragm arches of stone to support the panelled main ceiling. Finely carved FURNISHINGS of oak: presbyter's chair and lavish stalls at the N end, pulpit with mighty tester on the E wall, thin screen across the S end. STAINED GLASS by *Joseph Bell & Sons*, N wall (1889), *Shrigley & Hunt*, S wall (1890), and *W. Aikman* of *Powells*, side walls (1906–7). The HALL with its sturdy arch-braced roof is modest by comparison. The windows which externally seem to continue it westward are those of the Senior Common Room. But the LIBRARY with its ingenious timberwork is far from disappointing. Although there is one big roof over the whole, slim timber posts divide it into nave and aisles, the aisles being the reading cubicles. There is a gallery as well, exceptionally low. From the posts arched braces rise to collar-beams, arched braces from the collar-beams to the ridge, arched braces longitudinally from post to post, and raking braces to the aisle part of the roof. Champneys must have enjoyed designing it. The ceiling panels received their prettily painted foliage in 1896, from *Powells*. The route to the library begins, incidentally, at the rib-vaulted GATE PASSAGE, with its bust of Robert William Dale by *E. Onslow Ford, c.*1897.

The chapel now doubles uneasily as a dining hall, facilitated by *Rick Mather Architects'* KITCHEN of 2013–14 to its N. This has stone walls externally, and the glass-walled STAIRCASE in the angle with the hall goes with it. Somehow this glassy insertion is more obtrusive than a solid wall might have been. The old kitchens below hall and SCR have been converted to a café, with a sunk terrace alongside.

The JOHN MARSH BUILDING forms the S side of the quad. By *Thomas Rayson*, 1960–2: a late display of traditional architecture at Oxford. Long, low L-plan, restrained Cotswold ashlar, all somewhat reminiscent of Nuffield College. To the W a taller block of 2006, faced in pale stone. Glass-sided meeting rooms projecting below. By *Kieran Whiteman* of *Oxford Architects*. An earlier residential block, design-and-build of 1992 by *Brewer, Smith & Brewer*, on the central axis behind.

HANDS BUILDING, to the W. By *Rick Mather Architects*, 2016–17. Shared with the Bonavero Institute of Human Rights, part of the Law Faculty. In the basement is a sunken auditorium. Seventy-four student rooms above. Visually the building is weak: a long straggle of set-backs to the r., a poorly resolved mansard and an unsettling shift from all-glazed ground floor to ashlar facing above. An apparatus of ramps etc. in front. – STATUE of Eleanor Roosevelt by *Penelope Jencks*, 2018.

On the lawn, SCULPTURE by *Antony Gormley*, called Present Time, 2001 (installed 2013). A headless figure balances inverted on top of another.

For the ABLETHORPE BUILDING in Cowley Road *see* Perambulation 7, p.452.

MERTON COLLEGE
Merton Street

Merton is Oxford's earliest college, in the sense of an endowed, self-governing academic community in purpose-built accommodation. Balliol and University colleges can both point to older origins, but it was Merton, in the 1260s–70s, that became the collegiate model.

In 1262 Walter de Merton, lately appointed King's Chancellor and future Bishop of Rochester, obtained licence to vest the Surrey manors of Malden and Farleigh for the support of clerks 'in studio degentium' ('studying in a university'). Though not named, Oxford is clearly meant, and in 1263–4 Walter set up eight nephews here and made provision for more students not his own kin. A statute was approved in 1264, the first in either university. It names the figure of twenty and it names Oxford but adds 'or

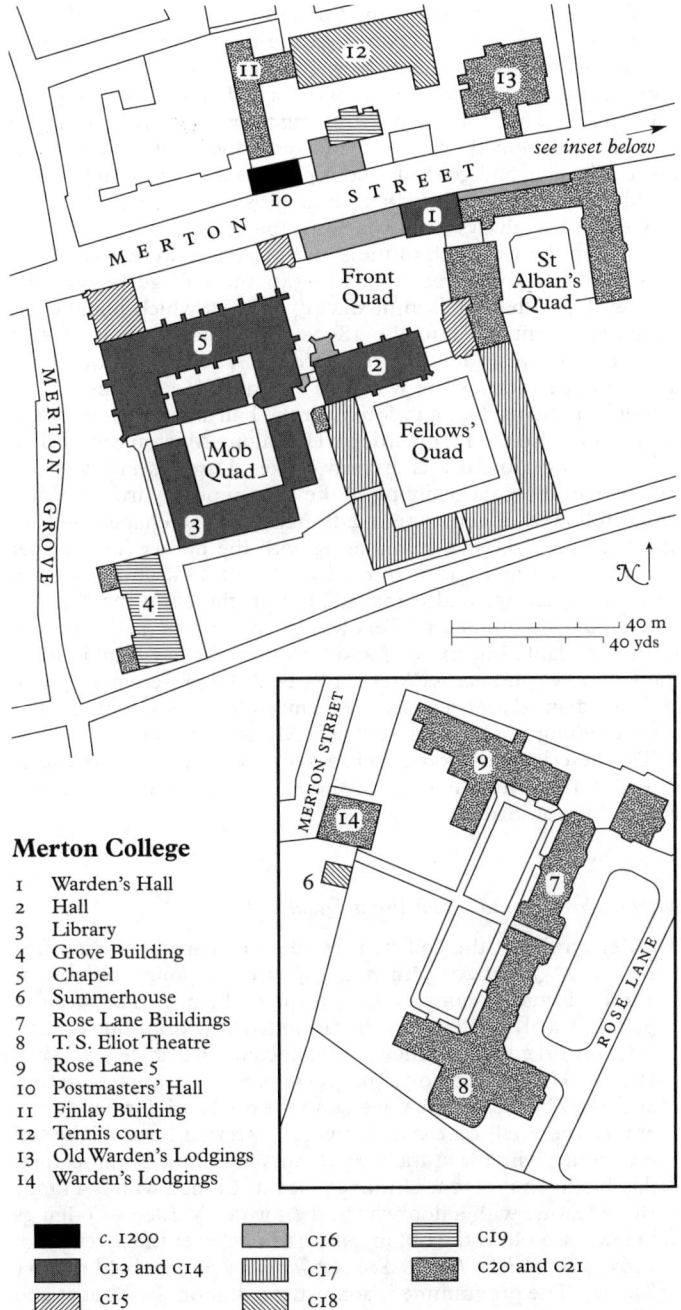

Merton College

1   Warden's Hall
2   Hall
3   Library
4   Grove Building
5   Chapel
6   Summerhouse
7   Rose Lane Buildings
8   T. S. Eliot Theatre
9   Rose Lane 5
10 Postmasters' Hall
11 Finlay Building
12 Tennis court
13 Old Warden's Lodgings
14 Warden's Lodgings

c. 1200
C13 and C14
C15
C16
C17
C18
C19
C20 and C21

somewhere else' ('vel alibi'). Initially, indeed, the foundation had its Warden and chaplains at the Surrey end. Then in 1266 Walter began to buy property in Oxford, including St John's church, and to enhance the endowment. New statutes in 1274 established a corporation of between thirty and forty Fellows, teaching the Liberal Arts while themselves studying for a higher degree. These statutes also imply the provision of a hall, chapel, library, lodgings for the Warden, and general accommodation. In 1280 Archbishop Peckham referred to the establishment as a *collegium*.

Merton has always been spacious, thanks to grants of Crown land up to the city wall, to the S and SE. There were early holdings N of Merton Street too. In 1549 the college bought the medieval St Alban Hall immediately to its E, which maintained an independent life into the 1890s. Finally in 1729 land E of the city wall was added to the gardens. The earliest buildings are therefore towards the W, where a remarkable amount of C13 evidence remains: first and foremost the hall and the choir of the chapel, but also the first Warden's Hall along Merton Street. The loose placing around a courtyard evokes a great secular house, rather than the tight planning of the contemporary friaries. Mob Quad followed, a complete quadrangle S of the chapel, built in stages up to 1378 and culminating with the library. The chapel acquired transepts and a tower in the C14–C15, and additions to Front Quad were also made. Then in the early C17 Warden Savile built the influential Fellows' Quad, S of the hall. The C18 is all but blank, but the C19 and C20 brought new buildings to the E and SW, and across Merton Street. The pre-eminent phase is Edwardian: *Basil Champneys*'s former Warden's Lodgings, and his rebuilding of St Alban Hall as a Mertonian quad.

The description is loosely chronological, following the quads in order, then the buildings in the eastern gardens, and finally across Merton Street.

Merton Street frontage and Front Quad

To Merton Street the college presents the chapel, standing free to the W (*see* p. 201), then a gap, then a long and much-altered frontage comprising two quads behind. The western part is FRONT QUAD, medieval and C16 within, but on this side reworked in a fancy and affected Dec style by *Blore*, 1837–8. His are the polygonal turrets, niche canopies, statues and gateway arch to the tower, and the oriel and dormer details etc. to the E, all renewed. Only the traceried head of the tall transomed window at the E represents a true medieval feature, datable to 1299–1300. Until 1937 it was framed within a fancy Blore feature with a doorway to the former Warden's Lodgings below. Also old is the oblong SCULPTURE over the gateway, of 1463–4 by *Robert Janyns Sen. & Janyns Jun.* (probably *Henry Janyns*). The programme is sophisticated: John the Baptist and Walter de Merton, respectively standing and kneeling r., with the Life of Christ represented emblematically by Unicorn,

Lamb, Pelican, Dove and Lion, amid a grove of trees. The central item is the Book of the Seven Seals from Revelation. Last restored 1954. Original doors below.

Joining on to the E is ST ALBAN'S QUAD, a composite of a two-storey frontage of 1599 below and an Edwardian gable storey and E section. The newer parts are of 1904–7 by *Champneys*, who swept away every other vestige of the former St Alban Hall.* The C16 doorway – rather crude, with coupled Tuscan columns and a small semicircular top feature – is Oxford's oldest surviving external show of a classical order. It probably owes something to the involvement of Sir Henry Savile, Warden of Merton. Window hoodmoulds linked by continuous horizontal strings, another early appearance for Oxford.

In FRONT QUAD it is the hall to the S, the chapel to the W that dominate. But first the NORTH SIDE, here of rubble masonry and Blore-free. The GATE TOWER with its projecting SW stair-turret is partly of 1416–18, with renovations *c.* 1455–71. Besides the sculpture already noted, these include the two bays of tierceron-star vaulting with carved bosses. To the W a single staircase of the C15, remodelled in 1631 and again in the 1830s; to the E a longer section rebuilt straightforwardly in 1589–91. But the projecting and crenellated E part of this range is of 1299–1300, perhaps incorporating some walls from a still older house, and was once the *parva aula* or WARDEN'S HALL, i.e. the hall of his Lodgings. It has longer windows than the rest, all renewed. The tracery has the same trio of convex-sided triangles as the N window already seen. The interior, now MIDDLE COMMON ROOM, is reached by a staircase and screens of 1937. In 1969–71 the roof was exposed and restored. It has tie-beams, shaped queenposts to collar-beams with arched braces, and crown-posts supporting upper collar-beams: the earliest-known example of this two-tier roof type (*see also* Introduction, p. 18).

To the S of here originally were the Warden's chamber and service quarters. This part, rebuilt in the C15, was replaced by *Champneys* in a very pretty free C16 style in connection with his St Alban's Quad (p. 207), with a twin archway through. In the SW angle more of the original WARDEN'S LODGINGS survive, as built or rebuilt for Warden Fitzjames (1483–1507). Crenellated, with mullioned-and-transomed upper windows of arched lights. The short S range connecting with the hall dates from 1497. It incorporates the GATEWAY to Fellows' Quad (p. 206). The passage is wide and low, with an excellent lierne vault with exceptionally good sculpted bosses of the Signs of the Zodiac. Virgo is especially attractive; so is Sagittarius. WAR MEMORIAL on the E wall, simple lettered panels of 1922, designed by *Comper*. The adjacent rooms here have on their S side a large through-storey bay window, externally renewed. The ground-floor room retains the C15 stone soffit

---

*The original dormer storey had been clumsily rebuilt with a C13 look in renovations by *John Gibbs*, 1863–6.

to this bay, panelled in a sophisticated pattern of tessellation. Also a late C18 copy of a Perp fireplace with quatrefoil frieze. Access to these INTERIORS is via a passage from the E side with a vault of plain cross-ribs and ridge ribs on carved corbels. Open-well staircase of the 1620s, compact in plan but lively in decoration: newels carved with square quasi-rusticated blocks, squared pendants, tapering squared finials, slim turned balusters. It connected with the Long Gallery originally made for the Warden within the E side of Fellows' Quad. In the circulation spaces also some amateurish Gothic doorways and plaster vaulting, done for the Tsar's visit in 1814. Other rooms show *Champneys*'s hand, with fine joinery in a free C17 style and plasterwork of slightly later inspiration.

The HALL is C13, albeit thoroughly restored by *Scott* in 1870–2. It was almost certainly in progress in 1270, and by 1277 was in use. There must then have been a detached kitchen, somewhere to the S. The hall is raised on an undercroft, vaulted in 1785. So the entrance – on axis with the gate tower, after the manner of secular mansions – is reached up steps. A porch-tower of 1579 encloses these. The front of this porch is *Scott*'s, but the higher stair-turret dates from *Wyatt*'s renovations of 1790–2. The hall windows were altered then too. Scott returned them to the C13 form indicated by fragments found built-in, i.e. slender transomed double lights with pointed trefoiled heads; but he also introduced ashlaring, buttresses and crenellations not shown in Loggan's C17 view. Inner doorway with double-chamfered continuous moulding. Large original DOOR with gorgeous ironwork, scrolls terminating in stamped rosettes, combined with hinges still of the older C-and-strap type. The INTERIOR is some 77 ft (23.5 metres) long. It retains the C13 window embrasures and stone seats. The fine roof is *Scott*'s, replacing Wyatt's plaster vault. It is of the original steep pitch and has sub-cusped-arched braces and wind-braces. Panelling etc. obviously also *Scott*; made by *Farmer & Brindley*. Heraldic stained glass by *Burlison & Grylls*, 1877–91. The window and doorway inserted in the screens passage W wall are early C16.

On the W side the hall is continued by a small recessed ARCHWAY or enclosed bridge of Warden Rawlins's time, i.e. 1508–21. The screens passage and hall were thereby connected with the turret stair of the chapel sacristy. This SACRISTY, now Choir Room, was begun in 1310. Its twin three-light windows put it among the earliest firmly datable English examples of tracery with reticulation units. The stair-turret projects to the SW, also apparently of original form. It may relate to an earlier covered route from the hall, possibly timber-built (cf. the four corbels on the hall's gable-end). In 1886 *Jackson* restored the sacristy, and the roof with side dormers is his, supposedly after the original form.

Until 1960 the passage to the S was filled with kitchen extensions etc. Now it is interrupted by a stone-faced half-octagon, housing a LIFT TOWER to the Senior Common Room. By

Berman Guedes Stretton, 2016–17. The w side is the E range of Mob Quad.

Mob Quad, with Grove Building

MOB QUAD is entirely late C13 and C14, the earliest complete   13
Oxford quad, though unlikely to have been projected as such at
the outset. It is of two storeys, and until 1874 it was roughcast.
The N part of the E range came first. It is through this sturdy
EXCHEQUER BUILDING that one enters the quad. Payment
for window locks was made in 1288, so it must have been
finished by then. The ground floor is divided equally between
two sections, each with two cells of quadripartite rib-vaults.
The S section comprises the entrance passage, formerly closed
with doors to E and W; the N section is fully enclosed as the
EXCHEQUER. Both parts have round abaci to the wall-shafts,
and vault-ribs with a broad fillet of typical profile. On the quad
side a canted projection with a broad spiral stair to the TREAS-
URY above. This occupies the entire floor. Roof of stone slabs
(renewed in Purbeck stone by *Robert Potter*, 1963–6), carried on
three plain stone cross-arches. The consistent use of stone was
to make the Treasury fireproof and secure. Two small windows
of 'Caernarvon' type; floor with the original plain tiles. The
older muniment cupboards are probably late C16.

The EAST RANGE continues as a plain range of lodgings,
probably the 'nova camera' begun 1299–1300. The NORTH
RANGE is of *c.* 1304–11. Here the living arrangements have
been deduced: chambers with three or four sleeping spaces off,
each with a small window, including one in the end wall. Both
these ranges are built of coral rag. The SOUTH SIDE and WEST
SIDE are of 1370–8, after a donation by Bishop Rede of Chichester, and use Wheatley stone. The first floor here includes
the library, i.e. it has a dog-leg plan. The master mason was
William Humberville of Taynton. With John Bloxham, Clerk
of Works and future Warden, Humberville went on preparatory inspection visits in connection, including to the London
Blackfriars. The model may descend from the Sorbonne library
in Paris.

The windows all round Mob Quad differ a great deal in
shape and date. The cusped single lights represent the C14,
of which those of the library are closely spaced. The straight-
headed, moulded two-light windows represent the C15 and
C16. One, S side, has kept its cusps. The big four-light library
dormers were added probably *c.* 1589, W side, and *c.* 1623, S side
(*see* interior, below). Arched lights and semicircular cresting on
these. On the other two sides the commonest dormer pattern
dates probably from 1874. Inspection of the outer sides to W
and S shows the upper lancets to have cusped ogee arches
under square frames. Also a larger window of two lights with
transom and Early Perp tracery, S side W, and a broad oriel of
1623 (renewed 1959) on the S side E face. This marks where the

library expanded into the chamber formerly there. Two Perp ground-floor windows, W side N, as late as 1928 (*T.H. Hughes*). The doorways also differ around the quad, and deserve study. The W range has a through-passage doorway corresponding to that on the E, but of broader proportions. The wall-shafts within have polygonal, not round, abaci to the capitals. But the most elaborate doorway is in the S range: moulded and shafted jambs, sub-cusped quatrefoils in the spandrels, plain C14 door. Until 1959 it was the library's principal entrance.

LIBRARY INTERIOR. Access is by a straight staircase with coarse vertically symmetrical balusters, i.e. probably of *c.*1623, emerging mid-floor. The panelled and canted ceiling was made by *John Fisher* in 1502–3, with small bosses partly carved, partly of metal. Above is the C14 trussed-rafter roof (carpenter *Robert Bath*). The FURNISHINGS are of Warden Savile's time, the W wing 1588–9 (joiner *Thomas Key*), the S wing 1623. Shelves, about 7 ft (2.1 metres) high, project at right angles between the window bays, separated by a middle passage. Reading boards attached to the shelves; low benches. Here then is Oxford's first library to adopt the stall system, i.e. with reading spaces defined by parallel bookshelves instead of the old, low lecterns. No earlier example survives anywhere, and it may indeed be the founding example of library stalls. Savile's friend Sir Thomas Bodley was quick to adopt them for his renovation of Duke Humfrey's Library (*see* p.335). Decorative motifs are modest and characteristic of the period. Against the end gables simple broad-banded plasterwork with vine scroll and grape bunches. Also some panelling, and the original N door. The charming arched portals to the shelved sections are probably of 1623, when the TILES of the floor were replaced with salvaged medieval ones. Some are patterned: rose traceries, a rabbit etc.

STAINED GLASS. The seven windows in the E wall of the W range contain late C14 glass with a trellis of patterned quarries, sundry borders, and in the upper part a roundel bearing the Agnus Dei or a dragon. There are four types of quarries and two sizes of roundels. Other windows contain C14–C16 fragments, including many inscriptions, pieces of figures and some complete tracery lights from the chapel. Of later glass the S range includes interesting C13-style designs of 1858 by *John James Laing*, sometime assistant to Ruskin, and made by *Powells* (MH). Also a nice scrapbook-ish memorial window by *R. Anning Bell*, 1925. But the big E window has twelve panels of Continental glass, probably Rhenish, in a setting of 1841. Each has a figure subject from the Passion, flanked by Virtues and Vices and set about with merchants' marks, shields of arms and a series of names with the date 1598.

The ground storey below is now MOB LIBRARY, converted for that use in 1904–7 and 1928, then remodelled by *S.E. Dykes Bower*, an old member, in 1958–9. The first-floor chamber of the W range, N end, was made the BEERBOHM ROOM in 1956. It has two little re-fixed frescoes by *Max Beerbohm* himself (another Mertonian), one illustrating his *Zuleika Dobson* (1911), the other of Rossetti, Swinburne and Jane Burden.

GROVE BUILDING stands detached, SW of Mob Quad. Of 1863–4 by *Butterfield*, but chastened in 1929–30 by *T.H. Hughes*, lately also busy at Corpus next door. The top storey was removed, two wings added to the W to compensate, and all faced or refaced in Cotswolds Tudor. Goodhart-Rendel, in *Vitruvian Nights* (1932), called the result 'something of the sort that Americans expect to find at Oxford...almost as slavishly Tudor as a modern public house'. Contrary to legend, Butterfield used plain stonework, reserving patterned brick for the staircase interiors. Earlier proposals for Butterfield to extend Mob itself, encompassing the demolition of its S side, were foiled by a general outcry.

Between the wings is a triangular OBELISK of 1931 with a carved flame on top. It commemorates the mountaineer Andrew Comyn Irvine †1924, and is by *Eric Gill*.

Chapel

The CHAPEL, for all its grandeur, is in one respect incomplete, for it was meant to have a nave and aisles. If it had, to any reasonable length, the whole would have been at least 200 ft and more probably 240 ft (61 or 73 metres). That is the size of a medium priory church. As it is, the C14 and C15 added transepts, crossing and tower to the C13 choir, but nave and aisles were never built. So Merton chapel came to correspond with the Oxford T-plan type introduced in the late C14 at New College – except that it has fully realized transepts by way of an antechapel, and a tower worthy of a great town church. The chapel did indeed double as the parish church of St John, an arrangement that ended only in 1891.

The CHOIR is well dated. Work started just before 1290 and roofing took place in 1296–7. Already in 1290 worked stone for the tracery was being bought. The window details fit such a date to perfection, and are one of the best late C13 sequences in the country. The E window is huge, of seven lights, all pointed-trefoil-cusped and with, in the head, a roundel of twelve spokes, all also pointed-trefoil-cusped. The three-plus-three side parts have intersecting tracery. This combination of intersecting tracery with a roundel destroying its even rhythm is typical of the latest C13. Exceptionally, the main lights also introduce elements of miniature architecture: open gablets with big finials inside the upper arch heads – a tracery motif taken from St Urbain at Troyes, begun 1262 – and slim pinnacles rising between these arches into the sharply stretched quatrefoils above. Sub-cusping also appears, echoed in the little triangular window in the gable. To each side is a gablet-headed buttress, ornamented with a motif of two blind lights with traceried gable and pinnacles at the sides.

The N side, which is the other show side, continues this buttress type, deployed within a tightly controlled, ashlar-faced design. Here the sills of the buttress lights are linked above the window heads as a running hoodmould, and the sills of the windows themselves are also joined across the buttresses – as too is the E window – by means of gabled set-offs. Windows of three lights, less intricate in their tracery than the E window. Spherical triangles appear, with unencircled trefoils, daggers and other Late Geometrical motifs. The patterns recur, A–B–C–D–A–B–C on both sides, with the lancets below finishing at different heights as required. Above is a finely carved string with heads alternating with foliage. Finally, at the level of this string the buttresses have giant human-figure gargoyles, horizontally projecting. Chief carver for the 1960s renewals here was *Percy Quick*.

The CROSSING was in progress in 1330/1. Parts of the SOUTH TRANSEPT may also date from the 1330s. Later in the C14 it was hemmed in by the W side of Mob Quad. Its present windows are early C15. For the NORTH TRANSEPT the recorded completion dates are 1419–21. Spectacular seven-light N window here, its design taken from the E window of Winchester College chapel (1387–95) by William Wynford. The key features include subdivision by two major mullions, and subsidiary arches with distinctively composed tracery defining each outer group of three lights. Extra motifs not at Winchester are the sub-cusping throughout, and brattishing to the transom. Elaborate canopied niches to l. and r. (restored 1901), with STATUES of the Virgin and St John the Baptist, more late C15 than *c.*1420 in style. The deeply modelled doorway below allowed access from the street for parishioners. In the gable a triangular window, below the main window a decorated string: both echoes of the C13 choir. Three-light windows to the transept sides. The main W window (six lights) is Perp too. (The more pointed arch above, and the lower arches to N and S, were meant for the C14 nave.) This W window may be the 'nova fenestra' mentioned in 1476/7. Here, as also in the S transept S window (five lights, *c.*1415), the main lights have ogee heads, the tracery has super-transoms, and sub-cusping is absent. Otherwise the designs are altogether different, nor does either match the N window – quite a contrast with the orderly antechapels of New College and All Souls.

The broad and stately CROSSING TOWER was erected only in 1448–52. *Robert Janyns Sen.* was in charge in 1448–9, and in 1451 was still called master of the works at Merton. Its lower stage is plain unmodulated ashlar. The bell-stage has to each side two three-light openings with super-mullioned panel tracery, of the type (also in the W window) that has cusped arches at the bottom as well as the top of each panel. A band of blind quatrefoils above, then an openwork embattled parapet with pinnacles placed at the corners and centrally.

INTERIOR. The usual entry is by the S transept. All is on a grand scale, very lofty and very spacious. The climax is the crossing.

The E arch here was in progress in 1294, and the other arches follow its design. Tremendous piers, six shafts to each side of each pier, except that those for the intended nave have only five. Bases and capitals and arch mouldings are all typically Dec. The choir windows are shafted inside, and there are also wall-shafts starting from the running hoodmould that links the springing of the window arches. Excellent corbels here, carved mostly with plants or human heads. The C13 roof, of scissor-braced paired rafters, has a replacement ceiling of 1849–50 by the young *Butterfield*. He took the design of canted boarding and cross-ribs from Grantchester church, Cambs. Its PAINT-ING with well-judged foliage and figure roundels is of 1850 by *J. Hungerford Pollen*, amateur artist, Pre-Raphaelite associate, Tractarian and Fellow of Merton until he turned Roman Catholic. Pollen returned in 1877 to decorate the walls, but this was purged in 1969. The ornate group of SEDILIA, PISCINA and S doorway was also largely renewed in *Butterfield*'s restoration. The pretty ringing gallery round the crossing tower above the arches is however of 1843–4, from an earlier phase of work by *Edward Blore*. That exposed the panelled wooden vault inside the tower, a sophisticated design like a hammerbeam roof folded square: tunnel-vaulted central axes, rib-vaults at the corners, angel bosses at the four main points, and a bell-rope hole in the middle. Possibly by a carpenter named *Grofe* or *Grove*, employed at Merton 1448–52. Transept roofs by *Blore*, in place of early C16 oak ceilings. High blank dado panelling to the N transept N wall. In the S transept is a DOUBLE PISCINA, its motifs puzzlingly more *c.*1300 than *c.*1330–40.

FURNISHINGS. ALTAR. The surround is *Comper*'s, 1923, Italian Renaissance, black and gold, as it seemed to suit the ALTARPIECE, a good Crucifixion of the school of Tintoretto. – Linenfold PANELLING of the sanctuary also by *Comper*, 1910–11. – STALLS by *Butterfield*, 1851. – CHAMBER ORGAN. Mid-C18; given 1968. Walnut case. Previously at Hawkestone Park, Shropshire. – LECTERN. Of brass, with an *orate* inscription for Richard Martock †1503. An outstandingly fine piece, not in the least showy. It is of the gabled, i.e. double-reading-desk type (like those of Eton and King's College chapels). – CANDELABRA. Two, of brass. Spanish. Acquired in the 1960s. – TILES. *Butterfield*'s choir floor mixes new encaustic tiles with reused black and white marble of 1671. – SCREEN. Designed by *Wren* and made by the Oxford joiner *John Ransford*, 1671–3. Dismantled by Butterfield, then in 1960 reinstated w of its original position, with some matching work. High, of three arches, with Corinthian columns or pilasters. Over the middle arch an open scrolly pediment.* – ORGAN, against the w wall and window. A Gothic extravaganza by *Dobson* of Lake City, Iowa, 2013. – FONT, N transept. With a big spired COVER. By

*The medieval screen also stood one bay E of the crossing. Parts of Wren's new stalls survive in Cuxham church (q.v.), and at Radley College, Berks. An early C18 PULPIT is now at Botley church, Berks.

Butterfield, 1851. – BOWL, moved from the Warden's Lodgings. A gorgeous piece of green Siberian malachite with an elliptical bowl. Given by Tsar Alexander I, it arrived in 1822. – CHALICE of engraved glass, in a case. By *Laurence Whistler*, in memory of T.S. Eliot (†1965). – STATUE, s transept. Mary, Seat of Wisdom. Gilded and painted wood. By *Peter Ball*, given 2014.

STAINED GLASS. The windows of the CHOIR constitute a united programme. Except for the two easternmost of the s wall, all fourteen LATERAL WINDOWS bear the name of the donor, Henry Mansfield (de Mamesfeld). He was a Fellow in 1288–96, later Dean of Lincoln, and died in 1328. The glass can be identified as the work of *William*, glazier of Thame, and dated from payments for deliveries in 1310/11, i.e. during Mansfield's time as Chancellor of the University (1309–12). This date is also consistent with the use of ogees for some of the canopy arches, as *c.*1290–1300 would not be. Likewise, the band type of composition used here was more widespread by 1310 than ten or so years before, when this form – which is of northern French origin – made an early appearance at York Minster. The band consists of gesturing figures under canopies, in rich coloured glass, offset against white glass with grisaille patterns. Here these groundwork patterns are geometric, painted with trails of ivy, oak or maple leaves; borders of ivy, maple or vine leaves, or an alternation of castles and fleur-de-lys patterns. In the middle of the main lights are mostly Apostles or Evangelists with their attributes, under crocketed and pinnacled canopies; in the lower and upper main lights are roundels with decorative designs or heads of kings and queens, also a head of Christ and a Pelican in her Piety. The main figures all turn towards the altar. Also there is a huge replication of pairs of scholar figures in hooded gown and cap of varied colours, barely smaller than the main figures towards which they kneel, and each with the inscription 'Magister Henricus de Mamesfeld me fecit' ('Master Henry Mansfield made me'). Much good restoration, very difficult to detect: by *Powells* in the 1850s, and especially by *Samuel Caldwell Jun.* of Canterbury 1931–3, but most of the figure panels are original. In the N windows the subjects are, E to W: St Peter; St Andrew; St Matthew(?); uncertain; St Bartholomew; St James the Less(?); uncertain. s windows, E to W: first two windows, saints (in the first an archbishop, St Paul, St Nicholas; in the second St Lawrence, St Simon(?), St Stephen). In the remaining five windows, central figures of St Thomas; St Mark (or Matthew?); St James the Great; uncertain; St John the Evangelist.

EAST WINDOW. Only the tracery glass is original and *in situ*, though much restored, particularly the decorative foliage lights. In the upper l. large quatrefoil is the Archangel Gabriel, forming a pendant to the upper r. quatrefoil with the Virgin Annunciate. At the centre of the rose three shields of arms, showing the advancing fashion for heraldry in the visual arts: the royal arms of England; a variant of the same; Clare (below). The seven main lights probably showed a Christological scene.

The present assembly here dates from 1934–6, devised by *Sir Walter Tapper*; again restored and re-leaded 1969–72. It gathers glass from the transepts and elsewhere, including armorial glass made for the hall and Warden Fitzjames's lodgings. In the lowest tiers fourteen shields of arms, chiefly later C15–early C16. Next tier, mostly early C15 panels from the transepts: Seraphim; Crucifixion, with the Virgin and St John (composites); Benedictine abbess saint; Virgin and Child; Benedictine abbess saint (Frideswide?); St John the Evangelist; Seraph, with Saint (composite). The four larger figures must be from the N transept. Although truncated, they are outstanding examples of glass-painting, very probably from the workshop or circle of *Thomas*, glazier of Oxford (*see* New College chapel). Next tier, shields of arms as below. Quarries, decorative roundels and borders largely 1930s.

ANTECHAPEL. What remains of the early C15 glazing here is gathered in the central WEST WINDOW, as reordered in the 1930s. Hard to see now, with the organ in the way. Canopy-work in the heads of the main lights, two main types, in varying stages of completeness. In the tracery lights mostly relocated figures. Beginning at the lower l., first tier: Apostle(?) (composite; head alien); St Christopher carrying the Christ Child; St John the Baptist; St Philip; St Bartholomew; St James the Less; St Simon; Apostle with alien female head; St Matthew; St Ethelbert; St George; Apostle (head alien). Second tier: a deacon saint; St Paul; St Peter; St Andrew; St James the Great; the Virgin; St Thomas; St James the Less; St Thomas of Hereford; a scholar. Third tier: fragments; figure at a parapet; St Barbara(?); Archangel Gabriel; Virgin Annunciate (pendant to the preceding); king; composite figure; fragments.

The NORTH TRANSEPT displays suspended panels from *William Price Sen.*'s former E window of 1702. W window, Crucifixion (across three lights); N window, Nativity, Last Supper, Baptism of Christ (two, three, two lights); E window, Resurrection and Ascension (two and two lights). Murky scenes, derived from Raphael and Tintoretto. Placed here in 2000.

BRASSES. N transept. (Richard de Hakeborne †1322. Bust only remaining, 14 in. (36 cm.).) – Robert de Tring †1351, tiny figure in the remains of an ogee octofoil. – John Bloxham, Warden, and John Whytton, priest and benefactor. Of c.1420. Two small figures (20 in.; 51 cm.) on a bracket under a double canopy. The bracket is on the top of a staff. – Warden Henry Sever †1471. Splendid figure 5 ft 8 in. long (1.72 metres), under a canopy. The orphreys with saints. – S transept. John Killingworth †1445. 9½-in. (24-cm.) demi-figure. – John Bowke †1519, 12-in. (31-cm.) demi-figure, alongside.

MONUMENTS. N transept. Sir Thomas Bodley, founder of the 42 Bodleian Library, †1613. Alabaster and marble. By *Nicholas Stone*, 1615, his first work at Oxford. It cost £200. Large hanging monument with an unusually sophisticated programme. Bodley's bust frontal in an oval recess. The surround has figures in relief, representing four of the Liberal Arts: Music, Arithmetic,

Dialectic, Rhetoric. To their l. and r. pilasters built up entirely of books laid flat one on top of the other, fore-edges outwards. The nude figure at the bottom, seated in relief, represents Grammar, the beginning of higher education. So she holds a key and on the l. is an open doorway to an ascending stair. Her elbow rests on books of the grammarians Donatus, Diomedes and Priscianus. On the pediment recline Geometry and Astronomy, their attributes at their feet. Minerva, standing, presides at the top. The identity of the outer standing figures is uncertain.* – Anthony (à) Wood, the Oxford antiquary, †1695. Small cartouche, supporting a crest. – Henry Jackson †1727. Bewigged bust in a big Corinthian aedicule. – Anne Wyrtle †1746, with Robert Wyrtle †1750. Not large. Nice allegorical figures; phoenix at the top. Attributed to *Sir Henry Cheere* (GF). – Dr J. Coleridge Patteson †1871, first Bishop of Melanesia. By *Woolner*, 1875. Tablet. Below he lies slain; above is his bust, and l. and r. Melanesian plants.

s transept. Sir Henry Savile, Warden of Merton, †1622. Large hanging wall monument. Frontal demi-figure, handling a book. Statuettes l. and r. of St John Chrysostom, Ptolemy, Euclid and Tacitus. Fame on top, and two small putti: one with a looking glass, the other writing in the Book of Life. In the lower zone crude but instructive paintings of Merton and of Eton (Sir Henry was Provost of Eton too, and is buried there). Also a half-globe showing the southern hemisphere, with Magellan's voyage indicated.† – Dr John Bainbridge, first Savilian Professor of Astronomy, †1653. Unusual inlaid black and white ledger slab, re-set against the w wall. – Alexander Fisher, donor of the chapel screen, †1671. Pedimented tablet with stumpy half-columns. Documented as by *Wood* of Oxford, mason; perhaps *Thomas Wood* of the Old Ashmolean (p.339). – Nathaniel Wight †1682. Oval inscription panel, two little girls on the pediment. – Frank Grimwood †1891. Green granite tablet, inset with his bronze profile against Art Nouveau mosaic. – G.N. Freeling †1892. Designed by *T.G. Jackson*. Bronze tablet, carved surround with angels. – W.W. How †1932. Tablet by *Eric Gill*, 1935.

(Choir. WAR MEMORIAL, a slate floor slab designed in 1922 by *Comper*, with sword and wreath.)

Fellows' Quad, St Alban's Quad and eastward

After the completion of Mob Quad nothing was done to enlarge the college until Warden Savile built FELLOWS' QUAD in 1609–10. The master mason was *John Akroyd the elder* of Halifax, in partnership with another Yorkshire mason, *John Bentley* of Elland. Akroyd had apparently been working in

---

* *See* Jean Wilson in *Church Monuments* 8 (1993).
† Attributed by Geoffrey Fisher to *James White* of Long Acre, Westminster.

the 1590s for Warden Savile's brother at Methley Hall near Leeds, a useful connection at a time when the University was at loggerheads with Oxford's own guildsmen. The carpenter, *Thomas Holt*, was recruited from Yorkshire too, as were other masons from the Akroyd and Bentley families. At just over 100 ft (30 metres) square the result is much larger than Mob, of even design, with three full storeys from the start – the earliest three-storey quad at Oxford. All windows still with arched lights, generally in a pattern of two–three–two lights facing into the quad, two lights facing out. The three-light windows are for the chambers, the two-lighters for the pairs of studies or bedrooms attached to each chamber, or for the staircases. Mostly running hoodmoulds. Broad gables on the outside of the ranges only, and pillar chimneystacks in groups between them. The composition to the s is perfectly symmetrical. Here the end bays are accentuated by broad oriels on the top floor, which is also the tallest floor. The evenness inside the quad is broken in the middle of the s side by a four-tier frontispiece of the full-columned type shortly after adopted at the Bodleian, and already deployed e.g. at Burghley House and at Stonyhurst, Lancs. The origin is mid-C16 French (Anet), via Old Somerset House in Westminster. Here its size is a little pinched. Paired columns in four tiers, the uppermost above the parapet. Tiny top pediment, and formerly also obelisks. Between the column pairs however are two ogee-headed niches on the second tier, then Gothic panelling above, but also two classical pilasters on the next tier up. The doorway too is four-centred-arched. This stylistic mixture, absent at Burghley and Stonyhurst alike, can only be deliberate. The battlements inside the quad (renewed) were added in 1622, with stepped-up centrepieces ending in a semicircle. The window spacing is closer for the KITCHEN, at the hall end of the w range. The SENIOR COMMON ROOM above it was designated in 1661, one of the first in an Oxford college. Handsomely panelled in 1680 by *Arthur Frogley*, in Flemish oak, with garlands and a swag in the overmantel. It is reached from the hall by a late C17-type staircase with twisted balusters.

ST ALBAN'S QUAD is a rebuilding by *Champneys*, 1904–7, retaining the old St Alban Hall street front already noted, while replacing part of the medieval Warden's Lodgings to the w. Free Tudor, very pretty, with Arts and Crafts touches. Oriels and gables galore. Weldon stone. The carver was *Robert Bridgeman*. Open to the gardens on the s side, with delightful RAILINGS across.

Access to the GARDENS is through the E range. Their s wall with its bastion is of course part of the medieval CITY WALL, which returns to the NE. In the gardens a SUMMERHOUSE of c.1706–7, a stone box, modest but dignified. Of the same date the long elevated TERRACE behind the wall. Further w the wall is much cut down, and railings appear instead.

Merton continues E of the wall with ROSE LANE BUILDINGS by *Sir Hubert Worthington*, 1939–40. Rock-faced stone (Bladon rubble), as at others of his Oxford buildings. A quasi-Palladian plan, with diagonal screen walls joining four Fellows' houses placed beyond the N and S ends, pavilion-fashion. Student common room across the long-stretching middle. Two-storeyed at first, bulked up with a mansard in 1989. Then in 2009–10 the T.S. ELIOT THEATRE was built between the houses to the S, and the screen walls there raised to full height. By *Ridge & Partners*. An earlier addition (1964–5) was *Carden & Godfrey*'s shapeless ROSE LANE 5 block, W of the NW house-pavilion. Of brick, now painted.

Plans for a new LIBRARY at the E end of the college site, to be designed by *Stanton Williams*, were announced in 2023.

Merton Street, north and east

Merton's presence N of the street dates from the C13. The former STABLES opposite the gatehouse are indeed older still, being the remains of a stone-built house of *c.* 1200 ('Edrich's house'): the earliest standing domestic building in Oxford. Mostly featureless rubble walls, but C18 and C19 views show twin two-light upper windows with early pointed heads. It almost certainly belonged to the type with a chamber or solar block over ground-floor storage; the hall range was at right angles behind. The present name, POSTMASTERS' HALL, refers to the college's postmasters or poor scholars. The r. part was rebuilt in 1580 as a house, later home to the C17 antiquary Anthony Wood. Rubble-stone walls, mullioned windows of three (some originally four) straight-headed lights. Stone dormer gables replaced in timber in the C19. Early C17 panelling and pilastered overmantel with arcading in one ground-floor room. The courtyard behind has *Allies & Morrison*'s FINLAY BUILDING for the college offices, 2004. Decent and discreet, faced in ashlar or rubble. Upright windows and boxy dormers on the E side, bigger apertures in the N return. This adjoins Oxford's last intact REAL TENNIS COURT (not part of Merton), of which the colleges had at least fourteen between them in the C17. This one is a rebuilding of *c.* 1798, big and plain, with something of the character of military or dockyard architecture. Rubble walls, continuous small-paned clerestories on the long sides. Half-hipped roof.

The OLD WARDEN'S LODGINGS, now the college's working LIBRARY, are next E. By *Champneys*, 1907–8; last and most lavish of the sundry new lodgings built up to 1914. It is indeed more assertive than any other principal's house in either university. High, symmetrical, in a mixed Jacobean–Carolean style, with a gateway and enclosed stair to the main entrance. The gateway has the alternate blocking of its columns which the Edwardians liked so much. Split-level plan, around a stair with oval motifs in the balustrade.

The replacement WARDEN'S LODGINGS stand some way E, facing down Merton Street where it bends N. *Raymond Erith*'s spirited Neo-Regency proposals of 1950 were judged too expensive. *Carden & Godfrey*'s unloved brick-faced Modernist building followed in 1965–6, reworked in 2012 by *Acanthus Clews* with a bland, quasi-traditional frontage.

For Nos. 20–22 Merton Street next to the Lodgings *see* Perambulation 1, p. 414; for HOLYWELL BUILDINGS, Holywell Street and Jowett Walk, *see* Perambulation 2, p. 417.

NEW COLLEGE
New College Lane and Holywell Street

William of Wykeham, Bishop of Winchester, founded Winchester College and New College at almost the same time, respectively in 1382 and 1379. The Winchester school and the Oxford college were the two parts of the same educational idea. They were founded, as New College's statutes say, to counter 'the fewness of the clergy, arising from pestilence, wars and other miseries', and so their object was to convert 'poor and indigent scholars' into 'men of great learning, fruitful to church..., king and realm'. Both foundations were unprecedented in scale and in the purposefulness of their statutes.

The college, properly St Mary College of Winchester in Oxford, was to be entered immediately after finishing at the school. There were to be a Warden and seventy Fellows, recruited in the first place from Winchester. In addition ten priests, three stipendiary clerks and sixteen choristers were to serve the college. Ordinary entrants would become full Fellows only after two years' probation, and their instruction was to be by senior Fellows. Higher degrees were not excluded – civil and canon law, astronomy, medicine and of course theology are mentioned – but were secondary to the basic arts course. Here the system effectively began of Fellows and students living together, instead of the old model whereby the Fellows made up the college and the students lived in halls.* The other great innovation was that New College – like its Winchester sibling – was built at one go, to a single monumental plan complete with hall, chapel, library and chambers. In both these respects, ambitious future colleges aimed to follow New College, including King's at Cambridge, founded by Henry VI together with Eton.

Wykeham's chosen site lay within the NE angle of the city walls, an area that had suffered especially from depopulation and decline during the C14. Work began in 1380, and by 1386 the quadrangle was ready for use. The cloister W of the chapel was

---

*At King's Hall, Cambridge, as re-founded in 1337, undergraduates already lived in college, though there was not yet tuition by the older Fellows.

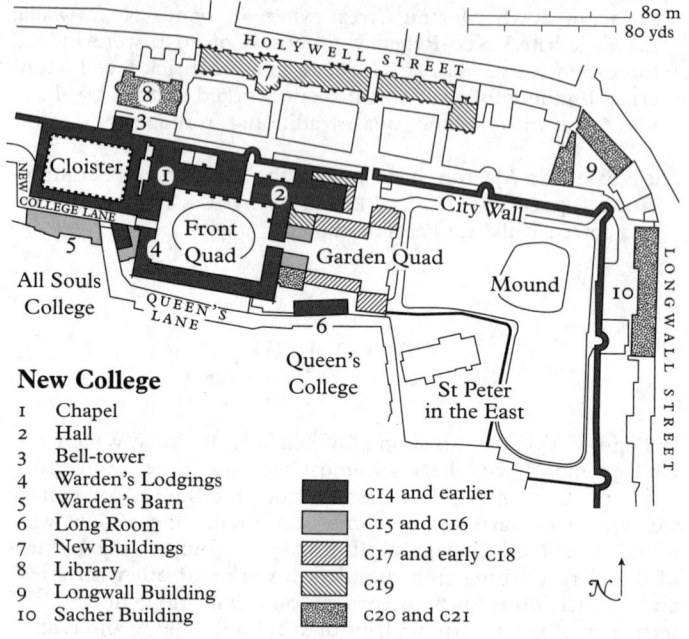

New College

1 Chapel
2 Hall
3 Bell-tower
4 Warden's Lodgings
5 Warden's Barn
6 Long Room
7 New Buildings
8 Library
9 Longwall Building
10 Sacher Building

- C14 and earlier
- C15 and C16
- C17 and early C18
- C19
- C20 and C21

begun *c.*1390 and consecrated in 1400; the adjacent bell-tower was built with it. Also preserved – amazing survivals both – are the late C14 Long Room (latrines) in the SE corner of the old parts, and the Warden's Barn to the W in New College Lane, of 1401–2.

Conception and plan in general may confidently be ascribed to Wykeham himself, but the epoch-making design of New College is attributed firmly to the mason *William Wynford*. He was named already in 1377–8 as master mason for all the bishop's undertakings, and is documented later as in charge at Winchester College, which has many personnel and details in common with the Oxford work. Wykeham's master carpenter was *Hugh Herland*, the genius of the Westminster Hall roof and the false vault at Winchester College chapel, although little of his work is left to see here. The royal master mason *Henry Yevele* also visited, and was presumably consulted on the design. The arrangement by which hall, chapel and chambers are marshalled into one composition derives crucially from Edward III's work of the 1360s in the Upper Ward at Windsor Castle, in which Wynford and Wykeham had both been involved. Chapel and hall at Oxford are in line along the N range, with a gate tower in the W range, on axis with a gateway out to the E. New College thus belongs, like Cobham College (Kent) and John of Gaunt's work at Kenilworth, to the movement in later C14 England towards formal planning, regular arrangements and monumental effects. The use of dressed stone on such a scale was also new for Oxford. Less obviously, the original chambers all had fireplaces.

The next major additions were to the E, in 1682–1707, making an open-ended quadrangle towards the gardens. Victorian and early C20 activity (*Scott*, then *Champneys*) was directed to the N and Longwall Street, post-war expansion to the E and NE. Both these areas lie beyond the magnificently preserved city walls that still traverse the college's enclave.

FRONT QUAD AND CLOISTER

The western approach to New College is unique. New College Lane, with its 90-degree kink and then the straight stretch between the mute walls of cloister (N) and Warden's Barn (S), with its baffling turn-off under the bridge (of 1676; *see* p. 220) towards Queen's Lane, takes one right out of the feel of a town centre. The GATE TOWER is a fitting introduction to the novelty of the college, as it is the first of Oxford's gate towers – but matched by the gate tower of Winchester College. It is of three storeys with a higher stair-turret in the NE corner. Archway with depressed four-centred arch and two big continuous hollow chamfers – the same moulding as appears frequently at Winchester. Above are two big transomed two-light windows, and above that niches for a figure of the Virgin and figures of the Angel of the Annunciation and the kneeling founder.* The inside towards the quad repeats that, but with a replacement Wykeham figure of 2012. Inside the archway are two bays of vaulting with diagonal and ridge ribs, sharply chamfered, and with bosses. The DOOR is original. Above the archway in the tower were the original Warden's Hall and Warden's Chamber, with his other rooms to the N (*see* p. 219).

Front Quad

FRONT QUAD is by medieval standards very large indeed, and it is a pity that the heightening of the chamber ranges tends to diminish the sense of space. Chapel and hall, it is true, are intact, and in the angle next to the hall is the MUNIMENT TOWER, four-storeyed, with the hall stair going up inside it. The archway has one big hollow chamfer and fine mouldings dying into the jambs. Above are again three niches with Virgin, angel and founder. The Virgin here is more heavily draped. All the tower windows heavily barred; sundial of 2000 on the S wall. The WEST, SOUTH and EAST RANGES had a third storey and battlements added in 1674–5 (refaced 1906–7), embracing earlier additions with gabled dormers which face the outer sides. The windows were sashed in 1718–21. The simple arched doorways remain, as does the rhythm of large

23

*The windows of this stage are restoration of 1947 by *R. Fielding Dodd*, after Loggan's depiction.

New College, from the west.
Drawing by E.H. New, 1912

and small windows, representing originally the large common bedchamber and small partitioned-off study cubicles. The closer window rhythm and lower string course on the E range indicate the Old Library. Here *R. Fielding Dodd* restored the first window on the l. to the transomed C14 pattern in 1950. The passage through the E range has another depressed four-centred arch, with one broad chamfer and again two bays of vaulting with sharply chamfered diagonal and ridge ribs.

The CHAPEL fills the greater part of the N side, with its antechapel cutting awkwardly into the W range. Four-light windows, with a six-light window (three plus three) in the antechapel E walls, and a central seven-light W window (two–three–two) and two four-light windows towards the cloister. All have transoms and developed panel tracery everywhere, the earliest Perp tracery to survive at Oxford. Pyramidal pinnacles on the buttresses, W doorway with leaf spandrels. Against the antechapel S wall a half-figure of a feathered angel, a modern copy after one from the oriel formerly on the Warden's side, removed in the C18 sashing. The HALL adjoins the chapel to the E – so the latter has no E window – and continues its roof-line. It is placed on the first floor, as earlier at Merton and also later at e.g. Christ Church. Its windows are again transomed but of only two lights, the tracery one broad Perp panel unit (really a straightened reticulation unit). On the E gable a pinnacle with niche and figure of St Michael, among the college's many re-carvings by *Michael Groser* from the 1960s refacing campaign.★ Earlier refacing of hall, chapel etc. by *Champneys*, 1899–1902.

★The original is now in Trinity College, President's Garden (p. 293).

The cloister is entered via the chapel passage. This PASSAGE and this whole corner are untidy – as at Winchester College. The doorway from the quad has a two-centred arch with quatrefoiled spandrels. Vault of two bays with ridge ribs and bosses, the ribs of a finer moulding than those met so far.

Cloister

The CLOISTER is datable to 1389–90 from the tree-ring evidence of its fine single-framed pointed wagon roof. No rooms open off it; the cloister garth was for burials, the walks apparently for just that. These have three-light openings. Immediately to the N, in place of one of the bastions of the town wall, is the BELL-TOWER, datable to 1394–7. Four-storeyed, plain, with straight-headed pairs of bell-openings. Original battlements and higher stair-turret. The walling is of Headington stone, Oxford's first documented example. Since 1996 the tower has held the library's special collections. With the gorgeous ilex tree in the NW corner, it forms an unforgettable group with the chapel, the lawn and the cloister walls.

In the cloister ten early C14 STATUES from the steeple of St Mary's church (p. 384), restored, but showing the original quality of draperies etc. Also many TABLETS of the C20, several with excellent lettering; those to Sir H. E. Richards †1922, Gilbert Bourne †1933 (E wall) and John Galsworthy †1933 (S wall) by *Eric Gill*. – Boer War memorial by *Alfred Drury*, S wall.

Chapel interior

The CHAPEL is the first to adopt the distinctive T-plan, later the model for Magdalen, All Souls and several other chapels at Oxford. (It invaded Cambridge only with Scott's St John's College chapel, 1863.) The antechapel is two bays deep from W to E. The theory that it was meant to be continued as a giant aisled nave across the site of the cloister has been disposed of by Roland Harris.* The tall piers have a section of four main and four thin diagonal shafts separated by shallow hollows. Capitals only to the shafts, those on the diagonals very small. Two-centred arches. Fine figured corbels of bishops and kings. The roofs themselves are of the restoration of 1877–81 by *Sir George Gilbert Scott*, completed by his sons *G. G. Scott Jun.* and *J. O. Scott*. Scott senior had proposed a tie-beam roof over the main vessel, but the college preferred a showier hammerbeam type. Thus perished the plaster vault from *James Wyatt*'s restoration of 1788–94, his most ambitious Neo-Gothic project

---

* First suggested by E. A. Gee in *Archaeological Journal* 109 (1952), and repeated in e.g. Howard Colvin, *Unbuilt Oxford* (1982). Central to the argument was Gee's incorrect belief that the W wall is deliberately not bonded in at the angles.

at Oxford. Wyatt had also restored the huge REREDOS from medieval traces but using mostly stucco, and *Scott* remade this in stone. It has four tiers of figures in niches, plus an invented top tier to fill the space created by the hammerbeam arch. This and the figure sculpture (mostly carved by *Nathaniel Hitch*) are of 1888–91, designed by *J. L. Pearson*. At the bottom a set of five very classical marble reliefs of the Life of Virgin by *Westmacott the elder*, survivors from the Wyatt reredos. (What remains of the medieval sculpture is now in the Song School – *see* p. 217.) By *Pearson* also the lavishly decorated SEDILIA and PISCINA.

FURNISHINGS. METALWORK. The CROZIER of William of Wykeham, in a glazed niche, N side. – STALLS largely by *Scott*, with carving by *Farmer & Brindley*, incorporating original late C14 seats, misericords and carved backs. The ELBOW RESTS have leaf-work, a pelican, a man fighting a monster, and a number of heads. Among the sixty-two MISERICORDS it is hard to make a choice. On the N one may wish to watch for a six-headed monster (8) and a gateway with portcullis and two knight's heads as supporters (11); on the S side for a peacock (1), a centaur musician (2), a lecture (8), more gateways with portcullis (14), a pulpit and architectural supporters (20), tumblers (22) and a monster hovering over two women (27); at the W end for a woman with a distaff (2, from N), fighting men (3) and a walled Gothic city with a bishop (Wykeham?) preaching (5). But there are also exquisitely done simpler themes: holly leaves (W7), a crowned head (N4) and flowers (N18). The workshop seems to have moved on to Winchester College, where the misericord style is very similar. – Also plain STALLS of 1636–8, now in the antechapel. Made by *William Harris* of St Cross. – SCREEN and ORGAN GALLERY by *Scott*, but in the screen the C14 DOORS with panel tracery and some original panels and spandrels. – ORGAN CASE. 1968–9 by *G. G. Pace*. Rather spiky for its setting. – SCULPTURE, antechapel. Lazarus, by *Epstein*, 1949–51. Swathed and throwing his head to one side. The main view is from the back, where profile and arms can play their part. Pevsner judged it 'impressive in its intense emotion, though no doubt hopelessly corny to the devotees of Anthony Caro'.

STAINED GLASS. One of the most important sequences in England for both C14 and C18 work, the latter having replaced the former and sometimes having derived some themes from it. The C14 work, now mostly concentrated in the arms of the antechapel, consists of large single figures under canopies of different perspective designs. All are more or less restored, and some are not *in situ*. The glass can be dated to the 1380s and attributed with confidence to *Thomas* of Oxford, who later worked at Winchester. Thomas's Winchester work already shows the advent of the International Gothic manner, possibly following designs from a Continental artist, and the same goes for his Tree of Jesse glass of the 1390s formerly in the chapel W window, but now partly reassembled in the choir S aisle at York

Minster.* So Thomas's remaining glass catches the medium on the eve of change.

Description of the C18 glass in the great W window and the chapel proper follows that of the medieval work in the antechapel, which is taken clockwise from the NW. The arrangement here is of Old Testament figures below prophets in the N and outer W windows, with Crucifixion groups below apostles in the E windows. Across the base of each window is an inscription, variously abridged: 'Orate pro Willelmo de Wykeham episcopo Wyntoniense fundatore istius collegii' ('Pray for William of Wykeham, Bishop of Winchester, founder of this college').

Antechapel N arm, W window. Lower tier, Adam (delving), Eve (spinning), Seth, Enoch; upper tier, Jeremiah, Isaiah, patriarch or prophet, Hosea; tracery, six angels representing Thrones (from the Nine Orders of angels). – N arm N wall, W window. Lower tier, Methuselah, Noah, Abraham, Isaac; upper tier, Amos, Joel, Micah, Zephaniah; tracery, angels representing Principalities. – N arm N wall, E window. Lower tier, Jacob, Judah, Moses, composite of Nahum and Aaron; upper tier, Daniel, Ezekiel, Obadiah, Habakkuk; tracery, angels representing Dominions. – N arm E window. Lower tier, female saint (incomplete and *ex situ*), remains of a crucifix panel with head of a female saint, St John the Evangelist, the Virgin, another crucifix panel, with part of an ecclesiastic, St John the Evangelist. Upper tier, St Peter, St Andrew, St James the Great, St John the Evangelist, St Thomas, St James the Less. Tracery, Wykeham kneeling before Christ, with angels below.

Antechapel S arm, E window. Lower tier, the Virgin, remains of crucifix panel with female saint inserted, St John the Evangelist, the Virgin, another crucifix panel with inserted female saint, St John the Evangelist. Upper tier, St Philip, St Bartholomew, St Matthew, St Simon, St Mathias, St Jude. Tracery, Coronation of the Virgin, with angels below. – S arm S window. Lower tier, St Athanasius, St Bernard, a bishop, a bishop; upper tier, a bishop, a pope, St Alphege, St Germanus; tracery, angels representing Cherubim. – S arm W window. Lower tier, St Martha, composite of female saint and bishop, a queen, composite of St Withburga and bishop; upper tier, St Mary of Egypt, Baruch, Jonah, St Mary Magdalene; tracery, angels representing Seraphim.

Great W window. Painted in 1778–85 by *Thomas Jervais* from the designs of *Sir Joshua Reynolds*, to replace nearly new glass by *William Peckitt* of York that was bumped to the chapel N windows (*see* below). The work is much more pictorial and painterly, with no attempt to re-create the medieval canopy settings. In the lower lights the Virtues: Temperance, Fortitude, Faith, Charity, Hope, Justice, Prudence. In the upper lights and tracery, the Nativity, after Correggio. Yet the outcome was

---

* More of the C14 glass (from the W tracery lights) has been identified at High Melton church, Yorkshire West Riding.

a grievous disappointment to Reynolds, and a major failure of post-medieval design. Horace Walpole found the right words when he wrote about the 'washy colours' of the Virtues, which made the darker colours (much brown) of the Nativity appear too dark. Mullions removed for the upper picture were reinstated in 1848.

Chapel s windows. Saints, patriarchs and bishops by *William Price Jun.*, 1736–40, incorporating C14 traceries and some canopy glass. The figure style is conventional C18 Raphael-esque, although the canopies nod to the C14 form. No names, but a few of the saints can be identified by their attributes, e.g. St Lawrence, second window from E, upper tier, far r. In the tracery from E to W, angels representing Cherubim, Domina-tions, Seraphim, Thrones, Principalities.

Chapel N windows. Apostles and prophets by *W. Peckitt*, again with some C14 traceries and incorporated bits. The first two windows from the E consist chiefly of figures made in 1772–5 for the W window. The much paler windows further W are of 1773, with figure designs by *Biagio Rebecca*. First window from E. Lower tier, St Paul, St Barnabas (these two by *Francis Eginton*, 1821), St Jude, St Mathias; upper tier, St Philip, St James the Great, St Andrew, St Bartholomew; tracery, six Wise Virgins (much restored). – Second window. Lower tier, St John the Evangelist, Christ, the Virgin, St Peter; upper tier, St James the Less, St Thomas, St Simon, St Matthew; tracery, Angels. – Third window. Lower tier, Jacob, Judah, Moses, Aaron; upper tier, Micah, Nahum, Habakkuk, Zephaniah; tracery, Archangels. – Fourth window. Lower tier, Methuselah, Noah, Abraham, Isaac; upper tier, Joel, Amos, Obadiah, Jonah; tracery, Virtues.   Fifth window. Lower tier, Adam, Eve, Seth, Enoch; upper tier, Baruch, Hosea, Daniel, Ezekiel; tracery, Powers.

BRASSES. The floor of the antechapel N arm is filled with brasses. Nearly all are C15 and none earlier; many represent Wardens of the college; and nearly all have a scroll above their heads. Only Cranley's (fourth row) is really outstanding. Here is the list in S–N rows, from W to E. First row. Richard Wyard †1478, 30 in. (75 cm.). – John Desford †1419, demi-figure, 16 in. (40 cm.). – Thomas Hylle †1468, 32 in. (82 cm.). – Walter Wake †1451, half-figure, 8½ in. (22 cm.). – Thomas Flemyng †1472, emaci-ated figure in shroud, 16 in. (40 cm.). – Second row. Walter Bailey †1592, 2 ft 5½ in. (75 cm.). – William Hawtryve †1441, 37 in. (94 cm.). – John London, Recorder of the University, †1508, 18 in. (47 cm.). – Richard Bedford †1509, in under-graduate dress, 13½ in. (34 cm.). – John Palmer †1479, 19½ in. (50 cm.). – John Frye †1507, demi-figure, 10 in. (25 cm.). – Third row. John Lowthe †1427, 34 in. (86 cm.). – Geoffrey Hargreve †1447, 3 ft (92 cm.). – Richard Malford †1403, 4 ft ½ in. (1.23 metres). – Anthony Aylworth †1619, sometime royal physician ('Hic iacet Hippocrates, hic Avicenna iacet' etc.), 31½ in. (80 cm.). – Fourth row. David Williams †1860, large cross, by *Messrs Skidmore*. – Walter Hill †1494, 4 ft 2 in.

(1.28 metres). – Thomas Cranley, Warden, and also Archbishop of Dublin, †1417; fine figure 5 ft 1½ in. (1.56 metres) long, under triple canopy. – John Young, Warden, and Bishop of Gallipoli, †1526, the '26' left blank; 4 ft 1 in. (1.24 metres). – John Rede †1521, 32 in. (82 cm.). – s arm e wall, Thomas Hopper †1623, plate with figures and geometrical designs, by the polymath *Dr Richard Haydock* (cf. Queen's chapel).

MONUMENTS. All in the antechapel. Dr Hugh Barker, demi-figure against a shallow black marble niche. By *Nicholas Stone*, 1632. – Robert Pinke †1647. Similar, with side scrolls. – Michael Woodward †1675, with stiff central demi-figure and Baroque cherubs to each side. – Richard Traffles †1703. Bust on top. Attributed to the *Townesend* workshop (GF). – William Gother †1764, with delicate musical trophy. – Dr Bowles †1765, signed by *John Townesend (III)*, more conservative. – John Oglander †1794. Signed by *Wyatt* as architect and *Westmacott (the elder)* as sculptor. Small tablet, delicately done. – Charles Burlson †1836. By *Humphrey Hopper*. Hanging monument with large female mourner. She has thrown herself on a tomb. – Alfred Robinson †1895, red marble tablet designed by *Lethaby*. – *Eric Gill* did the large memorial to those fallen in the First World War (1921; designer *Charles Holden*) and the small ones to German old members fallen on the opposing side (1930; s arm e).

N of the chapel are the VESTRY and SONG SCHOOL, late C14 rooms that may represent an early modification of the 1380s plan. – SCULPTURE. Five fragmentary scenes from the C14 reredos, on the same themes as those by Westmacott, are in the Song School. The carving is important because unrestored. – STAINED GLASS by *Rachel Thomas* of the *York Glaziers Trust*, mostly of C14 fragments artfully rearranged: Angel Trumpeter (vestry, W), 2008, and Tree of Life (Song School, E), 2006.

Other interiors (going clockwise)

HALL. The STAIRCASE in the Muniment Tower has a lierne vault, with the liernes opening and closing scissor-wise – a descendant of the Aerary Porch at Windsor – in which the lines of both ridge ribs and diagonal ribs are interrupted. The window contains C14 and C16 heraldic glass removed from the hall windows in 1865, the door is late C14 and original. Over the HALL itself is an arch-braced roof by *Scott*, 1862–5, again replacing a plaster vault by *Wyatt* (of 1786). The linenfold panelling was installed in 1533–5, makers *John Redyng* and a *Master Darnall* of London, probably as a bequest of Archbishop Warham. It has a thin top frieze with rather coarse and tentative Early Renaissance details: profile bust medallions, and shields supported by putti. *Scott* cut away the panelling where it continued across the window openings. The screen has linenfold panelling too. Above it a gallery made by *Champneys* in 1907. Stained glass by *Clayton & Bell*, 1860s, heraldic.

The panelling extends to the SCREENS PASSAGE. Central doorway to the kitchen, flanking doorways to buttery and pantry, l. and r. The former has in the spandrels of the panelling droll carvings of tankards and serving boys. A timber-framed stair runs straight down to the KITCHEN E of the hall, with *Herland*'s lean arch-braced roof with two tiers of wind-braces, datable to 1383, and timber-framed W wall. In the E wall two fireplaces of 1882 from *Wilkinson & Moore*'s restoration. They also did much to the low E addition of 1683, prominent in external views. Thorough renovation of 2014–15 by *Freeland Rees Roberts*, throughout the kitchen wing and spaces adjacent. Visible C14 features include the spiral stone stair down from within the buttery doorway to the BEER CELLAR, adjacent on the N and abutting the city wall. Rib-vault of four bays on a central octagonal pier. Diagonal ribs, with ridge ribs in one direction only. They have a long sharp chamfer. Top-lit student BAR to the W by *Freeland Rees Roberts*. On the first floor the BUTTERY, now merged with the space of the C14 pantry and a separate chamber or chambers to the E, where the wall is jettied out into the kitchen. Besides the *in situ* timbering there are also floor joists reused as rafters in 1726, when the attics were reconstructed to house the chaplains (the northern attics are of 1882–4 by *Wilkinson & Moore*). Tree-ring evidence shows that these reused timbers came from the 1380s hall floor, which *William Townesend* rebuilt in stone in 1722. His are the two parallel barrel-vaulted UNDERCROFTS that support it. The rib-vaulted PASSAGE to the W however was inserted by *Scott*, 1875, for easier access to the new Longwall buildings.

In the E range the MUNIMENT TOWER has rib-vaulted rooms on all four levels. That on the ground floor, again with ridge ribs of sharp chamfer, has very fine figured corbels. On the first floor the corbels have angels. The encaustic tile floors are specially well preserved.

Next on the ground floor the OLD BURSARY. Geometrical wooden ceiling with small bosses with ornaments of tin, identifiable as of the 1540s. Another room, called The Chequer, was added as an eastward projection in 1449, now subsumed within Garden Quad (*see* p. 220). Above the Old Bursary etc. is the OLD LIBRARY, the first to be fully integrated in a college complex. It is 70 ft (21 metres) long. Transomed C14 windows in the E wall where the addition joins on, exposed in *Fielding Dodd*'s stripping-out of 1949–51. The scar left by one of the lectern-topped medieval bookcases was also observed. These cases were superseded in 1602–6 by the full stall type. Bookless, the room now serves as the SCR DINING ROOM. To the E, above The Chequer, a room added in 1480–1 for a law library, later the SENIOR COMMON ROOM. Oak panelling with flat carved swags and an elaborate coat of arms, installed in 1678 (*Francis Butler*, joiner). A spiral stair just outside the room, probably part of the works in this wing by *Sir Charles Nicholson*, 1908–9 (also the PANTRY, N). It leads down to The

Chequer, which was used informally as a Fellows' common room as early as the c16.

The UPPER LIBRARY above the Old Library was formed in 1674 and remodelled in 1778–9 by *James Wyatt*, with *James Pears* as executant. Two end apses, arched window reveals, sparing Neoclassical decoration including painted swags. The STAIRCASE to its S was remodelled in 1722. It has an arched doorway into the Old Library with plain impost blocks and a shell carved at the top. Three STAIRCASES of similar date on the S side: open wells, twisted balusters.

WARDEN'S LODGINGS, BRIDGE AND BARN

The W side of the quad includes the WARDEN'S LODGINGS. They have expanded from their original suite, which in this range was confined to the tower and the first-floor rooms to the N. To the outside this enlargement means especially the roughly triangular or wedge-shaped additions of 1540–1 towards New College Lane, S of the gate-tower approach. These absorbed the c14 kitchen at the S end, originally detached, and created an irregular inner courtyard that has since been roofed over.

The approach is by the spacious STAIRCASE S of the gate passage. Made originally in 1675 by *Richard Frogley*, perhaps to *Byrd*'s designs, this occupies the former space of the c14 porter's lodge. It starts in two arms and returns on itself in one to reach the ground floor. Big dumb-bell balusters, ball finials to the newels. But the idiosyncratic newel props were inserted by *Caröe*, who remodelled the lodgings in 1903–4 for the celebrated Warden Spooner. He also took away the S wall and the first-floor W wall, in favour of matching balustrades. On the landings two internal windows with 1380s stained glass from the chapel traceries (Wise Virgins). The original Warden's Hall, now TOWER ROOM, is above the gateway. The room projected W of the frontage before additions were made alongside. That explains the two-light windows now adapted for internal doorways, one to the S, the other to the N. The ceiling of thin oak ribs is mostly *Caröe*'s matching work, but partly still 1540s (cf. Old Bursary, and the ante-room, below). Thin late c18 Gothick plaster frieze. Good panelling, mostly of *c.*1580. Big stone fireplace, c14 in its jambs, the rest *Caröe*'s. To the N the STUDY, originally with an oriel to the quad. Early c17 overmantel, not *in situ*. N of that a small ORATORY with a twin-slit squint into the antechapel. S of the staircase the present DINING ROOM, with a classical frieze. The room was made by *James Pears* in the 1780s, and restored to its original size when *Claud Phillimore* renovated the lodgings in 1958–60. Both this room and the GUEST BEDROOM above (panelled *c.*1700) were formerly Fellows' chambers.

Now E from the staircase, into a panelled ANTE-ROOM. In its present form this is chiefly *Caröe*, representing part of a longer E–W gallery made by him. The oak-ribbed ceiling with its little metal-leaved bosses is however partly of the 1540s, to a pattern of octagons derived from Serlio. The DRAWING ROOM ahead is the major interior within the C16 wing, formed by *Phillimore* but corresponding roughly to the Tudor gallery space. One tall two-light window and two sashed ones to the w. The flat, close-mullioned oriel in the N wall dates probably from the 1670s. On the ground floor is the former KITCHEN, its large fireplaces no longer visible, but with one original pointed-arched doorway. The back stairs etc. adjacent are *Caröe's*.

On the second floor the gate tower housed the WARDEN'S CHAMBER in Wykeham's time. Guest rooms were built on top of the range to its N in the C16. Then a storey was added at this level S of the tower. On the side towards the former inner courtyard here, now enclosed within a corridor, a blocked three-light window survives, apparently C17. This must have belonged to a dormer on the wall-head. Finally *Caröe* made an additional storey over this part, for servants' bedrooms.

The BRIDGE over New College Lane springs from the drawing room at its NW corner. It is of 1675–6, by *Byrd*. The arch is elliptical and has transverse ribs. For the so-called WARDEN'S BARN of 1401–2 – actually one long subdivided building, which provided the college's guest room and other functions – the name of *John Martyn*, mason, is recorded. Just a blank wall and two big broad gateways to the lane, but in the E wall by the bridge a cusped two-light window still with its shutters. This end was indeed used as living quarters. Matching window on the S side, towards the garden (originally the paddock for the Warden's horses). Other windows and openings of every date, a gloriously picturesque effect. They include the big barn doorway with a bargeboarded gable of timber, and another two-storey section at the W end. (Original crown-post roof.) – GARDEN HOUSE of *c*.1720, small but solid Oxford Baroque, attributed to *William Townesend*.*

GARDEN QUAD, LONG ROOM, CITY WALLS
AND LATER BUILDINGS

Garden Quad, Long Room and city walls

The germ of Garden Quad is the extension of 1449, when THE CHEQUER was built E of the Old Bursary in the E range, as mentioned above. Two blocked two-light S windows with cusped lights remain on the upper storey added in 1480–1, renewed externally (but intact behind panelling within).

This by way of preamble to GARDEN QUAD, which is not a true quadrangle, and moreover is open to the E. As so often, the impetus to expand followed the admission of gentleman commoners to the college (in 1679). The architect was *William Byrd*. Among his first proposals was a detached three-storey

56

*By Gervase Jackson-Stops, in the college history of 1979.

block placed some way E (cf. Wren at Trinity). Instead in 1682–4 he remodelled the C15 building with cross-windows, matched it by one opposite to the S, and provided offset blocks against the outer corners on both sides, so that the distance between the new eastern blocks is three times that between the western ones. All these façades have since been sashed. The E buildings are again castellated but have three storeys (that of the 1680s has only two, like The Chequer), six bays long, with on the main floor window pediments, alternating triangular and segmental. The model for this stepped, open-fronted plan may have been Wren's 1680s design for Winchester Palace, where Byrd also worked. His college elevations are less sophisticated however, with their wide variations in bay spacing and proportions of the window pediments. Each set within consists of two bedrooms opening off a shared chamber, Oxford's earliest consistent use of this system. Next, in 1700 (S) and 1707 (N), the quad was completed by adding two more wings each of three bays, again stepped back so as to touch the older work at the corners, but this time two rooms deep. *Richard Piddington* built the first of these blocks, *William Townesend* the second; each was subject to approval of the timberwork by the shadowy *Martin May*, a gentleman of Kidlington, who may have had a part in the design. They are also the earliest datable case at Oxford of domestic sash windows.* To the E the quad is closed by a gorgeous wrought-iron SCREEN with gates to the garden, beautifully curvaceous in plan; *Thomas Robinson*, smith, 1711. Railings renewed 1894 by *Lucy's* of Oxford.

The inner 1680s block included the first known JUNIOR COMMON ROOM at either university, now extended by *Champneys'* cross-windowed addition of 1912 on the outer, S side. The LONG ROOM stands to the SE behind, placed along Queen's Lane. It was built in the late C14 as the garderobe or lavatories for the college, with a cesspit on the ground floor that did duty until 1880. Seven bays, exposed crown-post roof, plain openings. Converted in 1974–5 for exhibitions and receptions by *Geoffrey Beard* of *Oxford Architects Partnership*.

The GARDEN was first made level in 1529–30. It is made picturesque not only by its planning but also by the marvellous artificial MOUND or mount, made in 1594, progressively enhanced up to the late 1640s and given its present steps in 1994, and most of all by the stretch of early to mid-C13 CITY WALL which is now inside the college. The most complete surviving section of the circuit, it shows the surprising grandeur of the defences of what was only a medium-sized settlement. The start is just N of the cloister, with walling standing up to full height (with renewed crenellation). The next bastion is just N of hall and chapel. This still has its wall-walk, battlements and loopholes. Equally well preserved are the bastions N of the garden and in

11

---

*In the contract of 1707 the term is not yet used. Instead it is specified that the windows should be 'hung on box pullies with hemp lines', whereas the 1718 contract for general re-windowing speaks of 'sashing'.

the NE corner, which was in fact the NE corner of the circuit. The stretch which follows, running s, also stands complete, with two more bastions. On the N and E sides there was once also an outer, much lower wall in this area. Unique among English urban defences, this suggests a second phase probably of the late C13 (murage grant 1285), perhaps under the influence of Edward I's concentric castles in North Wales, or of fortified cities overseas such as Carcassonne and Constantinople. Saxon ramparts – for Oxford was an Alfredian *burh* or fortified town – have been identified below the C13 wall line, most extensively in 2013, next to the kitchen.

Later buildings

Gates made in the wall in the early C18 and *c.*1875 lead N to the CI9 AND C20 BUILDINGS of the college. From here also one gets the view of hall and chapel from the N. The first new building – necessarily a substantial one, for the college grew rapidly after its venerable statutes were superseded in 1860 – came in 1872–7. *Sir G.G. Scott* was the architect. His range, the tallest at any Oxford college to that date, faces Holywell Street. Milton stone. Six staircases, with a tower placed between the second and third. The w part was a tutor's house. Building was continued to the E by *Basil Champneys* with the ROBINSON TOWER, more staircases and another tutor's house, the last in 1884–5 (offset at the E end of the range), the rest in 1896–7. It is rewarding to compare the collegiate of Scott, born 1811, with that of Champneys, born 1842. Scott is correct in his motifs – English Middle Pointed here – but their assembly, the general composition, the asymmetry of big, heavy elements: all these are mid-C19. The side to the college is less severe, though
p. 212
also asymmetrically composed. The contrast is also one of height, the college having insisted on four storeys from Scott. Champneys's range is of three storeys only and treats its Tudor motifs more freely, while avoiding Jacksonian mix-and-match. Plenty of pretty close-leaf decoration (carver *John McCulloch*). To the w is *Sir Hubert Worthington*'s LIBRARY of 1938–9. A formal, classical two-storey composition, but in small rock-faced stones – a match for the city wall – and with sparing detail in the Østberg-Paris-1925 categories, all much like the same architect's range for Merton. Pevsner diagnosed in it 'the timid modernity of so many English architects before the Second World War'. Different woods for the different panelled study rooms on the lower floor – mahogany, sycamore etc.

To the E, near the corner bastion of the city wall, the LONG-WALL BUILDING, 1980–1. By *John Fryman* of *Architects Design Partnership*, incorporating the Neo-Early Georgian red brick façade of *Tollit & Lee*'s Morris company garage of 1910 on Longwall Street. The new parts Neo-vernacular and symmetrical. (Altered in 2017–19 by *Marcus Beale Architects*, with a new single-storey wing.) Round the corner, also beyond the wall and also symmetrically composed, the SACHER BUILDING for postgraduates, of 1961–2 by *David Roberts* of Cambridge. Straightforward three-storey range with long bands of windows (renewed). Ashlar and slate facing. Only the bracket-like projecting white beam-ends pronounce the 1960s as against the International Modern of the 1930s. The Longwall Street front repeats the treatment, to monotonous effect. By the entrance, bronze SCULPTURE by *Barbara Hepworth*, called Garden Sculpture (Model for Meridian), dated 1958.

For BODICOTE HOUSE in Longwall Street *see* Perambulation 1, p. 415; for the WESTON BUILDINGS in St Cross Road and the GRADEL QUADS SITE, SAVILE HOUSE and CLORE MUSIC STUDIOS in Mansfield Road *see* Perambulation 2, pp. 420 and 421.

NUFFIELD COLLEGE
New Road and Worcester Street

Nuffield College was founded in 1937 as a mixed graduate college with emphasis on social studies and the cooperation of academic and non-academic people. The motor manufacturer William Morris, 1st Lord Nuffield, gave the land and £900,000. The buildings are on the site of the wharves and basin of the Oxford Canal (*see* Introduction, p. 46). By redeveloping these, Lord Nuffield also aimed to improve the approach to the centre of Oxford from the w. Building began in 1949 and was largely finished in 1958. Full collegiate status was assumed in that year.

The story behind these outlines is more complicated. The chosen architect was *Austen Harrison*, whose other works were all official commissions overseas. For Oxford he took into partnership *Thomas Barnes* and *Pearce Hubbard*. The designs presented in 1939 were markedly different from today's college in both treatment and extent. As to treatment, Harrison proposed a sort of elemental, flat-roofed fusion of ancient Greek and eastern Mediterranean forms, not unlike what he had provided for the Palestine Archaeological Museum in Jerusalem. As to extent, early plans included an ambitious Institute of Social Studies on the land w of Worcester Street. But the donor wanted his college to look more at home in his own home city, and in 1939 it was decided to redesign it on more traditional lines. What exists today is the result of further revisions, including cost-cutting after the Second World War.

The plan is a long L-shaped enclosure, placed sideways and roughly E–W, with the short axis at the E end and raised to a higher level. Overall the style is a sort of stripped Cotswold: walls of Clipsham ashlar in which are casement windows, entirely unmoulded and very slightly sunk, Collyweston-slated roofs with plenty of chimneys. The frontage to New Road is

112

symmetrical in its main extent – big gable, four small gables, big gable – and then the library as the link to the tower in the SE corner, and the hall behind the tower and projecting to the E. There is also an axial entrance through an archway in the short W side. From here a picture of the identical residential ranges of Lower Quad appears, their windows of three lights, very closely set, and a sheet of water in the gardened centre. Steps rise to Upper Quad, the E part of the space, with its focus on the upper big bay window of the Senior Common Room. Throughout, the relieving arches of the doorways are slightly pointed, as if to echo the Eastern ancestry of Harrison's rejected version.

As an assertive display of traditional building, Nuffield vexed those who hoped for something more up-to-date from post-war Oxford; J.M. Richards of the *Architectural Review* called it in 1952 'a missed opportunity of a really tragic kind'. Pevsner's verdict in 1974 was more generous: 'Much has been said to make [the buildings] appear ridiculous – Cotswold gables and Cotswold windows indeed…But as for the tower, I propose forgiveness. It has enough identity to be sure that one day it will find affection. That is more than one could say for the Harkness Tower at Yale – and would a tower like that of St Boniface in Basel be more acceptable, let alone likeable?* Harrison's tower is at the same time the library stack. So there are nine floors all with only three small windows to each side. But above that the square recedes, there are broaches, as it were, of original shape, and then the spire, deliberately thin after the mighty tower. Yes – it positively helps the famous skyline of Oxford. The inspiration incidentally must be Lutyens.'

Designs for alterations by *MICA Architects*, including a new formation of ramps and steps between the Upper and Lower quads, were approved in 2022. The college also has plans to expand on to the long-vacant site to the W.

INTERIORS. The HALL is four bays long, with pointed concrete arches subdividing a coffered ceiling painted with much red. Fireplace behind the high table with a very high hood, its coat of arms carved by *David Kindersley*. In the LIBRARY Oxford's best post-war mural, The Seasons, a collaboration by *Derrick Greaves* and *Edward Middleditch*, 1958. The surprising TOWER ROOM or common room within the tower top was restored in 2010. In it a spiral stair to the lantern storey, which features an orrery high overhead.

The CHAPEL was created in 1959–61 by *Thomas Barnes*, in the roof of one of the N–S cross-wings. It is remarkable for five STAINED GLASS windows by *John Piper* with *Patrick Reyntiens*. Abstract except for the ritual W (really N) window which has the Five Wounds of Christ, in whitish glass. The side windows

---

*Harkness Tower, Neo-Gothic of 1917–21 by James Gamble Rogers; Basel, apparently an error for St Anton, 1926–7, a Modernist church by Karl Moser. The final design of Nuffield's tower was made in 1954–5 by Hubbard's assistant *Keith Page*.

at this end have deep colours, those by the altar are lighter. PEWS and ALTAR also designed by *Piper*, likewise the decorative scheme. – REREDOS by *John Hoskin*. A welded-metal upright form, on a polished steel background, concave in the top-to-foot direction. Altar with crucifix standing free in front.

SCULPTURE. By the main entrance an abstract aluminium piece by *Hubert Dalwood*, 1962, set in a pool. To the N, Flayed Stone IV, 1999, one of *Peter Randall-Page*'s carved boulders.

MEWS BLOCK, added to the E by *David Beecher*, 1968. Other small interventions on this side. On the N side facing Bulwarks Lane a clashing addition of 2016.

ORIEL COLLEGE
Oriel Square and High Street

Oriel College architecturally is two colleges: Oriel to the S, and N of it St Mary Hall, incorporated only in 1902.* Oriel College was founded in 1324 by Adam de Brome, Chancery clerk and rector of St Mary's church (*see* p.385), but the titular founder was Edward II, who gave more ambitious statutes in 1326. The college was to have a Provost and at least ten Fellows, originally studying theology, canon law and arts. The familiar name derives from a late C12 house called La Oriole which belonged to the Crown and was acquired in 1329. St Mary Hall, the former rectory house of St Mary, came to Oriel already in 1326, Bedel Hall, s of it, in 1455, Martin Hall in 1503. Before 1326 the first scholars used Tackley's Inn on the High Street, to the W (p.412). All these were academic halls in the sense explained in the Introduction (p.8), but St Mary Hall managed to develop a distinct personality, and in 1545 its communicating door with Oriel to the S was blocked. St Mary Hall's architectural history must therefore be treated in its own right. It has in fact older remains than Oriel. At Oriel nothing medieval survives at all. At St Mary Hall there is at least some recognizable MEDIEVAL MASONRY: to the E along Magpie Lane, N of its former hall-and-chapel block; to the W along Oriel Street, on both sides of the doorway to the present St Mary's Quad. (A third stretch, along the S side of the quad's S range, is now hidden.) But no features add interest to the masonry.

The rebuilding at Oriel proper fell in 1620–42. Before that the main quad was smaller, with a chapel (licensed in 1437) partway along the S side, a vaulted gateway probably of 1410–11 on the W side, a library in the E range, and on the N side the main hall of c.1535.† In the C18 the walled garden between this rebuilt First

---

*Not to be confused with the C15 Augustinian foundation of St Mary's College in New Inn Hall Street, p.436.

†This hall, shown by Bereblock with a canted bay window, is a tantalizing loss. Advice on its construction was supplied by *Thomas Heritage*, a royal chaplain and former Fellow, who was also clerk of the works at Whitehall Palace.

Quad and St Mary Hall acquired buildings too, becoming Oriel's Second Quad. The N front to the High was rebuilt in 1909–11, but otherwise the St Mary Hall buildings have been treated kindly.

First Quad

The FIRST QUAD of Oriel College is of 1620–42: the W range 1620–2, the S range after 1622, the N range c.1640 and the E range with hall and chapel 1637–42. The man behind this ambitious enterprise was John Tolson, Provost. The WEST FRONT to Oriel Square and Merton Street is even, with a single bay at each end very slightly projecting and the gate tower placed centrally. This symmetry and the presence of three full storeys recall Wadham and Merton in the 1610s, but in other respects Oriel already goes beyond: in the uniformity of the windows, all of twin arched lights, and in the small but elaborate shaped gables on every bay, a fashion traceable to London and the 1600s (Holland House etc.). At Oriel they alternate between ogee-topped and round-topped profiles. The gate tower by contrast is all Gothic. It has the traditional spandrel decoration to the archway, canted oriel above, top crenellations, and a fan-vault inside. Continuous hoodmoulds step up and down over the window tops all round. Only the doors with their diamond patterning tell of Jacobean classicism. To Merton Street, S, thirteen standard bays are followed by the ANTECHAPEL and CHAPEL, necessarily placed at a slight angle. They have the posthumously Gothic tracery of early C17 Oxford. The motif remembered here is the 'mandorla', i.e. pointed ellipse, at the top. E window of 1884, in keeping. Along Oriel Street and Magpie Lane, Oriel's frontages are unmonumental and varied. Stretches of wall intervene, and the stretches of medieval masonry already referred to.

The INTERIOR FAÇADES of First Quad are largely the same as the exterior ones, except for the E range. The main difference on the other sides concerns the doorways, over which the hoodmoulds rise up in a form like those of the shaped gables. Shields of arms above the doors (renewed), with Mannerist-classical details. On the N side the window rhythm is broken towards the E, where the library formerly occupied the top floor. On the tower top a Gothic inset for a clock, dated 1820.

The EAST RANGE is a symmetrical composition comprising the antechapel etc., r., and hall, l., each with a louvre on the roof ridge, and the hall porch in the centre. As rebuilt in 1897, this represents the original form lost in the early C19. It is low and shallow and has a pierced cresting with the inscription 'Regnante Carolo' ('in the reign of Charles', i.e. Charles I) and strapwork. Such openwork lettering was a fashion at the time – see e.g. Felbrigg, Norfolk (c.1621–4) and Castle Ashby, Northants (1624). The origin is French (Notre Dame du Marais, La Ferté-Bernard, 1535–44). Above are two niches with statues of Edward II and Charles I(?) and one niche over

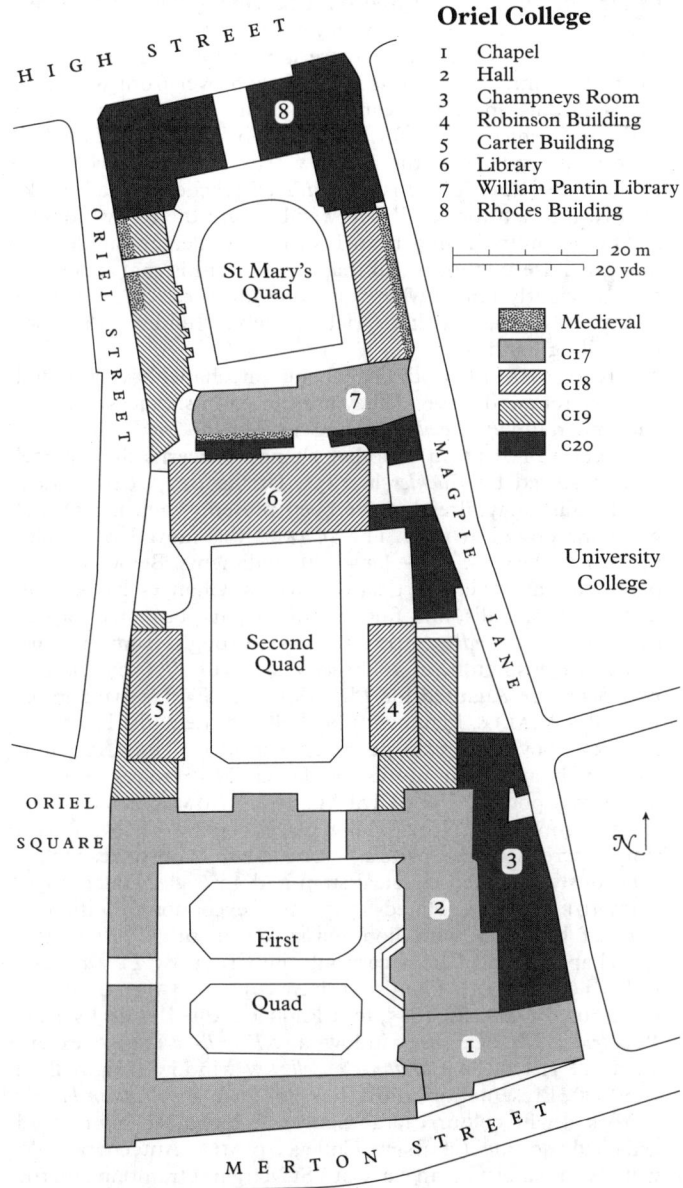

Oriel College

1 Chapel
2 Hall
3 Champneys Room
4 Robinson Building
5 Carter Building
6 Library
7 William Pantin Library
8 Rhodes Building

20 m
20 yds

Medieval
C17
C18
C19
C20

HIGH STREET

ORIEL STREET

St Mary's Quad

MAGPIE LANE

University College

Second Quad

ORIEL SQUARE

First Quad

MERTON STREET

N

with the Virgin and Child, the figures all renewed by *E. S. Frith* during 1960s refacing. The very top is remarkable in that it breaks the Jacobean tradition of the cresting motifs and goes classical, with pilasters, a shield with garlands, and a segmental pediment. The hall is raised on a basement. Its windows are like those of the chapel, and they are repeated for symmetry's sake r. of the porch, where there is no functional reason for them. This imposed symmetry was taken over from Wadham. The hall dais end has a canted bay window, transomed and entirely Gothic except for the strapwork cresting. The bay window is repeated at the r. end, where it belongs awkwardly to the antechapel. The chapel is indeed reached, equally awkwardly, through the small doorway beneath the bay window.

The accounts having been lost, the builder or builders of this quad are unknown. All that can be said is that its motifs are sufficiently unlike what was done up to c.1640 elsewhere in Oxford to suggest that Oriel was rebuilt under a different controlling hand.

INTERIORS. CHAPEL. Both chapel and antechapel have boarded ceilings, renewed c.1960. They are canted in six faces, painted with plain *trompe-l'oeil* coffering in *Marcus Beale Architects'* renovation of 2013–14. Another change concerns the chancel arch, restored by *Buckler* in 1858. Of the C17 WOODWORK, much (all?) may already have been present when the chapel was consecrated in 1642. The SCREEN was moved W in 1884 by *Sir T. G. Jackson.* Three bays with pediments. Below the side pediments are open, vertically set ovals. Changes by Jackson include extra stalls, and fine openwork parapet panels carved by *Farmer & Brindley.* – ORGAN CASE. Brought from St Mary Abbots, Kensington, in 1884; said to be of 1716 by *Christopher Schreider.* Adapted for *J.W. Walker & Sons'* instrument of 1987–8. – STALLS. Plain, with big balls on the ends. The PANELLING above has plain perspective motifs. Behind the altar the panels and their motifs are larger. No reredos as such, which may point to a pre-Civil War date. – COMMUNION RAIL. A very good job. Horizontally placed openwork ovals with simple scrolls in the panels. – LECTERN. Of bronze, with a generously moulded classical stem and an eagle. Dated 1654. – CANDELABRUM. Dated 1735. Also exceptional, with two tiers of branches with lion masks on them. – PAINTING, antechapel. Small Christ carrying the Cross. By *Bernard van Orley,* i.e. early C16 Flemish. Given 1911. – STAINED GLASS. E window by *Powells,* 1885, to a Raphaelesque design by *H.E. Wooldridge.* Chancel side windows also *Powells, c.*1885–7, except S side E, †1870, by *Clayton & Bell.* SW window (originally E window), Presentation in the Temple, 1767. By *William Peckitt* of York. Light colours, large figures. A technical failure, and artistically crude (cf. New College, p.216). Antechapel NW window, a panel with an early C16 St Margaret trampling on the dragon, and other fragments. W window, 2001, in memory of John Henry Newman. By *Vivienne Haig,* made by *Douglas Hogg.* – MONUMENT. George Carter, Provost, †1727. By *Sir R. Westmacott,* 1811. Aedicule on a strigillated base, simple and dignified.

The HALL has a hammerbeam roof, still with Gothic details. Some elements however must be restitution of 1827, when a plaster ceiling inserted in 1710 was taken out (cf. Corpus). Ceilings within the bay windows retain Gothic detail suggestive of 1827. The present screen and panelling, mixed classical and Gothic, are of 1910–11 by *Comper*. He also designed the stained glass, of 1911–26. Restored by *Richard Griffiths Architects*, 2020–1, with painting of the frieze. The BUTTERY, S, retains plain panelling of 1710; 'THE BOX' (Senior Common Room), N, panelling of 1676. To the E is the SCR's CHAMPNEYS ROOM of 1970–1 by *Geoffrey Beard* of *Oxford Architects Partnership*, the greater part of which projects as a sharp-edged ashlar volume to Magpie Lane. Here the boundary wall is cut down to allow its double oriel window to look out. On its S side another oriel, and a separately expressed servery. S of this are KITCHENS of 1920, proposed for replacement as part of *5th Studio*'s Brewhouse Yard scheme, approved 2021.

Best preserved of the C17 interiors is the TOWER ROOM, originally the Bursary. It has an uncommonly fine plaster ceiling of six subdivisions, and a plaster chimneypiece – Oxford's only example – with caryatids and panelling. The ceiling stucco has interlaced studded bands sprouting out into big flowers everywhere. Matching designs occur at Littlemore Hall in St Aldate's (p. 447) and in the Long Gallery at Chastleton House (*see Oxfordshire: North and West*), c. 1612 or later. Also on the W side, now within the enlarged PORTER'S LODGE, an early C17 painted overmantel with strapwork cresting in outline. STAIRCASES with open wells in the N and S ranges, the earliest ordinary college staircases of this type in Oxford. Those on the N side also include one in the Provost's Lodgings, for which *see* Second Quad.

Second Quad

SECOND QUAD has a totally different character, although the architectural scheme of First Quad is at least partially continued. The quadrangle is smaller, and its dominant feature is Wyatt's beautiful classical library, described below. The seven-bay W and E ranges continue the system of First Quad, whose N range here turns its irregular back. These side ranges comprise ROBINSON BUILDING of 1719–20, E, and CARTER BUILDING of 1729: even later than Radcliffe Quad at University College, where an early C17 formula was likewise reproduced. Oriel's Robinson shares the same builder and presumed designer with University College's Radcliffe, namely *William Townesend*. As often in the C18, the new buildings provided better-quality undergraduate accommodation than that available in the older parts.* The crenellated links with the S range are of 1815–19 by *Henry Hakewill*. He also doubled Robinson in depth, with a new range of four storeys facing Magpie Lane. On the W

---

*The *Almanac* engraving of 1736 shows the S side made symmetrical, presumably recording an aspiration to create a regular composition with the side blocks.

side the addition allowed Provost Coplestone to extend the Lodgings into Carter, where the ground-floor room became the PROVOST'S LIBRARY (now study). Hakewill's shelving here has a boxy Neoclassical look. Similar restrained classical detail by the architect in the Provost's other rooms, including a neat vaulted first-floor vestibule to communicate with the S range. The STAIRCASE here is early C17, plain by the standards of that at e.g. Merton's Lodgings. Slim balusters, slim column-props between the newels. Another *Hakewill* enhancement is the Gothic oriel window added to the Lodgings at the W end of the S range.

LIBRARY. By *James Wyatt*, built 1788–9 and finished internally in 1796. The stimulus was a donation of books by the 5th Lord Leigh. The mason was *Edward Edge*, the stone is Windrush ashlar. It is only seven bays long, and is separated from the W and E ranges by old trees looking in. Visually they are of the utmost importance. The library has a smoothly rusticated ground floor, an upper floor with unfluted Ionic columns, and an unbroken entablature. Ground-floor windows arched and recessed in larger blank arches, upper windows with straight entablatures and blank oblong panels above. Copper roof of 1949–50. Wyatt's roof was Welsh slate, an early occurrence for Oxford. The interior is 84 ft (26 metres) long, and plain except for the splendid E apse screened by two giant Corin-thian columns of green scagliola. A simple iron balcony runs along the two long sides and around the apse. The STAIRCASE, W, has a still plainer balustrade. Above it, reached from the library gallery, is the CEDAR ROOM, a panelled book-room with Corinthian pilasters and oak panelling of late C17 type. The source is said to be New College chapel, restored by Wyatt from 1788. If so, there must be a good deal of matching work too. Two SENIOR COMMON ROOMS on the ground floor, also plain. One has a fireplace with porphyry inserts, by *Westmacott Sen*. Decorative scheme by *John Fowler*, 1970.

The ARCHWAY E of the library is of 1930s, and leads to the Junior Library – but for the visitor this really belongs with St Mary's Quad, access to which is now gained from the NW corner of Second Quad.

St Mary's Quad

ST MARY'S QUAD is very attractive in the contrast of its regular shape with the variety of its buildings. The SOUTH RANGE sits close to the back of Wyatt's library. It contains in its E half the hall and chapel of St Mary Hall, arranged exceptionally with the former below the latter. The dates are 1639–40. Yet, again, all is Gothic. True, the windows of the chapel are round-arched, but the tracery – unlike Oriel's – is cusped throughout: an intersecting Perp-style pattern to the E, flowing Dec type to N and S. The hall windows below are straight-headed with cusped lights. The one bay of four storeys W of hall and chapel is original of *c.*1640 too. The range continues to the w, two-storeyed, with an extra timber-framed storey of *c.*1775–90. Loggan's view of 1675 shows close-set transomed windows along much of the first floor here, suggestive of a library, but these were replaced when the top storey was made.

The HALL is now the WILLIAM PANTIN LIBRARY, with fittings by *Marcus Beale Architects*, 2012. It retains the screen of *c.*1640, with pilasters and perspective panels. The upper pilasters and shell-hooded niche must be of *c.*1700. In the SCREENS PASSAGE the former buttery doorway, of wood with leaf spandrels. In 1923 incorporated in a war memorial by *H. S. Rogers*, with wreathed columns. To the s an addition with the former WRITING ROOM and curved passage from Second Quad, 1936 by *R. Fielding Dodd*. The CHAPEL is part of the JUNIOR LIBRARY. When still a chapel, in 1871–3, it was renovated by *J. C. Buckler*. The panelled and pointed-arched ceiling is his, and the plain entrance screen. Painted quarries in the side windows by *Lavers, Barraud & Westlake*, s, and *Powells*, N.

Poky LIBRARY EXTENSIONS of 1971–4 and 1987–8 fill the gap between the s range and the Wyatt library. In 1993–6 they were crowned by a well-judged top storey, designed without a professional architect. It shows externally as a slim gable to the w, a gable with a lunette (for the archive reading room) to the E.

The WEST RANGE is by *Daniel Robertson* and of *c.*1826. Gothic, with a vaulted entrance passage and two quite ornate oriels, all placed asymmetrically. One oriel is of six, the other of four lights. They are the best example in Oxford of pre-archaeological early C19 Gothic. Note especially the pretty, frilly details. In the N oriel tracery some stained glass said to be by *Willement*. The EAST RANGE is a quite uncollegiate seven-bay house built for the Principal of St Mary Hall, timber-framed and rendered, with a straight door hood on carved brackets. This is as late as 1743. And the NORTH RANGE is the back of the RHODES BUILDING, a mighty piece, dominating its stretch of the High Street, to which it turns its façade. Cecil Rhodes, an Oriel man, left £100,000 for it, and building took place in 1909–11. The architect was *Basil Champneys*, who was briefed to adopt 'the style which has become traditional in Oxford' – the Jackson manner, in other words. Here indeed is the last great Neo-Jacobean monument of Oxford, albeit already infused with free Baroque detail and other original touches. The front to the High is of nine big bays with the traditional mid-tower and gateway. The ground floor of the tower has pairs of alternatingly blocked columns; its first floor – very naughtily – has none, only two statue niches; but its second has columns in pairs again and one niche in the middle. In it the lately contentious statue of Rhodes, carved, with the other statues, by *Henry Pegram*. In the side pieces the ground floor is rusticated and has segment-headed windows in recessed smooth walling under round arches. Oriels and statues on the first floor, dormers with shaped gables above, picking up the Oriel theme. To the quad the design is similar, but with short,

81

non-matching extensions to each side. In *Marcus Beale Architects'* renovation of 2014–15 a storey of copper-clad dormers was added, marring the Edwardian proportions. Ground-floor windows also enlarged then, after the pattern of those in the end bays.

For O'BRIEN QUAD and the island site across Oriel Street, reached from the college by a tunnel of 1985–6, *see* Perambulation 1, pp.412–13; for JAMES MELLON HALL *see* East Oxford, p.499.

PEMBROKE COLLEGE
Pembroke Square and St Aldate's

Pembroke College was founded in 1624, on a site just within the southern city wall. Nominally the founder was James I, but the money came from the bequest of Thomas Tesdale, augmented by a gift from Richard Wightwick. Tesdale was an Abingdon malt-ster who made good and took an Oxfordshire estate at Glympton, where he specialized in woad for dyeing. Wightwick was a little-known clergyman, rector of East Ilsley in Berks. Tesdale had intended merely to enhance the foundation of Balliol, with precedence to candidates from Abingdon School. But the school itself petitioned successfully for a new college, to be based on Broadgates Hall, one of the longer-lasting of the medieval academic halls. There were to be ten Fellows and ten scholars (more or less), under a Master. The name was taken from the Earl of Pembroke, then Chancellor of the University.

The C17 quad is modest and was much altered in the C19, but the C18 chapel and C19 expansion in Chapel Quad to the w show increasing ambition. In the C20 additions were made to the E, including the annexation of Wolsey's C16 almshouses on St Aldate's, and to the N, including the old Beef Lane. Architecturally the results are unassertive, but the C21 has made up for this with *Berman Guedes Stretton*'s bold new Rokos Quad to the s.

Old Quad and Chapel Quad

Pembroke looks unpromising to the outside. Coming from St Aldate's, the visitor first encounters Wolsey's Almshouses (*see* p.236), with no obvious public entry. OLD QUAD lies behind and to the w, facing St Aldate's church (p.390) across Pembroke Square. This front range is of 1673–94, built by *John Townesend I*. But what one sees now is a Neo-Perp remodelling and heightening of 1829–30 by the builder-architect *Daniel Evans*. Townesend's GATE TOWER of 1694, tucked into the sw corner, had artisan-Baroque elevations before Evans got

Pembroke College

1	Former Master's Lodgings	6	Besse Building
2	McGowin Library	7	Staircase 12
3	Former Broadgates Hall	8	Macmillan Building
4	Chapel	9	Wolsey's Almshouses
5	Hall	10	Rokos Quad

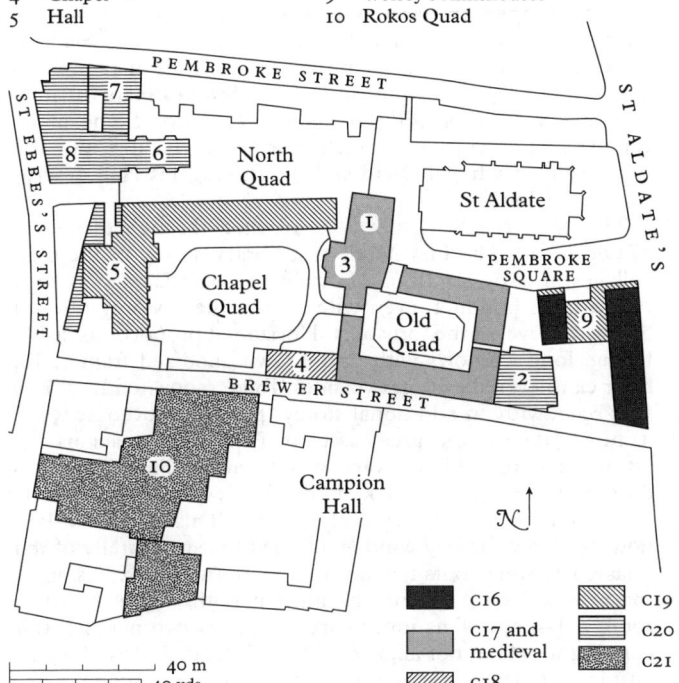

to work (cf. Exeter).* The big intricate oriel is a version of the
one on John of Gaunt's late C14 palace at Lincoln, a quotation
'ascribed to the taste of the Rev. C. Cleobury', Fellow. Tower
parapet rebuilt and simplified in 1879 by *Bodley & Garner*,
parapet to the s since simplified too. Looming up at right
angles to this tower are the former MASTER'S LODGINGS of
1695, also remodelled by *Evans* in 1829–30. They replaced the
late Elizabethan lodgings of the Principal of Broadgates Hall.
Obviously Victorian top storey, added *c.*1858.

After that OLD QUAD receives one with uniform sides and
friendly lawn. Two storeys plus dormers all round, except for
the pretension of the gate tower in its unhappy corner. The
fabric of the E, W and S sides is of 1626–70, refronted in
1829–30 or (E) 1838. This C19 refacing – itself since renewed –

*Loggan's engraving of 1675 shows a plain central tower instead, presumably as
then intended.

appears to have been faithful to the early C17 design. Doorways with flat, thinly detailed four-centred arches. Windows
of a rather neutral type, two or three lights, with chamfered
mullions and straight heads. Running hoodmoulds. The small
dormers have trefoil panels in the gables; the larger ones are
now flat-topped but were once gabled too. The N range had
plainer casements at first, but the windows were made to
match the other three sides in the C19. PLAQUE of 1896 in the
NW corner to James Smithson of the Smithsonian Institute,
by the US sculptor *William Ordway Partridge*. Some of the
walling in this corner is much older than the C17, but that
must wait for Chapel Quad and the Broadgates Hall description (*see* below).

The MCGOWIN LIBRARY is reached through the E side
of Old Quad. The first Modernist library at any of the older
colleges, it is by *Sir Leslie Martin* with *Colen Lumley*, 1972–4.
Not a large building, even with its basement storey fitted in
below the level of the forecourt. Horizontal proportions, ashlar
facing, long windows with dark-brown anodized frames. Top
floor cantilevered out on two sides. To be renovated by *Wright
& Wright*, with an additional storey (plans approved 2019).

CHAPEL QUAD is the great asset of Pembroke, spacious and
attractive all round in the variety of its ranges. The earliest is of
course the E range, the back of Old Quad, with at its N end the
former hall of BROADGATES HALL itself. This looks Neo-Perp
now, but only the bay window of *c.*1821 is structurally of that
phase. The walls to its l. and r. represent a 1620s extension for
the new college, and with the inner part they give the whole
room a T-shape. This inner part comprises two parallel walls
running W–E, but not aligned with Old Quad. A Perp doorway
visible in older views suggests a C15 date here. When a new
hall was built in the 1840s (*see* below) the old one became the
library, then in 1974 the SENIOR COMMON ROOM. It retains
a Jacobean-style frieze, looking 1820s too. The gabled storey
visible over the E part is of 1709, and housed the library when
its holdings were much smaller. Before that the college kept its
books in an upper room over the S aisle of St Aldate's church,
another arrangement inherited from Broadgates Hall.

The answering projection at the S end of the range is the
CHAPEL. Built by *William Townesend* in 1728–32, possibly to his
own design. It is a plain rectangle of five bays, totally rusticated
to the quad. The windows round-headed. Four Ionic pilasters placed between them in the central bays, which project
slightly. Entrance in the W bay, with hefty key blocks under a
broken pediment on brackets. Panelled parapet. The interior
now is essentially a Neo-Renaissance remodelling of 1884–5
by *Charles Eamer Kempe*, an old member (and former pupil of
G. F. Bodley), working with the architect *R. J. Johnson*. Kempe
is best known for his STAINED GLASS, nearly always Gothic,
but here in a kind of Holbein-Swiss-Renaissance style. Its dates
are 1884–93, plus 1921 for *Kempe & Co.*'s antechapel S window.

The ceiling on the other hand is Raphael style, with busy *grottesche*, as in the Logge of the Vatican. – REREDOS. Original, of marble, with paired Composite columns and a pediment. Underneath this are three putto heads. ALTARPIECE, a Risen Christ by *James Cranke*, given 1786, after Rubens's painting for the monastery of Discalced Carmelites, Antwerp. The ALTAR below is a modification of 1885. – SCREEN and simple STALLS, finished 1737. The screen is a fine piece, the centre wide open with two Corinthian columns set in and a pediment with an urn. The side piers have on the E face the two principal seats under ogee canopies. Probably made by *Jeremiah Franklin*, documented as working here. – ORGAN by *Messrs Létourneau* of Canada, 1995–6, in a case adapted from *Kempe*'s of 1894. Kempe in turn reused casework from *Harris*'s organ (probably *John Harris*) of 1726, formerly in the Sheldonian. – SCULP-TURE. Carved and coloured Apostles and Prophets in Baroque attitudes in niches between the windows, designed by *Kempe*.

The HALL is on the W side, an ambitious building, forerun- 84 ner to the grand Victorian halls at Balliol and Keble. It was built in 1847–8, under the expansive mastership of Dr Francis Jeune. The Master wanted Sir Charles Barry, who was too busy, so Barry's architect nephew *John Hayward* of Exeter stepped into the breach. The hall is detached, with a tall louvre-cum-lantern, four tall Perp windows, a shallow bay window to the l., a projecting porch-tower to the r., and stairs up to this porch on the inner side. The porch has a lierne vault, the hall a steep and weighty hammerbeam roof. Much heraldic glass by *Chance Bros*, 1850 onwards; also two windows each (E wall) by *Kenneth Banner*, 1955, and *Hugh Powell*, 1960. The long crenel-lated WALL across to the chapel, with a garden strip behind, is of 1847–8 too, but the KITCHEN is of 1869, a separate building beyond the hall. By *Buckeridge*; also Perp style. Before that the kitchens were in the hall basement.

The NORTH RANGE looks decidedly of two parts, but is the result of one campaign. It is also by *Hayward*, and of 1845–6. The E part is of three bays, Perp in detail, Barry-ish and sym-metrical in composition, with two canted bay windows l. and r. of the doorway. The larger W part is Perp also, but has four gables, and already assumes a Victorian-convent aspect.

North Quad

NORTH QUAD lies N of Chapel Quad, with the entrance at its E end. Until 1962 a street called Beef Lane ran E–W here, its alignment now indicated by the GATES at each end. By demolishing the houses on its N side, and annexing the houses of Pembroke Street immediately N, the college acquired prom-ising new territory. The new architecture unfortunately sells this short. First came the BESSE BUILDING of 1954–5 by *Sir Hubert Worthington*, one of M. Besse's benefactions to poorer colleges (cf. Keble, St Peter's, Worcester). A short range facing the old lane, symmetrical, three-storeyed, of ashlar, with mullioned windows and two canted bay windows. From *c.*1957 Pembroke's architects were *Simpson & Cleverly*, later *Moore, Simpson & Cleverly*. They added a SERVICE BLOCK with Gothick windows in the outer angle between the hall and Chapel Quad N side, and set about adapting the houses of Pembroke Street (*see* pp.444–5). That accounts for the Neo-Georgian hind parts of Staircase 17 (No.15); the rebuilding at Staircase 15 (Nos.19 and 20), with two broken-pedimented C18 doorways reportedly salvaged from demolitions at Lord Mildmay's Flete House in Devonshire; and the pretty raised terrace in front. In 1966–7 STAIRCASE 12 was fitted into the W side, designed by *C.P. Cleverly*. Copper-faced dormer storey, broad shallow-arched windows. The Pembroke Street side is dressed up to blend in there. Behind, separated by a raised court, is the MACMILLAN BUILDING, altogether a tougher proposition. Of 1973–6 by *Sir Leslie Martin*, executant architect *Colen Lumley*. Yellow-brown brick, the type of the architect's St Cross Building (p.382), and with a similar horizontal stress. Windows grouped in strips, with brown panels between. To St Ebbe's Street behind the block cantilevers outwards, with shops below. To the S one of Martin's characteristic external staircases all of brick.

Wolsey's Almshouses and city wall

WOLSEY'S ALMSHOUSES became the Master's Lodgings in 1928. They were begun by Cardinal Wolsey in 1525, across the road from his foundation of Christ Church. At first there were three ranges in a U-plan, open to the S and with the longest range fronting St Aldate's, E. The S end of this range may never have been finished; Loggan's map of 1675 shows it roofless. It was reconstructed in 1834 by *H.J. Underwood*, who also demolished the N parts and cross-range. So the present N fronts of the two remaining C16 ranges are his, as are the gables added towards St Aldate's. Other windows mostly of the original type, shallow-arched uncusped twin lights under individual hoodmoulds. Unrestored examples survive in the W range, protected within the present cross-range of 1877. In that year *Bodley & Garner* reconstructed the almshouses as a residence for the Rev. R.G. Faussett, Treasurer of Christ Church.

The almshouse subdivisions inside cannot now be traced. The E range does however retain part of a handsome display roof, probably the one recorded as in preparation in 1529. It has arch-braced collar-beams and two tiers of wind-braces. That suggests a first-floor hall here. Also original, but repositioned in 1877, are the moulded beams of the Oak Room on the ground floor. Panelling of *c.*1600 here from a farmhouse at Chalgrove, and two enriched doorways and an elaborate wooden chimneypiece from a house in Brewer Street. Its overmantel has clumsy herms and the arms reportedly of Oliver Smith, mayor in 1637. Another import is the back stair, brought from a house across St Aldate's and much modified to fit. Newels of the early C17 Oxford type with upward-tapering square finials. *Bodley & Garner*'s fireplaces mostly take after one C16 original with small-scale spandrel decoration, but their panelling, ironwork etc. already look to non-period, Aesthetic motifs.

The almshouses have their S end on Brewer Street, and then along Brewer Street the college continues as a wall. This was the CITY WALL, and parts appear to be medieval still, or at least early C16: see the Tudor Perp doorway towards the E. To the W are the picturesque upper parts of Old Quad, then the chapel with its arched windows and high parapet, both appearing much higher because of the falling ground. The wall continues under the footbridge and past the hall etc., leaving the city wall alignment where it returns N up St Ebbe's Street.

Rokos Quad

ROKOS QUAD is by *Berman Guedes Stretton*, 2010–13. It is linked to Chapel Quad by a glass-sided FOOTBRIDGE over Brewer Street – rather an elegant bridge, set on a slant, and counterweighted to avoid bearing on the city wall (engineers *Price & Myers*). The space is not a complete quadrangle, for the E side is open towards Campion Hall (p. 325), and the backs of existing buildings interrupt on the other three sides. The quad contains plenty of living accommodation, and sundry facilities of the kinds that colleges now require. What makes the grouping special is the sloping site. The bridge enters at a high level, and the buildings are laid out around a steep descending stair, with two small garden terraces opening off it on the way down. The facing materials are ashlar or pale soft yellow brick, a good rhyme for Lutyens's golden rubble across the way. For contrast there are dark, projecting window surrounds, and pitched, dark-coloured roofs. Stone is used for the HAROLD LEE BUILDING by the bridge, which features a tall oblong tower and a big adjacent meeting room. In the space below is a lecture theatre, with access from a ground-floor concourse that also opens to Brewer Street, and an art gallery. The W side includes a café on the ground floor and seminar rooms and outdoor terrace above. To the outside the buildings are separately articulated, with some minty green rendering towards Rose Place, S, and Littlegate Street, W.

For the SIR GEOFFREY ARTHUR BUILDING *see* South Oxford, p. 516.

THE QUEEN'S COLLEGE
High Street

Robert de Eglesfield, a Cumberland man, chaplain to Queen Philippa, established the college in 1341 and found it wise to call it Queen's College: partly as a counterpart to the king's (Edward III's) King's Hall at Cambridge, started in 1337 (a forerunner of Trinity College), partly in the hope that future queens would offer their patronage. There were to be twelve Fellows under a Provost, as well as 'poor boys' and chaplains, with a preference for those from the north-western counties. Building proceeded slowly: gateway 1352, chapel 1373–80 (with an E window of flowing tracery, an instance of late-lingering Dec), library c.1390, hall 1398–1402 (by *William Wynford*), antechapel 1516. The gateway faced E on to Queen's Lane, for architecturally speaking the medieval college had no High Street presence. But

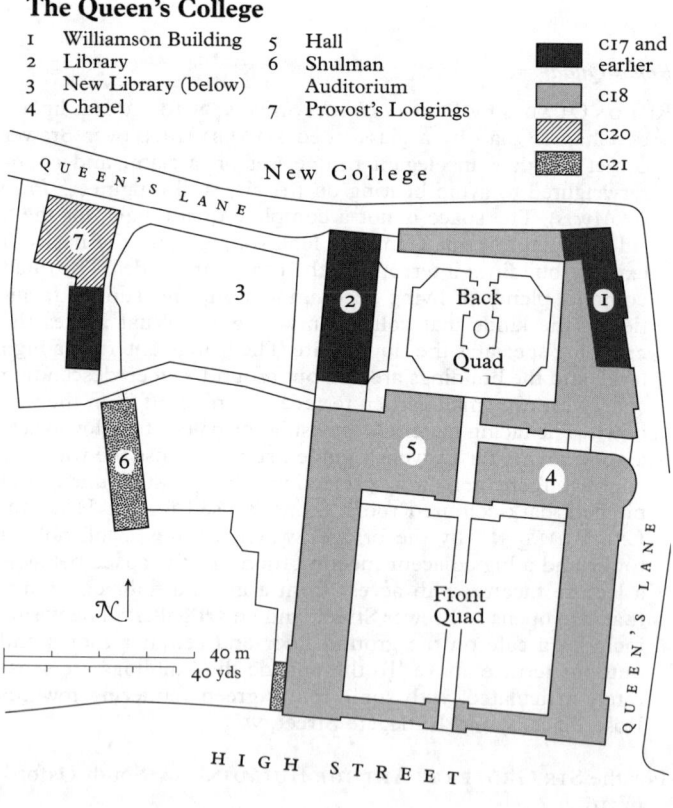

The Queen's College

1	Williamson Building	5	Hall
2	Library	6	Shulman
3	New Library (below)		Auditorium
4	Chapel	7	Provost's Lodgings

C17 and earlier
C18
C20
C21

all this has been swept away, for Queen's is the only old foundation with no buildings at all prior to the Restoration. In fact the
essential architectural history is condensed into the less than
a hundred years between 1671 and 1759: Back Quad in 1671–
1721, Front Quad in 1710–59. There is no early C17 hangover;
work was from the start classical in the Wren sense, and *Wren*'s
name indeed appears in connection with the first phase. But firm
authorship of the various parts is hard to establish at Queen's,
and suggestions will be commented on as we proceed.

Back Quad

Front Quad is so marvellous a feature of the High Street and in
itself that it may seem wrongheaded to start with BACK QUAD,
and doubly so with its outer E face to Queen's Lane. Yet this
is what chronology demands. This first building is the WIL-
LIAMSON BUILDING, i.e. the E range. It was built in 1671–4
to designs by *Wren*, as letters from Dean Fell of Christ Church
make clear. The Berkshire mason *Anthony Deane* was the
builder.* However, of that design we do not have much, since
the C17 building was lengthened, heightened and doubled in
depth towards the quad in the early C18. The best-preserved
part is the short N front. It has cross-windows, and the centre
is a blank niche. Originally there was a big hipped roof with
dormers, and a central E pediment.
    Sir Joseph Williamson – with Wren, one of the founders of
the Royal Society – spent £1,700 on this building. He also left
another £6,000 to continue by a N and a W range, thus creating
a new quadrangle N of the old one. Instead the quad now has
severely plain S, N and E façades, with simple pedimented doorcases and the windows vertically linked by plain apron panels.
The only accent is an archway with a broad broken segmental
pediment and a Venetian window in the centre of the S range.
As *John Townesend I*, the busy builder, was college mason from
1688 till his retirement in 1712, he may have designed these
ineloquent ranges. First to be built was the NORTH RANGE, in
1706–8. The SOUTH RANGE is of 1715–21, the EAST RANGE
in front of Williamson of 1719–21. By these years the rebuilding of the medieval college was in progress, with the kitchen
for the new hall in the S range, W part. In the E part here the
panelled WRITING ROOM, a common room for the college's
'poor boys' or Taberdars.
    The LIBRARY, however, occupying the W side, is another   57
matter. It is a detached building of 1692–5 with façades to the
quad and to the Provost's Garden behind, the latter the more
ornamental. Eleven bays, horizontally rusticated ground floor,
arched windows on both floors. Originally the ground floor

---

* Compare Deane's commissions at Holme Lacy, Herefs., and Horseheath, Cambs.,
with the architects Hugh May and Roger Pratt respectively as consultant and as
designer.

had open arches instead, with a range of rooms behind. *C. R. Cockerell* enclosed most of this loggia in 1843–5 to increase the book space. To the garden there is a solid wall below, which in its C17 form had doorways in the centre and outermost bays. The arrangement with two open bays at the S is Cockerell's doing, and the niches of the blind bays are now grouped 5:3 instead of 4:4. In them stand STATUES of benefactors: Henrietta Maria, Williamson, Bishop Barlow, Archbishop Lamplugh of York, Robert de Eglesfield, Edward III, Queen Philippa, Charles I. They were carved by *John Vanderstaine*. Also his the keystones, the eagles on the three-bay top pediments (renewed), and some parapet statues now lost. Relief SCULPTURE in the pediments: Wisdom with attendants to the quad, Queen Philippa ditto to the garden. Possibly by *William Townesend* (payments for unspecified carving from 1694), but greatly renewed.

The master mason of the library was again *John Townesend I*. He was paid in 1691 for plans of the existing college, and in 1692 for a visit to Cambridge, where Wren's library at Trinity stood as the new exemplar. Can the design have been his, and his alone? No architect is named on the two contemporary engravings that have survived, one showing the library as built, the other (dated 1693) a variant form. The latter was found in the papers of Henry Aldrich, Dean of Christ Church and amateur architect. Also, the library roof has flat-topped queenpost trusses with an additional central post, a distinctive type later used at All Saints' church (p. 388), whose attribution to the Dean seems sound. So there is a good case for *Aldrich* here, at least as a contributor to what may have been an essentially collaborative or consultative design.

INTERIORS. Entry to the library was originally via its S projection. This had to be rebuilt to integrate the library with the new Front Quad. The big 1690s STAIRCASE was retained, in a new configuration. The UPPER LIBRARY is gorgeous. Compartmented ceiling with foliage bands and panels by the plasterer *James Hands*, a late and very fine example of naturalistic work. The three principal panels were probably intended for paintings (cf. Trinity College chapel, also 1690s). Instead, in 1756 *Thomas Roberts* added his exquisite Rococo decoration. Above the windows to E and W runs a beautiful frieze of swags and garlands, shells, books etc., carved in stone; probably the 'fretwork' in the library for which *Vanderstaine* was paid in 1694. The S doorway is splendidly framed with Corinthian columns and a broken segmental pediment, on which are seated stucco figures of Arts and Science with their instruments, and the college arms above, borne aloft by eight cherubs and an eagle. Can this all be by *Hands* too? It looks more Flemish than English. The bookcases project to make stalls in the usual way, but the windows are not placed high enough to run the cases along the walls as well, as Wren had so ingeniously managed in Trinity library. The decoration of the cases is also outstanding. It includes enriched segmental pediments over four ends placed symmetrically, and openwork panels to screen the uppermost shelves. Openwork also are the big cupboard doors at the s (but originally at the N) end. The joinery was contracted for by *Thomas Minn, Sen. & Jun.* Eight of the window arches have C17 STAINED GLASS of portrait heads etc. from the old hall, attributed to *William Price Sen.* Also from there a STATUE of Queen Philippa, wood, probably early C17. Whoever the sculptor was, he went to the queen's effigy in Westminster Abbey for inspiration. Restored 1891. The Upper Library itself last restored 2013–14.

In the LOWER LIBRARY the arcade along the middle, the simple square-panelled ceiling and the bookcases are all *Cockerell*'s, as is the neat stair to the Upper Library, NE corner. Wrought-iron central gate of 1935 designed by *J. E. Thorpe*; also the paving, URN etc. in the quad. This storey now also gives access to *Rick Mather Architects*' accomplished NEW LIBRARY of 2014–17 (designs 2006–7; *Eckersley & Callaghan*, engineers), a complex subterranean volume that sits below the raised lawn to the w. The giveaways there are a giant skylight set at an angle, and two modest escape staircases descending to N and s.

In the passage through the s end of the library, WAR MEMO-RIAL panels: 1921 and 1950 (the latter by *Laurence Turner*). Alongside the library, s side, plate-glass infill by *Berman Guedes Stretton*, part of the new FELLOWS' DINING ROOM made by enclosing the upper space between the s range and the hall, 2008–10. A jolt to the eye amid so much stone. A new KITCHEN was made too, also by excavation.

Front Quad

So to FRONT QUAD at last. It rivals Peckwater at Christ Church as the grandest classical ensemble in the Oxford colleges, and it belongs entirely to the short phase which one has a right to name English Baroque, i.e. Baroque with English reservations. The High Street in particular has nothing else as rousing as the screen of Queen's; for the quad is open to the s in no more than a screen with a central gatehouse, an originally French scheme acclimatized already at Cambridge's Gonville and Caius College in the 1570s. Provost Lancaster, for whom the quad was rebuilt, said that the plan was based 'upon the plan of the Luxemburgh House [Palais du Luxembourg] in Paris' – which indeed has just such a domed gatehouse in its screen.

In detail, the situation at Queen's is this. The w range was built in 1710–11, the N, i.e. hall and chapel, range in 1714–15, the E range in two parts between 1733 and 1759, the screen and gatehouse in 1733–5. There is in fact quite a difference between the style of the 1710s and that of the 1730s. The architecture of the WEST and EAST RANGES, including their s ends to the High, is so severe as to be almost blunt. They are of ashlar, with the window bays set back slightly behind the totally unmoulded front face, and the second-floor windows have

The Queen's College, Front Quad.
Engraving by J. Le Keux after F. Mackenzie, 1834

aprons of a decidedly cubic character, again totally unmoulded.
The ranges are thirteen by three bays, and in their centre have
a three-bay attic storey surmounted by a broad segmental pediment with garlands and figure decoration. The ground floor
has a rusticated arcade all the way along. The GATEHOUSE on
the other hand has l. and r. of the entrance to s and N pairs of
columns with bands of vermiculated rustication, a much busier
motif, and on top an open, domed rotunda with a statue of
Queen Caroline beneath. Tuscan columns, two deep, and set
radially with their own slabs of entablature, carry the dome.
To the street the SCREEN WALL has five bays either side of
blank-arched aedicules set in rusticated niches, the rustication
running into the niches as in Wren's portal of St Mary-le-Bow
in London. The fine DOOR is part of the composition.* To the
quad the screen continues the horizontally rusticated arcading
of the w and E ranges.

That leaves the NORTH RANGE. It is not integrated with the
w and E ranges; yet there was no break in the building activity. The range has a middle gateway and passage with the hall
to the l., the chapel to the r. All this has an Oxford pedigree
(University College, 1637), although the arrangement with
central portico and turret descends from Wren at Chelsea
Hospital. The arched windows are set high up and separated
by giant Doric pilasters. The windows themselves appear to
stand on very high, totally unmoulded pedestals – again a way
to suggest layers of wall different in depth. The centre has giant

*A new MAIN ENTRANCE by *Burd Haward Architects* is under construction in the
gap between the front range and Nos. 33–38 High Street, w (2023).

attached Doric columns and a pediment with a figure composition. A cupola on top with pairs of columns, and these are
set diagonally, another Chelsea motif. But the details of the N
range are not Wren at all; they – and those of the other ranges
too – go more with *Hawksmoor*, Wren's principal pupil, than
anybody else. Indeed, drawings for the college in Hawksmoor's
hand include some that relate to the extant W and E ranges, as
well as others of more visionary character. There are marked
affinities too between the N range and Hawksmoor's contemporary Clarendon Building (p. 340). But other drawings for the
college exist by *Dr George Clarke* of All Souls, Hawksmoor's
ally and patron. What seems to have happened is that designs
supplied by Hawksmoor were selected and adapted by Clarke,
and that *William Townesend* also made adaptations as master
mason. As for the screen, the big wall niches are characteristic of *Hawksmoor*, and we know that the rotunda was indeed
designed by him, but was modified by *Townesend* in execution.

All the main fronts display SCULPTURE, now renewed or
heavily restored. Of the PEDIMENTS, that of the N front with
Britannia etc. followed designs by *Sir James Thornhill*; replacement by *Michael Groser*, 1982. W range, both pediments originally by *Garratt* and *Smith*; S pediment replaced by *E. J. & A. T.
Bradford*, 1965. E range, quad pediment by *John Townesend III*
and *William King*, *c.* 1759, Rococo, restored 1856 etc.; S pediment by *Sir Henry Cheere*, 1733, replaced 1968 by *Groser*. Of
the STATUES, *Cheere* supplied Queen Caroline in the rotunda
(1733), and the three (Law, Physic, Poetry) on the E wing S
front. Corresponding statues, W (Theology, Philosophy, Mathematics) replaced in Portland stone by *Thomas Knowles II*,
1847. Other episodes of RESTORATION include refacing the
N range S side in Bath stone in 1863, reconstruction of the
rotunda in 1909 (Portland stone) and the clock turret in 1910,
and a great deal in 1957–68 by the *Ministry of Works*, including
renewal of the S arcade piers.

For the INTERIORS it is harder to demonstrate Hawksmoor's
involvement, and it may be that *William Townesend* acted more
freely here. The CHAPEL is of impressive size and ends in an
apse to full height. The walls have giant Corinthian pilasters,
and these continue round the apse, where the middle two and
the wall between are marble-faced. The ceiling is coved and has
bold and strong stucco panels in the coving. The apse is treated
differently, with coffering in not quite regular hexagons. In the
apse ceiling a circular PAINTING of the Ascension by *Thornhill*, 1716. The present decorative scheme is *Quinlan Terry*'s,
1979.* FITTINGS largely of 1718–23: PANELLING, STALLS and
the superb SCREEN, the form that of a Venetian window. The
side parts have two pairs of fluted columns each side to W as
well as E. The top an open scrolly pediment and a big urn,
the sides scrolled and richly carved. – COMMUNION RAIL of

---

* In 1876 *J. P. Seddon* supplied proposals for extravagant redecoration with mural
figures etc.

wrought iron by *Richard Booth*, also of the very best quality.
– CHANDELIERS. Two, of brass, Baroque shape, given 1721.
William Cowdry made them. – LECTERN. Brass, with the usual
eagle. Signed by *William Borroghes* (*Burroughs*) of London,
1662. He did eagle lecterns also at Canterbury and Lincoln
cathedrals. – REREDOS. Copy of Correggio's La Notte, early
C19, by *James Craske*. – ORGAN by *Frobenius*, 1965, the case
designed by *Fin Ditlevsen*. Oxford's first example of the revived
classical type. – BRASSES, in the apse. Nicholas Hyenson or
Swinerton, priest, †1479, 13 in. (33 cm.), and Robert Langton,
priest, †1518, 3 ft ½ in. (93 cm.). Also two plates designed by
Dr Richard Haydock, each with kneeling subject and allegorical figures: Bishop Henry Robinson and Provost Henry Airay,
both †1616.

STAINED GLASS. A full complement. Most is C16 and C17
glass from the earlier chapel, re-set and adapted to fit. E
window by *Joshua Price*, 1717: Rest on the Flight into Egypt.
In the lunette, St Peter and St Paul and a view of a city. Also
by *Price* the lunettes of all the other windows: small biblical
scenes and shields of arms. Next four well-preserved windows
on each side, the work of *Abraham van Linge*, dated 1635.
N side, E to W: Last Judgment, repaired by *Price* (two windows,
originally one); Last Supper and Crucifixion; Annunciation
and Visitation. S side: Ascension; Resurrection; Adoration of
the Shepherds; Pentecost. The rest is early C16. One window
on each side with figures and some heraldic shields dated 1518
(the surrounding glass is later). N side, archbishop between two
bishops; S side, St Clement, St Peter as pope, a bishop. Finally
a window on each side with early C16 glass of more advanced
technique. N side, St Aldhelm, St Osmund, and St Lawrence
beneath the Annunciation with a crucifix on the lily. S side,
below, St John of Beverley, St Robert, and St Anne teaching
the Virgin to read; above, St Margaret, St Christopher, St
Edward the Confessor.

HALL. Entry is from the NW passage, without an intervening
screen. The architecture of the hall is worth close study. The
walls have giant Doric pilasters each with slips of entablature,
but the end walls have in addition on the W side three narrow
arched openings with wrought-iron balconies and blunt detail,
and above that level on the W and E sides short pilasters carrying a broad, low, broken segmental pediment. On the E side this
frames an urn in a niche, on the W an internal window. Severe
but Baroque fireplace. In the middle of the E side is what looks
like the Provost's throne but is merely a central feature. Entarsia
back; pediment on thick brackets. The ceiling is barrel-vaulted,
of big panels between cross-arches with plasterwork bands,
and over the dais an extra half-bay of coffering. STAINED
GLASS, 1909 by *Powells* to *Sir Reginald Blomfield*'s designs.
The windows incorporate more of the series of heads attributed to *William Price Sen.*, representing the founder, Queen
Philippa, kings Edward III and IV, Charles I, Henrietta Maria,
Sir Joseph Williamson and Provost Lancaster.

The VESTIBULE between hall and chapel is vaulted with one saucer-dome preceded and followed by two sail-vaults. In the passage, MONUMENT to Dr Joseph Smith †1756 by *William Tyler*, with bust. Another saucer-dome to the main GATEWAY. In the BUTTERY W of the hall, stained glass with the heads of Henry V and Cardinal Beaufort, mostly of *c.* 1640 but probably based on an earlier prototype, now lost. Above is the SENIOR COMMON ROOM, panelled and still in its early C18 state, with Corinthian half-pilasters framing the chimney-breast. In the E passage the three openings to the hall, and a re-set stone carved with angels supporting the arms of Bishop Langton, Provost in 1487–95. The OLD LODGINGS and other rooms to the S were burnt out in 1778 and reconstructed by *George Shakespear* under *Kenton Couse*, then burnt and rebuilt again (S end) in 1886–7.

Buildings to the west

The GARDENS lie to the W: the Provost's Garden behind the library, as already noted, the Fellows' Garden behind Front Quad. At the far end is the SHULMAN AUDITORIUM, reached down a lane with delightful countrified walls l. and r. By *Berman Guedes Stretton*, 2007–11. A successful combination of modern and traditional forms and materials: long, barn-like roof on steel trusses, rubble walling (the old W wall retained), plate-glass entrance projection to the S, and timber linings. The S and SW perimeter is made by annexed houses (DRAWDA HALL etc.), for which *see* High Street, pp. 413–14. To the NW the PROVOST'S LODGINGS of 1958–60, by *Raymond Erith*. A thoughtful essay in classicism, too original for the easy label of Neo-Georgian. The N side, to Queen's Lane, has no openings except the rusticated doorway and lunette emerging from the rusticated ground floor, two little windows l. and r., and two slits close to a niche in the first floor above. The influence is Sanmicheli, and the centralized plan with its barrel-vaulted N–S passage likewise owes much to Renaissance villa precedents. To E and W, totally sheer five-bay fronts under a hipped roof. The S approach passes GARAGES converted by *Erith* from the college brewhouse etc., with an applied timber colonnade and latticed doors.

There is not much more to add. A walk along Queen's Lane will show first the plain back of the E range, then the apse of the chapel with the windows set back slightly behind the sheer wall surface, then the Williamson Building with its additions, then the N side of the N range of Back Quad with much blunt wall and occasional bluntly framed narrow windows, then the library N window, a stretch of wall and the Lodgings to finish.

For DRAWDA HALL and CARRODUS QUAD, High Street, *see* Perambulation 1, p. 414; for the FLOREY BUILDING in St Clement's *see* Perambulation 7, p. 450.

REUBEN COLLEGE
Parks Road

see Radcliffe Science Library, p. 369

ST ANNE'S COLLEGE
Woodstock Road and Banbury Road

St Anne's originated in the late 1870s as the Society of Oxford
Home Students, which supported women students without a
college attachment. Its original character was thus to serve as
a base for members living at home or in lodgings. In the early
c20 it acquired or leased a few scattered properties, in 1932 it
bought part of the present freehold. Buildings began to go up

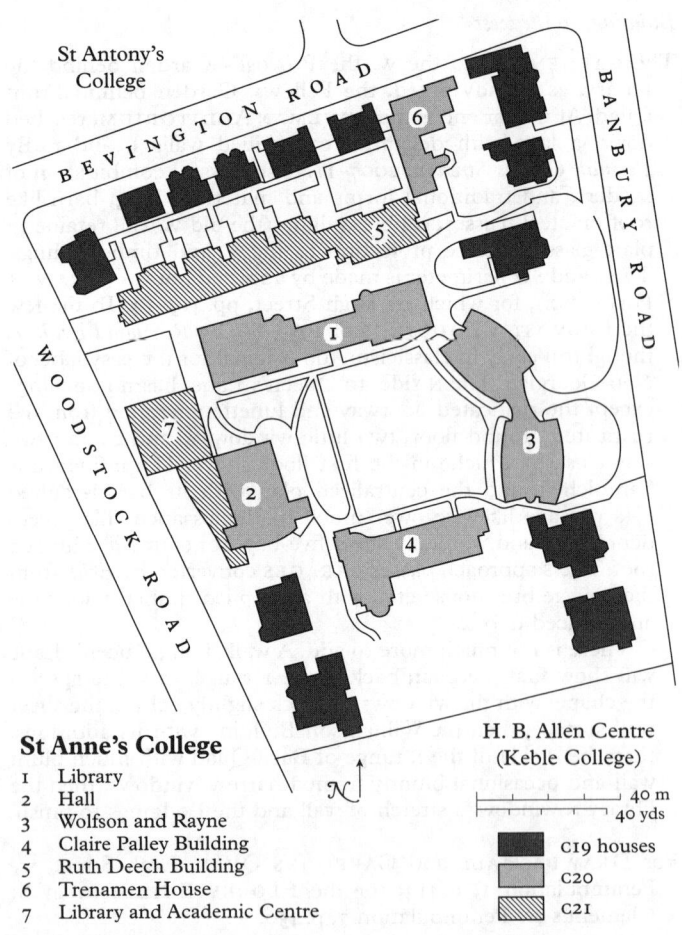

St Anne's College

1 Library
2 Hall
3 Wolfson and Rayne
4 Claire Palley Building
5 Ruth Deech Building
6 Trenamen House
7 Library and Academic Centre

H. B. Allen Centre
(Keble College)

N ↑

40 m
40 yds

C19 houses
C20
C21

here in 1937. In 1942 the Society became St Anne's Society, in 1952 St Anne's College.

The place to begin, because it lets the order flow chronologically, is the central garden. The N side of the garden belongs to *Sir Giles Gilbert Scott*. In 1937–8 he built the LIBRARY to the E, which now looks an appendix to the large HARTLAND HOUSE added to his design in 1949–51. The W part is as late as 1973, in keeping, but smaller than originally intended. Here altogether is another job all of squared Bladon rubble, and another job in that kind of squared-up traditional of which Oxford had so much in the 1920s–50s. Scott was not a historicist, and he liked decorative details of a curly Baroque kind, cf. the doorways to both his buildings. *E. S. Frith* was the carver. Hartland Building has two main accents, three-storeyed, where the rest is two-storeyed. These accents are expressed on the N side in apsidal ends (for that rounding of corners cf. Scott's New Bodleian). The parapets have stylized crenellations.

Then in 1958–9 *Gerald Banks* built the DINING HALL to the W, a very attractive job with full glazing to N and E. Much wood slatting inside, and an ample circular lantern with side-lighting and a low conical top. The high table is in a S recess made by an upper gallery, which serves as the SCR. Towards the garden a low projection with a large wild abstract MURAL by *Stefan Knapp*, in enamel paint on steel. The paving etc. here dates from *Fletcher Priest*'s renovations in 2010–12, when replacement KITCHENS were built along the Woodstock Road. These have a double-curved frontage of rubble walling, with intriguing clusters of little window holes at intervals.

Next, in 1960–8, came *Howell, Killick, Partridge & Amis*'s WOLFSON AND RAYNE BUILDINGS to the E, close to Banbury Road. *John Partridge* was the partner in charge, *A. J. & J. D. Harris* the structural engineers. The blocks are gently convex to E and W, and have three residential storeys, above the recessed glazed ground floors of common rooms and offices. Each window is boxed out, the surround canted l., r., top and bottom: a derivation from the architects' design for Churchill College, Cambridge, 1959 (cf. also St Antony's). The pre-cast concrete facings are of dark Cornish granite aggregate. The end towers and passages in contrast show the rough marks of concrete shuttering. The towers project as rounded shapes in the middle of the short N and S sides. They rise above the rest and are cleft vertically by recessed glass. One end has kitchens, the other an escape stair. Also a top-lit spiral stair within the thickness of each block. Structurally they depend on load-bearing brick cross-walls. A covered walkway links the pair, and this was meant to continue through four similar blocks to join the older buildings, enclosing a lake that was never made.

The CLAIRE PALLEY BUILDING on the S side, 1991–2 by the *Alec French Partnership*, is a well-crafted building in a lower key. Stone and brick, oak panelling above, and the small-scale detail of the Nineties throughout. Canted staircase bays. At the w end a cross-wing with lecture theatre and art gallery. The latter ends in an apse on the s side.

Kohn Pedersen Fox Associates' RUTH DEECH BUILDING of 2002–5 is N of the main garden group. A leap in scale: very long, with the entrance lodge within the w end, and function rooms below. These appear as an extra bottom storey where the land falls to the N. The residential part comprises eighteen bays of rooms in mirrored pairs in three upper storeys (the topmost set back), then a break for a glazed stair hall and lift tower, then seven more bays, residential on the ground floor too. Each room has silvered wooden panelling dividing a slim window from a recessed and part-glazed balcony, all within a stone frame. The bottom storey has a long hallway with internal bridges across from the glazed-in quad level. These bridges connect with staircases to the upper rooms, which also descend externally to the grassy strip behind the college's houses along Bevington Road, N. Closing the view to the E is TRENAMEN HOUSE, a sprawling pastiche of a North Oxford house by the *Wallace & Hoblyn Partnership*, 1993–5.

St Anne's newest addition is the LIBRARY AND ACADEMIC CENTRE by *Fletcher Priest*, 2010–16, s of the Woodstock Road entrance. A severe stone-faced block, nearly cubic, with upright deep-set windows; six bays per side, three storeys high. Angular skylights on the roof. Different treatment of the cast stone for the floor and wall parts. A subterranean passage connects it with Scott's library. The library replaced *Howell, Killick, Partridge & Amis*'s FOUNDER'S TOWER of 1965–6, Pevsner's 'building of wit', which made complex play with canted forms and steel-framed window bays.

For the college's houses on the Banbury and Woodstock roads and in Bevington Road *see* North Oxford, p. 460ff.

ST ANTONY'S COLLEGE
Woodstock Road

Founded in 1948 as a graduate college specializing in international studies. It was the chief benefaction to Oxford by M. Antonin Besse, a French shipping magnate, who also paid for additions or expansion at five other colleges.* St Antony's became a full college in 1965.

In 1950 the college moved into the OLD MAIN BUILDING, the former CONVENT OF THE SOCIETY OF THE HOLY AND UNDIVIDED TRINITY, built in 1866–8 by *Charles Buckeridge*.

*Keble, Pembroke, St Edmund Hall (High Street), St Peter's, Worcester.

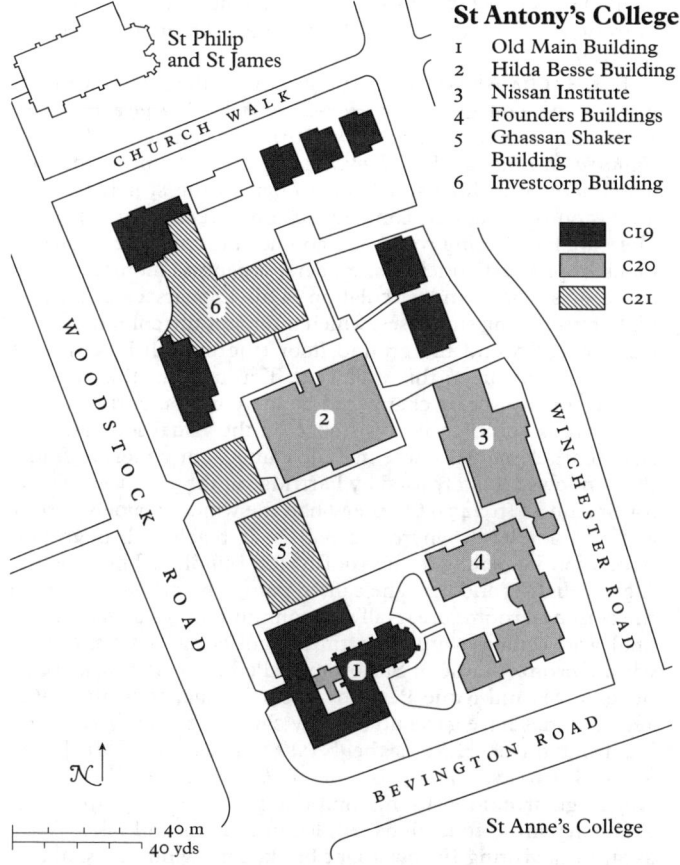

St Antony's College

1   Old Main Building
2   Hilda Besse Building
3   Nissan Institute
4   Founders Buildings
5   Ghassan Shaker
    Building
6   Investcorp Building

■ C19
▨ C20
⧄ C21

St Anne's College

40 m
40 yds

Its founder was Mother Marian Hughes, the first woman to take religious vows within the Church of England. *Buckeridge*'s initial design was planned in the visionary form of a Trinitarian symbol, with central chapel. What was built instead is rather grim, of rough hammer-dressed Gibraltar stone, with very blunt grouped or single lancet windows. The façade is symmetrical, with the same number of gables l. and r. on the long porch passage to the street. In 1891–4 the CHAPEL was added on this axis, of noble proportions and only slightly different from what Buckeridge had intended. The executant architect was *J. L. Pearson*. Five rib-vaulted bays plus apse, Geometrical tracery in the w window. The apse retains paintings by *C. E. Buckeridge*, the architect's son (central three), and *Ethel King Martin*. Two stained-glass lancets by *Hardman & Co.* (PC). The chapel is now the college's LIBRARY, with a glazed approach passage of 1971–2 by *Howell, Killick, Partridge & Amis*, and side galleries of 1995 by the *Architects Design Partnership*. UNDERCROFT below, with another, heavier, rib-vault. The N wing was raised to full height in 1900–1. – BUST in front, Andrés Bello †1865, Latin American liberator, signed *S. Polette*.

The HILDA BESSE BUILDING to the N, the first new building for the college, is by *Howell, Killick, Partridge & Amis*, 1968–70 (partner in charge *John Partridge*, engineers *Harris & Sutherland*; renovated by *Purcell*, 2019–21). Meant as the first instalment of a three-sided quad open to the S, it represents a revision of a big and compact scheme prepared in 1961–3.* Here are hall, dining room and common rooms, in a detached block of pre-cast concrete members, organized along a central spine of services and circulation. This appears externally as higher projecting staircases, which interrupt the colonnade and walkway all round the ground floor (the unbuilt blocks were meant to join on to this walkway). Throughout, the uprights are diagonally set or chamfered at the corners, and throughout there is an obsessive insistence on the visual separation of structural elements. These include canted-out panels to frame the windows, as lately used by Partridge at the practice's blocks for St Anne's (p. 247). On the W half the window panels appear at first-floor level, where the hall is. It reaches through two floors, i.e. its ceiling is the roof of the building. The E half is slightly higher, and here the canted panels are at the top, where the common rooms are. Hall and common rooms all have diagonal grid ceilings with inset timber coffering. – SCULPTURE within: bronze statue of St Antony of Padua by *Meštrovic*, 1953; busts of M. and Mme Besse by *Oscar Nemon*, 1955 and 1962. Later buildings have gone up roughly clockwise from here, starting from the E. Here is the NISSAN INSTITUTE OF JAPANESE STUDIES, 1991–3, by the *Architects Design Partnership*. An irregular composition, comprising a library for the Bodleian's Japanese collections (N), lecture rooms and offices, and a flat for a visiting Fellow. Light brick, dark windows, shallow-pitched roofs: muted echoes both of Frank Lloyd Wright and of traditional Japanese architecture. FOUNDERS BUILDINGS, S, 1999–2000, are by the same. Mostly residential, U-plan, with seminar rooms etc. in the S wing. Rubble stone below, brick above. Gables.

The GHASSAN SHAKER BUILDING (S) and GATEWAY BUILDING now make the college's main frontage. By *Bennetts Associates*, 2011–13. Five-storey blocks, with meeting rooms on the top. The articulation is by a crisp stone-faced frame with bronzed infill. – SCULPTURE in front of the S building: Solitary, by *Naomi Blake*, 1985.

The climax at St Antony's is the INVESTCORP BUILDING (Middle East Centre). Of 2013–15 by *Zaha Hadid*, with the structural engineers *AKT II*; developed from designs approved in 2008. One of relatively few British buildings by the influential Iraqi-born architect. A giant abstract volume stretching

---

*The successor plan (1973), for a building by the celebrated Brazilian Modernist *Oscar Niemeyer*, was likewise abandoned.

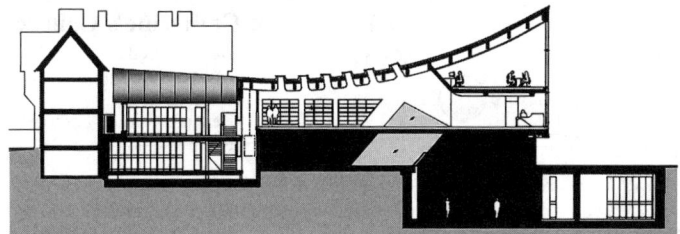

St Antony's College, Investcorp Building.
Section drawing, 2016

from N to S, clad mostly in mirrored stainless steel, and ending on the college side with a sleek wall of fritted glazing, as if cut off short. To Woodstock Road it appears like an unidentifiable segment of airliner that has somehow become wedged between two pre-existing houses. As to its uses, the top floor contains an archive room, the first (and largest) floor the main reading room, the ground floor a glazed-sided café and the entrance to a lecture theatre, which is sunk under the lawn to the E. The curving, shell-like exterior has its internal counterpart of impeccable white surfaces, unsettlingly depthless to the eye. They bend and fold around spaces that largely reject the distinctions between walls and ceiling, or between rooms and circulation areas. Also much fair-faced concrete, and oak linings drilled with holes. Circulation is by an oval staircase, around which the volumes flow unobstructed. Tear-shaped skylights puncture the library roof.

It is all undeniably a tremendous performance. But as one walks away, doubts may return as to the justification for such a song and dance around a fairly straightforward brief.

For the college's houses on Woodstock Road *see* North Oxford, p. 468.

ST CATHERINE'S COLLEGE
Manor Road

St Catherine's is the creation of the Danish architect *Arne Jacobsen*. Building began in 1960, and the main group was complete in 1964. It became a college proper in 1963. Since 1931 it had been St Catherine's Society, a later incarnation of the Society of Non-Collegiate Students instituted in 1868. The students lived in private lodgings, but communal buildings were provided in the 1930s on St Aldate's (later the Music Faculty; *see* p. 350), and before that on the High Street, in the 1880s (now Ruskin School of Art; *see* p. 348). The appeal for new buildings for a full college was launched in 1956.

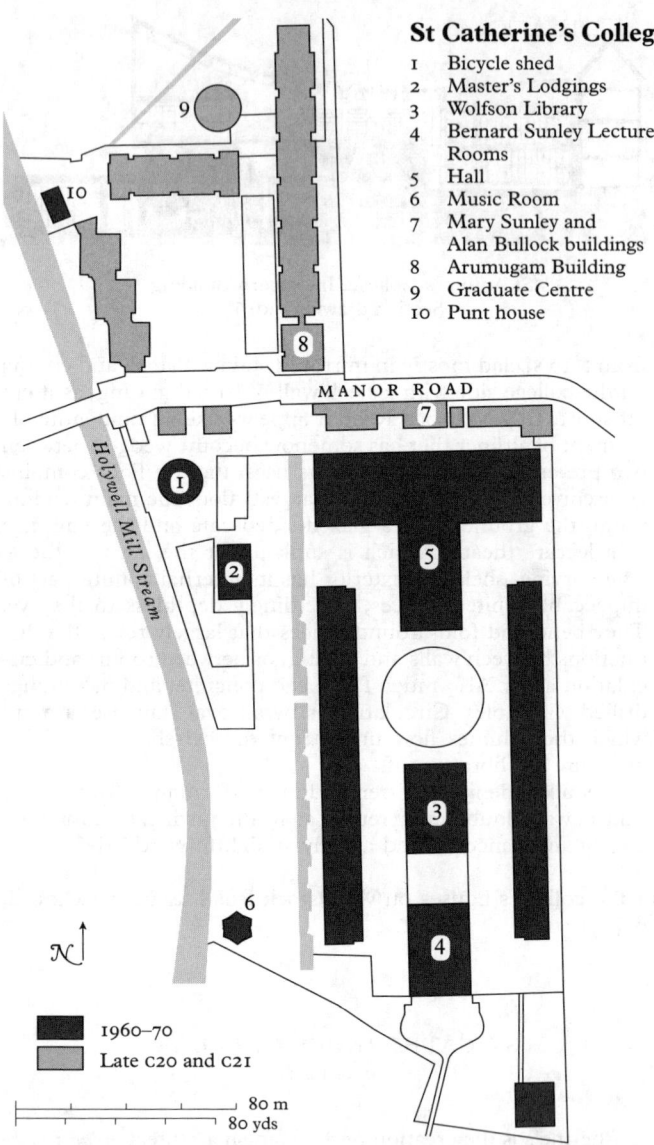

St Catherine's College

1 Bicycle shed
2 Master's Lodgings
3 Wolfson Library
4 Bernard Sunley Lecture
   Rooms
5 Hall
6 Music Room
7 Mary Sunley and
   Alan Bullock buildings
8 Arumugam Building
9 Graduate Centre
10 Punt house

MANOR ROAD

Holywell Mill Stream

N

■ 1960–70
▨ Late C20 and C21

80 m
80 yds

The first Master of this college was Alan Bullock. With other committee members, he had searched for the right architect among home-grown Modernists without success. Tours of the USA and Denmark were also made. By the late 1950s British architectural practice had become wholly home-grown, and the appointment of a foreigner caused a shock. (The provision that he should work with a British architect was soon dropped, although *Jack Lankester* as University Surveyor remained closely involved throughout.) Also novel in a mid-C20 British context were Jacobsen's meticulous methods; he liked to design his own landscaping and his own furniture and fittings, even down to the cutlery. The brief required him to leave one side of the quad open, to retain the Oxford staircase system, and to integrate Fellows' rooms with those of the students. The modest size of these student rooms was determined by funding from the University Grants Committee. Other donations paid for hall, library etc., on a grander scale. The princeliest donor was Dr Rudolph Light, who gave $1,000,000.

Jacobsen's college

Pevsner found St Catherine's at once an exemplar of Modernist design and a rich subject for debate. His account of 1974 follows, with a few adjustments indicated.

'Here is a perfect piece of architecture. It has a consistent plan, and every detail is meticulously worked out. Self-discipline is its message, expressed in terms of a geometry pervading the whole and the parts and felt wherever one moves or stops. The buildings are one long rectangle, 640 ft [195 metres] long. The major part of the long sides is residential, one range W, one   116 E. Between them, and much broader, and all identical in width, are lecture rooms, library, and hall. An area enclosed by low walls between the lecture rooms and the library contains the tower, the one part not placed axially, because it is a unique part. Between the library and the hall is a lawn, and the lawn is circular (though again one tree has been planted out of axis, because nature is nature). From the hall branch out the Senior Common Rooms to the W, the Junior Common Rooms to the E, identical in area. Outside the parallelepiped are only the Master's Lodgings, the Music Room, and the bicycle shed, and even the bicycle shed is a perfect circle in plan.* The geometry is made to tell yet further in the paving of paths through the garden areas inside and outside the parallelepiped, all of the same oblong slabs and never moving in an undulating way, and in the many screen walls, high or low, including those placed fin-wise to demarcate the gardens inside the parallelepiped from the more public circulation areas.

'Materials and structure are of the same clarity. Structure is concrete, and frame and beam-ends show. The beams which have to do the heaviest carrying are very large, in height only (5 ft) [1.5 metres], not in width. Infill is brick, a sand-coloured brick of a special two-inch [5-cm.] size and used in stretchers only.

'Entry is distressingly unmonumentally by an approach road at an angle....As it is, one passes the bicycle shed, the

*Also SQUASH COURTS, 1965, to the SE.

MASTER'S LODGINGS, placed as if it were a glorified porter's lodge, perfectly cubic and wood-slatted above, past the
beautiful water garden to the S with a piece of SCULPTURE by
Barbara Hepworth [Archaean, 1959] and the Music Room in
the distance, and so under the W range of rooms to the circular lawn. The two ranges of rooms are of three storeys, with a
receding ground floor, the concrete frame showing above, and
inside the frame glazing set in black metal, throughout, from
top to bottom of each room. The rooms are 10 ft [3 metres]
wide, and there is a spacious staircase for each ten rooms.

  'The WOLFSON LIBRARY again has its upper part projecting. The functional reason here is that the projecting part
represents the gallery. Inside here and everywhere brick is
exposed as it is externally. So are the high and narrow ceiling
beams. The spiral staircase of iron up to the gallery is treated
as thinly as possible in order not to interfere with the sense of
spatial order. The furniture is designed by the architect, here as
in most places. The BERNARD SUNLEY LECTURE ROOMS are
the same in outline, i.e. they have the same projection of the
upper floor – but here geometry has run away with the architect; for there is no internal justification for the projection. It
is simply framing exposed, and by means of a kind of shutters
along the front surface given a semblance of solidity. There is
a wavering here. In the square area between the two buildings
rises the tower, simply two high slabs of concrete connected
only twice across and a third time by the bell-platform. The
tower is 70 ft [21 metres] high. Also in this area bronze BUST
of Einstein by *Epstein* [1933].

  'The HALL N of the circular lawn faces it with a sheer brick
wall. Only two slits indicate the frame structure inside, and
along the W and E sides the high narrow beams project again.
The interior has cruciform piers of dark grey, an aggregate,
polished, carrying the beams. The furniture is light and simple.
Benches for the undergraduates. Only the high-table chairs
have shapely backs. Many little lamps on all the tables, and
some wall lighting. No chandelier is to interfere with the unity
of the space. Turn l. or turn r., the same passage with indoor
planting. If you turn l. you get into the Senior Common
Rooms, if you turn r. the Junior Common Rooms. There are
separate rooms for the Fellows, an open group of three for the
undergraduates. The furniture is again the architect's.

  'Finally the MUSIC ROOM [1965], another essay in geometry, but here more complex. It is a hexagon set across
another hexagon, seemingly windowless, because the windows
are only long slits in the bits of wall where the outer hexagon
meets the triangular bit of the inner hexagon which appears
outside. The broken surfaces, so different from those of the
parallelepiped, are an acoustic necessity, and the architect must
have felt them as a relaxation after all his right angles.

  'On the strength of this survey criticism and appreciation
can now be attempted. Criticism from the detail to the whole

of the conception. The undergraduates' rooms, as in so many new college buildings, are painfully small. They could have been larger here, if the staircases had been treated with less panache. That the staircase details are perfect too goes without saying. But what could have been trimmed off their size would have helped the bed-sitters. The glazing right down to the feet is at least open to doubt. Then, as for the apportioning of money, has not over-much been spent on the furniture, especially in the Common Rooms? And on the two-inch bricks made specially for the purpose? But let that stand. More serious is the criticism of the Junior Common Rooms. The upholstery is black, and the furniture is placed with such geometrical perfection that to move a chair seems a *lèse-majesté*. One remembers Adolf Loos's story of the Poor Rich Man to whom his architect says in the end: "Don't you realize, you are complete." Complete the furnishings indeed are, not made to be pushed around, and complete the college is.

'And so to the most sweeping criticism that has been made: "C'est magnifique, mais ce n'est pas un college." If a college to be a college must have a variety of moods due to a variety of style and dates of building, then St Catherine's is not a college, nor can any new college be, including Churchill at Cambridge. If a college must have a variety of moods merely due to a variety of sizes and shapes and vistas, then Churchill is and St Catherine's is not. But if a college is a college by having its own distinctive individual mood suited to be the surroundings for young people for their most impressionable years, then St Catherine's is a college. If young people don't like it, that may be an argument against them rather than against the college – always admitting that the Junior Common Rooms are alarming. My final verdict is that the college may have to wait until by the swing of the pendulum of history the ideal of self-permissiveness among students becomes once more the ideal of self-discipline. And let nobody say that St Catherine's, apart from being not a college, is un-English anyway. For if there is a relaxed, untotalitarian country it is Denmark.'

Half a century has brought no drastic change to St Catherine's, whatever the students may now get up to. The most obvious differences concern the planting. Hedges have grown to match the height of the screen walls, trees are larger and more common, creepers have crept (now covering the s wall of the hall), and since 1972 some areas of paving have made way for extra beds and lawns. RENOVATION by *Hodder Associates* in 2004–5 brought double glazing with integral Venetian blinds to the residential parts, set in dark bronzed metal to match the original. The cladding of the Master's House was also replaced. Less obviously, the same architects made a lecture room in the internal court of the Junior Common Room in 1995. Changes to the FURNISHINGS include replacement of the hall benches with Jacobsen chairs, and pragmatically ordinary pieces for the Junior Common Room.

Additions since the 1960s

Jacobsen's work left the entry to the college unresolved. More has been done here, without amending the frustratingly roundabout approach via the NW angle. In 1982–3 two low ranges for conferences etc. were added (MARY SUNLEY BUILDING, E, and ALAN BULLOCK BUILDING), N of and closely parallel to the common rooms and kitchens. Designed by *Knud Holscher*, Jacobsen's former assistant (with *J. Lankester*), and thoroughly Jacobsenian. – SCULPTURE alongside Mary Sunley, Unbroken Taichi Flow I by *Ju Ming*. Dated 1991.

Next, to the N, the college created a second open-sided quad, with *Hodder Associates* as architects. The work is sympathetic to Jacobsen, and uses many of his devices – thin yellow quarter-bonded bricks, the first-floor overhangs, the baffle walls and hedge-walls – without aiming at replication. Three storeys. W side of 1993–5; stepping back along the mill stream, with staircases expressed (whereas Jacobsen concealed his). N and E sides of 2003–5, detached from each other, and using more concrete and less stainless steel in the framing and cladding of the residential rooms. At the S end of the E side is the semi-detached ARUMUGAM BUILDING, with seminar rooms and porter's lodge. Timber *brise-soleil* here, and larger windows, and much steel facing. The grassed strip in front lines up with that of the 1960s water garden, i.e. the quads are staggered in relation to one another. In 2017–19 the E range was extended N by *Purcell*, and a new GRADUATE CENTRE built in front, i.e. behind the N range. A sober bronze-clad cylinder, standing free. Three storeys, glazed around much of the S curve and part of the N. Thin mullions, the staircase rising behind. Low clerestory. – In the NW corner the PUNT HOUSE of 1970, *Jacobsen*'s last work here. Like a miniature of the Master's House.

For ST CATHERINE'S HOUSE, Bath Street *see* Perambulation 7, p. 452.

ST CROSS COLLEGE

with PUSEY HOUSE

St Giles'

St Cross was founded in 1965 to provide a college home for non-attached academic staff and graduate students of both sexes. Its first site included the former St Cross School (*see* p. 419). In 1981 it moved to PUSEY HOUSE, an independent theological centre working in close collaboration with the University. This was established in 1884 as a memorial to the Oxford Movement luminary Edward Bouverie Pusey, whose library it inherited. Its founding Principal was Charles Gore, liberal Anglo-Catholic theologian and future Bishop of Oxford, who also established

St Cross College, Pusey House.
Elevation drawing, 1916

the Community of the Resurrection now at Mirfield in Yorkshire. At first a town house was used, adapted by *C.E. Kempe*, and extended in 1887 by *H.W. Moore*. New buildings had to wait until 1913–18, with *Temple Moore* – no relation – as architect. Additions of the 1990s and 2010s for St Cross have made a second quad behind, but it is as a major work of Temple Moore that Pusey House is most interesting architecturally. Those familiar with his exquisitely spare parish churches will find however that the buildings are closer to the poised and scholarly late C14 Gothic of Bodley or of George Gilbert Scott Jun., Temple Moore's own former master.

The front QUAD presents a two-storey range to St Giles', with a two-storey window treatment under the S gable and the big chapel E window under the N gable, but no grand entrance to prepare for the spacious quad behind. On its N side here the very large chapel with a real tower placed midway, on the W side the library range with the typical library windows, and below a handsome tripartite archway through to the back quad. The other two ranges are, or were, residential; the S side and part of the E side of 1924–6 by *John Coleridge*, in the same idiom.

The CHAPEL, complete by 1914, is large enough to recall some urban churches of the English friars, which it indeed resembles in plan. The choir, meant for the residents' daily services, is of three bays, the nave of five, with stone pulpitum and timber screen between. Four-centred-arched windows to the nave, two-centred to the choir, all of four lights. Both parts are vaulted, the choir with tierceron-stars, the nave with an odd pattern in which each square half-bay of the vault is crossed by diagonal ribs. Also a longitudinal ridge rib, and fragmentary transverse ridge ribs starting from above the windows. The lower walls of the nave have deep blank arches, two per bay, and these carry one of Temple Moore's narrow wall passages, *à la* Angoulême but in Gothic (provided to carry the heating pipes discreetly). The details are conventional English Gothic, but the conception shows resourcefulness. To the street the nave wall is treated between the shallow buttresses with a deep shelving batter to the nave, the choir with a narrow aisle-like passage. – CIBORIUM, 1937. 'By *Comper*, need one say? Who else would splash the gold about like that? Golden columns, and above an equally characteristic pretty-pretty foliage frieze of blue and gold' (Pevsner). The inspiration was Torrigiano's early C16 work at Westminster Abbey. Languid nude youths (Corinthians?) in the capitals, figures of the Resurrection on top. – Splendid gilt metal FRONTAL with foliage scrolls and the Annunciation. – STAINED GLASS. E window, Tree of Jesse, 1935. Unmistakable *Comper*. In the E cloister, windows to Temple Moore (†1920) and his son and intended successor *Richard*, lost at sea in 1918, who designed much of the detail at Pusey House. By *H. Victor Milner* (PC).

The LIBRARY has a sober barrel-vault of timber. COMMON ROOM in the S range, made in 1981 partly by taking in the cloister walk towards the quad, thus forming an interim hall for St Cross. In the E range two INTERIORS with Georgian features salvaged from houses previously on the site.

WEST QUAD began in 1991–3 with the S side, by *Philip del Nevo* of *Oxford Architects Partnership*. A little Temple Moore-style section to start off, then a deeper, cross-gabled part with HALL, kitchens etc., and student rooms over. Let down by the proportions: upper windows too horizontal, Venetian lower openings too big. The other two sides by *Níall McLaughlin Architects*, 2014–17. Each of the four staircase-sized sections is articulated by means of a system of big, sharply chamfered frames or window cells – aluminium replacements for the original glass-reinforced concrete, which proved faulty (2023). Library, lecture room etc. on the ground floor. The same system, but a less certain rhythm, on the outer faces, where the ranges overlook a (remade) rubble wall. To Pusey Lane, W, an engraved glass DOOR by *Alison Kinnaird*.

For the ANNEXE in St Cross Road *see* Perambulation 2, p. 419.

ST EDMUND HALL
Queen's Lane

St Edmund Hall, though now a college, was until 1957 the only surviving academic hall in the University, these halls being originally the lodgings or *hospitia* rented by Masters to house their students and teach them on the premises. In the mid C15 there

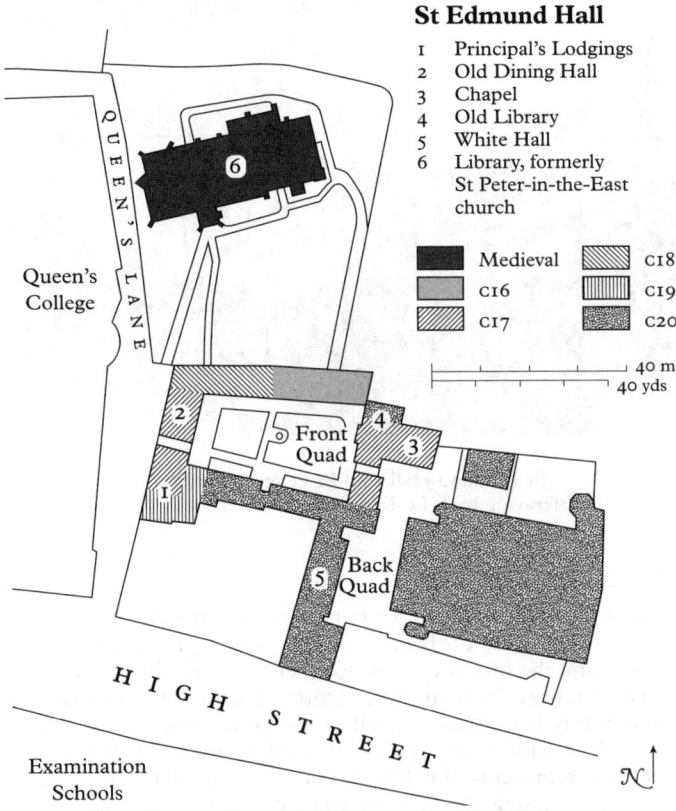

St Edmund Hall

1 Principal's Lodgings
2 Old Dining Hall
3 Chapel
4 Old Library
5 White Hall
6 Library, formerly
   St Peter-in-the-East
   church

Medieval   C18
C16   C19
C17   C20

40 m
40 yds

Queen's
College

Front
Quad

Back
Quad

HIGH STREET

Examination
Schools

N

were still seventy, by the early C17 only eight. Colleges were replacing them. St Edmund Hall stands by tradition on the site of St Edmund of Abingdon's house. Edmund lectured at Oxford in the early C13, endowed a chapel at the church of St Peter-in-the-East, and rose to be Archbishop of Canterbury. He was canonized in 1248. Anyway, the name St Edmund Hall first appears in the rental of Osney Abbey in 1317/18. In the C16 the hall passed to Queen's, as St Mary Hall passed to Oriel. But in contrast to St Mary Hall it was never swallowed up, and continued to exist independently as a property of Queen's, which reserved the right to appoint the Principal.

A single fireplace excepted, nothing survives architecturally from before the late C16, and nothing really ambitious from before the late C17. 'Teddy Hall' remained altogether a diminutive place well into the C20, completing the fourth side of its far from regular quad as late as 1934. In the 1960s, however, a big new Back Quad was begun, and the college took over the redundant St Peter-in-the-East for its library. Partly cleared and replanted, the churchyard now serves beautifully as a garden.

St Edmund Hall with St Peter-in-the-East.
Engraving by J. Le Keux after F. Mackenzie, 1836

Front Quad and Back Quad

FRONT QUAD presents its WEST RANGE and entrance to Queen's
Lane. The S part of this is of *c.*1635, the N part was begun in
1659, and the final N bay represents C18 rebuilding of the adjacent N range. There are three storeys plus a dormer storey, as
there were from the start. All the windows have arched lights.
But the façade is totally uncomposed. A big blank area in the
N part represents the hall within. Modest doorway, placed
off-centre alongside. With its steep pediment and lugs it suits
1659 better than 1635. The oriel in the S part originally rose
through two storeys. It belongs to the Principal's Lodgings.
This has been extended to the S, in ashlar: ground storey in
1800, second storey *c.*1833–5, top storey 1871. Three bays,
regular Gothic fenestration.

To the quad the W range is again higgledy-piggledy, but now
shows the three large windows of the OLD DINING HALL.
They are of two lights, with transoms and minimum Gothic
arches. Oriel over the passage added in 1880. Plain hall interior, very small even after extension in 1921, S, and 1934 (upper
gallery, N). The NORTH RANGE is the earliest part of the college,
or at least its E half to where the back of the retained C15 fireplace is. That part is of *c.*1596. Its third storey is an addition,
date unknown. The W half is a rebuilding of 1746–7, and the
faithful match is amazing.* Both parts are of rubble stone. The
windows have arched lights, and alternate regularly between
two and four lights. Dormers rebuilt 1932. All windows to
the N sashed. (Wall paintings: architectural overmantel and

---

*An engraved classical design for rebuilding the whole N side is in Williams's *Oxonia
Depicta* (1732–3).

strapwork overdoor in the Vice-Principal's study, *c*. 1600.) The SOUTH RANGE has first more of the ashlar-faced Principal's Lodgings, then a loosely early C17-style stretch in rubble stone by *Harold S. Rogers*, dated on rainwater heads 1926 and originally including the students' library.

Then a lower linking bay also of rubble, infilled above the ground floor in 1996 (*Montgomery Architects*). This joins on to, and unbalances the symmetry of, the CANTERBURY BUILDING of 1933–4 by *R. Fielding Dodd*. Canterbury in turn continues the motifs of *c*. 1600 of the house – one cannot call it anything else – which forms the S half of the EAST RANGE. But the N half is the one old building of St Edmund Hall with pretensions. It was built in 1680–6 and has a formal front of five bays, the centre bay singled out by giant attached columns from bottom to top, with Composite capitals. The windows are of the cross-type and pedimented on the ground floor, but have two transoms and no pediments above. These ones have on the other hand extra-broad, flatly stepped surrounds. The centre bay is treated differently. The doorway has another stepped surround and a pediment of double-curved shape placed on piles of books instead of brackets. That refers to the library, which is on the upper floor. The building was begun by *William Byrd*, who claimed authorship, and finished by *Bartholomew Peisley I*. That Byrd was indeed the designer is suggested by the slight projection of the wall face around the window bays, as at his additions to New College.

The lower floor contains in the middle the lobby to the CHAPEL behind, consecrated in 1682. It is small and has a plain segmental plaster vault, and modest but nicely detailed PANELLING, STALLS and SCREEN by *Arthur Frogley*. Of the STAINED GLASS, the E window is of 1865 by *Morris, Marshall, Faulkner & Co*. Its pictorial parts are by *Burne-Jones*, except for the Men of Galilee, middle r., and the Marys at the Sepulchre below, which are by *William Morris*, and the surprisingly conventional decorative parts, which are by *Philip Webb*. The central scene is a Crucifixion. This, and even more the smaller scenes are much more robust than Burne-Jones was going to be later. The tracery of the window too, with its plausibly late C17 tracery of three circles – two small, one large – is actually of 1865 and by *Webb*. In the side windows glass by *Clayton & Bell*, also 1865. *Street*'s designs for a medievalizing redecoration, submitted in 1861, were not acted on. – ALTARPIECE. Christ at Emmaus by *Ceri Richards*, 1957–8, German-inspired Expressionism, entirely convincing. – ORGAN LOFT of 1931.

The OLD LIBRARY is reached by a small stair lobby with two roundels of donated stained-glass fragments in its windows. The long low room with its gallery runs N–S. It is twice deceptive: first, in that the far N bay is a tactful extension of 1933–4 by *Fielding Dodd*; second, in that the shelving etc. in the older part is largely C19 and not C17. The library was incidentally the first in an Oxford college to have floor-to-ceiling shelves flat against the wall.

In the quad a medieval WELL-SHAFT, with a well-head of 1927.

BACK QUAD to the E is not experienced as quadrangular. Rather, it represents an ingenious expansion of accommodation and facilities into an area about as large as the whole old college. The main buildings are of 1968–70, by *Kenneth Stevens & Associates* (partner in charge *Gilbert Howes*).* Two parallel main blocks, connected by a raised deck. On the ground floor the W range has the new DINING HALL. Above it are four storeys of sets placed back to back, whereas the E range is half as deep and also lower, having no hall storey below. The buildings are of concrete. Where exposed it has the marks of shuttering, as on the high polygonal stair-towers placed NE, SE and SW. The walls otherwise are faced with grey blockwork. Motifs are less coherent than plan, from the rows of top gables of zinc-sheathed timber to act as a reminder of the C16 and C17 past to the segmental arches (Le Corbusier–Spence in derivation) on the W front of the hall. The arches run through as hanging vaults within the hall, which is lit also from the inner side by a clerestory above deck level. Spidery lighting rig, panelling etc. from *Gray Baynes & Shew*'s renovation of 2008. Common rooms in a lower projection N of the hall range. This part makes a pretty little garden of the NE corner, enclosed also by the city wall and New College garden wall. In 2007–8 a lecture theatre, the DOCTOROW HALL, was built on the upper deck. By *Montgomery Architects*.

WHITE HALL, S of the E end of Front Quad, is a budget block-work addition of 1974–5 with an C18-style front to the High Street (Nos. 46–47 there). Also by *G. Howes*. For other High Street houses now used by the college *see* p. 414.

Library, former church of St Peter-in-the-East

In 1968–70 the CHURCH OF ST PETER-IN-THE-EAST was emptied and converted for a LIBRARY for the college, by *J. R. Allen* of *Kenneth Stevens & Associates*. Little change was made to the older fabric, though some will seek out *Michael Groser*'s grotesques on the restored tower parapet.

St Peter's is without doubt the most interesting church from the Middle Ages in Oxford. It has work of all medieval periods from the C12 onwards, and is at once ambitious in its earliest phase and fascinatingly jumbled up. Excavations by David Sturdy during the conversion reportedly also found evidence of an aisleless C11 church of stone, and a still earlier church of stone and timber, consistent with the church having been a minster complex additional to that at St Frideswide's (Christ Church).

*A plan of 1962 for a 150-ft (45-metre) tower by *Louis Osman* fell foul of a promptly introduced ruling against tall buildings in central Oxford.

Concerning the C12 work, nave and chancel both belong to it. Closer dating depends on whether certain features in the chancel crypt are taken as evidence of an early C12 start, or as deliberately simple elements within a coherently conceived whole, which would imply a date in the mid C12.* This CRYPT is very large, a sign that the church was meant for something special. It is of five bays, with two rows of short columns along its length. The bays have groin-vaults, normally an Early Norman motif, and have steepish bases and capitals, two of two plain scallops, the others mostly with decoratively enriched scallops. But there are also foliage capitals and a figure scene, beasts and monsters. Capitals, vaults and general arrangement recall Anselm's Canterbury Cathedral crypt, i.e. an early C12 prototype. The W wall opens in three doorways, two to stairs from the nave, now lost, the middle one to a *confessio* or relic chamber: an arrangement known on the Continent but rare in England. Further E are two more doorways also formerly with stairs up into the chancel, which indicates separate access for the clergy. All this implies the provision for pilgrimage to a major shrine; yet no such cult is recorded here. The other doorways W, N and S share straight heads with plain tympana. A number of the original tiny windows remain. – FONT of *c.* 1842, a simplified copy of a large circular Norman font known from engravings. The original had twelve figures within the arcading.

Everything above ground is more ornate. The chancel has a billet frieze at the level of the window sills. A N and a S window survive, each shafted outside and in – also exceptional in a parish church – and with complex chevron arches. On the S side moreover are substantial remains of blank intersecting upper arcading, another Canterbury reminiscence, and on the N side original parts of the corbel table (all renewed, S side). The E window is Perp, but traces of the Norman predecessors can still be seen, and smaller Norman windows high up in the gable. The buttresses at the E corners are clasping. They represent stair-turrets, and in their walls too are small, blocked windows. Their tops are round and end in conical spirelets. The small windows indicate a two-storey system, and the chancel is indeed rib-vaulted inside, in two large bays, with a chamber formerly above. The turret stairs also connect with wall passages at sill level. Inside, the E vault bay is intact, with ribs uniquely decorated with a big chain motif. The W bay has a finer chevron, partly reworked or renewed in *John Plowman Sen.*'s repairs of 1836. There is also a pointed transverse arch with chevron, and a string course in both bays. These details too suggest a mid-C12 date, and an ambitious patron. Malcolm Thurlby identifies the rector and future courtier John, son of Henry, Sheriff of Oxford, as a likely candidate, which would narrow the date to *c.* 1155–60. Shafted C12 responds to the chancel opening, with cushion capitals; but the sharp double-chamfered chancel arch must be a C13

*For a fuller analysis *see* Malcolm Thurlby in *Oxoniensia* 83 (2018).

replacement. The (failed?) C12 arch may have been pointed too (cf. Dorchester Abbey).

The NAVE has Norman walling on the S side, with a S doorway. It has continuous orders of saltire crosses, beakhead and chevron. These motifs again point to a date *c.* 1150–60. A Norman window preserved above is visible from inside. Other, loose voussoirs with beakhead are displayed in the chancel. The nave W wall was originally 25 ft (7.6 metres) further E than the W wall is now, but the church was lengthened in the C14. Also of the C14 the NW tower, with its Early Perp top stage of oddly tapering outline. By that time a transeptal N chapel and a N aisle had already been made. It is a plausible as well as an attractive suggestion that this transept is the Lady Chapel built by St Edmund from the money he had received while teaching at Oxford. It has lancet windows to the E and a triple-chamfered arch on moulded capitals to the chancel. Its N window is Perp, of *c.* 1433 (*see* below). The aisle also has C13 origins, but is later, say *c.* 1230–40. It has a single arch to the transept. Three-bay arcade of quatrefoil piers with stiff-leaf capitals. In the C14 the aisle was rebuilt, with two Dec windows with flowing tracery (restored). A small chapel was later built out at its E end, probably in 1524. Of about the same time the NE vestry. The S porch is probably of *c.* 1498. This is storeyed, with a two-bay vault with diagonal and ridge ribs. Quatrefoil parapets were added to the church in the late C15 too. The nave S fenestration is wonderfully happy-go-lucky, especially the one huge Perp window: a reduced version of the five-light S transept window of Merton College chapel, i.e. early C15. The two-light Dec-style window to its W is of 1836, replacing a C17 one. Nave roof of 1844, by *John Plowman Jun.* On the chancel E wall remains of an *opus sectile* FRIEZE by *Powells*, 1897.

STAINED GLASS. Chancel E window. Introduced in 1837 by *John Absalom Edwards*. By him the main lights, the Four Evangelists, a good impersonation of C16 Continental work. Tracery, incomplete C15 figures, heavily restored. Lower lights, l. to r., St Christopher, female saint, small Crucifixion, Virgin and Child, bishop saint; apex, St Elizabeth of Hungary, St Dorothy. Chancel side windows: two by *Baguley*, 1873, one S (three lights, †1864) by *Clayton & Bell*. N transept N, remains of an important window set up by Vincent Wyking, vicar in 1433. The main lights originally contained canopy-work above figures. The upper parts remain of a deacon saint and St Vincent, with backgrounds and restored canopies. In the tracery a Coronation of the Virgin, with Christ to the r. (both heads modern), flanked by St Paul l., St Peter r. N transept E lancets, mid-C19, style of *Charles Hudson* (MH). N aisle W, 1850 by *Powells*; one scene derived from the Overbeck engraving that inspired Holman Hunt's Light of the World (MH; cf. Keble, p. 168).

MONUMENTS. Chancel. C12 grave cover and C13 coffin-lid. – Mayor Richard Atkinson †1574. Tomb-chest with cusped lozenges, and brasses on top. These are mostly palimpsests of one large early C16 Flemish brass featuring Early Renaissance architecture and putti. – N transept. Helen Low †1683. A pile-up of sculpted motifs with an urn on top. Rupert Gunnis attributed it to *John Bushnell* (GF). – William Levinz †1706. Pilastered big tablet on putti heads. – Mary Levinz †1730. Large tablet after a design by *Gibbs* (GF). With pedimented inscription plate, a bust in a round recess above it, and a segmental top pediment. – N aisle. Simon Parret †1584 (much restored); one of several Elizabethan and Jacobean pictorial brasses. – Elizabeth Dickinson †1670. Alabaster cartouche with two putti. – Prof. Robert Winstanley †1823, by *Robert Blore II*. With sarcophagus. – Nave. Daniel Fogg †1702. Leathery cartouche with skull. Attributed to *W. Woodman the elder* (GF).

The CHURCHYARD was partly remodelled in 2017 by *Gray Baynes & Shew*. The STATUE of St Edmund of Abingdon is by *Rodney Munday*, 2007. Of bronze, on a stone bench.

For the WILLIAM R. MILLER BUILDING in St Clement's *see* Perambulation 7, p. 452.

ST HILDA'S COLLEGE
Cowley Place

Last of the women's colleges in order of foundation, St Hilda's was established in 1893 by Miss Dorothea Beale, Principal of Cheltenham Ladies' College. She conceived it chiefly as a destination for Cheltenham girls, but access broadened later and in 1926 St Hilda's Hall became St Hilda's College. Architecturally St Hilda's was until recently the least ambitious of the women's colleges, and the most dependent on second-hand buildings. These chiefly comprise two much-extended riverside houses (now called Hall and South), divided until the 1950s by a public lane and river crossing. Additions from the 1950s to 1990s were made chiefly s of South. New buildings by *Gort Scott*, 2018–21, have given the college a central focus on the street side and also on the Cherwell, whose gently gliding presence is St Hilda's trump card.

Hall Building and Boundary Building

St Hilda's began life in the charming three-bay house of *c.* 1780, now the central section of HALL BUILDING, which one passes on the way to the entrance in Cowley Place. It was built for the botanist Dr Humphrey Sibthorp, near enough to the Botanic Garden, and originally (and confusingly) called COWLEY PLACE. It has an entrance projection of two storeys with niches l. and r. of the doorway as well as the principal window, and small Adamish motifs of decoration. Ramps etc. of 2012 in

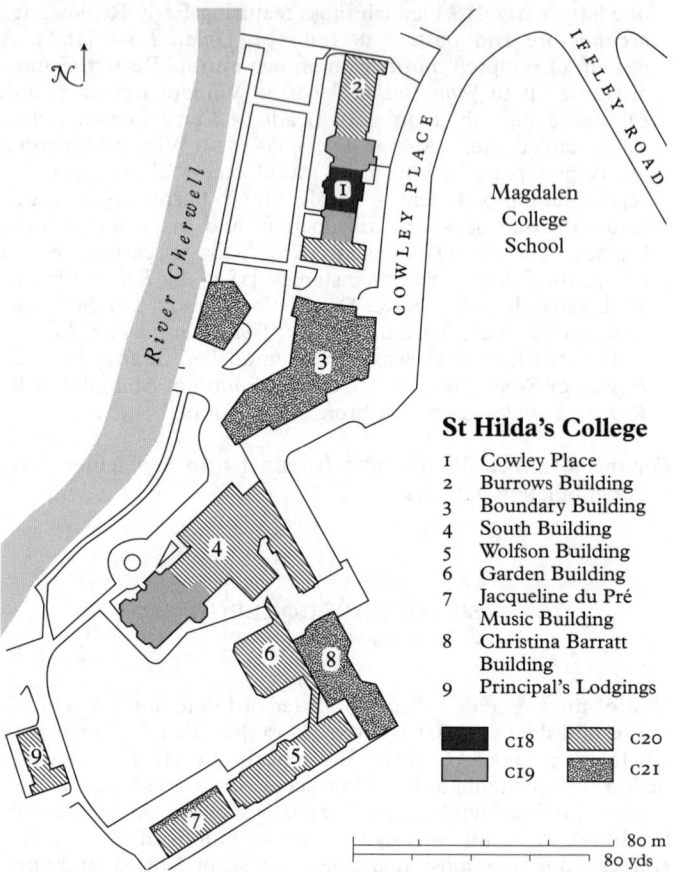

St Hilda's College

1   Cowley Place
2   Burrows Building
3   Boundary Building
4   South Building
5   Wolfson Building
6   Garden Building
7   Jacqueline du Pré
    Music Building
8   Christina Barratt
    Building
9   Principal's Lodgings

C18   C20
C19   C21

80 m
80 yds

front, by *Adrian James Architects*. The lower elevation however
is not C18 at all, but a restoration by *Robert Potter* of 1965–6. It
replaced a doughty Gothic porch by *Deane & Woodward*, added
for the chemist Sir Benjamin Brodie in 1862. Deane & Woodward's main extension is to the N, red and yellow brick Gothic,
i.e. most demonstratively different from the refined Georgian.
Attached to this is *Sir Edwin Cooper*'s BURROWS BUILDING
of 1933–4. In his simplified red brick Neo-Georgian manner,
with the handsome galleried LIBRARY behind the big round-
arched windows. Student rooms above. Cooper's daughter was
a Fellow. Small additions towards the street, brown brick and
rubble stone, with more underground; by *Blackwood Architects*,
2005. But before Cooper the college had already added to
Sibthorp's house on the s side: a neutral gabled range by *R.P.
Day*, 1897–8, and a cross-range of 1909 by *W.E. Mills*, of yellow
brick with red brick dressings, Georgian-looking windows, and
gables with Butterfieldian chequering. s porch and doors by
*Alison & Peter Smithson, c.*1970.

Next comes Boundary Building, but that must wait until the river side of Hall has been seen. The Georgian part has on the ground floor two Venetian windows, each with a fan-like super-arch. Central bay not original. Spacious entrance hall with ceiling plasterwork that mixes mid-C18 and late C18 idioms, suggesting a provincial hand. Likewise the awkward placing of the timber staircase, of slim elegant balusters.* The *Deane & Woodward* extension is chiefly one broad canted bay, with naturalistic leaf capitals. More rewarding are the capitals inside the link with the C18 house, reportedly carved by the *O'Shea* brothers. Top storey rebuilt by *Cooper, c.*1934.

So to *Gort Scott*'s BOUNDARY BUILDING, of 2018–21. This sets its own agenda visually, without obvious nods to the older ranges to each side. Pale brick speckled with dark. The walls mostly plain almost to harshness, but with some panels of ridged brickwork, most conspicuously at mid-height on the rectangular stair-tower by the street entrance. This rises to a big glazed lantern and viewing platform of concrete fins and bronzed framing, crowned with a garland of leaves fashioned from gilded aluminium. Loggia on the N side, by the porter's lodge; small central atrium. The rest of the big, irregular-shaped building is split between offices, Middle Common Room etc. on the lodge side and student rooms to the S, with similar square or near-square windows. Also a roof terrace, on which are two separately expressed enclosures, the smaller for a teaching room, the larger with a Fellows' set, guest rooms etc. Their dark bronzed materials recur in the big PAVILION for events and functions, on its own terrace by the river. An irregular pentagon, with sides of three, four or six bays defined by slim pale uprights. Shallow-pitched roof. The punt dock alongside is a nice touch.†

South Building and its neighbours

SOUTH BUILDING owes less to St Hilda's than Hall. The oldest part is the end of the main range: a house of 1877–8 called COWLEY GRANGE (later Cherwell Hall), of yellow brick, with gables and an Elizabethan porch. Its architect was *Wilkinson*, its patron Augustus Vernon Harcourt, tutor in chemistry at Christ Church. Inside, a chimneypiece on which naturalistic foliage is lavished, one of four carved for the house by *James O'Shea*. The house received dour EXTENSIONS to NE and N

---

*G.V. Cox, *Recollections of Oxford* (1868), claimed that Sibthorp bought the staircase and some windows when Lord Abingdon's Rycote Park (p. 719) was pulled down. There was a sale of furnishings there in 1779, but the house was not demolished until 1807.

†The new buildings replaced the polygonal LODGE and garages along Cowley Place by *Sir Albert Richardson & Houfe*, 1960; a COMMON ROOM added over the garages by *Robert Potter*, 1974; and by the river, MILHAM FORD SCHOOL, 1906, sub-Tudor brick, with improvements by *Richardson & Houfe*, 1959. Built in association with Cowley Grange training college, the school later housed the architecture department of the College of Technology, Art and Commerce, forerunner of Oxford Brookes.

in 1906 and 1911, for an Anglican teacher training college; the latter phase by *E.A. Fermaud*. St Hilda's took over in 1920. *N.W. Harrison* then converted the teachers' library of 1911 to St Hilda's HALL, infilled a small gap next to the C19 house, and added a hip-roofed block with kitchens etc. behind, all by 1925. Further extension in front by *Richardson & Houfe*, 1958. With its picture windows it gives South Building a Bournemouth look. Also by the architects an extension facing Cowley Place, 1954.

ADDITIONS next to South Building have made an open-sided quad facing the gardens. These can be taken chronologically. WOLFSON BUILDING is the long Neo-Georgian brick range parallel to South Building. Of 1961–3 by *Richardson & Houfe*, who had already, c.1950, sketched designs for a linking cross-range. Instead – and it must be a record long jump from Richardson – the college commissioned *Alison & Peter Smithson*. Their GARDEN BUILDING dates from 1968–70. It is nearly square, of four storeys of pre-cast concrete framing, and has rooms on three sides, wrapped round a service core of solid brick walls. Also covered walkways to r. and l. The canted corners recall the Economist group of 1962–4 in Westminster, another of the handful of completed projects by this influential and much-mythologized duo. But the main distinguishing feature is the diagonal timber bracing set in front of the façades proper, which the architects explained as both a trellis for plants and 'a kind of "yashmak"', for a building which was to be part of 'a girls' place'. Internally the rooms each have a separate miniature dressing room, rather than the costlier individual bathrooms proposed by the Smithsons.

The JACQUELINE DU PRÉ MUSIC BUILDING stands on the other side of Wolfson. 1992–5 by *van Heyningen & Haward Architects* (another wife-and-husband team). A tall oblong of brown brick, with a few small square windows and one big slot for the entrance. The brickwork has big sunk panels, and fine horizontals made by just-projecting courses that run right round. Also one cogged upper course. Above, the hipped roof of slate and raised leaded skylight. Inside are concert hall, practice rooms and recording facilities. In 2002 the architects added a long glazed foyer, at odds with the rough brick.

Batterton Tyack's CHRISTINA BARRATT BUILDING of 2000–1 is squeezed between Garden Building, i.e. the side without rooms, and Magdalen College School (pp.405–6): a cruel site for a residential block. The parts that show most have flush window bands. Ground floor largely open, for parking etc. Finally the PRINCIPAL'S LODGINGS, down the slope to the SW. A little Neo-Regency villa of 1954–5 by *Richardson & Houfe*, extended c.1981. A proposed replacement by *Design Engine Architects*, with two four-storey residential blocks alongside, was approved in 2022.

For JOCELYN MORRIS QUAD, Stockmore Street, *see* East Oxford, p.503.

ST HUGH'S COLLEGE
St Margaret's Road

Founded in 1886 by the Principal of Lady Margaret Hall, for poorer women students. In 1911 St Hugh's Hall became a college by name, in 1959 a full college by status.

North Oxford houses were used until 1914–16 (*see* No. 17 Norham Gardens, p. 461), when MAIN BUILDING was constructed. By *H.T. Buckland* of *Buckland & Haywood*, Birmingham. Symmetrical, large, neo-1700, of red brick except for the two front lodges, which are of stone. On axis with the lodges is the main doorway to the building, with a big decorated scrolly pediment and cupola above. In the angles to the wings octagonal stair-turrets with balustraded tops. To the s, i.e. to the garden, Main Building has two projecting wings and many pretty bow

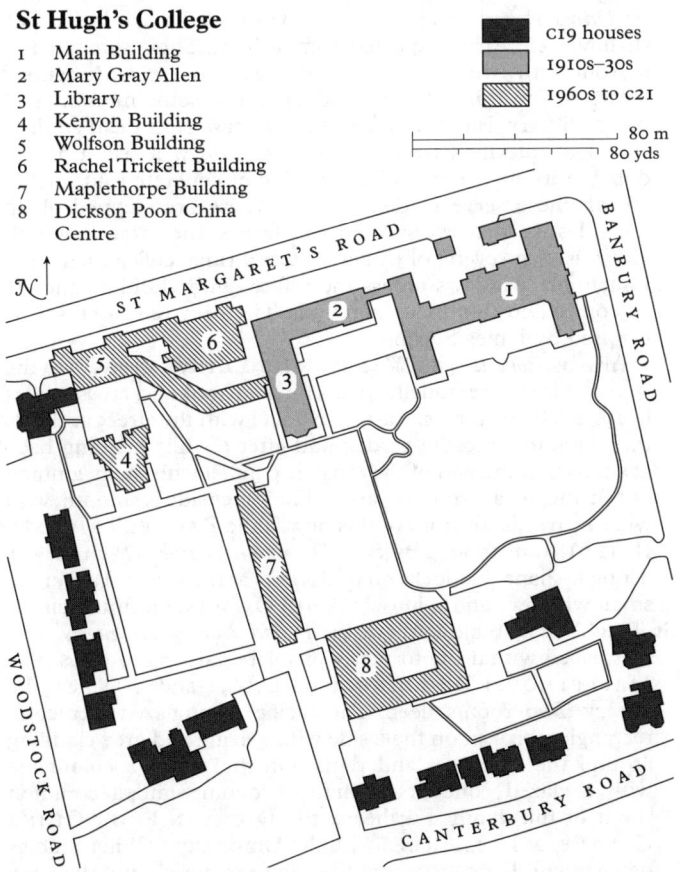

St Hugh's College

1 Main Building
2 Mary Gray Allen
3 Library
4 Kenyon Building
5 Wolfson Building
6 Rachel Trickett Building
7 Maplethorpe Building
8 Dickson Poon China Centre

C19 houses
1910s–30s
1960s to C21

80 m
80 yds

windows on the ground floor between, no doubt intended to add a feminine touch. Access to the rooms is throughout by corridors, not by staircases. The HALL is in the E cross-wing, which also has a low NW addition for a buttery, 1965–7. CHAPEL in the N part of the central block, a square cross-vaulted room on the first floor. Its decorative scheme is of 1964, by *Laurence Whistler*. Also a memorial panel of ENGRAVED GLASS by him, 1976, and a little window of *Powells'* STAINED GLASS (†1896) from a former chapel at Norham Gardens. – Stone baluster SUNDIAL of *c*.1700 in front on the S side, from Grove House, South Woodford, Essex.

An addition to the W, MARY GRAY ALLEN, was made by *Buckland* in exactly the same style in 1927–8, and a further one with the LIBRARY at right angles in 1935–6. The library is different in that it has broad giant pilasters of brick, with canted sides. Two storeys within, with much flush wood panelling. On the staircase two statues: St Hugh by *Esmond Burton*, Elizabeth Wordsworth probably by *William Bloye*.

St Hugh's most adventurous part is the KENYON BUILDING by *David Roberts*, 1964–6, placed W of the library in its own shallow well. An unexpected composition. Short symmetrical N front with two big pylons and a wide portal with canopy between. You think this introduces you to some monumental hall or library. But no, though the staircase runs dead straight with two intermediate landings, and though it has a glazed dome at its start, and a glazed ceiling of concrete grid further on, all these serve student rooms. These are stepped along the sides, so that every room can face S: the same sawtooth motif used at several of Roberts's Cambridge college schemes. Four more windows across the S face, with chunky concrete balconies and thin black handrails. The fiery red brick seems inspired by James Stirling.

Also by *Roberts* is the WOLFSON BUILDING of 1965–7 to the N, but this was remodelled with pitched roof and cross-gables in 1992. Three storeys, starting parallel with the street at the W, then bending into the garden and after a while bending back again so that the end of the range is parallel with the beginning but further away from the street. The street side is smooth, with window bands. In front of this now is the RACHEL TRICKETT BUILDING of 1990–2 by *Peter Thompson & Robin Pearce-Boby*, a long L-shape that locks on to Roberts at the W end. Red brick, small windows and a loosely North Oxford-conventual air.

St Hugh's C21 buildings are by *David Morley Architects*, and are placed within the formerly inviolate gardens to the S. The MAPLETHORPE BUILDING, 1998–2000, stands N–S near the library. Two rooms deep. The facing is unglazed terracotta rectangles, broken on the E side with glazing and grey cladding around the staircases and vents. On the E side a colonnade with a glazed concourse behind, widening into a common room of full depth. Further S, the DICKSON POON CHINA CENTRE, 2011–14, shared with the University's China Studies department. Here the multiplication of materials and the need to incorporate the various functions work against visual coherence. Main entrance to the S, slim spiral stair within the concourse. Open central court.

The GARDENS were largely created by *Annie Rogers*, 1920 onwards.

For the college's houses in Banbury, Canterbury and Woodstock roads *see* North Oxford, pp. 460ff.

ST JOHN'S COLLEGE
St Giles'

From St Giles' the college appears two, each with its traditional front with gate tower. Before the C19 St John's was indeed two, but divided W–E, not S–N. The W or Front Quad started life as St Bernard's College, founded by Archbishop Chichele in 1437. It was for Cistercian monks, to re-establish the order at Oxford after

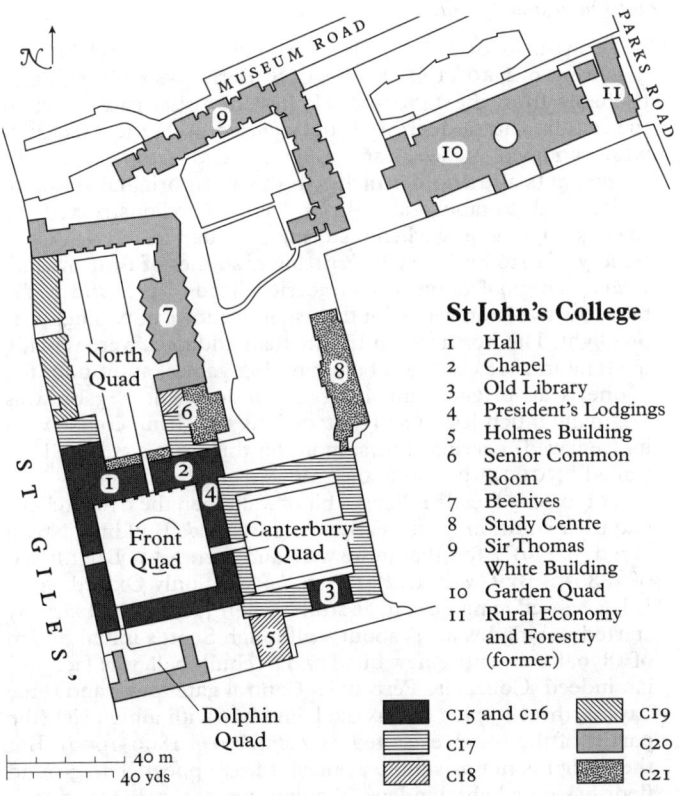

St John's College

1   Hall
2   Chapel
3   Old Library
4   President's Lodgings
5   Holmes Building
6   Senior Common Room
7   Beehives
8   Study Centre
9   Sir Thomas White Building
10 Garden Quad
11 Rural Economy and Forestry (former)

C15 and C16   C19
C17   C20
C18   C21

40 m
40 yds

the failure of their house at Rewley Abbey (p. 443). In 1479 the college was described as not yet half-built, and fresh agreements were made in 1502–3 with *William Orchard* for stone and construction. When the college – being a monastic foundation – was dissolved in 1539, the E range was still unfinished; but in 1555 Sir Thomas White, a London merchant, re-founded and completed St Bernard's as St John's College. It was to have a President and fifty Fellows, almost all of them from five nominated grammar schools, of which the Merchant Taylors' School in London had the lion's share.

A new library was built to the E in the 1590s, and in the 1630s this was assimilated into a coherent quadrangle, Canterbury Quad, given by the college's former President, Archbishop Laud. A third quadrangle, North Quad, grew piecemeal from the C17 to the 1950s. The 1940s brought the little Dolphin Quad, S of Front Quad. New buildings of exceptional ambition and quality followed to the N from the 1970s onwards, making use of the generous gardens; a further new quadrangle, Kendrew Quad, lies a little way N of the college (*see* Perambulation 3, p. 429).

Front Quad and St Giles'

The FAÇADE to St Giles' tells of a long architectural history. The front of FRONT QUAD, i.e. of St Bernard's College, dates probably from the 1470s–90s. It has the usual gate tower in the middle with a depressed four-centred arch, a canted oriel with canopied niches l. and r. above, and a top stage with single lights and another niche. In this is an original statue of St Bernard, suitably adapted. *J. J. Stevenson* reconstructed the tower's upper storey when restoring the quad in 1887–8. Oriel tracery of 1916 by *Harry Redfern*, lower statues of 1961 by *Alan Collins*. Original doors with traceried heads. To l. and r. the façade is two-storeyed, with the usual windows of two lights or one light. The dormers, an Elizabethan addition, were remade in stone in 1616. The end bays have big gables, and under the r. one is an original, much larger window. The l. gable was originally much less steeply pitched, as the string course with its (renewed) carving shows; more on this on p. 275. The low-walled ENCLOSURE along the front was made in 1576.

N of the C15 façade follows a bit of wall, then the C16 kitchens and their additions of the early C17 (*see* Cook's Building, North Quad, p. 279). After that more wall, and then NEW BUILDING of 1880–2. By *George Gilbert Scott Jun.*, his only Oxford work. It is a self-effacing design, at a time when Jackson had already started waving his arms about – although Scott's initial design of 1879, for an entire new quad and a rebuilt hall, was Jacksonian indeed. Collegiate Perp style. Central gate tower and three bays r., three l., plus one as the l. end bay with a big oriel (the part N of the tower executed by *E. P. Warren*, 1899–1900). But the design is not as simple as may at first appear. The ground floor has four-light windows, the first two of two lights in each of the six bays set further apart, and the gables have oriels, the one non-authorized motif. Or perhaps one should say that there are others: little lions' heads in many places and not set strictly axially, and tiny round-headed windows next to the gate tower.* It is really very subtle. Adopted buildings to the N are described with St Giles' (Perambulation 3, p. 428).

Going S from Front Quad, there is another stretch of wall, then the Neo-Georgian flank of DOLPHIN QUAD of 1947–8: the chief work among many contributions to St John's by *Sir Edward Maufe*, an old member. The contemporary Dolphin Gate, immediately adjacent to the S, is in fact by a different architect and belongs to distant Trinity College (*see* p. 297).

FRONT QUAD is entered under the original two-bay vault, with diagonal and ridge ribs and lively bosses. The tower has towards the quad in the top niche a statue of St John by *Eric Gill*, given by Maufe in 1936. (In the top room a stone corbel carved with an angel.) The quad is spacious, a perfect square of 117 ft (35.7 metres). Paving and lawn to *Maufe*'s design, 1954–5. Two-storey buildings, embattled in 1616–17. Windows sashed in the C18, but still indicating the C15 arrangement of a shared large sleeping room with small studies opening off it. The S range was in course of erection in 1438. (In a room of Staircase 5 some late C16 foliage painting.) The E range, never finished by the monks, included a first-floor library in its S part. On the N side are hall and chapel, both completed by 1517; but the three chapel windows now have Perp tracery from *Blore*'s restoration in 1843–4, and the hall has slightly pointed-arched windows with Georgian glazing of the 1740s. Between them the former antechapel, made into a passage through to North Quad by *Maufe* in 1936. Above its doorway a clock with carved surround designed by *N.W. Harrison*, 1919, and an ample rooftop louvre by *Blore*.

The CHAPEL is internally almost all *Blore*'s Neo-Perp of 1843–4, from the leggy hammerbeam roof to the STALLS and the wall panelling of Caen stone.† SEDILIA added in 1872 by *Buckeridge*, next to the President's discreetly recessed PEW, SE. To the NE, Blore inserted a two-bay arcade to the BAYLIE CHAPEL. This was made in 1662 for the reinstated President. Its handsome plaster fan-vault betrays the date only in the little cartouches. – FRONTAL installed in 1936, made up of C15 English embroidered work. – Main REREDOS by *Kempe*, 1892. Carved and painted wood. – PAVING. Black and white; mostly of *c.* 1670. – LECTERN. A delightful Rococo piece. An eagle on a baluster, holding in its beak a flower garland which twines round. Carved in 1773 by *Leonard Snetzler* of Oxford, brother of the organ-builder. – ORGAN. 2008, French, by *Bernard*

72

---

*For the lions cf. Lulworth Castle, an early C17 house in Dorset which Scott probably knew. Scott's carver was *John McCulloch*, later taken up by Bodley and by Champneys; the oriel at Warren's end has a carved shield and putti by *J.H.M. Furse*.
†*Adam Browne*'s COMMUNION RAILS of 1632 are now at Northmoor church (*see Oxfordshire: North and West*). Two columns from the SCREEN designed by *Wren*, *c.* 1670, are re-set in the stair landing of Painswick House, Glos.

Aubertin. Spectacular. – STAINED GLASS. E window by *Kempe*, 1892. Three by *Clayton & Bell*, 1870–2, N and S. Also two panels by *Ervin Bossányi*, *c*.1944 (given 1977). Baylie Chapel, heraldry by *Moira Forsyth*, 1936–7.

MONUMENTS. Nearly all in the Baylie Chapel. Richard Baylie †1667, with another Richard Baylie †1674/5. The chapel was built in anticipation of this monument, which is attributed to *Jasper Latham* (GF). Big standing base with two inscriptions in ovals. Running garlands above. Reclining effigy. Back panel with columns and a Mannerist entablature. Dismantled 1843, reinstated 1949. – Several Elizabethan brasses with kneeling figures. – Another with kneeler incised in stone, to John Wicksteed †1607. Strapwork shield above. – Ralph Hutchenson, President, †1606. The usual demi-figure with a book on a cushion. – Sir William Paddy †1634. A progressive piece for its date. Bust on a plinth with gristly surround. Two columns and an open scrolly pediment, and in this a triangle, like an inner pediment, formed by books. A skull in the triangle. The vocabulary has affinities with Canterbury Quad, and Howard Colvin indeed suspected *John Jackson* as the monument's author (GF). – William Levinz, President, †1698. Signed by *Thomas Hill*, 1699. White architectural tablet. Two columns, open segmental pediment. – William Holmes †1748. Large standing monument. Putti l. and r. Curly top pediment. On the base an amateurish relief of the Baptism of Christ. – Bishop Rawlinson †1755. An exquisite little heart-burial piece: a black marble urn in an oval recess with some drapery over; that is all. – Samuel Dennis, President, †1795. By *Westmacott Sen*. Elegantly decorated sarcophagus. – S wall. John Case †1600, Richard Latewar †1603, both with kneelers. – Cross-passage. William Bigmore †1631. Tablet, no longer Jacobean in style. Complicated pediment.

HALL. St John's hall was formed in 1555–6, where in the college of St Bernard the kitchen had been. (Of the latter the roof over the E part survives, above the plaster vault, with collar-beams, arched braces, and wind-braces.) In 1616–17 it was extended one bay to the W. The present mid-C18 appearance was achieved in stages, starting in 1729–30 with the simply panelled plaster vault. Grand marble fireplace of 1731, supplied by *William Townesend*, in place of an open hearth. The scagliola overmantel picture after Raphael's John the Baptist is by *Lamberto Gori*, and was brought from Italy in 1759. The hall panelling is of 1744 and again simple, though on the dais wall it has Ionic pilasters. The stone SCREEN was designed by *James Gibbs* and made by *John Townesend II* in 1742–3. Four unfluted Ionic columns, three arches – those of the sides blank except for circular openings – and enriched urns on top. Fine wrought-iron gates, made by *Thomas Stephens* of London. The screen now stands in place of the buttery E wall, having been moved one bay W by *Maufe* in 1936. The old screens passage thus became part of the hall space, and the room above the buttery became an overflow space for the hall.

The BUTTERY is of the Cistercian time, specifically of after 1494, when its vaulted CELLAR was still in progress – the best-preserved C15 work of the college. Four bays, with a round pier with octagonal capital. Vaults of diagonal and ridge ribs with a sharp chamfer. In addition one later support. C15 beams are visible within the buttery, which served as the college hall until the 1550s. Its low original roof pitch, two-storey arrangement and smallness in relation to the former kitchen are all difficult to account for; Howard Colvin suggested that a larger, northward-projecting hall may have been intended (cf. All Souls), after which the first hall would have reverted to use as a buttery. Instead, a replacement KITCHEN was built to the N. On its staircase are two detached fragments of Elizabethan wall painting, poor, as it usually is. Reused in the first-floor passage, a C15 cusped window head.

So much for the N range. The EAST RANGE has two broad doorways of 1633, made in connection with Canterbury Quad and preparing suitably for it. Big open scrolly pediments. The l. doorway leads into the President's Lodgings.

DOLPHIN QUAD is reached through the W end of the S range. It was designed by *Maufe* in 1942 and is attractive, though of course *retardataire* by the time of building in 1947–8. Short colonnades hide the walls and outhouses to E and W. The building itself is of seven bays, essentially Neo-Georgian, but with slightly squared-up details.

Canterbury Quad

CANTERBURY QUAD is a princely job, and by far the most impressive building of its date in Oxford – all the more so in that its construction appears to have involved more than one change of intention.* When Archbishop Laud, who had been President from 1611 to 1621, began the work, most of the present S range was already there, containing, as it still does, the library. This had been built in 1596–8, using materials from Oxford's Carmelite friary (*see* p. 431n.). Laud started in 1631, pulling down the cloister range that linked the library to Front Quad. By 1635 all was ready. p. 276

The passage through from Front Quad is fan-vaulted, a surprise after the pedimented doorway. One leaves it by a portal more sumptuous than the entry. Large decorated pediment; decorated frieze and 'leather faces' below. One then finds oneself in a long arcade of elegant columns leading nowhere l. and r. Opposite, the arcade repeats, and this range must first be described, as it is first seen. The columns are monoliths of Tuscan proportions, the spandrels have thick decoration and busts of Virtues, Liberal Arts etc. in roundels, beneath a rich quasi-Doric frieze. There are eleven bays altogether, the middle one being a showpiece. Two pairs of Roman Doric

---

* *See* Howard Colvin, *The Canterbury Quadrangle* (1988).

St John's College, Canterbury Quad.
Drawing by Gerald Gardiner, 1951

columns and an archway between, richly decorated too. Above,
two pairs of wholly detached very slender Ionic columns on
double-decked, thickly decorated pedestals. A niche with aedicule surround in the middle, composed of detached quasi-
Composite columns and an open pediment. The niche holds
the bronze statue of Charles I by *Le Sueur.* Sumptuous cartouche with shield beneath the niche, crouching beasts above
the king's head. Top pediment large and segmental, the tympanum recessed. A crown at the very top. All this is boldly done in
high relief. The w side of the quad, to which we can now look
back, is architecturally identical. Here the statue is Charles's
queen, Henrietta Maria. Le Sueur's price for the two statues
was £400, of a total cost for the quad of £5,553.

However, what has not been said yet is that the upper-floor
windows to E and W are of two arched lights in the C15 and

C16 tradition. This is indeed done throughout the N and S sides, without anything to make them match the two showpieces. There are also the traditional carvings of the string course beneath the battlements, and hoodmoulds of the type linked continuously between the windows – the latter almost certainly an alteration where the 1590s library block is concerned.* Of course Laud or his mason could have chosen instead to reface the library to a more thoroughly classical pattern, and it may also be significant that work began in 1631 to a brief with a balancing N range only, and just a cloistered walk to close the W side. However, novel juxtapositions of Renaissance and collegiate-Gothic motifs were in favour at both universities in the decade before the Civil War, and we cannot assume that a quad planned entirely from scratch would necessarily have followed a more classical path.

There seems also to have been a further change of direction after work began, as Colvin's analysis of the frontispieces showed. He explained the curious superimposed pedestals of the upper storey as a device to make up for the substitution of one order for two smaller orders at this level. In other words, the conventional vertical display of the orders, Doric–Ionic–Corinthian (cf. Merton and Wadham), was probably intended in the first design.

These complexities, coupled with a lack of close parallels elsewhere, make it hard to suggest a single designer's name for Canterbury Quad. Who the masons were, we know: first *Richard Maude* with *Hugh Davies* and *Robert Smith*, who together got into difficulties, as did their successor *William Hill*; then from 1634 a new team under *John Jackson* from London, who made his career in Oxford thereafter.† There is *Adam Browne* too, a master joiner who was paid £5 in 1633 for coming from London, '& drawing the Drafts, & making the Moulds'. He also negotiated with masons and carpenters on the college's behalf. Laud employed Browne at Lambeth and elsewhere, and he later became Surveyor to Westminster Abbey. Browne's appearance in Oxford may therefore be connected with the suggested redesign of the upper centrepieces, although he is unlikely to have been their author. The king's master mason Nicholas Stone has been suggested, but college records and Stone's own list of works do not support a connection. The work has nothing to do with Inigo Jones either. The closest parallels are to be found in the Baroque of the Low Countries around 1630, especially in the circle of Rubens: both in terms of such details as the animal skins on the lower plinths, and for the combination of columns and pediments and lush foliage in a three-dimensional and dynamic way. Colvin proposed another candidate in the person of *Sir Balthazar Gerbier*,

---

*The ground-floor window pattern was originally different, and the back is without running hoodmoulds on either floor.
†The *Strong* family, Burford masons, were also engaged in 1634, their first recorded Oxford project.

Charles I's agent in Brussels and an amateur architect of talent. Gerbier's stylistic personality is elusive, however, and even if a design for the centrepieces was procured from him, he may not have been its originator.

Alas, the rare Bletchingdon marble of the arcade columns was found to be splintering, and they were replaced with Swaledale Fossil limestone in 2022–3. As to the C17 carving, *Jackson* provided the great shields of arms and the sixteen busts, *Harry Ackers* and *Anthony Gore* most of the angel heads, friezes and strings. Much C20 re-carving by *E. S. Frith*, as well as general refacing, begun 1922, and more replacement work in 2022–3. Fine original rainwater heads by *James Fletcher*, plumber. Colvin's own MEMORIAL, E cloister, is a tablet by *Rory Young*, 2011. First World War memorial designed by *Selwyn Image*, 1921.

The garden side of the E range is neither as Gothic as the N and S ranges nor is it Baroque. It is embattled, with gables over the end bays, and it has five oriels, including the large one at the E end of the library. The zone below the windows of the oriels is decorated with strapwork, not with Laud's foliage and cartouches. The explanation is that the old library oriel of 1596–8 was re-set in the extended S range, and its details copied for the other oriels. The doorway however is from a recent Flemish source, Jacques Francart's *Premier livre d'architecture* (1617), with embellishments including more leather faces. Small oval windows originally in the lower storey are now blocked. The Study Centre now joins on to the N (*see* p. 281), so the N side of the N range no longer shows up from the garden side. It sports small Dutch gables, i.e. gables with pediments on ogee curves, not at all like the treatment of the other ranges. They are placed symmetrically in alternation with chimneystacks. The gable motif recurs at University and Jesus colleges, where *Richard Maude* also worked, and its use in Oxford may originate with him.

INTERIORS. The greater part of the S range comprises the OLD LIBRARY of 1596–8, Oxford's first new-built library with bookcase stalls, as lately introduced at Merton, rather than the old lectern-desk type. Originally barrel-vaulted; the canted roof of reused timbers was exposed in the 1880s. *J. J. Stevenson* added the nice ironwork ties then. Bookcases mostly original, but heightened 1736. Between them are benches, their ends still like plain Gothic bench-ends in churches. Some were probably saved from 1580s renovations to the original library in Front Quad. The E end, with the re-set E window and another large bay window to the S, is an addition of Laud's. Stained glass in these bays dated 1596, 1633 and 1636, the heraldic panels quite splendid. The 1630s extension or LAUDIAN LIBRARY continues at right angles into the E range, via a large stone portal with broken segmental pediment. It had cabinet-type cases made by *Adam Browne* with pedimented tops and doors with busily decorated openwork metal grilles (two surviving), placed flat against the walls. In 1838–9 *H. J. Underwood* made the present tall Perp-style bookcases, and the arch-braced roof with its plaster angels. On the ground floor below is the OTRANTO PASSAGE, now extended N to the Study Centre. Along one side is a linear artwork of 2015–16 by *Kirsty Brooks* inspired by the college's history, constructed of different types of glass. The Study Centre vestibule preserves part of the internal C17 framing as a feature.

Originally the library was entered at its W end. The 1630s continuation of the S range included a new STAIRCASE up to it, and this was rebuilt in stone by *James Pears*, 1796.

In much of the N range and part of the W range are the PRESIDENT'S LODGINGS, still with much 1630s work; joiner *David Woodfield*. The DRAWING ROOM (N range, first floor) has white-painted panelling and pilasters with strapwork decoration on their pedestals. Overmantel with twin niches flanking a panel with broken scrolly pediment. Mark Girouard suggested that Woodfield may also have made the moulds for the geometrical compartmented ceiling, with its pattern taken from Serlio: big octagons, Greek crosses, elongated hexagons. STAIRCASE with early vase-shaped balusters, its open well partly enclosed with Gothick glazing in 1764–5. In the W range the modest LONG GALLERY, an uncommon feature at Oxford college lodgings. C18 panelling. DINING ROOM below the drawing room, with decoration of 1778–80. The other residential rooms were sets for gentlemen commoners. Some good panelling, 1630s and mid-C18.

HOLMES BUILDING is reached through the S range of Canterbury Quad, by the Old Library staircase. Erected in 1794–5 by *Pears*, it is a battlemented five-bay block with hoodmoulds over the large sash windows. Sophisticated handling of the oval stair and entrance lobby, with doorway fanlights to the vestibules of each set. The S end now abuts the 1990s addition at Trinity (p. 296).

North Quad and later additions

NORTH QUAD is large and oblong and has two trees to give it its distinct character. It has buildings on all sides, and they are stylistically various. The older parts first. On the S side are hall and chapel, with *Maufe*'s flat-roofed passage of 1936 running across in front. The W side starts with a three-storey section, COOK'S BUILDING, whose stonework indicates a complex history. Its S part comprises the kitchens built in the 1550s, to an L-plan with its return and end gable on St Giles'. These were enlarged and a storey added in 1612, with rooms for renting to commoners. In 1642–3 an extension was built by *John Jackson* to the N, and the older gables made to conform. Their scrolly shapes ending in a little triangle, the lozenge openings in them and the occasional ovals of the façade are things that the Oxford architects of about 1900 must have delighted in. On the E side is the SENIOR COMMON ROOM, also of several phases: s part of 1673–6, builder *Bartholomew Peisley I*; three-bay extension by *Daniel Robertson*, 1826–7; projecting end bay of 1899–1900. The main storey has big sash windows with lugged surrounds all through, not a 1670s form, so perhaps made uniform by Robertson. Interiors and rear extensions are described below.

Completion of the quad began on the w side with *G.G. Scott Jun.*'s NEW BUILDING, started in 1880 and soberer here than on the street front, roughly symmetrical, but certainly not dull. The part N of the tower was carried out by *E.P. Warren*, 1899–1900. The N side is Cotswold C17 style by *N.W. & G.A. Harrison*, 1909–11. This range is known as RAWLINSON BUILDING. It was extended along the E side by *Maufe* in 1933–6, as far as the site of *Thomas Hardwick*'s stables of 1811. An approach was made to Maufe in 1956 to replace the stables with a residential block, but supporters of Modern architecture among the younger Fellows, notably Howard Colvin, had other ideas. The outcome was the first Modernist residential building at the Oxford colleges, the celebrated BEEHIVES, by the *Architects' Co-Partnership*, 1958–60 (architect in charge *Michael Powers*). By that time many younger English architects were bored with the rectangularity of the so-called International Modern of the 1930s, and some looked for inspiration to patterns from the natural world instead – though any parallel here (properly with the honeycomb, rather than the hive) is apparently coincidental. An elongated hexagon is the unit. The plan is strictly logical, the slit-windowed lanterns over the three staircases allowing the study-bedrooms to be arranged in such a way that they form a zigzag front and back. The many-angled frontage also bridges the conflicting alignments of the straight sections to its N and S, and the novelty of the forms is emphasized by facing them in Portland roach stone, an unfamiliar material for Oxford. Thus considerations of planning and aesthetic preferences merge. The range to the quad is not long, of two storeys over a basement – hence the external stair. Rooms to the w have their windows facing sw; those to the E have windows facing SE, and here a third full storey is made possible by split-level plan.

So to the Senior Common Room INTERIORS. The 1670s room has raised-and-fielded panelling, pedimented overdoors and very fine carved garlands on the overmantel. Gorgeous plaster ceiling by *Roberts*, made in 1742. The infilling of its compartments with closely spaced seashells – real ones, stuck on – must be later. The room of 1826–7 retains its original Neoclassical ceiling by *Frederick Crace*. N of the stairs, the 1900 extension was remodelled as a smoking room by *Maufe* in 1936, with a plain barrel-vault. Characteristic simplified-traditional panelling and fireplace. This space continues to the E as the SADLER ROOM, part of an extension of 1979–81 by *Sir Howard Colvin*, with *Walter Price* of Oxford Architects Partnership. L-shaped, the corner section of square plan under a faintly Soanian cross-vault, with window seats in twin oriels. The angle encloses the STAIRCASE which is all that remains of the addition of 1953–5 by *David Booth* of *Booth & Lederboer*. Both internally and externally indifferent, this was replaced in 2002–4 by *MacCormac Jamieson Prichard*'s spatially rich extension (job architect *Mark Hines*, structural engineers *Price & Myers*). Two storeys, pushing out as a glass-walled box within a structurally separate framework of composite steel-and-oak beams. The framework supports giant timber shutters, which pivot to help control the temperature inside. The chief space is the LUNCH ROOM, placed back to back with the C17 and C19 rooms, with kitchens below. Portal frames of concrete comprise the primary structure, from which the main floor is cantilevered out within the glass. Twin staircases tucked within the outer edges of the box descend to a bar and garden terrace on the ground floor. The 'solid' part of the roof serves as an upper terrace, with its own glass-walled pavilion at the old dormer level.

The Lunch Room now comprises one side of an open-ended enclosure for the President's Garden, facing across to the library extension or STUDY CENTRE attached to the Laudian Library. *Wright & Wright*'s building of 2014–19 is highly complex, with much use of split levels and borrowed light. Stone facing throughout. Towards the President's Garden it appears almost windowless and near-symmetrical, at least in terms of the central section between the two low stair-towers. 130 But the centre of the centre is a blind wall of almost full height, twice stepped forward, with slit windows facing N and S in the gaps between. Shallow abstract reliefs on the advanced walls, designed by *Susanna Heron* (repeated on their inner faces), pick up reflections from a moat-like pool in front. Beyond the towers the building rises higher to the N, and drops lower to the S by the junction with the C17 quad. Here is a segmental bulge – to house the reception desk – and a glazed-sided corridor link above. The interior arrangements are not easily deduced from outside. Below the pool and extending under the main range is a subterranean level for the college archives. The E side towards the main gardens also features a big blank wall, but here the wall is rubble and of C17 date. A tapering, part-sunk reading room has been made behind the old wall, spanned by shallow-pitched glazing and overlooked from the inner side by an intermediate storey or deck, placed slightly above ground level. The uppermost level rises high by means of a clerestory, and also has a continuous window along its E side, where the building overtops the old wall. At the N end the chief interior is an oak-lined seminar room, with a giant window angled round the NE corner and an open circulation space below. All this is rewarding to explore and consistently enjoyable to be in, thanks not least to the high standards of materials and finishes.

Buildings further north

After the Beehives the college's next step was the SIR THOMAS WHITE BUILDING of 1972–5, by *Philip Dowson* of *Arup*

Associates. It stands some way N of North Quad, one wing following the alignment of Museum Road behind, the other, not-quite-right-angled wing extending S and turning a little way W, partly enclosing a garden between. The competition-winning design of 1967 was for a much larger and more multi-functional complex, but despite subsequent scaling-down this is still the grandest of Arup's sequence of college buildings at the older universities, with 150 study-bedrooms and sets all told. Its closest cousin is the Leckhampton Building of 1963–4 for Corpus Christi, Cambridge: both have dramatic external framing composed of pre-cast concrete H-shapes, both include a sheltered circulation route where the ground-floor common rooms etc. are recessed, and both have the staircases and services expressed separately, betraying the influence of Louis Kahn. Here the stair-towers are windowless, faced in pale French limestone, and placed at regular intervals between the groups of rooms. Their chamfered angles make an especially bold rhythm on the skyline, where the fourth-floor penthouses are recessed between. To the W the ground floor opens up with a gate and entrance lodge. The N aspect is memorable for the way the piers of the frame are placed assertively just outside the old rubble boundary wall.

Across a smaller garden to the E of Thomas White are the MIDDLE COMMON ROOMS, created by *Berman Guedes Stretton* in 1997–8 as a steel-framed, pitched-roofed structure on top of *Arup Associates'* rubble-walled squash courts of 1972–5. Immediately behind is GARDEN QUAD of 1991–4, the most ambitious addition of that decade at any Oxford college. Like Thomas White, the project belongs in a sequence of outstanding collegiate work by a single practice, here *MacCormac, Jamieson & Prichard* (structural engineers *Price & Myers*). The basic concept is carried over from their Bowra Building at Wadham (p. 311): residential towers linked by an upper circulation level, over a separately accessed podium of public rooms. But where Wadham was contingent on filling in an existing quad, St John's creates its own formal and monumental world. Access is beguilingly discreet: a half-sunk passage along the S flank of the Middle Common Rooms, bridged over in two places by small annexes – each comprising a house for a Junior Fellow – into which the open stairs to the upper deck are inserted, one on either side of each house. Between the houses, the inner wall opens up unexpectedly with a wide segmental archway leading to a circulation court, which is spanned across by a flattened vault with a giant central oculus – now festooned with hanging greenery, like an Edward James jungle fantasy. Chain downpipes in each corner. The vault evokes Soane's Bank of England halls, and the reference is underscored by finely cast concrete rustication and other Postmodern classical details, an indulgence absent from MJP's works elsewhere. Screen walls of layered glass, made by the artist *Alexander Beleschenko*, divide the court from a lecture hall, l., and dining room, r. Each of these has its own saucer-dome, each with a little central lantern that rises as a feature in the formal garden terrace above. Here the interlinked residential towers already glimpsed from ground level appear in full array, four-storeyed all along the N side, three-storeyed on each of the short sides and the shorter returns to the S. The material is yellow load-bearing brick, giving way to precise concrete framing and shallow projecting roofs in the upper parts, with tight spiral staircases tucked in between. The centrepiece, placed over the lower arch, is a bow-fronted pavilion room or belvedere (the architects' term). As at Wadham, the ensemble resounds with echoes of Elizabethan Hardwick Hall, Japan and Frank Lloyd Wright, without reaching for the more explicit quotations of the ground storey.

Also part of the MJP buildings are the free-standing MUSIC ROOMS to the E, with an external stair, and the adjacent residential reconstruction of the former SCHOOLS OF RURAL ECONOMY AND FORESTRY, of 1906–14 by *N.W. & G.A. Harrison*. The inward façade is new, but the Edwardian frontage remains in Parks Road, a riff on the garden front of Canterbury Quad (the Schools were built by St John's for the University's use). Four bays, two storeys, ashlared, with pretty carving by *Gilbert Seale* on the sills of the oriels. Pedimented doorway in the S bay.

GARDENS. Informally landscaped in the 1770s, retaining a raised C17 terrace along the E side of the N part. The entry from Garden Quad is by an iron GATE of *c.* 1994 by *Wendy Ramshaw*, incorporating a glass lens, set in the C16 N wall.

For KENDREW QUAD, ST GILES' HOUSE and other college properties on St Giles' *see* Perambulation 3, pp. 428–30; for HART SYNNOT HOUSE *see* North Oxford, p. 468.

ST PETER'S COLLEGE
New Inn Hall Street

The college was founded in 1928 as St Peter's House. It became a full college in 1961. The foundation was at first decidedly Evangelical in character. The 'low' parish church of St Peter-le-Bailey became its chapel, the existing church institution of Hannington Hall became its hall. Two large Late Georgian houses and the former Central Girls' School of 1901 have also been annexed. The college's own new buildings fit into the spaces between and behind, on a constricted site largely within the NW course of the city wall. In consequence of this history the outside aspect is not remotely collegiate, so the New Inn Hall Street buildings are described here first, then what lies behind.

LINTON HOUSE contains the main entrance. It is a fine, plain house built by *Daniel Harris* in 1797 as the offices of the

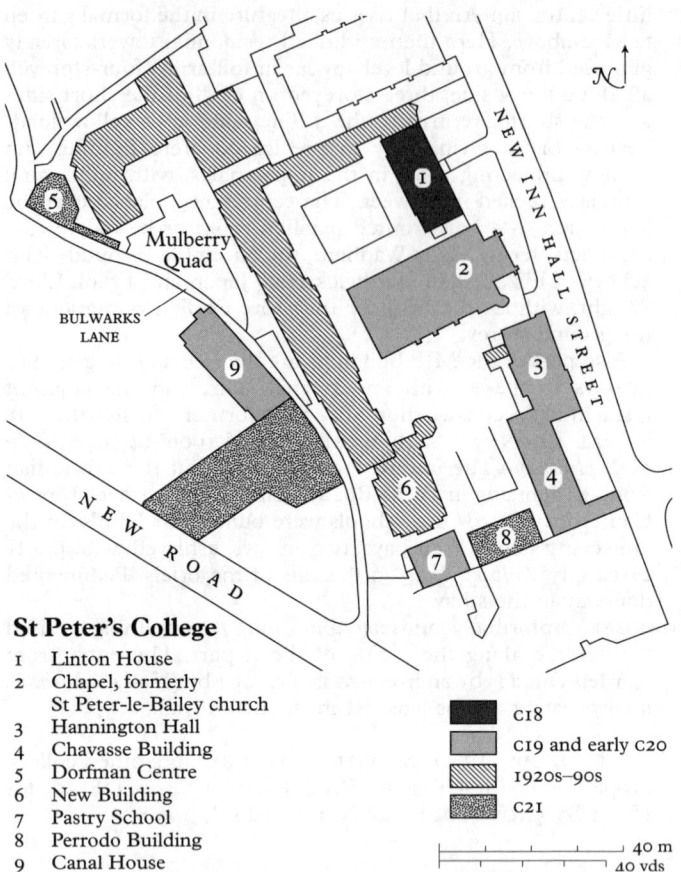

St Peter's College

1   Linton House
2   Chapel, formerly
    St Peter-le-Bailey church
3   Hannington Hall
4   Chavasse Building
5   Dorfman Centre
6   New Building
7   Pastry School
8   Perrodo Building
9   Canal House

■ C18
▨ C19 and early C20
▧ 1920s–90s
▨ C21

├─────────────────────┤ 40 m
├─────────────────────┤ 40 vds

Oxford Canal Company, adopted later as the rectory of St
Peter-le-Bailey, then sensitively reworked for the college. Three
storeys, with lower one-bay appendices and arched ground-
floor windows – all very smooth ashlar work. The porch with
Tuscan columns and open pediment is however of 1954
by *Thomas Rayson*, and he returned in 1959–60 to change
the upper storeys from three bays to five for the COLLEGE
LIBRARY, thus matching the rear façade. Its double-height, galleried space is neatly contrived. Modest staircase, no doubt of
*c.*1828 and by *Richard Tawney*, as the stair details at his Canal
House (*see* p. 287) match exactly.

The CHAPEL, i.e. the former CHURCH OF ST PETER-LE-
BAILEY, stands immediately s. An early work by *Basil Champneys*, 1872–4, it is economically done, with much plain wall
where the aisles were originally hemmed in. But the composition is forceful, the references to local Dec are nicely handled
– see e.g. the echoes of Merton chapel in the E window – and

the tracery of the bell-openings of the s porch-tower already shows enterprise. The material is Box Ground (i.e. Bath) stone. Plain arcades within, under a very plain roof. The upper tower space is open as a vaulted gallery. – FURNISHINGS. REREDOS. 1929, by F.E. Howard. Of wood. Much filigree carving, and sculpted scenes in a North German medieval idiom. Carvers A.R. Mowbray & Co. – PULPIT also by Howard. – FLOOR TILES by Godwin, some designed specifically for the church. – PAINTING. The Sacrifice of Isaac, late C17. Flemish? – FONT. An ambitious Neo-Norman piece of c. 1845 with circular reliefs on the sides, deriving from the Winchester Cathedral font. – ARCHITECTURAL FRAGMENTS (porch). C12 to C15, from old St Peter-le-Bailey church.* – STAINED GLASS. Expressionist E window by John Hayward, 1964. A large St Peter, with smaller scenes. The tracery glass remains from the window of 1874 by Henry Holiday, made by Heaton, Butler & Bayne, whose figures are now in the W window. Font window by Ervin Bossányi, made 1943, inserted 1997. Also several back-lit designs for other windows by Bossányi, N aisle. – MONUMENTS. Chancel, brasses to John Otworthe †1419(?), headless, 2 ft 2 in. (66 cm.), and Alice Sprunt, c. 1420, 17 in. (44 cm.). – Two time-shifting wall monuments: Mayor William Northerne alias Longburgh †1383 and wife, tablet of 1667 by Simon White; Thomas Grubb †1808, an appropriated early C18 cartouche with figured frame, including a reclining female writing. – Francis J. Chavasse, Bishop of Liverpool and co-founder of St Peter's Hall, †1928. Large plaster cast of 1932 from the front of his tomb, by David Evans, in Liverpool Cathedral.

HANNINGTON HALL is next, joined to the chapel by railings and gates, installed 1929. Of 1832 by Thomas Greenshields, and meant as part of something larger, the building is all that remains of New Inn Hall. This medieval academic hall was dissolved (strictly, absorbed by Balliol) in 1887. Front of five bays, ashlar-faced, with bays one and five flanked by giant pilasters. Inside was the hall of the Hall, as it were, and rooms for members. The ill-matched Free Style doorcase is by Walter K. Shirley, from alterations of 1897–8 for a short-lived Evangelical foundation that supplied the present name. In the N wall high up the Venetian window of the DINING HALL of the college, made in 1928–9 by R. Fielding Dodd. It is mid-Georgian in style, with Austrian oak panelling and a plaster barrel ceiling, and a handsome oak staircase up to it. Stained glass by C.C. Townshend & Joan Howson in the Venetian window. At the back an awkward lift tower of 1991.

Finally the CHAVASSE BUILDING, converted in 1985–6 from the greater part of Leonard Stokes's former CENTRAL GIRLS' SCHOOL of 1900–1. An impressive frontage, though not large. Nor is it really like other Oxford architecture of the period (cf. Stokes's contemporary Boys' School, p. 439). The

*This stood to the s, on the corner with Queen Street. Largely rebuilt 1728–40 and later, with William Chipps and then William Townesend as master masons.

centre with the schoolrooms is recessed and a little sunk. It is of two storeys with a cupola with diagonally set columns. The ground floor is a continuous strip of nine cross-windows, grouped in threes. Above, only three small four-light windows. The projecting wings are higher, and their doors are set into niches of banded rustication (*à la* Wren). Their upper rooms were for training male and female pupil-teachers. Carvings of pomegranates and doves over the side doorways.

LINTON QUAD lies behind Linton House. On the w side and extending s of the chapel are the college's own earliest buildings. By *Fielding Dodd*, 1929–31, with *Sir Herbert Baker* as consultant (who seems to have contributed next to nothing). Red brick with stone dressings in a free late C17 style, three-storeyed, with cross-windows and windows that go with these. Doorways with columns and pediments. They look 1900 rather than 1930. The N staircase in fact is later still, 1952–3 (*Fielding Dodd & Kenneth Stevens*), with only minor differences. Given by M. Antonin Besse, whose BUST by *Oscar Nemon* is within. Across the N side are part of MATTHEWS BUILDING (brick, four storeys plus leaded mansard, with much more behind) and the LATNER BUILDING (three storeys, board-marked concrete, with a lower, stone-clad salient alongside Linton House). Both by *Kenneth Stevens & Partners*, 1971–2 (partner in charge *J. R. Allen*).

Behind Matthews is MULBERRY QUAD, and on the N side of its garden another, angled *Fielding Dodd* block of 1929–31. Paid for by Lord Nuffield in memory of his mother, whose memorial BUST by *Alec Miller*, 1934, is displayed inside. At the back by the boundary wall, the DORFMAN CENTRE, a neat timber pavilion by *Lee/Fitzgerald Architects*, 2003. On the grass a big chunk of Neo-Gothic masonry from the Palace of Westminster, given 1934.

s of the chapel are two interlinked spaces at different levels. Facing the lower lawn, but with its stair-tower projecting neatly on to the upper level, is *Chamberlin, Powell, Bon & Woods*'s NEW BUILDING, 1987–9. Among the last works by this distinguished post-war practice (partner in charge *Frank Woods*), and rather good, even if the little tiled roof storey doesn't quite come off. A simple and efficient arrangement of mostly identical rooms, in a grid of four storeys and five bays. The slimmest brick-faced uprights, concrete floor bands, dark steel framework to the glazing of each room. Still more skeletal is the stair-tower, octagonal and glass – or glass-brick-walled, with the open-framed stairs climbing within. The PASTRY SCHOOL to the s is by *Stokes*, 1901, an outlier of his school opposite. Detached pavilion with pretty cupola. On the s side is the PERRODO BUILDING by *Design Engine Architects*, 2016–18, upright and sharply outlined.* Brown steel framing. The glazed

---

*A Postmodern design of 1991 for a law library here by *Paolo Portoghesi* was abandoned. Likewise, a utopian project of 1971 by *Buckminster Fuller* and *Norman Foster* for an underground theatre hidden below the quad.

parts alternate with thin cream-coloured rods in an irregular pattern. Top floor set back. In front, hard landscaping runs amok – paving, dwarf walls, ramps, steel rails etc. The architects have made over Linton Quad too (2016).

The MASTER'S LODGINGS are in the picturesquely narrow Bulwarks Lane which runs between walls to the W, part of the former circuit of the castle bailey. Originally CANAL HOUSE, second headquarters of Oxford's canal company; the basin and wharves were where Nuffield College now is. By *Richard Tawney*, 1827–8. Ashlar, with low Greek Doric tetrastyle portico on the short side. On its apex a *Coade* stone plaque: Britannia with barge, Radcliffe Camera and St Mary's church. The building is of three storeys, including the rough rusticated lower floor towards the former canal site (best seen from New Road, S). The main storey on that side is articulated by pilasters. To the lane just blank red brick. To the E, new STUDENT ROOMS by *Design Engine Architects*, comprising two irregularly shaped blocks on a shared podium, are in progress in 2023.

For ST GEORGE'S GATE in Tidmarsh Lane and the PARADISE STREET ANNEXE *see* Perambulation 5, p. 441.

SOMERVILLE COLLEGE
Woodstock Road and Walton Street

Founded as a women's college in 1879, and named after the scientist Mary Somerville (1780–1872). The foundation was non-denominational, and represented an alternative to Lady Margaret Hall's Anglican restrictions. Somerville Hall adopted the name Somerville College in 1894, although like the other women's colleges it was granted full collegiate status only in 1959. For a home it chose Walton House, an early C19 villa approached from Woodstock Road, E, with extensive gardens to the W. The college has since built two small quads along the eastern approach, and placed its other buildings mostly around the single splendid lawn beyond. Architecturally there is no coherent plan – which for a college with such firm intellectual traditions is surprising – but much to enjoy in the individual parts.

The north-eastern quads

DARBISHIRE QUAD fronts Woodstock Road as a round-arched gateway with some wall l. and r., a single-bay house to the l., and a three-bay house on the r., neither of which seems entirely to belong. Actually this is the frontage of a little three-sided quad, quite handsome in a squared-rubble, neo-1700 way, and beautifully planted. It was built to *Percy Morley Horder*'s design in 1932–3, replacing a modest 1890s gateway.

Somerville College

1   Walton House
2   Library
3   Park
4   Wolfson
5   Penrose
6   Catherine Hughes
     Building
7   Vaughan
8   Margery Fry and
     Elizabeth Nuffield House
9   Chapel
10   Maitland
11   Hall
12   Dorothy Hodgkin Quad
13   ROQ Buildings
14   Darbishire Quad

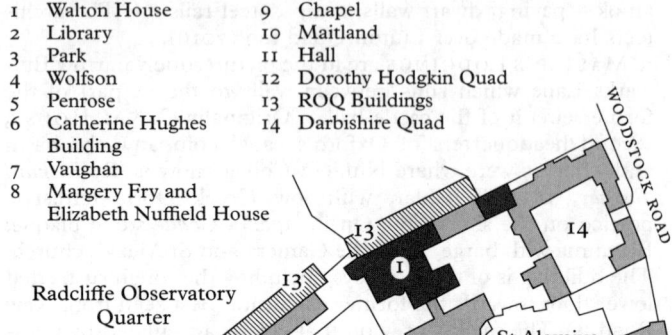

Radcliffe Observatory
Quarter

Main
Quad

St Aloysius

WOODSTOCK ROAD

WALTON STREET

LITTLE CLARENDON STREET

C19
C20
C21

40 m
40 yds

An archway in the w side leads into a SECOND QUAD, this one unfortunately asphalted and shapeless. It has on the s side the view of the bleak Victorian church of St Aloysius (p. 398), on the E side the brick back of Morley Horder's stone range, and on the N and W sides a jumble. The most interesting element of this is *Jackson*'s range, added in 1881–2 to HOUSE, alias Walton House (*see* below), and enlarged by *Walter Cave* in 1892–3. Not big, it is of grey stone trimmed with red brick. Shaped gables, and between two projecting wings to the E a proper Oxford frontispiece, treated in the free Jackson way, but here alas sadly pinched. *Cave* was responsible for the ground-floor extension here, and for the N wing and the turret crowding next to the frontispiece, with top details typical of 1892 not 1881. Moreover, House is continued to the E by HOSTEL, a neutral five-bay brick link of 1948–50 by *Geddes Hyslop*, and by a plain range of 1896 by *Cave*, with a pediment, symmetrical once, but now half-swallowed by the Morley Horder buildings. s of Jackson's building and on the main axis is a tripartite brick ARCHWAY by *Horder*, 1938, into Main Quad.

Main Quad and Dorothy Hodgkin Quad

MAIN QUAD is too expansive and intermittent to be a true quad, with its lawns and fine trees, and buildings which have enough space. In the NE corner is WALTON HOUSE, and now one sees how Jackson simply added to it. It is a plain stone house of *c.*1829 with one tripartite pedimented W doorway remaining, but otherwise worked over by *Cave* in 1892–3 with new interiors, bay window, mansard etc.

Onwards, anti-clockwise, to the NORTH SIDE. Next to the house is a gateway with a glimpse of the ROQ Buildings of 2009–11, but these can wait for now. Then, dominating the N side, the LIBRARY by *Champneys*, 1903–4. Red brick with stone dressings. Eleven bays with attached upper Ionic pilasters, oriels nicely distributed, and in the centre an arched loggia below, applied columns above and a segmental pediment at the top. A pity that Champneys's intended lettering of the frieze with the college motto was countermanded, and that the loggia has been crudely glazed in. Long upper room with a gallery added in 1924 along the N side, and a plaster barrel-vault with windows also in its N side. Low E continuation, housing a staircase. Its W counterpart was demolished for HOLTBY, a squared Neo-Georgian link of 1951–6 by *Hyslop*. Concrete-arched loggia in front, student rooms above. Then the long L-shape of PARK, 1886–94 by *H.W. Moore*, the largest building up to that date. Elizabethan style, not opulent, with five gables (clumsily repointed) and three oriels on the S front. Like the early phases of Newnham College, Cambridge, the building required students to live, study and dine together under close supervision – hence also corridors, rather than staircases, inside. To Walton Street it has an asymmetrical façade with gables and oriels too, and a little brick LODGE of 1888 in front, also by *Moore*. The adjacent Neo-Tudor building at the N corner here is the former ST PAUL'S GIRLS' SCHOOL, 1848 by *T. Grimsley*. Stone and render. Now the college's DAY NURSERY.

The WEST SIDE of Main Quad is closed by WOLFSON, 1964–7, the latest of the 1960s buildings for the college by *Sir Philip Dowson* of *Arup Associates*. Five bays, four storeys. 'The rooms each have a squared oriel almost fully glazed with very large sheets, and the concrete frame demonstrated by the verticals sticking up above the necessary and the beams sticking out beyond the necessary. Brutalism among the ladies' (Pevsner). The same facing Walton Street. The staircases and service rooms are isolated in twin flanking towers of sheer-sided brick, with raking tops. In front is the BRITTAIN-WILLIAMS ROOM by *Niall McLaughlin Architects*, added 2012. Low, of big timber framing, and generally quite sympathetic to Dowson.

The SOUTH SIDE begins with PENROSE, opposite Park. The purest piece of conventional plain brick Neo-Wren, 1926–7 by *Harold S. Rogers*. E-shaped, eleven bays, hipped roof. Rogers's former sanatorium wing behind, 1932. In the angle, standing end-on, is *McLaughlin Architects'* CATHERINE HUGHES BUILDING, 2017–19. Tall and slim, four to five storeys. Red brick, closely stepped around the full-height openings in which the windows are grouped two by two. Bronzed metal framing here, but the inner structure is of giant cross-laminated timber panels (cf. the architects' buildings for Balliol in St Cross Road, pp. 418–19). The kinked plan preserves the little Gothic hall of the former BEDFORD HOUSE SCHOOL on Walton Street; 1875, builder *Joseph Hall*. Then *Dowson* returns with VAUGHAN and MARGERY FRY & ELISABETH NUFFIELD HOUSE and their linking podium, 1958–66. Here, as Dowson also did for Corpus Christi in Cambridge, the whole concrete frame is in front of the windows and detached from them. The inner corners of each cell within the frames are rounded. Vaughan, for undergraduates, has eleven narrow bays to its framing; Fry–Nuffield, for graduates, eight broader bays. The latter block is offset and placed close to Little Clarendon Street, which can be reached through the brick-walled podium by a low gateway passage. The podium houses storerooms etc., and in its w part also shops facing the street, recessed behind a cloister of segmental concrete arches: one of several echoes of contemporary ideals in urban planning.* A glazed student BAR was added to Vaughan in 2013. Also on the podium, SCULPTURE of 1979 by *Polly Ionides*, a carved stone figure called Gymnast.

Next on the s side the CHAPEL, 1933–4 by *R. Courtenay Theobald*. At this non-denominational college it was a controversial addition, even though there is no dedication to a specific creed. Classical, ashlar, of three main bays with narrower E and W projections. The classical motifs, subtly battered profiles and thin, sharp set-backs all evoke the late works of Lutyens. Inside at the E end no altar, only STAINED GLASS by *Reginald Bell*. Also SCULPTURE, a della Robbia-style tympanum of the Annunciation, over a side door. STALLS and ORGAN CASE by the architect, in late C17 style.

Finally the EAST SIDE. Two Neo-Wren buildings here, rare works by *Edmund Fisher*, a former Champneys pupil who lost his life in the First World War. MAITLAND is of 1910–11, big and unified, of fourteen bays. Three storeys and a parapet. Next to it a columned and recessed loggia, on top of which *Morley Horder* added rooms in 1930. Then the HALL, 1912–13, of seven bays and two storeys with pediment. The hall is on the first floor, not very easily getatable. It has high dark panelling with columns on the long sides. Plaster tunnel-vault, but bays one and seven lower and flat-ceilinged. Then the archway through which we came in.

* *See* Alistair Fair in *Architectural History* 57 (2014).

SCULPTURE on the lawns. SE corner, Triad, 1971, big angular abstract by *Wendy Taylor*. NE corner, Elipsodrome, 1963 by *Friedrich Werthmann*.

DOROTHY HODGKIN QUAD lies at the W end of a garden S of St Aloysius's church. By *Geoffrey Beard* of *Oxford Architects Partnership*, 1988–91. Quite an imposing E range, with a residential storey raised up over two big, non-matching rooms for the MARGARET THATCHER CONFERENCE CENTRE. Between them an open staircase to an upper terrace, from which the student rooms and staircases are reached. Informal, small-scale architecture here, of friendly motifs and materials: stone blockwork, lead, stained timber, pitched slated roofs. Older houses on Woodstock Road are also incorporated, with one discreet rebuilding at the N end there (No. 25).

Finally the ROQ BUILDINGS, facing N towards the Radcliffe Observatory Quarter (*see* p. 361), with their back walls against the former college perimeter. By *Niall McLaughlin Architects*, 2009–11. One range of three storeys, the other, W, of four. A white concrete plinth of battered profile sits under the latter where the ground slopes away. For the rest the material is red brick, here with oak for the sixty-eight rooms with their boxed-out windows and for the imposing glazed stair enclosures at the ends. Recessed strips of white rendering separate the sections. The stair enclosures are framed in a narrow upright rhythm, and rise up as slim oblong lanterns.

TRINITY COLLEGE
Broad Street

The story resembles that of St John's. A monastic college was dissolved and shortly afterwards rose again as a private benefactor's new foundation. The first college in this case was established in 1286 by the Durham Cathedral priory, i.e. it was Benedictine. It was called Durham College, and – as at St John's – what little survives of it is late medieval, after endowment by Bishop Hatfield in 1381. The college then provided for eight *socii* or Fellows and eight *pueri*, i.e. secular undergraduates. The quad corresponded to the present Durham Quad and had chapel, hall and library in the places where they are now. Final confiscation of the college took place in 1545. Its replacement, the demonstratively named College of the Holy and Undivided Trinity, dates from 1555, under Queen Mary (again, as at St John's). The founder was Sir Thomas Pope, former Treasurer of the Court of Augmentations, which had dispersed the monastic lands.

Pope's college had twelve Fellows and twelve Scholars, who made do with the adapted older buildings. The hall was replaced in 1618–20, the chapel – much more demonstratively – in 1691–4. By then *Wren* had already made a start on a North Quad, duly completed in the C18. Key events after that are *Sir T. G. Jackson*'s

Trinity College

1   Durham Quad   6   Kettell Hall
2   Hall   7   President's Lodgings
3   Chapel   8   War Memorial Library
4   Staircase 18   9   Levine Building
5   Dolphin Gate   10   Cumberbatch Buildings

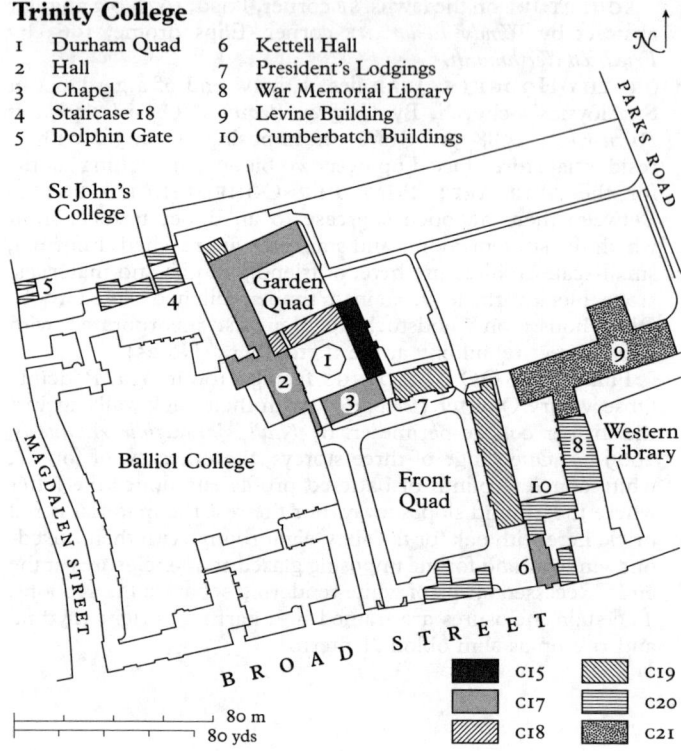

additions of the 1880s to the SE, *Maguire & Murray*'s of the 1960s behind these, and the partial replacement of the 1960s work by *ADAM Architecture* in 2018–22. Jackson's work especially is enhanced by the garden setting, for Trinity's core buildings lie far back from Broad Street, from which they appear seductively embowered by trees. Description begins with the old quad, alias Durham Quad.

Durham Quad and chapel

The S side of DURHAM QUAD comprises the chapel and the real gate tower of the college, a single building of 1691–4. But first the remains of the Durham College of the monks, on the EAST SIDE. This range is essentially that built in 1417–21, but with later ground-floor windows. The library was above, where the paired close-set lights are (altered), with a vestry and treasury below and chambers to the N. Dormers renewed during the refacing of 1964–9 to match the form of 1602, when the roof storey was created. Some of the non-library rooms became the first President's Lodgings, but were remodelled c.1687 by Ralph Bathurst (who also added a new range to the S, since replaced). Of this C17 phase the two large gabled stair projections thrown out towards the President's Garden behind. The C15 forms have lasted better on this side: one three-light ground-floor window and several transomed two-light windows, all straight-headed with lights with two-centred arches and cusping. Against the NE corner buttress on this E side is a decayed late C14 niche with a STATUE of St Michael, in a contorted stance: brought c.1830 from the old pinnacle over the hall gable at New College.

INTERIORS. The present Bursar's Office and other ground-floor rooms preserve PAINTED DECORATION datable to c.1555, exposed in 1986 and partly left visible behind hinged or glazed panels. Vigorous rather than sophisticated, it includes a giant roundel on a partition filled with the assertively Catholic IHS motif. Red and white, on a ground of crude brocade pattern. Elsewhere much tendrillage and foliage. STAIRCASES, one late C17, the other (N) elegantly replaced c.1824. The OLD LIBRARY has cases of 1625, heightened after 1850; quite plain. Its STAINED GLASS is chiefly early C15, of high quality, probably from the old chapel. The glass was restored c.1765, 1878 etc. In the E windows figures under canopies and shields, some shown with kneeling monks as donors, and most with speculative name inscriptions added. First window: St Frideswide (all restoration, head and r. hand excepted); canonized king; crowned female saint (very restored), perhaps St Hilda; 'St Placidus' (all restoration, head excepted). Second window: 'St Swithun'; St John the Baptist; 'St William of York'; 'St Benedict', with donor labelled Johannes Tokot. Third window: 'St Augustine'; 'St Dunstan'; 'St Gregory'; St Thomas Becket. Fourth window: the four Evangelists (St Luke very restored). S window: tracery, in situ shield of arms of Thomas Hatfield, Bishop of Durham 1345–81, with three angel supporters. In the main lights a C15 archbishop saint of the main series; small C14 figure of an archbishop; C15 Virgin and Child; other material introduced 2005. E windows, C17 oblong quarries with ten Virtues and six Apostles, not so good.

The WEST RANGE contains the HALL, completely Perp, though of 1618–20; rebuilt after the medieval hall collapsed when a cellar was dug. Canted bay window, S. Above the entrance *Mark Batten*'s copy of the C17 three-quarter carved figure of the founder, installed 1955. The top storey is not an addition but was built as sets together with the hall, which therefore was flat-ceilinged from the start. The Jacobean parapet had small shaped gables, replaced c.1681 with castellations, then given a bald straight profile c.1960. The SCREENS PASSAGE preserves a medieval wall to the N, but the openings are C16. The HALL INTERIOR is more modest than most, but it is no longer C17. The panelled and coved stucco ceiling is a design of 1772, replicated in 1960; the screen and dais panelling with Doric pilasters and metope frieze are C18, of unknown date. Redecorated after an early C19 scheme in *Original Field*'s renovation of 2022–3, replacing marbled paintwork of 1987 by *Alec Cobbe*. Gothic fireplace inserted in 1846, picking up details from the C18 Doric overmantel, which has quatrefoils in its metopes. The stained glass includes some Swiss C16 panels (bay window). The fierce dragon-headed object on clawed feet is a lectern, given 1723.

The KITCHEN as rebuilt in 1676–7 is in line with the screens. It has chambers over, and is much modernized.

Immediately S of the hall is another monastic leftover. The renewed two-light window on the first floor with transom, straight top and a little panel tracery is of late C14 type. In the tracery glass a most unusual design of hands holding scrolls, inscribed 'Dominus Willelmus Ebchester Custos huius collegii'. This William was Warden in 1419–28. The window may have lit an oratory, although the fabric now behind is mostly identified as early C17 by the RCHME. Top storey added 1811. On the ground floor is the OLD BURSARY, made in 1665 as a senior common room, and panelled by *Arthur Frogley* in 1681. Fine scrolled overmantel. The E end panelling was hinged in the early C19 to make document storage for the bursar. STAIRCASE of early C18 type, as is the SENIOR COMMON ROOM above. White-painted panelling here, with a tripartite arrangement of the end walls as arched doorways or blind panels. Other rooms with panelling and carved overmantels to the E belong to the gate tower.

So to Dr Ralph Bathurst's GATE TOWER and CHAPEL of 1691–4 on the S side, the first Oxford chapel to break completely with Gothic tradition. The views from N and S are the same in all but a few details. The gateway has Ionic pilasters; above is a large overarched window with very unusual decoration. The tumbling putti and draperies of the middle cartouche especially are not like any older Oxford work. The tower stage – in plan a deep oblong – ends in a blind balustrade, with renewed statues of Geometry, Astronomy, Theology and Medicine. The CHAPEL has four big arched windows, the arches rising from moulded imposts, the bays separated by large Corinthian pilasters. Top blind balustrade and flaming urns. Quoining at both ends, so that the whole building is expressed as a single mass. Over the passage a flat moulded ceiling – no longer the fan-vault motif.

Much has been argued about this design, which is known in several engraved or drawn versions. It cannot have been by *Wren*; he was consulted in 1692 by his friend Dr Bathurst, but no more. Wren liked the design he was shown 'in the maine very well', and advised some modest changes to the mouldings and parapets, and to planning within the tower, but building was already under way by then. *Hawksmoor* drew an unexecuted variant elevation, but there is no reason to think that he was the originator either. The chosen master mason *Bartholomew Peisley II* can be ruled out too, the design being too sophisticated, as can his fellow mason 'Kemster' (*Christopher Kempster*), the likely designer of the Town Hall at Abingdon, who offered advice but proved too expensive. Professor Martin Kemp has put the case for *Bathurst* himself, who referred once to 'our whole design', and ended up paying for the fabric. A stronger academic candidate is *Dean Aldrich* of Christ Church, one of the three 'able judges in architecture' consulted before Bathurst decided to rebuild. As James Campbell has noted, the original roof used here was of a distinctive type also employed at All Saints' church (p. 338) and Queen's College library, both of which can be connected to the Dean.*

INTERIOR. Trinity chapel is one of the most perfect and most sophisticated late C17 ensembles in the whole country – even more so, since its sympathetic restoration in 2015–16. Architecturally it is simple enough, a single tall oblong chamber with a coved ceiling, subdivided by an organ screen at the w. What makes it stand out is the display of the best craftsmanship in wood and plaster, as well as some figurative religious painting. This is by *Pierre Berchet*: an Ascension in the ceiling centre, and two smaller panels within a strongly compartmented but thickly ornamented stucco design with much illusionistic detail. Stucco between the window arches too. As to WOODWORK, stalls, screen, reredos, all are there, variously veneered with much use of walnut and Bermuda cedar, and some carving in limewood, as so often for prestige jobs of the period. The chief joiner was *Arthur Frogley*, and the London carver *Jonathan Maine* is also named. But the limewood carving of the REREDOS is so exquisite that one hesitates to think of anybody but *Grinling Gibbons* himself. His involvement is not documented, but Celia Fiennes noted that the work was by the same hand as that at Windsor, and there we know that Gibbons was responsible. Big segmental pediment, its centre jumping back, and on it two reclining Evangelists. The SCREEN is of the same elements and motifs. The side pieces here have openwork panels of rich foliage and cherub heads; the Evangelist figures on top, like those of the reredos, gaze up at the ceiling image. The COMMUNION RAIL has openwork panels too. The STALLS are simpler, but even they have raised centrepieces with an urn and cherubs. The ORGAN above the screen has a triangular centre projection. Case designed by *S. E. Dykes Bower*, 1965. – PAINTING. Copy after Andrea del Sarto, w end. – Otherwise nothing jars but the Holbein-Renaissance STAINED GLASS, mostly of 1885–6 by *J. W. Brown* of *Powells*, but also one NW window by *Mayer*, 1874 (reinstated 2016). Even Sir Thomas Pope's MONUMENT of *c*. 1567 is tucked away in a kind of sash-windowed cupboard N of the altar. Two recumbent effigies of alabaster on a tomb-chest with pilaster-like strips and laurel wreaths. The answering s enclosure was for female members of the President's household.

The NORTH RANGE is a rebuilding of 1728 by *William Townesend*. Two and a half storeys; windows round-arched, segment-arched, near-square. Its form is determined by the rest of Garden Quad, below.

* Martin Kemp, *The Chapel of Trinity College Oxford, 1691–94* (2013); James Campbell in *Building Histories: Proceedings of the Fourth Conference of the Construction History Society* (2017).

In the centre of Durham Quad a big raised grassed octagon designed by *Peter Shepheard*, 1980.

Garden Quad, and buildings to the west

GARDEN QUAD started life as a single building, designed by *Wren* for Dr Bathurst and built in 1665–8 (mason *Thomas Strong I*, carpenter *Robert Minchin*). It survives, but nobody would recognize it. It is the N range and originally had two storeys, a large and novel French mansard roof with dormers, cross-windows, and a three-bay pediment. The central shell niche and the recess alone are as Wren left them, and the design has been repeated – as he anticipated – in a W range and opposite in a S range, to make a quad of three ranges, with railings across the garden side. Both ranges are two rooms deep, the earliest at Oxford to adopt this plan. Thus Oxford acquired its first double-pile college range, and then its first open-sided quad (though that concept was to Wren's mind 'a lame one somwhat like a threelegged table').* The W range was built in 1682, the S range is the back of *Townesend*'s of 1728. Furthermore, the mansard storey was rebuilt with upright walls by *William Wilkins Sen.* in 1801–2, and no pediments accepted. The windows here were given different proportions in the refacing of 1958–66. Wren provided each chamber with two small rooms opening off behind, but his letter of 1665 identifies these as bedroom and studies respectively, i.e. not yet the early C17 innovation of shared study and separate rooms for sleeping. In the NW angle a doorway of 1851; the outer NW angle here was infilled with a four-storey block in 1864.

The quad displays four fine C18 lead VASES, given 1957. Also a BUST of Cardinal Newman by *Abraham Broadbent*, 1915, against the E range. Four French lead STATUES of the C18 are in the President's Garden.

The GARDENS were once Oxford's most ambitious example of the formal early C18 manner. The axis from Garden Quad still terminates at the far E end in the exquisite IRON GATES of 1713 towards Parks Road, by *Thomas Robinson* (cf. New College). Their Baroque GATEPIERS (rebuilt in 1966) are L-shaped with three urns each on top. In the SE corner, facing the road, the PRESIDENT'S GARAGE, *c.* 1936 by *Sir Giles Gilbert Scott*. A miniature companion to Scott's New Bodleian (Weston Library) to the S (p. 344). Rubble stone; Rustic Baroque doorway to the flat above. A good C13 ARCH is re-set in the garden S wall, visible from behind the Weston.

Also easily overlooked is the back entry to the college, from St Giles' to the W. The way is round the N side of North Quad, and then beneath the flattened archway of *Gray Baynes & Shew*'s gauche STAIRCASE 18 BUILDING of 1992. Along

---

*Wren's earliest surviving plan (1664) was for a detached block on his preferred site, S of Durham Quad. At Cambridge the detached type had appeared as early as 1640–3 (Christ's College, Fellows' Building).

the lane beyond are *R.B. Gray*'s chunky SQUASH COURT of 1974, some staff flats of 1959, then *Sir Hubert Worthington*'s DOLPHIN GATE of 1947–8, quite a nice little piece. This is confusing to the street, where one thinks at first that it must be the end of Balliol; then one realizes that the building of the same cornice height next door is Dolphin Building, a separate job for St John's (p. 275). The openings are similar to those of Worthington's New College library of 1939.

Broad Street, and buildings to the east

The iron GATES to Broad Street and next to Balliol are largely of 1886, smaller but similar in style to those of 1713 already mentioned. Then a range of what many will take for late C17 COTTAGES – the same cottages which William Morris helped to save from destruction in 1880 – but which in reality are replicas of 1969 by *Pinckheard & Partners*. Old stone was reused in the front wall, and stone slates on the roof. Next the more prominent KETTELL HALL, built *c.*1620 on his own account by Ralph Kettell, President of Trinity, and taken over by the college only in 1898. It has mullioned windows and gables and is three storeys high, over a sunk kitchen basement. To the w are five even gables, to the s are three. On this side the projecting entrance bay, with the original wicket door. Irregular, pragmatic plan. Blackwell's, the bookshop, follows, and it is relevant to mention that (*see* below).

So much for the frontage. FRONT QUADRANGLE one sees first through a variety of trees – cedars, a catalpa, a *Magnolia grandiflora* and so on – with the old college to the NW, on the

Trinity College, Front Quad.
Drawing, 1887

w side Balliol, with its chapel, and to NE and E a detached house and a long N–S range. These date from 1883–7, under the reforming President, John Percival, and are – inevitably – by *Sir T.G. Jackson*. A specially lavish version of his characteristic style, i.e. mainly with English C17 motifs, but also in this case with gables derived from Elizabethan Kirby Hall, and all put on thick. A gateway connects the E range with the N building, which is the PRESIDENT'S LODGINGS, replacing Bathurst's range of 1687.

Going E and then S from that gateway leads into LIBRARY QUAD. Its beginning is the WAR MEMORIAL LIBRARY of 1925–8 on the E side. By *James Osborne Smith*, architect of the London Library, to outlines specified by the then President, *H.E.D. Blakiston*. Its present appearance – a Neoclassical block of only five bays and one storey, with attached columns, American McKim style – is deceptive: a S extension was anticipated, and an entrance bay to the N was demolished in the 1960s, when a balustraded parapet was also lost. *Maguire & Murray*'s square, somewhat pagoda-like replacement block of 1964–6 to the N has in turn made way for the much bigger LEVINE BUILDING of 2018–22, by *Hugh Petter* of *ADAM Architecture*. It too is classical, but astylar. Ashlar, all the edges very sharp, and handled like the modernized Neo-Georgian of the 1930s, with e.g. bronze casement windows. The N range continues some way w on the garden side, with a two-storey projection, on the far side of which squared rubble takes over as the New Bodleian is approached. *Maguire & Murray*'s work, collectively known as the CUMBERBATCH BUILDINGS, survives on the S side of Library Quad, comprising a small quad fitted in next to Kettell Hall to the SW, some facsimile rebuilding of No. 53 Broad Street (p. 425), and large underground showrooms for Blackwell's beneath the open centre of Library Quad. The upper walls are of grey cubic concrete blockwork, with concrete floor bands and blue brick below. In addition there are boxed-out wooden oriels, some of double height, where the sets have sleeping decks inside. Whatever the weaknesses of Cumberbatch as an ensemble, the idea of expanding underground has since been widely taken up in Oxford, including another collaboration with Blackwell's at Wadham (p. 312; cf. also Trinity College, Cambridge and Heffers).

For Trinity's student accommodation in Rawlinson Road and on the Woodstock Road *see* North Oxford, pp. 466n. and 467.

UNIVERSITY COLLEGE
High Street

William of Durham, a scholar who had joined the migration from Paris in 1229 and had been Archdeacon of Caux for some years, left, when he died in 1249, 310 marks (£206 13s. 4d.) to the

University for the purchase of property to maintain ten to twelve Masters of Art. Properties were bought in 1253 (Little University Hall, now part of the Brasenose site), 1255 and 1262 (Brasenose Hall). Only in 1280 was a document drawn up to regulate the foundation. It was to have four M.A.s to start with, all studying theology. Further statutes were made in 1292 and 1311. In 1332 and 1336 property on the present site was purchased, and by the 1360s 'the Great Hall of the University of Oxford' had its new home here. In 1398 a chapel was consecrated. The mid c15 made this part of a quad, with a new hall and a gate tower. But nothing of all this has remained.

The architectural history of the present University College begins only in 1631, with the decision to rebuild the main quadrangle on a grander scale. This replacement quad grew slowly and was completed in 1676. It was followed by the Radcliffe Quad of 1716–19, immediately to the E. Later additions and acquisitions stand in all directions, W, E and S, but none can challenge these two quads for prominence.

University College

1	Chapel	8	Kybald House
2	Hall	9	Parsons' Almshouses
3	Kitchen	10	Master's Lodgings
4	New Buildings	11	Durham Buildings
5	Shelley Memorial	12	Goodhart Building
6	Library	13	New Library (former
7	Mitchell Building		History Faculty Library)

C17
C18
C19
C20
C21

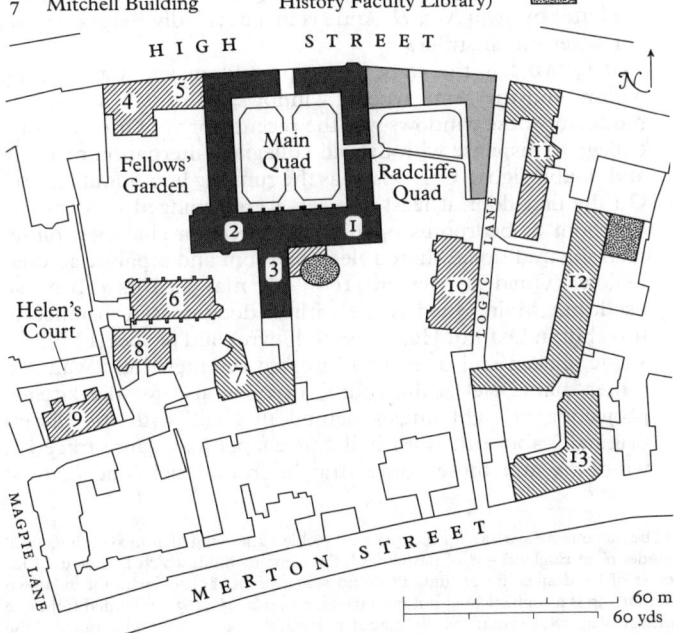

Main Quad and Radcliffe Quad

Main Quad was begun in 1634, with *Richard Maude* as master mason. He may also have provided the design, although his sometime partner *Hugh Davies* is a candidate too.* Small parapet gablets of matching type – ogee-curved, and finishing with a little cross-bar and a rounded top – certainly appear on two other 1630s projects of Maude's: Canterbury Quad at St John's and Second Quad at Jesus. But the most astonishing thing architecturally about University College is that Radcliffe Quad of 1716–19 continues this 1630s design essentially unchanged. The resulting FRONTAGE to the High Street is a very long, symmetrical three-storey façade of twenty-three bays. The windows still have depressed-arched lights, and their hoodmoulds are connected by a continuous string course, stepping up round the windows. Each quad has its own gate tower, and these too are a close match: battlemented, with first-floor oriels and a top storey with central niche between transomed two-light windows. The centre of the whole composition is a big three-storey bay window, and this must be an addition of 1716–19. Only the doorways differ much, the earlier one with elaborate Perp mouldings, the E one with more summary, post-Gothic forms. The DOORS are also identical, and their style is that of the mid C17. Designs for doors were procured in 1637/8 from *John Jackson*, another of the masons employed at St John's, so they may be his. Jackson was also paid for advice on the tower. The STATUES in the niches above are of Queen Anne (E), 1709, and Queen Mary II (W), 1719, the latter by *John Nost II*. Anne is in a decidedly Baroque pose, her sister much stiffer.

MAIN QUAD has the same elevation system and top cresting within, and the same type of windows, all of two lights. The model for these windows was the recent work at Oriel, the first college to dispense with the old collegiate alternation of single and double lights. Oriel also has the running hoodmould motif. On the first floor at least, the sets were arranged as a smaller bedroom or bedrooms opening off the main chamber, rather than the traditional shared sleeping room and separate studies. Fellows' Quad at Merton (1609–10) may also have been so used, but Main Quad is the earliest documented instance of this shift in Oxford. Hall (r., with louvre) and chapel (l.) fill the s side, placed end to end and treated symmetrically. Wadham rather than Oriel is the source here, as also for the kitchen projecting at right angles behind the hall, with the library originally above it. Both hall and chapel have large traceried windows, and these come straight from Oriel. The pointed

---

*The incomplete MODEL for the quad – the oldest surviving identified architectural model from England – is of pasteboard, the same medium which Davies used for most of his designs for an unbuilt grand staircase for the Bodleian. Of unknown authorship is a sophisticated but impractical proposal of *c.*1632, recorded from one drawn plan, with symmetrically placed porticoes on the E, W and S sides of the quad.

oval or almond shape at the top is the obviously post-medieval motif. But the Gothic centrepiece with two-storey oriel and niches is a remodelling of 1802 designed by *James Griffith*, Fellow and later Master of the college. The C17 frontispiece was classical, of three stages and somewhat confused in detail: double doorway with wide open segmental pediment, but the top with a segmental gable or parapet, not a pediment. Griffith also replaced the top cresting on this side with battlements, and put blind panelling below the windows. More changes followed when the S side was refaced in 1957–8: a lower parapet of modified design, and Griffith's pinnacles removed (architect *S.E. Dykes Bower*).* The tower entry has a fan-vault, though with typical mid-C17 cartouches. Towards the quad here a STATUE of James II in Roman dress, put up in 1687. Katherine Esdaile attributed it to *John Bushnell*. It displaced one of King Alfred, legendary founder of the college.

Finally some construction dates: W range 1634–5; N range 1635–7; S range, walls raised 1639–42, hall finished 1656–7, chapel consecrated 1666, library in use *c.*1671; E range, 1668–76. By the 1650s *John Jackson* was master mason, and the lost frontispiece of the S side may have been his design.

INTERIORS. The CHAPEL is internally mainly of the time when *Scott* gothicized it in 1861–2. His are the corbels, all naturalistic foliage (richly carved by *J. Birnie Philip*), his the pointed barrel-vaulted timber roof and his the five-light Dec E window, breaking the evenness of the three-light windows of the C17. But his polychromatic stone REREDOS is now hidden, and curtains conceal his SEDILIA and other decoration of the E end. So the dominant elements are again the C17 woodwork and stained glass. – WOODWORK. The PANELLING and the STALLS (with big balls on the ends) are of 1665–6, by *Arthur Frogley*. The stall backs have pilasters, mostly coupled, and in the frieze little swags and garlands. The present REREDOS is a reconstruction of 1924, using parts of the one made by *Frogley* in 1682. The handsome pelican and garlands between the Corinthian pilasters seem an addition of 1695. By then, in 1694, a new SCREEN had been made one bay W of its predecessor, with matching extra stalls to fill the gap. The joiner was *Robert Barker* of London, who however promised that the carving would be done by 'a skilful artist'. Detached Corinthian columns and a foliage frieze at the level of the capitals. Two angels and four urns on top. Outer bays with openwork panels of leafage. – Black and white marble FLOOR of the same period. – COMMUNION TABLE. Early C17. – Bronze eagle LECTERN, mid-Georgian most probably. – CHANDELIERS. Two, of brass, Baroque shape. Given 1747. – ORGAN CASE designed by *Sir Albert Richardson*, 1955.

The original STAINED GLASS is by *Abraham van Linge* and of 1641–2, having survived the Civil War and Interregnum in

* Chief consultant architect for the 1950s–60s refacing was *R.B. Gray* of *Pinckheard & Partners*, with *T.A. Bailey* of the *Ministry of Public Building and Works*.

storage. It is his *magnum opus*, rich in colour and exuberant in the telling of the stories. The figures, undeniably crude, mostly move in landscape settings. From W to E: S side, Cleansing of the Temple, Christ in the house of Martha and Mary, Sacrifice of Isaac, Adam and Eve lamenting the Fall, with Abraham and the angels; Temptation and expulsion of Adam and Eve. N side: Jacob's vision; Elijah and the Fiery Chariot, with Elisha below; Jonah and the Whale (signed and dated). In the traceries an angel with heraldic shield in each central panel, lesser female figures seated in profile at the sides. The first E window came later, in 1687 (by *Henry Giles*). Its replacement is by *O'Connor*, 1864. Two-light SE window by *Clayton & Bell*, 1866.

MONUMENTS. In the choir, B. Freeman Willis †1774 and J. Webb Willis †1778. Twin urns in front of obelisks and above them drapery and Faith in relief. – In the antechapel several monuments by *Flaxman*. Foremost is the large one to Sir William Jones †1794, made 1796–8 and at first intended for Calcutta. Heavily detailed, with a relief of Sir William writing his digest of 'Hindu and Mohammedan laws'. He is seated, and opposite him are Indians. At the top a lyre, two gourds, a caduceus and a vinar or vinod (an Indian musical instrument). – Also by *Flaxman* Sir Robert Chambers †1803. An original design. Four tall fasces. No figures. – Nathan Wetherell, Dean of Hereford, 1808. *Flaxman* again, with a good, if small, allegorical trio at the top. – *Flaxman*'s Matthew Rolleston, 1818, has two indifferent allegorical figures l. and r. – Cecil Boyle, a Boer War casualty, 1904. Bronze portrait by *Henry Pegram*, alabaster frame with angels. – First World War memorial, W wall. 1921. With a tablet of late C17 type. – A. J. M. Melly †1936, W wall. Beautifully lettered tablet by *Eric Gill*.

The HALL was originally reached by a short r. turn before the screens passage and buttery, as at Wadham. The current arrangement reflects C19 and C20 changes. In the hall the hammerbeam roof preserves the C17 form, with much old timber incorporated. One beam has the carved date 1656. Reconstruction of the roof dates from *H. Wilkinson Moore*'s campaign of 1903–5. He lengthened the hall by two matching bays to the W, added the lower roof pendants and installed the present panelling. The bay window in the second bay from W (rebuilt *c.*1963) shows where the C17 dais was. The Neo-Jacobean CHIMNEYPIECE dates from 1904 too, but incorporates a Gothic surround and quatrefoiled top circle with a head of King Alfred carved by *Richard Hayward*. These are relics of the remodelling of the hall undertaken by *Henry Keene* in 1766, the first complete antiquarian-Gothic interior in Oxford. His panelling and plaster fan-cum-barrel-vault were casualties of 1903. Keene's project was instigated by the amateur medievalist Sir Roger Newdigate M. P., an old member. The STAINED GLASS is mostly *Powells*, 1904–7; heraldic.

The KITCHEN WING projects S of the hall. On the W side it cuts against one of the hall windows. The 1630s plan would have left the window clear by means of a set-back on this side. The same plan stipulated an open ground-floor passage here, and a covered bridge to the library above, served by a staircase enclosure in the E angle. Instead, the wing was built with a straight W wall and the staircase inside and at the NW (reassembled, with some old materials). The FORMER LIBRARY above has windows to E and W of the same type as those in Main Quad. The S oriel however has been altered from the arch-transomed form recorded in a drawing of 1674.* In 1956 Sir A. Richardson converted the space to the ALINGTON ROOM, an additional dining room, with panelling and a thickly coffered cedarwood ceiling. A rib-vaulted BUTTERY of 1860 by Scott is attached E of the wing, and this has been greatly extended by Freeland Rees Roberts, 2007–8. Theirs is the oval drum, stone-faced below, timber-slatted and standing free above, with a lead roof and oval top lantern. The upper floor houses the BUTLER ROOM, for functions.

The W range of Main Quad has the WINTER COMMON ROOM, panelled by Robert Barker in 1697. S of this room the SUMMER COMMON ROOM, with panelling dated 1575. It came from No. 88 High Street, demolished in 1901 for the Durham Buildings (see p. 305). The panels have the typically Elizabethan blank arches. Frieze with carved emblematic scenes, twenty-eight of them. Twenty of the designs have been traced to the 1547 edition of Alciati's Emblemata. The chimney-piece has gawky caryatids and atlantes. Adjacent, the PAYNE ROOM, with some of Keene's Gothic panelling from the hall.

Now E to see RADCLIFFE QUAD, named after Dr John Radcliffe. 63 His bequests to Oxford included £5,000 to build it and for Fellowships to fill it. The gate tower duly has a lead STATUE by Francis Bird of Radcliffe holding a caduceus, put up in 1719. Bird was paid £70 for it. Apart from the oriel and some details of the gateway's very late fan-vault, the architecture is repeated from Front Quad. The fact is explained partly by Radcliffe's stipulation that the frontage be 'answerable' to the C17 one, partly no doubt by conservatism and esprit de corps. The quad is open to the S, i.e. has here only a wall with a gateway, now blocked. Even this, with its four-centred arch and its top like a shaped gable, harks back to the earlier C17. The quad was built by William Townesend & Bartholomew Peisley III, with some undefined involvement by Dr George Clarke. Clarke also came up with a classical design for new Master's Lodgings here, but in the event these were provided within the E wing. Some ground-floor rooms in Staircase XI preserve plaster rib-vaulting, a Gothic fireplace etc. designed by Griffith, resident here as Master from 1808.

*This drawing also depicts an unusual shelving arrangement: tall cases coming out from the walls in the usual C17 way, but also lateral galleries along the walls above (cf. Jesus library, slightly later.)

C19 and C20 additions

The additions to 'Univ.' are of all shapes and sizes. The most sensible treatment is topographical, leaving the eastern outliers till last.

w of Main Quad is the FELLOWS' GARDEN. On the N side are NEW BUILDINGS, Tudor Gothic of 1841–2 by *Sir Charles Barry*. His only substantial work at Oxford or Cambridge. Three storeys, disappointing from the garden, but more assertive to the High Street: symmetrical, of three bays, with two tall oriel windows and an extra gable storey. Dormers added by *Moore*. To the w are houses in college ownership (*see* p. 413), to the E a low attachment with a leaded dome. This is by *Champneys*, 1892–3, to house the SHELLEY MEMORIAL. The monument itself is a major work by *E. Onslow Ford*, originally conceived for the Protestant Cemetery in Rome. It shows the white marble effigy of Shelley drowned, represented not as a classical ideal but emphatically as a naked corpse. He lies on a substructure of coloured marbles, supported by bronze figures of the Muse of Poetry, two lions and a tangled fruit tree. It is all extremely lush. Originally the setting was more secluded, but in 1933–4 the enclosure and railings were altered for ease of viewing from outside.

The LIBRARY stands s of the garden, still on the w outskirts of Front Quad. 1859–61 by *Scott*. A tall stone vessel, Middle Pointed, with stair-turrets at opposing angles. The curious, quite original side windows have shouldered transoms, straight tops and on the N side also ballflower surrounds. Roof with timber vaulting of the same type of trefoil section as San Zeno in Verona, but pointed at the top. Scott's interior was divided horizontally by *A. S. G. Butler*, 1937. Of that time the NE staircase and the tracery of the w window. In front of this window a SCULPTURE of 1842–8: seated marble pair of the brothers Lord Eldon and Lord Stowell, by the Cumberland sculptor *Musgrave Lewthwaite Watson*, unfinished when he died in 1847 and completed by *George Nelson*. Stern figures in legal robes, the features craggy, the hands over-large. The piece was intended for New College, but rejected; the 2nd Earl of Eldon's trustees then offered £5,000 for a new library here instead, on condition that it be housed within. Ground floor refitted 1992 by *Frank Bradbeer*, with a new N doorway.

s of the library the MITCHELL BUILDING, a cute little brick building by *John Fryman* of the *Architects Design Partnership*, quite ingeniously inserted in 1968–71. The open-sided staircase goes up to the Middle Common Room, which stands on pilotis partly over a lane beyond the old wall. The building's hind parts here contain workshops, kitchen offices etc. To the w is *H.W. Moore*'s KYBALD HOUSE, built as a tutor's house in 1887. Red brick, shaped gables and Arts and Crafts detail

– quite pretty. It faces Kybald Street. Also there is a big C17 GATEWAY, relocated from W of the High Street front.

Further W, and reached round the far end of the library, is HELEN'S COURT. On the S side a college acquisition of 1959, PARSONS' ALMSHOUSES, built 1816. Two-storeyed, Tudor, six bays, with two entrances. Main front again to Kybald Street. On the N side a former BARN, converted for college use in 1963 by *Booth, Ledeboer & Pinckheard*.

Now E, back to Radcliffe Quad. S of the S wall here, with a front to Logic Lane, are the MASTER'S LODGINGS. These are by *Bodley & Garner*, in a sumptuous Jacobean style, and date from 1878–9. Symmetrical façade to the Master's Garden, with three shaped and two smaller straight gables. Canted bay windows in the outer bays, ending in segmental pediments. Big bow window under the middle gable. This gable has uncommonly lively decoration. The drawing room (S) and a larger dining room-cum-library are on the garden side, with a big stair hall behind. Big plaster friezes, and a grand 1630s-style overmantel in the dining room. The mid-C18 bookcases of Dr Browne's library were kept from the previous lodgings.

LOGIC LANE has become a visual part of the college entirely. On the W side DURHAM BUILDINGS, 1895–6 and 1901–3 by *H.W. Moore*. Brick and render with timbered gables to the lane, more assuming to the High Street, where the building is connected to Radcliffe Quad by a covered bridge of 1905. Stone façades here, four bays and three storeys. Two gables with two-storey oriels under, balancing Barry's oriels at the W end. Close blank four-centred-arched arcading on the ground floor with small windows in all of them. The S part – the first phase, i.e. 1895–6 – lost one gabled bay when the GOOD-HART BUILDING went up, 1960–1 by *Robert Matthew & Stirrat Johnson-Marshall*. Long main range, set back E from the lane. It was white-rendered in *Freeland Rees Roberts*'s renovations and extensions of 2014–15, but the slim pilotis, restless fenestration and zigzag skyline still tell of the 1960s. At the S end, left intact, a small two-storey cross-range with a seminar room above. Copper roof of a long, shallow and a short, steep pitch, glass spirelet on the apex.

Immediately S is the college's latest acquisition, the former HISTORY FACULTY LIBRARY (latterly Philosophy), of 1954–6 by *Sir Hubert Worthington*. Since 2016 the NEW LIBRARY, offices etc. The design is of 1938–9, and that it was not set aside after the Second World War speaks volumes about the architectural conservatism of mid-1950s Oxford. Squared rubble, with a rounded corner to Merton Street with portal surmounted by fancy decoration. Four bays, the upper windows mullioned.

For the college houses on the High Street, Merton Street etc. *see* Perambulation 1, pp. 413–15; for UNIV NORTH ('Stavertonia') in Woodstock Road *see* North Oxford, p. 467.

WADHAM COLLEGE
Parks Road

Wadham was the first wholly new college to be established after the Reformation. The founders were Nicholas and Dorothy Wadham of Merifield in Somerset, elderly landowners of considerable wealth; the site was that of Oxford's house of the Austin Friars, already demolished.* There were to be fifteen Fellows and as many Scholars, under a Warden who was not to marry. Building began in 1610, after Nicholas's death, and was complete in 1613. Such consistency in planning and architecture was not seen again in a complete Oxford college until the later C19.

A plain block (Staircase 9) was added S of the street frontage in 1693–4. Minor enhancements from 1871 fell to *T. G. Jackson*, an old member and Prize Fellow of the college, but building on a large scale did not resume until after the Second World War. Notably ambitious and resourceful works by *Gillespie, Kidd & Coia, MacCormac, Jamieson & Prichard* and *AL_A Architects* have followed, S and E of the C17 quad. The college's key additions and annexations along Parks Road and Holywell Street are also described here.

Front Quad and gardens

FRONT QUAD, of 1610–13, remains virtually unchanged but for the refacing of 1957–66. Planning and outlines show a commitment to college traditions inherited from the C16, refreshed by an enhanced concern for symmetry and by selective classical episodes. The designer can be identified as the Somerset master mason *William Arnold*, called by Dorothy Wadham 'an honest man, a perfectt workman, and my neere neighbour'. Arnold had worked on the design of Lord Salisbury's Cranborne House in Dorset, and is also credited with Montacute House and with work at Dunster Castle in his home county. His supervision of the work earned him £1 a week, besides what he got for his own share of the fabric. Under him was a team of other masons and artisans brought from Somerset, just as Yorkshire artisans had carried out Sir Henry Savile's works at Merton not long before. *Edward* or *Edmund Arnold*, probably Thomas's son, took charge in 1612, as work was finishing.

The FRONTAGE of Wadham follows the innovations of Merton's new quad two years before: three full storeys and strict regularity of fenestration, here combined with the usual higher gate tower with the customary oriel. The end bays are gabled, and have their own canted bays through all three storeys. The window lights read across 4:2–2:3:2–2:tower:2–2:3:2–2:4. Only the mouldings of the tower archway are clearly post-Tudor. But the gateway has its established fan-vault, though the pendant and corbel details and the idiosyncratic centre are

---

*Tracery fragments of C15 type were found in the 1970s reused in a boundary wall.

Wadham College

1 Chapel
2 Hall
3 Old Library
4 William Doo Centre
5 Dr Lee Shau Kee Centre
6 Library
7 Bowra Building

8 Holywell Music Centre
9 Staircase 9
10 Blackwell's Music Shop (former)/ Holywell Court

■ C17
■ C18–C19
▨ C20
▨ C21

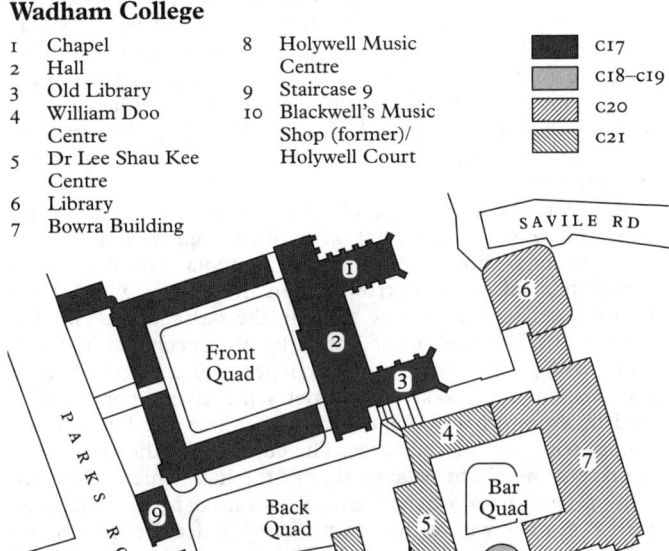

SAVILE RD

Front Quad

PARKS ROAD

Back Quad

Bar Quad

Weston Library (New Bodleian)

HOLYWELL STREET

N

30 m
30 yds

post-medieval. The DOOR, incidentally, is one of several historically spurious Perp-style interventions at Wadham by *Blore* (1832). No pinnacles, but the gables, chimneys and parapet battlements give plenty of incident high up.

Within, Front Quad shows on all sides the same fanaticism for symmetry. The N and S sides have three doorways each with a two-light window over, and then between the first and second and the second and third it goes 3:1:1:3. Dentil cornice above, and indeed all round. The W side is symmetrical too (though the tower has a square higher stair-turret here), and the E side makes a grander symmetry of chapel and hall, with some ingenious planning behind. The front has four large windows l. and r. of a four-tier classical frontispiece exactly contemporary with the yet higher one in the Schools Quadrangle. These windows have tracery not correctly Gothic but Gothic in mood, with one upright and two squashed ovals, linked by blocks like flat clasps which may once have been painted. The FRONTISPIECE is another echo of Merton, including the use of a panel for the top stage above battlement level. It has first an order of coupled Roman Doric columns, then two Ionic pairs, and between them in two niches founder and foundress,

copies after the original statues by *William Blackshaw*. They
have over their heads ridiculous flat, horizontally placed shells.
Then paired Corinthian columns and also pilasters, framing
a statue of James I under a Gothic canopy, and a matching Corinthian top storey with coat of arms. At the very top
a near-segmental motif with quatrefoils and Gothic cresting.
E.S. Frith was the carver entrusted with the frontispiece in
the refacing.

Between the outer pair of windows on each side of the
frontispiece is a big portal with open segmental pediment
and urn, and above each portal is a cupola. The r. portal is
completely false and narrower than the l. one, which leads
into the chapel (entry now through the passage, l.). This has
the Oxford T-plan. So one enters by an antechapel, the four
windows belong to that, and the chapel itself projects E behind
the quad. For the sake of symmetry the chapel wing had to
find its counterpart behind the hall, and so the kitchen and
library wing was placed there. The cupola over the antechapel
is present merely to balance that of the hall, which was originally a true open louvre. The hall is raised up, so one must
turn r. at once within the central entry under the statues and
ascend steps to get into it. Behind the frontispiece itself is the
buttery, and this explains the dead wall within the entry. The
little CLOCK FACE dated 1671 on the chapel side is associated
with *Sir Christopher Wren*, who was at Wadham under Warden
Wilkins, one of the founders of the Royal Society.

The EAST FRONT is at once less symmetrical and more
expressive. As to symmetry, the wings are not placed quite centrally against the main quad, though this is less apparent than
the differences in fenestration. As to expression, the chapel, N,
has big windows of impeccable Perp tracery, quite unlike the
antechapel. The mason here was not Arnold but *John Spicer*,
which may be significant or may not. The library E window has
the teardrop shape of its uppermost lights as its only non-Perp
motif. Simple cusped windows to the sides, uncusped ones
like those of the quad to the kitchen below. The two wings are
connected below the antechapel and hall windows by a cloister walk, the BUTTERY PASSAGE. Three-light windows with
cusped lights here. Symmetry lapses above, where one near-
central window appears with single lights to either side. The
sash and timber mock-tracery to this window, which lights the
Senior Common Room, are of 1826.

Facing S, the main hall window is of six lights, doubling
the standard window pattern under tracery with more playful
scrolly forms l. and r. of the top oval. Also a bay window to the
E for the dais, with simple cusped lights. The outer S side of
the quad is symmetrical once more, but with four big gables.
Likewise the outer N side, except at the W end, where the
WARDEN'S LODGINGS have caused some changes. What is
obviously Victorian here is of 1871–6 and by *T.G. Jackson* – his
first academic commission – including an elevated conservatory and a link to the former STABLES, N.

The GARDENS owe much to expansion to the N under Warden Wills (1783–1806), whose gardener was one *Shipley*. The informal planting and senior specimen trees are of this time. Raised walk to the NE, identified as part of the Civil War defences. Between chapel and Old Library, STATUE of Maurice Bowra, a seated half-figure by *John Doubleday*, 1977.

INTERIORS. First the CHAPEL. The antechapel follows the New College model of two bays' depth from W to E. The slender piers have still the standard Perp section of four shafts and four hollows, but external symmetry required the aisles to be cross-gabled rather than roofed parallel to the nave. In consequence the roof here rises higher than that of the chapel proper. The carpenter of the C17 roof was *Edward Thornton*, work now hidden by *Blore*'s ceilings of 1831–2. That of the chapel proper has stucco panelling with a Perp motif. The misguided REREDOS and Perp stone panelling round the chancel are *Blore*'s too. Other FURNISHINGS of 1612–13, an early instance of the post-Elizabethan movement towards well-appointed dignity in worship: STALLS (but with *Blore*'s poppyheads in place of the C17 balls), PULPIT (on one foot) and SCREEN. The last was made by *John Bolton*, and is the best at Oxford of that date. Slender columns, finely decorated arches and big openwork cresting derived from engravings by Vredeman de Vries. On its W side two pew enclosures for the college servants. – COMMUNION RAILS of *c.*1670. Upright ovals and openwork spandrels. – Marble PAVING of the same date. – LECTERN. 1691. Brass; very big balusters and small cruel eagle. – Elaborate Renaissance ORGAN CASE by *Jackson*, 1886. *Farmer & Brindley* were the carvers. – SCULPTURE, antechapel. Dependent Beings, by *John Robinson*. Polished metal Möbius strip, *c.*1980.

STAINED GLASS. The earliest of Oxford's C17 ensembles, showing a revived confidence in the validity of religious art. E window signed by *Bernard van Ling[e]*, 1622. It cost £114, and is the van Linge brothers' earliest-known English work. Passion scenes, the Crucifixion not excluded, with Old Testament antetypes above. Much of the imagery was copied or adapted from engravings after Martin de Vos, published 1595. The side windows have clear glass in the upper tier, three large figures each in the lower: the original arrangement, with some C19 swapping-about. On the N side Prophets, on the S Apostles. The former are by *Robert Rudland* of Oxford (much restored), 1613–14, the latter – two of them dated 1616 – partly by *Louis Dauphin*. The antechapel figures, obviously later but still decidedly pre-Victorian in style, are by *David Evans*, 1837–40, to designs by *John Bridges*. Also some heraldic glass of the period, re-set 1885–6.

MONUMENTS. One standing monument: Sir John Portman †1624. Reclining youth. Twin black columns l. and r. Back wall arched with two Victory figures. Top with open pediment with two reclining putti and statuettes of Virtues, ending with Father Time. – Many tablets. Thomas Harris †1614, one of the founding Fellows. Composed fictively of books (cf. Bodley's monument at Merton). – John French †1668. With bay garlands and two dolphins. – Thomas Farmer †1672. Similar bay garlands, broken pediment. – John Upton †1686. With two putti and drapery. – Wardens Wills (†1806) and Tournay (†1833), Gothic designs by *Blore*. – Many wall monuments designed by *Jackson*; the earliest by commemoration date is J.E. Farnell †1870, Aesthetic in mood (Martin Jones). – Thomas Bruce Joy †1915, with bronze portrait by *A. Bruce Joy*. – Frederic Harrison †1923 and wife, black cinerary urn in architectural surround. – Rev. Francis Kilvert †1879, lettered slate by *R. Boulton*, 1991.

HALL. Very large, at 82 ft (25 metres) long; of the older college halls, only New College and Christ Church are longer. The hammerbeam roof is original, i.e. of 1612–13. The carpenters were *Thomas Holt*, one of the Yorkshire artisans then lately employed at Merton, and one *Tesely*, otherwise unrecorded. It has pendants, and S-braces within the trusses, from which fleurs-de-lys and scrolls stick out. Original louvre. Screen made by *John Bolton*, closely akin to his chapel screen. Columns, much small-scale strap decoration, and panels with the usual blank arches and also the type of four centripetal L-panels. Big openwork cresting, again deriving from Vredeman de Vries. Fireplace of 1826 by *Daniel Robertson*, with small-scale Jacobean motifs. The heraldic stained-glass panels are by *Willement*, 1826, re-set in 1898. (CELLAR with round piers and groin-vaulting.)

SENIOR COMMON ROOM. Reached by a spiral stair behind the quad frontispiece. Its panelling is said to date from 1724–5, but the present use of the room is earlier, and the work certainly has a late C17 look. Very sumptuous above the fireplace, with carved palm fronds and above broad, flattish garlands. Swags and festoons at the top of the panelling of the walls. Ceiling with just one oval wreath of stucco, also of late C17 type.

OLD LIBRARY, now SCR LUNCH ROOM. Over the barrel-vaulted kitchen; reached from the buttery passage by stairs inserted in 1806 by *Daniel Harris*. Converted by *Robert Potter*, 1986. A spare, light room, stripped of woodwork save for the big late C18 doorcase. New ceiling modelled on that of the antechapel.

WARDEN'S LODGINGS, in the NW corner. Formerly extending to the room over the gateway, New College fashion: Oxford's final instance of this arrangement. Some C18 panelled rooms and a reconfigured mid-Georgian staircase with turned balusters.

Bar Quad and Back Quad

Back Quad is the enclosure with fine old trees s of Front Quad. Mixed and informal in character, it is composed mostly of annexed buildings that face the streets to W and S, as described below. Its E side is shared with BAR QUAD, created from the late C20 onwards, and here Wadham has lately been bold. For the quad's NW angle was rebuilt by *AL_A Architects* in 2017–20, not in any traditional materials or idiom but in a taut, shimmering combination of aluminium and etched-glass panelling, with through-storey glazing for the shallower link where the wings meet. The result is surely the most radical intervention at the pre-C19 colleges since the St John's Beehives in the 1950s – and that alone may be too much for some. The wings are clearly differentiated: the WILLIAM DOO UNDERGRADUATE CENTRE (Junior Common Room etc.) on the N side with more horizontal proportions, the DR LEE SHAU KEE BUILDING, W side, with narrow upright panels, and irregularly spaced windows on the two upper floors of student rooms. The ground floor here includes the Access Centre, designed to welcome school groups and thus to encourage more diverse applications to the college. Internal circulation is by a moulded vermilion-red staircase in the W wing, vivid enough to register externally even on a bright day (but surely too insistent at night). The ground floor of the glazed section next to it is left open, making a passage through to the re-landscaped quad, where the N side is recessed behind thin piers. Demolished to make way for the new work was the undistinguished Goddard Building, 1951–3 by *Henry Goddard*, an old member: pitched-roofed and squared-rubble-faced in the interwar way, with some tamely handled Modernist motifs in its fenestration.

The genesis of Bar Quad continued after Goddard with the tall LIBRARY of 1973–7 by *Gillespie, Kidd & Coia*, i.e. *Andy Macmillan* and *Isi Metzstein*. It is reached from the W via a raised terrace with steps, the latter rebuilt integrally with the new Undergraduate Centre. The library adopts the chunky forms and angular leaded roofs of late Brutalism, as embraced by Basil Spence, Casson & Conder *et al.* Yet the concrete is stained yellow to look more like Clipsham stone, and the horizontal faces have sunk panels: a detail that anticipates the architects' revival of historically charged motifs at Robinson College, Cambridge not long after. The main volume is expressed by means of smoked frameless glazing to near-full height next to the entrance. Two leaded top storeys with student rooms, introverted around their own little court in a way suggestive of sky burials or some such secluded ritual. To the S is a lower residential wing, the stub of an intended longer range. Inside the library entrance, stairs lead both up and down within a symmetrical but nicely intricate space, its decks and levels unified by good pale woodwork.

Work resumed in 1988–92 with *MacCormac, Jamieson & Prichard*'s BOWRA BUILDING. This extends from the 1970s stub, continuing its access deck to the S, but is almost as different in its materials and expression as AL_A Architects' are from both. Eighty-five student rooms are grouped into nine house-like units that rise tower-like from the deck: four on the

W side, three placed at offset intervals on the E side, and two more overlapping the E side at both ends, together forming the E part of Bar Quad. Within the ground storey are various communal rooms, some with skylights that double as features on the deck. The towers have twin shallow-pitched-roofed silhouettes, evocative at once of Elizabethan great houses (Hardwick especially) and domestic Frank Lloyd Wright. The materials combine pale yellow brick and cast stone with darker window detailing. External staircases up to and down from the deck – one of them lopped off for the new building – encourage exploration and discovery. Especially striking is the S aspect from the deck, where the towers line up in steep perspective like the back scenery of Italian Renaissance theatre, with the bell-tower of New College as a borrowed view-closer. Tightly compressed and richly suggestive, the scheme is a worthy successor to the architects' Sainsbury Building at Worcester (p. 323), and draws also on ideas from MJP's second, unbuilt project for that college (1986).

The S side of Bar Quad is interrupted by the rubble-walled apse of the HOLYWELL MUSIC ROOM. Constructed in 1742–8 for the sole purpose of musical performances, the first such building in England. *Thomas Camplin*, Vice-Principal of St Edmund Hall, provided the design. To Holywell Street it looks very like a large Nonconformist chapel, with its white pedimented three-bay front. A lower projection with arched windows, added probably in 1822, houses the gallery staircase. Portal by *John Melvin*, 2009. *Carden & Godfrey*'s renovation of 1959–60 is responsible for the present interior, based on an C18 account. Organ of 1790 by *John Donaldson* of Newcastle upon Tyne (installed 1985; from Belvedere House, Dublin). Two chandeliers, made to hang in Westminster Hall for the Coronation banquet of George IV (1820). The GREEN ROOM, W, was added by *Gillespie, Kidd & Coia*, 1982–3.

Finally to BACK QUAD. Its W side is straightforward. STAIRCASE 9 is a five-bay, three-storey ashlar block built next to the C17 quad in 1693–4, mason *Bartholomew Peisley II*. Sashes on this side, but the Parks Road front has cross-windows, put back in *Robert Potter*'s refacing of 1968–9. Next to this two stone houses of 1797 and 1801, taken over by the college in 1828. The larger house (STAIRCASE 11) was built as a foundry and warehouse for the University Press.

The Holywell Street side, S, is best explained chronologically. The key to Wadham's presence here is the former BLACKWELL'S MUSIC SHOP and associated additions of 1969–71 by *Gillespie, Kidd & Coia*. Its shopfront to the S (by No. 38) is a stepped-out, tile-roofed wedge with glazed entrance below and ribbon window above. The shop is now part of the McCALL MACBAIN GRADUATE STUDY CENTRE, after adaptations and additions by *Lee/Fitzgerald Architects*, 2008–12. On the college side the 1970s work is tucked away behind an older rubble wall, now with a terraced walk and pergola on top, approached by steps or ramp from either end. The walk allows a view of the small, all-glass atrium of the former shop, and a larger but still diminutive court called HOLYWELL COURT, placed within the rear angle of the King's Arms (p. 416). This has Fellows' rooms on N and E sides, with large windows and lead facing. Also of the 1970s phase is the tall back part of college rooms above the shop, dressed up with pitched roof and period windows in 1992. *Lee/Fitzgerald* assert themselves with an enigmatic stone box or tower with intersecting bronze-clad lift shaft, placed at the E end of the terrace. Inside is a bony open-framed staircase of steel, rising to a little seminar room at the top. But the stairs also descend a storey, to allow entry to the back of the Music Shop. Its reconfigured spaces will unsettle anyone who remembers the shop in its heyday, but the finely crafted 1970s shelving etc. looks surprisingly at home in these unusually generous Graduate Common Rooms. Closing the quad at the SE, STAIRCASE 15 is a mock cottage of *c.*1955 designed by the college Clerk of Works, *Roy Cozier.*

For MERIFIELD off Marston Ferry Road *see* North Oxford, p. 470; for the DOROTHY WADHAM BUILDING on Iffley Road *see* East Oxford, p. 503.

WOLFSON COLLEGE
Linton Road

Wolfson College means *Powell & Moya.* It is their last work at Oxford, concluding the sequence begun at Brasenose in the late 1950s, and their most ambitious at either of the ancient universities. The college was founded at Iffley as Iffley College in 1965, and renamed after Lord Wolfson gave the princely sum of £1,500,000 and the Ford Foundation a similar amount. The foundation was for graduates, with an emphasis on the sciences, and an initial complement of 250 students of both sexes. It also increased the availability of fellowships to University staff without an existing college connection, and made some provision for families. Fellows and students have belonged to a single common room from the start, and altogether the traditional Oxford hierarchies are not much in evidence here.

The first Principal was Sir Isaiah Berlin, who invited *Powell & Moya* to compete at the suggestion of Nikolaus Pevsner. (Also shortlisted were *Gordon Bunshaft* of *Skidmore, Owings & Merrill* of Chicago and *Heikki & Kaija Siren* of Finland.) Work began in 1968, making good use of the mature trees that came with the riverside site. The structural engineers were *Charles Weiss & Partners*, the landscape architects *Powell & Moya* themselves. In 1974 the college buildings were completed. Nothing was built after that until the 1990s.

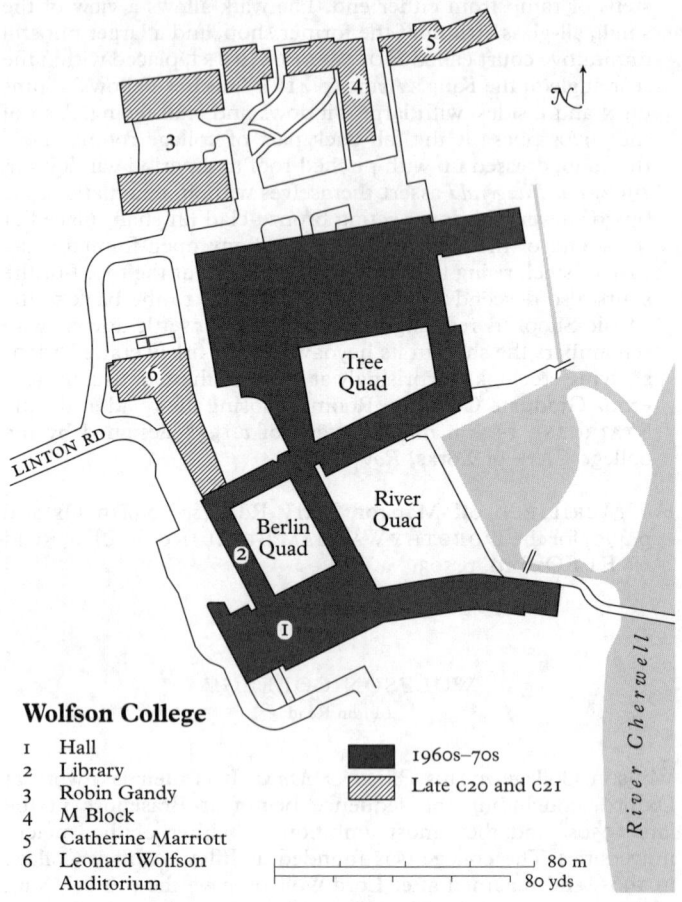

Wolfson College

1   Hall
2   Library
3   Robin Gandy
4   M Block
5   Catherine Marriott
6   Leonard Wolfson
    Auditorium

1960s–70s
Late C20 and C21

80 m
80 yds

Powell & Moya's college is discouragingly blank towards the
Linton Road approach – though less so now that the new
entrance quad (*see* p.316) has been made at the NW angle.
The design begins to unfold within the original main quad,
now BERLIN QUAD. Communal facilities are grouped here:
hall on the S side, common rooms and seminar rooms on the
longer E and W sides, library on the W side upper floors, and
sundry offices. The hall is made prominent by a pyramid roof
– there are no other dominating accents. Here and throughout the elements are all quite simple, and the mastery shows
in the composition. Reinforced concrete construction, faced
not with the Portland stone of the architects' earlier Oxbridge
projects but with big pieces of crushed grey granite in pre-cast
concrete panels. Reveals and back walls are painted white,
windows and metalwork are black anodized aluminium, vertical supports are circular in section. A cloister unifies the quad

below, and extends outwards at the same level through the complex. The HALL – square in plan, and with no dais – is lined with chestnut, and boarding continues within the roof pyramid, twice interrupted by horizontal slots for natural light. The apex is also glazed, and a clerestory runs round at the base. The usual entry is via a spatially exciting STAIR HALL with much pale grey marble facing and open-sided stairs and landings on the quad side. The LIBRARY has the novelty of carrels for individual use, thirty-six tiny cubicles each with its own door, arranged in two storeys towards the quad. The main space is thus left as a long narrow double-height volume with white walls and an angled skylight above. In 2013 the library expanded into the N side.

To the E the land slopes down towards the River Cherwell, with a lawn and an artificial punt-harbour, between the two residential wings of RIVER QUAD. The N wing joins on to Berlin Quad at right angles, bending back acutely at the end; the S wing is angled outwards, and curves back gently midway – a refinement decided on by Isaiah Berlin, whose inspiration was the celebrated harbour of Portofino. The cloisters are here placed along the front of the S wing, along the back of the N one, where there is also an open staircase at the far end that comes down and through to the harbour. On both wings the uprights are flat-fronted, representing the ends of cross-walls. Balconies with angled fronts of dark tinted glass. The maximum height is five storeys, including the set-back penthouse flats with intermittent horizontal canopies. A big arched FOOTBRIDGE links the S side with the meadows on the other side of the river.

The rest of Powell & Moya's residential accommodation is behind the N wing, which itself forms two sides of the irregular TREE QUAD. The N and W sides here are lower, and have much car parking in the bottom storey. On the podium thus created are two- and three-bedroom houses intended for couples with children, arranged for seclusion as terraces that form two inward-facing courts. The terraces are white-walled and flat-roofed, and each has an angled skylight enclosure running from end to end. Also there are some two-room flats in a spur block projecting E, and more flats in the E side of Tree Quad proper. Otherwise the residential parts are chiefly composed of study-bedrooms, planned in groups with communal kitchens etc. Much use is made of glazed-in walkways for access, rather than the traditional staircases with rooms opening off, or the spine corridors of the older women's colleges. So the different needs of Wolfson's members are given firm but humane architectural expression – not for nothing did Powell & Moya begin as designers of innovative social housing – and blended with some of the communal and monumental traditions of college architecture, as well as the special capabilities of the riverside site. All this makes Wolfson a formidable achievement.

(Discreet re-glazing in 2021–2 by *Original Field*, part of an ongoing decarbonisation project.)

ADDITIONS began in the 1990s with isolated blocks to the N. To the NW, ROBIN GANDY, two-storey flats facing each other across a paved court. Stone facing, but the floor bands treated with aggregate *à la* Powell & Moya. By *Oxford Architects Partnership*, 1991–3. To the E are SQUASH COURTS and the L-shaped M BLOCK, 2000–3, then CATHERINE MARRIOTT, slightly cranked, 2004–9. These are by *Berman Guedes Stretton*, and closer to the Powell & Moya idiom. A new block by *Penoyre & Prasad* is proposed for S of Berlin Quad (2023).

Finally back to FRONT QUAD, also *Berman Guedes Stretton* – which is to say the well-judged new front range, making an open-ended quad with Powell & Moya to E and S. The N end with the LEONARD WOLFSON AUDITORIUM (2011–13) is signalled by a slim white ventilation tower, with the asymmetrical grey roof sloping up in three steps to meet it. The auditorium roof structure shows inside as concrete beams raking dynamically outwards from one corner, with timber slats between. The two-storey ACADEMIC WING (2014–16; lodge, café, study rooms etc.) adopts more from Powell & Moya, but without mere replication. Curving stone benches and paving in the quad enclosure, suggesting a memory of the cylindrical cycle shed that formerly stood at the entrance.

WORCESTER COLLEGE
Worcester Street

Worcester College until 1714 was Gloucester Hall or Gloucester College, founded in 1560. This in turn was a re-foundation of Gloucester Hall, established in 1283 by the Benedictines of St Peter's Abbey, Gloucester: one of the monastic colleges of Oxford, like St Bernard's College or Durham College (*see* pp. 271 and 291), or Magdalene College in Cambridge. In 1320–1 the site lately vacated by Oxford's Carmelite friary (*see* p. 431n.) was added to the holding. Individual chambers were built at the college in the C15 by and for individual monasteries, and a good few of these remain, but much fewer of the buildings held in common.

The present college is named for Sir Thomas Cookes, a Worcestershire landowner who in 1701 left the University £10,000 and the option to build and endow 'an ornamental pile'. Work began in 1720, steered by *George Clarke* of All Souls, in collaboration with *Hawksmoor*. They envisaged a college on a novel plan, with two open-sided quads or courts – one small, one very large – placed back to back. Work dragged on to *c.*1790 without replacing all the medieval work. Then the buildings remained as they were for more than a century; for Worcester is unique too among Oxford's older colleges by its absence of any major C19 or early C20 building. Additions around the expansive grounds and gardens began only in 1939, and have continued in the C21.

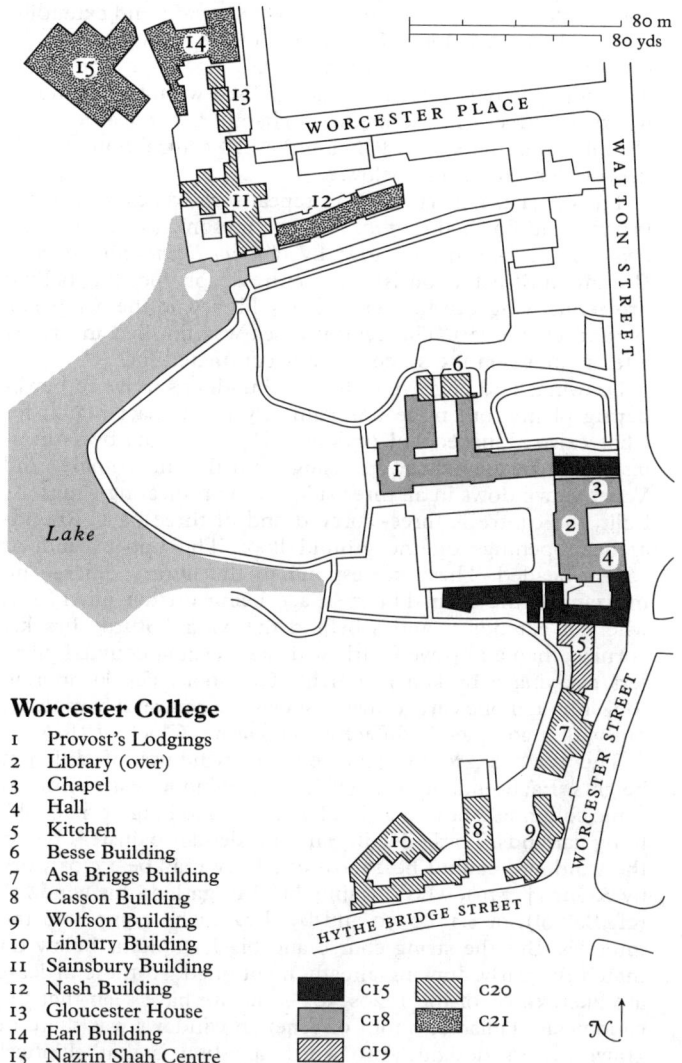

Worcester College

1 Provost's Lodgings
2 Library (over)
3 Chapel
4 Hall
5 Kitchen
6 Besse Building
7 Asa Briggs Building
8 Casson Building
9 Wolfson Building
10 Linbury Building
11 Sainsbury Building
12 Nash Building
13 Gloucester House
14 Earl Building
15 Nazrin Shah Centre

C15 C20
C18 C21
C19

The medieval and c18 college

The C18 parts are the starting point for exploring the college. Their history however is complex. The design seems to have been provided by *George Clarke*, Fellow of All Souls and benefactor of Worcester, working closely with his old associate *Hawksmoor* in matters of planning and detail (cf. Queen's College). Clarke's PLAN comprised a U-shaped central building facing E in which chapel, library and hall were combined, and parallel ranges set a little way to the N and S and extending back a long way behind. The far end of the N range was to be the Provost's Lodgings. Of these side ranges only the N one was built, partly to a later C18 design, and without continuing up to the street. So the medieval chambers survive here and also all along the S side, flanking the C18 central building. Of these older parts more below.

The CENTRAL BUILDING, to repeat some dates, was begun in 1720 and finished c. 1790. The first mason was *Bartholomew Peisley III*, followed after 1727 by *William Townesend*. Towards Beaumont Street it consists of a centre deeply receding behind projecting wings. In the centre is the library, in the wings hall (S) and chapel (N). The central block was finished in or just after 1736, when the SE corner was contracted for.

Drawings and engravings for this building survive in bewildering plenty, but none unfortunately is an exact match for what exists. Unexecuted options include designs by *Hawksmoor* with octagonal towers rising from the inner angles and Venetian windows in all three sides of the projecting wings. As built, the centre is three-storeyed and of three bays. Round-arched openings on the ground floor. The upper windows square-headed. These correspond to the library offices and mezzanine, the main library space being on the inner side, where it extends N and S behind the wings. Sturdy bracket cornice, then an upswept attic with short, squat coupled pilasters carrying a broken pediment. This looks Hawksmoorian too, although one early drawing shows the centre as completed but with a completely different top feature. Clock of 1856.

The WINGS are two-storeyed, i.e. windows of different heights. Each ends in a large Venetian window with unfluted Ionic columns. Above it a circular recess, and long horizontally hung garlands. These details, and the slender balusters below the windows, cannot be 1720s–30s. They may be 1770s work by *Keene* (†1776), who certainly liked to garland his windows (cf. Balliol), or c. 1780–90 and by *Wyatt*, who completed the interiors. But the string course and big flat quoins below do match the early drawing already mentioned, so these at least are likely to be of the 1720s–30s – and we have seen that the canonically Palladian motif of Venetian windows was there in Hawksmoor's designs. Also worth mention is that elliptical recesses in the N and S fronts were observed during the 1960s refacing work, apparently infilled from inside later in the C18. So the wings may have stood as shells before being finished with the fashionable new motifs of the late C18. Railings and GATES of 1951 across the centre by *R. Fielding Dodd*, after a design left by the C18 smith *Thomas Goff*.

To N and S the MEDIEVAL BUILDINGS appear. To the N the end gable of a rubble-stone range and then a broad four-centred-arched gateway, infilled with a smaller arch. This gateway was the main entry to Gloucester College, via a lane on the N side; i.e. there was no gate tower. It probably belongs with work of the 1420s for St Albans' Abbey (shield above), and may be by the mason *Thomas Wolvey*. To the s a whole range, the windows of which are mostly sashes on this side. Also one mullioned C15 window, missing its tracery.

The main QUAD is open as well, open at the far end to the famous gardens of the college (*see* p. 322). The E and N sides are C18, but the NE portion and the whole s side are medieval. It is lopsided, no-one would deny – and the C18 design had of course foreseen *tabula rasa* for the s range too – but of enormous appeal. The CENTRAL BUILDING here is demonstrably *Hawksmoor*, or *Clarke* and *Hawksmoor*, matching as it does the engraving in Williams's *Oxonia Depicta* (1732–3). A stately arcade or cloister all along the ground floor, with groin-vaults on very broad basket arches, and big, plain, unmoulded blocks instead of capitals for the piers. Symmetrically placed doorways to chapel and hall. Above the arcade the composition divides into a three-bay centre with arched windows and coupled Ionic pilasters surmounted by a pediment, and three-bay side parts of simpler treatment. An annotation by Hawksmoor identifies the source of the pilasters and arches as the Roman 'Arch of Saintes' (Arch of Germanicus), in the Charente-Maritime. WAR MEMORIALS in the cloister: 1921 by *Macdonald Gill*, 1947 by *E. R. Bevan*.

The NORTH RANGE was finally begun in 1753–9, to a design left by *Clarke* (two E staircases), and completed along with the W pavilion – the Provost's Lodgings – only in 1773–6. For the latter work the architect was *Henry Keene*. The range itself is nineteen bays long and of three storeys to the front, which, however, as it has a terrace in front raised substantially above garden level, makes four storeys at the back. Three-bay pediment, arched ground-floor windows set in blank arches. In the side parts the wall surface is cut back vertically on each bay. Squared aprons of the second-floor windows here. Attic storey added 1926.

The PROVOST'S LODGINGS have their main façade to the gardens, i.e. the W, where all four storeys appear. *Keene*'s is a curious composition, animated but just a little disjointed, with its rusticated ground floor and the rusticated broad buttress-piers flanking the centre triple bay. Action is concentrated here; the side parts have just one window on each floor and all the rest blank wall. But in the centre between the rusticated buttress-piers is the doorway, reached by an outer staircase in two curved flights, and then, above, the piers become smooth and carry pairs of unfluted Ionic pilasters, and between them is the climax motif, a tripartite window with Ionic columns and a garland and finally above that a tripartite lunette with vertical garlands and a pediment. Only the bracket cornice is carried on from the earlier parts. The spacious but plain top-lit staircase originally went no higher than the first floor.

Projecting N of the N range and built in connection with it are the former PROVOST'S KITCHEN and the STABLES, now converted for other uses. *R. Fielding Dodd & Kenneth Stevens*'s BESSE BUILDING of 1952–5, the gift of M. Antonin Besse, makes a closed court across the N side. *Carden & Godfrey's* little timber colonnades of 2008 are a pretty touch.

Less spectacular but no less interesting than Worcester's C18 architecture is the MEDIEVAL WORK. The centre of Gloucester College lay where the central building of the college is now. It had a small quad, with chapel on the N side, hall on the W and library in the E range, and in addition the domestic ranges, much of which survive. These are special in that they were not just sets but *camerae*, i.e. each unit was the responsibility of an individual Benedictine monastery within the Province of Canterbury. Coats of arms over doorways identified them, although some have since been moved.

The SOUTH RANGE is two-storeyed, and entirely of the C15. Though nearly all the windows have lost the arches and cusping of the original lights, the state of preservation is astonishing. Enough also remains to show the very deliberate differences between the chambers, which are of two or three bays. Windows, doorway spandrels (trefoils, quatrefoils, shields or foliage), hoodmoulds and hoodstops: all differ from part to part. The chamber furthest E (Malmesbury) has the widest doorway – serving the kitchen passage – and squared recessed windows. In the upper room, now part of the JUNIOR COMMON ROOM, a C15 wagon roof with thin moulded ribs. This space served as the college chapel for much of the C18. No. 11 has a central doorway, No. 9 very shallow boxed-out bay windows. No. 8 alone has a window still with arched lights. It is recessed a little and has blank panelling between this and the (altered) upper window – like a negative of the bay window of Grevel's House at Chipping Campden. Above the doorway of No. 7 (Pershore) is a tiny image niche. The final *camera* has gone, exposing a timber-framed gable to which a pretty bargeboard was added *c.* 1821–4. Of the same date most of the dormers etc. on the unfeasibly picturesque rear parts. The Perp-style doorway through the garden wall beyond is of 1856.

Also medieval is much of PUMP QUAD, in the SE angle. Here are more doorways to *camerae* (Bury St Edmunds E, Glastonbury S). One is set across the SE corner. One other window of one light with a cusped arch looks acceptable. The courtyard ranges were heightened in 1824. The sashing of most windows may also have been done then, but the outer windows are Neo-Perp. The S side continues to the W as the OLD KITCHEN, probably built in 1423. This sits behind the *camerae* and must be seen from the gardens, where its enormous chimney-breast appears. Converted to rooms in 1844, when a new KITCHEN was built at right angles to the S. Extensions of 2013–14 by *Freeland Rees Roberts*, in a Cotswold manner.

More CAMERAE survive N of the centre (St Augustine's Canterbury etc., now mostly SENIOR COMMON ROOMS), i.e. continuing the C18 range to the E. On the N side again a few cusped one-light windows amid the sashes, and again some eye-catching 1820s dormers.

INTERIORS. Of principal interiors in the central building the LIBRARY must be taken first. It fills the whole of the W length above the cloister, and is entered midway on the long side (cf. All Souls and Christ Church). Access is by a spacious spiral STAIRCASE behind, begun in 1736, with stone walls and dome and a graceful iron railing. The pattern repeats in the library itself, for the balcony railing. The balcony runs along three sides, with bookcases placed flat against the walls. This shelving was provided to *Clarke*'s specification, and his books were moved in from All Souls in 1736. On the short sides the cases cut across the windows, a decidedly maladroit arrangement. In the middle of the inner wall the balcony rests on two full-grown Corinthian columns, inserted in 1825 by *R. Wyatt & Son*. They also did the modest Neoclassical ceiling plasterwork, and the graining of the upper bookcases. The lower ones were painted white in *Emil Godfrey*'s redecoration of 1960. The library has expanded into the storey over the hall (1928–9) via a neat extension of the staircase landing, and subsequently over the lower library and chapel.

The CHAPEL was dedicated only in 1791. Its designer was *James Wyatt*, commissioned in 1783 after Keene's death. However, *William Burges*, one of the most potent High Victorian architects, redecorated it from 1864 onwards.* He did not obliterate Wyatt's work but he swamped it. *Wyatt*'s are the screen of Ionic columns between vestibule and chapel, the characteristic fan-like coving by the arches over the windows, and much of the ceiling plasterwork with its delicate foliage patterns in the four coved corners and little central dome. But nearly all the rest is *Burges*. His interventions follow an exhaustive theological programme, of a kind fashionable for college chapels just then. The WALL DECORATION is Raphaelesque, remarkable in so convinced a Goth as Burges (he dismissed C18 classicism as 'the vilest Renaissance of George III's time': *The Builder*, 1 January 1876). The gold-ground figure frieze was painted by *Henry Holiday*, as was the decoration at window level (the Te Deum, 1864–70). The painters *Ellis Wooldridge* and *F. Smallfield* were also employed. In the little ceiling panels the Fall of Man and Expulsion from Eden, with Virtues and Prophets. A more Roman or Pompeian style prevails in the vestibule. – STAINED GLASS. Life of Christ, designed by *Holiday* too, and made by *Lavers & Barraud*, 1864–5. *Millais* was originally asked, but Burges rejected his first (and only) design. Holiday's is earthier than Morris glass, with sturdier figures and less subtle colours, though the faces are Pre-Raphaelite. – The STALLS with the intarsia inlay and exotic beasties on the ends are *Burges* indeed. They were made by *Harland & Fisher* of London (*Robinson*, carver). – MOSAIC FLOOR with saints, made by the same, 1865–8; Early Christian, not Renaissance. – STATUES in the rounded corners. The Evangelists, by *Thomas Nicholls*. – Nicholls also modelled the gorgeous alabaster LECTERN in a pure Quattrocento, carved by *Jacquet* of London. It is dated 1865, as are the two alabaster

---

*Chosen as a cheaper alternative to *Scott*'s designs for renovation, submitted 1863.

CANDLESTICKS, equally Quattrocento. The chapel interior was cleaned and restored by *Carden & Godfrey* in 2001–2.

The HALL was decorated by *Wyatt* in 1783–9, with another entrance screen of columns, then partly redecorated by *Burges* in 1876–9, toned down in 1909 and forcibly made Wyatt again by *Emil Godfrey* in 1966–7. Discreet wall panels (the detailing best not looked at too closely), delicate plasterwork on the ceiling. Also a new white marble fireplace. 'Exit Burges. They will be sorry in fifty years, but for the time being they have for their daily use a more pleasing hall.' Thus Pevsner in 1974. And some *Burges* has indeed been brought back: his delicate E window with pictures of feasts, made by *Saunders & Co.*, was reinstated in 2003.* (Below the hall a tunnel-vaulted CELLAR.)

The gardens, with the C20 and C21 buildings

Of all the colleges, Worcester has the best GARDENS of the naturalistic landscaped type. Its LAKE was made in 1813. The path around it goes through an ARCH reportedly brought from the monastic buildings. The Provost's domain includes a ROSE GARDEN designed by *Alfred Parsons* in 1901 (restored 2006–7). In it two carved HEADS, one C17 and one C19, from the series around the Sheldonian (p. 339).

Worcester has understandably placed its NEWER BUILDINGS around the garden perimeter. They vary wildly in ambition and attainment.

S of the old buildings is the ASA BRIGGS BUILDING of 1938–9 by *W.G. Newton*. Nine bays, squared rubble, only two floors, but a big hipped roof with dormers. A gift of Lord Nuffield, it is Cotswold-Georgian-inspired, and has no special message beyond that. Then an open-sided court formed by the CASSON BUILDING, 1959–61 by *Sir Hugh Casson, Neville Conder & Partners*, W, and the WOLFSON BUILDING, 1969–71 by *Peter Bosanquet & Partners*, E. The Casson Building was reduced by around a third at its N end when the Linbury Building was added (*see* below). Three storeys of light brown Crowborough brick, plus a storey of split-level rooms in a recessed mansard. Pevsner noted this mansard and the little square oriel windows as 'an appeal for elegance' in the terms of 1961. Also canted sills to these oriels, and a few very tall slit windows. Brick type, window projections and mansard profile are echoed in the Wolfson Building, which has three storeys altogether and is roughly crescent-shaped.

On the far, W side of Casson and joining on to it, *Maguire & Murray*'s LINBURY BUILDING of 1988–90.† Really it is two buildings, a chevron-shaped cluster of meeting and function

---

*The fireplace is now at Burges's Knightshayes Court, Devon.
† Chosen in place of a costlier design of 1986 by *MacCormac, Jamieson & Prichard* (*see also* below), ideas from which recur in the architects' Bowra Building at Wadham, p. 311.

rooms to the N, taller residential range to the S, and small court between. From Hythe Bridge Street the S part appears as a stepped and staggered composition of pale rendered walls, rising from W to E, and punctuated by staircase towers with belvedere top storeys under shallow pyramid roofs. It is an effective way of animating a necessarily defensive frontage. The N part has shelving roofs too, with a complex culmination of squares and diagonally rotated squares over the Governing Body Room in the centre.

Later expansion looked N, to the end of the lake. The first arrival was *MacCormac, Jamieson & Prichard*'s masterly SAINSBURY BUILDING of 1980–3. An intricate but coherent diagonal composition, rising from a low, prow-like terrace that pushes out into the water. The dominant material is yellow-buff brick, with pale concrete for the upper terrace deck and some squared-rubble walling around the edges. Darker accents in the boxed-out window frames and in the slated mono-pitched roofs of the rooms, deployed singly or in split pairs, as they mount up. The residential rooms are arranged not quite symmetrically in five L-shaped groups of three, with a kitchen for every six rooms. A function room faces the terrace prow, sunk slightly below the waterline, while a little gatehouse-like extension to the N makes the link to Worcester Place and the streets outside.

With its open circulation areas, cross-passages and ingenious internal and external staircases, the whole is rewarding to explore. In addition it is richly suggestive of earlier architecture, from late Arts and Crafts to Alvar Aalto (the projecting stair enclosures in the NW angle) to Frank Lloyd Wright, not to mention the classical echoes in the roofs like split pediments – on the gatehouse especially. A pity, then, that wire safety fences have gone up on the terrace, the external steps and the stone-slab bridge across the little water garden on the S side. A FOOTBRIDGE across the lake just to the S is also proposed, designed by *Colvin & Moggridge* (2022).

The nearest neighbours are not in the same league. Immediately E of Sainsbury, a wedge-shaped space made by two yellow brick ranges with grey detailing, not altogether bad, but without finesse. It is a design-and-build project by the *Leadbitter Group* with *ADP Architects*, 2005–8. The S range is the NASH BUILDING. The plainer N range incorporates some Victorian house frontages to Worcester Place behind, and has an imitative extension there. Lesser Victorian buildings alongside, also adapted for the college. N of Sainsbury is GLOUCESTER HOUSE, 1978 by *Phippen, Randall & Parkes*. Red-brown brick. Built as graduate flats, modified as single rooms in 2007. Then the bulkier EARL BUILDING, 2006, more of the yellow brick mode already seen.

Niall McLaughlin Architects' NAZRIN SHAH CENTRE to the NW, 2014–17, shows a return to the highest form. Several disparate functions – lecture theatre, dance studio, seminar rooms and study area – are assembled here. Externally the

most legible elements are the theatre, rising as a quadrant
of stone fins above the flat-roofed main block; the studio,
facing towards Sainsbury as a sheer ashlar box with a giant-
windowed end overlooking a pool; and the two seminar rooms,
which frame a skeleton loggia on the long s side. The stone
is Clipsham, used as facing on the giant chamfered uprights
and lintels, and combining with beautifully calculated timber
slats and ceiling grids inside. Here the spaces are unified by a
single free-flowing concourse, designed to open both outwards
to the loggia and inwards to the theatre, as required. The light
falls beautifully throughout, and the surfaces are a pleasure to
the touch as well as to the eye. Only the N side is looser, but
this is not normally seen.

The loggia of Nazrin Shah faces the cricket pitch, made
in 1897–1900. Timber PAVILION by *Thomas Tyrwhitt*, an old
member of the college. At the far W end the CANAL BUILD-
ING, design-and-build of 1994. Vaguely Neo-Victorian; fortunately screened by trees.

PERMANENT PRIVATE HALLS

BLACKFRIARS
St Giles'

A Dominican priory founded in 1921, the 700th anniversary of
the order's first arrival in Oxford; a Permanent Private Hall
since 1994 (for the medieval priory *see* p.449). Buildings of
1921–9 by *E. Doran Webb*, rear addition and tower of *c.*1951
by *T. Rayson*. Domestic-looking frontage of late C17 character,
with mostly cross-windows and a pediment not in the centre.
Statue of the Madonna over the entrance by *Thomas Rudge*,
inscription below by *Eric Gill*. Rusticated s doorway, a near
copy of one on the C18 house formerly on the site. Behind the N
part is the CHAPEL, with altar to the W. It has a three-bay nave
and a narrower four-bay choir, under an arched ceiling of plain
plaster. The forms are C15 Perpendicular Gothic, the mood
spare and sober. Plain STALLS by *Colin Fleetwood-Walker*, 1963.
Of SCULPTURE there is *Eric Gill*'s little St Dominic statue and
a C15 English alabaster panel with the Annunciation, second
and third side chapels respectively, and fervent STATIONS OF
THE CROSS carved in low relief by *Fr Aelred Whitaker*. Low s
tower, hardly visible externally. It faces a small quadrangle.
Other elevations in an early C17 style except on the E side,
where the CHAPTER ROOM on the first floor is also Gothic.
REFECTORY in the s range with a ceiling patterned with thin
ribs of early C16 inspiration. The full-height STAIRCASE in the
1950s tower is worth a look. In the street range, first floor,
the LIBRARY (N) and a room with a brought-in Elizabethan
overmantel with herm pilasters.

CAMPION HALL
Brewer Street

Campion Hall is *Lutyens*'s only Oxford building. It came about when the celebrated Fr Martin D'Arcy consulted him in 1933 as to who should design the Jesuits' newly relocated Oxford house, of which D'Arcy was the incoming Master. The Society of Jesus had been licensed to open a Private Hall at Oxford in 1898 (a Permanent Private Hall from 1918). Work began in 1934, and the buildings were opened in 1936. Lutyens was used to bigger budgets and broader margins, certainly, but the commission brought out to the full his gift for marrying playful invention with seriousness of purpose.

The Lutyens buildings make an L-shape, the short side along Brewer Street, the long side extending s from its e end. Additions to make a full quadrangle were intended, and partly realized, for which *see* below – but not by Lutyens (whose tantalizing outline drawings survive). The material is squared coursed rubble. Coming w from St Aldate's one sees first the polygonal apse end of the chapel elevated above a ground floor with two round arches. Alongside is a round-arched two-light window with a circle over, for a side chapel. Higher up and set back is a slim gable with an oculus, for an upper oratory. Tight up against this are the twin end gables of the w range, a more conventional affair with simple stone-mullioned and mullion-and-transom windows of C17 Cotswold type. Along the top floor to Brewer Street the two-light chapel windows reappear. The fenestration then continues in a way one would at first call random but recognizes after a while to be of a carefully worked-out irregularity. Also here is the deep portal with its stepped round arch. The w end is an incorporated older house (MICKLEM HALL), of stone too, with a Late Georgian doorway with Tuscan demi-columns and triglyph frieze. It has a tile-hung *Lutyens* top storey. Part of a Tudor-arched fireplace inside. Behind, facing a surprisingly large garden, the e range presents a pilastered central doorcase of Lutyens's Delhi order. The CROSS-RANGE, s side, was added in 1957–8, designers *J. O. Armes* and *Lawrence Shattock*. Tile-hung rather than stone gables here. Across the garden wall to the w is now Pembroke College's Rokos Quad (*see* p. 237).

INTERIORS. The atmosphere remains intensely that of the socially elevated, intellectual Catholicism of Fr D'Arcy's day. Yet *Lutyens*'s hand is everywhere evident too. The main STAIRCASE has balusters of nicely non-period bulbous profile around its open well. LIBRARY in the e wing, lined with plain bookcases, with clever steps and other furniture designed by the architect (as also in the REFECTORY). The CHAPEL has a smooth white barrel-vault and a very original arched BALDAC-CHINO, of wood and with slim columns, that seems to merge with the apse. PEWS and cardinal's-hat LIGHT FITTINGS, also

110

characteristic late Lutyens. – STATIONS OF THE CROSS, 'xylo-graphs' (lithographs on wood) by *Frank Brangwyn*. – Ante-chapel, REREDOS by *Daphne Pollen*, a Calvary; STATUES by *Arthur Pollen*. – LADY CHAPEL to the S, of half-height, with two sail-vaults. It has touching MURALS by the little-known *Charles Mahoney*. Contemporary 1940s dress, visionary moods; echoes of Piero della Francesca, also of Stanley Spencer. The ORATORY, also barrel-vaulted, has a squint down to the main chapel.

SCULPTURE. On the main staircase a small panel by *Eric Gill*, 1935: St Martin of Tours in modern uniform. Near the staircase foot a large painted southern Spanish wooden sculpture of St Ignatius and followers, early C17, after the iconography of the Mater Misericordiae.

REGENT'S PARK COLLEGE

Pusey Street and St Giles'

Founded in Stepney in 1810 as a training college for Baptists. It moved to a house in Regent's Park in 1856, then set up in Oxford in 1927. In 1957 it became a Permanent Private Hall of the University.

The MAIN QUAD is largely of 1938–40 by *Thomas Harold Hughes* of the Glasgow School of Architecture (W side and N side), much engaged in Oxford. That applies to the N side and W end only, where the hall is. To Pusey Street the hall has its short side, five bays wide, with a three-bay centre with coupled giant pilasters and pediment, above a Gibbs doorcase – this for direct access when in use for lectures. Ashlar. Lower, two-storey S wing of 1966–8 along the street. Behind is the long narrow quad. The hall presides, its giant antae turning to Ionic pilasters in the middle bay. Attic storey above, with side ranges stepping up to meet it. The style close to early C19 French classicism. Across the E end a kind of pergola of pillars, behind which are the houses of St Giles'. The design published in 1958 encompassed the rebuilding of these, but a contextual rear addition was made instead, and not until 1985–7. It includes the facsimile rebuilding of the SE corner house, No. 56 St Giles' (now WHEELER ROBINSON HOUSE), reusing the old shopfront. The hall also expanded modestly N: the BALDING BLOCK, NE, 1961, and ANGUS HOUSE and GOULD HOUSE for married students, N and NW, straightforward brick, 1977. All the 1950s–80s designs are by the practice founded by T.H.'s daughter *Frances Heather Hughes*, i.e. *Hughes & Lomax*, then *Hughes Lomax & Adutt*. The PRINCIPAL'S LODGINGS are at No. 55 St Giles', of *c.* 1800 (p. 426).

WYCLIFFE HALL

Banbury Road

see North Oxford, p. 462

CENTRAL OXFORD

UNIVERSITY BUILDINGS

The University buildings are arranged as follows: first the old
centre around Broad Street and Catte Street, in chronological
sequence; then grouped clockwise, E and S, W and NW, N and NE.
For buildings outside the central area *see* pp. 453ff.

1. THE OLD CENTRE
around Broad Street and Catte Street

The area by the Radcliffe Camera and the Bodleian is unique in
the world, or, if that seems a hazardous statement, it is certainly
unparalleled at Cambridge. The Old Schools at Cambridge
shrink to insignificance compared with the Schools Quad; Great
St Mary is dull if one has just seen Oxford's St Mary; the Senate
House and the Old Library are fine, as good perhaps as the
Sheldonian, the Clarendon Building and the Old Ashmolean;
but it is the closeness and compactness, the absence of anything
merely a foil, that is true only of Oxford.

BODLEIAN LIBRARY
WITH DIVINITY SCHOOL AND CONVOCATION HOUSE
Catte Street and Radcliffe Square

The University's library is named from its benefactor Sir Thomas
Bodley, who in 1602 re-established the medieval foundation in
its original C15 home. That building always had a dual function,
serving also as the University's Divinity School or lecture room.
The ambitious early C17 additions likewise included both
library rooms and school rooms, as well as serving some of the
University's administrative, ceremonial and judicial functions.

Architecturally the results are more harmonious than this story may suggest, for the C17 took close account of the C15 work, combining classical novelties with motifs drawn from Oxford's wider medieval traditions.

Gifts of books to the University are recorded from the early C13. In 1320 Bishop Cobham of Worcester founded its first library, in the upper storey of the Congregation House added to St Mary's church (p. 384). In the late C15 the books were moved to the upper storey of a new building, also with a vaulted ground floor, but all to a much grander scale. This much-delayed C15 building survives as the main W arm of the present library, comprising the Divinity School below and Duke Humfrey's Library above. The name is from Humphrey, Duke of Gloucester (†1447), who presented important collections of classical manuscripts during his lifetime.

This library, however, was dispersed at the Reformation, and it was thanks to the energy and liberality of Sir Thomas Bodley (1545–1613) that a new library was got together and made usable. Bodley had been a Fellow of Merton, lecturer in Greek and Hebrew, and the Queen's Ambassador in the Netherlands in 1588–97. His library opened in 1602, with 2,000 books. Shortly after, in 1610–12, Bodley added a new cross-wing E of the C15 part. When he died in 1613 he had already prepared plans for more space, to be provided in a top storey at the new Schools Quadrangle which the University was about to build on to the E. This magnificent addition was externally complete by c. 1620. It replaced the patched-up Schools or lecture rooms of 1440, a long two-storey range which stood N–S, some way E of the Divinity School. The final instalment of Bodley's plan was a W cross-wing to balance his first addition. As achieved in 1634–7 this housed yet more library space above, and a Convocation House for the University below.

The library as originally conceived was thus entirely on the upper floors, as those of the colleges generally were. That changed as its holdings grew, swelled by donations and by copyright agreements requiring the free deposit of a copy of each new book. From the late C18 the Bodleian therefore progressively colonized the lower storeys of the Schools Quad, and the University built or found new lecture rooms and examination rooms elsewhere. In the 1860s the hitherto independent Radcliffe Library was annexed as the Radcliffe Camera (p. 341), after the scientific books had been sent to the new University Museum (*see* Radcliffe Science Library, p. 369). The C20 brought underground additions, and in 1936 a giant new building was begun N of Broad Street, now the Weston Library (p. 344), also with access by tunnel. Later growth has been managed by off-site storage, culminating in the depository built in Swindon in 2009–10.

Divinity School wing, with Proscholium and Convocation House

EXTERIOR. The DIVINITY SCHOOL WING is best seen externally from the N, where it faces the Sheldonian. In 1423 it was

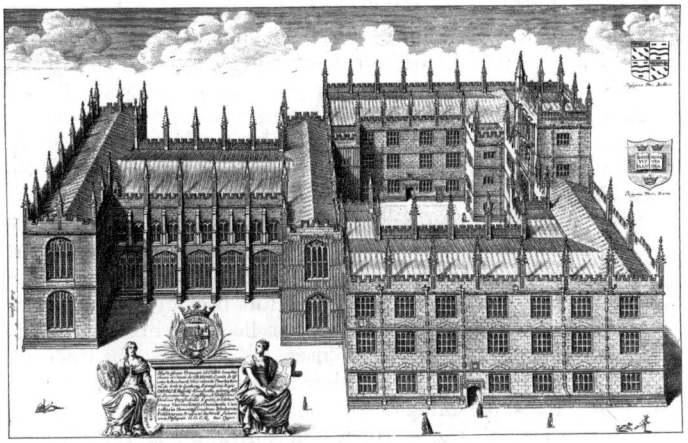

Divinity School and Bodleian Library.
Engraving by David Loggan, 1675

described as 'now begun'; in 1427 its walls were 'now rising';
and in 1430 the mason *Richard Winchcombe* is recorded as in
charge. Formerly in royal service, Winchcombe had already
rebuilt the chancel of Adderbury church (*see Oxfordshire: North
and West*), on behalf of New College. A legacy of 500 marks
came from Cardinal Beaufort in 1448, the building was first
roofed in 1458 (tree-ring date) and glazing was paid for in
1469–70. Bishop Kemp's gift of 1,000 marks over the years
1478–82 allowed the installation of the Divinity School vault,
and in 1485–6 the roof was reconstructed at a higher level. By
1488 books were at last being chained to the shelves.*

The building is a rectangle, five bays long. It has a base
frieze of quatrefoils, giant six-light windows with close panel
tracery under flattened and straight-sided arches, deep and
richly panelled buttresses, and twice as many upper, i.e. library,
windows, each transomed and of two lights. Above these a
large area of blank wall, apparently a legacy of the decision to
raise the roof higher in 1485–6. Then follows the usual string
with carvings, battlements and square pinnacles. The central
doorway is an insertion of 1669 (*William Byrd*, mason). That is
a remarkable date; for it is decidedly Gothick and looks with its
ogee gable and finial fifty years later. The design is attributed
to *Wren*, whose initials it bears (as 'CWA'), in connection with
his Sheldonian entrance to the N. Reused CI5 DOOR.

The W end originally had twin stair-turrets, giving access
to the library level. These were lost when the cross-wing was

---

*Some C20 commentators suggested that both the library storey and the vaulting
were afterthoughts; yet the deep buttresses and integral springer stones indicate that
a lower vault and a substantial upper storey must always have been intended.

built here, the second of the C17 projections to the E and W which give the building its H-shape. The eastern one houses the PROSCHOLIUM or vestibule of 1610–12, with the Bodleian's Arts End above (*see also* below). Much bare wall, divided by four elegant friezes of little pointed arches – the legacy of early refacing in which the original all-over panelling was not fully renewed. Two four-light windows in the N end, two in the S, with details taken from the C15 library windows. The rather bleak pointed-arched portal of the N arm to the W looks early C18. The WESTERN PROJECTION houses Convocation House and Chancellor's Court, with the Bodleian's Selden End above, and dates from 1634–7. Convocation previously met in St Mary's church, and the new facility reflects Archbishop Laud's drive to relocate such secular uses. It has four-light traceried windows to N and S too, but they are round-arched, and there are no friezes, panelling or side buttresses. Fine classical portal in the N arm to the E: rusticated surround, Doric pilasters, segmental pediment with garlands, and cartouche with Bodley's arms, carved by *James Partridge*. Only the DOOR has any Gothic touches.

Now back to the PROSCHOLIUM, this time to the E front, facing the Schools Quadrangle. As already noted, the range was built shortly before the quadrangle, and independently of it (the rest of the quad, and questions of authorship, must wait for now). The façade takes its cues from the old E front of the Divinity School, which partly survives inside, now of course hidden by the Proscholium. There are four tiers of high panels of narrow blank cusped arches, then a crenellated parapet with pinnacles in the C15 way. But the pinnacles have no buttresses in line with them, and so the single-minded panelling appears especially relentless across the flat front – even more so, no doubt, in the interval before the stair enclosures were added in front of each end.* Just one doorway, with leaf spandrels, and the most curious of gables: fancy in shape and fancy in decoration, with some Gothic and some post-Jacobean foliage, closer in spirit to the 1660s doorway or even Hawksmoor than to the 1610s. Above this doorway just one seven-light window, more strongly Gothic. It is probably of the same size as the lost E window of Duke Humfrey, of which Bodley wrote in 1612 to ask the dimensions. The tracery has an early C17 flavour, especially the squashed uppermost tracery light.

INTERIORS. Inside, the PROSCHOLIUM has a lierne vault of five bays with plenty of bosses. The pattern comes from the late C15 Fitzjames archway vault at Merton, Bodley's own college (p. 197). Strong transverse arches. The main E doorway from this side has a Gothic-panelled head, and wrought-iron doors of 1962, copied from those elsewhere in the quad. Also in 1962 two doorways were inserted for access to the stairs, thus allowing the Proscholium to double as the main library entrance.

---

*The inner walls of both enclosures preserve areas of panelling, with intact string-course carvings above.

The W doorway (to the Divinity School) is true C15 work, with little brackets and canopies for statuettes, and the original DOOR. Remains of stone panelling from the old W front to l. and r., in two planes.

The interior of the DIVINITY SCHOOL would be nothing without the vault of 1478–82, one of the marvels of Oxford. To speak of it, one has to start by describing the end walls. They each have three blank arches with straight shanks, and buttress-shafts between. The middle arch, with the doorway, is narrower and lower. The areas are panelled, and a sweeping four-centred super-arch goes over all three. For the vault is first of all a matter of four strong transverse arches plus these two wall arches. They begin as flying arches with open tracery above, then halfway up they have a pair of pendants each, and the whole vault with all its complicated ribs appears to issue from these pendants – which of course for structural reasons it can't. In fact the pendants are just bold arch voussoirs, and the vault is a lierne vault with its weight pressing on the arches, the outer walls and the buttresses. The vault is very much like a fan-vault, but it isn't, as the ribs are too prominent. So a lierne vault it ought to be called. As such, it looks back to the late C14 lierne-and-pendant vault at Christ Church Cathedral (*see* p. 123). *William Orchard*, master mason of Magdalen, was the executant – though not necessarily the originator, as he may simply have carried on with an older design. His initials appear five times among the 455 bosses of the vault. Others with monograms, a lion, a horse, a pelican, a wheatsheaf, vine and grapes, and so on. Major patrons are commemorated on the central boss of each bay (E to W): Bishop Kemp of London, Archbishop Kemp of Canterbury, Edward IV, Archbishop Bourchier of Canterbury, Chancellor Woodville.

In addition to the bosses there is much SCULPTURE, all under canopies: tiny statuettes within the pendants; larger ones of angels, clerics and bishops along the two wall arches, eight on each; groups over the end doorways with the Virgin and Christ Child with a book, and the Four Evangelists (W), the Virgin and St John with St Peter and St Paul below, and a gap for a missing rood at the top (E). These groups belong with the 1480s work, although some of the drapery folds are still rounded in the tradition of the early C15. Other draperies are in the succeeding and more angular manner.

One other detail should be noted. On the S side the buttresses lack panelling, and the window surrounds are much plainer, their lesser shafts represented only by abandoned or incomplete work low down. The change can be linked to the appointment of *Thomas Elkin* as the new chief mason in 1440. We know this because Elkin was ordered to adopt a plainer style, avoiding pointless enrichments ('supervacuam talem curiositatem dicti operis'), to which 'several magnates of the kingdom and other wise men' had taken objection. That may merely be a gloss on the necessity for economies, rather than part of the wider programme of aesthetic reform suggested by John Harvey. Either way, when funds arrived for a vault, economy went out of the window again.

Besides lecturing, the Divinity School was used for the academic disputations that preceded the practice of written exams. That explains the balustraded PLATFORMS of 1668–9, made by *William Cleer* and carved by *Richard Cleer*, both then also busy with the Sheldonian.

48,
p.32
The W doorway opens to the CONVOCATION HOUSE, in the cross-wing of 1634–7. It is lined with extremely fine PANEL-LING with pedimented arches with elementary perspective effects, just as at Oriel and Corpus, and also the 1630s pulpit at Balliol, and has BENCHES and STALLS with balls on the ends, again just as at Oriel and Corpus. The THRONE has the perspective motif on the backplate. Its hexagonal canopy is supported by two slim columns. *Thomas Richardson* was the joiner for all this. The doorway to the Chancellor's Court has a steep pediment with two badly carved reclining figures. Overhead is a stone fan-vault of big, somewhat thin forms, suggestive of C17 Gothic but actually installed in 1758–9 by *John Townesend III*. It replaced the earliest-known plaster vault in Oxford, and probably copies its form. At the same time the vault of the CHANCELLOR'S COURT ROOM or Apodyterium to the N appears to have been replaced. What date are the big pedimented stone doorcase, the panelling and the room's other fixtures? The 1630s are too early, the 1750s too late. Pete Smith suggests *Wren*'s hand here, *c.* 1670, and *William Cleer* as joiner.*
The room also served for robing, and for the weekly meetings of the Vice-Chancellor and heads of houses.

Bodleian Library and Schools Quad

The SCHOOLS QUADRANGLE, considering its date, 1613–*c.* 1620, is a formidable building and without parallel in the secular architecture of those years. As with the Proscholium wing the conception appears to have been Bodley's own, and his nominee Sir John Bennet was its principal fundraiser and overseer. While he lived, Bodley also worked closely with his friend Sir Henry Savile, Warden of Merton. Savile had lately brought in the Yorkshire masons *John Akroyd* and *John Bentley* to build Merton's new quad, after which they moved on to the Bodleian: first for the Proscholium, then for the rest. The carpenter at Merton, *Thomas Holt* of York, came with them, and ended by overseeing the final stages. The precedent of the Merton quad is especially clear in the Schools Quad, with its three-storey form and classical frontispiece. Bodley regarded Savile himself as having 'the judgment of a mason', though the artisans no doubt made their own contributions. Quadrangles of lecture rooms at Continental universities (Pisa, Padua, Bologna, Salamanca, Alcala de Henares, Wurzburg etc.) may also have been an influence on the basic form.

* *Georgian Group Journal* 18 (2010).

EXTERIOR. The building is to the outside an unrelieved block, very nearly square. Three storeys high, with widely spaced identical straight-headed four-light windows, formerly transomed, with cusped round arches in all the lights. The windows are thus Gothic in intention, and Gothic are the carvings of the top frieze, the battlements and the pinnacles. The last are again without accompanying buttresses; nor do chimneys appear, Bodley having prohibited the introduction of fire to his library. In the middle of the E side, again in the Oxford tradition, stands a tower, two more storeys high. The outer archway (with the original panelled DOOR), though round, has Perp mouldings. Spandrels decorated with strapwork and foliage. In the middle of the first and second floors is an oriel, mostly Gothic in detail, its windows with one transom below, two above. The top of the tower has a parapet with two tiers of Gothic piercings, not to any medieval pattern, and eight pinnacles. On the N and S sides there is no central tower, only a smaller doorway placed not quite in the middle.

The E archway has a one-bay lierne vault with big bosses displaying more post-medieval drapery than Jacobean strapwork, and a diamonded and studded exit-arch into the quad. One should on arrival turn back at once; for such a FRONTISPIECE 43 as this one will never see again. With five tiers it is the biggest of England's so-called towers of the orders, and that means the biggest anywhere. Such frontispieces are Italo-French Renaissance in origin, coming from France via Somerset House in the 1550s, then at Burghley House, Hatfield House – dated 1611 – and so on. Few have more than three tiers, but Savile's quad at Merton has four, and the new Wadham College had recently followed suit. Bodley's was carved at least in part by *Michael Bentley*, younger brother of John Bentley. It starts with a plain stage of coupled Tuscan columns. Next slim Roman Doric pairs, with a broad band of mixed strap and foliage motifs also round the pedestals of the columns. From here upwards the columns all have their lower two-fifths decorated. Six-light transomed window. Top frieze of strapwork and bucrania. Next stage Ionic columns with decorated plinths; six-light window with two transoms. Next stage Corinthian columns, and between them a big panel showing James I seated in a niche under a canopy which, taking in the niche, is round in plan, and to his l. Fame, to his r. the kneeling University. This is an early afterthought, done to commemorate the king's gift in 1620 of his own works in Latin, and carved originally by *John Clark*, son-in-law of John Akroyd. Above and reaching into the top stage three statuettes. Finally Composite columns with strapwork plinths and frieze, another six-light window and a big pierced strapwork cresting. The corners have thickly crocketed pinnacles except at the NW, where a big octagonal stair-turret, like that at Magdalen tower, throws the composition off-kilter.

That frontispiece is the one piece of display in the QUADRANGLE. The passages to N and S are small. They have big-leaf spandrels to the doorways and tierceron-star vaults. The walls of the E, N and S sides are treated like the exterior; only in the angles spacious square blocks project, and they have small three-light windows making it clear that these are for staircases. The W ones carry on the panelled finish of the Proscholium, the E ones are plain. For the rest, no distinction is made between the schools windows of the lower storeys and the gallery of Bodley's library above. Over the doorways in the staircase projections and in the walls between, the names of the SCHOOLS to which they originally gave access have been repainted: Logic, Astronomy, Rhetoric, Music, Natural Philosophy, Medicine, Jurisprudence (Law), Moral Philosophy, Grammar, History, Languages, Geometry, Arithmetic and Metaphysics.* Much renewal of stonework, in 1877–84 under *Sir T.G. Jackson* (Clipsham stone; tower and top storey especially), and more in 1959–68.

STATUE in the quad, close to the Proscholium entrance. The 3rd Earl of Pembroke, Chancellor of the University. Of bronze, attributed to *Le Sueur*, c.1630. It came from Wilton (Wilts.) in 1723. Placed here in 1951, with marble plinth and railings from its old setting in the upper gallery.

INTERIORS. Open-well STAIRCASES survive in the W enclosures only. They have spiral balusters, a form not current before c.1650, and one newel post has been tree-ring dated 1697. Their flights also cut across the heads of the first-floor doorways. So the original arrangement here must have been different. Bodley had proposed a grand library staircase within the W wing, for which the Oxford mason *Hugh Davies* made models from 1625 onwards, but that wing was shortly built without one.

The LOWER READING ROOM comprises the partially knocked-through schools in the middle storey. Its present panelling, fittings and plain concrete-and-steel floors belong to *Sir Hubert Worthington*'s post-war renovations. He had begun in 1940–1 with the former CURATORS' ROOM on the ground floor to the SE (now shop; some reused C17 panelling), and finished in 1955. The UPPER READING ROOM preserves the sober panelled ceiling installed by *Sir Robert Smirke* in 1830–1. The space here is continuous (tower arches excepted), much like the long galleries of great houses of Bodley's time, and it was indeed first used for the display of pictures and artefacts. The painted FRIEZE dates from 1618–19 and is by *Thomas Knight*. It comprises 202 portraits of authors, Aquinas and Wyclif, Huss and Luther among them, with emblems etc. between. Late C16 engravings provided the sources. The painting is very basic, and includes much restoration and gap-filling by *Clive Rouse* and assistants, 1950–4, after the frieze was rediscovered. Worthington also exposed the early C17 painted ceiling in the tower space. Roundels and small panels of late

---

*The Seven Liberal Arts, it will be remembered, were the Trivium of Grammar, Rhetoric and Logic, and the Quadrivium of Arithmetic, Geometry, Music and Astronomy.

C16 and C17 STAINED GLASS in all the windows, and in the tower room of the floor below. On the debit side, Worthington destroyed *Thomas Roberts*'s pretty plasterwork of 1753 around the tower arches, saving only the Rococo ceiling centrepiece, now remade in the upper Archives Room in the tower.*

The western library rooms are preserved closer to their historic condition. ARTS END, of 1610–12, has galleries along the W and E sides, the earliest English example of wall-shelving as against stall-shelving. The ultimate source is the library at the Escorial (1584). The galleries rest on thin columns, and have thin colonnettes for their fronts and also for the benches below, which face towards the bookshelves. *John Bolton* and *William Bennett* were the joiners. Two open staircases in timber cages on the W side, copies made in 1919 after the arrangement shown in Loggan's engraving. Top frieze of stone with carvings in a consciously late medieval manner. The roof compartments have repetitive painting of the University coat of arms by *William Davies*, and the shallow-pitched trusses have decorative painting.

DUKE HUMFREY'S LIBRARY opens to the W by a big arch. On it are two BUSTS, on the l. Bodley, given 1605, on the r. Charles I (by *Le Sueur*), given 1636. The comparison repays. Bodley is stone, Charles bronze; Bodley is in an arched niche, Charles in an oval recess with garlands, carved in 1641 by *John Jackson*. That is the change within four decades. Roof with major kingpost trusses on mostly C15 corbels. Much of its fabric is still that of 1458, but the arch braces and wall-posts are chiefly from the heightening of 1485–6. Of that date also the secondary trusses inserted between. The ceiling panels and moulded secondary rafters belong to Bodley's renovation (tree-ring dates 1598), and the painted University arms and other painted decoration are as in Arts End. The BOOKCASES are Bodley's too, though somewhat restored in the 1870s, and now without the original arrangement of closets etc. in the end bays. The system of lofty stalls was taken over from Savile's recent installation at Merton library. Chairs replaced bench seating in 1756.

At the far exit archway are two more ambitious pieces of woodwork with classical details that may belong with SELDEN END itself, i.e. of 1634–7. Named for the jurist and orientalist John Selden, a benefactor of the library, who died in 1654. Here the balconies are on stronger-looking columns (in fact, hollow drums) carrying elliptical arches, and the gallery balusters are of dumb-bell shape. The joiner was *Thomas Richardson*. Most of the present woodwork actually dates from the restorations of 1960–3 by *Robert Potter*, who also contrived the four discreet gallery staircases. Those on the W side fill the embrasures of two big windows that were walled up in

*Also discarded was the unique tower floor, composed of a self-supporting lattice of short timbers after a pattern from Serlio. It also featured plain plastered corner quadrants shaped like fan-vaults, a peculiarly English touch.

1753. Potter replaced the failing floors throughout the w parts with an H-frame installation of concrete and steel, extending into the buttress cores (engineer *E.W.H. Gifford*).* Compartmented timber ceiling, flat this time. Its fifty-two painted panels with strapwork surrounds were brought from the Old Library at Christ Church (p.134). In the end windows roundels of mostly Flemish and German C16–C17 STAINED GLASS; in the w window mostly English glass, including two excellent C15 panels (Louis of France greeting Thomas Becket, and The Penance of Henry II).

A BOOK STORE was excavated below Radcliffe Square in 1909–12, after designs by *Edmund Woodthorpe*. Its iron-framed sliding bookcases were supplied by *Lucy*'s ironworks (cf. those specified by Gladstone for his library at Hawarden, Flintshire). Converted in 2010–11 as the GLADSTONE LINK, with access by the original tunnel from both the Bodleian and the Radcliffe Camera.

SHELDONIAN THEATRE
Broad Street

2   The Sheldonian is *Wren*'s second work of architecture. It dates from 1664–9, just a little later than his chapel at Pembroke College, Cambridge. Wren's master mason was *Thomas Robinson*, with *William Byrd* as chief stone carver. The proposal to erect a new home for the University ceremonies then held at St Mary's church originated before the Civil War, in Laud's time. Laud wanted to build it roughly where the Radcliffe Camera now stands. The idea was resurrected in 1663 by Lord Clarendon as the incoming Chancellor, and paid for by his successor, Archbishop Sheldon, who gave the necessary £14,470. In 1636–48 Sheldon had been Warden of All Souls, where Wren was later a Fellow. As the son of a dean and nephew of a bishop, Wren also had many other connections with both chancellors through Royalist-clerical circles. Moreover, in 1664 he was already Savilian Professor of Astronomy and a Fellow of the Royal Society, with an outstanding reputation for mathematics and geometry.

The plan is an elongated D-shape, with the main façade and ceremonial entrance towards the Divinity School and its inserted doorway, s (p.329). The façade is classical of course, as no previous Oxford building had been, so for Oxford it may be called revolutionary; but nationally speaking this has nothing of the purity of Inigo Jones's masterpieces. In fact it is, as a beginner's job, just a little confused, and poorly related to the sides. Seven bays, two storeys. The middle three bays emphasized by engaged Corinthian columns below, as against

---

*Duke Humfrey's floor had already been raised in 1876, by the engineer *Douglas Galton*. Potter also removed extensions to the s buttresses added when *Wren* strengthened the fabric in 1701–2.

the pilasters to each side, and by Composite pilasters above. Pediment over the centre with garlands in the frieze below, and the never wholly satisfactory motif of half-pediments over the sides. Arched lower windows, and in the outer bays shell niches, where the staircases are. The upper windows are of two lights, mullioned, and are divided by a subsidiary order of short broad pilasters which interpenetrate with the pilasters. In the upper window heads and next to the scrolls that terminate the half-pediments is odd fish-scale-like decoration, an imitation of Roman *opus incertum* technique. Much small-scale carving of the entablatures.

The sides and back are plainer. They abjure a fully expressed order in favour of superimposed piers: broad ones arranged in an arcade of channelled rustication on the high ground floor, shorter ones above like those of the s façade, with the same two-light windows. Fenestration of the ground floor is limited to glazed lunettes and curiously narrow lights within the blank infilling of the arcade. Basement windows below, where the University Press was housed (the roof-space served as its book warehouse). The N end is not curved, but is taken round in nine facets; the only true curves in the entire plan are within the staircase enclosures. Balustrade all round. Wren's roof had big oval dormers, omitted from *George Saunders*'s replacement of 1801–2. The lantern is of 1837–8, by *Blore*, well detailed but larger than the original. Other changes date from refacing and renovation in 1958–61 under *W. Godfrey Allen*. Windows of C17 type, including a version of Wren's ingenious tilting circular panels within the lunettes, replaced the sashes which *Henry Keene* introduced in 1767–8. The splendid carving over the N doorway was also re-created (by *E. S. Frith* and *E. J. & A. T. Bradford*).* This comprises a slightly concave recess with broad trophies l. and r. Big garlands and a cartouche above. The doorway itself has a straight cornice on console brackets and a bay-garland frieze.

There were no obvious precedents for such a building, and Wren freely mixed motifs ancient and modern with his own invention. The s façade's half-pediments recall the Basilica of Maxentius as reconstructed by Palladio. The blind arcading on the sides may evoke Roman theatre loggias, but its detailed form is markedly French; see especially the pavilions of the Château de Vaux-le-Vicomte by Louis Le Vau (1657–61). A general comparison in Wren's grandson's memoir *Parentalia* (1750) to the Theatre of Marcellus in Rome refers not to the executed building but to a costlier preliminary version. This may correspond to a surviving drawn plan by Wren for a building with a full theatrical stage and an outlandish oval-polygonal auditorium. As executed, the Sheldonian is closer to C16–C17

---

*Destroyed when a niche was inserted in 1735 for a statue of Charles II, by *Sir Henry Cheere*. This is now stored in the basement, with other STATUES by Cheere (Sheldon and the Duke of Ormonde) from niches in the s front.

Sheldonian Theatre, interior.
Engraving by J. Skelton after J. Buckler, 1820

court theatres, with the characteristic curved end and elonga-
tion of the sides of the 'D'.

The INTERIOR is treated as one large hall with tiered seating
below and in a gallery. The gallery rests on wooden Composite columns, and continues across the s wall where one might
expect the stage to be. Within the 'D' the tiered seats come
right down to floor level. In the centre here is the CHANCEL-
LOR'S THRONE with its winged sphinxes; over the side doors
are the rostral boxes for the Proctors, carved with bundles of
fasces in the mouths of lion masks. Excellent joinery by *William
Cleer*, carved by his brother *Richard Cleer*. Redecoration in
2010 reinstated the C17 colour scheme of stone-grey plinth,
cedar-brown seating, white gallery fronts and purple ('rance')
column shafts. ORGAN CASE of 1876–7 designed by *Sir T. G.
Jackson* in the revived late C17 style, and carved by *Farmer
& Brindley*. Side sections removed 1963. Other C20 changes
include a concrete floor of 1958–61, and steel reinforcement
of the galleries by *R. Fielding Dodd*, 1937.

The CEILING is painted too, an ambitious scheme of
Baroque illusionism by *Robert Streeter* or *Streater*, the king's
Serjeant-Painter. Streeter's reach was greater than his grasp
– James II regretted that Verrio had not done it instead, and
even Verrio was not a master of the first rank – but the ceiling
nonetheless remains one of the grandest English exercises of
its kind. The subject is the Triumph of the Arts and Sciences
(including Architecture) over Envy, Rapine and Ignorance;
the composition is an illusionistic ring of figures in a dark
cloudscape, identified by Anthony Geraghty as deriving from
the masque designs of Charles I's court. Cherubs push back

curtains around the edges, a playful reference to the rope-like divisions of gilded wood that are intended to simulate the *velarium* of a Roman open-air theatre. But what most impressed contemporaries was Wren's roof construction above, which was lost in the 1830s work. It spanned some 70 ft by 80 ft (21.4 by 24.4 metres) without intermediate support, achieved by means of trusses spliced or scarfed together both lengthways and vertically, and reinforced with iron plates and bolts.

The N semicircle of the building is repeated by the SCREEN WALL with its famous 'termaines' of uncouth Imperial heads on the piers. These are by *Michael Black* and of 1969–72, replacing decayed heads of 1867–8 by *Edwin Gardiner* of Oxford, successors in turn to *Byrd*'s heads of 1666–9.* The source is again Vaux-le-Vicomte. The side walls were truncated when the Old Ashmolean and Clarendon Building went up, but a part remains S of the former (the archway an 1860s insertion). Originally the wall displayed Roman inscriptions and reliefs, mostly from the Arundel collection.

OLD ASHMOLEAN MUSEUM
(HISTORY OF SCIENCE MUSEUM)
Broad Street

Built in 1679–83 by the Oxford master mason *Thomas Wood* (styled '*T. Wood Archt.*' on a contemporary engraving). Combining the functions of museum, University lecture room and laboratory, it fulfilled for the first time the aspirations in scientifically inclined English circles to raise an institution dedicated to research and instruction. Wood's model may well have been an unexecuted design of 1668 by *Wren*, known from descriptions, for a home for the Royal Society in London.

The building is very different from the Sheldonian next door, less learned and with display fronts only to the N and E. The N front is of five close-set bays, with a top balustrade and cross-windows on both upper floors. They have hollow-moulded surrounds and alternating triangular and segmental pediments, and are linked vertically by shallow projections (cf. New College, Garden Quad). The doorway has its segmental pediment on consoles, and a display of fine ornament in the mouldings. But the ceremonial entrance is from the Sheldonian side. In this short side there are no side windows, only a large portal with pairs of Corinthian columns and a segmental pediment of which the middle part of the base jumps back. The doorway itself has an open scrolly pediment. A cross-window flanked by tall panels of fat festoons above. At parapet level a triangular pediment. Carving, much renewed by *E. S. Frith* in

---

*The sequence was continued in the 1680s in front of the Old Ashmolean (these first replaced 1875). Deposed Emperors may be found in some Oxford gardens, *see* e.g. Worcester College, p.322.

1959–61, again both delicate and abundant. Along the N side the Emperors' heads of the Sheldonian palisade are carried on.

The N entrance is up a steep staircase, with side flights down to the basement. This is *W. Godfrey Allen*'s re-creation of 1957–8, the old one having been removed in alterations of 1863–4 by *Buckeridge*. Entry is made directly into the old lecture room, as remodelled by *Underwood* in 1833 with two rows of Greek Ionic columns on the long axis. Ahead is the staircase, a big open-well example with turned balusters, filling most of the rear projection. Commemorative stained glass by *Powells*, 1927 etc. The descending flights are *Buckeridge*'s matching work, cutting through a C17 vault. The smooth plain barrel-vault of the basement room remains intact. It served as both laboratory and anatomy theatre originally. Across the E end some pedimented BOOKCASES of 1746, displaced from the Upper Reading Room of the Bodleian. The top-floor room housed the museum, including the collection presented to the University by Elias Ashmole in 1677, on condition that a new building should be provided to house it. Most of these specimens and artefacts he had taken over from that odd and mysterious character John Tradescant Jun., gardener to Charles I, and son of the original collector. The elder Tradescant had travelled as far as Arkhangelsk and Algiers, always on the lookout for plants, coins, costumes and other curiosa.

The present designation of the museum dates from between the wars. In 1999–2000 the building was restored by *TPS Dangerfield*. New auxiliary rooms were tucked beneath the front pavement, showing as glass-brick-fronted projections in the basement area.

CLARENDON BUILDING
Broad Street

The Clarendon Building was erected as the new home of the University Press in 1712–15, partly from the proceeds of the publication in 1702–4 of Lord Clarendon's *History of the Great Rebellion*. The designer was *Hawksmoor*, in consultation with *Dr George Clarke*, with *William Townesend* as mason, and the building shows Hawksmoor's grave but unfettered imagination throughout. The N side has in the middle a far-projecting portico of four giant Doric columns, of unorthodox slim proportions, with a wider interstice in the middle and three-quarter columns to meet the wall. There are two main storeys, but they are placed on a high basement. So one reaches the portico six steps up, and steps then continue between the column pedestals – another unorthodox touch. The windows in the three bays each side are segment-headed and set deeply in broad, flat, projecting bands, instead of the luxuriance of any moulding. Just one upper window on each side has a key block and an intersecting architrave, of wholly original form. In the first and third bays of these side sections the windows are placed within a recess set back a little behind the smooth front surface, an effect which Hawksmoor anticipated by a year or two at Queen's College. Only in the middle, behind the portico, are the openings round-arched. The S side is the same, except that the portico here has engaged columns and a different configuration of niches between. Pediments also across the short sides, each with the same unmoulded half-round opening as in the main porticoes. On these sides it is the central bay which is recessed. The cornice continues all round, the attic storey showing as little windows between its triglyphs. The skyline is finished by pedestals and lead STATUES of the Nine Muses, designed by *Sir James Thornhill* (two are replacements of 1974 by *Richard Kindersley*). In the niche on the W side also a lead STATUE of Clarendon by *Francis Bird*, 1721. Originally over the S archway, where its former niche now has a concave window made in 1933. The arched passage below runs through from S to N, on axis with the Schools Quad, with side recesses that cut powerfully into the barrel-vault. Outstanding wrought-iron GATES by *Richard Booth* at the N end. The two sides were for the 'Bible press' and the 'learned press', each with its own staircase.

One noble INTERIOR, to the SW, still the meeting room of the Delegates of the Press. Panelling with fluted Corinthian pilasters, and arches between (*Thomas Minn*, joiner). BUSTS of Laud and Clarendon by *Sir Henry Cheere*. Entry through a memorable doorcase with huge triglyphs in lieu of capitals. The Press otherwise moved out in 1830. *Sir Robert Smirke* then fitted up the interiors for other University uses. Original small twin STAIRCASES with twisted balusters, behind the side bays of the N portico.

As at the Sheldonian, the SETTING received considerable care. Railings (of Swedish iron, with foundry stamps) run round the W, N and E sides, between sturdy stone piers with doubled cornices. The GATE into the precinct from Catte Street, E (much restored 1925) has an ornamental overthrow. Answering gates and railings to the W, i.e. in front of the Sheldonian, were removed in the C20.

RADCLIFFE CAMERA
Radcliffe Square

Dr John Radcliffe, sometime Fellow of Lincoln College, was the most successful physician of the late Stuart years. On his death in 1714 he left most of his fortune to Oxford, including £40,000 for a new library. In the event this money became available only in 1736, by which time several proposals had come and gone. *Hawksmoor* made multiple schemes in the 1710s, and in 1720 he was one of the eminent architects approached for ideas (with Wren, Vanbrugh, Hawksmoor, Gibbs, Archer, John James and Thornhill). Hawksmoor's is the idea of a rotunda, but his was to stand further N, either as an attachment to the Selden End of the

Bodleian – with Exeter College having use of the ground storey – or against the s side of the Schools Quad. A model for the latter site is preserved, made in 1734–5, when a start seemed imminent. It features a square base, with quadrant corners. Around the same time fees were also paid to *James Gibbs*, who supplied a rectangular design that owed something to Wren's library at Trinity College, Cambridge. After Hawksmoor's death in 1736 the younger man was appointed. He then adopted the concept of a rotunda, but of a more urbane and Italianate treatment than Hawksmoor's hyper-rusticated version. A precedent for a round library interior existed at Wolfenbüttel (1705–10, dem.), and Wren too had toyed with the idea for Cambridge.

The site having been cleared of houses, the building was begun in 1737 and opened in 1749. Significant changes were made in the early stages. Columns replaced the giant pilasters shown in the first engraved version, and the dome, which was meant to be all of stone, was instead built of timber sheathed with lead. (The stone model that was made for the stone dome can be seen at St Giles' House, p. 429.) The ground floor is rusticated; smooth, wide-jointed blocks of Headington hardstone. There are eight large arched and pedimented bays all originally open – till 1863–4 – and eight intermediate bays with niches. The flight of steps and inserted N doorway are of 1863–4 too (by *Sydney Smirke*). Originally one went in by the great arches. These were made secure by the handsome grilles and gates, made by *Robert Bakewell*. The upper floor has coupled Corinthian columns, and the bays now alternate between windows and niches. Both are in two tiers. The large windows above have pediments, echoing the bigger pediments below, the small ones below have lugs top and bottom. The lugged form is repeated in the bays with the niches, which also have swags at the level of the capitals. Top with balustrade and urns, and then the drum and the dome, the chief distinctive mark of the Oxford skyline. The drum has segment-headed windows between plain buttress-piers, with more urns on top. The dome is more elongated than that of St Paul's, i.e. rather of the St Peter's type. Pronounced ribs; small domed lantern.

Gibbs's MASONS were of two great dynasties: *Francis Smith* of Warwick, succeeded in 1738 by his son *William Smith*; and *William Townesend*, succeeded in 1739 by his son *John Townesend II*, who probably supplied the capitals and swags, and latterly by *John Townesend III*. The carved swags remain externally, but the partial refacing and renewals of 1965–8 have replaced the C18 capitals and main cornice.*

Entry is now from the S, to the LOWER READING ROOM. Finishes all of stone: central saucer-dome with a pattern of moderately decorated compartments, surrounding bays with

---

*Architect *W. Godfrey Allen*, with *A. Llewellyn Smith*; capitals carved by *E.J. & A.T. Bradford*, other carving by *Michael Groser*. Earlier stonework repairs of 1886 by *Waterhouse*, who also strengthened the main floor in 1877.

smaller saucer-domes of three different designs, big piers with deeply coved arches. Ahead, N, is a big pedimented door-case with Doric columns, for the STAIRCASE. This makes two complete revolutions in its oval well, which continues to full height overhead. Wrought-iron handrail, with thickly ornamental detail, by *Thomas Wagg*.

The UPPER READING ROOM is magnificent. It too has eight stone piers, here with attached twin Ionic pilasters, and they carry fully expressed arches. The decoration is stone-carved, except in the dome, where it is stucco. Splendid cartouches in the arch spandrels. Ornate frieze with metopes and console brackets. Hanging garlands between the drum windows. A gallery runs all the way round, halfway up the piers. The dome has hexagonal coffering between the ribs, and a little prettifying decoration. The chief plasterers were *Joseph Artari* and *Charles Stanley*, one Italian, the other Danish, and both among the best in England. Stanley worked with *Thomas Roberts* of Oxford, as good as any; their share includes the staircase ceiling and the gallery underside. The London carpenter *John Phillips* constructed the dome, and supplied some of the joinery and the mahogany FURNITURE, jointly with *William Linnell*. Central desk by *Worthington*, 1935. The original way up to the gallery was by two discreet spiral stairs, next to the main stair. STATUE of Radcliffe by *Rysbrack*, 1745–7 (cost £220), in the pedimented niche above the entrance. Outside the staircase doorway a BUST of Gibbs also by *Rysbrack*, wigless in the Roman manner. 1726; given 1845.

Radcliffe's foundation was separate from that of the Bodleian, and the building's precise purpose was at first uncertain. Only in 1863 was it adopted as a reading room for the Bodleian. The scientific books went to the University Museum: the genesis of the present Radcliffe Science Library.

The SETTING realized aspirations for an open space between the Bodleian and St Mary's that went back to Laud and the 1630s. The Camera was originally set about with obelisks topped by lamps, then from 1828 by railings, removed in 1936. The present RAILINGS date from 1993.

OXFORD MARTIN SCHOOL (former INDIAN INSTITUTE)
Broad Street and Holywell Street

The Indian Institute was the brainchild of Sir Monier Monier-Williams, the Professor of Sanskrit. It was built in 1882–4 (N part) and 1895–6 (s part of Broad Street front), to a single design by *Basil Champneys*. The aim was to promote understanding of India, including among students destined for the Indian Civil Service. But Champneys's building is in a mixed C17 style, its mission signalled only in a few details, such as the elephant weathercock with a howdah and some carved animal heads on the rounded corner stair-turret. With its cupola, this makes an excellent *point-de-vue* at the E end of Broad Street. Detached columns and projecting pieces of entablature below the cap, and originally also a ring of finials. Below, some decoration in a kind of Cornelis Floris style, but with Indian faces to the herms. Along the w side s of the tower five bays with oriels rounded in plan and bulgy in outline, each originally with strapwork above. Other decoration with late-C17-inspired cartouches. Taynton stone. The carver was *William Aumonier*. Raw brick behind. The original arrangement had a double-height library on the first floor, with a larger museum behind, both with galleries high up. Groin-vaulted corridors. Mostly mixed C17 details, but the stair balustrade of wrought iron and of C18 form.

After 1968 the building served the History Faculty. Adapted in 2013 by *Berman Guedes Stretton* for the Martin School, a new foundation which addresses cross-disciplinary problems in the contemporary world. Regrettable plate-glass doors to Broad Street.

WESTON LIBRARY
(NEW BODLEIAN LIBRARY)
Broad Street and Parks Road

Built in 1936–40 as the Bodleian's overspill library, to designs by *Sir Giles Gilbert Scott*, his grandest Oxford work. Reconstructed internally by *Wilkinson Eyre*, 2010–15, with an emphasis on reading rooms, exhibition spaces and public access over on-site storage of books.

For Pevsner in 1974, Scott's building was 'neither in an Oxford tradition nor modern for its date…It is not Neo-Georgian by any means, yet it seems undecided how far the safe anchorage in history might be loosened.' Yet the use of rough-faced squared Bladon rubble stone (as Baker had introduced it to Oxford at Rhodes House, p. 379), combined with classically detailed portals and small ashlared areas, puts the library in the mainstream of 1930s Oxford architecture – for all that this *via media* soon came to look like a dead end. The library also suffers by comparison with Scott's University Library at Cambridge (1931–4; likewise made possible by funds from the Rockefeller Foundation), with its compelling axial sequence of circulation spaces and reading rooms. By contrast, Oxford's was conceived largely for bulk shelving, with a mass of artificially lit stacks at its core – a plan-type taken from recent US designs such as the Library of Congress Annex or the Sterling Memorial Library at Yale.* Only on the N side was a spacious reading room provided. A tunnel mechanism carried books back and forth to the old Bodleian.

The plan is near-square. Three storeys, to respect the height of the surrounding buildings. The third storey slightly recessed. Behind, placed in such a position that it appears only from the SE and at some distance, is the slit-windowed former stack

---

* *See* David Frazer Lewis in *Bodleian Library Record* 29 (2015). Also removed in the renovation was the Reading Room of the Indian Institute Library by *Robert Potter*, added to the rooftop in 1966–8.

block, which is quite considerably higher. Short projecting W wing to Broad Street, with the service entrance. At the E end two rounded corners, and between them a ceremonial doorcase with Bodley's bust, placed on the same axis as the passages through the Clarendon Building and Bodleian proper. Upright main windows with stepped jambs and aluminium-alloy glazing bars. Along the Broad Street front a colonnade of square piers, now opened up as an entrance loggia with glazing behind. Originally it was part-blind, and was preceded by an equally forbidding raised terrace, now replaced by steps. This setting back was Scott's way of making a more formal setting for the Clarendon Building. Cartouches above the colonnade (carvers *H.H. Martyn & Co.*). Readers' doorway on Parks Road, also in C17 classical style.

The chief interior of *Wilkinson Eyre*'s renovation is the BLACKWELL HALL, a sort of indoor agora, made possible by the banishment of the Scott stacks. An impressive space, combining complexity with invitation. Polished floor; pale surfaces; partial top lighting. Café and shop are placed to the W, exhibition galleries and lecture theatre open off to the N. A glass-fronted gallery runs round at first-floor level, continuing as glazed bridges on the E and W sides where the main space runs through, with books nicely illuminated on its back wall. The enclosing walls are punctuated by little study-oriels of playfully varied angle and form, opening off the other concourses. Above the gallery level a slatted volume projects into the space, comprising the lower part of a new concrete-box structure which rises through several floors (*Pell Frischmann*, engineers). Its full extent is visible to the N, where a tapering void runs right up within the old upper stack wall.

One older feature marks the readers' entrance, though it has nothing much to do with Bodley or indeed with Oxford: an early C17 GATEWAY of stone, with strapwork cresting and C18 ironwork tympanum, from Ascott Park, Stadhampton (q.v.).

The top floor of the stack now houses the DAVID READING ROOM. *Scott*'s first-floor reading room survives as the RARE BOOKS READING ROOM, with its ceiling of different woods. The 1930s finishes in the eastern corridors and staircase have also been restored.

2. EAST AND SOUTH

EXAMINATION SCHOOLS
and RUSKIN SCHOOL OF ART
High Street and Merton Street

The EXAMINATION SCHOOLS of 1877–82 are *T.G. Jackson*'s [98] most noteworthy building in Oxford, because they are his first and because they are such a passionate challenge to what Oxford University architecture had been in the hands of Butterfield,

Scott, Waterhouse and the others. Here was a mature man of supreme confidence handling with undeniable panache a style no longer Gothic or Tudor but licentiously fabricated out of elements from the Quattrocento to the mid C17, with the main stress on the impure classical of the late C16 and early C17. He won the job in 1876, in competition with Neo-Gothic designs from *Bodley*, *Champneys*, *T.N. Deane* and *John Oldrid Scott* – the third such competition, after two earlier goes failed to produce an acceptable design.* That meant being in charge of the largest job of these years of large jobs – the final cost was around £180,000 – and being at once allowed into the limelight of the High Street. It also established him as the favoured architect of the University's progressive party, for whom examinations were central to the wider mission of reform.

The Examination Schools can show at once fully fledged Jackson's way of mixing. His *Recollections* tell how he was led by 'the haunting vision of Elizabethan and Jacobean work, and especially of those long mullioned-and-transomed windows at Kirby Hall', and how he adopted it because he found it 'more elastic' than Gothic or classical. 'It seemed to me', he continued, 'that it was possible to refine the English Renaissance by avoiding its eccentricities, retaining the Gothic feeling which gave it life, and instead of imitating the gross ornamentation to which it was prone, looking rather for example to the lovely decorative work of the early or Bramantesque Renaissance in Italy.'

98 After reading all this the façade to the High remains a shock. Five bays of monumental scale, the middle one with a deep porch with the Venetian-window motif for the entrance and a very elaborate louvre-like turret on the roof ridge behind. To l. and r. one huge six-light window with three transoms, the tops of the lights elliptical-arched. The end bays with windows the same, but divided by blank or carved panels to indicate floors. For the two windows l. and r. of the porch indeed light one room of huge height. What is it? The GREAT HALL, the *salle des pas perdus*; and there the roof is a complex arch-braced affair suggestive of old English hammerbeams, but the walls have a free Italian Renaissance character, hard to describe. Thus the facing wall has deep coffered and depressed arches, projected forward on huge brackets below an upper gallery; the end walls have a blank architecture high up of large columns, arches and, above the higher middle arch, a pediment. *Mazzioli* of Paris provided the floor's mosaic panels.

So much for the overture, for the opera itself takes place in a QUAD open to Merton Street, round the corner to the E, but

* *Street* and *Deane* were invited to compete in 1867. After two years' delay Deane was declared the victor, but was asked to redraft his design. His new versions were then rejected, and a re-run ordered in 1873, now pitting Deane against *Blomfield*, *Waterhouse* and *John Oldrid Scott*. Scott was chosen, but Convocation promptly rejected his design too. In the third and final contest, Jackson and Champneys were enlisted only after Norman Shaw and E.M. Barry had declined the invitation to compete (William Whyte, *Oxford Jackson* (2006)).

closed there by gates and gatepiers of 1888. The climax here is a tower-of-the-orders frontispiece in the Oxford tradition but detailed as none had been detailed before. Especially the top stage is the least disciplined design of Jackson's. The windows all round are again transomed, and the larger, upper ones have arched lights. But the frieze above them is heavy with garlands *à la* Wren's time. The ends of the two wings, which project by seven bays, have a six-light window each with a pediment, and in the big gable a tiny Venetian window. Wherever has one seen such impudence or such courage?

What an image of examination such a building creates: the puny candidates and the Moloch of the testing machinery. Still, something of this is what those who chose Jackson's design must have wanted to convey.

The building also owes much to its fine craftsmanship and materials, within and without. Jackson specified Clipsham ashlar from Rutland, its first use in Oxford for a new building. The contractor was *Albert Estcourt* of Gloucester. Much carving by Messrs *Farmer & Brindley*, including the putti holding shields of the colleges around the quad, two little reliefs in modern dress on the High Street porch (done by *Pomeroy* and *Jenkins*), and the Liberal Arts as represented in the arcade brackets of the Great Hall, the last added in 1906–9. The same firm did the marblework of the circulation spaces, including the monolithic columns of the NE and NW lobbies (Breccia and Cipollino respectively), where the CORRIDOR awkwardly changes direction twice around the three wings. On the inner side are the smaller rooms, for *viva voce* examinations. But then on the outer W side is the STAIRCASE, with a pierced balustrade of alabaster and marble, somewhat like early Italian *cancelli*. It rises in two flights to a sumptuous LANDING with columned and arcaded walls of coloured marbles, both under coved ceilings of red and green chequerwork, inspired by that of San Zeno in Verona. The larger rooms, for written exams, open off it; no corridors on this floor. The NORTH SCHOOL turns out to be huge. It is L-shaped and fills half the W range and most of the N range. The SOUTH SCHOOL is T-shaped. It fills proportionately less of the S range, so as to allow for a second STAIRCASE (concrete barrel-vault, plasterwork decoration) and its landing, and the EAST SCHOOL beyond, of four windows' length. All three schools have coved ceilings with the beams showing and plaster panels between them, those of the North School with big animal reliefs. Many FIREPLACES with tiled insets, several by *De Morgan*; big electric CLOCKS in every room, an early use. Altogether the state of preservation is extraordinary, enhanced by a return to some of Jackson's colour schemes since 2012.

The THRONE in the North School is a genuine piece of *c.* 1700, origin unknown, with squared Composite pilasters supporting columns supporting an open pediment. Its TESTER, an elongated octagon, is from the former throne of the refurnishing of 1668–9 at the Divinity School (*see* p. 332). On its underside a painted glory in the style of *Streeter* (cf. Sheldonian, p. 338). In the South School, THRONE with columns and a canopy, also looking *c.* 1700; said to come from St Mary's church, i.e. the former Vice-Chancellor's throne there.

RUSKIN SCHOOL. The huge Exam Schools are not all that *Jackson* did. In 1886–7 at the corner of Merton Street and the High, a building for the SOCIETY OF NON-COLLEGIATE STUDENTS was added (*see* St Catherine's College, p. 251; later the Registry; since 1975 the RUSKIN SCHOOL OF ART). This is quieter, and largely of squared rubble instead of ashlar, but just as original as its neighbour. Two storeys, with three gables and beneath them just three upper windows of two main lights with a bit of 'debased' Perp panel tracery, i.e. the kind of tracery a learned man like Jackson could find in country churches of the C17. The windows are pedimented, and their lower lights are surrounded by panelling which covers this whole floor. The ground floor has none of it. Here is an Elizabethan doorway, quite small, and a top frieze of naturalistic foliage with little beasts and birds. At the SE corner a polygonal oriel juts out. In the S wall an Oxford-1630 tracery window, i.e. uncusped ovoid shapes.

Finally, in 1895–7 Jackson provided a long, narrow building for the LOCAL EXAMINATION DELEGACY on the S side, end-on to Merton Street (No. 12 there), with a shaped gable, attached pilasters, and a bow on the first floor. Toothed masonry shows that an E continuation was intended. The addition joins on awkwardly next to the arcaded SOUTH PORCH of Jackson's Schools – but lucid planning was never his forte.

BOTANIC GARDEN
High Street

The oldest botanic garden in Britain, founded in 1621 as a physic garden for the University by Henry Danvers, 1st Earl of Danby. He leased the site from Magdalen College, walled it round, laid it out and left a Yorkshire living to the University in his will to maintain it. The three GATEWAYS were raised in 1632–3, the earliest fully classical buildings in Oxford. The mason was *Nicholas Stone*, who recorded in his diary in 1631 the commission 'to mak 3 ston gattes in to the phiseck garden'. His nephew or great-nephew Charles Stoakes later asserted that Stone designed them too. However, the wording of Stone's own notebook entry seems to distinguish between the Oxford project as a matter of execution only, and his 'desine' of the house he built for Danby at Cornbury in the same year (*see Oxfordshire: North and West*). Then there is a marginal note by Inigo Jones elsewhere, which refers to 'sum mathematitians of Oxford that desined for a gate for ye garden of simples, lam[e]ly'. Yet a recent source for many of the motifs of all three gates can be identified in the Haarlemmerpoort at Amsterdam (dem.),* by Stone's own father-in-law,

---

*As noted by Adam White, to whom this account is indebted.

Hendrick de Keyser, of which a timely engraving was published in 1631 – which is not to rule out the involvement of Jones's donnish amateurs.

The MAIN GATEWAY is highly ornate, and of a profusion that   50
is a world away from the austere Palladian classicism of Inigo Jones. The fountainhead in terms of C16 sources is indeed not Palladio but Serlio, specifically the *Extraordinary Book* of doorways (1551), which shows the same delight in the alternation of smooth and heavily rusticated parts. Here the rustication is not rock-faced but vermiculated. The gateway is in three parts, the middle being the arched passage. It has to the N three pediments, the main one half-hidden by the two lateral ones. The four engaged Doric columns have bands of vermiculated rustication, the archway and the side niches have the alternation too, but offset from that on the columns. In the niches are the (later) STATUES of Charles I and a Romanized Charles II. In the main pediment two armorial cartouches, and a smaller niche with the BUST of Danby himself. The sculpture, much restored, is by *John Vanderstaine* (payments 1694–5).

To the S the design is quite different. The lateral parts here have each two tiers of two niches, loosely reminiscent of the Arch of Janus in Rome, and the pediment goes right across with a thin segmental pediment set in and some more rustication. Rustication also on the big radiating voussoirs of the arch. The design is carried round the sides, as that of the N side is also. Yet, inside, the gateway has the plainest tunnel-vault and arched recesses, in which are niches no less plain. GATES apparently made from tomb railings of early C15 type, introduced in the C19.

The two minor GATEWAYS of 1632–3 in the E and W walls are also rusticated, and distinctive for the way in which the main pediment has a smaller, segmental pediment superimposed at the top. The actual arches are segmental too.

So to the C18 and after. Just E of the main gateway is a small pedestrian DOORWAY, again with alternating rustication, and formerly with a counterpart to the W. The date is probably *c.*1733–5, when *William Townesend* built two single-storey PLANT HOUSES against the N wall. That on the E is best preserved, with canted ends, canted projecting centre and vermiculated panels and key blocks; but its upper storey is an addition of 1834–5 by *H.J. Underwood* for the remarkable Charles Daubeny, Professor of both Chemistry and Botany. The rest of Underwood's new house (now owned by Magdalen College) faces the High Street behind, Grecian here, of five bays with on the upper floor four fluted Ionic columns. The upper windows have bracketed entablatures, and there is a parapet.

The W plant house is now part of the much larger DAUBENY BUILDING. Here the Townesend treatment has been used throughout the many extensions. Most notable is the heightening and squaring-off of the C18 part in 1848, with a new N range behind. This part housed Daubeny's own lecture room-cum-laboratory. (Of double height, with a thin balcony all round; of special interest as Oxford's oldest surviving laboratory interior.) Converted for Magdalen by *Ivor Smith & Cailey Hutton*, 1975. To the E the Vines Wing of 1910–12 etc., to the W the MANLEY LABORATORY, 1902 (*A. Mardon Mowbray*) and 1932.

The garden's S wall is now breached by a big opening with C18 urns on the end piers. Beyond is a ROCK GARDEN of 1924. Further S, a fine C18 URN carved with pan pipes etc., in an informally planted area annexed from Christ Church Meadow in 1944. The GLASSHOUSES against the E wall on the riverside are successors to those begun by Daubeny in 1851. To the N, by the High Street, a commemorative ROSE GARDEN with formal hedges of box and yew, 1953, designed by *Sylvia Crowe*.*

<h2 style="text-align:center">MUSIC FACULTY</h2>
(originally ST CATHERINE'S SOCIETY)
St Aldate's

Erected for St Catherine's Society, the non-residential predecessor of St Catherine's College (*see* p. 251). The buildings lie back from the street, to preserve the view of Christ Church from the S. By *Sir Hubert Worthington*, 1935–6. His usual squared Bladon rubble, but more domestic-cum-vernacular – or late Arts and Crafts – than his other Oxford jobs. Two storeys, big hipped and tiled roofs. Right-angled ranges freely planned, without quad-making. The HALL with tall and narrow windows with segmental heads is to the r. of the entrance. LIBRARY in the upper floor of the N wing. To the NW a separate block apparently of the 1950s, with minor differences in treatment, currently housing the BATE COLLECTION of historic instruments. Before that, in 1962–77, the buildings served as the first home of Linacre College (p. 174).

<h2 style="text-align:center">HISTORY FACULTY LIBRARY (former)</h2>
Merton Street

see University College, p. 305

<h2 style="text-align:center">UNIVERSITY SPORTS CENTRE</h2>
Iffley Road

see South-east Oxford, p. 497

*Williams's *Oxonia Illustrata* (1733) shows a concave-ended forecourt wall and gates added in front of Danby's gateway. An imposing Townesend-Baroque range along the street, built in 1728–34 as Professor Dillenius's house and library, was pulled down to widen the Magdalen Bridge approach in 1790. It probably incorporated the plant house illustrated by Loggan in 1675.

3. WEST AND NORTH-WEST
including the Radcliffe Observatory Quarter

OXFORD UNION SOCIETY
St Michael's Street and Frewin Court

The University's student debating society was founded in 1823. In 1852 the present site was bought, with a three-storey late C18 house and large garden. Much of this red brick HOUSE remains, of L-plan: a N–S wing one room deep, and W-projecting wing with a canted end. Entrance from the S in the angle, with a sturdy closed-string open-well staircase with tall turned balusters. In the W room remnants of strongly moulded plasterwork, notably a roundel depicting a dog and a goat. Little S office added by *David Warr*, 2005.

The W wing joins on to the LIBRARY, designed as the Debating Room by *Benjamin Woodward* and built in 1856–7. It is a simple elongated octagon in plan, the E and W sides being twice as long as the rest, with a steep slated roof – one of several parallels with Woodward's University Museum (p.364). The material is brick, red with some yellow stresses; the style is Gothic, and Woodward used cut bricks to fringe his two-light lower windows with a kind of sawteeth. The lower windows stone-dressed, with mid-shafts. There are upper windows as well, and they are sexfoils. They light the gallery, and the parapet of this again has sawtooth decoration. Rugged timberwork inside, with much notching and billet, dogtooth etc. Also the celebrated WALL PAINTINGS by the Pre-Raphaelite circle of scenes from the Morte d'Arthur, all around the sexfoils above the gallery bookcases. They were painted chiefly in summer 1857, but so amateurishly, as far as technique is concerned, that they are hard to make out today, even after the well-informed restoration of 1986. Yet in 1857 Coventry Patmore could call them 'so brilliant as to make the walls look like the margins of a highly illuminated manuscript'. Subjects and artists are as follows: E wall: Arthur's Wedding, with the White Hart, *William Rivière*, 1875 (entrance bay); Sir Lancelot's Vision of the Sangreal, *Rossetti* (next bay S). S end: Sir Pelleas and the Lady Etarde, *Val Prinsep* (SE); Arthur receiving Excalibur, *Hungerford Pollen* (S); Arthur's First Victory with the Sword, *Rivière*, 1875 (SW). W wall: Tristram and Iseult, *William Morris* (S bay); The Death of Merlin, *Burne-Jones* (N bay). N end: Sir Gawaine and the Damsels at the Fountain, *Spencer Stanhope* (NW); The Death of Arthur, *Arthur Hughes* (N); The Education of Arthur by Merlin, *Rivière*, 1875 (NE).

By contrast, the *Morris* foliage decoration all over the roof panels and on the arched braces can be fully enjoyed. This, however, is not as it was done in 1857. It was repainted in 1875 to what Morris called 'a new and lighter design', executed under his supervision by *F.R. Leach* of Cambridge, and itself since renewed in 1986. The original was, we are told, darker and had a prodigious number of 'all kinds of quaint beasts and birds'. As it is, the decoration of the roof is a sheer delight. In the middle of the room is a double fireplace of marble with an underfloor flue. Also, easily missed, a stone tympanum over the S vestibule doorway outside, King Arthur and the Knights of the Round Table. Designed by *Rossetti*, carved by *Alexander Munro*, and originally coloured.

After Woodward's death, in 1862–3 *William Wilkinson* added a two-storey block of reading and writing rooms, now BAR (below) and GLADSTONE ROOM (above), and that is the room E of the library which also has a canted projection. Here buttresses appear, and the windows have more stonework, with dogtooth surrounds and some little foliage at the top. On the N window the head of Shakespeare. Some decoration in vitrified dark blue brick. The Gladstone Room has a steep pointed ceiling with painted decoration of college shields, a remnant of *G. F. Armitage*'s romantic Smoking Room scheme of 1888. Lesser offices etc. of 1862–3 were replaced in 1910–11 by a much larger wing extending N, designed by *W. E. Mills*, completed posthumously by *J. E. Thorpe*. Conventional Tudor Gothic, with three through-storey bays. Some rich panelled interiors: LIBRARY below, MACMILLAN ROOM above with grand stone fireplace and intricate plasterwork barrel-vault. The separately expressed N part is the former STEWARD'S HOUSE.

Across the garden to the W, *Waterhouse* in 1878–9 added a new building for a new and larger DEBATING HALL. This is a much smoother job than Woodward's and Wilkinson's. Red brick, with decoration in yellow terracotta – an uncommon choice of material for Oxford. Cross-windows with Waterhouse's distinctive glazing. One can't really call such a building Gothic. The hall itself is architecturally disappointing.

ASHMOLEAN MUSEUM AND TAYLORIAN INSTITUTION
Beaumont Street and St Giles'

The competition of 1840 was won by *C. R. Cockerell*, the most learned but also one of the most original architects of his generation in England, against a largely underwhelming field.* Entries were to be 'of a Grecian character', and had to provide both for the University's collection of antiquities and pictures, and for the institute endowed in 1788 by the bequest of Sir Robert Taylor, the architect, 'for teaching and improving the European languages', funds for which had finally been released. Building followed in 1841–5, to a slightly revised design. The contractors were *George Baker & Son* of Lambeth, the cost £49,373. In the 1890s some of the collections from the Old Ashmolean Museum (p. 339) were transferred, and in 1908 what had been known hitherto as

---

*Judged by Sir Robert Smirke. *George Mair & E. H. Browne, John Plowman Jun.* of Oxford, *Henry Hakewill* and *Anthony Salvin* were also shortlisted.

the University Galleries formally adopted the older name. Since Cockerell's time the most important episode by far is the rear extension by *Rick Mather Architects* of 2006–9, replacing accretions of more than a century.

Cockerell's building is one of the most typical ones of the transition from the strict Grecian to something freer and more eclectic. Towards Beaumont Street it presents a broad centre and two projecting wings, with a raised and balustraded courtyard between. The centre of the centre is a tetrastyle portico of Ionic columns of that variety found within the Temple of Apollo at Bassae in Greece, which Cockerell had been among the first to study. The capital is inelegant when compared with those of other C5 B.C. exemplars such as the Erechtheion or the Temple of Nike in Athens, but it has more force, and Cockerell evidently wanted a forceful building. Yet the façade within the portico is Renaissance rather than Antique: two shallow rusticated niches, flanking a big doorcase with an Italian Mannerist architrave. Above, the portico has a frieze with an unusual Hellenistic basket-weave motif which runs right round the building. All the architectural carving, most of which survived the refacing works of 1965–71, is by *W. G. Nicholl*, who also did the pediment sculpture. On top of it is a seated figure of Apollo. To the l. and r. of this frontispiece is apparently windowless wall, articulated by giant antae. Between them like a membrane is rusticated wall below, and above a tier of very short half-antae pushed close to the giant ones, and the panels with wreaths. Overall the impression is French, and Cockerell was *au courant* concerning Parisian architecture. Closer inspection shows that the panels of the middle tier to the l. of the

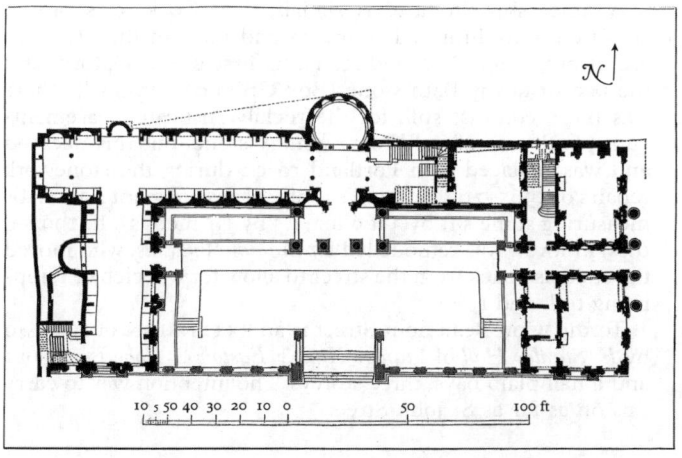

Ashmolean Museum and Taylorian Institution.
Plan, 1846

portico are of ground glass rather than ashlar, for side-lighting the gallery within.

The wings have two full storeys plus high and heavy attics, deeply shelving bracket cornices after Vignola, and shallow hipped roofs. All of this makes them taller than the centre, always a visual risk to take, and here particularly so, as the difference is not great. But in the fronts of the wings towards the forecourt Cockerell took a further risk. To understand it one ought to look first at the side of the Taylorian wing facing St Giles', to the E. There are here four giant detached Ionic columns with the frieze and the whole entablature projecting boldly above each of them. They carry statues by *Nicholl* representing France, Italy, Germany and Spain. Between these entablatures, i.e. within the attic storey, appear three round-headed windows: a favourite juxtaposition of Cockerell's, deriving from a now lost Roman temple at Bordeaux.

This St Giles' front, then, is powerful and perfectly integrated. But to use the same system throughout – only with demi-columns, and hence the entablature fragments coming forward much less and urns on them instead of statues – led to a crisis in the corners between centre and wings. The demi-column here stands right in the corner. That can neither be enjoyed nor justified. The ends of the wings to Beaumont Street have only two giant demi-columns each, of the same kind and likewise unfluted. They in conjunction with the high attic and its round-arched window create a discord – but that discord Cockerell surely wanted. He also wanted the aggressiveness of all his projecting slabs of entablature, and the depth of relief which they give confirms that here (and in Basevi's slightly earlier Fitzwilliam Museum at Cambridge, which Cockerell helped to complete) the way is shown from the classicism of the early C19 to the Baroque traits of the later C19.

Another shift in taste is signalled by Cockerell's use of structural polychromy. The orders and most of the dressings are of near-white Portland stone, its first use in Oxford, and the rest of tawny Bath stone (Box Ground). Originally there was more contrast still, for the rockily rusticated basement-cum-plinth was of red-brown Whitby stone, but this decayed and was replaced with Portland roach during the stonework repairs of 1965–71. Cockerell's roofs survive, of giant slate slabs measuring some 5 ft by 3 ft 6 in. (1.5 by 1.1 metres). In 1994–6 the TERRACE was remodelled by *Stanton Williams*, who moved the staircase back from the street to allow for wheelchair ramps rising to l. and r.

To the W on Beaumont Street is an EXTENSION of 1939–40 by *E. Stanley Hall* of *Stanley Hall & Easton & Robertson*. Four and a half plain bays, three storeys. The intention was to carry this on as far as St John Street.*

---

*An earlier version published in 1933 included a recessed centre, to balance the C19 composition.

Cockerell's INTERIORS are leaner than the exterior may suggest.
The entrance hall has to l., r. and ahead screens of Greek Doric
columns used – a solecism – in terms of the Venetian window,
i.e. with a middle arch. Cockerell was an experienced archae-
ologist; he knew what he was doing. Originally the screen
ahead opened to a blind apse or exedra with niches in which
statues of the Nine Muses were placed. *H.W. Moore* replaced
this in 1892–4 with the present straight-sided lobby, leading
to a rear extension since replaced by Mather. To the r. is the
roomy STAIRCASE, climbing in three unequal flights. Walls
ordered with niches and sunk panels, a copy of the Bassae
frieze above, plain barrel-vault with a round top light. To the
l. the RANDOLPH GALLERY, which ends in another Doric
screen. It has the side-lighting high up already noted externally,
and niches containing the Arundel marbles, formerly displayed
in a room in the Schools Quad. Original green Connemara
insets in the floor. The WEST GALLERY, at right angles to the
far end, is entered through a screen of doubled columns, but
this is *Stanton Williams*'s insertion of 1994–6. Also of 1994–6
is the apse on the W wall, facing the museum's side portal:
a reinstatement of Cockerell's apse lost in 1908, made this
time to house new stairs down to the basement. To the W are
EGYPTIAN GALLERIES of 1956–7, renovated by *Mather* in
2011. The BASEMENT has groin-vaulting on a central row of fat
simplified Doric columns, renovated in 1994–6. Of the same
date the HEADLEY LECTURE THEATRE and other extensions
under the courtyard.

   Of Cockerell's FIRST-FLOOR GALLERIES those of the
main range remain, but the grand double-height gallery in
the W range was floored across and subdivided in 1923–8
by *E. Stanley Hall*, who added a new STAIRCASE in connection. Detailing all sympathetic to Cockerell. Also by Hall
the WELDON GALLERY (Gallery 46), 1933, immediately NW
of this W staircase. Of later interventions, the MCALPINE
GALLERY remains (Gallery 52), added above the Egyptian
galleries in 1972–3 by *Yorke Rosenberg Mardall*, as does *Robert
Adam Architects*' SANDS GALLERY on the first floor at the
extreme E, provided in 2001 as part of the rebuilt Griffith
Institute (*see* p. 357).

So to *Rick Mather Architects*' EXTENSION of 2006–9. It replaced a
maze of *ad hoc* structures and dead ends – over twenty phases
of addition or alteration are recorded in this area – with a
much roomier complex, rising a storey higher than the front
range, but remaining invisible from the street. Most of this
volume comprises galleries and circulation spaces, organized
on a governing idea of routes of exploration and cultural connection – a determined contrast with the old division into
geographical and typological fiefdoms. The chief circulation
space is a full-height void to the E, white-walled, with a staircase of criss-crossing, partly curved flights stacked up on the
r. side. Its elegance is undermined by the conflicting lines of
glass balustrades and attached handrails. To the W is a lesser

stair void with similar detail, here with a giant through-storey window. The galleries occupy most of the space between, of both major and mezzanine heights, with displays designed by *Metaphor*. Cross-views and glimpses abound, and the visitor's experience is of spatial flow as much as of a sequence of discrete rooms. Along the N side, the previously separate CAST GALLERY of 1958–9 by *Easton & Robertson, Cusdin, Preston & Smith* has been incorporated, its external wall frankly showing. Also retained is *van Heyningen & Haward Architects'* split-level CHINESE PAINTINGS GALLERY of 1999–2000 along the E side, squeezed into the slip of space behind the Taylorian extension (*see* below). The Mather building includes a NE wing for education and office spaces, showing its brick facing and sawtooth window projections to the service lane to St Giles'; galleries for temporary exhibitions, and a top-floor restaurant and terrace looking towards Beaumont Street.

TAYLORIAN INSTITUTION. *Cockerell*'s original entry from St Giles' is brilliantly conceived, a doorway with stairs under an open barrel-vaulted passage to the courtyard terrace, lined with small paired antae, shallow rustication with niches, and twin Greek Doric doorways. The N doorway leads to the main staircase and so up to the MAIN READING ROOM, a richer space than any of the Ashmolean interiors. A cube of nearly 40 ft (12 metres), tall enough to embrace the lunette windows. A thin balcony runs round, canted diagonally across the corners, and the ceiling cove echoes this octagonal shape. Elongated bracket cornice as on the exterior; linings of light-coloured wood, rich fireplace surrounds of beaten-copper foliage by *Thomas Potter* of South Molton Street, London. EASTERN LECTURE ROOM with inset Ionic columns at the podium end, other lecture rooms plainer. Painted panels by *George B. Hill*, 1876, after the Parthenon sculptures. These rooms extend some way into the main E–W range, a division which Cockerell's courtyard front blithely ignores. Along St Giles' is an EXTENSION by *T.H. Hughes*, built 1931–2 and 1938 (the two N bays). Nicely in keeping; an appreciative job. The upper of the two floors has seven large oblong windows set in a blank arcade with broad, heavy piers. Narrow bays l. and r. with decorative urns. Staircase likewise in the Neo-Grec taste, interconnecting with the landings of Cockerell's staircase alongside.

SACKLER LIBRARY AND GRIFFITH INSTITUTE
St John Street

By *Robert Adam Architects*, 1997–2001, for the Classics and History of Art faculties. The design evolved from one part of a grandiose project, published in 1995, for rebuilding all the way behind the Ashmolean and Taylorian, through to a new portal on St Giles'. What resulted is more in the pragmatic Oxford manner of exploiting backland sites, yet it also represents the University's chief venture into the latter-day classical revival.

Adam's classicism stands somewhere between the robust schematic Postmodern of late Stirling and John Outram and the more traditional approaches of John Simpson or Quinlan Terry. Tradition is to the fore in the ENTRANCE VESTIBULE, a neat ashlar drum clasped between single-storey projections. Two fat Doric columns of the Bassae variant (a homage to Cockerell's Ashmolean) flank the doorway. A full cornice all round. Bands of bold colours on the walls within. The entrance axis leads via a rear door to a formal external staircase down to a small sunk courtyard, with the GRIFFITH INSTITUTE (Egyptology) ahead. A tall rendered façade of elongated proportions, the lowest floor rusticated and arcaded, the attic with a huge bronze RELIEF by *Alexander Stoddart*. The style like Flaxman's, done with conviction. The subject is 'a commentary on libraries'.

The LIBRARY itself rises immediately to the l., a giant rendered drum with small stark upright windows. Asplund's 1920s library in Stockholm is the chief reference, but the ideal penitentiary projects of the Enlightenment also come to mind. Five storeys all told, from basement to Doric cornice. Two non-matching office attachments on Pusey Lane to the N, of red brick. Entry is via a lobby off the entrance drum, an unsatisfactory space with a lopsided aisle. No dome or top lighting within; instead, every library floor has a square central enclosure for the book stacks, defined on each side by four primitivist Doric columns. Reading spaces around the perimeter, alternating with smaller enclosures for offices, staircases etc. The logic is clear enough, but the low ceilings, utilitarian finishes and unresolved spaces between perimeter and core are disappointing after the external fanfares.

ORIENTAL INSTITUTE
Pusey Lane, N of Beaumont Street

1958–60 by *Easton & Robertson, Cusdin, Preston & Smith*. A rather mannered façade, with its decoration round the entrance and its two-storey oriels (re-windowed) projecting triangularly for the office rooms. Shorter wings extend behind. Sweeping oval staircase inside. Provision was made for a top storey, eventually added in 1999–2000. The hideaway location in this former mews is explained by the proximity of the Ashmolean: the Cast Gallery immediately behind (p. 356) was part of the same project, and a covered bridge formerly crossed to the back of the museum.

HISTORY FACULTY
(former HIGH SCHOOL FOR BOYS)
George Street

1880–1 by *T. G. Jackson*. A non-denominational foundation, conceived by the Balliol philosopher T. H. Green, for which the architect's progressive, post-Gothic style made a good match. It is a monumental stone pile, though of five bays only. Centre with bold projection encompassing a triple-arched porch. Typical Jackson gable with two tiers of pilasters, feathery leaf decoration, and an open scrolly pediment in front of a gable. Windows range from the type with arched heads for the lights to the Ipswich type. Carving by *Farmer & Brindley*. Also a lovely octagonal spirelet with two glazed and lead-faced stages. Two spatially complex staircases with column-newels. The upper floor is one big hall, with a ceiled kingpost roof. W extension of 1895 by *Jackson*, continued by *W.H. Castle* with a cross-wing etc. of 1915 using Jackson motifs, but not to his plan. Jackson also designed an unbuilt headmaster's house, meant to stand by the street to the NE.

The former playground to the S is bounded by a surviving section of the CITY WALL with one big bastion, all largely reconstructed.

SAÏD BUSINESS SCHOOL
Park End Street

Founded in 1996 with an endowment from the financier Wafic Saïd, as the successor to the Oxford Centre for Management Studies (*see* Green Templeton College, p. 151). The new home by the railway station, designed by *Jeremy Dixon & Edward Jones* (*Dixon Jones*), followed in 1997–2001, on the site of the old London & North Western Railway terminus (*see* p. 407n.). Some features were carried over from the architects' proposals of 1996 for a site on Mansfield Road, but the design is altogether different: formal and quadrangular, of pale yellow brick with ashlar facing wrapped around the entrance end, and with a dominant N–S axis offset by an eccentric twelve-stepped ziggurat turret of patinated copper by the SW corner. The E side is less formal, with a long slanting lean-to for service rooms. Other motifs – the striped brick-and-stone colonnade and open cornice high up on the station side to the W, the plain slab-like piers of the cloister colonnades, the unexpected amphitheatre formed on the roof of the round-ended students' common room at the N end – belong with the Postmodern return to evocative primal forms. For the big horizontal *brise-soleil* canopy of steel that shelters the S entrance, however, Norman Foster (Nîmes etc.) looks like the source, while the huge FOYER with its rows of thin columns aligns the building with the world of corporations rather than Oxford's college traditions (the school indeed has no resident students). Above the foyer is the elliptical-roofed, two-storey LIBRARY, also copper-roofed; behind the foyer the CLOISTERS run N. That on the E side is open-sided and has white-walled courtyards of smaller rooms extending off it; that on the W side has glazed openings and courtyards raised up on the first floor, with lecture theatres (U-shaped seating, Harvard style) below. Open steel staircases within each cloister walk. The central court is exotically planted with flowering Paulownia trees. The E range ends to the N with the GARDEN ROOM, a copper-roofed lean-to added by *Dixon Jones* in 2017. In the GARDEN are features marking the former site of Rewley Abbey (*see* p. 443). – SCULPTURE. In a recess on the W front, *Olivia Musgrave*'s bronze ox of 2002, an eyecatcher for those arriving by train. Bust of Wafic Saïd in the foyer by *Michael Rizzello*, 2004. W cloister, First Light, a wall-mounted abstract by *Nigel Hall*. E cloister, Shapes in the Clouds, four polished marble forms on rough oak plinths, by *Peter Randall-Page*, 2005.

In 2010–12 the school was extended to the NW (THATCHER BUSINESS EDUCATION CENTRE), also by *Dixon Jones*, for programmes for senior executives. The treatment is accordingly more introverted and exclusive, with some costlier-looking materials. Ashlar front to the S, with a rather Art Deco polished black plinth that steps up and over the doorway. The other façades non-committal. Marble-lined foyer, from which a straight and narrow top-lit staircase climbs slowly to the N end. The LOUNGE opens off to the E on the first floor; separated by big sawtooth-plan glazing from a terrace and pergola. DINING ROOM on the second floor, its N part with a low pyramid roof with a truncated top. Externally the pyramid is copper-clad, and this gives the wing its skyline feature.

For the school's Business Education Centre *see* West Oxford, power station, p. 517.

UNIVERSITY OFFICES

Little Clarendon Street and Wellington Square

By *Sir Leslie Martin* with *David Owers*, 1970–3; designed together with the residences at No. 25 Wellington Square, immediately W (p. 433). Executant architect for both was *Douglas Lanham*. A dry and dutiful building. Four storeys, the lower two recessed behind plain piers. Bands of windows with uniform mullions alternate with bands of plain concrete. Expansive external stairs to the first-floor entrance.

OXFORD UNIVERSITY PRESS

Walton Street

Built in 1826–32, largely to the design of *Daniel Robertson*, but completed by *Blore* (N wing and W side) after Robertson's imprisonment for debt in 1829. Builder, *Charles Smith* of London. £48,977 was spent on the structure, which is of remarkable size and ambition for an early C19 factory, and vastly larger than the Press's previous home in the Clarendon Building (p. 340). The original quadrangle consists of a representational front range, two very long, absolutely plain three-storey side wings (for the Bible Press, S, and Learned Press, N), and a W range with the two supervisors' houses, all of Bath stone ashlar. If it were not for the lawn with its round

Oxford University Press.
Engraving by H. Le Keux after F. Mackenzie, 1832

basin and two copper beeches, one might think of barracks. But the FRONT RANGE makes up for the dourness of the back. It is unmistakably Late Classical in style and has a highly monumental centre and monumental ends as well. Centre and ends are of three bays each, and they are connected by one-storey links with windows (originally blind) and simple pilaster strips. The end blocks have three bays with giant angle pilasters and two giant three-quarter columns. Big attic on top. But the centre has a triumphal-arch entry, treated as a large barrel-vaulted archway for vehicles and two small groin-vaulted ones for pedestrians, and it goes on triumphally with four giant Corinthian columns, grouped as two and two and carrying each its own projecting piece of entablature. The Arch of Constantine is the model, except for the slabs of attic that here project like fins.

The QUADRANGLE has some original window frames of cast iron, as also was much of the internal structure. The design is not in its original state. On the w side, *Blore*'s plain semi-detached houses (designed 1831) with their side porches are flanked by a later C19 printing-house façade, l., and a round-arched two-storey range, r., from the 1990s renovations (*see* below). On the s side an engine-house projection of 1872; all along the E side an addition of 1960–1 by *T. H. Hughes*, Oxford-Belated classical, the side parts given an extra storey c. 1965.

Book printing on site ceased in 1989, and the other EXTENSIONS now consist of adapted print works etc. and office ranges. To the s, the ROBERTS BUILDING, three-storey offices, end-on to Walton Street. The concrete-and-brick upper storeys are by *John Fryman* of *Architects Design Partnership*, 1974–6, and were constructed on wide-span frames above press buildings that continued in use throughout. Reconstructed c. 1992 with a replacement ground floor. Also new linking ranges, glazed to full height where they face the small quad behind. The w side here (formerly the boiler house) is of 1866, architects *Wigg & Oliver*, and matches the Robertson elevations. To the N, a small classical coda (*Hughes*, 1930s?) to Robertson's street range. The long structure behind it is the former MAILING SHED, 1920s, renovated by *Berman Guedes Stretton* in 2006.

So to the mighty REAR EXTENSION, which pushes back into the streets of Jericho. The renovation of 1990–3 was by *AMEC Design & Management*, working with the architect *Roger Stretton*. Its basic structure is mostly *Fryman*'s concrete-framed print works of 1966–7 and later, refaced with yellow brick below (context for the C19 housing), mirror glass on a small square grid above. Main entrance up steps on the N side, set back from Great Clarendon Street and next to the old quadrangle, with a N-projecting wing alongside. Behind the entrance is the 'fairway', a generous linear atrium. Pitched-roofed glazing supported by two rows of slim white columns. White walls. Little historicist details elsewhere, e.g. fat sub-classical columns. Also an inner courtyard with part of the OLD BINDERY of *c.*1900 as its s side, here refaced in red brick. This shows as three plain storeys behind the houses of Walton Crescent.

RADCLIFFE OBSERVATORY QUARTER
Woodstock Road and Walton Street

A confusing name (familiarly the 'ROQ') for the former Radcliffe Infirmary quarter, to which the Radcliffe Observatory is next-door neighbour to the N (*see* Green Templeton College). The University bought the ten-acre site in 2003. The three major Infirmary buildings on the Woodstock Road side have since been adapted for new uses. To the w, most of the huge hospital complex has been cleared. Its redevelopment has been dogged with false starts and wrong turnings. Early proposals included a neo-Beaux Arts project by the US architects *SLAM Collaborative*, with a grand diagonal boulevard aligned on the Observatory. A competition for a masterplan was won in 2005 by *Rafael Viñoly*. This too envisaged a series of low-rise urban blocks, but multiplied the number of radial boulevards. Much criticism and revision followed, during which time the only buildings to appear were *Niall McLaughlin*'s accommodation ranges for Somerville College along the s side (p.363). Designs for the two largest elements on the site were approved in 2010: *Viñoly*'s own Mathematics building, opened in 2013 (p.291), and *Bennetts Associates*' Humanities building and library, intended as the centrepiece. The latter has been superseded by a more comprehensive design by *Hopkins Architects*, to be called the Schwarzman Centre for the Humanities in honour of its benefactor, and begun in 2022. All the new buildings so far completed are commendably ambitious and distinctive, the spaces between less so.

RADCLIFFE INFIRMARY, now RADCLIFFE HUMANITIES, Woodstock Road. The Infirmary was built from the funds of the Radcliffe Trustees in 1759–67, to a contract price of £5,692, and opened in 1770. It follows the C18 English hospital convention of a long, symmetrical astylar front with a pedimented centre. The architect was *Stiff Leadbetter*, who seems to have drawn heavily on *Luke Singleton*'s design for Gloucester Infirmary (1755–61, dem.), where Leadbetter had been the contractor. Leadbetter died in 1766, and *John Sanderson* oversaw completion. The building is three storeys high plus a mansard storey (heightened 1826), and thirteen bays long, the two outer bays at each end being in slightly projecting wings, where the main wards were. The central doorway and window above it are an alteration of 1933 by *Stanley Hamp*. Originally there was a double external stair to a first-floor doorway. Inside, Hamp created a double-height ENTRANCE HALL, cutting through the first floor and making a balcony all round. On the first floor behind is the COMMITTEE ROOM, with a canted end (as at Gloucester), and adorned with gilt-lettered panels naming benefactors. Big fireplace with console brackets. Stone-vaulted corridors run laterally between, provided as a fire precaution, with a triple-arched opening on the hall side. Main STAIRCASE also of stone, actually a replica from *Purcell*'s conversion of 2011–12. Victorian accretions behind were removed.

In the forecourt a triton FOUNTAIN, a version of 2012 of *John Bell*'s original, made in *J. M. Blashfield*'s terracotta in 1857 (original now at Castle Mill, by Port Meadow). The inspiration is Bernini's famous Triton fountain in Rome.

CHAPEL (former), N side of the forecourt. 1863–5 by *Arthur Blomfield*, presented by Thomas Combe (*see* St Barnabas, p. 391) and dedicated to St Luke. Aisleless and steep-gabled, in the style of 1300. W rose, three stepped E lancets with bar tracery. S vestry with a canted end and a stone bellcote riding above. S porch with a relief of Christ as Good Shepherd, carved by *Thomas Earp*. Arch-braced roof. (– SCULPTURE. Three relief figures by *Laurence Bradshaw*, salvaged from *Collcutt & Hamp*'s former Nurses' Home of the 1930s on the Walton Street side.) – STAINED GLASS. E window of uncommonly good quality, by *Henry Holiday* for *Heaton, Butler & Bayne*. W rose, 1869, by the same firm.

The S side is the former OUTPATIENTS' DEPARTMENT, 1910–13 by *E. P. Warren* with *Dr D. J. Mackintosh*, Director of the Western Infirmary, Glasgow. Brusquely converted in 2014–16 by *Niall McLaughlin Architects* as the RADCLIFFE PRIMARY CARE BUILDING. Warren's façades are mid-Georgian: twin pedimented wings to the forecourt, a looser composition to Woodstock Road. The gap between the wings is now filled with a plain stone ground floor and a big glazed atrium set back above, its concrete framing visible. New W end of yellow brick. On it a re-set mother-and-child SCULPTURE by *Laurence Bradshaw*, from *Collcutt & Hamp*'s demolished Maternity Wing of 1931 (cf. his sculptures now in the chapel). Progressive style for the date.

ANDREW WILES BUILDING (MATHEMATICAL INSTITUTE).
Directly behind the Infirmary, and angled around it to the
NE and E. By *Rafael Viñoly Architects*, 2010–13; structural engineers *Pell Frischmann*. A complex building that repays attention. Two unequal sections, stepping up from three storeys at
the outer ends to five in the diagonal middle part, which is
sundered by a wedge-shaped, glazed entrance and through
route aligned on the Observatory tower. This viewing axis was
carried over from Viñoly's otherwise very different design and
masterplan of 2005. Square grids of pale cast-stone members
define the elevations. Each square has a dark-bronze-coloured
solid centre between upright panes, and a movable screen of
bronzed slats in front, of about one-third of the square's width.
The upper part of the entrance wedge houses the common
room. Big staircase down from the entrance lobby to a deep
basement, much of the building (lecture theatres included)
being subterranean. Daylight reaches the circulation areas here
via two angular skylights of mathematically interesting forms
cutting through the ground-floor concourse, one in each wing.
Above each is a top-lit atrium. Square service towers with
slatted sides rise through the atriums, breaching their pitched
glazed roofs. Running around and across these white-walled
atrium spaces are balconies, bridges and staircases, all with
wood-slatted fronts.

Four bold ARTWORKS. By the entrance, polished PAVING
designed by *Prof. Sir Roger Penrose*, of 'non-periodic' symmetry.
Within the entrance, SCULPTURE by *Mat Chivers*, Axiom, a
brain-like form, and abstract MURALS by *Antoni Malinowski*
composed of coloured flecks, called Spectral Flip. Outside to
the NW, SCULPTURE by *Simon Periton*, The Alchemical Tree.

HARKNESS BUILDING and GIBSON BUILDING (behind), to
the NNW. Leftovers from the Radcliffe Infirmary, respectively
of 1970 and 1945 (upper storeys 1964).

NEW RADCLIFFE HOUSE, to the NW. By *Hawkins/Brown*,
2011–12. Pleasing and inventive. An oblong, placed N–S. Two
storeys of University offices above ground-floor GPs' surgeries.
Brown brick facing, with some patterning. The fronts are
gently cranked back and forth, and the parapets slope up and
down in counterpoint. Upper-floor windows placed at varying
heights; some deep-set, others boxed out. Glazed entrance
recess with applied silhouetted tree forms by *Oona Culley*,
continued on interior surfaces. The waiting area has a scatter of
round skylights, with glimpses of the elliptical light well within
the upper storeys, lined with white-glazed bricks.

BLAVATNIK SCHOOL OF GOVERNMENT, Walton Street, S of
St Paul's church (p. 397). A postgraduate institution founded
in 2010 with funds from the Soviet-born businessman Sir
Leonard Blavatnik. *Herzog & de Meuron*'s building followed
in 2013–15 (engineers *Pell Frischmann*). It is the most original
C21 addition to Oxford's architecture so far, from a Swiss
practice notable not for any signature look or motif, but for
the ability to generate freshly conceived outcomes for each
new commission. Their building achieves true novelty of form,

125

while respecting traditions of formal symmetry, vertical walls – not slanting or blob-like – and an emphasis on the entrance portal. But these thoughts come only after one has registered the iconoclastic shape and materials: the shape a diminishing stack of six storey-height discs, modified with a cutaway for the entrance and a square-cornered finish to the first floor above; the material a faceted, reflecting curtilage of upright glass panes, with slim concrete floor slabs between. A closer look at the upper floors shows that the outer panes form screens with slim gaps, behind which are the windows and walling of the interior proper. The cutaway part by contrast is faced in oak, including the framing of the huge-paned picture window under the second-floor overhang. Nor are the floor drums concentrically placed: at the back they all align vertically at a single point on the main axis. All this captures and beguiles the eye from any angle. Only at night does the effect falter, when artificial light puts the irregular-shaped rooms and uneven window rhythms on display.

The INTERIOR is conceived around a single circulation space, from the forum in the basement with its surrounding lecture theatres etc. to the oculus piercing the topmost drum. The floors between are almost all open to this space, to which they present concrete balconies with rendered front faces. But these circular voids are offset from storey to storey, and the balcony fronts slide away from the horizontal to take open staircases down to the basement and up to the first floor. A smaller staircase twists down from the ground floor at the back. So the impression is one of motion, displacement even, rather than repose. Palette and motifs are again consistent: much fair-faced concrete, much stained oak. The light fittings and acoustic panels on the ceiling slabs are circular too. The cumulative effect is of a world apart – for all that the stated design principles are transparency and openness.

The project had a difficult birth. A competition in 2009 was tied between *Dixon Jones* and the classicist *John Simpson*. Neither proposal reportedly enthused the patron, and *Robert Stern*, Dean of Yale's architecture faculty, was appointed instead. The final choice of Herzog & de Meuron was announced in 2011.

SCULPTURE. To the N, a giant fountain pen poised on its nib, outlined in magenta-coated steel. By *Michael Craig-Martin*, 2021.

4a. NORTH AND NORTH-EAST
University Museum and Science Area

UNIVERSITY MUSEUM
Parks Road

The initiative for a science building and museum of natural history with lecture rooms and laboratories came from a group of leading Oxford scientists including Dr (later Sir) Henry Acland, distinguished medical practitioner and Reader in Anatomy. A memorandum was drawn up in 1847 for a museum to display 'materials illustrative of the facts and laws of the natural world'. Convocation voted in favour in 1849, and the new Honour School of Natural Sciences was founded the year after. The project was therefore central to the broader movement to modernize the University's curriculum. In 1853 a site was identified, in 1854 a competition was held. The specification was for a courtyard plan of two-storey ranges, with a glazed-all-over roof: a type already exemplified by Barry's Reform Club and Pennethorne's Geological Museum in London. Subsidiary wings were to be provided for Chemistry and Anatomy, and the main building was to allow for extension on one side.

Over thirty entries were received, of which just twelve were Gothic – the style already proposed by *Street*, who published his own proposals independently, but then chose not to compete. The final shortlist consisted of just two: one described as 'Palladian', by *E. M. Barry*, the other 'Rhenish Gothic', by *Sir Thomas Deane, Son & Woodward* of Dublin – or rather *Benjamin Woodward*, shy, silent and modest, and soon to die. The competition was to all appearances anonymous, but it may be that Deane's connections with Acland helped to steer the commission to the Irish firm, who were then already busy with their museum at Trinity College Dublin. Oxford's museum was duly erected in 1855–9, to a revised and slightly simplified design, with the Oxford architect *W. C. C. Bramwell* as clerk of works.

The other key person in the story is Acland's friend John Ruskin. The two had been undergraduates together at Christ Church, and Acland had been with Mr and Mrs Ruskin and Millais on the momentous journey to Scotland in 1853. It happened that the building contractors, *Lucas Bros* of London, were to be paid for the basic construction only, and Ruskin took an intense interest in directing and raising extra funds for carving and decoration. In its carved detail especially the museum exemplifies Ruskin's concern for the supreme importance of the workman's hand and of nature as the source of all worthwhile ornament. Before long his enthusiasm waned, partly on account of the use of iron-and-glass construction for the central atrium, but not entirely so; as he wrote to his father, 'The real fact was, I couldn't make up my mind what was at fault in the Museum.' Yet there are few buildings anywhere that illustrate so well the neo-medieval ideals he had expounded in *The Stones of Venice* (1851–3). More than this, the commission was a crucial episode both in the rise of modern Gothic for public architecture, and in the story of iron-and-glass construction. In its ornament and iconography, the museum also represents the contemporary tension between religious and materialist interpretations of the natural world.

So the building is Gothic, but not of English derivation, nor especially Italian either, except for the use of coloured stone – chiefly red Bristol sandstone, in bands and voussoirs in the Bath stone ashlar. It is a large building of symmetrical outline,

University Museum.
Engraving by W.E. Hodgkin after R. Sly, 1855

originally standing entirely on open ground. The w front has a
tower in the middle, crowned by the steepest of hipped roofs,
a motif neither Italian nor English but suggestive rather of the
great medieval town halls of the Low Countries. To l. and r.
are six bays in two storeys. The roof is large and steep too, and
the wooden dormers are absurdly steep triangles. The upper
windows are large and have foiled Geometrical plate tracery; so
have the tower windows; the lower windows are lancets, mostly
paired, and placed with a freedom that is at first not conspicuous. The front range shows its gabled ends, beyond which are
spired and canted projections for the twin stair enclosures, and
then the gable-ends of the N and s ranges. Of these, the N side
is partly three-storeyed and of greater depth, to accommodate
the chief lecture room. Originally this section had bold patterning to the roof slates, lost in mid-C20 renewals (likewise the
two chimneys that rose through the roof of the main tower).

The architectural sculpture is also in a class of its own.
Round some of the upper windows is a profusion of carving
– animals as well as foliage and flowers. On the ground floor
fewer have received their due; others are still wholly uncut. The
story of all that carving is familiar, how the red-bearded brothers *John* and *James O'Shea* and their nephew *Edward Whelan*
were brought in from Dublin, how they set about doing the
job with great zest, and how they carved monkeys and cats
as well as foliage. Acland later propagated a legend that they
began to caricature University notabilities and so were got rid
of; the humdrum truth is merely that in 1861 the donations
for carving ran out. The loss can still be felt, for the carvers
really represented Ruskin's ideal come true. He had written
to Acland: 'Your Museum is literally the first building raised

in England since the close of the fifteenth century, which has fearlessly put to new trial this old faith in nature, and in the genius of the unassisted workman, who gathered out of nature the materials he needed.' Besides their own inventions, the O'Sheas followed one design supplied by *Ruskin* himself: it is for the ground-floor lancet pair, second r. from the portal (and directly below the celebrated 'cat window'). For the portal itself, which was meant to be treated especially lavishly, the designer was *Hungerford Pollen*, funds having proved insufficient to build Woodward's intended shallow-projecting porch. The never-finished carving here is by the sculptor *Thomas Woolner*, including the marble section of the arch with its little figures of Adam, l., Eve, r., and at the apex an angel holding out the Book of Nature and some living cells. Doors of 1862, designed by *T.N. Deane*, i.e. after Woodward's death.

INTERIOR. The VESTIBULE has a rib-vault, with steps up to another portal. The capitals with animals and birds date from 1879, when *James O'Shea* came back for more. And so one enters. The MUSEUM COURT is almost square, and surrounded 89 like an Italian cloister by an ambulatory and an upper gallery, with the doors to the departmental rooms. The whole centre is glass and iron. Acland in 1855 looked forward to finding out 'how Gothic art could deal with these railway materials – iron and glass'. That is interesting; for Ruskin wavered violently on the question of whether these materials should ever be the vehicles of art. His *Seven Lamps of Architecture* (1849) had allowed that a new system of laws for metal construction would be necessary one day. In similarly positive mood, in a letter to Acland early in 1859, he drew an iron spandrel with horse-chestnut leaves; for wrought iron as a decorative material was in itself hallowed by many ancient uses.

As for the glass and iron of the museum, it consists of three parallel glass roofs, excessively steep again, supported by pointed arches on piers made up of four linked shafts and pointed-arched iron braces, the bolts all showing with perfect frankness. Of the three naves, as it were, the middle one is much higher, and has aisles composed of additional arcades placed partway along each roof slope. The capitals of the piers and the bigger spandrels have the most exuberant wrought-iron decoration, culminating in the W and E ends of the middle nave. The exquisitely delicate palm branches in particular had no parallel anywhere before Art Nouveau. They are much more elaborate than anything Viollet-le-Duc was drawing or doing in France, and they were completed before his *Entretiens* came out. The roof was designed and made by *Francis Skidmore* of Coventry, the first great work by the best English craftsman in iron. Skidmore was no engineer, however, and his first version collapsed when its wrought-iron piers proved too weak to support the glazing. *Sir William Fairbairn* then advised the introduction of more substantial piers and braces of cast iron, leaving Skidmore to rebuild the roof and reuse what he could.

The arches are painted with schematized patterns. In 2011–14 the roof was restored by *Purcell*.*

The STONEWORK is almost as admirable. On the capitals of ambulatory and gallery again there is the most gorgeous display of true-to-nature foliage species. Of the original phase are those of the ground floor and w gallery, carved by the *O'Sheas* and *Whelan*. Some of Ruskin's correspondents supplied designs for capitals, including Pauline, Lady Trevelyan, and the artist William Bell Scott, but the carvers preferred to work from wild specimens instead. The rest of the upper capitals were done in 1905–12, by craftsmen from *Farmer & Brindley*. It is characteristic of the museum that the polished columns are every one of them a specimen as well, of marble, of granite and so on. Deane & Woodward had done something similar in their Dublin museum, but the total at Oxford – 126 shafts, from across the United Kingdom – far exceeded it. At Oxford the scheme for stones and capitals alike was devised by the museum's Keeper *John Phillips*, also Professor of Geology. In addition, the brick surfaces above the lower arcades were to have been plastered and painted with narrative scenes, an idea which may now seem distracting. Ruskin even hoped to persuade Rossetti to contribute. In the event the only MURALS were done by the *Rev. Richard St John Tyrwhitt*, vicar of St Mary Magdalen, in the Geology Lecture Room (now subdivided as director's office etc.), ground floor, s side. The subjects are *Mer de glace* and Lava Stream, both of 1859, in style like the Pre-Raphaelite landscapist John Brett. The lower cloister has brick vaulting, also surprisingly rough. Much notched and zigzag woodwork throughout, on the wonderfully inventive doors with their foliate lock-plates, and the open roofs of some upper rooms. Some surviving painted decoration on walls and ceilings, much of it stencilled and by *Swan* (probably Morris's friend *Joseph Swan*, cf. No. 33 High Street, p. 414), e.g. in the former HOPE ENTOMOLOGY ROOM, first floor s side. Here also a fireplace carved by *Whelan* with foliage and creeping insects.

STATUES of great scientists stand around the courtyard. Of Caen stone. The earliest are contemporary with the building, and include works by the Pre-Raphaelites *Alexander Munro* – who also worked at the Oxford Union (p. 351), where others of the Brotherhood were busy painting – and *Woolner*. In the central aisle is the Prince Consort by *Woolner*, 1864. The rest are described anti-clockwise. NW corner: Hippocrates, by *Munro*. w side: Harvey, by *Henry Weekes*, 1864; Sydenham, 1886, and Hunter, 1894, both *H. R. Hope-Pinker*; Aristotle, by *H. H. Armstead*; Francis Bacon, by *Woolner*; Roger Bacon by *Hope-Pinker*, 1914; Priestley, by *E. B. Stephens*. SW corner, Davy, by *Munro*. s side: George Stephenson, by *Joseph Durham*, 1867;† Watt, by *Munro*; Oersted (plaster), 1886, after *J. A. Jerichau*. SE corner, Leibniz, by *Munro*. E side: Euclid, by *Durham*;

* Sadly, the original wood-framed display cases were replaced in 2020.
† Stephenson qualified as a scientist, such was the Victorian equation of scientific discovery and technical invention.

Galileo and Newton, both *Munro*; Darwin, by *Hope-Pinker*, 1899. NE corner, Linnaeus by *J. L. Tupper*. N side, again by *Munro*, the moving relief BUST of Woodward, who died in 1861. The surround is of green Connemara Serpentine, as too are the polished piers to l. and r.

In 1885–6 the PITT RIVERS MUSEUM was added NE of the Museum to house the anthropological collections of Lt-Gen. Henry Lane Fox Pitt Rivers. The architects were *T. N. Deane & Son*. A blatantly economical building. Superimposed galleries all round a single tall space, originally top-lit. Token Gothic patterns in the iron gallery fronts and roof trusses. Externally it shows to the N as a windowless wall with giant blind Gothic arches, yellow brick with some red brick voussoirs. In 2006–9 the museum was renovated by *Pringle Richards Sharratt*, who added to the S a big wing with stone-faced ends and a glazed centre. Blunt hip-roofed lantern over the top-floor interior, library floor below. The extension marked the final abandonment of a long campaign to carry off the marvellously crowded collections to a new home, of which the concrete-mesh-domed project of 1966 by *Powell & Moya* with *Pier Luigi Nervi* was the most utopian incarnation. Instead, part of the intended site was used for a small annexe at No. 60 Banbury Road, now part of Kellogg College (p. 463).

The University Museum proved to be the vanguard building for the present Science Area (*see* p. 370), into which *Woodward*'s two outlying ranges are now subsumed. The most notable remnant is the former CHEMISTRY LABORATORY to the S. It is a version of the Abbot's Kitchen at Glastonbury, i.e. a sturdily buttressed Gothic square with an octagonal pyramidal stone roof, here with stone chimneys on their own little pyramids at the four corners. Windows reworked in 1902 by *H.W. Moore*, who floored across the main space. The present arcaded two-storey link to the Museum is a rebuilding of 1949. An EXTENSION for Chemistry was provided in 1877–8 by *Deane*, also Gothic, across the far side of the (now infilled) courtyard behind; visible from the present courtyard of Inorganic Chemistry, adjacent to the S (p. 374). The former ANATOMY COURTYARD survives to the N, facing Dorothy Hodgkin Road; likewise much altered and extended.

Demolished in 1955 was the CURATOR'S HOUSE to the SE, also *Woodward*, 1857–8; a forerunner of North Oxford's legions of Gothic villas.

RADCLIFFE SCIENCE LIBRARY
WITH REUBEN COLLEGE
South Parks Road and Parks Road

The library originated with the transfer of scientific books from the Bodleian and Radcliffe Camera to the new University Museum in 1863. In 1898–1900 a bold new building was given by the Drapers' Company of London, and this is the present SOUTH WING that extends W from the former Chemistry Laboratory S of the Museum (*see* above). Unmistakably by *Sir T. G.*

Jackson. Irregular T-plan, three-storeyed, the cross-range at the E. Six main bays to the main range. To South Parks Road the cross-range appears as a slight projection with giant pilasters, a pediment and a large upper Venetian window. The rest has buttresses and mullioned-and-transomed windows bound together with arches at the very top. The entrance was in the cross-range to the NW, now replaced with a plain window. In 1934 a new doorway was made to South Parks Road with lettering over it by *Eric Gill*. The main entrance moved to the WEST WING of 1933–4, placed at right angles along Parks Road. This is – equally unmistakably – by *Sir Hubert Worthington*. His first Oxford use of the characteristic squared Bladon rubble, here with Clipsham ashlar below. N and S ends slightly convex, E and W sides with very shallow canted projections. The ashlar decoration is no longer period, but not Modernist either. The forms probably derive from that arsenal of the *Moderne*, the Paris Exhibition of 1925. In 2009 *Pringle Richards Sharratt* rebuilt Worthington's intervening STAIRCASE in glass-box form: a sore thumb to South Parks Road especially.

The library built a huge UNDERGROUND EXTENSION in 1971–5, by *Jack Lankester*, University Surveyor, with *A.M. Milne* and *E.J. Powell*. Of two levels, planned as interlinked rectangles which correspond to the paved courtyard and the S half of the University Museum lawn. The escape stair surfaces in the lawn by the original front boundary wall, and is detailed to match. Huge ceilings with a dominant grid of big circular recesses. Colonnades of slim, widely spaced piers. Later used as museum stores; in 2022 under conversion to a shared Teaching and Research Centre for all the University's museums.

INTERIORS. Jackson's STAIRCASE in the cross-wing rises around a cage of stone arches with wrought-iron balustrades. First-floor READING ROOM with aisles of slim columns playfully interpenetrating the bookcases. The UPPER READING ROOM has a big compartmented barrel ceiling of Jacobean-style plasterwork. In the 1930s wing the first-floor office has paired sliding DOORS of oak designed by *Eric Gill*, with openwork panels depicting Oxford scientists (the two Bacons and Hooke, l.; Harvey, Wren and Dillenius, r.). The sculptor was Gill's pupil *Donald Potter*. Also a CLOCK inside the office with carved angels.

The lower floors, with the University Museum's former Chemistry Laboratory (*see* p. 369), are now home to a new graduate college, REUBEN COLLEGE, founded 2019. Architects for the conversion *FJMT*.

SCIENCE AREA
South Parks Road and Parks Road

The main Science Area was designated in 1937, an area E and N of the University Museum (*see* p. 364). The land was formerly part of the University Parks (*see* p. 378), hence the inclusion of the Old University Observatory, established there in 1874. A

Science Area and Keble Triangle Site

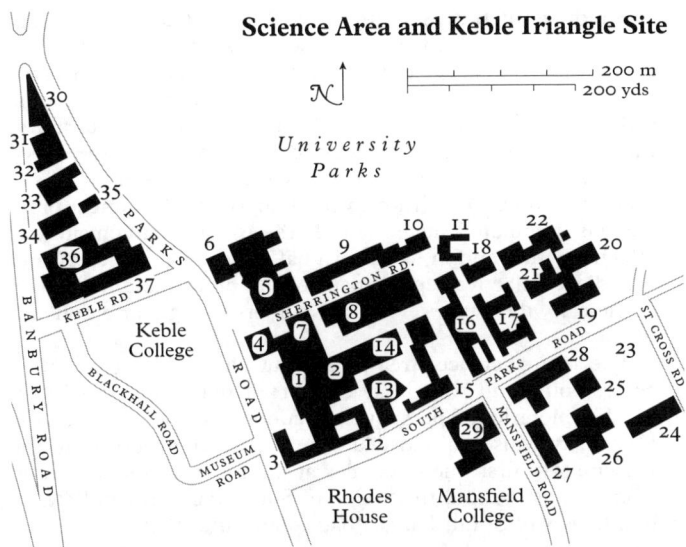

University Parks

200 m
200 yds

Keble College

Rhodes House

Mansfield College

1	University Museum
2	Pitt Rivers Museum
3	Radcliffe Science Library/Reuben College
4	Robert Hooke Building
5	Clarendon Laboratory
6	Beecroft Building
7	Atmospheric Physics etc.
8	Biochemistry
9	Sherrington Building
10	Henry Wellcome Building
11	Old University Observatory
12	Inorganic Chemistry
13	Earth Sciences
14	Le Gros Clark Building
15	Dyson Perrins Building
16	Physical Chemistry
17	Plant Sciences
18	Rodney Porter Building
19	Pathology
20	Edward Abraham Building
21	Molecular Pathology Institute
22	Medical Sciences Teaching Centre
23	Life and Mind Building (site)
24	Chemistry Teaching Laboratories
25	Peter Medawar Building
26	Pharmacology
27	Tinsley Building
28	Biomedical Sciences
29	Chemistry Research Laboratory
30	Jenkin Building
31	Information Engineering
32	Engineering and Technology
33	Holder Building
34	Thom Building
35	Hume-Rothery Building
36	Denys Wilkinson Building
37	Wolfson Building/E-Research

plan for most of the area not yet built upon had already been made in 1934, and the 1937 designation ruled out any further intakes of park land. Post-war expansion therefore looked w, to the established Keble Triangle site (p. 377), and to the s side of South Parks Road, replacing its Victorian villas and the N part of Merton's cricket ground – all as recommended in *Lord Holford*'s report of 1963.*

*A radical proposal of 1960 by *Chamberlin, Powell & Bon* to rebuild the main Science Area with deck-access blocks was soon shelved. Also rejected was their wildly impractical design of 1961 for a tapering Zoology tower 240 ft (73 metres) high, meant for the eastern edge of the Science Area.

Buildings of the 1870s to 1920s followed the various historical styles favoured by their architects. In 1935 *T.A. Lodge* of *Lanchester & Lodge* was appointed architect to the Science Area, and the partnership's symmetrical, stripped-traditional style – much employed also in Cambridge's science quarter in the mid C20 – is easily recognized in buildings up to *c.*1955. In that year the Modernists *Ramsey, Murray, White & Ward* took over, doing much up to the mid 1960s. No single practice has dominated since then. By the 1990s the main site was effectively full, and in its eastern half especially congested and muddled. Selective replacement of the older buildings began in the early C21, with several newcomers of high ambition and quality.

The main Science Area is laid out chiefly along two E–W access routes, in ways that do not all make for straightforward exploration. The sequence adopted below starts at the University Museum and takes the N and NE group up to the Observatory first, then resumes at the museum for the group along or just behind the N side of South Parks Road. Science buildings S of South Parks Road follow after that.

North and north-east

The wing coming forward NW of the University Museum, balancing the Radcliffe Science Library (p.369) to the S, is the ROBERT HOOKE BUILDING (now Computer Sciences etc.). Largely of 1946–8 by *Lanchester & Lodge*, built for Geology and Mineralogy; one of their squared-rubble, squared-up quasi-classical pieces. It includes a drastic reconstruction of the original CLARENDON LABORATORY (Physics) by *T.N. Deane*, 1869–71, i.e. a continuation of the C19 museum group. All that now shows of this externally is a Gothic bay window and some trefoil-headed openings on the N side. (Gothic-arched staircase enclosure inside; some capitals with naturalistic carving.) E part clashingly rebuilt in 1963 (*J. Lankester*) with grid-like concrete framing. Next to this a patterned brick section of *c.*1990.

On Parks Road just to the N is MUSEUM LODGE, a pretty stone fantasy of 1888 by *H.W. Moore*.

The present CLARENDON LABORATORY stands to the N. Multiple phases here, for the most part at odds architecturally. First, facing W, the former ELECTRICAL LABORATORY (now TOWNSEND BUILDING), 1908–10 by *Jackson*. Bright red brick and stone, William-and-Mary to Queen Anne in style. The Jackson office was moving with the times. Symmetrical front with shallow-projecting wings. Cross-windows, centrepiece with attached columns and a pediment, too low for effect (as at Hampton Court). Thick garlands, carved by *Farmer & Brindley*. Given by the Drapers' Company, like Jackson's Radcliffe Science Library; the main staircases have an affinity. Rear attachments of 1949 (NE), stone, and 1962 (E), i.e. the *Lanchester & Lodge* and *Ramsey, Murray, White & Ward*

eras respectively. To the N is *Lanchester & Lodge*'s NEW CLAR-
ENDON LABORATORY (now LINDEMANN BUILDING), 1939–
40, best seen from the Parks. Pale brick with a little stone;
shallow rebates and square panels in the brickwork for interest.
The W front is now partly obscured by the BEECROFT BUILD-
ING of 2015–18 by *Hawkins/Brown*, with *Peter Brett Associates*,
structural engineers. A rich building, with a distinctive and
coherent vocabulary. Oblong plan, not of uniform height. The
exterior shows close-set bronze horizontals and fins in staggered vertical alignments, i.e. the common early formal C21
device, here with the refinement of extreme slimness. Sombre
colours between: dark glazing, copper-mesh screens. On the
blind ground-floor section to Parks Road a big diagrammatic
RELIEF on aluminium panels by *Bridget Smith*, called Thinking
Light. Five above-ground storeys, another five below. The latter
are so placed both to respect height restrictions and to help
reduce vibrations in the laboratories, which rest on their own
dampening systems. Circulation from ground floor upwards is
via a full-height atrium, at once spectacular and visually coher- 129
ent. It has rounded corners, and is crossed by freely placed
flying stairs and by big landings hovering at half-heights,
serving as informal discussion spaces. Much use of wood,
including balustrades of close-set dark-brown timber slats – an
Aalto motif. The same on the bridges that cross the slanted
glass-walled entrance lobby on the Lindemann side. Finally the
MARTIN WOOD LECTURE THEATRE of 1998–2000, a wedge
in the gap between Jackson and Lanchester & Lodge. Symmetrical curved front. Stone uprights make a colonnade below,
and frame panels of red brick above. Glass-fronted foyer, r.

Now E, along the accidental and shapeless Sherrington
Road, between Clarendon (N) and Robert Hooke (s). On the
s side ATMOSPHERIC, OCEANIC AND PLANETARY PHYSICS,
the main part built as the MORPHOLOGICAL LABORATORY
(Comparative Anatomy) in 1898–1901. By *J.J. Stevenson &
Harry Redfern*. Three storeys, of stone, with cross- and two-
light mullioned windows and some larger ones with Gibbs
surrounds. Brick W addition 1937, added top storey.

Next on this side the new BIOCHEMISTRY. *Hawkins/Brown*
again: W part 2004–8, larger E part and main N entrance
2019–21. One giant block, four storeys high (the maximum
planning rules allowed), plus two below ground. Curtain
walling of pale grey-blue with flush window bands, brought to
life by the application to the upper storeys of coloured-glass
fins of different depths; purple and brown chiefly, also yellow
and orange. The SW corner is set back to form a small paved
square. Here the fins are omitted, and the curtain-wall glazing
has clear patches in Rorschach-like patterns, designed by the
artist *Nicky Hirst*. Other artworks include *Annie Cattrell*'s flock
of coloured cast-resin birds suspended in the atrium. This
WEST ATRIUM is of irregular plan, lined partly with grooved
timber, with stairways and bridges that cross and climb at
exciting diagonals. Write-up rooms etc. are placed around

the perimeter, laboratories around the outer walls. Structural engineers *Peter Brett Associates* for the w part, *Pell Frischmann* for the e part, in which the laboratories are located next to the atrium instead. The combined site formerly housed four interlinked blocks, 1880s to 1960s.*

On the n side of Sherrington Road, the SHERRINGTON BUILDING (PHYSIOLOGY etc.) of 1949–53. A long symmetrical front of light brown brick – *Lanchester & Lodge*, needless to say, here reworking a design of 1937. Top storey added, centre originally less high; NW extension, 2005. The Parks elevation has pylon-like attachments of Giles Gilbert Scott type in the middle. The e attachment is the HENRY WELLCOME BUILDING OF GENE FUNCTION, 2003 by *RMJM Ltd*. Sleek curtain walling. Pilotis below, and a passage through to the Parks.

The OLD UNIVERSITY OBSERVATORY is just beyond. Of 1873–5 by *Charles Barry Jun.*, who was a friend of the Rev. Charles Prichard, Savilian Professor of Astronomy. Built after an estrangement between the University and the trustees of the Radcliffe Observatory (for which *see* p. 151). Lecture room, library etc. added 1877–8. Yellow brick, vaguely Italianate detail. Much extended and altered.

North side of South Parks Road

The start is just e of the Radcliffe Science Library (p. 369), facing Rhodes House on the s side (p. 379). The main building of INORGANIC CHEMISTRY is by *Lanchester & Lodge*, 1954–7, but after pre-war designs. A symmetrical façade, three- and four-storeyed. Squared rubble above ashlar. Georgian proportions, though not Georgian windows. Enclosed courtyard with the *Deane* laboratory of 1877–8 as its w side (*see* p. 369).

Next EARTH SCIENCES, 2008–10 by *Wilkinson Eyre*, usually an extrovert practice, as indeed here. The structural engineers were *Pell Frischmann*. L-plan, with an eastward projection for the offices etc. to the n. The laboratory range, stone-faced and set end-on to the street, features a 'narrative wall' along the inner side. Bands of polished or glass-laminated limestones here, in angled arrangements suggestive of folded and faulted strata, with a touch too of Deconstruction *à la* Daniel Libeskind. Ribbon windows between, likewise slanting up and down, narrowing and widening. The other windows mostly square. Office wing with aquamarine cladding, cantilevered out on two sides. Full-height atrium in the angle between, behind a tall *brise-soleil*.[†]

*The original PHYSIOLOGY to the e, 1884–5 by *T.N. Deane & Son*, with Jacksonian C17 details, extended 1907–8; BIOCHEMISTRY, low and white with upper pilasters, by *Redfern*, 1924–7 and 1936–7; the HANS KREBS TOWER, w, an eight-storey slab of 1961–3, and MICROBIOLOGY, 1959–60, both *Ramsey, Murray, White & Ward*.
[†]Replacing PHARMACOLOGY, a smart curtain-walled block by *Gollins, Melvin, Ward & Partners*, 1959–61, s, and *J.A. Souttar*'s original PATHOLOGY LABORATORY, 1899–1901, N.

The rear parts face a kind of quad with the LE GROS CLARK BUILDING (Physiology, Anatomy and Genetics) on the N side. Pale brick, four- and five-storeyed, utilitarian; E part by *Lanchester & Lodge*, 1954–6, W part of 1917 etc. Incorporated behind is the original HUMAN ANATOMY BUILDING, 1891–3, stone, Free Renaissance, with a fancy pyramidal turret over the theatre. By *H.W. Moore*. Anatomy joins on to the Pitt Rivers Museum to the W, for which *see* p. 369. The E side of the quad is the back of the DYSON PERRINS BUILDING EXTENSION (Organic Chemistry), 1940–1, *Lanchester & Lodge* and pale brick again, but in their earlier, squared-up Georgian style. A third storey added *c.*1958, with other extensions. The link to the S range was rebuilt in 2004, further obscuring the attached portico of giant pilasters of the original DYSON PERRINS LABORATORY. This is by *Paul Waterhouse*, 1913–16 (E wing 1920–2). Fifteen bays along South Parks Road, dark red brick and ample stone dressings, the doorway not strongly marked. The specifications were based on those of the architect's John Morley Laboratories at Manchester (1908–9). Attached at the W a lecture theatre, separately treated. On the E side of the 1941 extension is its main entrance, and to its N an addition which incorporates the LECTURE ROOM of 1957–9 by *Ramsey, Murray, White & Ward*. Later infilling of its sloping underside, where the raking concrete piers were originally exposed.

Next E, aligned N–S, is PHYSICAL CHEMISTRY. 1938–41 by *Lanchester, Lodge & Davis*, paid for largely by Lord Nuffield. The same style and materials as the Dyson Perrins extension but not the same details; and bigger. Three storeys and an added fourth. Attached to the SE, a straightforward and attractive block by *Ramsey, Murray, White & Ward*, 1958–9. White ashlar wall to the street. The N attachment is the REX RICHARDS BUILDING (Molecular Biophysics), 1984. Brick bands with canted brick sills and corner. Mansard roof. The link cuts across one of the E–W streets of the 1930s Science Area plan (*see* pp. 370–1).

PLANT SCIENCES stand immediately E. Two interlinked H-plan blocks, originally Forestry (S) and Botany, built 1947–50. Another of the squared-rubble and squared-up ashlar jobs, here distinguished by blunt canted profiles. The style is like that of the 1930s Radcliffe Science Library addition (p. 370), and the architect is the same: *Sir Hubert Worthington*. Handsome garden between the blocks, originally accessible through the pergola screen of stubby columns on the E side. Inside Forestry a fine complement of finishes and fittings using woods from across the Commonwealth. To the N, the ponderous RODNEY PORTER BUILDING (Glycobiology etc.), 1989–91 by *D.W. Bending*, University Surveyor. Pale brick, window bands, hipped roof. *p. 138*

PATHOLOGY marks the E end of the Science Area. To the S, generously set back behind gates amid its own trees and lawns, the SIR WILLIAM DUNN SCHOOL OF PATHOLOGY, 1926–7. By *E.P. Warren*, a late work; comparable to his slightly earlier Pathology building at Cambridge and funded from the same legacy. William-and-Mary style. Long, symmetrical brick front with stone dressings. Short projecting wings. Big door hood, perron stair. Another perron to the W side. An octagonal lobby where the cross-corridors meet inside. On axis behind, the EDWARD ABRAHAM BUILDING, 2001–2 by *Llewelyn Davies*. An excess of materials: main E–W range with steel *brise-soleil* above brick; timber cladding on the end wall; shapeless linking range housing a canteen, glass-walled or green-copper-clad. The main range is prolonged to the W by the MOLECULAR PATHOLOGY INSTITUTE, by *Make* with *Nightingale Associates*, 2009–11. White walls, and extensive glazing to N and S with intermittent *brise-soleil* of red terracotta. It replaced a block of 1967–9 by *Sir Leslie Martin*. Further N, also linked on axis, the MEDICAL SCIENCES TEACHING CENTRE (NE), 2001–2. Dark cladding; slit windows; but partly curtain-walled towards the Parks. The enigmatic red brick block to its W is PATHOLOGY SUPPORT, 1995–7.

Science buildings south of South Parks Road

University science jumped across to the S side of South Parks Road with the Tinbergen Building (Zoology and Psychology) along St Cross Road, demolished in 2020. A major work of *Sir Leslie Martin*, 1965–70, with *Colen Lumley* (executant architect *Douglas Lanham*): a Brutalist concrete citadel, stepping up from the ends towards an E–W circulation spine. Scheduled for refurbishment, it was found to contain so much asbestos that demolition was ordered instead. *NBBJ*'s designs for a replacement LIFE AND MIND BUILDING were approved in 2021. This will join on to the CHEMISTRY TEACHING LABORATORIES added along the S perimeter in 2017–18 by *FJMT*. A row of five big cast-stone-faced boxes with mostly louvred fronts and big light-scoops above. The fourth box is left void, with a flight of stairs up to a glazed section across the back.

To the W, originally linked to Tinbergen by covered bridges, the PETER MEDAWAR BUILDING FOR PATHOGEN RESEARCH, 1996. This steps down to the W, echoing the former Tinbergen profile in a steel-framed, sharper idiom. Curtain-walled upper floors with projecting horizontal screens, vertically linked. Close by to the S is PHARMACOLOGY, 1989–94 by the *Architects Design Partnership*. Big, on an irregular cross-plan, the N and S arms extending laterally as pavilions. Yellow-brick facing, with a system of major and minor uprights. The major ones project, and support the projection of the top floor. Wrightian shallow hipped roofs. The same brick is used for the architects' TINSLEY BUILDING alongside to the W. Of 1978–81, for Virology; since 2011 the Centre for Neural Circuits and Behaviour. A vigorous, chunky design, expressing the subdivision into secure sections. Two unequal main parts, each with a two-storey slated mansard roof. Between them a pair of canted-ended, windowless stair enclosures. The other corners also canted. Ground floor recessed, with an entrance ramp and steps on the Mansfield Road side. To the N is BIO-MEDICAL SCIENCES, 2003–8. More yellow brick, with areas of green curtain walling and silver cladding, clumsily composed.

The CHEMISTRY RESEARCH LABORATORY stands to the w, across Mansfield Road. By *RMJM*, 1999–2003, to concentrate the research work of Oxford's three historic departments of chemistry. Logical and legible, but little more. The main bulk is on South Parks Road, with glazed staircase enclosures as end stops. Between is the pale green curtain walling of the laboratory storeys. Cast-stone panels on the ends. Along the s side a tall glass-walled concourse box, with the refectory and wall-climber lifts. Bridges span the void to the much smaller s block, for offices and meeting rooms. Also the main entrance, placed curiously remotely to the sw.

KEBLE TRIANGLE SITE
between Banbury Road and Parks Road

The University acquired this elongated triangle from 1912 onwards, after an early attempt to take land in the Parks was rebuffed (*see* Science Area, pp. 370–1). First on the site was the JENKIN BUILDING (Engineering), at the sharp N apex. 1914 by *W.C. Marshall*, architect also of Cambridge's Engineering buildings. Jacobean, brick with stone dressings, shaped gables. Symmetrical to Banbury Road, as completed by *E.P. Warren*, 1927. N front with a gable finial of a boy riding a tortoise. Utilitarian extension to Parks Road, 1931 by *G.P. Baynard*. Next on Banbury Road INFORMATION ENGINEERING, by *RMJM*, 2002–4. Mostly curtain-walled, sharp and clean-lined, with a glazed staircase enclosure and atrium entrance to the s. The brick block adjacent is ENGINEERING AND TECHNOLOGY, *c.*1989 (*D.W. Bending*, University Surveyor). Window bands, canted corners.

The 1950s–70s buildings further s form a distinctive group, interlinked by deck access raised above a service podium. The first masterplan was provided in 1957 by the New Zealand-trained Modernist *Basil Ward* of *Ramsey, Murray, White & Ward*, previously of the notable interwar partnership Connell, Ward & Lucas, but was never strictly followed. For the later buildings *Arup Associates* were the architects, including the HOLDER BUILDING (Engineering and Metallurgy), 1973–6. Reinforced concrete. Clear spans are achieved for the laboratories by placing the piers externally to the N and s. The floors with their ribbon glazing are jettied out E and w. Circulation and services in separate vertical enclosures to the N, with canted corners. Also a slim office tower to Parks Road, on stilts, with an entrance below. To the sw is the THOM BUILDING (Engineering Science), 1960–2 by *Ramsey, Murray, White & Ward*. A broad eight-storey tower, with projecting floor strings clad in small tiles. The butterfly roof-line adds a note of the arriving fashion for peculiar shapes. Nothing so tall was

allowed in central Oxford after that. To the SE of the Holder
Building, the HUME-ROTHERY BUILDING (Metallurgy), also
by *Ramsey, Murray, White & Ward*, 1957–9. Four storeys, lightweight aluminium cladding. The bow-sided shape recessed on
the Parks Road side is for a lecture theatre. Finally the DENYS
WILKINSON BUILDING (Nuclear Physics, etc.), by *Sir Philip
Dowson* of *Arup Associates*, built in phases 1963–71. Two near-
square courtyards, placed so that they intersect at one corner.
The main accent is the fan-shaped tandem accelerator with
unwindowed ribbed N and S walls, conspicuous to the NW:
a high point of the New Brutalism in Oxford. Otherwise a
powerfully horizontal composition. Post-and-lintel concrete
construction, with much demonstrative bracketing where the
top floor or floors project over the circulation deck. These have
dark, reflective curtain walling of exceptional precision. The
deck is bounded by slabs of heavily tooled white concrete, the
ground floor is treated as a battered plinth of shuttered concrete with window bands with closely set irregular mullions.
So the vertical progression is from rawness to refinement. A
broad open-tread staircase leads up to the circulation deck
from Keble Road. A domed OBSERVATORY was added over
the junction of the courtyards in 2005.

An intended third courtyard, to the SE, remained unbuilt.
Here instead is COMPUTER SCIENCE. The WOLFSON BUILD-
ING of 1989–93, extending from the big Victorian houses of
Keble Road (p. 430), defers to their pale brick and gabled
outlines. To the N, E-RESEARCH by *Oxford Architects*, 2006.
Two segment-roofed blocks, glazed link between.

4b. NORTH AND NORTH-EAST
outside the Science Area, with the Parks

UNIVERSITY PARKS
Parks Road, E side

Laid out from 1864 onwards by *William Baxter*, Curator of the
Botanic Garden, to a plan in which playing fields and informal
planting are intermixed. Gothic NORTH LODGE by *Deane*,
1862, to the NW. The SW entrance has ornate iron GATES of
1853, origin unknown; installed here 2004. In the park the
UNIVERSITY CRICKET PAVILION, 1880–1 by *T. G. Jackson*.
Oxford's most conspicuous introduction to the tile-hanging
and half-timbered gables of Norman Shaw *et al*. The SOUTH
LODGE on South Parks Road (SW), 1893 by *Drinkwater*, shows
the influence. – TENTORIUM (facilities building), 2002 by
Gray Baynes & Shew, faced in timber slats.

The parks extend E beyond the Cherwell and its branches.
Two footbridges of note. RAINBOW BRIDGE, 1923–4, with
a soaring concrete arch, is by *J. E. Wilkes*, City Engineer. The

very shallow-arched PARSON'S PLEASURE BRIDGE of 1949, not spectacular, is one of the earliest pre-stressed fixed-arch concrete bridges anywhere. By *Alfred Goldstein* of *R. Travers Morgan & Partners*, structural engineers.

ARCHAEOLOGY. Dr Plot, Keeper of the Ashmolean Museum, was the first to notice the Bronze Age ROUND BARROWS in the University Parks in the mid C17 (although he did not recognize them as such), and they can still be seen from the air in dry weather conditions.

DEPARTMENT OF STATISTICS
Nos. 24–28 St Giles', E side

1964–6 by *Jack Lankester*, University Surveyor, as the Mathematical Institute. Modest and sensible. Low, square block, intersecting a taller oblong slab to the S. Light brick. Leslie Martin is the influence. Brown ventilation panels in the ribbon windows, inserted in *Hawkins/Brown*'s sympathetic renovation of 2015.

AGRICULTURAL ECONOMICS RESEARCH INSTITUTE (former)
No. 9 Parks Road, W side

A minnow among the University's buildings: an early C19 house extended S by *Morley Horder* in matching fashion, 1925. Painted brick, shutters. Rear extensions by Horder, 1932 and 1938. Now departmental offices.

SCHOOLS OF RURAL ECONOMY AND FORESTRY (former)
Parks Road, W side

see St John's College, p. 283

RHODES HOUSE
South Parks Road

Established under the will of the arch-imperialist Cecil Rhodes (†1902) and in his memory, for an intended elite of postgraduate scholars from overseas. Initially there were to be ninety-six from the United States, sixty from the British Empire, and fifteen from Germany. The site was formerly part of Wadham's gardens. *Sir Herbert Baker* designed the building, which was constructed in 1926–8. Rhodes had been his early patron in South Africa, and for Baker the torch of his memory burned bright.

The result is a curious wedding of high-roofed Cotswold mansion and classical copper-domed rotunda. The mansion is H-shaped, the rotunda set between the two N wings. The mansion is large, the rotunda much less so, yet it is impressive in terms of scale.

The mansion has mullioned and mullioned-and-transomed windows, a balustrade, a hipped roof and an open cupola on eight thin columns; the rotunda has a tetrastyle Ionic portico two columns deep, and then the rotunda itself with its shallow copper-clad dome and bronze doors. Baker argued that the rotunda should not be 'out of place ... in the seat of classical scholarship', and that the Cotswold features represent the 'traditional craftsmanship of the stone-building shires of Oxford and Gloucester'. Architects are so good at finding rational justification after the event; but in truth the building was first designed without the rotunda, which was conceived as a memorial to Viscount Milner, chairman of the Rhodes Trust, who had recently died. Over the doorway a roundel of a ship carved by *Cecil Wheeler*; other carving by *Laurence Turner*. The rotunda centrepiece is linked to the mansion by corridors that go sideways from the ante-room behind. The E cross-wing contains the Warden's House. The main material incidentally is squared, rough-faced Bladon rubble, and Rhodes House started thirty years of that fashion in Oxford.

INTERIORS. The ROTUNDA is a lofty and powerful space, ashlar-lined under its more roughly finished stone dome. Paired Doric columns are inset at each high-set window, and at the recess over the doorway that houses *Wheeler*'s bust of Rhodes. Baker called this space the *Heroön* (heroes' shrine). From the rotunda one moves into a second ANTE-ROOM, a square with its own shallow dome on four segmental-arched openings with Doric columns. Ahead is the MILNER HALL for dining, with a W gallery and an E apse that is three sides of an octagon, and hence covered with three sides of a domical vault. Baker liked such unexpected little touches. The roof is open, a steep, muscular affair of arched braces and crown-posts. The proximity of this bluff Old English feature to the classical column-screen under the gallery and to the openwork Cape Dutch fanlights is disconcerting. Likewise the placing of the bay window, not by the dais, but centrally. Stylistically unstable juxtapositions in the smaller rooms too: dark ceiling beams on polished columns, carved Zimbabwe birds etc.

Ultimately, then, this beautifully crafted building is an oddity, but it has personality enough to rouse affection in some. The one whose affections were strongest was Sir Herbert Baker, who in his memoirs quotes Sir Michael Sadler's calling it 'the most inspiring place in Oxford' (*Architecture and Personalities*, 1944).

RENOVATION by *Stanton Williams* began in 2020. The basement is being reconfigured for a conference centre, excavating below the S garden terrace, with access from a new staircase descending inside the rotunda. The E garden will become a sunken residential court, and a large new pavilion will be built in the W garden. Amended versions of Baker's little lodges, l. and r. of the main building, are to be reinstated in reused materials.

ROTHERMERE AMERICAN INSTITUTE
South Parks Road, SE of Rhodes House

By *Kohn Pedersen Fox*, 1998–2001 (structural engineers *Dewhurst MacFarlane*), following a competition in 1993. Designed chiefly as a receptacle for the Vere Harmsworth Library of books on US history, politics and government, with additional offices, teaching rooms etc. The site overlooks the garden of Mansfield College to the S (p.192), and the design aims to reflect that. Structurally it comprises a steel-framed, glass-walled atrium towards the garden, interlocking with a concrete-framed part to the N, faced mostly in Bath stone ashlar. These solid walls continue on the W and E sides, and the SE corner with the entrance recess is singled out by a round-ended, glass-walled lift tower. An oversailing steel canopy and external louvres of fritted glass slats screen the library glazing from the sun. Below is a half-sunk storey with the smaller rooms at the level of the gardens, to which steps descend at each end.

The main interior is a complex but orderly combination of split levels and open library decks. Two of these decks face the S atrium, their concrete construction exposed as a series of big grey scalloped vaults. The upper deck projects less far, and above it the long clerestory shows, designed for natural ventilation. Some finishes of American oak, but mostly a late High Tech aesthetic of neutral greys and sharp lines.

OXFORD UNIVERSITY CLUB
Mansfield Road, E side

By *Maguire & Co.*, 2000–4. Curvaceous in plan, with pointed ends. Walls of square concrete blocks. The Mansfield Road side is enigmatic, with a few openings below, a round-ended staircase projection and a slim cylindrical stair-tower to the r., linked by glass bridges. Also a row of little porthole windows on the first floor. Steep glazed roof ridge, like a keel. On the playing fields side are runs of upright windows set very close, with a long veranda below, steel-framed and projecting far out above the basement storey, and a shallower balcony to the storey above. Top floor with a ribbon window under the eaves. The inside disappoints because the spaces seem to have been fitted in anyhow; the top glazing brings light down only to the S part, and that not very well; and so on.

QUEEN ELIZABETH HOUSE
(DEPARTMENT OF INTERNATIONAL DEVELOPMENT)
No.3 Mansfield Road

Mainly the house of 1897–8 by *C.J. Phipps* and his partner and son-in-law, *A. Blomfield Jackson*, for Dr J.H. Mee of Trinity. Cotswold gables and mullioned-and-transomed windows, buttressed Gothic porch. Absurdly huge chimney-breast to Jowett

Walk, s. Grand stair hall with a stone fireplace hood, also huge, and tie-beam roof. Brick N extension of 1966–8 by *Lankester*, for the library of the former Geography Faculty (fenestration reworked 2014–16). On Jowett Walk, *Hawkins/Brown*'s gabled extension of 2007–9 for the current occupants, replacing *Sir H. Worthington*'s Geography lecture hall of 1938. Something of a mis-step, with its bronze link section and its bronze window surrounds against rendered walls. The chimney-like features, bronze-clad too, are for passive cooling.

ST CROSS BUILDING
St Cross Road

Of 1961–4 by *Sir Leslie Martin & Colin St John Wilson*, with *Patrick Hodgkinson*; executant architect *Douglas Lanham*. The first post-war University (as against college) building in Oxford of international calibre, it was also the chief architects' most important collaboration. The brief of 1958 required an innovative combination of three faculty libraries – Law, English and Statistics, of which Law was by far the largest – with shared lecture rooms and other facilities. The great achievement was to lock everything together with such conviction and formal ingenuity. A comparison with *Peter Shepheard*'s designs of 1956 for a Law Library here, of pitched-roofed blocks weakly linked, shows how great a leap was taken.

Visually the building presents itself as a low, spreading composition with great emphasis on the contrast between long dark-framed window bands and sheer windowless cubes. The material is pale sand-faced Ibstock brick, used everywhere with each third course slightly raised, except in the three cubes which stand up above the rest. These represent the three skylit reading rooms. Altogether this is a cubic design. Projections of some of the banded parts for instance help to stress that. As against St Catherine's (p. 251), less than five minutes away, where the historical antecedent is Mies van der Rohe, here it is much of the progressive architecture of the 1920s. That is where one first finds these massive cubes and these sweeping bands of low windows. Yet there is a more recent influence too, and that is Alvar Aalto and especially his Säynätsalo Town Hall with its approach by external staircase and terrace. For in spite of its relative lowness and its complexity of grouping this is also a monumental building. The route up to the Law Library establishes that at once: a wide, open staircase rising into the heart of the building, first by seven steps to a spacious platform and then between the mid-storey walls l. and r. by another nine to another platform, and by ten, a landing and ten again to the entrance platform and terrace. It has the splendour of Persepolis.

The LAW LIBRARY READING ROOM is square, with a gallery, and the gallery widens above the issuing desk to form a square in the corner of the reading room square – a diagonal emphasis which had later issue in Wilson's British Library reading rooms. The room is white, with cork flooring and furniture of pale wood, and has a deep concrete grid as its ceiling, seven bays square. Around the two outer sides is a perimeter of shelving, then an outer zone of research desks or carrels. The other two READING ROOMS are of similar configuration, only smaller, and at different levels: English is reached from the lower landing, Statistics (now in other uses) originally from the ground-level doorway to the r. of the staircase. Within the lower levels are also three large, square LECTURE ROOMS, two of them going through two storeys. Teak linings and steeply raked seating within. While the reading rooms are light and happy, the CORRIDORS at these levels have a strange, frowning monumentality. They are low, and the brick is exposed – *architecture parlante* to a haunting degree.

MANOR ROAD BUILDING (SOCIAL SCIENCES)
Manor Road, E of the St Cross Building

By *Foster & Partners*, after a competition in 1995–6. Built in 1998–9 (S) and 2003–4 (N), bringing together Economics, Politics, Sociology etc. A broad rectilinear building, of three tall storeys rising to four in Phase Two, with a set-back entrance by a branch of the Cherwell to the SE. The pale grey concrete frame dominates externally, on a 5.4-metre grid determined by the bookstack units within. Each opening is filled with four upright glazing panels set flush, largely in a random pattern: clear (and openable) or opaque blue-grey. To the N the system changes to include half-width aluminium panels. At the entrance recess the rectangular plan is completed by carrying the roof across on a tall corner pier, a favourite Foster device.

Fair-faced concrete finishes and flush glazing continue, and dominate, internally. The entrance lobby is overlooked from the N by an internal café deck. From here a grand circulation route ascends to the upper storeys, rather as if the staircase of the St Cross Building had been taken indoors. First a straight stair climbing back to the W, where it ends with some bathos at a mere office corridor. A glass-sided bridge crosses the space, which rises to a long clerestory. At the second landing a broad passage extends to a square first-floor atrium within the N part, with its own lantern or clerestory, under which an open dog-leg staircase continues to the floors above. The ground floor is mostly open, with library stacks in the middle and reading spaces round much of the perimeter – serviced space, rather than a grand interior.

PLACES OF WORSHIP

Church of England

CATHEDRAL OF ST FRIDESWIDE. *See* Christ Church, p. 119.
ST MARY THE VIRGIN, High Street and Radcliffe Square.   22
    Oxford's chief parish church, and the place where the University held its ceremonies and kept its library in its early stages,

is stately by any parochial standard. It has a nave six bays long and a chancel five bays long, and a total length of about 175 ft (53 metres). It is chiefly a Perp church, except for some elements on the N side which are older: an outer aisle chapel, the steeple and the old Congregation House to the E.

In order of time one must start with the TOWER, a firm design with deep angle buttresses with repeated set-offs. This must have been started in the late C13; perhaps the work of *Richard of Abingdon*, mason, who was working at the church in 1275. N window from the restoration of 1861–2 by *G. G. Scott*, in place of one with simple intersecting tracery. He took the new Geometrical design from the infilled head of the former tower W window, now seen only inside. Also visible there the large arch to the S, with three orders of shafts and moulded capitals, clearly of the same late C13 date. This opened originally to a lost N transept, of which the gable line shows on the tower S wall, above the present aisle roof. A lower but still substantial shafted archway to the E, also visible only on the outer face, is interpreted as a preparation for a chapel that may never have been built. Above it is an early C14 window with ogee forms. The bell-stage has three-light openings with intersecting tracery. Then follows the SPIRE, one of the most spectacular in England. Its date *c.*1310–30 is determined by the lavish use of ballflower. The buttresses, one pair projecting at right angles at every corner, have ogee-canopied niches on all three sides, most of which house a statue. Set back behind them and placed diagonally against the spire are uncommonly large oblong pinnacles, each outer side with steep twin gables, and each setting back to a smaller, square pinnacle on top. To add to the profusion, four large lucarnes start from the foot of the spire on each cardinal face, again ending in a steep gable. The present arrangement of the inner pinnacles is of 1893–6 by *Sir T. G. Jackson*, who reversed a different restoration by *J. C. & C. A. Buckler*, 1849–51. All but one of the STATUES are Jackson's replacements, by *Sir George Frampton*.* The top 48 ft (14.6 metres) of the spire were renewed too. The total height is 191 ft (58.2 metres).

The CONGREGATION HOUSE was begun in 1320 by Bishop Cobham of Worcester, to provide the University with a meeting house and chapel (below) and a library (above). It is thus the oldest surviving University building in England. But the work was incomplete when Cobham died in 1327, and a wrangle followed with Oriel College, owners of the church, over its furnishing and use. Only after 1410 was the upper room finally fitted up, and here the University's books were kept, before the move to Duke Humfrey's Library later in the C15 (*see* Bodleian, p. 328). Congregation – the University's governing body – then moved upstairs, continuing to meet here until the Selden End of the Bodleian was completed in 1637.

---

*Originals now in New College cloister, p. 213.

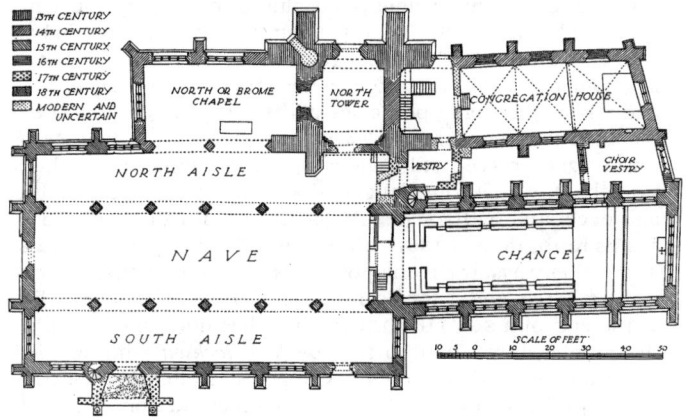

13TH CENTURY
14TH CENTURY
15TH CENTURY
16TH CENTURY
17TH CENTURY
18TH CENTURY
MODERN AND
UNCERTAIN

NORTH OR BROME CHAPEL

NORTH TOWER

CONGREGATION HOUSE

NORTH AISLE

VESTRY

CHOIR VESTRY

NAVE

CHANCEL

SOUTH AISLE

SCALE OF FEET

St Mary the Virgin.
Plan, 1939

The building is of three full bays and one lesser bay to the W, to link it with the tower. The Perp windows, four lights under four-centred arches, were made *c.*1507 to match those of the rest of the church, disguising the two-storey internal arrangement. In the skewed E wall this arrangement is still clear, with Dec windows: three lights above, two lights below. Entry through the W bay, remodelled *c.*1676 with a new doorway and oval upper window. The open-well staircase here is a replacement of 1758 (tree-ring date). The remaining bays of the Congregation House preserve the C14 rib-vaulting, on very short and very thin wall-shafts. Ribs with a long, sharp chamfer; good foliage bosses. In 1871 the space was adapted by *Scott* for a chapel for 'unattached' students, i.e. the body that became St Catherine's College in the C20. He restored the two-light S windows. After other uses, *Maguire & Co.* converted it to a café in 1992. Close-set lancets in the upper room (blocked on the N side) show the C14 arrangement, like that used later at Mob Quad library at Merton (p. 199). Its roof and elaborately decorated ceiling with flat foliage bosses date from *c.*1507, made by *John Fusting*. Of the same time the W vestibule screen, uncovered in 1963 and originally traceried, and probably also the pretty S oriel. In medieval times the entry was to the S, via an external stair. A C16 VESTRY fills the gap between chancel E end and Congregation House.

W of the tower is the N aisle chapel, alias ADAM DE BROME'S CHAPEL: built *c.*1328 by the rector, who was also the founder of Oriel College (p. 225). This too was remodelled with four-light Perp windows, *c.*1510–20.

As to the rest, the chancel is of *c.*1462–7, the nave and aisles of 1487–*c.*1500. The former was paid for by Bishop Lyhert of Norwich, a former Provost of Oriel, the latter by subscriptions from distinguished alumni begged by the University. The CHANCEL has very high windows of three lights, with two-centred arches, and transomed. They look spectacular from the S, i.e. the High, where there are no accretions and where the many pinnacles add to the feel of festiveness (actually the work of *T.G. Jackson*, 1897–1902). E window of seven lights, placed still higher up. To continue along the S side, the NAVE has four-light windows with four-centred arches and decorated battlements, the latter to a design recovered in *Scott*'s restoration of 1861–2. The pinnacles are again *Jackson*'s. Two S doorways, the E one post-1675, the other with undercut leaf spandrels and a four-centred arch. But that doorway lies at the end of a SOUTH PORCH which has not quite its par in the country. It was built in 1637 by *John Jackson*, who received £272 for the work, although its design has often been attributed – probably incorrectly – to the eminent mason-architect-sculptor *Nicholas Stone*.* It has a round-arched entrance and twisted columns l. and r., the so-called Salomonic motif, with connotations of sacred kingship. Rams' heads on the plinth like those at Canterbury Quad, St John's (pp. 275ff), where John Jackson had lately been working. Outside the columns are big volutes like the set-offs of buttresses. The columns carry a wild superstructure of classical elements, fragments of a segmental pediment ending in scrolls and with angels sitting on top, and, squeezed between them and dropped to just above the arch, a shell-topped niche with a STATUE of the Virgin and Child, and another pediment above the niche. (The present statue dates from 1895, the replacement angels by *Michael Black* from 1970s restoration.) But inside the porch – a telling fact – is a fan-vault still. The porch was given by Morgan Owen, former chaplain to Archbishop Laud and future Bishop of Llandaff, and the inclusion of the Virgin's statue was made one of the indictments at Laud's trial in 1644. GATEPIERS, alternately blocked, of the same date, with good wrought-iron GATES of the early C18. When *Scott* restored the porch in 1864–5 he refused to submit to pressure to destroy all these. Seven-light nave W window, renewed 1790–1. The design is taken from Winchester College chapel, i.e. a late C14 source (cf. Merton chapel N transept). Nave N doorway dated (15)69, with original DOOR.

Perp is the total impression of the INTERIOR. Very light chancel with its high windows. The NE window comes down with blank panelling nearly to the ground. Excellent SEDILIA on the S side. The nave arcades are high, the piers with a typical Late Perp section: thin triple shafts in the main directions, a wide hollow with a thin set-in shaft in the diagonals. Octagonal caps with concave sides. Two-centred arches. Similar chancel arch. A carved frieze with angel busts runs along the sill of the clerestory windows and turns down l. and r. of the W

---

*Starting with Stone's kinsman, Charles Stoakes. Stone's candidacy has been upheld by Russell Taylor in *Georgian Group Journal* 23 (2015).

window. Roofs C15 or early C16, but the chancel roof largely reconstructed in concrete by *Fielding Dodd & Kenneth Stevens*, 1947, after a fire. The C14 date of the Brome Chapel can be recognized in the two-bay arcade of two broad continuous hollow chamfers. (Now concealed, an arched C14 opening in the N aisle E wall, formerly the E wall of the lost N transept. Two colonnettes with moulded capitals.) Gothic WEST GALLERY of 1827–8 by *Thomas Plowman* of Oxford. One E bay of his NORTH GALLERY also survives. The other arches to the N chapel here were opened up in 1930 by *Sir Charles Nicholson*. PANELLING of 1733 survives on the inner walls of the chapel, with seating and a THRONE (W), all done for the Chancellor's Court and all now painted. The court entrance was the Baroque stone doorcase in the tower opening. The present OFFICE under the W gallery, with translucent walls of greenish glass slabs, belongs with renovations by *Caroe Architecture*, 2011–12.

OTHER FURNISHINGS. CHANCEL. Of the C15 REREDOS one row of seven canopied niches remains. STATUES inserted 1933, one or more by *Esmond Burton*. – Below is wooden PANELLING from the refurnishing of 1673–5, with Corinthian pilasters. – ALTARPIECE. Virgin and Child of the Column by *Simon Vouet* (1590–1649), lent by the Ashmolean. – COMMUNION RAIL. 1673–5, of openwork foliage panels. – STALLS. The original C15 stalls. Simple blank tracery panels on the fronts; small poppyheads on the ends. Plain backs, the pretty cresting added in 1900 by *Jackson*. – CHANCEL SCREEN of stone, Gothic, 1827–8 by *Plowman*, pierced with two extra doorways in 1926. The timber columns on the E side seem to be of *c.*1600. – ORGAN above by *Metzler* of Switzerland, 1986–7, its C17-style case designed by *Bernhardt Edskes*. – STAINED GLASS. E window, C15 and C16 fragments. – MONUMENTS. Many tablets and cartouches. – s wall. Thomas Gurney †1661, carved like a beast's skin. Attributed to *Thomas Cartwright I* (GF). – Charles Holloway †1679, s wall. Large columned tablet with open scrolly pediment and a big urn. Signed *William Stanton*. – N wall. Charles and Alice Holloway, both †1695. With convex inscription panel. Presumably by *Thomas Hill*, cf. the Levinz monument at St John's College (GF).

NAVE. By *Plowman*, 1827–8, the wooden PULPIT, the THRONE under the W gallery for the Chancellor or Vice-Chancellor, and the small octagonal Neo-Perp FONT in the N aisle. – SCULPTURE. Plaques of the Precious Blood by *Bernard Johnson*, inspired by Eric Gill. Installed 2012. – STAINED GLASS. Two windows designed by *Pugin*, s aisle E (1844, made by *Wailes*) and s aisle s, second from E (1848, made by *Hardman*). Also here, from E to W, windows to Keble by *Clayton & Bell*, 1866, to the Rev. Charles Marriott by *Hardman*, 1867, and to Isaac Williams, 1870, again *Clayton & Bell*. N aisle, old heraldic glass, installed 1933. W window, Tree of Jesse by *Kempe*, 1891.

MONUMENTS. s aisle. Fine anonymous tablet with a big urn, garlands and skull-and-crossbones. – Dr John Wallis, Savilian Professor of Geometry, †1703. Demi-figure preaching.

Attributed to *William Townesend*. – Dr David Gregory, Savilian Professor of Astronomy, †1708. Also *W. Townesend*. Bust with much animation and excellently carved. Relief of three putti with astronomical instruments. – N aisle. Malina Boys †1584, stone arched panel with brasses of kneeling groups. – Elizabeth Cary †1723. Very Italian and Baroque. Bust in relief in an oval, set against black drapery. A putto at the top. Design attributed to *George Clarke*, carving to *Francis Bird* (GF). – Sir William Jones, 1801 by *Flaxman*. With an Indian and an allegorical female figure l. and r. of the inscription. (*See also* University College chapel, p. 302.) – Martyrs' monument, lettered slab designed by *Martin Jennings*, 2008. – N chapel. Tomb-slab of Adam de Brome †1332. Indents of a brass cross with Virgin and Child at the foot. Base of 1940 by *Caröe & Passmore*. – R. and R. Playdell †1690 and †1693 (NW corner). Cartouche attributed to *Edward Pearce* (GF). – Mrs Eveleigh †1799. By *Sir R. Westmacott*. Big tablet without figures. Elegantly carved sarcophagus. – Tower. Over the S doorway, C15 stone slab with little angels and brackets for shafts. – Edmund Croston, Principal of Brasenose Hall, †1507, above. Small kneeling brass figure and figure of St Catherine, re-set between carved pieces of Croston's chest tomb, made by *J. Fusting*. – Henrietta Luisa Fermor, Countess of Pomfret †1762. Signed *John Townesend Jun.* (i.e. *III*). Delightful early Gothic Revival, as also adopted by the countess for her London house. Tripartite, the middle with an ogee arch. In the side parts two weeping cherubs.

ALL SAINTS (former), High Street. Since 1975 the LIBRARY of LINCOLN COLLEGE, just to the N (p. 175). Rebuilt in 1706–10, after the medieval church tower collapsed. Its authorship has been a favourite puzzle of architectural history. *Dean Aldrich* is named as designer in the *Pocket Companion to Oxford* (1756), and Aldrich was also one of the trustees of the rebuilding fund. In addition, the same distinctive type of flat-topped queen-post roof truss appears earlier at Queens' library (*see* p. 240), another building in which Aldrich had a hand.* So there may seem little reason to look further, except that early engravings of the design show a markedly different treatment of the upper tower and spire, left unbuilt when Aldrich died in 1710. There exist alternative drawings and a sketch by *Hawksmoor* for the tower, all different, but these are even less like what was eventually built in 1718–20. Instead, an unknown hand appears to have combined elements from both proposals, as will appear.

All Saints is one of the most perfect English churches of its date, and important too as a forerunner of the grand London churches that followed the Act of 1710. By comparison with the London group, it has none of the Baroque violence of Hawksmoor's churches, and yet more force than Gibbs's. The church consists of a straightforward oblong body without aisles

* *See* James Campbell in *Building Histories: Proceedings of the Fourth Conference of the Construction History Society* (2017).

or separate chancel or apse, and a w tower wholly projecting, i.e. not rising seemingly out of the body of the church
as Gibbs allowed it to happen. The tower is square below,
with channelled rustication to its lowest stage, and provided
with plain arched windows. The aprons of these windows have
something of Vanbrugh's and Hawksmoor's bluntness. Above
is a transitional stage with a big oculus on each side, answering
to the attic level of the church, and then the bell-stage. The
openings here are arched too, with the curiously old-fashioned
detail of intersecting tracery. The arches stand on imposts that
run through to the broad angle pilasters, where the channelled
rustication is repeated. Then follow the balustrade, corner urns
and low drum, all after *Aldrich*, the rotunda with its detached
columns after *Hawksmoor* (taken from Sangallo) and the top
stage with its octagonal spire adapted from Aldrich, where
Hawksmoor had proposed a little stone dome. Rotunda and
spire play an important role in the skyline of Oxford.

The sides of the church have in the westernmost bay a big
portico of paired Corinthian columns with a pediment to N
as well as S. The rest of the sides, and the end wall as well,
have plain arched windows between paired pilasters of the
same order. There is an attic too, with short, segment-headed
windows. Much refacing: of 1971–5, when *Robert Potter* converted the church for the college, and before. Indeed the spire
was first rebuilt (by *E. G. Bruton*) as far back as 1874. C18
RAILINGS survive to the E and N.

The INTERIOR has giant pilasters all round, of the same
Corinthian order as the outside but fluted. They stand against
half-pilasters, forming attractive clusters. Broad flat ceiling
with penetrations from all the attic windows and stucco panels
with wreaths, palm fronds and the like within its big grid of
compartments. In the conversion the W gallery was removed,
and the floor of all but the W part raised to the level of the
bases of the pilasters. A lower level was excavated beneath
this, lit by opening some of the blank lunettes in the plinth.
Lincoln's old SENIOR LIBRARY was then moved lock, stock
and barrel into the E part. It features Doric pilasters and heavy
entablatures of 1739, veneered on to the C17 oak presses. The
shelves etc. of the upper level incorporate WOODWORK from
the church, pierced panels etc., as well as late C17 work originally from the choir and altarpiece of Magdalen chapel. Also
woodwork from *T. G. Jackson*'s restoration of All Saints as the
City Church in 1895–6.* – REREDOS. Given by Lord Crewe
in 1717, and plausibly attributed to *Hawksmoor*. Of stone,
pedimented, with paired cherubs' heads and drapery against
tapering piers. – CHANDELIER. Also early C18. – ROYAL ARMS,
carved. Queen Anne. – MONUMENTS. William Levins †1616.
Recumbent effigy, praying. The surround has disappeared.
– Edward Tatham, †1834. By *H. Weekes*, 1843. Very large wall

*The C18 pulpit is now at Holy Trinity, Reading.

monument; it cost £800. Seated figure at a desk, hands folded. – Also several cartouches.

ST ALDATE, St Aldate's. A pre-Conquest foundation. The name may derive from 'old gate'. Heavily rebuilt by *J.T. Christopher*: in 1862–3 the arcades with their typically High Victorian piers of pink Aberdeenshire granite with naturalistic capitals, the aisle extensions alongside the chancel, the NW vestry and the W part of the S aisle; in 1872–3 the W tower and recessed spire, near-copies of what was there before. Earlier, in 1832 or 1843, *H.J. Underwood* extended the N aisle by one E bay, since pierced with a two-bay arcade in *Batterton Tyack Architects*' reordering of 1999–2002. This goes with an assertive new porch-cum-baptistery, glass-walled with a patinated copper roof and stone-built flank. *J.M. Surman*'s flat-roofed meeting rooms, vestries etc., of 1961, wrap round the tower. Local scenes carved in the parapets. The rest is as follows: N chapel with Perp windows, added *c.*1456 by Philip Polton, Archdeacon of Gloucester, and now open to the nave; late medieval chancel (E window probably *Underwood*'s); and the three E bays of the S aisle, built as a chapel by John of Ducklington before 1334. Restored Dec windows here. The reticulated tracery of the original chapel E window was successfully reused in 1862–3, as a screen above the arch to the chancel S extension. Ducklington's chapel has a CRYPT beneath its two eastern bays, now a heating chamber. (Quadripartite vaulting rising right from the floor, sharply chamfered ribs.) From at least *c.*1530 to 1843 the S aisle had a hefty upper storey, built originally to house the library of Broadgates Hall next door, the predecessor of Pembroke College. Until 1732, when it built its own chapel, the college also used the S aisle for worship. In the chancel N aisle, E, a length of re-set and restored C12 arcading previously in the chancel N wall. An early origin is indicated by a piece of C10 cross-shaft found in 1999 in the nave S wall.

FURNISHINGS. Not much, after reordering. – FONT. C15. Lions and leaves on the foot, quatrefoils with faces on the body, a frieze of angel heads with wings above. (Octagonal C17 COVER, spire-shaped, with paintings.) – SCREENS, now at the W end. One designed by *P.S.P. Morter*, 1929–30, with carved scenes of work and making. The other designed and carved by *Evelyn Wybergh* of Overton, Flintshire, 1926. It depicts hedgerow creatures. – STAINED GLASS. E window, in memory of the Rev. A.W.M. Christopher, rector and cousin of the architect. *Burlison & Grylls*, 1913. – MONUMENTS. John Noble, Principal of Broadgates Hall, †1522. Alabaster. Tomb-chest with angels under narrow canopies. Damaged effigy. – Three pictorial brasses, †1597–†1613. – John Woolly †1690, *et al.*, small tablet with putto heads and garlands. – John West †1696, with wife and daughter (tower). Wall monument with three frontal demi-figures as if at a balcony. Short columns l. and r. and an impure pediment. – W. Chipps, mason, †1730. Draped tablet. – Rev. Samuel Stockford †1809, by *Thomas Knowles I*. Neoclassical.

RECTORY, Pembroke Street. *See* Perambulation 6, p.444.

ST BARNABAS, Cardigan Street. Built in 1868–9 in the workers' suburb of Jericho at the expense of Thomas Combe, Superintendent of the University's Clarendon Press, High Churchman and early patron of the Pre-Raphaelites. The first Pre-Raphaelite picture which William Morris saw was one of Combe's purchases. Combe dressed and behaved picturesquely and was a client of precise demands. He turned to *Arthur Blomfield*, as he had done a few years previously for the Radcliffe Infirmary chapel (p. 362). At this date Blomfield had not yet become *arrivé* and conventional. In the architect's words, the stipulation was 'strength, solidity and thoroughly sound construction in every part; and not a penny was to be thrown away on external appearance and decoration'. In another account: 'All methods of construction should be the simplest...and...a solemn internal effect should be aimed at by proportion alone, and by the addition, by degrees, of coloured decoration applied to the surface of the walls.' Indeed Blomfield intended at the beginning to build the whole structure of concrete (not yet reinforced concrete of course). However, he found that rubble walls cement-rendered would be cheaper, and this is what the church became – rendered, with brick bands and other small brick features as the chief ornament. Where concrete was indeed used it is unobtrusive, e.g. the lintels and sills. The church thus completed cost £6,492. The campanile followed in 1871–2 (re-roofed in 1965; the original had a steeper pitch). *Joseph Castle & Co.* of Oxford were the builders. The NE chapel is of 1888 by *Blomfield*, the SE chapel of 1919–20 by *C. G. Hare*, the NW chapel (former porch) by *Paul Waterhouse*, 1912.

Blomfield's basic conception is an Italian Romanesque basilica, i.e. arcades with round arches, clerestory windows round-headed, an apse, and a campanile rising on the S outside the aisle (connected high up by an organ loft, in 1887). Besides the added SE apse there is also a W apse, serving as the baptistery. The bell-openings however are Gothic, with Geometrical tracery. The low aisle windows and those of the vestry W of the campanile are very odd, neither correct Romanesque nor correct Gothic. They are very low, of two lights with a stumpy dividing column. The columns of the arcades are vaguely French Early Gothic, very fat, with freely treated foliage, near to waterleaf and near to crockets (carver *E. F. Knowles*; faces of Blomfield, Wilberforce etc. on the capitals of the baptistery arch). Shallow-pitched open roof of quite elaborate carpentry, with *Blomfield*'s decoration. A low-walled choir enclosure comes forward of the altar steps, originally finished with iron screens, and reminiscent of the Italian *cancelli*. The DECORATION of the E end is Blomfield's too, executed originally by *Heaton, Butler & Bayne* but redone with much gilding in 1893. The apse semi-dome has the great Pantocrator like the Romanesque churches of Sicily. The other walls have achieved some of the extra surface decoration foreseen in 1869, notably on the N side: *opus sectile* decoration of the arcade spandrels, and long rows of saints and martyrs – *à la* Ravenna, but of course much more humane – between the

91

clerestory windows. All this by *Powells*, 1905–11. That on the s side was never executed.

FURNISHINGS. St Barnabas has what is claimed to be the first BALDACCHINO in an Anglican church, an original *Blomfield* feature. Italian Trecento Gothic style. – Hanging metalwork CROSS, 1869, i.e. also very early. – PULPIT. 1887. Designed by *Blomfield*, executed by *Heaton, Butler & Bayne*. Renaissance-Jacobean, on columns and with a sounding-board. Painted figures of the Apostles by *Floyce*. – ALTAR and REREDOS, NE chapel. 1873 by *Blomfield*, with figures by *Heaton, Butler & Bayne*, who added more in 1906. – WAR MEMORIAL, *c.*1920, s aisle. From St Paul, Walton Street. Designer *F.C. Eden*. – BRASS. Rev. M.H. Noel †1929, designed by *C.G. Hare*.

ST CLEMENT, Marston Road. The old church stood just E of Magdalen Bridge. Its replacement on this new site is of 1825–8, by *Daniel Robertson*. It cost £6,530. John Henry Newman was curate at the time of building. 1828 is a remarkably early date for Neo-Norman. The w tower and the whole church are Norman, though patently Georgian Norman. The tower is very square, the windows are tall, and there are symmetrical doorways in the first and last of the six bays – all Georgian characteristics. Square E end; no structural division between nave and chancel. Six-bay arcades with columns. Richly carved capitals, clearly modelled on those of the Cathedral, and more plausible than might be expected for the 1820s. Grotesque bust corbels and wall-shafts above. Canted ceiling. Of the refurnishing by *E.G. Bruton* in 1871, the FONT and some PEWS remain, both also Neo-Norman. – STAINED GLASS. E window by *I.H. Russell* of Oxford, 1846–7, with stories in small medallions. N aisle E, *Powells*, 1907. Four N windows of 1865 by *A. & W.H. O'Connor* with scenes told in large figures, from St Martin, Carfax (p.408). – Several Neo-Norman MONUMENTS. – WAR MEMORIAL (churchyard). Delicate Gothic cross. 1921.

ST CROSS (Balliol Historic Collections Centre), St Cross Road. The church still has the character of the village church next to Holywell Manor, even though its neighbours now include prominent University buildings. It was first built *c.*1100, and of that time is the plain chancel arch, unmoulded, on plain imposts carved with a grid of small St Andrew's crosses. The next surviving part is the w tower. Its doorway of three continuous chamfers is from *J.M. Derick*'s work of 1843–4, but the arches into the N and s aisles in their bases and capitals point to the C13. So the church already had aisles then, and they embraced the tower. The upper tower is of 1464, after a collapse. Both aisles are Early Victorian rebuildings: the s aisle of 1843–4, with round arcade piers, the N aisle of 1837–8 by *John Plowman* (*Sen.* or *Jun.*), who reused some old Perp windows. Chancel restored and NE vestry added in 1876, by *H.J. Tollit*. Excellent conversion for the present use by *Montgomery Architects*, 2009–11, leaving the chancel intact. Their lofty wooden CASES now fill most of the aisles.

OTHER FURNISHINGS. PAINTING of the chancel ceiling by *Henry Strachan*, 1898, of the nave ceiling to designs by *E.P. Warren*, 1893. The Crucifixion over the chancel arch is by *Leslie Pimm*, 1940, replacing angels of 1893 by *Reginald Hallward*. – STAINED GLASS. E window by *Hardman*, 1874; also s aisle s, two, 1871. s aisle E (Sir John Stainer memorial), *Powells*, 1901. N aisle N, *Baguley*, three, 1870–2. N aisle w, 1855, but moved and garbled. By *Horwood Bros* of Frome. Good vestry E window, †1865. – WAR MEMORIAL, *opus sectile* by *Powells*, 1924. – MONUMENTS. Brass to Elizabeth Franklin of the King's Arms inn, †1622, in childbed. Canopy above her head with looped-up curtains. Probably by *Richard Haydock*. – G. Freeling †1892, tablet designed by *E.P. Warren*, carved by *Lawrence Turner*.

The churchyard blends into Holywell Cemetery: *see* p.419.

ST EBBE, St Ebbe's Street. First recorded *c.*1005, when it was given to Eynsham Abbey (*Oxfordshire: North and West*). The oldest visible work is C12, namely the w doorway, as restored and reassembled here in 1904. Two orders of colonnettes, decorated scallop capitals, an inner arch order of beakhead, and an outer order of point-to-point chevron. It must be of *c.*1150–60. The lower part of the tower seems C13 – see the w lancet – but the rest is chiefly C19: first the Oxford builder-developer *William Fisher Sen.*, 1814–16, then *Street*, 1862–6. Fisher's is the N side with the typical early Gothic Revival windows – intersecting and Y-tracery – and the next stage of the tower. Street's are the added s aisle, the arcades, the chancel and the stonework of the E and w windows. Tower top and bell-openings by *A. Mardon Mowbray*, 1904. Finally the balancing N doorway at the E end, and the rubble-walled s projection with some re-set Street windows, 2017 by *Quinlan Terry*. They go with new GALLERIES, three-sided in the Georgian way, even down to the steeply raked panelled benches. Nave roof ceiled in connection. Earlier reordering left only *Street*'s REREDOS, and the FONT given *c.*1810–20. This is octagonal, generally Perp, crisply and neatly carved. – STAINED GLASS. E window, 1905 by *T.W. Camm*. Chancel s, †1918, partly photo-realist. s aisle, first from E, C15–C17 heraldry and fragments, including part of a C15 figure of St James. Second from E, much restored Virgin and Child (heads original), a composite figure of St Ebbe (mostly), and other fragments, assembled 1904. Third from E, *Wippell & Co.*, *c.*1920. – MONUMENTS. Cartouche to Robert Whorwood †1688, near-twin of the Upton monument at Wadham chapel. Also a vigorous framed tablet to Frances Whorwood, 'Virtuous Gentlewoman', †1678.

CHURCH CENTRE and VICARAGE are attached to the SW, workaday designs by *K.C. White & Partners*, 1971–4, extended by the *MEB Partnership*, 2003–4. For the former rectory *see* Paradise Square, p.440.

ST GILES, St Giles'. First mentioned *c.*1123–33. The existence of the Norman St Giles is proved by the remains of two (formerly

more) blocked, round-arched clerestory windows on the nave
N side, and by two re-set Norman shafts with cushion capitals
in the chancel S wall. The lower part of the tower is pre-1200
too, with a pointed arch on gross waterleaf capitals. In the early
C13 the tower was finished and given its twin bell-openings
with the curious little lancet openings in the tympana. Early
C13 also the nave arcades, of well-wrought round piers, quite
tall, with round abaci and double-chamfered arches, and the
tower-embracing aisles with their windows, lancets, paired
lancets and a stepped triplet of lancets. A strange feature is
the round-arched recesses with shafts inside the lower aisle
walls. The N aisle is richer, and of exceptional form: detached
shafts with a few stiff-leaf capitals separating the lancet groups
inside, cross-arches from the piers, and cross-gables externally, suggesting a sequence of discrete chapels. The S porch
belongs, though much restored. The chancel roof has been
tree-ring dated 1288. It comprises collar-rafter couples with
ashlar pieces, giving the effect of a canted wagon roof. Contemporary chancel N window, of two lights with a lozenge in
the tympanum. The E window of three stepped lancet lights
represents an adaptation in 1894 of a window by *J.M. Derick*,
1840. The S chapel is mid-C13, its E window with Geometrical tracery restored in 1838–9, its S wall rebuilt in C13 style
in 1851–2, both by *H.J. Underwood*. Are the simple shallow
imposts of the chapel's unmoulded W arch C13 as well? The
RCHME thought they might be C12, reused. Lastly the nave
clerestory, late medieval, with trusses of 1850. Victorian embellishments were partly expunged by *Harry Redfern*, 1920, and
Sir Charles Nicholson, 1949–50.

FURNISHINGS. PULPIT. 1840 by *Derick*, copying late C14
woodwork found within the old pulpit. – FONT. C13. Square
with angle colonnettes, on one fat and four thin shafts. Plenty
of dogtooth in vertical strips. – SCREENS. Lady Chapel (SE),
1995 by *Allan Doig*, with other chapel furnishings. W, 1999–
2000 by *Christopher Rayson*, detailed after a *Redfern* screen of
1933. – SCULPTURE. Small polished disc by *Philippine Sowerby*,
suspended in the internal chancel window. 2011. – STAINED
GLASS. E window, *Burlison & Grylls*, 1894, with lower panels
of 1920. Chancel N lancet, *Clayton & Bell*, 1866. N aisle E,
†1854, Seven Works of Mercy, unusual in treatment and iconography. Style of *William Miller* (MH). N aisle N, one window
with detached scenes by *Clayton & Bell*, 1862, another by
Hardman, 1881. S aisle S, two dark panels designed by *H.J.
Moberly* for *Powells*, 1862. S chapel E, *Ward & Nixon*, 1851.
– MONUMENTS. Henry Bosworth, erected 1635. Kneeling
figures only, reassembled on the W screens in 2004. – Thomas
Rowney †1694, handsome cartouche. Attributed to *William
Woodman Sen.* (GF). – Bartholomew Peisley III †1727, master
mason, 'in re ARCHITECTONICA peritus artifex' (skilled prac-
titioner in architectural matters). Big plain tablet. – Sir Charles
Nourse †1789. Tablet with large fluted urn and palm fronds.
– Laura Bickmore †1980, idiosyncratically lettered, by *David*

Kindersley. – Churchyard. C15 tomb-chest of Walter Barow and wife. Quatrefoil panels. Ejected from the church. – John Townesend I †1728, a sturdy Baroque tomb, attributable to his son *William Townesend.*

CHURCH HALL, *see* Woodstock Road, p.431.

ST MARTIN (former), Carfax. *See* Carfax Tower, p.408.

ST MARY MAGDALEN, Magdalen Street and St Giles'. A confusing exterior and a confused interior. The church is wider than it is long. It has a nave and aisles, a chancel which hardly projects, and an outer S aisle or chapel. The whole N aisle was rebuilt by *Scott & Moffatt*, 1841–2. It is called the Martyrs' Aisle and was paid for with funds left over from the Martyrs' Memorial just to the N (*see* p.426), with which it shares a courtly 1290s vocabulary (now missing some pinnacles). It is of considerable importance as the most advanced attempt at archaeologically correct Gothic in Oxford to that date. Scott's *Recollections* admit his debt to Pugin in these early strivings. Also of 1841–2 the E wall of the chancel and inner S aisle, with comparable windows. The outer S aisle is another unified piece. It is of *c.*1320–30, with windows mostly with reticulated tracery, an openwork parapet and elaborately decorated buttresses to the S (renewed, and with statues of 1914 designed by *H.W. Moore*). The W window of the inner S aisle has cusped intersecting tracery. Below it is a storeyed early C16 porch. The W tower, embraced S and N, was rebuilt in 1511–31. Decorated plinth, plainish otherwise. Reused C14 W window. Battlements rebuilt in 1890 by *Moore*. Much refacing since then. Inside, *Scott & Moffatt* removed the Norman chancel arch and put in two piers to match the existing Perp ones. They are octagonal. More interesting is the arcade to the outer S aisle. This has piers and arches of continuous mouldings with sunk chamfers. The N aisle has blind arcading of 1841–2, displaced from the chancel E wall. No clerestories, which makes the church dark. All the roofs ceiled. Further restoration by *Wilkinson*, 1874–5, and by *Moore* at various dates. The glass-fronted vestries etc. at the W end are of 2003, by *John Perryman.*

FURNISHINGS. Much evidence of High Church tastes. – REREDOS, 1894 by *Moore*, with painted wooden figures of saints. – Two RELIQUARIES, Baroque, Continental (Italian?). – SCREEN to S aisle, 1886 by *Moore*. – SCULPTURE. Large wooden St Mary Magdalene, C17, perhaps German (S aisle). – CHEST. Datable *c.*1315–20. Of unusual design, similar to German or Scandinavian examples. Blank Geometrical tracery. The front stiles l. and r. with identical monsters in three tiers are an antiquarian restoration. – FONT. A highly decorated piece, mid- to late C14. It was one of four examples taken in 1841 as models for the miniature fonts made for the Cambridge Camden Society. – STAINED GLASS. E window, *Burlison & Grylls*, 1894. N aisle E, †1870, *Clayton & Bell*. N aisle N, grisaille, style of *O'Connor*, *c.*1855–60 (MH). Inner S aisle, *Wailes*, 1844. Outer S aisle E, *O'Connor*, 1862. By the same, S aisle S, *c.*1865. Also a S window with late C16–C17 panels, given 1834, with the heraldic glass above. W window, compellingly naïve work of 1898, designed by *Elizabeth Wigram*. – MONUMENTS. Brass to William Smith †1580 (S aisle). Kneeling figure; inscription in distichs. – William Pickering †1635. Bust in an oval niche with auricular frame. Books behind him, more books piled pyramidically above. – Ann Seborne †1675, with two standing cherubs. – Caroline Strettell and Anne Elizabeth and Maria Taunton †1843–8. Gothic diptych, much adorned.

ST MICHAEL AT THE NORTH GATE, Ship Street and Corn-market Street, just within the old city wall. The W tower is late Anglo-Saxon, *c.* 1010–60, built possibly as a stand-alone defensive lookout. Rough coral ragstone, long-and-short quoins (renewed, SW), and two tiers of twin bell-openings with bulgy balusters supporting through-stones. Also two little oculi or sound-holes in the upper N wall, and a blocked W doorway. It appears to have belonged to the Anglo-Saxon tower-nave type, in which the main liturgical space was within the tower itself (cf. Oxford Castle tower, p. 401). When constructed, the tower also had some connection to the ramparts themselves (upper doorways in the W and N walls). Space to add a conventional church to the E became available only after the Conquest, when the adjoining city gate and defensive wall were rebuilt further to the N. The length of this church is attested by the present chancel, of the early C13. It has twin lancets to the S and a close-set triplet of lancets to the E, all heavily restored by *Street* in 1853–4. A little later than the chancel is the SE chapel. Its date is indicated by the S window with three stepped lancet lights. A second S chapel followed W of this, with reticulated tracery, i.e. early C14 Dec. The two are now one S aisle. The S porch is C15, with a re-set C13 entrance arch. The N side has a NE chapel and N transept of the early C14 (see the chapel N window), but the transept was largely rebuilt in 1833 by *John Plowman Sen.* The nave N aisle is Perp and C15, as the windows show. Both arcades also C15, with octagonal piers. In the E responds image niches. Tower arch of the same date, and the open-spandrelled arch to the transept on its W side. Chancel arch by *Street*, but the pointed-arched ceilings are from the anti-Victorian restoration by *Gilbert Flavel*, after a fire in 1953. Plain Perp chancel SEDILIA with C14 arch into the N chapel. The W opening of the N aisle was unblocked and filled with intersecting tracery in 1994, when *John Perryman*'s little glass-fronted porch-cum-shop was added. Earlier, in 1986, the tower was restored and the visitors' staircase inserted (*Peter Bosanquet & John Perryman Associates*). The CHURCH CENTRE fitted against the N side is largely *Flavel*'s addition of 1974. St Michael is now the City Church, in succession to All Saints, and St Martin, Carfax before that.

FURNISHINGS. REREDOS, N chapel. Original C15 work, with three recesses. The gilding, painting and statuettes by *Harold Youngman* are of 1939–42. – SCREEN, chancel N. By *Street*, incorporating panels from a parclose screen of *c.* 1400. – PULPIT. Little, of Perp work. – MACE REST. Wrought iron. Is it C18? – FONT. Late C14, originally from Carfax church. Octagonal, without foot or stem. Against the lowest stage defaced statuettes. – SCULPTURE. A sheila-na-gig from the tower W wall, C11 or C12, displayed within the tower. – STAINED GLASS. Chancel E window. Four late C13 panels, set against white 1950s quarries: St Nicholas, St Edmund of Abingdon, Virgin and Child, St Michael. The quality of design is exceptional, with some affinity to the slightly later glass in Merton chapel. N chapel E, three C15 tracery panels (damaged by fire, 1953): two Seraphim, and part of an Annunciation with a lily Crucifixion. S aisle, *Powells*, 1904, 1903, 1913. N aisle, 1921, designed by *Beatrice Cameron*. – MONUMENTS. Ralph Flexney †1578 and wife, pictorial brass (S aisle). – William Guise †1683. Large cartouche, elaborately carved and signed by *William Byrd*. – Anne Harris †1685, another good cartouche (chancel).

ST PAUL, Walton Street. Closed 1963; since 1988 FREUD'S café. 1835–6 by *H.J. Underwood*, the only Neoclassical parish church in Oxford. Tetrastyle portico with fluted Ionic columns, very eroded now. Plain sides with big oblong windows. The apse was added in 1853 by *E.G. Bruton*, the NE vestry in 1892–3 by *H.W. Moore*. Austere interior with compartmented ceiling, antae on the E wall, gallery on slim Doric columns at the W. The present cornice and the arrangement of pilasters around the apse are, surprisingly, alterations of 1908 by *F.C. Eden*, together with the extra N windows inserted high up. – STAINED GLASS. Six Neo-Renaissance windows by *Kempe*, 1888–94. Also one each by *Cox, Buckley & Co.*, 1888, N side westernmost, and by *Heaton, Butler & Bayne* (PC), S side easternmost. E window by *Eden*, 1910. – MONUMENT. Rev. W.B. Duggan †1904, with oval portrait in marble relief. Signed *F.J. Williamson*. – Superior original RAILINGS in front.

ST PETER-IN-THE-EAST, Queen's Lane. *See* St Edmund Hall, p. 262.

ST PETER-LE-BAILEY, New Inn Hall Street. *See* St Peter's College, p. 284.

ST THOMAS, Becket Street and St Thomas Street. Founded shortly after 1189 by Osney Abbey, initially as a chapel within the parish of St George, of which the church was within the Castle (*see* p. 401). Visible remains of this Norman church include three small round-headed windows in the chancel N wall, very restored. Dec E window. Small priest's doorway, S, of C13 appearance. Its DOOR is covered with large ironwork palmette scrolls – five tiers between the hinges – of late C12 type. Late Perp W tower. The nave is largely rebuilt. Much of the S wall is of 1825, including probably the paired lancets to the W. Two Perp windows to the E, the larger one original. Porch between, added in 1621 by the Rev. Robert Burton, of *The Anatomy of Melancholy*. N aisle rebuilt larger in 1846–7 by *J.P. Harrison* (but the W vestry of 1898, by *C.B. Hutchinson*). Harrison also rebuilt the chancel arch. Canted roofs, renewed 1898. Ceiling under the tower of 1996 by *Alan Frost*, curving down to a pendant with dove carved by *Rachel Shorter*.

FURNISHINGS. REREDOS. Neo-1700, of 1915. Designer *M.C. Hack.* – CHANDELIER. 1705. Of brass with two tiers of arms, a fine piece. – PULPIT, designed and carved by *James Rogers*, after 1875. – ROYAL ARMS, 1832, on canvas. – STATUE, Madonna and Child by *Martin Travers*, 1945. – STAINED GLASS. All done under the Ritualist vicar Thomas Chamberlain, author of *The Chancel: An Appeal for Its Proper Use* (1856). He introduced daily services, Gregorian chant, incense, vestments and the veneration of saints. The N aisle E window of 1860, fine early work by *Clayton & Bell* after a suggestion by *Street*, captures Chamberlain's fervent, hieratic character. N aisle N also *Clayton & Bell*, †1862, †1864, *c.*1875. By *O'Connor* the E window, 1853, chancel lancets 1847 and 1848, a S window there of *c.*1860, and nave S, first from E, 1866. Nave S otherwise all *Lavers & Barraud*, 1870s. W window, 1879, early *Kempe*. – MONUMENT. Draped cartouche to James Funnell †1701, with cherubs' heads and skull.

VICARAGE, N of the churchyard. By *C.C. Rolfe*, 1893, a very sensitive design. – E of the church, the former JOHN COMBES'S SCHOOL, named from its donor, an Oxford master plasterer who later worked in London. The inscription provides the date 1702. The original windows still mullioned, but typical of the last stage, i.e. of two lights, upright not horizontal in shape, with raised flat surrounds instead of mouldings and attached to a platband running all round from the steeply pedimented W doorcase building (cf. Stone's Court Almshouses, p.452). Attached to the S in Osney Lane, the plain replacement BOYS' SCHOOL, 1838–9. The lane ends at a brick ARCHWAY with sculpted figures: all that remains of *Rolfe*'s extensive works of 1886 onwards at OSNEY HOUSE, a convent of the Sisterhood of St Thomas's, established here under Chamberlain's influence and demolished in 1958. For former St Thomas's Schools nearby, *see* Perambulation 4, p.442.

Roman Catholic

ST ALOYSIUS, Woodstock Road. 1873–5 by *J.A. & J.S. Hansom*, for the Jesuits; Oratorian since 1990.* A grand church, though well short of the soaring, magnificently towered design originally supplied. The orientation is reversed. Yellow brick, mostly with lancets, but a big rose in the façade wall and a polygonal turret to its l. The interior, though all the forms are Gothic, is not a medieval interior. It is wide, as Hansom *père* liked it. Narrow passage aisles, but not low. They have large arches, very slightly pointed, and above, high up, are the clerestory lancets. The pier shafts were replaced in grey marble in the 1880s–90s. Pointed barrel-vaulted roof. Equally wide apse, the

*For an earlier project for an ostentatious R.C. church for Oxford, intended for St Aldate's, *see The Dublin Builder*, 15 January 1861; architect *James Castle*.

REREDOS curving round with it. Two tiers of statues of saints, an angel frieze, then roundels with heads looking out. The arcading was carved by *Farmer & Brindley* in 1878, the sculpture by *A.B.Wall* of Cheltenham, up to 1888. – FURNISHINGS. A rich haul, including the many side altars and chapels. Fine COMMUNION RAILS of iron. – PULPIT, 1888, with statues by *Wall.* – ALTAR, Sacred Heart Chapel, ritual NE. Italian C17 style. Designer *Robert Kerr* of *ADAM Architecture*, 2020. – STATIONS OF THE CROSS, *c.*1910. Designed by *Basil Champneys* and brought from the Convent of the Holy Child Jesus (now Linacre College). – FONT, Decorated Gothic, thickly sculpted. – WALL PAINTING, W end. Jesuit saints. By *E. Percival*, 1977–9. Also sympathetic redecoration of the Lady Chapel, ritual SE, 2007. – RELIC CHAPEL, ritual S side, an interesting Baroque installation of 1908. – STAINED GLASS chiefly by *Hardman*, dates into the early C20, but the apse windows by *N.H.J.Westlake*. – MONUMENTS. Philippa Fletcher †1914 and war memorial 1921, both by *Gabriel Pippet*. Eric Gill is the influence.

On the S side of the church, a new CHAPEL in Italianate classical style is proposed, by *ADAM Architecture* (2022).

The church is set back behind a forecourt with an ARCH of 1925, with a carved Crucifixion by *Pippet*. The PRESBYTERY (No.25 Woodstock Road), next to Somerville College on the N side, is by *Wilkinson*, 1877–8. Also of yellow brick and Gothic, with diapering. Extended 1911 by *Fr Benedict Williamson & Beart Foss.*

CATHOLIC CHAPEL (former), St Clement's Street. *See* Perambulation 7, p.452.

Nonconformist

WESLEY MEMORIAL METHODIST CHURCH, New Inn Hall Street. 1877–8 by *Charles Bell*. A demonstrative building in Decorated Gothic style, with a very prominent NW steeple aligned on St Michael's Street. Cross-gabled aisles with galleries. Arcades with piers of polished granite, and varied capitals naturalistically carved by *Henry Frith*. Reordered 1978. – PULPIT and SCREEN behind by *N.W. & G.A. Harrison*, 1913. – STAINED GLASS. E and W windows, patterns and emblems by *Thomas Cox*. S windows of 1879, style of *E.R. Frampton* (PC), and 1906 by *T. W. Camm*. – HALL to the N, *c.*1933, with a glazed link between by *Gray Baynes & Shew*, 2021.

NORTH GATE HALL (former Methodist), St Michael Street. *See* Perambulation 5, p.438.

NEW ROAD BAPTIST CHURCH, Bonn Square. Oxford's senior Baptist church, for a congregation traceable to 1653. Rebuilt in 1798, enlarged and refronted by *John Hudson* in 1819. Three bays, ashlar. Quoins of even rustication below, and a porch treated as a small Doric portico. On the upper floor in the middle a big stilted lunette between attached columns. Niches

l. and r., pilasters at each end. Not a well-integrated composition. Three-sided gallery. – CRUCIFIX, 1982–4 by *Heather
Harms*. A powerful piece, carved from African woods.

ST COLUMBA'S UNITED REFORMED CHURCH, Alfred Street.
By *T. Phillips Figgis*, 1914–15, originally for Presbyterian
members of the University. Its Free Perp frontage and entrance
arcade were lost in 1960, when *E. Brian Smith*'s uncompro-
misingly modern front and lobby were added. Broad interior,
with good STAINED GLASS (one window) by *Margaret Voelcker*
and *Theodora Salusbury* (PC). – Adjacent CHURCH HALL, 1933.
    The predecessor CHAPEL (dem. 1969) stood behind. By the
Rev. William Jenkins, 1817–18, classical; latterly converted for
accommodation for St Peter's College.

FRIENDS' MEETING HOUSE, St Giles'. *See* Perambulation 3,
p.427.

CHRISTIAN SCIENCE CHURCH, St Giles'. *See* Perambulation
3, p.427.

Other faiths

SYNAGOGUE (OXFORD JEWISH CENTRE), Richmond Road,
Jericho. Rebuilt as a multiple-use complex by *David Stern*,
1971–5, renovated and extended 2001–5 by *Simone Bloom* of
Herbert & Partners. Stern's parts are in darker brick, including the prayer hall with asymmetrically divided roof to the E.
Additions and refacings in paler brick, with strenuous swooping roofs of green copper. Stern's design reportedly drew on
sketches for a synagogue by *Arne Jacobsen*, made shortly before
his death in 1971. Oxford's chief medieval Jewry was at the N
end of St Aldate's.

PUBLIC BUILDINGS

Oxford Castle and Prison

CASTLE, New Road. A prison until as recently as 1996, Oxford
Castle is now a unique combination of historic attraction and
unconventional hotel. Its regeneration in 2004–6 was steered
by the Oxford Preservation Trust, based on a masterplan of
2001 by *Alan Baxter Associates*. The site is remarkable for its
CII monuments and late CI8 and Victorian penal buildings,
and for the exceptional continuity of uses that this date-span
implies. Excavations during the work revealed much about the
medieval site.
    The castle was built for the Conqueror by Robert d'Oilly in
1071. Of this time is the tree-topped MOTTE or mound, now
clipped by New Road, of 1769–70. It is *c.*250 ft (76 metres)
across and *c.*64 ft (19.5 metres) high, and was originally surrounded by a moat. In the CI3 a ten-sided shell keep was built

on top, of which there is no visible trace. What survives of the
C13 is a rib-vaulted hexagonal WELL CHAMBER within the top
of the mound. The ribs have one, rather slight chamfer.

s of the mound is the one high remaining TOWER. The
Norman castle incorporated this in the defences, but its alignment and form point to an earlier origin, as a stronghold close
to the w gate in Oxford's Anglo-Saxon defensive circuit. The
C11 tower of St Michael at the North Gate (p. 396) offers a
parallel, but the scale here is much larger, and the tower is less
likely to have been meant for ecclesiastical use, especially if it
belonged with the Anglo-Saxon hall and chamber identified
in excavations some 90 yds SE. Four stages, slightly receding.
High up are the remains of large round-headed windows. In
the w wall a window with a transom lighting two internal levels.
Later attachment for a staircase, set diagonally at the SE angle.
An internal floor, tree-ring dated 1552, appears to replicate the
close-joisted form of the early floor it replaced. Top lantern by
Richard Griffiths Architects, 2004–6; VISITOR RECEPTION at
the base by *Panter Hudspith*.

What is certain is that this enigmatic tower was adapted
as part of the collegiate ST GEORGE'S CHURCH, founded
by d'Oilly and Roger d'Ivry in 1074. That explains the plain
Romanesque tower arch, unmoulded and with the simplest
imposts. It opened originally to an aisleless nave with apsidal
chancel. The CRYPT of this chancel is partly preserved, having
been reconstructed in the 1780s on the initiative of the antiquarian gaol-keeper Daniel Harris. It sits beneath the prison's
D Wing, which extends E and aslant from the tower. The crypt
is low, with aisles, and is now three and a half bays long. Originally it had an apse. Short round piers carrying big capitals,
several crudely carved with what must be meant as large,
broad, ribbed leaves, one in each diagonal. The present groin-
vaults are of course replacements.

So to the buildings of the PRISON. Oxford was among those
gaols rebuilt on reformed lines by *William Blackburn* after the
Penitentiary Act of 1779, and now has the most intact survivals of his work.* Before that time the accommodation was
improvised from what remained of the castle after its slighting
at the end of the Civil War. The builder was *Edward Edge* of
Gloucestershire, succeeded by *Daniel Harris* himself. D WING,
of c.1785, embodies the new regimen of individual vaulted
cells off a spine corridor, here with lunette windows linked
externally by impost blocks and blank arcading. The upper
floor was the infirmary. The E end, rounded and crenellated
and carried up two more storeys, was the DEBTORS' TOWER,
with timber enclosures where indebted prisoners were held
under less strict conditions. An unusual triangular staircase
here. Conversion for display by *Panter Hudspith*, including the
viewing deck to the E.

---

*Besides this, the County Gaol, Blackburn also designed the CITY GAOL at
Gloucester Green, 1786–9 (dem. 1879).

Now beneath the deck, and S. Ahead, two matching hip-roofed blocks with low oblong windows. They comprised *Blackburn*'s HOUSE OF CORRECTION, for petty offenders. Converted for hotel use by *Architects Design Partnership*, with a fussily treated new block between, where the C18 gaol-keeper's house once stood. Immediately W, low TREADWHEEL HOUSE, of before 1850. To the E, aligned N–S, is C WING, also now part of the hotel. *Blackburn*'s work is recognizable below. Again a rounded end, here resting on rubble foundations of the medieval Round Tower. Upper storeys of 2004–6 by *Architects Design Partnership*, faced in Bath stone, replacing post-C18 rebuilding. Joined on at the N and stretching a long way E–W is A WING, 1852–6 by *H.J. Underwood*, carried out after his death by *J.C. Buckler*. Here the inspiration was the new model prison at Pentonville in North London (1840–2), where similar wings radiate from a central hub. Three storeys. The distinctive feature inside is the full-height, iron-galleried central void, signalled externally by the giant round-headed window in each end wall. *ADP* and *Jestico & Whiles*'s conversion required making bedrooms from groups of three cells, indicated by cutting down the third window neatly below string-course level. Also some modifications to form a foyer and staircase on the N side, where a cross-wing projects to join a shallow, stylistically muddled E–W range of 1870–1 etc. The N frontispiece here appears as a symmetrical composition of square turrets. At the W end of this range is the GOVERNOR'S HOUSE, of 1847–8 by *Benjamin Ferrey*, placed just outside Blackburn's perimeter wall. An upright crenellated box, with a lesser block set back, W. Perp-collegiate windows. The smaller, detached block just E of A Wing was the GOVERNOR'S OFFICE, of after 1878.

Finally the other NEW BLOCKS of 2004–6. By the New Road entrance is a block housing hotel rooms, restaurant etc. by *Dixon Jones*, broad and low, with pale, plain ashlar arcading on the long sides and an awkward white-rendered end by the road. The wrong finishes amid so much penal squared rubble. N of St George's Tower is *Panter Hudspith*'s LEARNING CENTRE. Brick above stone, windows boxed out at an angle (also to Tidmarsh Lane, behind). To the SW, cranked along the perimeter line, APARTMENTS by *Architects Design Partnership*. The basement of one of these displays part of a ragstone retaining wall from the ANGLO-SAXON TOWN RAMPART, probably of the late C9 or early C10.

City walls

Substantial parts remain of the CITY WALLS of Oxford, as rebuilt in 1226–40. They are best seen and best understood at New College, where the NE angle of the defences survives almost intact, including six of the bastions (p. 221). Following the circuit clockwise, the next section to survive runs through the gardens of Merton and Corpus Christi, overlooking Christ

Church Meadow to the s (pp. 207 and 145). To the w of St Aldate's the wall appears again along the s side of Pembroke College, facing Brewer Street (p. 237). Some fragments, not easily seen, remain in the section between Littlegate Street and the Castle, where the precinct of the Greyfriars (p. 450) breached the wall shortly after its completion. On the N and s sides of the Castle the walls were again interrupted to allow for the moat. The next exposed length is from the NW sector, behind the former High School for Boys in George Street (p. 358). A few bastions and sections of walling remain behind the houses on the N side of St Michael's Street and Ship Street (p. 403). Continuing E, the wall ran exactly where the s façade of the Sheldonian now is. The four main GATES were demolished between the C16 and the 1770s, but the church of St Michael at the North Gate survives to mark the position of one of them, and the early C16 octagonal chapel that is now part of Hertford College (p. 159) records the location of Smith Gate, one of the three lesser gates.

Civic and municipal

COUNTY HALL, New Road. 1839–41 by *John Plowman Jun.* A   82
Romantic period piece, like a Meyerbeer opera. The intention must have been to defer to the Castle immediately to the w (*see* p. 400). Castellated, with unmilitary Neo-Norman detail – the same recipe as e.g. Penrhyn Castle (Gwynedd) – but of old-fashioned symmetry. Seven bays, the centre with a castellated porch and a castellated top with two castellated turrets. Two large arched windows in the side parts, where the courtrooms were. Nook-shafts with varied capitals of C12 type. Yet the main hall is classical, with giant pilasters and an oblong lantern with flat coffering. By way of an overture, cast-iron STANDARDS stick up in front, fashioned as fasces with axeheads. EXTENSION (New County Hall) to the E of 1973–6, by *Albert E. Smith*, County Architect. A mute slab, angled around the corner with Castle Street. Five aggregate storey bands, dark-framed ribbon windows set flush. Entrance forecourt on the inner side, where a round-arched range runs W to join old County Hall.

TOWN HALL, St Aldate's. 1893–7 by *Henry T. Hare*, partly on the site of the town hall of 1751–2 etc. (*see* below). Hare won the competition in 1892, aged just thirty. A busy career in public architecture followed, but nothing quite so unashamedly showy. For Hare gave Oxford town what Jackson for fifteen years had given Oxford gown. There are the alternately blocked columns, the transomed windows with arched lights, the gables *à la* Kirby. Did Jackson chuckle or foam? The façade is entirely symmetrical with its crowning louvre-like spirelet, with the exception of the s corner turret. External sculpture by *William Aumonier*. Roofs and floors are steel-framed, and the building was electrically lit (chief contractor *Parnell &*

Son of Rugby). To Blue Boar Street, s, Clipsham ashlar gives way to Bladon rubble, with separate entrances for the former public library (lower parts used since 1975 by the MUSEUM OF OXFORD), and the court house and police station.

The INTERIOR is sumptuous too. The staircase up to the Main Hall ends in an arcaded lobby with columns and a lot of Jacobean-style plasterwork. The MAIN HALL itself is 95 ft 9 in. (29.2 metres) long, galleried on three sides, apsed to the E, with an organ by *Henry Willis*, under a barrel-vaulted ceiling. Sculptured decoration and stuccowork wherever one looks, including Michelangelesque personifications in the spandrels by *F. E. E. Schenck*. Other plasterwork by *George Jackson & Sons*, internal stone sculpture by *Butcher & Axtell*, wood carving by *G. Hawkings*. (In the MAYOR'S PARLOUR to the N, panelling and overmantel with blank arches and caryatids, saved from the parlour of the Council House of 1615–19.) COUNCIL CHAMBER, N, and tall ASSEMBLY ROOM, w, with coved ceilings combining big timbering with enriched plasterwork. In the latter a stone fireplace romantically incorporating a musicians' gallery. Also the former REFERENCE LIBRARY, s of the Assembly Room. (Underneath the N extension of 1932 (*see* Carfax, p. 409) is the Plate Room, a vaulted CELLAR, probably C15, retained from the former tavern at Knap Hall. Three bays. Wall-shafts with moulded capitals, ribs with one long, sharp, hollow chamfer. Blocked w doorway.)

PREDECESSORS. The Town Hall of 1751–2 was a Gibbsian-Palladian design by *Isaac Ware*, originally with an arcaded Corn Exchange below, and with the retained Council House of 1615–19 attached to the NE. Also demolished in the 1890s were *S. L. Seckham*'s replacement Corn Exchange of 1861–3 to the E, and Nixon's Free Grammar School to the N, a timber-framed building of 1659 with interesting Artisan Mannerist details. Ware in turn replaced two much-altered properties, one comprising the stone-built late C13 town hall.

OXFORDSHIRE REGISTER OFFICE, New Road. A nice two-storey corner composition of 1911–12 by *W. A. Daft*, with a big two-transom window at the entrance and a pediment and cupola over. Contrasting stones. Behind and along Tidmarsh Lane, Macclesfield House, now OXFORD CENTRE FOR INNOVATION. Former County Council offices by *Albert E. Smith*, 1967–9. Vigorously framed pre-cast concrete, with sills canted in at the top.

PROBATE OFFICE (former), New Road. *See* Perambulation 5, p. 441.

CROWN COURT AND COUNTY COURT, St Aldate's. What looks like a grand interwar court house is in truth the retained façade of MORRIS GARAGES, by *Harry W. Smith & Son*, 1932–3. Ashlar, classical, with a concave sweep on the ground floor, it faces and outdoes the police station (*see* below). Servicing and repairs were handled at street level, with public garaging above (ramped access from behind) and a showroom for second-hand cars on top. The rest of 1982–5 by the *Property*

Services Agency, including the long s extension. Some horizontals carried through; ground floor recessed behind piers. Relief portrait of Lord Nuffield high up by *Martin Jennings*, 1989.

MAGISTRATES' COURTS, Speedwell Street and Albion Place. By *Douglas Murray*, City Architect, 1966–9. Large and excessively defensive. Base faced in rough yellow brick, projecting upper floor with an alternation of large reeded concrete panels and pairs of recessed windows.

POLICE STATION, St Aldate's. 1936 by *H.F. Hurcombe*, City Estates Surveyor. Ashlar, thirteen bays, two and a half storeys, blankly classical. s extension of *c.*1988, rather mannered, by *D. Colin James* (Department of Planning and Property Services, Oxfordshire County Council). In Floyd's Row behind, former LABOUR EXCHANGE, 1936 by *P.M. Stratton* of the Ministry of Works, s side, and small CORONER'S COURT and MORTUARY, 1939. The squared-rubble Cotswold manner.

FIRE STATION, Rewley Road. By *Douglas Murray*, City Architect, 1968–71. A sequence of interlinked blocks, strongly articulated by concrete framing. The uprights are carried up to make an open parapet.

OLD FIRE STATION, George Street. *See* Perambulation 5, p. 438.

POST OFFICE, St Aldate's. 1878–80 by *E.G. Rivers* of the Office of Works. A tall Gothic building of Chilmark stone, intricately carved in places. Extended s *c.*1910. At the same time the entrance tower was reworked with a steep copper-clad roof, replacing a clumsy earlier heightening.

Colleges and schools

CITY OF OXFORD COLLEGE, Oxpens Road. An adult education college, instituted to provide for less advanced courses than those taught at the Polytechnic (*see* Oxford Brookes University, p. 477). The earliest buildings are at the N end, ASH, BRENT and CHERWELL, of 1968–72 by *D. Murray*, City Architect. Yellow brick and concrete panels, with blocky corner eminences and strangely unfinished-looking parapets. DORN, to the s, is later and blander. Subsequent blocks include GLYME and JERICHO (1986–8), w, with bright trim in the High Tech mode; by *Bilham Woods* for Oxfordshire County Council.

RUSKIN COLLEGE (former), Walton Street. *See* Perambulation 4, p. 432.

CHRIST CHURCH CATHEDRAL SCHOOL, Brewer Street. *See* Perambulation 6, p. 446.

MAGDALEN COLLEGE SCHOOL, Cowley Place and Iffley Road. The school's early buildings now belong to Magdalen College (pp. 190 and 415). The present group began with the building just E of Magdalen Bridge, with its garden down to the Cherwell and two white wooden Chinese Chippendale bridges. It is by *Sir Arthur Blomfield* and was built in 1893–4, partly for boarders. Rock-faced, in a dutiful English C17 style. Mullioned-and-transomed windows, some of them pedimented and with gables to Cowley Place and gables to the N, where there is also the main doorway with coupled pilasters.

Across Cowley Place to the SE are the C20–C21 buildings, an incoherent group. BIG SCHOOL, i.e. the hall, is by *Pinckheard & Partners*, 1964–6. An elongated hexagon in plan, of purple-brown Sussex brick. Concrete-framed windows high up, and much variety of outline. The former chapel end, N, has abstract stained glass by *Lawrence Lee*. By the same architects (as *Booth, Ledeboer & Pinckheard*), 1955–8, the SCIENCE BUILDING immediately S, and the older part of the COLIN SANDERS BUILDING across the playground, which was doubled in depth on that side in 1997–8, by *Architects Design Partnership*. The Science Building has a shelving-roofed S addition along Iffley Road by *Ivor Smith & Cailey Hutton*, 1971–3, meant (with the S end block) as the first part of a much longer sequence. The *Oxford Architects Partnership* designed its S continuation in 1990, with a few Postmodern touches, and the 1980s QUINCENTENARY BUILDING next along Iffley Road. The cluster to the SW includes the *Architects Design Partnership*'s SPORTS COMPLEX (1999–2001), and *Buttress Fuller Alsop Williams Architects*' MICHAEL PEAGRAM BUILDING (2006–8), stone-faced with copper-green trim and a plain double-storey colonnade for the main entrance. The link between has storeys added by *Original Field*, 2011–14, largely of structural timber. The colonnade motif is picked up in the SIXTH FORM CENTRE immediately NE, 2015–17 by *Tim Ronalds Architects*. Its stone-faced framing yields to pale brick in the upper storeys.

NEW COLLEGE SCHOOL, Savile Road. *See* Perambulation 2, p. 421.

FORMER SCHOOLS. High School for Boys, George Street, *see* History Faculty, p. 357. High School for Girls, Banbury Road, *see* Perambulation 3, p. 430. Central Boys' School, Gloucester Green, *see* Perambulation 5, p. 439. Central Girls' School, New Inn Hall Street, *see* St Peter's College, p. 285. South Oxford Schools, *see* Perambulation 6, p. 448. Other former schools are also described with the Perambulations.

Markets, transport and communications

COVERED MARKET, High Street and Market Street. In origin an open-air market with blocks of stalls, built in 1772–4 to designs by *John Gwynn*, together with Nos. 13–16 High Street (p. 410). Rebuilt, enlarged and put under cover incrementally by the Victorians, keeping the C18 plan of N–S avenues, but with beguiling irregularities. The oldest part is now the City Surveyor *Thomas Wyatt Jun*.'s enlargement to the NW, 1839.* Lightweight iron trusses here, like those of contemporary train sheds, marked with the name of *Messrs Dewer*'s foundry,

---

*Unexecuted designs for complete rebuilding were supplied in 1836 by the market specialist *Charles Fowler*.

London. Stalls 46–48 were restored by Oxford Preservation Trust to the original design, 2020. The rest of 1881–98, successively by *Codd*, *Bruton* and *W.H. Castle*. All of timber, lit from clerestories above the two-storey shops, with great variety in the trussing. The SW part is *Codd*'s extension of 1881; the thickly timbered middle crossing and the hip-roofed, slanted ends facing Market Street to the NE are *Bruton*'s, 1886–7; the triple-gabled, Georgian-looking N wall alongside is from *Castle*'s completion of the NW quarter, 1897. In 1986–7 extended to the W by *Dunthorne Parker*, into Golden Cross Yard (*see* p. 422). A renovation of the market by *Gort Scott* is proposed (2023).

TELEPHONE EXCHANGE, Speedwell Street. Huge. The greater part of 1954–9 by the *Ministry of Works*. Three-sided, of brown brick with window bands of different heights. Rubble end walls. S range of 1972–5 by the *Department of the Environment*, changing to cast stone and slit windows above brown tile facing.

RAILWAY STATION, Park End Street. Main building of 1987–90 by *British Rail Western Region Architect*. Long, of yellow brick. Pitched roof, stepping up as a clerestory over the circulation area. W platform building of 1972, as utilitarian as the predecessor Great Western stations of 1891 and 1852; Cambridge did better. In 2023 the rebuilding of the W side was begun. The earliest station, of 1844, was some way to the S.*

FOLLY BRIDGE, S of St Aldate's. 1825–7 by *Ebenezer Perry*, spanning the Thames or Isis with three rusticated arches. Distinctive railings supplied by the builder *Hugh McIntosh*, later a pioneer railway contractor. The name comes from the hefty medieval gate tower which stood until 1779 on the predecessor bridge. GIRDER BRIDGE of 1888 across the channel S of Folly Island. For the medieval Grandpont causeway *see* Abingdon Road, South Oxford, p. 515.

MAGDALEN BRIDGE, High Street. One of the great Georgian bridges, though the setting hinders its appreciation. The crossing was rebuilt in 1772–8 to the design of *John Gwynn* of Shrewsbury, architectural writer, bridge specialist and Surveyor to the Commissioners under Oxford's Improvement Act of 1771 (*see* Introduction, p. 46); contractor *John Randall*. The raised approaches make for a near-level deck. Two groups of three semicircular arches, plus a dry elliptical central arch on the island in the River Cherwell. Mask key blocks and rusticated voussoirs, their channelling carried through on the underside. Half-columns with alternating blocking, and an aedicule in the centre of each side. Good sturdy balustrades. Gwynn wanted sphinxes to stand on the parapets, but these and his intended central pediments remained unexecuted. The

---

*Oxford's other STATION (Rewley Road), of 1851 for the London & North Western Railway branch from Bletchley, stood just E of the present one. Of special interest as a structure by *Fox, Henderson & Partners*, contractors for the contemporary Crystal Palace, with which it shared the use of *Sir Joseph Paxton*'s modular system of prefabricated iron and timber. Closed 1968, dismantled 1999, reconstructed at the Buckinghamshire Railway Centre, Quainton Road, Aylesbury.

quadrant sweeps on the W approach were completed in 1790, after Gwynn's death. S side rebuilt wider in 1882–4, to make room for trams (*W.H. White*, City Engineer).

OSNEY BRIDGE. *See* West Oxford, p. 517.

GASWORKS BRIDGE, off Dale Close. 1886–7, engineers *T. & C. Hawksley*. Built to serve Oxford's gas works, when this acquired a railway feeder from the SW. Two lattice-girder spans. Now used as a footbridge.

PERAMBULATIONS

1. East: Carfax and High Street

CARFAX. The perambulations to the four main compass points all begin at Carfax, the highest point within the walled town. Its name is from *quadrifurcus*, 'four-forked', for this was the original crossing of the roads to the four town gates (*see* Introduction, p. 4). The buildings that once marked it as a civic space have all disappeared now.* CARFAX TOWER remains to the NW: the late medieval tower of the church of ST MARTIN, extant by the early C11. Doorway, buttresses, bell-openings, stair-turret and parapets all from restoration in 1897–8 by *T. G. Jackson*; also the classical surround to the clock. Below it, replicas of the quarter-jacks of *c.* 1621–4 from the old church, between Doric columns. The church itself, as rebuilt in 1820–2 in looming Gothic by *Daniel Harris & John Plowman Sen.*, was demolished to widen the cross-roads in 1896.[†] Its function as the City Church passed to All Saints, then to St Michael at the North Gate.

The Gothic churchyard GATEWAY alongside St Martin's tower is by *H. T. Hare*, 1896. He proposed to Hareify the tower

---

[*]The CONDUIT installed in 1617 has been reconstructed at Nuneham Courtenay (p. 708), displaced by road widening in 1787. PENNILESS BENCH, constructed in 1545 against the E end of Carfax church as a meeting place for citizens (rebuilt with a loggia in 1667), lasted until 1747. The SW corner had the BUTTER MARKET of 1709–13, built probably by *John Townesend I*: an L-plan colonnade, in front of a substantial assembly room for the mayor and councillors.

[†]Reused fabric includes stained glass now at St Clement (p. 392). Also windows built into Windlesham House School chapel at Brighton, then relocated again when the school moved to West Sussex, 1934.

too, but a widespread outcry prevented this. The rest of Hare's corner scheme of 1896–7 went ahead. The HSBC BANK on the NW corner is his, a lively design with all kinds of elements arranged in a random way, hoodmouldings but round arches, big gables and an angle turret lower than they, stubby Venetian windows in the gables and so on. Originally Frank East, drapers; the ground floor is an alteration for the bank, 1914. Also by *Hare* is TOWER HOUSE, W of the tower. The SW corner, SANTANDER (originally Glyn, Mills Bank), by *Ashley & Newman*, 1930–2, is much chaster. Their SE corner, the TOWN HALL EXTENSION (with *H.F. Hurcombe*, City Estates Surveyor) is contemporary and of almost the same design, but the NE corner, LLOYDS BANK, beats the others and indeed takes some beating. It is by *Stephen Salter* (*Davy & Salter*) of Oxford, 1901–4, and shows the consequences of seeing too much Jackson about every day. There is nowhere that motifs don't sprout: alternately blocked columns, Ipswich windows, big, steep shaped gables. Carving by *W.H. Feldon*. The banking hall replicates the fine ceiling of *c.* 1600 from No. 2 High Street, a match for that in Corpus Christi gate tower (p. 142); the original was installed at The Shrubbery, No. 72 Woodstock Road (p. 468).

The HIGH STREET is one of the world's great streets. It has everything. It is on a slight curve, so that vistas straight ahead always change. It has plenty of good and impressive buildings of large size, mostly of course colleges but also two churches, all set off by just enough houses, and it has a few trees. As one walks along, one recognizes at once the essential part played by the trees, by the two church spires and, as the final beacon, if one walks E, by Magdalen Tower. And while most of the houses now have ground-floor shopfronts, and few have fabric older than the C16, the medieval urban pattern is not hard to recover – on the S side especially, where houses on long, narrow burgage plots are punctuated by the narrowest lanes and alleys. The other big theme, not always immediately apparent, is the annexation or replacement of many houses by the colleges.

Starting on the N SIDE, No. 5 is Late Georgian, ashlar, five bays, with the mid-window pedimented. Nos. 6 and 7, ashlar too, appear of similar date but are facsimile rebuildings of 1959. No. 6 is an interesting design, with a Venetian window, its super-arch reeded, and with pairs of pilasters on the second floor. No. 9, modern Georgian of 1934 by *G.T.F. Gardner*, for Mowbrays' the publishers. Nos. 10–11 reportedly retains C15 fabric behind an C18 front, but the upper storey and C17-style oriels are from *Codd*'s heightening of 1883, for the City Drapery Stores.

On the S SIDE, *Wills & Kaula*'s Nos. 139–140, 1938, and *Gardner*'s No. 136, 1933, carry on the Carfax widening scheme. Between, No. 137 has a timbered Old English front of 1884 for the Swan Brewery offices (Messrs Hall's). No. 135, late C17 or early C18, is characteristic of many timber-framed High Street houses: stuccoed and updated with later sashes, set flush. Three bays. At No. 134 an ashlar house of 1790 with pedimented first-floor aedicule, at No. 133 a freakishly tall and thin rebuilding of 1937 by *Gardner*, for William Rose, photographer. Then Nos. 131A and 132, again refronted, but still with some C15 or C16 studding and a complete timber doorway exposed in the passage. The rear part is the CHEQUERS INN, of late medieval origin, with C17 windows. In the bar a reused length of C15 stone, three panels with enriched quatrefoils and a carved figure. No. 131, C18, introduces another timber frontage type, with a through-storey canted bay. At No. 130 the late medieval two-storey form survives in front, with a jetty and twin gables. Rear part largely from the City Council's restoration of 1930. A passage with a four-centred-arched wooden doorway, l., leads to KEMP HALL, a 'passage-type' house built by Alderman William Boswell in 1637, unusually well preserved inside and out. Five timber-framed bays with two jetties, one room deep against a stone rear wall. The doorway has a little canopy, and on the middle floor are oriels carried on scroll brackets. Central staircase with pierced splat balusters; original panelling, doorways, fireplaces and one overmantel. A s cross-wing of 1611 has gone. Nos. 127–129 were sumptuously rebuilt in 1897, including the WHEATSHEAF pub behind. No. 126 has been identified as the survivor of a triple-jettied pair built by Henry Mychegood, Squire Bedel of the University (†1501); but the present façade is late C17 and of uncommon quality, Oxford's best survivor of the type; probably added by the mercer Robert Pauling, mayor in 1679–80. Four storeys, with a broad, shallow through-storey upper bay with rounded corners. On the first floor it has a large Ipswich window, on the second an overlapping version of the same motif. The top storey is given a split pediment framing one tall arched light under a pediment of its own. But if one watches the gable against which this pediment is set, one notices the original richly carved bargeboards and even a little pargeting. (Tie- and collar-beam roof with queenstruts.) Re-set in the passage, framing and a timber-mullioned window from a near-contemporary rear wing, demolished 1972. Nos. 123–125 are mostly plain timber-framed of 1790, for the former Bear Inn; No. 124 preserves the carved frontage of Acott's music shop, 1912.

Back to the N SIDE, where Nos. 13–16 are *John Gwynn*'s front range of 1773–4 to the Covered Market (p. 406), created under the town's Improvement Act of 1771. A long symmetrical ashlar composition of fifteen bays, with tripartite windows in the end and middle bays and a seven-bay pediment with a tripartite lunette. Next follows the MITRE INN, a property of Lincoln College since the C15, its upper storeys student rooms since 1969. Called 'recently new fronted' in 1803. The usual stucco and canted bays, but renovation in 2018–20 confirmed that the main range is structurally C16, with a back wall of stone. Against this wall a grand double-jettied accommodation range was added in 1631 (date on a window bracket), facing the inn yard behind. Restored and embellished by *Richardson & Gill*,

1922. C17 staircase with turned balusters. (Vaulted tavern cellar partly surviving, probably early C14. Single-chamfered ribs, shafts with moulded capitals. One room under the 1631 gables has ceiling beams plastered with running ornament of foliage and pomegranates, and re-set square panelling of *c*.1600. C16 fireplaces in several S rooms.) The stable ranges etc. facing the long inn yard were rebuilt in 1925 as the Mitre Tavern, Old Englishry by *J.R. Wilkins*. Access is from Turl Street, E, where the college has closed the entry with a little GATEHOUSE by *TSH Architects*, 2018–21. Stone-faced, minimal Perp style.

TURL STREET now has houses on the W side only, a nicely varied and shop-fronted foil to the colleges, Lincoln and Exeter, E, and Jesus, W. N of the Mitre yard, Nos. 11–12 (WALTERS etc.), with shallow jetties and central passage, was the Maidenhead Inn; probably C18. No. 14 is C17, with grotesque gable brackets. Lincoln College added a back annexe in 1967–8 (*K. Stevens & Associates*), and LINCOLN HOUSE (No. 15) is Lincoln overspill too, 1938–9 by *Sir Hubert Worthington*, executed by *G.T.F. Gardner*. Handled very like a run of rendered C18 Oxford houses, with through-storey bay windows above shops. Here Brasenose Lane runs E to Radcliffe Square, still with the medieval form of a central gutter. For Ship Street, W, and the Georgian N end of Turl Street *see* Perambulation 3, p. 424.

Now to the HIGH STREET, S side, once again. The former LONDON & COUNTY BANK is of 1867–8 by *F. & H. Francis*, Gothic for Oxford, just like their bank for the same company in Cambridge. It cost £9,000. Yellow brick and Bath stone dressings, Middle Pointed, i.e. the style of the late C13. Windows with cusped lancets, portal with naturalistic capitals. Steep stepped gable and polygonal angle turret. The three-bay E part originally housed Russell's music warehouse. Extension down Alfred Street by *Norman Bailey, Samuels & Partners*, 1964–5. Stone-faced, with semi-random relief patterns.

In ALFRED STREET, St Columba's church (p. 400), and on the SE corner the big former OXFORD GYMNASIUM, a remarkable building of 1858–9 by *William Wilkinson*. For Archibald Maclaren, a pioneer of physical education. Red-brown brick (the cornices too), with round-arched windows under slightly pointed extradoses. Octagonal lantern over the pyramid-roofed central part, which had a through-storey void to provide for rope- and mast-climbing. The arrangements served as a model for several military gyms built in the 1860s. Office conversion by *Perry Associates*, 1989. The little BEAR pub, W, is probably C17.

Continuing E along the High, a nice, unassuming row follows, facing All Saints (p. 388) and the tree E of All Saints. No. 119 has a timber front of 1703, with on the first floor two pedimented windows linked by a thick full cornice. Good Neo-Georgian shopfront by *Gardner*, 1930. C16–C17 behind. (No. 118, of the C16, has superior wall paintings in a rear first-floor room, treated as red fictive patterned tapestry. Suggested as the work of *Walter Wilkins*, goldsmith, who leased the house in 1621.) Nos. 116 and 117 have matching fronts of *c*. 1810, at No. 117 concealing a late medieval former hall house. This was of the small kind with an upper chamber or gallery, and only the smoke-bay (floored across in the C16) rising to the roof. Nos. 113–114 are largely plausible rebuilds of 1932–4, by *J. E. Thorpe*. The corresponding row on the N side, Nos. 19–23, three- or four-storeyed, are all late C18. Then the first college, the S range of Brasenose (pp. 107–8).

Opposite is KING EDWARD STREET, a new formation cut through Oriel College property in 1872. It might be a street of any Victorian town centre. Four-storey houses, predominantly drab yellow brick Italianate by *Codd*, 1873–4; the corner buildings with capitals carved by *Samuel Grafton*. No. 8, last on the W side, with a Gothic oriel of stone, is by *George Jones*, builder, 1879. On No. 6 a RELIEF commemorating Cecil Rhodes's residence, by *Onslow Whiting*, 1906. Nos. 9–10 opposite completed King Edward Street in 1884. Behind the W side is another Lincoln College outpost, the BEAR LANE site. Access is through the plain building of *c*. 1835 for Quartermain's Stables on that lane. Modest red brick blocks by *Geoffrey Beard* (*Oxford Architects Partnership*), 1975–7, quite intricate in plan. (Bulkier infill of 1993–5 by *Lee & Ross Architects* to the W, with white-rendered upper storeys and eaves projecting.)

p. 19

Back in the HIGH STREET, still on the S side. Nos. 106–107 belong with TACKLEY'S INN, an early academic hall (*see* Introduction, pp. 9 and 19), although one would not expect it from the two stuccoed C18 fronts with their shallow canted bay windows. Built between 1291 and 1300 by Roger le Mareschal, parson of Tackley, Oxon; acquired as an investment after 1324 by Adam de Brome for his new Oriel College, and restored by Oriel in 1986. Originally it fronted the street with five shops, each with a solar above. Three and a half bays of a rib-vaulted cellar of tavern type survive under the street range. The ribs have a sharp chamfer and rise from short wall-shafts without capitals. The C13 hall remains behind No. 107, of stone, its S wall with a two-light window, the Y-tracery not original. (Re-roofed with collar-beams on arched braces and with wind-braces by *Robert Carow*, *c*. 1512–14.) The E part (No. 106) was reworked as a separate house, probably in 1465–6. In No. 104, first floor, a small late C16 plaster ceiling with patterns of thin ribs and little Bourbon lilies. Nos. 102 and 103 were built *c*. 1714, the former with more classical detail than average. It stands at the corner of ORIEL STREET, the line of which is likely to follow the original eastern limit of the first Anglo-Saxon *burh*. A row of unpretentious early C18 timber-and-stucco houses curves nicely down the W side, facing the walls of Oriel. Mostly of shallow plan, with angled fireplace stacks etc. Nos. 9–10 are structurally C17; No. 12 comprises a former pair of houses of *c*. 1730 in front, each with a very tight staircase, and an originally independent rear wing largely of rubble stone, *c*. 1600, with a bay window and central staircase. All gently adapted as Oriel's O'BRIEN QUAD in 1982–91, with rear circulation and a tunnel link to the college. Also behind is a long and large former REAL TENNIS COURT. Tree rings date it to 1637. Clerestory and roof are late C18 replacements. Now floored across for a lecture theatre etc., with an external staircase. The houses continue along the N side of ORIEL SQUARE, where the gabled frontage is a facsimile of c. 1950–2, and goes with *W.H. Godfrey & Russell Cox*'s formal Neo-Georgian block for Oriel (Middle Common Room etc.), l.

Back once more to the HIGH STREET. The houses facing the W end of St Mary the Virgin are described with Brasenose, p. 108. On the S side, after Oriel's Rhodes Building, houses resume at No. 94. The front to the High Street is a fancy performance of 1902–3 by *Stephen Salter*, but behind is a roughcast timber-framed house facing MAGPIE LANE, its jettied S part with the carved date 1588. No. 2 alongside has a double jetty, and a date 1613. Handsome top oriel on brackets to the N. Further down Magpie Lane again a varied sequence. No. 5, C17, has a straight C18 door hood on carved brackets, and Nos. 6–9 are a Late Georgian terrace, stuccoed. Then follows *Powell & Moya*'s block for Corpus Christi (p. 145), and round the corner in Kybald Street the almshouses now part of University College (p. 305), facing KYBALD TWYCHEN, a rubble-walled house of c. 1600. One original five-light stone-mullioned window. Two timber-framed C17 gables, with oriels.

High Street again, and now facing All Souls. Nos. 92 and 93 (THE OLD BANK) are each ashlar-fronted, four storeys and four or five bays, and uncommonly dignified. No. 93, r., built c. 1775 for William Fletcher, mercer and banker, has arched first-floor windows. No. 92, of 1798 for Fletcher's banking partner John Parsons, has windows with alternatingly shaped pediments. In 1904 the ground floor at No. 93 was 'brought into agreement' with its rusticated and round-arched neighbour, but that may not be the C18 form. Hotel conversion by *Berman Guedes Stretton*, 2000. No. 91, five plain bays, is of stuccoed timber above, ashlar below. No. 90 (now with University College) was built in 1612 by John Williams, apothecary, but its elaborate timber-framed front has been reworked in Georgian stucco. Three upper storeys with two canted bay windows. Below, a double shopfront between Doric columns, all of c. 1812. Two first-floor rooms with identical early C17 plaster ceilings with decorated beams and cartouches framed in the compartments, panelling with Ionic pilasters, and original overmantels, one with allegorical figures, supported on pilasters with herms. Second-floor rooms with less enriched ceilings (also panelling and overmantels). S addition of c. 1812 with two minimum Venetian windows.

Then the long front of University College proper, and opposite, E of All Souls, the sycamore tree which deserves to be called the pivot of the High Street. The N side's houses resume with a nice stuccoed group (Nos. 33–38, now with Queen's College), three, four, four and two-and-a-half storeys high. No. 33 is C17 behind, and has in a first-floor room some amateurish but very engaging Pre-Raphaelite oil-painted decoration: a leaf scroll on the beam, some medallions with heads over the fireplace, and scrolls and two figure scenes on the door. The work was done almost certainly by *Joseph Swan*, a young Irish artist. He had worked with Morris and his fellows on the original roof of the Oxford Union, and in 1865 married Kate Feldon of DRAWDA HALL, the passage-type house attached to rearward. Late C17, timber-framed, with some older fabric. The name is from William of Drogheda, a C13 owner. Nos. 37–38 has two canted bays and two gabled C17 dormers with brackets for oriels.

Back to the S side for Nos. 86–87, early C17 timber, but with the most formal shopfront on the High. Of stone, with seven Greek Doric columns; by *John Plowman Sen.* for himself, 1832 or just after. The iron-balconied Nos. 83 and 84 were early C19 extensions of the great Angel Inn, otherwise demolished from 1876 for the Examination Schools (p. 345). No. 84, *c.* 1815–20, includes the former coffee room (now Grand Café), with Grecian Ionic columns of brown scagliola. Later shopfront with Corinthian half-columns, no less fine. At No. 83 a quasi-Venetian window on the first floor and giant pilasters l. and r., their capitals decorated with bacchic heads. On the N side, after the grandeur of Queen's, the enchanting back route of QUEEN'S LANE, past St Edmund Hall and New College, where it becomes New College Lane (Perambulation 2, p. 416). The houses that follow include much replication or imitation for the colleges. Nos. 40–43 now go with Queen's small CARRODUS QUAD, formed in 1967–9 by *Marshall Sisson* to house two Fellows and fifty students. Access is from Queen's Lane, through near-facsimiles of the old houses there. Sisson's loosely Neo-Georgian buildings, of buff brick, four floors high, and invisible from the street, extend by corridor access along the N and E sides. To the front, Nos. 40–41 are little more than a retained façade, but Nos. 42–43 is intact, a double-gabled C17 timber house with two short gabled wings picturesquely offset behind. At Nos. 44–45 *Sisson* imitates an Oxford C18 front quite plausibly. Nos. 46–47 are coarser impersonation, by *Gilbert Howes*, 1974–5, pushing through from St Edmund Hall behind (p. 262). Then Nos. 49–52, a long stone-and-roughcast Tudor range of lodgings over shops, 1900–1 by *E. P. Warren*. Built as an investment by Magdalen, but colonized from 1950 by St Edmund Hall with funding from Antonin Besse. Also by *Warren*, of similar materials but C17 in style, is the EASTGATE HOTEL opposite, 1899–1900. On the front a coloured relief by *George Simonds* of the medieval East Gate as rebuilt in 1711 (dem. 1771).

The hotel extends down MERTON STREET, where Nos. 20–22 are *Warren* too, built for rent by Merton College in 1901–3. Three of an intended terrace of five. Long and high, thirteen bays altogether, the middle five recessed. Stone again below, render with brick quoins above. Cross-windows. At the back, higher still, white, with three big gables. Next door, Merton Warden's Lodgings (p.209) face down the lovely cobbled E–W part of Merton Street, with the college garden wall on the S side. On the N side a run of mostly stone-built houses, C17 to C19. Nos.13–15 for example, built in the last years of the C17, are chiefly of large, squared blocks, not ashlared. Then the former Local Examination Delegacy (*see* Examination Schools, p.348) and former History Faculty (*see* University College, p.305). By Logic Lane, No.9, early C19. Two bays, with a channelled ground floor and a Victorian oriel. The rest of the street on this side is described with Merton and with Corpus. A last return to the High Street, with not many more houses still to come. On the N side the finish is Georgian ashlar, from the street improvements of 1771–2: No.57, with plain tripartite windows, and *John Townesend III*'s No.58, of five bays, the middle windows distinguished by straight entablatures. The C18 motifs are echoed by Magdalen's residential LONGWALL ANNEXE next door, of 1935–6 by *J.E. Thorpe*.

On the S side more nice variety of heights and materials. Nos.69–70 was an exceptionally prominent instance in Oxford of good mid-C18 brickwork, with stone quoins and Gibbs surrounds; stuccoed and neutered in 1932. No.65 onwards were all rebuilt after 1771 in connection with the new Magdalen Bridge, but not to any standard design or material. No.64, with pretty small-scale decoration by the first-floor window heads, was built by *Stephen Townesend*, c.1783. On No.63 another good balcony. The end is MAGDALEN GATE HOUSE, the High Street's grandest, facing Rose Lane and the Botanic Garden. Of 1802 for Thomas Roberson, later Town Clerk. Three storeys, with a very high first floor, central window aedicule and three-bay pediment. Rusticated end pilasters. Plain S wing, raised by one storey after c.1890. Opposite, N, is Magdalen itself, where the front lawn with trees in front of the C19 buildings is visually wonderfully happy. It makes one feel at once a loosening of the street coherence as one gets near the river. The bank can be gained via Rose Lane to Christ Church Meadow, past MEADOW COTTAGES, stone, c.1700; tile-hung dormer storey, looking Victorian.

Finally LONGWALL STREET, and the houses facing Magdalen's boundary wall. LONG WALL HOUSE, 1856–7, and the slightly later additions behind were built for boarders at Magdalen College School (*see* p.405). Nos.1–3, late C17, is the street's one remaining jettied and gabled house. At No.8 a pretty C18 fanlight. BODICOTE HOUSE (No.8A) is New College accommodation of 1968–9 by *Geoffrey Beard* (*Oxford Architects Partnership*), a strongly articulated concrete frame with boxed-out upright windows. The timber-framed Nos.9–14 were leased in 1812 as 'lately erected'. For the Sacher Building next to it, and the former Morris garage round the corner, *see* New College, pp.222–3.

2. North-east: Holywell Street to St Cross

To the NE, pre-Victorian Oxford begins and largely ends with Holywell Street. Spaced out further N are late C19 and C20 colleges (Harris Manchester, Mansfield, Linacre, St Catherine's), outliers of older colleges (Balliol, Brasenose, Merton, New), much University building, playing fields, and the medieval outlier comprising St Cross church and Holywell Manor.

HOLYWELL STREET runs E from the E end of Broad Street, just N of the city wall. The land in front of the wall is still shown as clear on Agas's map of 1588, but Loggan in 1675 depicts houses along both sides. Despite Victorian and C20 losses, the street still has Oxford's best concentration of C17 houses, allowing of course for much Georgian heightening, stuccoing and re-windowing, and also the selective rebuilding of back parts after annexation by the colleges. The S side starts with the unabashed display of the former Indian Institute (p. 343), followed by part of Hertford College. On the N side, the KING'S ARMS inn, called 'rebuilt and greatly enlarged' in 1791. Stuccoed timber. An unassuming five-bay W front with a pedimented mid-window. To Holywell Street an early C18 four-bay continuation. The Georgian stucco façades break for the former Blackwell's Music Shop (*see* Wadham College, p. 312). The first stone-fronted house is No. 37, C18, four storeys. No. 35 is different. It is partly timber-framed, and of the broad-fronted, one-room-deep type. Two storeys plus three dormers. On the first floor two oriels on original carved brackets, dated 1626. Late C18 ground floor of stone. Then the Holywell Music Room, another Wadham property (p. 312). Houses now start on the S side too. The first are all late C17, but with rear parts rebuilt for Hertford's 1970s quad; Nos. 53–55 ashlar-fronted, with two-light mullioned windows.

Next the picturesque little BATH PLACE runs S between smaller C17–C18 houses, turning E through a passage to the lovable enclave of the C18 TURF TAVERN, under the city walls by New College bell-tower. From here, St Helen's Passage leads W and S to NEW COLLEGE LANE, with the Bridge of Sighs (p. 159). Houses on the N side here, between the colleges. No. 5, plain red brick, early C19. The former NEW COLLEGE SCHOOL, E, is ashlar, in C14 Gothic style. By *Field & Castle*, 1874. Set back, Nos. 6–7, with a stuccoed C18 front. The rooftop platform was made in 1705 for the observatory of Edmund Halley, lately appointed Savilian Professor of Geometry. No. 8, red brick, must be mid-C18. Stone quoins and key blocks.

Back in Holywell Street, No. 56 comprises tutors' flats for Merton, 1938, Neo-Georgian by *T. H. Hughes*. The little No. 57 preserves the timber-framed mid-C17 form: jetty, square bay, gable. On the N side, No. 33 is of three bays, Early Victorian; No. 32 is largely C17 behind an early C19 five-bay ashlar front; No. 31 is timber-framed early C18, with pilastered doorway and scroll-bracketed hood. No. 30, C17, also timbered, incorporates the largest of Holywell Street's several entrances to former rear courts or yards. Opposite, Nos. 59–60, 1900 by *Castle, Field & Castle*. Ashlar with tripartite windows, their lights having rounded top corners. Nos. 61–62, early C18, again have straight door hoods on carved brackets. The N side from No. 29 is stuccoed and taller, with the canted bays of so many Georgian Oxford houses. (In No. 29 an early C17 splat-baluster staircase, in No. 28 an overmantel dated 1661.) Of the next group on the s side, No. 65 has an oriel bracket dated 1639, but is probably a C19 reconstruction. Nos. 66–67 is a replacement of 1952 for New College, the Victorian N range of which follows beyond. On the N side, No. 25 is joined to PYE HALL behind, a stone-built C17 house with two renewed four-light mullion-and-transom windows; now with Harris Manchester College.

The houses resume after Mansfield Road, cut through in 1893 (*see* p. 421). No. 20 has the carved date 1635 inside. (One modestly ornate plaster ceiling, a pilastered overmantel, and another splat-baluster staircase.) No. 19 formerly had a patterned floor made of knucklebones with the dates 1701/2, but the plain stone front looks later. The Yorkshire carpenter *Thomas Holt* lived at No. 17 in the early C17, and David Sturdy identified the doorway with fleur-de-lys chamfer-stops as his. No. 13 stands out with its early C17 rubble-stone front, two storeys plus two high dormers, each with an ovolo-moulded three-light window. No. 7, early C19, was once one house with the jettied No. 6, of C17 origin; the C18 gatepiers, l., mark the entrance to its garden, now part of Merton's Holywell Buildings (*see* below). No. 3 is early C17, stone-fronted (restored 1972), one room deep. Squared window hoodmoulds, one asymmetrical canted bay, central Tudor-arched doorway under a straight hood with carved brackets of *c.* 1700. (Good staircase of mid-C18 type: slim turned balusters, swept rail, tread-ends with brackets and dentils.) The s side resumes with Nos. 96–98, a timber-framed C18 group. The last group is stone, of which No. 99 is twin-gabled early C17; then Longwall Street (Perambulation 1, p. 415). No. 2 opposite is early C17 timber-framed, top storey reworked, but still with two jetties and with oriels on decorated brackets. Finally No. 1, probably a later C18 re-casing. Rendered, with a pedimented mid-window over a doorway set in a niche in a curious way.

N into ST CROSS ROAD. On the w side is HOLYWELL COTTAGE, actually a substantial five-bay rubble-walled house of *c.* 1700. Renewed timber cross-windows. JOWETT WALK runs back w alongside, the place to see what the colleges have done behind Holywell Street. The s side is Merton's HOLYWELL BUILDINGS, 1992–4 by *Architects Design Partnership*. Two medium blocks then a large one, altogether too big to suit the unenterprising collegiate-domestic detail. The N side belongs to Balliol. First, to the w, JOWETT BUILDINGS by *MacCormac Jamieson Prichard*, 1992–6 and 2004. Not all of the intended scheme was built, but enough to make the concept clear. Five

Jowett Walk, Jowett Buildings.
Perspective drawing by Peter Hull, 1992

square pavilions – nine were originally projected – all faced
in tawny brick striped with single courses of blue-black. They
are placed in such a way that three are linked diagonally at the
corners. One side of each pavilion has a broad lower opening,
to accommodate a cross-route parallel with the street. The
ground level is partly sunk, forming a series of courtyards
around the public rooms in the lowest storeys (theatre, seminar
rooms etc.). Above are the students' rooms, grouped round
top-lit cantilevered staircases. These have their own intercom-
munication route by means of slim bridges, which run through
within each big opening at first-floor level. The upper parts
break out as slim, dark-framed diagonal oriels and canted
bays, and the parapets likewise finish plainly and sharply, for
which the architects claimed Lutyens's Castle Drogo as inspiration. Other echoes are of Postmodern pioneers of the 1980s
– Mario Botta or James Stirling for the stripes, Aldo Rossi for
the square basement windows to the N – and the whole retains
the freshness and suggestiveness of the best Postmodern work.
The diagonally accented square units, and their offset grouping
along a linear circulation axis, also look back to MJP's Burrell's Field scheme for Trinity College, Cambridge, of 1991–5.
  Balliol resumed building in 2017–21 with the MASTER'S
FIELD scheme by *Niall McLaughlin Architects*, on the E corner
and N along St Cross Road. Eight flat-roofed residential blocks,
oblong or L-shaped, loosely grouped N and s of a replacement

pavilion for sports etc. on the playing-field side. The blocks are three- or four-storeyed, of cross-laminated timber walling cased in variegated pale brown brick and storey-height cast panels with a basket-weave motif. Sharp arrises and stepped profiles, familiar now from the practice's other Oxford projects. The PAVILION is broad and low, fronted by a simple open colonnade. A paved terrace at the outer angle by the road. Admirable clarity of detail throughout, though the cumulative effect is repetitious; early proposals included a gabled assembly hall, a regrettable omission. Between the blocks some Balliol tutors' houses remain, of 1897 by *Sir Ernest George & Yeates*: No. 7, hip-roofed with square bays added in 1919–20, and a similar pair, Nos. 9–11.*

Now the E side of St Cross Road. Opposite No. 7, set back, is the ST CROSS ANNEXE, shared by St Cross and Brasenose colleges. Two big buildings by the *Wallace & Hoblyn Partnership*, 1995–6, with a central lawn. Arts and Crafts inspiration, big tiled roofs, free detail. A plan of 1966 for a wholly new St Cross College here, to an angular and jagged design by *Stout & Litchfield*, foundered on lack of funds. This reprieved the former ST CROSS SCHOOL to the N, a modest one- to two-storey building of stone by *Buckeridge*, 1858. One large Gothic window with plate tracery. Its N side joins on to the former LODGE of 1850 to HOLYWELL CEMETERY, a fascinating work by the Oxford builder and sculptor-modeller *Thomas Grimsley*, who patented various forms of timber-free construction. Its N porch has mullion-like stone uprights and tracery, a brick-built gable masked by an early instance of tile-hanging, and an iron-framed roof of interlocking diagonal tiles, exposed inside. The nicely three-parts-wild cemetery has against its N wall the family plot of the Rev. J.W. Burgon, latterly Dean of Chichester, †1888, with Burgesian detail. – Henry Bird, a chorister, †1856. Open-sided table tomb housing an effigy by *Earp*. – Prof. Sir John Rhys †1915 and wife. Terracotta, clearly by *Mary Seton Watts* of the Compton Pottery, Surrey. – Dr Hastings Rashdall, philosopher and Dean of Carlisle, †1924. A cross with strikingly good figure reliefs, loosely of Anglo-Saxon inspiration.

The cemetery joins on to the graveyard of St Cross church (p. 392), now another Balliol colony. The WALL to its N with windows of Geometrical tracery is a relic of the time when the Clewer Sisterhood (from Clewer near Windsor) had their 'Female Penitentiary' at Holywell Manor, to rescue women from the risk of prostitution. It belonged to the penitentiary's

*The McLaughlin scheme replaced *Maufe*'s Nos. 1–5 and Eastman House, 1960, and *Sir Leslie Martin*'s MARTIN BUILDING of 1965–7, for graduate students of Balliol and St Anne's. This shared the horizontal proportions and pale brick facing of Martin's St Cross Building opposite. Projected as Phase 1 of a mixed postgraduate foundation, the project was overtaken by the general opening of the colleges to both sexes after 1974. Also Balliol's DELLAL BUILDING, 1984–6 by *Barnett Briscoe Gotch*.

chapel of 1862 by *James Castle*; later buildings by *Moore* (1891) and *C.C. Rolfe* (1896–1900) have gone.

HOLYWELL MANOR, the manor house next to St Cross, stands at the corner of Manor Road. The original house dates from 1516, when *Richard Gelys* or *Gyles* of Winchester and *Thomas Phelypp* of Oxford rebuilt it for Merton College. End ranges added between *c.*1555 and 1572. It too became part of the Penitentiary, then was adapted for Balliol students in 1931–2, the first fully fledged residential outstation for any of the colleges. What remains of the C16 is L-shaped, with ranges stretching N and E. Windows with arched lights, and hoodmoulds on the ground floor. A big buttressed projection towards the church. The hall was in the E–W part. (One room with a minor chimneypiece with three blank arches in the overmantel.) To the W a large, open-sided quad was added in 1931–2 by *Kennedy & Nightingale*, of whom *George Kennedy* was a Balliol man. Mildly Neo-Georgian, rendered with a big mid-window. A first-floor ante-room has MURALS of 1934–6 by *Gilbert Spencer*, entirely in his brother Stanley's characteristic style. They tell of the life of John de Balliol. The quad and garden have abstract sculpture, and a FOUNTAIN by *Peter Lyon*, 1965. N of the 1930s part a further extension by *Architects Design Partnership*, 1992–3. Most of its motifs nod to 1932, but also some timber-framed glazing to the small circular courtyard within.

MANOR ROAD continues W, with the St Cross Building (p.382) and Social Sciences Building (p.383) on the N side. The S side and MANOR PLACE then present an unexpected enclave of big, plain red brick terraces of 1893–*c.*1898 by *Castle, Field & Castle*, built as a speculation by Merton. St Catherine's College follows, but Manor Road carries on through it to Merton's sports ground, with its PAVILION of 1966–8 by *Michael G.D. Dixey* with *Richard Sudell*, landscape architect. Dark brick and board-marked concrete slabs, with a cantilevered balcony to the S. On the road side are two squash courts, windowless, with a covered bridge between. The building holds its own so close to Arne Jacobsen.

St Cross Road continues N. Just beyond the St Cross Building, extending from the E side, are the WESTON BUILDINGS of New College. Graduate accommodation of 1997–9 by *Initiatives in Design*, comprising interlinked pavilions sheltered by shallow hipped roofs. Diagonal oriels at the corners may invite unfavourable comparisons with Jowett Walk, but the whole is pleasing and composes well. In the middle is an interruption, New College's SPORTS PAVILION, *c.*1956 by *R. Fielding Dodd & Stevens*, of traditional outline. Then the University buildings of the Science Area (pp.370ff), and also Linacre College at the NE corner with SOUTH PARKS ROAD. All that remains in the latter road from before the University takeover are two huge brick villas by *Wilkinson* on the S side, No.2 of 1865–6 (originally Park Grange), the plainer No.1, W, 1868–9.

That leaves MANSFIELD ROAD, specifically its s part, by Holy-well Street. On the w side here, between Mansfield College and Harris Manchester, SAVILE HOUSE. A New College property comprising a tutor's house of 1897, sober stone Neo-Tudor, plus one matching N bay from *N.W. Harrison*'s extension for student rooms, 1935, r. Attached to the latter, New College's CLORE MUSIC STUDIOS by *John McAslan & Partners*, 2016–19. A Portland stone box, the front composed rather like an upright Ben Nicholson relief, above a glazed ground floor. Entrance link glazed to full height, also the set-back attic. (A section of RAMPARTS from the Civil War defences of 1642–3 behind; also a bastion N of The King's Mound, *see* below.)

To the s and w, the GRADEL QUADS are taking shape in 2023. A big scheme by *David Kohn Architects* with *Purcell*, shared between New College and NEW COLLEGE SCHOOL, and approved in 2018. Published designs indicate a new aesthetic for Oxford, curiously like 1920s free-form Expressionism, with a tall tower. Landscape design by *Todd Longstaffe-Gowan*. What remains of the school's older buildings is SAVILE ROAD. No.1 here is another tutor's house, 1901–2 by *Nicholson & Corlette*. They also designed the original SCHOOL of 1903–4 to the NW, comprising headmaster's house as well as classrooms and dormitories. Mild, rambling Cotswold-manorial. Steep roofs, slim chimneys. Closer to the road, domestic-looking GYM etc. by *TSH Architects*, 2005–7. Pale ashlar.

On the E side of Mansfield Road, No.3 is now the University's Queen Elizabeth House (p.381). The other houses were built by Balliol. Nos.5 and 7 are by *E.P. Warren*, rendered Neo-Georgian with hipped roofs, 1924. Finally, set back, THE KING'S MOUND (No.9) by *Jackson*, built for A.L. Smith in 1892–3. Demonstratively monumental, with shaped gables, mullion-and-transom windows, and two big bows on the s side. The giant size is explained by Smith's household, which included many college entrants and overseas Balliol students.

3. North: Cornmarket Street, Broad Street and St Giles'

CORNMARKET STREET formerly had a covered market, built in the wide roadway in 1536 and destroyed in the Civil War. It now starts with the profusely expressed blessing of the banks at the Carfax corners (*see* p.409), and is largely a commercial Victorian and C20 street indeed. The start on the E SIDE is No.1A (now with Lloyds), the former Jolly Farmers pub, slim half-timbering of 1876 by *H.J. Tollit*. The next buildings of note are C15, C16 and C17. At No.3 the four-bay Georgian front hides a multi-phase timber house with a late C15 core, originally part of the Bull Inn. In a second-floor room are the best Elizabethan WALL PAINTINGS in Oxford. One full wall and part of another with interlaced reticulation units, a little as in thin-ribbed stucco patterns, against a red ground. In the

35

units flowers or grapes. The frieze has black-letter devotional inscriptions. Over the fireplace a large (earlier?) IHS. Contemporary work in a rear room, now destroyed, suggested John Tattleton, resident 1564–81, as the patron. The other front room has re-set C16 panelling, with some painted strapwork.

The GOLDEN CROSS INN, immediately N, has medieval and C17 evidence of much interest. All this is in the yard, reached through a C15 timber archway at No.4. The N range is a dormitory wing of 1534/5 (tree-ring dates), with original, finely moulded oriel windows and an underbuilt ground floor. The S range is later C17, built as two houses. Two-storey oriels, the larger ones all with Ipswich windows. Four gables of three different sizes. The E range is early C19. Various added ground-floor projections to N and S. The whole eminently picturesque ensemble was restored in 1986–7 by *Dunthorne Parker*, with a new passage of shops through to the Covered Market. In the opened-out first floor of the N range (now PIZZA EXPRESS) are more WALL PAINTINGS. Two walls have white-on-black designs of big candelabra with symmetrical foliage, putti and other 'antique' motifs of *c.*1550–60, partly overpainted with a band or frieze of coloured foliage, fruit, birds etc. between 1595 and 1604. So the lower part must have been hidden behind panelling by that time. Also one wall with tapestry-like designs of *c.*1570–80, again one above the other, and painted partly on cloth. No.4, incidentally, may have Oxford's first architectural design by a female architect, a Modernist refronting of 1957 by *Nadine Beddington*. Nos.6–7 next door are commercial Free Style of 1907 by *John R. Wilkins*.

The W SIDE starts with *H.G.W. Drinkwater*'s Nos.59–61. Built as the Metropolitan & Birmingham Bank in 1890–1, when it was called the 'first instalment' of the intended Carfax improvements. Nice carving by *McCulloch* on the oriels. THE CROWN, set down a passage, originated as C19 stables for the lost inn of that name. Next the former Littlewood's, 1962–4 by *D.M.C. Roddick*, architect to the firm, rather showy, with its vertical fins (demolition proposed). The tall Nos.53–54 originated as the Shakespeare Hotel (the two l. bays) by *Thomas Wyatt Jun.*, as early as 1864; matching r. extension and bank front for BARCLAYS, 1922–3 by *Alfred Foster*. Then the former WOOLWORTH'S, 1956–7, with a façade by *Lord Holford*. Stone-faced, with a little grooving of the window grid. Infill of slate panels or of squared Bladon rubble, an interwar echo. Converted to the CLARENDON CENTRE in 1983–4, with a shopping arcade through to Queen Street (p.435). The predecessor was the former Clarendon Hotel, a largely mid-C16 inn with a late C11 vaulted cellar, concealed by a stucco front of *c.*1783.

On the E side opposite is MARKET STREET, with the former ROEBUCK pub, S side. Nicely composed Neo-Georgian by *Thomas Rayson*, 1938. N of Market Street is Jesus College's new Fourth Quad, with shops below (*see* p.164). On the w side, Nos.47–51, a picturesque pile-up by *Codd*, 1879–80. A corner tourelle by FREWIN COURT, the passage to the Oxford

Union (p. 351), and formerly to Frewin Hall (Perambulation 5, p. 436). Also a well-judged infill scheme of *c.* 1988 by *Barnett Briscoe Gotch*, in a sort of Postmodern Victorian Gothic, with brick polychromy and triangular arch heads. Back on the E side, No. 22, W. H. SMITH. Tudor, four-storeyed, 1915. No. 23, and Nos. 41–42 diagonally ahead, have fronts of the stuccoed C18 type of four storeys with two canted bay windows which is so frequent on the High Street. No. 24 is five-storeyed, ashlar, gabled, with quite an attractive treatment of Free Style motifs. By *R. H. Kerr*, 1904–5, for the Capital & Counties Bank.

Then a major survival, the former NEW INN. Built from 1386 by John Gibbes, vintner, or his son, in a pragmatic combination of timber and stone. Three of the original five shop-houses remain in front, of standard late medieval framing, with a double jetty. Collar-beam roof with clasped purlins, dragon beam at the angle with Ship Street. Also a retained earlier stone wall inside, N–S. Restored in two phases: No. 28 (N) in 1950–2 by *T. Rayson*; Nos. 26–27 in 1986–7 by *F. W. B. Charles*, with *John Fryman* of *Architects Design Partnership*, for Jesus College. Rayson added plausible oriels and bargeboards, and also cusped windows on the N side, taken from Buckler's C19 drawings; Charles placed a purist emphasis on the structural frame. (Early C17 wall painting at No. 26, fictive panelling framing coloured strapwork.) The inn proper was behind (cf. the Golden Cross). What chiefly survives is part of the entrance range, the stone-fronted No. 26 Ship Street. Mullioned windows of correct late C14 type, probably inserted when *Bruton* restored the building as his offices in 1867. The inner wall is of stone on the ground floor only, with a doorway

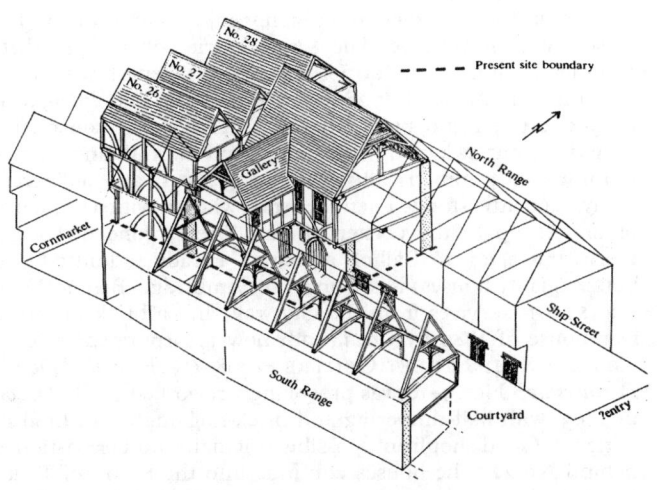

New Inn, Cornmarket Street.
Reconstruction drawing, 1992

with two-centred arch. (Jettied upper floor, probably a dormitory. The surviving part includes one two-light timber window with tracery modelled on that of New College hall. Crown-post roof, the tie-beams and wall-plates moulded. A partly surviving gallery crossed behind the shops, linking N and S ranges; the latter was timber-framed, against a rear stone wall.)

SHIP STREET has the stone-built former Ship Inn of *c.*1756 at Nos. 1–5. An unspoiled stretch of modest C17–C18 houses follows, mostly timber-framed and jettied, facing Jesus College. No. 11 retains C18 mock-rustication of timber on the ground floor. Originally the street was part of the circuit that ran just within the old city wall. St Michael's church on the N corner with Cornmarket (p. 396) stood next to the former North Gate, which doubled as the town's Bocardo prison; demolished with the other gates in 1771. No. 35 Cornmarket Street (W side), a truncated late C18 ashlar front with a Venetian window under a relieving arch, marks where the gate stood. Further S, by St Michael's Street, THE PLOUGH (No. 38), formerly dated 1665. Low, timber-framed, with a seven-light window below two small gables treated pedimentally. Taller gable behind. Much restored in 1925 by *Rayson*. He made the little niche, N, from discovered fragments. No. 30, E side, has a commercial Free Style front of 1904 by *Herbert Quinton*.

The end of Cornmarket Street is also early C20 commercial. On the George Street corner, W, tall and busy classical by *Homer & Lucas*, 1910–11. Curving into Broad Street, E, WATERSTONES, 1914–15 by *N.W. & G.A. Harrison*, with *Payne Wyatt* of London. Built for William Baker & Co., cabinet-makers. The Selfridges model: giant columns between bronzed framing, squared-off detail. The l. bay never received its intended attic storey.

BROAD STREET is another street highly enjoyable for the walker in search of townscape. The S side carries on Cornmarket-commercial at first, the former BOSWELL'S department store, now THE STORE hotel. 1928–9 by *North, Robin & Wilsdon*, with Lutyens's pupil and biographer *A. S. G. Butler* as consultant. Grandiose but awkward, with stalky giant Corinthian pilasters framing two symmetrically placed entrances, and an excessively plain attic storey. Then the street widens, with a sequence of houses up to the corner of Turl Street, none of special merit, but a foil to Balliol, as King's Parade (admittedly of better-quality houses) is to King's at Cambridge. Behind No. 6 a BASTION survives from the city wall, and a brick furniture warehouse of 1882 by *Codd*, both now incorporated in Jesus College's SHIP STREET CENTRE (2008–11, *Architects' Design Partnership*). Nos. 9–10 was provokingly reworked by *Wilkinson* in 1863, with half-timbering and brick-nogging of un-English patterns. Good shopfront, possibly original. Another bastion is behind No. 22. The houses continue into the N end of TURL STREET, here consistently of 1787–9, when the street was widened (some sixty years after the old Turl Gate was taken down). Three have good big radial fanlights.

The s side of Broad Street goes on with Exeter College. Then the great University conclave begins, with the Old Ashmolean, Sheldonian and Clarendon Building (pp. 339, 336 and 340), and the former Indian Institute beyond (p. 343). On the Balliol side, Trinity follows, including Kettell Hall (p. 297). Then another stucco group, though not much is old. No. 53, BLACKWELL'S MUSIC SHOP, has a facsimile front of 1967–8 by *Maguire & Murray*, and goes with their Cumberbatch Buildings for Trinity behind (p. 298). The WHITE HORSE (No. 52) is C16 or C17, refronted in 1951 probably by *J. E. R. Leed*. The front of BLACKWELL'S is genuine Georgian at Nos. 50–51, imitation of 1938 by *F. E. Openshaw* at Nos. 48–49, from when the New Bodleian (p. 344) was built next door. The back and underground parts are 1960s, also shared with Trinity. The E end of Broad Street on this side is the King's Arms, described with Holywell Street (Perambulation 2, p. 416); the houses to its N belong with Wadham College (p. 312).

Back w to the corner with Cornmarket, where MAGDALEN STREET runs N. More late C19 and early C20 commercial façades here (lately Debenham's), facing St Mary Magdalen and its islanded churchyard. The corner building with turret is of 1894–5 by *Drinkwater*. Nos. 3–4 were Taphouse & Co.'s music shop, by *G. H. Blatherwick* and *M. V. Treleaven*, Gothic, and as late as 1913; the upper storeys housed the YWCA. Elliston & Cavell, drapers, built Nos. 7–12, of which Nos. 9–12 are more by *Drinkwater*, mixed Georgian of 1894–5, the rest by *H. Quinton*, 1899–1900. Then back to the C20 with a bang: OXENFORD HOUSE, 1965–6 by *Fitzroy Robinson & Partners* with *Brett & Pollen*, a very mannered piece of façade design. It looks like a concrete frame of pre-cast parts, except that the mullions are broken off every time the sill bands of black glass run through, so that the seeming mullions are stuck on in front of the real frame. The narrow, mongrel front at No. 19 is the ODEON cinema of 1922–4 by *Frank Matcham & Co.* with *James C. Leed*. Barrel-vaulted auditorium, little altered. (Concealed behind acoustic curtains, two murals of 1924 by *G. Rushton*: Modern Sport, Early Learning.)

The RANDOLPH HOTEL next, Oxford's one grand hotel from the railway era. Of 1864–6 by *William Wilkinson*, contractors *Kirk & Parry* of London. Wilkinson was also surveyor to the Norham Manor Estate from 1860 (p. 460), and in both he rubs in the message that Georgian is abysmally dull and Second Pointed the one and only salvation. The hotel is high and large, and was so even before the w extension of 1951–2 (by *J. Hopgood*) which decided to keep to the Randolph characteristics. Four storeys. Yellow brick with stone dressings, iron balconies along most of the first floor. The entrance front is nearly symmetrical, i.e. the end bays with oriels and pointed roofs are the same and the centre has the portal, the oriel over, the gable and the pavilion roof behind (not Gothic, that) all in the middle, but l. and r. are some differences. Some capitals of the French Early Gothic foliage type, others Ruskinianly naturalistic. Iron porch by *H.W. Moore*, 1889 (also the ball-room, SW); ground-floor bays adjoining the entrance extended forward by *Collcutt & Hamp*, 1923. The central oriel formerly had its own steep roof, as did the big canted bay which terminates the E front. Vaulted entry. Open-well staircase with looping iron balustrade and lancet windows, climbing to full height. The latest additions, facing Friars Entry, are by the *Bell Slater Partnership*, 2002–4.

So ST GILES' is reached, the widest street of Oxford, and with its plane trees on both sides and the refusal of both sides to run parallel a visually most attractive space. Its S focus is the MARTYRS' MEMORIAL, N of St Mary Magdalen. The project was devised in 1838 by a Low Church group to commemorate Cranmer, Latimer and Ridley, burnt to death in Broad Street in 1555–6 under Queen Mary. It was thus also read by many as a challenge to the Tractarians. The cross was erected in 1841–3 to the design of *George Gilbert Scott*, proof at once that almost as early as Pugin (whom he admired – martyrs or no martyrs) he had seen the light of Gothic perfection revived by strict archaeological accuracy. The three competitors had been instructed to base their designs on the Eleanor Cross at Waltham, Herts., but to be 15 ft (4.6 metres) taller. Mansfield stone. The plan is hexagonal; there is the decorated lower part, the upper part with statues (by *H. Weekes*), and the elaborate spire. Other carving by a Mr *Cox*; builder *Kirk* of Sleaford. The details are all impeccably of *c.*1290 except for the nodding-ogee canopies of the statues, which bring in the early C14. Restored 2002–3 by *Donald Insall Associates*. Also part of the memorial project is the N aisle which Scott added to the church (p.395).

Going N, St Giles' on the E side is for a long way almost all colleges: Balliol, a little of Trinity, then St John's. On the W side, first the Taylorian and Ashmolean (p.352), stretching down Beaumont Street (p.431). Then No.66, of 1869, built by *George Wyatt* for himself. All of stone, Deane-and-Woodward Gothic, the details, caricature heads etc. devised by Wyatt's own men. No.65 is early C18, remodelled probably by *Henry Keene*, who took the lease in 1768. (Plausibly Keene's, the open-well staircase with Chinoiserie balustrade and a chimneypiece with Ionic columns.) Gothic shopfront of the 1860s, partly reinstatement of 2005–7, when *van Heyningen & Haward* converted both houses for the STELIOS IOANNU CENTRE (Classical and Byzantine Studies). Rear atrium with a giant slatted north-light roof, angled steeply downwards. A new four-storey wing along the S side, partly open to the atrium. The old house backs look untidily in. After that, Blackfriars and St Cross College (Pusey House), up to Pusey Street.

The N part of St Giles' has its own character, with Oxford's greatest assembly of good Georgian houses on both sides. The street also widens even more, so each side is described separately. On the W SIDE, after Pusey Street, the first houses belong with Regent's Park College (p. 326): No. 56 a 1980s facsimile, No. 55 of *c.* 1800, plain painted stone, five bays, with a columned doorcase. At Nos. 53–54 a stone-built C16 or C17 house. Two storeys, with canted bays rising to gabled timber dormers. Small depressed-arched passage doorway, r. No. 52, tall, slim Lombardic, was designed by *R.C.E. Tanner*, a surveyor in the Oxford office of Charles Buckeridge, 1868. The EAGLE AND CHILD pub, heavily modernized, retains a late C17 cross-window behind. Then the entry to WELLINGTON PLACE, an unanticipated pocket of mid-C19 stucco villas. Nos. 45–46, *c.* 1840, also stuccoed brick, the first-floor windows arched and with iron balconies. Porch with square pillars. No. 43 is dated 1660 and has three bays. Rendered rubble; the windows originally no doubt mullioned. Some re-set pierced flat balusters. The FRIENDS' MEETING HOUSE sits behind, 1951–5 by *T. Rayson*. The E view is almost all stone-slated roof, above a simple Tuscan loggia. Rubble walls. Canted ceiling to the meeting room. At No. 42 a superior early C19 iron balcony. No. 41 is a fine ashlar house of *c.* 1700, refaced in 1956–7. Four bays and three storeys, with tightly spaced windows. They have linked straight entablatures, except those on the second floor, which are pedimented – the outer pediments triangular, the inner segmental – against a steeply gabled parapet. Late Georgian doorway with Doric columns and open pediment. (Close-string staircase with turned balusters.) Lying back from the street, No. 40 is of multiple phases, early C17 onwards, and partly timber-framed. (Original stucco-decorated ceiling beam in one first-floor room.) No. 39, stone Tudor Gothic, probably of 1850; the Diocesan Registry was here.

The tall Georgian frontages resume with No. 38, originally two houses, of *c.* 1830. Eight-bay front, rendered, with arched ground-floor windows. Iron balcony along the first floor, good lotus-head railings in front. Matching fourth storey of 1910. From 1923 to 2022 No. 38 was the home of St Benet's Hall, founded in 1897 as the Oxford house of the Benedictine order and made a Permanent Private Hall of the University in 1918; now owned by St Hilda's College. St Benet's started in 1897 as an Oxford house for the Benedictines of Ampleforth. It became a Private Hall in 1899, a Permanent Private Hall in 1918, and moved here in 1923. CHAPEL in the garden, 1911 by Canon *A.J.C. Scholes*, for a convent preceding the Benedictines.

No. 37A dates from after 1808, old-fashioned, with alternating first-floor window pediments. (Extensive rear additions, 1959 and 1998.) No. 37, five bays, ashlar, with a columned and pedimented Doric doorcase, was built by the carpenter *Vincent Shortland* for himself, *c.* 1789. The last grand houses are Nos. 34–36, 1828–9 by the builder *Daniel Evans*, presumably to his own design. Three bays each, three storeys, arched ground-floor windows, nicely subdivided first-floor balcony. Evans lived at No. 34. Behind the houses, a paved court with the CHRISTIAN SCIENCE READING ROOM and CHURCH, 2003–4 and 1996, by the *Bozeat Partnership*.

These last houses are level with St Giles's churchyard, which begins by *Rayson*'s WAR MEMORIAL of 1921. A slim Gothic cross on a stepped base, answering to the Martyrs' Memorial. The churchyard marks the fork where most non-connoisseurs of Oxford always forget which is the Woodstock and which the Banbury road. Both roads now belong as much to central Oxford in their southern stretches, which are therefore included below (pp. 430–1).

The E SIDE of St Giles' has been much affected by the expansion of St John's. The college's main front ends at No. 9, of *c.*1600. Squared rubble, timbered dormer gables. Dolled up for the college in 1905 by *N.W. Harrison*, then restored in 1962 after Buckler's view of 1821. Next MIDDLETON HALL, built in 1663 by Thomas Tudor, lawyer (refaced 1903). Windows of four narrow lights, under running hoodmoulds. Through-storey porch with a later doorway, formerly finished with a balustraded balcony. The top balustrade remains. Stair enclosure projecting behind. In 1857–8 *Benjamin Woodward* added a Gothic brick SE wing for the Rev. Bartholomew Price, Professor of Natural Philosophy. It has a steep gable and trefoiled lancet windows with spiky sawtooth surrounds of cut bricks. The window shape is Venetian Gothic. (Inside, crazily patterned doorcases and a splendid stone chimneypiece with foliage, birds etc., attributed to *O'Shea*.) The LAMB & FLAG is of *c.*1830 in front, with a C16 or early C17 rear wing.

The inn passage leads past St John's to MUSEUM ROAD. On the N side two semis for married tutors, 1938, in *Edward Maufe*'s modernized Neo-Georgian, then three big Gothic pairs of the 1870s, then Keble College. The S side is earlier: plain stucco terraced houses of *c.*1850–60. Parallel and behind, the EPA SCIENCE CENTRE, accommodation etc. for Lincoln College. 2002–3 by *Architects Design Partnership*. Treated as linked, angle-fronted units, with sharply folded roofs. The SE corner is No. 10 Parks Road, 1862 by *C. Buckeridge*. Red brick with severe Gothic stone detail. Off Museum Road to the N, where BLACKHALL ROAD runs behind Keble, Nos. 15–17, three flat-roofed houses by *Michael Powers* of the *Architects' Co-Partnership*, 1962–3. Built for St John's as tutors' houses, in effect the last flourish of this Oxford type. Pale grey brick with concrete storey bands, quite tough. Each is planned around a core comprising fireplace and curved-ended stairwell.

Back to St Giles. No. 14 looks mid-Georgian, still with Townesend-Baroque details, e.g. the rusticated ground floor with key blocks and the second-floor aprons. Four storeys, middle window with a pediment. No. 15, also ashlar, was called 'newly erected' in 1820. Four bays, three storeys. Doorway with Ionic columns in the fourth bay.

So to No. 16, ST GILES' HOUSE. Built in 1702 for the elder Thomas Rowney M.P., and the best house of its date in Oxford; a property of St John's since 1966. The builder was probably *Bartholomew Peisley II*. Seven-bay ashlar façade with quoins, and a central three-bay projection. Originally there was a central dormer, so the present pediment over this projection must be later.* It may belong with the rather dull doorway with Doric pilasters and a straight entablature. Gatepiers with gorgeous urns. At the back an equally gorgeous decorated plaster shell-hood, the finest in Oxford, and a pragmatically asymmetrical s wing. The front originally also had a shell-hood. A grand panelled stair hall runs from front to back, through a broad arch framed by Ionic pilasters. On its r. side an open-string staircase on a country-house scale, climbing to a first-floor landing in two flights. Twisted balusters, grouped in fours at the newels. Plaster ceiling with a fine rich oval wreath of flowers and foliage. Full-height back stair to the s. Some early C19 updating inside too, from when the dukes of Marlborough had the house, e.g. reeded fireplaces. Also the cut-down windows of the N bays. – In the garden a charming SHELTER with four unfluted Composite columns, the middle ones carrying a pediment, incorporating an older stone dome and lantern. This is identifiable as a model for the top-lit stone dome *Gibbs* intended his Radcliffe Camera to have, even down to the coffered underside.

Next house of note is No. 20, rendered early C19. Rounded bow in front. Another bow behind, facing St John's KENDREW QUAD of 2007–10. The last major Oxford work by *MJP Architects*, i.e. the *MacCormac, Jamieson & Prichard* practice, this shrugs off the Postmodern details of their Garden Quad at St John's main site (p. 282) in favour of boldly articulated, well-crafted Modernism. The quad sits some way back, and is open across its s side. Four storeys. Entry is by a symmetrically composed projection on the W side, beyond openwork steel GATES designed by *Wendy Ramshaw*. The central space is grassed, with a big old beech tree. The inward-facing sides are symmetrical too, the fine white concrete framing making a grid for the warm brown timber-panelled student rooms with their *brise-soleil*. Top storey of Fellows' flats with dark-framed continuous glazing, set back. Across the N side a café enclosure with a terrace on top. Its centre is raised as a tall oblong clerestory, making a formal emphasis with the balancing open staircases up to the terrace. But the most distinctive feature is the circulation: four slit-windowed, cylindrical staircase enclosures – two within the N angles, two pulled out at the ends of the E and W ranges – with spiral staircases around central lift cores, and bridges to the residential corridors. The N staircases start from the first floor only, the entire enclosure being suspended from the central core (structural engineers *Price & Myers*). The rest of the ground floor houses teaching rooms, archive, law library (in the deeper E wing) etc. Other ARTWORKS include *Alexander Beleschenko*'s glass screen wall to the café frontage, *Ian Monroe*'s screen on its back wall, and *Langlands & Bell*'s sculpted column in the W forecourt.

---

*As observed by Nick Wright. In the restoration of 2019 the roof was found to contain much reused timber, including late C16 or early C17 moulded beams.

Next to the entry to Kendrew is No. 21, BLACK HALL, a big, high late C17 stone house, much renewed.* Three-storey canted bay window, its top window not simply mullioned but arched in the centre, Ipswich-fashion (i.e. Sparrowe's House). Late C18 s porch. The N wing with its running hoodmoulds was added for the bookseller Joseph Parker, c. 1830. Open-well staircase with distinctive turned balusters and plain newels, tree-ring dated 1674. To the N a small barn also of 1674, making a small courtyard with an outlying studio block from MJP's quad. St Giles's last houses are the humbler Nos. 22–23 and No. 30, also C17, flanking the Department of Statistics (p. 379).

KEBLE ROAD runs E here, named from the college on its s side. The N side has the big bang of the Nuclear Physics building (p. 378), then a monster Gothic terrace by *Wilkinson* (eleven houses), 1868–71, of convent-like austerity. Yellow brick. The end is again PARKS ROAD, where two Gothic villa pairs survive amid the science buildings to the N, Nos. 12–13 (*Codd*) and Nos. 14–15, 1868 and 1869.

Now to the s end of BANBURY ROAD. On the w side, the OLD PARSONAGE of St Giles's church (to the s; p. 393). Early C17, stone, the central doorway dated 1659. Mullioned windows, two gables with ball finials. Now a hotel, and much extended. Next PARK VILLAS, a sequence of good Italianate stuccoed villas. Three designs. Nos. 7–9 and 11–13 probably by *S. L. Seckham*, c. 1850–5; Nos. 15–19 by *Henry Dixon*, 1847. All now joined behind by the University's I.T. SERVICES BUILDING, 1969–74. No. 21 was originally the HIGH SCHOOL FOR GIRLS, 1879–80 by *T. G. Jackson*. A pretty five-bay building with hipped roof and square cupola. Red brick against render, but the decorative elements all of fiery red *Doulton*'s terracotta, e.g. the Cinquecento upper columns; a rare material for Jackson. At No. 23 a raw red brick villa by *Bruton*, 1867. Then the H.B. ALLEN CENTRE, a very large satellite quad for Keble College (*c.* 240 postgraduate rooms). Of 2016–19 by *MICA Architects*, successors to *Rick Mather Architects*, developing Mather's designs of 2006–9. The site is the old Acland Hospital, a nursing home founded in 1882 by Sir Henry Acland. A disappointingly neutral frontage, stepping out and in a little. Four storeys, faced in thin brown bricks. Dark panels by the windows. A gap for entry at its s end, with a little quasi-Butterfieldian patterning on the end wall. The quad is composed around the only retained hospital element, *Jackson*'s block for paying patients of 1895–6 on the N side. Formerly the centrepiece of a larger range, this has a scrolly Dutch gable against a high mansard roof. Red brick and render. The adjacent new parts are fully glazed and recessed on the ground floor, a visually unstable conjunction. Glazed inner angles, also awkwardly handled. The central space has been excavated, and a lecture

---

*Formerly home to QUEEN ELIZABETH HOUSE, now at No. 3 Mansfield Road (p. 381). Attached buildings of 1961 by *R. E. Enthoven* were demolished for Kendrew Quad, and the house restored by *Dunthorne Parker Architects*.

theatre, laboratories etc. lie below. To Woodstock Road, w, a
detached block for offices and a café, its first floor fully glazed
and boxed out, screened by onyx-patterned glass slats. For the
rest of Banbury Road *see* pp. 460ff.

WOODSTOCK ROAD can now be followed from its s end. The
start by Little Clarendon Street is modest three-storey houses
with shops, C18 or C19. The E side then has *Moore*'s ST GILES'S
CHURCH HALL, 1887–91. The hall part, with dormers and big
brick buttresses, close to Arts and Crafts; porch and two-storey
N part with some free Perp stone tracery. More Arts and Crafts
detailing at the former BIG GAME MUSEUM, a true freak of
1906 by *J. R. Wilkins*, to house Mr C. V. A. Peel's trophy collection. Originally lit only by the flat-topped clerestories in alternate bays; other windows and floors inserted 1990. Opposite
is St Aloysius's church and presbytery (p. 398), then Somerville
College gate, then the Radcliffe Observatory Quarter (p. 361).
The E side goes on with ST GILES' TERRACE (Nos. 14–36),
c. 1800, which shows how well the Oxford timber-framed tradition could adapt to Georgian conventions. Mostly mirrored
pairs, rendered and scribed. The rear wings of red brick look
later. *Wilkinson & Moore*'s Nos. 38–40, 1886, are the first villas
of North Oxford type encou431
ntered here. After the ROYAL OAK pub, C17 and timber-framed,
the H. B. Allen Centre again (*see* above). The description of
Woodstock Road continues on pp. 467–9.

4. North-west: Beaumont Street to Jericho

Oxford's NW quarter developed in earnest in the C19. Industry
was attracted by the canal opened in 1790, notably Lucy's ironworks and the relocated University Press, and housing for the
workers was provided in the new district of Jericho. Closer to
the centre, a smart enclave of terraced houses took shape in the
1820s–30s, with which the perambulation begins.

BEAUMONT STREET runs w from St Giles', between the Ashmolean and the Randolph Hotel (pp. 352 and 425). Laid out
in 1822 by the surveyor *Henry Dixon*, across the site of the
medieval Beaumont Palace.* Together with the streets to the N,
it makes the finest Georgian ensemble of Oxford. The development belonged largely to St John's College, thus foreshadowing
its later activities across North Oxford (*see* p. 460), but the initiative started with Worcester College at the w end. Long terraces of three-storey houses, fronted with Bath stone. Designs
for the houses by *William Garbett* were not used, and the
happy variety of frontage details (also the diverse house plans)

---

*Built by Henry I as a walled enclave in the early C12, BEAUMONT PALACE fell
from royal favour after the mid C13. In 1318 it was granted to Oxford's Carmelites,
already established on part of the site of Worcester College, who adapted the buildings as their new home. One small C12 structure survived into the 1820s.

were left to the individual builders. Some door surrounds with columns and open pediments, many iron balconies, a few houses with verandas instead, i.e. canopied balconies. Of the last, Nos. 34–36 (N side) are by *Thomas Wyatt Jun.*, as are Nos. 22 and 23 (S side), which share the same close-barred fanlight type. ST JOHN STREET running N, formed at the same time, has smaller houses and less ornament; also the Sackler Library (p. 356). Behind the W side is BEAUMONT BUILD-INGS, with plain or chequered brick-fronted houses, irregularly placed. All three streets were substantially complete by 1836. Tucked away in Beaumont Buildings are the former BRITISH COUNCIL OFFICES, 1966–7 by *John Fryman* of *Architects Design Partnership*. Small and handsome. Concrete and close-set brick fins. Three different heights. Also some parts of Perp windows, re-set on the garden wall of No. 28 Beaumont Street.

Some of Beaumont Street's houses have since fallen to the expanding Ashmolean and Randolph, and in 1937–8 THE PLAYHOUSE replaced part of the S side, with an elevation by *Sir Edward Maufe*. The architect did the only possible thing and did it well, neither hiding the function of his building nor rubbing it in. *Eric Gill* carved the lettering. The rest is by *F. G. M. Chancellor*, whose own façade design had not found favour. Streamlined auditorium, sympathetically refurbished in 1996 by *Bryan Martin* of *Michael Reardon & Associates*. Facing Gloucester Street behind, SW, a plain brick addition (the BURTON TAYLOR STUDIO), 1972–5 by *Jack Lankester*, University Surveyor; now used as a student theatre. Residential addition for Worcester College behind Nos. 5–7 Beaumont Street, 2006–8, by *Gray Baynes & Shew*.

From the W end of Beaumont Street, WALTON STREET runs N. On the E side No. 172, a much-altered early C17 lobby-entry house; then stuccoed, three-storey mid-C19 terraces. The W side has Nos. 1–2, endearing stone-built Georgian cottages below the present roadway level, then the COHEN QUAD of Exeter College, or rather the original front part of RUSKIN COLLEGE, which is what Exeter has taken over. 1912–13 by *Joseph & Smithem*, for the working men's college established in 1899 (now based at Headington, p. 481). Red brick and Bath stone, Neo-William-and-Mary, much like work of those years at Lady Margaret Hall or St Hugh's College. Eight-bay front with a steep pediment in the centre. On the flank to Worcester Place a segmental pediment, and four bays of the N side of the intended quadrangle. *Alison Brooks Architects*' new work of 2013–17 replaced later additions, squeezing in a great deal by means of deft planning and complex sections. The results are undeniably bulky, not disguised by the bold fish-scale tiles of the rounded-topped upper parts (also on the pavilion roofs added to the 1910s section), but are carried through with conviction. The new part is stone-faced to the street, with a diversity of differently splayed window openings to the communal areas. S-shaped plan, stepping down to the W, and making enclosed courts to the S and N. At the far end a glazed-sided lecture hall with a skewed, incurved clerestory roof of laminated timber. Main circulation axis framed by multiple diaphragm arches, first of knotty timber then of concrete, another example of the interesting use of materials throughout.

Walton Street continues N with early C19 brick terraces on the W side, of the Beaumont Buildings type, but here with front gardens and also some iron balconies (e.g. Nos. 13 and 15). On the E side the former CLARENDON PRESS INSTITUTE, 1892–3 by *H.W. Moore*, for the families of workers at the University Press. Brick and stone, symmetrical, Free Jacobean, with three shaped gables. Then glum four-storey terraces of 1869–71 (Nos. 132–150), part of the Wellington Square development (*see* below). The end houses were replaced in 1973–5 by the University's GRADUATE ACCOMMODATION, by *Sir Leslie Martin* with *David Owers* (executant architect *Douglas Lanham*), meant as part of a much larger scheme. This stretches along LITTLE CLARENDON STREET, where it lines up with the same architects' University Offices immediately W (p. 359), and *Hening & Chitty*'s office block of 1968–70 at No. 55 beyond, all dominating the street's mostly friendly and small-scale N side. The graduate block is of cream blockwork and ribbon windows between board-marked concrete storey bands, partly stepping down from the W end. Its S side is set behind a raised terrace to WELLINGTON SQUARE. Here was Oxford's Workhouse, by *John Gwynn*, 1772–5; after its removal to Cowley Road (*see* p. 497), *E. G. Bruton* laid out the ground for houses in 1869. His too is the former St Anne's School in the SE corner, 1872–3; founder, the Rev. Thomas Chamberlain of St Thomas's. Yellow brick front, red brick for the extensive rear ranges. *Thomas Rayson*'s classical doorcase was added in 1926–7 when the school became REWLEY HOUSE, the University's DEPARTMENT FOR CONTINUING EDUCATION (*see also* Kellogg College, p. 463). Enlarged behind in 1983–6 by *Bradley Burrell Architects*, with a sunk courtyard, lecture theatre etc. and a plain new entrance block in St John Street, w. The other houses followed in 1873–6 and are less stark, if not by much. Those in the Rewley House range with open-traceried doorways are by *J. C. Curtis*, with a relief of the Duke of Wellington on the flank by *Samuel Grafton*; those on the W side of St John Street by *T. Jones*; those on the square's E and W sides by *G. Shirley* (*Galpin & Shirley*, builders).

Back to Walton Street, and N again. The NE corner with Little Clarendon Street, plain commercial of 1877, is now Lincoln College accommodation, with a new L-shaped range behind showing on both streets; by *Oxford Architects*, 2011–13. Then a break in the houses, with on the E side Somerville College, followed by the Radcliffe Observatory Quarter (p. 361) and the former St Paul's church (p. 397), on the W side Oxford University Press (p. 359).

This is a good point to enter JERICHO, by one of the earliest of its grid of streets, GREAT CLARENDON STREET, on the axis of St Paul's. The name comes incidentally from Jericho

Gardens, first mentioned by Anthony Wood in 1688. To the W begin to appear the simple two-storey brick terraces that are the suburb's prevailing type of *c.* 1830–60. The dates further S and N are mostly later, with larger houses set back from the street, e.g. Walton Crescent, S, *c.* 1869; Juxon Street, N, *c.* 1876. Also small areas of low-rise rebuilding throughout, much of it council housing by the *City Architect*, under the enlightened policy of 'gradual renewal' adopted in 1966 – a retreat from the wholesale clearances that had swept away most of St Ebbe's. The largest and earliest council group is in Cranham Street (Nos. 68–73, with Venables Close, 1969). Later enclaves tend to follow the pavement edge, e.g. Nos. 45–47 Great Clarendon Street, flats of 1974–5 with integral garages. These sit next to the former St Barnabas School (originally St Paul's School), by *Street*, 1855–6. A long, introverted front of rubble stone, with little lancets and only a few full plate-traceried windows. St Barnabas's church (p. 391) is in Cardigan Street, to the NW. At the SE corner with Canal Street here, the St Barnabas Parish Institute, 1892, designed by its builders *Symm & Co.* Honest red brick, approaching Arts and Crafts simplicity. Redevelopment along the canal side has long been argued over; the latest proposals (2021) are by *Stride Treglown*. Well to the SE in Walton Lane, Nos. 1–2, a powerfully compact semi-detached pair by *Adrian James Architects*, 2008–10.

Back in Walton Street, W side, the Jericho Tavern (No. 56) is Italianate of 1866, the adjacent Phoenix Cinema as early as 1913, by *G.T.F. Gardner*, but with a plain front of 1939 by *F.G.M. Chancellor*. Opposite, a shop terrace of 1887 by *Moore* (Nos. 112–118), divided by banded giant pilasters. By No. 78 is the path to St Sepulchre's Cemetery, entered through a forthright Gothic lodge by *E.G. Bruton*, probably 1850s. A Neo-Norman chapel of 1848 by *H.J. Underwood* was demolished *c.* 1972. Where Walton Well Road branches NW, No. 1, old-fashioned free Italianate by *J.C. Curtis*, 1891. The fancy iron balcony and railings were reportedly supplied by *Lucy's*, i.e. Lucy's Eagle Ironworks, the other big industrial enterprise in Jericho. Beyond are Lucy's eagle-topped gatepiers and its unpretending red brick offices by *George Gardiner*, 1905 etc. The company redeveloped the rest of the site for rented housing in 2007–9 (*Berkeley Homes*, with *John Thompson & Partners*). Mostly red brick slabs, some with a slight warehouse look. Then substantial front-gabled terraces. Nos. 11–25, S side, are *Curtis* again, 1883, with delicate tympana carved surprisingly with the story of Elijah. The last terraces on both sides are more *Moore*, 1885–8 – his characteristic string courses – as is the little Drinking Fountain by Longworth Road, 1885.

Beyond, two Bridges – over canal, of *c.* 1789, and railway, of 1885 – then the expanses of Port Meadow. The latter bridge gives a view of Oxford's most divisive C21 project, Castle Mill (Phase 2), along the railway line to the S. Graduate accommodation, commissioned by the University from the *Frankham Consultancy Group*, 2011–13. The bland, economical architecture, arranged in pavilion blocks of up to five storeys, is the lesser offence; the greater by far is its intrusive position, walling off the view of Oxford's spires from the meadow. Such was the outcry that the University Congregation had to hold a vote on whether the blocks should be reduced in height. Instead, in 2019 they were given some palliative foliage cladding, and their white render was toned down. So they endure. The comparatively innocuous Phase 1, s, is by *Oxford Architects*, 2004.

ARCHAEOLOGICAL REMAINS on Port Meadow are visible as slight earthworks in very dry conditions or when the Meadow starts to flood; others can only be seen from the air. These include Bronze Age BARROWS and at least three IRON AGE HOUSE SITES with adjoining rectilinear and irregular enclosures. The trace FORTIFICATIONS at its s end were made (perhaps by Parliamentary forces) during the siege of Oxford in the mid C17. In the N part a race course was laid out in the later C17, and the BRIDGES linking the course with Wolvercote Common can still be seen.

5. West and south-west, from Queen Street

To the w of Carfax the University and colleges count for less, the town and its former industries for more. The low-lying sw area has its own character, with multiple streams passing between the buildings.

QUEEN STREET, the site of Oxford's chief meat market until the Covered Market was built, is a modern shopping street like Cornmarket. From the E, the newest arrival is *Wright & Wright*'s Nos. 4–5, 2014–18, on the s side. Ashlar-faced, plain but well made, with traditional proportions. The upper storeys and extensive rear parts are student accommodation for Christ Church. On the N side, Tower House (No. 45) goes with the Carfax group (p. 409). At Nos. 39–41 the s end of *Gordon Benoy & Partners*' CLARENDON CENTRE of 1983–4, the mall roof replaced 1998–9 by *Architects Design Partnership*. In 2023 under demolition, to make an open lane in place of the mall walk (*Marchini Curran Associates*). Nos. 36–37 were surprisingly the early showroom of Morris Garages, 1912, by *Herbert Quinton*. Loose C17 style, with a half-timbered top storey. Next door, the former Wilberforce Temperance Hotel of 1888, by *F. W. Albury* of Reading. A Tudor Gothic slab, red brick and stone. Nos. 31–32 were the warehouse of Thomas Hyde & Co., outfitters; 1877–8 by *F. Codd*. Four storeys. Very consistent fenestration: a close row of segment-headed, a close row of round-arched, another close row of segment-headed windows. Facing Shoe Lane behind, Hydes' factory of 1869, long and narrow red brick, also *Codd*. On the s side of Queen Street, MARKS & SPENCER (Nos. 13–18) by *Lewis & Hickey*, 1975–8, utterly nerveless. Nos. 20–21 were the offices of Hall's City brewery, by *Wilkins & Jeeves*, 1914–15 (*see also* No.30 Pembroke Street, Perambulation 6, p.445). Moderate Free Style, with two shallow curved bays. Now a façade only, included with *Leach Rhodes Walker*'s coarse red brick development of 1996–7, r.

Queen Street ends at BONN SQUARE, the former churchyard of St Peter-le-Bailey (*see* p.285n.). Paved over in 2008 by *Graeme Massie Architects*. The obelisk MONUMENT of 1900, by *Inigo Thomas*, commemorates the Oxfordshire Light Infantry's losses on the north-west frontier of India. It looks almost convincingly Georgian. On the N side the Baptist church (p.399), and a complex of offices, café etc. by *Peter Reynolds Architects*, 1980–2. Slick smoked glass, set back from a brick entrance. SCULPTURE in front, Knowledge and Understanding, by *Diana Bell*, 2009. Bronze piles of books.

NEW INN HALL STREET runs N here. What survives of New Inn Hall (w side) now belongs to St Peter's College, as also do the former Girls' School, St Peter's church etc. On the E side a run of smaller houses introduces FREWIN HALL (belonging to Brasenose College). This preserves something of St Mary's College, founded in 1435 for Augustinian Canons using a much older house, of which more below. The place to start is the remains of the GATEHOUSE by Nos.32–34, originally storeyed. The four-centred-arched gateway (renewed) is probably late C16, for it rises above the medieval vault level indicated by traces of two-bay vaulting on the S wall inside. On the N side within, a rubble-walled outbuilding, largely C17. Beyond is a pleasant lawn, and FREWIN HALL proper, comprising two ranges at right angles. The name is from Dr Richard Frewin, who leased it in 1721, and the range facing S appears of his time, with a columned porch. The date 1888 on the sundial above points to *Jackson*, who added the upper storey for Dr Charles Shadwell of Oriel. (But the ground-floor walls of the front range are of *c.*1582–4, and the vaulted basement below them is the retained lower storey of a stone-built Norman house, datable from its barrel-vault and plain imposts to the late C11 or C12: Oxford's oldest identifiable vault. It has an insertion of two supporting arches on a column with scalloped capital of late C12 type. Original windows in the w bay. One ground-floor room with a late C16 plaster ceiling with thin ribs forming geometrical patterns and small foliage motifs, the details matching those at Corpus Christi's gate-tower ceiling. Chimneypiece with tiers of blank arches with caryatids, contemporary panelling.) The E range is 1720s, plain, two-storeyed, with a heavy doorcase. Some C17 framing retained. The approach to the house from Frewin Court, E, is through a doorway with a hoodmould, formerly with the date 1666. Changes made by Brasenose since 1960 include the taller S extension to the E range, 1996–7 by *Carden & Godfrey*. A small, three-sided student quad by *Lee/Fitzgerald Architects* is due for completion on the S side in 2023, with restoration of the main house.

The form of ST MARY'S COLLEGE was first reconstructed by John Blair.* It appears to have comprised a small, probably cloistered quad, its s side aligned with the gatehouse. The Norman house was incorporated as an E projection; an E–W extension from the NE corner housed the chapel (foundations identified 1977; cf. the plan of Corpus, 1512–18). The roof of that chapel, unmistakably of early C16 form, was reused at Brasenose's chapel in the 1650s. Roof type and plan-form both correlate with an initiative by Wolsey in 1518 to achieve the long-delayed completion of St Mary's buildings. Nos. 22–24 New Inn Hall Street also include earlier single-storey framing on the ground floor, interpreted as part of a s range of unheated lodgings for St Mary's College, placed along the street.

Of the other old houses, Nos. 26–30 are prettily grouped round a cobbled entry and have Victorian fronts, though basically C17. Nos. 32 and 34, probably C17, served from c.1780 as a Methodist chapel. N of the gateway all is Victorian brick, No. 38 with an inventively articulated polychrome façade with carved stone capitals. The houses' rear parts were replaced with big staircase projections by *Architects Design Partnership*, 1976–7, also for Brasenose.

ST MICHAEL'S STREET runs E beyond, with the Wesley Memorial Church (p. 399) closing the view from Cornmarket Street. More Brasenose accommodation at Nos. 13–15, s side, indeterminate traditional of 1974–5 by *J. Fletcher-Watson & Partners*, set back between timber-fronted C17–C18 houses. Then on the N side two ashlar-fronted houses of special interest, now united as a hotel, with a retained C18 stone front between. No. 24 is early C18, with two Dutch gables (also behind), and a Vanbrughianly heavy doorway. Much C17 timber-framed fabric within. The major house is No. 20, VANBRUGH HOUSE. Here the front was rebuilt c.1721 by *Bartholomew Peisley III*, one of Vanbrugh's master masons at Blenheim, and is almost a parody of that house. This was the Peisley family house, and no involvement by Vanbrugh himself need be inferred.[†] Ashlar, five bays and three storeys, with a slight one-bay projection. The top windows are segment-headed, the first-floor windows have squared aprons. But the Brobdingnagian spirit of Blenheim – Vanbrugh and Swift represent the same generation – inspires the centre bay only. Two broad giant pilasters each with a bit of entablature on top – just one triglyph – carry a cornice as deep as though it were a canopy and existing only in that bay. Above it the second floor runs through as if nothing had happened. The doorway and the window above it have big triple keystones. Awkward plan, indicative of partial rebuilding of an older house. C18 staircase with twisted balusters. In the ground-floor front room a buffet alcove painted with a bowl of flowers under a shell head, with a marble slab and Delft tiles below. (The city wall runs through the basement;

64

---

* *Oxoniensia* 43 (1978).
[†] No. 34 Broad Street of c.1710, dem. 1882, made similar use of Blenheim motifs.

No. 32, w, is built over one of its bastions.) Next door is the former NORTH GATE HALL, 1870–1 by *J.C. Curtis*. Originally the United Methodist Free Church above, schoolroom below. Stone and pale brick. Five bays. Three-bay pediment, arched upper windows. Nos. 4–10 remarkably are of *c*. 1560, under Late Georgian stucco or Victorian brick. On the opposite side, after the Oxford Union (p. 351), the THREE GOATS HEADS pub (No. 5), originally offices of 1876 by *Codd*. Vigorous Gothic frontage, nicely adapted by *Broadway Malyan*, 1988.

New Inn Hall Street was extended N in 1872 through to GEORGE STREET. Here is Oxford's best concentration of interwar commercial architecture, though highlights are few. Going E, on the N side the NEW THEATRE. Rebuilt in 1933–4 – a lean period for grand theatres – by the specialist architects *W. & T.R. Milburn*. Ashlar and brick, with bitty classical detail, on a steel frame. *T.P. Bennett & Son* designed the Art Deco interior, with big bands and stripes zooming around the proscenium arch. Also two tightly composed panels of shallow-relief figures. Opposite, the former Twining Bros, grocers (Nos. 17–19, now a hotel), Neo-Georgian brick by the prolific *G.T.F. Gardner*, 1924. THE GRAPES (No. 7) is a sweet little pub by *H.G.W. Drinkwater*, 1894. Terracotta against a red brick gable. It faces the former YMCA, rebuilt behind, but retaining most of *F.W. Albury*'s asymmetrical elevation of 1891. w extension 1914.

w of New Inn Hall Street, George Street's biggest presence is the ODEON of 1936 by *Robert Cromie*, originally the Ritz cinema. Blockish Deco, two tones of red brick. Entrance, E, under a figure relief by *Newbury Trent*. Long thin stone stripes along the blind flank, facing the former Boys' High School, the city wall behind it (p. 358), and minor Georgian brick (Nos. 41–45, plus imitations). Then the OLD FIRE STATION and former CORN EXCHANGE, w: one long building by *H.W. Moore*, 1894–5, now an arts centre. Red brick and stone, loose Northern Renaissance. Shops below; off-centre tower with steep hipped top. The Corn Exchange hall sits behind (*see also* below). On the s side, No. 59, the ladies' clothing factory of W. F. Lucas & Co., 1890–2 by *Drinkwater*. Ruthlessly plain. A festive contrast next door, *Frank Mountain*'s former OXFORD CO-OPERATIVE SOCIETY department store, 1908–9. Much stone striping, jaunty shaped gable. Extended 1929 by *F.J. Cooke*, l., a small-scale recapitulation.

GLOUCESTER GREEN lies N of George Street. The underemployed open space here was redeveloped in 1987–9 with *Kendrick Associates*' mixed-use scheme, after a competition in 1983. Oxford's largest Postmodern episode by far, undeniably patchy in effect, but in its best aspects done with relish and conviction. The planning is successful too. A tall barrier block of offices along Worcester Street, w, encloses an open-air bus station. A second, L-shaped range divides this space from a market square to the E, with the Odeon forming its s side; a new entrance was also provided to the Old Fire Station at the SW angle here. All of red brick, with bands of yellow and black, cast-stone dressings, and plenty happening along the skyline. References range from Elizabethan, especially the outer SW angle with its Burghley turrets, to *fin-de-siècle* Free Style, especially around the market square. The spirit of T.G. Jackson also comes and goes, e.g. at the staircase enclosures on the inner W side.

Two older buildings also play their part. N of the bus station, the former CENTRAL BOYS' SCHOOL, 1900–1, by *Leonard Stokes*. Small in scale, to harmonize with the cottages which surrounded it. Only the centre is ashlar-faced. It has two shallow canted bays with mullioned windows but curiously a pointed doorway, with beautifully handled reliefs above. Big roof of Westmorland stone slates, and a square cupola. Stokes was a first-rate school designer (his father was one of the first Inspectors of Schools). The bay windows light the cloakrooms; the brick sections were originally windowless, to cut out noise from when the market was held here. The plan is ingenious, to suit the irregular site. Four classrooms open off a cupola-lit central hall which has weird flattened pilasters (Stokes's partner George Drysdale later said that he had 'no appreciation for the orders'). At the back a fine hooded doorway to a stair-turret, for access to the manual instruction classroom above the E flank. To the E, in Gloucester Street, the RED LION, a superior Arts and Crafts-influenced pub of 1905 by *J.R. Wilkins*. The main part on an ample curve, its ground floor of stone and brown-glazed tile with shallow arches on half-columns.

Now S, back to Bonn Square. On the S side here is the WESTGATE CENTRE, a retail complex of 2014–17, incorporating about two-thirds of its smaller predecessor of 1969–72 by *Douglas Murray*, City Architect. The latter accounts for the flanks to St Ebbe's Street, E, and the realigned Castle Street, W. The new masterplan and shared areas are by *BDP* (executive architects *Chapman Taylor*, structural engineers *Waterman*, landscape architects *Gillespies*). Separate architects were engaged for the four main buildings. The results are architecturally much better than average for this notoriously un-neighbourly building type, externally as well as internally, for all that they lord it over a much larger area of the city than before. Time will tell whether Oxford can sustain quite so much generic retail space.

So to the 2010s work. Facing Bonn Square, *Dixon Jones* added new frontage, a big concave sweep of squared rubble above ashlar, pierced with a central oculus. At the r. end a plain brick tower with a polygonal glass lantern designed by *Daniela Schönbächler*, which lights up at night. Facing Castle Street, windows to the retained CENTRAL LIBRARY have been punched through at intervals between the 1970s concrete uprights. Inside, the old mall has been reworked with a cool white barrel-vault with circular openings. Dixon Jones's new buildings follow to the S, ending at MIDDLE SQUARE, by the cross-route of Turn Again Lane, with a big rounded W projection externally. Beyond is *Allies & Morrison*'s section,

102

adopting a two-level arrangement as the ground falls, with full top glazing across the spectacularly large atrium. Part of the C13 encaustic-tiled PAVEMENT of Greyfriars (*see* p.450), excavated from the site, has been re-set on the E side, by the escalators. These lead up to a roof terrace, with unfamiliar views across Oxford. The S end of the atrium is LEIDEN SQUARE, placed E–W. The S side here is by *Panter Hudspith*, notable externally for patterning of the brick and irregular dotting with windows and louvres where it faces the main road, internally for escalators to a rooftop terrace of restaurants etc. Immediately W, a covered bridge spans to *Glenn Howells Architects'* JOHN LEWIS, an atrium block faced in syncopated rhythms of diagonally stepped yellow brick. W of this, a residential block by *Hawkins/Brown* (No. 1 Abbey Place) sits over the entrance to the centre's underground car park.* Also part of the scheme is the adjacent walkway along Castle Mill Stream, with a bridge to the City of Oxford College (p.405).

s of Oxpens Road here is *Nicholas Grimshaw & Partners'* ICE RINK of 1982–4, grimy now, but a key monument of early High Tech (structural engineers *Ove Arup & Partners*). It combines the slick-skinned, lightweight 'big shed' form carried over from the 1970s, exemplified by Norman Foster's Sainsbury Centre for the University of Norwich, with the growing interest in tensile forms and dramatized structure. Two steel masts, each 30 metres (98 ft) high, take the weight of the central spine beam by means of thin diagonal rigging, avoiding the need for deep foundations for the walls. The beam and its ground-anchored rigging project some way to N and S, an unmistakably nautical effect. The N wall is nearly all glass, giving views in from the main road; little porthole windows on the other sides.

The return N is up Norfolk Street, along the W side of the West-gate Centre. To the W in PARADISE SQUARE, on the N side, is the former RECTORY of St Ebbe's, 1853–4: an early work by *Street*, who later restored the church (p.393). Of stone, picturesque, with plain mullioned windows. Typical and valuable Street the E front and the NW stair-turret. In 1868 additions in brick and stone were made by *J.T. Christopher*, including the W porch and the bay at the W end of the S front. The square was first built up in 1838–c.1850. Other old houses have been cleared, and on the W side now is one of the *City Architect's* decent terraces, 1981. On the N side, the PREMIER INN, *Allison Pike* and *Rick Mather Architects*, 2017–21, stepping up to the E. The W side runs N to PARADISE STREET. On the E corner the JOLLY FARMERS pub, C17, jettied, above a stone ground floor. Next to it is a courtyard with two rendered houses, formerly and misleadingly called GREYFRIARS. The arched doorcase in the courtyard wall has ears and garlands and, free-standing on the wall, a rich foliage cartouche under a curly top and flanked by volutes. It must be later C17, as also is the larger house, E.

---

*Successor to *Vernon Gibbs & Associates'* belligerent multi-storey car park of 1974, s of Turn Again Lane.

Here a splendidly decorated shell-hood doorcase with a spray of flowers. Early C18 sw projection. (Two pretty overmantels. One is framed by huge over-sized scrolls; the other, on the first floor, has thick plaster foliage and drops rather in the Roberts style, i.e. a generation or two later than the house.) The w house is of *c.*1700, heavily altered. (One plasterwork ceiling with an oval wreath of flowers.)

To the e is CASTLE STREET, with the thoroughly half-timbered CASTLE pub of 1892 on the sw corner, one of *Drinkwater*'s Old English hostelries. The realigned street rises to the N (in the 1960s plan it was to smash on through to Gloucester Green), with the 1970s County Hall extension on the w side. At the top is NEW ROAD, Oxford's first significant post-medieval street, formed in 1769–70 to improve the western approach. On the N side the former PROBATE OFFICE of 1862–3, by *Buckeridge*. Small, in later C13 English Gothic style, not symmetrical. An extension of St Peter's College by *Design Engine Architects* is under construction to the w in 2023. The rest of New Road is Nuffield College on the N side, County Hall and Castle etc. on the s side (pp.403 and 400), then the Register Office etc. (p.404) at the corner with TIDMARSH LANE. On the lane's w side a former maltings of 1823, with a taller, all-brick N part of 1884 by *Drinkwater*, still with its lucam. Adapted by the UNIVERSITY SURVEYOR'S OFFICE for its own use, 1958–9 (*Jack Lankester* with *N. Riley*): early for the conversion of an industrial building for offices. To its s, by the side entrance to the Castle and facing the Castle Mill Stream, ST GEORGE'S GATE, accommodation for St Peter's College by *Marcus Beale Architects*, 1994–5. Plain brick with five gables, then a common room of timber, s, by the Castle tower. Balconies projecting over the stream. Quaking Bridge crosses to the w bank, i.e. the top end of PARADISE STREET, with the bulky MARRIOTT HOTEL, 2016–19 by *Urban Innovations* of Belfast. Red brick. Paradise Street continues SE, past early C21 flats and back over the stream, to another ST PETER'S COLLEGE ANNEXE on the N side. By *Anthony Rickett Partnership*, 2003–8, architecturally more diffuse than St George's Gate.

The little iron bridge here is QUAKING BRIDGE, of 1835, signed by *Cort & Co.*, Leicester. Going w, a prosperous red brick house of *c.*1798 on the NW corner of Paradise Street (No.1 FISHER ROW), for the brewer Edward Tawney. Nos.2–3 alongside, with a shared pediment and inscription, were built as almshouses under Tawney's will of 1800. The westward route is ST THOMAS STREET. On the s side, the low hip-roofed building is a former HORSE HOSPITAL of 1887. *Drinkwater*'s former Brewery Gate pub next door, 1896, heralds the remains of the LION BREWERY (Tawney's, then Morrell's), adapted for residential use by *Jewell & Co.* from 2003. *Drinkwater* also designed most of the original buildings around the U-shaped courtyard, now largely replaced with flats; retained parts include the brewing shed E of the main gate (1879) and the offices immediately to the w (1892). Nice iron gates with lion finials. To the sw a big chimney of 1901. On the N side of the street a large and complicated mixed-use development of 2002–4 by *Oxford Architects*, including private flats and student rooms. Similar developments of low-rise flats follow, now the default post-industrial type in this district. Woodbine Place, s, still has Victorian houses, and also The Hamel, alias CHRIST CHURCH OLD BUILDINGS, a unique survival in Oxford of 'industrial dwellings' of the London type. Christ Church built them in 1866–8, to designs by *E. G. Bruton*, to replace a notorious patch of bad housing.* Three-storeyed, of red brick striped with yellow. Access is via open staircases, with crude pointed arches. The other ranges face s, to Osney Lane, and E, forming an inner court which served as a playground and drying yard. Each of the thirty-six dwellings had its own scullery and water closet. Also on the E side, facing the street called The Hamel, an orthodox terrace of houses by *Bruton*, 1869. Extra flats with Postmodern touches were added to the Woodbine Street range *c.*2001, by *The Oxfordshire Practice*. Also in OSNEY LANE, s side, the former ST THOMAS'S SCHOOL, 1904 by *Philip Appleby Robson* of London (son of 'Schools' Robson). Cheap, but with a festive Baroque frontispiece of striped brick, behind Art Nouveau railings.

St Thomas Street continues w to St Thomas's church and its adjacent school (p. 397). Before the churchyard, HOLLY-BUSH ROW crosses N–S. On its w side part of the Neo-Tudor ST THOMAS'S GIRLS' SCHOOL of 1841, a minor work of *H. J. Underwood*. Now part of HOLLYBUSH LODGE, post-graduate housing of 2006–8 for Brasenose, a shouty design by *Oxford Architects*. The latest development of this type is the 515-bedroom STUDENT CASTLE complex on Osney Lane by the railway, 200 yds sw (*FJMT*, 2018–20). On the E side of Hollybush Row the Chequers Inn, a well-crafted former pub of 1913 by *Wilkins & Jeeves*.

So to PARK END STREET, N, part of the New Road route of 1769–70. Going E, the ROYAL OXFORD HOTEL of 1934–5 turns its alien Yellow Guiting stone front towards the station. By *J. C. Leed*, in a flattened version of the style of *c.*1700. The s corner is the big KING CHARLES HOUSE, Postmodern offices of 1989–91 by *Covell Matthews Wheatley Architects*. Then Nos. 36–39, CANTAY HOUSE, formerly Archer, Cowley & Co.'s furniture warehouse. By *Tollit & Lee*, 1901; extended 1908, w. Notable for its early use of steel framing, but the brick and stone frontage is orthodox 1900s commercial. Behind, a much-adapted extension of 1920 by *G. T. F. Gardner*, reportedly Oxford's first concrete-framed building, and the LAMPL BUILDING, a residential outpost of Corpus Christi College by *TSH Architects*, 2012–14. Next to Cantay is the N end of *Oxford*

---

* Other blocks intended by Bruton were not built. The four-storey CHRIST CHURCH NEW BUILDINGS to the sw, 1891 by *Elijah Hoole*, were demolished *c.*1987.

Architects' scheme of 2002–4, already seen in St Thomas Street. Then PACEY'S BRIDGE, rebuilt wider in 1922 (*J.E. Wilkes*, City Engineer). On the N side here a long Neo-Georgian commercial range, its E end by *Gardner*, 1925. No. 14, refronted in 1934 with plain giant pilasters, is a survivor of the street's several interwar garages.

Continuing W, the S side of Park End Street faces FRIDESWIDE SQUARE, the greatly widened thoroughfare in front of the Saïd Business School (p. 358). No. 27 is the former factory of FRANK COOPER, whose famous marmalade was made here from 1903. By *Herbert Quinton*, a high point of his easy Free Style. Nice carving over the doorway. Fruit was cut up on the second floor, the first floor was for bottling, and boiling was done in the outhouse behind. Corner extension 1925. Then lesser houses, all by *Moore*, 1897, except No. 23, the Castle Temperance Hotel of 1888 by *E. G. Cobb*, with iron roof cresting.

The older route into Oxford from the W was via Hythe Bridge Street, along the N side of the Royal Oxford Hotel. At the corner with Rewley Road, N, is the very large former BEAVER HOUSE, built as the headquarters and mail-order office of Blackwell's, the booksellers, 1970–2, by the *Oxford Architects Partnership*. The pivot is the diagonally set stair-tower at the angle, of reeded concrete. The rest is chiefly dark mirror glass, the ground floor retracted on the S side, the top floor only projecting to the W and N. To Rewley Road the ground floor is reeded concrete with six widely spaced windows. Well-handled heightening of *c.* 1978.

Continuing N in REWLEY ROAD, the Fire Station (p. 405), then REWLEY ABBEY COURT, interlinked residential blocks of *c.* 1995 for Green Templeton College (*Oxford Architects Partnership*), followed by much quasi-traditional private housing. By the Castle Mill Stream path behind the 1990s blocks is all that is left standing of REWLEY ABBEY: part of the precinct wall, and a C15 doorway with a two-centred arch and quatrefoils in the spandrels. The abbey was Cistercian, founded in 1281 by Edmund, Earl of Cornwall. From 1292 until at least the mid C14 it also served as the order's academic college at Oxford. Excavated remains indicate a cruciform church with an aisled nave and a cloister to the NW. A mound in the garden of the Saïd Business School marks the site of the church crossing, just visible from Rewley Road through a slot in the garden wall, W. 250 yds N, the road gives a view of the disused SWING BRIDGE of 1850–1 by the railway, still with its original manual mechanism. Designed by *Robert Stephenson* to carry the London & North Western's line to its former station to the S (*see* p. 407n.). A rare survival; restored in 2021 by Oxford Preservation Trust. To the E here is the Isis Lock on the OXFORD CANAL of 1790, and its ROVING BRIDGE of 1844 by *Frederick Wood*, with a delicate wrought-iron span.

HYTHE BRIDGE STREET was named from a hithe or wharf, first recorded in 1233. On the N side by the Wareham Stream is *Bruton*'s former BOATMEN'S CHAPEL of 1868, also used as a school for children of those working on the boats. Painted brick. One big plain pointed-arched window. Opposite is a former COLD STORE of 1912 by *J.R. Wilkins*, with blind arcading along the top; very altered. Between the streams, on the S side, the former Nag's Head, 1939. Manorial in yellow brick, the pub style of *J.C. Leed*. Just after Hythe Bridge, N side, is the end of the canal as truncated in the C20. Beyond, Worcester Street leads N to Beaumont Street (*see* Perambulation 4).

6. South: St Aldate's, with St Ebbe's

St Aldate's is the C19 name for the long street running S from Carfax to Folly Bridge. To its W lies St Ebbe's, a former working-class suburb of largely C19 housing and industry, almost entirely supplanted by redevelopment and road-widening in the 1960s–70s.

ST ALDATE'S begins on the E side with the Town Hall (p. 403), on the W side with big-townish, between-the-wars commercial Neo-Georgian. Most notable here are *G.T.F. Gardner*'s Nos. 117–119, 1938–9 for the Oxford & District Gas Co. (now part of the development of student rooms with Nos. 4–5 Queen Street, p. 435) and Nos. 114–116 for Barclays Bank, 1931–2. The balcony ironwork of the gas offices features the marketing mascot 'Mr Therm'. At No. 108 the ST ALDATES TAVERN of 1897, *H.W. Moore*'s spirited imitation of a fancy mid-Georgian frontage. Multiple Venetian windows, Gibbs surrounds. The nondescript Victorian front of No. 107 conceals fabric from a house of *c*. 1600. For the Post Office *see* p. 405. Nos. 6–7 opposite is double-gabled early C17 timber, originally the Unicorn Inn. No. 8, urbane ashlar of *c*. 1830. Just to the N, beyond the S flank of the Town Hall, BLUE BOAR STREET has at No. 5 the former official residence of Oxford's Chief Constable. Simplified Tudor by *W.H. Castle*, 1899.

Continuing S, Christ Church takes over on the E side. The W side goes on with ordinary houses and routine later Victorian commercial, up to PEMBROKE STREET. On the N side here two Victorian intrusions. Nos. 41–42, commercial Old English of 1900 by *Castle, Field & Castle*, were built as a house and a pub, the Leden Hall. Now part of THE STORY MUSEUM, renovated in 2020 by *Purcell* with *Ramboll UK*, structural engineers. No. 40 is ST ALDATE'S RECTORY, 1877–8 by *J.T. Christopher*. Yellow brick, timber Gothic porches. Nicely varied older houses on the S side, co-opted by Pembroke College's North Quad behind (*see* pp. 235–6). Nos. 13–14 are of considerable interest, both in front and at the back. The house was built by Richard Hannes, brewer, in 1641. Four storeys, painted rubble below, timber-framed above. To the street a middle projection with a later doorway with pulvinated frieze and big pediment. A vertically placed oval over. Canted bays to l. and r. To the s there is a deeper middle projection for the staircase, and this on the first floor has a two-light w window with arched lights. To l. and r. are canted bays too, here flanked by little pendant arches under the second-floor jetty. Gable storey also jettied. Staircase with pierced flat balusters. (On the second floor a contemporary draught lobby with decorated pilasters and pediments.) No. 15, *c*. 1830, has details matching *Thomas Wyatt Jun.*'s houses in Beaumont Street. Nos. 17–18 are a pair of *c*. 1600, of rubble, with two canted bays. Doorways with four-centred arches. The timber-framed Nos. 23 and 24 are early c17, one with an oriel with ornamented mullions. Three imitation fronts of 1966–7 follow, part of Pembroke's Staircase 12 building (p. 236).

On the N side, Nos. 38 and 39 are a timber-built pair of *c*. 1690 with a stone rear wall, incorporating an older chimney stack. (Reused early c17 panelling inside No. 38, of unusual lozenge and concentric square patterns.) Nos. 36–37 are c18, timber, of five major bays, formerly with door hoods. MODERN ART OXFORD at No. 30 was adapted in 1965–6 by *Trevor Green* from part of Hanley's City brewery stores, of 1888 by *H. G. W. Drinkwater* (later Hall's; *see also* Nos. 20–21 Queen Street, pp. 435–6). An early instance of the conversion of an industrial building to display art, here using the upper floor as the main gallery. Twice expanded since, taking over more brewery buildings, including the sharp-roofed central tower, 1882 by *Arthur Kinder*. Frontage restored in 1986 by *Andy Macmillan* of *Gillespie, Kidd & Coia*, circulation reworked by *Block Architecture*, 2002. In 2010 *dRMM* moved the entrance w to the 1990s building in St Ebbe's Street, with a brightly striped new doorway and passage designed by *Richard Woods*. The corner between has the ROYAL BLENHEIM pub, a showpiece for Hall's, half-timbering and tile-hanging above good brick. By *Herbert Quinton*, 1898. Nos. 33–36 on the w side of St Ebbe's Street are Free Style by *A. J. Rowley*, 1900.

ST EBBE'S STREET continues s, past St Ebbe's church on the w side (p. 393). Facing the back of Pembroke is LITTLE-GATE HOUSE, yellow brick offices by *Collins, Stonebridge & Bradley*, 1972–6, extending over the pavement. An inscription on the front records the excavated site of the Little Gate (Little South Gate) in the city wall here. Immediately s is No. 15 Littlegate Street. Mid-c17 timber-framed to the N, with an c18 doorway on scrolled brackets; stone-built early c18 to the s, the central bay raised as a pedimental gable. Round the corner in TURN AGAIN LANE, three gabled stone houses also of the c17 (Nos. 8–10), saved from the St Ebbe's clearances by Oxford Preservation Trust, and restored in 1972. They face traditional houses of 1987 by the *City Architect*. Beyond is the expanded Westgate Centre (p. 439), preceded by a little garden with monolithic SCULPTURES of 2018 by *William Cobbing*.

Back N and E to St Aldate's, via BREWER STREET. The N side
here is bounded by the city wall and by Pembroke College,
which now has a high footbridge across to its Rokos Quad
(p. 237) on the S side. Nos. 7 and 8 alongside, C17 timber-
framed houses, were restored and incorporated with the quad
(*see also* Introduction, p. 23). Next is Campion Hall (p. 325),
also with an annexed house, and CHRIST CHURCH CATHE-
DRAL SCHOOL, set back behind a little garden. 1892–4 by *H.W.*
Moore. Brick, asymmetrical, not tall, with mullioned windows.
The front range was the master's house. Rear addition by
Broadway Malyan, 1993–4. No. 2 is of *c.* 1620, rendered, with a
top storey from *Coleridge, Jennings & Soimenow*'s reconstruction
of 1933. (Good plaster ceiling with decorated beams making
four compartments, each with thin-rib patterns in major and
minor registers.) No. 1, originally three-storeyed and gabled,
is intriguingly like a section of a college range of the early
C17. Ashlar, with arch-headed mullioned windows linked by
running hoodmoulds. The RCHME records the carved date
1596 inside, but 'of doubtful authenticity'.

ST ALDATE'S resumes with Christ Church and its Memorial
Garden (p. 118), which was created as part of clearances and
widening all along the E side from the 1920s onwards. So from
here onwards, older houses appear on the W side only. No. 91,
late C18, has some minor Adamish doorway details. (Some
plasterwork and two chimneypieces in the Adam style too.) It
belongs with ST ALDATE'S QUAD of 1982–6, a mixture of old
and new by *John Fryman* of *Architects Design Partnership*, for
Christ Church. Of the other houses, No. 89 was demolished in
favour of a near-facsimile front. Well-handled ranges of yellow
brick behind, the upper storeys partly of dark-stained wood
under slightly projecting roofs.

Then, at right angles with its front to Rose Place, the
so-called OLD PALACE, since 1919 the CATHOLIC CHAP-
LAINCY. The main part was built in 1622–8 by Thomas Smith,
brewer and mayor, as an addition to a slightly earlier house,
W. The 1620s E part has five gables, the lower W part two.
Pargeting in imitation of quadrant-braced panels on the E part
only. Both parts are jettied, with pendant valancing on the E,
and both also have oriels on figured brackets, the liveliest in
Oxford: sphinxes, satyrs and others, some turning this way or
that. Other bracket figures from *F. Russell Cox*'s restoration of
1952–4, when a disfiguring N addition was removed and the
pretty Neo-Georgian shopfront added. Cox also renewed the
ashlared St Aldate's façade. Its big, unusually shaped gable
follows the old design, but the window arrangement is new.
Inside, some specially good plaster ceilings, the chief one (E,
first floor) having broad strapwork bands with – an uncommon
feature – their rims raised, and flower bunches and cartouches.
In the older part, the adjacent W room has a quieter design,
with decorated beams and symmetrically arranged smaller
sprays in the panels. Two staircases, the W one with late C17

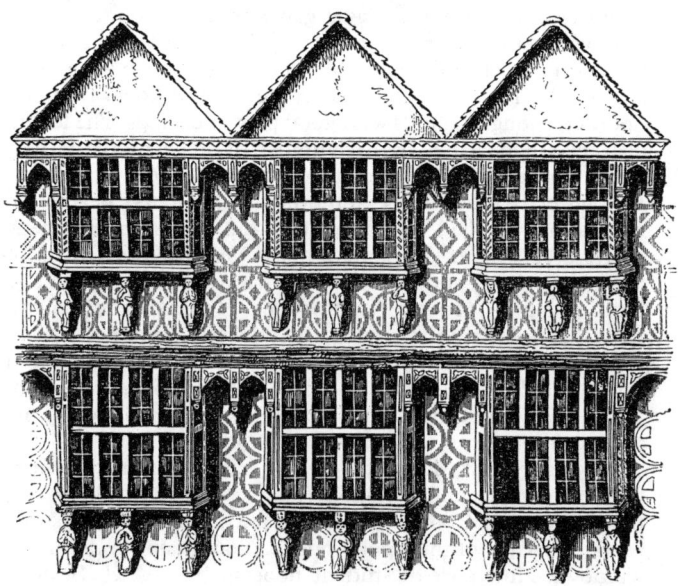

Old Palace, detail of front.
Engraving by Orlando Jewitt after W.A. Delamotte, 1847

balusters. One big second-floor room with plasterwork, w, formed in the 1950s.

The EXTENSION along Rose Place to the w is by *Ahrends, Burton & Koralek*, 1970–2, based on proposals of 1965. It is of buff brick and emphasizes, in purposeful contrast to the Old Palace, large, bare, windowless surfaces. The transition from old to new is a group of bay windows, each stepping a little more forward, above an angled brick plinth (cf. the architects' work at Keble, p. 169). They house the library, and above that study-bedrooms. The blank curve which follows houses the baptistery, the blank straight wall a chapel. s of the chapel is the Newman Room, the largest space; lit by round skylights, twelve of them, and designed for flexible use, performance etc. as well as worship. The house beyond is C18, and faces Clark's Row, s, with two bay windows. (Chimneypiece with a pretty relief of Summer.)

Continuing s, No. 84 St Aldate's is Late Georgian in front, C16 and C17 behind. Restored by *Julian Harrap*, 2005–7. (First-floor room with re-set early C17 panelling and columned chimneypiece.) Its rear wing, tree-ring dated to 1637, was reconstructed using the original timbers under *Dan Miles* in 2020–1 (*see also* Introduction, p. 22), when tall, flush-windowed flats were built at the far end. LITTLEMORE HALL at Nos. 82–83 is C15, but with mostly C17 features. Of rubble, two-storeyed, with two dormers and a bigger gable on the r. Pointed-arched doorway from restoration in 1965 by *Llewellyn Smith & Waters*, based on a Buckler drawing. Mullion-and-transom windows to either side. Those of six lights on the ground floor and upper floor, l., belong to rooms with good plaster ceilings. The former has decorated beams and a number of small motifs in each panel, above a cornice of rustic unicorns between lion masks. The latter is much more sumptuous. Decorated beams too, but the panels filled with interlaced thin bands growing fleur-de-lys everywhere. The same moulds were used in Oriel College's gate tower and at Chastleton House, Oxon, which suggests a date *c.*1610–25. SPEEDWELL HOUSE ends the row, three- and four-storey offices of concrete framing, upright windows mostly boxed out. By *Olins John Associates*, 1972–4. Speedwell Street, greatly widened in the 1960s, leads w to the Magistrates' Courts and the Telephone Exchange (pp. 405 and 407).

Staying with St Aldate's, the E side has the Faculty of Music followed by the police station (pp. 350 and 405), the w side the Crown and County Courts (p. 404). Next to the last, the retained façade of the Apollo pub, *c.*1866. Plain round-arched windows. Now part of student housing by *Oxford Architects*, 2010–12. Postmodern 1980s offices follow on both sides, then SOUTH BRIDGE ROW, council housing of the same date, turning its back to the road to make pleasant spaces on the Christ Church Meadow side, E. Its Neo-Georgian neighbour, meant to echo demolished early C19 houses here, is part of Hertford College's WARNOCK HOUSE. By *Knowles & Son Design & Build*, 1994–5; the larger component, detached to the w, dismayingly nondescript.

So to Folly Bridge (p. 407). The river bank to its E has the HEAD OF THE RIVER pub, the former house and warehouse of the boat-builder Isaac King, 1827. Both of plain ashlar, three-storeyed, and set at right angles; the house part with segmental-arched ground-floor windows. Balconies etc. on the warehouse from the very successful conversion of 1977 by *Ronald Lloyd* and *Ken Smith*. On the bridge's w abutment a pretty Italianate TOLL HOUSE of 1844, by *Thomas Wyatt Jun.* as City Surveyor.

THAMES STREET, widened and extended in 1968 as part of the continuation of the sw relief road, runs w from the end of the bridge. On the s corner is FOLLY BRIDGE COURT, private housing of 1983 onwards by *John Spratley & Partners*, with lower-rise houses to the w and along the river (Nos. 50–82 Thames Street).* A similar aspect to the council housing – brown brick, pitched roofs, broken skylines, backs turned to the road – and likewise looking good, in an undogmatic way, forty years on. The N side has the former SOUTH OXFORD SCHOOLS, 1910, by *W.H. Castle* as City Estates Surveyor. An interesting design, clearly influenced by Leonard Stokes. Brick;

---

*The site was meant for a giant hotel by *Sir Philip Dowson* of *Arup Associates*, begun in 1971 then abandoned.

two storeys – girls above boys – under a rooftop playground, now with an added storey. Square-topped end towers, and between a lively movement from small windows to large windows. Then an unwelcome splosh of colour, student housing by *Yurky Cross*, 2012–17, part of a larger scheme including lumpen private flats to the w. The low-rise council housing of BUTTERWYKE COURT beyond, 1982, embraces WHARF HOUSE, a neat stone box of *c.*1830 facing w. To the sw across Thames Street, in FRIARS WHARF, the earliest post-war housing of St Ebbe's: maisonettes by the *City Architect's Department* (*E.G. Chandler*, succeeded by *D. Murray*), 1959–62, on part of the gas works site. Unimaginatively arranged in slabs around two squares, and meant as the first phase of an area plan which would have been some five times larger. Instead, the setting to N, s and w is later, low-rise housing, both public and private. 1978–83 by *Architects Design Partnership* (Dale Close, Trinity Street etc.), with green spaces and interconnecting alleys handled with unusual care. Also one block of flats end-on to the riverside, called RIVERCOURT, designed in 1985 by *Phillips Cutler Phillips Troy*.

Finally the area N of Speedwell Street. ALBION PLACE is mostly 1970s and yellow brick. On the w side BROOKS-TAYLOR COURT, strongly articulated retirement flats by *Oxford Architects Partnership*, designed 1979, and the curvaceous former Salvation Army headquarters by *John Fryman* (*Architects Design Partnership*), now HOGREFE HOUSE, 1970–1. Fryman's round-cornered windows are echoed at *Marshman, Warren & Taylor*'s office group at Nos.1–6 Cambridge Terrace, E side, of 1972–*c.*1980. Here Albion Place turns w, with NORFOLK HOUSE (No.11 Littlegate Street) at the far end. Small flats by *Douglas Riach*, 1999. Favourite 1990s motifs: glass bricks, segmental roofs. Immediately s, an older complex including a seriously altered former BAPTIST CHAPEL of 1832 by *William Fisher Sen.*, and an attached stone-built house with through-storey porch on the E side, dated 1647 above the inner doorway. Porch rebuilt in heavy restoration of 1968, when the interior proved to contain part of the GATEWAY to the late C13 Blackfriars: two jambs of the major gate, and a pedestrian archway to the s. Latterly the group served a centre for the deaf. Conversion for community uses is proposed, with partial rebuilding as a hotel (2023). To its s is LUCY FAITHFULL HOUSE, medium-rise housing by *Levitt Bernstein*, 2019–22.

The two chief FRIARIES of Oxford are now better known, thanks to multiple excavations over the years. The BLACKFRIARS or Dominican house stood some way s of the gateway. As a teaching body the Dominicans had a special mission in Oxford, and this was their most ambitious friary outside London, with the status of *Studium Generale* (place of study) for the order in England. The first house, soon outgrown, was founded in St Aldate's in the 1220s. Its replacement of 1245 onwards featured two complete cloisters s of the church, aligned N–S and with a shared cross-range, and what was probably a service court beyond. The church was 240 ft (73 metres) long, plus an additional w bay added to its aisled nave in the early C14, and had the customary cross-passage and tower between nave and choir. Less common features included a chapter house projecting E of the N cloister, and a later covered passage across the nave W front. The GREYFRIARS or Franciscan friary was to the NW, for which the city wall was breached in 1245 to allow expansion from the original site established after 1234. Its church was where the older part of the Westgate Centre now stands. Completed only c. 1330, it included a substantial N transept almost as long as the nave. To its S was a cloister with an L-shaped S attachment for the dormitory and reredorter. Separate buildings, identified as kitchen/storehouse and refectory, stood to the w. A salvaged section of tiled chequerwork PAVEMENT from the main cloister walk is displayed within the Westgate Centre (p. 440).

7. East of Magdalen Bridge: St Clement's and The Plain

St Clement's parish was absorbed by the city only in 1835. Its population grew in earnest from the early C19.

The parish church (p. 392) originally stood on THE PLAIN, the open space just E of Magdalen Bridge, now a traffic island with trees. Also the VICTORIA FOUNTAIN, with its little stone-slated shelter with Tuscan columns and a clock turret, of 1899 by *E. P. Warren*. On the S side is Magdalen College School (p. 405), with St Hilda's College behind. On the N side, the WAYNFLETE BUILDING of Magdalen College, 1960–1 by *Booth, Ledeboer & Pinckheard*. The first great Modernist disappointment among Oxford's college commissions. Exceedingly neutral, with a six-storey range rising from a riverside terrace, joined by a glazed entrance and staircase to a four-storey street range. Concrete framing faced in Portland stone, brick infill panels almost flush. The windows in them are vertical. The top floor to The Plain has the frame without the infilling, as the rooms are set back; the ground floor has shops, also recessed. The river terrace was meant to continue to other college satellites upstream, on which *see* below. Otherwise minor C19 houses and commerce, including the CAPE OF GOOD HOPE pub on the tapering corner between Cowley Road and Iffley Road, SW. By *H. G. W. Drinkwater*, 1893, a prestige job for Morrell's brewery. Brick, stone and half-timber, with big mullion-and-transom windows.

ST CLEMENT'S STREET runs E from The Plain. First a concentration of social housing of c. 1970–80. On the N side, the FLOREY BUILDING sits behind, of 1968–70 by *James Stirling* for Queen's College (structural engineer *Frank Newby* of *F. J. Samuely & Partners*). The last of the three Stirling buildings now widely canonized as the 'Red Trilogy', with close affinities especially with the History Faculty building at Cambridge

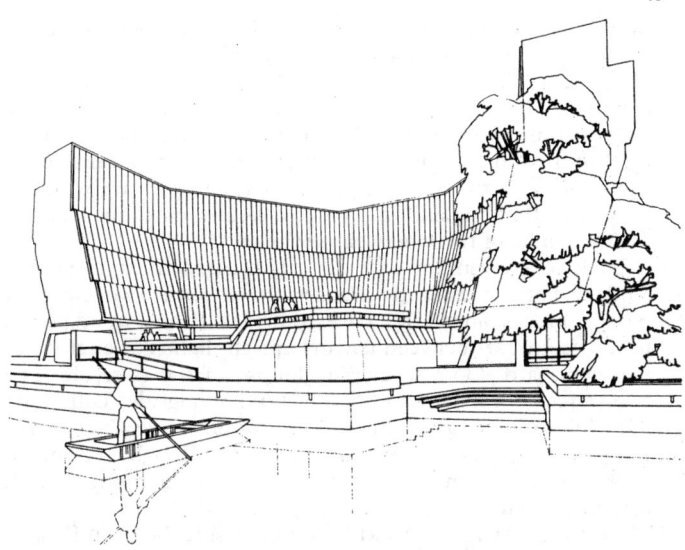

Queen's College, Florey Building
Perspective drawing, 1970–5

(1964–8).* Both make rigorous use of diagonal planning; both are faced in harsh red brick or tile, contrasted with dramatically slanting glazed elevations on the inner sides; both have also proved problematic in use, and burdened with technical shortcomings – to such an extent that in 2023 the building sits empty, awaiting viable refurbishment. Yet its bloody-minded originality, and the rigour with which form and structure are derived from the concept, still make the Florey Building one of Oxford's most compelling Modernist landmarks.

The plan comprises five sides of an irregular polygon, the rooms facing inwards to W, S and E. A spacious courtyard, also of course irregular in plan, remains in the middle. To the N it is open, to give all the rooms a view of the Cherwell and the town. The main block is of five storeys. There are some eighty student rooms, those on the top two floors of the two-level type. The lower three floors step progressively back from the courtyard, and have walls that also slope markedly backwards. Only the double-height top section, meant for postgraduates, is vertical. These inner walls are nearly all aluminium-framed patent glazing. As if all this were not enough, the whole block is lifted up on slim concrete trusses of A-frame type, with a perimeter wall running all round between the legs, placed so as to create an inner and an outer cloister. For access to the residential floors there is a free-standing gate tower on the St Clement's side, comprising staircases and lift enclosure, with glazed bridges across to the strip-windowed corridors that run

*The third is the Engineering Building at Leicester University, 1961–3 (Stirling & Gowan).

unbroken round the outer sides. Finally, in the courtyard there is the Breakfast Room, a structurally independent square, set diagonally, with one chamfered corner and the one opposite rounded. The room is sunk, so that its roof and weathervane vent are only two feet above the courtyard and its floor is at the level of the footpath along the river. Reached by a ramp from the courtyard, this was meant originally to join up with the Waynflete Building and with other college outstations planned for the banks of the Cherwell (*see* below).

Back to convention with ALICE HOUSE, next E, private student flats of 2014 by *Hodder & Partners*. Two close-set parallel blocks, linked by a covered bridge. Brown wood panels to the rooms, set between narrow upright lights, or angled out like cupboard doors to give a glimpse of the riverside. The two ranges of ALAN BULLOCK CLOSE alongside, University flats for married graduates by *Oxford Architects Partnership*, 1973–6, are more generously disposed. Rough red brick, broken outlines, monopitch roofs. The living rooms face a central garden.

Back to ST CLEMENT'S STREET, on the S side the OLD BLACK HORSE pub. C17, roughcast rubble. C18 W extension. DAWSON STREET, alongside, has the WILLIAM R. MILLER BUILDING for St Edmund Hall, 2002–4 by *Oxford Architects*. A vernacular-cum-Neo-Victorian frontage with, of all things, brick-nogged oriels. Immediately S and mostly hidden, the ABLETHORPE BUILDING for Mansfield College, *c.*1996, another courtyard scheme by the same practice, with access from Cowley Road. Incorporated there are some older houses, including Nos. 35–39, C18 stone.

STONE'S COURT ALMSHOUSES, a little further E on St Clement's Street, are dated 1700. Builder *Bartholomew Peisley II* (contract 1697). A range of eleven bays and two storeys with a hipped roof and in the middle the doorway, a cross-window and a pediment. The windows are of one light with a plain raised band as the surround and attached to an equally plain band across the façade (cf. John Combes's School, St Thomas Street, p. 398). Major restoration of 1957–8 by *Thomas Rayson*, whose rear extensions were replaced in 2009 by *Montgomery Architects*' partly timbered additions. Also by *Rayson* the two rear blocks, 1957–9, E, and 1964, W (extended 2017), in keeping. On the N side, ST CLEMENT PARISH BUILDINGS are part free Gothic, part Old English. 1887–91 by *H.W. Moore*. The PORT MAHON INN, S side, is early C18 stone, with a pedimented central niche with upswept parapet (cf. No. 15 Littlegate Street, p. 445). Then the former CATHOLIC CHAPEL (No. 82), set well back. Built of stone in 1793, heavily altered. The roundel is the one original feature in the façade. By the street, the chapel's former SCHOOL of 1909, also stone. Free classical, with Venetian windows to the front and side. To the N in Bath Street, ST CATHERINE'S HOUSE, graduate accommodation for that college, 1971–3 by *Architects Design Partnership*.

1.   Oxford, St Michael at the North Gate, tower, early c11 (l., p. 396) and New Inn (former), 1386 onwards (r., p. 423)
2.   Oxford, Broad Street, with Clarendon Building (l.), by Nicholas Hawksmoor, 1712–15 (p. 340), and Sheldonian Theatre (r.), by Sir Christopher Wren, 1664–9 (p. 336)

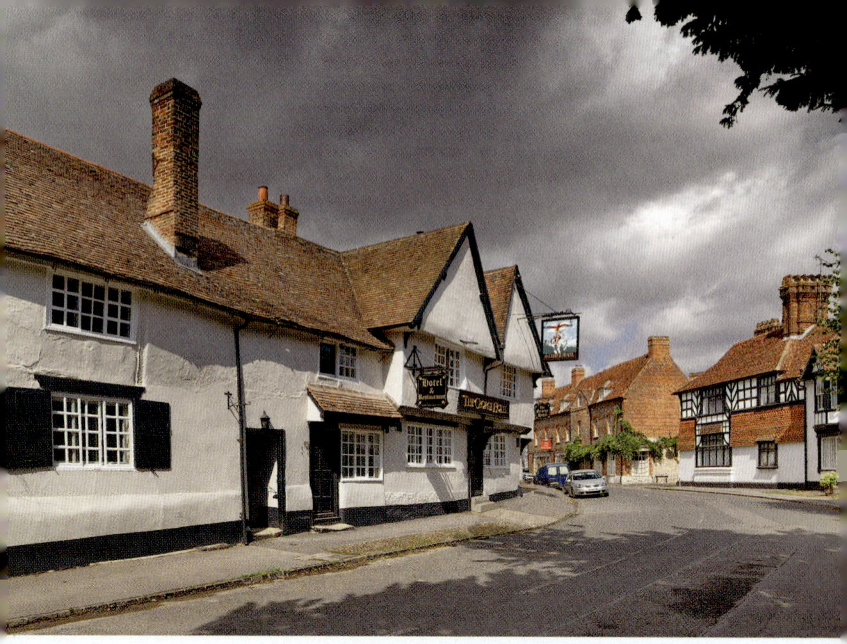

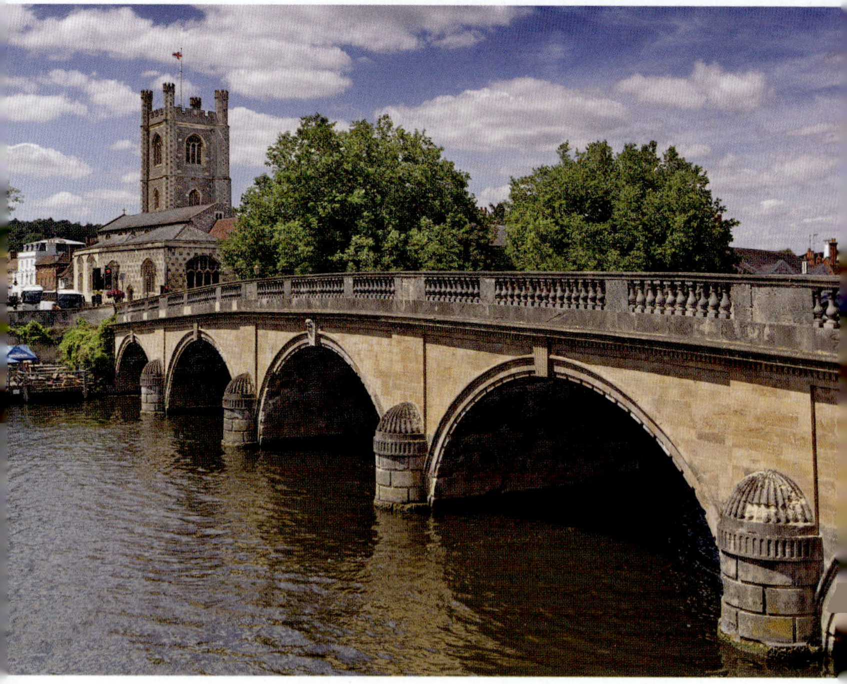

3. Dorchester, High Street (p. 630)
4. Henley-on-Thames, bridge, by William Hayward, 1782–6 (p. 667) and St Mary, medieval (p. 662)
5. Oxford, St Peter-in-the-East (now St Edmund Hall), chancel crypt, early to mid-C12 (p. 263)
6. Oxford, Iffley, St Mary, late C12, W front (p. 505)

3 | 5
4 | 6

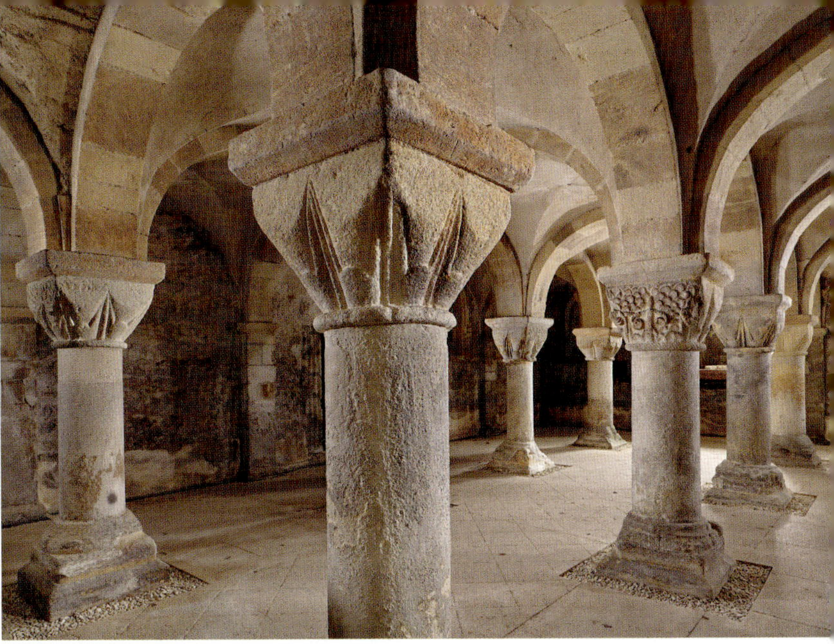

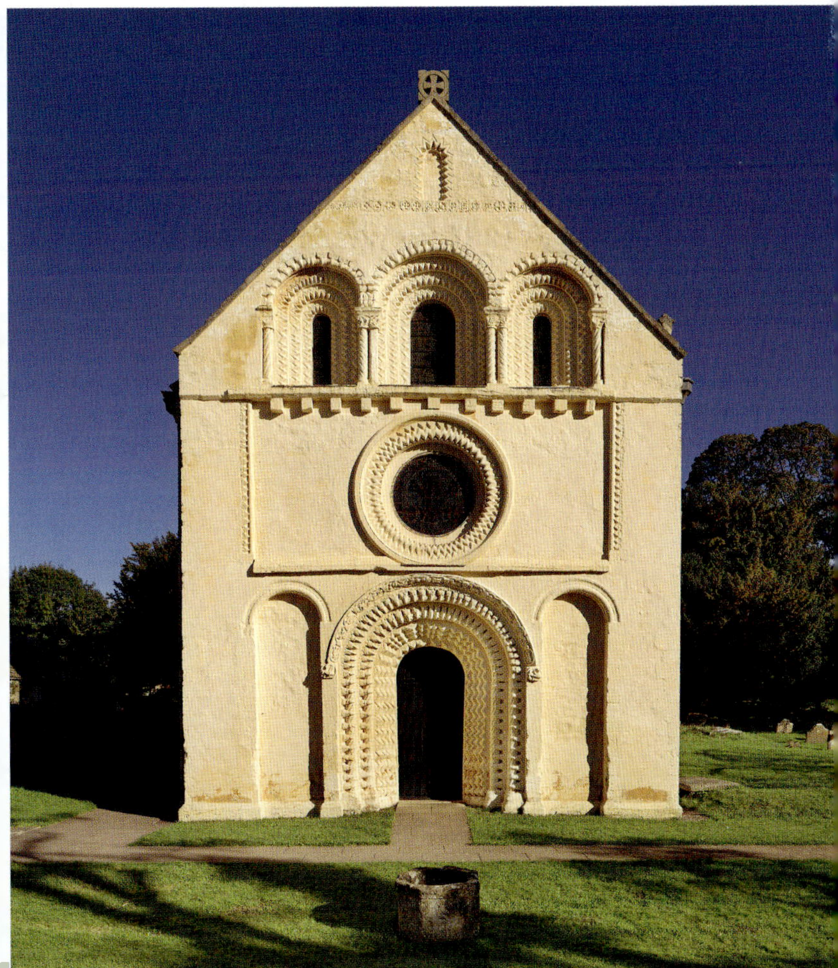

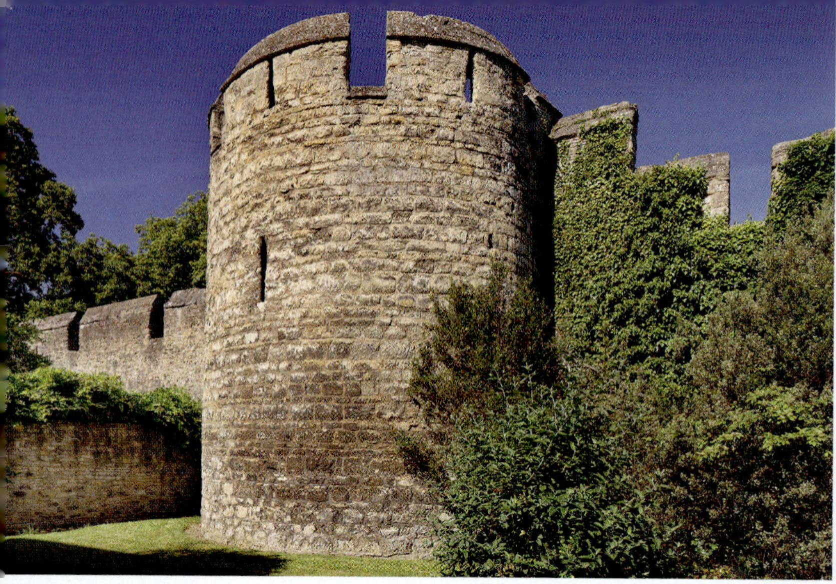

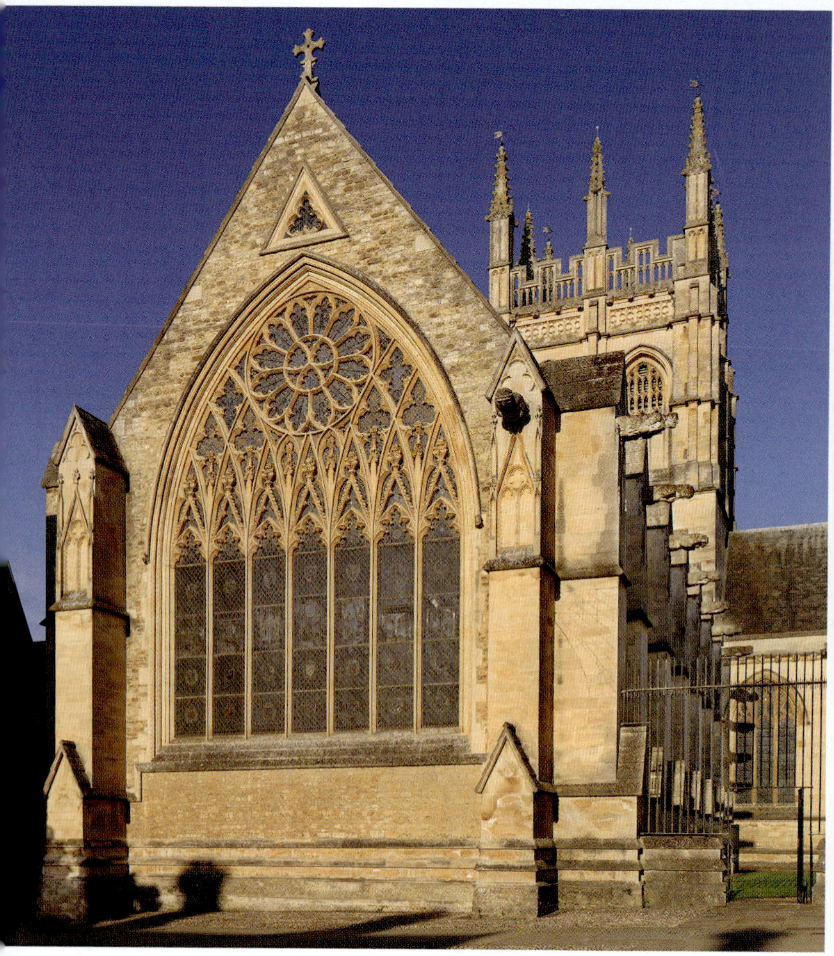

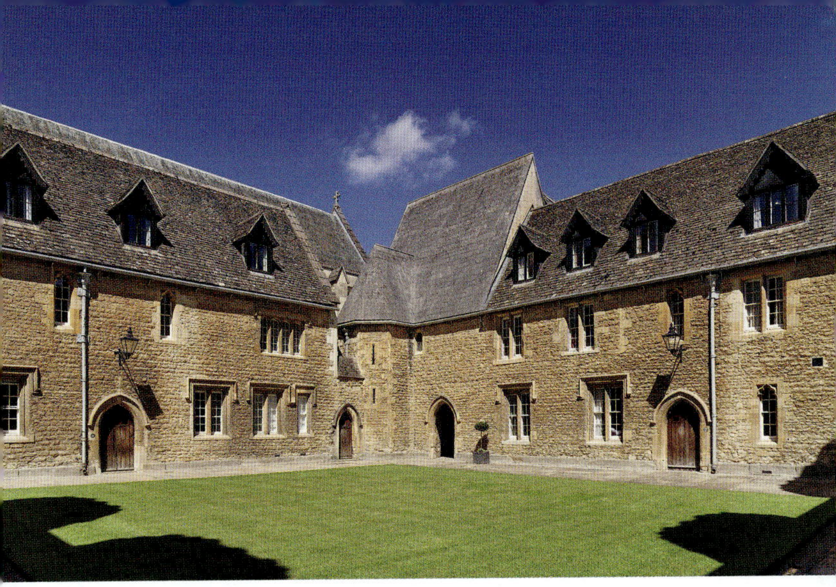

11. Oxford, New College, city wall, early to mid-C13 (p. 221)
12. Oxford, Merton College, chapel, choir, *c.* 1290–1300, and crossing tower, 1448–52 (pp. 201–2)
13. Oxford, Merton College, Mob Quad, late C13 and C14 (p. 199)
14. Oxford, Christ Church, Cathedral, Latin Chapel, St Frideswide's shrine, *c.* 1289, detail (p. 130)
15. Oxford, Merton College, chapel, choir N window, stained glass, St Matthew(?), by William of Thame, 1310/11 (p. 204)

11	13	
12	14	15

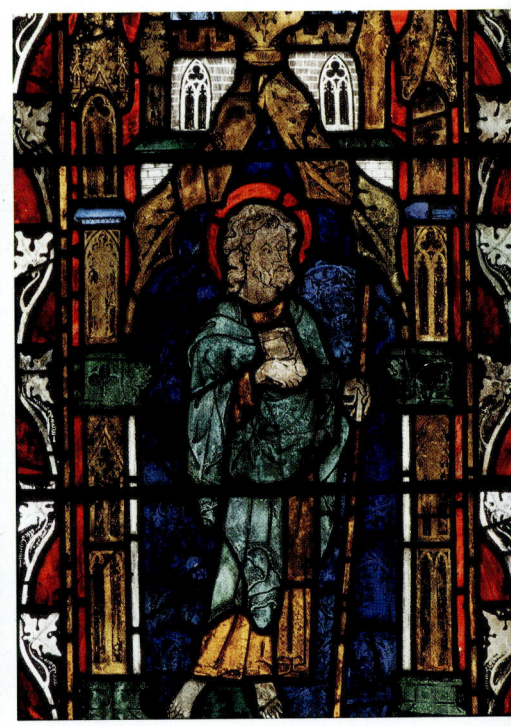

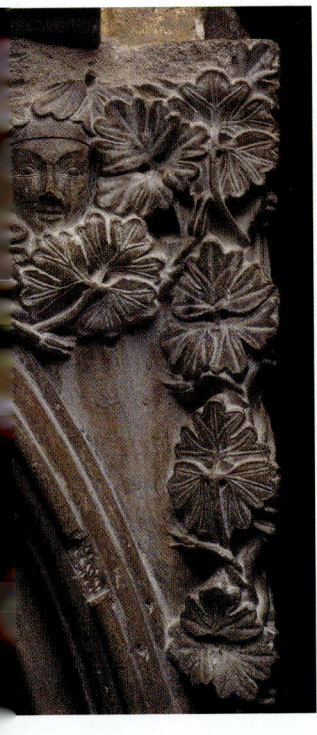

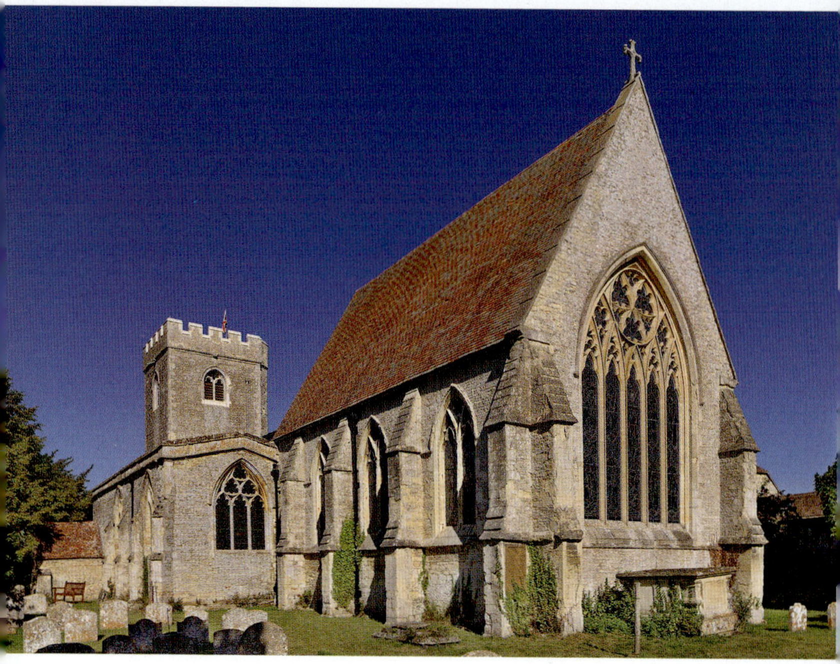

16. Great Haseley, St Peter, C13–C15 (p. 650)
17. Dorchester Abbey, monument to William de Valence the younger †1282 (p. 628)
18. Dorchester Abbey, interior, mostly C14 (p. 625)
19. Dorchester Abbey, sanctuary N window (Jesse Window), *c.* 1340 (p. 626)

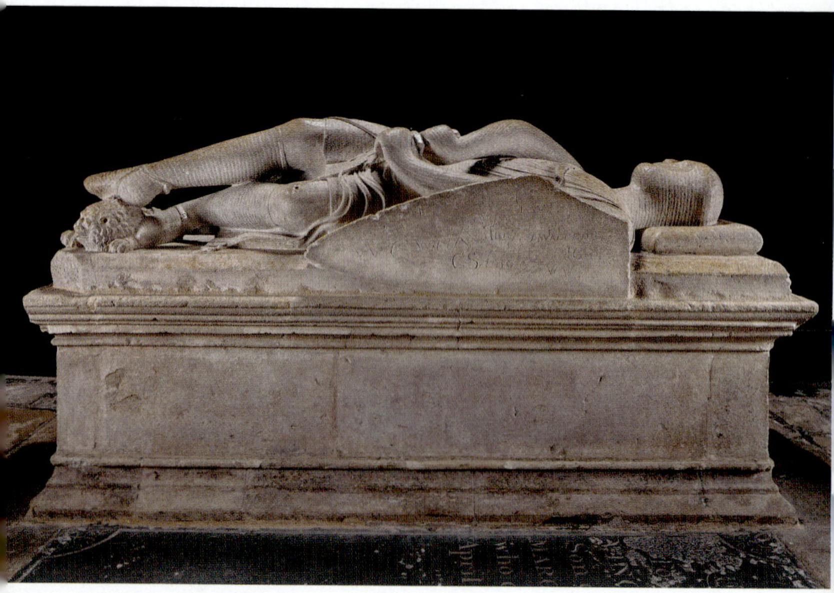

16 | 18
17 | 19

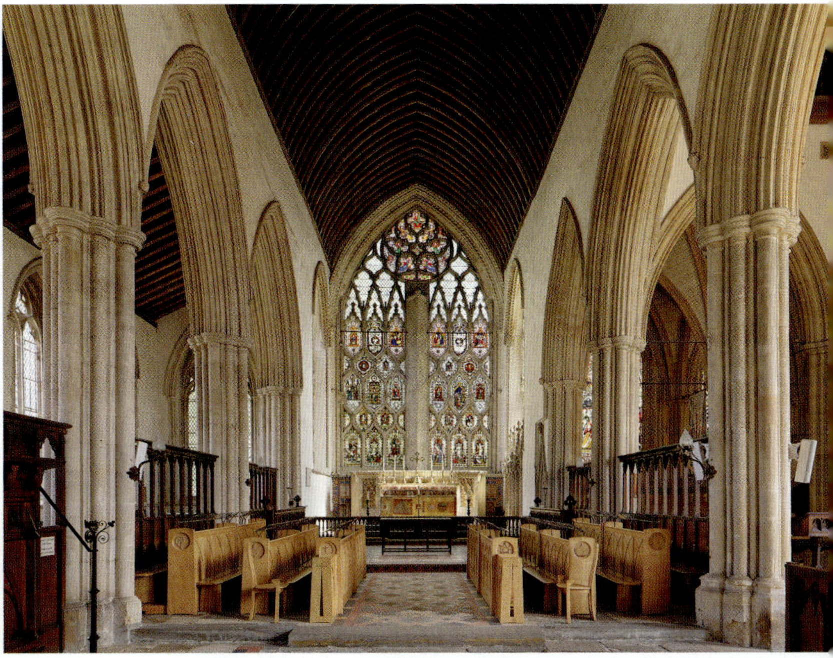

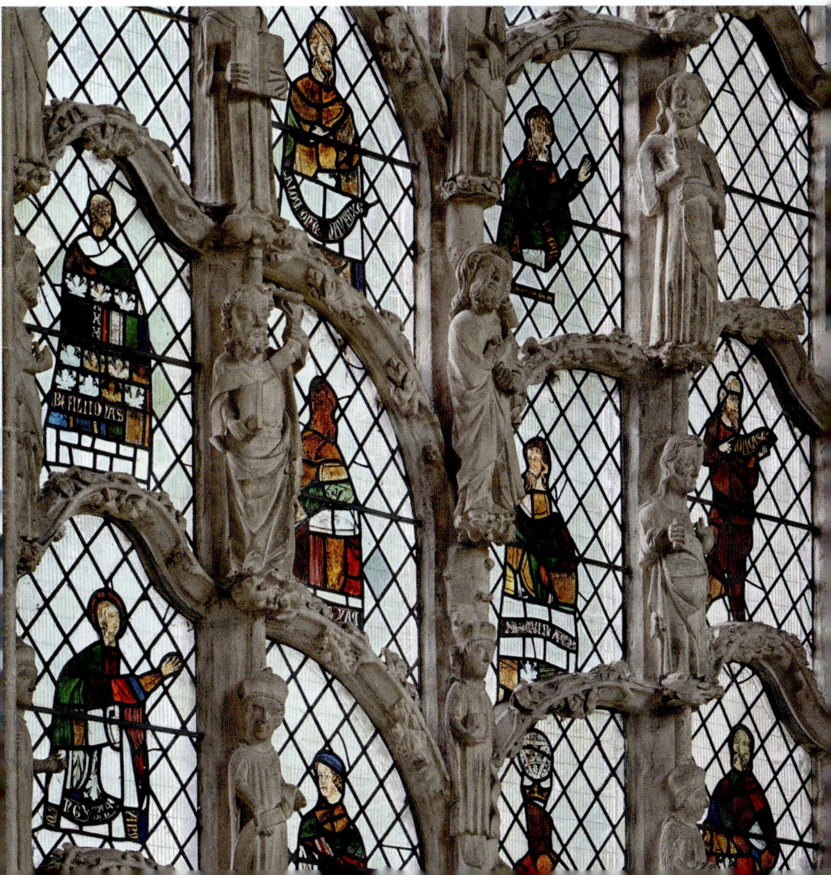

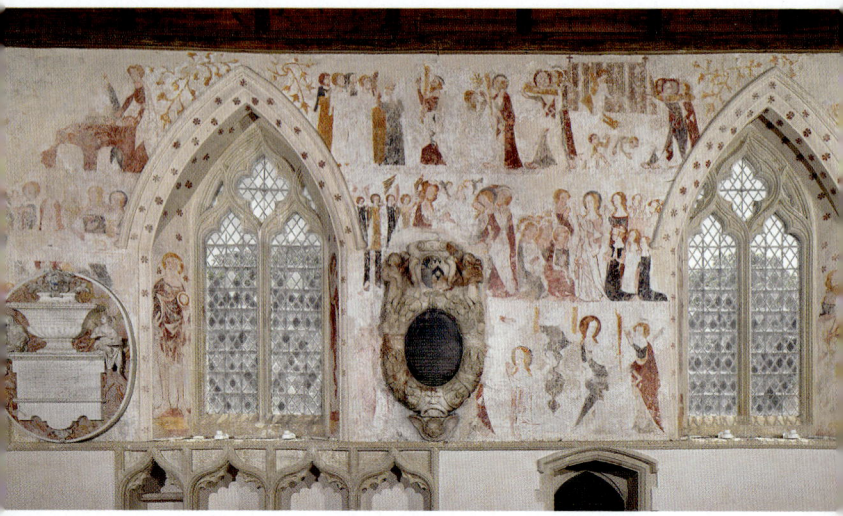

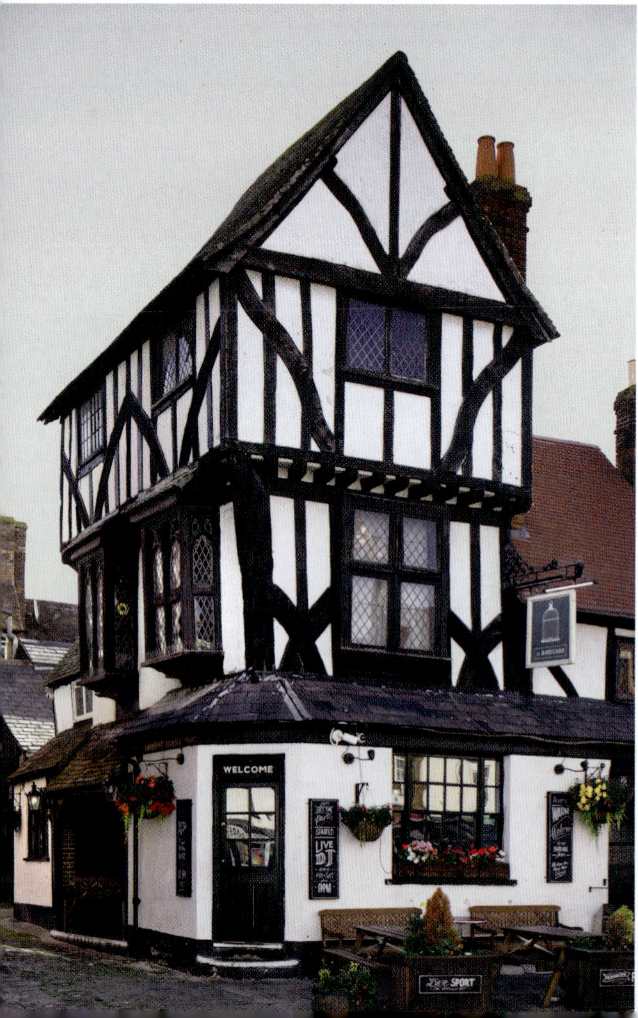

20. Chalgrove, St Mary, chancel S wall, wall paintings, *c.* 1320–30 (p. 598)
21. Thame, The Birdcage, C14 and later (p. 750)
22. Oxford, St Mary the Virgin, C13–C15 (p. 383)
23. Oxford, New College, Front Quad, begun 1380, W range, with chapel and hall (N) (p. 211)

20 | 22
21 | 23

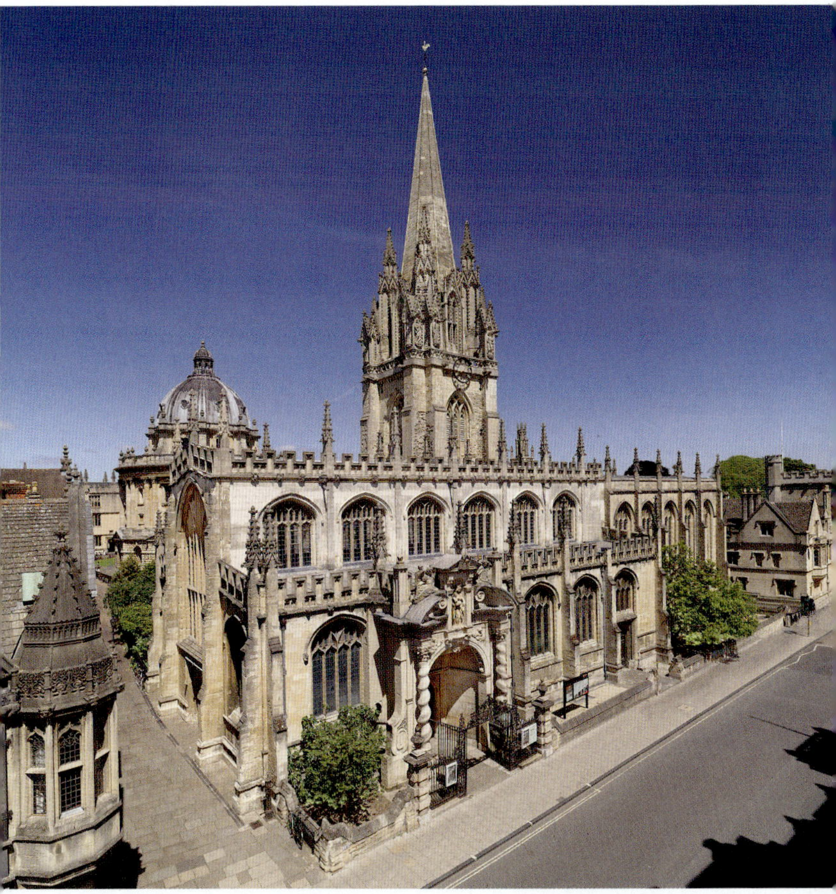

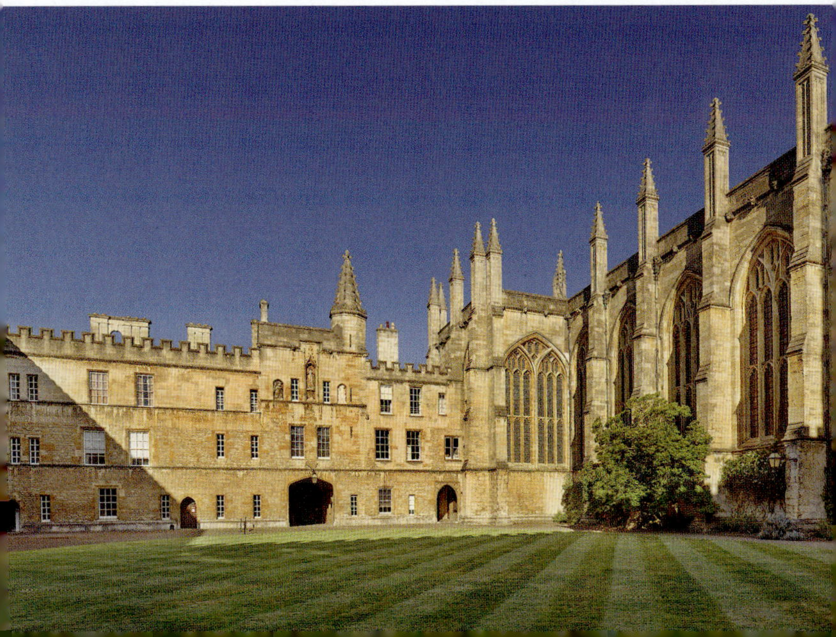

24. Oxford, Worcester College, *camerae*, C15 (p. 320)
25. Oxford, All Souls College, chapel, reredos, mostly *c.* 1493–1511 by John Fusting, restored 1870s by Sir George Gilbert Scott (p. 89)

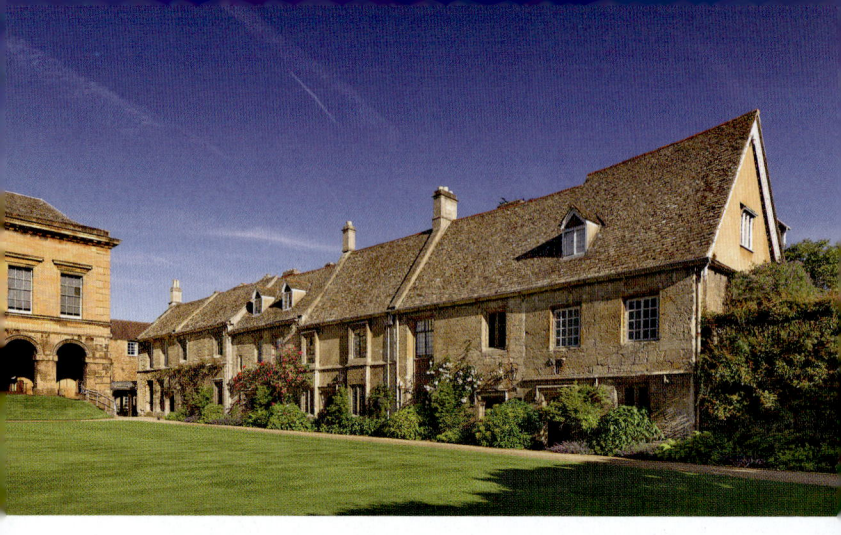

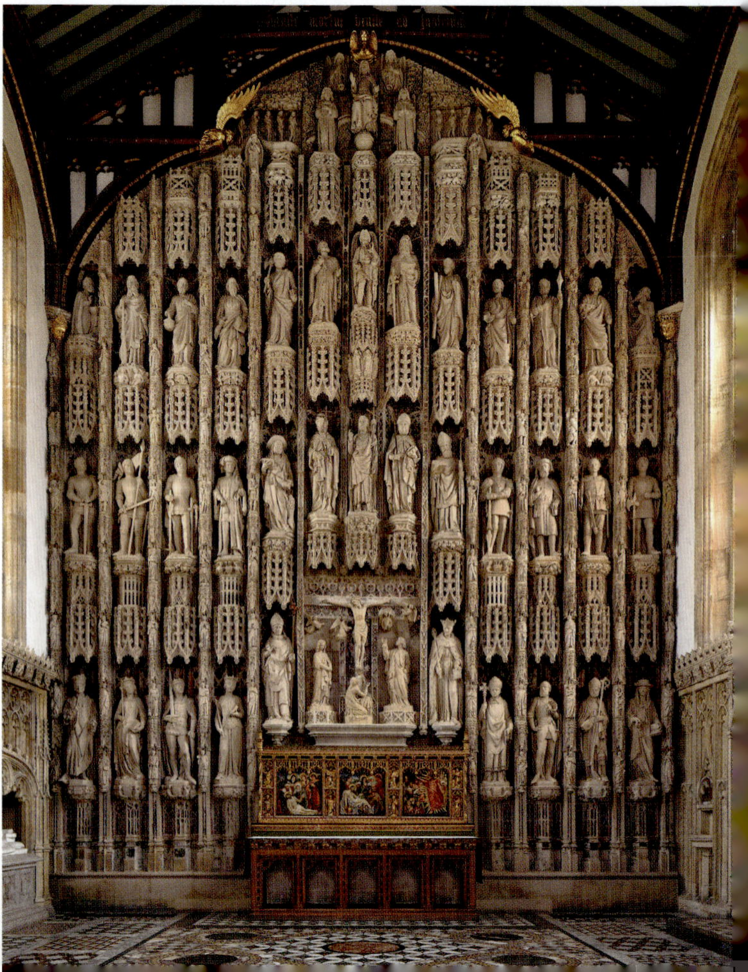

26. Oxford, Magdalen College, begun 1474, Cloister Quadrangle, with bell tower (behind) and Founder's Tower (r.) (p. 179)
27. Oxford, Divinity School, begun by Richard Winchcombe, 1423, vault by William Orchard, 1478–82 (p. 331)

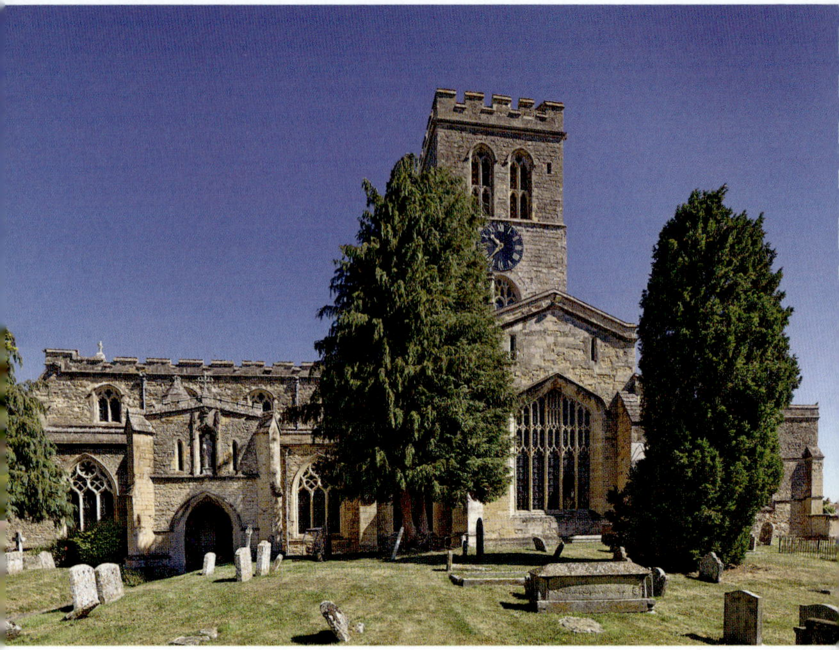

28. Thame, St Mary, C13–C15 (p. 742)
29. Ewelme, God's House, founded 1437, with N porch (p. 638)
30. Ewelme, St Mary, monument to Alice, Duchess of Suffolk †1475 (p. 638)
31. Rycote, Chapel of St Michael, founded 1449, with C17 furnishings (p. 718)

28 | 30
29 | 31

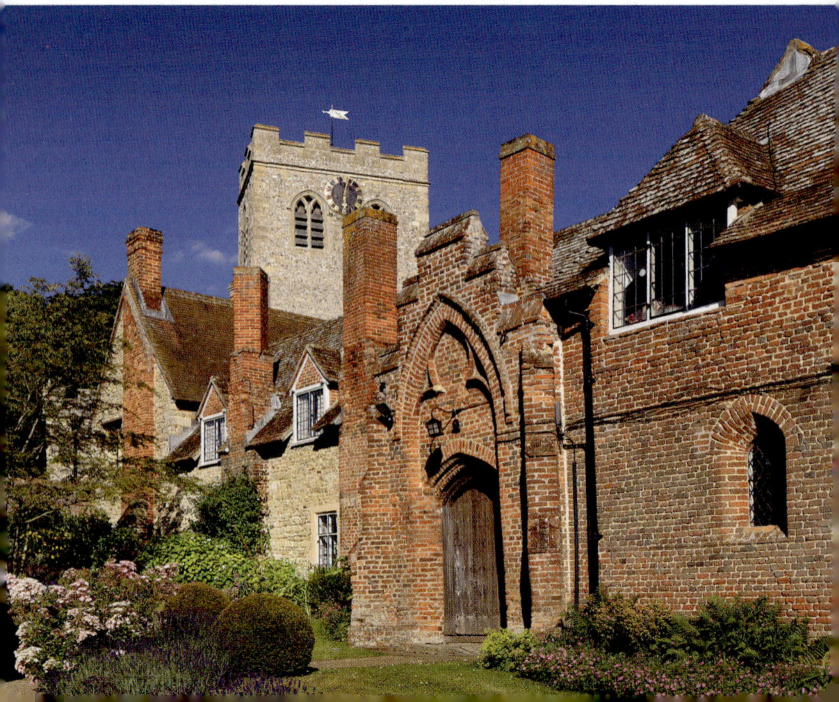

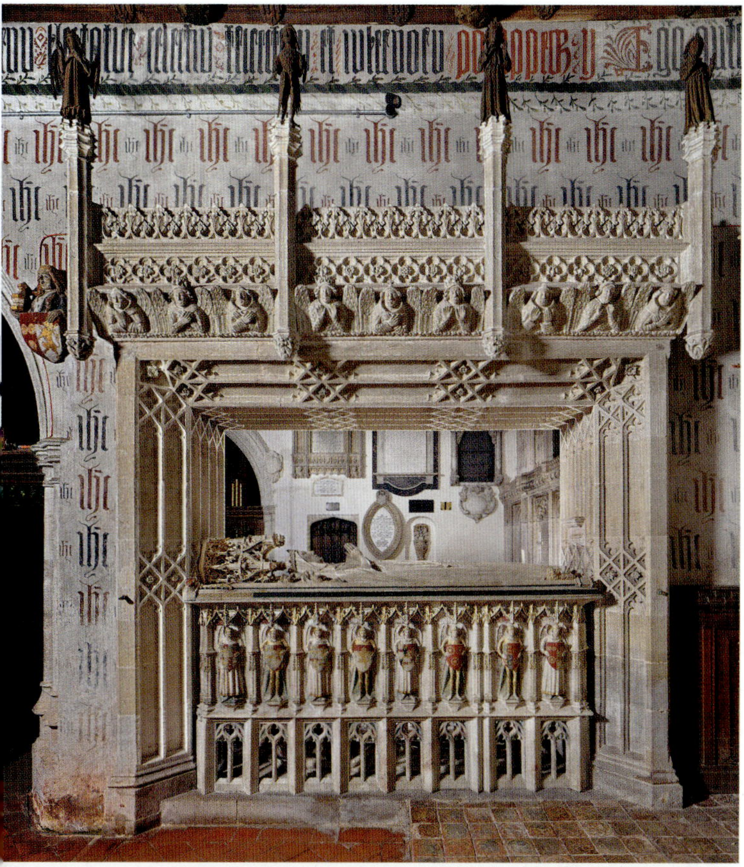

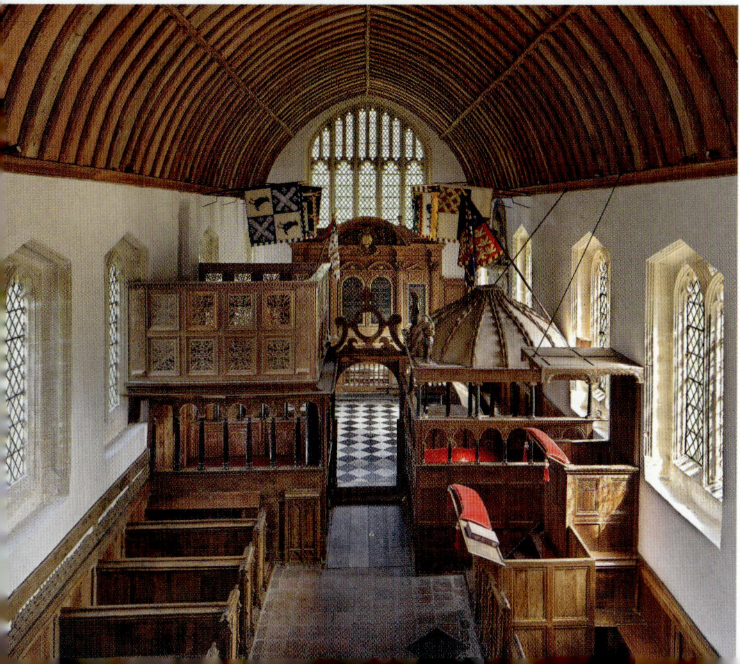

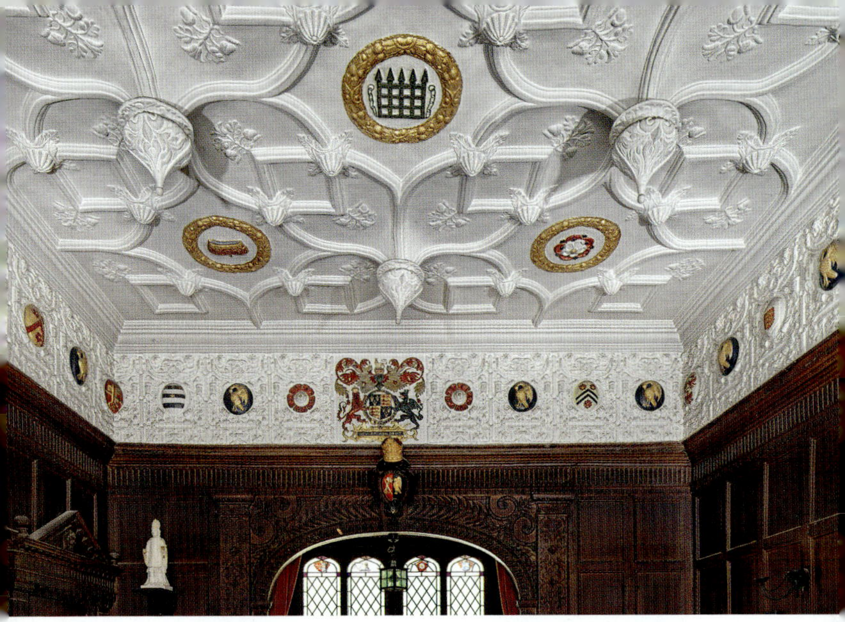

32. Oxford, Christ Church, Tom Tower, by Henry Redman, *c.*1525, completed by Christopher Wren, 1681–2 (p. 112)
33. Oxford, Christ Church, hall, by Henry Redman and Humphrey Coke, begun 1525 (p. 116)
34. Oxford, Corpus Christi College, gate-tower room, ceiling plasterwork, late C16 or early C17 (p. 142)
35. Oxford, No. 3 Cornmarket Street, wall painting, late C16 (p. 421)
36. Thame Park, Abbot's Parlour, panelling, wall decoration and internal porch, *c.*1530 (p. 755)

32 | 34
33 | 35 36

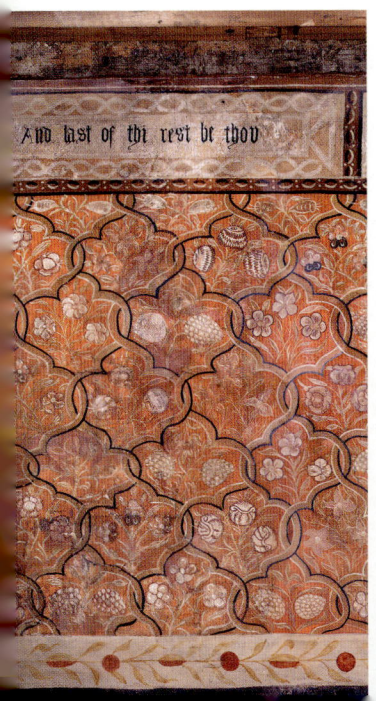

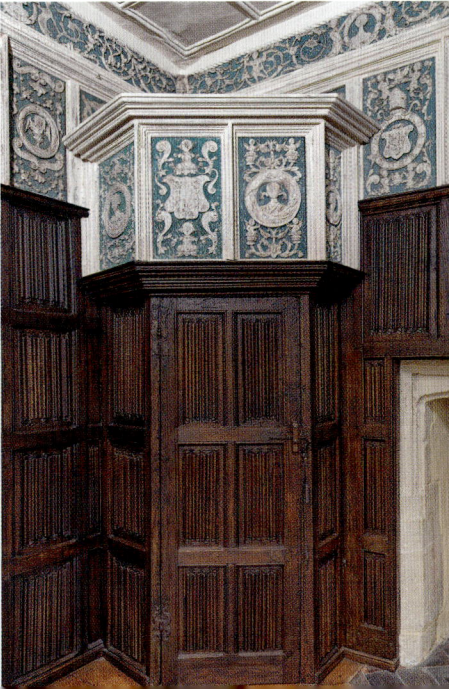

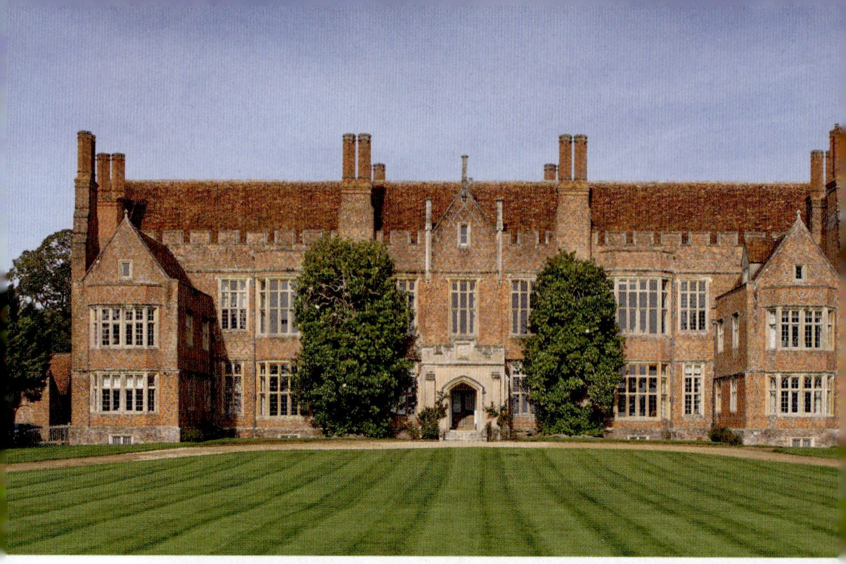

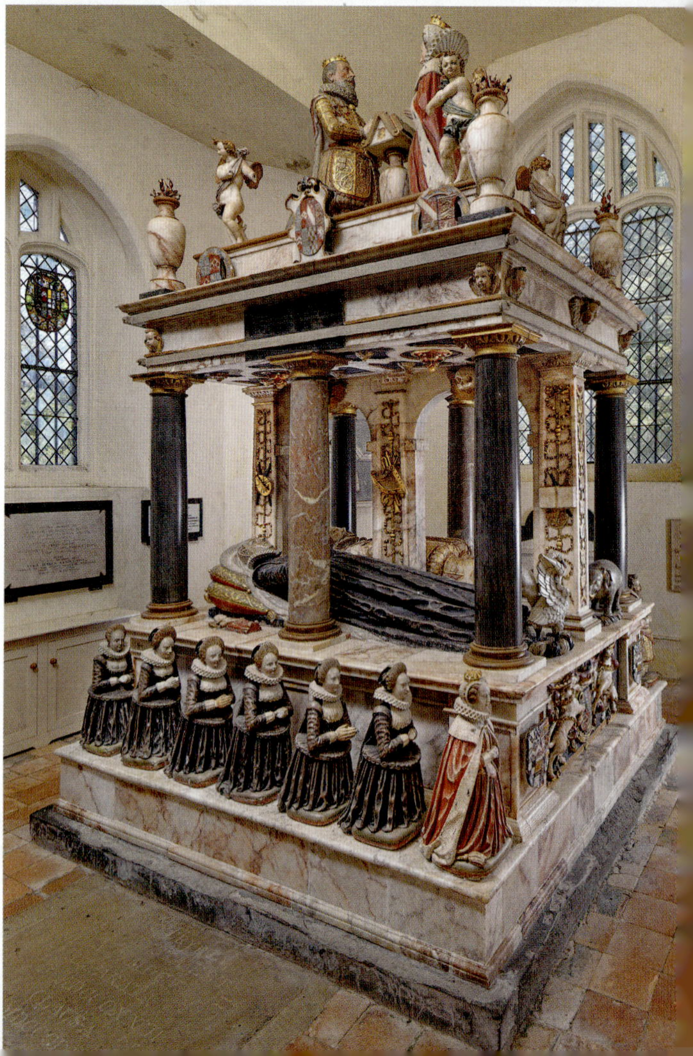

37 | 39
38 | 40

37. Mapledurham House, 1609–12, E front (p. 688)
38. Rotherfield Greys, St Nicholas, Knollys monument, 1605 (p. 711)
39. Oxford, No. 126 High Street, late C15, with late C17 front (p. 410)
40. Dorchester, No. 55–59 High Street, formerly Bull Inn, 1610 (p. 631)

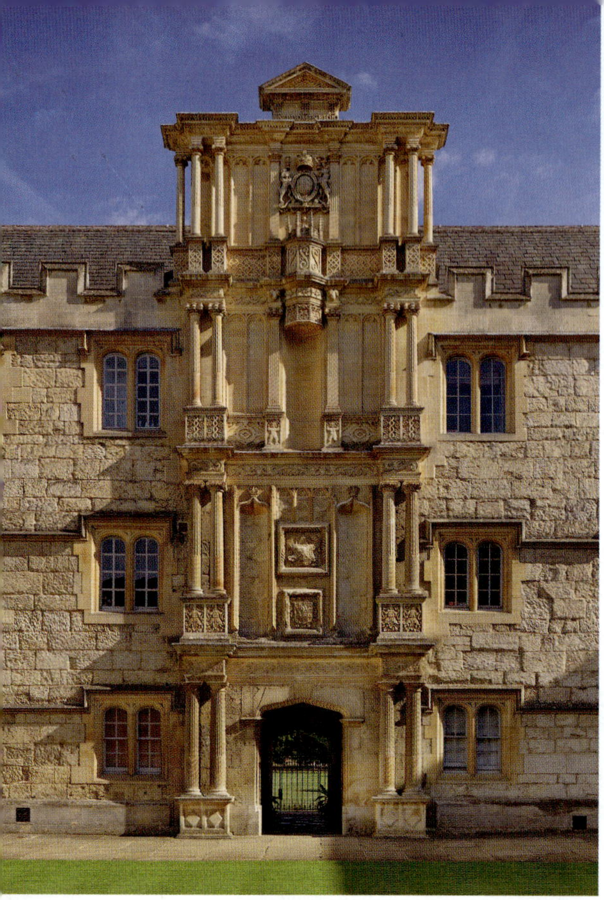

41. Oxford, Merton College, Fellows' Quad, by John Akroyd the elder and John Bentley, 1609–10 S side (p. 207)
42. Oxford, Merton College, chapel, monument to Sir Thomas Bodley, by Nicholas Stone, 1615 (p. 205)
43. Oxford, Bodleian Library, Schools Quad, by John Akroyd and John Bentley, 1613–*c.* 1620, E side with tower (p. 333)
44. Oxford, Bodleian Library, by John Akroyd and John Bentley, Arts End, 1610–12, interior, joinery by John Bolton and William Bennett (p. 335)

41	43
42	44

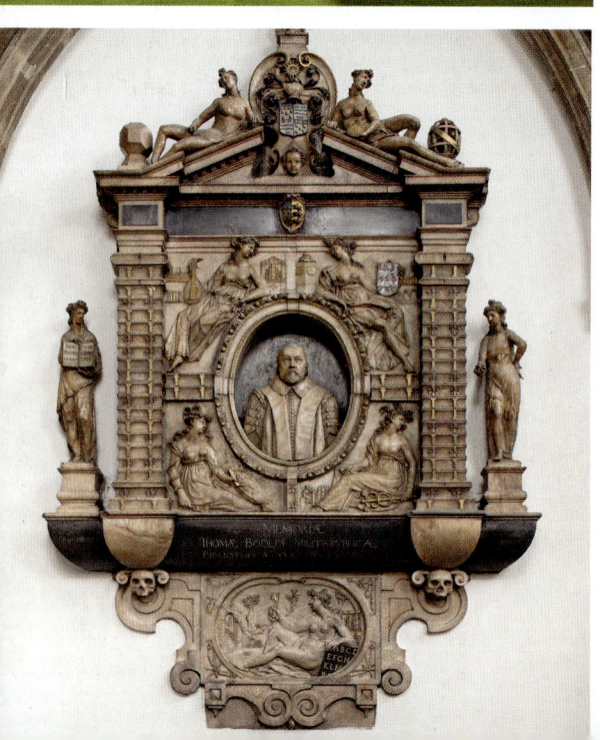

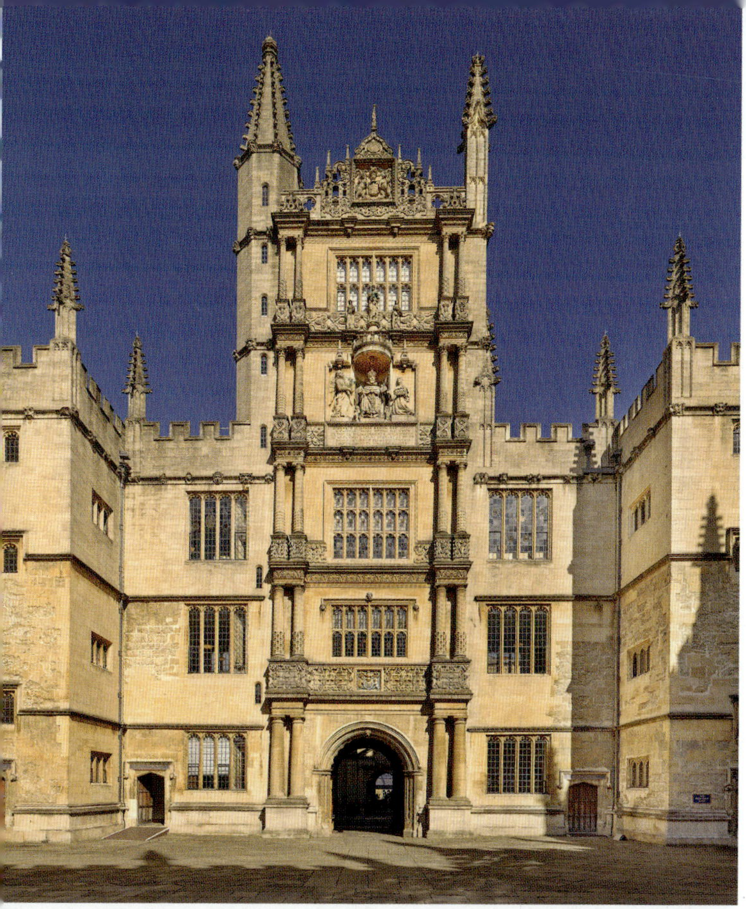

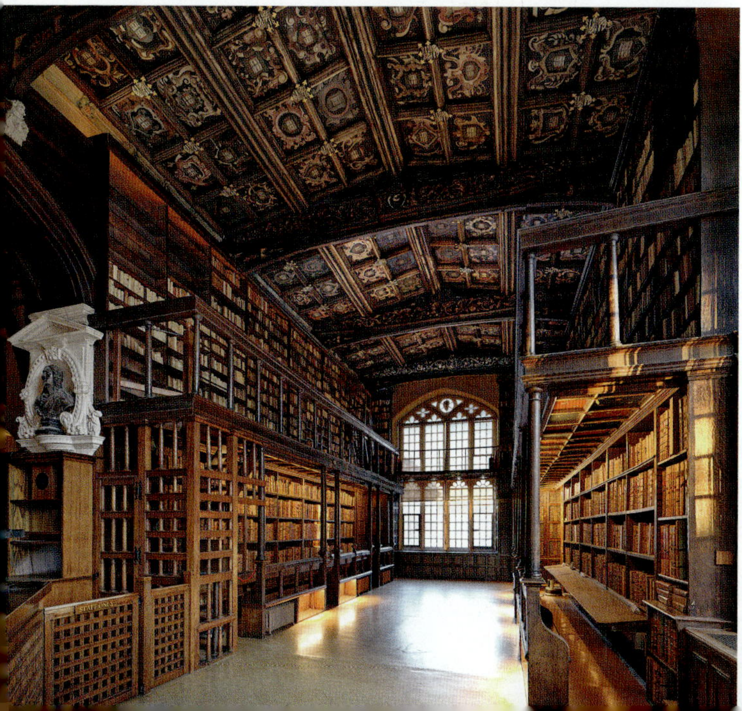

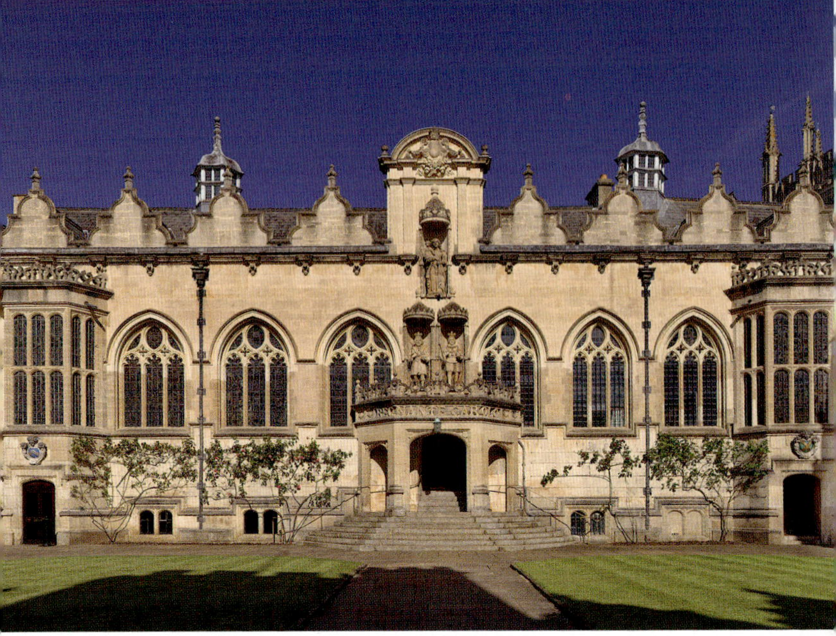

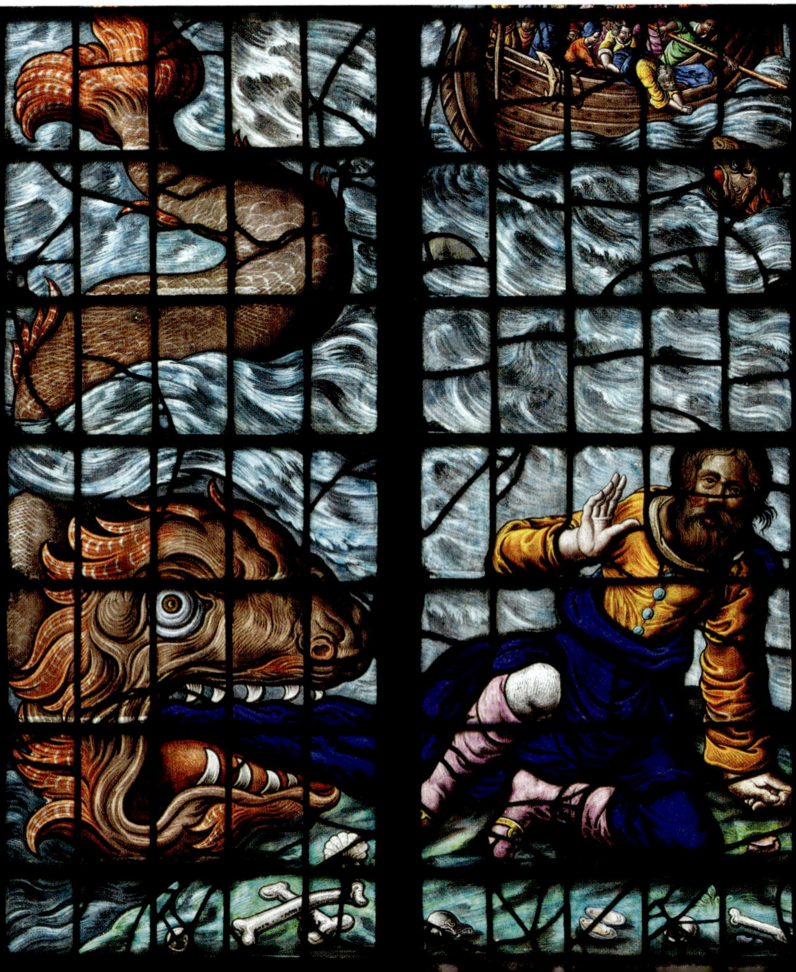

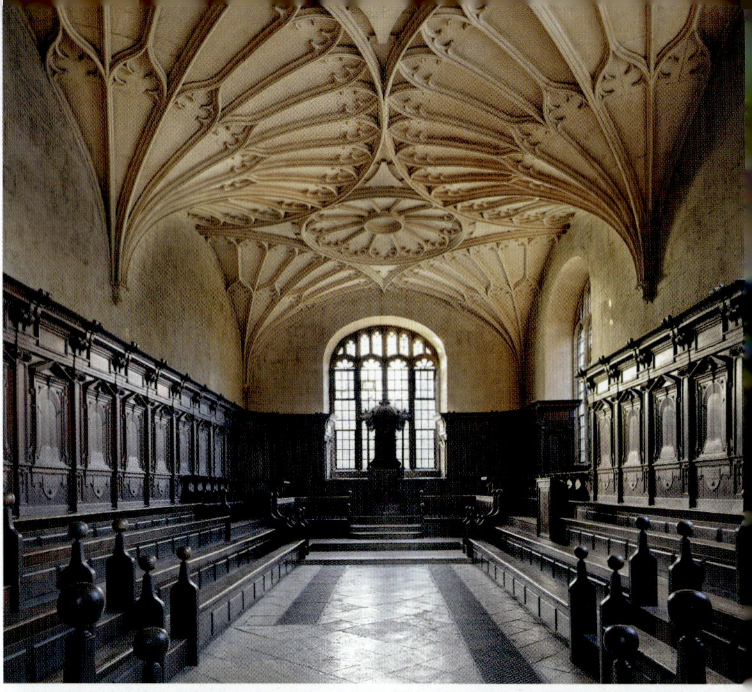

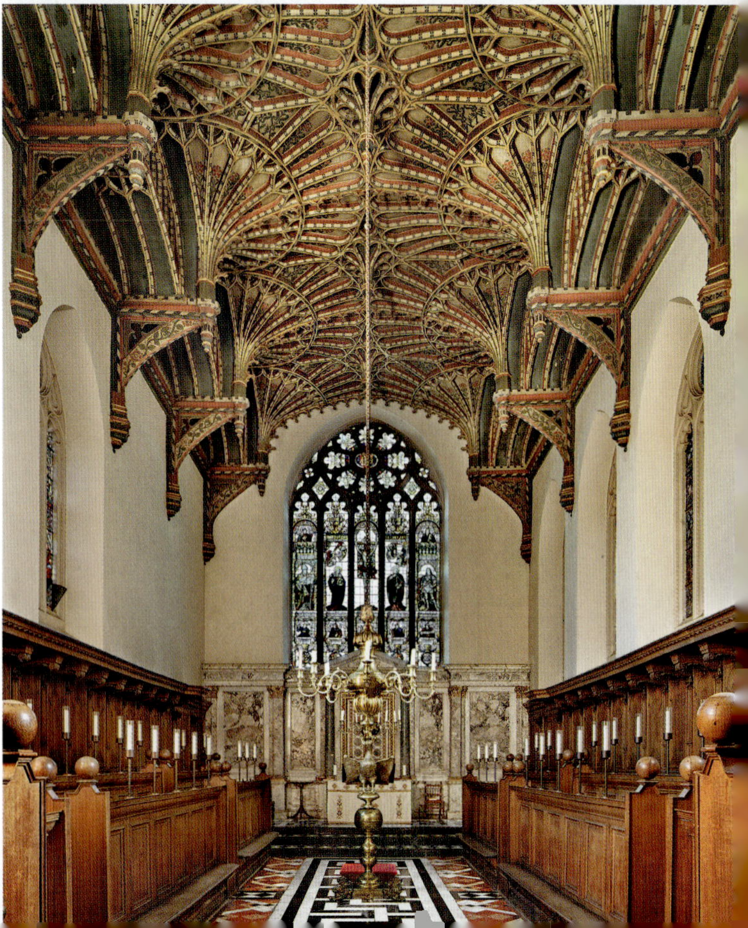

48. Oxford, Bodleian Library, Convocation House, 1634–7, interior, fan-vaulting by John Townesend III, 1758–9 (p. 332)
49. Oxford, Brasenose College, chapel, by John Jackson, 1656–9, interior (p. 106)
50. Oxford, Botanic Garden, gateway, by Nicholas Stone, 1632–3 (p. 349)

48
49 | 50

51. Watlington,
    town hall,
    1664–5 (p. 763)
52. Warborough,
    St Laurence,
    w tower,
    1666 (p. 758)
53. Great Milton,
    St Mary,
    monument
    to Sir Michael
    Dormer,
    attributed
    to Samuel
    Baldwin, 1618,
    detail of relief
    (p. 655)
54. Brightwell
    Baldwin, St
    Bartholomew,
    Stone family
    memorial,
    c. 1670 (p. 593)

55 │ 56
   │ 57
   │ 58

59. Oxford, Clarendon Building, by Nicholas Hawksmoor, 1712–15 (p. 340)
60. Oxford, All Souls College, Great Quad, by Nicholas Hawksmoor, E range and towers, 1722–35 (p. 92)
61. Oxford, The Queen's College, hall, probably by Dr George Clarke and William Townesend after designs by Nicholas Hawksmoor, 1714–15, interior (p. 244)
62. Oxford, All Souls College, library, by Nicholas Hawksmoor, 1716–51 (p. 93)

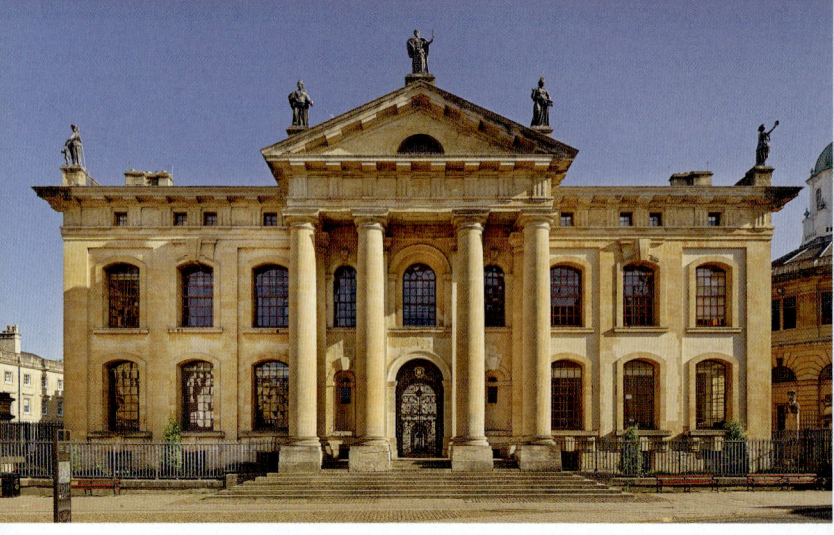

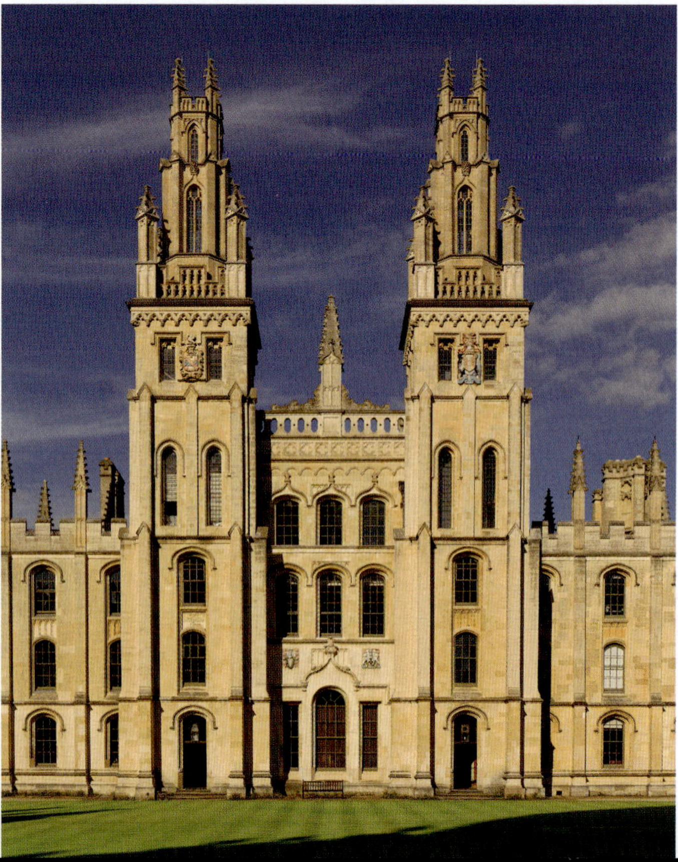

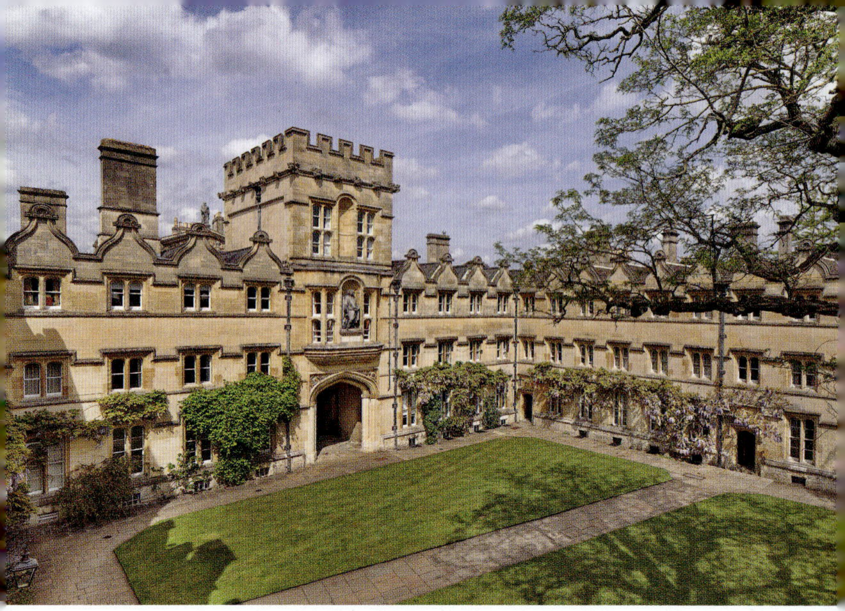

63. Oxford, University College, Radcliffe Quad, by William Townesend and Bartholomew Peisley III with Dr George Clarke, 1716–19 (p. 303)
64. Oxford, Vanbrugh House, front, by Bartholomew Peisley III, *c.* 1721 (p. 437)
65. Oxford, Radcliffe Camera, by James Gibbs, 1737–49 (pp. 341–2)
66. Oxford, Christ Church, Cathedral, monument to Dean Aldrich, designed by Dr George Clarke, sculptor Sir Henry Cheere, 1732 (p. 131)

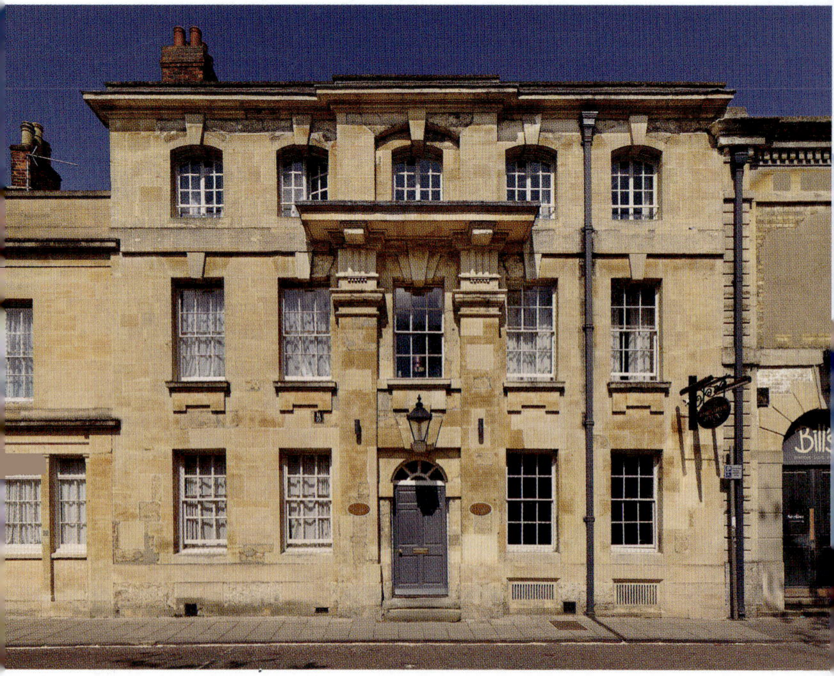

ALDRICH.S.T.P.ÆDIS.CHRISTI.DECANVS.ET.GRANDE.TOTIVS.ACADEMIÆ.ORNAMENTVM
VIXIT. VIR. CLARISSIMVS. ANNIS LXIII
OB. XIX. KAL. IAN. MDCCX.
NE. CINERES. DEFVNCTI.
SINE. NOMINE. ET. TITVLO.
DIVTIVS. NEGLECTI. IACERENT.
GEO. CLARKE. QVI. VIVVM. COLVIT ET. AMAVIT
AM. B. M. FECIT. A. D. MDCCXXXII

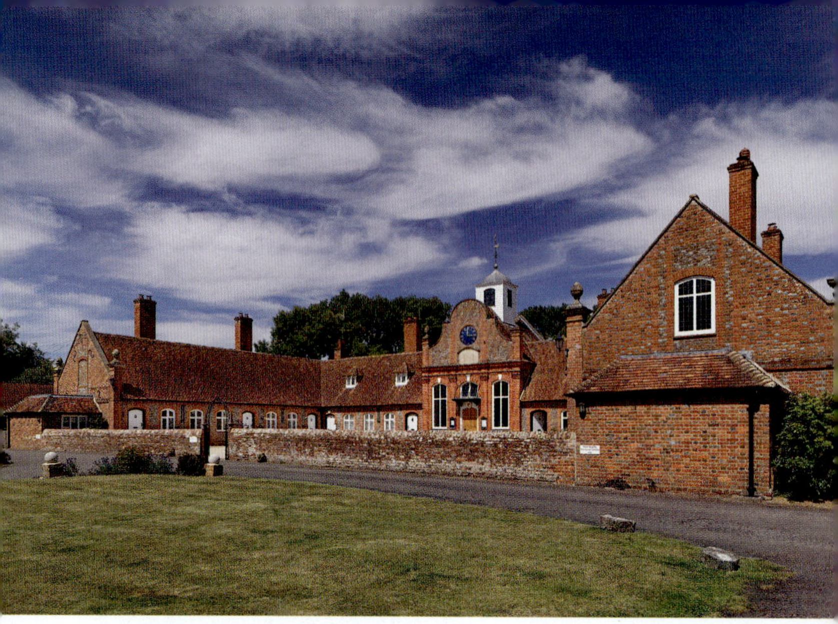

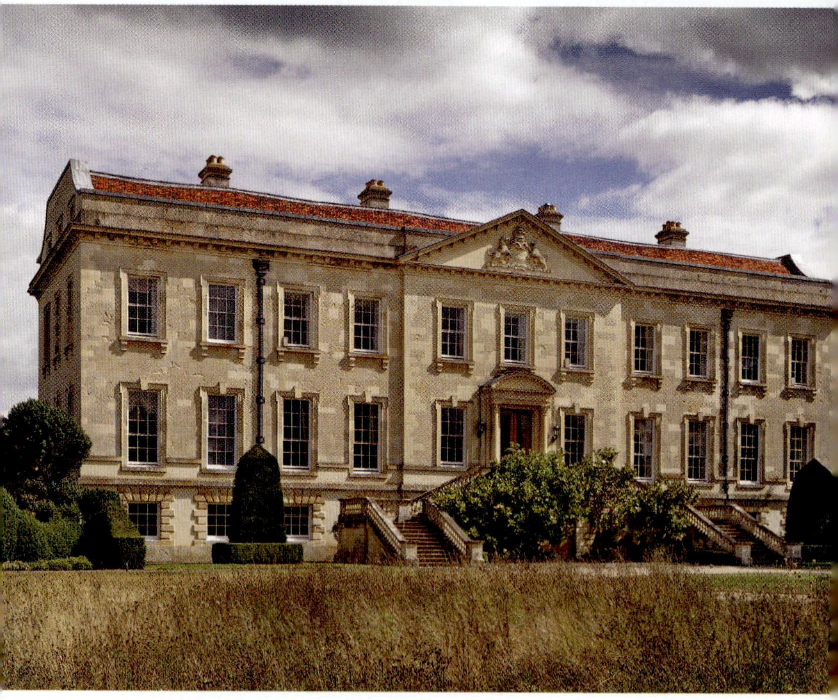

67. Goring Heath, almshouses, 1725–6 (p. 648)
68. Thame Park, W range, by William Smith, *c.* 1745–50 (p. 753)
69. Chiselhampton, St Katherine, 1763 (p. 606)
70. Henley-on-Thames, New Street, Camden House (l.), 1729, and Bishop's House (r.), early C18 (p. 674)

67	69
68	70

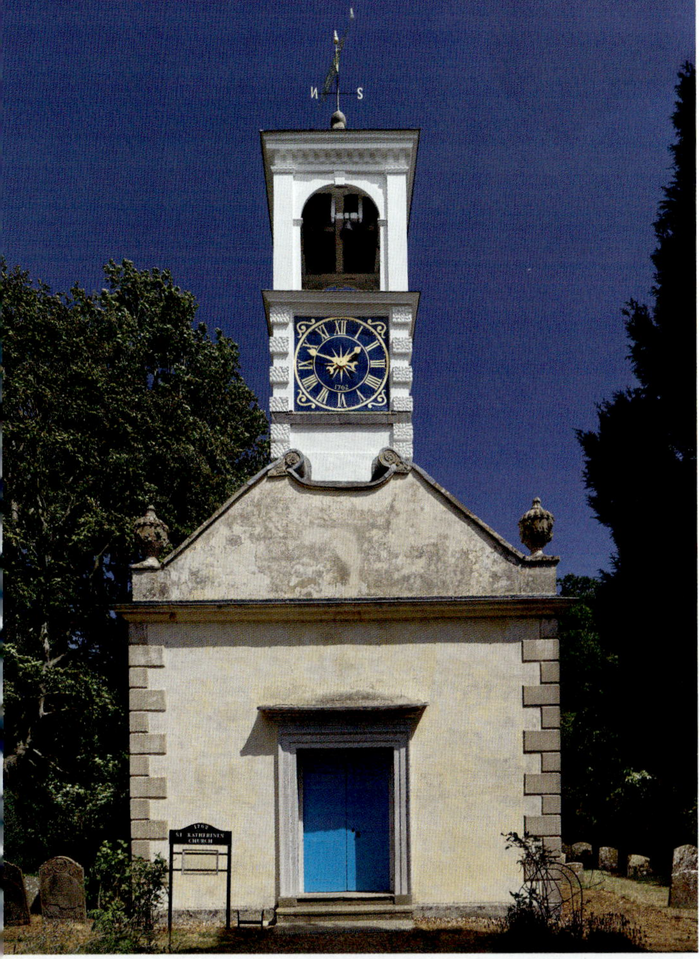
1762
ST KATHERINES
CHURCH

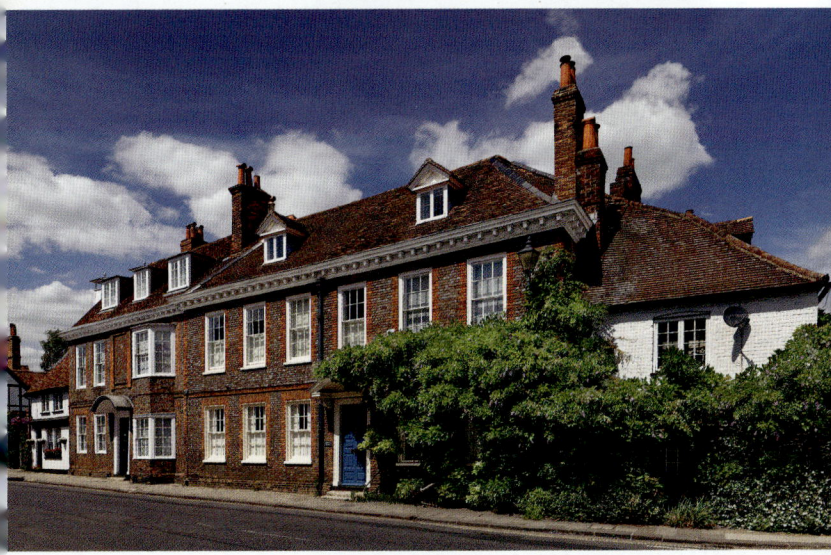

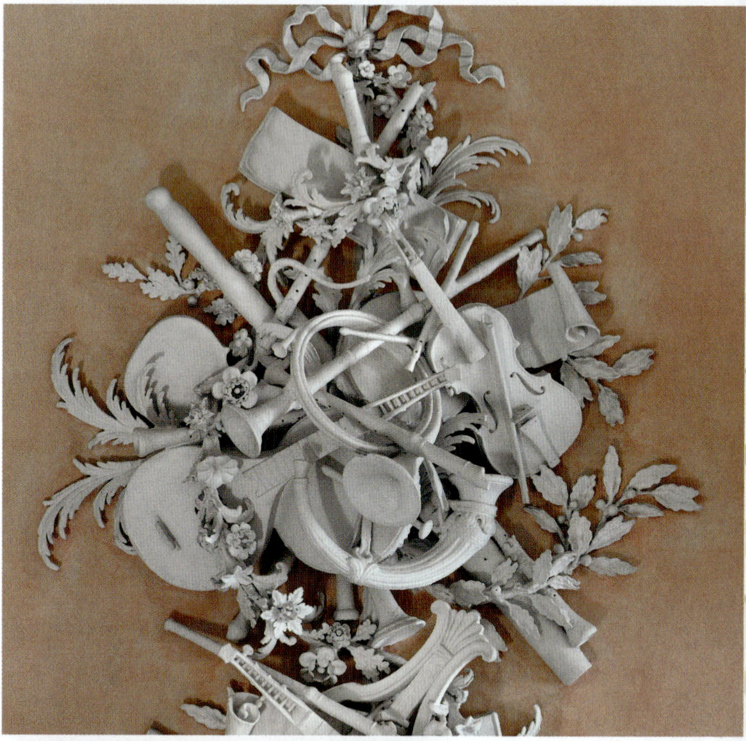

71. Oxford, Christ Church, Upper Library, stucco-work by Thomas Roberts, *c.*1760, detail (p. 137)
72. Oxford, St John's College, chapel, lectern, by Leonard Snetzler, 1773 (p. 273)
73. Oxford, Oriel College, library, by James Wyatt, 1788–9 (p. 230)
74. Oxford, Green Templeton College, Radcliffe Observatory, by James Wyatt, 1773 to mid-1790s, Observatory Tower interior, with railing and stair by John Mackell, 1796 (p. 153)

71 | 73
72 | 74

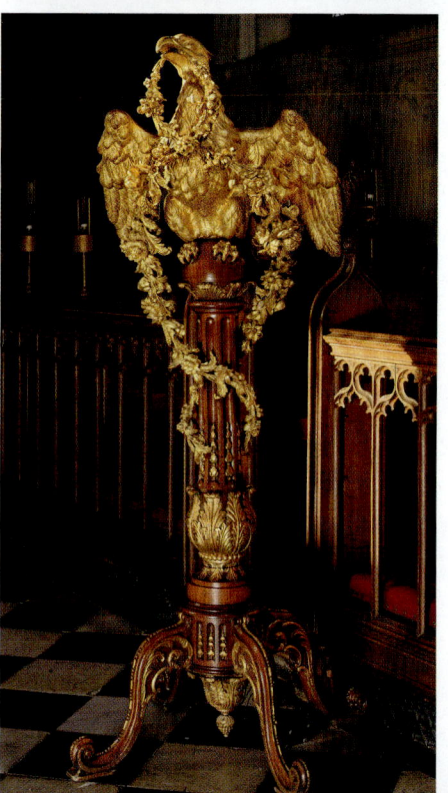

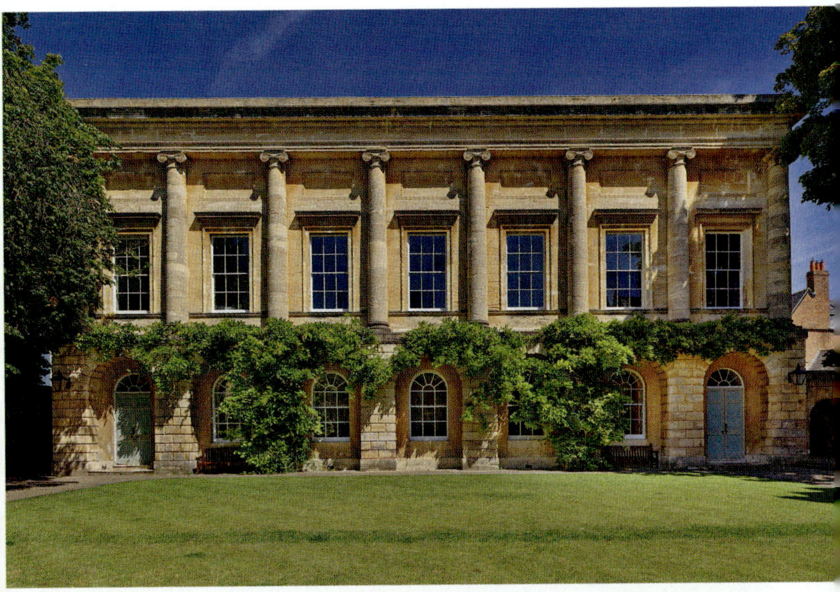

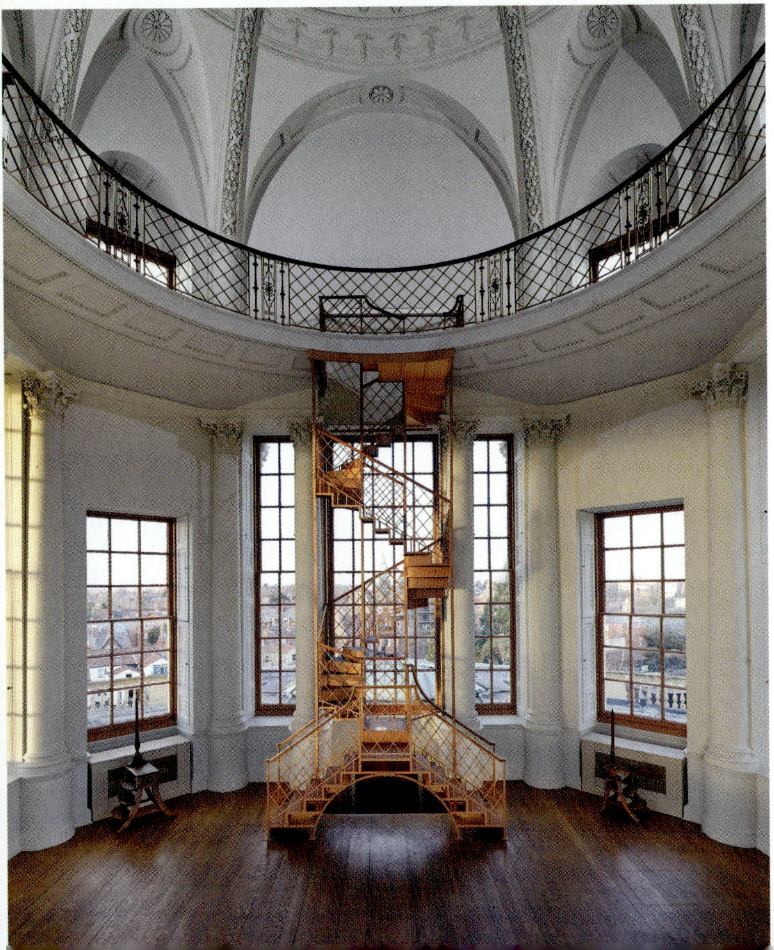

75. Nuneham Courtenay, All Saints, by Simon, 1st Earl Harcourt and James Stuart, 1763–4 (p. 706)

76. Nuneham Courtenay, Nuneham House, staircase, by Henry Holland and Capability Brown, 1781 (p. 704)

77. Ipsden, Braziers Park, s range, by Daniel Harris, after 1794 (p. 680)

78. Mapledurham House, chapel (R.C.), 1796–7, plasterwork by Samuel Kerridge (p. 691)

79. Oxford, Gaol (former), D Wing, by William Blackburn, *c*.1785, with St George's Tower (Oxford Castle), early C11, r. (p. 401)
80. Oxford, High Street, No. 84, shopfront, early to mid-C19 (p. 414)

81. Oxford, Oriel College, St Mary's Quad, w range, by Daniel Robertson, c.1826 (p.231)
82. Oxford, County Hall, by John Plowman Jun., 1839–41 (p.403)

83. Oxford, Ashmolean Museum and Taylorian Institution, by C.R. Cockerell, 1841–5 (pp. 352–3)
84. Oxford, Pembroke College, hall, by John Hayward, 1847–8 (p. 235)
85. Oxford, Park Town, crescent, by Samuel Lipscombe Seckham, mid-1850s (p. 464)
86. Oxford, Headington Hill Hall, by John Thomas, 1856–8 (p. 478)

83	85
84	86

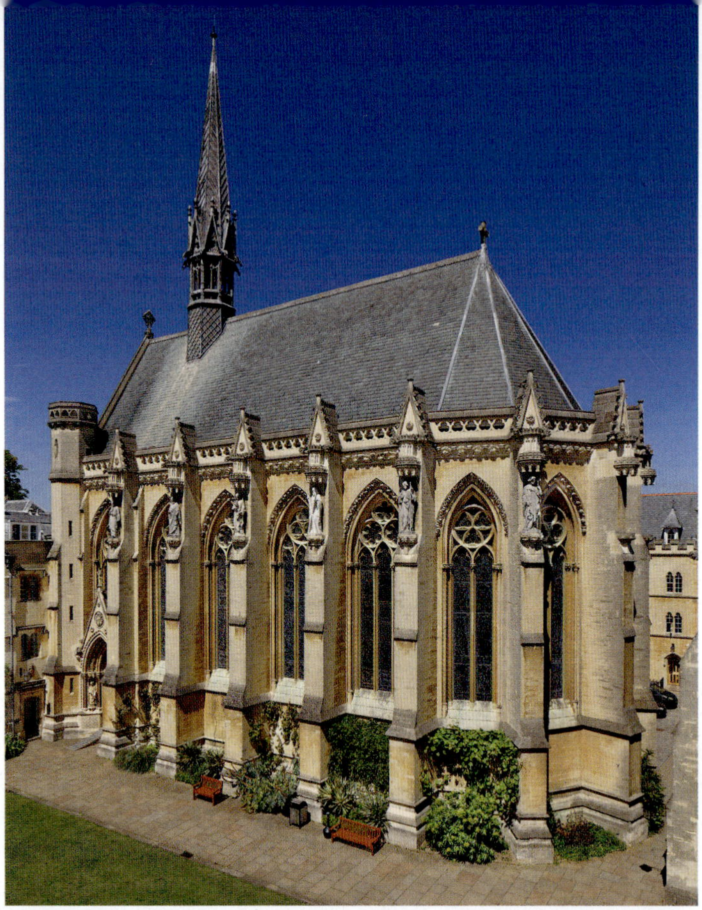

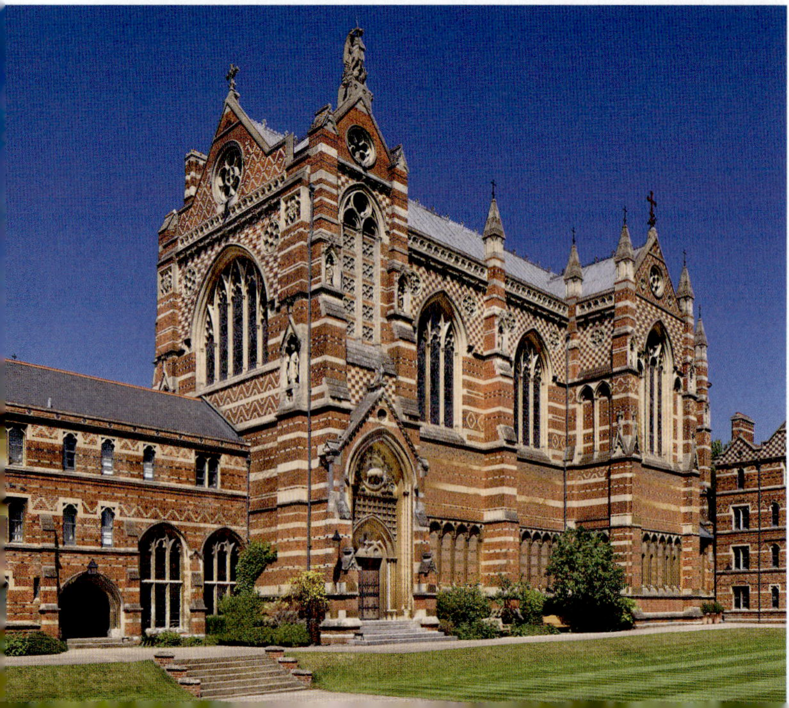

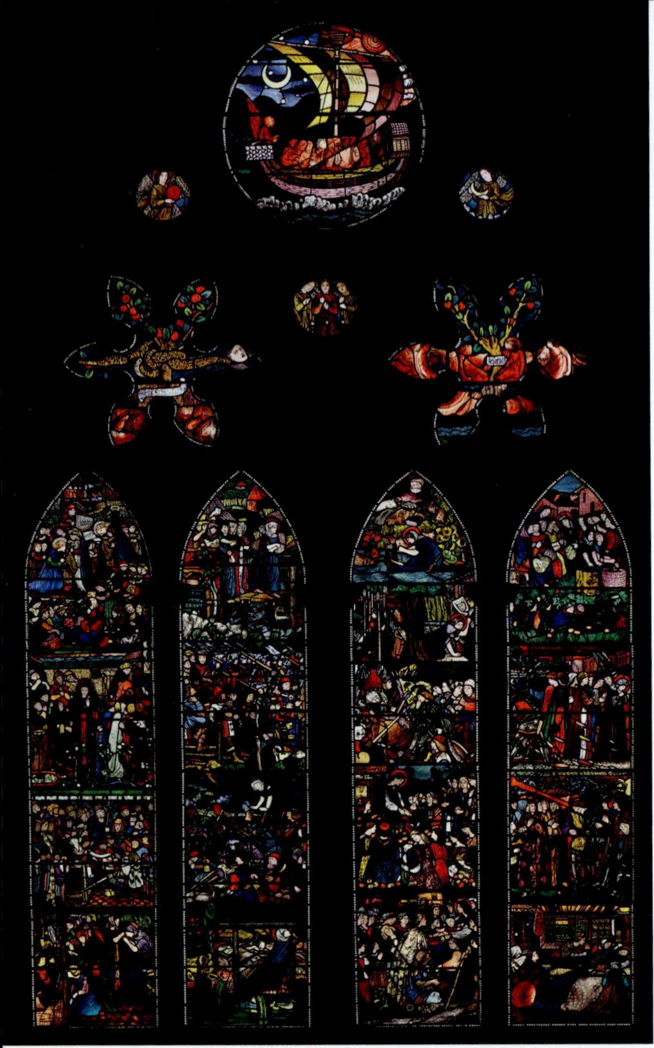

90. Oxford,
Christ
Church,
Cathedral,
Latin
Chapel,
E window,
stained glass
by Edward
Burne-Jones,
made by
Powells,
1860 (p. 127)

91. Oxford,
St Barnabas,
by Arthur
Blomfield,
1868–9,
interior,
(p. 391)

92. Oxford, No. 62 Banbury Road (Kellogg College), by E. G. Bruton, 1864–5 (p. 463)
93. Oxford, No. 29 Banbury Road, by J. J. Stevenson, 1880–1 (p. 460)

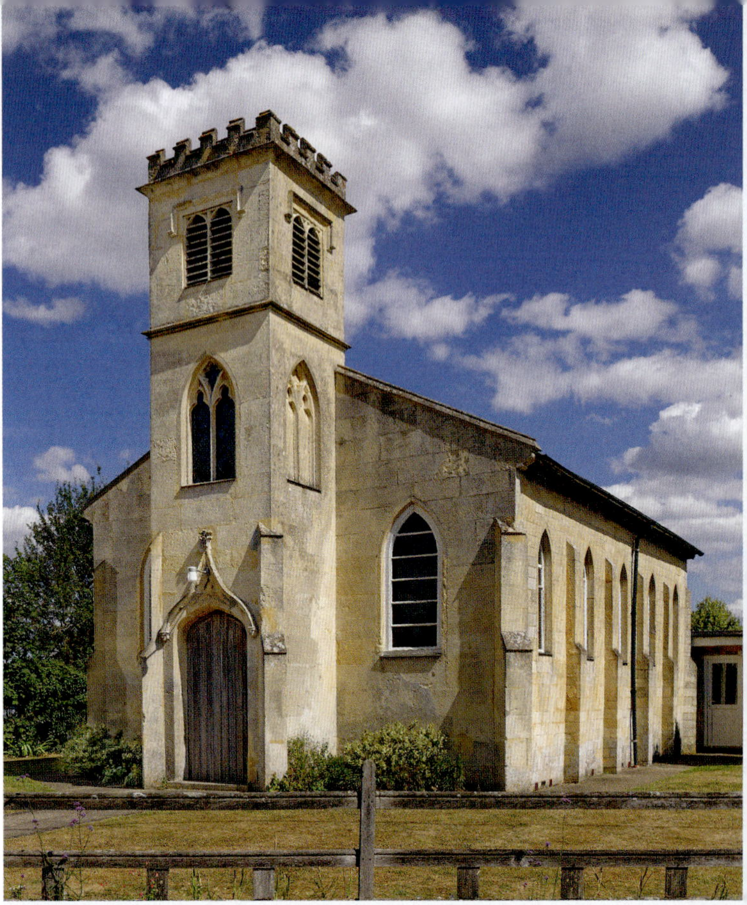

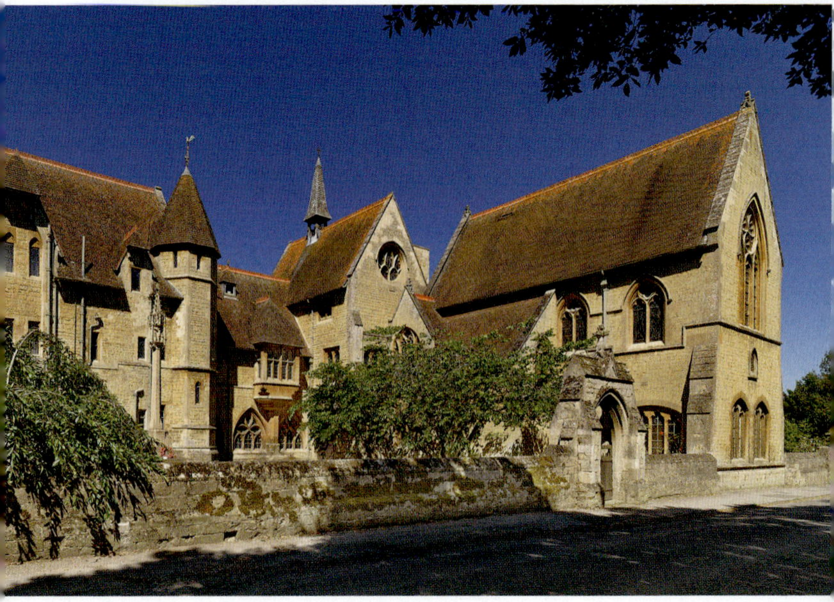

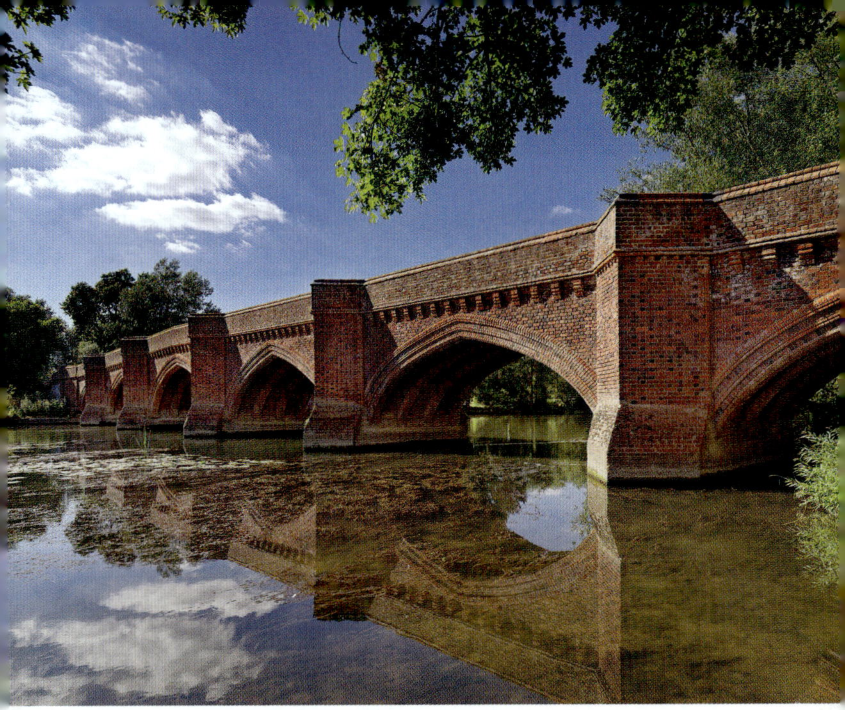

94. Binfield Heath, Congregational chapel, 1835 (p. 590)
95. Cuddesdon, Ripon College Cuddesdon, by G.E. Street, 1853–4 and 1874–5 (p. 614)
96. Clifton Hampden, bridge, by G.G. Scott, with Homfray, engineer, 1864 (p. 610)
97. Rotherfield Peppard, Wyfold Court, by G. Somers Clarke, 1873–6, garden front (p. 716)

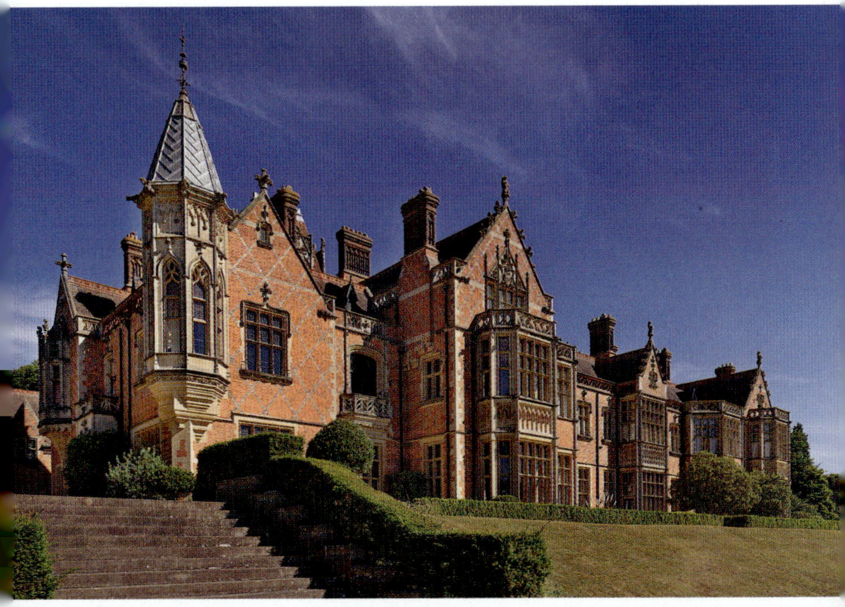

94 | 96
95 | 97

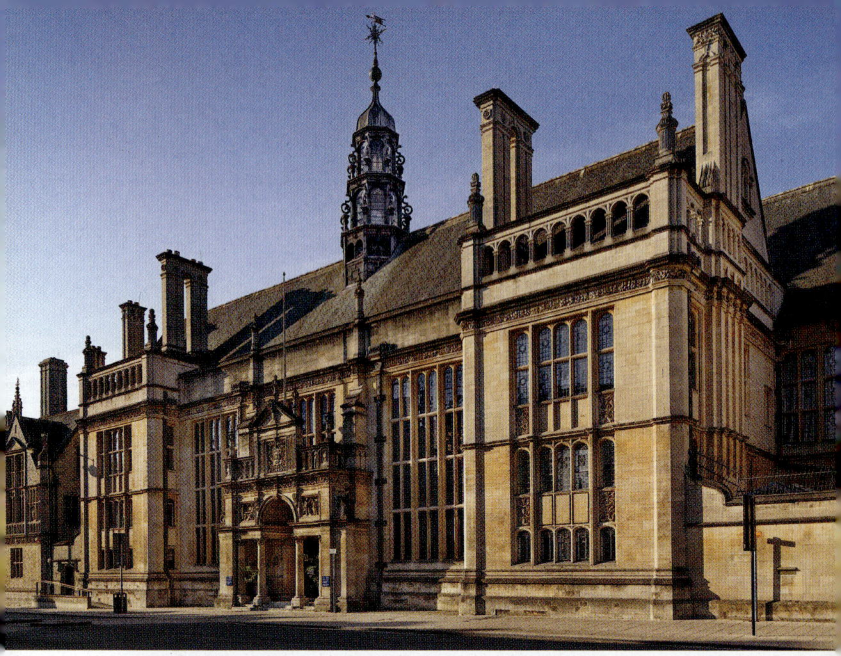

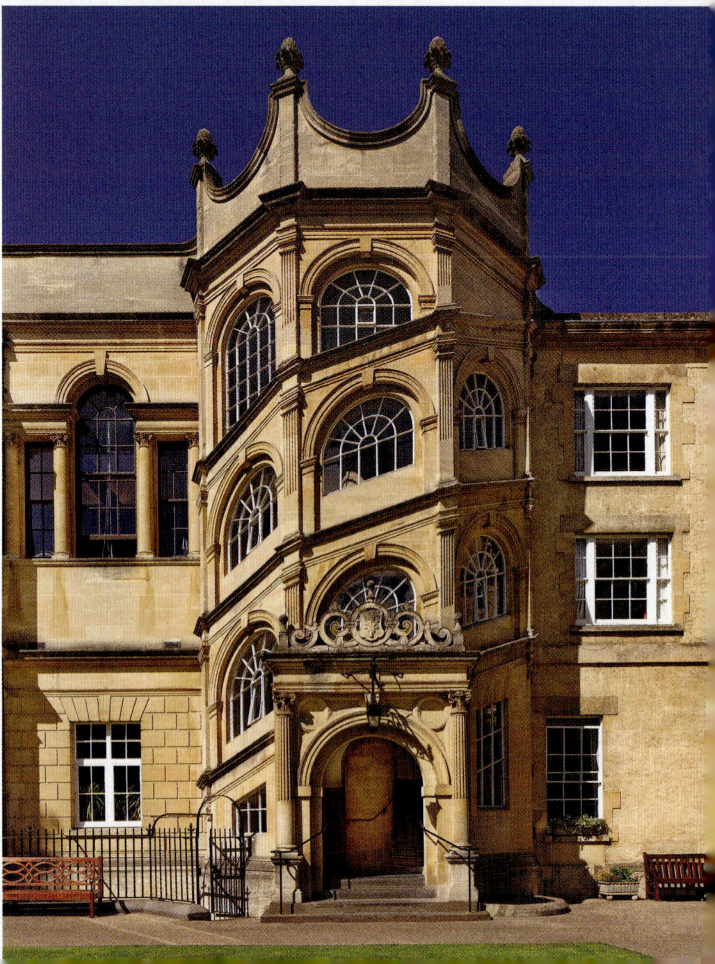

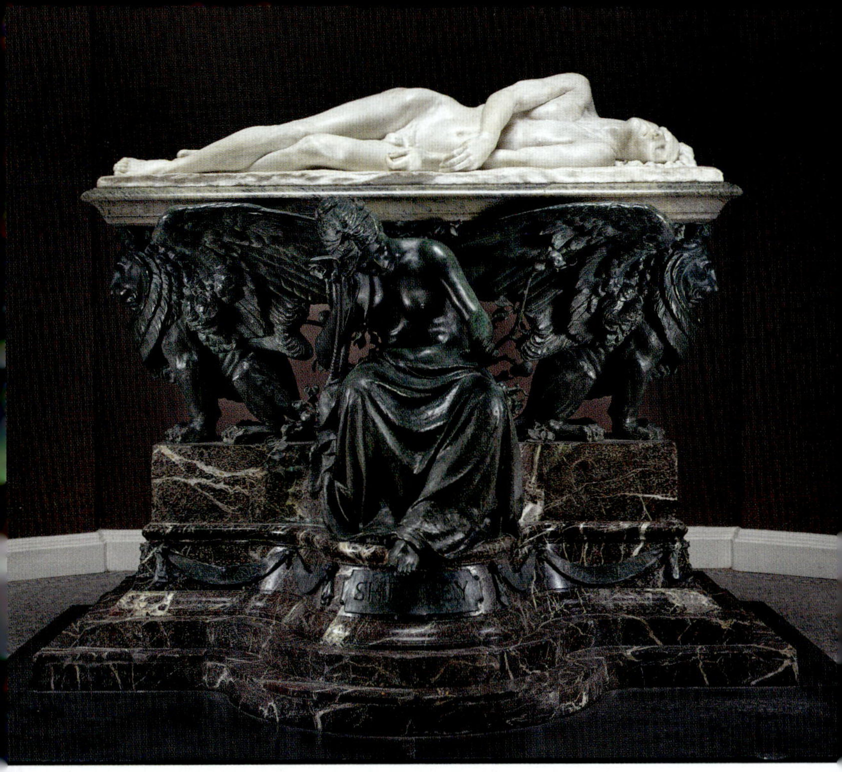

98. Oxford, Examination Schools, by T.G. Jackson, 1877–82 (p. 345)
99. Oxford, Hertford College, Old Buildings Quad, stair-tower, by T.G. Jackson, 1887–8 (p. 157)
100. Oxford, University College, Shelley Memorial, by E. Onslow Ford, 1892–3 (p. 304)
101. Oxford, Town Hall, by Henry T. Hare, 1893–7, Main Hall (p. 404)

98 | 100
99 | 101

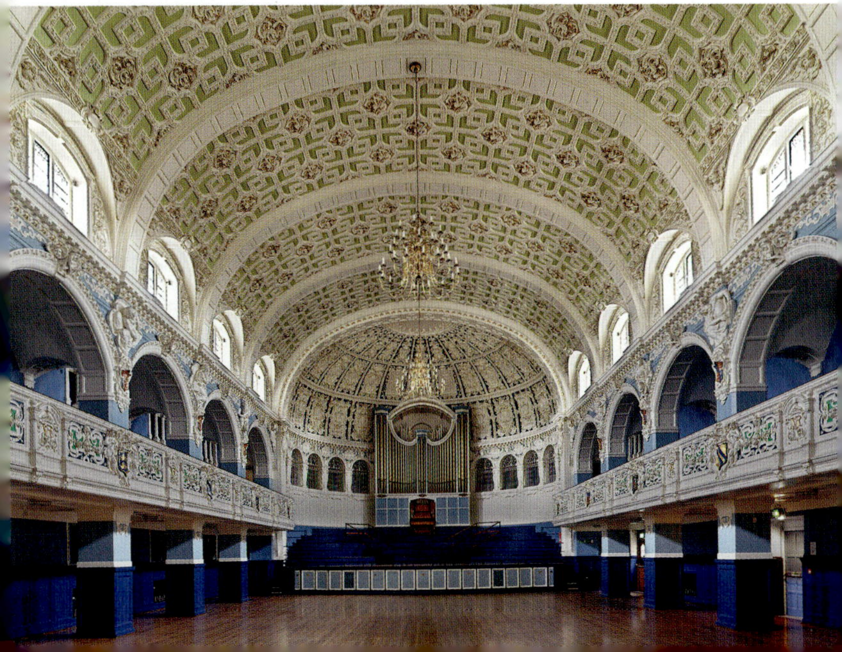

102. Oxford, Central Boys' School (former), by Leonard Stokes, 1900–1 (p. 439)
103. Oxford, Frank Cooper factory (former), by Herbert Quinton, 1903 (p. 443)
104. Oxford, Lady Margaret Hall, Wordsworth (l.), 1896, Talbot (c.), 1909–10, and Toynbee (r.), 1914–15, all by Sir Reginald Blomfield (pp. 171–2)

105. Goring Heath, Flint House, by Ernest Newton, 1913, garden front (p. 649)
106. Oxford, St John's Home, chapel, by Sir Ninian Comper, 1905–7, interior
    (p. 493)

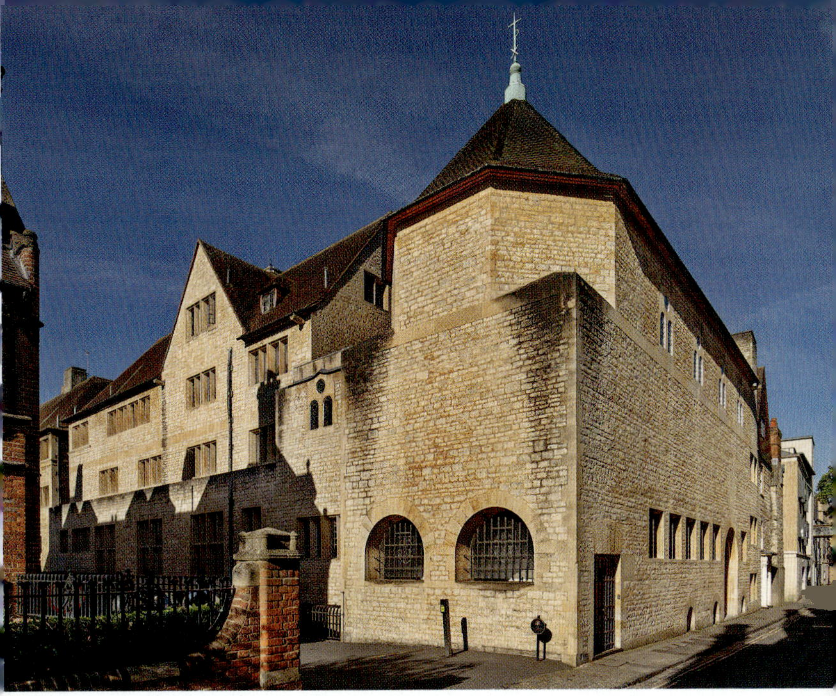

107. Oxford, Lady Margaret Hall, chapel, by Sir Giles Gilbert Scott, 1931–2 (p. 172)
108. Oxford, Holywell Manor, mural, by Gilbert Spencer, 1934–6 (p. 420)
109. Oxford, New Theatre, 1933–4, interior, by T. P. Bennett & Son (p. 438)
110. Oxford, Campion Hall, by Sir Edwin Lutyens, 1934–6 (p. 325)
111. Oxford, Regent's Park College, main quad and hall, by T. H. Hughes, 1938–40 (p. 326)

107	110
108	111
109	

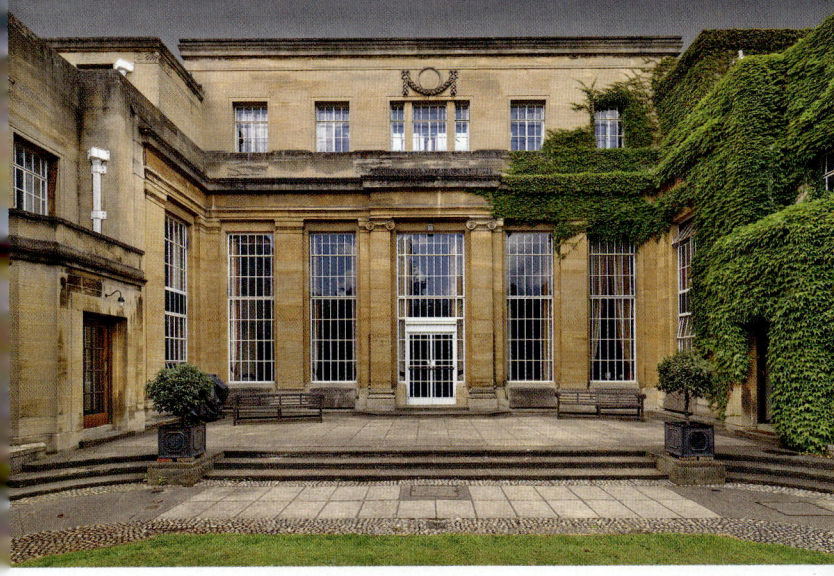

112. Oxford, Nuffield College, by Austen Harrison with Thomas Barnes and Pearce Hubbard, 1949–58 (p. 223)

113. Oxford, New College, chapel, Lazarus sculpture, by Sir Jacob Epstein, 1949–51 (p. 214)

114. Oxford, St John's College, 'Beehives', by the Architects' Co-Partnership, 1958–60 (p. 280)

115. Oxford, Somerville College, Vaughan and Margery Fry & Elisabeth Nuffield House, by Sir Philip Dowson of Arup Associates, 1958–66 (p. 290)

| 112 | 114 |
| 113 | 115 |

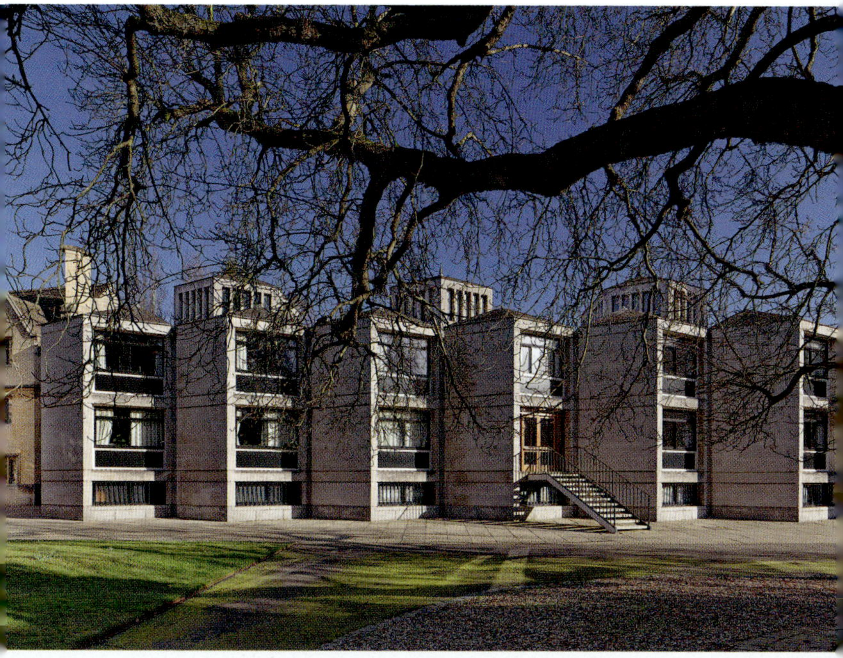

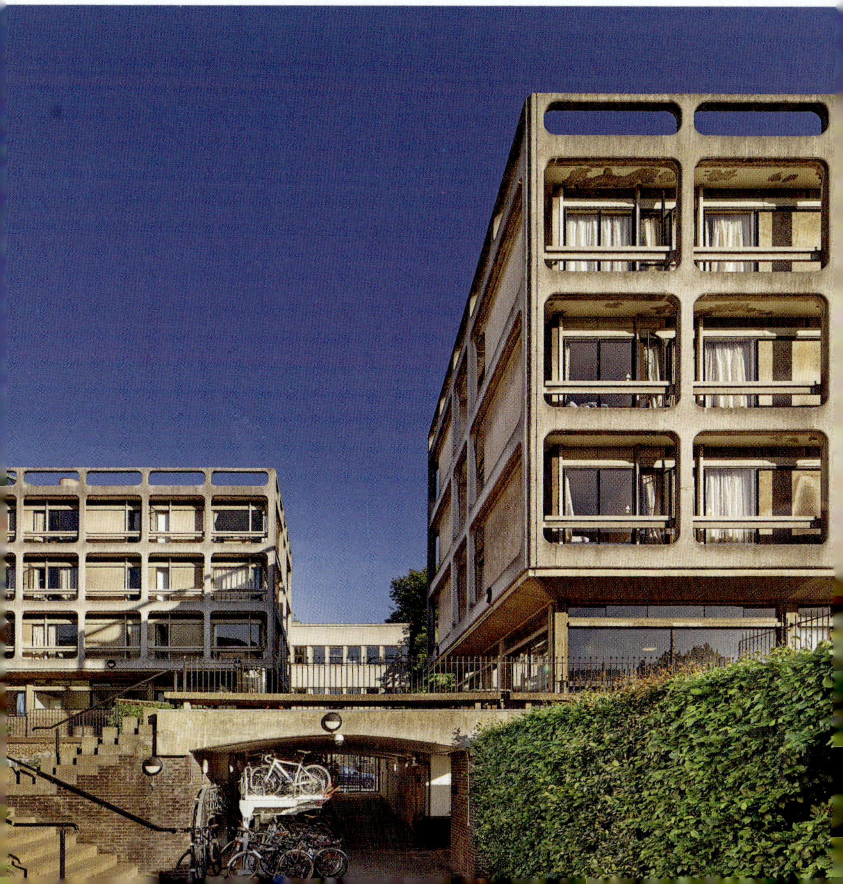

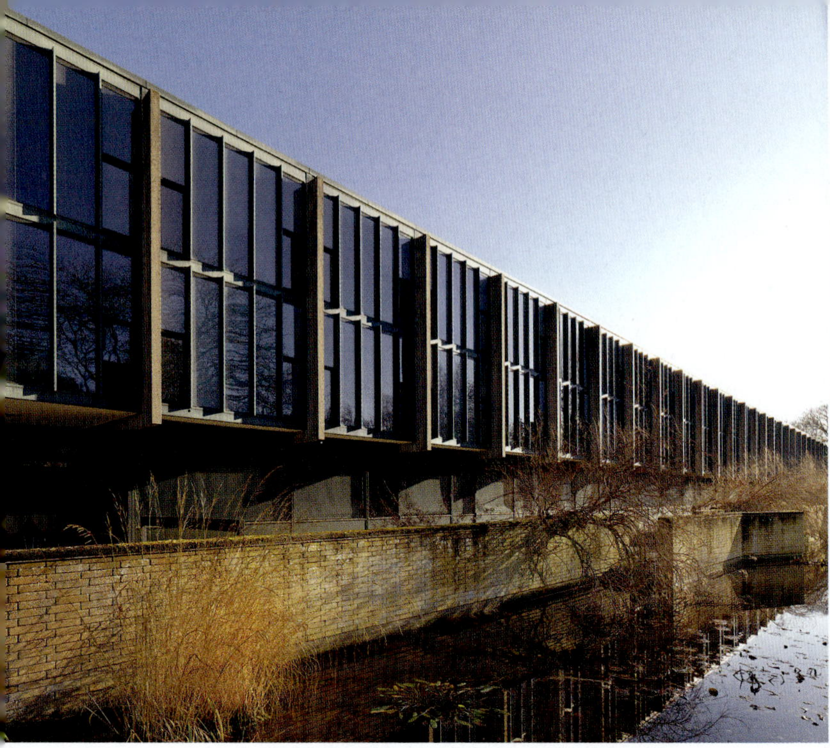

116. Oxford, St Catherine's College, by Arne Jacobsen, 1960–4 (p. 253)
117. Henley-on-Thames, Past Field, by Patrick Gwynne, 1959–60 (p. 678)
118. Oxford, St Cross Building, by Sir Leslie Martin and Colin St John Wilson, 1961–4 (p. 382)
119. Oxford, St Antony's College, Hilda Besse Building, by Howell, Killick, Partridge & Amis, 1968–70, hall interior (p. 250)

116 | 118
117 | 119

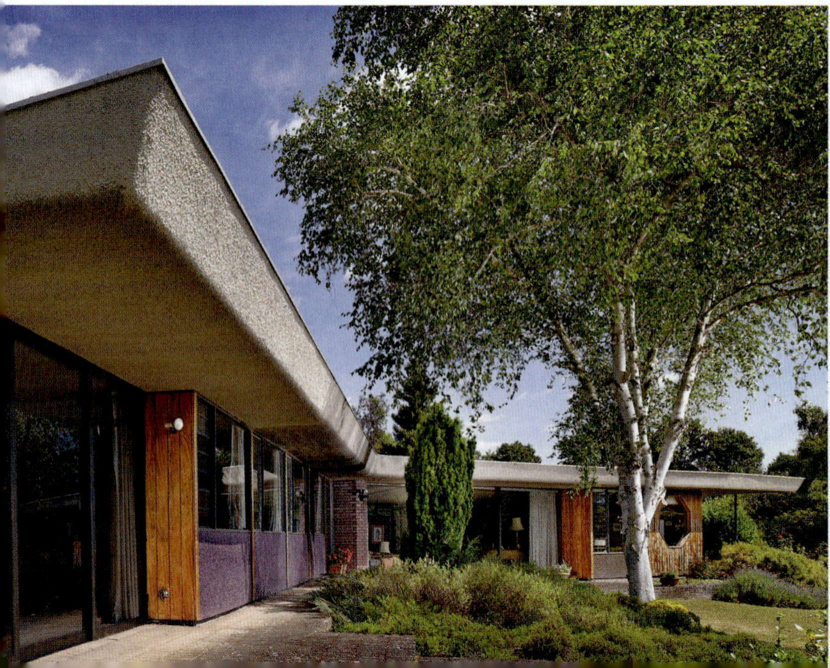

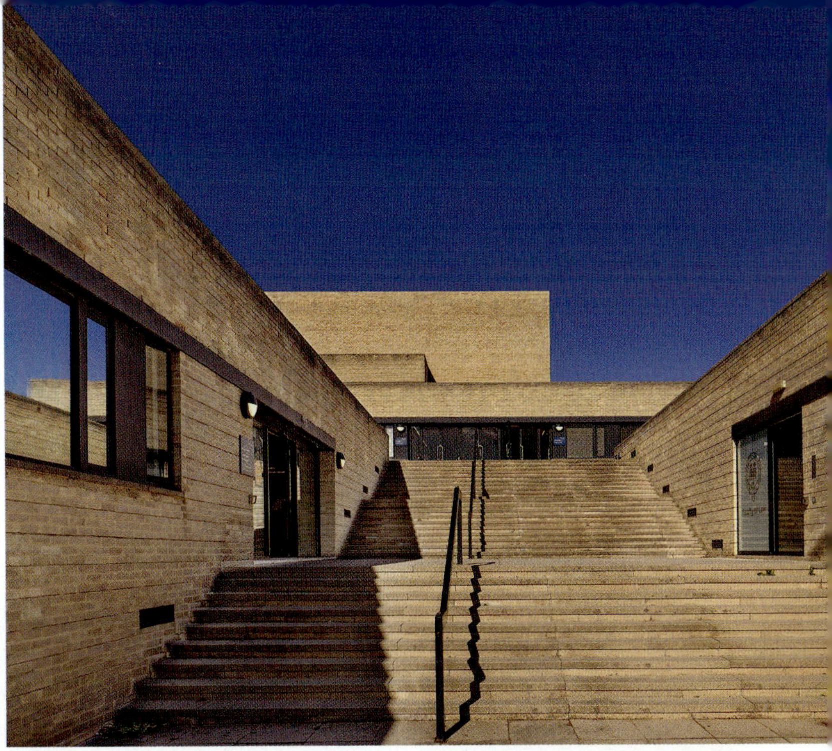

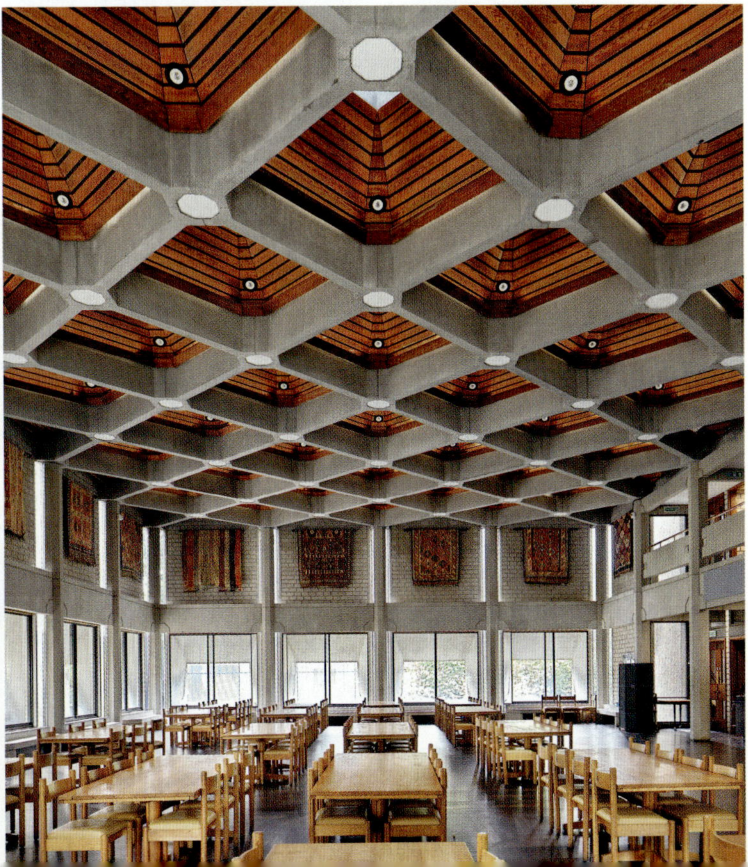

120. Oxford, Wolfson College, by Powell & Moya, 1968–74, River Quad (p. 315)

121. Oxford, Keble College, De Breyne Quad and Hayward Quad, by Ahrends, Burton & Koralek, 1970–7 (p. 169)

122. Oxford, Worcester College, Sainsbury Building, by MacCormac, Jamieson & Prichard, 1980–3 (p. 323)

123. Oxford, Sackler Library, by Robert Adam Architects, 1997–2001 (pp. 356–7)

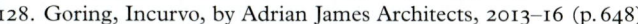

127. Cuddesdon, Ripon College Cuddesdon, Edward King Chapel, by Níall
     McLaughlin Architects, 2011–13, interior (pp. 615–16)
128. Goring, Incurvo, by Adrian James Architects, 2013–16 (p. 648)

129. Oxford, Beecroft Building, by Hawkins/Brown, 2015–18, interior (p. 373)
130. Oxford, St John's College, Study Centre, by Wright & Wright, 2014–19 (p. 281)

Two chunky yellow brick-faced blocks set at an angle. Open ground floor, open staircase. The terrace in front looks like part of the intended riverside walkway.

At the end of St Clement's Street is LONDON PLACE, by the start of Marston Road and Headington Road. A terrace of houses not uniform, but of a generally Late Georgian character. The only slightly more ambitious ones are Nos. 11–13, of one bay each with giant pilasters with sunk panels. Other houses Gothic brick, of 1875 etc.; more of these in GLEBE STREET, S, c.1885. MORRELL AVENUE runs SE here, made 1929–31. Mostly council houses (architect *H. Kellett Ablett*, under *J.F. Richardson*, City Engineer), but at the start also Nos. 2–12, a formal Neo-Wren composition dated 1932, built for sale. They face SOUTH PARK, which has on the Headington Road side a PILLAR of 1935 commemorating the acquisition of the park. It is by *Eric Gill*.

OUTER OXFORD

OUTER OXFORD: NORTH

PLACES OF WORSHIP

ST ANDREW, Linton Road. 1906–7 by *A. R. G. Fenning*; North Oxford's one Evangelical parish church. Norman, of all the improbable styles. Rock-faced (Stamford stone), large and rather mechanical-looking. Along the front a pentise-like addition of 1985–90 by *Maguire & Murray*, with offices etc. They also completed Fenning's front symmetrically, where a NW tower had been intended. Aisles of compound piers with waterleaf capitals and cross-arches. False vault to the nave. Cedar-panelled apse with rich STAINED GLASS by *Powells* (*W. Aikman*). Major additions by *MEB Design* to the S, 2013–15: two storeys with meeting rooms and a hall, separated from the church by a linear atrium and gallery.

ST MARGARET, St Margaret's Road. 1883–91 by *H.G.W. Drinkwater*, but the SW porch-tower by *Bodley*, 1898–1902. The tower was never continued. The porch with its inner transverse arch dying into the walls is ashlar, the rest is rock-faced. The style is *c.*1300–30, turning early Perp for the W window. Lofty aisled interior, with a large SE chapel. Chancel arch or division of oak rather than stone, the chief unconventional feature. Vestries to the NE, built integrally with the VICARAGE, 1908–9.

Lavish FURNISHINGS. The ROOD SCREEN is by *Bodley* (gates 1896, rood 1904–7). Cresting added 1915. – PULPIT, small, Perp, with a tester, also by *Bodley*. – REREDOS and AUMBRY by *C.G. Hare*, 1908. The aumbry has fine, embellished Gothic doors, rather Spanish, and painted figures within; the reredos is of wood, with many painted and gilt statues and a Nativity scene. – Elaborate REREDOSES in the S chapel, by *Hare*, 1925, and N aisle, by *F.E. Howard*, *c.*1930. Also a brought-in reredos, S chapel, looking C18 French, with an oval painting of Virgin and sleeping Child. – FONT with elaborate timber cover, 1913–14, again by *Hare*. – CHANDELIER of brass from Cuckfield church, Sussex, given 1891. – STAINED GLASS mostly by *F.C. Eden*, in a variety of styles, dating from *c.*1900 to at least as late as 1935; the earlier windows made by *James Fisher* (†1915). Also chancel N by *Bell & Beckham*, 1886, and several clerestory windows by *Burlison & Grylls*, *c.*1907. – MONUMENT. Capt. Edgar Hester †1917. A statue of St Martin, 1920, designed by *Hare*. – WAR MEMORIAL W of the porch, 1919–20. A Calvary in a free-standing shelter.

ST MICHAEL AND ALL ANGELS, Lonsdale Road, Summertown. 1908–9 by *A. Mardon Mowbray*. Conservative C13-style Gothic. Only chancel, transepts, S chapel and one nave bay were built, all large enough. Mowbray also projected a SW tower with an open crown spire. Two bays to each transept; the arcades run high across them inside. The S chapel E window has mullions rising from carved angels like hammerposts, a Burgesian throwback. Narthex with kitchen, toilets etc. added by *Adrian James Architects*, 2014–18, of brick. The low, elliptical volume, with a copper drum around its central roof-light, redeems the makeshift W front. – FONT, probably the one provided by *Street* in 1857 when he enlarged the predecessor church (St John, 1831–3, by *H.J. Underwood*). – Hanging ROOD GROUP, 1949. – STAINED GLASS. E window by *J.C. Bewsey*, 1922, Christ in Majesty, with French and English saints. S chapel, two by *Christopher Webb*, 1934 and †1937; another †1930, probably by *C.C. Townshend & Joan Howson*.

St Philip and St James.
Engraving by O. Jewitt & Co., 1872

ST PHILIP AND ST JAMES (former), Woodstock Road. Since
1986 the OXFORD CENTRE FOR MISSION STUDIES. 1860–2
by *Street*; the steeple 1864–6. The builder was *Joseph Castle*. St
Philip and St James was to be the parish church for the new
Gothic North Oxford, and hence is a big church of considerable ambition. Street's is not an engaging but a very powerful
design. It is in the C13 style, then accepted as the ecclesiastical
ideal, but Street uses lancets predominantly, and lancets in
the way he handled them made for severity; so does the plate
tracery which he preferred to the more widely favoured late
C13 Geometrical tracery. Take the commanding tower above
the chancel with its big bold paired lancet bell-openings. (This
is one of only two cruciform churches by Street with a central

tower, with the much later Kingston in Dorset.) The tower is oblong, and has a spire with very large broaches and one set of large lucarnes starting at a level that overlaps the tops of the broaches. Street gave the w front lancets and a rose window over, the N transept lancets and an almond-shaped window over, the apse plate tracery, and the s transept alone a large and elaborate rose. The aisles have small cusped lancets, but the clerestory an alternation of lancets with plate tracery and large quatrefoils – the only busy motif. All the walls are hammer-dressed, with bands of red sandstone: an Italian motif, although the accent of the rest is French.

The nave is wide, and its width appears even greater because the arcades are very widely spaced. There are only four bays, with round piers of polished pink Aberdeenshire granite and very big capitals of the French Early Gothic foliage type, carved by *Earp*. Here lies really a statement of principle – maximum visibility of the altar, not of the parson or the pulpit. The bend-in of the E bays of the arcades was meant to increase this focus on the chancel. The effect is most odd from the outside; this was much objected to at the time, as was the lack of relation between clerestory windows and nave arcades. A man like, say, Scott would not have done that, nor the unconventional arcade spacing. The roof is pointed, with stencilled and painted boards, above horizontal ties with kingposts. In the transepts and apse there is more conventional rib-vaulting and plenty of black Devonshire marble shafts, looking like Purbeck marble, and shaft-rings. The s transept was enlarged in a gentler spirit in 1920–1 by *Sir Charles Nicholson*. He added the small apse and the twin openings from the s aisle. Advent Chapel, N side, converted from the original vestry; NE vestry 1876–7, extended 1912.

FURNISHINGS, now mixed in with the Mission Centre's things. REREDOS by *Street*, carved by *Earp*, and altered with new frames in 1884 by *Burlison & Grylls*. – Also by *Street* the STALLS, LECTERN, PULPIT (carved by *Earp* too), FONT and FONT COVER (1867). – TILES by *Minton* in the apse. – COMMUNION RAILS, 1899 by *F.C. Eden*, late C17 style; also the chancel FLOOR. – ROOD. 1896 by *Micklethwaite & Clarke*. Added figures by *Laurence King*, 1960. – WAR MEMORIAL over the vestry door. 1921, designed by *Nicholson*. – STAINED GLASS. Apse, by *Clayton & Bell*, 1861–74. Aisles, 1865 etc., by the same. By *Burlison & Grylls* the s transept lancets, 1884–90, the clerestory and the s transept rose of 1912, after Van Eyck's Adoration of the Lamb (PC). Nave w windows, *Kempe*, 1905–6. – Timber MEETING ROOM at the w end by *Robert Franklin*, c.1992, with upper level by *Andrew Stone*, c.2010.

ST GREGORY AND ST AUGUSTINE (R.C.), No. 322 Woodstock Road. Arts and Crafts work by *Ernest Newton*, 1911–12. Commissioned by Charles Robertson of Field House, to the E, where Newton also worked (p. 471), and meant to revert to use as a hall once a new church was built in front. A small

white-rendered rectangle with a cupola. W window with a
gently curved head. Plaster tunnel-vault inside with tie-beams.
Newton's pleasingly simple FURNISHINGS were enhanced in
2008–10 by *James Gillick*'s PAINTINGS on the reredos, saints in
an uncannily convincing Spanish C17 style. – PARISH ROOMS
behind by *Sandy & Norris*, 1949.

HOLY TRINITY AND ANNUNCIATION (Greek Orthodox),
Canterbury Road. By *Ganter & Kershaw*, 1972–3. Enigmatic.
Octagonal, of yellow brick, with lower attachments to E and W.

SUMMERTOWN UNITED REFORMED CHURCH (formerly Con-
gregational), Banbury Road. 1893–4, designed by its builder
T.H. Kingerlee. Red brick, Perp W window. E extension and
HALL by *F. W. Troup*, 1909–10, with Free Style touches.

UNIVERSITY BUILDINGS

EWERT HOUSE (now Department for Continuing Education),
Ewert Place, off Banbury Road. 1963–5 by *J. Lankester*, University Surveyor, with extensions. Two-storeyed, of yellow
brick, with canted corners. Repeated tall windows between
slim brick piers. Replacement proposed.

KELLOGG COLLEGE, Banbury Road. *See* Perambulation 1,
p.463.

WYCLIFFE HALL, Banbury Road. *See* Perambulation 1, p.462.

SCHOOLS

CHERWELL SCHOOL, Marston Ferry Road. A former secondary
modern, its main building by *D. Murray*, City Architect,
1960–3. Curtain walling and brick.

D'OVERBROECKS' SCHOOL, Banbury Road. *See* p.470.

OXFORD HIGH SCHOOL, Belbroughton Road. An independent
girls' school, relocated from No.21 Banbury Road (p.430)
to *Ramsey, Murray, White & Ward*'s curtain-walled complex of
1955–7. The low courtyard range, W, was partly rebuilt in 2011
with a new entrance, linked to an assembly hall, refectory
etc. All by *GDST Property Department*, Estates Director *Zoe
Smith*. (SCULPTURE in the court, *Epstein*'s Deirdre, 1957. A
bronze bust with arms.) To the E, the ADA BENSON BUILD-
ING, 2017–20 by *Ellis Williams Architects*. Long and low, with a
diagonal plan which is bisected by a concourse aligned NE–SW.
The cladding is silvery stainless steel, with a pierced openwork
parapet formed by angled strips that continue as an irregular
pattern on the walls below.

ST EDWARD'S SCHOOL, Woodstock Road and South Parade.
A public school, founded in 1863 by the Rev. Thomas Chamberlain, vicar of St Thomas's. The school moved to its present
site in 1873. The original buildings around the central quad
are by *Wilkinson*, followed by *Wilkinson & Moore*. They are
of red brick and of course Gothic, of the type of Wilkinson's
North Oxford houses. The MAIN BUILDING (1872–3; now

APSLEY) is on the N side, a long three-storey range, just a little asymmetrical. Dormitories on the upper floors. Flat-roofed front extension of 1928–9 by *Herbert Kitchin*. The Warden's Lodging in the W wing was enlarged in 1886. On the W side is the broad GATEHOUSE of 1879, on the E side BIG SCHOOL and the OLD LIBRARY of 1880–1, with an open cloister below. The cloister runs N to join the school's spectacular CHAPEL of 1873–7, in the NE corner. It is of rock-faced stone, mostly with lancet windows, and has an apse. Steep arch-braced roof, and a SW tower the size of a substantial church tower, with a spire and four spirelets also of stone. The whole has something of Pearson's Anglo-French manner. (Impressive interior, the walls below the high windows originally left bare for intended decoration, *à la* Keble chapel. The apse lancets are shafted. Stained glass: apse and nave S by *Kempe*, 1882 onwards; nave N window by *Herbert Bryans*, 1910, also two by *Christopher Webb*, 1937.) CALVARY to the S outside, a war memorial by *H.S. Rogers*, 1919, carved by *Alec Miller*.)

On the S side of the quad, to the W, is MACNAMARA'S HOUSE, by *Wilkinson & Moore*, 1882. Work then stalled until 1924–5, when TILLY'S HOUSE by *H.S. Rogers*, still Gothico-Tudor, was added to the E. Next, the typically late turn to Neo-Georgian: the WORK BLOCK (Class Building) by *Brook Kitchin*, 1931, eight bays long. COWELL'S HOUSE further E, a twenty-one-bay range of 1936 by the same, is Neo-Georgian too. Between these blocks and also of red brick is the CHRISTIE CENTRE, part of an ambitious and responsive complex of 2016–20 by *TSH Architects*. The N–S section joins a taller cross-range, placed end-on to the quad. Here it appears as a steep gable-end of evenly spaced concrete uprights, rather in a Níall McLaughlin mode, with full-height glazing behind the upper floors. The top-storey reading room has a bold exposed roof structure of laminated timber, with top lighting along the ridge. A plain cloister links up with Big School to the N, behind which appears one end of the OLIVIER HALL, a big oval volume faced in plain stone and ringed by windows at the height of its upper balcony. A ground-floor foyer joins the hall to the buildings to the S and W.

Many other buildings, including some in the surrounding streets. *Fielding Dodd & Stevens*'s former MEMORIAL LIBRARY, between the Olivier Hall and the chapel, shows Neo-Georgian still current in 1953–4. Immediately to its E is ART, DESIGN AND TECHNOLOGY by *Schofield & Partners*, 1986–8, with a clerestory in its shallow-pitched roof. Along the drive S of the main quad, the W range of PHYSICAL SCIENCES, added in 1956–7 by *Brett, Boyd & Bosanquet*, marks the arrival of Modernism. BIOLOGY, next E, is by *TSH Architects*, 2006–8. Finally two buildings in South Parade, placed for ease of public access. On the main school site is the NORTH WALL ARTS CENTRE. Of 2003–6 by *Haworth Tompkins*, architects with a distinguished record in reworking older arts buildings with sensitivity to materials and textures. Here the starting point was the school's swimming baths of 1887–8 (the red brick structure to the w, now the auditorium), and the adjacent squared-rubble boundary wall through which the new entrance is made. The added part (dance studio, gallery etc.) has a roof slope which rises to a slightly higher ridge. Walls faced in shingles and plain slats of oak, with a few big, stark windows. One of these lights the foyer, which has finishes of polished concrete and coloured plywood panels. Opposite is the OGSTON MUSIC SCHOOL, 2014–17 by *Tim Ronalds Architects*. A long N–S range of red brick, fronting the street with a handsomely plain four-bay return with flush stone dressings.

Other school houses are in a cluster on FIELD SIDE, amid the playing fields W of Woodstock Road. CORFE HOUSE, with a broad tile-hung gable towards the road, is by *Moore*, 1890. To the W is a quadrangle of which the N and W ranges (SING'S and FIELD HOUSE) are by *Sir Robert Matthew, Johnson-Marshall & Partners*, 1963–5. The N side has boxed-out bays and oriels with canted glass tops and canted sills – decidedly mannered. Completing the quad, the *Architects Design Partnership*'s L-shaped KENDALL, 1989–91. Separately treated pavilions at the angle and the ends, echoing the 1960s composition. To either side, facing S, JUBILEE HOUSE (2012–13) and the co-educational COOPER LODGE (2018–20). Both by *TSH Architects*, both of pale brick, the latter with sharp-gabled cross-wings. *John Pawson*'s PAVILION of 2008–9, in the SW corner of the playing fields, is by contrast studiedly horizontal.

WYCHWOOD SCHOOL, Banbury Road. *See* Perambulation 1, p.464.

CUTTESLOWE PRIMARY SCHOOL, Wren Road. 1939. Red brick. Flat roofs, and a tall chimney treated as a streamlined feature.

DRAGON SCHOOL (preparatory), Bardwell Road. The original parts are of 1894–5, by *Charles Lynam* of Stoke-on-Trent, whose son was headmaster: the W part of the LODGE, and the OLD HALL in the NW angle of the main quadrangle. Plain brick, white-painted sashes. Of the remainder, the E range comprises *Pinckheard & Partners*' gym of 1970 at the N end, sharply detailed brick with a thin clerestory, and *MEB Partnership*'s block of *c.*1992 for art, design etc., fancier, with an octagonal SE tower. On the N side of the road, set back, the BOARDING HOUSE of 1909–10. *Lynam* again, in a more explicit 1700 style, but using the butterfly plan then fashionable for superior villas.

SUMMER FIELDS SCHOOL (preparatory), Mayfield Road. Named from a villa of 1820 at the S end of the site, heightened and much extended both before and after 1864, when the school took over. Early additions include CLASSROOMS of 1888 and the CHAPEL of 1896, long and low blocks placed parallel and to the N, Jacobean and Gothic respectively. (Stained glass in the chapel by *Holiday*, 1897 and 1913.) On the street side, W, the former GYM and the HALL perpendicular to it, plain red and yellow brick, early C20. Incorporated to the N here is the former ST GILES' WORKHOUSE of 1824. Plain stone, pedimental gable. Six bays plus a central blind bay. Directly behind it is the ART DEPARTMENT, and further E the SPORTS HALL, pitched-roof designs by *Oxford Architects Partnership*, 1990–5. The latter has a more demonstrative S addition (SALATA PAVILION) of 2014–15 by *BBLB Architects*, its SE corner treated as a glass-walled quadrant. Notable among the free-standing buildings is the Neoclassical BEECH HOUSE (headmaster's house) to the N, 1971–2 by *Francis Johnson*, most of whose works are in his native Yorkshire. A full-width pediment with a plain lunette across each end.

PERAMBULATIONS

Most of quintessential 'North Oxford' – the area developed largely by St John's College in the years after the mid C19 – can be explored in two consecutive perambulations, starting on Banbury Road and returning S down Woodstock Road (Perambulation 2, p. 466).

1. Banbury Road, Norham Manor and Park Town

The University and the colleges having rebuilt so much of the southern fringe, the North Oxford character does not appear in strength until some way up BANBURY ROAD. The place to start is the junction with Parks Road, 300 yds N of St Giles' church. On the W side, Nos. 27 and 29 were the first true 'Queen Anne' houses in Oxford, a splendid pair of 1880–1 by *J. J. Stevenson*; for the philosopher T. H. Green, and for Thomas Omond, bursar of St John's and brother-in-law to the architect. Red brick with richer moulded and rubbed-brick dressings, crowning balconies, and window frames of wood, white-painted. The quality and sophistication of these in comparison with other North Oxford houses is striking. No. 29 is now the Principal's Lodgings of St Anne's College, adjacent (p. 246). Opposite are the University Parks' gate and North Lodge (p. 378).

From this point Norham Gardens begins its gentle curve N and E. It marks the entrance to the NORHAM MANOR ESTATE, laid out by *William Wilkinson* from 1860, and still largely intact. Stringent regulations forbade roughcast or cemented exteriors and high boundary walls between the plots, and demanded high standards of workmanship and sanitation. An early perspective for the estate included Italianate villas as well as Gothic ones, but Wilkinson as overseer came with the bias generally felt at that time in Oxford for modern Gothic, and Gothic of a kind remained the predominant style in the area well into the 1870s. All this contributes to the atmosphere of leafy sobriety. The houses of these years have much in common. They are all large, mostly raised on half-basements, and steep-gabled. The red or yellow brick is set off by prominent stone dressings in nearly every case, with a passion for stop-chamfers, and columns with carved capitals where a little more was to be offered; the early ones are particularly severe.

NORHAM GARDENS, the first new road made on the estate, is of special interest. The villas on its S SIDE are exceptionally grand and generously spaced, with bay windows to the rear. Originally they enjoyed direct views over the Parks, as is less apparent now that the trees have grown up and so many of the gaps between have been diminished by extension or infill. The process began in the later C19 and early C20, with the addition or enlargement of reception rooms etc. Colleges, convents and University bodies also took over a good few of the houses, and further building followed. Yet not one house has been lost. No. 1 is by *Wilkinson*, 1864–5, red brick, double its original size. No. 3, by *Charles Buckeridge*, 1865–6, is yellow brick, with some elaborate Dec tracery. W additions by *H. G. W. Drinkwater*, 1895. No. 5 (1863–5) and No. 7 (1860–2 and 1867) are again *Wilkinson*'s, the latter remodelled and made larger still in 2015. No. 9, for the historian Professor Montagu Burrows, is the most characterful house: by *Buckeridge*, 1862–3, red brick, stern and ecclesiastical in mood, with plate tracery at front and back and a half-tourelle on the W side. *Wilkinson*'s No. 11 (1866–7) has clumsy post-war extensions, initially for use as a hostel for St Anne's students. No. 13 (1868–70), also by *Wilkinson* and originally the road's largest house, was admired and illustrated by Viollet-le-Duc, together with others of Wilkinson's works. NW addition dated 1879. Extended further and classicized internally by *N. W. & G. A. Harrison* in 1906–7 for Professor Sir William Osler, the physician. Beyond, Nos. 15–19 are by *Frederick Codd*, 1871–6, all Wilkinsonian in character. At No. 15 a NW wing was provided in 1888 by *Tollit*. Additions on the garden side for the Department of Educational Studies, chiefly an abruptly plain block by *J. Lankester*, University Surveyor, *c.* 1960. No. 17 served from 1887 as the first home of St Hugh's Hall (later college), for whom *H. W. Moore* extended it to the E in 1892. It later passed to St Stephen's House, responsible for *Stevens, Flavel & Beard*'s ugly E extension of *c.* 1963. Now a graduate colony of St Edmund Hall, as also is No. 19, with 1980s–90s additions between and behind. The pretty two-storey timbered addition at the SW corner of No. 19 is by *A. H. Moberly*, likewise the covered passage of 1915 to the W. This joins on to the simple former CHAPEL of St Hugh's Hall, 1909 by *N. W. & G. A. Harrison*. Then the gates of Lady Margaret Hall (p. 170).

On the N SIDE are more detached houses giving way to pairs. Nos. 2–8 and 14–18 are all by *Codd*, 1870–3; Nos. 20–30 by *George Shirley* (*Galpin & Shirley*), 1873–6. Behind No. 26 nine neat little terraced houses of 1975–7 by *Maguire & Murray*, for married students at St Stephen's House.

BRADMORE ROAD runs N from the W end of Norham Gardens, and continues its style. Houses of 1870–4, mostly *Codd* (Nos. 1–2, 13–17) or *Galpin & Shirley* (Nos. 7–12, 18–20). The Paters lived at No. 2 – they introduced *Morris* wallpapers to Oxford – and the Humphry Wards at No. 17. Post-Victorian additions include *Hyde & Hyde*'s awkward appendage of 2020 to No. 18, E side, and the less assertive expansion of No. 13 for New College graduates by *Oxford Architects Partnership*: S side 1973, E side, facing Norham Road, *c.* 1986. Otherwise No. 13 is typical *Codd*, with pointed surrounds to the upper windows and an attractive lean-to wooden porch.

NORHAM ROAD, with FYFIELD ROAD and CRICK ROAD to the S, is less exclusive, with pairs preponderant. Gothic detail gives way to debased Jacobean in places, in accordance with the later date of the houses, mostly *c.* 1874–84. An earlier group, opposite Bradmore Road, was demolished for the MAISON FRANÇAISE, 1965–7 by *Jacques Laurent* with *Brian Ring/Howard & Partners*. Crisp, elegant and not showy, well composed of various parts, very pale buff brick, with much plain wall. SCULPTURE on the front lawn, *Maillol*'s Flore, *c.* 1912. Of what remains in Norham Road, the highest score belongs to *Wilkinson* (Nos. 14–26, 30–35). Off its E end, in BENSON PLACE, are some tightly designed yellow brick terraces of two storeys by *Brett & Pollen*, 1966–7, with the integrated garden walls fashionable then.

Back to BANBURY ROAD, and S again, to where Norham Gardens begins. The E side here was the show front of the Norham Manor Estate, and includes some houses built to suit the whims of individual clients. The first two, Nos. 52 and 54, now belong to WYCLIFFE HALL, an Evangelical theological college founded in 1877. No. 52 is another typical *Codd* house, 1869. No. 54, by *John Gibbs*, 1867, is a high, round-arched-windowed house, built for the tutor Thomas Arnold Jun., son of Dr Arnold of Rugby, big enough to house his residential pupils. Storey bands of black brick or encaustic tiles. Slightly plainer additions for Wycliffe Hall: to NE, 1877–8 and later, and S, 1881 by *Wilkinson & Moore*, with a ground-floor lecture room. Between Nos. 52 and 54, in 1896, *William Wallace* added the Perp-style CHAPEL with its SW turret and linking corridors. The chapel was extended E probably *c.* 1906. In front of No. 54 a DINING HALL of 1912–13 (now lecture room), similarly low and Perp, by *A. R. G. Fenning*. A new dining hall was added behind in 1979–80, by *Peter Bosanquet & John Perryman Associates*. Wycliffe Hall became a Permanent Private Hall of the University in 1996.

No. 56 is WYKEHAM HOUSE, commissioned as a speculation by an Oxford draper, Henry Hatch. Also by *Gibbs*, 1865–6 (extensions 1884, S, and 1894, N, with tower), but quite different, a yellow brick nightmare castle with plate tracery, and statue of William of Wykeham by *W. Forsyth* of Worcester. Porch also of 1894; conservatory added by *Moore* in 1900, S. Rear addition for Oxford University Careers Service, 1992–3 (*D. W. Bending*, University Surveyor). No. 58 is again by *Gibbs*, 1865–6, back at the round-arched style which he called 'a development of the ancient Romanesque'. Darker brick than at No. 54, and more characterful, with solid window heads, cable-moulded and chamfered. In the garden is the University's PAULING CENTRE (Human Sciences), a modest pyramid-roofed building by *J. Lankester*, 1979–81.

KELLOGG COLLEGE, a graduate college of the University, occupies Nos. 60–64 and the buildings behind. The name and college status date from 1994, but the college has deeper roots in the C19 movement for wider access to the University, hence its previous home at Rewley House (p. 433). The present site was acquired in 2004. The HOUSES first. No. 60 is by *Wilkinson*, 1865–6, the only intact survivor of the four North Oxford villas published in his *English Country Houses* (1870 and 1875). Luckily it is his best; yellow brick, a cleverly balanced composition with a small tourelle just r. of the doorway and unusual capping to the roof on the l. Equally interesting is No. 62, 1864–5 by *E. G. Bruton*. Built for the Rev. R. St John Tyrwhitt   92 of Christ Church, artist, author and disciple of Ruskin, who helped Morris paint the original Union ceiling and did murals at the Museum (pp. 351 and 368). It is distinguished by the steep-gabled tympanum of the porch, carved with foliage, a seated king above a lion, a goat, a greyhound and two birds. The source is scriptural (Proverbs 30.29), but the mood is very close to that of the carving at the Museum.* Finally No. 64, 1868–9, also *Bruton*, but dull by comparison. Extended behind by *Gerald Horsley*, 1891. Of the ADDITIONS, the most notable is the DINING HALL behind Nos. 60–62. It originated as the major part of the Pitt Rivers Museum's former outstation, designed by *Lankester*; built in 1978, opened in 1986 (for the 1960s plans for the site *see* p. 369). Low, with a distinctive 'eggbox' roof of steep hipped and tiled roofs, rectangles rather than pyramids this time, in two rows of three. Deftly adapted in 2008 by *Berman Guedes Stretton*, with inserted full-height windows and slatted timber linings. Between Nos. 62 and 64, the HUB by *Feilden Clegg Bradley Studios*, 2015–17, providing a common room and café. A low, free-standing block, designed to 'Passivhaus' standards of energy efficiency. Red brick walls, thick roof of grey steel. Along the side of the roof a frieze of bifurcating forms like stylized trees. s side fully glazed behind a shallow colonnade. Paths extend behind to Nos. 7–12 Bradmore Road, also owned by the college. Last in the row of houses is No. 66, not part of the college. *Codd* again, 1869, with a tall turret. Parapets reinstated 1990. Neo-Georgian extension of 1959–61 by *Thomas Rayson* for Wolsey Hall, sublimely indifferent to the Victorian context.

Now the W SIDE of Banbury Road. After St Anne's, the houses resume with *Codd*'s Nos. 35–41, 1865–8. BEVINGTON ROAD, w, has Nos. 1 and 8–10 by *Codd*, 1868–9, and Nos. 11–13 by *Wilkinson*, 1870–4. More by the latter in WINCHESTER ROAD, N from Bevington Road: Nos. 5–10 and 22–26, 1875 onwards. A very large scheme by *Níall McLaughlin Architects* for the E

---

*No firm evidence can be found for the local attribution of the carving to Hungerford Pollen, nor is it in the O'Sheas' style.

side and the back land behind, to be shared by the University and Hertford College, was announced in 2023. Continuing on Banbury Road, Nos. 43 and 45 are of 1868–70 by *T.E. Collcutt*, designed when he was still 'a gentleman in Mr Street's office'. *Codd* returns at Nos. 55 and 57, 1870, yellow brick with courses of red and black (also the similar Nos. 81–87), and the unusual 'Old English' No. 59, 1871, tile-hung and brick-nogged. GEE'S restaurant (No. 61A) is a florid greenhouse of great size by *Moore*, built for a nurseryman in 1897. Gee's is the prelude to a group round the end of NORTH PARADE AVENUE, smaller-scale houses and shops running through to the Woodstock Road, developed from 1833. The stuccoed villas at Nos. 77 and 79 belong with these early outliers. Then comes CANTERBURY ROAD, with houses mostly of 1873–6 and by *Codd*, who went bust as a speculative builder in the latter year. THE LAWN (No. 89, set back) is another villa, *c.*1840–5, of ashlar with pilasters, unsympathetically extended at each end by *Gerald Horsley*, *c.*1895. His white-painted, small-paned window frames and Voyseyesque eaves brackets are characteristic.

Opposite this, the PARK TOWN ESTATE, laid out in 1853 as North Oxford's first planned development, and completed *c.*1860. It made intelligent use of a quite narrow parcel of land, lately bought from New College as a site for the city's new workhouse (eventually built on Cowley Road instead). The private trust created for the development promised 'elegant villas and terraces' and 'ornamental gardens and pleasure grounds well stocked with trees and flowering shrubs'. What it became is this: two three-storey CRESCENTS N and S of an elliptical central garden with trees and shrubs, ashlar-fronted and still in a Late Classical style, all suggesting the influence of 1820s–30s developments at Cheltenham; PARK TERRACE, a curved terrace in two parts across the E end, dated 1855, of light brick with a rendered lower storey; and between this and the crescents, as well as between the crescents and Banbury Road, large, vaguely Italianate VILLAS with bracketed eaves. In addition there are symmetrically arranged STABLES between Park Terrace and the western villas. The designer throughout, excepting only a few of the villas, was the builder-architect *Samuel Lipscombe Seckham*, who in 1853 had just been appointed City Surveyor. Most of the villas are rendered or stuccoed, but among the western group No. 7 (N) and Nos. 8 and 10 (S), apparently not by Seckham, point the way to the standard North Oxford brick with stone dressings. The GARDENS owe their layout to *William Baxter*, Curator of the Botanic Garden.

Continuing N from Park Town, the St John's estates continued from 1881 to 1903 under the supervision of Wilkinson's nephew *Harry Wilkinson Moore*, working until 1886 as *Wilkinson & Moore*. On the E side of BANBURY ROAD, Nos. 72 and 74 are typical *Wilkinson & Moore* houses, 1884 (joined in 1960 for WYCHWOOD SCHOOL). Red brick and stone with characteristic small areas of carved Renaissance decoration.

BARDWELL ROAD, E, has more subdued villas by *Moore* (Nos. 1, 13–17 etc.), 1891 onwards, by now without basement storeys. The road also introduces half-timbered gables, at e.g. Nos. 10 and 12, by *Radclyffe & Watson* of Birmingham, and Nos. 14 and 16, by *Herbert Quinton*, all also of the 1890s. At the far end, the Dragon School (p. 459). In NORTHMOOR ROAD, off Bardwell Road to the N, *Moore* himself began to stir half-timbering and tile-hanging into the mix (Nos. 4–12 and Nos. 5–19, 1901–4). Of other houses here, the superb No. 2 is by *E.W. Allfrey*, 1902–3 for C.H. Firth, reforming Professor of Modern History. Upright, free Queen Anne, with a double-storey bow over the porch, and different types of dormers. Just S of St Andrew's church (p. 453), *Frank Mountain*'s Nos. 14–16, 1912, boast squared-rubble walling and buttresses.

The adjacent roads do not comprise a straightforward per-ambulation. CHARLBURY ROAD and CHADLINGTON ROAD, both to the E of Northmoor Road, are well populated with houses by *N.W. Harrison*, Moore's pupil and successor as St John's estate surveyor after 1903, who favoured rendered walling. More individual are *Stephen Salter*'s Nos. 2–4 Charl-bury Road, 1908–9, where the central timbered gable flirts with Art Nouveau patterns, and *Mountain*'s No. 11 Chadling-ton Road, 1910. At the S end of Chadlington Road, a path leads E to the CHERWELL BOATHOUSE (now restaurant), built in 1904 by Thomas Tims, boat-builder and waterman to the University Boat Club. Three big tile-hung gables, each with some lively carving inset, bracketed out over the long central recess. LINTON ROAD, running through E–W, shows *Harrison*'s more venturesome side at No. 14, 1905, and *Moore* at his best at No. 2, 1895, both on the S side. No. 7 is of 1903 by *A.H. Moberly*, in the accomplished Neo-Georgian of his dons' houses in Cambridge. The Arts and Crafts way with rendering appears opposite at No. 8, 1899–1901 by *E.J. Marriott*, and at several houses by *George Gardiner*, especially Nos. 19–27, 1908–12. Further N, Neo-Georgian brick predomi-nates in BELBROUGHTON ROAD, developed from 1924, espe-cially from *Christopher Wright* (Nos. 1–7, 4, 10, etc.). His No. 1 (1925–6) stands out, with its front of three giant arches. Also by Wright are Nos. 22–26 (1925) in the N part of NORTHMOOR ROAD. No. 20 here, simply rendered, is by *F.E. Openshaw* for the bookseller Basil Blackwell, 1924; later home to Professor J.R.R. Tolkien.

On BANBURY ROAD, most of the houses on the E SIDE up to Belbroughton Road are by *Moore*, lease dates 1890–1904 (Nos. 82–120).* On the W SIDE the authorship is more varied. No. 105 is by *Wilkinson & Moore*, 1886, and its mixing of tile-hanging, leaded windows with mullions, and freestone Jacobean ornament in the style of Jackson is adept if a little

---

* No. 78, 1885 by *Pike & Messenger*, was taken by Dr James Murray, editor of the *Oxford English Dictionary*, which was compiled in a flimsy 'scriptorium' in the garden; the POST BOX in front was placed there for his huge correspondence.

affected, and quite original. N of Rawlinson Road, No. 109 is a huge affair by *J.W. Messenger*, 1889, half-timbered on the first floor, tile-hung on the gables. At No. 117, THACKLEY END, *E.A. Ould*'s house of 1904–5 was replaced in 1972–3 with four blocks of concrete-framed flats by *Bernard Hartley & Partners*, facing outwards in different directions from the access court. Finally there is No. 121, an excellent and sophisticated house of 1902–3 by *H.T. Hare*, without any of the profuse ornamentation of his Town Hall. The composition is horizontal in accent, with strings of windows under the eaves and no gables breaking into the eaves. Projecting bays on the garden front. To either side and behind, boxy timber-clad pavilions for ST CLARE'S private college by *Hodder Architects*, 2008–15.

2. Woodstock Road and Walton Manor

The route returns S towards St Giles', starting from where Perambulation I finishes on the W side of Banbury Road.

ST MARGARET'S ROAD (1879–86) and RAWLINSON ROAD (1886–9) both connect the Banbury and Woodstock roads, and both have copious examples of *H.W. Moore*'s easily recognizable work; STAVERTON ROAD, next N and just beyond St John's estate, has a few more (Nos. 6–12, 1900). The S side of St Margaret's Road has been changed by the presence of St Hugh's College (p. 269), but its continuation W of Woodstock Road and up to St Margaret's church (p. 454) is mostly undisturbed. Rawlinson Road is also still intact, and as charming as any of West London's Bedford Park, despite the lower architectural standards; the half-timbered and tile-hung houses here are by *H. Quinton* (Nos. 6–8, 1889, and 11–15, 1890–3).*

   W of Woodstock Road and to the N, *Moore* was the architect in POLSTEAD ROAD (1888–94), excepting *Drinkwater*'s St Philip and St James's (later St Margaret's) PARISH INSTITUTE, 1889–90; in CHALFONT ROAD (1889–99), excepting Nos. 1–7; and in FRENCHAY ROAD (1895–8). The houses in these streets are increasingly plain and closely spaced. Also, parallel to Polstead Road to the W, HAYFIELD ROAD is all *Moore*, 1887–8, workers' terraces this time, a project of the Oxford Industrial and Provident Land and Building Society. Even here the doorways are surmounted with Moore's favourite device of little paired scrolls, the houses' only ornament. At the S end is THE ANCHOR pub, 1937–8, in *J.C. Leed*'s stripped Tudor manner. Earlier terraces continue S along much of KINGSTON ROAD, where Nos. 114–138 and Nos. 149–164 were built in 1870–3 to the designs of *C.C. Rolfe*. Only one and a half storeys high,

---

* Behind Nos. 16 and 18 are FLATS by *Pinckheard & Partners*, built *c.* 1976 for married Trinity College graduates. An earlier proposal to demolish the houses was rejected at a public inquiry in 1973, a turning point in the campaign to defend Victorian North Oxford.

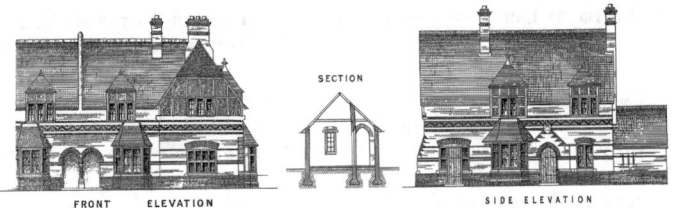

SECTION

FRONT ELEVATION

SIDE ELEVATION

Kingston Road, cottages.
Elevation drawing by C.C. Rolfe, 1870

but true North Oxford Gothic, with Butterfieldian patterning in the brick. Nos. 114–118 have timbered and brick-nogged dormer gables, the rest have hip-roofed dormers and ground-floor bay windows with steep tiled roofs.

WOODSTOCK ROAD in this section also has much by *Moore*, though plenty of houses have been lost to piecemeal redevelopment, especially in the 1960s–70s. Starting at the end of Staverton Road, E side, No. 106 was rebuilt as FLATS for Trinity College, a Postmodern North Oxford parody of 1988–92 by *Gray Baynes & Shew*. S of the corner is UNIV NORTH ('Stavertonia'), the annexe of University College. By *Sir Philip Dowson* of *Arup Associates*, an old member, though not at his best at this insufficiently resolved project of 1970–3. Four three-storey buildings, two of a fat T-shape placed close to the road, the other two each composed of a pair of residential blocks linked by an octagonal stair-turret. Blockwork cross-wall construction, with facing panels of pre-cast ribbed concrete. Projecting frames surround the big horizontal windows. In three places the fronts are of stepped section, making shallow balconies for the upper storeys. Designs by *Níall McLaughlin Architects* for seven additional blocks in the gardens were approved in 2020. Of the houses following, No. 94 is by *H. G.W. Drinkwater*, 1888, with pretty half-timbered twin gables, Nos. 88–92 are by *Quinton*, 1891–2, with some gimmicky porches. Opposite are *Moore*'s Nos. 145 and 147, 1888–9, linked between the wars by a CHAPEL and connecting passages for the former Notre Dame convent. Now Trinity College accommodation. No. 80 (*Wilkinson & Moore*, 1881) is another which sports Dutch gables, rather than the more usual straight form. Opposite is RUSSELL COURT (Nos. 137–141), on the S corner of St Margaret's Road. Private flats of red brick, the front range with footbridge access over a sunk garage storey. By *Elsworth Sykes & Partners*, designed in 1969 together with the former YWCA, immediately S. Red brick again, here with much stepping back, and with windows placed in the outer corners. Now a property of Reuben College and renamed FARNDON COURT.

The neighbouring complex on this side is STEVENS CLOSE, 1973–5, student flats for Jesus College. By *John Fryman* (*Architects Design Partnership*) and perhaps the most restless of his Oxford buildings, which is saying something. It also illustrates the 1970s trend for re-engaging with historical forms – pitched roofs, mullioned windows, pointed-spired staircase tops – with decidedly mixed results. Yellow brick, four to five storeys. The plan is half a bisected hexagon, with spur blocks off the outer corners. Their storeys are cantilevered out in alternating directions, so that they intersect at right angles. Within the angles are the stair enclosures, with disruptive, inward-sloping glazed sides. The next houses, Nos. 121–123 of 1856–7, are a relic of the first plans for the WALTON MANOR ESTATE, as projected c. 1855 by *S. L. Seckham*. They are stuccoed, semi-detached and classical, rather in the style of his Park Town (p. 464). A revised plan by Seckham followed in 1860, with provision for lesser houses in Leckford and Farndon roads behind, none of which he designed himself. BUTLER CLOSE is next, private flats by *E. L. Preston*, designed in 1968. Five blocks, with pattern-making window arrangements, set behind retained trees.

The houses on the E SIDE opposite include No. 72, THE SHRUBBERY, now the Principal's Lodgings for St Hugh's. Greatly expanded from a villa of c. 1840, notably with the N addition of 1900, where the plasterwork ceiling of c. 1600 rescued from No. 2 High Street (p. 409) was installed. (The motifs match those in Corpus Christi gate tower, p. 142, but Claire Gapper observes that the frieze design with tritons is apparently unique.) The house's GATES are in Canterbury Road, s, a Miami-esque design of swans by *Laurence Whistler*, 1986. No. 70 is representative *Codd*, 1872. Then St Philip and St James's church (p. 455), and its former VICARAGE at No. 68, half-timbered and tile-hung. By *Drinkwater*, 1886–7. St Antony's College immediately follows, including the former Holy Trinity convent (p. 248). Back on the W SIDE, the houses show the change after the arrival in 1860 of *William Wilkinson* as surveyor to the St John's estate. No. 111 of 1866, brick and Gothic, is one of his. Behind the houses here, with access from Leckford Road, is HART SYNNOT HOUSE, graduate accommodation for St John's. Of 1971–4 by *R. B. Gray* of *Pinckheard & Partners*. Yellow brick. A forbidding entrance front with twin stair-towers and windows of somehow unpleasing shapes. Nos. 91 and 93–97, modest two-storey stucco, represent Oxford's early northward expansion, c. 1830–40; Nos. 83–89 are an informally composed terrace by *Moore*, 1890–1. PLANTATION ROAD alongside, where development began shortly before 1830, also has a few early houses (e.g. No. 75), and more *Moore* too, Nos. 2–14 at the far end, built in 1884 for the Oxford Cottage Improvement Society, and quite demonstrative for a cottage terrace. By the Woodstock Road end, No. 50 is the self-designed house of the architectural historian *Sir Howard Colvin*, 1969–70. Of brick, pragmatic and independent-minded, without historical motifs.

Woodstock Road carries on with Nos. 71–79, another stucco terrace of c. 1830, and No. 69, formerly the HORSE AND JOCKEY, which *Drinkwater* rebuilt in 1880 to look nothing like a pub. BELSYRE COURT next door, 1934–6 by *E. R. Barrow*, is a one-off for Oxford: a big U-shaped complex of flats with a colonnade of shops wrapped around the near side, like a stray from Maida Vale. St Bernard's Road, just N, has good, plain mews terraces by *Oxford Architects Partnership*, designed in 1972 and called ARTHUR GARRARD CLOSE. S of Belsyre Court, OBSERVATORY STREET is mostly small stucco terraces of *c.* 1837 onwards, but also has the former St Paul's vicarage at No. 1A, free Neo-Georgian by *F.C. Eden*, 1905–6. Last on this side before the colleges begin is the unusually accomplished ST JOHN'S TERRACE, three storeys of red brick, recorded from 1826. The E side here has later houses, surviving on either side of St Anne's College (p. 246): Nos. 58 and 60, Gothic semis by *Codd*, 1872; No. 50 by *Wilkinson & Moore*, 1881, for *Alexander Macdonald*, the Ruskin Master of Drawing, who 'furnished the outline of the design'; No. 48, 1882 by *Drinkwater*, with an ogee-arched doorway. For the road further S *see* p. 431.

3. Summertown and further north

SUMMERTOWN was developed after 1820 as a modest satellite of Oxford, on two oblong enclaves N of the St John's College estate. Coming from the S on BANBURY ROAD, the early C19 houses first appear on the E side with Nos. 194–200, two- or three-storeyed, with the stuccoed DIAMOND COTTAGES behind. Further N, most of the houses on this side have been replaced by 1960s–70s offices and shops, but more survive behind in Summerfield Road and Mayfield Road, including the workhouse of 1824 (*see* Summer Fields School, p. 459). The EASYHOTEL (Nos. 276–280), weighty red brick by *Seven Architecture*, 2018–21, marks a fresh cycle of rebuilding. Next is the former TWINING'S (No. 294), a superior grocers' with a gaily ornamented tympanum; of 1901 by the Oxford builder *T.H. Kingerlee*, who also provided the Congregational chapel next door (p. 457). It faces SOUTH PARADE, another part of the original Summertown.* Of the early houses here, the best is No. 23 (N side, now NORTHERN HOUSE ACADEMY), 1824. Three bays, with a pedimented porch. On the S side opposite, St Edward's School (p. 457) dominates. Also ROBERT SAUN-DERS HOUSE further E, a postgraduate hall of residence for St Anne's College; 1996 by *Knowles & Son Design and Build*, and harmless enough. Off South Parade to the N is MIDDLE WAY, rightly so called, as it runs midway between Banbury Road and Woodstock Road. MARTIN COURT, private flats designed in 1962 by the *Oxford Architects Partnership*, appears monu-mental in this small-scale street. Purple-brown brick, the two entrance recesses with sheer-walled stair-towers and glazed links to connect the parts. The same architects' mews terrace in HOBSON ROAD, E (Nos. 4–15), designed in 1979, shows the

*Confusingly, Summertown's South Parade is 1 m. N of Oxford's North Parade Avenue (p. 464).

return to pitched roofs and continuous street frontages. Also in Middle Way, W side, No. 12 is a boxy former Congregational meeting house of 1844, floored across and refronted.

Continuing N on BANBURY ROAD from South Parade, No. 269 (BBC OXFORD etc.), chunky and angular yellow brick, is by *Lyons+Sleeman+Hoare*, 1986–8. At Nos. 275–277 a symmetrical two-gabled Tudor stone cottage of 1831. Diagonally opposite, ST MICHAEL'S CHURCH HALL by *G.T.F. Gardner*, built in 1925 with stone from St John the Baptist, Summertown, which St Michael's replaced (*see* p. 454). Simplified Tudor, but with Gothic buttresses on the E side, recognizable salvage from *Street*'s additions to the old church (1857–8, 1875–6). In the garden a WAR MEMORIAL of 1921, of the cross-and-sword design by *Sir Reginald Blomfield*. The sturdy flats immediately E in Portland Road are by *Adrian James Architects*, 2017–19. D'OVERBROECK'S SCHOOL at No. 333 occupies a rather grand Italianate villa, ashlar, with an Osborne-type tower. It originated as a house of 1823, but everything now visible must date from refacing and expansion after 1846, for James Ryman. Further additions made after 1954 for Oxford's Freemasons have been replaced by *TSH Architects*' school buildings of 2016–18: a long E–W range joining on to the villa, with a loggia or cloister along its S side, facing a free-standing HALL with an apsidal W end. Variegated brown brick with cast-stone trim, and lively detailing to the windows. At the same time the school built ISLIP HOUSE at No. 376 opposite, a boarding house also by *TSH*, more vertical in emphasis. No. 380 is RITCHIE COURT, many-balconied retirement flats of 1973–6 by *Philip del Nevo* of *Oxford Architects Partnership*, on an irregular U-plan. SUMMERTOWN HOUSE (No. 369), facing Apsley Road, is another early C19 villa. Interesting for its cyclopean E doorcase and for the full-height ground-floor windows of the pedimented S front. In 1962–6 it became the centrepiece of a three-sided group of UNIVERSITY FLATS for graduates with small families, three- to five-storeyed, by *Howell, Killick, Partridge & Amis*. The concrete beam-ends show, as these architects liked to do it, and the floors project slightly one above the other to gain flats of increasing size, but since 2001 the original cladding of square concrete tiles has been replaced with render or unglazed terracotta. Enlivening the A40 roundabout is HARLEQUIN HOUSE, flats of 2010–13 by *Adrian James Architects*, black brick and white render used in brazenly piebald alternation. ⅓ m. N, a substantial TOLL HOUSE survives at No. 566 Banbury Road. The road here was turnpiked in 1754, but the detail looks *c.* 1820–40. Canted front bay, mullioned windows with hoodmoulds.

Architectural interest E of this long stretch of the Banbury Road is modest. Just S of Summertown, Marston Ferry Road has MARSTON FERRY COURT, flats designed in 1981 by *Oxford Architects Partnership*, another broken-up composition like their Ritchie Court (*see* above). Off to the N in Ferry Pool Road, the MERIFIELD annexe of Wadham College, 1996–8 by *Architects*

Design Partnership. An informal quadrangle of shallow hip-roofed blocks of flats, yellow brick changing to blue cladding on the top storey; a variant of the firm's designs for Jesus College off Cowley Road (p. 500). N of the Summertown strip, to the E of Kings Cross Road, *Peter Reynolds*'s HAWKSWELL GARDENS shows the early 1960s suburban ideal: a picturesquely arrayed enclave of private houses and three-storey flats, sharing a front-garden strip. Of individual houses, KINGS CROSS ROAD has No. 11 by *Alan Drury Architects* (2014), with twin slat-guarded oriels of timber; WATER EATON ROAD has No. 4 by *R2 Studios* (2018), a brusque block of dark grey brick, partly patterned with raised headers. Also screens to some windows made by 'hit-and-miss' gaps between the bricks.

CUTTESLOWE, to the NE, includes a large City Council estate of 1931–4. The notorious CUTTESLOWE WALLS, built in 1934 across Aldrich Road and Wolsey Road to prevent the council's tenants from crossing into the private development further W, stood until 1959. By the primary school (p. 459) in Wren Road, E, is the COMMUNITY CENTRE, *c*. 1989 by *Reginald James*. Big monopitch-roofed wedges facing three ways. Red brick.

WOODSTOCK ROAD in this sector is largely residential, except where playing fields remain to the W. These include St John's, with a PAVILION of 1896 by the ubiquitous *H.W. Moore* (extended 2009 by *Gray Baynes & Shew*), visible from Bainton Road. Also in Bainton Road, N end, No. 105 by *Acanthus Clews*, 2003. Notable for its wavy glazed front. Just off Woodstock Road to the E, LATHBURY ROAD has No. 26, wholesome Arts and Crafts by *P. Morley Horder*, 1913. Chapel attached, built for Bishop Vernon Herford of the Evangelical Catholic Church (1866–1938). N of Summertown, down a long drive to the E, THE LODGE (No. 304). The core is a villa of *c*. 1830, expanded and remodelled in 1862 for the grocer Owen Grimbly, with stucco pilasters, veranda, balancing conservatories etc. Off Squitchey Lane, next N, is THE PADDOX of 1965, one of *Eric Lyons*'s SPAN developments of private housing. Four three-storey slabs around a garden square, of yellow brick and white weatherboarding, enlivened by complex butterfly-section roofs. Separate garaging, as usual with SPAN. Another twelve such blocks were projected to the W, likewise in the former grounds of FIELD HOUSE. This plain villa of 1830 (originally called Apsley Paddox) survives to the N, with access from Field House Drive. In 1910 it was extended in matching style by *Ernest Newton*, for Charles Robertson, patron also of Newton's R.C. church at the Woodstock Road end (*see* p. 456). Newton gave the house his favourite external shutters, since removed. The next drive leads to WOODSTOCK COURT, two big blocks of Metropolitan-style mansion flats by *R. Fielding Dodd*, 1933–5; four blocks were intended. No. 358 is *T. Lawrence Dale*'s own house, neat Neo-Georgian brick of 1928. In DAVENANT ROAD, No. 26 is by *Clough Williams-Ellis*, 1923. White-rendered and demure. Finally to BLANDFORD AVENUE, where No. 26 is an early response to the need for energy efficiency, 1993–5 by *Sue Roaf & David Woods*. Commonplace in front, but the s side has a roof of integral photovoltaic cells and a glazed annexe for passive solar heating.

WOLVERCOTE

The village was annexed to Oxford in 1929. Of two parts: the old centre around the parish church, and Lower Wolvercote on the lower ground w of the canal and the railway, with the Thames and Godstow Abbey beyond.

St Peter, First Turn. C14 w tower, of three stages, with bell-openings of two ogee lights and a quatrefoil over, and a C15 w window and doorway. In 1859–60 the rest of the church was rebuilt by *C. Buckeridge*, to a conventional design in C13 style. All the side windows with identical Geometrical tracery. N aisle. Chancel arch in Transitional style, echoing its demolished predecessor. Squat N vestry by *Lawrence Dale*, 1934. – PEWS by *Buckeridge*, plain but shapely. – ORGAN by *Robin Jennings*, 2016. Case with Gothic details. – FONT. C12. A precise tub shape, finely incised with diapering and a concentric band. – STAINED GLASS. E window by *Heaton, Butler & Bayne*, 1887 onwards. Chancel s window head and tracery, early C14-style grisaille with a design of oak leaves and acorns. Reputedly from Merton College chapel, but is it good 1860 imitation? Nave s, The Calling of Peter, 1860, *Clayton & Bell* in their early heyday, given by Buckeridge. Also windows by *Ward & Hughes*, 1881, and *John Piper* and *Patrick Reyntiens*, 1976 (Palm Sunday), with inscription tablet by *Will Carter*. – MONUMENTS. Sir John Walter, Chief Baron of the Exchequer, †1630, and two wives. Recumbent effigies with three sons and three daughters kneeling at their heads and feet. Alabaster. Now squeezed into the N aisle; of its original grand canopy only the shields of arms survive, re-set above the arch. – David Walter †1679. Marble wall monument with a fine bust on a pedestal. Attributed to *John Bushnell*.

CHURCH ROOMS, attached to the NW by a glazed corridor. By *Adrian James Architects*, 2008–10. With three wonky-shaped tapering roof-lights. They join on to the former NATIONAL SCHOOL N of the church, dated 1831 inside. Elementary hoodmoulds.

BAPTIST CHAPEL, Godstow Road, Lower Wolvercote. Of 1886, to 'plans provided by Mr *Martin*' (*Jackson's Oxford Journal*). Yellow brick, superannuated Gothic details.

PRIMARY SCHOOL, First Turn, opposite the church. Extended from *George Castle*'s former infants' school of 1898, w. The central part with cupola and diamond shapes on the gables is by *Sidney Stallard*, County Surveyor, 1912–13. Red brick.

CHURCH FARM, First Turn, w of the church. Plain C18 front range, refronted in the C19. Reused four-centred-arched C16 doorway with shields in the spandrels. Also a salvaged C16 fire-place in one room, with a late C16 overmantel of three double-arched bays divided by herms and decorated with strapwork and foliage. Older parts behind, C16 or C17. N of the church in MERE ROAD, No.3 is an unconventional house by *Peter Boston* (*Saunders Boston*), 1964. Square plan, with timber-clad upper storeys of A-frame construction, on a ground storey of brick.

LOWER WOLVERCOTE. The once-dominant PAPER MILL, re-built for Oxford University Press in the 1950s–60s, closed in 1996. Its replacement is housing of 2017–22 by *Glenn Howells Architects*, flats and short terraces of strongly urban character, N of MILL ROAD. In that road are some stone-built C18 and C19 terraces. Nos.12–15, N side, probably belong with an earlier rebuilding of the mill in 1856 by Thomas Combe. (Nos.49–63 Godstow Road, set back on the S side, are locally rare BACK-TO-BACK HOUSES, 1880s or 1890s.) WEBB'S CLOSE, off Godstow Road to the SW, was built from 1967 for mill-workers' families. By *Booth, Ledeboer & Pinckheard*. Well designed and grouped: three-storey flats of grey brick by the road, two-storey terraces behind. These are slate-hung with some white pebbledash, materials of the most sombre colours. Immediately S is TOLL BRIDGE, rebuilt 1876. On its approach wall, a TABLET commemorates two pioneer airmen killed in a crash in 1912.

TROUT INN, Godstow Road, further SW. Beautifully placed below the weir at Godstow Bridge. Plain stone, mostly of 1737. The BRIDGE alongside has a pointed N arch, possibly medieval. S arch rebuilt 1892. Also a FOOTBRIDGE of Chinese Chippendale pattern, late C19 or early C20, joining the inn to an island in the river. On an orchard wall by the roadside entrance is another commemorative TABLET, this one lettered by *Eric Gill*, 1940.

GODSTOW ABBEY, Godstow Road, just W of the Thames path. A Benedictine nunnery founded *c.*1115, dedicated to St Mary and St John the Baptist. The church was consecrated in 1139 and enlarged or rebuilt between 1176 and 1188, when Henry II made donations. At the Dissolution in 1539 the abbey passed to Dr George Owen, the king's physician. He adapted part of the buildings as a dwelling, wrecked in the Civil War in 1645.

The remains, with nothing obviously earlier than the C15, comprise a roughly rectangular walled enclosure, of which the SE angle can be recognized as the shell of a chapel. Much rebuilding of the other walls, and no trace of the church. This stood immediately N, as C17 and C18 drawings show. It had a NW tower of which the remains lasted into the late C18, and an outer or guest court to the W. The nuns' cloister was S of the church, within the present enclosure; part of its arcade survived in 1710. The SE chapel has a three-light E window with uncusped lights and straight-sided arch, later C15 or C16, and two two-light S windows at different heights, indicating a former W gallery. High in its N wall is a squint which must originally have opened to the first floor of an attached building. These arrangements suggest a domestic chapel, but the location is anomalous in terms of the normal placing of the abbess's lodgings at or near the main gate. Other details include a large blocked archway with a straight-sided four-centred arch in the outer face of the W wall of the enclosure.

FOOTBRIDGE, ⅓ m. NW. Timber-built, to an economical tilting design particular to the Oxford Canal. The S section (Banbury to Oxford) was cut in 1786–90.

CEMETERY, Banbury Road, ½ m. NE. Of 1892–3, with CHAPEL and LODGE identical to those at the contemporary Botley (Berks.) and Rose Hill cemeteries. By *W.H.White*, City Engineer.

OUTER OXFORD: EAST AND NORTH-EAST

Headington, a royal manor from Saxon times, is the chief medieval settlement on the heights NE of Oxford, still with a recognizable village centre despite incorporation with the city in 1929. The neighbouring village of Marston, also well preserved, was annexed in 1991. It was briefly the Parliamentary headquarters during the Civil War. Around 1790 the present route through Headington to London was formed, succeeding the old route over Shotover Hill. Villas followed, culminating in the 1850s with the enlarged Headington Hill Hall. The workers' settlement at Headington Quarry is first recorded in the C17, but has no surviving buildings as old. Closer to central Oxford, New Headington and New Marston are suburban developments, C19 and C20. In those centuries the area also became a stronghold of hospitals, colleges and schools, including what is now Oxford Brookes University. Marston and the overspill district of Barton are treated separately, pp. 488–90.

HEADINGTON, HEADINGTON QUARRY, NEW HEADINGTON AND NEW MARSTON

Places of worship

ST ANDREW, St Andrew's Road. The parish church of old Headington. Much of the chancel must be structurally C12, with later features. Chancel arch of *c.*1160, with two orders of continuous chevron and one between with colonnettes. The l. shaft decorated basket-fashion, unplaiting into a spiral as it rises. The r. shaft is restoration. Simple block capitals, imposts with chip-carved saltires. C13 relieving arch above. Lean C15 chancel roof with collar-beams on arched braces, supported on corbels with unsophisticated heads and busts. Two Perp S windows. Cusped C13 PISCINA. E window of reticulated tracery from *J.C. Buckler*'s restoration of 1863–5. The nave was enlarged by a two-bay S aisle and a SW tower in the mid C13. The arcade has a round pier and round abacus and double-chamfered arches. Aisle E window of cusped grouped lancets. Drastically restored single lancets, S. The tower has triple-chamfered arches to aisle and nave. So the old nave was no doubt lengthened too. The upper part of the tower is Late Perp. Distinctive square stair-turret, set diagonally. The rest is chiefly *Buckler*, who rebuilt the nave with two more W bays, and provided a N arcade. In 1880–1 the anticipated N aisle was added by *Wilkinson*. Big Perp-style meeting room, N, from the reordering by *Carden & Godfrey*, 1996–7. Also the vestry extension, NE. – ORGAN by *Kenneth Tickell & Co.*, 2008–9, nicely divided at the W window. – STAINED GLASS. E window and S aisle E both by *Henry Holiday* for *Powells*, 1891 and 1866. A telling contrast between lush Renaissance and early Pre-Raphaelitism. Chancel S, late C19, by *H. G. Murray*. W, *A. K. Nicholson*, 1932.

CROSS in the churchyard. Octagonal C15 base with quatrefoils, each originally with an open book in the middle. Top renewed 1961.

ALL SAINTS, Lime Walk, New Headington. 1909–10 by *Arthur Blomfield & Sons*. The chancel 1937 by *N.W. Harrison*, in keeping. Quite a large church, of conservative design. Red brick; no tower. The windows are lancets or groups of lancets, at the W end three stepped, at the E end five stepped. Interior all exposed brick. Short piers and broad arches. No capitals at all. Wagon roofs, ceiled and chequered red and green over the chancel. It is an exceptionally impressive interior. – STAINED GLASS. W window by *John Hayward*, 2000. Lady Chapel E, 1955 by *J.E. Nuttgens*; also one figure, S aisle. Other aisle windows by *Christopher Webb*, 1959–65.

HOLY TRINITY, Trinity Road, Headington Quarry. 1848–9 by *George Gilbert Scott*, an early work, though of course later than the Martyrs' Memorial and Martyrs' Aisle (pp. 426 and 395). Dec style. Nave and chancel, N aisle, S porch. Big bellcote on a buttress between the two W windows, a favourite Gothic Revival arrangement (cf. Scott's Chantry church, Somerset, 1843–6). A large N extension is planned (2022). Many original FUR-NISHINGS, including stone PULPIT and low wooden SCREEN. – STAINED GLASS. E window, Christ in Glory by *Comper*, 1951. Chancel S, 1925, by *Lilian J. Parsons*, incorporating some late C19 work (PC). N chapel, framed Crucifixion by *Heaton, Butler & Bayne*, from the old E window of *c.*1868. Nave S, angel, by the same, 1910. Nave N, C.S. Lewis memorial, engraved glass by *Sally Scott*, 1991. – WAR MEMORIAL, churchyard. A cross, quite delicate. 1920 by *F.E. Howard*, carver *Alec Miller*.

ST FRANCIS OF ASSISI, Hollow Way, Headington. By *T. Lawrence Dale*, 1930–1. Built as a church hall. Dale's sketch of the intended grand enclosure with church and vicarage is displayed inside. White-rendered front. Arch over the doorway, pushed up into the pediment in the Alberti manner. The trusses have an unfinished scheme of PAINTINGS of the Creation and of the Life of St Francis by *Leslie Davenport*, who taught at Oxford

School of Art. Three colours, evocative of book-jacket design of the period. – HANGING CROSS, 1964. Designed by *A. Hawkesley*. T-shaped, of steel and coloured glass.

St MICHAEL AND ALL ANGELS, Marston Road, New Marston. 1954–6 by *T. Lawrence Dale*. Yellow sand-lime brick. Otherwise, not at all as if it belonged to the 1950s, with its repeating motif of very elongated elliptical windows, its portal, and its thin SW tower, vaguely Italian Renaissance. Inside, it is true, brick and concrete transverse arches. Sculpture on the W front by *Michael Groser*, also a relief over the doorway by *John Bunting*. W end subdivided *c.*1976. E extension for meeting rooms etc. by *Gray Baynes & Shew*, *c.*1995. – Unusually ambitious FURNISHINGS for a 1950s church. REREDOS, fresco of the Resurrection of Christ with hovering angels, below STAINED GLASS, his Ascension. Its background sneaks in Dale's project for a boulevard relief road through Christ Church Meadow (*see* Introduction, p.68). Both by *Leon Underwood*, who also did the Lady Chapel reredos, N. – ROOD with carved figures by *Bunting*. – Other SCULPTURE by *Groser*: statue of St Michael, biblical reliefs on the nave piers.

St NICHOLAS (now Russian Orthodox), Ferry Road, New Marston. Simple hall of 1911 with lunette window, built as a chapel of ease to St Nicholas, Marston. Slim yellow brick campanile in the style of *T. L. Dale*, added in 1936–7. (Rich Orthodox furnishings and decoration, 2010 onwards.)

CORPUS CHRISTI (R.C.), Margaret Road, Headington Quarry. By *G.T.F. Gardner*, 1936–7 and 1953 (E end). Red brick. Square-headed windows carried up through the eaves. – STATIONS OF THE CROSS. Inventive bronze-resin plaques by *Faith Tolkien*, 1987–8. – STAINED GLASS. E window, *dalle-de-verre* by *Leslie Sheels*, 1970.

St ANTHONY OF PADUA (R.C.), Headley Way, Headington. 1959–60 by *Jennings, Homer & Lynch* of Birmingham. Brick, T-plan, moderately Modern. – SCULPTURE of Christ by *Faith Tolkien*, 1975, over the W doorway. – ORGAN. 1815 by *William Gray*, brought in. – CHURCH HALL by *Towle Spurring Hardy*, 2003–4, E. Porthole windows.

LIME WALK METHODIST CHURCH, New Headington. *Cripps & Stewart*, 1932. Simplified round-headed tracery. Porch replaced *c.*2000. The CHURCH HALL, facing New High Street behind, is the original chapel of 1889. Y-tracery.

CORNERSTONE CHRISTIAN CENTRE (formerly Methodist), Quarry High Street, Headington Quarry. Of 1859–60, enlarged 1874 (Sunday School) and 1931. Plain stone hall. Cusped straight-headed windows.

BAPTIST CHURCH, Old High Street, Headington. Rebuilt by *David Grindley*, 2006–7. Pragmatic and unchurchy. Ashlar, with some timber panelling. The entrance, l., is recessed, with glazing that gives glimpses of the interior. Meeting rooms etc. in the storeyed front part, worship space under a split-pitch roof with clerestory.

UNITED REFORMED CHURCH (formerly Congregational), Marston Road. 1939. Plain brick, small round-arched windows.
UNITED REFORMED CHURCH (formerly Congregational), Collinwood Road, Risinghurst, E of the by-pass. 1958–9 by *H. O. Bailey.* Brick, with trusses of Douglas fir.
CEMETERY, Dunstan Road, Headington. Very pretty CHAPEL, 1884 by *H.W. Moore* (*Wilkinson & Moore*). Delightful free Gothic, with small-scale decoration on bellcote and doorway.

Oxford Brookes University

Oxford's second university, previously the Polytechnic (1970–92), College of Technology (1956–70), College of Technology, Art and Commerce (1952–6), Schools of Technology, Art and Commerce (1932–52), and separate Technical Schools and School of Art, the former with a building of 1893–4 by *Moore* in St Ebbe's (dem.), the latter going back to the drawing school founded in 1865 at the Taylorian Institution (p. 352). The name honours John Henry Brookes, Principal of the merged college from 1934 to 1956, who oversaw the post-war move to Headington Hill. The expanded university includes Headington Hill Hall, N, and halls of residence to the N and W.

HEADINGTON CAMPUS, Headington Road. The C21 has transformed the main campus quadrangle by rebuilding and renovation. The buildings of the municipal era are, or were, designed by the City Architect *E. G. Chandler* (1953–63) and his successor, *D. Murray* (to 1976), straightforward exposed concrete frame or straightforward curtain wall, with a main entrance in Gipsy Lane, E. Now there is instead an entrance forecourt on Headington Road, N, made in conjunction with *Design Engine*'s JOHN HENRY BROOKES BUILDING of 2010–14. A bold and confident design, which engages with the retained older parts while also opening up to the outer world. The forecourt rises to an entrance at first-floor level, where there is a glass-walled atrium of full height. To the l. a lean colonnade faced in cor-ten steel, fronting a block housing shops, café etc. The cor-ten runs on through the main circulation route inside, coming out at the slimmer SW end as a web-like pierced screen and as cladding for the chimney. Otherwise dark grey stone and cladding dominate, offset variously by pink fins and by sawtooth slats of etched glass at the library windows on the top floor, W side. The atrium-cum-forum flows through to the multi-level heart of the building, with another glass wall facing the courtyard on the E side. Pushing through the glass is a giant hovering box containing an auditorium, which has timber ribs on its indoor faces. The courtyard's N side (ABERCROMBIE) has a random pattern of dark upright panelling and narrow windows, chopped away at the NW where an open concrete staircase slants up to the forecourt. This N range stands parallel to one of the remaining older blocks (1953–5, including the architecture school), from which it is separated by a long atrium with bridges of coloured structural glass angled across. The other sides, CLERICI (E) and SINCLAIR (S), are structurally of 1953–61, re-clad and variously reworked in 2015–17 by *Berman Guedes Stretton*, sympathetic in materials and treatment to the rest. Clerici also acquired a replacement MAIN HALL projecting to the E, where its foyer faces N towards the former library block added in 1968. – SCULPTURE. Courtyard, Assembly by *Saad Qureshi*, 2008, droll perching birds. Forecourt, Rain Pavilion, 2015, from a design by two Brookes architecture students, *Alexandra Horsman* and *Charlotte Birch*. Tall leaf-like structures in a group.

OTHER BUILDINGS. Flanking the entrance, two white-clad blocks with external framing by *Gotch, Saunders & Surridge*, the MEDIA CENTRE (W), 2001, and BUCKLEY (E), 2003–5. Down the lane W of John Henry Brookes, TONGE, 1982–7. Built when *Oxfordshire County Architect's Department* were responsible for the Polytechnic's buildings. Rough brown brick below, gables and dark boards above, with a near-continuous window strip. Courtyard behind, completed to the NW *c.*1997. S of the main courtyard, GIBBS, 1972–4, with a pattern of raised blocks on the storey bands. FULLER (catering), SE, dates from 1966–7.

HEADINGTON HILL HALL, N of Headington Road. Oxford's greatest private mansion, taken over by the university in 1993 with its gardens and outlying buildings. The HOUSE faces W, towards the city. By *John Thomas*, 1856–8, for James Morrell Jun., the brewer. Should one call it Italianate or rather Louis XIII? Thomas, really a sculptor, was not a disciplined designer of buildings. Five bays, mostly Bath stone ashlar, with some contrasting small-coursed stonework on the entrance front. Short *porte cochère* with alternatingly blocked columns and pilasters. Channelled superimposed pilasters all round; also a full complement of blind boxes. Mansard roof. Along the garden sides runs a colonnaded veranda, with diagonal projections to N and S for the bay windows. On top is a pierced parapet and promenade walk. Service wing to the N, incorporating the plain house built for James Morrell Sen. in 1824.

The INTERIOR was reportedly remodelled by *Wilkinson* in 1872 for G.H. Morrell, but the chief ceilings are likely to be the 'very elaborate' ones noted in 1858. A pilastered top-lit hall is at the centre of the plan. An imperial staircase opens off it, returning to the first-floor gallery. Enriched coving around the roof-light. On the ground floor, plasterwork with a bust of Diana between hounds, above a portrait tondo of J.H. Brookes by *Leonard McComb*, 1993. The staircase window has hideous stained glass by *Nehemia Azaz*, Samson at the Gates of Gaza, installed by the publishing magnate Robert Maxwell (resident 1959–91). Marble chimneypieces carved with thick garlands in the main rooms. Also one of *c.*1800 from Fitzroy Square, London.

The GROUNDS were laid out in 1858 by *William Baxter*, Curator of the Botanic Garden. Steps run down S and E from the house. The lower slopes are now Headington Hill Park (p.485). Main LODGE to the W, *c.*1859 by *Thomas*. To the NE the former STABLES, by *Wilkinson*, 1877, now the RICHARD HAMILTON BUILDING; the courtyard infilled with offices *c.*1987 for Robert Maxwell's Pergamon Press. Extension of 1997. Across the drive to the S, a new STUDENT CENTRE is proposed.

CLIVE BOOTH STUDENT VILLAGE joins on to the grounds to the NW. The earliest and best buildings are on the higher slopes, intricately planned and rather villagey, with varied pedestrian routes around and through. Purple-brown brick. By *Mervyn Bennett*, 1975–8 (replacement by *MICA Architects* approved 2022). The rest mostly by *Gotch, Saunders & Surridge/GSS Architecture*, 2001–8. Many interlinked square or double-square blocks, in right-angled groups. Also the POSTGRADU-ATE CENTRE, in the angle between Marston Road and John Garne Way. A four-storey quadrangle, stepped and staggered along the E side. Yellow brick, timber cladding, recessed glazed-walled staircases. In the courtyard is a timber-slatted pavilion for the common room, set by a pond.

CHENEY STUDENT VILLAGE. W of the main campus and S of Headington Hill Hall, from which *Wilkinson*'s bridge of 1877 runs across. *Gotch, Saunders & Surridge*, 1998–2004. Four-storey blocks, tiringly repeated. Only one deviates, with an octagonal centre, open below. To the E the CENTRE FOR SPORT, 1995.

Other higher education buildings

OXFORD CENTRE FOR ISLAMIC STUDIES, Marston Road. An independent residential institution with close links to the University; founded in 1985 by Dr Farhan Nazami. Built on the present site from 2001, structurally complete by 2005, but opened only in 2017, a delay explained in part by the extreme care taken with finishes and decoration. The building is wholly of traditional materials and load-bearing construction, and as such is consistent with other works by its Egyptian-born architect *Abdel-Wahed El-Wakil*, notably his many mosques in Saudi Arabia. This approach also points up the Centre's many affinities with the Western revival of classical and traditional forms in the late C20. The final cost was some £100 million, plus donations of material and work in kind from countries across the Islamic world. *Blampied & Partners* were the executive architects.

The basic form is a square quadrangle, with projections from all four corners. The most conspicuous of these by far, because of its height, treatment and closeness to the lodge on

Marston Road, is the MOSQUE at the SE, all ashlar-faced, with its surmounting drum and leaded dome. Because of its orientation, the mosque stands at an angle to the main quad and to its own minaret, which breaks out at the top into two balconies corbelled out on rich *muquarnas* vaulting. Also on the E side a finely carved through-storey portal, facing the ISTANBUL FORECOURT, and the attached MALAYSIA AUDITORIUM, separately expressed as a gabled hall with triple pointed-arched doorways below an enclosed wooden oriel of *mashrabiya* type. Fountains in the two forecourts, of granite and marble. The other main elevations and wings are chiefly of light brown brick, with large and small crowstepped gables. Stone dressings, the windows consistently showing their relieving brickwork arches above the lugged architraves. All the details very sharp. Otherwise the walls are mostly unmodulated, even slab-like. Lavish bronze door furniture. The central QUAD or courtyard reverts to ashlar. On the N and S sides the ground floor has an open cloister with exposed brick vaults and depressed pointed arches on stocky columns. Another sunk fountain in the middle. The garden side, W, has an extra storey where the land falls away, overlooked by the residential wings and the attached DIRECTOR'S HOUSE, NW. The PRINCE CHARLES GARDEN evokes the fourfold symbolism of Islamic tradition, with formal rills converging on a fountain, within a raised perimeter walk.

INTERIORS. The double-height MAIN ENTRANCE strikes the keynote, with patterned stone floors and a transverse timber bridge enclosed with carved screens, *mashrabiya*-fashion. More carved woodwork around the dais in the AUDITORIUM, much of it in traditional Malysian forms. Open-trussed roof, its metalwork exposed and polished. On the E side, the OMAN HALL, a communal dining hall in the collegiate tradition, but with the unfamiliar feature of aisles – necessary here to support the guest rooms (BAHRAIN SUITE) above. Square piers, cool white groin-vaulting with flat cross-arches. The MOSQUE, funded by Shaikh Zayed of Abu Dhabi, comprises a square between two half-squares, plus an entrance bay with the women's gallery above. Its dome shows the concentric brickwork construction, spanning 10 metres (33 ft). *Prof. Jacques Heyman* of Cambridge, expert in shell structures, was the consulting engineer. Brickwork is also exposed below the drum. Delicately patterned stained glass, delicate carving of the marble *mihrab* and the cross-arches. Polished panelling of red and green marble lines the lower walls.

Anyone familiar with Oxford's colleges will pick up multiple echoes in a tour of the building, intermixed with the parallel traditions of the Islamic madrasa. Overall, though, the Centre's nearest affinities in Oxford are – unexpectedly – with Rhodes House (p. 379): for the merging of motifs across traditions, the attempts at reaching out to Oxonian forms and moods, and the close identification between building and institution.

EF INTERNATIONAL LANGUAGE CENTRE, Pullens Lane. Modest buildings of *c.*1976 onwards by *Broadbent, Hastings,*

Reid & New, for the former Plater College. Alterations and additions by *West Waddy ADP* from 2007, including the entrance range with glass-walled foyer.

RUSKIN COLLEGE, Dunstan Road, Headington. Founded in 1899 to provide education for working people, a major force in the early history of the Labour Movement. For its original building in Walton Street *see* p.432. Since 2012 the college's Oxford activities have been concentrated in Headington, where THE ROOKERY was acquired as an auxiliary site in 1946. The house has a plain s range of *c*.1810, five bays and three storeys. Open-well staircase, no less plain. Behind, standing N–S, the older part. It has both C17 and C18 features, much overlaid with embellishments and attachments of the later C19 and 1910 (the latter by *N.W. & G.A. Harrison*). Substantial E addition of 2009–12 by *Penoyre & Prasad* (library etc.), its cast-stone front picking up the early C19 plainness. A glazed section links it to the house. Auxiliary residential buildings, including *Peter Bosanquet & Partners*' BOWEN HOUSE, NW, 1964–5, with a neat half-butterfly arrangement of walls where the paired windows are canted outwards. WALLED GARDEN N of the house, dated 1731, with a zigzagging end wall.

In 2021 Ruskin College became part of the University of West London.

Schools

CHENEY SCHOOL, Cheney Lane, Headington, just s of Oxford Brookes. Incorporating the former boys' Technical School of 1952–4, S, and Central Girls' School of 1957–9, N, both by *E.G. Chandler*, City Architect. Yellow brick and curtain walling.

HEADINGTON SCHOOL, Headington Road. A private girls' school. Main building by *Gilbert T.F. Gardner* and *Thomas Rayson*, 1928–30. Very long, of brick, Neo-Early Georgian, with a cupola. Plain additions of 1985–*c*.1989 at each end by the *Falconer Partnership*, also engaged for some of the buildings behind. Earlier BOARDING HOUSES along Headley Way by *Booth, Lederboer & Pinckheard*, *c*.1963. (ARTS CENTRE by *Lyons+Sleeman+Hoare*, 2017–21, N.) By Pullens Lane, 400 yds WSW, DAVENPORT HOUSE, a large villa of red brick, bought by the school in 1920. Said to date from *c*.1847, though its quasi-Tudor manner looks somewhat later.

MILHAM FORD SCHOOL (now Oxford Brookes University, Faculty of Health and Life Sciences), Marston Road, New Marston. A former girls' school, probably by *H.F. Hurcombe*, City Estates Surveyor. Planned from 1928, completed 1939. By that time the full Ionic portico must have seemed old-fashioned. Brickwork of unusual chevron pattern. Quadrangular plan.

THE SWAN SCHOOL, Marston Ferry Road, New Marston. Secondary school by *ADP*, completed 2021. Main building of muted colours and mixed materials, including close-set timber slats.

HEADINGTON QUARRY SCHOOL (now a nursery), Quarry Hollow. Robust Gothic by *James Brooks*, 1863–4. Additions, 1882 by *Codd*, W, in keeping; 1892 by *Drinkwater*, N, plain.

WOOD FARM PRIMARY SCHOOL, Titup Hall Drive, New Headington. By *Jacobs*, 2011–14. Brick, punctuated by windowless projections in different colours.

Hospitals and medical research buildings

CHURCHILL HOSPITAL, Roosevelt Drive, S of Old Road, New Headington. Built in 1939–40 as an emergency hospital, architect *R. Fielding Dodd*. The early low-rise buildings are making way for more ambitious blocks, notably *Steffian Bradley Architects'* HOSPITAL of 2005–11. Bulky and boxy. Pale cladding in various shades, grey, beige etc., and silver for the Cancer and Haematology section, N. Just NW, tiny by comparison, the MAGGIE'S CENTRE, 2009–14 by *Wilkinson Eyre* (structural engineers *Alan Baxter Associates*). A drop-in centre to support those affected by cancer, one of a growing national network. Of timber, and placed by a wooded slope, with access by footbridge. Three-pronged plan, all the angles skewed or deflected, under a gently folded copper roof. A single space inside, with subdivisions to make resting spaces etc. Calming views out to the trees, screened partly by criss-cross lattices of oak. The concept is admirable, but the giddying geometries may feel at odds with the brief.

s of the main building, SOBELL HOUSE (hospice). Mainly by *Nightingale Associates*, 2001–3. A near-semicircle, pitched-roofed, with a central top-lit concourse. Red brick or white render. S extension by *Gray Baynes & Shew*, 2019. Older parts to the E, 1970s–80s. (The CHAPEL has re-set stained glass by *J. Bell* of 1867 from the old Cowley Road Hospital chapel, p. 497.) To its E, *Sheppard Robson*'s OCDEM BUILDING, also 2001–3. A heavy presence. White- or pink-rendered walls. Triangular atrium court within. The FULBROOK CENTRE (Elderly Mentally Infirm), S, is a gentle complex of yellow brick, the taller entrance range with a split-pitch roof. By *Carnell Green Nightingale*, 1995–6.

ROMAN POTTERIES. Extensive remains of potters' workshops with kilns, excavated at the hospital, represent one of a number of centres of this major industry in East and South Oxford.

JOHN RADCLIFFE HOSPITAL, Osler Road, Headington. Successor to the Radcliffe Infirmary (p. 362), which in 1919 bought the Headington Manor estate with future expansion in mind. In 1963 planning began for a new teaching hospital here, with *Yorke, Rosenberg & Mardall* as architects. The main buildings form a roughly oblong group, aligned NW–SE. Phase I, SE, is the Maternity Unit (now WOMEN'S CENTRE), 1968–72. A notable instance of the post-war hospital type with a multi-storey slab for the wards, set on a larger podium containing clinical departments, outpatients etc. Five storeys for the slab, two for the podium, which is planned around three inner courtyards. Two big *portes cochères*, one for a first-floor entrance where the land rises. YRM's rigorous modular design allowed for all-over cladding in standard white tiles, here applied upright. Phase II (MAIN HOSPITAL), immediately NW, 1976–9, has instead of a single upper slab a huge white near-square, with cross-ranges that form four internal courtyards. Also by *YRM* the lower ranges along the NE side between (ACADEMIC CENTRE etc.). Additions include modest extensions by *YRM*, 2001 etc.; *Capita Symonds*'s WELCOME CENTRE of 2012–15, closing the originally open-fronted space between Phases I and II; and the windowless and enigmatic ACCIDENT AND EMERGENCY block by *RMJM*, 2018–20, placed along the SW front.

YRM's Phase III was never built, and the rest of the group are mostly early C21. Going NW, the HEART CENTRE, 2006–9 by *Nightingale Associates*, with projecting tall blank bays; a new CRITICAL CARE block, begun 2021; and *RTKL*'s interlinked CHILDREN'S HOSPITAL and WEST WING, 2003–7, with lots of big coloured surfaces, clumsy-looking after YRM. Also some lesser additions behind, i.e. along the NW side.

Other buildings stand around the main group. An unlikely survival is the estate's MANOR HOUSE just to the E, now hospital offices. By *Henry Keene* for Sir Banks Jenkinson, 6th Bt, 1773–4. Ashlar, of five bays and two and a half storeys, with a three-bay pediment on consoles. Lower wings, set back. Porch with Tuscan columns. STABLES, E, with a simplified version of the pedimented S front. Further E, WILLIAM OSLER HOUSE, the medical students' social club. The core is a white-walled, flat-roofed house of 1932 by *Stanley Hamp*, for Arthur Sanctuary, Administrator of the Radcliffe Infirmary. Horizontal windows, but also round-arched ones, i.e. not yet the full Modernist programme. Partly restored and sympathetically extended by *Wildblood Macdonald*, 2008–9. The owner is commemorated to the S by ARTHUR SANCTUARY HOUSE, staff accommodation of 1955. Brown brick, quadrangular, at the prettier end of the Fifties spectrum; by *W. H. Watkins, Gray & Partners*. To its W, *AEW*'s RONALD McDONALD HOUSE, 2018–20, for short stays by families of children being treated in the hospital. Rough brick, the ground floor recessed and green-glazed. Finally the smart WOLFSON BUILDING (neuroscience research etc.), on its own at the N, by the utilities block. By *FJMT*, 2018–19. Grooved grey-brown terracotta panelling, slit windows, above a fully glazed basement storey that slides into the rising ground. Entrance end with a giant window recessed within a wooden surround.

MANOR HOSPITAL (private), Beech Road, N of London Road, Headington. By *Kendall Kingscott*, 2000–4. Terracotta-faced, the windows few and small. Relief sculpture on the front by *Diana Bell*.

NUFFIELD ORTHOPAEDIC CENTRE, Windmill Road, New Headington. Largely rebuilt by *RTKL*, 2001–6. Main part an incomplete circle on plan, its wards radiating in wedge shapes from a glass-sided entrance hub. To the SE a smaller rotunda (Physiotherapy). A yet smaller rotunda by the road entrance. Some ranges from *R. Fielding Dodd & Partners'* predecessor of 1931–9, given by Lord Nuffield, remain to the SW.

OLD ROAD CAMPUS (University of Oxford Medical Sciences), Roosevelt Drive, New Headington. Just N of the Churchill Hospital (p. 482). Rebuilt since 1997 with a succession of bold, vividly distinguished buildings. The first was *Anshen/Dyer*'s WELLCOME INSTITUTE FOR HUMAN GENETICS, W side, 1997–2000. Red brick, white upper walls. To the W a glazed half-rotunda. Immediately S, facing the road, the RICHARD DOLL BUILDING by *Nicholas Hare Architects*, 2006. All white, with plentiful *brise-soleil*. Laboratories form the spine, from which three office wings project to the S. Two atriums between the wings, which increase in length from E to W.

The middle row is all by *Make*. By the road, the RESEARCH BUILDING, 2004–8. Green cladding of different shades, rounded corners. A scarlet stripe across the entrance recess, NE. KENNEDY (Rheumatology), 2011–14, also has a NE entrance recess, but is crisply rectilinear. Big black panels with yellow lining, changing to thin light-green framing on the E side. Then two blocks comprising the LI KA SHING CENTRE (Big Data, S, and NDM Building, N), 2012–17. Both have dark-brown or bronze cladding and close *brise-soleil* screens, and both finish with sharp prows to the E. Big Data has in addition a slot-like atrium running back from the entrance, and a sunken garden area on the N side. Its foundations comprise a system of concrete beams and passages, allowing low-energy regulation of the building's air temperature (structural engineers *Griffiths & Taylor*). Between the two, SCULPTURE, Origin, by *Julian Wild*. A giant red truss-like arch, its centre fusing or disintegrating into mirrored blocklets.

In the E row, the INNOVATION BUILDING is *Make*'s too, 2015–19, designed for start-ups. A strange hybrid: the N end with thin uprights and windows in alternate bays, and cladding of the same light green-blue used on some other buildings here; the S end all open-framed car parking, screened with twisted aluminium uprights. (All the Make buildings feature atriums with cantilevered staircases, variously timber-clad, concrete or all white.) Finally the IDRM BUILDING, 2019–22, by *SRA Architects*. Glazed below, rusted cor-ten steel panels above.

WARNEFORD HOSPITAL, Warneford Lane, New Headington. Founded in 1813 as the Oxford Lunatic Asylum, for private patients; renamed in acknowledgement of donations of £70,000 from the Rev. Dr Samuel Warneford. The plain original building of 1821–6 is by *Richard Ingleman* of Southwell (Notts.). It reproduces the arrangement of tall central block and long ward wings, male and female, deployed at his The Lawn asylum, 1817–20, at Lincoln. Plain three-bay pediment.

Wings extended 1852 (*J.C. Buckler*) and later, including the SE end block by *N.W. Harrison*, *c.*1926. The approach is through the large NE extension of 1876–7 by *Wilkinson*, built after designs by *J. Oldrid Scott* were set aside (*Building News*, 15 January 1875). Florid centre, already, it seems, inspired – or should one say bowled over – by Jackson. Porch with coupled pilasters, windows with radiused corners, clock tower with a steep pyramid roof. Two originally identical wings (the SE one added by *H.W. Moore*, 1887–9), so purely Georgian and so restrained that they might mislead one. All Bath stone ashlar. The little rounded bows derive from the 1820s building, of which those on the SW front appear to be additions of after 1846. In the entrance hall a seated STATUE of Dr Warneford by *Peter Hollins*, 1843–6.

Close by to the NW, the former NURSES' HOME by *N.W. & G.A. Harrison*, 1913–14. A few Anglo-Baroque touches. Beyond, the CHAPEL, given variously to *Underwood* and *Thomas Greenshields*. Built 1841–3, not completed until 1852 (by *J.M. Derick*). Simple E.E. style. Strangely abrupt entrance front with three tiny trefoil openings. The little Free Gothic building next to Warneford Lane here is the former MORTUARY CHAPEL, 1891 by *Moore*. S of the 1820s building, PSYCHIATRY (University of Oxford), a complex mostly of low-rise brown brick of *c.*1979 etc. The HIGHFIELD UNIT for adolescents, SE, is by *Gray Baynes & Shew*, 2009–13. Big split-gabled timber centrepiece, looking rather Alpine, until one sees how markedly the roofs are skewed. To the N, *Porphyrios Associates'* POWIC building, 2000–3, with a fanciful miniature *porte cochère* of attenuated Postmodern-Egyptian columns.

Other buildings: Headington and New Marston

Described roughly from W to E.

The main through route is HEADINGTON ROAD, which to the E becomes in due course London Road. The route was adopted *c.*1790 as the main turnpike road to London. Up Headington Hill, its N side has a RAISED FOOTPATH originally made *c.*1700. Also HEADINGTON HILL PARK, with James Morrell's ostentatious cast-iron GATES (restored 1996) and LODGE of *c.*1859. The decorative cast-iron BRIDGE across the road is of 1877 by *Wilkinson*, for the Morrells' private road. For Headington Hill Hall *see* Oxford Brookes University, p.478. Opposite the main approach to the hall, on the S side, HILLTOP, a neat early C19 villa. Three bays, channelled ground floor. The N side beyond has Headington School (p.481).* After the main Oxford Brookes site on the S side, BROOKSIDE (No.26 London Road), 1886 by *Wilkinson & Moore*, with a

* (No.14 Woodlands Close, E of Headley Way, is an early C20 house by *Herbert L. North*.)

huge mullion-and-transom staircase window. Now the PRE-PARATORY SCHOOL for Headington School, with an extension by *Morse Webb Solway Brown*, 2012–13. Continuing E, student halls of residence dominate: BEECH HOUSE, 2015–17 by *Carey Jones Chapman Tolcher*, with windows in a yellow brick grid, and *Oxford Architects*' DORSET HOUSE, 2006–12, mostly timber-faced. On the N side No. 69, *c.*1924 by *Thomas Rayson*, with tile-hung gable but a Neo-Georgian shopfront. THE BRITANNIA pub, S side, is C18, with a platband, though the shutters give it an interwar look. Next S is New High Street, with modern Headington's most famous sight: the fibreglass SHARK apparently crashing head-first into the roof of No. 2. Sculpted for Bill Heine by *John Buckley*; called 'Untitled 1986', but installed tellingly on the anniversary of the bombing of Nagasaki. Amid the shops further E, No. 77 (N side), vigorously articulated with flats above, by *Riach Architects*, 2005–7. At No. 105, a former BARCLAYS BANK, *c.*1930. Early Georgian style, mannered proportions. Beyond the shops, Nos. 209–247, N side, are early COUNCIL HOUSES for Headington RDC, 1919–20 by *James Wells*. Semis of generous size. More in Barton Road, N, to a gable-fronted design by *W. Page-Webb*, 1925. On the S side facing the roundabout, COLEMANS HILL, flats and maisonettes treated as a barrier block. By the *City Architect*, designed 1975.

MARSTON ROAD runs N from St Clement's. The Centre for Islamic Studies (p. 479) on the W side is its first big event. Immediately N, where the playing fields begin, *R. P. Jones*'s PAVILION for Magdalen College, 1903, with extensions. Quite rustic, yet with a small portico. The lane alongside leads W to KING'S MILL, a small late C18 house which must once have been larger. The E side has Oxford Brookes's Clive Booth Student Village (p. 479), then *Frank Edward Whiting*'s nice Arts and Crafts SCOUT HALL at No. 238, 1913. (In William Street immediately E, No. 30, a terraced house dated 1877, eccentrically ornamented with much stone carving.) To the N are the former Milham Ford School (p. 481), Jack Straw's Lane (*see* below), then the road's two churches (pp. 476–7).

PLOWMAN TOWER, Westlands Drive, NE of Marston Road. 1965–7 by *D. Murray*, City Architect. A twin to Forester's Tower (p. 488), together comprising two of Oxford's four 1960s tower blocks. Fifteen storeys, two offset squares in plan. Re-clad by *BM3*, 2018. Just NE, BETTY HOUSE. Eye-catching flats by *Allford Hall Monaghan Morris*, 2013–18, commissioned for Kevin McCloud's HAB company. White brick, flush windows. Very bright metal balconies, turning from yellow to red, and irregularly placed. The centre is hollow, with a suspended deck for access to the upper storeys from behind. By the same architects DORA CARR CLOSE, just NW. Also white brick, but here making front-gabled terraces with spiky permutations of roof pitches: acute, equilateral, obtuse, monopitched.

PULLENS LANE. A shady private drive off Headington Road, forming the E border of the grounds of Headington Hill Hall.

PULLEN'S GATE, E side, with wavy bargeboards, is probably 1840s. The giants are further N, built mostly for dons from *c.* 1880. Opposite the EF Centre (p. 480), on the W side, THE VINES of 1889–90 by *H.W. Moore*, good and sober. The E side then has two houses now taken by Rye St Anthony School. THE CROFT, 1881–2, characteristic red brick Gothic with straight-topped windows, is *Waterhouse*'s only domestic work in Oxford. The other house, LANGLEY LODGE of 1886–7, is extraordinarily large, with lots of tile-hanging, big wooden balconies and a jolly little lookout tower. Many buildings for the school behind and between. HIGH WALL opposite is by *Walter Cave*, dated 1910, a very handsome big house in free early C17 style, for Miss Katherine Feilden. The gardens laid out by *Harold Peto c.* 1912 survive in part. To its N is COTUIT HALL of 1890–1, again by *Moore*. Flat-roofed porch with little pilasters. Hostel blocks of 1960–2 and *c.* 1968 behind, from when the house was owned by Oxford College of Technology. The road continues as JACK STRAW'S LANE, which turns W. FIELD HOUSE (No. 28) is a late work by *Herbert L. North* of Llanfairfechan, *c.* 1930. Rendered, with plain mullioned windows. The understated handling recalls Baillie Scott. Opposite is No. 69A, an L-plan Modernist house by *Spratley Studios*, 2016. No. 10 is by *Yorke, Rosenberg & Mardall*, 1953–6. White walls, flat roof, as if it were 1935.

OLD HEADINGTON is the mercifully unspoiled village centre, centred on St Andrew's church (p. 474). Simple stone-built houses, C18 and early C19, face the church on ST ANDREW'S ROAD. W of the church, a substantial cottage terrace by *R. Fielding Dodd*, 1938. Brick chimneys with shallow modelling in the Lutyens way, set on the roof ridge. Behind the old wall opposite, LAUREL FARM CLOSE, good infill housing by *J.K. Billingham*, City Architect, 1983–6. Just W, beetling over the Osler Road corner, ST ANDREW'S HOUSE, plain stone Gothic of 1862. Here the road turns NW, continuing as DUNSTAN ROAD. The VILLAGE HALL, s side, is late *Thomas Rayson*, 1957–9. Beyond Ruskin College (p. 481), also on the s side, MANOR FARM HOUSE. C17 main range, porch and fancy-gabled rear projection from *Stanley Hamp*'s reworking for R.H. Rose-Innes, 1932. Then the cemetery (p. 477), facing which are Oxford's most original 1960s houses, by *Ahrends, Burton & Koralek*, 1967–8. Five interlinked dwellings, largely of white reconstructed stone blocks, fortress-like to the outside, all playing on the motif of diagonality and canting. All have a nearly entirely enclosed garage courtyard in front. The main view is to the NE.

Going E from the church, St Andrew's Road turns s into OLD HIGH STREET. At the N end and facing s, MATHER'S FARMHOUSE, C17, with hollow-chamfered mullions. Just E in Barton Lane, EMDEN HOUSE, sheltered flats of 1979–81 by *Philip del Nevo* of *Oxford Architects Partnership*. A long, pitched-roofed ramble, the lowest resting on the old garden wall. On the High Street, the Baptist church (p. 476) faces THE PRIORY.

A strange house. The carcase mostly C17 and rubble-built, reconstructed by *Drinkwater* in 1880 for Maj.-Gen. Desborough, Governor of the Military College (p. 500), with red brick window surrounds in random-looking arrangement. No. 67, stone and half-timber, was built as the British Workman, a Temperance club, in 1880. On the W side in its own grounds, HEADINGTON HOUSE, built after 1775 by William Jackson, proprietor of *Jackson's Oxford Journal*. Two and a half storeys, five bays. Rusticated ground floor and porch, quoins, eaves cornice with modillions. Remodelled *c.* 1936 by *Austin Durst*, adding a low E wing and single-storey rear bow. Finally BURY KNOWLE HOUSE, off to the E, where the grounds are now a public park and the house a public library. Built *c.* 1800 for Joseph Lock, goldsmith. Three bays, plus single-storey wings. Central pedimented projection with perron stair to an Adamesque doorway. Behind the pediment a single-bay attic storey, also pedimented. Relieving arches to the ground-floor windows. Later C19 red brick additions behind the Georgian double pile.

Other buildings: New Headington and Headington Quarry

NEW HEADINGTON has some C19 houses but is chiefly C20. In addition, CHENEY FARM survives on the S side of Cheney Lane, with an C18 barn. Of COUNCIL HOUSING, the Gipsy Lane Estate of 1926 onwards shows the turn to Neo-Georgian details under *J. F. Richardson*, City Engineer (*H. Kellett Ablett*, architect). S of Old Road, amid the 1950s blocks of the Wood Farm Estate, is FORESTER'S TOWER, a tower block of 1965–7 by *D. Murray*, City Architect. Re-clad in 2018 by *BM3* (cf. Plowman Tower, p. 486). (Just N of Old Road, Nos. 3 and 3B York Road, houses of 2013–14 by *Original Field*. Interesting shapes and use of materials.)

HEADINGTON QUARRY also has few buildings of note, but a rewardingly intricate streetscape, formed in the C19 and C20 within and around the old quarry pits (*see* Oxfordshire Introduction, p. 528). Also memorable are the substantial rubble-built BOUNDARY WALLS. Quarry Road has the former PARSONAGE of Holy Trinity (p. 475), plain stone by *Arthur Blomfield*, 1867–8. Further S, Douglas Downes Close leads to SCIENCE OXFORD, an educational charity. Straightforward timber-clad buildings by *ADP*, 2017–19.

BARTON

Spillover development N of the Ring Road. Council housing began in 1937, resuming rapidly after 1945. Early post-war houses included many PREFABS (*BISF*, *Howard* and *Orlit* types), mostly since replaced. Expansion resumed in the 2010s with the Barton Park development, W, and is set to continue on the Wick Farm site (*see Oxfordshire: North and West*) in the 2020s.

ST MARY, Bayswater Road. A late work by *N. F. Cachemaille-Day*, 1956–8. Nave, low aisles, and a triangular sanctuary with a lower chapel E of it. Brick with brick-mullioned windows which form a continuous band in the clerestory. Extensions to the aisles by *Purcell* are proposed (2023).

(BARTON MANOR, Barton Village Road. Late C17, behind an C18 front. Formerly windowless to the street; first-floor windows here reinstated 1992. Late C17 staircase.)

BARTON PARK. A joint venture between the City Council and Grosvenor Developments, begun in 2015 and extending N up to the Bayswater Brook. Phase I, W and NW (Barton Fields Road), is by *Alison Brooks Architects* and *Pollard Thomas Edwards*, with landscape design by *TEP*. Like much recent development on the Cambridge outskirts, where these architects have also worked together, the forms and materials are startlingly urban, notably Brooks's close-set blocks of flats. Five storeys, black- or partly speckled buff brick facing, plain cut-out window openings. Along the N edge, PTE's interlinked houses, with simple gabled profiles. The landscaping includes a linear green corridor running SE–NW.

BAYSWATER MILL, 300 yds E of Bayswater Road, just N of the city boundary. Probably C18, on an older site, of which walling remains to the S. Two tiers of plain windows, N. The S side has tall round-headed windows. Adapted for partial operation by steam in 1835 (timber dates), with a big chimney, W. Domestic conversion 1985.

MARSTON

The old village centre is N of Marston Ferry Road.

ST NICHOLAS, Church Lane. Chancel, clerestoried nave, aisles, and low W tower with a battlemented parapet and gargoyles. Unpretentious exterior, almost entirely Late Perp. Only the main E and W windows have tracery. The others mostly of two cinquefoiled lights. Those of the chancel have square hood-moulds with square carved terminals, some with the monogram IHS (renewed). The priest's doorway has in addition carved foliage in the spandrels. S doorway of *c.* 1300, reused (also one C15 window) when the S aisle was rebuilt in 1562. Two Elizabethan S windows of plain twin lights, plain S porch. Inside, E.E. arcades with circular piers and double-chamfered arches. Those on the N have lower square bases, suggesting an earlier date. The E.E. chancel arch may be Norman work re-cut, as an early impost remains on the SE side. The sill of the chancel SE window forms SEDILIA. Plain PISCINA. Nave roof Perp; also some moulded medieval beams in the N aisle. S aisle roof double-pitched, with queenpost trusses. Chancel roof from *H. G. W. Drinkwater*'s restoration of 1883. Perp-style N vestry of *c.* 1978, extended by *John Perryman c.* 2004.

FURNISHINGS. Late C17 COMMUNION RAILS. – TILES in the chancel. C15, with floral and heraldic patterns. – STALLS with poppyheads (chancel) and plain oak BENCHES (nave), largely C15 or C16. – PULPIT and TESTER. Jacobean. Shallow-relief arches and decoration. – SCREEN, in the tower arch. Also Jacobean. Pierced flat-baluster patterns. – WALL PAINTING. Over the chancel arch, royal arms, apparently late C16 or C17, imperfectly surviving. Also sprigged and foliage patterns. – WEST GALLERY, 1962. – STAINED GLASS. Interesting E window of 1903 by *F. C. Eden* with *James Fisher* (MH), late medieval in mood and incorporating C15 quarries. More of these, with sundry scraps of old glass, in other windows. Also in one chancel N light a geometric pattern of small bosses linked by a trellis frame. If it is original C13 work, this is most unusual. – MONUMENT. Richard Croke †1683. A late Artisan Mannerist composition, double-pedimented. Alabaster.

CHURCH HALL, Elsfield Road, E. The old village school of 1851 by *H. J. Underwood*, with extensions. Neo-Tudor.

HOUSES. Nos. 15 and 17 Mill Lane originated as one house, built by the lawyer Unton Croke and used not long after as General Fairfax's headquarters when Parliament laid siege to Oxford in 1645. No. 15 (MANOR HOUSE), r., now has a C19 front range. At No. 17 (CROMWELL'S HOUSE) the C17 frontage survives, with dormers added probably in 1912, the date of the set-back kitchen wing to the l. Inside is a little *ex situ* C16 woodwork and mid-C17 ovolo-moulded panelling. ALAN COURT immediately SE, C17 but 1930s behind, was the home farm. COURT PLACE, No. 33 Oxford Road, is early C16 in its main N–S range, but much Victorianized.

OUTER OXFORD: SOUTH-EAST

COWLEY, WITH IFFLEY ROAD AND ROSE HILL

Places of worship

ST JAMES, Beauchamp Lane. The parish church of Cowley village, and still with the feel of a village church. Unbuttressed C15 W tower, funnily stunted-looking, because *Street*, when he restored and all but rebuilt the church in 1864–5, heightened the nave roof. The medieval nave S wall and chancel remain, now rendered. St James came to Osney Abbey in 1149, and the remaining Norman parts may well be of shortly after that. They are chiefly the re-set S doorway with one order of columns with scallop capitals and with a roll moulding in the arch; the re-set N aisle doorway with a round, slightly chamfered arch; and the responds of the chancel arch, also with one order of columns, but with single-scallop capitals. Their original painted treatment survives, renewed – spirals on one, little lozenges on the other – and part of a thin foliage scroll close to the N column. There was much more in 1864, mainly figures. The chancel itself was rebuilt in the C13: see the three fine stepped E lancets and the PISCINA with a shouldered lintel. The straight-headed chancel windows are C13 too, one of them a lowside window. Nave s windows straight-headed, C14 and C15. The N aisle and chapel are all *Street*'s. Piers with dogtooth in the abaci. – REREDOS, STALLS and cylindrical PULPIT also by *Street*. The reredos is oblong with a raised pointed arch in the middle. Small slabs of various marbles and small areas of gilt mosaic. – TILES by *Godwin*. – ORGAN from St Martin, Carfax, installed 1896. – Norman FONT, a plain drum. – STAINED GLASS. E window and two s by *Baguley* of Newcastle, 1868. Also one s by *Clayton & Bell*. – MONUMENTS. N aisle w, Col. W. J. Lindsey †1922. With flimsily draped mourner, rather Belle Epoque.

ST ALBAN, Charles Street, Cowley St John. 1928–33 by *T. Lawrence Dale*. Simple brick mission church. Diocletian windows to the s, also a small transept. Bellcote. Relief over the s porch by the many-sided *John Henry Brookes*, then Principal of Oxford School of Art, later part of Oxford Brookes University. Tripartite chancel arch. Kingpost roof, the beams painted with the Instruments of the Passion. – MURAL by *Peter Greenham*, 1946, E wall. – Incised STATIONS OF THE CROSS, some by *Eric Gill*, the rest by his workshop, 1938–41. – Square HALL by *Associated Design Partnership*, 1985–6, attached SE.

ST LUKE (now OXFORDSHIRE HISTORY CENTRE), Oxford Road, Temple Cowley. 1937–8 by *H. S. Rogers*. The gift of Lord Nuffield, whose Morris motor works then lay just to the E. Large, of sheer yellow brick, with a blunt tower at the ritual NW. Vaguely Gothic windows. Gothic interior with an elliptical ceiling, partly floored across in the conversion of 1999–2000. The REREDOS with *Alec Miller*'s painted figures survives.

ST MARY AND ST JOHN, Cowley Road, by Leopold Street. By *A. Mardon Mowbray* for Fr Richard Meux Benson, founder of the Cowley Fathers (*see* p. 494); built 1875–8 (chancel), 1882–3 (nave), 1892–3 (tower). Rock-faced stone, with Geometrical tracery. There are transepts, but they barely project. Big, broad w tower, with higher stair-turret, but lacking the intended spire. Much foliage and figure carving, the E wall outside by *Grafton*, the inside mostly by *McCulloch*, to a theological programme by Benson. The N transept's angel busts were done as late as 1938. Most of the capitals and corbels of the nave have been left uncarved. Barrel-vaulted chancel and nave. The aisles are treated unexpectedly. They have half-arches across, and triplets of low lancets, the rere-arches on very big corbels. The chancel was designed surprisingly as part of a much smaller, towerless church, intended to double as a cemetery chapel for the burial ground donated by Benson, to the s. E vestries added 1911–12. – REREDOS, 1918–22, coloured in 1938. Designed by *C. G. Hare*. The ROOD BEAM of 1921 is his too. – Italian SANCTUARY LAMPS, given 1885. – STATIONS OF THE CROSS, Oberammergau Baroque work of 1911–13. – STAINED GLASS. E window, 1891–2 by *Burlison & Grylls*. The Vision of St John, partly after Van Eyck's Ghent altarpiece. By *Comper* the s transept, 1892, N transept, 1913, and Lady Chapel, 1922. Aisles, figures by *Burlison & Grylls*, 1886–1923; also one by *Lawrence Lee*, N, 1949. NE chapel, beautiful small-scale windows by *M.E. Aldrich Rope*, 1924 (three lights) and †1929.

CROSS in the churchyard, in memory of Father Benson. By *Comper*, 1916–17. A small calvary group at the head.

PARISH ROOM, E, by *Bucknall & Comper*, 1892–3. Squared-rubble walls. Early Perp style, with a broad traceried N window. Attached to the S end, the VICARAGE, 1901–2, by the same. Steep red-tiled roofs, white-rendered walls, stone-mullioned windows with slim sashes. Beyond the churchyard is St John's Home (p. 493).

OUR LADY HELP OF CHRISTIANS (R.C.), Hollow Way, Cowley. By *Patrick J. Sheahan* of Limerick, with *Ballard & Beese* of Oxford, 1961–2. The well-worn longitudinal type, with a campanile. Brick. (– REREDOS by the *Irish Mosaic Co.* of Roscommon.) N addition 2010.

ST EDMUND AND ST FRIDESWIDE (R.C.), Iffley Road. *See* Greyfriars, p. 496.

COWLEY ROAD METHODIST CHURCH. 1903–4 by *Stephen Salter*, for Wesleyan Methodists. Rock-faced Gothic, with a SW turret. Typical of *c.* 1900 in the playful gable shapes and other such details.

ROSE HILL METHODIST CHURCH. 1835. A plain rectangle originally. Arched windows, echoed in extensions of 1940–1. Rear addition 1957–8.

JOHN BUNYAN BAPTIST CHURCH, Beauchamp Lane, Cowley. By *Peter Reynolds*, 1963–4. It slants up to a brick entrance wall between angled-back glazed sections. Triangular clerestory over the pulpit. Hall etc. of 1938–41 attached, E.

GRACE CHURCH (formerly Congregational), Oxford Road, W of St Luke (*see* p. 491). 1929–30 by *G. Smith*. Old-fashioned churchy Gothic, with a tower. Brick.

SEVENTH DAY ADVENTIST CHURCH, Chester Street, W of Iffley Road. 1970–2 by *Oxford Architects Partnership*. Decidedly unchurchy. Shallow lateral projections with narrow windows.

CENTRAL OXFORD MOSQUE, Manzil Way, N of Cowley Road. By *Mohammed Ehsan*, 2001–2, reduced from a design of 1996. Quite large even so, with a dome and a minaret with domed lantern.

ROSE HILL CEMETERY, Church Cowley Road. 1892–3. One of three contemporary municipal cemeteries (with Wolvercote, p. 474, and Botley, Berks.), each with an identical Gothic LODGE and CHAPEL designed by *W.H. White*, City Engineer.

Religious houses

BARTLEMAS (ST BARTHOLOMEW'S HOSPITAL), Cowley Road. Founded as a leper hospital by Henry I in 1126–8. In 1329 it was granted to Oriel College. The city used the hospital as almshouses from 1536. Three buildings, deep in a green enclave up a lane between Southfield Road and Bartlemas

Close. The CHAPEL must date from *c.*1330. In 1913 *Comper* restored the windows to their original length. The very odd and unusual Dec details are original. Also conventional Perp windows, e.g. the s window to the w. Perp w doorway. Steep roof, renewed in the C17. Below is a ceiling of lower pitch, re-created by *Comper* in 1924. It incorporates timbers from the ceiling made by *Robert Carow* in 1522. – SCREEN, given by Oriel. Dated 1651. Triple arches on each side of the entry, divided by two columns and two pendants. – LIGHT PENDANTS by *Comper*, 1936.

BARTLEMAS HOUSE, N of the chapel, is the hospital's former main range, rebuilt by Oriel in 1649 after Civil War ruination. Two storeys, twin doorways. Plain chamfered window surrounds, one to three lights. Restored by *H.S. Rogers*, 1922. (Some original doorways and fireplaces.) Also ST BARTHOLOMEW'S FARM HOUSE, SW. No datable masonry features, but tree rings from the main roof timbers match records of work at Bartlemas by *Carow* in 1510.

CONVENT OF THE INCARNATION, Fairacres Road and Parker Street, behind the terraced houses. The Sisters of the Love of God, an Anglican order, moved in 1911 to FAIRACRES HOUSE, a T-plan Italianate villa of the 1830s. To its s, a white-rendered residential range (ST MARY'S) and CHAPEL were added in 1922–3 by *Paul Waterhouse*. The chapel is Spanish Baroque, barrel-vaulted, with a pyramid roof over the E end. (In 2019–21 a full CLOISTER was created by *MEB Design*, with a new N range and cross-walk joining on to the s range of the 1950s and 1990s.)

ST JOHN'S HOME, St Mary's Road. Begun in 1873 by Father Benson (*see* St Stephen's House, below) and Miss Frances Sandford as a home for the infirm aged, s of Benson's St Mary and St John's church (p.491), and still in use for its intended purposes. A huge Gothic design was supplied by *Buckeridge*, comprising a cloistered quadrangle with two eastward-projecting wards to the E and a giant chapel-cum-district church intersecting the w range, so that patients could follow services from their beds. All that was done of this – executed after Buckeridge's death by *Pearson*, 1873–5 – comprises part of the two-storey s end of the main N–S range, with some Venetian-looking tracery in the upper bay window. Charlbury stone. The home then grew more modestly as funds allowed, abandoning the aspiration to provide free wards for poor patients. From 1880 it was run by the Society of All Saints Sisters of the Poor, for women only. Additions by *Pearson* were made in 1880, 1882–3 and 1888–90, mostly three-storeyed and in a more relaxed Tudor. Then in 1905–7 *Comper* added a further wing, and the CHAPEL across the N end, a major work.★ 106 It deserves to be better known. East Anglian Perp, of white

---

★ Strictly the credit should be *Bucknall & Comper*, the work having been commissioned in 1902; their parting of the ways was hastened by the discovery of Bucknall drunk on site in 1904.

stone, very tall inside and out. Some inventive wiry tracery in the E window. Octagonal rood-stair-turret to the N. Steep arch-braced roof, all white, but handsomely decorated. In the chancel each panel has a little pendant (plasterwork by *McCulloch*). To the S a lower chapel, with an entry from the home. The sisters' choir has its windows set high, and is enclosed by a superbly carved ROOD SCREEN of the palest stone (carver *Gough*). – By *Comper* the ENGLISH ALTAR, elaborate STALLS and his typical STAINED GLASS: E window 1907–11, S chapel 1914, W window 1946.*

In 2013 Conventual Franciscans took over the chapel and N part of the buildings, and the sisters moved into separate quarters to the S. Two new structures here, designed in 2004 by *Jessop & Cook*. The BROWNLOW BUILDING is an arresting zinc-roofed shape suggestive of a great hall (though two-storeyed within), its upper walls clad in grey-weathered timber. To its N an elliptical building with meeting room and CHAPEL. Brownlow joins on to a former SCHOOL on St Mary's Road, plain brick Gothic of 1868, N extension 1898. The boundary wall and GATEWAY on this side are by *Pearson*, 1891. – N of the Comper chapel, HELEN HOUSE. Of note as the world's first children's hospice, opened 1982. Architect *John Bicknell* (*Bicknell & Hamilton*).

ST STEPHEN'S HOUSE, with ST JOHN'S CHURCH, Iffley Road and Marston Street. The complex was built for the Cowley Fathers, properly the SOCIETY OF ST JOHN THE EVANGELIST, an austere order founded by Richard Meux Benson in 1866. The first Anglican order for men which endured, it soon established daughter houses in the United States, India and South Africa. Benson's mission house of 1868 survives in Marston Street. After he stepped down, the order acquired more demonstrative buildings in 1894–1907: the church by *G. F. Bodley* on Iffley Road, and the cloister and new accommodation for the order, placed between church and mission house and attached to both. Significant additions were made in 1933–8 by *Comper*, who had already designed for the order overseas. Membership later dwindled, and St Stephen's House, a theological college with High Church traditions, took over the buildings in 1980. St Stephen's was a Permanent Private Hall of the University between 2003 and 2022.

The first MISSION HOUSE was built by *Joseph Castle & Co*. No architect is recorded, and Benson may not have engaged one. After 1901 it served as the guest house. Modernized in 1961 with banal enlarged windows and a new doorway and staircase. Upright front section of three and half storeys with plain gables, taller rear part with a steep-roofed chapel (FOUNDER'S CHAPEL) right on top. This has to the W a rose

---

*Pevsner in 1974 referred to the windows harshly as 'some of that stained glass which has done so much damage to stained glass in England, until Evie Hone [1894–1959] first broke the spell of this pretty-prettiness'.

window, to the S a shingled bell-turret, to the E a big niche with a carved Calvary group. Inside, the chapel has been truncated at the W end. Three bays remain, with a basic kind of aisles with posts and angle braces. Simple stalls. Altar with tester, surely *Comper*. Mid-C20 painting on the W wall, the Martyrdom of St Stephen, brought from the chapel at the old St Stephen's House in Norham Gardens (p.461). Other rooms originally included a refectory, libraries, a parish room for public business, and twenty-six individual cells.

The second MISSION HOUSE is of 1900–1. *Bodley* was the architect in charge, but he passed most of the design to his former assistant *William Maynard Shaw*, who had joined the Society as *Brother Maynard*. Though large, it presents to the world no more than the modest, rendered entrance front set back to the r. of the 1868 building, and even here the top storey is an addition of 1929 (*F.E. Howard* and *T. Rayson*). Free Gothic doorway, but windows of plain mullioned C17 type. Hipped red-tiled roof. Similarly austere ranges beyond, on an axis perpendicular to the entrance range. The planning does not conform to monastic tradition. U-shaped main building, its arms extending W (properly, SW), and housing the dining hall, common room and library. Cross-range with an extra dormer storey, for the offices and accommodation. Two small courtyards between the wings, divided by a central walk. Projecting midway from the cross-range on its E side is the HOUSE CHAPEL. It has the plainest pointed barrel-vault and a slim painted frieze. The stalls and other woodwork are plain and without Gothic motifs, like mature Arts and Crafts work. But the transeptal altar end is an addition of 1938 by *Comper*, and here pointed vaults are developed into exaggeratedly steep groined forms. In conscious contrast, one of Comper's Quattrocento ciboriums stands over the altar, this one understandably painted all white.

The main CLOISTER is entered from the covered walk between the small courts. Simple Gothic detail here, the windows glazed in 2012. The W side communicates with the E end of St John's church (*see* below). – SCULPTURE by *Paul Vanstone*, 2011. A winged head, of streaked marble.

Across the garden to the NE, MOBERLY CLOSE, 1980 by *Philip del Nevo* of *Oxford Architects Partnership*, for St Stephen's staff and married students. L-plan, brick, one wing stepping upwards. Round-headed perspex door hoods.

ST JOHN THE EVANGELIST, Iffley Road, was the church for the Cowley Fathers' public services, in succession to an iron church of 1859 in Stockmore Street, N. It is by *Bodley* (properly, *Bodley & Garner*) and was built in 1894–6, the tower in 1902–3, the porches in 1907. *Brother Maynard* was clerk of works. Bath stone. The tower, the climax of the church, was intended to be higher, but it looks splendid as it is, in its sturdiness, with the broad middle buttress and the thin corner buttresses also facing W. The middle buttress has a Calvary group carved

just below the battlements. No W doorway. The tower's twin
W windows are Dec, the aisle W windows of a free Gothic
with Geometrical and Perp motifs. The aisles embrace the
tower. Seen from the side, the long, high, uninterrupted roof
of nave and chancel is equally splendid. The aisles have flying
buttresses, and two flying buttresses, less happily, support the
chancel from the E. The buttresses have obelisk pinnacles,
another tellingly plain detail. The E window of five stepped
and cusped lancet lights is placed high up, as Bodley liked
it, for the sake of the reredos. A crucifix is carved below. The
gable is echoed by that of the N chapel for weekday services,
with its own bellcote. Further W on this side is a lesser attachment, originally for the song school. In 2012 the church was
adapted for shared use as a performance space (SJE ARTS),
by *Montgomery Architects.*

The INTERIOR is high, and the near-uninterrupted ceiling is
again the finest feature. Its painted decoration is by *Maynard*,
who had worked for Kempe before his time with Bodley.
Where there are flying buttresses outside, there are transverse
stone arches inside. The nave arcades are conventional Dec,
except that the W and E arches die into the imposts. The
same for the arches under the tower, which is open below.
Plain plaster finishes. English medieval friars' churches are
the closest model, as with other late churches by Bodley. Differences from the standard parochial arrangement include the
unusually long chancel and the twin doorways in the E wall
for access from the mission house. Chequered paving at the
E end. Bodley planned a grand coloured reredos as a climax.
Instead, there is *Comper*'s REREDOS of tester and embroidered
hangings, 1934. – By *Bodley* the ORGAN CASE high up on the
N wall, the unusual square PULPIT, and the ROOD SCREEN
with its Oberammergau figures. – STATIONS OF THE CROSS
painted by *E.A. Fellowes Prynne*, 1918–20. – CIBORIUM and
iron SCREEN of 1935 by *Comper* in the Blessed Sacrament
Chapel, converted from the song school. – STAINED GLASS
by *Kempe*, 1897–1905. E window (the earliest), the True Vine,
with monastic saints; W windows, missionary saints; clerestory
scheme not completed.

SONG SCHOOL etc. (former), N of the nave. By *Comper*, 1935.
Mullioned and cross-mullioned windows. The work includes a
little cloister for circulation from the E.

GREYFRIARS, with ST EDMUND AND ST FRIDESWIDE (R.C.),
Iffley Road. Church of 1910–11 by *Fr Benedict Williamson* with
J.H. Beart Foss, friary of 1930–1 by *G.T.F. Gardner*, adjoining to
the S (ritual E). The church was built for the Jesuits, then passed
to Capuchin Franciscans who moved from the St Kenelm's
School site (p.501). Greyfriars was a Permanent Private Hall
of the University from 1957 to 2008. Both parts are large, and
both – why on earth? – are of black knapped flint with red
sandstone dressings. Also both are Norman in style, with few
C20 convolutions. The church has a big W tower whose saddleback roof with a needle spirelet is the most original feature. The

interior is more attractive than the exterior. Arcades with plain cylindrical piers of Corsham stone, simplified cushion capitals, open roof. – STATIONS OF THE CROSS in *opus sectile*, 1938, reportedly designed by *Williamson*. – FRAGMENT. A moulded C13 capital from the medieval Greyfriars (p. 450), set in the credence table of the N chapel. – STAINED GLASS. E windows, very good late work by *J. E. Nuttgens*, dated 1978. Figures of saints. – Gardner's friary was designed to have a cloister to the S, where the elevation relaxes into Tudor. Instead, a HALL was built there not long after.

NAZARETH HOUSE (former). *See* Cowley Road, pp. 498–9.

Public buildings

POLICE STATION, Oxford Road, Cowley. By *D. Murray*, City Architect, 1963–6. Blockish, of black brick between white-painted concrete floor bands.

COWLEY LIBRARY, Temple Road. 1939–40. Streamlined and stylish. Entrance recessed between forward-projecting wings.

ASIAN CULTURAL CENTRE, Manzil Way, N of the mosque. By *William Fisher Jun.*, built in 1866–7 as the chapel of the Cowley Road workhouse of 1863–4, later in hospital use (dem.). Transepts, apse, Geometrical tracery. Adapted in 1987–9 by *Architects Design Partnership*, with parallel N range and link of yellow brick.

IFFLEY ROAD SPORTS CENTRE (UNIVERSITY OF OXFORD). Opposite St John's church. A running track was first made here in 1867. Cantilevered GRANDSTAND of 1961–2 by *D. Armstrong-Smith*, N side. Brick boxes for the MAIN GYM, 1964–6 by *J. Lankester*, W side, and in the NW corner the ROSENBLATT POOL by *Nigel Grayshon & Partners*, 1996–2003, and ACER NETHERCOTT SPORTS CENTRE by *FaulknerBrowns*, 2016–18. (The last has the UK's first 'smart glass' floor, with markings that change electronically for different sports.)

OXFORD SPIRES ACADEMY, Barracks Lane, Cowley. Originally Southfield School (boys), 1934–5 by *H.F. Hurcombe*, City Estates Surveyor. One- to two-storey Neo-Georgian, with a cupola. Additions include the REUBEN BUSINESS CENTRE, E, with dolly-mixture-coloured mullions. By *Nightingale Associates*, 2012–14.

ST GREGORY THE GREAT SCHOOL (R.C.), Cricket Road, Cowley. A former middle school, expanded as a secondary by *Towle Spurring Hardy*, 2003–7. The eyecatcher is a hollow three-storey drum with flame-coloured cladding (brick-faced and with a cloister walk within. Alongside, a small CHAPEL of rounded plan).

EAST OXFORD PRIMARY SCHOOL, Union Street, Cowley. Of 1900–1, one of *Leonard Stokes*'s three highly individual Oxford schools (cf. pp. 285 and 439). Main building of broad U-plan. Steep roof, brought forward between square-topped corners on the wings. Banded brick. Centre infilled later. The delightful infants' school, w, has a long row of gables at the back.

ROSE HILL PRIMARY SCHOOL, The Oval. Of 1950–2, representative of *E. G. Chandler*'s era as City Architect. Red brick. Long and low, windows in bands, parapets projecting.

ST MARY AND ST JOHN PRIMARY SCHOOL (former), Hertford Street, Cowley. By *Bucknall & Comper*, 1895–6 and 1899 (SE). Warm red brick. Upper windows mostly with depressed pointed arches, under three-quarter-hipped gables. Immediately NW, the INFANTS' SCHOOL (now Comper Foundation Stage School), 1902–3, by the same. Symmetrical this time, with cross-gabled ends. Castellation along the parapet. Behind, two big half-timbered gables, their windows cutting into a pointed-barrel-vaulted hall.

EAST OXFORD HEALTH CENTRE, Cowley Road. By *Hunter & Partners*, 2005–7. The bulk is leavened with a few fashionable motifs: wavy roof, crossed-over raking struts.

ST BARTHOLOMEW'S MEDICAL CENTRE, Manzil Way, just behind the Health Centre. By *Sutton, Griffin & Morgan* of Newbury, 1989–90. Unusual and inventive. A four-pointed star in plan, with corner entrance. The roof ridges steeply glazed, over passages that meet in the centre.

Other buildings

Cowley cannot easily be perambulated. There is too much of it. One can still sense that it was several communities until the C20. Cowley St John, with the churches of St John and of St Mary and St John, was an eastward extension of Oxford, created a parish in 1868. To the w are the old centres of Cowley village, alias Church Cowley, and nearby Temple Cowley, named from an early preceptory of the Knights Templar: both detached from Oxford, and more or less detached from one another, but added to the city in 1929. The main interest is along Cowley Road, in these older centres, and along Iffley Road.

Perambulations

1. Cowley Road and streets adjacent

COWLEY ROAD, coming SW from the St Clement's end, is humdrum until the Methodist church (p. 492) and the former ELM TREE pub on the opposite corner of Jeune Street, genial Voyseyesque by *H. T. Hare*, 1899–1901. Twin gables, skewed away from the centre. Just N in Jeune Street, the ULTIMATE PICTURE PALACE of 1910–11, designed for the pub's owner by *John R. Wilkins*. A rare early cinema restored to its intended use. Rudimentary front with a segmental gable and Doric colonnade, sheltering a central paybox between twin doorways. Next w, the former children's wing of NAZARETH HOUSE, a

Roman Catholic home for the poor founded in 1875. Of 1901–2 by *Edward Goldie*. Partly Tudor, partly Georgian windows. The chapel (1876–8, *F.W. Tasker*) has been demolished, and Goldie's wing is now part of Oriel College's JAMES MELLON HALL. The greater part is *David Morley Architects*' distinctive round-ended building of 1999–2000, set back in the garden. Four storeys, red brick, with a colonnade round most of the ground floor, where the communal rooms are. Stainless-steel-clad top storey. Lesser L-shaped block in the angle behind. Also part of the complex are the mid-C19 Larmenier House in Rector Road, and *Brown Matthews*'s underwhelming addition of 2007–9 there. On the s side, white paint disguises *H.W. Moore*'s Nos. 106–114, 1889–90, with the former EAST OXFORD CONSTITUTIONAL HALL behind (subsequently music hall, theatre and cinema). On the N side again, the corner with Princes Street has the EAST OXFORD COMMUNITY CENTRE, originally Cowley St John Boys' School, 1870–1 by *Buckeridge*. Simplified Gothic, with nice tumbling-in of the plain brickwork. N addition 1902.

The next N turning is Union Street, with East Oxford Primary School (p. 497), and to its E three slabs of student flats by *Brookes Architects*, 2014–18. On the s side beyond, down Bullingdon Road, the workshops and projects building of the University's RUSKIN SCHOOL OF ART, by *Spratley Studios* of Henley, 2013–15. The main part brick-walled and barn-like, its zinc-clad roof flattened at the top. Big street-side window on to which pictures can be projected from within. Recessed entrance, l., and a lower section clad in grey panels, cut asymmetrically by the gable. Nos. 190–196 Cowley Road are the former CO-OP, now O2 Academy, dated 1907. By *Frank Mountain*? (cf. his George Street Co-op, p. 438). Beyond St Mary and St John's church, the CITY ARMS pub (No. 288), stripped Elizabethan of 1938 by *J.C. Leed*. On the opposing corner is the former REGAL CINEMA of 1936–7 by *Robert Cromie*, now a church. Placed sideways to the main road, like Cromie's Odeon: another echo from George Street. The flank has a defile of thin Deco pilasters, repeated between the powerful angle towers of the entrance front, where they frame the central windows. Full Ionic columns in the foyer. (Undivided auditorium with slim columns and ribbed coving.) Magdalen Road, between cinema and pub, has at No. 14 the former ST MARY AND ST JOHN MISSION HOUSE, *c.* 1891, apparently *Bucknall & Comper* (cf. their schools, p. 498). Good red brick, symmetrical. Small-paned windows under chamfered shallow-pointed arches.

COUNCIL HOUSING. Nos. 434–472 Cowley Road, with Shelley Road and Milton Road. Of 1920–1 by the *Oxford Panel of Architects*, then in charge of municipal housing, under the generous terms of the Addison Act of 1919. Rendered, many with shared gables that slope down to intersect with the porches.

HERBERT CLOSE, Barracks Lane, N of Cowley Road. A spacious residential enclave of Jesus College, overlooking its playing fields and *R. England & Sons'* PAVILION of 1906. Along the N side, HUGH PRICE HOUSE, 1989–90, friendly blocks of flats by the *Architects Design Partnership*. Each comprises two asymmetrical brick- and timber-faced parts at different heights, linked by a glazed-sided staircase. Twinned near-pyramidal roofs, broken by a window band. To the E and NE, the same architects' LEOLINE JENKINS HOUSE, 1987–8, a more complex L-shape, and THELWALL HOUSE of 1997–8, flats for couples (the latter replacing accommodation by *John Fryman* of the practice, 1965–6). Due S of Leoline Jenkins is HAZEL COURT, 2000–1 by *Maguire & Co*. A more spare and reductive design, with motifs – plain little windows, chimney-like vent stacks – that look back to the firm's Liddell Building on Iffley Road (p. 502). U-plan, subdivided into ten houses. Inside they are arranged like college staircases, two rooms per floor, except for the top storey, where a thin horizontal window lights the kitchens and common rooms.

HILL TOP ROAD, off Divinity Road, N. *Adrian James Architects'* No. 6, 2009–11, appears raw and angular amid the interwar houses. Entirely of concrete-panel construction, exposed inside.

2. Temple Cowley and Cowley village

Cowley Road continues roughly SE as OXFORD ROAD. On the N side after the churches, the much-reused buildings of the MILITARY COLLEGE by *Sir T. G. Jackson*, 1880–1 and 1877–8 (facing Hollow Way, E). The boarding school had an optimistic brief to prepare boys for the Army or for the University, but its never-completed buildings evoke neither: three storeys, red brick dressings against originally white render, a Dutch gable to the E, and on the inner sides an applied order of superimposed terracotta pilasters decorated with graceful Quattrocento detail, putti etc. Between Jackson's wings are annexed buildings for an earlier failed school, Cowley College: conventional stone Neo-Tudor of 1852 on the corner, a chapel of 1870 by *Bruton* with C13 detail attached to its W. The gap between the latter and Jackson, occupied until its demolition in 1957 by Cowley's late C17 manor house, is architecturally terrible infill from the residential conversion of 1996–9. Also a plain S addition of 1931 to Jackson's S wing, for the Nuffield Press, an offshoot of the Morris motor company which bought the complex in 1912. The first production-line Morris cars were built in the E wing in 1913, and William Morris kept his office in the 1852 building thereafter. Opposite is the ORIGINAL SWAN pub, 1930. Long, with half-timbered gables.

TEMPLE ROAD runs N between the churches. On the E side the CRICKETERS ARMS pub, 1936. Waney-edged boarding in the gable. Opposite, a big vernacular stone house, apparently C18. Next to it a former Congregational CHAPEL, polychrome Gothic, dated 1878. A *Mr Beasley* was the 'honorary architect'. Where the road bends w, No. 74, plain C18. Plat-band carried up as an arch over the doorway. No. 76 (s side, down a lane) is dated 1761. Unusual banded stone, ashlar alternating with rubble. Window surrounds with key blocks, of broad vernacular proportions. Further w, the former ST CHRISTOPHER'S SCHOOL. Red brick Gothic in the Street manner by the young *Mardon Mowbray*, 1876 and 1884. To the N at the angle of Junction Road and Crescent Road, the former SALESIAN COLLEGE. Not built for them, but for the short-lived St Kenelm's School, 1880 (centre of the w wing, *Wilkinson*) and 1883 (extensions and N wing, *Wilkinson & Moore*). Red brick, the later part with fewer stone dressings. Its E end was the chapel, extended in 1906–7 by the Franciscans, who later moved to Iffley Road (p. 496).

BETWEEN TOWNS ROAD runs SW and w from Oxford Road by St Luke's church, towards Cowley centre. Mostly big blocks, starting with *Hodder & Partners'* BETWEEN TOWNS COURT, student halls of 2016–19. Three parts, linked by distinctively treated open-sided staircases. All of pale brick, with concrete floor bands. Nos. 21 etc., round-ended offices of deep red brick, are by *Fletcher, Ross & Hickling*, 1980 onwards. On the N side is intelligently composed housing by *Levitt Bernstein* for Oxford City Council, 2019–22. Purple-brown and white brick. A linked group of units encloses a small garden behind.

TEMPLARS SQUARE is just beyond: the renamed Cowley Centre, built in 1960–5 by the City Council to serve fast-expanding East Oxford. By *E. G. Chandler*, City Architect, completed under *D. Murray*. Only its location well away from the historic centre distinguishes it from other city shopping centres of the period. There were two main pedestrian spaces, a square (E) and an oblong, both glazed over in 1989. The junction between is marked by a slab block of flats with curtain walling. Also multi-storey car parks to S, W and E, of which the last is part of an addition of 1975–6 by *P. Bosanquet & R. Diplock Associates* that includes the white-tile-faced shops on Barns Road. To the N is a supplement for larger shops, TEMPLARS RETAIL PARK, 1986–7 by *Neale Associates*. Its chief architectural interest is the relocated gable-end of the former Oxfordshire Steam Ploughing Co. against the w wall. Dated 1900, with a little relief of a traction engine. To the E, down the convex curve of Barns Road, a block by *Allford Hall Monaghan Morris*, 2013–16, commissioned for Kevin McCloud's HAB company (cf. Betty House etc., p. 486), and replacing the 1960s community centre. Upper floors of very white brick, each flat with a recessed balcony and two upright windows, combined in a strong pattern.

BEAUCHAMP LANE, just w of the Cowley Centre, has what remains of old Cowley village. Thatched COTTAGE at the N end, probably C17. S of the Baptist church (p. 492), the former Rectory Farm House, partly C17. Gable with kneelers and ball finials. Beyond St James's church, Nos. 10–14, a cottage terrace built for Christ Church. Listed as early C17, but the banded masonry and broad windows make a tell-tale match for No. 76 Temple Road (above), of 1761.

OXFORD BUSINESS PARK, Garsington Road, just E of Oxford Road. Opened in 1994, on the site of the original Morris motor factory. No building stands out. In JOHN SMITH DRIVE, S, the architects were *Lyons+Sleeman+Hoare* to 2001, followed by *Frank Shaw Associates*. By the latter e.g. JUBILEE HOUSE and its neighbour, *c.*2003, with rounded cast-stone uprights. ALEC ISSIGONIS WAY, N, began with *Thorpe Architecture*, U-shaped buildings 7200–7799, NW, designed 1993. 8000 and 8050, facing the N–S axis, are by *Aukett Europe*, *c.*2004. Glass-box entrances.

HOLLOW WAY runs N towards New Headington. On the E side facing the golf course, one block remains from COWLEY BARRACKS, 1874–6 by *Capt. Hurt* of the Royal Engineers. Built for the Oxfordshire and Buckinghamshire Light Infantry, as part of the Cardwell reforms of the Army. Squared rubble, three-storeyed with two storey wings. Chamfered window lintels are the only non-functional touch. On each side, PAUL KENT, halls of residence for Oxford Brookes by *Towle Spurring Hardy*, 1997–9, echo the 1870s gables. More halls N of James Wolfe Road, UNITE STUDENTS PARADE GREEN, 2017–19 by *Broadway Malyan* (885 rooms!). The flat-roofed block at the corner is meant to evoke the former 'Keep' of the barracks, demolished in 1971.

PLANT OXFORD, E of the Eastern By-pass. The current name for the motor works, now concentrated on the former Pressed Steel Fisher site, making Minis for BMW. Its most prominent buildings are the sequence of 1950s–60s office blocks facing the by-pass, re-liveried in smart black *c.*2013. The six-storey office slab at the Unipart depot to the SE, 600 ft (180 metres) long, is by *Harry Weedon & Partners* of Birmingham, 1965–6.

3. Iffley Road, with Rose Hill

The Oxford end of IFFLEY ROAD opened in 1778, linking the rebuilt Magdalen Bridge with the turnpiked route to Henley. The dominant presence at the Oxford end is Magdalen College School (p.405). On the E side mostly later Victorian terraces, mostly quite ambitious. Also at No.43 the former CRICKET-ERS' ARMS, a semi-Modern pub by *G.T.F. Gardner*, 1938, with a relief of a batsman. Opposite is the LIDDELL BUILDING, actually a group of residential blocks shared between Christ Church and Corpus Christi. By *Maguire & Co.*, 1989–92. A domestic image, deferring to THE RED HOUSE (No.60), a don's house of 1892 with the unusual motif of shaped gables. The new buildings stand at a distance, two large blocks and two small, the latter a pair of identical plan but mirrored and set at right angles. Pale purple-brown brick with contrasting varnished woodwork and red-tiled roofs, interrupted by square dormers with distinctive flat hoods and by chimneys with vents in their sides. Other windows small and unpredictably placed. Here and there a double-shouldered gable, placed frontally. The echoes are of the high Arts and Crafts of *c*.1900, but of a mood a world away from the Neo-Voysey marques of the early C21 housebuilder. A separate COMMON ROOM and a delicate, copper-roofed PORTER'S LODGE attached to No.60 complete the group.

Terraces of interest back on the E side include two polychrome brick groups of *c*.1864–5, Nos.65–73 with sexfoil discs, and the eye-watering Nos.85–93, symmetrically composed and ingeniously modelled. It overlooks the University's Sports Centre (p.497). Behind Nos.77–87 is the JOCELYN MORRIS QUAD of St Hilda's College, created in 2016–18 by *TSH Architects*. Chiefly infill and extension around *Oxford Architects Partnership*'s little lead-roofed block of postgraduate flats, 1976–7, in Stockmore Street, N. Past St John's church (p.495), No.137, *c*.1880, has a splendid iron balcony on the first floor. It faces BANNISTER CLOSE, a civilized interpretation of the terrace form by the *Oxford Architects Partnership*, 1980–2. Then a stretch of *c*.1887–95 between Henley Street and Stanley Road (Nos.189–223) which looks entirely North Oxford. Some are still Gothic, i.e. they are late for their appearance. Nos.1–7 Stanley Road are earlier, *c*.1863, on ground broken by the short-lived Conservative Freehold Land Society, and clearly by the same hand as Nos.85–93 Iffley Road. No.225, a free design in brick with tile-hanging, is a villa and studio house by *H.W. Moore* for the painter Walter Tyrwhitt, 1903. A favourite Moore detail, a thin string course rising as a pair of interlinked scrolls (cf. Walton Well Road, p.434), appears at Nos.220–242 opposite, one house dated 1901, which may be his too; also at Nos.283–287.

EXETER HOUSE, for Exeter College's postgraduates, embraces Nos.237 and 239, two late Italianate villas built *c*.1865 by *James Castle*, with new accommodation by *Anthony Pettorino* of *McLennan Architects* behind and between, 2007–10. The additions continue the villas' stucco finishes and shallow-pitched roofs, but with pragmatic fenestration. Near-full glazing towards the little quad behind the front entrance lodge. Also converted were buildings behind No.239 from ST BASIL'S HOME for aged women, *c*.1895 (with the former chapel, N; attributed by Peter Howell to *C.C. Rolfe*) and *c*.1915–20. These are a poor exchange for *Jackson*'s ambitious Gothic design for the home, exhibited 1913. In Magdalen Road alongside, the PEGASUS THEATRE for young people, 1973–5; the front end reworked by *Feilden Clegg Bradley Studios* in 2008–10 as a big copper-clad box.

The DOROTHY WADHAM BUILDING of 2017–19 at Nos.265–277, for Wadham College undergraduates, is *Allies & Morrison*'s first accommodation for an Oxford college, after much comparable work at Cambridge. Like a traditional quad, symmetrical and with a formal entrance via the glazed middle section, except that the ranges sit back behind little front gardens on three sides, and have gaps where they face the side streets. Pale, rather undercooked-looking brick, timber window uprights. The lower windows at the front also have steel guards or cross-mullions set in front. More extensive glazing – for kitchens and staircases, as at Exeter's scheme – on the inward faces. A single-storey common room closes the E side. Further S, changes in the design of early COUNCIL HOUSING can be traced between the *Oxford Panel of Architects'* work of 1920–1 at Nos. 298–304, with Addison Crescent etc., and the cheaper short terraces of 1925 onwards in Meadow Lane etc., SW.

BEDFORD STREET, W of Iffley Road. No. 16 is the only work at Oxford or Cambridge by *Ernö Goldfinger*. For the physicist Prof. Hans Motz of St Catherine's College, 1963–4. Small, but full of ideas. Two parts, flat- and monopitch-roofed, linked by a short first-floor bridge. Brick, with concrete floor slabs. The flat-roofed part sits over an old stone wall, which is interpenetrated by its support piers.

FLORENCE PARK ESTATE, between Iffley Road and Cowley Road. By *G.T.F. Gardner*, 1933–7. Oxford's largest enclave of interwar private housing, archetypal 1930s suburbia built by *Nathaniel Moss & Son* of Cardiff, initially for rent. The PARK was the gift of Mr F.E. Moss, in memory of his sister.

WAR MEMORIAL (Oxon and Bucks. Light Infantry), corner of Church Cowley Road and Rose Hill. By *Lutyens*, 1923. Obelisk on a subtly stepped plinth.

ROSE HILL COMMUNITY CENTRE, Carole's Way, off Ashhurst Way. A large building by *ADP*, 2013–16. Plain yellow-brown brick, given interest by the cranked front and the angled and recessed entrance.

ASHHURST WAY in Rose Hill has BUTLER HOUSE, sheltered housing for the Oxford Cottage Improvement Society, a late work by *T. Rayson*, 1958–61. Three-bay centre with pediment. Also good social housing of 2019–21 by *Levitt Bernstein* at No. 60 etc., and to the W in THE OVAL. Strongly domestic forms in contrasting shades of plain brick.

BLACKBIRD LEYS

A planned suburb SE of the Ring Road, built to provide especially for the huge workforce of Oxford's motor industry. The plan was adopted in 1953, the first houses of an intended 2,800 finished in 1958. The whole is uninspired, but no worse than that, and as an environment Blackbird Leys does not deserve the disparagement it has often attracted from outsiders. Most of the communal buildings are within the oval of Balfour Road–Pegasus Road–Merlin Road. Greater Leys, to the S, is chiefly private housing of 1990 onwards.

HOLY FAMILY, Blackbird Leys Road. 1964–5 by *Colin Shewring*. Radical in form and also in concept, as a shared church for

Anglicans and Nonconformists. Brick, all the walls curved, the roof a hyperbolic paraboloid, with a forward altar below. Listed in 2019, the church awaits demolition in 2023 after repairs were judged unaffordable.

LIBRARY, Cuddesdon Way and Blackbird Leys Road. 1965–8 by *D. Murray*, City Architect. Yellow brick, pyramid roof.

CITY OF OXFORD COLLEGE, Cuddesdon Way, by the library. The college's Technology Campus, opened in 2016 with new buildings by *ADP*. The rest is mostly the old Redefield School (Secondary Modern), 1960–2 by *E.G. Chandler*, City Architect.

PEGASUS PRIMARY SCHOOL, Pegasus Road. 1962–5 by *Murray*, City Architect. Some interesting angles in the roof.

(WINDALE PRIMARY SCHOOL, Dunnock Way. Designed 1994, to serve the expansion to S. By *Oxfordshire County Council Architects*. Courtyard plan, kept low, under big pantiled roofs.)

COMMUNITY CENTRE, just N of Holy Family church. Designed 1962, City Architect *Murray*. – SCULPTURE in front, Glow Tree, plaited steel by *Neil Wood*, 2006.

(THE BARN, Long Ground. C18 or C19, from the original Blackbird Leys Farm. Adapted from 1993 as part of a community centre for Greater Leys, by *Phippen, Randall & Parkes*.)

HOUSING. Two fifteen-storey tower blocks, WINDRUSH TOWER, 1960–2, and EVENLODE TOWER, 1962–4, within the central oval but not well integrated. Windrush is of specialist interest as the first example of the contractor *Laing*'s much-multiplied standard design. Both towers re-clad by *BM3*, 2017–18. (FRY'S HILL ESTATE, 1995–7 by *PRP Architects*, comprises a large part of the private housing to the S.)

SCULPTURE, Watlington Road, NE. A family group by *Diana Bell*, 2007. Bronze resin.

IFFLEY

ST MARY, Church Way. A magnificent C12 parish church, lavishly decorated with sculpture, and very well preserved. Built probably in the 1160s, almost certainly by Geoffrey de Clinton II, a connection by marriage of the local St Remy family. Externally the doorways are the showpieces, apparently executed by the workshop also responsible for those at the Cathedral chapter house and St Ebbe's church (pp. 132 and 393). Their chevron and beakhead motifs have links with sculpture from Reading Abbey, the beakhead also with Kenilworth Priory in Warwickshire, another de Clinton foundation. A closer parallel is the church built by the de Clintons at Stewkley in Buckinghamshire, likewise a property of Kenilworth, with which Iffley shares features, including a three-stage W elevation, a type more common in C12 Normandy and Aquitaine than in England.★

★*See* the excellent guidebook by Geoffrey Tyack and Mark Pythian-Adams with Malcolm Thurlby, 2018.

The plan of chancel, central tower and aisleless nave is original. The E end was rebuilt *c.*1220–30, replacing what was almost certainly an apse. Subsequently the nave roof was lowered, destroying part of the W gable, and the crenellated parapet was built on the S side. Its inscribed date 1612 may well be a later addition, referring to other renovations. C19 campaigners made careful attempts to restore the original design of the WEST FRONT, a combination less apparent since the application in 2017 of an all-over shelter coat of lime. Of its three stages, only the lowest is wholly C12. The upper gable was rebuilt in 1823, instigated by the Oxford bookseller Robert Bliss. The frieze and small blind window, and also the top parts of the side windows to below the level of the outer capitals, are thus entirely C19, and unusually sympathetic restoration for the date. The central window is wider, and likewise deeply recessed. All three windows are ornamented with chevron and beakhead and divided by shafts with carved capitals. The nave roof behind was rebuilt in 1843–5 by *R.C. Hussey*, to its original pitch but of kingpost form. In the middle stage, the oculus window with chevron mouldings is also C19, inserted by *J.C. Buckler* in 1856. He was guided by the outline of a blocked round window which had been replaced by a Perp one. The W doorway below is flanked by two tall blind roll-moulded arches. It has three continuous orders of carving, i.e. no shafts or capitals: a wide inner order of fourfold stepped chevron set parallel to the wall, typical of *c.*1160–70, and two outer orders of beakhead over a spiral roll moulding. On the hood a motif of beaded chain links, connected by flat masks. The links frame reliefs of Signs of the Zodiac and symbols of the Evangelists.

This W entrance was probably used for ceremonial occasions, the usual entry being on the SOUTH DOORWAY. Like the N doorway, this is placed in a projecting section of walling, a feature most common in England among the C12 churches of Worcestershire. The S doorway was protected by a porch until 1807 and is unusually well preserved. Its decoration is no less exuberant than that on the W doorway. The inner order is continuous, a roll with a hollow on either side filled with rosettes, fantastic beasts, quatrefoils and heads. The two outer orders have arches with chevron and a roll with an outer band of sawtooth decoration. They are carried on shafts with chevron and diaper patterns. Five faces of the capitals have lively carving. To the r., two horsemen fighting and Samson with the lion. To the l., a male centaur trampling a sheep, while also apparently feeding a female centaur on the next face who is herself suckling her young; also a lion killing a horse. The NORTH DOORWAY is simpler. Arch with an outer order of roll moulding and sawtooth under a beaded hood, inner order of a roll with repeated chevron. Plain jamb shafts with scalloped capitals.

Round the entire NAVE runs a corbel table of plain square blocks. It was presumably intended to be carved, but only two blocks on the S were completed. The N and S walls each have two windows flanking the doorways, large windows by C12 standards, linked with a running hoodmould. The western-most windows retain their arches, decorated externally with chevron, and inside with more chevron and a roll moulding. Larger windows were inserted in the eastern window openings in the C15, with depressed straight-sided arches, but the C12 mouldings partly remain. TOWER of three stages with shallow clasping buttresses below. In the bell-stage on all sides two arched openings divided by pilaster strips under a corbel table of alternating triangular and round arches, all harshly renewed in 1975–7. The original square blocks were probably intended to be carved. The decoration of the bell-openings is also incomplete. Each has an arch of three recessed orders, the central arch on shafts with scalloped capitals. Only the SW arch is carved, with chevron and beakhead, likewise renewed. On the NW a stair-turret with slit windows and a top stage treated like clustered shafts. The renewed battlements have gargoyles carved by *M. Groser*. On the ground stage C15 windows have been inserted in the original openings. The CHANCEL is C12 in the W bay, but with later C13 two-light windows with quatrefoil tracery inserted in the openings. E of this, the early C13 chancel extension. Very large single lancets without tracery. On the E wall clasping buttresses with angle shafts. The other buttresses are C14 to N and S, mid-C19 to the E. Small reused C12 window in the gable. A blocked arch in the S wall has been explained as the doorway to the vanished cell of a documented C13 anchoress named Annora.

The INTERIOR shows a marked rise in levels from W to E, including unusually a step within the nave: a powerful effect when combined with richly decorated tower arches. On their W faces these have octagonal shafts of black Tournai marble, an exceptionally rare material in English architecture, in which the less dark Purbeck marble did similar duty more widely after *c.* 1170. The decoration of both arches is similar. On the W side two bands of chevron and a wide outer order with a large stylized flower motif. The E face of both arches has chevron only. The bottom stop-chamfers of the W arch on the nave side are carved with a bird on the S, a beast on the N. On the E arch the abacus returns against the nave wall, explained as early evidence for provision of a rood beam. The W bay of the chancel has a quadripartite vault, the ribs with chevron. At the centre an unusual boss with a winged serpent, four animal masks and four diagonal pine-cones. The vault springs from clustered shafts, the hollows between them filled with rosettes; and on the S is a nesting bird, a charming detail which looks forward to Gothic naturalism. The C13 bay of the chancel has a quadripartite vault of roll-moulded ribs. Shafted windows also with roll mouldings. The C12 apse would have been divided by a round arch. Its position is marked by a wide band on the vault, and on the walls a section sloping towards the C13 vaulting shafts. The C13 designer provided a narrow blind pointed arch with chevron at this junction to make a smooth transition. Double PISCINA in a recess with a shouldered arch. Projecting bowl on a half-shaft. Also later C13 SEDILIA with three tre-foiled arches on shafts, blocking the anchoress's doorway. The present chancel floor is of 2011.

FURNISHINGS, from W to E. Original FONT, a mighty piece, again of Tournai marble. Square bowl, roughly cut, on a squat shaft. Corner shafts with spiral fluting. The one plain shaft is C13. LID of 2014, designed by *Roger Wagner*, sculptor *Nicholas Mynheer*. – SEATING from *Caroe & Partners'* restoration of 1995 around the font. – ORGAN by *W. Hill*, 1875. – PEWS, 1843–5 by *Hussey*. – SCULPTURE, N wall. A C13 roundel of the Agnus Dei, of high quality. Originally the head of the churchyard cross (*see* below). – REREDOS. An enriched blind arcade of pointed arches, 1864 by *J. C. Buckler*. – AUMBRY, inserted in one piscina opening in 2011. Figures carved by *Mynheer*. – STAINED GLASS. Lingering C15 bits in the eastern-most nave window tracery. N side, mostly *in situ*, foliage, Tudor roses, angels, cherubim and lesser fragments. S side, fragments including two late C15 quarries, each painted with a bird. Also in the main centre light C15 quarries and the shield of John de la Pole, Duke of Suffolk †1491. – The rest is C19 to C21. W windows by *Hardman*, 1856. Nave S, Nativity window by *John Piper* with lamb and birds, maker *David Walsey*. Installed 1995. Nave N, Flowering Tree, by *Roger Wagner*, 2012. Tower N and S, a pair, †1875. Chancel N and S by *Clayton & Bell*, 1864. E window by *Christopher Webb*, 1932. – MONUMENT. On the N wall a Purbeck slab from a tomb-chest with indents of brasses.

In the churchyard to the SE, the base and slim shaft of a C13 CROSS. The replacement head was carved by *Earp* from a design by *Street* in 1857. – W of the church the octagonal bowl of a probable C15 FONT.

PARSONAGE, NW of the church. Medieval, and as such a rarity among Oxfordshire parsonages. Gabled, of stone, with lofty diamond-shaped brick chimneystacks and mostly red-tiled roofs. The main range runs N–S. Its S part includes the walls of a C13 hall, to which a timber-framed upper storey, subse-quently rebuilt in stone, was added in the late C14. The solar wing, projecting E, followed probably in the C15. Around 1500 the main range was continued or rebuilt to the N, with rooms of higher status. This part is taller. Four six-light and two three-light windows on its garden side, W. All the lights uncusped. NE stair-tower. In the sitting room a late C16 plaster ceiling with shallow ribs in a pattern of elongated squares and octagons, enclosing small lions' masks. C17 panelling, probably brought in. (In the SE wing is a re-set C13 opening of exceptional quality and unusual form. Two lights divided by an elongated shaft with a moulded base. Jamb shafts with richly moulded and carved capitals and moulded bases. It may have come from the anchoress's cell at the church.) The S end was reworked by *J. C. Buckler* in 1857–8, with a new kitchen and housekeeper's quar-ters. Restored and subdivided by *Philip Jebb* for the Landmark Trust in 1979–80, when a corridor added along the E side in 1819–20 was demolished.

COURT PLACE, S of the church, has a re-set datestone of 1580 on the N wall. Small C16–C17 gabled wing at the rear, but the main house is Georgian. Perhaps built by the mason *John Townesend III* (†1784), who lived here. COURT PLACE GARDENS to the S and E is an enclave of family housing for University postgraduate students. Originally mid-1970s semis, being replaced from 2022 with grouped terraces by *FJMT*.

CHURCH WAY, N of the church. SCHOOL (now church hall), dated 1838. A long, thatched range of stone. Miniature bell-cote. Diagonally opposite, the former DAME SCHOOL, a square stone house with the inscription 'Mrs Sarah Nowell's School 1822'. Behind No.96, the MALT BARN, with a collection of built-in Gothic windows and carved fragments. At least one of these, an ogee-headed single light of C14 type, appears medieval. Also a large eroded figure of a bishop (C17?). The TREE HOTEL at No.63 is by *Drinkwater*, 1882. Three matching bays, brick-nogged and tile-hung. At No.44 a stone-built house by the *Oxford Architects Partnership*, designed 1972, of two unequal monopitch-roofed parts.

MANOR HOUSE, Mill Lane, W. Somewhere within the comical mash-up of C19 and early C20 additions – crenellations, two-storey cross-wing with upper veranda r., rounded bay l. – is the fabric of a C17 house.

GROVE HOUSE, No.44 Iffley Turn, at the N edge of the village. Stuccoed Italianate villa of 1832–3, most memorable for *Gerald Banks*'s unique addition of 1962. This displayed the collection of dolls' houses assembled by Mrs Vivien Greene, estranged wife of the novelist Graham Greene. A Neo-Regency rotunda with a little open lantern and plain through-storey arcading, it might have come from Clough Williams-Ellis's Portmeirion. A covered bridge links it to the house.

BEECHWOOD, Anne Greenwood Close, off Iffley Turn. By the *Oxford Architects Partnership*, *c.*1968. A well-designed three-storey block of flats for old people. Dark red brick. Windows around corners or in tall slots.

IFFLEY LOCK. The second channel from the E includes some walling from the POUND LOCK first recorded in 1632, one of the earliest such locks on the Thames. The reconstruction of 1923–4 is unexpectedly idyllic: charming timber SHELTERS over the lock walkways, a ROVING BRIDGE of stone with balustrades of C18 type, and a LOCK COTTAGE of Cotswold inspiration, not the standard Thames brick type. By the Thames Conservators' Chief Engineer *G.J. Griffiths*, with *H.S. Fleming*, architect.

LITTLEMORE

ST MARY AND ST NICHOLAS, Cowley Road. Founded by John Henry Newman, whose living of St Mary the Virgin included Littlemore, before his conversion to Rome in 1845. The church as first built in 1835–6 comprised the present nave only, a chaste and severe E.E. hall of striking proportions, with tall narrow lancets, and until 1885 also a w bellcote. The architect was *H.J. Underwood*. Newman's brother-in-law, the Rev. Thomas Mozley, supplied sketches of the C13 chancel of his own church, Moreton Pinkney in Northants, as a model.* The result was widely admired, and its publication in 1840 and 1845 by Oxford's own Society for Promoting the Study of Gothic Architecture encouraged others at home and abroad to take it as a prototype. Ecclesiological correctness required a separate chancel, duly added by *Joseph Clarke* in 1848, with the NE tower. The intended splay-foot spire was never supplied. Clarke reused Newman's triple E lancets and blind arcading along the altar wall, the latter upgraded with Purbeck marble shafts and later richly painted. Also Newman's Gothic-panelled stone ALTAR (slightly enlarged). Another challenging gesture by Newman was the cross carved in the wall above it, now no longer visible. The SEDILIA with three trefoiled canopies are Clarke's. Nave roof of giant cusped-arched braces, of uncertain date but clearly mid-Victorian. Underwood's roof was a thin pseudo-hammerbeam design. NE vestry by *F.E. Howard*, 1918. Reordering by *Conservation Architects*, 2019–20, with a new floor of polished stone and a WEST GALLERY with offices below.

OTHER FURNISHINGS. CHANCEL SCREEN of 1913, by the Cheshire craftsman-scholar *F.H. Crossley*. ROOD GROUP above carved at Oberammergau; the crucifix presented 1901. – PULPIT, also *Crossley*, with tester. – FONT. C13 bowl from St Mary, Oxford. Blind arcading of elongated trefoiled arches with roll mouldings, separated by fleur-de-lys. The COVER, in East Anglian style with tiers of crocketed pinnacles, is of 1924 by *Crossley*. – LECTERN. Eagle type, of wood. Probably that supplied when J.R. Bloxam was curate, 1837–40. – STAINED GLASS. The windows of Newman's church were originally plain, except for a single suggestive red quarry in the E window. Glass by *Thomas Willement* followed from 1839, of which the chancel side windows (four, with Willement's monogram) and the nave W and two S windows survive. E window of 1900 by *Louis Davis*, a Crucifixion, with much gradation of the white glass. Nave NE and SE, single figures set in plain quarries, 1887 by *Morris & Co*. The next two on the N are of 1900 by *Shrigley & Hunt* of Lancaster. – MONUMENTS. Jemima Newman, John Henry's mother, †1836. By *R. Westmacott Jun*. Like an Annunciation, with figures of Mrs Newman (holding a plan of the church) and a standing angel. The church building in progress in low relief behind. – Rev. David Nicholls †1996. Brass by *Michael Black*. – LYCHGATE by *Clarke*, c.1848.

BLESSED DOMINIC BARBERI (R.C.), Cowley Road. 1965–9 by *Peter Reynolds & Partners*. A diagonal-square-plan church of the

---

*T. Mozley, *Reminiscences, Chiefly of Oriel College and the Oxford Movement* (1882). Underwood's own St John the Baptist, Summertown of 1831–3 (dem.) was very similar in style, so he may have needed little guidance.

type encouraged by the Liturgical Movement (cf. Reynolds's John Bunyan church, Cowley, p. 492), here with the gimmick of a cluster of glass pyramids making the clerestory. Buff brick. Porch and rear hall rebuilt by *PCA Architects*, 2002–5.

OXFORD ACADEMY (secondary school), Sandy Lane West. Largely rebuilt in 2009–11 by *White Design*, with specially indigestible combinations of dazzle-pattern cladding.

JOHN HENRY NEWMAN C. OF E. PRIMARY SCHOOL, Grange Road. Blocks by *Oxfordshire County Council Architects*, designed 1992 and 1994. Big roofs with glazed ridges or apexes.

ST JOHN FISHER CATHOLIC PRIMARY SCHOOL, Sandy Lane West, ½ m. ENE. By *Oxford Architects Partnership*, 1965–6. The flat-roofed hall pushes up amid the classrooms.

EMMANUEL CHRISTIAN SCHOOL, Sandford Road, by the churchyard. Enlarged from the simple building erected by J. H. Newman in 1838.

INFANTS' SCHOOL (former), Sandford Road, further s. Of 1904, by *E. P. Warren*. Straightforward and honest.

LITTLEMORE HOSPITAL, Sandford Road. The former County Lunatic Asylum. After closure in 1998 the main complex on the E side of the road was converted to housing, under the alias of ST GEORGE'S MANOR. A N–S spine just short of 1,000 ft (305 metres) long, from which four cross-wings extend to the W and (not so far) to the E. The entrance courtyard is closed on its E side by the central administrative section, of eleven bays with three shallow-eaved projections, and two octagonal towers where the cross-ranges run through. All this is of 1844–6 by *Robert Clark* of Nottingham, with enlargements of 1847–52 at the outer ends of the ward blocks. The latter are by *H. J. Underwood*, or perhaps by the Oxford contractors *Plowman & Lock*, whose 'plans and specifications…approved by the Secretary of State' were tendered for in 1847. Completed by *J. C. Buckler*. Oblong water towers in the two outer courtyards. LODGE by the road, more explicitly Italianate. Behind the original building is a parallel range of HOUSING inserted by *Towle Spurring Hardy* after 1998, replacing service blocks etc. Immediately E, now in other uses, a parallel HOSPITAL RANGE, of 1902–5 by *H. J. Tollit*, County Surveyor. Faintly Vanbrughian in style, with quoins, corner towers and ball finials. The central part, now reconstructed, was the asylum's recreation hall. Also by *Tollit* the big CHAPEL of 1882–3, s. Norman style, with chancel, nave, W porch and bellcote.

A MENTAL HEALTH CENTRE remains in use on the W side of the road. C20 low-rise buildings of no special note. Among them, parts of an isolation hospital by *Tollit*, 1902.

VILLAGE CENTRE. The crossing by the church is dominated by BLEWITT COURT, a quasi-manorial roadhouse for Hall's brewery, built as the Marlborough Head in 1939–40. In Cowley Road, r., humble L-shaped stables and cottages, converted in 1842 by John Henry Newman into a chapel, library and six sets of rooms for 'THE COLLEGE', his own ascetic community. They are linked along the back by a simple veranda or cloister.

Restored after 1951 as a memorial to Newman. In Sandford
Road, SW of the church, CORPUS CHRISTI FARMHOUSE (W
side). Dated by its tree rings to 1424, and identified as originally two dwellings of equal status, each with an open-roofed
upper hall. No early details in the stonework. Next S, the
MANOR HOUSE, possibly C15 but much remodelled. Through-
passage plan, with a curtailed cross-wing, l. The canted bay is
probably from alterations by *G. F. Turner* (*Who's Who in Architecture*, 1926). S of the church down David Nicholls Close,
LAWN UPTON HOUSE. Built *c.*1846 for Charles Crawley, a
friend of Newman's, on land which the latter had acquired for
his projected religious community. Coursed rubble, Elizabethan style. Late C19 additions, N.

DORMER CROFT, No. 28 Cowley Road. C17. (Dated 1657 on a
quoin, 1630 in plasterwork in the cross-wing.)

OXFORD SCIENCE PARK, Grenoble Road, ⅓ m. SE. Developed
by Magdalen College from 1989; Oxford belatedly catching
up with Cambridge, where Trinity College had established
Britain's first US-style science park in 1972. Masterplan and
landscaping by *Robert Rummey Associates*, making use of the
Littlemore Brook as a feature. The first instalment was *Ian
Ritchie Architects*' NORTHBROOK HOUSE, 1990–1, N of the
E–W road. Three storeys, all white, left open for car parking
below. The roof beams project, and mesh screens hang from
them. Of the rest, JOHN ECCLES HOUSE, by the SE entrance,
is interesting: austere blockwork to the E, open-framed services
and blue vent nozzles to the S, timber screens on the entrance
side, W. By *Proctor Matthews*, 1997–9. Newer and larger blocks
at the W end. The HINSHELWOOD BUILDING, 2001, and
NOMINET are by *Nicholas Hare Architects*. Mostly white, the
former with a thin portico of pole columns, the latter with one
side recessed under a giant pergola. Islanded in the loop, the
forceful SCHRÖDINGER BUILDING by *Bogle Architects*, 2016–
18. Irregular diagonals in the plan, making a glass-fronted
entrance atrium where the office wings splay out to the E. The
other sides have mushroom-grey cladding and sharp exposed
steel framing. *Hamilton Associates*' WINCHESTER HOUSE and
FLETCHER HOUSE, N, designed in 2005, make one continuous block, dark-clad, with a bold central entrance void. Further
N, a building by *Perkins & Will* is due in 2023.

LITTLEMORE PRIORY (MINCHERY FARM), Grenoble Road,
½ m. ESE. The small Benedictine nunnery was founded in the
mid C12 and dissolved by Wolsey in 1525. The remains consist
of the E range of the cloister garth as remodelled *c.*1600, with a
small gabled projection for the stairs on the W side. The dormitory would have been on the first floor, and the chapter house
etc. below. The earliest surviving details are late C15. They
include two doorways, two windows with two arched cusped
lights under square heads, and probably the five similar single
lights. (C17 staircase with flat pierced balusters and newel posts
with lantern finials and pendants. Queenpost roof with clasped
purlins.) Derelict in 2023.

OUTER OXFORD: SOUTH

ABINGDON ROAD, GRANDPONT AND NEW HINKSEY

The coverage of South Oxford begins just S of Folly Bridge. It takes in the area W of the Thames, transferred to the city in 1889 from Berkshire parishes including North Hinksey and South Hinksey.

ST JOHN THE EVANGELIST, Vicarage Road, New Hinksey. By *Bucknall & Comper*, 1899–1900. Comper projected a lavish hall-church based on late medieval East Anglian models, as realized not long afterwards at his St Cyprian, Clarence Gate in London, but there was money only for the nave. In 1937 he added one more bay to make an interim chancel. Red brick, stone dressings. The N windows large in a distinctive mixture of Perp and flowing elements, the S windows simpler. Bavarian churches inspired the plain bottle-glazing. White walls inside. Arcades on tall quatrefoil piers. The roofs ceiled, with handsome original painting. They were meant to run right through to the chancel, with a rood and screen at the division. The church replaced a school-chapel by *Bruton*, 1869–70. – ALTAR of 'English' type, supplied by Percy Dearmer's *Warham Guild*, 1900. – Giant CRUCIFIX above, c.2005. – VICARAGE, W, also of red brick. By *H.W. Moore*, 1887–8, with minor amendments by *J. Oldrid Scott*. Long, low and unusually memorable for Moore, especially the W front with its row of five not quite identical gables.

ST MATTHEW, Marlborough Road, Grandpont. 1890–1 by *J.T. Christopher & E.E. White*. Grandly sized, but hemmed in by houses. Rock-faced, Perp, without a tower. Nice details round the S porch with its turret. No clerestory. Wagon-roofed nave, ceiled barrel-vault over the short chancel. Octagonal arcade piers. Reordered, keeping the nicely detailed PULPIT. – CHURCH CENTRE by *Carnell Green Nightingale*, 1992–4, N.

HOLY ROOD (R.C.), Abingdon Road. 1959–61 by *Gilbert Flavel*. An early instance of the Liturgical Movement's impact on church design, showing the influence especially of Maguire & Murray's St Paul, Bow Common, London (1956–60). Rectangular plan, most of which is filled by a taller octagon. On it a square lantern consisting of four glazed gables cutting into a pyramid roof. Porch glazed almost to full height. Undivided interior, with a W gallery for the organ and a platform for the forward altar. Slim windows to N and S light the chancel recess behind. The FURNISHINGS include much from pupils or followers of *Eric Gill*, whose own sculpture of Christ on the Tree of Life forms the ALTARPIECE of the low-ceilinged S chapel. It came from the chapel of Pigotts, his house in Buckinghamshire. The free-standing main ALTAR and the FONT have lettering by *Kevin Cribb*. Big CORONA over the altar, and bronze SCULPTURE of Christ Pantocrator on the wall behind, by *Michael Murray*. – Abstract STAINED GLASS by *Charles Ware*, S chapel.

PUMPING STATION (former), now SOUTH OXFORD COM
MUNITY CENTRE, Lake Street, New Hinksey. Opened 1856.
Designed by Oxford Corporation's waterworks manager *James
Jones*. Red brick. Round-arched windows, sparing classical
detail. A taller, single-bay engine house was added to the W in
1862, for a *Butterley Co.* rotative engine. Smaller additions for
more engines to the NW (1884, 1890). The GROUNDS are now
a public park. HINKSEY LAKE, W, was formed by 1850 from
the extraction of ballast for use by the railway. The open-air
SWIMMING POOL to the N was adapted in 1936 from former
filter beds.

DONNINGTON BRIDGE. By *R. Travers, Morgan & Partners*,
1960–2. One very shallow concrete arch.

BOATHOUSES. Downstream from Folly Bridge, mostly on the N
bank beyond Christ Church Meadow, but easily viewed from
the S towpath. Unlike at Cambridge, the college boat clubs
used special moored barges until the mid C20, commonly
designed by architects; the boats themselves were stored elsewhere. The replacement buildings include several matching
pairs, and are mostly shared between colleges. From W to E: (1)
Wadham etc., clean-lined brick with a pyramid roof, 1987; (2)
Pembroke and St Edmund Hall, linked, 1968–9; (3) St John's
etc. and (4) Jesus etc., by *Bridgewater & Shepheard*, 1962–3,
with bow-fronted balconies and open staircases; (5) Brasenose etc., also (7) Balliol etc., by the same, 1956–9, with far-
projecting balconies; (6) Queen's etc., *Henry Goddard*, 1956–7,
with a dark weatherboarded top storey; (8) Merton etc. and
(9) Magdalen etc., near-twins of 1939–40, blockish brick; (10)
Christ Church, 1935 by *G.C. Drinkwater*, also brick, with a
plain Venetian window and no front balcony.

The S bank has the big UNIVERSITY COLLEGE BOAT
HOUSE, by *Belsize Architects*, 2005–7. An excellent design, if
unexpectedly sombre by comparison with *J. Oldrid Scott*'s
burnt boathouse of 1880–1 for the Oxford University Boat
Club on the same site. Black brick, the viewing deck sheltered
under a lean, far-projecting cantilevered roof. In the middle
of the upper level hovers a sharp glazed box for the clubroom.
Off-centre entrance void to the r. below. The rest of the upper
storey contains student rooms and a keyworker's flat.

FOLLY ISLAND, in the Thames or Isis at the S end of Folly Bridge
(p. 407). On the W side by the roadway, NORTH HINKSEY
HOUSE, a bit of a joke. Built in 1849 for Joseph Caudwell,
accountant. Red brick, only one bay wide in front, with a
rusticated doorway and window surrounds of raised bricks,
cast-iron and stone statues in niches l. and r. of the first-
and second-floor windows, and crenellation on top. Behind is
another tall house, 1875 by *George Shirley*, but its crenellations
are no older than 1974. The E side is SALTERS' boat company,
notably the Picturesque building of 1900–1 by *Stephen Salter*
(of the family), facing N. To the S, a slab-sided warehouse of
1835–6 by *Thomas Greenshields* for an earlier boatbuilding firm,
designed for conversion to houses if required.

ABINGDON ROAD is the main thoroughfare, running s from Folly Bridge. It overlies part of GRANDPONT, the late CII stone causeway built by Robert d'Oilly to raise the s approach to Oxford above the meadows and marshes. Later widenings account for the causeway's present stone flanks and arches, which show especially well by the inlet on the w side.

The E side of the road starts with HERTFORD COLLEGE GRADUATE CENTRE, 1997–2000 by *Oxford Architects Partnership*. Of U-plan, enclosing a dock. Yellow brick, blue or leaded trim. Oversailing flat roofs, and several round-ended staircases of glass brick to the fore. Elegant FOOTBRIDGE on the towpath alongside, of 1953 by *Donovan H. Lee*. Next, set back down a path, GRANDPONT HOUSE, built *c.*1785 for William Elias Taunton, City Solicitor and Town Clerk. Three storeys, the major façades rendered. To the river two canted bays, a central doorway with a Venetian window over it and a tripartite window over that, all awkwardly proportioned. On the w side, the N corner of Western Road begins with a superior Gothic-windowed house of 1888 by *G.T. Sessions*, part of the Grandpont Estate of streets begun in 1880. The s corner has been rebuilt as ABINGDON HOUSE, another Hertford College project by *Oxford Architects Partnership*, 1988–90. Something between a house-type and a staircase-type treatment, to go with late CI9 houses incorporated to the s. Next PEGASUS GRANGE, retirement flats etc. of after 1992 by *Denning Male Polisano*, with some arch collegiate detailing. The OLD WHITE HOUSE is a consciously un-pub-like pub by *H.T. Hare*, dated 1897. Stone below, rendered above, symmetrical, with some typical 1900 decoration in the pedimental gable.

Opposite, Brasenose's playing fields conclude with a CRICKET PAVILION of 1896 by *A.J. Rowley*, who may also have done the nice Free Style cottage by the gate. Further E is the PAVILION for Queen's, cosy Arts and Crafts of 1901 by *E.W. Allfrey*. GRANDPONT VILLAS (Nos. 65–85) follow, boxy villa semis of *c.*1860, then the Brasenose SQUASH COURTS of 1937, windowless of course, with a faintly Deco stepped parapet. Some 300 yds s, a lane leads to the OXFORD SPIRES hotel, a Neo-vernacular ramble of 1998–9 (*Oxon Planning Partnership*), and the remarkable survival of EASTWYKE FARMHOUSE. Early to mid-CI7 stone, T-plan, with a few original windows. Another 200 yds s, another CRICKET PAVILION: for University College, 1914, by *Clough Williams-Ellis*. With a miniature portico and a toy-like stepped clock tower *à la* Portmeirion.

The w side of Abingdon Road here has a stretch of older houses, from the early development along Vicarage Road and Lake Street; No. 202 is dated 1849. Then more Late Victorian terraces, Nos. 238–246 with a distinctive two-storey timber veranda all along the front. Further s and in the side streets around Weirs Lane, a concentration of 1920s council houses, built partly for people displaced by the St Aldate's clearances (*see* p. 446). Much variety of treatment: some of concrete block, others rendered or with tile-hung upper storeys, others still with quasi-Georgian cast-stone surrounds to the doorways (Nos. 360–412 etc.).* On the E side facing, the plain LODGE of the former City Isolation Hospital of 1884–5 (builder *T.H. Kingerlee*), otherwise demolished.

SIR GEOFFREY ARTHUR BUILDING (Pembroke College), Baltic Wharf, Grandpont. An unusually large college satellite, of 1986–90 by *Maguire & Murray*. From the towpath it appears almost like a Baltic citadel, plain-walled and steep-roofed, with square projections at intervals. Flush windows and simple blockwork construction, economical but not impoverished. The plan is an irregular S-shape, forming two open-ended quads. Until 2020 there was also a separate L-shaped building for shared facilities enclosing the SE corner, but this has been demolished for a new, taller graduate block by *MICA Architects*. A little pavilion at the NW corner has gone too, replaced likewise by a taller block. Goodbye, then, to Maguire & Murray's carefully balanced composition.

RIVERSIDE COURT, Long Ford Close, just SW. Old people's flats by *Oxford Architects Partnership*, designed 1985. A cranked U-shape of yellow brick, humanely handled.

OUTER OXFORD: WEST AND NORTH-WEST

OSNEY AND BOTLEY ROAD

The boundary with inner Oxford is the railway. The small Thames-side suburb of Osney preserves a little of the abbey of that name but is mostly Victorian, with some good recent infill. Botley Road is the main through route; Botley itself belongs with pre-1974 Berkshire.

ST FRIDESWIDE, Botley Road. By *S.S. Teulon*, 1870–2, and typical Teulon in its ruthlessness. Early French Gothic, aisleless, with a canted apse and also with a very low octagonal central tower, intended to rise above the broaches and to carry a spire. Stunted N transept, lower, squeezed in between mighty buttresses and with a lean-to roof. Balancing organ chamber, s. The nave windows are pairs of short lancets. But the w side and the apse have windows with over-dimensioned plate tracery, the w side in a group. Walls of rough Charlbury limestone. The Bath stone dressings were meant to have much more carving, but much has been left uncarved, and these raw blocks suit the style of the church. Designs to finish the tower by *H.G.W. Drinkwater* (1876) and *J. Oldrid Scott* (1888) were likewise not taken forward. Long, narrow interior lined with

---

*No. 436, wrecked by a falling tree in 1996, was the last of Oxford's curious paper-roofed houses, here with the extra novelty of card-clad walls. Built in 1844 for John Towle, extended up to 1875.

brick, now painted except for the vault under the tower. The W and E arches here stand on stumpy shafts which in their turn start as corbels. Arch-braced nave roof.

FURNISHINGS. ALTAR probably designed by *Teulon*, PULPIT and FONT certainly so. The altar front is sculpted with the symbols of the Evangelists. – REREDOS by *James Rogers*, 1906. – TILES by *Maw*. – DOOR (nave NE). Carved as a sanctuary door for St Frideswide's mission, Poplar, London, by 'the *Misses Liddell*, daughters of the Dean of Christ Church' (*Oxford Times*, 18 July 1891). That points to the unmarried *Rhoda* and *Violet Liddell* rather than Lewis Carroll's Alice, who became Mrs Hargreaves in 1880. – SCULPTURE. Fourteen Victorian wooden angels, brought in 1955 from the Clewer Sisters' latter-day home at Littlemore (Lawn Upton House, p. 512). Probably made for their original chapel at Holywell Manor (pp. 419–20), perhaps designed by *C. C. Rolfe*. – WAR MEMORIAL. 1922. Designer *F. E. Howard*, carver *Alec Miller*. – STAINED GLASS. Apse, 1905 by *Herbert Davis*, except the two outer lights, 1930 by *J. E. Nuttgens*, and the tracery lights, style of *Kempe & Co*. N transept W, also *Kempe & Co.*, 1922. Nave, six re-set lights by *Geoffrey Webb*, from St Thomas's Convent (Osney House, p. 398), some dated 1931.

VICARAGE, S. By *Drinkwater*, 1876, joined to the church by a covered passage.

RESTORATION CHURCH, Botley Road. A former Railway Mission hall of 1904, by *H. Quinton*. End window with the simplest tracery.

WEST OXFORD COMMUNITY PRIMARY SCHOOL, Ferry Hinksey Road. By *W. H. Castle*. Dated 1913 in a terracotta panel. Two storeys, four big plain gables, flat-roofed centre.

POWER STATION (former), Arthur Street. A rare survival of a late C19 installation, greatly expanded in the C20. In 2023 under reconstruction as an education centre for the SAÏD BUSINESS SCHOOL by *John McAslan & Partners*, retaining the chief façades. The oldest of these comprises the two gabled sections facing the river, W, with two tiers of close-set windows and blind arches of polychromatic brick: 1891–2 by *A. P. Brevitt*, for the Electric Construction Co. of Wolverhampton. Matching third gable, N, and the adjacent oriel and Russell Street front by *Herbert Quinton*, 1904–5. To the S, a stripped-classical section probably of *c.* 1933. To Arthur Street, E, towering brick enclosures of 1925–8 (*F. H. Francis*, Chief Engineer).

BRIDGES, Botley Road, E to W. OSNEY BRIDGE, over the main Thames channel, was rebuilt by *W. H. White* as City Engineer, 1887–9. A shallow-arched 60-ft (18-metre) cast-iron main span, with looped openwork parapet. Two stone arches for a relief channel, W. ST FRIDESWIDE'S BRIDGE dates from 1767, when the road was turnpiked and given new bridges designed by *Sir Robert Taylor*. Seven plain arches. Widened to the S in 1906. BULSTAKE BRIDGE and BOTLEY BRIDGE were also rebuilt in 1923–4 (*J. E. Wilkes*, City Engineer). Flat concrete decks, Chinese-Chippendale-style balustrades.

PERAMBULATION. Just W of the railway bridge, BOTLEY ROAD has a former toll house of 1850 by *Underwood* (N side), with twin canted bays. E extension of 1902 by *J.R. Wilkins* for the Old Gatehouse pub. Big houses of *c.*1873 on the S side. To the N in Abbey Road, No. 29, by *C.C. Rolfe*, 1886–7. A pretty and characteristic red brick house, Gothic going Arts and Crafts. Built for the Rev. W.H. Smythe, Warden of St Thomas's Convent (p. 398).

To the S, MILL STREET has the former KITE pub (No. 68), Free Jacobean by *W. Drew & Sons*, 1900. To the W here is the former power station (*see* p. 517). N of it, some interesting later housing. The boldly patterned, terraced echelon facing the river is by *Roland Huggins* (*City Architect's Department*), 1985–7. To its N, *Adrian James*'s own residence, No. 81 Mill Street, 1995–6. Almost a tower house, finished with a giant segmental near-pediment. Red brick over lightweight steel framing. The approach is via a sturdy little annexe with a domed copper roof, added in 2001. Immediately E and also by *James*, Nos. 79A–E, a terrace of tiny 'live/work' houses, 2004–5. Brick below, timber-clad and backward-sloping above.

OSNEY LANE crosses Mill Street further S. On its N side, the long, slim plot by the railway has CHERWELL HOUSE, sixth-form housing for Cherwell College, 2012–14 by *Paul Brookes Architects*. Its sawtooth-profiled inner side gives all the rooms a SW aspect. Enlargement is proposed (2022). To the S, OSNEY CEMETERY, opened 1848. Chapel by *Underwood* gone, original LYCHGATE remaining. Further down Mill Street, the BISHOP'S GATE flats were Pickford's Depository, with a 1930s Neo-Georgian front block.

In MILLBANK, W of Mill Lane, is OSNEY MILL. Of L-plan, early C19. The E–W range across the mill leat is of stone and brick; N–S range all of brick, apparently later; top storey added 1905. Burnt out in 1946, converted to flats in 2012 by *Oxford Architects*. Theirs is the coarse W addition, and the garage block making a forecourt. Just to the W by Osney Lock is the early C19 OSNEY MILL COTTAGE.

OSNEY ABBEY, which owned the medieval mills here, has its one surviving structure immediately S. Founded in 1129 by Robert d'Oilly the younger for Augustinian Canons, the abbey had a church 332 ft (101 metres) long, with a central tower and W tower, and a C14 Lady Chapel N of the presbytery. Henry VIII made it a cathedral in 1542, but four years later switched the designation to St Frideswide's priory church instead, i.e. what is now Christ Church. It is depressing to see how little is visible now – just a truncated oblong outbuilding of 1409 (tree-ring date), from the abbey's former waterfront range. Ashlar E wall with a blocked two-light E window, straight-headed, with cusped lights. Also a remaining stub with a broad, flat-arched doorway. Rubble-stone W wall; N wall partly C19 brick. (Wind-braced roof of 'raised-aisle' type, i.e. with crown struts and an upper collar above the main collars.)

Continuing w on Botley Road, the next s turning is BRIDGE STREET, the spine of OSNEY TOWN, a distinctive enclave wholly surrounded by waterways. Laid out in 1851, and built up mostly with modest but varied terraces of Jericho type. One grander exception at the NE corner, No. 1 East Street, a Gothic villa of 1881 (now clubhouse), by *T.C. Tanner*. At No. 16 the VISHUDDHA YOGA CENTRE by *Adrian James Architects*, 2019–22. Copper-faced infill, with windows in turquoise-coloured splayed recesses. In North Street, the tiny house with a close-slatted frontage (No. 4A) is by *McLennan Architects*, 2010. On Botley Road opposite St Frideswide's church (*see* p. 516), the WEST OXFORD COMMUNITY CENTRE, reminiscent of a Romano-British reconstruction drawing, with its pantiles and shallow-pitched, broad-eaved roof. By *Stanhope Wilkinson Associates*, 1999–2000. On the s side, the end of FERRY HINKSEY ROAD has council houses of 1921, of which Nos. 101–104 are of concrete-block construction, the design of *J. E. Wilkes*, City Engineer. The former OSNEY ARMS pub at No. 45, pretty Domestic Revival of 1899 by *H. Quinton*, ends Botley Road's notable buildings.

OSNEY MEAD is an industrial estate at the s end of Ferry Hinksey Road. One notable building, likely to disappear under plans for an 'innovation quarter' here. It is the former OXFORD MAIL AND TIMES of 1968–71, an example of *Arup Associates'* way of deriving bold forms from an analysis of process and use. A perimeter wall of cream-coloured brick, with an opening on axis with the offices, a large, low, plain rectangle with a concrete frame. Its entrance leads to a spine corridor originally dividing the large, mostly open-plan side from smaller, separate offices. The spine is emphasized by the beams reaching higher, to contain the service ducts. Rising to the w is the press hall, encased in cream brick. Later press hall added by *Oxford Architects*, 2003–7, taller still.

BINSEY

A rural oasis in the low-lying farmland NW of Oxford. The village consists of little more than a few farmhouses facing a wide green. The church is ½ m. further NW, approached along an avenue.

ST MARGARET. Small and rustic, with chancel, nave, and bell-cote between. S doorway of *c.* 1170, the arch with one order of roll moulding overlapped by a band of chevron and a hood with two rolls flanking a band of dogtooth which terminates in heads. The capitals are carved with foliage which creeps over on to the jambs. The door jambs of the C12 porch are original, the capitals and arch probably from the moderate restoration of 1875. Bellcote also renewed then, of C13 form. In that century the Norman church was remodelled and the chancel arch built, with unusual corbels carved as knots. Original lancets in the chancel s wall (a partially blocked 'lowside') and high in the W wall. The present nave S lancet is not shown in early views. Other windows appear simple late C14 or C15. Rebuilding of the E wall is recorded in 1833. That the entire N wall is windowless and near-featureless implies rebuilding there too. In the chancel a C13 PISCINA in a recess with a hollow-chamfered arch, the bowl carried on a small half-shaft. Chancel roof C14, arch-braced and partly ceiled. Nave roof of late medieval form, but very crude; explained by the re-roofing of 1718 recorded by Hearne. – PULPIT. 1875, with a figure of St Margaret carved by *John Chapman*. – FONT. Tub-shaped, C12, on a restored C13 shafted base. – ROYAL ARMS of Queen Anne, painted. – STAINED GLASS. Medieval fragments collected in the E window. Six panels of late C15 quarries below. Above, l. to r., mid-C14 head; C14 figure holding a cross (Edward Grim, from a martyrdom of St Thomas Becket?); composite figure, the head of St Margaret or St Frideswide(?) with an incomplete torso from another figure, C15.

WELL, in the churchyard. Restored 1874. Dedicated to St Margaret and connected with the legend of St Frideswide, whose community used Binsey as a place of retreat. Buildings probably associated with pilgrimages here were noted by Anthony Wood in the C17. The large sub-oval EARTHWORK of uncertain date that enclosed the settlement is identifiable as the *Thornburi* mentioned in a late C12 life of the saint.

MEDLEY FOOTBRIDGE, SE of the village. 1865. Designed by *James Castle*, Engineer of the Upper Thames. Wrought-iron latticed sides.

(MEDLEY MANOR HOUSE, by the bridge. C17, with a much larger late C18 wing to the NW. This part probably incorporates material from the short-lived Medley House, built after 1722 for Benjamin Sweet, former army paymaster and County Sheriff. Also a late medieval DOORWAY re-set in the garden wall.)

SOUTH-EAST OXFORDSHIRE

INTRODUCTION

Definitions first. What follows is an account of the SE part of the historic county of Oxfordshire, broadly as it was constituted between the CIO and 1974. In the general overhaul of local government in the latter year, a large part of Berkshire W of the Thames was transferred to Oxfordshire. Nationally, many of the changes made in 1974 have been revised or even reversed, but those affecting Oxfordshire and Berkshire have not, and relatively few people in the 2020s can have adult memories of when the Thames still divided the counties from the outskirts of Oxford all the way to Henley. But the *Buildings of England* series has largely remained loyal to the old boundaries – no revised volumes on the Metropolitan Counties designated in 1974, nor on the mayfly creations that were Avon, Cleveland and Humberside. So the coverage here corresponds to the historic SE area, as described by Jennifer Sherwood in the 1974 edition of *Oxfordshire*.*

A few exceptions should be noted. The settlements of Barton, Binsey, Iffley, Littlemore, Marston and Wolvercote are included in the gazetteer with Oxford, although their older buildings are discussed with the rest of the county area below. Also, the districts of Emmer Green and Lower Caversham were transferred in 1977 to Reading, which had already annexed Caversham on the Oxfordshire side of the Thames in 1911. Those areas have therefore been included in the revised *Berkshire* volume.

Accounts of Oxfordshire tend to dwell on its inconsistent character, or, more positively, its variety. Much of that variety is supplied by the SE area, comprising as it does both the Chiltern uplands and the less elevated country to the W. To the S, the Chilterns extend right up to the Thames – these are the tree-covered slopes familiar to travellers on the Great Western main line W of Reading – with only a narrow interval at Goring, where the Berkshire Downs descend to the opposite bank. Greater elevations are found further N, in the thickly wooded and folded country that merges into the Buckinghamshire Chilterns to the E; the highest point in Oxfordshire is Bald Hill at Aston Rowant

---

*The division with Alan Brooks's companion volume *Oxfordshire: North and West* runs eastward from the Oxford boundary across the old hundred of Bullingdon, s of the parishes of Horspath, Wheatley, Holton and Waterperry.

(843 ft, 257 metres). To the W, a rolling expanse of open country runs northward from Ipsden and South Stoke to the Miltons and the Haseleys – with a localized rise to the NW, where Cuddesdon and Garsington sit side by side on their hills – and also to the W, where the Thames makes a big wavering loop towards Abingdon, with Culham near the tip.

The area's settlements reflect this diversity of terrain. Nucleated villages prevail in the low-lying parishes, as they do in the rest of the county. (A caution here: many historic parishes had very different boundaries from those of today, typically comprising long and narrow strips with both upland and lowland ends.) The Chilterns show a more scattered pattern, with a multitude of hamlets – names often concluding with Green, End or Row – and isolated farms, reflecting woodland clearance. The area's towns are few, partly on account of the closeness of Reading, Wallingford and Abingdon on the Berkshire side. Thame and Watlington are well-preserved market towns, not large. Henley is in a different league: always the area's largest and most prosperous town, enriched by river-borne trade and by brewing, then greatly enlarged in the railway era and especially from the late C19, when rowing and boating became fashionable pastimes. Other Thames-side settlements, Goring especially, were also boosted by the railway and the expansion of the London commuter belt.

The influence of Oxford on the area's buildings is less apparent than might be expected. Reading-based architects found much to do here, especially in the C19 and early C20, and the red brick and small-scale decoration of many Late Victorian buildings have a decided Reading character, especially along the Thames. Elsewhere, the variety of local materials and their many permutations are constant sources of interest and visual pleasure: good red or grey brick, whole or knapped flints, freestone, stone rubble, chalk, timber framing, and red tiles or thatch for roofing. It is a similar mixture across large parts of Berkshire, which shares much of the area's geology and the easy navigation offered by the Thames.

GEOLOGY AND BUILDING STONES
BY PHILIP POWELL

Geology, topography and mineral resources

The rocks of Oxfordshire are a series of limestones and clays which originated as beds of sediment in the seas of the Jurassic and Cretaceous periods (200–65 million years ago). They pass laterally into adjoining counties as part of the sweep of strata that extends across southern England from Dorset to Yorkshire. In Oxfordshire the pile of beds is tilted slightly to the SE so that the edges of the layers appear at the surface as NE–SW trending bands. The beds are therefore progressively younger towards the SE. Broadly speaking the strata comprise three clay formations alternating with three limestone formations. The limestones, being more resistant to weathering, form higher ground, while the clays underlie the intervening vales. The basic simplicity of this arrangement has of course been greatly modified by the variation in character and extent of individual beds, and by the sculpting action of streams and rivers.

The LIMESTONES vary in physical and geological character. Some are rubbly, some are splintery and some are susceptible to attack by frost. Others are durable, workable rock that make good building stone. Details of these are noted in the second section, below.

The oldest rocks are the Jurassic clays of the LOWER LIAS FORMATION. They form the floor of the upper valley of the River Evenlode in the NW of the county and of the River Cherwell as far S as Somerton (*see Oxfordshire: North and West*; hereafter *ON&W*). They also form the floor of the tract of heavy pasture land W of Deddington (*ON&W*). The clay was formerly exploited for brickmaking at a number of sites.

Next in the succession are the MIDDLE LIAS beds, consisting of sands overlain by a reddish-brown limestone. This rock, usually called MARLSTONE or HORNTON STONE, forms the plateau country in the Banbury district (*ON&W*) which culminates in the escarpment at Edge Hill in neighbouring Warwickshire. It is also called the Banbury Ironstone: a reminder that between 1850 and 1967 this stone was exploited as iron ore.

Above the Hornton stone, the thin clay beds of the UPPER LIAS form narrow outcrops which once supported a number of brick pits. Springs and marshy ground mark its junction with the overlying sandy beds of the INFERIOR OOLITE Group. The main areas of outcrop of these sands are around Tadmarton and Sibford Ferris (*ON&W*). Nearby, isolated remnants cap rounded hills such as Fern Hill and Hob Hill. Eastwards the sands become ferruginous and develop into the Northampton Sand Ironstone.

In later Inferior Oolite times the CLYPEUS GRIT was deposited. This is not a true sandstone grit but a rubbly, coarse-grained, shelly limestone named after *Clypeus*, a bun-shaped fossil sea urchin which is locally abundant. Its main area of outcrop is in the valley of the Evenlode and its tributaries.

Next, the GREAT OOLITE GROUP of beds form the upland limestone country across north Oxfordshire from Burford to Bicester (*ON&W*). This tract is characterized by arable fields and by villages built of pale limestone. Beds of clay occur within the limestone sequence. This combination of materials is ideal for cement manufacture, and was formerly exploited in the Cherwell valley in works at Kirtlington and until recently at Shipton-on-Cherwell (both *ON&W*).

The limestone belt of the Great Oolite dips down southwards below the OXFORD CLAY. This clay covers a broad tract of low-lying country across the middle of Oxfordshire. It underlies Oxford city and the valley of the upper Thames. North-eastwards, it carries the River Ray and forms the wet lands of Otmoor (*ON&W*). In the C19 it supported the many brickworks

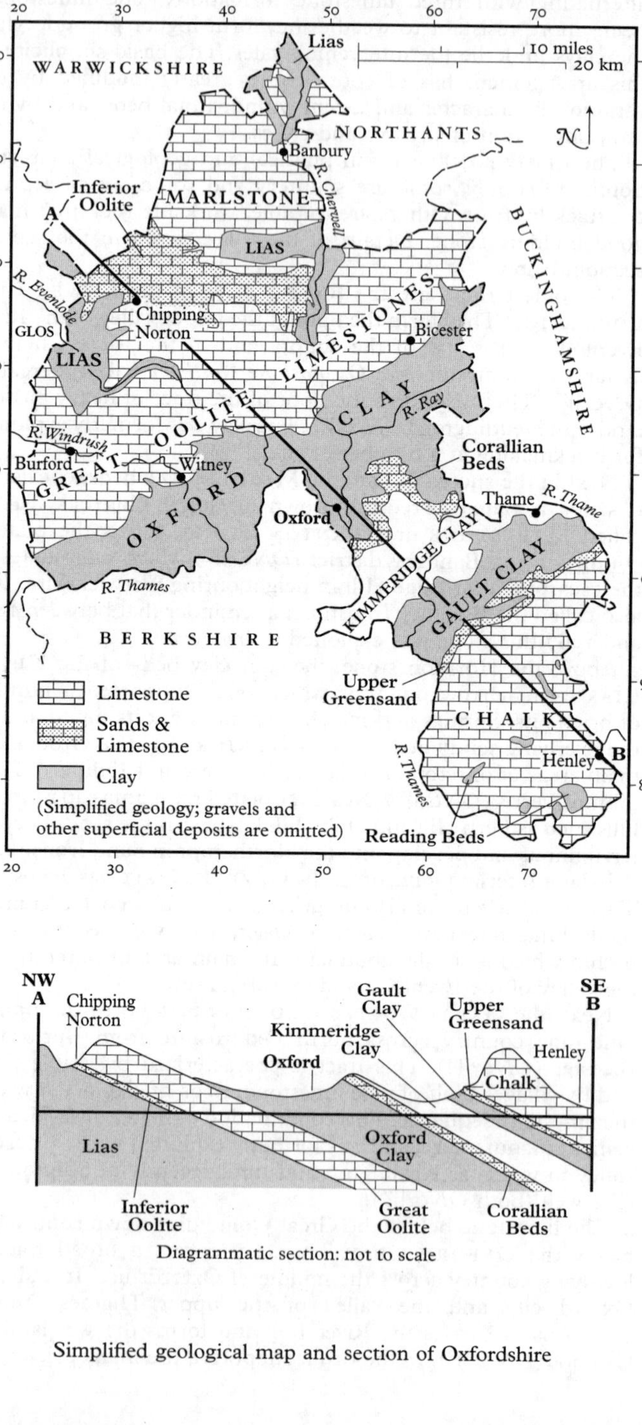

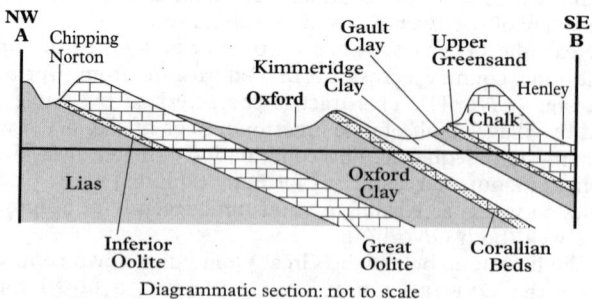

Simplified geological map and section of Oxfordshire

which sprang up to cater for the housing of the expanding population, especially that of Oxford itself.

Overlying the Oxford Clay, the sands and limestones of the CORALLIAN FORMATION make up the high ground E of Oxford, around Elsfield, Beckley (both *ON&W*) and Headington (Oxford). They continue as far as Wheatley (*ON&W*), after which the formation becomes clay and merges with the Oxford Clay and the Kimmeridge Clay.

The KIMMERIDGE CLAY follows the Corallian and occupies the slopes of the hilly areas from Shotover, Forest Hill and Wheatley (all *ON&W*) to Garsington and the Baldons. It forms the channel of the River Thame and continues NE past Thame into the Vale of Aylesbury. The clay was dug for brickmaking in pits at Shotover and Wheatley. There, the sands of the upper part of the formation were mixed with the clay to reduce shrinkage on firing.

The PORTLAND FORMATION, which in Dorset provides the famous white building stone so extensively and prominently displayed in London buildings, is represented in Oxfordshire mainly by only a few metres of ochreous sands and rubbly limestones. These form the sandy tract between Nuneham Courtenay and Toot Baldon and the higher parts of the ridge that extends from Garsington to Wheatley and Shotover.

The top of Shotover and the Garsington to Wheatley ridge are capped by deposits of Lower Cretaceous age known as the WHITCHURCH SANDS. On Shotover these include beds of high-quality ochre and white pipe clay. Near Wheatley the upper layers are a purple sandstone, once dug as iron ore.

The coarser sands of the succeeding formation, the LOWER GREENSAND, occur as thin patches around Tiddington (Albury) and in the triangle between Nuneham Courtenay, Burcot and the Abingdon loop of the Thames. At Culham the rock is a white grit which provided stone for querns from Iron Age to medieval times.

After this comes the GAULT CLAY, which makes a low-lying belt of land across the middle of south Oxfordshire, parallel with the foot of the Chilterns from Wallingford (Berks.) to Thame. It is a grey silty clay which was dug for brickmaking at Culham, Thame and other smaller pits. At some levels within the clay are layers of black nodules rich in phosphate. During the C19 many pits were opened across Buckinghamshire and as far as Towersey in Oxfordshire to obtain the nodules for conversion to fertilizer.

The UPPER GREENSAND grades upward into the CHALK, the soft, white porous limestone that forms the Chiltern ridge and underlies the rest of the county to the SE. The Chalk can be divided into three main units on the basis of its composition. The LOWER CHALK is a white chalk without flints. It forms the gentle lower slopes of the Chilterns, making a shelf on which Shirburn, Lewknor and Chinnor are built. This chalk has a considerable content of clay, which makes it the ideal raw material for cement manufacture. It was exploited for this purpose at Chinnor. The MIDDLE CHALK is white chalk without flints, and forms the main part of the Chiltern escarpment. At certain levels, fractured hard bands allow water to permeate, and to issue as springs such as those that feed the cress beds at Ewelme. The UPPER CHALK caps the escarpment and forms the dip-slope down to Henley. It is pure white chalk with abundant flints.

At the end of Chalk times the pile of Jurassic and Cretaceous rocks was raised up to form dry land. Erosion, rather than deposition, was now the dominant geological process, and subsequent deposits are sparse and thin. The oldest of these are the READING BEDS: sands and clays laid down about 60 million years ago by SE-flowing rivers. This cover was subsequently eroded, leaving scattered remnants on the hilltops at Russell's Water (Pishill), Nuffield, Nettlebed, Stoke Row and Greenmoor (South Stoke). At all these localities the sands and clays have long been exploited for making bricks, tiles and pottery.

Sedimentary debris from the erosion of the Reading Beds mixed with flints from decomposition of the Chalk makes up the deposit known as CLAY-WITH-FLINTS. This is the red-brown earth that stretches along the crest of the Chiltern ridge. Other remnants of the Reading Beds are represented by masses of indurated sandstone, or sarsen stone, scattered along the top of the Chilterns.

The final sedimentary deposits were laid down in the PLEISTOCENE EPOCH, which began about two and a half million years ago. During this period the climate swung several times from glacial to warm temperate conditions, with many lesser fluctuations between the extremes. Although Oxfordshire was not invaded by an ice sheet, there were times when permafrost extended to a considerable depth. At times, intense freeze-and-thaw created mixtures of shattered rock and clay that sludged downslope into valley bottoms. These deposits are called HEAD, or COOMBE ROCK if formed from Chalk. At other times heavy rains along with frozen ground swelled rivers into torrents that swept vast quantities of rock debris along to form spreads of sand and gravel. The oldest of the gravels are the WALLINGFORD FAN GRAVELS, which are spread along the foot of the Chiltern escarpment between Ipsden and Watlington. They include the chalky, flinty gravels which have been exploited for aggregate at Turners Court (North Stoke) and Oakley Wood (Benson) and nearby localities. Pits near Ewelme yielded finely made flint implements representing different periods of human occupation.

In NW Oxfordshire, patches of a clayey, pebbly deposit called NORTHERN DRIFT or Plateau Gravel lie on the high ground along the sides of the Evenlode valley and onwards past Oxford. The deposits are characterized by their abundant cobbles of brown quartzite, or indurated sand, which were derived from rocks in the West Midlands. The alignment and composition of the deposits indicate a powerful river ancestral to the Evenlode/Thames drainage, reaching far to the NW. The quartzite gravels can be traced across the Chilterns and on into the London Basin.

The most extensive spreads of gravel lie within the modern river valleys. In the upper Thames region the main component is derived from the Jurassic limestones. Below Dorchester and the confluence of the River Thame, flint pebbles predominate. These gravels are commercially important sources of aggregates, and many worked-out pits are now lakes or landfill sites. Deposition took place at four stages during the last 470,000 years or so. Each mass of gravel would be periodically abandoned and a new level begun as the river cut down its channel in response to continuing uplift of the land. The gravels record evidence of climatic fluctuations over thousands of years, as well as of the accompanying fauna, which include early people.

Building stones

Northern Oxfordshire is well supplied with a range of limestones suitable for building, while in southern Oxfordshire good stone – apart from flint – is not so readily available, and brick and timber are more important. The character of vernacular building across the county thus reflects the differences in the underlying geology.

In the Banbury district (*ON&W*) HORNTON STONE (MARL-STONE) has long been the principal building stone, both as free-stone and as rubble for every type of building, as well as for gateposts, fireplaces and flagstones. In the C19 it was widely used in Oxfordshire for gravestones. For many buildings the stone was dug on the spot, as can be seen at Chastleton House (*ON&W*). Today the stone is quarried at Hornton and Great Tew. As a building stone its warm gingerbread colour gives a distinctive charm to the villages of the district.

The CLYPEUS GRIT is a rubbly limestone mostly worthless for building. However, the basal bed in a deep quarry in the park at Cornbury (*ON&W*) provided a fine freestone, full of the characteristic fossil sea urchins, from which much of the house at Cornbury Park and of Blenheim Palace (*ON&W*) were built.

In north Oxfordshire the limestone strata of the Great Oolite Group include a number of good building stones. The basal member is the CHIPPING NORTON LIMESTONE, which varies from white, shelly oolite to hard, brown, sandy limestone. Chipping Norton and Charlbury (both *ON&W*) and nearby villages are built of it. Numerous small quarries all over the outcrop provided stone for cottages, barns and field walls.

A little higher in the sequence is the TAYNTON STONE. This is a brown, coarse-grained oolite with prominent bands of shell fragments, whose durability is attested in buildings such as the C14 Taynton church (*ON&W*). Stone from the quarries has been supplied for Oxford colleges, Windsor Castle and Blenheim Palace, and for the dressings and carved work of many churches in Oxfordshire. BURFORD STONE is a paler variety of Taynton stone. In Oxford, for example, it makes the quoins of the NW corner of the Anglo-Saxon tower of St Michael at the North Gate.

The STONESFIELD SLATE occurs as lens-shaped bodies of calcareous sandstone within beds of Taynton stone age at

Stonesfield (*ON&W*). The celebrated roof tiles came into production in the C17, when it was found that exposing the freshly
dug stone to frost enabled it to be split into thin sheets. The stone
is also famous for its fossils of dinosaurs and early mammals.
Stone tiles of the same geological age have also been made at
Taynton and at Fulwell (near Enstone; *ON&W*), but not so
extensively as at Stonesfield.

The FOREST MARBLE lies near the top of the Great Oolite
sequence. It is not a true marble but a coarse-grained flaggy
limestone packed with shell debris, mainly of oysters. The name
comes from its occurrence in Wychwood Forest, where it was
quarried for walling stone, flagstones and gravestones. Huge old
pits are still visible at East End, near North Leigh (*ON&W*).
Forest Marble was also quarried in the Cherwell valley at Bletchingdon (*ON&W*) for fireplaces, paving, and the original columns
in the arcades of Canterbury Quad at St John's College, Oxford,
of the 1630s. Under the name of BLADON STONE it was dug in
the pit at Long Hanborough (*ON&W*) in the late C19 and C20
for use as a coursed rubble in buildings such as the Examination
Schools and Rhodes House in Oxford.

The Corallian Formation includes sandy, shelly, rubbly
limestone which can be studied in the City Wall. The top bed is
a pale, tough rubble called CORAL RAG. The towers of Oxford
Castle and of St Michael at the North Gate are largely built of
it, and their condition demonstrates its durability. The Coral
Rag grades laterally into different varieties of stone. At
Headington (Oxford) it passes into thin bands of very hard
white limestone called HEADINGTON HARDSTONE, which
was used for kerbstones and steps, and as a plinth for nearly
every old building in Oxford. Another variation is the coarsely
granular shell-fragmental limestones of WHEATLEY STONE
and HEADINGTON STONE, both providing valuable freestone
since the C13. Headington stone is seen mainly in Oxford, while
Wheatley stone is widely distributed across the county in churches
and houses. Gravestones made from Wheatley limestone at the
Lye Hill quarries near Wheatley (*ON&W*) are seen in many
Oxfordshire churchyards.

The upper part of the PORTLAND beds, around the Miltons and
Haseleys, contains a bed of sandy limestone formerly quarried as
freestone, while CHALK (or clunch) as a building stone appears
only in a string of villages roughly from Warborough to Adwell.

Southern Oxfordshire has no good building stone apart from
FLINT. As flint cannot be shaped for corner stones, door jambs
and so on, it needs support from other materials. In older
churches the framing is Wheatley stone; in C19 churches Bath
stone is usual. In other buildings brick is used.

BRICKS have been made from all of the clay deposits that
occur across Oxfordshire. The principal strata that have supported important brickworks are the Lias, Oxford Clay, Kimmeridge Clay, Gault Clay and Reading Beds. TILES for floors
and roofs seem to have been produced earlier than bricks. In
the mid C14 thousands of tiles for Wallingford Castle were being

made at Nettlebed. The industry there has been an important producer of bricks, tiles and pottery continuously down to the C20. The clays and sands used there are from the Reading Beds, plus a few metres of a patch of overlying London Clay. In the early C15, bricks from the kiln at Crocker End near Nettlebed were brought for building at Stonor Park. The bricks for the important group of buildings from the 1430s–40s at Ewelme may have been made from Gault Clay near Great Milton. In the north of the county, where good building stone was readily available, the earliest important building in brick was Hanwell Castle (*ON&W*), begun *c.*1498.

These high-status buildings made bricks fashionable and started a trend that gradually percolated down the social scale, mainly in the Chilterns and the Gault Clay belt. By the C18 brick was the fashionable material for building or refronting town houses, and many fine examples are to be seen in Watlington, Thame and Henley.

In the C19 many new brickworks were opened to supply the needs of an expanding population for houses, schools, chapels and so on. Towards the end of the century various factors began to reduce the number of brickworks. One of these was the competition from the Fletton brick industry in Bedfordshire. This process used Lower Oxford Clay, which has a high content of organic matter that burns during firing and reduces the amount of fuel needed. The effects of the world wars and other adverse economic conditions during the C20 resulted in further closures; now no working brick pits remain in Oxfordshire.

OXFORDSHIRE IN PREHISTORY
BY GILL HEY

Our earliest HUMAN ANCESTORS were present in Oxfordshire at least 400,000 years ago, in the Hoxnian Interglacial, as represented by a handaxe from Hanborough and occasional quartzite tools from gravel quarries at Stanton Harcourt and Yarnton (all *ON&W*). By this time the River Thames was flowing more or less along its modern valley system. Stone tools from hunting activities dating to a more recent interglacial, at *c.* 200,000 years ago, were found in the Dix Pit gravel quarry at Stanton Harcourt (*ON&W*), in the same early channel deposits as a remarkable collection of mammal bones, particularly mammoth, bison and horse. From that time on, traces of hunter-gatherers have been detected at all periods warm enough for human occupation.

As the climate warmed after the last Ice Age (in the eleventh or tenth millennium B.C.), hunter-gatherers returned from the Continent when the sea level was still low and before Britain became an island. Their MESOLITHIC tools are found throughout the area, but particularly near to the Thames and its tributaries and on the Cotswold uplands, where they hunted game, particularly deer, trapped birds and perhaps fish, and gathered wild fruits and nuts in an increasingly wooded environment. Evidence for their activities has emerged mainly by field-walking or in gravel quarries, as is the case with much of what is known about prehistoric occupation.

The first structures and monuments, however, were built in the NEOLITHIC period, by people who brought domesticated plants and animals, pottery and new stone tool technologies into Britain c. 4000 B.C., and/or by people who adopted their customs. The earliest HOUSE or HOUSES so far discovered in Oxfordshire lay beneath the Ascott-under-Wychwood long barrow (*ON&W*) and were small rectangular structures of the later fortieth or early thirty-ninth century B.C. The much more substantial, hall-like building (70 by 35 ft, 20 by 10 metres) found on the Thames floodplain at Yarnton (*ON&W*) was constructed a little later, c. 3800 B.C., and a small, circular Early Neolithic house dated to c. 3600 B.C. was found on the same site. All these structures were built with earth-fast posts and probably had wattle-and-daub walling and some kind of thatched roof.

The earliest evidence for formal burial of the dead also belongs to the Early Neolithic period. LONG BARROWS of earth and stone could be of substantial size, although their burial chambers were usually small. Ascott-under-Wychwood, for example, was 150 ft (46 metres) long, E to W, and up to 50 ft (15 metres) wide. Trapezoidal in shape, it was built around two pairs of stone chambers, entered from either side of the monument. Around twenty-one individuals were buried there. The barrow was dismantled in the early 1970s, but the fragmentary remains of similar monuments of Cotswold–Severn type survive e.g. at Chastleton, near Leafield, and at Lyneham near Sarsden (all *ON&W*).

PORTAL DOLMENS, simple permeable chambers formed of upright stone slabs and roofed with a single large capstone, are found in the Cotswold–Severn area and are also believed to have been used for burial. An upright standing in the 'entrance' or 'portal' is one of their defining features. The best surviving example in Oxfordshire is the Whispering Knights, part of the Rollright Stones complex in the very north of the county, but remains of another can be seen at Enstone (*ON&W*). Some small ROUND BARROWS, e.g. the Hoar Stone near Steeple Barton (*ON&W*), enclosed megalithic chambers and may also be of Early Neolithic date.

Our first public monuments, CAUSEWAYED ENCLOSURES, are of the thirty-seventh to thirty-sixth century B.C. These large circular monuments, roughly 100–200 yds (90–180 metres) across, were defined by one or more ditch-and-bank circuits. The ditches were dug in segments, leaving causeways which would have facilitated access to the interior, and their fills often contain deposits of fine objects with food remains, perhaps the remains of feasts, and sometimes human bone. In Oxfordshire these sites are mainly positioned on the southern slopes of the Cotswold hills and adjacent gravel terraces. Another example was found in the narrowest part of the Goring Gap during pipeline work. They are only visible today by remote sensing techniques such as air photography; a recently discovered enclosure to the W of Thame demonstrates that even in the modern era such substantial features can escape detection. The permeability of causewayed enclosures suggests inclusion and communal participation, and they are believed to be places where the wider community gathered to commemorate the dead, exchange goods (including exotic objects such as polished stone axes from the west of Britain), exchange breeding animals and undertake other social activities.

In the middle of the fourth millennium B.C., monument-building spread on to the gravel terraces of the Thames and its tributaries. These generally small earthwork enclosures were very varied in form, with rectangular, U-shaped, oval and circular monuments all present. They can be as small as 40 by 35 ft (12 by 10 metres) or as large as 210 by 80 ft (65 by 25 metres), and were often modified through time. Sometimes they are found associated with human remains. They seem most likely to be the ceremonial sites of small communities or family groups, who built their monuments to meet individual and specific situations, selecting from a range of commonly employed architectural techniques. Notable examples were found in advance of gravel extraction just N of Dorchester and at North Stoke.

These monuments were constructed at a time of increased mobility, when there was less emphasis on cereal cultivation and more on animal rearing. No DOMESTIC ARCHITECTURE has been found from this time until the very end of the Neolithic, c. 2500 B.C., and settlement is instead evidenced by pits, often in small clusters, and by scattered post-holes. Not infrequently the pits contain pottery, fancy stone tools, food remains, and, occasionally, small quantities of cremated human bone. Such feature groups are thought to be the remains of mobile pastoralists who repeatedly returned to the same sites but never remained for long, and who marked the opening and closing of their periods of occupation and other important events in their lives with formal deposits in pits.

Monument construction on a grand scale continued through-out the Neolithic, demonstrating a degree of social cohesion over this period. For reasons that remain uncertain, circular cause-wayed enclosures were abandoned in Oxfordshire early in the second half of the fourth millennium, and long linear rectangular enclosures known as CURSUSES (or cursūs) were built instead. The C18 antiquary William Stukeley named them thus, believing they were early Roman or British chariot-racing courses; today they are commonly thought to be processional routes, often associated with and/or linking monuments to the dead. They can stretch considerable distances on the gravel terraces of the Thames Valley, the longest being at Dorchester: just over a mile long, and c. 200 ft (60 metres) wide. They are defined by ditches, and would have had internal banks parallel to the ditch. Those known in Oxfordshire are concentrated around Dorchester;

they often attracted later monument-building and, in the case of Dorchester, unusual CREMATION CEMETERIES that can be paralleled at Stonehenge.

As in the Stonehenge landscape, HENGE MONUMENTS were constructed in the first half of the third millennium B.C. Major monuments of this type have been found at Dorchester (next to the cursus), in Oxford (recently discovered beneath St John's and Keble colleges) and at the Devil's Quoits at Stanton Harcourt (*ON&W*). Thence they can be traced from Westwell up the Windrush valley (*ON&W*). Their ditches, which were over 330 ft (100 metres) in diameter, had external banks and opposing entrances. In the case of Dorchester Big Rings, another ditch lay beyond the bank. Unlike other Neolithic ceremonial monuments, the Devil's Quoits remained visible in the landscape until the Second World War. Professor Grimes noted at that time the presence of a slight bank, and supervised the removal and burial of the single conglomerate stone which remained *in situ* from an internal circle of twenty-eight stones. The only henge in Oxfordshire known to have had a stone circle, it has now been reconstructed, partly using original stones found during later excavations; the surviving ditch has been partially excavated and the bank reconstructed.

An absence of building stone in most parts of the county explains the rarity of Neolithic and Bronze Age megalithic architecture, although rings of post-holes such as those excavated at Dorchester and at Mount Farm, Berinsfield, represent the remains of timber circles of similar type. The King's Men stone circle at Rollright Stones (*ON&W*) is an exception. Its small size and closely spaced oolitic limestone uprights most closely resemble stone circles of Cumbrian type.

Throughout the *c.* 1500 years of the Neolithic, there is nothing in the settlement or burial record to suggest complex social structures or hierarchies, although the construction of large ceremonial monuments demonstrates that people could come together to accomplish communal building projects. It is possible, however, that the more complex forms of henge monuments presented opportunities for individuals to win prestige and wield power. The rich contents of very early BEAKER GRAVES of BRONZE AGE date, which are sometimes associated with henge monuments (as at Dorchester), indicate that by the middle of the third millennium B.C. some people had accumulated wealth and were buried with ostentation, marking them out from the norm. These powerful individuals deployed Continental-style Beaker pots and, most importantly, metalwork (gold, copper and, later, bronze); they could themselves have been incomers. There is a notable concentration of Beaker burials in the county, some of which were covered by round barrows, following a period when burial practices left little archaeological trace.

ROUND BARROWS are a characteristic feature of the Early Bronze Age, and at a time when occupation evidence remains scarce they provide our best indication of settlement patterns. They are found singly and in small groups, and sometimes formed significant BARROW CEMETERIES, particularly within the Thames Valley itself, e.g. near Stanton Harcourt (*ON&W*) and at North Stoke. Many barrows were constructed in grazed grassland, demonstrating widespread woodland clearance by this time, and the importance of stock rearing. It is rare for them to have survived above ground in Oxfordshire; they are usually recognized from the air as ring ditches of between 60 ft and 120 ft (20 and 40 metres) across. (Dr Plot did, however, notice circular cropmarks when riding his horse across the barrow cemetery that lies beneath the University Parks, Oxford, in the mid C17, although he thought they were fairy rings or the result of lightning bolts.) A number of barrows continued to be used as places of burial in the Middle to Late Bronze Age, when CREMATION BURIAL became the norm. Some cremated individuals were buried in funerary urns; an important and extensive urnfield was excavated at Standlake (*ON&W*) in the mid C19 and mid C20.

From the beginning of the Middle Bronze Age (mid second millennium B.C.) there is evidence for increasingly permanent settlement. This includes the presence of POST-BUILT HOUSES, waterholes, larger quantities of occupation debris in pits, such as weaving equipment, and a greater emphasis on cereal production. The small circular buildings are dispersed across the valley bottom landscape (individually, in pairs or small groups), and seem most likely to represent single-generation households.

Ditched FIELD SYSTEMS, which are typical of the Middle Thames at this time and are often found near Late Bronze Age high-status sites, although rare in the north of the county, are more common s of Oxford. There is little evident settlement hierarchy at this time, but a rich island site lay just across the river near Wallingford, and the Iron Age hill-fort of Castle Hill, Little Wittenham (Berks.), overlooking Dorchester, had Late Bronze Age antecedents. The deposition of hoards and metalwork in rivers is also not as prevalent as in the Middle Thames, but caches of Middle Bronze Age metalwork have been recovered from Leopold Street and Burgess Meadow, Oxford, and Late Bronze Age metalwork, including weaponry, has come from the Thames at Days Lock, between Dorchester and Little Wittenham.

At the end of the Bronze Age some settlements began to be inhabited for extended periods, with houses rebuilt on the same plots, and greater organization of features, such as pits, four-post structures and waterholes, within the settlement. A good example lay to the SE of Cassington (*ON&W*). This presages the establishment of unenclosed settlements of round houses associated with clusters of pits, mainly on the river terraces but also on higher areas, at the beginning of the IRON AGE, a time of rising water levels on the Thames flood plain. These sites are comparatively numerous and long-lived, being inhabited into the Middle Iron Age and sometimes beyond. They indicate a more populous landscape, with self-sufficient farming communities managing their arable land and stock more intensively within recognized (if not always bounded) land holdings.

More specialized PASTORAL SETTLEMENTS within ditched enclosures, some with very long and elaborate funnel-shaped entrances, are also evident from at least the Middle Iron Age (*c.* 450 B.C.). They are mainly found in more upland areas in the N of the county, for example around Upper Heyford (*ON&W*), but also in low-lying parts of the valley, such as on Port Meadow, Oxford, and at Farmoor (Cumnor, Berks.), where their use seems to have been seasonal. There are hints at some that metalworking was also taking place, but finds assemblages do not indicate any difference in status from other occupation sites.

Enclosed settlements do not appear to have had a defensive function, and the frequency of open sites does not suggest widespread warfare. Nevertheless, HILL-FORTS were constructed in Oxfordshire, particularly on the Cotswold uplands, which would have been both impressive and defensible, such as the multivallate fort at Madmarston, Swalcliffe (*ON&W*); on the Berkshire side, the hill-fort on Castle Hill, Little Wittenham, dominates the Dorchester landscape. A valley fort is also known at Burroway near Clanfield (*ON&W*), where traces of burnt wooden ramparts have been found in the waterlogged soils. There has been limited excavation of these sites, but evidence from elsewhere suggests that they were not for permanent occupation but had a range of other economic, religious and political roles; they could have been refuges at times of uncertainty. They do, however, symbolize political control, at a time when there is little other evidence for social stratification.

Towards the end of the first millennium B.C. hill-forts were abandoned, and new political centres were created on or near to the tribal boundaries indicated by Late Iron Age coin distributions. They include the massive LINEAR EARTHWORKS of the North Oxfordshire Grim's Ditch (Ditchley Park), Aves Ditch (Middleton Stoney, *ON&W*) and the South Oxfordshire Grim's Ditch (Crowmarsh Gifford and Nuffield), the enclosure at Cassington Mill (*ON&W*), and the *oppidum* at Dyke Hills, Dorchester (*see also* Roman Oxfordshire, below). 110 acres of dense settlement were enclosed here, within substantial earthworks at the confluence of the Thames and Thame. Together, these earthworks represent major engineering projects and statements of political control on the eve of the Roman invasion.

ROMAN AND ANGLO-SAXON OXFORDSHIRE
BY PAUL BOOTH

The Roman period

The pre-1974 county of Oxfordshire covers an area which in the Roman period formed parts of the territories of three of the major tribes or *civitates* of Britain: the Catuvellauni, centred on Verulamium (St Albans, Herts.) to the E, the Dobunni, centred on Cirencester (Gloucs.) to the W; and the Atrebates, with their centre at Silchester (Hants) to the s. These units were perhaps not formally constituted before the later CI A.D., and the extent to which they related to pre-Roman polities is uncertain, but at the end of the Iron Age the linear EARTHWORKS of Aves Ditch, w of Bicester (Middleton Stoney, *ON&W*) and the South Oxfordshire Grim's Ditch at Crowmarsh Gifford and Nuffield may have partly defined the territory of the Catuvellauni in relation to the Dobunni and Atrebates respectively. At the same time there were major local centres – so-called ENCLOSED OPPIDA, defined by very substantial earthwork enclosures – on the Thames at Cassington (*ON&W*), Abingdon (Berks.) and Dorchester. Further N, the discontinuous earthworks of the North Oxfordshire Grim's Ditch at Ditchley Park and elsewhere defined a much larger area, the significance of which remains uncertain.

The impact of the ROMAN INVASION of A.D. 43 was immediate and substantial. Alchester (at Wendlebury, near Bicester, *ON&W*) was established as a major military base, possibly a fortress of the *Legio II Augusta*, as early as A.D. 44. It was placed at a strategically important junction of a s–N route from Chichester and Silchester up to the Midlands with an E–W one (Akeman Street) forming a direct road between Verulamium and Cirencester and indirectly linking the region with the new provincial centre of Colchester. These routes became formalized as the main ROMAN ROADS through the county, and in due course NUCLEATED SETTLEMENTS grew up along them. Alchester and Dorchester – the latter also the site of a fort, but one perhaps not established until after the rebellion of Boudica in A.D. 60/61 – eventually developed as walled towns, military occupation meanwhile having ceased before the end of the CI. Alchester became the largest settlement in the county, covering an area of around 100–110 acres. w of Alchester was a series of settlements on Akeman Street, at Sansom's Platt (N of Woodstock), Wilcote and Asthall (all *ON&W*). Further settlements grew up on other elements of the road system, for example in the N of the county at Swalcliffe Lea on the road from Towcester to Stratford-upon-Avon, while there may have been a minor settlement at the crossing point of a N–S road over the Thames at Oxford. There were other nucleated settlements in locations not obviously served by the major road network, such as Chipping Norton and Gill Mill (South Leigh) (both *ON&W*).

These sites varied considerably in size and character. STONE BUILDINGS were common for example at Alchester, Sansom's Platt, Asthall and Swalcliffe Lea, and at Alchester included temples, a bath building and houses as well as the town walls, while at Swalcliffe Lea at least one building contained four mosaic pavements. At both Alchester and Dorchester there were significant areas of settlement outside the defensive circuits. Elsewhere, for example at Gill Mill, which has been extensively excavated, no more than five stone buildings are known, of simple rectangular plan, although again the existence of a temple is likely here on the basis of other evidence. SHRINES OR TEMPLES were probably key features of all the major settlements, though rural temple complexes are also known, with a particularly important one at Woodeaton (*ON&W*) and another at High Wood, Harpsden. The presence of a shrine at Dorchester is suggested by an inscription, erected by an officer who may have been based at a *mansio*, or official posting station. The provision of such services, and of temples and markets (these two often associated), was among the major functions of the nucleated settlements; over the long term, an intimate relationship with surrounding agricultural communities was the most important characteristic of these sites.

The great majority of the population was based in RURAL COMMUNITIES already in existence at the time of the Roman conquest; there is almost no evidence for disruption of settlement in the mid C1 except in the vicinity of Alchester. With the passage of time, distinct variations in settlement pattern began to emerge. Much of the Thames Valley was occupied by FARMSTEADS of simple character, sometimes in small clusters. Further N, on the Cotswold dip-slope, there were more VILLAS, some, like North Leigh, Stonesfield and Wigginton (all *ON&W*), ultimately very substantial establishments indeed, richly furnished with mosaic pavements and painted walls. There was a notable concentration of villas within the area of the North Oxfordshire Grim's Ditch, several of which seem to have been established unusually early, in the later C1; elsewhere, villas did not normally appear before the mid C2, and sometimes rather later. The division between areas of settlement dominated by villas and those dominated by farmstead sites of different sizes was not a simple one, however, and in areas such as the Thames Valley below Abingdon both types were interspersed. The extent of lower-status rural settlement in the northern part of the county is largely unknown because of the limited amount of work that has been carried out there. Across the county, evidence for rural buildings is scarce apart from the villas. It is likely that a pre-Roman tradition of construction of round buildings using cob was widespread, but evidence for such structures is very difficult to identify archaeologically.

A notable feature of the Thames Valley is a phase of widespread disruption of the settlement pattern in the early C2. Many sites were abandoned or relocated at this time; their successors often have a more regular rectilinear layout than previously, and are associated with ditched trackways. These sites often continued in use through the Later Roman period. The reason for this development is unknown; it suggests large-scale reorganization of land-holding, but it does not seem to have affected the villa sites in the north of the county.

Most settlements were involved in MIXED AGRICULTURE, for which the best evidence comes from the Thames Valley. Processes of intensification of production during the period included the introduction of 'corn-drying ovens' and animal- or water-powered mills, and the exploitation of hay meadows as a means of overwintering increased numbers of animals. The large settlement at Gill Mill (*ON&W*) is thought to have been a specialist centre for cattle rearing. There is no evidence for large-scale industry, with the important exception of POTTERY PRODUCTION: a major industry centred on modern-day East Oxford (but with component sites ranging from Noke in the north to Dorchester in the south) was one of the largest in Roman Britain from the mid C3. Its specialist products – gritted mixing bowls and fine red-surfaced table wares – were very widely distributed, particularly across central and southern England. A locally important pottery industry was probably based near Wilcote on Akeman Street, while iron working is attested at Asthall and may have been of more than immediately local significance at Swalcliffe Lea (all *ON&W*).

The evidence for BURIAL PRACTICE shows that the conventional view of dominant cremation traditions being replaced by inhumation from the later C2 is too simple, although it is broadly true for cemeteries associated with the major settlements. Rural traditions were varied, and while they included inhumation in the Early Roman period, rural burials are scarce at this time and many may have involved a rite that did not result in formal placement of human remains in graves. Late Roman burials, mainly inhumations, are much more commonly found in all settlement contexts, and include variant rites such as decapitation and prone burial. Richly furnished graves are very rare. Rural cemeteries rarely contain more than about forty graves, whereas those associated with the larger settlements, particularly Dorchester, can be much larger.

Many (but not all) settlements of all kinds were occupied up to the end of the C4, but dating the FINAL PHASES of 'Romano-British' activity is highly problematic once supplies of coins and pottery ceased to be renewed – around A.D. 400 for the former but at a less certain (and disputed) date, perhaps early in the C5, for the latter. Dorchester was an important focus of very late Roman activity, with large associated cemeteries and evidence for the presence of military personnel and possibly sub-Roman mercenaries. Environmental evidence suggests that use of the countryside continued with relatively little change in the C5. This must indicate the survival of a significant Romano-British population in the first instance; but whether they were supplanted by immigrants, or became acculturated in the course of the C5, adopting 'Anglo-Saxon' building techniques, artefacts and (up to a point) burial practices, remains highly contentious. The chronology and exact nature of these developments are unclear, though it is certain that Anglo-Saxon material culture was dominant in the region by the later C5.

The Anglo-Saxon period

SETTLEMENTS of Early Anglo-Saxon type were usually modest in size, and within the region are best known in the Thames Valley. They typically comprised small timber buildings with a sunken element (*Grubenhäuser*), sometimes with a few larger post-built structures. The largest local examples are at Radley and Sutton Courtenay in Berkshire, but extensive, sometimes dispersed, settlement is also likely elsewhere, for example around Eynsham (*ON&W*). Some of these sites are closely associated with earlier Roman settlements, but imprecise dating evidence makes it uncertain whether occupation sequences were continuous (as environmental evidence tends to suggest).

Early Anglo-Saxon graves commonly contain objects that can be quite closely dated, so CEMETERIES often provide a better indication of the chronology of early settlement. Early cemeteries contained both cremation and inhumation burials. The latter are more common, and of a general character quite similar to that of the Late Roman period, but are more frequently distinguished by a distinctive array of grave goods, including weapons for men, and beads and brooches for women. Adjacent Late Roman and Early Anglo-Saxon inhumation cemeteries outside Dorchester and at Berinsfield have been shown by radiocarbon-dating to present a continuous sequence of burial, with hints of an overlap roughly in the middle of the C5. Like the settlements, the early cemetery evidence is best known within the Thames Valley, and there are few later C5 or early C6 cemeteries in Oxfordshire upstream of Standlake (*ON&W*). Differences in individual status in this period seem to be expressed more clearly in burial provision than in settlement architecture, though the practice of furnished burial seems to have declined sharply in the late C6, in line with a nationally observed trend.

By this time, however, a few sites in the region with very substantial timber HALL BUILDINGS suggest a different manifestation of the increasing stratification of society. These are associated with the Gewisse, a polity based in the upper Thames region and thought to have formed the basis of the later kingdom of Wessex. Heightened social distinctions are also suggested by the appearance in the C7 of small numbers of rich 'princely' burials, sometimes under BURIAL MOUNDS, as at Asthall (*ON&W*) and (probably) at Cuddesdon. A variety of other burials (by this time entirely inhumations) with grave goods continued to occur, including a small number of well-appointed female graves, among which a bed burial from a substantial C7 cemetery at Ardley (*ON&W*) is notable, but the practice finally ceased towards the end of the C7.

The question of whether this trend was related to the growth of CHRISTIANITY in the region is debated, but there is no clear connection, and the later C6 decline in provision of grave goods pre-dates the conversion of the region. In about 635, however, Birinus was established as the first Bishop of Wessex at Dorchester, which thereafter periodically remained the seat of a bishopric until the C11. No direct evidence of Birinus's church survives, though Early and Middle Saxon structures have been found immediately N of the present abbey, which probably lay outside the Roman defended circuit. Other broadly contemporary structures known from inside the Roman walls possibly related to the episcopal complex, although none are ecclesiastical in character. Other early churches in the region are mostly known or inferred from historical rather than archaeological evidence, but there is excavated evidence for parts of the important early minster/ monastic complex at Eynsham from at least the C8 onwards, and less extensive remains from Bampton (*ON&W*), Bicester (*ON&W*), with a Middle to Late Saxon cemetery that may have been associated with a minster, and Oxford.

The main early ecclesiastical centres were established under noble or royal patronage, and the locations of a number of important ROYAL MANORIAL CENTRES are known, though none are directly attested archaeologically. They are likely to have contained substantial timber hall buildings like those mentioned above. Domestic settlements of the Middle and Later Saxon period are also poorly known, being much less commonly found than their equivalents of the C5–C7. A small site at Black Bourton (*ON&W*) is notable for a long sequence of occupation, including the Middle Saxon period. The first example to be extensively excavated is at Yarnton (*ON&W*). Its C8 and C9 timber halls, representing one or two farmsteads, were much more substantial than earlier buildings, and were set within enclosures with subsidiary structures. The disappearance of these structures by the C10 suggests movement of population towards a settlement focus at or near the present village of Yarnton. In turn this may reflect the wider establishment of NUCLEATED VILLAGES and open field systems, eventually widespread across England (but not universal in Oxfordshire, where more dispersed settlement patterns are also found). The chronology of this process is still debated, but that village formation was underway in the C10 seems very likely. There is, however, almost no relevant archaeological evidence from the county. There are slight traces of features related to probable Late Saxon manorial centres: elements of a timber structure or structures of uncertain plan at Cogges (*ON&W*) appear to be of this date, and an enclosure bank and a fragment of stone wall at Middleton Stoney (*ON&W*) may reflect part of another such complex, but a pre-Conquest date is not certain. Equally, the beginnings of towns are hard to detect away from the major centre of Oxford, but may be hinted at by Late Saxon timber buildings at Bicester. These lay near the likely minster site, supporting the view that a close association between minsters and markets encouraged the growth of a number of towns in the region, though the clearest evidence for this comes mainly in the post-Conquest period.

For the early history of Oxford *see* pp. 3–4.

THE MIDDLE AGES

Anglo-Saxon and Norman churches

The ANGLO-SAXON CHURCH has left little to see in southeast Oxfordshire. Only the ancient episcopal seat of Dorchester Abbey has any standing fabric, and this comprises no more than an area of late Anglo-Saxon walling on the N side of the nave, with the outline of a possible *porticus* opening. Earlier churches from the Anglo-Saxon see at Dorchester cannot now be located. Nor have any physical remains been found of churches at three other important pre-Conquest centres, Benson, Goring and Thame, although the street plans at the latter two places appear to perpetuate Anglo-Saxon enclosures. SCULPTURE with a likely origin in the period is limited to a re-set sundial at North Stoke church.

Dorchester and Goring also became MONASTIC CENTRES, with churches that were kept for parish use after the Reformation. At Dorchester a post-Conquest rebuilding of the church was followed by more ambitious reconstruction after *c.* 1140, when an Augustinian abbey was established. Its one remaining auxiliary building is of C15 date and domestic in character, but the development of the church into the C14 was shaped by the need to provide a claustral complex, and also to provide for the cult of St Birinus (*see* p. 538). Goring acquired an Augustinian nunnery, first recorded in 1135. Here too the present church shows the marks of attached conventual buildings, now lost. Also established around 1140 was the greatest monastery in the area, the Cistercian house of Thame Abbey (later Thame Park). Foundations from its vanished C12–C13 church have been recorded, and part of what was probably its infirmary remains, with mid-C14 detail; the lavish quarters of its C16 abbots are discussed on p. 550. Minor buildings have been left by the Benedictine nunneries at Littlemore and at Godstow, near Wolvercote (both Oxford), and from the great Benedictine abbey at Osney, which belongs with the story of Oxford and its diocese (p. 24). The only other religious houses were the preceptory of the Knights Hospitallers at Sandford-on-Thames, from which a probable chapel of C15 date survives, and the vanished C12 leper hospital at Crowmarsh Gifford.

Dorchester remains the greatest of the NORMAN CHURCHES in the area in terms of extent, although its form is no longer easily appreciated. Its partial rebuilding for the abbey preserved the cruciform and aisleless plan, from which the nave N wall survives, with the retained Anglo-Saxon fabric. The crossing lacked a tower – the three intact crossing arches are too lightly built for that – and the chancel had a straight E end with pilaster buttresses. Carved stones assembled in the pentice gallery give an idea of the quality of the lost C12 parts. Two other Norman CRUCIFORM CHURCHES in the area date from the end of the C12: Cuddesdon, a property of Abingdon Abbey, with a full crossing tower, and Lewknor, where one transept has been replaced by an aisle. Otherwise the standard regional plan-form throughout the C11 and C12 for churches large or small consisted of a chancel and an aisleless nave, with or without a tower.

Intact Norman TOWERS are uncommon. Goring has a powerful w tower of the early C12, vaulted below and with paired bell-openings; at Garsington the w tower dates from the late C12. The alternative arrangement with the tower placed between nave and chancel occurs only at Iffley (Oxford), at once the most sophisticated and the most intact of the area's Norman churches. Iffley is also one of the few early medieval churches in SE Oxfordshire which can be dated with confidence, its architectural motifs and its connections with the de Clinton and St Remy families placing it in the 1160s. Links can also be traced to the workshop responsible for the mid-C12 doorways of St Ebbe's church and St Frideswide's chapter house in Oxford, which share Iffley's distinctive chevron and beakhead motifs, and to Reading Abbey as the regional source of the mid-C12 beakhead fashion. Iffley's other special features include a coherently composed W front, echoed at the de Clintons' contemporary church at Stewkley in Buckinghamshire; a vaulted chancel; very large round-arched windows, with chevron ornament inside and out; and the extraordinary use of Tournai marble for the jamb shafts of the tower arches. A much simpler C12 W elevation is at Crowmarsh Gifford, with its upper window flanked by little oculi.

This is to run ahead a little, because the area also has notable Early Norman churches at Checkendon and Swyncombe. These closely related buildings both retain apsed E ends, and display herringbone-pitched masonry of C11 type. Goring, Mongewell and Woodcote also have APSES, but these are Victorian re-creations based on old foundations. Apsed chancels co-existed with square-ended ones, as the ruined early C12 church at Bix and the E end at Rotherfield Peppard both demonstrate. Many other churches retain Norman fabric amid later enlargements and rebuilding, typically doorways (often re-set) and side walls of naves and chancels. Cuddesdon and Great Milton preserve the outlines of round-headed C12 windows in nave walls since pierced and enclosed by arcades and aisles.

Norman DOORWAYS are too many to list here, but some notable features may be picked out. Unlike the rest of Oxfordshire, SCULPTED TYMPANA are absent – the outstanding examples at Tetsworth having been destroyed in 1855 – and even more simply decorated examples are rare. Those at Dorchester and Watlington show diapering, and an *ex situ* tympanum at Shirburn has interlace carving. Also *ex situ* is a door lintel at Clifton Hampden with a boar hunt in shallow relief. FIGURED CAPITALS are scarce too. The S doorway at Iffley has the best examples, just as its W doorhood arch has the area's only coherent SCULPTURAL SCHEME, showing Signs of the Zodiac and symbols of the Evangelists. Pyrton has another sculpted door hood, with motifs of leaves and fruit. Capitals with figures or heads elsewhere include those on the doorway at Checkendon and in the chancel at Ipsden, while capitals with interlace or basket-weave patterns appear on doorways or chancel arches at Checkendon, Cuxham and Pyrton. The favourite Early Norman type of cushion capital is best seen in the cross-vaulted tower at Goring.

By the late C12 much of the work in the region's churches is of TRANSITIONAL character, typically combining Gothic pointed arches with Late Romanesque motifs such as roll mouldings (of plain or keeled section), point-to-point chevron, square abaci, and waterleaf or upright-leafed capitals. The pointed w crossing arch at Dorchester and the combination of rich round-arched doorways and pointed crossing arches at Cuddesdon are harbingers of the change. Good work from these decades is well distributed, including nave arcades at Chalgrove and Great Haseley, the w tower at Garsington (another mixture of pointed and round-arched openings), and the chancel arches at Lewknor and Rotherfield Peppard. The late C12 chancel at Ipsden also deserves mention for its leaf and volute capitals and its early use of Purbeck marble shafting.

No significant wall paintings survive from the period, and CHURCH FURNISHINGS are largely limited to FONTS. The cluster of lavishly sculpted or shaped Norman examples centred on Aylesbury (Bucks.) does not extend this far westward, where most early fonts are of simple tub shape. Lewknor and Berrick Salome have patterns of raised intersecting circles with beaded ornament, clearly from the same workshop. Other decorative treatments are generally modest: spirals at Mapledurham, diapering at Wolvercote (Oxford), scalloping and cable moulding at Harpsden. Rotherfield Peppard's font has a mid-band of cabling and is more pronouncedly chalice-shaped; that at Crowmarsh Gifford has elaborated arcading; the plain tub at Nuffield has a Lombardic inscription. Of special interest are the lead fonts at Dorchester and Warborough, both of the late C12, on which the arcading frames seated figures of bishops, abbots or Apostles. Warborough's has a sibling at Long Wittenham (Berks.) where some of the moulds recur. The mighty font at Iffley is in a class of its own, a square bowl of Tournai marble on a squat shaft, with spiral-fluted shafts to support the corners. PILLAR PISCINAS of the C12 appear at Swyncombe and Towersey, and early PISCINAS in the chancel walls at Crowmarsh Gifford and Harpsden. Good early IRONWORK survives on doors at Cuddesdon and Great Haseley.

8,
p. 759

Churches c.1200–c.1540

The area has relatively little to show from the first half of the C13, the period of mature EARLY ENGLISH GOTHIC. The best example is not a parish church but the elegant domestic chapel of c.1240 at The Prebendal at Thame (see also p. 548). On a larger scale, the town churches at Henley and Thame were both rebuilt to cruciform plans in the C13. Henley has preserved less of this incarnation than Thame, where the nave arcades of quatrefoil piers remain intact. There is also the mid-C13 chancel at North Stoke, with its Purbeck marble shafting and accomplished stiff-leaf capitals. Smaller churches of the period include Toot Baldon and the partial rebuilding at Binsey (Oxford), both with bellcotes renewed in Victorian facsimile. Individual features of superior quality are the lavish doorway of five orders at Great Haseley and the extension of the sanctuary at Iffley, its vaulting made continuous with the C12 work.

28

The prevailing Gothic window type up to the mid C13 was the lancet, chiefly used singly, sometimes grouped in threes (e.g. Cowley (Oxford), Newnham Murren, Shiplake S aisle). Tracery begins with openings pierced in the spandrels above paired or grouped lancets, the form known as PLATE TRACERY, represented by a side window at Warborough. The succeeding form is bar tracery, developed in France and first used in England in the 1240s. Foiled circles and varied groupings of circles are the dominant motif of its first phase, known as GEOMETRICAL TRACERY. The best examples in the area are in the N aisle of the chancel at Dorchester, of two different dates from the second half of the C13, and the E window at Thame (with late C19 restoration). Intersecting tracery and Y-tracery with or without cusping became common from the late C13 up to c. 1300, appearing together in the chancels at Emmington (renewed), Garsington and Shirburn. In the same period more complex and diverse tracery patterns began to supplant older Geometrical formulae, enlivened with fresh motifs such as split cusping and sub-arching. At the chancel at Great Haseley and the chancel S aisle at Dorchester, the source is clearly the new chapel of the 1290s at Merton College: a rare medieval instance for the area of direct imitation of an Oxford academic commission. Similar sub-arched tracery forms also appear in the early C14 chancel at Lewknor, though the internal sculptural details here suggest a date after c. 1320.

These developments introduce the DECORATED STYLE, which brought novel forms and enrichments to all the elements of Gothic architecture. At Dorchester this includes the unparalleled windows of the new sanctuary added c. 1330–40. In all three of these windows the tracery patterns extend below to cover the entire opening, and some of the mullions and transoms display small-scale sculpture on the inner face. In the N window the theme is the Tree of Jesse, with carved foliage and figures of the ancestors of Christ, linked to subjects in the stained glass (*see* p. 547). The closest parallels in the county are the W window at Bloxham and the E window of the N aisle at Ducklington (both *ON&W*), both rather less ambitious; also the Lady Chapel at St Albans (Herts.), where the figures are confined mostly to the jambs. The S window tracery and the lower part of the E window look forward to the panel patterns of the succeeding Perpendicular style.

At other churches the FLOWING TRACERY of the first half of the C14 takes more familiar forms. The full Decorated repertoire of flowing leaf-like shapes scarcely appears; the S aisle E window at Brightwell Baldwin is the best example. Instead, the most widely distributed shape is the reticulated type of cusped circles or ovals with ogee tops and bottoms, used singly or together. The chancel N chapel at Henley presents what may be one of the earliest datable instances. All the windows in the chancels at Chinnor (consecrated 1326) and its near-contemporary at Chalgrove are of this type. In the S aisle at Great Milton, reticulated tracery is combined with a Late Geometrical window of trefoil pattern and an E window of complex major and minor reticulations. Also reticulated are two spectacularly large nave

16

18, 19

19

windows at Dorchester, examples of the square-headed type widely employed for side windows from the mid C14 onwards. CLERESTORIES for aisled churches become more common from around the same time. The C14 examples at Garsington and Great Milton have distinctive circular windows.

C14 work in the area typically comprises enlargements or partial rebuildings, of chancels and aisles especially. The only near-complete C14 CHURCHES are the modest Easington and Emmington, the latter with a W tower with a saddleback top. The tower at Chinnor also has a gabled C14 summit; that at Marsh Baldon has an octagonal top stage, suggestive of an intended spire. The sole medieval SPIRE is at Newington, of c.1300. Of internal features, ARCADES in the area's churches mostly have plain octagonal piers, in succession to the round type that prevailed in the C13. The exceptions are once again led by Dorchester, where the late C13 chancel arcades feature many-shafted compound piers and richly moulded arches, albeit with plain moulded capitals. The simpler four-shafted pier type may be seen in the chancel aisles at Henley, with wave-and-hollow mouldings of characteristic Dec type in the arches.

VAULTING is barely seen. That in the chancel S aisle at Dorchester is Victorian reinstatement, and there is a vaulted crypt below the nave S aisle. Storeyed porches with vaults occur at Dorchester, Great Milton and Thame, and there is a single-storey porch with a vault at Chinnor. Gothic tower vaults are represented by the Perpendicular example at Henley.

The best architectural SCULPTURE of the Gothic centuries is again concentrated at Dorchester. In addition to the sculpted figures of its sanctuary windows, the associated sedilia make a spectacular display of pinnacled canopies encrusted with ballflower, foliage, animal heads and yet more small figures: a fusion of architecture and carved decoration characteristic of the period, in contrast to the C13 use of sculpture to define rather than conceal the structure. Also of note is the large early C14 corbel on one pier of the nave S aisle, carved with sleeping monks and foliage. The characteristic foliage type of the early to mid C14 is of wavy or blobby form like seaweed, as seen here and also at Lewknor, which has the most lavish of the SEDILIA and PISCINAS in the area's other churches. At Chalgrove and Chinnor the sedilia and piscinas are of purely architectural form, treated with refinement and carefully integrated with the C14 chancel interiors.* Those at Great Haseley are at once bolder and less closely related to the architecture, though they clearly belong with it, as too does the elaborately cusped TOMB RECESS alongside. The twin tomb recesses in the N chapel at Aston Rowant likewise indicate a C14 patron or patrons. Other enriched examples are at Newington (c.1300), South Weston (a Victorian copy), Watlington (C14) and in the S aisle at Great Haseley (three of the C14, with indented cusping similar to that on the recess in

---

*The sedilia at Great Milton are *G. G. Scott*'s re-creation of the early C14 design, based on fragments found.

the chancel). The scanty remains of the early C14 SHRINE of St Birinus at Dorchester, recovered and re-set in the 1960s, are of the same class of small-scale Dec architecture.

The PERPENDICULAR style replaced the ogee curves of the Decorated period with patterns more dependent on vertical and horizontal lines It arrived in Oxford at the former Canterbury College, built from c. 1370, and at New College, founded in 1379. In the rest of the county it flourished most in the Cotswolds, where many churches were remodelled in the C15 from the profits of the wool trade. The nearest equivalent in the SE area is the church at Ewelme, rebuilt in stages from the 1430s to the 1450s mostly by William and Alice de la Pole, courtiers who ended as Duke and Duchess of Suffolk. Here the S aisle windows have affinities with contemporary Oxford work, the Divinity School in particular; but the completed building adopts the East Anglian arrangement in which the nave arcades and clerestory run through into the chancel, with screens to mark the division. Another distinctive feature at Ewelme is the use of brick for the parapets, also employed for the almshouses and school alongside (*see* p. 550). Elsewhere, brick makes an early appearance at Stonor Park, for the tower which was added to the plain C14 flint-walled chapel some time in the C15. The other intact private chapel is at Rycote Park, consecrated in 1449 and modelled more obviously on a small parish church, except for the absence of a structurally distinct chancel. Its E window shows Perpendicular panel tracery in its maturity, and the side buttresses are carried up as pinnacles in the manner of a greater church. *p. 639* *p. 735* 31

Datable Perp work at other CHURCHES includes the chancel at Cuddesdon (probably c. 1375–6) and the S aisle or chantry chapel at Mapledurham (period 1381–95), the former with depressed pointed-arched side windows, the latter with straight-headed windows even at the E end. From the other end of the period there are the remaining parts of Waterstock church as rebuilt from c. 1480 to the early C16, where the N arcade has the Late Perp variant of octagonal concave-sided piers. In the towns, communal and mercantile patronage sponsored the Perp rebuilding of the transepts at Thame from 1442, with *John Buckley* of Headington as master mason, and the new crossing tower there. This is typical of Oxfordshire in its plain treatment, with none of the panelling or elaborate pinnacles of the West Country or East Anglia. At Henley the nave aisles and crossing were reconstructed and a new tower provided at the NW, with flint and stone chequering and octagonal angle turrets; the date may be late C15, although a C19 tradition has an early C16 Bishop of Lincoln as the tower's donor. 28 4

Most other churches have some Perp features, generally of predictable standard forms. At the largest scale these include W towers, commonly with diagonal buttresses (Checkendon, Lewknor, South Stoke etc.). At the smallest scale, sedilia and piscina have repetitive trefoiled or cinquefoiled arches, and none is elaborately carved. The mid-C15 SE chapel at Watlington is an exception, with unusual attached round shafts on the window mullions and chancel arcade. There is little architectural

SCULPTURE of note; the best work is the sequence of angels and a king on the nave hoodmoulds at Ewelme. At Rycote the chapel has carved greyhounds instead of pinnacles at the E end, now replaced with copies.

To complete the survey of CHURCH TOWERS, the area has two timber examples from the C15, at Berrick Salome and Drayton St Leonard. The former has the tree-ring dates 1428–9. It projects from the W wall, but was thoroughly disguised in a restoration of 1890. The tower at Drayton St Leonard stands within the w wall, and is weatherboarded. It represents a much larger group of internal timber W towers and bellcotes known from C19 views, nearly all of which were replaced with Neo-Gothic stone designs by Victorian restorers.

The best of the medieval church ROOFS in the area is the compartmented ceiling of the Chapel of St John at Ewelme from the 1430s, i.e. the chapel of the almshouse foundation there, with its complement of carved broad-winged angels. Other roofs offer variety rather than grand spectacle. Newnham Murren has a C14 crown-post roof in the nave. The N chapel at Ipsden displays many-cusped wind-braces in its C14 or early C15 roof, which combines cambered ties and arch-braced collars. The similar but plainer nave roof at Mapledurham has yielded the tree-ring date 1446. Sydenham nave has a C15 hammerbeam roof, Thame nave a restored C15 tie-beam roof with queenposts braced to the purlins. Rycote chapel is wagon-roofed, with a pointed profile; the C15 nave roof at Benson has solid spandrels with shallow carving above the ties.

Church furnishings and monuments, C13 to early C16

Most medieval churches in the area have something to show from before the Reformation in terms of furnishings or monuments, if only on a modest scale. To the early FONTS already described may be added those of the C13 at Aston Rowant and Rotherfield Greys, the former octagonal and of Purbeck marble with shallow arcading, the latter square and with angle shafts. There is also the elaborately arcaded C13 font bowl at Littlemore (Oxford), brought from the city's chief parish church of St Mary. Of later fonts only the mid-C15 example at Ewelme stands out: an enhanced version of the standard Perp type with octagonal bowl and stem, with a towering spired COVER in the East Anglian manner, made more ornate by C19 embellishments. Ewelme also has a good array of encaustic TILES, and these are widespread in churches across the area, thanks no doubt to the proximity of the Buckingham-shire tile-making industry. Most have been re-set, including the large collection in the reconstructed chapel at Thame Park. Late medieval CHOIR STALLS may be seen at Dorchester, Marston (Oxford), Rycote and Thame, none with misericords. Thame is also good for SCREENS, notably the chancel screen of 1529 (contemporary with the stalls), with early post-Gothic motifs, and a displaced C14 screen with octagonal shafting. The C14

p. 605

screen at Chinnor is older still, with round shafts and Geometrical tracery. Ewelme's several screens are almost intact, including the main chancel screen with its rare iron mullions. No medieval pulpits or lecterns remain in the area, but several CHESTS survive, of which the late C14 example at Brightwell Baldwin is painted with St George and the Dragon.

WALL PAINTINGS include an impressive C13 example in the apse at Checkendon, comprising the Apostles in single file with Christ in Majesty above. The two remaining narrative sequences are both of C14 date, in the nave at North Stoke and the chancel at Chalgrove. Of these, the latter is both more coherent and more accomplished artistically, reflecting the likely patronage of Sir Drew Barentin II in the 1320s. Among the paintings at Dorchester are a restored C14 Crucifixion and a late medieval St Christopher. Ewelme also deserves mention, not for any ambitious pictorial work but because its painted patterns and monograms play an important part in the C15 ensemble.

STAINED GLASS remains the largest category of medieval figurative art in the area, although most of what is left comprises later compilations of C14 and C15 remnants, some heavily restored (Binsey (Oxford), Brightwell Baldwin, Marsh Baldon, Waterstock etc.). What survives of the early C14 glazing of the sanctuary at Dorchester has a special interest as part of the integrated scheme of two- and three-dimensional decoration, already mentioned; besides the Tree of Jesse sequence there are some exquisite little windows in the pierced heads of the sedilia. From the same period, Chinnor retains figures of saints and scenes from an Acts of Mercy sequence, and Great Milton has two small narrative scenes depicting Lazarus. Marston (Oxford) has some patterned C13 glass which may be *in situ*. The late C15 and early C16 are represented by a window at Newington with donor priests and some re-set saints at Mapledurham, and there is a valuable collection of French monastic glass from the same period at Shiplake, plus a few French pieces at Bix. Two pieces of SCULPTURE stand out: a roundel with the Agnus Dei from the C13 churchyard cross at Iffley, and an early C15 Assumption of the Virgin at Sandford-on-Thames. The latter was probably made for one of the region's lost monastic churches, which must have influenced the architecture and artistic production in the parishes in ways which can no longer be traced.

Medieval CHURCH MONUMENTS in the area include two works of the highest quality, at Dorchester and at Ewelme. Dorchester has the cross-legged effigy of a knight identified as William de Valence the younger †1282, carved with exceptional vigour and force. At Ewelme the great presence is the canopied tomb of Alice, Duchess of Suffolk †1475, its alabaster effigy, attendant angels and architectural setting all extraordinarily intact, with much original colouring, and the extra feature of the only surviving female cadaver sculpture in England, in its own enclosure below the tomb-chest.

There is nothing of comparable importance among the monuments elsewhere, but much of interest. The sequence of effigies begins with an early C13 priest at Thame, and continues with two C13 knights in chain-mail at Great Haseley and a third at Chinnor. There are several C13 and early C14 TOMB-SLABS or coffin-lids carved with foliated crosses, including two good examples at Great Milton. Adwell has a small monument from a heart burial of *c.*1300, carved with a knight holding his heart above a shield. The earliest alabaster effigy is at Dorchester, probably representing Sir Hugh Segrave †1387, with tomb-chest intact. A less costly form consisted of a tomb-chest, with or without enrichment by diapering, shields and other devices, with effigial brasses set into the top slab. There is one example at Ewelme (Thomas Chaucer and wife, †1434 and †1436), and no fewer than four at Thame, the latest of which (†1539) stands under a mural canopy. The tomb-chests at Brightwell Baldwin and Great Haseley dispense with effigial brasses, and are made wholly or partly of Purbeck marble.

BRASSES appear more commonly as independent memorials, of which the most lavish are those of Sir Robert de Grey †1387 at Rotherfield Greys and the very similar brass to Sir Robert Bardolf †1395 at Mapledurham (originally on a tomb-chest). Good groups of lesser brasses may be seen at e.g. Chalgrove, Checkendon, Ewelme and Thame. The Cottesmore memorial at Brightwell Baldwin (†1439) is important as the earliest known English mural brass, and the Beauchamp brass of *c.*1430 at Checkendon uniquely depicts a soul carried heavenward by angels. The oldest survival in the area is at Chinnor, the head of a priest in a foliated cross of *c.*1290, and there are matrices for lost early brasses or brass inscriptions at Aston Rowant, Garsington and North Stoke. A rarer type is the incised EFFIGIAL SLAB, represented by a late C13 monument to a priest at Pyrton and by Abbot Smith †1535 at Dorchester.

Medieval secular buildings

Timber-framed houses survive in the area from at least the early C14, barns from earlier still, and these are covered in the chapter on vernacular buildings (pp. 550–6). The chronology of GREATER HOUSES goes back further, although it is difficult to draw a coherent picture of the early centuries. The oldest remains are at the de Greys' seat of Greys Court (Rotherfield Greys), a large fortified courtyard house of many periods. Its earliest identified fabric comprises some walling in the Great Tower, of C12 or even late C11 origin. The rest of the tower, with the adjoining mural towers and the curtain walling between, is of the late C13 to C14, and some timber-framed C15 lodgings survive elsewhere on the site. Also clearly legible is The Prebendal at Thame, a well-preserved clergy house comprising a C13–C14 solar block, a chapel of *c.*1240, and the remains of a hall between, all raised on undercrofts, and a replacement hall of C15 date to the N, with tall transomed windows. A lost fourth range made the house quadrangular. Camoys Court at Chiselhampton is

much less complete, the hall having disappeared, but the early
C14 solar window and garderobe tower remain. Harpsden Court
and Fifield Manor (Benson) both incorporate well-concealed
solar or storeyed chamber blocks of c.1200. At Harpsden the
block was latterly part of a large courtyard complex noted by
Leland in the 1540s, but this was substantially rebuilt not long
after. Fifield Manor also includes a storeyed section of c.1300
with a tall transomed window, though the relationship between
the medieval parts is unclear. The shell of an early C13 hall and
a re-set C13 two-light opening survive within the many-phased
parsonage at Iffley (Oxford).

The former royal residence at Henley has left no traces, and the
only CASTLE is at Shirburn, datable from Lord de Lisle's licence p.727
to crenellate in 1377. Despite extensive Georgian rebuilding the
C14 form remains: a symmetrical quadrangle with rounded
corner towers, standing within a moat. The type is familiar from
Bodiam Castle in Kent, begun a few years later. Earthworks of a
mid-C12 siege castle at Crowmarsh Gifford have been identified
in excavations; it was raised by King Stephen against Matilda's
forces across the river at Wallingford Castle (Berks.), one of three
chief medieval strongholds in the region together with the castles
at Windsor and Oxford.

All the houses so far mentioned are stone-built, though some
must have included timber-framed parts since lost. This combination of MATERIALS survives at Stonor Park, where there is a p.735
four-bay stone arcade from a C13 aisled hall enclosed within later
walling. It was followed in the C14 by a second aisled hall, this
time of timber; and much of this hall and its cross-wings also
survives within the later brick and stone shell. Further additions
of the C14 and C15 at this dizzyingly complicated house variously
adopted stone, flint, timber framing, brick infill or structural
brick: a reminder of the diversity of the area's building materials. At Blounts Court in Rotherfield Peppard there are encased
elements of what was a large C15–early C16 house of mixed stone
and timber-framed construction, and the remaining section of
the early C16 North Weston Manor (Thame) combines timber
framing with brick. A more consistent use of brick appears at
the Manor House at Ewelme, the C15 palace of the Chaucers
and de la Poles, although its double courts are reduced to a
single truncated lodging range. Another curtailed mansion is
the Barentins' Haseley Court (Little Haseley), which retains a
storeyed stone-built range of C15 date; it may have included an
upper hall. The late medieval house at Rycote Park must also
have been a great establishment, but this was wholly rebuilt in
the C16.

Such was the rate of rebuilding in later centuries that the
standard type of late medieval MANOR HOUSE with central hall
and cross-wings is surprisingly scarce, even when partial survivals
are included. Chalgrove Manor (*see also* p. 553) is the best timber-
framed example. Mapledurham has a re-cased manor house tree-
ring dated to 1448, but here the hall is on the first floor. Of
stone-built manor houses, *John Sewy's* hall range of 1474–7 at

Great Milton survives between replaced cross-wings, and the misnamed Elvendon Priory at Goring includes what appear to be elements of hall and solar ranges. Culham Manor retains one C15 wing from a former grange of Abingdon Abbey, of timber framing above a partly stone-built ground floor.

By far the grandest domestic survival from the RELIGIOUS HOUSES of the area is the battlemented and bay-windowed Abbot's Lodging at Thame Park, of several early C16 phases. The parlour made here for Abbot King after *c.*1527 is an especially precious survival, with panelling and other decoration that includes some of the earliest surviving Renaissance ornament in an English secular interior, as well as a very early internal porch.

A few other building types are represented. At Ewelme, the de la Poles' cloistered mid-C15 ALMSHOUSE foundation (God's House) displays sophisticated planning and inventive brick details, clearly influenced by the Low Countries, and their adjacent two-storey SCHOOL is likewise remarkable for its architecturally ambitious brick construction. One major medieval BRIDGE remains, built across a branch of the Thames at Culham in 1416–22, as well as remnants of the C12 bridge at Henley. For the C15 bridge from Culham to Abingdon *see The Buildings of England: Berkshire.*

VERNACULAR BUILDINGS IN
SOUTH-EAST OXFORDSHIRE
BY DAVID CLARK

The vernacular buildings of SE Oxfordshire have been relatively well researched over the years. All the parishes in the area have now been covered by the *Victoria County History*, and each volume has a section on its buildings. Over a hundred buildings in the area have been tree-ring dated. There have also been studies of individual places such as Dorchester, Henley and Benson, while some village histories contain useful information about buildings (*see* Further Reading). An ongoing Oxfordshire Buildings Record project to survey all the older houses in Chalgrove has so far produced thirty individual reports. Dan Miles has dated forty-one building phases in Mapledurham, and thanks to the tenacity of Ruth Gibson and the Henley-on-Thames Archaeological and Historical Group seventeen houses in that town have been dated and written up. More recently, Stephen Mileson and Stuart Brookes's ground-breaking study of Ewelme Hundred included detailed surveys of fifty-three houses.

The task of pulling these studies together is complicated because it is in the S and E of the historic county that the diversity of its traditional buildings is most apparent. This is partly due to the underlying GEOLOGY, which includes the Kimmeridge and Gault clays to the S and E of Oxford, with their outcrops of limestones including Corallian beds around Wheatley (*ON&W*),

36

29,
p.639

exploited from the C14, and the creamy limestones at the Haseleys and the Miltons. These form the rubble-stone walls of many cottages in the N of the area, though they probably replaced an earlier timber-framing tradition using crucks. Bands of large and small stones alternate as a decorative effect in a few places, such as Marsh Baldon. To the s comes a band of Greensand below the Chilterns where chalk (clunch) and flint predominate. Neither of these is used on its own; brick is generally included to give the buildings structural stability, but in some places, for example Ewelme, clunch is an infill material in timber-framed houses. There are also a few standing buildings built in cob (packed earth), including two former Nonconformist chapels, a summerhouse and cob walls in Dorchester. Near the Buckinghamshire border, the local variant of witchert (white earth) is found e.g. in a barn at Towersey, but is also used as an infill material in timber-framed houses, such as in Thame. In 1819 it was reported that some recently demolished houses in Watlington were made of mud thrown on to wattle hurdles, 'a method common in the district'.*

The traditional vernacular ROOFING MATERIAL was wheatstraw thatch. Two survivals of smoke-blackened medieval thatch have been recorded in this area, at No. 1 Priest End, Thame, and in Ewelme – the latter sadly destroyed in a fire in 2022. Plain red tiles appear in building accounts for higher-status medieval houses, and in due course they were the favoured replacement in this area for the traditional thatch of the vernacular cottage. The use of stone slates is rare, though some can be seen in Garsington. In Sandford-on-Thames is a terrace with a low-pitched roof characteristic of the use of tarred paper, promoted by J.C. Loudon in the early C19. The paper was made at the nearby mill.

The area's long thin parishes, with a variety of landscapes from riverside grazing to pasture and woodland in the Chilterns, gave each a source of building timber, mainly oak or elm, and TIMBER-FRAMED HOUSES are found throughout. Both box- and cruck-framing traditions are present, with a surprising number of cruck survivals in the market towns (Dorchester, Henley, Thame). Cruck buildings do not lend themselves easily to extension, and usually the economics of town-centre space led to their replacement. The contrast with N and W Oxfordshire is clear, where there are few (if any) cruck survivals in the market towns.

ROOF CARPENTRY follows the general pattern in southern England. Crown-posts provide lateral stability in the C14–C15, with purlin roofs dominating thereafter. But in SE Oxfordshire and the adjacent counties there are also local traditions. For example, there are some ten instances in the area of the 'type W' cruck apex found in the region centred on Oxfordshire, including Orchard End at Waterstock, while other apex forms follow nationwide distributions. Another local feature is the ogee-curved scissor-braced truss. In Henley there is a smokeblackened example at No. 25 Market Place, of 1471. Also from the

* J.N. Brewer, *A Topographical and Historical Description of the County of Oxford* (1819).

mid C15 is the 'crown-strut', a single vertical timber between tie-beam and collar. Examples have been recorded in Ewelme (alms-houses, founded 1437), Henley (The Bear, and No. 13 Gravel Hill, 1454), South Stoke (Corner House) and elsewhere. From this century, too, are examples of the 'butt-purlin pretending to be a clasped purlin' at Dorchester Abbey guest house (1445) and Crown House, Great Haseley (1448–50). Also found at No. 55 East St Helen Street, Abingdon (Berks.), this was a short-lived local experiment that did not catch on due to its inherent struc-tural weakness.

In the Nettlebed area, the exploitation of BRICK CLAY in the C15 was encouraged by the Stonors for their house and chapel, where the brick work was carried out by 'lez Flemyngges'. The de la Poles used brick for their school and almshouse complex at Ewelme, being familiar with the material and its decorative possi-bilities through their East Anglian and Continental connections. The Blounts at Mapledurham, having built their magnificent new brick house in the early C17, appear to have reused materials from Reading Abbey in their contemporary outpost at Chazey Court (Caversham, now in Berks.), while their dispersed tenants continued to live in medieval timber-framed houses, gradually improved by the addition of chimneystacks and upper floors. As a largely agricultural area (with woodland and pastoral farming), Mapledurham was sheltered from the rebuilding pressures to the E of the Chilterns, and the result is a remarkable collection of cruck-framed houses. Mill Farm Cottage (1335) serves as a likely model for the peasant house in the chalk area, as documents from c. 1300 confirm that these were timber-framed, with wattle-and-daub infill and thatched roofs. It is of three cruck-framed bays, with a two-bay hall in which the seating for the smoke louvre survives. Re-thatching allowed a detailed analysis to be made of the timbers, which showed that 111 trees of various sizes had been used, varying from a 24-in. (61-cm.) diameter hedgerow tree for one of the crucks and other roof parts, to twenty 4-in. (10-cm.) diameter woodland trees used to make rafters. The walls are of wattle-and-daub, and the frame sits on a dwarf stone plinth. The recent discovery of shutter grooves in the wall-plate forces us to rethink the common view of the medieval peasant living in a cold and draughty house.

The other DATED BUILDINGS that survive from before the Black Death (1348) are mostly of high status, such as the barns at Towersey Grange (1294) and Church Farm, Great Haseley (1313), the latter unusual for its assembly marks in Arabic numer-als. The aisled hall of 1341 at Crowmarsh Gifford (now the Queen's Head) and the raised aisle roof at the former rectorial farmhouse in Lewknor of around the same date are important domestic survivals. There are two dated early town buildings, also timber-framed: the cross-wing of 1315 at No. 7 Butter Market in Thame (where the cruck-trusses of the hall survive in the adja-cent building), and the Old Bell of 1325 in Henley, which has a crown-post roof. The market in Thame was established by 1215, and a number of the buildings of the market infill between the

narrow Butter Market and the Cornmarket are also likely to be
C14, indicating that by this time there was pressure on the available commercial space. These include the enigmatic Birdcage
Inn, which may date from the C13/C14, based on documentary
history and the presence of saltire framing within. Of later C14
buildings, what is now Cromwell Lodge at Upper Assendon
(Stonor) has a cruck-framed hall from 1394, and an open hearth
with pitched tiles partly surviving inside. The roof covering is
plain red tile, and brick replaced wattle-and-daub in a post-
medieval remodelling when a chimneystack was inserted, backing
on to the through passage.

21

Some twenty-two houses in the area have been tree-ring dated
to the C15, including seven in Henley and four in Mapledurham.
All the town examples have box frames, with features common
to the period such as arch braces, crown-posts or crown-struts,
while one (No. 9 Northfield End, Henley) is a rare, late aisled
hall (1472). In the rural areas, crucks continued to predominate.
At Whittles Farmhouse, Mapledurham, the cross-wing of 1413 is
box-framed – though, as the present hall is later, its predecessor
probably had crucks. One of the dated structures (Russetts at
Roke, Berrick Salome, of 1466) seems to be a former detached
kitchen. Once likely to have been a common type, these rarely
survive, though there is a good example at Willoughby House,
Dorchester, and a possible one at Cranmer Cottage in the same
place.

From the C15 we also have two phases of Chalgrove Manor, the
N wing (1457) and the hall (1488). The latter has its smoke-louvre
seating *in situ* and must have replaced an earlier hall. With the
addition of a new cross-wing in 1505, we see an example of the
process of alternate rebuilding of hall and cross-wings. It is also
possible that there was 'end reversal', by which the old service
wing was replaced by a new parlour/solar and the services moved
to the other end of the house.

One continuing interest of historians of vernacular buildings is
the phenomenon referred to as the 'great rebuilding', the process
of modernizing medieval open-hall houses by inserting chimneystacks and upper floors. Glimpses of the process can be seen
in SE Oxfordshire. For example, in Mapledurham, Mill Farm
Cottage got its fireplace in the late C16, and around the same
time the occupier of Three Chimneys (1457/8) was clearly keen
to adopt the new technology. Pithouse Cottage, however, built
around the same time, did not get a proper fireplace until the
C17. In Chalgrove, Pyke Barn Cottage, a two-bay cruck house
from 1556, has a lightly sooted roof, suggesting that its first
floor was inserted after only a few years as an open hall. On the
other hand, Fairleigh Cottage (No. 159 High Street) in the same
village seems to have been started as a hall house in the early
C17, but was given a chimney, lobby entry (*see* below) and upper
floor during construction. Also transitional are The Thatch in
Cuxham, Crucks at Great Haseley and Fulbrook House at South
Stoke. Among the modernized medieval buildings in Henley,
Baltic Cottage in Friday Street includes a two-bay hall house of

1537 with a smoke-blackened crown-post roof. In contrast, the former Brook Cottage in Benson of 1538 seems to have had a stair-tower when first built.

The early C17 also saw the development of new PLAN-FORMS. In his seminal work on vernacular houses, Eric Mercer used The Forge, Mapledurham (1691) as an example of the popular LOBBY-ENTRY form of the period.* The central door opens to a lobby, which is typically in front of the central chimneystack, with the staircase behind. This pattern is found in many places, for example The Lamb in Chalgrove (1610), Old Rectory Cottage, Cuxham, the Old Forge in Dorchester, and the so-called Bishop's Palace in Thame. Lobby-entry plans were also produced by inserting the chimneystack into the (off-centre) through passage of medieval houses, as at the Six Bells in Warborough.

At a lower social level, the SINGLE-ROOM HOUSE with gable-end stack and staircase built against it was another common form, particularly where stone was available to build a gable wall. The Thatch at the edge of Cuxham is placed at right angles to the road, allowing the stack to be a prominent feature. April Cottage, Chalgrove, which began as a two-bay cruck house around 1600, also has a stone gable with a stack, though it was another sixty years before it gained a first floor, staircase and second chimneystack.

From the later C17, exploitation of the local brick clays allowed owners of timber-framed houses to replace their wattle-and-daub infill with a more permanent material, for example in 1691 at the White Hart in Dorchester, where the date appears in the brickwork. Some encased the entire house, as at No. 1 Brook Street, Benson, where Richard Arthur clad his cruck cottage in brick, stone and flint in 1747, and put this date on a brick. At No. 13 Rotten Row in Dorchester, works in 1984 revealed a complete medieval hall house with a rare internal jetty within the facing brickwork.

The decorative use of BRICK appears in two main forms in SE Oxfordshire. On their own, grey glazed headers alternate with deep red stretchers in the almost ubiquitous use of Flemish-bond brickwork, though glazed headers laid in header bond are found in high-status houses such as Easington Manor and Golder Manor Farm (Pyrton). In flint areas, alternating bands of flint with brick or clunch are characteristic, though rarely with chequerboard patterns; one exception is the E end of the de la Poles' church at Ewelme, a building with known East Anglian influences. Where flint predominates in an elevation, as in a number of houses in Goring, brick is used for quoins and dressings. Glazed headers were used in the C16 and into the C17 to create diaper patterns in brickwork, and in the 1860s–70s a Chalgrove builder used them to insert dates in the gable walls of four buildings in the village. Brick was the material of choice for chimneystacks, as it avoided the difficulty of rainwater reacting with warm limestone, while also allowing for decorative effects.

* *English Vernacular Houses* (RCHME, 1975).

All the towns in the area retain their medieval STREET PLANS, and in many cases the burgage plot boundaries. There is also much surviving medieval fabric, most visible in Thame, less so in Watlington, while Henley was where London fashions had the greatest following. The pressure on town-centre sites can be seen where houses are gable-end to the street, perhaps with a side passage to the rear of the plot.

Some of the settlements on the major roads have good surviving examples of early INNS. The George in Dorchester is C15, and has a galleried range along one side of the rear courtyard. The former Old White Hart in Henley has a hall and lodging range dated to 1531, but the front part has a crown-post roof of 1391. Also in Henley, the Bull and Bear inns in Bell Street retain medieval features. These inns were modernized over the centuries, but at the Bull in Dorchester a massive new timber-framed lodging range was built alongside in 1610, with two jetties and evidence for impressive rows of oriel windows facing the street. In Benson, however, such was its importance as a coaching stop on the London to Oxford road that its medieval inns were almost completely replaced between *c.*1680 and *c.*1750. The Crown, Old Red Lion and Castle inns all show the latest classical styles, with brick the material of choice, and sash windows in profusion. Thame was likewise well provided with inns, including the Swan, with its rare surviving painted ceiling of the late C16 or early C17.

In Friday Street, Henley, are a number of early timber-framed buildings likely to have been associated with the RIVER TRADE. Coal wharves at the town were noted from the 1680s, suggesting that its fireplaces and chimneystacks were adapted to burn this fuel much earlier than elsewhere in the county, where the main driver was the opening of the Oxford Canal in 1790. Also around the town are a number of MALTINGS, mostly brick-built and from the C18.

There are some early MILLS in the area. At Mapledurham, a water mill on an early site was rebuilt in 1626 and extended in 1746 and thereafter. Mills on the Thame and its tributaries include C17 or C18 examples at Overy (Dorchester), Chalgrove, and Cuxham (two, including Cutt Mill), but of these only Chalgrove is potentially operational. The tall stone tower windmill of *c.*1760 or later at Great Haseley has been restored, and the post mill at Chinnor is a modern reconstruction reusing some timbers of 1789.

As well as some important C13 and C14 BARNS noted above, there is the C15 six-bay aisled barn at Drayton St Leonard that now houses the Aston Martin Owners' Club. The five-bay timber-framed and partially aisled barn at Manor Farm, South Stoke, represents the C17, with a double queenpost roof. The prosperity of post-Enclosure agriculture is expressed in a remarkable collection of large barns, of which the twenty-four-bay C18 brick barn at Ipsden Farm is perhaps the most impressive, though the early C19 barns at Fifield Manor near Benson and the other Newton family complex at Preston Crowmarsh in the same parish are close behind. From the mid C18 we see a new – and relatively local – type of barn with cranked inner principal roofs, twenty-eight dated examples of which from c.1740 to c.1800 have been identified in SE Oxfordshire.* Some have inevitably been converted to domestic use, for example the two at Manor Farm, Chalgrove, both with elm timbers. The jury is out as to the purpose of this form of construction; it certainly provides additional space for managing unthreshed grain in the upper part of the roof, but may simply have been a way of using bent timbers.

In this area, too, are some of the largest DOVECOTES in the county. The largest is at Culham Manor, dated 1685, with some 3,300 nests. At Manor Farm, South Stoke is a brick example from the C17, with about 1,500 nesting holes, while the stone dovecote bearing the date 1767 at Fifield Manor, Benson has 1,100. Others now stand alone in the parkland at Brightwell Baldwin (c.1632; 1,180 nests) and at Ascott Park near Stadhampton (680).

The population of the area began to rise steeply from the mid C18. The pattern was not uniform; in 'closed' communities there was a limited amount of better HOUSING, controlled firmly by the landowner, and the dispossessed had to move to more 'open' ones and make the best of what they found there. But some landowners also provided modern houses for their tenants and workers. At Nuneham Courtenay, where Lord Harcourt demolished the medieval village in the 1760s, he rehoused the entire population in purpose-built cottages along the main road. He described them as 'good and not expensive', and they were indeed far superior to much rural accommodation of the time.

REFORMATION TO RESTORATION

Secular buildings

The DISSOLUTION OF THE MONASTERIES in the area is illustrated by the transformation of Thame Abbey into the mansion called Thame Park. The twist here is that the same Abbot King who commissioned its early Renaissance interiors continued to enjoy them into the 1540s in his new Protestant role as the first Bishop of Oxford, before the property passed into lay hands. The other surviving monastic enclaves – at Sandford, and at Godstow (Wolvercote) and Littlemore, both now in Oxford – show various adaptations for domestic use.

p.719   The foremost GREAT HOUSE of the mid C16 was Rycote Park, as rebuilt for the same Sir John Williams (later Lord Williams of Thame) who acquired Thame Park. It was of brick, with several courtyards, a centrally placed gatehouse, and fashionable embellishments such as octagonal turrets with ogee cupolas. A damaged section of the gatehouse is all that remains, together with some of the service ranges, from which a larger house was fashioned in the C20 and C21.

*See David Clark in *Vernacular Architecture* 35 (2004).

There is no comparable ELIZABETHAN great house in the area, but several older houses saw significant investment in the period. At Harpsden Court the main range was reconstructed in 1568–72, apparently replacing the medieval hall with storeyed accommodation, in line with later C16 preferences. Around the same time, the giant huddle of components that made up the late medieval Stonor Park was given a regular, many-gabled brick façade and a central frontispiece dressed with largely classical detail. Its Marian iconography, together with the reconstruction of the chapel roof in 1578, illustrate the Stonors' commitment to Catholicism. At Greys Court (Rotherfield Greys), the medieval accommodation was extensively reworked by the fiercely anti-Catholic courtier Sir Francis Knollys. Subsequent losses make it difficult to tell all that was done, but a substantial gable-fronted residence or superior lodging range of 1575–6 remains, with other additions. These include an octagonal corner tower clearly meant to preserve the overall symmetry, and a remarkable well-house of 1587 with its donkey wheel intact. NEW HOUSES on a smaller scale include the Lybbes' seat at Hardwick, in its first incarnation around 1580, and The Priory at Great Milton, a stone-built gentry house of similar date. Its front has regular cross-gables with fashionable finials, but the windows are still asymmetrically placed.

p. 735

New houses from the JACOBEAN period and into the 1640s make a greater contribution. The outstanding example is the Blounts' brick-built Mapledurham House, now shown from analysis of its timbers to date entirely from 1609–12. Many of its features reflect Georgian amendments followed by partial restoration to a Jacobean appearance in the early C19, but the C17 outlines remain clear. The plan is an elongated H-shape, with a great chamber placed above a ground-floor hall in the central range, and a long gallery under the roof. The spacious open-well staircase survives, with early shaped balusters. Some muddles at the landings and upper levels suggest the hand of an inexperienced carpenter; but there are also some deftly concealed priest holes, Mapledurham being another Catholic stronghold. Several original ceilings survive, with broad ornamented ribs and plenty of portrait medallions in the compartments, clearly by two different workshops. Some of these plasterwork elements recur at nearby Hardwick House, as enlarged and partially rebuilt around 1610–15. The Great Chamber at Hardwick also has contemporary panelling and an ornate fireplace carved from clunch, with an overmantel relief of Abraham and Isaac: the only sculpted overmantel of the period in the county. Other INTERIORS with notable work include a room at Iffley parsonage (Oxford) with a shallow-ribbed late Elizabethan ceiling and a passage at Stonor Park with *trompe l'œil* painted panelling of the mid C17. There is a later example of this economical device in a room at Chalgrove Manor, of *c.* 1680.

37

Lesser GENTRY HOUSES of ambition from the early C17 include Pyrton Manor, brick-built on an E-plan in the 1600s, the more compact Checkendon Court of *c.* 1622, and the primary phases of

Baldon House (Marsh Baldon). The rebuilt hall range at Culham Manor has an attractive porch dated 1610, and the Manor House at Great Milton acquired a gateway with a shaped gable, worthy of a much larger house. In a class of its own is Garsington Manor, built in the 1630s. Its strongly symmetrical façades have arched window heads and running hoodmoulds: features not generally current by that date, but here clearly related to contemporary work at the Oxford colleges a few miles away. The compact plan is of an advanced type: rooms arranged as a so-called double pile, separated by a transverse passage, and provided with a back stair. The house may also have featured shaped gables originally. More widely, the plain-gabled type of lesser gentry house remained current into the late C17, as at Cuddesdon Manor. Among town houses, Stribblehills at Thame (1647) was originally faced with pargeted plaster, a feature now absent from the area. For other houses of the period, and for inns, mills, dovecotes and barns, see Vernacular Buildings, pp. 553–6.

PUBLIC BUILDINGS of the period are few. The only SCHOOL is the substantial two-storey example at Thame, built in 1569–70 from a bequest by Lord Williams. He also rebuilt the adjacent almshouses, which are timber-framed. Smaller ALMSHOUSES are at Mapledurham (1616–17) and Stonor (c. 1620, much altered). The BRIDGE over the Thame at Chiselhampton is late C16, and elements of an early POUND LOCK survive at Iffley, an important aspect of the Thames navigation story (another is at Culham). Parts of the ornate CONDUIT of 1617 that stood at Carfax in Oxford now make a feature in the park at Nuneham Courtenay, reconstructed as an ornamental feature for Lord Harcourt in the late C18.

Church architecture, furnishings and monuments

Barely any new CHURCHES were built in England in this period, and church work in the area typically takes the form of partial rebuildings and lesser additions. Medieval models are generally followed, with some simplification or coarsening. That applies to the partial reconstructions at Marston (Oxford; 1562) and Stadhampton (1588 and 1600), the Henley-type tower of c. 1602 at Dorchester, the Knollys funerary chapel at Rotherfield Greys with its simplified Perp tracery (1605), the rebuilt tower at Mapledurham (1608), the tower top at Cuddesdon (1630) and the brick and flint porch at Ipsden (1634). At Sandford-on-Thames the porch of 1652 has the running-hoodmould motif of the Oxford colleges. A comparable parallel is the nave roof dated 1615 at Berrick Salome, with thin but elaborate timbering like that of the open roofs at some early C17 college halls and chapels.[*]

CHURCH FURNISHINGS show a faster uptake of classical decorative forms. PULPITS are the most common survival, and

[*] At Denton House (Cuddesdon) the original windows from the Gothic-cum-Baroque chapel of the 1650s–60s at Brasenose College have been re-set as garden features.

most of these are of the early C17, many with carved arcading and foliage panels in shallow relief. At Brightwell Baldwin, Marston and North Stoke the tester also survives. Great Haseley and Newnham Murren have pulpits with cartouche motifs suggestive of the mid C17. PEWS include the two sumptuous enclosed examples in Rycote chapel, one double-decked, the other ogee-canopied, datable respectively to c. 1610 and 1625. The pulpit and the WEST GALLERY at Rycote are also Jacobean, and original decorative finishes are much in evidence throughout. Henley has a stocky octagonal FONT dated 1626, Marston a Jacobean SCREEN at the tower end. The only counterpart of the early C17 ensembles of PAINTED GLASS at the Oxford colleges is some minor heraldry at Brightwell Baldwin and Culham. Early ROYAL ARMS appear at Stadhampton (of Elizabeth, carved, brought in) and Marston (a wall painting), plus the restored C17 Prince of Wales's arms at Warborough.

The first of the CHURCH MONUMENTS of Oxfordshire to display Renaissance decoration is that of Lord Williams of Thame (†1559) and his wife, a tomb-chest with recumbent effigies and pilasters with ribbonwork trophies, plus some later embellishments. Another aspect of Renaissance influence is the greater realism of its effigies, which are precisely and delicately carved. The sculptor is unknown, but is unlikely to have been English. After that there is a gap until the early C17, and the grand canopied installations at Rotherfield Greys (1605) and Great Milton (1618). Each features multiple effigies representing two generations, of the Knollys and the Dormer families respectively, and like the Williams monument they are both of alabaster. One of the Southwark workshops established by Netherlandish sculptors is the likeliest source of the Knollys monument, possibly that of *William Cure II*, but the Dormer monument is attributed to *Samuel Baldwin* of Gloucestershire. Both are populated by a supporting cast of lesser figures, and the Dormer tomb-chest features an especially fine relief of a military scene. The double monument of Sir Richard Blount (†1628) at Mapledurham lacks a canopy, and the canopies of the Walter monument at Wolvercote (Oxford; †1630) and of the twinned double monuments of the 1620s at Lewknor have been lost.

All these monuments have recumbent effigies. The arrival in the early C17 of reclining effigies is illustrated by the monument to Dame Elizabeth Periam †1621 at Henley, which also shows a new simplicity and clarity in its architectural surround. Geoffrey Fisher attributes it to the Flemish-born sculptor *Maximilan Colt*.

WALL MONUMENTS of the early C17 may display small kneeling figures (Richard Lybbe †1599 and wife, Whitchurch-on-Thames; Lady Hobbee †1618, Aston Rowant) or frontal busts or demi-figures, a type often favoured for scholars and lawyers (Blunden †1607 and Plowden †1652, Shiplake; Croke †1641/2, Waterstock; Higgs †1659, South Stoke). At Newington, the Dunch monument of 1650 has two busts in shrouds, a fashion set by John Donne's monument at St Paul's Cathedral; it is attributed to *Thomas Cartwright I*. The oval surrounds, the use of black and white marble, and the architectural motifs associated with the Artisan Mannerist style (e.g. broken pediments and side scrolls) are all characteristic of mid-C17 classicism. The Howard monument at Ewelme (†1647) is a nice conceit, with angels assisting the shrouded subject's resurrection from a shapely urn.

SOUTH-EAST OXFORDSHIRE, c.1660–c.1840

Great houses, gardens and landscapes

The grandest Late Stuart and Georgian COUNTRY HOUSES in Oxfordshire are in the N and W parts of the county, and the SE territory has nothing to rival Blenheim, Heythrop House or Ditchley Park. Nor did the great works of the period at Oxford raise many echoes in the area's domestic architecture, though a few connections may be pointed out. Overall, too, the tally of LOSSES from this period is considerable. Sir William Dormer's Ascott Park (Stadhampton), the first big country house to appear after the Restoration, burnt down in 1662 before completion, and its appearance is unrecorded. Other casualties include William Cadogan's Caversham Park of 1718–23 (now part of Reading, Berks.), by an unknown architect, its original form recorded only on a plan of the house and park in *Vitruvius Britannicus*; Medley House at Binsey (Oxford), 1720s; Wheatfield House, Early Georgian, burnt in 1814; and Mongewell House, late C17 and late C18, demolished 1890. The C20 losses came after the Second World War: Badgemore House (Rotherfield Greys), by the London master carpenter *Richard Jennings*, probably 1710s; Aston House, late C18 and early C19; Burcot House, C18 and C19; *S.P. Cockerell's* austere Waterstock House, 1787–90; and all but fragments of Brightwell Park, c.1790, Whitchurch House, c.1715, and *J.W. Sanderson's* Coombe Lodge (Whitchurch), 1794–5.

Another lost house, the Bishop's Palace at Cuddesdon (1679–80, burnt 1958), introduces the earliest surviving group of POST-RESTORATION HOUSES. It was the work of two Oxford artisan builders, the carpenter *Richard Frogley* and the architect-mason *Thomas Wood*.* Legal records from a dispute between the two allow us to identify them as the builders of the closely contemporary Newington House and Great Haseley Manor, both of which survive. The former is a plain but well-proportioned rectangle of double-pile plan, with a later C18 top floor; the latter is also plainly treated and two rooms deep, but has forward-projecting wings (one rebuilt), similar to the arrangement at Cuddesdon. Haseley Court (Little Haseley; 1709–10) is likewise undemonstrative, with simple window surrounds and an unembellished pediment, as is the frontage of c.1720 at the Great House at Great

---

* *Wood's* finely ornamented doorcase from the palace survives at Christ Church, Oxford.

Milton. Haseley Court also shows the early C18 preference for a full attic storey in place of the hipped roofs of the late C17.

The early C18 is associated nationally with the BAROQUE manner. The nearest equivalent in the area is Lord Macclesfield's partial reconstruction of Shirburn Castle from 1720, which combines a medieval silhouette with simplified classical openings in ways reminiscent of certain projects by Sir John Vanbrugh and Nicholas Hawksmoor. There is also Britwell House (Britwell Salome; 1727–8), an astylar design which belongs to a group of houses attributed to the Oxford master mason and architect *William Townesend*. Its distinctive features include the assertive Doric details and open-pedimented fireplace in the entrance hall and the pilastered first-floor vestibule, both of which echo some interiors by Hawksmoor, a regular collaborator with Townesend in Oxford. Another brick-built house is Crowsley Park (Binfield Heath; 1734), a curiously elongated design with wings of different depths.

Britwell House consists of a villa-like block with a pediment, linked by quadrants to right-angled service wings: an arrangement associated with the succeeding PALLADIAN style. A less assured (and more altered) version of the plan-type is Woodcote House of c. 1733. The Palladian formula of a *piano nobile* or chief storey placed over a rusticated basement appears at the ashlar-faced w wing of c. 1745–50 at Thame Park, by the Midland architect-builder *William Smith*, although its proportions are closer to the mid-C18 average than to the exact hierarchies of Lord Burlington and his followers. Thame Park also has the richest and most expansive mid-Georgian INTERIORS in the area, especially the hall with its lavish naturalistic woodcarving and opulent plasterwork in the manner of *Thomas Roberts* of Oxford. Watlington Park (c. 1755) is a late example of the Palladian villa type; Chiselhampton House (1767–8, by *Samuel Dowbiggin* of London) is a three-storey brick villa with an applied Ionic portico. The best interior at Watlington Park also has plasterwork in the ROCOCO style, and there is more in this playful manner in mid-C18 interiors created at Greys Court (Rotherfield Greys), Hardwick House and Harpsden Court.

The C18 house with the strongest claim to national importance in SE Oxfordshire is Nuneham House (Nuneham Courtenay), begun for the 1st Earl Harcourt in 1756 with *Stiff Leadbetter* as architect. The template was again the Palladian villa with wings and quadrant links, and there was initially an external staircase to the *piano nobile*. But before the house was complete Lord Harcourt brought in *James Stuart*, fresh from his investigations of the antiquities of the eastern Mediterranean, to provide some novelties of detail. Thus the Venetian windows display features borrowed from Hellenic and Roman monuments in Athens, and some of the fireplaces have other freshly observed Antique motifs. Such innovations herald the NEOCLASSICAL manner, but Stuart's interiors also draw on the home-grown designs of Inigo Jones. Some of his contributions are not easily distinguishable from those of *Capability Brown* and *Henry Holland*, who in

p. 727

68

p. 704

76

1781 remodelled and enlarged what was clearly an impractically arranged house. Other motifs from the Hellenistic world appear in the plasterwork of a room at Greys Court, taken from Robert Wood's *The Ruins of Palmyra* (1753).

Later Neoclassical interiors are characterized by small-scale motifs and rectilinear compartments, familiar nationally from the closely related styles of James Wyatt and the Adam brothers. *Wyatt* himself contributed the plain ashlared s wing at the Great House in Great Milton in 1788, with its characteristic cornices and fireplaces. The double-height saloon of *c.*1780 in one of the lateral extensions at Haseley Court may also be his, and a grand Neoclassical saloon was added around the same time at Woodcote House. The oval Catholic chapel built on to Britwell House in 1767–9 has plasterwork which juxtaposes the Adamesque fashion with looser Neoclassical motifs.

A parallel story concerns the rise of NEO-GOTHIC design. The earliest firmly datable example in the area is at Stonor Park. This had a general mid-C18 renovation in which the exterior was regularized with orthodox sash windows. Inside, the C14 aisled hall was subdivided by *John Aitkins*, who introduced a Gothic screen and a big ogee-headed fireplace, similar to William Kent's pioneering 'Gothick' designs of the second quarter of the C18. Harpsden Court has a contemporary fireplace with the same profile, presumably installed when the house was refronted with mixed classical and Gothic openings. Medieval Catholic associations no doubt explain the adoption of Gothic for the plaster-vaulted chapel added to Mapledurham House in 1796–7, and for the similar vaulting installed in *James Thorp*'s remodelling of the chapel at Stonor Park in 1796–1800. The medieval range at Haseley Court was also vamped up with Gothic extras in the late C18. Among the wholly post-medieval houses, Ipsden House and Baldon House (Marsh Baldon) each has a late C18 extension with Gothic openings; at Baldon House this joins on to a folly tower incorporating medieval stonework from old Nuneham Courtenay church. At Braziers Park (Ipsden), *Daniel Harris* added a charmingly stagey Gothic extension with good surviving interior work. The antiquarian resurgence of the early C19 steered the renovation of Shirburn Castle, probably to designs by *John Nash*, and the restorations to idealized versions of older styles at Mapledurham House (1828–31, by *Thomas Martin*), The Prebendal at Thame (1837, by *H.B. Hodson*) and Hardwick House (1839).

The area's major GARDENS and DESIGNED LANDSCAPES have sometimes outlived their houses. The formal aesthetic of the late C17 and early C18 is represented by the remains at Ascott Park, with its intersecting avenues and its octagonal brick dovecote and granary probably inherited from an earlier layout. Other formal avenues appear at Crowsley Park, Haseley Court (re-created) and Shirburn. The less regular and more pictorial taste that came to prevail by the mid C18 found expression in the first phase of work at Nuneham Courtenay, with its temple-like church (*see* p.565) and other classical garden buildings. Greater naturalism was promoted by *Capability Brown* and his followers, and Brown was duly called in to adapt and extend the park at Nuneham in 1779–82, as well as working at Thame Park and Rycote Park. *Humphry Repton,* Brown's inheritor in many ways, was engaged at Coombe Park and probably also at Brightwell Park towards the end of the C18. Elsewhere, the lakes remain from depleted landscaped parks at Aston House and Mongewell House, and there is naturalistic landscaping on a smaller scale at Adwell House and Baldon House. Nuneham Courtenay also had an influential flower garden, created for the 2nd Earl Harcourt in 1771–2 by the versatile poet-gardener *William Mason,* and restored in the late C20. Its more intimate scale and contemplative mood reflect the influence of Harcourt's friend, the philosopher Jean-Jacques Rousseau. The early C19 revival of terracing and formal enclosures is represented at Nuneham too, where the architect *Robert Smirke* and the artist and landscape designer *W. S. Gilpin* worked for Archbishop Harcourt in the 1830s. Further from the house, Gilpin also created an extensive pinetum (now arboretum).

Fashions in GARDEN BUILDINGS are also well represented. As well as those at Nuneham, the classical properties of the mid-Georgian period are represented at Shirburn (temple, rotunda and orangery, woefully neglected) and at Britwell House (obelisk and column). There is a grotto and an early rockery at the Flower Garden at Nuneham, and a specially good flint-faced grotto at Crowsley Park. The derelict C18 walled garden at North Weston Manor (Thame) is centred on a summerhouse with an Ionic temple front. Mapledurham has a Gothick fern house, also derelict. On a more modest scale, the former grounds of Hardwick House retain a rudimentary Gothic eyecatcher, now incorporated into an early C20 house, and a very early example of the *cottage orné* type in the form of Straw Hall, a thatched pavilion for taking tea, in place by 1756. Some of the LODGES at the entrances to grounds and parks are also memorable: refined ashlar boxes with Neoclassical detail on the edge of Henley, thought to be outliers of *James Wyatt'*s works at Fawley Court (Bucks.); stagey castellated designs of the early C19 at Shirburn Castle (probably by *Nash*) and at Thame Park; thatched *cottages ornés* of *c.* 1820 at Little Milton Manor; minimal Greek Doric at Nuneham Courtenay, of 1838 by *Smirke.*

Other buildings in town and country

The HOUSES of the area's towns and villages from the period display the usual adoption of motifs and conventions from 'polite' architecture. Frontages become symmetrical, classical doorcases appear (first with carved brackets, then pilasters, then sometimes columns), and windows change from horizontal to upright proportions. The wooden cross-windows favoured in the late C17 and early C18 survive e.g. at Courtiers in Clifton Hampden, but most were replaced with sashes in the C18 and C19. Benson is a good place to study the change from thick glazing bars and flush sash-boxes in the early to mid C18 to thin bars, recessed sash boxes and panes of taller proportions later in the C18. For

the full picture of Georgian development, Henley has fine and
well-preserved houses of all periods, including good c18 brick
and some stucco villas from the second quarter of the c19.

Outside the towns, PARSONAGES are a reliable index of architectural fashion, from the lingering steep gables and brick diapering at Britwell Salome (1675–6) to the neat white box at
Whitchurch (*Richard Billing II*, 1835). The Neo-Tudor rectory of
*c.*1819 at Albury stands out as an early return to medieval motifs.
Some of the ESTATE COTTAGES built by improving landlords
from the mid c18 onwards also make a show, although the type
begins with studious plainness at *Lord Harcourt*'s new roadside
village for the tenants displaced by his park-making at Nuneham
Courtenay (1760–1). The 1830s additions at Nuneham by *W. S.
Gilpin* are more ornamentally treated, and Stonor has some distinctive early c19 pairs with banded pilasters. The outstanding
ALMSHOUSES of the period are those of 1725–6 at Goring Heath,
an isolated enclave with shaped gables and a central chapel, given
by a former Lord Mayor of London.

The three towns each have one major PUBLIC BUILDING of
the period. Watlington retains its brick-built and gabled TOWN
HALL of 1664–5, of the widespread type with an open lower
storey for marketing. Its architectural details belong to the vernacular classicism of the mid c17. WORKHOUSES survive at
Henley and at Thame. Henley's is of 1790–1 by the local builder
Henry Bradshaw, and is also markedly vernacular in character. That at Thame, of 1836 by the workhouse specialist *George
Wilkinson*, observes the standard provisions of the new Poor Law
Act. Purpose-built VILLAGE SCHOOLS began to proliferate in
the same decade; those at Lewknor (1836) and Iffley (Oxford;
1838) are thatched. Among the BRIDGES across the Thames
the outstanding design is that of 1782–6 at Henley by *William
Hayward*, of five elliptical arches. Its predecessor had timber
spans, and there were timber bridges of c18 date at Shillingford
(Warborough) and Whitchurch, and another of 1837 at Goring.
Shillingford's was the first of these to be rebuilt, superseded
by *John Treacher Jun.*'s stone bridge in 1826–7. The patched-up
stone bridge at Dorchester was also replaced, by *Francis Sandys*
in 1812–15.

A few COMMERCIAL AND INDUSTRIAL buildings stand out.
Henley, the largest town, acquired a small theatre as early as
1805. In the same street are some interesting brewery buildings,
including William Brakspear's house and office of the 1820s.
The brickmaking industry at Nettlebed is commemorated by an
impressively large kiln, probably late c17.

INNS, MILLS, DOVECOTES and BARNS of the period are discussed with vernacular buildings, pp. 555–6.

Church architecture, furnishings and monuments

Only three CHURCHES in the area were wholly replaced in this
period, but piecemeal rebuilding was widespread. The simplified

Perp manner of the early C17 was sustained after the Restoration for the Dorchester-type tower of 1666 at Warborough and the big w window dated 1672–3 at Thame. Cuxham church was rebuilt around 1685, mostly of reused materials. Fully classical designs did not appear until the C18, starting with the modest w tower at Culham (1710). Later towers and tower tops vary in style: classical at North Stoke (1725) and Stadhampton (*c*.1737); broadly medieval at Brightwell Baldwin, Chalgrove (after 1727), Nettlebed, Ewelme (1792) and Aston Rowant (*c*.1812). A juxtaposition of styles appears in the two-part rebuilding at Benson (1765–81), from the hands of two successive members of the *Townesend* dynasty. The charming renovation of the little medieval church at Wheatfield around 1730–40 combines a Venetian E window and a pedimented porch with fat battlements. The Georgian remodellings at Stoke Talmage and Waterstock were reworked in Victorian times, as was that at Mongewell, now semi-ruinous, which retains its Gothick eyecatcher tower of 1791. Early C19 interventions show increasing deference to medieval forms, as at Shiplake and Shirburn in the 1820s, and the scholarly restoration of the upper w front at Iffley in 1823.

That leaves the fully rebuilt churches, which nicely exemplify three different approaches. The tiny church of 1763 at Chiselhampton is classical of an engaging vernacular kind, and preserves its contemporary fittings from carved reredos to w gallery. *Lord Harcourt* and *James Stuart*'s Nuneham Courtenay church was begun in the same year and stands just three miles away, yet it comes from a different world. It serves both as a showcase for Athenian classical detail (the Ionic order of the Temple on the Ilissus) and as an ornament in the Arcadian park landscape, with its shallow central dome and twin porticoes. Finally there is little Albury church, rebuilt in 1830 under the reported direction of *Thomas Rickman*, best known as the pioneering analyst of the development of Gothic.

The best ensembles of CHURCH FURNISHINGS are at Chiselhampton, already noted, and the similarly full provision at Wheatfield, where the characteristic Georgian arrangement of pulpit, reading desk and box pews survives intact. Also largely intact is the almshouse chapel at Goring Heath, where busts of the founders look down from the apse. Older work includes an unsophisticated post-Restoration FONT at Chalgrove. Berrick Salome has a balustraded WEST GALLERY of 1676, Rycote chapel a superior classical REREDOS dated 1682, of the type provided at Wren's London churches. Both churches preserve representative COMMUNION RAILS of the period, the former with spiral balusters, the latter with a more modest turned type. There are spiral-twisted rails of *c*.1700 at Thame, which also has a fine inlaid PULPIT and tester. Around a dozen ROYAL ARMS of the period survive, including a double-sided set at Chinnor of Charles II and George II. Chinnor also has imported PAINTINGS by *Sir James Thornhill*, produced in 1721–2 as designs for a stained-glass rose window at Westminster Abbey. Another C18 exile is *Pompeo Batoni*'s altarpiece at Marsh Baldon, brought from Oxford after

52

69

75

it was displaced from the chapel at Corpus Christi College. *John Plowman Sen.*'s pulpit and pews of 1832 at Ewelme and the contemporary stone reredos there show the increasingly serious intent of the GOTHIC REVIVAL. By contrast, Nuneham Courtenay church has Italian furnishings from the Renaissance and Baroque centuries, installed in the early C20.

Provision for CATHOLIC worship was made at the great houses at Stonor and Mapledurham, as described. The area's oldest NONCONFORMIST chapel is at Goring, a meeting house of 1793 for the Countess of Huntingdon's Connexion, now heavily altered. The archetypal early C19 brick box is represented e.g. at Stoke Row (Independent, 1815), with round-headed windows, and at South Stoke (Countess of Huntingdon, 1820), with oblong ones. Binfield Heath has an ashlar-faced Congregational chapel of 1835, notable for its precocious adoption of Gothic forms.

There are no great CHURCH MONUMENTS to compare with those of previous centuries. The architectural compositions in favour in the post-Restoration decades are represented by the extraordinary Blake monument of *c.*1670 at Brightwell Baldwin, with its flaming alabaster urns offset against dark marble and a black-painted surround. Another standing monument is at Newington (†1686), with a garlanded urn. Bewigged portrait busts appear on monuments at Wolvercote (Oxford; †1679), attributed to *John Bushnell*, and at Great Haseley (†1709), a rare signed work by the Oxford sculptor *John Piddington I*. The only full-scale statue is on the anonymous monument to John Sanders †1731 at Mongewell, represented in a turban and loose draperies, reclining on a sarcophagus. Sarcophagi and urns in relief are commonplaces of C18 wall monuments, appearing in some of the mid-C18 works attributed to the prolific *Sir Henry Cheere*, who liked to introduce backings of coloured marble (Thame †1749, Lewknor †1752, Chalgrove †1766). The bust on the Earl of Abingdon's monument set up in 1767 in Rycote chapel may also be from his hand. Minor signed monuments by leading London-based sculptors appear at Wheatfield (*Peter Scheemakers*, †1739), at Rotherfield Greys (*Westmacott the elder*, †1781) and in the chapel at Thame Park (*Westmacott*, either *the elder* or his son, later *Sir Richard*).

VICTORIAN AND EDWARDIAN

Religious buildings and their furnishings

Oxfordshire is an especially interesting county in the architectural history of the CHURCH OF ENGLAND. This is due in large part to theological, antiquarian and pastoral initiatives from Oxford. On the theological side, the High Church party associated with John Keble, John Henry Newman and the *Tracts for the Times* (published 1833–41) were generally conservative and ascetic in their attitude to architecture. Thus Newman's own church at Littlemore (Oxford), of 1835–6 by *H.J. Underwood*, was built as a single cell with plain lancets. Enthusiasts for things medieval were represented by the Oxford Society for Promoting the Study of Gothic Architecture (later the Oxford Architectural Society), founded in 1839 and led by the antiquary and publisher J.H. Parker. Its preoccupations mirrored those of the more activist and dogmatic Cambridge Camden Society (subsequently the Ecclesiological Society), which was founded in the same year. Fascinated by every aspect of medieval church buildings, the Ecclesiologists sought to restore them to an ideal form, and to purge them of post-Reformation furnishings such as galleries and box pews. They also exalted the Gothic styles of the C13 and C14 above all that came after, licensing the replacement of late medieval features with 'correct' equivalents. This moralizing approach was shared by the Catholic convert A.W.N. Pugin, a Neo-Gothic architect and designer of genius. Pugin was an especially scornful critic of almost every convention of Late Georgian architecture, from its stylistic pluralism to its use of 'dishonest' materials such as stucco and cast ornament.

The progress of the GOTHIC REVIVAL after *c.*1840 was steered by these powerful ideals and personalities. It also coincided with wider concerns about the state of Anglican parish life, from the condition of church buildings to the need for a resident clergy and the state of education in the parishes. The energetic Samuel Wilberforce, appointed Bishop of Oxford in 1845, ensured that the diocese was in the forefront of reform. His first commission was to *Benjamin Ferrey*, Pugin's friend and future biographer, to add a chapel to the Bishop's Palace at Cuddesdon in 1846. (*Ferrey* also designed the area's only C19 church for a new urban district, built in Henley in 1847–8.) Two COLLEGES followed. The training of teachers for the diocese was taken care of by *Joseph Clarke*'s convent-like Culham College of 1851–3. By then Wilberforce had already appointed *George Edmund Street* as Diocesan Architect, and Street's first major commission followed, in the form of the theological college at Cuddesdon (1853–4 and 1874–5). Its buildings illustrate the movement away from native medieval forms after *c.*1850, drawing here on early French Gothic for both the details and the dramatized, slab-sided composition. A short-lived third college, for training missionaries, has left buildings of 1884–6 at Dorchester and a chapel of 1913 by *E.P.Warren*, transplanted to its second site at Burcot.

Street's own office was in Oxford between 1852 and 1855 – the young William Morris and Philip Webb were among his assistants there – and he remained Diocesan Architect until his death in 1881. Unlike (say) T.H.Wyatt in the neighbouring Salisbury diocese, he took a relatively restrained share of Anglican commissions in his territory, and none of his five Oxfordshire churches is in the SE area. Partly as a result, and partly no doubt because of its easily accessible situation between Oxford, Reading and London, a great many different architects – at least forty-five – were engaged on the area's PARISH CHURCHES during the period. A few of these commissions were for previously unprovided-for Chilterns settlements, but most concerned the restoration or the partial or complete rebuilding of existing churches. Nearly all the leading London-based church architects are represented, sometimes by minor commissions only, as well as *Charles Buckeridge, J.C. Buckler, E.G. Bruton, James Cranston, H.G. W. Drinkwater, James Johnson, C.C. Rolfe* and *H.J. Underwood* among the Oxford contingent, *John Billing, J.B. Clacy, Joseph Morris, S.S. Stallwood* and *William Woodman* from Reading, and a few outliers such as Wolverhampton's *Edward Banks* (Chinnor, restored 1865–6).

Much of this work comprises unexceptional essays in English Gothic of the approved period. Typical examples include the Dec-style replacements of small medieval churches at South Weston (*R.C. Hussey*, 1860–1) and Britwell Salome (*Buckeridge*, 1867). The stylistic range extends to Neo-Norman, at *J.M. Derick*'s W tower of 1840 at Sandford-on-Thames, and at Woodcote church as rebuilt by *Underwood* in 1845–6. Larger churches were less likely to be replaced, and there are relatively few new towers or steeples; the boldest is by *John Hayward* of Exeter, for his rebuilt church at Little Milton (1843–4 and 1861). The mid-C19 fashion for 'structural polychromy' – patterned or juxtaposed materials of deliberately contrasted colours – barely appears externally, though the local combination of flints with stone dressings offers a more sober equivalent. *A.W. Blomfield* introduced some striped walling when he restored Lewknor church (1863–4), and *William Butterfield* embraced the existing early C17 chequerwork when he rebuilt the W tower at Mapledurham in 1863, but that is all.

A change of mood is detectable after *c.* 1870–80, from strict archaeology towards a certain latitude of design, even to the point of prettiness. Examples include *Walter Cave*'s cottagey chapel of ease at Christmas Common, *A. Mardon Mowbray*'s reworking of the C15 timber tower at Berrick Salome, and the Arts and Crafts-inspired N aisle by *J.T. Micklethwaite* at Marsh Baldon, all of 1890, and *Rolfe*'s free Gothic chancel at Cuxham (1895). Few churches remained in their pre-Victorian condition by that time, and late restoration work often shows a more self-effacing approach, represented by *William Weir*'s work at North Stoke and Rycote chapel under the aegis of the Society for the Protection of Ancient Buildings (1902 and *c.* 1912).

The many earlier CHURCH RESTORATIONS include some of unusual interest. Keen to promote good practice, the Oxford Architectural Society sponsored *J.M. Derick*'s well-informed restoration of the chancel at Great Haseley in 1840–1, and Derick also began to restore Cuddesdon church, completed after Bishop Wilberforce's arrival by *Ferrey*, then *Street*. The Society's greatest project was Dorchester Abbey, initiated in 1845. Here the first architect to be engaged was *James Cranston*, soon replaced by *Butterfield*, then by *George Gilbert Scott*, the most discriminating restorer among the premier Victorian church architects. His interventions include the re-created vaulting of the SE chapel. Other restorations by *Scott* include Great Milton (1850) and the transformation of the little C12–C14 church at Clifton Hampden (1843–4 and 1864–6).

Clifton Hampden is also one of the best places in the area for CHURCH FURNISHINGS. With funds from the very rich Gibbs family, one of whom was vicar, *Scott* provided the chancel with a brass screen made by *Hart & Co.*, brass coronas, a mosaic reredos executed by *Clayton & Bell*, and an effigial monument to another Gibbs family member: an ensemble of rich and mysterious effect. The most memorable pieces elsewhere tend to be those by national architects with a bold personal style, less constrained by period precedent: *Butterfield* at Dorchester and Mapledurham, *Street* at Shiplake and Waterstock, and *Henry Woodyer* at Harpsden, Toot Baldon and Whitchurch, all of which also display his distinctive spiky aesthetic in the rebuilt architectural parts. The turn to later medieval English models and small-scale detail is represented e.g. by *C.E. Kempe*'s pulpit at Cuddesdon (1896), *J.N. Comper*'s side altar at Ewelme (1904), and some elaborate rood screens, especially those of the 1910s by *Percy Stone* at Goring, by *F.H. Crossley* at Littlemore (Oxford) and by *Walter Tapper* at Swyncombe. The chancel at Henley has the best PAINTED DECORATION, done in the 1890s to designs by *Comper* and others, and enhanced by *J.D. Sedding*'s fine wrought-iron screens. There are also some exposed sections of *Clayton & Bell*'s 1870s murals in the second chapel at Cuddesdon College, otherwise painted over in the anti-Victorian C20 backlash.

There is much in SE Oxfordshire to illustrate the development of Victorian STAINED GLASS. Garsington church has delicate heraldry of 1845 by the Oxford maker *I.H. Russell*, and some 1830s windows at Thame Park chapel may also be his. The versatile medievalist *Thomas Willement* also produced heraldic glass, as well as boldly coloured pictorial designs with small figure scenes in the C13 manner, as installed at Littlemore in the late 1830s. There is later work by him at Great and Little Milton, Sandford and Waterstock, and Willement also restored and re-set the French glass at Shiplake. Pictorial windows on a larger scale include work by the Birmingham firm of *John Hardman & Co.* at some sixteen churches, of a consistently high standard. Two especially vivid Hardman windows are at Henley, both designed by Pugin's son-in-law *John Hardman Powell*: one at the parish church (1868), the other at its C20 Roman Catholic counterpart. Here there is a salvaged reconstruction of the altar and E window which *Pugin* himself designed for a domestic chapel in Buckinghamshire in 1851. Another major firm is that of *Clayton & Bell*, founded in 1855. Their lucid and bright early work is represented at Wolvercote (Oxford) and Waterstock. Later C19 and early C20 windows by the firm commonly look to late medieval or Northern Renaissance art for inspiration (Ipsden, Thame etc.), as does the contemporary work of *Burlison & Grylls* (Great Haseley, Kidmore End). *Clayton & Bell* also deserve mention here for the skilful restorations of medieval glass at Chinnor and Dorchester, and for the late 1850s sequence at Great Milton, apparently designed by *J.R. Clayton* and made by

Heaton & Butler, with whom Clayton & Bell initially shared a studio. The great *William Morris* firm is represented by minor works only, at Lewknor (1873–7) and Littlemore (1887), plus 1920s windows at Thame and at Friar Park, Henley. Other secular glass of note is at Henley Town Hall, by *Henry Holiday*.

The most influential late C19 stained-glass maker was *C.E. Kempe*, whose muted palette and small-scale details appear e.g. at Crowell and Watlington. Characteristically lighter work from the early C20 by his former assistant *Herbert Bryans* is at Albury, Clifton Hampden, North Stoke and Lewknor, and Henley has windows by another ex-Kempe hand, *J.C. Bewsey*. Designs by *Comper* show a similar preference for lighter grounds and C15–C16 models (Drayton St Leonard, 1897–8). The most important window of the Arts and Crafts school from the period is *Louis Davis*'s magisterial Crucifixion at Littlemore, of 1900. Other windows worth seeking out are those by *Charles Hudson* at Clifton Hampden and Swyncombe (†1846 and *c.*1850), one by *Ion Pace* also at Clifton Hampden (†1879), and the E window of 1903 at Marston (Oxford) by *F.C. Eden* with *James Fisher*, incorporating C15 quarries.

As stained-glass memorial windows became general, the popularity of CHURCH MONUMENTS declined. The best locations for these are Lewknor, with late C19 works by *Boehm* and *Bazzanti* of Florence, and Nuneham Courtenay, where the Harcourt memorials include portrait sculpture by *Alexander Munro* and *Matthew Noble*.

There are two Victorian ROMAN CATHOLIC churches: at Dorchester, Puginian Dec of 1849 by *W.W. Wardell*, and at Goring, begun in 1897–8, by *W. Ravenscroft* of Reading. The modest resources of many NONCONFORMIST congregations are illustrated by two cob-walled former chapels at Dorchester from the late 1830s – the architectural obverse of Binfield Heath's assertive Gothic chapel of 1835 (*see* p.566). First prize among later churches and chapels goes to the Congregationalists at Henley, extrovert Late Gothic by *H.W. Pratt*, 1907–8. *Cooper & Howell*'s Free Church of 1893 at Goring and *C. Smith & Son*'s Quaker meeting at Henley of the following year are domestic-looking designs by Reading architects.

Public, commercial and industrial buildings

SCHOOLS are the most widespread public building type. Early Victorian examples mostly make little show, and many were no doubt designed by their builders (e.g. Aston Rowant, 1844). Exceptions include Garsington, a Neo-Tudor display piece of 1840–1 by *Underwood*, supported by public subscription, and *Joseph Clarke*'s school of 1847 at Clifton Hampden, with its added clock tower. *Street* as Diocesan Architect is represented only at Chinnor (1859–60, altered). The School Boards established under the Education Act of 1870 weakened the Anglican hold, and undertook some larger buildings; Brightwell Baldwin and

Garsington School.
Engraving by Orlando Jewitt, 1846

Chalgrove have late 1870s examples by *Morris & Stallwood* of Reading. The area's only purpose-built Victorian boarding school is that of 1877–9 for Lord Williams's establishment at Thame, neutral Tudoresque by *William Wilkinson*.

The largest PUBLIC BUILDING by far is the Oxfordshire LUNATIC ASYLUM at Littlemore (Oxford), begun in 1844 by the specialist *Robert Clark* and latterly converted to apartments, including the hospital range of 1902–5 by the County Surveyor *H. J. Tollit*. Also now residential are the Victorian additions at Henley's WORKHOUSE, by various local architects. Two of the area's three TOWN HALLS were rebuilt. Thame has a weak, small-scale design of 1887–8 by *Tollit*, Henley a proto-Baroque essay by *H. T. Hare*, of 1899–1901. Thame also has a neat little COURT HOUSE of 1861, now the town's museum. The area's first VILLAGE HALL (so named) is that by *Percy Stone* at Goring, 1900. A private benefactor gave Nettlebed a *de luxe* WORKING MEN'S CLUB in 1912–13, an appealing Arts and Crafts design by *C. E. Mallows*. An earlier gift to a Chilterns parish is the ornate WELL of 1863–5 at Stoke Row, presented, implausibly, by the Maharajah of Benares.

RAILWAYS begin with the Great Western main line of 1838–40. This crosses in and out of the county w of Reading, by means of *Brunel*'s original Thames bridges outside South Stoke and Goring. The line from Didcot (Berks.) to Oxford opened in 1844, and Brunel's neat Neo-Tudor station at Culham survives on its Oxfordshire section. The Henley branch came next, in 1857. Lines in the Chilterns followed, but did not last: the route to Oxford via Thame closed to passengers in 1963, a branch to Watlington succumbed in 1957. The railways transformed the fortunes of many Thames Valley settlements, Goring and Henley especially, although the original station buildings there

96   have gone. Another BRIDGE across the Thames was built for road
traffic at Clifton Hampden in 1864–5, a Gothic-arched design by
the inexhaustible *G. G. Scott.*

There are few COMMERCIAL AND INDUSTRIAL buildings
of note. The first purpose-built BANK is at Thame, of 1889–90
by *C. P. Ayres.* The nicely composed run of BOATHOUSES at
Henley and the larger single boathouse by *Percy Stone* at Goring
bear witness to the Late Victorian boom in waterborne leisure,
as does Henley's riverside GRANDSTAND (1913, by *F. G. Sainsbury*). HOTELS also appeared at Henley, most notably *William
Theobalds*'s Old English pile of 1896–7. Henley also has substantial buildings of the period for Brakspear's brewery, and a showpiece pub of 1900 for the same, probably by *W. G. A. Hambling.*
A LIME KILN of *c.*1908 has been preserved from the former
works at Chinnor.

Domestic architecture

Few of the area's older country houses were rebuilt in the
period, and its Victorian and Edwardian GREAT HOUSES were
mostly commissioned by incomers. The sequence begins with
J. H. Hakewill's Howbery Park at Crowmarsh Gifford, a Neo-
Jacobean house for the M.P. for Wallingford across the Thames,
begun around 1848.* The only house of the first rank for size and
97   display is Wyfold Court at Rotherfield Peppard, a French Flamboyant extravaganza of 1873–6 by *George Somers Clarke*, for the
Lancashire M.P. and cotton magnate Edward Hermon. The late
1880s are a turning point, as the Thames Valley and the Chilterns
both became fashionable locations. The riverside saw the first of
p.724   this new wave, in the form of Shiplake Court (1889–91): one of
Ernest George & Harold Peto's best houses, in a relaxed and genial
Tudor Gothic style, also of patterned red brick. Neo-Tudor or
Jacobean modes in stone or brick, with or without timbering,
remained current to the end of the period. Examples by London
architects include *Frank Verity*'s Shillingford Court (Warborough)
from the 1890s; *C. R. Baker King & C. Harold King*'s Joyce Grove
(Nettlebed), *Paul Waterhouse*'s Bozedown House (Whitchurch)
and *Oswald P. Milne*'s Huntercombe Place (Nuffield) from the
1900s; and *Frank Pearson*'s Great Oaks (Goring Heath) from
the 1910s. Mongewell House, of 1890–1 by *R. S. Wornum,* is in
the free William-and-Mary manner pioneered elsewhere by W. E.
Nesfield, and late French Gothic was adopted by the otherwise
little-known *Robert Clarke Edwards* at Sir Frank Crisp's Friar Park
(Henley), 1890–5. Around this lavish and eccentrically detailed
house, Crisp also created the best GARDENS of the period, a fabulous realm with formal and informal landscaping, lakes, caves
and grottoes.

*An earlier Neo-Jacobean house of comparable size was Swyncombe House, built
*c.*1840 and demolished in 1978.

The relaxation of stylistic categories was encouraged by the ARTS AND CRAFTS MOVEMENT. Not many of its greatest names are represented in the area, but the influence is clear in a group of houses marked by pragmatic planning, simplified detail and well-wrought materials. The best examples are deep in the hills: *Walter Cave*'s Ewelme Down House of 1905, and two houses of 1913, *Ernest Newton*'s Flint House (Goring Heath) and *L. Stanley Crosbie*'s Ewelme Park (Swyncombe). Smaller dwellings include *Halsey Ricardo*'s Eyot House (Dunsden; 1902), with tilework panels by *William De Morgan*, and the intriguing White House of 1908 at Shiplake by *George Walton*, close in spirit to some designs by Mackintosh or the Viennese Secession.

Edwardian fashion also encouraged the sympathetic EXTENSION of older houses, where previous generations might have remodelled more or rebuilt entirely. The results may be seen at Checkendon Court, Elvendon Priory (Goring), Great Milton Manor, Heath End (Checkendon) and Rycote Park, all enlarged between 1905 and *c.*1912. *W.E. Mills*'s addition at Braziers Park (Ipsden) shows this respectful treatment extending even to Georgian Gothic. Woodcote House, altered by *Detmar Blow* around 1913, belongs in a different class, with its brusque but creative treatment of the Early Georgian fabric.

PARSONAGES in the area follow national lines of development for the type. Tudor Gothic or Late Perpendicular styles tended to prevail in the 1840s, as at two giants by *G.G. Scott* at Clifton Hampden (now the Manor House) and at Great Haseley, where the hall roof from the late medieval predecessor is incorporated. Deference to English medieval precedent is first set aside at *G.E. Street*'s Cuddesdon vicarage of 1853–4 and later, a forerunner of Street's college buildings there. Parsonages of the familiar High Victorian type, steeply gabled and with mostly minimal Gothic references, followed through the 1850s–70s; architects represented include *A.W. Blomfield* (Great Milton), *David Brandon* (Dorchester), *Buckeridge* (Benson and South Stoke), *Codd* (Garsington) and *Woodyer* (Toot Baldon). One later example worth mention is *W.D. Caröe*'s Arts and Crafts essay of 1906 at Whitchurch Hill.

The numbers of LESSER HOUSES rose especially steeply in the Thames-side settlements along the railway. Goring was a prime spot for VILLAS, of which the best remaining sequence is by *T.W. Cutler* (1906–7). Henley, more densely developed, has a street of intriguingly fancy villas of the 1890s by the local builder *Charles Clements*, and lively detail including sgraffito decoration on a few late C19–early C20 semis elsewhere. Outside the towns, there is good ESTATE HOUSING at Burcot (*Howard Martin*, 1889–90), Checkendon (*Maxwell Ayrton*, a timber-framed Arts and Crafts extravagance of 1906), and Preston Crowmash at Benson (1909, architect unknown). *William Wilkinson*'s MODEL FARM for Lord Macclesfield at Shirburn (1856–7) should also be mentioned, not for its dwelling but as an early instance of farm buildings with integral steam-powered equipment.

INTERWAR, POST-WAR AND TWENTY-FIRST CENTURY

Between the wars

The interwar years in SE Oxfordshire were architecturally un-eventful. COUNCIL HOUSING was the most widespread innovation, and as elsewhere, the earliest projects were the most generous in scale. Henley has some well-handled terraces of 1919–22 by *H.T. Hare*, and *F.G. Sainsbury* designed a formally grouped enclave of 1920–2 outside Dorchester, for Crowmarsh Rural District Council. The same body also commissioned some thatched (now tiled) houses at Crowmarsh Gifford, of 1930–1 by *J.E. Thorpe*. Of comparable houses built privately, some of the best are *Goodhart-Rendel*'s emphatically roofed farm and cottages of 1937 at Rycote Park.

With LARGER HOUSES the picture is similar to that of the Edwardian years, but with a marked shrinkage in scale. Additions are generally modest, as demonstrated by *Goodhart-Rendel* at Rycote Park and *Philip Tilden* at Britwell House (Britwell Salome). Only at Chippinghurst Manor (Cuddesdon) does the tail wag the dog, here a C17 manor house inflated by *R. Fielding Dodd* of Oxford (1932–4). The wealthiest patron to build for himself in the area was Lord Nuffield of Morris Motors, but his expansion of *Oswald P. Milne*'s renamed Nuffield Place from 1933 is essentially suburban in its scale and aesthetics. The outstanding GARDENS of the period are at Garsington Manor, created largely by *Lady Ottoline Morrell* during the Morrells' eventful years there (1915–28), inspired by both English and Italian traditions.

The influence of MODERNISM on interwar houses takes some finding. Unlike in neighbouring Buckinghamshire, the Chilterns parishes did not attract many enthusiasts for the new architecture. Oxfordshire's first fully Modernist house appeared near the Thames at Mongewell, in 1938. Designed for two unmarried women by *George Nuttall-Smith & David Booth* (later of Booth & Ledeboer), it was lightly built and proved short-lived. That leaves Kibes at Highmoor, a streamlined, white-walled composition of 1939 by *Florence H. Gibb* and *Margaret Low*, now altered and extended. The embrace of simplified or reductive forms also marks Pond House at Stoke Row, of 1938 by and for *Jock & Elizabeth Shepherd* (refaced in 2011), which is otherwise of traditional gabled outline. The prominence of female patrons and designers in these commissions is noteworthy.

Other SECULAR BUILDINGS include a better-preserved Mod-ernist design, the range added to the Culham College quadrangle in 1938–9, by the obscure *A. Brace*. Another training establishment was the farm school at Turners Court (Nuffield), from which the assembly hall and clock tower of 1930 remain. On the COMMERCIAL side, Henley acquired an unusually good branch bank by *T.B. Whinney* in 1924, and in the 1930s Brakspear's brewery built roadhouse-type pubs to designs by *A.E. Hobbs*; those at Henley and Bix survive in domestic use.

The only new CHURCH of note is again at Henley: *A.S.G. Butler*'s Sacred Heart (R.C.) of 1935–6, simplified Gothic in deference to its salvaged altar end and E window by *Pugin* and *Hardman*. New STAINED GLASS includes designs at Chinnor, Lewknor and elsewhere by the long-lived *Powells* firm, also represented in the area by earlier work; good 1920s windows by Kempe's pupil *Geoffrey Webb* at Great Haseley and Thame; work by *A.J. Davies* of the *Bromsgrove Guild* at Crowmarsh Gifford and Warborough; and fine memorial lancets by two other Arts and Crafts practitioners, *Margaret Agnes Rope* at Clifton Hampden (1920) and *Marion Thompson* at Harpsden (1929). There are FURNISHINGS of interest at Cuddesdon church, a test-bed for High Church initiatives from the adjacent theological college: an early nave altar and accompanying screen by *S.E. Dykes Bower*, 1940–1. The one notable CHURCH MONUMENT, minor war memorials excepted, is that to Lady Ottoline Morrell at Garsington, of 1939 by *Eric Gill*, otherwise represented in the area only by lettered tablets.

From 1945 to the C21

The post-war era introduced PLANNING on a large scale. The Town and Country Planning Act (1947) reined in the sort of ribbon development that trails along the road to Garsington, but there was no special protection for the landscape until 1965, when the Chilterns were designated an Area of Outstanding Natural Beauty.* New ROADS came in the form of by-passes, e.g. at Dorchester and Crowmarsh Gifford, and the M40 motorway to Oxford cut through six parishes at the N of the area, opening in 1974 (N extension 1991). No NEW TOWNS were designated in Oxfordshire, but a local initiative established Berinsfield, a smaller-scale settlement at a former airfield near Dorchester. A plan by *Sir William Holford* was adopted in 1957, but no noteworthy architecture followed at Berinsfield, nor at the nearby atomic science centre at Culham, opened in 1960. Among existing villages Chalgrove has grown mightily, and the exurban settlements at Sonning Common and Woodcote continued to expand.

So to PUBLIC BUILDINGS. The largest of these, the *Architects Design Partnership*'s OFFICES of 1979–81 at Crowmarsh Gifford for the newly created South Oxfordshire District Council, fell vacant and were demolished after a fire in 2015. The design of SCHOOLS and LIBRARIES remained the responsibility of the *County Architect's Department* into the 1980s, headed successively by *G.R. Hutton*, *Albert E. Smith* and *M. Dutton*, all of whom produced decent but unexceptional work. The area's most interesting school buildings are those of the former Carmel College, a Jewish boarding school at Mongewell. This was planned and largely designed by *Tom Hancock* after 1960, with contributions

---

*For a critical assessment of C20 developments up to that time *see* Lionel Brett, *Landscape in Distress* (Architectural Press, 1965).

from others including *John Urwin Spence* of *Sir Basil Spence*'s practice; the latter's pyramidal exhibition hall of 1969–70 and *Hancock*'s spectacular glass-walled synagogue are due to be preserved when the site is redeveloped. Of the area's COLLEGES, Culham has extensions of decidedly mixed quality by *Seely & Paget* from *c.*1960, Cuddesdon a sequence of contextually minded late C20 additions, then a clean break in the form of *Hopper Howe Sadler*'s bold residential block and *Niall McLaughlin Architects'* luminous Edward King Chapel, both of 2011–13. Not strictly a college is the *Architects Design Partnership*'s Institute of Hydrology at Crowmarsh Gifford, 1969–72 and later; it resembles some Oxford educational buildings of the period in its expressive use of pre-cast concrete framing. Henley has a key early work by *David Chipperfield* in the form of the MUSEUM dedicated to rowing and the river (1989–97), a harbinger of the embrace of more tactile materials and archetypal forms at the turn of the C20. On a smaller scale, HEALTH CENTRES – a relatively new building type – are represented by strong but altered designs by reliably original architects at Chinnor (*Peter Aldington*, 1966–8) and Henley (*Patrick Gwynne*, 1968–70); the latter has a worthy companion alongside, of 1991–3 by *Sutton, Griffin & Morgan*.

COMMERCIAL ARCHITECTURE is mostly an out-of-town story. The service station by the M40 at Waterstock by *JWA Architects*, 1993–8, and the business-park offices at Howbery Park (Crowmarsh Gifford) by *Scott Brownrigg & Turner*, 2003–9, are better than average examples of these genres. The headquarters building for Bremont at Harpsden, by *Spratley Studios* of Henley (2017–21), also makes use of full-height glazing, and shares a broadly High Tech aesthetic.

The chapel at Cuddesdon excepted, the CHURCHES have not produced much new work of interest in the area since 1945. There are economical 1960s buildings at Berinsfield, Sonning Common and Woodcote, all more or less Modernist; the Catholic church of the same period at Littlemore (Oxford) by *Peter Reynolds & Partners* has lost its distinctive original roof. Another new Catholic church is at Watlington, a resourceful design on a more modest scale, by *Peter Bosanquet & John Perryman Associates*, 1988–90. Older church buildings have been updated with added vestries, meeting rooms, lavatories etc., in traditional or contrasting modern styles; Rotherfield Peppard shows both approaches (1965 and 1981–2). REORDERING has transformed some church interiors, sometimes introducing new furnishings of interest, as at South Weston (*Maguire & Murray*, 1982–3). Stadhampton has been more drastically cleared, for joint use as a village hall (2011–13).

Post-war STAINED GLASS falls broadly into two schools: the continuing pictorial tradition, represented e.g. by *Michael Farrar Bell* at Warborough and Swyncombe, and a Modernist embrace of more abstracted forms, in which *John Piper* – living at Fawley Bottom, just over the Buckinghamshire boundary – and his collaborator *Patrick Reyntiens* were leading figures; Nettlebed and Pishill have windows by them of the 1960s–70s, and there are more at Iffley and Wolvercote (Oxford). A window of 1961 at

Crowmarsh Gifford by *Charles de Vic Carey* is a convincing Modernist collage of smaller images and texts. Makers working somewhere between these approaches include *Morris Meredith Williams* (Rotherfield Peppard, 1948–62). Checkendon has engraved glass of 1963 by *Laurence Whistler* in memory of the artist and sculptor *Eric Kennington*, whose work is represented by a MONUMENT in the same church, rather in the Eric Gill manner.

DOMESTIC ARCHITECTURE is largely a tale of individual commissions, though *Lawrence Dale*'s early post-war council housing at Thame shows a surprisingly confident Neo-Georgian spirit, and there are creditable developments of small private houses at Henley, Goring, Little Milton and Warborough of the 1950s–70s. Henley also has larger enclaves, notably *Raglan Squire & Partners'* terraces and multi-storey flats of 1966–8 at Ancastle Green. On the debit side, several COUNTRY HOUSES were demolished in the post-war decades (*see* p. 560), but the area's good connections encouraged the adoption of others as centres for business, research or recreation. The list includes Blounts Court (Rotherfield Peppard), Bozedown House (Whitchurch), Flint House (Goring Heath), Howbery Park (Crowmarsh Gifford) and the Manor House at Great Milton, now a celebrated restaurant. Other houses were reduced for their owners by demolishing C19 and early C20 extensions, as done by *Seely & Paget* at Hardwick House and at his own Watlington Park by *Lionel Brett*, later 4th Viscount Esher. More modest reductions were made at the two great Catholic houses, Mapledurham and Stonor, when these were sympathetically restored in the 1960s–70s. Other restorations, at Chalgrove Manor from 1977 and at the National Trust's Greys Court (Rotherfield Greys) in 2002–8, have transformed understanding of those houses, aided by dendrochronology.

Two major houses in the area were taken by leading interior decorators: Haseley Court (Little Haseley) by *Nancy Lancaster* of *Colefax & Fowler* in 1955, Britwell House (Britwell Salome) by *David Hicks* in 1960. The former's nostalgic INTERIORS have survived better than their bolder counterparts at Britwell, but both houses retain inventive formal GARDENS created by their owners. There are more gardens by *Hicks* at Brightwell Grove (Brightwell Baldwin), to which he moved in 1980. Other gardens of note include those created at Greys Court by the Brunners, and *Christopher Bradley-Hole*'s of 2009–10 for Haseley Manor (Great Haseley).

New post-war HOUSES in the area are readily identifiable as Modernist or traditional. The latter experienced a modest revival on the Britwell estate under *David Hicks*. In 1971 he commissioned *Raymond Erith & Quinlan Terry* to design a farmhouse at Berrick Salome, and later co-designed other Neo-Georgian houses at Britwell Salome, as well as a replacement for Swyncombe House. Harder to classify is Upper Pindars at Rotherfield Greys, an intriguing pyramid-roofed house by *Green, Lloyd & Son*, c. 1961. *Philip Jebb*'s grandiose Oakingham House at Nuffield, designed around 1988 in late C17 style, belongs with a new wave of incoming wealth. For the most part this has since tended to settle on older properties, many of which are increasingly invisible behind security gates and barrier planting.

Notable MODERNIST houses of the post-war years begin with a cluster of single-storey designs of the late 1950s. The best of these, and the best preserved, is *Patrick Gwynne*'s Past Field at Henley, an American-influenced design carefully integrated with its sloping site. Also in Henley is *Francis Pollen*'s own The Walled Garden, now drastically altered. Another patio-type house is *Philip Dowson*'s White Acres at Goring Heath, which preserves more of its original form. Pollen shortly formed a partnership with *Lionel Brett*, whose singular brick-built tower house of 1967 at Christmas Common shows the decade's readiness to embrace new forms. Other novelties include *David Tapp*'s own house of 1969 in Henley, partly cantilevered over the garden, and a post-partnership design by *Pollen* at Ipsden called Bibury, of six-armed radial plan (1976–*c.*1983). The steel-framed Bridge End House at Dorchester by *Julia Feilding & Donald Morrison* and *Douglas Lanham*'s Grange House at Burcot are two 1960s designs which remained faithful to the single-storey rectilinear model.

Interesting dwellings continue to arrive in the C21. Jacob's Ladder at Chinnor is an early work by *Niall McLaughlin* (1999–2001), a homage to the steel-framed Case Study houses of post-war California. *Avanti Architects*' Long View of 2004–7 at Henley is an imaginative reworking of motifs from Past Field next door, *Pippa Nissen*'s hip-roofed Mount House of 2011 is a well-judged insertion at Ewelme, and *Adrian James Architects*' Incurvo of 2013–16 at Goring more than justifies its name. Two larger houses of ambition outside village centres are *Aldington, Craig & Collinge*'s introverted Oakwood Farm at Checkendon, 2007–11, and Rowan Atkinson's conspicuous Handsmooth House of 2010–16, a white Neo-Corbusian mansion by the American architect *Richard Meier*.

SE Oxfordshire has entered the 2020s with most of its historic buildings in good shape; if anything, over-restoration can be more problematic than neglect. Of the great houses only Shirburn Castle is in an uncertain condition, and much of the decay at lesser historic buildings which Lionel Brett deplored in 1965 has been halted or reversed. Relatively few parish churches have been made redundant, and four of these have a secure future with the Churches Conservation Trust. Now the area seems set for further large-scale building, notably on the southern fringes of Oxford and on the airfield site at Chalgrove. Is it too much to hope that some of this will be of architectural value?

FURTHER READING

Oxfordshire was rather poorly served by LOCAL HISTORIES before the *Victoria County History* (VCH) began its coverage in the C20. When the original Oxfordshire volume of the *Buildings of England* series was published in 1974, only three VCH volumes with coverage of the present area had appeared (vols V, VII and VIII, published between 1957 and 1964). The remaining districts have since been magnificently surveyed under the editorship of Simon Townley (vols XVI, XVIII and XX, the last in 2022). Work continues on some remaining areas in the N and W of the county, but for the S E area the VCH should be the first port of call. Except for the most recent volumes, they are all, most helpfully, available online at *www.history.ac.uk/research/victoria-county-history/ county-histories-progress/oxfordshire/vch-oxfordshire-publications*. Also recommended is *An Historical Atlas of Oxfordshire*, edited by K. Tiller and G. Darkes (Oxford Record Society vol. 67, 2010), an amazing compendium of summaries of a wide variety of Oxfordshire topics, all with most useful maps, as well as extensive suggestions for further reading.

Earlier COUNTY HISTORIES are of more limited value. The first, Robert Plot's *Natural History of Oxfordshire* (1677), occasionally includes antiquities, but is more concerned with 'natural curiosities' than architecture. There is nothing more until Joseph Skelton's *Antiquities of Oxfordshire* in 1823, useful for illustrations of buildings before C19 restorations. For the later C19 and early C20, much information can be gleaned from Kelly's Directories and similar publications, and from the expanding online coverage provided for subscribers to the British Newspaper Archive at *https://www.britishnewspaperarchive.co.uk*. Some GENERAL BOOKS such as the Oxfordshire volume of the *Little Guides* series (1906), by F. G. Brabant, are useful. Slightly later is the *Shell Guide to Oxfordshire* by John Piper (1938, 2nd edn 1953), one of the best of that series, much enhanced by Piper's own drawings.

Recommended works for EARLIER PERIODS are Martin Henig and Paul Booth, *Roman Oxfordshire* (2000), and John Blair, *Anglo-Saxon Oxfordshire* (1994). These can be supplemented by the three Oxford Archaeology Thames Valley Landscapes monographs on *The Thames through Time: The Archaeology of the Gravel Terraces of the Upper and Middle Thames*: no. 32 on early prehistory to 1500 B.C. (A. Morigi, D. Screve, M. White, G. Hey, P. Garwood, M. Robinson, A. Barclay and P. Bradley, 2011); no. 29 on late prehistory (G. Lambrick with M. Robinson, 2009); and no. 27 on the early historical period, A.D. 1–1000 (P. Booth, A. Dodd, M. Robinson and A. Smith, 2007); and by H. Hamerow, 'Anglo-Saxon Oxfordshire, 400–700', *Oxoniensia* 64 (1999).

One older book still of great value for CHURCHES is the scholarly *A Guide to the Architectural Antiquities in the Neighbourhood of Oxford* (1846) by J. H. Parker, a founder of the Oxford Society for Promoting the Study of Gothic Architecture, later renamed the Oxford Architectural and Historical Society (*see* p. 567). Briefer accounts of all the county's churches are provided in Parker's *Ecclesiastical and Architectural Topography of England: Diocese of Oxford* (1850). More recent surveys are Jennifer Sherwood, *A Guide to the Churches of Oxfordshire* (1989), and Richard Wheeler, *Oxfordshire's Best Churches* (2013). For NONCONFORMIST CHAPELS the best summary is the Oxfordshire section in *Nonconformist Chapels and Meeting-houses: Central England*, compiled by Christopher Stell (RCHME, 1986). On medieval STAINED GLASS there is the *Corpus Vitrearum Medii Aevi, Great Britain, vol. I: The County of Oxford* (1979), by Peter A. Newton. He also provided the medieval glass entries for *The Buildings of England: Oxfordshire* in 1974, on which the coverage in this revised volume has been based. For C19 glass there are no similar local studies; the best general introduction remains *Victorian Stained Glass* by Martin Harrison (1980). For CHURCH MONUMENTS, details of sculptors can be found in Ingrid Roscoe, *A Biographical Dictionary of Sculptors in Britain 1660–1851* (2009). BRASSES are comprehensively covered by the late Jerome Bertram in *Oxfordshire Brasses and Slabs* (2019), medieval SCREENS by F.E. Howard in *Archaeological Journal* 67 (1910).

Of PERIODICALS generally, the reports of the Oxford (later Oxfordshire) Architectural and Historical Society began in 1840. Its journal, renamed *Oxoniensia* in 1936, has the most thoroughly researched articles. The Oxford Historical Society publications of 1884 onwards deal mainly with the city. Also useful is the *Berks, Bucks and Oxon Journal*, from 1889 onwards. Detailed accounts of assorted and varied VERNACULAR BUILDINGS from the area can be found in J. Steane and J. Ayres, *Traditional Buildings in the Oxford Region c.1300–1840* (2013), and in S. Mileson, 'People and Houses in South Oxfordshire, 1300–1650', *Vernacular Architecture* 46 (2015). W. Foreman, *Oxfordshire Mills* (1983), is a useful, well-illustrated summary. For BUILDING MATERIALS, W.J. Arkell, *Oxford Stone* (1947), still provides a first-rate account. Most large COUNTRY HOUSES have been written up in *Country Life*. Several Oxfordshire houses are also covered by Anthony Emery in *Greater Medieval Houses of England and Wales 1300–1500, vol. III: Southern England*, 2006. Lively accounts of many of the area's gardens are provided by Tim Mowl in *The Historic Gardens of England: Oxfordshire* (2007). A stimulating discussion of PLANNING from a 1960s perspective is Lionel Brett's *Landscape in Distress* (1965).

For details of INDIVIDUAL ARCHITECTS the essential source remains the *Biographical Dictionary of British Architects, 1600–1840*, by Howard Colvin (4th edn, 2008). Sidney M. Gold, *A Biographical Dictionary of Architects at Reading* (1999), covers the period up to 1930 and includes much from the area, as well as from Oxford. Alan Powers, *Francis Pollen: Architect* (1999), is a useful monograph on a locally based designer.

A general survey of TOWNS is provided by Kirsty Rodwell (ed.), *Historic Towns in Oxfordshire* (Oxford Archaeological Unit, 1975). Individual studies include Simon Townley, *Henley-on-Thames: Town, Trade and River* (VCH, 2009) and J.H. Brown and W. Guest, *A History of Thame* (1935). Among the many accounts of VILLAGES, two with good architectural coverage are Kate Tiller (ed.), *Benson: A Village Through Its History* (1999), and Sheila Llewellyn, *The View from the Bridge: The Story of the Thames-side Villages of Clifton Hampden and Burcot* (2000). The area's two most important medieval buildings are admirably covered by early C21 MONOGRAPHS: Kate Tiller (ed.), *Dorchester Abbey:*

Church and People 635–2005 (2005); Warwick Rodwell, *Dorchester Abbey* (2009); John Goodall, *God's House at Ewelme* (2001). The college at Cuddesdon has histories by Owen Chadwick (1954) and Mark D. Chapman (2004). Older studies include Percy Stone on Goring church and priory (1893), and two books on Thame: by H. Lupton (1860) and F. G. Lee (church, town and abbey, 1883).

For still wider reading, a BIBLIOGRAPHY by E. H. Cordeaux and D. H. Merry of printed works related to Oxfordshire was published by the Oxford Historical Society in 1955. A comprehensive update is provided in the *Historical Atlas of Oxfordshire*, mentioned above. ONLINE SOURCES besides the VCH include the updated National Heritage List for England at *https://historic england.org.uk/listing/the-list.*

SOUTH-EAST OXFORDSHIRE

St Mary. Rebuilt in Dec style in 1865 by *A.W. Blomfield*. He reused the late C12 s doorway, with an arch with roll-and-hollow mouldings on jamb shafts with bell capitals. The church is aisleless, with small transepts. Extravagant bell-turret corbelled out from the w wall, with gargoyles, gables on the diagonals, and a spirelet. – STAINED GLASS. E and w windows by *Ward & Hughes*. – SCULPTURE. Two late C19 angels in high relief, apparently cut down from a larger piece. – MONUMENTS. Knight, *c.*1300. From a heart burial. The small figure holds up his heart, everything below covered by a shield. – Frances Webb †1846 (vestry). Gothic, with a thin canopy and pinnacles.

ADWELL HOUSE, NE of the church. Largely of *c.*1790. The s front of the main block is rendered, of five bays, with a thin cornice and parapet. The centre bay breaks forward and has a Doric porch, its side-lights inserted in 1960. The r. extension housed a billiard room. (Fine staircase of *c.*1820 with an ironwork balustrade, under a dome flanked by two ribbed half-domes. Interior decoration by *John Fowler*.) – GROUNDS landscaped with lakes and ponds in the late C18 and early C19.

RECTORY (now Rectory Cottages), facing the church. C17 main range of lobby-entry type. Some Gothick glazing bars.

with TIDDINGTON

St Helen. A small aisleless church, rebuilt in 1830 for the Hon. and Rev. Frederick Bertie. J.H. Parker's *Ecclesiastical Topography* (1850) states that the work was done 'under the direction of Mr Rickman', i.e. *Thomas Rickman*, architect and pioneering authority on Gothic architecture in England. Yet in archaeological terms the details are somewhat hit-and-miss. All the openings have a single chamfer, the windows with prominent hoods with large headstops carved in an antiquarian spirit. The tracery, a kind of minimal Perp, lacks the expected cusping, and the porch has a most un-medieval treatment of the hollow moulding of the arch, which is returned around its sides. Square w turret with a pyramidal spirelet. Vestry added in a restoration of 1891–2 by *A. Mardon Mowbray*. Bony open roof and w gallery. – ROOD SCREEN. 1917. – FONT. C12. An irregular drum with an unusual pattern of linked scalloping, a roll moulding and a lower band of chevron. – STAINED GLASS. All by *Herbert Bryans*. Some windows are dated, 1913–18.

RECTORY, s. Rebuilt *c*.1819 by *John Ackerman*, reusing old materials. Stone, collegiate Tudor style, with square hoodmoulds. Staircase with a thin Gothic balustrade.

TIDDINGTON, ⅓ m. w, is the main settlement. Mostly C20 houses. At the s end is TIDDINGTON HOUSE. Early C18, with cut-brick lintels; the lower frontage largely reinstatement after *Morris & Stallwood*'s elaborate porch of 1883 was removed. HILL COTTAGE, 100 yds N, is a timber-framed former farmhouse of *c*.1600. Is the canted oriel original?

ASTON ROWANT

ST PETER AND ST PAUL. The nave is of *c*.1100, with side chapels of the C14. A small round-headed window remains high up in the s wall, now within the porch. Also in the N chapel N wall a Norman window and doorway, re-set when *E. G. Bruton* extended the chapel to the w in his restoration of 1883–4, and now blocked by an extension of *c*.2012. C13 s doorway of one chamfered order. The chancel arch similar. Around 1400 the nave received a clerestory and a new roof, from which the corbels remain, below a plain ceiling of 1831. Early C14 chancel, the side windows with plain Y-tracery mostly of 1883–4. One window of lowside type on the s. Dec-style E window of 1856. C14 w tower with angle buttresses. The w doorway (renewed) and the tower arch both have typical C14 wave mouldings, but the top stage was rebuilt *c*.1812 by *Isaac Stone* of Thame, with strange banded pinnacles. The chapels each open to the nave through a two-bay arcade with double-chamfered arches and an octagonal pier. In the N chapel are two unusual Dec TOMB RECESSES. Each has a sharply triple-gabled canopy enclosing quatrefoils, supported on brackets carved with rosettes. The rood stair remains N of the chancel arch; also a squint to the chancel. One chancel N window is blocked by the vestry of 1884. Next to it a TOMB RECESS with an arch supported on small half-columns, and big cusping carved with a head and a rosette. The label has headstops. On the s a PISCINA and CREDENCE in a trefoiled niche.

FURNISHINGS. The ALTAR has a medieval mensa, re-set in 1932. – PULPIT. Composed of C17 woodwork. – FONT. C13. Purbeck marble. Octagonal bowl with a blind arcade of lancets, on an outer ring of shafts. – STAINED GLASS. N chapel E window, traceries with C14 fragments including two female heads and border pieces of crowned Ms, with Christ in Majesty (incomplete) above. Nave N, later C15 pieces in the tracery, including an angel harpist and a seated Christ. E window and N chapel N by *Clayton & Bell*, 1908. – MONUMENTS. Coffin-lid with a foliated cross, C13 (chancel). – Near the chancel step the matrix of a large brass to Sir Hugh Blount †1327. – S wall, mid-C15 brasses to Ralph and Isabel Copoite, †1438 and †1455. 17¼-in. (44-cm.) figures. – Nave floor, part of a C15 brass of a woman with a group of daughters. – N chapel wall, Eleanor Eggerley †1508. Brass; 6½ in. (17 cm.) remaining. – Lady Cicill Hobbee †1618. Small wall monument with obelisks, shield of arms, and a figure at a prayer-desk. – Frances Thornehill †1640, an architectural piece. – Routine C19 memorials, including Susan Mangin †1826 and two other Mangins all by *Humphrey Hopper*, and Reuben Mangin †1846 by *Bedford*.

OLD VICARAGE, E. Of *c.*1808. Neat chequer brick.

(ASTON HOUSE, S. The grand but poorly recorded mansion was demolished after a fire in 1957. It was mostly late C18 and early C19, with a thirteen-bay garden front. The large LAKE remains from its landscaped park, with to its W an enclave of 'executive' houses of 1961–3.)

SCHOOL, Aston Green, ¼ m. ENE. 1844 and later. Flint and brick, elementary hoodmoulds.

COPCOURT, 1¾ m. NW. Mostly mid-C18, with some older fabric behind. The steep hipped roof is memorable. S front of four bays and two storeys in chequer brick. Doric doorway with fanlight and pediment. The house sits within a moat, with three bridges of C18 and later; brick, with small piers. – Good weatherboarded farm buildings, including an C18 GRANARY.

CHALFORD MANOR FARMHOUSE, 1⅓ m. NNW. Probably early C17, of unusually tall proportions. Through-passage plan, with a N cross-wing. The framing is infilled with brick, but plenty of timber mullion-and-transom and cross-windows remain.

BENSON

6090

The centre of an important royal estate in mid- to late Anglo-Saxon times, Benson had a second heyday in the C18 and early C19 as a coaching halt on the road between Oxford and Henley. The old London road was severed in 1937 when RAF BENSON was established, now with its own settlement 1 m. to the E.

ST HELEN, Church Road. Georgian W tower, medieval nave and Victorian chancel. The tower was begun in 1765 by *John Townesend III*, with round-arched openings and squat diagonal buttresses, and completed in 1781, when *Stephen Townesend* added the Gothick battlemented bell-stage and pinnacles.

Heavily altered nave, now rendered externally. The aisles were remodelled in the C14. Two Dec windows remain in the s aisle, but its w window is Victorian. Its Transitional E window was found at the E end of the N aisle when the vestry was built, and was re-set in the corresponding position here. s clerestory with oblong windows, probably of 1628. The N aisle N wall was rebuilt in 1808–9 by *John Philips* of Wallingford. Schematized Gothic windows: plain middle mullions, no tracery. Inside, both arcades are C13 with double-chamfered arches and round piers, three with stiff-leaf capitals. The fourth bay, w, is now largely filled by the tower. Single-chamfered C13 chancel arch with a roll hood, the imposts re-cut in the C14 or C15. Late C15 nave roof with straight tie-beams and solid upper parts with carving. Chancel rebuilt in early C13 style by *Charles Buckeridge*, 1861–2. Flint and stone, with a N vestry and organ chamber. PARISH ROOM attached N of the tower, a low square stone block by *David Birkett*, 1997–9. – FONT. Tub-shaped, C13, with a C17 cover. Placed in the N aisle in the reordering of 1971–8. – STAINED GLASS. Chancel, *Clayton & Bell*; the E window of 1868, designed by *F.R. Pickersgill*. s aisle s, Annunciation by *A.K. Nicholson*, 1936. s aisle w, lancet by *G.E.R. Smith*, 1951.

PRIMARY SCHOOL, Oxford Road. By the Oxford builder *George Wyatt*, 1851. Chequered brick, Tudor windows. Extended w in 1901, and again in 2002–4 by *W.S. Atkins*, a long block with timber-framed monopitch-roofed shelters at the entrances.

The VILLAGE is best explored from CASTLE SQUARE, 200 yds E of the church. At the w end is the former WHITE HART INN, probably late C18 but stuccoed in the 1830s. Conspicuous to the w is the OLD VICARAGE, 1869–70 by *Charles Buckeridge*. Flint and red brick, trefoiled Gothic window lights. To the E, N side, the former CASTLE INN, part of a cheerful Georgian group at the road junction. Its main range is late C17, with an early C18 frontage of stone dressed with brick. Two pedimented doorways. Mid-C18 extension, l., with a tower-like semi-cylinder of red and silver-grey brick. The INN SIGN retains its C18 wrought-iron frame of scrolls with a pineapple finial.

HIGH STREET continues E, with on its s side the former OLD RED LION. Its refronting began in the late C17 when a five-bay façade was applied facing Mill Lane, E. Coursed rubble, with brick strings and dressings; broad sixteen-pane sashes. The High Street frontage followed *c.*1720–30; all brick, with segment-headed windows. Its two w bays are a matching addition of 1752. On the N side, Nos. 11–15, a U-shaped stone house dated 1704. KINGSFORD HOUSE, diagonally opposite, shows the broad striping of red and grey brick in vogue *c.*1830–40. Again going diagonally, COLLEGE FARMHOUSE (set back): of two C16 phases, with a hefty brick chimneystack, l. On the s side, Nos. 26–32 look like a consistent C17 cottage row, but the r. end (Nos. 26–28) began as a cruck-built house of *c.*1450 with a two-bay open hall. Banal shopping parade of 1963–4 opposite. No. 37 is the former FREE CHURCH of

1879, another permutation of red and silver-grey brick. Then the CROWN INN, refronted in brick and stone in 1709 (date in the cornice), but now painted.

BROOK STREET just beyond starts with No.1 (N side), prettily refronted in 1747 in stone and flint bands dressed with brick. Its E wall shows remnants of cruck framing, possibly as early as c.1300. On the S side by Observatory Close, the former BROOK COTTAGE has been dated to 1538 for its N bays (which possibly included a stair-tower), and c.1550 for the two-bay extension with the framing exposed. 300 yds E is BROOK FARMHOUSE (Nos.66–68), largely C17. (Early C17 painted frieze and some graining inside.) Finally Nos.74–76, a C17 farmhouse of unusual and memorable form. Rendered stone, with brick end stacks and a central stair-tower. A red-tiled catslide roof slopes down over low outshuts on either side. Entrance at the back.

FIFIELD MANOR, 1 m. ENE. A medieval house of stone, heightened and refronted in stucco around 1840 for Robert Newton, son of Thomas (*see* Preston Crowmarsh, below). 2:4:2 bays, the middle four with console brackets in the cornice. Porch of four Tuscan columns evenly spaced. The E end may have begun as a storeyed or tower house, indicated by single-chamfered doorways exposed inside: on the ground floor to the E, in a now internal wall; in the corresponding wall of the room above; and at two levels in a former porch and stair enclosure to the S, also internal. The date must be c.1200. The W end appears to be of c.1300, with a solar above. Was there then a hall between? A fine transomed upper window survives in the W wall, fully exposed in late C20 restoration by Dr Francis and Christine Brown.* Twin cinquefoiled lights, under a plain circle in the head. Rebates and hinges for shutters internally. Alongside it is a cambered-headed opening, probably an entry from a lost stair-turret. Rooms with mid-C18 panelling on the ground floor, centre and W; a good introduced fireplace of the period with carved ornament in the solar. Compact open-well staircase of c.1840, with a scrolled iron balustrade.

BARNS to the W, now residential. 1825–7. They form an L-plan with seven projecting openings through, each with a hipped roof. Residential conversion c.1990. At the NE angle a row of cartsheds, extending to a Tudor-style LODGE. – S of the house, the shell of a large oblong DOVECOTE dated 1767. Of clunch; upper parts rebuilt in flint, with a new lining of brick.

PRESTON CROWMARSH, a riverside hamlet ½ m. S. Notable for CROWMARSH BATTLE FARM at the S end, transformed c.1800–30 by the improving tenant farmer Thomas Newton. The FARMHOUSE was refronted but the rest is older, with reused medieval timbers. Grand enclosure of weatherboarded BARNS, expanded by Newton from an C18 core. On the N side are C18 STABLES, of stone, flint and brick. All converted for

---

*A cusped light in the ground-floor S wall was introduced in the restoration, ex-Magdalen College, Oxford.

offices by the *Spratley Partnership*, 1998–2002. Also a weather-boarded C19 GRANARY next to the house, and an octagonal brick DOVECOTE behind, formerly dated 1684 inside.

MILL COTTAGES (Nos.35–41) and PRESTON HOUSE (No.43), ¼ m. N of the farm. Built in 1909 by George Denison Faber M.P. of Howbery Park (*see* Crowmarsh Gifford), for his estate workers and bailiff. The local vernacular of rubble walls patterned with brick and flint, artfully interpreted by an unknown architect.

OLD MILL HOUSE, next N. Of *c.*1700. Five handsome brick bays. Is the doorcase early C20?

BERINSFIELD

A small new town established in 1957 by Bullingdon Rural District Council, on the site of a former airfield. The plan was supplied by *Sir William Holford*, and the first residents arrived in 1959. Expansion beyond the original W and NW areas was approved in 1963, again mostly for council housing.

Jennifer Sherwood's assessment for *The Buildings of England* in 1974 was not positive. 'The result cannot be called a failure, but is an opportunity missed. From the start there seems to have been no attempt at planning or attention to the design of the buildings. In fact, the town is little more than a huge council estate, with brick semis and terraces of the most dismal kind, sprawled out aimlessly along dreary streets with no positive landmark to pull the scheme together. There is a central green, but nothing has been done towards landscaping or grouping the buildings effectively around it.'

'Dismal' may go too far, but the charge of indifferent planning and design still stands, nor have steps been taken to provide a more convincing focus. The church of ST MARY AND ST BERIN sits at the W edge of the green, of 1962 by *Harold Best*, vicar of Dorchester, who had trained as an architect before ordination; a simple stone box, now without its flèche. The SCHOOLS by the S approach are of 1959 and 1964, standard one- and two-storey designs with weatherboarding and blue panelling. A HEALTH CENTRE followed in 1968–9, in Fane Drive N of the church. Monopitched roofs with slate-hung half-gables. By *Albert E. Smith*, County Architect.

BERRICK SALOME

ST HELEN. A church like no other in Oxfordshire. Timber bell-towers or bellcotes were provided in the late Middle Ages across the region, of which the tower at Drayton St Leonard (q.v.) has survived Victorian rebuilding. The key difference here is that the tower stands proud, w of the nave wall. Its tree rings supply the dates 1428–9, but what meets the eye is *A. Mardon Mowbray*'s showy restoration of 1890. Short and dumpy, with a pyramid roof, wooden arcading for the bell-louvres, and alternating bands of fish-scale tiles and wooden shingles around the middle. The rest of the church is unexpected too, rendered and with mostly Jacobean arched windows of brick, that of the s transept with older stone mullions. Plain Norman s doorway. Also a small Norman window in the nave s wall made from bits found in 1890, a re-set C13 lancet in the transept E wall, and an early C14 chancel with trefoiled lancets and an E window of restored intersecting tracery. *Mowbray* supplied the N vestry, the fancy bargeboarded dormers and the banded tile roofs, and dressed up the medieval timber porch.

The interior is a festival of C17 woodwork, dominated by the elaborate nave roof. A framed panel on its E face gives the date 1615, and the churchwardens' names, John Hambelden and Henry Wisse. Tie-beam and double-collar trusses, arch-braced at all three levels, with two registers of queenposts and central pendant posts with openwork drops. The closed trusses to E and W are different again, with a display pattern of curved braces. Curved wind-braces too. The transept roof is older, probably C15. In the chancel a C14 PISCINA and AUMBRY. Some medieval TILES in the chancel, mostly with the familiar quadrant pattern making up circles. – COMMUNION RAILS of *c.*1700. – PEWS of 1636, cut down and rearranged. – ROYAL ARMS. George II, on board. – Norman FONT, tub-shaped, carved with intersecting beaded circles (cf. Lewknor). – WEST GALLERY dated 1676. Skittle-shaped balusters. Re-set on whimsically carved corbels in 1890.

GRACE'S FARMHOUSE, ¼ m. SW, where the road forks. Behind a C19 extension, an L-plan house of the C17. (Splat-baluster staircase. Internal dates 1655 and 1663.)

LOWER FARMHOUSE, down a lane W of Grace's Farmhouse. Timber framing behind added walls of clunch rubble, with a handsome s front of four equal gables. The three W bays have been dated to 1550, the E parlour range to 1613. Later in the C17 a cross-gabled stair-tower was added to the NE.

ROKE is a hamlet ½ m. S. RUSSETTS in Chapel Lane is of three strongly contrasted phases: a thatched and cruck-framed W part built as a detached kitchen, tree-ring dated 1466; a short two-bay cross-wing of box framing to the E, dated to 1550; and a middle of *c.*1600, perhaps replacing an open hall.

HARE HALL, ¾ m. SE. Neo-Georgian farmhouse designed in 1971 by *Raymond Erith & Quinlan Terry*, for David Hicks's estate (cf. Britwell Salome).

BINFIELD HEATH

A civil parish formed in 2003 from parts of Shiplake and of Eye and Dunsden. There is no Anglican parish church.

CONGREGATIONAL CHAPEL. 1835. One of a group built by the
94   Rev. James Sherman of Reading, unusual for their early adoption of Gothic for Nonconformist buildings (cf. Wargrave and Woodley (Reading), Berks.). Narrow battlemented w porch-tower with a doorway with an ogee hood and finial. All the other windows plain lancets.

HOLMWOOD, ½ m. ENE. A long Georgian house of several phases, much altered in the C19 and C20. The w part corresponds to the house built for Col. William Boyle shortly after 1721. The *Guide to Henley upon Thames* (1838) records 'very considerable alterations and improvements' from 1813 onwards by Rear-Admiral Lord Mark Kerr and his successor, the 4th Earl of Antrim. That accounts for the three-bay projection on the N side, with a pediment enclosing an oval window. The clumsy re-windowing of the l. bay is of *c.*1963 by *Aubrey Jenkins* (*Phillimore & Jenkins*); also the round and oval recesses over the ground-floor windows. Porch of *c.*2010. (Ashlared garden front, *c.*1813–15.) The four-bay E extension is chiefly early C19; a taller w attachment was demolished *c.*1963. Steep roofs of the 1860s–70s, done for Admiral Charles Swinburne, father of the poet A.C. Swinburne. Extensive STABLES of *c.*1813–15 to the w; also a COACHHOUSE of 1836 with two huge windows, inserted probably for projected use as a Catholic chapel by the Hon. Charles Stonor, Lord Antrim's successor.

(BARN, Barn Grounds, 1 m. NNW. Built in the C18, reusing an arch-braced cruck structure tree-ring dated to *c.*1454.)

COPPID HALL, ¾ m. NW. A long, rambling house, of red brick with stone dressings, half-timbered gables and profuse diagonal chimneys. The oldest part is to the SE, of 1863 by *Henry Clutton* for Sir Robert Phillimore. Extended for the Phillimores in similar style, 1874, 1901 and 2004–5 (VCH). – U-plan STABLES, 250 yds SE. By *Walter Cave*, the design published in 1901. Arched entrance framed by pilasters with stone bands.

CROWSLEY PARK, 1½ m. NW. A strange house, built for Francis Heyward in 1734 (rainwater head) and made odder around 1800, when crenellated parapets and a three-bay w porch were added. Chequered brick. The E side comprises a five-bay block composed 2:1:2 from which four-bay wings step back in stages, each of a single bay and three outer bays. At the N end the outermost bays are barely 10 ft (2.4 metres) deep. Seen from the w, this wing is an asymmetrical appendage, and has two tiers of upper windows rather than one. The other bays on this side are grouped 1:8:1, on a different central axis from the E, of which the angle bays project. Uneven spacing of the window bays and the awkward plan suggest an enlargement, but what was its scope? Windows straight- or segment-headed, also a few pointed heads to the N. Embellishments for Henry Baskerville after 1845 include the crest on the W parapet, a gross quasi-Jacobean E doorcase, and heraldic tread-ends on the staircase. This is of dog-leg plan, with fine spiral balusters. Good 1730s fireplaces and panelling, and one SE ceiling of compartmented plasterwork. Attached to the S is a conservatory of *c.*1997 in a modern style, on the site of demolished services; by *Sutton, Griffin & Morgan* for the clothes designer Jeff Banks.

To the SW an octagonal C19 GIN GANG or donkey-engine house, and a COACHHOUSE and STABLES dated 1758. U-shaped and smartly handled, the arched openings without key blocks. A small pediment on each inner side.

The PARK has partially surviving AVENUES, radiating E, W and WNW from the house. In woodland 300 yds SSE a fine C18 GROTTO. Flint front with two upper niches and a central open oculus above the entrance. Inside, a rib-vault on corbel heads. Four arched recesses in each side wall; end wall partly lined with shells. Also a prodigious early C21 STUMPERY.

BIX

7080

with ASSENDON

A high Chilterns parish, with scattered hamlets.

ST JAMES, Bix. 1875 by *John Gibson*, best known as a designer of banks. The 6th Earl of Macclesfield paid for it. Flint and stone. Chancel, nave, N aisle and organ chamber. C20 NE vestry and a small NW addition of 2022. Cheerful interior with exposed brickwork, patterned in black and white. – Fragmentary FONT and PISCINA from the old church (*see* below). – STAINED GLASS. E and W windows by *Ward & Hughes*, 1878 and 1883. Chancel S, *Clayton & Bell*, 1892. N aisle, two windows with panels of good early C16 French glass, Joseph meeting Jacob(?) and the Miracle at Cana. Nave S, lancets by *G.E.R. Smith* of *A.K. Nicholson Studios*, *c.*1938, and *James Hogan* of *Powells*, 1945.

THE FOX on the A4130, 350 yds W of the church, is a specially elaborate former Brakspear's roadhouse by *A.E. Hobbs*, 1936 (cf. the Old White Horse at Henley, p.673). To the S, BIX MANOR has C17–C18 BARNS with notably neat herringbone brick infill. NW of Bix Hall, LITTLE BIX BOTTOM FARM is a good example of a C17 lobby-entry house of brick and flint, with a twin-gabled N addition dated 1741.

BIX HALL, ⅓ m. N. The former rectory. Largely of *c.*1790, of a broad U-plan (the red brick front of the SE return is an addition). Full-height bow on the S flank. Some retained C17–C18 fabric at the N end. In the garden a charming C18 ROOT HOUSE with Gothick windows.

MIDDLE ASSENDON FARMHOUSE, ¾ m. NE. A C16 hall house with a later cross-wing. Framing all infilled in brick.

BERE-ERN, Middle Assendon. An early architect-designed barn conversion, 1976 by *Donald Lacey*. The barn is C18, weatherboarded, with two mid-streys.

OLD CHURCH, 1 m. N. Abandoned in 1875. J.H. Parker described it in 1850 as 'a small poor church', of chancel and nave with a wooden W bellcote. Its ruin was consolidated in 2015–16. The early C12 chancel and most of the nave side walls remain. In the nave N wall a small round-headed Norman lancet; another in the chancel N wall. Also Norman the plain round-headed S doorway and chancel arch. The latter is flanked by a later altar recess, N, and niche, S. Perp four-centred-arched E window and nave S window, patched in brick. Of the W wall there remains only slumped C18 brick buttressing.

CEMETERY, Lower Assendon, 1 m. SE. *See* Henley-on-Thames, p. 665.

UPPER ASSENDON. *See* Stonor.

BRIGHTWELL BALDWIN

ST BARTHOLOMEW. The aisled nave and chancel are of the early to mid C14. In the C15 the W tower was rebuilt, retaining the semicircular C13 stair-turret, S. In it a little quatrefoil opening, with a fragment of Norman nailhead moulding re-set above. Tower of three stages, the two-light W window and doorway grouped under one arch with canopied niches in the jambs. The battlemented top stage with its blank oculi is an C18 rebuilding. All the aisle windows are Dec. In the S aisle identical side windows of two lights, and a three-light E window with good flowing tracery. In the N aisle the side windows are again consistent and of two ogee lights, but have square heads. N and S doorways with shallow continuous mouldings. The chancel has reticulated tracery in the E window; segment-headed Dec S windows, plus one straight-headed and transomed window with Perp elements to the W. Mid-C15 N chapel of equal length to the chancel. Its windows are also straight-headed, with unusually compressed panel tracery. The E window (now vestry) of three simple cusped lights looks a little later. The chapel had a smaller predecessor of *c.* 1300, indicated by a blocked arch in the chancel N wall. To its E the head of a deeply splayed C13 lancet is exposed. Four-bay nave arcades with standard C14 octagonal piers and double-chamfered arches. The chancel arch is similar. Trefoil-headed PISCINAS in the S aisle and chancel N wall. Moderate restorations by *J.W. Hugall*, 1868 (chancel), and *S.S. Stallwood*, 1895 (nave; also the renewal of the S porch in 1905).

FURNISHINGS. STALLS and stone REREDOS of 1868. – CHEST. Late C14. Plain timbers, but with the front painted with St George on horseback, advancing on a (barely legible) maiden and dragon. Thin foliage scrolls at each end. – ROYAL ARMS, over the chancel arch. Hanoverian; repainted in 1895, an unusually respectful gesture for the date. – Jacobean PULPIT and TESTER. – BOX PEWS. – FONT. C14, octagonal. Pyramidal C17 COVER. – Medieval TILES re-set by the font.

STAINED GLASS. A notable medieval collection, skilfully restored c.1895. Vestry, inserted panel of Christ on the Cross between the Virgin and St John, early C15. – N chapel, first from E: St Paul and (much restored) the Virgin Annunciate, against coloured grounds; matching canopies. Mid-C15. In the traceries contemporary shields of arms: Stody, Barentin, Bereford; Waters (C19 copy). Second from E: St Peter and St Paul, gesturing (lower parts mostly restoration); c.1325–50, with canopies. Traceries with more C15 shields: unidentified; Conyers for Norton(?); a stag couched; a lion. In the lower l. panel a naked soul in a balance being dragged down by a devil, C15, against modern quarries. – Chancel S, fourth from E: set against quarries in the main lights, the Archangel Gabriel and the Virgin Annunciate, the latter inside-out; mid-C15. Tracery, two archbishop saints, one of c.1500 with restoration, the other a C19 copy; outer lights, part of a canopy, l., and shield of Bereford, r., both C14. Below the transom, post-medieval shields of the sees of Durham and Oxford, with the arms of bishops Howson (Oxford, 1619–28) and Corbet (Oxford, 1628–32). – S aisle E window: C14 fragments collected in the traceries and window heads. At the apex an early C14 female saint. S aisle first from E: Virgin Annunciate, mid-C14, finely drawn.

MONUMENTS. Chancel, a rare double brass to Sir John Cottesmore †1439 and wife Amice. On the N wall their kneeling effigies and scrolls (8-in. and 8½-in. figures, 20.5 and 21.5 cm.), a representation of the Trinity between them missing, with a long encomium below. This is the earliest-known English mural brass. The couple are also splendidly commemorated on the chancel floor, with 38½-in. and 37¾-in. figures (98 and 96 cm.) under canopies, with eighteen children below. – William Paul, Bishop of Oxford, †1665. Incomplete. Inscription panel and flanking column shafts of black marble. – N chapel. Below the windows, two monuments reusing late medieval Purbeck marble tomb-chests: Anthony Carleton †1575/6 and wife, E, and John Carleton †1547 and wife. Both have fronts decorated with lozenges and quatrefoils enclosing shields. Brass inscriptions. – Stone family. The entire E wall is occupied by a Baroque *tour de force*, erected by John Stone c.1670 partly to commemorate family monuments lost in the Fire of London. Four draped and flaming urns in black-painted niches framed with dark marble, each with a cartouche of arms above. The climax is a giant cartouche with a little skull below, the wall behind painted with black shadowing like a Rorschach blot (meant for smoke?), spreading on to the plaster vault. The latest commemoration date is 1739, r. The corresponding urn and niche are of white marble, presumably replacing C17

54

alabaster. – Edward Stone †1696. With a border of flowers, flamed by drapery held up by two cherubs. – Francis Lowe †1754 and family. Large. Four pilasters frame the inscriptions. Broken pediment and cartouches with arms above, formerly also with painted shadows. – William Lowndes Stone I †1772. Signed *Westmacott*, i.e. *Richard Westmacott the elder*, 1790. Finely carved marble urn and bay wreath. – N aisle, brass to John Smith, *c.*1370. Inscription only. Notable for using English, a very early occurrence. – Porch, Richard du Cane †1904, tablet carved by the young *Eric Gill*.

BRIGHTWELL PARK. The medieval manor house, remodelled in the late C16 or early C17, was demolished after fire damage in 1788. Only the roofless ground floor remains of its successor, built by William Lowndes Stone II and dismantled in 1948–9. It was of five bays, with a one-bay pediment to the entrance front. The nondescript service range remains to the NW, heightened by two storeys in 1874 and re-roofed after 1948; now called the DOWER HOUSE. Further NW are the former stables, now BRIGHTWELL HOUSE. (Pedimented centre to the courtyard, and small pedimented lodges at the entrance; some stonework reused from the main house *c.*1949.)

The PARK was landscaped in the late C18 in the naturalistic manner, probably by *Humphry Repton*, whose watercolour of Brightwell was engraved and published in 1797. It has a conspicuous DOVECOTE of *c.*1632, of stone with red brick-mullioned windows and a hipped and tiled roof. The plan is a compact rectangle with shallow E and W projections. Also an elliptical-arched BRIDGE of *c.*1790 to the E of the house, with openwork balustrades of cast iron.

VILLAGE. Opposite the church, the LORD NELSON INN. Of C17 origin, U-plan, with a later veranda between the end projections. Its doorways and windows display fine late C17 wooden mouldings, carved with bay-leaf and acanthus; said to come from the manor house demolished after the 1788 fire. To the E, GLEBE FARM. Also C17 but thatched and timber-framed, with some herringbone brick infill. Small early C19 STABLE behind; flint and brick, with Gothic windows. Beyond, the OLD RECTORY. 1804. Stuccoed, of three bays, with an M-shaped mansard roof. Doorway and ground-floor windows set in shallow arched recesses.

UPPERTON, ½ m. s. The hamlet includes THE ROW, a roadside terrace of six dated 1801. Down a lane to the E, IVY COTTAGE is C15, a former hall house of four bays, reduced to three. Cruck construction.

SCHOOL (former), 1 m. s. Shared with Britwell Salome. By *Morris & Stallwood*, 1878–9. Like their school at Chalgrove (q.v.), but better preserved. Assertively diapered brickwork. Chimneys linked by an arch, for a bellcote.

BRIGHTWELL GROVE, 1¼ m. s. An early C19 farmhouse adapted by *David Hicks* in 1980, after he moved here from Britwell House (*see* Britwell Salome). The stuccoed front is his, a restrained Neo-Regency design. A shallow-pitched gable, the centre recessed under deep eaves, the side bays with their own pedimental gables, linked by a reduced Doric entablature on two fluted columns. (Rear room lined with grisaille murals of trophies and landscapes by *Rex Whistler*, 1937, painted for Lord and Lady Mountbatten's penthouse flat at the 1930s incarnation of Brook House on Park Lane, Mayfair; removed previously to Britwell House by David and Lady Pamela Hicks (née Mountbatten). The extensive GARDENS are also by *Hicks*. Much axial and symmetrical planting, the compartments and vistas punctuated by statues and urns. The architectural features include a Neo-Gothick GAZEBO.)

BRITWELL SALOME   6090

ST NICHOLAS. Rebuilt in 1867 by *Charles Buckeridge*. Flint and stone, with chancel, nave and w bellcote. Uninspired Dec style. The chancel wall has a facsimile of the Norman s doorway from the nave, reusing a few old stones: some billet moulding in the hood, and the scalloped and zigzag-patterned capitals of the jamb shafts. – PAINTING. Christ carrying the Cross. Spanish, C17. – FONT. C12 or C13, cup-shaped. C17 ogee-domed COVER. – STAINED GLASS. Chancel windows all by *Clayton & Bell*, from cartoons by *George Daniels* (†1888, †1892, †1914); bright nave s window by *Preedy*, *c*.1867 (MH and PC). – BRASS. John Mores or Maurice, priest, †1492. 13-in. (33-cm.) effigy.

OLD RECTORY, s. Early C18 front of brick, five bays, with a segmental door hood. The steep gable with its blue brick diapering indicates that the house is earlier, built by James Stopes in 1675–6. (Open-well staircase with a closed string, turned balusters and ball finials on the newels.) At the back a C17 timber-framed wing.

BRITWELL HOUSE, ¾ m. SW. A medium-sized country house built in 1727–8 for the Roman Catholic bachelor Sir Edward Simeon, 2nd Bt. The rainwater heads are dated 1728. It has a Palladian plan with the main house linked by quadrants to L-shaped pavilions. Red brick with stone quoins and dressings, the windows segment-headed. Three-bay pediment with a broad lunette, which replaced a little Venetian window recorded in photographs of *c*.1912. The garden front to the NW is all but identical, but the sides are treated differently; they are of red and blue brick, the windows plain, and the centre carried up as an attic that encompasses the chimneystacks. There are many similarities with Woodperry House (*see Oxfordshire: North and West*), begun in 1728, and carried out by William King. King had been an apprentice of the Oxford master builder *William Townesend*, who is the likely designer here. In 1767–9 an oval chapel was added on the SW side. According to his chaplain, 'the whole plan both within and without was contrived by *Sir Edward Simeon* himself'. A two-storey extension with a sacristy came later. The present quadrant corridors to the wings may also be late c18. Early c20 changes include the upper storey added to the quadrants around 1920 and the two-storey extension to the NE, the latter among alterations by *Philip Tilden* for Major G. C. Whitaker, 1932–5. The house was bought in 1960 by the interior designer *David Hicks*. His improvements include the bellcote on the c18 STABLES to the SW, after the one on Chiselhampton church (q.v.).

Inside, the bold decoration and massive forms recall the work of Hawksmoor, Townesend's regular collaborator. Especially powerful is the ENTRANCE HALL, with its deep triglyph frieze and stone fireplace with a scroll pediment surmounted by a plasterwork vase of flowers. It is flanked by arched keystoned doorways, and in the wall opposite is an aedicule with a shell niche. All is outsize. The doorways burst out of their allotted space with their heads against the cornice and the whole is vigorous rather than elegant. More conventional is the capacious STAIR HALL to the r. of the hall, the stairs climbing in two flights, with twisted balusters and fluted Corinthian columns as newel posts. Bold blue-and-white wallpaper designed by *David Hicks*, whose major decorative schemes have otherwise gone. The DRAWING ROOM behind the entrance hall has a fireplace of *c.* 1740, carved with flowers and a head in a sunburst. To its r. is a small OCTAGONAL ROOM with 1920s Rococo plasterwork, to the l. a room with a sturdy marble fireplace of the 1720s. The bedrooms open off a very spacious panelled LANDING of T-plan, with Ionic pilasters and pedimented or round-arched doorways all of wood. The extravagant use of space for circulation is another affinity with Hawksmoor, notably his Easton Neston (Northants). But the most splendid interior is that of the CHAPEL of 1767–9, the dining room since the 1920s, half a storey down from the main house. The chimneypiece, in the position of the former altar, is framed by coupled Corinthian columns, answered on the wall opposite by pilasters and pedimented doorways. The ceiling has a shallow dome or coving with plasterwork by an unknown maker. Adamesque elements in the central panel, surrounded by more thickly interlaced Neoclassical work in low relief with acanthus scrolls, garlands, urns, and pairs of cherubs supporting chalices at the cardinal points. In the NORTH-EAST WING the main interior is now of double height, with a gallery, panelling and pilasters of *c.* 1991 designed by *Peter Luck & Associates*.

The GARDENS include formal elements introduced by *Hicks*, including the slim CANAL between double avenues on the NW axis. Opposite the entrance front is a stone COLUMN, more properly a tall pier with four applied Corinthian pilasters, crowned with an urn; set up by Sir Edward Simeon in 1764, and inscribed in memory of his parents. (In the woods to the N a slim octagonal OBELISK with a pineapple finial, probably of similar date.)

VILLAGE. HOME FARM is c16, cased in flint with roughcast above. To the E, BROADLANDS COTTAGE with its hoodmoulds and Gothick windows shows the hand of *David Hicks*, and bears his emblem of four Hs. N of the corner, the OCTAGON HOUSE of 1974–7 by *Hicks* with *Colin Golding* (*Golding, Baker & Guy*); like a Regency stucco lodge. By the lane to the church, ¼ m. NE, THE PRIORY is Regency indeed, of 1826. Five broad bays, added open-pedimented porch.

BURCOT

5090

Clifton Hampden

ST MARY (former). 1869 by *Sir G. G. Scott*. Built as a school-chapel for the Rev. William Macfarlane of Dorchester. Informal and domestic, red brick, with wood-mullioned windows. Half-timbered lean-to W porch, shingled conical bell-turret. The polygonal E end alone is churchy, with trefoil-headed lancets.

BURCOT HOUSE, SW. Demolished 1956. It was C18 and C19, with clumsy embellishments of *c.* 1887 for the genial financier, M.P. and fraudster Jabez Balfour. In the 1920s Dorchester Mission-ary College took over, and in 1929 the college's simple CHAPEL of 1913 by *E. P. Warren* was dismantled and moved here. Brick and stone, shingled W turret, Perp-style windows. On the lane from the main road is GRANGE HOUSE, designed in 1966 by *Douglas Lanham*, an associate of Leslie Martin. Single-storeyed on an L-plan, rigorously detailed and sparingly windowed.

ESTATE COTTAGES along the main road. Of 1889–90 by *Howard Martin*, for Jabez Balfour. Unusually generous pairs, plain brick with timber porches.

CHALGROVE

6090

Chalgrove has expanded mightily since the 1960s. Add-ons and infill housing now dominate both sides of its high street, two-thirds of a mile long. A by-pass was made to the N in 1966–7, and a new town is proposed on the site of the airfield immediately beyond.

ST MARY, Church Lane, S of the High Street. Externally Dec and Perp, but the nave arcades are older. The S arcade came first, *c.* 1200. It has round piers with waterholding bases, on square plinths with corner spurs. The piers have corner volutes; waterleaf capital to the W respond. Pointed arches with one roll moulding and a continuous hood. At the E end a half-sized bay with similar details, apparently an early extension. It dates probably from the mid C13, when the N arcade was added. This has round piers and single-chamfered arches. One moulded capital, the other carved with stiff-leaf. The S aisle preserves the original narrow width. It has a PISCINA with a plain chamfered arch, and a two-light Dec E window. The N aisle W window is also C14 Dec. Other aisle windows Perp. Those of the N aisle are mid-C15, with casement-moulded surrounds and straight-sided arches; most likely the work of Sir Drew Barentin III (†1453), who made bequests to a 'newly repaired' N chapel at the church. As enlarged, the aisle extends alongside the chancel. Late Perp S porch. The chancel is entirely Dec, a coherent design outside and in. It was rebuilt probably by Sir Drew Barentin II (†1329), or else by Thame Abbey, which held the living from 1319. Chancel arch with a filleted convex moulding on major and minor half-round shafts. In both side walls are two two-light windows, plus a priest's door and a lowside window on the S. Three-light E window, the tracery reticulated. A string links the sills, and also the fine PISCINA and triple SEDILIA under four sub-cusped ogee arches. In the N wall a rare double SQUINT, facing the altar and the S wall (*see* wall paintings, below). The W tower collapsed in 1726/7 and was rebuilt by the mason *Richard Belcher* of Little Milton. The consistent quoins on its three stages suggest that little medieval walling remains, but the Y-traceried bell-openings and the N doorway may be reused. Crenellation, skimpy angle pinnacles, and round W window in the middle stage all C18. In 1882–3 *Morris & Stallwood* restored the church, replacing the roofs. Further restoration by *Caroe & Partners*, 2015–16.

WALL PAINTINGS. In the chancel, one of the most complete and coherent series in the country, probably of *c.*1320–30 and given by Sir Drew Barentin II. Arranged mostly in three tiers, and executed in earth colours of red, yellow and black; also red stars all round the window arches. Artistically they rank as 'competent though unexceptional provincial work' (David Park). Restoration in 2015–16 by *Madeleine Katkov* helped to clarify the subjects, although some are now barely legible.* Three scenes (N and E walls) have added bands of Latin texts.

On the NORTH WALL at the W end a Tree of Jesse, filling two tiers. The smaller scenes are of the Life of Christ. They start between the windows with the Nativity (W) and Adoration of the Magi. Over these, the Slaughter of the Innocents (W) and Presentation in the Temple. The top tier runs through W–E above the windows: Judas, the Betrayal, Jesus before Annas, the Mocking of Jesus, the Scourging, Jesus bearing the Cross, the Crucifixion. Below the last, the Descent from the Cross (middle tier) and the Anointing of the Body. The E wall continues with the Harrowing of Hell (bottom tier), Resurrection and Ascension (top). The window splays are painted with taller figures. From W to E: Gabriel and the Virgin; St Helen and St Mary Magdalene; St Peter (E window).

The SOUTH WALL begins at the W with a full-height Last Judgment and Resurrection. The three-tier scenes beyond show the Death and Assumption of the Virgin, an exceptionally

*See the excellent guidebook by R.W. Heath-Whyte (2016).

full cycle drawn from the *Golden Legend*. Between the windows, the bottom tier has the Presentation of the Palm (W), the Virgin at Prayer, and a damaged scene (the Virgin, the widows and St John?). Middle tier: the Virgin's farewell to the Apostles, with virgins and widows (W), Death of the Virgin. Top tier: Funeral of the Virgin (W), Conversion of the Chief Priest, Conversion and Healing of the Jews, Burial of the Virgin. Below the last, the Apostles at Table (middle) and a destroyed scene. The E wall has St Thomas receiving the girdle (bottom), the Assumption, and the Coronation of the Virgin (top). On the window splays, W to E: St Bartholomew, St Lawrence, St John the Evangelist, St John the Baptist, St Paul (E window). – In addition, the N aisle E wall has a big C15 painted niche and canopy.

OTHER FURNISHINGS. STALLS of 2016. – IRONWORK of the C14 on the chancel S doorway, with one intact scrolled hinge. – Late C17 COMMUNION RAILS, re-set under the chancel arch. Twisted balusters. – PULPIT. Jacobean, polygonal. The conventional blind arcading. – HANGING LIGHTS made by *Michael Jacques*, 2016; also the steel Tree-of-Life GATE, S porch. – FONT. Probably *c*.1660. Cup-shaped, octagonal, on a spiral-fluted shaft. On the bowl the royal emblems of rose, thistle and fleur-de-lys. – CHEST. Dated 1674 in nailheads. – C18 COMMANDMENTS BOARDS etc., now on the nave walls. – BANNER of the Chalgrove Friendly Society, 'Established July 6th 1840' (nave). – STAINED GLASS. N aisle, two mid-C15 angel heads drawn from the same cartoon. – BRASSES. Sir Drew (Drugo) Barentin III (†1453) and two identical wives, †1437 and †1446. 34½-in., 32-in. and 32½-in. figures (87, 82 and 83 cm.). – Reginald Barentin †1441, alongside. 36-in. (90-cm.) figure. – MONUMENTS. Benedict Winchcombe †1623 and family. Slate with incised pictures, alabaster surround. Attributed to *Francis Grigs* (GF). – Rev. Francis Markham, dated 1679. Inscription in a rustic Baroque oval frame of alabaster. – Robert Quatremaine, 1692 (W wall, moved from the N aisle). A painted depiction of an oval wall tablet. Clumsy putti and cherubim in the spandrels. – Katherine Lewis †1766. Attributed to *Sir Henry Cheere* (GF). An urn and pedestal in shallow relief against coloured marble, within an oval frame. Sculpted female mourners sit on the pedestal. One has a book with the text 'I know that my Redeemer liveth'.

PRIMARY SCHOOL, High Street. Greatly expanded from *Morris & Stallwood*'s Board School of 1876–7.

CHALGROVE MANOR, Mill Lane. A notable timber-framed house of the mid C15 to early C16; sympathetically restored from 1977 by Paul and Rachel Jacques, after long neglect. The form is the familiar H-plan with jettied cross-wings, the centre having been built as an open hall. Tree-ring evidence suggests the phased replacement of the manor house recorded from *c*.1240, for the earliest dates obtained were in the N wing, of *c*.1457 (range 1447–68). The hall followed in 1488, the S wing in 1505 (dates 1503–5), with parlour below and chamber above. Removal of late C19 render has exposed the framing: tension bracing on both wings, used with close studding on the s, and mortice holes for a lost two-storey porch on the hall, of which the upper room was reached by a doorway from the N wing. The N wing has a braced collar-beam truss in the gable; the s gable was rebuilt and an attic room made in the later C16. Around the same time the open hall was floored across and ceiled, and a brick chimneystack inserted at the former dais end, s. A second stack is attached at the N end. This side formerly had a garderobe projection and an external stair enclosure, replaced by an internal stair; another garderobe was on the s side. Late C16 additions to the cross-wings behind, largely of elm-wood framing.

The finest element of the interior is the generously timbered ROOF over the former hall, with moulded arch-braced and collar-beam trusses. The truss at the dais end is larger than the others; a fifth bay was lost to the inserted stack. Two tiers of wind-braces. In the N wing the three-bay arch-braced roof to what was probably the SOLAR is exposed. The rooms below would have provided services to the hall, but the ceiling beams of the front room seem too richly moulded for the purpose. Was this the parlour when first built, if the previous hall had its services at the s end? A staircase was inserted alongside the s wing in the C17. Some rear walls refaced in brick in the C18. Among the rarer internal features is the reused SCREEN at the hall entrance, perhaps as early as the C13. Some slim buttresses with simple tracery patterns remain. Possibly salvaged from the second manor house at Chalgrove, under construction c. 1230–50 and demolished probably c. 1485. Two walls of the PARLOUR were painted c. 1680 in imitation of walnut panelling, and one bedroom in the former hall space displays a unique combination of timber studs and late C16 fictive timbering, both coloured with the same grey paint.

GATEHOUSE to the road, timber-framed, of 1994. It replaces one of the C15–C16, demolished after accidental damage c. 1975.

VILLAGE. The HIGH STREET still offers rewards, despite the loss of many thatched cottages in the 1960s. Starting from the Church Lane end, PYKE BARN COTTAGE (No. 122) is a late open-hall house, tree-ring dated 1556 (smoke-blackened rafters). Thatched C17 cottages follow at No. 118 and Nos. 110–114. On the N side, FAIRLEIGH COTTAGE (No. 159) was apparently begun as a hall house in the early C17, but was floored over and chimneyed during construction. Cottages by THE GREEN, s side, include a late C16 hall house with curved braces at No. 1, floored only a decade or so after completion. GRANNY'S (No. 123) is C17, with an end wall of stone, rising from the brook that runs alongside the street. The RED LION (No. 115) is C15 or C16, with crucks showing inside. Another former hall house at No. 113; two bays, early C16. The weatherboarded PARISH HALL is an early work by *G. Berkeley Wills*, 1906. The POST OFFICE (No. 109) is boldly dated 'JULY 1869' in the brickwork. No. 97 is the OLD VICARAGE, 1702. A regular stuccoed façade of seven bays and two storeys. Coved cornice, door hood on brackets. Of the thatched cottages further W, Nos. 59 and 61 are a C17 pair built in line; LIMMERIDGE (No. 37A) is C17, incongruously dressed up with Perp-style windows. APRIL COTTAGE (No. 1) began around 1600 as a two-bay cruck-framed hall house with a stone gable and chimneystack. MILL LANE runs S opposite, by THE LAMB pub of 1610 (tree-ring date). A medium-sized lobby-entry house, its roof largely of elm. One original upper window with a sill on shaped brackets. Gray's Close, off Flemming Avenue to the E, has APPLE TREE COTTAGE (No. 46). A storeyed cruck-built house of the C15 or C16, i.e. with dormers from the beginning. Further down Mill Lane is Chalgrove Manor (*see* p. 599), with timbered BARNS in front, converted to houses in 1988–9; the C18 ones show the local use of cranked inner principals (*see* Introduction, pp. 555–6). THE MILL, E side, comprises a mostly C17 house with the mill to the r., its brick extension dated 1871. One overshot wheel of iron. Beyond, a pyramid-roofed LODGE, late C17 brick, remains from the C16 Langley Hall, largely demolished 1980. Finally JOHN HAMPDEN COTTAGE (No. 73), a tiny two-roomed house of *c.* 1700 perhaps built by squatters, and Nos. 68–70, a cruck house of *c.* 1500, later raised and floored.

HAMPDEN MONUMENT, Monument Road, ²⁄₃ m. NE. 1843. It commemorates the Parliamentary leader John Hampden, fatally wounded at the Battle of Chalgrove Field in 1643. A square stone pillar 18 ft (5.5 metres) high, to which a blunt obelisk was added in 1863. Portrait relief by *W. Scoular*. On another side the donors' names are prominently listed.

ROFFORD HALL, 1⅓ m. NW. A generously sized mid-C18 three-bay farmhouse. Rubble stone and brick. (To its NE, ROFFORD MANOR is of *c.* 1700, extended to a T-shape *c.* 1730–40. Notable gardens, created by Jeremy and Hilary Mogford from the 1980s onwards.)

CHECKENDON

ST PETER AND ST PAUL. A well-preserved and superior Norman church of *c.* 1100. Nave, chancel and apsidal E end with one original window, much renewed. Flint and stone, laid herring-bone-fashion (cf. Swyncombe). The S doorway has one order of roll moulding and jamb shafts with capitals carved with eagles and monsters. Diaper-and-pellet pattern on the inner order of the arch, scales on the outer order. Tympanum and bases from *E. G. Bruton*'s restoration of 1868–9. C15 porch with two-light windows to the E and W and a holy water stoup. W tower also C15, three undifferentiated stages, coarsely detailed. The other windows are Dec and Perp; one Dec window in the chancel continues below a transom, on the pattern of a lowside

window. Inside, two grand Norman arches divide the nave,
chancel and apse, forming an impressive vista. Both have two
orders of roll moulding towards the W, and capitals decorated
with palmettes or very rich beaded interlace. The chancel arch
has half-round responds, an outer order of jamb shafts and a
super-arch of billet and chevron; the apse arch has two orders
of jamb shafts. Perp nave roof of shallow profile, much renewed
in 1956–7 by *J.C. Shepherd*, with some replacement bosses by
local carvers under *Eric Kennington*.

FURNISHINGS. WALL PAINTINGS. A procession of Apostles
flanks the E window, with Christ in Majesty on the half-dome
above. C13; repainted 1869, restored 1954. Red ochre on a
white ground. Leaf-crocketed canopies distinguish St Peter
and St Paul. Some Apostles lost to the C14 window on the S
side. Pedestals with architectural motifs. Circles and rosettes
on the dado. Also C14 remnants on the chancel N wall, discovered in 1998. The lower scene shows a man in armour
behind a horse. – A few medieval TILES on the sanctuary
steps. – FONT. Octagonal, Perp. – STAINED GLASS. E window
by *Clayton & Bell*, 1869. Nave, memorial window of 1963 to
Eric Kennington (†1960), engraved by *Laurence Whistler*: two
knightly Virtues and the Grail, over a landscape. Also windows
by *John Hayward*, 1987, and *Debora Coombs*, 1995. – BRASSES.
John Rede, Serjeant at Law, †1404. 47-in. (1.18-metre) figure
under a triple canopy. – Walter Beauchamp, *c*.1430. A unique
instance of an English brass with the figure of a soul borne
by angels as its main subject. – Anne Bowett †1490, 28½-in.
(74-cm.) figure. – MONUMENTS. Christian Braybrooke †1629.
Wall monument with kneeling effigies. Attributed to *Francis
Grigs* (GF). – Henry Knappe †1673. Rustic Artisan Mannerism,
with a segmental pediment and cherubs. – Temple and Grace
Stanyan, †1751 and †1768. Obelisk and statuette of Fame
above a round-ended inscription panel with little birds carved
in the frame. – Two *opus sectile* memorials by *Powells*, 1919 and
1932. – Herbert and Maud Rothbarth, 1960, by *Eric Kennington*. Big hieratic sculpted angel framed by a Norman aedicule.

LYCHGATE by *Guy Dawber*, 1920. With little tracery panels.

SCHOOL, N of the churchyard. Expanded from a plain four-bay
building of 1840.

VILLAGE HALL, NE. By *Frank Pearson*, 1913–14. Flint and brick,
after the local vernacular.

CHECKENDON COURT, 200 yds WNW, in accomplished formal
gardens. Substantially the plain red brick manor house begun
by Leonard Keate (†1622/3), who directed his executors to
complete it. Plain triple gables to N and S. The NE part is a
good match by *Maxwell Maberly Smith* for F.S. Oliver, *c*.1906,
originally with loggias to the E and S; since enclosed or built
against by *Chapman Taylor Partners'* SE addition of *c*.1981–3.

VILLAGE HOUSES. Opposite the church a picturesque group
with undulating roofs. They include FOUNDRY HOUSE,
with a three-bay cruck frame dated to 1467/8. (Exceptionally
long purlins, the full 30-ft (9-metre) extent of the roof. A

flying collar takes the place of a central cruck.) To the s are
LANGTREE COTTAGES, excellent Romanticism of 1906 by
O. Maxwell Ayrton of *Simpson & Ayrton*, for Sir Edward Busk (cf.
Heath End, below). Framed in local oak, with steeply pitched
roofs, clustered chimneys and a front-gabled projection to the
r. Further sw the former FOUR HORSESHOES pub, late c15
and cruck-framed in the centre, between late c17 and early c19
sections. The OLD RECTORY beyond was refaced by *Bruton*
in 1865–6. Complex fabric behind: a four-bay timber-framed
house of *c.*1530–50, expanded to the se not long after by two
gabled s projections, now under Georgian brick, and enlarged
to the sw in 1823–4.

SCOT'S FARM HOUSE, ½ m. N. L-shaped, of three phases, all
c15. Close-studded framing, partly concealed by brick or
render. Cross-range with gable-end chimneystacks to e and w.
On its N side a rare survival, a moulded window frame and sill
bracket. Another sill bracket on the N range, which may have
included an open hall.

NUTHATCH COTTAGE, Uxmore Road, ½ m. NE. Two-bay cruck
house tree-ring dated to 1425.

NEAL'S FARMHOUSE, 1¼ m. E. By *Henry Drake* of Reading,
1844. Still Late Georgian in manner. Flint, with especially bold
red brick quoining.

HEATH END. Deep in woodland, ⅔ m. SE. A house of *c.*1851,
reworked and extended after 1905 by *O. Maxwell Ayrton* for Sir
Edward Busk's own use. Low-lying and cosy, of brick and flint.
Ayrton's additions include the N bow and the stables close by.
The house had murals by *Arthur Hacker*, whose adjacent studio
house of 1902 by *Ayrton* is no longer recognizable as such.

OLD SCHOOL, Hook End, 1¼ m. SE. By *G. Somers Clarke*,
dated 1874. Given by Edward Hermon of Wyfold Court (*see*
Rotherfield Peppard), with diapering to match.

OAKWOOD FARM, ⅔ m. SSE. By *Aldington, Craig & Collinge*,
2007–11. Described by the architects as a 'stockade'. The
house's three ranges enclose an axial oblong courtyard. Zinc
monopitched roofs.

HOOK END MANOR, 1 m. SSE. Greatly aggrandized after 1921 by
Collcutt & Hamp. Half-timbering and brick-nogging in plenty,
but also plain brick gables with a more interwar look.

CHINNOR

A large village, swollen by c19–c21 housing. The chief c20
employer was the cement works just to the s (1908–2000).

ST ANDREW, Church Road. Almost entirely early c14 externally
and very uniform in style. A consecration of 1326 allows a
date for the chancel. Windows of two lights in the side walls
and of three lights with reticulated tracery at the e end of the

chancel. S porch and doorway also early C14, the porch with a quadripartite vault springing from corner shafts, the doorway with three orders of roll-and-fillet moulding and small jamb shafts. The W tower has a shallow saddleback roof and C14 bell-openings. Late C13 lower stages with a plain W doorway, three-light window and tower arch. Nave arcades also C13, of five bays, the W bay cut by buttresses added later to the tower. Circular piers with square bases, arches of two orders. The N arcade is earlier, with only one order chamfered. The hoodmould terminates in heads in the spandrels. S arcade with double-chamfered arches and alternating octagonal and round abaci. In the C14 the aisles were extended W beside the tower. (On its S wall is a string course, once external.) In the S aisle a TOMB RECESS with an open-cusped arch. C13 PISCINAS in the N aisle and the nave S wall. Perp nave clerestory. The chancel arch has two orders of wave moulding and half-quatrefoil responds. PISCINA and triple SEDILIA grouped in ogee-headed recesses, the latter with clustered shafts. Also a square lowside window in an arched recess, S. The steep-pitched roofs of nave and chancel date from the restoration of 1865–6 by *Edward Banks* of Wolverhampton.

The remarkable PAINTINGS in nave and chancel deserve to be better known. There are sixteen canvases by *Sir James Thornhill*, made in 1721–2 as cartoons for Joshua Price's N rose window at Westminster Abbey. Twelve have upright figures of Christ and Disciples, four show the Evangelists reclining with their symbols. Plain blue grounds with the outline of cusped compartments. Given probably soon after Thornhill's death in 1734, they were restored in 1993 after the correct identification was made by a retired teacher, June Cray of Sydenham. The ALTARPIECE, an Entombment of Christ loosely after Titian, is probably also *Thornhill*'s.

OTHER FURNISHINGS. Chancel PANELLING designed by *Herbert Read* of Exeter, 1911. – ROOD SCREEN. A fine early C14 example with slim ringed shafts and tracery formed by quatrefoils in circles. Original doors. – PULPIT of Caen stone, 1865. Intricate reliefs of the Parable of the Sower were carved on it in 1899. – FONT. Octagonal; C14. – ROYAL ARMS. Double-sided: Charles II, painted in 1660 by *William Goldfinch* of Chinnor, and George II. – STAINED GLASS. E window, 1865 by *Clayton & Bell*. They also restored with great skill the glass of *c.*1326 in the windows alongside. Chancel S, St Lawrence, with gridiron, and St Alban, with inscription, under matching can-opies. Borders of grotesque beasts in a serpentine foliage trail. Tracery, Clothing the Naked, from a Corporal Acts of Mercy series. Chancel N, a bishop and an archbishop, canopied as in the S window. Borders of vine foliage and roses. Tracery: Giving Drink to the Thirsty. N aisle E, C14 tracery lights with Christ in Majesty above censing angels; main lights 1920 by *Powells* (*A.F. Erridge*) (PC). S aisle E, *Clayton & Bell*, *c.*1880. S aisle S, *Powells* (*Erridge*), 1930. N aisle furthest W, an early C14 shield of arms of Zouche, on white glass with oak-leaf trails. Also

Chinnor, St Andrew, rood screen.
Drawing by F. E. Howard, 1910

four nave windows by *William Aikman*, 1937–47. – BRASSES.
One of the largest collections in the county; since 1935 mostly
mounted on the chancel walls, stamp-album fashion. N wall:
head of a priest in a foliated cross-head, *c.*1290. – Reynald
de Malyns and two wives, *c.*1385. Figures of 43 to 45½ in.
(109 to 116 cm.). – Esmoun and Isabel de Malyns, late C14.
Half-figures, 17 and 16½ in. (43 and 42 cm.). – John Cray
†1392. 56½-in. (143-cm.) figure in plate armour, a lion at his
feet. – Widow or nun, *c.*1390. 16½-in. (42-cm.) half-figure.
– Reginald Malyns †1430. Headless half-figure, 13 in. (34 cm.).
– S wall: John de Hotham or Botham, rector, also Provost of
Queen's College, Oxford, †1351. 24-in. (60-cm.) half-figure,
*c.*1388. – Alexander Chelseye, rector, †1388. A companion
half-figure to Hotham. – Nicholas atte Heelde, *c.*1410. 16-in.
(41-cm.) figure. – Robert and Katherine atte Heelde, *c.*1410.
15½-in. (40-cm.) headless wife with the feet of her husband.
– Folke Poffe †1514 and wife, with child. 12-in. (30-cm.)
figures. – MONUMENT. Truncated effigy of a knight in chain-
mail, late C13.

METHODIST CHAPEL, Station Road. 1873. Red brick, with pediment and round-headed windows; porch added 2017. Probably
by the Chinnor engineer *Spencer Jackson*; cf. his READING
ROOM of 1878 in the High Street.

CHINNOR COMMUNITY CHURCH (formerly Congregational),
High Street. 1805, enlarged 1811 and subsequently heightened.
Stuccoed front with round-arched windows. Flint and brick
sides. Sunday School added behind, 1885.

SCHOOL (former), Oakley Road. 1859–60 by *Street*. Plain brick,
half-hipped roofs.

HEALTH CENTRE, off Station Road. By *Peter Aldington*, 1966–8.
An early example for a village; greatly extended E in 1999.
Stock brick and timber, originally stained black. The distinctive

element is the cylindrical tower rising through the foyer roof, cut diagonally to form a skylight for the lavatory within.

HOUSES. Few of note. The HIGH STREET has two boldly composed builder's Gothic terraces at Nos. 28–34 and 58–64, c. 1880. The design recurs at Ewelme (q.v.). PINNATT'S (No. 41) is a neat three-bay house of c. 1830, of chequer brick with a shelving hipped roof. LOWER FARM, No. 90 Oakley Road, box-framed with some brick infill, has the date 1717 on one brick.

(LIME KILN, Kiln Avenue, ½ m. S. A relic of the cement works of 1908. About 20 ft (6 metres) tall.)

(JACOB'S LADDER, Chinnor Hill, ¾ m. SSW. An early work by *Niall McLaughlin*, 1999–2001. Influenced by the glass-walled Case Study houses of mid-C20 California, both for its spare framing and for its placing on a hill-slope, with entry by bridge to the first floor.)

WINDMILL, Mill Lane, ½ m. WNW. A post mill, dated 1789 on the main post. The only surviving English example set on six supporting piers or feet. Four sails. Reassembled from c. 1990 using some old parts, near the original site.

CHISELHAMPTON
Stadhampton

ST KATHERINE. Rebuilt in 1763 by Charles Peers of Chiselhampton House.* Here is the best-preserved Georgian parish church in Oxfordshire, complete with original fittings. Small and unsophisticated, it shows an odd interpretation of classical detail by an unknown builder. Stuccoed exterior. The w gable, disguised as a broken scroll pediment of strange proportions, is flanked by urns. Above the diminutive volutes at its apex rises a wooden clock turret with vermiculated quoins and a square cupola with angle pilasters, its roof upswept. W doorway with simple mouldings and a plain cornice. Four arched keystoned windows in the s wall. A shallow E projection for the altar, originally with a three-light window of intersecting tracery. The side walls are divided internally by pairs of plain pilasters between the windows and the answering recesses on the N side. Their bases rest awkwardly on scroll brackets just above pew level. Another oddity is the treatment of the capitals, which are formed by simple projections of the dentil cornice. A gallery on stretched Tuscan columns occupies the w bay. The ceiling, cut away in 1882, was reinstated in *Oswald Brakspear*'s gentle restoration of 1953.

The pulpit excepted, the FITTINGS are entirely Georgian. The REREDOS has texts written unusually in black on a gold ground, with the Tetragrammaton and painted cherub heads

---

*The clock face has the painted date 1762.

over. Well-carved swags and festoons above and to the sides, and under the pediment a flourish of Rococo scrollwork with a basket of foliage. – COMMUNION TABLE with a stone top and fashionably decorated frame and legs. – Thin-balustered COMMUNION RAILS. They make a three-sided enclosure, i.e. the normal post-Restoration form, but also extend W to make additional compartments against the N and S walls, probably for communicants. – High BOX PEWS. – CLERK'S DESK, and READING DESK integrated with the Jacobean PULPIT. – Very rustic FONT, a plain marble pudding basin on a wooden base. – CHANDELIERS. Late C19 copies. – MONUMENTS mostly of the Peers family. That to Sir Charles Peers, Chief Inspector of Ancient Monuments, †1952, is a design by *Frederick Etchells* in the style of *c.*1700.

CHISELHAMPTON HOUSE, S of the church. Built in 1767–8 for Charles Peers, the son of a lord mayor of London. It is one of the few known works by the London surveyor and master joiner *Samuel Dowbiggin*, whose son *Launcelot* also signed some of the drawings. A tall, plain villa of red brick and stone dressings, the chief embellishment an applied W portico of four stone Ionic pilasters and a pediment with cartouche and coat of arms. Porch of *c.*1820 with Greek Doric columns *in antis*. On the S front two canted two-storey bay windows. An early C19 drawing shows these with balustraded parapets, now gone. (Rainwater heads dated 1768.) The N side had similar bays, but around 1963 these were infilled between. Garden front of five bays, completely plain. (Entrance hall combined with the stair hall, which has a fine curved staircase within the D-shaped N side, galleries at first- and second-floor levels, and a glazed umbrella dome. Two other rooms have plaster friezes. Some good marble fireplaces of *c.*1820.)

(The setting was transformed in 2004 by *John Brookes*. The ground was lowered to the SE, and a lake made beyond. To the N, a grid-patterned TERRACE was laid out between the house and the pedimented STABLES of the 1760s. The iron-framed CONSERVATORY to the NE is of *c.*1820, five-sided, with ornamented main members and an elegant half-round roof. 200 yds E of the house is the walled KITCHEN GARDEN, near the site of the late C16 manor house of the Doyley family. Estate maps of the 1740s show an E-plan mansion with plain gables and irregular windows.)

COACH AND HORSES INN. 400 yds S of the church. Late C17 or early C18. Limestone rubble, ashlar quoins, brick window surrounds.

BRIDGE across the River Thame, S of the inn. Eight low cambered arches. The E side is late C16, with diagonal cutwaters and refuges. It replaced a bridge of five timber spans on stone piers, noted by Leland around 1540. W side widened 1899.

CAMOYS COURT, ⅔ m. S. A moated stone-built house of the C14, with extensions. It may correspond to the house at Chiselhampton which Sir Richard de Louches was licensed to crenellate in 1318. The N front has two storeys and two big gables, roughly equivalent but of unequal pitch. To the E an early C19 lower range and a single-storey addition of 1995. Doorway in the original position, the porch with Doric columns probably also of the early C19. The w gable belongs to a C17 extension, of which the w flank was rebuilt in brick *c.* 1880. Two canted bays on this side, of different C20 dates. The medieval form appears best from the s, where the upper floor has a C14 solar window of two cusped ogee lights. The mullion is C20 restoration, as possibly is the vesica-shaped opening in the head. Also of the C14 is the oblong SE attachment, thought to have included a garderobe. The medieval hall is thus most likely to have stood to the w. (Crown-post roof to the main C14 section, three bays long and with roll-moulded main timbers, above a modern ceiling. Arched braces reaching to the crown-plate. The roof is ceiled between the braces, which may be an original feature.)

CHISELHAMPTON LODGE. *See* Cuddesdon.

7090

CHRISTMAS COMMON
Watlington

CHURCH OF THE HOLY NATIVITY (former). An early work by *Walter Cave*, built as a chapel of ease in 1890–1. Now a house. Simple brick hall with tile-hung gables. Gothic detailing is limited to the bellcote openings and some tracery in the flat-headed wooden windows. s vestry added 1937. – STAINED GLASS. w window by *Powells*, 1908.

THE TOWER, in woods 200 yds SW. Built in 1967 as a weekend retreat by *Lionel Brett* (*Lord Esher*) of *Brett & Pollen*, after he moved from Watlington Park (p. 765).* Purple-brown brick. Four storeys; firmly Modernist, allowing for the steeply pitched roof and the gabled turret for the lift on one side. The living room on the first floor has a large window opening on to a balcony. The remaining windows smaller and irregularly spaced. Since 1997 a swimming pool has replaced the original moat, and the sheer outlines have been blunted by additions.

5090

CLIFTON HAMPDEN

A Thames-side village, notable for the architectural patronage of the Gibbs family in the Victorian and Edwardian years.

---

*Also on the Watlingon Park estate, ¼ m. SSW, was HIGH WOOD, of 1939 by *Brett* for his parents, the 3rd Viscount and Lady Esher. An interesting transitional design, informal Neo-Regency with a weatherboarded upper storey (*Country Life*, 8 July 1939). Replaced in 2022 with a house by *Spink Partners*.

St Michael and All Angels. This church has a theatrical quality, both from its position on a steep little ridge overlooking the Thames and from its drastic restoration and extension by *G. G. Scott* for the Gibbs family in 1843–4 and 1864–6. It is approached from the sw by a stairway of thirty-three steps, made in 1909–10 together with the memorial cross at the top to Henry Hucks Gibbs, 1st Baron Aldenham (†1907), all to designs by *W. E. Tower*. The campaign of 1843–4 added the s porch and replaced a wooden w bellcote with an elaborate stone turret, pierced by four nodding-ogee arches and carrying a tall spirelet. In 1864–6 the n aisle was extended e with a vestry and organ chamber. Most of the windows are also *Scott*'s, but c13 lancets remain at the w end of the s aisle and another in the n aisle. The e window of the s chapel is a c14 trefoiled lancet. Nave and chancel are under a continuous roof, with two dormer windows of 1899.

Inside, there is much more evidence of the earlier church. s arcade of *c.*1180 with three pointed unchamfered arches and piers with leaf capitals. The bases are now nearly 2 ft (60 cm.) high and form seats. c13 piscina with a chamfered arch. The fourth, easternmost arch of this arcade is Dec and goes with a small Dec s chapel. c14 n arcade, its arches and piers with continuous shallow mouldings. In the chancel n wall is a c13 lancet, now opening to the extended aisle. The chancel itself was transformed by *Scott* into an opulent 'founder's chapel', glittering with mosaics and polished brass, in memory of G. H. Gibbs, whose legacy paid for the 1840s restoration. His tomb is on the n side under a rich crocketed canopy, facing elaborate sedilia and a piscina.

fittings mostly designed by *Scott*, including the pulpit and screen. The latter is of 1864, completed in 1867 with clustered brass shafts and arches with cusping formed by iron scrolls and flowers (makers *Hart & Co.*). On it are gilded figures of St Michael and angels by *J. F. Redfern*. – Stone reredos of 1873–4 with a mosaic of the Last Supper, designed by *C. Buckeridge* and executed by *Clayton & Bell*. – Brass coronas. – Exceptionally rich floor tiles. – Square Neo-Norman font of 1844, also designed by *Scott*, 1844; carved by *Cox* of London. – sculpture. Built into the s chapel wall inside is a c12 relief of a boar hunt, previously in the n aisle wall. It probably came from a doorway lintel, although the subject is ostensibly secular. – stained glass. A memorable collection. Much by *Clayton & Bell*, including the e window (1873). Chancel s windows by *Kempe*, 1880, and his pupil *Herbert Bryans* (w), 1913. s chapel e window, Good Shepherd, †1879 by *Ion Pace*. n aisle: war memorial lancet by *Margaret Agnes Rope*, 1920 (pc), and Gibbs memorial windows by *Hardman*, †1856, and *Charles Hudson*, †1846, finely drawn (mh). Also two s aisle windows with diverting assemblies of medieval and later faces and fragments, given in 1993 by the antique dealer Christopher Gibbs, then of the Manor House (*see below*). – monument. G. H. Gibbs †1842. Designed by

Scott, with a recumbent stone effigy by *Samuel Manning II.* Heraldic glass by *Willement* in the back wall opening, reinstated *c.* 2018.

LYCHGATE of wood, 1843–4. Probably by *Scott.*

VICARAGE, NE of the church. The S front is C18 brick, the rest a rebuilding of 1923–4 by *A.S.G. Butler,* with pointed-arched glazing bars to the windows.

SCHOOL. N of the church, well sited on rising ground. By *Joseph Clarke,* 1847. The donor was William Gibbs, brother of G.H. Gibbs. Steeply pitched roof, mullioned windows. The cross-gabled clock tower is said to be an early addition, attributed to *Scott.*

MANOR HOUSE, E of the church. Built as the parsonage in 1843–6 by *Scott,* for a younger son of the Gibbs family. Stone, with a red-tiled roof and gables of different heights. Enlarged in 1864–5 by *Buckeridge* and again in 1905 by *Woodd & Ainslie,* who added the mullion-and-transom windows in big crenellated bays.

BRIDGE across the Thames, 150 yds S. Of 1864 by *G.G. Scott* for Henry Hucks Gibbs. A later memorandum by Gibbs also names an engineer, the otherwise unrecorded *Homfray.* Victorian Gothic river bridge of red brick, a rare sight. Six four-centred arches, ribbed beneath. Plain TOLL HOUSE on the Berkshire side.

VILLAGE. Many cottages of the Gibbs era, mid-C19 to early C20. Older houses include LOWER TOWN FARMHOUSE, ½ m. WSW. Timber-framed, C17, with a brick front dated 1771. Windows still of vernacular proportions. To its SE is THE ORCHARD, a C16 cruck-framed house heavily restored in 1982. COURTIERS, in Watery Lane 300 yds N of the church, is an unusual early C18 gentry house. Three tall storeys, six bays wide, but only one room deep. Cross-windows of wood. Later Georgian doorcase, C19 hipped roof.

CROWELL

ST MARY. A small church of flint and stone, almost entirely rebuilt in 1878 by *H.J. Tollit* and *Edwin Dolby.* They followed the medieval plan and reused some old work. The wooden W turret was replaced by a stone bellcote and a N vestry added. Norman N doorway with a chamfered arch and jambs. C13 S doorway with a pointed chamfered arch. Windows in C14 style, mostly with cusped Y-tracery. In the chancel a reused square-headed lowside window, a C14 PISCINA re-set in a trefoil-headed recess, and SEDILIA of the same date with simple moulded arches. Chancel arch responds partly of the C13. – REREDOS, a stone relief of 1878. – Medieval TILES behind the communion table. – STAINED GLASS. E and W windows by *Kempe*, 1885 and 1895. – BRASS to John Payne, priest, †1469. 8½-in. (22-cm.) demi-figure.

OLD RECTORY, E. 1822 by *John Biagio Rebecca* of London. White-painted brick with a shallow-pitched roof. The central bay projects and has a doorway with a segmental fanlight.

ELLWOOD HOUSE, N of the church. C17 brick towards the road, of different phases and with exceptionally irregular casement windows. Some have ovolo-moulded stone mullions. The rear is gabled and partly roughcast, concealing C16 timber framing. Two large chimneystacks each with three diagonal stacks.

CROWMARSH GIFFORD

Crowmarsh

6080

A linear Thames-side village, immediately E of the bridge to Wallingford (Berks.).

ST MARY MAGDALENE. A small Norman church, established by 1139.* Mostly rendered. The treatment of the nave w wall is unusual, with two small oculi flanking a central arched window. W doorway of three orders, the inner arch plain, the central roll-moulded, the outer with peltoid decoration. On the imposts and the hood chip-carved saltire-in-square decoration. The central order has jamb shafts, with one weathered carved capital remaining. Nave side walls each with two Norman windows high up. Shallow grooved mouldings to the heads. Also a blocked s doorway with roll-moulded arch and jamb shafts. Single Norman-style lancets to the w from restoration by *J.H. Hakewill*, 1868. His timber w bellcote was given arched sides by *Hugh Vaux* in the mid C20. Norman-style chancel windows and interior details of 1840–1. On the E wall a recess formed from pieces of Norman carved work, reportedly from the sanctuary interior and re-set here *c.*1894. A N transept was added *c.*1200. Original chancel arch, wide and high, of two plain orders. Unusually early PISCINA with a round-arched opening and projecting ribbed bowl. Double-chamfered and pointed transept arch. – PULPIT. Neo-Jacobean, acquired 1904. – FONT. Cylindrical C12 bowl with a blind arcade of twisted columns. – STAINED GLASS. E window by *J.W. Brown* (*Powells*), 1895 (MH). Chancel N, 1961 by *Charles de Vic Carey*, collaging small images and texts; interesting and original. Transept, introduced fragments, C16 and later. Nave w, 1924, and N, 1940, both by *A.J. Davies* of the *Bromsgrove Guild* (PC).

OLD RECTORY, N. By *Hakewill*, 1845. Ashlar. Simplified Tudor.

*Nothing remains of the LEPER HOSPITAL first recorded in 1142. Traces of an earthwork SIEGE CASTLE raised by King Stephen against Queen Matilda's forces at Wallingford around the same time were excavated near the bridge in 2011.

THE STREET. Nos. 17–19 are of 1435–8 (tree rings). Six structural bays, tension-braced. The building has the unusual combination of a storeyed upper end, l., and a former open hall. The QUEEN'S HEAD includes a cruck-built aisled hall dated to 1341, floored across as early as 1454. The aisled form shows in the framing on the l. flank and inside, the floor having been removed in the 1980s. C14 ogee-headed internal doorway. In Benson Lane opposite, the little former SCHOOL of 1844, doubtless by *Hakewill*. Diapered brick; altered.

NEWNHAM HOUSE, The Street, further E. A tall plain box of *c.* 1760–80, much extended and embellished in a Tudor style from the 1850s onwards. – STABLES, W, probably 1850s. With a big radial lunette.

(SOUTH OXFORDSHIRE DISTRICT COUNCIL OFFICES, Benson Lane. The large complex of 1979–81 by the *Architects Design Partnership* was demolished after an arson attack in 2015.)

CENTRE FOR ECOLOGY AND HYDROLOGY (formerly Institute of Hydrology), Benson Lane. Low-rise courtyard complex of 1969–72 by the *Architects Design Partnership*, who extended it in 1978 and *c.* 1999. The 1970s parts are of distinctively handled pre-cast concrete, with white finishes and slit windows in the uprights. Attached to the N end a timber-clad laboratory block by the *RH Partnership*, 2008–10.

HOWBERY PARK, Benson Lane, further N. A business park developed from the former Hydraulics Research Station, of which 1950s–60s *Ministry of Works* buildings survive on the N side. To the W, the HOUSE called Howbery Park. By *J.H. Hakewill*, built from *c.* 1848 for William Seymour Blackstone, M.P. for Wallingford. It bankrupted him, and was sold unfinished in 1858. Red brick and stone Neo-Jacobean, rather rigid. Shaped gables and twin through-storey bays on the S front. Double-height entrance hall with a balcony. Service wing, W, with a slim octagonal tower finishing in an ogee roof. The STABLES, to the N, are latest C19 or earliest C20, friendly and partly timbered. Between, the FOUNTAIN CENTRE by the *Architects Design Partnership*, 1983–6, in High Tech mode. Corrugated cladding and big porthole windows over a glazed ground floor; central concourse under bright green tubular framing. By the road entrance, RED KITE HOUSE and KESTREL HOUSE, cranked-plan office blocks by *Scott Brownrigg & Turner*, 2003–9. Meant as low-energy designs, using brise-soleil canopies mounted with solar panels. Facings of terracotta and slate. The giant SHEDS alongside house wave basins and similar installations.

COUNCIL HOUSES, Crowmarsh Hill, ½ m. E. 1930–1, by *J.E. Thorpe* for Crowmarsh RDC. Originally thatched, as the raked dormers suggest.

COLDHARBOUR FARM, 1 m. E. Probably C18, expanded and prettified in the 1840s. Twin bargeboarded gables, twin verandas, and an inset Doric loggia between.

GRIM'S DITCH. A substantial E–W boundary bank with ditch to the S, originally extending almost up to the Thames N of Mongewell. Excavated evidence suggests a late Iron Age date.

CUDDESDON

An Oxfordshire village like no other, with the Anglican theological college as its dominant presence.

ALL SAINTS. A handsome church which belonged to Abingdon Abbey. Rebuilt *c.* 1180–1200 to a cruciform plan, with a central tower and wide transepts. The aisles are C13 additions, the chancel a Perp replacement. Later the church was taken in hand by Oxford antiquaries and High Church clergy, and restored by *J.M. Derick* from 1843, by *Benjamin Ferrey* from 1849 (chancel), and finally by *G.E. Street* from 1851. Some of the fine Norman detail may have been sharpened in the restorations.

Impressive W entrance with a wide porch, round-arched but with detail of *c.* 1300. An unusual Dec window with tracery transom above. To the sides the two C13 W lancets (N aisle restored). The nave has pilaster-buttresses with angle shafts, a detail which also appears on the corners of the N transept and again on the top stage of the strongly projecting square stair-turret on the NW corner of the tower. Entirely Perp chancel, probably of *c.* 1375–6, when 50 s. was spent on stone for it. Side windows with depressed pointed heads, E window by *Ferrey* in Early Perp style. The tower has set-back buttresses which stop short of the top stage, which was rebuilt in 1630 with twin arched bell-openings. Embattled parapet. Norman W doorway with a chamfered arch in a broad plain surround framed by two richly carved orders, the inner with a keeled roll moulding and dogtooth decoration, the outer of point-to-point chevron with cut-out centres under a hood with beasts'-head stops. The capitals of the jamb shafts exemplify the transition from Late Norman stylized upright leaves to something approaching the more free E.E. stiff-leaf. C13–C14 S porch with another Transitional doorway, reused when the aisle was built. Arch again with a broad plain surround, order again with keeled roll moulding and dogtooth. Capitals of the jamb shafts carved with embryo stiff-leaf and a head on the E. One small Norman window remains in the N transept E wall. Group of three low lancets in the S aisle, showing its original lower height, under a two-light Victorian insertion. The other windows Dec (aisles and probably the nave clerestory), Perp (transepts) or 1850s (S transept S, in a wall rebuilt in the C17).

Inside, the most spectacular details are the richly ornamented pointed arches of the crossing. These have an orderly system of decoration. The arch facing the nave has a hood with dog-head stops, an outer order of chevron and an angle roll, and an inner order with a larger roll. On the other three arches the outer faces are of two simple orders with angle half-rolls. The inner faces of all four arches again have a band of chevron (vertical face only) and an angle roll, and a plain inner arch with a big angle roll. The capitals of the jamb shafts are fluted on the E piers, but on the W there are beasts' heads, waterleaf and crocket capitals. The quadripartite tower-vault is *Street*'s reinstatement of 1851. Below the Norman window in the E wall of the N transept an arched recess and a blocked doorway. A similar recess in the S transept. Evidence that the Norman church was aisleless appears in the remains of pilaster-buttresses over the nave arcades in the aisles. In the N aisle also the heads of small round-arched windows. C13 arcades of three bays, with double-chamfered arches and octagonal piers with vigorously moulded capitals. An unusual detail in the chancel is the big blind arches framing the side windows.

FURNISHINGS. The ALTAR is of 1921 and 1933, retaining carved figures by *Earp* from the Victorian predecessor. – Big CHOIR STALLS, probably by *Ferrey* and of 1849. – CHANCEL SCREEN of 1940–1 by *S.E. Dykes Bower*, of steel painted black and gold, designed as a backing for the nave altar (an early example). Classical and Gothic detail. – C18 CANDELABRA above. – PULPIT. 1896, designed by *Kempe*. – FONT. Big plain tub with a moulded base. Late C12 or C13. – IRONWORK on the W door. Orderly late C12 straps and C-hinges. – STAINED GLASS. E window of 1882 by *Kempe*; also windows in the S aisle (rather good) and N aisle, 1891–1901. Chancel side windows by *Powells*, 1852, with shields of arms of the bishops of Oxford amid stamped quarries. W window also 1852, by *Hardman*. Two *Clayton & Bell* windows, *c.*1870s, N aisle and S transept. One bright lancet in the S aisle by *J.A. Nuttgens*, 1986.

Good LYCHGATE, after 1877. Presumably *Street*.

CUDDESDON HOUSE, N of the church. A bland modern house of 1960–1 by the *Church Commissioners' Official Architect*, built to replace the BISHOP'S PALACE of 1679–80, demolished after a fire in 1958. This was a broad-fronted house of banded stone with shallow-projecting wings and a hipped roof, a typical later C17 composition. Built for Bishop Fell by *Richard Frogley*, carpenter, and *Thomas Wood*, mason, both of Oxford.* The CHAPEL added to its N end in 1846 has survived. By *Benjamin Ferrey* for Bishop Wilberforce, in Dec style. Three bays, W bellcote. (– STAINED GLASS. Shields by *Willement* in four windows.)

RIPON COLLEGE CUDDESDON, on the W side of the main street. Named from the merger in 1975 of Cuddesdon College and Ripon Hall, formerly at Boars Hill W of Oxford. Cuddesdon's college was founded by Bishop Samuel Wilberforce, who appointed a principal in 1851. It was conceived on the model of other diocesan theological colleges of the period, allowing graduates to spend a year preparing for ordination. Building followed in 1853–4: the first important project by *G.E. Street*, whom Wilberforce had appointed Diocesan Architect for Oxford in 1850. Picturesque and strongly influenced by French Gothic, it was praised by Sir Charles Eastlake in *The Gothic Revival* (1872) and also by *The Ecclesiologist*. The original part stands N–S, parallel to the road. Planned with

*Its fine doorway is now at Christ Church, Oxford (*see* p.140).

future enlargement in mind, its design relied for effectiveness on proportion and skilful grouping, not on elaborate ornament. The residential part has Street's characteristic half-hipped dormer gables on the top floor. It ends with an octagonal stair-turret. Then a two-storey section with arches for the entrance, later filled in by Street with Dec tracery, under the chunky oriel of the original common room and library above. Next to this a tall block at right angles with the gable and rose window of the original chapel high up and a flèche on the roof ridge. In 1874–5 *Street* added an L-shaped extension including a chapel on a more ambitious scale, overlapping the NE corner of the first chapel and projecting E towards the road. This new chapel is at first-floor level, with a lecture hall (now refectory) below. E window with Geometrical tracery, traceried two-light side windows. Street's aesthetic prevailed when *Spencer Slingsby Stallwood* added a long W range (RASHDALL BUILDING) behind the chapel in 1904–5, but the SE addition making a three-sided forecourt to the road is simple Neo-Tudor, of 1919–20 by *A.H. Hart & P.L. Waterhouse* (GORE BUILDING). A broad canted bay was thrown out to the S in 1937–8, at the junction with the 1850s range. Service wing of 1925 at the N end, enlarged by *Architects Design Partnership* in 1998–2000. The forecourt still has its stone GATEWAY by Street, 1854. Also a war memorial CROSS of 1918, designer *F.E. Howard*.

Inside, the 1870s CHAPEL has a carved screen, forming an antechapel, and a panelled roof with painted patterns by *Clayton & Bell*. They also provided rich wall paintings (recently re-exposed in part), the reredos and stained glass (1876); the little W window is by *John Piper*, 1965. Black and white floor of 1899, designed by *F.C. Eden*. In the 1850s chapel a lively rose window by *Hardman*, 1855. Probably by the same the two-light window of *c.* 1876 on the staircase (MH and PC).

LATER BUILDINGS start at the NW with the RUNCIE BUILDING for married students, a nerveless gabled affair by the *Architects Design Partnership*, 1988–90. HARRIET MONSELL HOUSE, in line with the 1904–5 wing, marks a fresh start. By *Hopper Howe Sadler* (later *Sadler Brown Architecture*), 2011–13. Three residential storeys faced in silvered wood slats, above largely glazed teaching rooms on the ground floor. No eaves, so the slats continue uninterrupted up to the rounded roof ridge. Stone-faced lift tower to the S. A contrasting but sympathetic companion to Street.

The counterpart to the S is the EDWARD KING CHAPEL, also of 2011–13, by *Niall McLaughlin Architects*.* Not large, but compelling both internally and externally. The plan is an oval, with a slim open bell-frame of timber and a plain stone-faced vestibule to the S. The chapel is stone-faced too, of plain Clipsham ashlar below and with a spare clerestory of the thinnest mullions above. Between is a tall zone of small

---

* Unexecuted designs for a new chapel by *H.R. Goodhart-Rendel* were approved in 1935.

cogged courses, an effect suggestive of basketry or weaving (the architect cites Gottfried Semper's theories on primal structural methods here). Three lesser projections, all different. By the bell-frame is a rounded top-lit enclosure for the sisters of the Order of St John the Baptist, for whom a separate convent was originally intended alongside. A smaller tabernacle enclosure projects on the N side. To the W is a tapered nozzle-like oriel with a 1960s look. The INTERIOR is pale and evenly lit, the central space with its opposed altar and lectern held within a beautifully realized cat's cradle of laminated timber. Each tapering pier divides in three high up, the middle member curving back across the ambulatory to touch the clerestory, the outer ones intersecting to support the flat roof (structural engineers *Price & Myers*). The space is charged with Gothic and Baroque echoes, and the boat-like and forest-like forms provide underlying metaphors, all held in equipoise. – TABER-NACLE of coloured stones by *John Maine*, installed 2022.

COLLEGE HOUSE, to the S. The former VICARAGE, 1853–4 by *Street*. So placed because the vicar of Cuddesdon was also Principal of the college. Gabled and churchy, with a NW enlargement of 1859–60 and a projecting roof added over the door in 1861. To the E a triplet of pointed windows to a former oratory. It was divided from the entrance hall by a wooden screen pierced with quatrefoils, now moved a little to the W. Gothic fireplace beyond. Distinctive stair balusters like chamfered slats. 100 yds S by the entrance to the church is a picturesque red brick COTTAGE HOUSE, built in 1877 for college students.

CROSS, The Green, behind College House. Steps and stump only.

MANOR HOUSE, S of The Green. Late C17, L-plan, plus exten-sions. Simple gables. The S front is said to date from 1805.

CUDDESDON MILL, ¾ m. ESE. Three-storey C19 mill, very plain. Datestone of 1716, re-set. Separate MILL HOUSE, reportedly with a datestone of 176(?).

DENTON HOUSE, ½ m. SW. A tall and compact C17 house remodelled in the C18, possibly in 1757 (date on the rainwater heads). Five-bay S front with platbands, the windows grouped 2:1:2. Doorway with an elliptical head under a bracketed stone hood. The first-floor windows include two C20 insertions flanking the middle one. On the W front the moulded C17 strings remain. Through hall on the ground floor with an open-well staircase at the back. Splat balusters of mid-C17 pattern, also some mid-C18 balustrading higher up. Brought-in woodwork at the bottom with the date 1614. Some fireplaces of C16 type: conservatism, or evidence of older fabric? One ground-floor room has C18 panelling of chestnut and elm.

Late C17 GATEWAY to the lane, with a broken segmental pediment enclosing a cartouche. In the garden walls, re-set WINDOWS from *John Jackson*'s additions of the 1650s–60s to Brasenose College, Oxford, displaced by restoration in 1845. The most spectacular is the former E window of the chapel, of five lights, with a huge oval rose in the head. The other six, from the library, are of two cusped lights. Another in a wall by the stable yard, across the lane. The STABLES are a square block with a hipped tile roof and octagonal lantern, formerly a dovecote. Depressed-arched and keystoned doorways like those of the main house, i.e. of earlier C18 type, but not impossible for the 1750s.

CHIPPINGHURST MANOR, 1¼ m. S. The late C16 house was extended and 'practically reconstructed' in 1932–4 by *R. Fielding Dodd* for Robert McDougall, of the self-raising flour dynasty (*The Builder*, 9 November 1934). U-plan, open to the N. Plain mullioned windows with hoodmoulds. Servants' wing of 1932–4 in line with the W side.

CHISELHAMPTON LODGE, 1¾ m. SSW. By *Robert Adam Architects*, 2005–7. A big house uneasily mixing mid-Georgian and Regency motifs.

CULHAM

5090

The parish is largely bounded by the loop of the Thames towards Abingdon (Berks.).

ST PAUL. W tower rebuilt in 1710 (date on leadwork, now inside). Plain oblong openings. The rest is Victorian: aisled nave and S transept of 1852 by *Joseph Clarke*, apsed chancel of 1872–3 by *R. Phené Spiers*. Plain C13 style throughout. – Original FURNISHINGS; also a REREDOS of 1910 with painted figures. – ROYAL ARMS. Queen Victoria. – STAINED GLASS. Mostly *Clayton & Bell*, 1860s–70s. The heraldic shields of the 1630s in the N aisle N window go with re-set MONUMENTS to Edmund Cary †1637 and Judith Cary †1638. Identical designs, with shields and ribbon borders.

CULHAM MANOR. S of the church, behind splendid topiary. A U-shaped house of the C15 and early C17 that was formerly larger. N side all of roughcast stone. Both wings project slightly. On the l. wing a porch with the date 1610 and the initials of Thomas Bury. The cross-range of one broad bay's width is probably his, unless an older hall was re-cased and re-roofed then. Ovolo-moulded mullion-and-transom windows with square hoods. The porch has an arched doorway with pierced spandrels, a frieze of little brackets, and lesser ornamental mouldings that are echoed on the mullioned windows on either side. Carved brackets supporting small obelisks above. It was probably once the centre of a symmetrical façade, as the foundations indicate a matching L-shaped part to the l. This was partly re-created when Sir Esmond Ovey restored the house after 1933. He added the gabled N–S range with reused C17 mullioned windows to the E, which makes the front roughly symmetrical. The W range is substantially C15, part of a grange of the abbots of Abingdon. Strong timber framing with downward braces, above stone walling on the w side. Inner side all timber-framed, the openings largely post-1933. The E range is shorter, also timber-framed and partly stone-faced. The wall that encloses Ovey's water garden between the wings looks early C17. Re-set in a garden wall to the E is an incomplete two-light cusped C15 window of uncertain origin.

The WEST WING is the most interesting inside. Its kingpost roof with arched braces is partly exposed. Much panelling, chiefly brought in by Ovey, who provided bathrooms *en suite* throughout the first floor. One bedroom is lined with linenfold, and also a section of six panels carved with foliage and heads in medallions, of *c.*1530–50. One original STAIRCASE, a single straight flight with treads of solid rectangular oak blocks. In the E wall of the large ground-floor room at the N is a kitchen fireplace with an immense stone arch. To its r. a former serving hatch. Much C16 and C17 stained glass on both floors, mostly Flemish or Dutch roundels with scenes in grisaille and yellow stain, previously at Culham House (*see* below). The cross-range also has much panelling, and in the DINING ROOM a chimney-breast painted after 1933 copying the Elizabethan patterns at No.3 Cornmarket Street, Oxford (pp.421–2). In the next room a staircase with late C17 balusters taken from a house in Worcester. The main bedroom has a wooden Elizabethan chimneypiece with arcaded overmantel.

In the front garden a C17 SUNDIAL on a round C13 column. To the w a mighty double-chambered DOVECOTE of 1685, rectangular, of stone with brick dressings. Cross-gables midway on the long sides. 3,329 nesting places have been counted.

CULHAM HOUSE, NE. Mid-C18, probably by the London builder *John Phillips*, whose house this was. Originally of five bays; extended two bays to the r. *c.*1800, when the doorway with its Gibbs surround was moved to the new centre bay. The original house is of blue brick with red brick dressings, the addition is of a chequer pattern. Hipped roof. (Original staircase and some C18 fireplaces.)

OLD BRIDGE, ½ m. N, across a backwater of the Thames. Widened and much altered, but recognizable as the bridge built in 1416–22 by the Abingdon Guild of the Holy Trinity. Five pointed arches of different sizes.

CULHAM COURT (former vicarage), ⅓ m. NE. Built *c.*1758, but the serpentine front, with three great curved three-storey bays, is of *c.*1816.

CULHAM COLLEGE, now EUROPA SCHOOL, ¾ m. ENE. Founded by Bishop Samuel Wilberforce as a diocesan teachers' training college, an advanced institution at this date, and built in 1851–3. *Joseph Clarke*'s original buildings, for up to 125 students, are in C13 Gothic style and more convent-like than collegiate. They make a three-sided courtyard, with a cloister formed by a lean-to roof on wooden or stone supports. Small slit windows for the dormitory cubicles, lancets for the upper hall on the s side. The N side was closed in 1938–9 with a white-rendered Modernist range by *A. Brace*. Also a tile-hung

NE extension with laboratories etc. by *J. G.T. West* of Abingdon, 1901–2.

Clarke's CHAPEL is attached to the SE. Late C13 style, with traceried windows; in 1954–5 extended by *Seely & Paget* to the N and given a nasty foreshortened E tower with the old altar window re-set. Stripped interior; the bishop's throne of 1853 remains. Stained glass by *Powells*, 1858, *Percy Bacon Bros*, †1903 (both S), and *O'Connor*, †1871 and 1875 (w). Also of 1853 is the PRACTISING SCHOOL (now Art Block) to the NE, a weightier version of a village school, used for teaching practice with the local children.

N of the main courtyard are many ADDITIONS by *Seely & Paget* from *c.*1960 onwards, including residential ranges and dining hall, culminating in a four-storey teaching block designed in 1969. Since the college closed in 1979 the buildings have been used as a secondary school. The PRIMARY SCHOOL to the NW was added *c.*1985, by the *Property Services Agency, Wessex Design Team*. A pleasing design of yellow blockwork with pyramid roofs, grouped round its own low cloister.

STATION, 1¾ m. E, on the Great Western line to Oxford. A delightful small building of 1844 by *I.K. Brunel*. Neo-Tudor, red brick, with a deep timber canopy projecting on all four sides. The sole survivor of four stations to this design. Adjacent STAFF HOUSES of 1898 ('C' type), plain red brick, and RAILWAY HOTEL, simplified Tudor of *c.*1845.

CULHAM SCIENCE CENTRE, 2 m. E. Opened in 1960 under the aegis of the UK Atomic Energy Authority. The main complex for fusion energy (CCFE) is of 1961–5 and later, by the Authority's architect *R.B. Philpott*. Interlinked low-rise blocks planned on a grid, with much curtain walling. (SCULPTURE by *Geoffrey Clarke*, called Plasma Stabile, by the conference centre entrance.) The Joint European Torus building (JET) was added in 1978–83, architects *Gordon Graham & Partners*. Designs for a NUCLEAR FUSION PLANT by *AL_A Architects*, approved in 2023, include a giant glazed drum with spiralling diagonal framing.

CUXHAM

An especially attractive village, its older houses irregularly spaced along the main street, the mill stream running alongside.

HOLY ROOD. The medieval church was rebuilt *c.*1685, reusing old materials. Squared limestone rubble in thin courses. Plain W tower of two stages with a pyramid roof. Its W doorway has a C12 round arch of two plain orders, impost blocks missing. The capitals of the jamb shafts do not fit. The shafts are spiral-fluted, the capitals are carved with eroded interlacing scrolls. Two small C12 round-headed lancets in the ground stage; the plain windows above may be C15. Round tower arch with re-set voussoirs with pieces of chevron decoration. Aisleless nave with two C14 N windows, each of two square-headed lights with ogee tracery. The plain S windows must be 1680s. Also of two lights, with summary hoodmoulds, all of rendered brick. Roof with tie-beams, double or superimposed queen-struts, and arched wind-braces. How much is reused medieval work? In 1895 *C. C. Rolfe* rebuilt the chancel. It has a Dec-style S window and an uncanonical E window, a triplet of exaggeratedly tall squared lancets under linked pointed-arched hoodmoulds. – PULPIT. Jacobean or Carolean. – PANELLING in the nave from the refurnishing of 1671–3 at Merton College chapel, Oxford (p. 203), dismantled in 1851; installed here 1923. The CARVINGS of two wooden swags on the chancel wall appear to have come from the pediment of *Wren*'s contemporary screen at the chapel. – PEWS. Some with buttresses; probably C16. – Plain tub FONT. – BRASS. John Gregory †1506, with two wives and children. 18-in. and 17½-in. figures (46 and 44 cm.). The achievement of arms is probably a C17 insertion.

SCHOOL, now village hall, by the church. 1849, extended 1911. Chequered brick; Gothic windows of biscuit-coloured brick dressings.

OLD RECTORY, 200 yds WNW. 1823. Ashlar. Three central bays with a Doric porch to the l., projecting one-bay wings. Hipped roof with bracketed eaves. Contemporary STABLES and coachhouse by the road, remodelled from a timber-framed barn dated 1750.

Of the smaller houses, THE THATCH (N side) is a cottage of *c.* 1600 with a gable-end chimneystack and staircase alongside. To the E, the early C17 OLD RECTORY COTTAGE reuses smoke-blackened timbers, probably from a medieval hall house. Lobby-entry plan. Set back on the S side, WHEELWRIGHTS, probably later C16. Thatched and with brick-infilled framing. Further E, YEW TREE COTTAGE has at its centre a two-bay timber-framed house of *c.* 1500–30, its open hall floored over *c.* 1600. CUXHAM MILL opposite (S side) is mid-C18, of chequered brick. The E projection of chalk rubble may be earlier.

CUTT MILL, ⅔ m. NNW. House and mill in line, both mid-C18. The mill roof half-hipped at one end.

5090

DORCHESTER

In the Neolithic and early Bronze Age (*c.* 3650–1600 B.C.) Dorchester became a prestigious CEREMONIAL CENTRE in the Thames Valley. The earliest monuments at Dorchester were quite small and seem to have been associated with funerary rituals, but between around 3400 and 3200 B.C. a long and impressive linear ditched enclosure known as a CURSUS was constructed, linking a number of the earlier sites. This stretched for over a mile between the rivers Thames and Thame across the neck of land to the N of the present settlement. Its purpose remains uncertain, but it was probably associated with ritual processions. The cursus provided the focus for further small enclosures and circles of pits of post-holes, many with cremation burials. The BIG RINGS HENGE was constructed just S of the cursus at the end of the Neolithic period (c. 2700–2500 B.C.). This substantial earthwork monument comprised a bank over 550 ft (170 metres) in diameter between two concentric ditches, with entrances to N and S. It would have provided a huge arena for people to congregate, and to witness and participate in ceremonies and rituals. The area remained a place to bury important dead throughout the Early Bronze Age (c. 2200–1600 B.C.), most obviously within round barrows.

The importance of the area was re-emphasized in the Late Bronze Age and Iron Age by the establishment of a defended enclosure and later hill-fort on Castle Hill, Little Wittenham, immediately across the Thames (Berkshire), and then by an enclosed centre at Dyke Hills, on the river terrace just S of Dorchester (see p. 633). The importance of this site and the related crossing of the Thames by the S–N Silchester to Alchester road determined the location of a subsequent ROMAN SETTLEMENT on the present site. Early Roman settlement was partly displaced by a fort, perhaps occupied c. A.D. 60–75, and after c. 160 its central area was defended with a rectangular EARTHWORK enclosing about 13½ acres, with a secondary N–S road as its central axis. Substantial areas of occupation lay outside, particularly alongside the main road SE of the River Thame. In the later Roman period the earthwork defences were supplemented with a stone wall, and a wide DITCH associated with the wall may still be seen to the SW. The axial road was partly lined with buildings, best known from the area of allotments; fragments of mosaic pavements and a stone altar are known from antiquarian observations. Substantial late Roman CEMETERIES lay outside the walls, the closest to the S in the Wittenham Lane area. Intensive intramural activity in the early C5 may reflect the presence of late Roman military personnel. This was followed by widespread early and mid-Saxon occupation, represented by sunken-featured buildings and later by other timber structures perhaps associated with palisaded enclosures.

In 635 St Birinus established a bishopric here, and Dorchester remained an important medieval RELIGIOUS CENTRE even after the Normans moved the see to Lincoln in the 1070s. Leland in 1542 states that it formerly had three parish churches, which suggests that Dorchester followed the early Anglo-Saxon model of multiple churches within a religious precinct. William of Malmesbury described the town c. 1125 as 'obscure and unfrequented', but also found 'the beauty and state of its churches very remarkable'. The main church became an Augustinian abbey not long after, and in the C13 the cult of St Birinus was revived. A steady pilgrimage trade is suggested by the cluster of medieval inns along the winding picturesque High Street, part of the main Oxford–Henley road until the by-pass to the E opened in 1982.

The present character is that of a well-preserved linear village with remarkably few post-Georgian buildings.

ABBEY CHURCH OF ST PETER AND ST PAUL

A former monastic church which has survived in parish use with little architectural loss. The medieval fabric is mostly CII to CI4, but the site is very much older. Bede records that Dorchester was given in 635 to the missionary bishop St Birinus by Cynegils, king of the Gewisse. The bishopric was large: it originally included the future see of Winchester, and later extended N as far as the Humber. No certain traces of the C7 church have been found. The earliest identified fabric is late Anglo-Saxon, retained when the church was rebuilt by Remigius, the first Norman bishop.* The bishopric was transferred to Lincoln in 1072/3, but around 1140 Dorchester became an Augustinian abbey. The usual monastic accommodation was added, here placed N of the nave. The monks completed the church around 1170 and rebuilt its E end, retaining the simple cruciform CII plan. The cult of St Birinus revived after 1224/5, and the transepts and E end were enlarged and marvellously enhanced from the mid CI3 to c.1340. Shortly after, the nave acquired a S aisle. Following the Dissolution in 1536 the monastic buildings were largely lost. The chancel was purchased by Richard Beauforest, 'a great riche man' of Dorchester (Leland), who bequeathed it to the parish in 1554. The W tower was rebuilt c.1602.

The church and its contents became a favourite antiquarian subject from the mid C17 onwards, and Victorian restorations proceeded with care. First, the Oxford Architectural Society sponsored work by *James Cranston* (1845–6), then *William Butterfield* (1847–c.1854). A new incumbent, William Macfarlane, engaged *George Gilbert Scott* in 1858–74 to complete work on the E end and restore the nave. A few later interventions are described below. The now lost 'great slatted barns' noted by Anthony Wood in 1657, one of which was a CI4 base-cruck threshing barn, are recorded in photographs and CI9 drawings.

EXTERIOR. The tall proportions, long plan and lavish provision of traceried windows show straight away that Dorchester is not an ordinary parish church. The sanctuary bay at the E end is especially distinctive, rebuilt c.1330 by a designer of great originality whose use of sculpture combined with tracery is without parallel on this scale, not only in England but in Europe.

The Norman church, cruciform and aisleless, is still represented by almost the entire N wall of the long and narrow NAVE. It has round-headed windows of c.1170 high in the walls: one complete example, with the jambs of two others E and W of it. String course at sill level, continuing along the W wall of

---

*The dating of this account follows Warwick Rodwell, *Dorchester Abbey Oxfordshire* (2009).

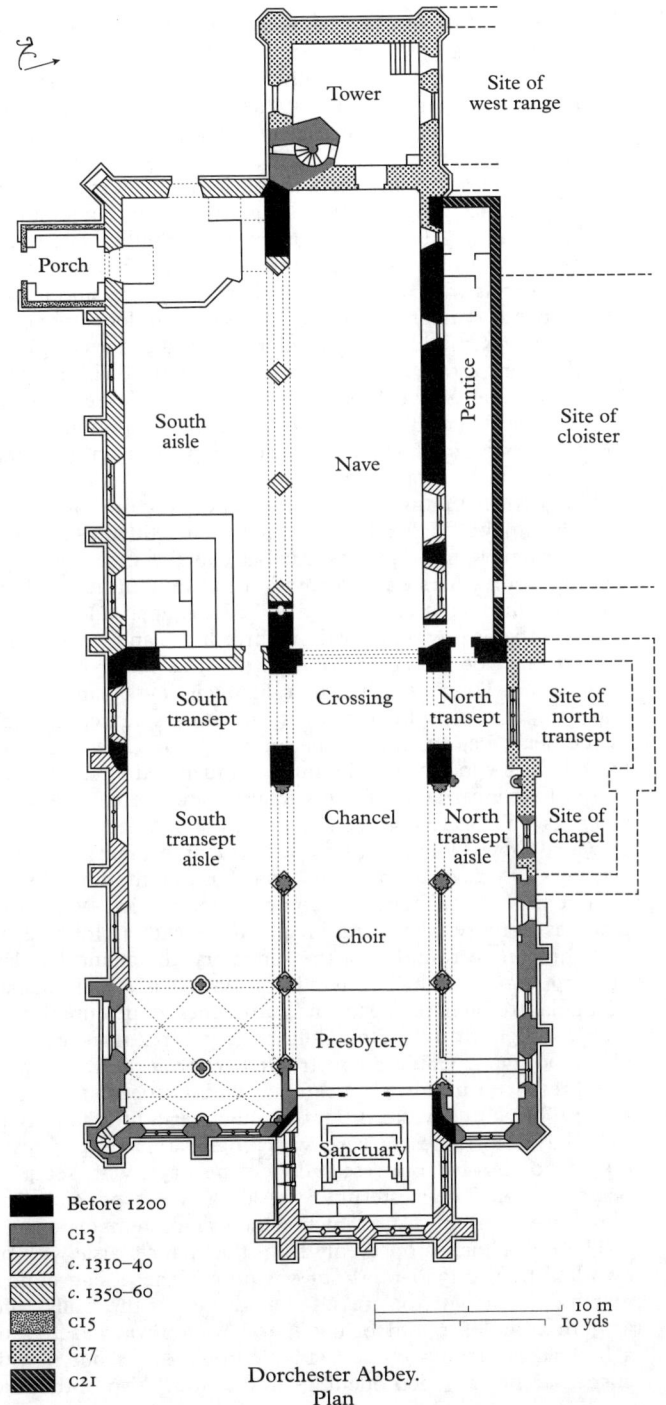

Tower

Site of
west range

Porch

South
aisle

Nave

Pentice

Site of
cloister

South
transept

Crossing

North
transept

Site of
north
transept

South
transept
aisle

Chancel

North
transept
aisle

Site of
chapel

Choir

Presbytery

Sanctuary

Before 1200

C13

c. 1310–40

c. 1350–60

C15

C17

C21

10 m

10 yds

Dorchester Abbey.
Plan

the former N transept. Just below the string is *Martin Ashley*'s nicely judged PENTICE of 2005, of timber with Gothic openings. The wall behind it is sufficiently different in character from the upper parts to indicate an earlier date, identifiable with the reconstruction for Bishop Remigius after 1067. In addition, the masonry towards the transept end includes an even earlier section in which is the infilled outline of a big archway, its size and position suggestive of an Anglo-Saxon *porticus* opening. Also within the pentice is the fine late C12 W doorway from the N transept to the lost cloister. Single order of shafts, capitals with deeply carved beaded foliage, and a shallow-diapered tympanum above the segmental doorway arch.

Whatever Remigius may have done at the E end was replaced shortly after 1140 by a new Augustinian chancel with pilaster-buttresses, one of which is exposed in the angle between the chancel N aisle and the sanctuary. In the corresponding angle to the SE is a small section of another pilaster with a shaft, partly hidden by a rainwater head.

The CHANCEL makes a complicated picture on the N side. From the W, the first bay represents tidying-up when the Norman N transept was cut back in the C17. Four-light window with a harsh approximation to Gothic tracery above the transom. The lost transept also had E chapels added in the C13, and the next window with its three lights and wheel in the tracery must be of *c.*1280, re-set when the outer chapel was taken down. Then a smaller three-light window of similar type and date, *in situ*, and two more each with a spherical triangle in the head, i.e. an earlier type, of *c.*1250–60. These and the three-light E window with its three cinquefoiled circles belong to the first incarnation of this N aisle, and were heightened when its walls were raised twenty years or so later, as internal evidence shows. The sanctuary with its extraordinary traceried windows of *c.*1330–40 must also wait for the interior view. Its E gable is *Butterfield*'s restoration of 1847, and its NE buttress includes a reused late C12 image niche with pointed head and chevron surround. S of the sanctuary, the chancel S aisle presents two three-light E windows. Each has a split-cusped triangular trefoil in the head, and sub-arches to the outer lights: motifs straight from Merton College chapel (p. 201), suggestive of *c.*1290–1300. Gable reconstructed by *Scott* in 1872. The S side presents a uniform appearance, with cusped intersecting tracery. The three western bays are however a little later than the E bay, and represent early widening of a narrower S aisle, *c.*1310–20. Gabled buttresses divide the bays, with sculpted beasts on top. The westernmost aisle bay corresponds to the Norman S transept, from which some walling remains.

The NAVE carries on evenly from the chancel aisle with its own S aisle of *c.*1350–60. Four S windows, the design almost matching, but with buttresses that die in to the walls, and a more complex plinth below. S and W doorways each with a hollow-moulded arch set with fleurons; C15 S porch with cusped-arched wooden openings to the sides. Also of the mid

C14 the two big square-headed nave windows on the N side, with reticulated tracery. The s aisle W window is harder to account for, as the tracery type is like that of the SE chapels, i.e. *c.* 1290–1300. It may have come from a s chapel that was swept away when the aisle was built, evidence for which survives inside. Certainly re-set is the elaborate diagonal buttress at the SW corner of the aisle, with two tiers of niches with stiff-leaf capitals, all clearly C13. It presumably came from the SW angle of the old s transept. Carved heads added in 2000–5 commemorate two notable figures in the late C20 and early C21 restorations.

The WEST TOWER was rebuilt in the C17; it bears the date 1602 and the initials JW near the top of the SW turret. Small openings, Y-traceried or round-arched. Angle turrets of flint and brick in a chequer pattern, as on the late medieval tower at Henley (q.v.). In the SE corner a stair-turret was incorporated from the previous tower, late C13 or C14. Pyramid roof by *Scott*, 1868–9.

INTERIOR. The bare NAVE preserves the tall Norman propor-   18
tions, with the internal string course on the N and also on the s, to E and W of the three-bay C14 arcade. At the W end here are the jambs of another C12 window. One arcade pier has a large corbel carved with sleeping monks and oak leaves, clearly meant as a shelf for a statue or image. The E end of the aisle is raised over a cross-vaulted crypt. SEDILIA(?) in the sill of the SE window, and an adjacent PISCINA. A solid E wall divides the space from the chancel s aisle. In the wall is a small, re-set C14 doorway with wave mouldings. Also a big blank niche high up, with a painted cross within it, overlaid on earlier painting. This niche, which is older than the present s aisle, must mark the position of a lost altar and timber gallery from an earlier aisle or chapel here. The roofs are by *Scott*, whose pupil *J. M. Bignell* restored the W window in 1883.

Of the C12 CROSSING only the W arch survives in its original form. It is of *c.* 1170, almost the full width of the nave, and too lightly built to have carried a crossing tower. Pointed, unmoulded arch on responds with slender shafts and capitals with palmette leaves. The round, unmoulded N and s crossing arches are narrower than the W arch. Origi-nally they must have enclosed superimposed sub-arches. They were opened up in the late Middle Ages, cutting into the C12 strings, and making ledges for altar settings on their E sides.

So to the splendours of the CHANCEL. The first enlarge-ment of the Norman church must have followed the papal authentication of St Birinus's bones in 1224/5, with permis-sion to translate them to 'a more worthy place'. It comprised two chapels on the E side of the N transept, probably mirrored by corresponding chapels on the s side. Of the N chapels there remains a finely moulded C13 arch on stiff-leaf capitals where the former transept opens to the chancel's N aisle. Its N respond is actually a half-exposed pier, free-standing until the C17 demolitions. (Also the r. side of the arch of a PISCINA, and a blank half-trefoil in the spandrel facing W, both now hidden by the organ.) The N aisle, representing a further C13 extension, still betrays its original height of *c.*1250–60 in the wall-shafts. They must have been meant for a timber vault, most likely the setting of the saint's shrine. Two shafts with dogtooth capitals remain on the N wall, and part of a third in the NE corner. Also in the N wall a niche with a flue, probably for a wafer oven, and three plain locker openings. These face a PISCINA with a damaged cusped arch and a projecting bowl with stiff-leaf decoration. Windows with shafted openings, heightened *c.*1280–90 when the chapel was made taller. At the same time the N arcade was magnificently rebuilt, out of alignment with the mid-C13 buttresses outside. Three bays, the piers with four major and four minor shafts. Elaborately moulded arches with hoodstops carved as heads or foliage.

The S arcade is very similar to the N arcade and only a little later, *c.*1290–1300. Differences include more complex bases, and thin shafts rather than hollow chamfers between the eight main shafts. The stylish PISCINA just to the E is of the same phase. It has a steep crocketed gable with a finial. Two openings with straight-sided heads, diamond-shaped quatrefoil tracery. The S arcade belongs with the twin SE chapels, each two bays long. Their lost vaulting and dividing piers were deftly reinstated by *Scott* in 1874, using the original wall-shafts. In the SE corner an elaborate doorway to the angle stair-turret, with a cusped head and pinnacled ogee canopy. Above it, the vaulting shaft is supported by a corbel carved as the head of a so-called green man, biting foliage. To the r. a PISCINA with a similar canopy and reticulated tracery on tiny side shafts. The W extension of the S aisle was never vaulted, and the space over the vault may have served as a watching loft when St Birinus's shrine was relocated there. Roofs of the E end by *Butterfield* (chancel E), completed by *Scott*.

Finally the SANCTUARY or eastern extension of the chancel of about 1330–40, the most remarkable part of the whole church. All three windows – E, N and S – are different from each other, and different too from all other Decorated windows in England. The tracery, instead of being confined to the window heads in the usual way, is extended over each whole opening, and combined with figure sculpture that originally formed a coherent sequence with the stained glass (*see* p. 628; cf. Ducklington church, North Oxon). The great E window fills the entire wall. Its arch is decorated with ballflower. Seven lights originally, but at an early date the central light was filled with a buttress to strengthen the whole. This stops below a rounded compartment of flowing tracery in the head, inserted when *Butterfield* reinstated the top in 1848 (in spite of evidence that the original form was a more regular rose or wheel). Cusped and crocketed tracery below, deriving ultimately from Merton chapel, but with a line of sculpted figures against the mullions portraying scenes from the Passion and Resurrection of Christ. The N window is the Jesse Window, a unique treatment of a popular C14 subject. The lower tracery, carved with foliage, forms a tree springing from the recumbent figure of Jesse on the sill. On the mullions between the wavering branches are figures of the ancestors of Christ (above), and at sill level the Angel Gabriel (l.), the Magi (two plus one, flanking a lost Virgin and Child on the middle upright), and King David (r.). The s window has panel tracery, almost Perp in style, except that the lower and upper tiers are offset by the width of one half-light. On a transom bar stand six carved figures or groups of saints and monks carrying the bier of St Birinus. Below are the SEDILIA, and these are no less original. They are magnificently canopied, with four crocketed spirelets over small rib-vaults. The canopies, of openwork tracery, are thickly populated with small figures of saints and with human and animal heads. The wall below is pierced with four small triangular windows of curvilinear, almost Rococo form, decorated with ballflower and filled with stained glass. Restored by *Cranston* in 1845–6, with the s window.

FURNISHINGS, roughly from E to W. REREDOS of 1874 by *John Medland*, a pupil of Scott. Incomplete, and fortunately never carried higher. It has tiles by *Godwin*. – Behind is a simpler REREDOS by *Butterfield*, composed of *Minton* tiles applied to the wall. – COMMUNION RAIL. Early C18, with turned balusters. – COMMUNION TABLE. C18. Simple quasi-Gothic openings. – STALLS. Two with poppyheads given in the early C16 by Abbot Beauforest, whose crozier is carved on one of the ends, with a scroll bearing his name. Others by *Philip Koomen*, 2012, of clashing pale wood. – PULPIT of wood by *Butterfield*, 1852–3. – SCREENS in the chancel designed by *Butterfield*, with a few salvaged C14 arched heads, s side. – BENCHES also by *Butterfield*. – SE chapels, REREDOS painted by *Rebecca Hind*, 2013, called Moon Rising, and Gothic RETABLE by *F.E. Howard*, 1922, from the Missionary College (*see* p. 630). – BIER dated 1685. – Between nave and s aisle, the lower part of a C14 SCREEN. – TILES, s aisle. A few of the C14 and C15 against the screen. – FONT. Of *c.*1170. One of the best-preserved lead fonts in the country, and the only one belonging to a monastic church to survive the Reformation. It has eleven seated figures of the Apostles under an arcade and bands of foliage around the top and bottom. Plain base by *Butterfield*, replacing an ornate Perp predecessor. – PROCESSIONAL CROSS, nave s aisle. Made from steel by *Brian Catling*, 2007. – INNER PORCH, 2003. By *Peter Scott* of *Martin Ashley Architects*. Engraved glass designed by *Jane McDonald*. – SCULPTURE. On a nave windowsill, the head provided by *Scott* for the churchyard cross *c.*1875, with small figures under canopies. In the pentice, excellent displays of capitals, voussoirs, beakhead and other gathered fragments, especially of the C12 and C13. Likely sources include a former W doorway, and a cloister arcade apparently of the early C13. – WALL PAINTINGS. SE chapel, syrupy work by *W.T. Beane* of *Clayton & Bell*, 1893–4 (restored 2006). Chancel s aisle, a big late medieval St Christopher, uncovered in 2006. s aisle, a C14

Crucifixion with a diapered background, heavily restored by *Clayton & Bell* in 1863. Early C15 brocade patterning below. In the niche above, the plain C14 cross already mentioned; probably the backing for a carved figure.

STAINED GLASS. Most of the medieval glass can be associated with the late C13 and early C14 rebuilding of the E end. The most unusual feature is the combination of glass and sculpture in a unified iconographic programme (*see* above). The present setting is largely of 1806–7, when the bulk of what remained was gathered in the sanctuary windows. The EAST WINDOW was again restored in 1966. Starting at the bottom, the first two tiers are by *Clayton & Bell*, 1870. Third tier from l. to r., all scenes also with small roundels of mostly crowned heads: Annunciation; St Michael spearing the dragon; donor figure of Radulphus de Tiwe; St Lawrence holding a gridiron; St Birinus preaching; composite figure of a bishop. Fourth tier: fragments; head of a monk in a roundel; Virgin and Child; fragments; fragments; Christ in Majesty; emblem of the Trinity and the Agnus Dei in a roundel; fragments. Fifth tier: mostly *Clayton & Bell*, 1874, but also large medieval heads of a king and queen. Rose, glass designed by *Butterfield* in 1847–8 and executed by *O'Connor*. – JESSE WINDOW, N. Tantalizing fragments of the Tree of Jesse: sixteen heads of kings and prophets on bodies made up of fragments, one almost complete figure of a prophet, and bits of the original inscriptions, with curious spellings of some of the names. – SOUTH WINDOW, mostly C14 shields of arms, with some restorations. Probably originally in the E window, where they were recorded in the C17. Six tiers. From the bottom, l. to r.: Bigod, Earl of Norfolk; part of a C14 panel of Jonah and the Whale; Foliot; Tyes; Segrave; Edward, Prince of Wales; Geneville; Edmund, Earl of Cornwall; quarterly Leon and Castile; Grey of Rotherfield; Fitzalan; De Vere; Ferrers; Bigod; Fitzwalter; Toni; Ferrers; Hastings; Wake; Latimer; Toni. In the heads of the sedilia below, from l. to r.: foliage fragments; a Mass scene, mid-C14, probably from a series of the Seven Sacraments; two late C13–early C14 roundels with an archbishop and a pope, each seated in benediction. – Chancel N aisle E window, roundel with St Birinus consecrated as bishop by Asterius, Archbishop of Milan, *c.*1230–50. – Nave N, collected C14 fragments of quarries, borders and canopy designs, and three early C14 shields of arms: England, Earl of Cornwall, Earl of Lancaster. Also the Macfarlane memorial window, 1887 by *Hardman*. – Chancel S aisle. Two E windows by *Hardman*, 1874, two S by *Mayer*, 1899.

MONUMENTS. Chancel S aisle, SHRINE of St Birinus. Of 1964, designed by *F. Russell Cox*. Under bright paint in its niches are elaborate rib-vaulted canopies, found in the C19 in the infill of the N transept W doorway, and identifiable with the new shrine recorded in 1320 by the C14 chronicler Higden. – William de Valence the younger †1282. One of the great works of English medieval sculpture. Well-preserved limestone effigy of a knight, described by *Kelly's Directory* as of 'a most determined countenance', cross-legged and vigorously drawing his sword. – John Stonor, chief justice of common pleas, †1354. Effigy in legal robes on a low tomb-chest with the Stonor arms. – Weathered effigy of a bishop, early C14. Identifiable as the 'Bishop Aeschwyn' recorded by Leland, and made probably to commemorate one of Dorchester's Anglo-Saxon bishops. – Sir Hugh Segrave(?) †1387. Alabaster effigy on a three-sided tomb-chest with small buttresses and blank shields, probably made to stand in a wall recess. – Sir John Drayton †1417 and wife. Brass, male figure only, minus legs; originally 60 in. (151 cm.). – Headless woman, c.1490. 15-in. (38-cm.) brass. (– Margaret Beauforest †1524 and two husbands. Brass. 15-in. (38-cm.) figures, one husband missing.) – Indents for other brasses, two or three still with shields of arms, including Drayton c.1470 and one with a late C15 wool merchant's mark. (– Chancel. Abbot Richard Beauforest, c.1510, 31-in. (79-cm.) brass. – Abbot Roger Smith †1535, a worn incised alabaster slab.) – Nave s aisle. A ledger stone commemorates Mrs Sarah Fletcher, who in 1799 'sunk and died a martyr to excessive sensibility'.

CHURCHYARD. SW of the church, a C14–C15 stone CROSS-SHAFT. – S of the nave, an early CHEST TOMB (John Drayton †1634), still with trefoil-headed panels. – LYCHGATE of massive kingpost trusses by *Scott*. Designed probably in 1861, completed 1867.

ABBEY GUEST HOUSE (now Museum), W of the W tower. The only surviving monastic building; converted into a school c.1654. The building must have joined on to a lost gatehouse or gate tower at the W end of the church. Tree rings have dated it to 1445. Stone S front, timber-framed behind. In the S front a blocked square-headed upper window with two trefoiled lights. At its SE corner is the l. jamb of an archway, originally providing access between the outer court and the main monastic complex to the N. Over it the jamb of a lost window. On the N side the first floor is jettied for a gallery, with the outline of a blocked doorway suggestive of a former external staircase up to the lodgings. Herringbone brick infill below. Queen-strut roof.

OTHER BUILDINGS

ST BIRINUS (R.C.), Bridge End. A small church by *W. W. Wardell* in mid-C14 style, consisting of nave and chancel only. Built in 1849 at the expense of John Davey of Overy, who was generous, as it has elaborate carving with the statue of St Birinus under a canopy on the W wall, and the Virgin in the gable of the porch. (Richly furnished chancel with traceried SCREEN, canopied sedilia and piscina, and a gilded roof. – ORGAN by *Bernard Aubertin*, 2021. – STAINED GLASS. 1849 by *Ward & Nixon*. – BRASS. John and Elizabeth Davey by *Hardman*, 1856.) SCHOOLS (former), Queen Street. The girls' and infants, S (now VILLAGE HALL), is a bold design of 1871–2 by *G. G. Scott*.

Red brick. Gable-end facing the road with a rose window, two pointed-arched windows with tile-hung heads. Scott's missing arched bargeboard may be reinstated. The boys' school, N, is post-Gothic. 1895–6 by *Samuel Johns* of Wallingford.

BRIDGE, across the River Thame. 1812–15 by *Francis Sandys*, superseding a medieval bridge downstream. Five arches, approached by long causeways. Seats over the middle piers, balustraded parapet between.*

THE VILLAGE

The HIGH STREET, still with cobbled pavements, runs irregularly across the NE corner of the Roman town enclosure. Starting from the entrance to the churchyard, the GEORGE INN stands opposite. C15, single- and double-jettied, now rendered and with horizontal-sliding sashes. The carriageway through the set-back part, r., shows tension-braced framing. Behind, the original hall and kitchen project from the l. part. Attached is a timber-framed lodging range with an external staircase to an unenclosed first-floor gallery.

From here the description runs N, then returns S. THE PRIORY, N of the Abbey gateway, is apparently of two Early Georgian phases, front and back. Façade of four bays, with keystones, a brick dentil cornice, and a high parapet with outlines of blocked windows. On the S corner of Queen Street, CHURCH HOUSE, built in 1884–6 for the missionary college founded by the Rev. William Macfarlane (*see also* Burcot), and designed by Sir G. G. Scott's pupil *J. M. Bignell*. Brick, with red fish-scaled tile-hanging and half-timbering, now aggressively painted white and black. Big clustered chimneystacks, and the porch in a polygonal turret at the side. The college also used the mid-Georgian range on the N corner, now THE OLD COLLEGE. Red and grey brick, red-tiled roofs and six bow windows, added *c.*1951 for an antique shop. Loosely Gothic rear range added for the college in 1878, also by *Bignell*.

Queen Street leads to Manor Farm Road, r., and the VICARAGE built for Macfarlane and his spinster sister in 1856–7. By *David Brandon*, heavy Gothic, of stone, with trefoiled windows. Extended 1866. To its NE is the MANOR HOUSE, timber-framed and probably early C17 in origin. The casing is of rendered C18 brick, with a hipped roof with castellated parapet, a porch to match and Gothick windows. Early C19 garden range, not matching. Attached to the N is a plain, taller Late Georgian house.

Continuing N along the High Street, No. 31 is C17, its timbers exposed on the jettied first floor. At No. 33 a Georgian refronting, roughcast. Two bay windows flank a doorway with pilasters. Nos. 37–39 originated as three timber-built late medieval workshop houses, each two bays deep, with later heightening of

---

* Scars in the recesses show where the seats were 'sloped up' in 1847, in response to a complaint from the ladies of Dorchester concerning the 'nuisances' committed on them.

the fronts. No. 37 preserves a Late Georgian shop window. On the E side, the WHITE HART HOTEL has the date 1691 picked out in the brick infill of the timber framing. That date must also apply to the rendered and triple-gabled top storey, and to the removal of some big timber oriels from the façade, as scars in the framing show. A late medieval timber gallery survives at the back. Long, low Georgian wing of whitewashed brick to the N. At No. 30 a C17 lobby-entry house with herringbone brick infill to the first floor and an end jetty.

Opposite, placed well back but still too high for the setting, BEECHCROFT, three-storey housing by the *Dry Halasz Dixon Partnership*, designed 1972. To the l. is MALTHOUSE LANE, with a terrace of eight thatched cottages along the S side, some timber-framed, some rendered, some entirely brick; the oldest probably C17. Those at the N end were converted from a malthouse. Nos. 55–59 High Street were formerly the BULL INN. The l. part is remarkable: a double-jettied wing of lodgings, dated '1610 IH' on one upright. The small mullioned windows placed symmetrically under the jetties are original; the larger casements replace four big oriels, of which scars remain on the posts and under the jetties. Big stack with four diamond chimneys, set in the front roof slope, and originally answered by a stair-tower behind. Original console brackets carved with sophisticated classical detail. The lower ranges, r., are late medieval, the central one with carriageway and single jetty. No. 63 is a C17 tea-cosy cottage, timber-framed and thatched, set back in a garden. Opposite. No. 52, the former CROWN INN, C16, with a Georgian brick front. Bow windows of *c.*1960, and a brought-in carved doorcase r. of the carriageway. Rear wing with an intact C17 oriel, simply detailed. WATLING LANE COTTAGE, facing N on the W side, is C17, thatched, the framing with brick infill. Beyond, WILLOUGHBY HOUSE (No. 73) has a Late Georgian rusticated and stuccoed front, three bays wide. Whimsical Victorian porch, matching N addition (No. 75). The structure however is timber-framed and late C15, probably a hall house, with the service end to the l. C17 stair-tower behind. Also a small timbered KITCHEN, placed E–W and originally free-standing, one of several in Dorchester. To the r. some thatched COB WALLING, partly C19.

Beyond this the houses become sparser. THE OLD FORGE (No. 72) is a C17 lobby-entry house, with three diagonal stacks like those at The Bull. No. 76 includes a late medieval hall house at its centre, probably cruck-built. To the W, set back, BISHOP'S COURT FARM has a timber-framed core, probably C16, behind early C19 fronts. Two timber GRANARIES, one thatched, on staddle-stones. Further N, CRANMER COTTAGE (No. 90, E side) includes what may be another detached timber-framed kitchen. Before all these, in MARTIN'S LANE to the E, No. 9 looks like a C16–C17 storeyed house, but smoke-blackening of the roof timbers suggests older origins.

Now S from the Abbey gateway. S of The George, Nos. 13–19 are a late medieval cruck-framed row, heavily disguised. The FLEUR DE LYS is another inn, likewise late medieval and cruck-framed.

Part of one cruck blade exposed in the carriageway. The original lower height shows from behind, and also at THE PIGEONS next door, another cruck house. ROTTEN ROW, the cul de sac to the S, probably represents the encroached former market place. Largely C17 cottages, but THE OLD COTTAGE (No. 13) is early C15 behind the brick front. (Remains of a screens passage with internal jetty over, l. Later stair-tower behind.) No. 14 is mid-C18, chequer brick with clunch walling behind.

S of the churchyard is a former TOLL HOUSE, part-octagonal, c. 1816. Red brick. Then BRIDGE END HOUSE, 1965 by *Julia Feilding & Donald Morrison*, for themselves. A rare British example of a steel-framed house *à la* Mies, here elevated on stilts above the flood plain, with access by a raised walkway. BRIDGE END, leading to the pre-C19 crossing point, continues S. No. 12 has a front with banding in stone and flint, dated 1715, but is probably C17 behind, with a later l. extension. MOLLY MOP'S COTTAGE in Samian Way, off Watling Lane to the SE, has the renewed date 1701. This is thatched and even more decorative, with flint and brick set in stripes and diamond shapes. Continuing S, BRIDGE END CLOSE, dated 1797 over the doorway. Three bays wide. Grey brick dappled with red, the windows and doorways with red brick trim. BRIDGE HOUSE opposite has an earlier type of sash frame but must also be late C18. Porch with colonnettes, delicate fanlight. Grey brick with red window surrounds in front, chequer brick on the flank. At the end is a small triangular green with humble squatters' cottages, mostly early C19. Also a cob-walled former PRIMITIVE METHODIST CHAPEL of 1839. Broad oblong windows in thick walls, the corners rounded.

WATLING LANE, running W then N, follows the outer line of the Roman enclosure. Attached to Orchard Cottage (No. 26) is another cob-built former CHAPEL, of 1837, for Baptists. Also cob-walled is the little Gothic-windowed SUMMERHOUSE at Port House (No. 25), probably early C19.

OVERY

A small settlement S of the River Thame, ¼ m. SE. The home of the recusant Davey family in the C17–C19. The MANOR HOUSE has a datestone of 1712 with the initials WHD. Low two-storey range of chequer brick. A taller Late Georgian addition in parallel to the E, red and silver-grey brick with a canted bay window. Former FARMHOUSE to the W, of clunch and red brick (scratch-dated 1704), still with casements and cross-windows. To the NNE beyond, MILL HOUSE. A long, picturesque range. The C17–C18 water mill is timber-framed and weatherboarded with a red-tiled roof. Adjoining house of two builds, c. 1700 (l.) and c. 1750. Red and silver-grey brick.

COUNCIL HOUSES, Henley Road, ¼ m. further SE. 1920–2 by *F. G. Sainsbury*, for Crowmarsh RDC. Rendered, generous in scale, and formally grouped.

DYKE HILLS

An area of some 114 acres, ⅓ m. sw, defined by the Thames
to the w and s and by the Thame to the e; enclosed on the
n and ne by a massive double rampart, partly levelled in
the C19, with a ditch between, possibly intended to channel
water. A Late Iron Age date (perhaps CI B.C.) is presumed
but not proven, as are high-status functions. Earlier activity is
indicated by features within the earthworks known from aerial
and geophysical surveys. Three important early C5 burials in
the inner rampart, two found in 1874 and a third in 2010, were
probably of members of the late Roman military community
in Dorchester.

DRAYTON ST LEONARD   5090

St Leonard. Low w tower with a pyramid roof, almost entirely
timber-framed, unusual in Oxfordshire. It was restored in
1884 and faced with shingles, replaced with weatherboarding in 1983. Inside it is composed of massive timbers with
arched braces, probably C15. Roughcast Norman nave with
a red-tiled roof, C13 w lancet and C13 n chapel. C14 chancel,
largely reconstructed in 1859 by *G.E. Street*. Nave s doorway
Norman, its external arch lost and the lintel replaced. Original
internal arch, jambs and imposts. Corresponding n doorway,
with a chamfered arch and jambs and plain imposts, now
within a vestry of 1932. Original deeply splayed window in
the nave n wall, part of the rere-arch of another to the e, and
the e jamb of a third in the s wall near the pulpit. Opposite
this, in the n wall, the openings to the n chapel, apparently
the beginnings of an intended aisle. Two very unequal arches
on a substantial round pier. Slightly pointed chancel arch,
probably late C12. The square-headed s windows are Perp. In
the chancel a cusped C14 PISCINA and some re-set medieval
TILES. – COMMUNION RAILS and depleted CHOIR STALLS by
Street. – PULPIT. 1898. Designed by *J.N. Comper* and brightly
painted and gilded. – FONT. Perp. – C18 PANELLING, reused
on the tower partition. – STAINED GLASS. Chancel n window,
St Leonard, mid-C14. The lower part, background and canopy
are all *Clayton & Bell*'s restoration of 1861. e window and nave
se by *Comper* in C15 style, 1897 and 1898. The latter is based
on a painting by Dirk Bouts in Louvain Cathedral.

OLD RECTORY, 100 yds SE. 1862 by *J. Billing*, extended
and altered.

The VILLAGE has no definite centre. At the junction on the w
side the WAR MEMORIAL, a cross by *Sir Aston Webb*, 1923.
Down a lane to the s is a fine BARN, *c.*1400 or a little later. Six
bays, aisled on all four sides. Steep tiled roof with gablets. The
trusses have straight braces and curved queen-struts. Adapted

in 1999–2001 by *Architecture plb* for the Aston Martin Owners' Club. Silvered oak boarding, discreetly treated openings and no affected rusticity. Immediately s is WATERSIDE HOUSE, C16 or C17, partly timber-framed with herringbone brick infilling. In Water Lane to the E, GUYS and GUYS COTTAGE represent one large timber-framed C17 farmhouse, the w half now brick-clad. Other C17 timber houses include GARDEN COTTAGE and the tiny LITTLE GARDEN COTTAGE, along a lane to the SE.

LOWER GRANGE, ½ m. s. Mid-C15 and substantial, of six timber-framed bays. (C17 open-well stair, the newels with acorn finials.)

DUNSDEN
Eye and Dunsden

ALL SAINTS. Nave of 1842 by *John Turner*, with a w bellcote. Silver-grey brick with stone dressings. The sides have single lancets divided by shallow buttresses. A graduated triplet to the w, repeated at the E end when the 1840s chancel was rebuilt in 1872 by *John Goldicutt Turner*. – PULPIT. 1853, from Sonning church, Berks. Stone. By *Woodyer*, with flat Gothic carving by *Messrs Wheeler* of Reading. – STAINED GLASS. Mostly *Hardman*. – MONUMENT. Plaque of 1978 by *Reynolds Stone* to the war poet Wilfred Owen (†1918), lay assistant at Dunsden in 1911–13.

ROWLANE FARMHOUSE, s. Late C17, with superior brickwork. Five bays, the wide central bay projecting slightly and framed by superimposed brick pilasters. Moulded brick platbands to the side bays. Two blind windows with cut-brick lintels on the flank.

GLEBE HOUSE (former vicarage), 300 yds NE. By *J. G. Turner*, 1870 and 1876. Grey and red brick. Steep-roofed, with bands of fish-scale tiles.

VILLAGE HALL, ½ m. ESE. The former school. 1869, extended 1879 and 1893 (Kelly). Grey and red brick. (Immediately N, DUNSDEN FARMHOUSE. Mainly C17, but the l. cross-range survives from a late medieval house.)

EYOT HOUSE, Sonning Eye, 1½ m. SE. By *Halsey Ricardo*, 1902, for Reginald Blunt, general manager of the De Morgan Pottery, where Ricardo had been a partner and designer from 1878 to 1888. White-rendered and tiled-roofed, informal and relaxed plan. In the rear loggia a TILE PICTURE by *William De Morgan*: two sailing ships against a Mediterranean coast with classical buildings. De Morgan tiles also in the sitting-room overmantel.

MILL HOUSE and BRIDGE, 1¾ m. SE. *See The Buildings of England: Berkshire.*

BISHOPSLAND FARMHOUSE, ¾ m. NW. Brick. Big chimney-stack with three diagonal shafts where the main ranges join. A late C16 origin is likely.

EASINGTON

Cuxham

A shrunken village at the end of a lane, with manor house and dower house close to the church.

ST PETER. One of the least interfered-with small medieval churches of South Oxon. Limestone rubble. Continuous C14 nave and chancel with no chancel arch. Trefoiled lancets, and an E window with reticulated tracery. Late C12 N doorway, re-set. It has a rounded chamfered arch with a truncated roll hoodmould. Square imposts, incompletely carved with squared quatrefoils. Two plain s windows in the nave are probably C18 or early C19. Their hoods are improvised from re-set medieval mouldings, including two bits of C12 chevron. Blind W wall with a central buttress. The tie- and collar-beam roof looks C15 or C16. Its westernmost truss is later, presumably put in when the little weatherboarded bellcote was made. Ogee-headed PISCINA. – C14 TILES in the chancel. – PULPIT with tester. Made up in 1916 from pieces of C17 woodwork, one with the carved date 1633. – PEWS. Probably early C19. – FONT. Plain tub. – WALL PAINTINGS. A patch of damask-like patterns in red and dark blue on the E wall; late C15–C16? Also fragments on the ceiled truss where nave and chancel join. – STAINED GLASS. In the E window twelve C14 rosette quarries, and a C14 roundel in the tracery, all set inside-out.

EASINGTON MANOR, NE. A late C18 front mostly of grey header brick. Disorderly fenestration at the r. end betrays the inclusion of older fabric, from which a C16 chimneystack shows at the back.

DOWER HOUSE, immediately N. Of c. 1800 and c. 1830 (l.). Chalk rubble dressed with brick.

EMMINGTON

Chinnor

ST NICHOLAS. Redundant since 1987, now privately maintained. A small church, originally entirely of the early C14. W tower with saddleback roof and square-headed bell-openings with ogee tracery. Aisleless nave, its two-light windows again square-headed. In 1873–4 its s wall and the whole chancel were rebuilt by *Charles Buckeridge* (completed by *J. L. Pearson*), reproducing the C14 forms. E window of three lights with intersecting tracery, chancel N and s windows with cusped Y-tracery. Original chancel arch of two chamfered orders. (Two original PISCINAS, SEDILIA of 1874.) – FONT. Cup-shaped, on a moulded base; C13.

RECTORY (former), N of the church. Enlarged to the SW in 1874 by *Bruton*, in colourful flint and red brick, with pointed-arched bargeboards.

EWELME

Prettily situated in a valley of the Chilterns with watercress beds along the stream. At the centre of the village is a magnificent C15 group of interlinked church, almshouses and school, the gift of Alice, granddaughter of Geoffrey Chaucer, and her third husband, William de la Pole, Earl of Suffolk (†1450; Duke of Suffolk after 1448). In the early C16 the property of the de la Pole family was seized by the Crown, including their C15 palace here. Only a small part of this remains, but the school and almshouses are little changed and continue to function.

ST MARY. An earlier church dedicated to All Saints was rebuilt in stages, mid-C14 tower excepted, during the C15. The result is a long, low church with a continuous clerestory: an arrangement which resembles that of churches in East Anglia, including Wingfield in Suffolk, the site of the de la Poles' castle. Its architectural motifs and use of materials are also unusually sophisticated. Generally respectful restorations in the C19 and C20 have left most of the furnishings intact.

The tower has angle buttresses and an unusual plan, much broader than it is deep. Single bell-openings to N and S, pairs side by side to E and W, with cusped Y-tracery. The details are likely to date from rebuilding of the upper stage in 1792. C15 W window. Double-chamfered arch with half-round responds to the nave. Rebuilding began with the S aisle and nave arcade, probably under Thomas Chaucer, father of Alice, not long before 1435. Rubble stone; three-light windows with straight-sided arches brought to a sharp point, a type lately employed at the Divinity School at Oxford (*see* p.328). Its embattled parapet is contrastingly of brick, repeated on the rest of the rebuilt church. S porch of timber with traceried openings at the sides. Next came the Chapel of St John the Baptist S of the chancel, i.e. the chapel of the almshouse foundation, complete by 1438. Wider than the aisle, it has the same window type to the S but is flint-walled, changing to flint-and-stone chequer on the E wall. Chancel, N chapel and N aisle followed, chequered across the whole E end. The N side shows flint or flint-and-stone rubble (originally rendered), with plain limestone for the W part of the clerestory only. Windows with depressed four-centred-arched heads and panel tracery, plus straight-headed twin lights to the NE vestry and the clerestory. N porch rebuilt in 1832, reusing the original openings.

The continuous clerestory and arcades, unbroken by any chancel arch, create a strikingly spacious and unified INTERIOR. The only subdivisions are by screens. Arcade piers of standard type throughout, of four shafts and four hollows at the diagonals. The mouldings of the nave S arcade are less elaborate than the rest, and its hoodmould stops are plain shields. On the N side and to the E the shields are held by angels (those over the chancel screen are of the 1840s), except by the font, where a superbly carved head of a king appears. Two statue corbels on the westernmost piers may represent almsmen. The roof rests on figure corbels: grotesques in the nave, more angels with shields in the chancel. E window of five lights. The easternmost arch to the S chapel has painted hoodstops of crowned helmets with unicorn crests over shields with the arms of the Roets and the Chaucers.

The CHAPEL OF ST JOHN is an impressive display of Late Gothic ornament. The altar is flanked by canopied niches and the walls are diapered with the IHS monogram, repainted in 1843 then toned down in the early C20. The monogram is repeated on bosses and shields on the compartmented wooden ceiling, which is enlivened by feather-bodied angels with outspread wings at the intersections. On the N side is the tomb of the Duchess of Suffolk (*see* below), with much carving, painted and gilded; the hoodstops to the arch W of it are heraldic demi-virgins bearing shields.

FURNISHINGS. Stone REREDOS of 1832, unusually including a stone ALTAR. Probably designed by *John Plowman Sen.* (*see* below). – STALLS. 1876. – DOORS to the vestry and N and S porches, all C15, with blind panel tracery. – SCREENS. All C15. Narrow openings with ogee heads and panel tracery. The chancel screen and its continuations exceptionally have iron mullions. Central section lowered in 1844 and restored to original height in 1924. Parclose screens to the side chapels with wooden uprights. – ALTAR in St John's Chapel by *Sir Ninian Comper*, 1904. Frontal and reredos painted with holly scrolls and figures on a gold background. Two riddel-posts with angels supporting candles. – C15 TILES in the chapel, mostly with the Burghersh lion for Alice's mother's family. Also some fragments around the font. – WALL PAINTINGS. The IHS motif of St John's Chapel is continued in restored form around the chancel. – PULPIT and PEWS of 1832, Gothic, by *J. Plowman Sen.* Also PEWS of 1901 in St John's Chapel. – FONT. An octagonal bowl on a buttressed base panelled with blind ogee arches, with a spectacular wooden COVER, 10 ft 6 in. (3.2 metres) high. This was originally plainer, of crocketed fins pierced with cusped arches, stepped back in four stages (cf. Salle, Norfolk). After 1825 the fins were linked with rings of ogee-crested arches. The counterweight is carved with a rose. – STAINED GLASS. Medieval remnants gathered into the chapel E window in 1832. Mostly C15; a few C14 bits, including two heads near the top of the light furthest to the r. Several roundels of heraldic beasts, chiefly lions and yales, originally in the S aisle traceries. Also floral quarries and fragmentary figures of saints, male and female. Shields of arms in the tracery, including Roet (with wheels; for Chaucer) impaling Burghersh, sixth light from the l. – E window, a Crucifixion of 1882 by *Clayton & Bell*.

MONUMENTS. In St John's Chapel, Thomas Chaucer †1434 and Matilda Burghersh, his wife, †1436. Tomb-chest of Purbeck marble, with brass figures, 39 in. and 38 in. (99 and 96 cm.).

Brass inscription band renewed in 1843, with most of the shields around the sides. These have heraldry indicating a date no later than 1438. The tomb must have been relocated not long before, as its N side was originally carved and meant to be seen. – Alice, Duchess of Suffolk †1475. A magnificent installation, filling the first bay between chancel and chapel. Much of the colouring is original, and the carving is of the highest quality. Effigy and tomb-chest of alabaster, probably from a London workshop. She has long aristocratic features, like a horse's, and wears a coronet and simple robes with the Order of the Garter on her l. arm. Pillow supported by four angels, under an exceptionally intricate hexagonal canopy formed from a single block. Angels too under nodding-ogee canopies along both sides of the tomb, robed or feather-bodied, all holding shields. The lower register has traceried openings to show a sculpted female *gisant* or wizened cadaver, only partly covered by its shroud: a grim example of the Late Gothic love of the macabre. On the ceiling over it are paintings of St Mary Magdalene and St John the Baptist with the Lamb. The tomb-chest has been shortened by one bay, so that the uprights second from the E are doubled; done probably because it was too large for the setting when first made. The canopy has canted and panelled sides with bands of blind lozenge tracery, and a deep frieze with half-figures of angels, wings outspread, under a band of quatrefoils and cresting. Four octagonal uprights project from the canopy on each side, bearing wooden figures of angels, again alternately feathered or robed.

Chancel. Catherine Palmer †1599. Brass with kneeling figures. – Henry Howard †1647. An odd little wall monument. A naked figure in a shroud is pulled from an urn by two angels at the Resurrection. – John Howard †1663. Inscription with a little drapery, between columns on lions'-head brackets. Attributed to *Thomas Cartwright I* (GF). – Francis Martyn †1682. A Baroque cartouche with draperies and two swords. Attributed to *William Stanton* (GF). – Nave. Mostly brasses. John Bradstane, rector, †1458. 11⅜-in. (29-cm.) demi-figure. – Henry Morecote, rector, †1467. All but identical. – William Branwhait, master of the hospital, †1495 (S aisle). The same formula; probably an appropriated brass of *c.*1460. – John Spence, also master, †1517. 24-in. (60-cm.) figure. – Thomas Broke †1518 and wife. 29-in. and 27-in. figures (73 and 69 cm.), turning towards each other. – Grenville Hampden †1881, with marble portrait roundel.

GOD'S HOUSE. Founded in 1437 by the Earl and Countess of Suffolk, to house thirteen poor men under the care of a master and two chaplains. Its endowment in 1442 probably gives the completion date. The almshouses are down the slope W of the church, placed at an angle, so that the brick-walled porch and linking passage between meets the church tower at a diagonal. They are one of the earliest English examples to be built on a formal plan around a quadrangle. The outer wall is 84 ft (25.6 metres) square, of plain rubble stone, originally

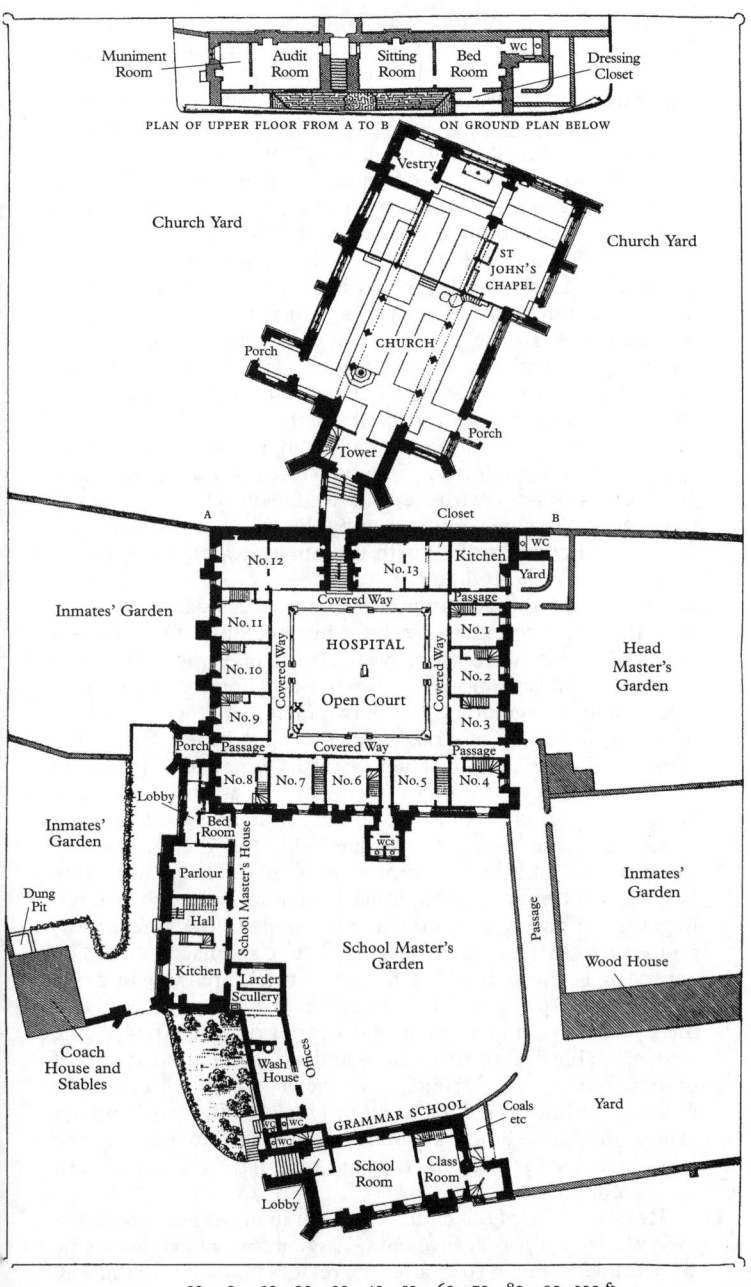

Ewelme, God's House.
Plan by F.T. Dollman, 1858

rendered. Timber framing within, planned mostly in 13-ft or 9-ft (4- or 2.7-metre) units. Brick is the other material, still a rarity in Oxfordshire at this date. Externally it is used as her-ringbone facing for the E wall N of the passage to the church, for the chimneystacks spaced along the N, S and W walls, and for the step-gabled N porch, with its pointed arch and diag-onal buttresses. In the porch gable a large sunken panel with a trefoiled head in moulded brickwork, an ensemble close to work of the same date in Bruges (cf. the brickmaking at Net-tlebed for Stonor in 1416–17, and the employment of Flem-ings there). Internally, brick is used as patterned infill for the framing around the cloister walks, which have posts to carry the tiled roof. In the centre of each side an arched opening under a gable with fretted bargeboards, original on the W side, and three ogee-traceried lights. Much that meets the eye here dates from C19 restoration or from the renovation of 1970. Each dwelling originally comprised a single room plus another in the roof, lit by a dormer. Two full storeys on the E side only, also a cross-passage with steps up to the church entry. On the upper floor the steps are flanked by the master's accommoda-tion, S, and common hall with muniment room, N, under an open roof with braced collars.

SCHOOL, SW of the almshouses. The building dates probably from the 1440s and may have been finished only after Suffolk's murder in 1450. Walls all of brick. Two storeys, with diagonal buttresses and two massive sheer chimney-breasts on the High Street side. Irregularly spaced two-light windows, of stone, with tracery mostly of straight-sided cusped heads. Four label stops are in the form of angels bearing renewed shields. On the N flank a gabled porch of two storeys with the original W door of the church, very worn. Originally there was a balancing attachment with a staircase on the S side. (In the main upper room a fine arch-braced timber roof of six bays and three tiers of wind-braces.) Additional classrooms of 1999 behind. Beyond the porch, a Georgian stone-walled attachment joins on to the former SCHOOLMASTER'S HOUSE, placed E–W. The approach is through a C15 moulded brick archway under a battlemented parapet. The house has a S front probably of the 1770s but retains much mid-C15 fabric, including a fine stepped gable facing the school and an internal structure of timber framing. An L-shaped annexe to the W, with a brick-framed window of one light and original C15 timber doorways inside, links the house to the almshouses. Too big for one schoolmaster, the combined range may have included guest accommodation.

OLD RECTORY, SE of the church. Rebuilt in instalments between the 1760s and 1791–2. Five bays. Large informal extensions by *W.D. Caröe*, added *c.*1927 after the rectory was sold. In the wall towards the church a C15 stone DOORWAY.

MANOR HOUSE, S of the High Street. All that remains of the late medieval palace of the Chaucers and de la Poles is a modest three-bay house of C15 brick, still ending in stepped diagonal buttresses to the r., but now with sash windows and a porch added after 1821. It represents the surviving w end of a lodging range from the outer or base court, shown in its full step-gabled extent in Buck's engraving of 1729. The buttressed end housed the staircase to a timber gallery along the front, for access to the separate chambers of the upper storey. (Roof of five bays, those over the former staircase with two tiers of wind-braces.) It probably belongs with enlargements of the 1430s–40s by Alice Chaucer and the Earl of Suffolk. In the C16 the house was sometimes used by Henry VIII.* Reported as in poor repair in 1612, it was mostly demolished soon after.

VILLAGE. Several prosperous houses of the late C17 to early C18. Opposite the school, FORD'S FARMHOUSE is of limestone rubble with brick dressings, perhaps late C17; the windows not yet symmetrically placed. A good retinue of farm buildings behind, including a converted C18 BARN of nine bays. In Parson's Lane w of the church, SAFFRON HOUSE. Mid-Georgian, of two phases. Chequered brick. FIELDS END beyond, flint-walled with brick dressings, betrays much reconfiguring of the windows. Between these two is MOUNT HOUSE, an original and well-composed design of 2011 by *Pippa Nissen*. Red brick. A low single-storey entrance links two unequal pavilions, pyramid-roofed, with recessed gutters in place of eaves. To the w is MEAD HOUSE by *Ivor Smith*, then of *Morton, Lupton & Smith*, designed 1965; angled extension also by *Nissen* (then of *Nissen Adams*), 2004–6. Near the corner of Parson's Lane and High Street, a former WESLEYAN CHAPEL of 1826. Simple pedimented front. Going w, SUFFOLK HOUSE by the stream comprises additional dwellings for the almshouse foundation, 1976–7. Then WATERCRESS COTTAGES and WATERFRONT COTTAGES, 1880s. Four houses each, with cheerfully approximate Gothic detail. The same design appears at Chinnor (q.v.).

OLD MILL HOUSE, Brook Street, 250 yds further w. Hidden within late C19 additions and re-casing is a late C15 hall house of three bays. (Raised-cruck trusses.)

EWELME DOWN HOUSE, 1½ m. SE. Romantically placed on the wooded scarp. Of 1905 by *Walter Cave* for Frank Lawson, son of a co-owner of the *Daily Telegraph*. Plain Neo-Elizabethan, of stone. Three gables to the w. Midway along the entrance front, N, a broad castellated tower like a northern pele. (Panelled interiors in C16 and early C17 styles, freely interpreted. – 200 yds E, a large MOTOR HOUSE on the pattern of a stable courtyard, with upstairs accommodation for the chauffeurs. Rendered and Voyseyesque.)

EWELME PARK, 2 m. SE. *See* Swyncombe.

---

*Leland described it in 1542: 'the base court of it is fair and is buildid of bryke and tymbre. The inner part of the house is set with in a fair mote, and is buildid richly of brike and stone. The haul [hall] of it is fair and hath great barres of iren overthu-art it instede of crosse beams.'

COTTESMORE FARM, ¾ m. WNW. One BARN has been tree-ring dated 1602. Up the lane, AMERICA FARM is a white Neo-Regency house of 2013–16 by *Nichols Brown Webber*, for India Hicks and David Flint Wood. It replaced farm cottages by *Erith & Terry*, 1971–2.

5000

GARSINGTON

On a hill 1 m. SE of the Oxford outskirts, with fine views to the S.

ST MARY. The W tower is Transitional work of *c.*1200. Plain parapet with corbel table. Pointed twin bell-openings with a roll moulding and jamb shafts with carved capitals, now much weathered. Small round-headed windows in the middle stage. The W window of the ground stage also has a round head, set in a pointed relieving arch carried on slender shafts. Flat clasping buttresses. Inside, the tower arch is almost fully developed E.E., of one order, with a big keeled roll moulding, a fillet and a hollow. The capitals of the jamb shafts are still Transitional, with square abaci; stiff upright leaves on the S, embryo stiff-leaf on the N. The N aisle is E.E., but its richly moulded N doorway and the parapet gargoyles belong with *Joseph Clarke*'s restoration of 1848–9. N arcade with round piers, moulded capitals and double-chamfered arches. Dec S aisle, with a restored S doorway and a Victorian porch. Arcade with octagonal piers, E window of three lights with flowing tracery. PISCINA alongside. The side windows in both aisles are also Dec, of two ogee lights under a square head, as are the clerestory windows in the form of foiled circles. *Clarke* reinstated the chancel arch responds, matching those of the N arcade. The chancel is entirely of *c.*1290–*c.*1300 (a papal indulgence of 1291 may relate to its rebuilding). Plain Y-tracery in the side windows, intersecting in the E window. The SW and NW windows extend below a transom to form lowside windows, and the sill of the SE window is dropped to form SEDILIA. Integral PISCINA with a trefoiled arch.

FURNISHINGS. Medieval ALTAR SLAB. – REREDOS of carved wood, with Crucifixion. By *James Rogers & Sons*, 1912. – PULPIT. 1849. Leaf carving by *George Jarrett*. – FONT, *c.*1845. A more ornamented version of the E.E. font at Weston, Lincs. – SCREEN in the tower arch. C15, moved from the chancel arch and reduced. Six traceried openings remain, now glazed. – STAINED GLASS. E window, high-quality work of 1862 by *Clayton & Bell* from St Giles, Oxford (p.393), moved here in 1894. Heraldic shields of 1845 in the chancel side windows by *I.H. Russell* of Oxford. Tower, a good *ex situ* panel (Aaron) of *c.*1850, early C13 style. – MONUMENTS. In the chancel floor a slab with the indent of a foliated cross and remains of an inscription, interpreted as 'Isabele de Fortibus gis ici:

Deus de sa alme eyt merci' (Isabel de Fortibus lies here: may God have mercy on her soul). She died in 1293 but is buried elsewhere. – Brass to Thomas Radley †1484 and wife. 9-in. and 9½-in. figures (23 and 24 cm.), plus groups of children. – Lady Ottoline Morrell, a late work by *Eric Gill*, 1939. Profile relief between pilasters. Hopton Wood stone.

OLD RECTORY, set back opposite the churchyard entrance. 1872 by *F. Codd*. Yellow brick, of North Oxford aspect. By the road a Perp-style DOORWAY, probably from improvements of 1827 to the previous rectory by *Daniel Harris & J. Plowman Sen.* for James Ingram, rector and also President of Trinity College, Oxford.

OLD SCHOOL, The Green, W side. A model building of 1840–1 by *H.J. Underwood*. It cost some £1,500. Matching girls' and boys' schoolrooms, linked by the house for the master and mistress. Tudor style with stone slates, exaggerated chimney-stacks and a cupola. *p.571*

GARSINGTON MANOR, Southend, S of the church. Exceptional among the county's early C17 manor houses for its sophisticated planning and elevations, and also celebrated as the home between 1915 and 1928 of Philip and Lady Ottoline Morrell. The house and its gardens feature in the recollections of numerous guests from that period, people who were often illustrious or otherwise gifted, if not all grateful or appreciative; others cherished their time at Garsington, a stimulating retreat that was also 'a habitable work of art' (Juliette Huxley).

The house was built on an older site for William Wickham, probably in the 1630s. Its motifs echo Oxford college work of the period, of which Richard Maude's rebuilding of University College (1634 onwards) offers the closest match. That applies to the running hoodmoulds and arch-headed lights – old-fashioned for houses by the 1630s – and also to the pronounced symmetry of the main fronts, N, S and E. The N front faces the road, flanked by dark yew hedges as high as the house and forming a small courtyard with the low front wall and handsome late C17 gateway. Two storeys, plus big gabled attic dormers. Mullioned windows in the pattern 3:2:1:2:3 above. The same below, excepting the central doorway with its late C17 stone hood on ornamental brackets. In the middle the pointed top of a roof turret. To the garden, S, the first-floor window pattern is 3:1:1:1:1:3, the ground floor 4:1:1:1:4, with a basement storey below. On the E front between the big chimneystacks it is 2:1:2, and the hoodmould skips up above an oval overdoor window lighting a former passage between the N and S rooms. The short two-storey additions flanking the N front may be late C17 or early C18, likewise the two-storey SW addition, all with matching windows. Further E is an arcaded LOGGIA and terrace by *Philip Tilden*, added for the Morrells in 1925–6.

INTERIORS. The N doorway now opens into the Hall, where there must have been an entrance passage originally. The lateral E–W passage has also largely gone, and the HALL to the l. has seen much alteration. To the r. is the DINING ROOM, which must be the original kitchen, judging by the plain fireplace with its wide arch. To the W the lateral passage ends at the main STAIRCASE, a dog-leg with turned balusters and newel posts with square finials. The first two flights have a continuous newel in the form of an Ionic column. Two parlour rooms to the S, of which the OAK ROOM to the SW has C17 panelling – painted Venetian red with gold lining in the Morrells' day – and an original fireplace. Between the parlours was a back stair, intact only from the first floor upwards. From the upper cross-landing a separate stair climbs to the timber-framed ROOF TURRET, which opens to a viewing platform within the roof ridges. Could the turret, and the dormer gables too, be late C17 alterations? In the SW extension, the upper room is fitted up as a STUDY with pilastered bookshelves, probably part of *F. E. Openshaw*'s refurbishments of 1915.

The beautiful GARDENS were designed by *Lady Ottoline Morrell*, inspired partly by her aunt's gardens at Villa Capponi near Florence. Below the lawn to the S of the house is a large oblong POOL (regularized from an old fish pond), enclosed by clipped yew hedges and set about with classical statues. Another statue reclines on the central island platform. By the pool's edge is a small classical PAVILION of timber, brought from the Morrells' previous house at Rotherfield Peppard (q.v.). The kitchen garden E of the house and loggia became a formal FLOWER GARDEN of small box-hedge compartments.

To the W of the house a BAKEHOUSE with two open fireplaces, C17 and C18. To the E, downhill from the flower garden, is a square, hip-roofed DOVECOTE with the internal date 1714.

The VILLAGE has some C20 sprawl but good older houses also remain, including several former Oxford college farmhouses. N of the main crossing is the octagonal base of a medieval CROSS on three stone steps, and near it the WAR MEMORIAL of 1922, a stone cross probably by *H. S. Rogers* (cf. Stadhampton). To the NW, OXFORD ROAD has LIBRARY FARMHOUSE, C16, of stone, with a central cruck-truss. In the rear wall a re-set C17 oval opening. THE OLD KENNELS (No. 30) is a distinctive late C17 house built of alternating bands of ashlar and squared rubble. Four irregular bays, the end gables with ball finials. In PETTI-WELL to the SW, PETTIWELL HOUSE (No. 15) is C16–C17, of regular timber framing. LANESRA COTTAGE (No. 21) has late medieval cruck framing in the l. part, and THE MALT-HOUSE (No. 22) includes a C17 maltings range behind. SOUTHEND, to the SE, has two three-bay early C18 farmhouses, MANOR FARMHOUSE (No. 4), with a square DOVE-COTE dated 1762, and HOME CLOSE just beyond the Manor, with a timber-framed GRANARY by the road. ¼ m. beyond, SEVEN BELLS COTTAGE (No. 93), set end-on. Late C16 or C17, thatched and mostly timber-framed, with a wooden-mullioned window in the ground-floor stone facing on the N side.

GORING

Attractively situated amid the wooded hills of the Goring Gap, where the Thames slips through between the Chilterns to the E and the Berkshire Downs to the w. The river was first bridged here in 1837. Three years later the Great Western main line arrived, but the village remained small until the later C19, when big villas began to proliferate. Many of these have been replaced since the 1960s by tidy enclaves of terraced houses, and more run-of-the-mill C20 housing has also spilled w and NW, taking in the upstream hamlet of Cleeve. The river crossing with its lock and weir preserves much of its picture-postcard appeal in the early C21.

St Thomas of Canterbury. Probably the successor to an Anglo-Saxon minster, which would account for the large curving enclosure within which the church sits. By 1135 the parish church was shared with a priory of Augustinian nuns, and the present building is likely to date from not long before that time. It consists of a big w tower, a tall and originally aisleless nave, and a chancel with an apsidal E end. The present apse is a reinstatement on the original foundations, the early C12 apse having been replaced c.1180 by a separate church for the nuns. This had N and s walls in line with the existing nave, and a straight E end 96 ft (29.3 metres) from the springing of the present apse. A wall with a small doorway in it was built to divide the two churches, and this lasted until *Benjamin Courser* returned the E end to its original form in his restoration of 1887–8.

The tower is of three C12 stages, with a short Perp upper bell-stage and a later parapet. The C12 bell-openings have double arches divided by octagonal shafts with volute capitals. w doorway with an unusually high arch with two orders of roll mouldings on jamb shafts with cushion capitals. Much of it, including the cross in the tympanum, must date from *Wyatt & Brandon*'s interventions of 1847–8, when a house attached on this side was taken down. NW stair-turret, changing from square to round for its upper stages. It has a stone cap, small circular windows at the top, and a round-arched lancet below. Adjoining it on the N side of the tower is a shallow C12 lean-to of unknown purpose, which reaches the sill of the bell-openings. It has another circular window and a small lancet, shafted inside. Was this addition also provided for the priory? Certainly there were priory buildings attached to the s and w walls of the tower, as shown by the rough blocked openings at upper-storey level there. In the ground stage of the tower a cross-vault with ribs of double-roll section, on angle shafts with cushion capitals. The arch to the nave is impressive, of particularly massive members: a giant roll moulding, big imposts, responds with cushion capitals with cable necking.

The nave was of four bays with windows set high. These remain intact on the S side, above corbels which supported the roof of the former cloister. Around 1200 a N aisle was built, roofed continuously with the nave, so that three of the C12 windows here survive only internally. A fourth remains entire to the E. Arcade of triple-chamfered arches on powerful short round piers with moulded capitals and bases. C14 Dec aisle windows and N doorway, C14 or C15 N porch. The N organ chamber is of 1887–8, reusing as its N window the former three-light E window of the aisle, Dec, with cusped intersecting tracery. Thin nave roof probably of 1847–8. In 1937 *T. Lawrence Dale* added the arcading around the apse wall inside, and in 2008–9 the church was reordered by *Acanthus Clews*. Their CHURCH ROOM along the nave S side uses traditional materials – oak boarding, lime-rendered panels – but the contrast is still jolting.

FURNISHINGS. ROOD SCREEN of 1909–10 by *Percy Stone*, the figures carved by *Nicholls Bros.* – PULPIT, chief survival of the 1888 fittings. – FONT. A plain C12 cylinder. Scalloped base of 1937 designed by *Bernard Miller* of Liverpool, COVER carved by *Alan Durst*. – BELL, nave W wall. Late C13, signed by the Essex bell-founder *Richard de Wymbish*. – STAINED GLASS. Apse E and N aisle N windows both by *Hardman*, 1888. – MONUMENTS. Brass to Elizabeth Shilford †1401, chancel wall. Effigy of 22½ in. (57 cm.), with netted headdress. Canopy and marginal inscription. – William Whistler(?) and wife, *c.* 1600–5. Detached brasses, nave wall. – Mary Higgs †1770. Cherubs, skull and hourglass in low relief framing the inscription.

PRIORY. Percy Stone's excavations in 1892 showed that the nuns' church was transeptal, and located the foundations of the cloister, 86 ft (26 metres) square, S of the nave. On its E side was the dormitory range, with vestry, chapter house and parlour on the ground floor. Foundations of the refectory range were found adjacent to the S wall of the churchyard. The medieval range that joined on to the W of the tower has been plausibly interpreted as the prioress's lodging.

WAR MEMORIAL in the churchyard, a stepped cross designed by *G.F. Turner*, 1921. To the E a C17 LYCHGATE with a queen-post roof.

OUR LADY AND ST JOHN (R.C.), Ferry Lane. 1897–8 by *William Ravenscroft*; nave completed 1938. Red brick, stone dressings. Small octagonal NE tower, the base of which forms a chapel. Twin Gothic windows in the E and W walls, straight-headed cusped windows along the sides. The interior is effective: exposed brickwork and a brick chancel arch, white-painted coving, boarded wagon roof. Attached hall, W, 2021. – STAINED GLASS. All *Hardman*, 1898, 1938 and (N chapel) 1951.

FREE CHURCH, corner of Manor Road. *J.O. Cooper & W.R. Howell*'s church of 1893 is of red brick, in domestic style, on an irregular plan, with half-timbered gables. Attached behind is the former meeting house of the Countess of Huntingdon's

Connexion, 1793, unsympathetically re-windowed by the Victorians. Plain MANSE of 1823 at the back.

PRIMARY SCHOOL, Wallingford Road, Cleeve, ½ m. NE. 1959–60 by *Hilton Wright Associates*, extended 1967–8. Of lightweight timber construction, with a square cross-gabled hall.

BRIDGE. Rebuilt 1922–3. Of reinforced concrete (*Kahn* system) with oak braces and railings; meant to preserve 'as far as possible' the appearance of the timber trestle bridge of 1837. Two parts, spanning to an island. Designed jointly by the County Surveyors of Oxon and Berks., respectively *A.E. Cockerton* and *Lieut-Col. J.F. Hawkins*.

VILLAGE. The MILL stands just S of the bridge. Largely C18 brick, with C19 and C20 alterations. The mill-race section appears to have been rebuilt in connection with the adjacent WEIR of 1937, which is of the 'paddle and rymer' type unique to the Thames. The LOCK to the N retains its KEEPER'S HOUSE of 1879. By the bridge on the N side of HIGH STREET is the former BOATHOUSE of the boat-builder Samuel Saunders, 1894 by *Percy Stone*, with a big half-circular entrance. On the S side beyond is the VILLAGE HALL of 1900, also by *Stone*. Red brick, with a steeply pitched roof and clock turret with small flying buttresses. On the N side at the corner opposite the Free Church, the picturesque MILLER OF MANSFIELD HOTEL. C18 brick with two-storey canted bay windows added, and an informal extension to the r. by *W. Ravenscroft*, 1899. The adjacent GLEBE COTTAGE, l., is C17 and of flint, cross-gabled, with ogee-hooded Georgian Gothick windows and brick extension.

From here MANOR ROAD curves round SW to the mid-C17 OLD VICARAGE. Probably brick, now roughcast. Symmetrical front with three small tile-hung gables and a two-storey porch, the entrance with a square hood. Replacement VICARAGE to the S, 1984–6 by *D.T. Rathbone*, with historical touches. Behind and facing towards the churchyard are LYBBE'S ALMSHOUSES. A later inscription dates them to 1714, but they were finished only *c.*1725. Two storeys, plain brick, casement windows. Originally four dwellings, combined as two in 1967. Manor Road turns E into STATION ROAD, where the CATHERINE WHEEL INN is probably late C17. Timber-framed in part, with a flint and brick C18 forge incorporated on the road side. Opposite is the little TEMPERANCE HALL of 1878, now the library, and to the E the former SCHOOL of 1855 and later, now the community centre. The OLD FARMHOUSE, reportedly dated 1809, is a tall brick box with a Doric porch and arched tops to the sash panes.

Other HOUSES of note stand further to the S or N. Off the S part of Manor Road, THE GRANGE is a *ci-devant* example of the Thames-side monster villa, 1919 by *W.R. Howell*. N of High Street in Thames Road is ORIEL HOUSE, dated 1906. An enjoyable compendium of Free Style motifs and materials. Giant arched wooden door hood, sloping buttresses, flat-topped bay windows, and a tile-arched garden loggia. THE PAVILION to the N is by the *Nash Partnership*, 2019–22. Long and low, of black weatherboarding, with a flint-faced bulge for the staircase. In Cleeve Road to the E is REST HARROW by *W. Ravenscroft*, 1884–8 and later. The sites of similar late C19 mansions are represented by low-rise private enclaves such as GLEBE RIDE to the E, designed in 1975 by *Ernest Chew & Associates*. The best Edwardian group remaining is on the heights of Icknield Road (LANGTON LODGE, FERREBY etc.), pebbledashed and inventively composed, with steep shelving roofs; all *T. W. Cutler* of London, 1906–7. Also INCURVO, a powerful and original house designed by *Adrian James Architects*, 2013–16. Irregular and almost wholly curved in plan, of warm orange-red brick with some ribbed black panelling.

CLEEVE MILL, Cleeve Road, ½ m. NNE. Partly C17, with obvious contributions from its domestic conversion some time after 1887.

ELVENDON PRIORY, 1¾ m. ENE. Never a priory. W front of flint and stone, three gables, with a narrow higher block to the S. Mostly plain mullioned windows of late C16 or C17 pattern, but also two apparently of the C15 or early C16 on the ground floor, with three arched cusped lights: *in situ*, or re-set? The house deserves a detailed survey, as it is possible that the present large hall to the r. of the entrance was the hall of a medieval house with the solar to the S. Around 1910 the 4th Earl of Cottenham added a stair enclosure at the back and a wing at right angles to the W front, forming an L-plan. Stained glass of 1926–7 to the staircase by *T. W. Camm* of Birmingham.

GATEHAMPTON MANOR, 1 m. SE. The timber-framed NE wing is probably late C16, the rest C17 but made regular in the late C18 (scratched date 1780). S extensions and porch *c.* 1900. Late C17 BARN to the NW.

RAILWAY BRIDGE, Gatehampton, 1 m. SE. *Brunel* carried the Great Western main line across the Thames here in 1838–40. Four elliptical arches, duplicated in widening of 1891–2.

GORING HEATH

Scattered settlement on the high land E of Goring.

ALMSHOUSES. Founded by Henry Allnutt, Lord Mayor of London, and built in 1725–6. A lettered panel formerly inside the chapel lantern (now in the chapel) names *James Breach* as carpenter, *Moses Avery* as bricklayer. The almshouses stand back in a woodland setting, approached along a short avenue. One-storey dwellings, originally numbering twelve, around three sides of a courtyard. The fourth side is closed by a low wall with a contemporary wrought-iron gate, the gateposts with wooden obelisk finials. The centrepiece is the chapel, which has a shaped gable of silver-grey and red brick with stone acorns. It bears an inscription and a clock. The lower part is of good rubbed red brick with four pilasters and a moulded cornice. Two tall narrow windows flank the doorway, which has a wooden hood on carved brackets. On the roof a lantern with an ogee cupola and weathervane. The almshouses have steeply pitched roofs, the gable-ends again flanked by stone acorns. Silver-grey brick walls with red brick dressings. Cross-windows throughout. The chapel retains the original two-decker PULPIT and COMMUNION RAILS, also modified PEWS. On either side of the apse, BUSTS of Henry Alnutt and his executor Richard Clement, the latter of plaster.

ALLNUTT HOUSE, to the r., was built for the chaplain in 1742. Small and formal, with banded brick quoins and side doorway, deep parapet and hipped dormers.

SCHOOLS, to the l. Of 1878, enlarged in 1894 by *Joseph Morris*; 'a horrible parody of the style of the almshouses' (Jennifer Sherwood, 1974). Converted for almshouses 1989.

POST OFFICE (former), at the crossing 300 yds SE. Built c.1900. With steep roofs and much tile-hanging, and originally weatherboarding too.

ABBOT'S TOWER, ¼ m. NE of the almshouses, on the B4526. A slim brick water tower of 1902, circular and with a witch's-hat roof. Now part of a house.

THE ORATORY PREPARATORY SCHOOL, 1 m. WNW. The main building is GREAT OAKS, of 1914 by *Frank Pearson* for F. G. Lomax. Very large, composed freely around a courtyard. Brick, stone, and close-studded half-timbering. The Oratory (*see* Woodcote) took over in 1970 from an R.C. girls' school; the CHAPEL projecting at the SW corner, with a windowless end wall, is by *Lassetter & Judd*, c.1959.

WHITE ACRES, Cold Harbour, 1½ m. WNW. An early work by *Philip Dowson*, 1958. A simple design of some authority. To the lane a blank brick wall. In it a doorway to a small courtyard or patio, with the central living-room block directly opposite. It has a pyramid roof with wide eaves projecting over a clerestory. The garden front is half glass, half brick. Flanking the centre are the bedrooms and offices, altered and extended in the C21.

FLINT HOUSE, 2 m. WNW. A large house by *Ernest Newton*, built in 1913 for F.N. Garrard. The architect's son W.G. Newton called it 'a harmonious summary of much of the work of the previous thirty years'. Flint and stone in minimal Tudor style, symmetrically composed on an elongated H-plan, with small windows and brick chimneys irregularly placed. Two-storey porch with a little patterning of the flint, ashlared canted bay on the r. gable-end. The central axis has another canted bay on the garden front. An open-well staircase is placed alongside this axis, and a cross-axis of corridors runs along the s side of both floors. The service wing, E, has been subsumed in *Broadway & Malyan*'s additions of 1986–8 for the POLICE REHABILITATION CENTRE. Other extensions and large additions followed by *Bickerdike Allen Partners* from 1994, in a broadly similar style. Newton's formal GARDENS are largely lost. [105]

WHITCHURCH HILL. *See* Whitchurch-on-Thames.

GREAT HASELEY

St Peter. An impressive church for a small village, with many fine details, especially of the C13 and C14. Mid-C15 W tower of three stages, with a rich re-set doorway of *c.* 1200, the chief external evidence of the earliest phase. It has a pointed arch with three orders of keeled roll moulding and a band of dog-tooth. The jamb shafts have stiff-leaf capitals and the whole is almost full E.E. style, except for the Transitional square abaci. Re-set S doorway of matching style and quality, but of two orders. High tower arch to the nave, which has three-bay arcades of *c.* 1200, again good examples of the Transition from Norman to E.E. The pointed arches with keeled roll mouldings and thin running hoodmoulds are more advanced, but the flat soffits, the large square projecting abaci, and the capitals, some with flat upright leaves, others with a weak version of stiff-leaf, are still Norman (cf. Christ Church Cathedral, p. 122). A fourth bay to the E on both sides is C14 and has an arch of two chamfered orders and irregular six-sided piers. Yet the chancel arch has details of the same period as the arcades – two orders of keeled roll moulding on square abaci, capitals with sprigged leaves, corbels with a band of dogtooth – so it is hard to say what these eastern nave bays may have replaced. C15 clerestory and nave roof. The entire chancel, Early Dec work of very high quality, must have been built by the unknown benefactor whose elaborate tomb recess is in the S wall. Merton College chapel (1290–7; *see* p. 201) was clearly the inspiration, for the great E window especially, and the absence of ogees in any of the details suggests a date not long after 1300. The E window is of five lights under sub-arches organized 2:1:2, and has a rose in the head enclosing three cusped spherical triangles. N and S windows of uniform design, of two cusped lights with an elongated trefoil above, and a quatrefoil in the head between. Over the windows inside is a continuous hood, and above this a frieze of ballflower and vine scroll. Blocked lowside window with a trefoiled head.

Along the S wall are the SEDILIA, PISCINA and TOMB RECESS, *en suite*. All have refined cusped arches divided by pinnacles, and over two sedilia arches are gables with sharp-pointed cresting and finials. The tomb recess is likewise unusual in its detail, with cresting above the arch and deeply undercut cusping below, modelled at the points to form a series of trefoils. Squints to both aisles from the W corners of the chancel. The S aisle has a three-light E window with spherical-triangle tracery, i.e. the style of the chancel, but also some elaborate Dec details of slightly later character, including a PISCINA with a nodding-ogee head under a crocketed arch with side pinnacles on head corbels. Along the E window sill is the battlemented cresting of the original reredos. Image niche with crocketed canopy on the E wall between, little ogee-headed niche to the W. Further W is a row of three TOMB

RECESSES with cinquefoiled arches, the cusps indented. Two s windows with simplified tracery of C17 type. C14 N aisle with doorway and flowing Dec windows to the w, Perp windows to the E. On the E wall inside two moulded image brackets, to the N a four-centred-arched TOMB RECESS of the C15, with mutilated pinnacles at the sides and apex. A later addition is the mortuary chapel of *c.* 1710 on the chancel N side. Originally of brick, it was refaced probably in *J.M. Derick*'s pioneering restoration of 1840–1 onwards for the Oxford Society for Promoting the Study of Gothic Architecture. The tracery of the C14 window opening from the chancel was also reinstated then. In 1897 *Thomas Garner* restored the chancel, with red and white marble paving. s aisle roof restored 1901–3 with *Bodley* as consultant.

FURNISHINGS. ALTAR of the 1930s by *Geoffrey Webb*, richly adorned. – STALLS by *Garner*, 1897. – PULPIT. Hexagonal, each panel carved with a cartouche, i.e. *c.* 1630–40. The legs look late C19. – PEWS of 1840–1, copied by *Derick* from some medieval survivals. – TILES on the walls in the w part of the s aisle, C13–C14. – IRONWORK. Two early C-strap hinges on the s door. – FONT. A plain C12 tub. – STAINED GLASS. Tree of Jesse, E, and other chancel windows all by *Hardman*, 1853–4. Several by *C.A. Gibbs* in the aisles and tower, 1872–5. Transfiguration window (s aisle E), and N aisle N by *Burlison & Grylls*, 1906. Also a s window by *G. Webb*, 1927, and N aisle E by *Stewart Bowman*, 2000. – BRASSES. Thomas Butler †1444, chancel. 18-in. (45-cm.) figure. – William Leynthall †1497, s aisle. 19-in. (48-cm.) figure in a shroud. – Mary Huddleston †1581, nave. 18-in. (45-cm.) figure with five children. – MONUMENTS. C13 slab with a foliated cross, introduced to the chancel tomb recess. – Effigy of a knight in chain-mail, sword drawn and legs crossed. C13. – A second, similar effigy, badly mutilated. – Sir William Barentin. Early C16 tomb-chest, now in the N aisle. Side panels carved with cusped lozenges enclosing shields. – George Blackall †1709, in the mortuary chapel. By *John Piddington I* of Oxford. Exuberant Baroque with a podgy bust beneath trumpeting cherubs on a pediment. A remarkably accomplished production by a local sculptor. – Lieut. Roger Gelderd-Somervell †1915. Bronze plaque with portrait roundel by *Hamo Thornycroft*.

MANOR HOUSE, NW of the church. A late C17 H-plan house, identifiable from a dispute of 1680–1 between two Oxford master builders, the mason *Thomas Wood* and the carpenter *Richard Frogley*, as the house at Haseley on which they had lately worked for 'Esquire Lenthall' (William Lenthall, †1702).* Banded ashlar and rubble stone, as at Wood and Frogley's lost Cuddesdon Palace of 1679–80. Tuscan doorcase with a segmental pediment. The cornice breaks into a pediment above. Elaborate dormer windows with pediments and side scrolls, added after 1816. The l. wing was rebuilt for Thomas Blackall

* *See* Catherine Cole in *Oxoniensia* 24 (1959).

around 1770–80 with three full storeys, also of banded stone-work. Long service wing added to the E. (Early C17 open-well stair, apparently brought in, with a flat strapwork balustrade. In the dining room a late C17 marble fireplace with a swagged frieze and side scrolls. The late C18 interiors have enriched cornices and doorcases, and a fireplace with a relief panel by *William Collins*.) The fine GARDENS in front are of 2009–10 to designs by *Christopher Bradley-Hole*, for Julian and Brooke Metcalfe. A broad pool is set lengthwise to the house, and new gates in traditional style breach the wall by the church path. A clairvoie opposite extends the vista some 70 yds to the S, with an avenue edged by block-like hedges arranged in right angles.

The former STABLE BLOCK E of the house is mid-Georgian, two-storeyed, with a pediment. Four Venetian windows on the ground floor, another in the centre of the first floor. To its S a pyramid-roofed outbuilding, possibly a converted C17 dovecote.

TITHE BARN, E of the stables. Built in 1313. Of stone, but-tressed all round, with a half-hipped roof. High gabled porch with a double-hollow-chamfered segmental arch; on its l. side another small doorway. Six bays remain of the original nine, the W end having been taken down in 1811. Of the aisled timber structure within, two bays preserve the C14 form, an unusual combination of base crucks and arched braces, with added timbers from repairs of 1811. The three E bays were replaced in 1495–6, with queen-strut trusses and curved wind-braces. The barn belongs with CHURCH FARM to the S; main house by *Stephen Mattick*, *c.* 1998, in Cotswold manor style.

OLD RECTORY, Rectory Road. Rebuilt in 1846 by *G. G. Scott* for the Rev. William Birkett, on a grand scale. Irregular plan, with a two-bay loggia at the E entrance and a gabled S projection with a canted bay. Square-headed windows with cusped lights, late C14 or C15 style, some said to be medieval and reused. The C15 hall roof from the previous rectory was incorporated at the NE (arch-braced trusses, two tiers of arched wind-braces).

The VILLAGE is attractive, the older houses mostly of rubble, several still thatched. Of the timber-framed houses, the most interesting is CROWN HOUSE in Thame Road, w of the Manor House. A tight U-shape with stone-faced ends, the wings apparently an addition, but yielding the same tree-ring dates of 1448–50 throughout. It may represent the reconstruction of a longer galleried range, as suggested by David Clark. In Rectory Road, S side, CRUCKS is a two-bay house of the mid C16, one cruck-truss exposed to the E. It faces CHURCH FARMHOUSE, early C18, of three full storeys. To its l., THE FARM has an unusually large GRANARY by the road, dated 1762. Further w is SUNDIAL HOUSE, early C18, with Baroque giant pilasters at the ends and a blind niche above the doorway. Victorian two-light windows and porch. 300 yds w is MILL LANE, an especially pretty cluster of thatched cottages, C16 to C18.

LATCHFORD HOUSE, ¾ m. E. The N–S range is C16, timber-framed, with to the E a four-centred-arched doorway and part of a jetty. C17 cross-range of stone, S. C18–C19 additions to the N.

WINDMILL, ½ m. NW. A large tower mill of stone, restored in 2013–14 with an ogee cap and four sails. Dated to 1760 by the SPAB, to the early C19 by the *Victoria County History* (date-stone of 1806).

NORTH WESTON MANOR, 3¼ m. NE. *See* Thame, p. 752.

GREAT MILTON

6000

A large village with an unusually full complement of manorial and prebendal houses.

ST MARY, Church Road. A substantial aisled church dating from the C12 to *c.* 1400. The thorough restoration of 1850 by *G. G. Scott* found evidence of damage by fire in the early C14, after which the nave had been largely rebuilt.* The aisles and storeyed S porch are entirely of this date, but the C13 arcades survived the fire, and there is also visible Norman fabric. In the chancel N wall is a tiny round-headed C12 lancet; a matching blocked lancet is in the S wall opposite. The chancel was remodelled in the early C13: there is a tall lancet in the S wall, and the chancel arch is E.E. The chancel appears to have been extended in the early C14, with two-light Dec side windows and a four-light E window with dagger tracery patterns; this extension mostly rebuilt in facsimile by *Scott*. Reused in the N aisle is an elaborate C13 doorway. It has a sharply pointed arch of highly complex roll-and-hollow mouldings, on five orders of shafts with stiff-leaf capitals. The windows in this aisle are all Dec and of the early C14 rebuilding. The S aisle has more elaborate windows of the same period, with reticulated tracery; its E window makes play with major and minor reticulations. Also one three-light S window with unencircled trefoils in the tracery, a throwback to late Geometrical patterns. Canopied image niches on the buttresses and on the octagonal stair-turret of the porch, which has a rib-vault with a central boss. S doorway with characteristic early C14 wave mouldings. Big but plain W tower with early Perp detail and a plain parapet, plausibly the work at the church for which a papal indulgence was granted in 1398.

Inside, the outlines of two blocked Norman windows in the spandrels of the N arcade suggest that the C12 church was aisleless. The westernmost bay of the S arcade is Transitional work of *c.* 1200 with a simple chamfered arch. The other aisle bays must be a few decades later, with round piers and fully moulded arches with roll mouldings; they may have been

---

*Some moulded stones from the C14 parts proved to have burnt C13 mouldings on the reverse.

altered after the fire, as the mouldings and capitals are not uniform. One mystery is the presence of what look like reused sections of cylindrical piers at the springing of the arches, facing the aisles. The head of a woman in a C14 square head-dress is carved on the E respond of the S arcade. C14 clerestory windows in the form of quatrefoils. Perp window over the chancel arch, to the l. of which is a rood-loft doorway. In 1592 the nave roof was repaired or partially renewed (date on the E tie-beam). Perp-style SEDILIA of 1851 by *Scott*, based on original fragments. Further E is a C14 square-headed PISCINA cutting into an earlier one, which looks C13. In the chancel N wall a recess containing a circular bowl, thought to be an ACOUSTIC JAR placed to increase the resonance of music. Elaborate DOUBLE PISCINA in the S aisle, also by *Scott*, again derived from recovered fragments.

FURNISHINGS. REREDOS of 1875. Designed by *A.W. Blom-field*, figures carved by *Earp*. – Two standing CANDELABRA of brass, 1897. – STALLS designed by *Scott*, based on those at Dorchester (q.v.). They incorporate two C15 BENCH-ENDS, one carved with a chalice and two cruets. – C14 TILES by the chancel arch. – CREED and LORD'S PRAYER on boards by the chancel arch, and ROYAL ARMS in the N aisle, all painted in 1958 by *Janet Truda Lenton*, directed by *E. Clive Rouse*: a curious revival of Georgian conventions. – PULPIT. Given in 1640, but looking Jacobean. – Plain FONT, C12 or C13. – STAINED GLASS. E window by *Willement*, 1852. Chancel side windows, Prophets, Apostles and a Tree of Jesse. Style of *Heaton & Butler* with figures by *J.R. Clayton* of *Clayton & Bell*, c.1858–9, from when these firms shared a studio (MH and PC). N aisle E window with early C14 narrative scenes in two tracery lights, death of Lazarus (l.) and Lazarus begging (r.); main lights by *Heaton, Butler & Bayne*, 1915. W windows: N aisle by *O'Connor*, 1868; tower by *Hardman*, c.1855–60; S aisle by *Charles Castell*, c.1850–5. S aisle S, panel by *M. Farrar Bell*, 1957.

MONUMENTS. N aisle, two slabs with finely carved foliate crosses; late C13 or C14. – S aisle. Fragments of a C14 effigy. – Brass to the children of Robert and Katherine Eggersley, c.1510. Two 6-in. (15-cm.) figures, two others lost. – Joan Meetkerke †1695. Alabaster, of a type common in Oxford. Oval inscription framed with cherubs, masks and flowers. – Tower, Sir Michael Dormer, his wife and his father, Ambrose Dormer. A large alabaster monument of 1618, painted and gilded; moved from the S aisle to its present position in 1860. Adam White attributes it to the Gloucestershire tomb-maker and carver *Samuel Baldwin*. The carving is of the highest quality. The three effigies lie under a pilastered and arcaded canopy with a coffered soffit, on which stand elegant personifications of Youth, Death, Age and Time, with achievements of arms between. More heraldry on the cornice and on the sides of the tomb-chest, repainted in *E. Clive Rouse*'s restoration of 1956. Details of costumes are picked out in gold, intricate patterns on the armour, and embroidery on Lady Dormer's dress. On the shield of Sir Michael is a magnificent relief of the Sun in Splendour. The reliefs in the spandrels of the arches include King David, Death with his dart, and trumpeting angels of judgment. At the foot of the tomb-chest is a fine relief of Sir Michael at a military encampment during the Spanish wars. Relocation to the s aisle is proposed (2022).

WESLEYAN CHAPEL, High Street. 1842. Brick and stone, with two lancets and a later porch.

OLD SCHOOL, High Street. Incorporating a front-gabled house of c.1600 on the l., with mullioned windows under hood-moulds and a doorway on the inner side. The cross-range and schoolroom in similar style were added in 1854.

MANOR HOUSE (BELMOND MANOIR AUX QUAT'SAISONS), S of the church. The hall range remains of the house built for William Radmylde in 1474–7, by the Reading mason *John Sewy*. Both cross-ranges have been rebuilt, the s around 1600, the N in the late C17. In 1908 the s cross-range became the main entrance when the house was doubled in size for Mrs Anne Thomas. The architect was *E.P. Warren*, who used dressings of an alien orange-yellow stone. Also in the C17 the hall section was made deeper to the E, represented by two middle gables on that side. Ovolo-moulded mullioned windows on both floors here. Traces of the C15 screens passage remain, leading to a wooden E doorway with a four-centred head. (Also some tie-beams and posts of the medieval hall, now floored over.) In the N wing an adapted mid-C17 staircase, the newel posts with ball finials. Various extensions of the 1980s–90s at the N end, for the restaurant and hotel established by Raymond Blanc in 1983.

The GARDENS include a C17 wall with baluster-mullioned viewing openings. Probably also of the C17 is the DOVECOTE s of the house, circular, with a conical roof. In the wall by the road, alongside *Warren*'s gates of 1908, a fine Jacobean GATEWAY with a shaped gable, obelisk finials, and diamond ornaments to the arch. Integral pedestrian doorway to the r., four-centred-arched. – In 2022 permission was granted for thirty-one new hotel and spa buildings within the gardens, to be designed by *Purcell*.

THE GREAT HOUSE, opposite the church. Seven-bay front of c.1720, the two outer bays at each end projecting slightly. Boldly moulded cornice. Doorcase with fluted Doric pilasters. Sash windows with thick glazing bars and aprons below the sills. Later C17 behind, with a panelled entrance hall. The N end extends to the rear as a wing of C16 or C17 origin, with Georgian windows. Set back on the s side is a balancing ashlar-faced wing dated 1788 on the rainwater heads, by *James Wyatt* for Sir John Skynner, Chief Baron of the Exchequer.* Two storeys, with a full-height bow to the drawing room. A Doric column-screen at the entrance from within the front range. The main interiors have plaster friezes of delicate design. Two

---

*Described as 'by the late Mr Wyatt' in Thomas Ellis, *Some Account of Great Milton* (1813).

fine marble fireplaces with classical relief panels and distinctive Wyatt details to the uprights, e.g. urns on triangular plinths; probably supplied by *Westmacott the elder*. Wyatt also reformed the circulation by means of a rear corridor to the front range, including a second staircase to the N.

(ROMEYNS COURT, NW of the Great House. Late C17, of regular H-plan. Rubble stone with quoins and intermittent bands of ashlar.)

OLD VICARAGE, Church Road, N of the church. 1867 by *A.W. Blomfield*. Minimal Elizabethan style.

THE PRIORY, Church Road, NE of the church. Elizabethan; said to have been built for Dr Herbert Westfaling of Christ Church, Oxford, who served as Vice-Chancellor of the University in 1576–7. Flat frontage with cavetto-mullioned windows spaced unevenly, under three gables with finials. Some Victorian enlargement of the ground-floor windows. Two large C16 fireplaces back to back on the ground floor. Extended behind in the early C17, forming an L-plan. Kitchen addition by *Bosinney Architects*, *c.*2001, with mildly Gothick windows.

MONKERY FARMHOUSE, N of The Priory, on the opposite side of the road. Early C17, with a Georgianized front. Three storeys. A three-light ovolo-mullioned window survives at the back. SW wing probably of the 1650s. – C18 DOVECOTE behind.

The centre of the village, where three roads meet about ½ m. N of the church, is a triangular GREEN with C17 and C18 thatched houses. In Lower End, a further ¼ m. NE, MILTON LODGE. Early C18, five bays. Later wide Tuscan porch with a pediment.

GREYS COURT *see* ROTHERFIELD GREYS

HARDWICK HOUSE
Whitchurch-on-Thames

An expansive and picturesque house of red brick, of several phases between the late C16 and late C17, with plenty of amendments since. The basic form is an elongated H-plan, built over cellars on falling ground, N to S; but the mid-section has been extended laterally and *ad hoc*, so the whole lacks the orderly symmetry of Mapledurham House a mile or so to the SE (q.v.). Viewed from the E, the oldest visible part comprises the southernmost gable of the central section, from the house built probably *c.*1580 by Richard Lybbe I. The two gables to its N stand forward, and these appear to represent early C17 reconstruction to a deeper plan, for Richard Lybbe II. The more northerly gable has windows at irregular heights, where the staircase rises. This bay is returned at the l. against an earlier wall, evidence that the extension was done in phases. The deeper cross-wing at the N end was also constructed separately; it must have followed shortly after, say *c.*1615. Around 1660 a cross-wing at the s was built by Anthony Lybbe, replacing one that may have been damaged in the Civil War. In a deed of 1672 this is called the 'new building'. It broadly resembles the older work, with mullioned windows and three s gables facing the Thames, but is more regular. Moulded brick string courses, and blind oval recesses in the gable-tops. The chimneys also differ: rectangular blocks with panelled sides, instead of diagonally set square stacks. The windows of the main floors are largely restorations of 1839 in place of C18 sashes. They have mullions and some transoms, and they include the reinstated through-storey bay projecting from the N range.*

The entrance is on the E side of the widened section. Over it was built in 1719 a small brick clock tower with angle pilasters, little oculi and an ogee cupola. Linked to this wing is the compact DOWER HOUSE of *c.*1700–15, two parallel gabled ranges of chequer brick with reinstated mullion-and-transom windows. A panel dated 1964 over the tower doorway records downsizing by *Phillimore & Jenkins*. They removed a two-storey infilling (of 1839?) from the courtyard between main house and Dower House, refacing the walls thus exposed. Also taken down was a substantial W extension of the s range, added in 1893 for the banker and sportsman Charles Day Rose, future baronet and M.P.

INTERIORS. Entry is made into the STAIR HALL. The open-well stair and ground-floor finishes are a later Victorian re-creation, probably the 'noble staircase' noted in 1885. A galleried landing at the top. The early C17 ceiling remains, of broad decorated ribs extending from a big central pendant. Lush frieze composed of mermaids in pairs, strapwork, swags and festoons. The stair leads up to the GREAT CHAMBER in the N wing, a *tour de force* of affluent Jacobean decoration. Plaster ceiling of square and barbed-quatrefoil compartments, with small turned pendants, and medallions with profile portraits identified as Joshua, Julius Caesar, Jeroboam and Fame ('Fam'). Also three frontal female busts with extravagant headdresses, perhaps warrior queens or goddesses (a fourth bust, in the bay, is C19). An identical Caesar's head also occurs at Mapledurham in a ceiling dated 1612 (*see* p.690), and a more refined version of the foliage sprays on the staircase ceiling appears there too. So the Hardwick ceilings were probably done slightly later and in emulation, whether or not any of the Mapledurham artisans were involved. Hardwick's female heads, winged cherub heads and some of the trails and beasts on the compartment ribs also recur in ceilings at Dorton House (Bucks.; 1626) and Castle Ashby (Northants), identified by Claire Gapper as products of the same South Midlands workshop. Thick strapwork frieze. The panelling below has blind arcading articulated by pilasters ornamented with strapwork and arabesques, and a wooden doorcase with herm

*An engraving of 1842 shows the windows of the E and N fronts largely in their present form.

pilasters. Chimneypiece of local clunch, the overmantel with strapwork cresting and a shield of arms. In the centre a relief of Abraham and Isaac with the angel carried on a cloud enclosing the sun, moon and stars, flanked by figures of Hope and Faith in shell niches. One BEDROOM has contemporary plastered beams ornamented with vine trails.

Below the Great Chamber is the LIBRARY, with an Adam-style fireplace of 1778 and mechanical Neo-Jacobean decoration of uncertain date. S of the stair hall is the DINING ROOM, with panelling and decoration of 1742. Overdoors with scrolls, swags, flower baskets and masks, and an overmantel with pretty, slightly rustic Rococo plasterwork of scrolls framing a crowned and bearded head in an oval medallion. The W wall is actually a timber passage-screen with Doric pilasters, for access to the KITCHEN, S. (In the S wing another big open-well STAIRCASE, and a TURKISH BATH in the basement, made for Charles Day Rose.)

Hardwick House was the home of Caroline, Mrs Lybbe Powys (1736–1817), the celebrated diarist. A later *habitué* was Henry James, who took the house as his model for Gardencourt in *The Portrait of a Lady* (1881).

STABLES to the W, with the date 1724 on a weathervane. Immediately S is a hulking REAL TENNIS COURT of 1906–7. Built for Charles Day Rose by the specialist *Joseph Bickley*, who had patented an internal plaster finish to facilitate play in damp weather, with *William Weir* as architect. Steep cross-gables of C17 profile. An earlier and plainer TENNIS COURT by *Bickley* (1896), now derelict, stands 250 yds W. A further 300 yds W is the STUD FARM established by Rose in the 1880s. Stables with a half-timbered central part sporting gables of different sizes. C17 farmhouse with 1880s enhancements.

STRAW HALL, ¼ m. ENE. A little thatched building with pointed windows and a veranda of thin tree trunks to one side, built for Philip Powys of Hardwick House. An inscription shows that it existed by 1756, which makes Straw Hall a forerunner of the Late Georgian *cottage orné* mode. It served as a pavilion for taking tea rather than as a dwelling.

THE BAULK, ½ m. WNW. A one-off. The SE end is an C18 Gothic eyecatcher built of whole flints, with two square towers topped by pyramidal pinnacles. Attached to it is a quite substantial house by *F.L. Pearson*, 1909, largely of the same material.

HARPSDEN

ST MARGARET. A small medieval church of flint, restored and enlarged by *Ferrey* in 1848–52. He lengthened the nave to the W, and added the N aisle and N tower, placed midway. N vestry of 1844, probably also Ferrey's. Chancel and nave S walls medieval. Late C12 nave S doorway of one order. An original

C14 window opening W of it. Four reused medieval tie- and collar-beam trusses in the nave roof. In the chancel S wall a round-headed PISCINA of the C12, a C14 TOMB RECESS and a taller recess or blocked opening. *Woodyer* restored the chancel in 1879, and the thorny cusped arch to the vestry must be his. – Chancel TILES (*Minton*) and STALLS from *Woodyer*'s furnishings, otherwise purged in 1953. – FONT. C12. Tub-shaped, with scalloped decoration above a cable moulding. – TILES, re-laid in the N porch. C14? – STAINED GLASS. E window, 1879 by *Hardman*; also a nave S lancet of 1897 with Queen Victoria kneeling. Chancel S, Resurrected Christ, 1929. A rare work by *Marion Thompson*, who emigrated to the USA. Chancel S, the Evangelists, and nave S, Baptism of Christ, both with stamped quarries. By *Powells*, 1848 and 1853, to designs by *John G. Howe* (MH). Nave W, two by *Wailes*. Nave N, shields of Forster and Forster impaling Stonor(?), and the head of a man, all C15. Tower, heraldic painted glass signed *John Wycot*[-], with a cropped C18 date. – BRASSES, some wall-mounted. Mother Forster *c.*1460. 14-in. (36-cm.) figure. – Sir Humphrey and Alice Forster, *c.*1465. 37 and 36 in. (95 and 92 cm.). – Walter Elmes, rector, †1511. 15 in. (38 cm.). – Sarah Webb †1620. A late effigial brass. 17-in. (44-cm.) figure. – MONUMENT. Early C14 effigy of a knight, clumsily carved.

CHURCH ROOM, attached S. 1973–5, by the *Architects Design Partnership*. Canted ends. – ORATORY in the churchyard. Converted in 1993 from the displaced porch of the medieval church. Some timbers look C15.

HARPSDEN COURT, S of the church. An Elizabethan house with substantial medieval fabric and many later alterations and embellishments. Tree rings from the roof indicate construction in 1568–72, but the rendered N front shows no C16 features. Startlingly unembellished window openings of both C17 and C18 outline, the latter both classical-Venetian and ogee Gothick. To the l. a late C19 through-storey porch. Three gables with mostly blank oculi, arranged symmetrically. The middle gable (reinstated in the restoration of 2020–1) is false. Its elongated shaped profile places it with the mid-C18 windows. Also largely of the C18 is the r. cross-range (roof dated to 1722), with window openings of narrower proportions. Brought-in rainwater heads, i.e. the dates do not signify. To the W are Georgian and post-Georgian service ranges; to the SE a four-bay brick addition of *c.*1800, steep-gabled in sympathy with the main front. On the E side here the C16 range shows a Gothick canted bay, its ground floor rebuilt larger in the late C19. Also C19 is the timber-mullioned window in the gable above, where older views show a blank lunette to match the SE bays. Three genuine gable windows of similar type, now blocked, survive on the S side. Also on the S is the Elizabethan stair projection, hip-roofed and of box-framed construction, engulfed in lower post-C17 additions.

Not externally apparent is the incorporation in the main range of a two-storey tower of *c.*1200, roughly corresponding to the width of the shaped gable. A lancet window from its E wall and a formerly external pointed-arched doorway in its W wall are visible inside. It may have comprised the solar block to a hall placed to the E. Blagrave's drawing of 1586 shows an anomalous N doorway in the easternmost bay of the range, suggestive of a screens passage, as well as courtyard ranges of medieval appearance to the S. Leland indeed recorded a 'manor place with dobil courtes' at Harpsden in the 1540s. So the C16 range may perpetuate an older hall as its chief ground-floor room, for which these lost courts would have provided the services.

The interiors have much square panelling of Elizabethan type, not all *in situ*. The chief features otherwise are mostly mid-C18, both Gothick and Rococo, and compatible with a date *c.*1750–60. In the hall a big bold ogee-headed fireplace, a match for the one in John Aitkins's work of *c.*1758 in the hall at Stonor Park (q.v.). The main staircase opens to the S, a dog-leg Victorian replacement, under a coved ceiling with delicate Rococo foliage sprays and C-scroll compartments. Over the hall is the Music Room, of square plan and low C16 proportions. Delightful plasterwork on its walls and shallow dome. Trophies of musical instruments flank the fireplace, which has garlanded ornament and a pier-glass surround with fully modelled sprigs and flowers. Paintings of cherubs in some of the compartments, the smaller ones possibly C18.*

GATEWAY, E of the churchyard. Neo-Jacobean, dated 1908. W of the church, a weatherboarded BARN with a red-tiled roof, dated HHE 1689 around the doorway. Across the road, a C19 CARTSHED and STABLES with three gable-ends clad in C19 wooden wallpaper-printing blocks, applied *c.*1924.

BREMONT, ⅓ m. E. 2017–21 by *Spratley Studios* of Henley. Headquarters and factory for a luxury watchmaking company. Two interlinked buildings. The eye-catching part is a rising convex shape, its front fully glazed behind pairs of raking roof struts. A smart work in the spirit of late C20 High Tech.

LOWER BOLNEY FARM, ½ m. SE. Regimented complex of polo stables by the *Architects Design Partnership*, 1994–7 and *c.*2013. Vernacular materials including knapped flint panels.

CRAY HOUSE, ½ m. S. 1911 by *M. Maberly Smith*. Loosely in a late C17 style. Brick, with brick quoins and small wooden casement windows. Hipped roofs and big chimneystacks. Symmetrical to the S, with a central through-storey bow to the 'sitting hall'. Service wing to the NE.

BELLEHATCH PARK, I m. SW. Timber-framed rear part, probably C16 or C17. Early C19 main range with narrow incised pilasters. (Five-bay S front. Doric porch with arched fanlight. – In the garden wall a pedimented Doric SUMMERHOUSE.)

---

*The *Victoria County History* suggests the Rev. Humphrey Gainsborough of Henley as the ceiling's designer, but Gainsborough was an amateur engineer-inventor, and not a likely author of decorative schemes.

HARPSDEN WOOD HOUSE, ½ m. WSW. A very large house of 2015–17 by *Jonathan Lees Architects* in an Edwardian Arts and Crafts manner, encompassing *M. Maberly Smith*'s own home of 1909 as its E–W range.

HUNT'S FARM, 1¼ m. WSW. The hip-roofed main part origin-ated as a three-bay late medieval cruck house. C19 flint and brick front. – Weatherboarded BARN, r., C17 or earlier.

OLD PLACE, 2 m. WSW. Large timber-framed house. The oldest part is on the N side, two bays with the porch, probably late C16. To the NW a close-studded BARN, brought from elsewhere *c.*1995.

VILLAGE HALL, ½ m. W. By *G. Berkeley Wills*, 1937. Late Arts and Crafts. Opposite, the former SCHOOL of 1856–7, the teacher's house partly tile-hung.

OLD RECTORY, Harpsden Bottom, 1 m. W. Rebuilt in 1617 (VCH). Mid-Georgian S range with a canted centre.

Riverside houses. *See* Shiplake.

HENLEY-ON-THAMES

7080

Henley has always had strong links with London. The town was almost certainly a late C12 royal foundation, alongside an existing river crossing. Its basic plan is a classic arrangement of burgage-plot streets around a market place. Henley later became a port for the supply of timber, corn and malt by river to London. By the late C15 the Thames was more difficult to navigate further upstream, and a boom in transhipment trade followed. Tree-ring dating has identified a good number of buildings from this period.* Malting proved a more enduring industry, though Brakspear's celebrated brewery closed in 2002. From the late C17 the town also became a coaching halt between London and Oxford, and there was much rebuilding or refronting of its timber-framed houses into the early C19, so that the local red and grey brick shows to advantage. The railways vanquished the coaches, but C19 Henley increasingly prospered as a river resort, especially for rowing. The famous regatta was founded in 1839, and boathouses proliferated in the Late Victorian decades, when the town also expanded substantially to the S. A second wave of speculative building followed the arrival of the M4 motorway in the 1960s. Overall, however, post-war pressures have been well managed, and Henley retains its distinctive atmosphere as a historic Thames-side market town with river pursuits as an additional allure.

---

*Detailed building reports are available on the Henley Archaeological & Historical Group website, *https://hahg.org.uk*.

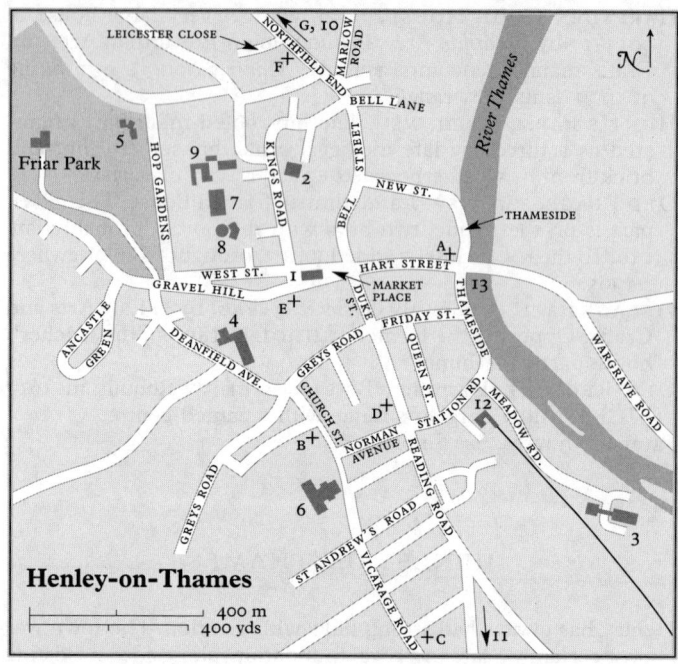

Henley-on-Thames

400 m
400 yds

A	St Mary	1	Town Hall
B	Holy Trinity	2	Library
C	Sacred Heart (R.C.)	3	River & Rowing Museum
D	United Reformed church	4	Henley College
E	Baptist church	5	Badgemore Primary School
F	Friends' Meeting House	6	Holy Trinity School
G	Fairmile Cemetery	7	Townlands Memorial Hospital
		8	Surgeries
		9	Workhouse
		10	Smith Hospital
		11	War Memorial Hospital
		12	Railway station
		13	Bridge

CHURCHES

ST MARY, Hart Street. A big town church with a cheerful Late
Gothic exterior. The tower occupies the NW angle of an originally C13 church, which consisted of chancel, nave, aisles and
probably transepts. Externally there is no work of this date,
though the W doorway is an apparently faithful renewal of
an E.E. predecessor, done in *Benjamin Ferrey*'s restoration of
1852–4 (albeit with Serpentine marble shafts).* In the C19 the

---

*An enriched doorway of *c.*1160–80, salvaged *c.*1800 from a house in Hart Street
and now part of an ornamental dairy at Fawley Court, Bucks., may have come from
an earlier church.

tower was said to have been given by John Longland, a son of Henley and Bishop of Lincoln in 1521–47, though the octagonal angle buttresses, embattled pinnacles and broad three-light bell-openings could as well be late C15 as early C16. Also, two bosses on its lierne vault appear to display merchants' marks (as noted by John Goodall), which implies funding from within the town. The vault has angle shafts, set on corbels with the symbols of the Evangelists. The nave arcades have E.E. detail – double-chamfered arches and round piers with moulded capitals – but the proportions are wrong. They were probably heightened in C15 remodelling (cf. All Saints, Wokingham, Berks.). Also, the two E piers with octagonal capitals and bases are Perp, the chancel arch too. As this eastern nave bay is close to a square in plan, it probably replaced an earlier crossing tower. Perp capitals also on the two W bays of the S aisle and the N aisle bay next to the tower arches.

Before then, in the early C14, a NE chapel had been added. It opens from the chancel by a two-bay arcade with a pier of quatrefoil section, arches with two orders of wave mouldings, and a hood with headstops. If this is the 'newly built' Chapel of St Mary mentioned in 1311, the windows have some of England's earliest datable reticulated tracery (cf. Merton College chapel sacristy, 1310, p.198). Five lights to the E window, with a six-light wheel at the top. Chancel E window of equally vigorous C14 Dec tracery, possibly an invention or improvement by *Ferrey*. Off the NE chapel a shafted four-centred archway opens to the smaller Chapel of St Leonard, built by the Henley merchant John Elmes (†1460) and restored in 1910. All stone externally, with a battlemented parapet with grotesques. Very flat-arched windows with panel tracery. Vaulted niches in the E wall (two) and N wall inside. W window originally external.

The SE chapel may be the work for which the royal mason *Thomas Wolvey* was engaged in 1397–8. It too opens to the chancel by a two-bay arcade. Perp windows with wide, flattened arches and panel tracery. They were reused when the walls were rebuilt with flint-and-stone chequering in 1789, apparently the inspiration of the builder, *William Bradshaw* of Henley. The chapel extends W of the chancel arch to what was probably a transept. The arches to the nave S aisle here are of 1852–4, replacing a solid wall. To the W a wedge-shaped vestry extension of *c*.1820, again with re-set C15 windows. The smaller pointed-arched W window of this extension has the look of pre-scholarly Gothic, but the head at least appears to be older. *Ferrey* provided the outer N aisle, Dec style with windows of reticulated tracery imitated from the former N wall; screened off in 1970. Also his are the nave clerestory, most of the roofs, and the SEDILIA and PISCINA in the chancel.

FURNISHINGS. CHOIR STALLS and wrought-iron SCREENS to the chancel sides, rich and unusual designs by *J. D. Sedding*, 1890; the screens made by *Henry Longden* of the Phoenix Foundry, Sheffield. – ROOD SCREEN. 1920, designed by *G. H.*

Fellowes Prynne. – WALL PAINTING of the Adoration of the Lamb around the chancel arch, 1891 by the *Rev. E. Geldart,* executed by *Cox & Buckley.* Chancel roof painting, 1890, also designed by *Geldart.* The coloured shields and grey stencilled pattern on the side walls are of 1895, designed by *Comper.* – PULPIT of marble, 1897. Given by Lady Crisp of Friar Park (p.676). – C18 brass CHANDELIER in St Leonard's Chapel. – FONTS. One with a bulbous octagonal bowl, dated 1626 (S aisle). Under the tower, *Ferrey*'s C14-style font of 1854. Its setting is of 1880, by *W. Scott Champion.*

STAINED GLASS. Spectacular E window in the Lady Chapel, of 1868 by *Hardman* (*J. Hardman Powell*), with elegant flame-like figures; also the NE window. The rest mostly *Lavers & Westlake*: chancel E window 1889, SE chapel and S aisle 1886 onwards, clerestory 1887, W window and two in the outer N aisle 1897 (hidden) and the Nurse Sparkes memorial (†1892). N aisle going E, *Heaton, Butler & Bayne,* 1872, and saints by *O'Connor,* probably also 1870s (MH). Tower N and W (1883) by *Clayton & Bell.* St Leonard's Chapel, 1910–13 all by *J. C. Bewsey,* formerly with the Kempe firm.

MONUMENTS. C13 coffin-lid with floriated cross (tower). – Dame Elizabeth Periam †1621 (N aisle). Simple and classical for this date. Alabaster and black marble, with a well-carved recumbent effigy in an arched recess with Doric columns. Decoration is confined to large simple strapwork around the crest and inscription. Work of high quality, attributed to *Maximilian Colt* (GF). – Dr John Cawley †1709 (SE chapel). By *Francis Bird*; architectural. – Elmes family, *c.*1775 (SE chapel). Tabulated names under a weeping cherub. – William Hayward †1782, designer of Henley bridge (tower). Graceful Neoclassical motifs. – Richard Hayward, brewer, †1797 (tower). A fine big cartouche with cherub heads, archaic by that date. Was a blank early C18 piece dusted down?

HOLY TRINITY, Greys Hill. Puginian Dec of 1847–8 by *Benjamin Ferrey,* a Henley resident in these years. Flint and stone. Triple W bellcote. In 1890–1 *W. T. Lowdell* added aisles, SE vestry and NW baptistery, but his intended W tower never happened. Heavily reordered. – STAINED GLASS. E window and one S (†1873) by *Clayton & Bell.* – VICARAGE, S. 1848–9. Chiefly of flint.

SACRED HEART (R.C.), Vicarage Road. 1935–6 by *A. S. G. Butler.* Arts and Crafts Gothic in red brick, with a low tower over the chancel. STATUE over the doorway by *A. Ryan.* Neat extensions at the W angles by *Peter Brownshill,* 2005–7. The main attraction is the E end, with its salvage from the chapel commissioned in 1851 by Charles Scott-Murray from *A.W.N. Pugin* for Danesfield House, Medmenham, Bucks. (demolished *c.*1901). It includes the magnificent window with reticulated tracery and STAINED GLASS by *Hardman* (*J. H. Powell*). Women of the Old Testament below, the Immaculate Conception in the tracery. Elaborate REREDOS with the Virgin and Child under a canopy, between reliefs of the life of St Charles Borromeo. On either side are larger figures in canopied niches, St Charles and St Elizabeth of Hungary. *E.W. Pugin* completed the ensemble in 1853–6 after his father's death, and added the HIGH ALTAR and RELIQUARY CHEST. – SCREEN of etched glass, w. By *Graham Jones*, 2007. – PARISH HALL behind by *Francis Pollen*, 1968–9.

UNITED REFORMED CHURCH (formerly Congregational), Reading Road. Rebuilt in 1907–8 by *Hampden W. Pratt*. Big, blowsy Gothic, red brick with Bath stone dressings. The gable window has elaborate tracery. SE tower given by Sir Frank Crisp of Friar Park (p.676), with clock, lantern of traceried windows, and small spire. Well preserved inside, with opposed galleries for congregation and choir. Pseudo-hammerbeam roof. – Original LIGHT FITTINGS with copper trim. – Art Nouveau STAINED GLASS in flamboyant colours, made by *J. Hooker* of Croydon. – Large CHURCH HALL adjacent, 1903–4, also by *Pratt*. The connecting concourse goes with the CHRIST CHURCH CENTRE by *HSD Architects*, 1995–2000. – MANSE, N. A C19 remodelling of two C18 cottages.

BAPTIST CHURCH, Market Place. *See* Perambulation 1, p.669.

FRIENDS' MEETING HOUSE, Northfield End. 1894. By *C. Smith & Son* of Reading, and with a Reading look.

FAIRMILE CEMETERY, at Lower Assendon, 1½ m. NW. Opened 1868. CHAPELS of flint and stone with Dec tracery. According to the *Victoria County History* the architect was *Barry*, but which one? The C. of E. chapel has a tower with an octagonal belfry E of the porch.

PUBLIC BUILDINGS

TOWN HALL, Market Place. 1899–1901 by *Henry T. Hare*, in free Neo-Wren style.* Red brick and Bath stone. Neat, square front with an applied Ionic portico pushed high above the doorway. Broken pediment, filled with a well-carved royal arms which surmounts a columned Venetian window below. Hipped roof; cupola also, with attached columns. The front is deceptively small, as the building runs back ten bays in depth. Stone banding *à la* Norman Shaw on the flanks. Another portico in relief at the back. Pleasingly intact interior. A steep imperial STAIRCASE serves the upper floors. Stained glass by *Henry Holiday* in the Venetian window, column-screens to the side landings at the summit. The top floor has the big barrel-vaulted HALL with pilasters framing the dais. COUNCIL CHAMBER below, panelled in late C17 style.

LIBRARY, Ravenscroft Road. 1979–81 by *Oxfordshire County Architect's Department* (*M. Dutton*). Low brick pavilion with a hipped roof.

RIVER & ROWING MUSEUM, Mill Meadows. The first major building by *David Chipperfield*; initial designs 1989, completed

---

*The portico and other parts of *William Bradshaw*'s predecessor of 1795–6 were saved by the Henley builder *Charles Clements*, and incorporated into his house at Crazies Hill, Berks.

1997. Two major parts, placed on low concrete decks and
linked by a covered bridge at first-floor level. The E part houses
the main museum, the w the town's museum, education facilities etc. The museum has a fully glazed ground floor, with the
galleries in two parallel gabled volumes above. Their roofs are
very steeply pitched, with flat tops to allow skylighting. Added
pictorial displays have since spoiled the look of the ground
floor, but the bold, simple masses, achieved in sober, tactile
materials – weathered oak slats, polished concrete, roofs of
dull grey terne-plated steel – point forward to some enduring
themes of early C21 architecture.

HENLEY COLLEGE (Sixth Form). Two sites. N of Deansfield
Avenue, a complex with the former NATIONAL SCHOOL of
1849–50 by *J. Billing* at the core. Bleak flint and brick with a
central gabled residence flanked by two large classrooms. Of
the later blocks the best is D1, by the road: brown brick, upright
proportions, with blue-grey window enclosures deployed in
lively ways. By *Oxfordshire Dept of Planning*, designed 1984.
ROTHERFIELD COURT, ¼ m. w in Pack and Prime Lane,
began as a mansion by *Woodyer* for T.B. Morrell, 1861. Red
brick banded with flint. Two-storey bay windows with gargoyles
flank a central Gothic loggia. Enlarged 1876 (rainwater head),
and again in 1928, for Henley Grammar School.

BADGEMORE PRIMARY SCHOOL, Hop Gardens. 1974–7 by
Oxfordshire County Architect's Department (Project Architect
Derek Wareham). Friendly, informal buildings of brick with
shallow-pitched roofs, clustered amid mature trees on the edge
of Friar Park.

HOLY TRINITY SCHOOL (former), Greys Hill. By *Albert Pinck-
ney* of Cheltenham, 1893. Red brick. Tudor-type chimneystacks.

TOWNLANDS MEMORIAL HOSPITAL, York Road. By *AHR*,
2014–16. Interlinked brick units with grey steel brise-soleil.
It replaced the first example of the *Oxford Regional Hospital
Board*'s widely adopted steel-framed building system, 1963–4
(architects *W.J. Jobson* and *J.P.B. Bosanquet*). Just ssw, the
very basic little PESTHOUSE of Henley's former workhouse
(*see* below), *c*.1791.

SURGERIES, York Road, s of the hospital. HART SURGERY is by
Patrick Gwynne, 1968–70, for Dr Salmon of Past Field (p.678).
An inventive design, since altered and extended. Round plan,
with consulting rooms set radially around the greater part of
the circumference. Each has a spur-like outer wall for greater
visual privacy. BELL SURGERY alongside is of 1991–3 by *Sutton,
Griffin & Morgan*, segment-shaped in response to Gwynne's
curve. Glass-fronted, of blockwork and rugged steel framing.

WORKHOUSE (former), off Mount View. Now LAUREATE
GARDENS, a conversion for retirement flats by *Nick Baker
Architects*, 2017–20, with some new building. Especially valuable as a well-preserved town workhouse from before the 1834
Poor Law. The oldest part is of 1790–1, designed by the Henley
builder *William Bradshaw*. It might be a century earlier. U-plan,
facing s, with a round-arched loggia on simple square piers in

the cross-range. Plain brick, vernacular window proportions. The E ward range has been repeatedly extended: across the S end, with angle pilasters (*William Cooper*, 1837); dining hall-cum-chapel along the inner flank, also a master's room with canted bay for surveillance (*J. Billing*, 1847); lavatory cross-ranges on this same side (*W. Wing*, 1886); central S projection with canted sides, for the Board Room (*C. Smith & Son*, 1895). To the N, the former INFIRMARY, mostly 1841–4 by *Billing*; to the NE, former SCHOOLS with upper dormitories by *Frederick Haslam*, Borough Surveyor, 1871–2.

SMITH HOSPITAL (former), Fair Mile, 1½ m. NW. An isolation hospital of 1891–2 by *Keith D. Young*, given by W. H. Smith. Single-storey ward blocks amid commercial offices by *Hamilton Associates*, 1999 onwards.

WAR MEMORIAL HOSPITAL (former), Harpsden Way, ¾ m. S. Two-storeyed, domestic. By *C. Smith & Son*, 1922–3.

RAILWAY STATION, Station Road. The branch opened in 1857. Modest replacement building of 1983–4 by *British Rail Architects*.

BRIDGE. Rebuilt in 1782–6 from designs by *William Hayward* (†1782). Contractor *John Townesend III* of Oxford, succeeded by *Stephen Townesend*. Five handsome elliptical arches – the central one 'regulated', in Horace Walpole's words, by General Conway of Park Place (Berks.), one of the Bridge Commissioners – and a balustraded parapet. Heads of Thames and Isis on the central keystones carved by *Anne Damer*, the general's daughter. – Plain late C12 ARCHES from the previous bridge survive alongside, on both banks. Henley's is now in the cellars of the Angel Inn (*see* below).

4

PERAMBULATIONS

1. Hart Street, Market Place and west

Starting from the bridge, a spectacular entry to the town. On the Berkshire side is a background of wooded hills; on the other, St Mary's church tower framed by two inns. On the l. the stuccoed ANGEL INN, C16–C17 and *c.*1800, with canted bay windows on both parts. On the r. the grand RED LION HOTEL (now THE RELAIS), Georgian brick. The oldest C18 part, *c.*1720–30, comprises six riverside bays with segment-headed windows and a moulded string course. Canted corner, and a long, plain range facing S, probably of 1780; porch of 1889. Attached at the W end, close to St Mary's chancel, is a timber-framed range, tree-ring dated to 1462. On the riverside going N also the former stables, refronted in the late C18 with blind through-storey arches and a central pediment.

The W end of the church faces a Gothic DRINKING FOUNTAIN of 1885 by *James Forsyth*, moved from the central cross-roads. Red granite and stone, with a crocketed spirelet. The CHURCHYARD behind is enclosed on the W by a stuccoed terrace of twelve ALMSHOUSES in Tudor style, built in 1830:

replacements for those provided *c.* 1538–47 by Bishop Longland on the s corner by the bridge. On the e are single-storey brick almshouses in similar style, originally 1660s but rebuilt in 1846. Just NE of the church, the so-called CHANTRY HOUSE, built as a medieval merchant's premises. Tree rings yielded the date 1461. Two storeys here, with a jettied first floor and a broad arched doorway, but three storeys on the lower ground facing the Red Lion courtyard, with a short e projection. Arch-braced corners. Brick-nogging, painted in *Oxley Conservation*'s restoration of 2003–4. The top floor is now one long former schoolroom, with inserted aisle-posts and an impressive wind-braced roof. Originally the space was ceiled, and had separate lodging chambers and a landing, connected by a corridor along the e side. The lowest floor as built was open-fronted, to store river-borne goods.

HART STREET, the spine of the town, runs w from the bridge to the Market Place and Town Hall, widening as it goes. The houses appear predominantly Georgian, but many fronts hide earlier work. On the n side next to the churchyard is LONGLANDS (No. 39), *c.* 1730–40. Handsome elevation, five bays and three storeys, of local red and yellow London brick. Panelled parapet, angle pilasters, segment-headed windows. Pedimented doorway with fluted pilasters and a fanlight. Older timber-framed rear wing. Opposite are Nos. 48–50, early C17, and the SPEAKER'S HOUSE (No. 44), C15–C16, both gabled and jettied, but prettified in the C19. No. 44 was probably the chamber cross-wing for a lost hall to the e. Behind is a former SCHOOL, plain flint and red brick by *Ferrey*, 1857–8. No. 40 is of C16 origin, but with bogus timbering above early C19 shopfronts. Better half-timbering at No. 38, built after 1905 as the off-licence of Brakspear's brewery; probably by *W. G. A. Hambling*. No. 30 is C16 timber, with a taller Georgian refronting to the r. Good Early Georgian at Nos. 26–28, of five asymmetrically grouped bays. Cut-brick upper window heads, dentil cornice, hipped roof. No. 24 is C16 and later, stuccoed, with an intact jetty. At No. 22 the timbers are exposed, braced at the lower corners. It probably began as the cross-wing to a late medieval house of which No. 20 was the hall, now refaced in Georgian brick. (Blocked trefoil-headed timber window in the e wall of No. 22.) On the n side, Nos. 31–33 is mid-Georgian red brick, with angle pilasters and a modillion cornice. Doorway with a fanlight and a hood on scroll brackets. To the l. a modern shopfront. No. 29 of *c.* 1830 is stuccoed. Ground floor with channelling, pedimented first-floor windows, doorcase with antae. Then the former OLD WHITE HART at Nos. 19–23. Its front range, antiqued for Brakspear's by *A. E. Hobbs* in 1931, retains parts of a crown-post roof, tree-ring dated to 1391. (Barrel-vaulted, chalk-lined cellar of *c.* 1300 below.) Timbers in the courtyard ranges behind are datable to 1531. Original features here include the projecting passage along much of the first-floor lodgings, and the jettied two-bay hall with S-curved bracing on the w side. The ground floor all round is of brick, the earliest datable use in Henley. Some diapering on the unpainted outer w side. The n side has weatherboarding over a carriageway. A Tudor-arched timber doorway to the r. probably served stairs to the upper chambers.

Back on the s side, No. 18 is substantial Early Georgian, of silver-grey brick headers laced with red. Six bays. Hipped roof and modillion cornice, door hood on shaped brackets. Substantial maltings behind, the end part dated 1768. BARCLAYS (Nos. 10–12) began as Simonds & Co.'s bank, by *C. Smith & Son*, 1895–6. Mixed Elizabethan, with a bold half-timbered gable towering above its neighbours, a valuable emphasis at this point. The white-painted CATHERINE WHEEL HOTEL opposite occupies No. 17 (r.), Early Georgian like No. 18, and No. 15, where early C19 stucco conceals C16–C17 timber construction. No. 17 also has an artisan-Baroque doorcase. At the crossing, the NE corner house dates from widening in 1814, the SE is a former restaurant of 1893 by *S. Slingsby Stallwood*, with Dutch gables.

In the MARKET PLACE the pleasant variety of houses and shops continues. MACHIN'S (No. 7, s side) shows curved bracing set in squares, probably an early C17 enhancement to an older structure. On the n side the single-storey former Midland Bank (HSBC) at No. 6, a late work by *T. B. Whinney* (*Whinney, Son & Austen Hall*), 1924. Gentlemanly Neo-Georgian, praised as an exemplar by the *Architect's Journal*. Nos. 16–18, NATWEST (formerly London & County Bank) is of 1891–2 by *W. Campbell Jones*. Red brick above flint and stone, with half-timbered gables. No. 20 is of *c.* 1740, silver-grey brick with red trim, modillion cornice and three-bay pediment. Good internal details, an open-well staircase with carved treads and also balustraded light wells in the landing corners, and a ground-floor back room with a tripartite window and a fireplace with foliage frieze. The timber-framed service wing is older. No. 17 opposite, dated 1749 on a rainwater head, is also of grey and red brick, with a hipped roof and modillion cornice. Early C19 brick at No. 25 hides a house tree-ring dated to 1471. (Ogee-curved scissor-braced truss in the rear wing.) At No. 26 (n side) the framing is C16, behind an early C20 mock-antique front. Past where the Town Hall (p. 665) comes in, the KING'S ARMS BARN behind Nos. 32–36, tree-ring dated 1602, is mostly weatherboarded, the upper floor apparently meant for domestic use. On the s side of the Town Hall, Nos. 37–39, dated 1755, with panelled parapets. The builder *Charles Clements* lived and worked at No. 43 *c.* 1868–*c.* 1901, and its mixed fancy details are his. Timbers at Nos. 45–47 give the date 1353/4. Partly jettied first floor. The enlarged central carriageway has a pointed-arched doorway on its E side, from the former screens passage. (Crown-post roof partly intact.) C18 alterations and brick infill. At No. 57 the narrow-fronted BAPTIST CHURCH, 1878–9 by *J. O. Cooper & Son*. More red and silver brick, but Gothic. Behind No. 59 a timber-framed outbuilding, C17 or early C18. (An inserted kiln roof indicates later use as a malthouse or oast.) Closing the view to the w, a very conservative short terrace (Nos. 62–66) of 1864.

GRAVEL HILL climbs westwards from here. No. 1, brick with a concentric-arched doorway, looks *c.* 1840. The row behind the raised walk beyond includes one big cross-wing (No. 13), tree-ring dated 1454. Powerful exposed truss, with a central post and curved side-struts to the collar. Its E attachment originated as an earlier double-hall house, built probably for market-related trades. No. 19 is Late Georgian chequered brick. Then a former National School, firmly Gothic. By *W. Wing,* 1879. 100 yds on is HOPE CHAPEL (now a house), with arched windows and doorway, of 1873 but looking more like 1830. Opposite was Paradise House, C18; replaced behind its garden wall with tile-hung and weatherboarded dwellings after *c.* 1970. Beyond is ANCASTLE COTTAGE, a C16 lobby-entry farmhouse, jettied behind. Framing infilled with painted brick. Down Paradise Road, s, another C16 timber house, PARADISE FARM. Porch of two storeys, C18 rear extension.

On Gravel Hill opposite are the lodge and gates to Friar Park (*see* p. 677), and HOP GARDENS, running N, with mostly Victorian houses. FONTHILL is tile-hung brick, *c.* 1880–90, of very picturesque intent. Then SURREY LODGE, 1866, brick Gothic of North Oxford type. Next door, the TAPP HOUSE, by *David Tapp* for himself, 1969. A showcase for the architect's own prefabricated timber system, including a first-floor living room boxed out on the garden side. Nos. 5–16, plain and decent cottage pairs of flint and brick, around a green. By *W.M. Fawcett* of Cambridge, 1872–3.

WEST STREET leads back to the centre, parallel to Gravel Hill. On the N side opposite the fire station is ADWELL SQUARE, 1967 by *C.H. Elsom & Partners,* a good small development in scale and character with this part of the town. Concrete-framed cottage terraces with brick or flint infill and red-tiled roofs. Larger houses follow. ALBION PLACE (Nos. 6–14) is a rendered terrace of *c.* 1800–10; No. 4, *c.* 1700, with a pedimented and swagged doorcase, stuccoed *c.* 1830 and given a mansard roof and pedimented dormers. Finally No. 2, mid-C18 brick, six bays, with a coved wooden cornice. Additions of *c.* 1900 to its r. side, with a Dutch gable and oriel.

2. Bell Street and north

BELL STREET, the main shopping street, runs N from the central crossing. No. 16, E side, was built *c.* 1790, probably as ASSEMBLY ROOMS. Stuccoed, with a central carriage arch flanked by doorways, a Palladian window above, and a full-width pediment on superimposed pilasters. The OLD BELL at No. 20 next door is of special interest as an early C14 house or house-wing (tree-ring date 1325). Three bays, set end-on to the street, where the gable has been cut back. (Crown-post roof with octagonal post and moulded capital to the truss. Framing of a Gothic

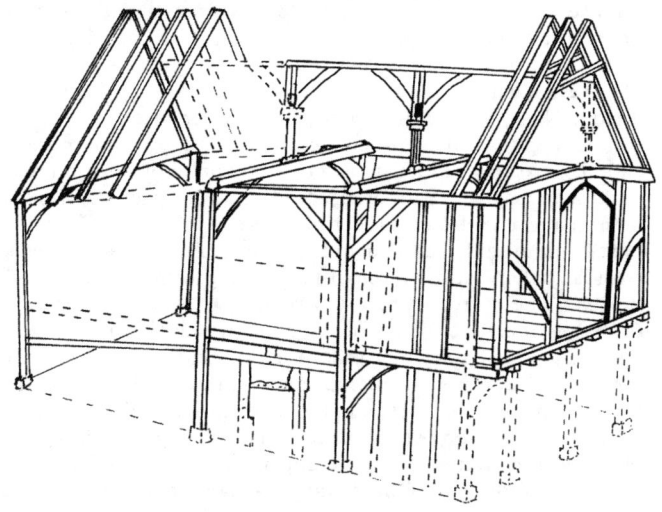

Henley, No. 20 Bell Street.
Reconstruction drawing by Ruth Gibson, 2011

first-floor doorway, now blocked.) At No. 32 a big mid-C18 house of seven bays with a dentil cornice, altered *c.* 1830 with a new doorway, stuccoed ground floor, and Soanean gatepiers, r. Much rebuilding of the 1990s opposite, when a supermarket and a CINEMA were provided behind, the latter of 1996–7 by *Daniel Lelliott Krauze*; all red brick. Nos. 46–50 are probably Bell Street's 'newly built' houses mentioned in 1785. Big, of red and grey brick. The BULL INN (Nos. 57–59, w side) is C15. Arch-braced timber framing. Three gabled first-floor bay windows with arched central lights, typical of *c.* 1650–80. Rear ranges including a weatherboarded barn. No. 61, a smaller C15–C16 house, has exposed framing to its cross-range, with tension braces and a truss with queen-struts. No. 65 is early C19, but with *Robert Cromie*'s pseudo-Adam doorcase of 1957. It faces down New Street (*see* p. 673), to which the SE corner is a late C15 house with a long jetty on its N side. First-floor windows of original proportions here.

Continuing N, No. 71 is early C19, with some of the best Late Georgian detail in Henley. Stuccoed, with a central bay window and ironwork balcony above. To the l. a Doric doorway with fanlight, to the r. the carriage entrance. On the first floor a fan-headed tripartite window. At No. 73 a C15 former hall house, much disguised. The former BEAR INN (Nos. 77–81) has four rendered gables, the l. pair C15 with crown-strut roofs, the r. pair late C17, with canted oriels. Exposed framing on the flank. At the rear is a two-bay open hall tree-ring dated to 1438. This was extended N by the unusual means of re-roofing to greater height and width (rafters dated to 1589/90), probably for use as a kitchen. The long timber-framed and weather-boarded s range of the inn courtyard, its rear part datable to 1454/5, shows beyond. ADAM COURT alongside is creditable Neo-vernacular infill by *Eric G.V. Hives & Son*, *c.*1983. On the E side, Nos. 70–72, Late Georgian chequer brick. Doorcases (one a copy) with an open pediment and urns in place of capitals. Nos. 74–78 began as a two-bay hall house with cross-ranges, the hall now floored across, and all again concealed behind the C18 front. Tree rings date it to 1405. (Principal posts with moulded capital and attached pilasters. Arch-braced trusses, collar- and principal-rafter roof with cusped wind-braces.) The s cross-range was rebuilt in 1569. (Rear ranges probably of *c.*1800, when Brakspears' principal maltings were here.) Nos. 82–84 are of *c.*1680–1700, including some refronting. Dentil cornice, segmental-pedimented doorways, and a canted bay between surviving cross-windows on the first floor. At Nos. 93–95 opposite, a date range of 1436–44 has been obtained for the two s bays, comprising a hall or solar; the N bays are a little later. (Richly hollow-chamfered ceiling beams and wall-plates here, and a roof with cusped wind-braces. Rear range datable 1758/9.)

The road widens as the fork approaches, with handsome Georgian fronts on both sides; the w side continues as North-field End (*see* below). Staying on the E side, COUNTESS GARDENS (No. 86) is one of the grandest, of *c.*1740. Silver-grey and red brick, six bays, three storeys, with a straight parapet. Segment-headed windows, doorcase with fluted pilasters and triglyph frieze. (Reused timbers datable to 1611 in the roof.) Next door is RUPERT HOUSE, ten years or so later. Three bays, with a late C18 extension, l. Doorcase with Ionic half-columns, pediment, and a fanlight of *c.*1800.* The row at Nos. 92–102 is early C17 behind early C19 stucco, with two bow windows. Next N is chiefly RUPERT'S ELM and two adjoining houses, forming a long terrace set back behind gardens. They originated in the C17 as the Bell Inn, which received a stucco front probably *c.*1790. Main part of sixteen unevenly spaced bays, with a bracketed modillion cornice and modest pediment. Doric porch with a balcony over it. The taller s addition of three bays is DENMARK HOUSE, C18.

Back now to the w side of NORTHFIELD END. First OLD BELL HOUSE (No. 9), its C18 stucco frontage with four schematic Palladian windows on the first floor and a wooden Tuscan porch. (Rear wing tree-ring dated 1472: originally a late aisled hall, of two bays, with smoke-blackened queen-strut roof.) NORTHFIELD HOUSE is stuccoed and tall, of three storeys plus basement. Two curved full-height bays flank a Greek Doric porch with a fanlight, approached by a flight of steps. (Date-stone 1812 at the rear.) SYDNEY HOUSE (No. 15) has a late C18 front range of white-painted brick. Bracket cornice, canted bay

---

*At the far end of Bell Lane here is THE WALLED GARDEN, *Francis Pollen*'s own house of 1959, altered beyond recognition in 2022.

windows. No. 17 is similar. BEULAH LODGE (No. 39) is mid-c18, grey brick with red brick dressings. Doorcase with fluted pilasters and bracketed hood. Next door, OXFORD LODGE is early c19 stucco. Central two-storey bay window, Doric porch. 1960s developments follow, LEICESTER CLOSE with genteel little Neo-Georgian houses of 1965–7, FAIRMILE COURT with Neo-Georgian flats by *Robert Cromie*, designed 1957. Between them, on the NE side, HAWKS VIEW HOUSE is a former Brak-spear's pub (the Old White Horse), an emphatically domestic job of 1938 by *A. E. Hobbs*.

The road continues NW as FAIR MILE. Nos. 1–15, OXFORD VILLAS, are tall semi-detached pairs of 1863 onwards. Italian Gothic style, yellow brick banded in red. Gabled porches with fat stone columns and carved capitals. All have side extensions of *c.*1980. Nos. 2–4 and 6–8 represent an earlier villa fashion, stuccoed sub-Tudor of around 1840.

Coming back SE, MARLOW ROAD goes off to the N. It passes between square stuccoed LODGES of *c.*1770–80, each with a finely detailed Doric cornice and Palladian windows set in blind arches. Linked gatepiers with reeded saucer-shaped caps. Attributed plausibly to *James Wyatt*, who in 1771 was working for Sambrook Freeman of Fawley Court (Bucks.), ¾ m. N. Immediately E is the drive to PHYLLIS COURT. The irregular stuccoed Italianate house of *c.*1845 was greatly expanded as a country club on the American model, chiefly in the 1920s. Some colonnaded interiors by *Waring & Gillow*, but the intended classical transformation by *J. J. Joass* never happened (shown in *The Tatler*, 1928). The previous house was largely c16 and early c17, possibly on the site of the c12 royal residence at Henley. By the river bank here is a steel-framed GRANDSTAND for watching the regatta, of 1913 by *F. G. Sainsbury*; glazed in and renovated 2013–16.

Back towards the town centre, and E into NEW STREET, a pretty residential street with prosperous houses. Beyond the Bell Street cottage on the S side, BARNABY COTTAGES, in origin two mid-c15 houses with crown-strut roof trusses. A plaque records William Barnaby's gift of 1582 and a subdivi-sion in 1788, a likely date for the white-painted brick refront-ing, r. Framing exposed on the E flank. Opposite is CLARENCE HOUSE (No. 11), early c18. Chequer brick, four bays, plus a carriageway, l., under a canted bay window. Door hood on shaped brackets. Next door, SARAGOSSA HOUSE, *c.*1700 under early c19 stucco. Four bays plus a blind half-bay on each side. Hipped roof. (The service wing is older, and timber-framed.) Nos. 15–17, a pair built 1805, are of unusual design. Three arched recesses, the central arch lower and contain-ing the doorways. The outer arches frame both storeys. Small ground-floor bay windows here. Then the little KENTON THEATRE, also of 1805. One of the earliest surviving theatres in the country, though only the shell is old. *William Parker* of Henley was the builder. Except for the modern canopy, the red brick front is entirely domestic; indeed, the r. bay was a separate house originally. Round-arched side windows. Interior mostly of 1965–7 by *David Tapp* of *Maurice Day & Associates*. No. 40 opposite shows C16 framing in the side passages, behind an C18 grey and red brick front. C18 chequer-brick cottages in the rear court. Nos. 25–27, N side, are a later C18 brick pair with tripartite windows. REDCLIFFE HOUSE (No. 31), early C19, three bays and three storeys, has a concentric-arched doorway with a fanlight. On the S side again, the front of No. 52 is a stucco equivalent of *c.* 1820, with angle pilasters, channelled ground floor and a doorcase with antae. (Rear downpipe dated 1719.) ANN BOLEYN and TUDOR COTTAGES originated as a C15 house. Framing exposed, jetty intact. The central arched cross-passage now leads to a row of diminutive C19 cottages.

The former HENLEY BREWERY (Brakspear's) is next door. Buildings of many phases, illustrating the growth of brewing from its domestic origins. First a long range of 1897–8 (tun room etc.) with pedimental gables, partly two-storeyed, boldly trimmed in black brick. Two adjoining early C19 houses, the l. one built as the brewery office by 1826, when William Brakspear began living here. It has an ample through-storey bow with a reeded doorcase. The brewery yard behind has buildings dated 1898 (W), 1903 (SW, with lucam) and 1857 (boiler house, S). Closed 2002; converted for the HOTEL DU VIN by *Compton Lacey*, opened 2011. The older buildings on the E side are rear ranges to No. 86, the very grand OLD BREWERY HOUSE, built probably by the brewer-maltster Benjamin Sarney, *c.* 1735. Five bays, three storeys, hipped roof. Rusticated doorcase with fluted pilasters and a triglyph frieze. Brakspears' largest building is opposite: the former MALTHOUSE of 1899, with two kilns with pyramid roofs and wooden lanterns. Just to the W here is a broad entrance with square piers leading to RADNOR CLOSE, 1970–1 by *R. Cromie Architects*, red brick flats in a watered-down Georgian style. Continuing E, No. 51 is C16 with brick infill. CAMDEN HOUSE (No. 53), dated 1729 on a downpipe, is of silver-grey brick with red dressings. Segmental door hood, and a blind aedicule above it. Hipped roof. BISHOP'S HOUSE (No. 55) of a few years earlier is very handsome, of six bays. Staircase placed behind the main rooms. Last on the S side is a small courtyard group, the S side comprising brewery stables. Its river range (No. 28 Thameside etc.) includes a mid-C15 framed house, one end rounded off and brick-faced in the early C19.

THAMESIDE has ravishing river views, enhanced by the festively treated two-storey BOATHOUSES of Henley's heyday as a resort. To the N, a cluster of five with fancy bargeboards, begun *c.* 1885 by *H. E. Hobbs & Sons*. WATER'S EDGE, more domestic, was built for Sir Frank Crisp of Friar Park in 1893–4. Going S, the LITTLE WHITE HART HOTEL is a Brakspears' showpiece of 1900, probably by *W. G. A. Hambling*, with balconies in its three steep gables. Next to the Red Lion are former granaries converted in 1888–9 for the boat-builder Tom

70

Shepherd. The twin pediments have delightful red sgraffito decoration showing rushes, water lilies and herons.* And so to the bridge.

3. South of the bridge

THAMESIDE continues s from the bridge. Facing the Angel Inn (p.667) is the OLD RECTORY. Scratched dates 1701 and 1716 are recorded. Red and yellow brick. Hipped roof and bracket cornice. Seven bays, the s bay and rear wing an early addition. Tile-hung gables behind. Now w into FRIDAY STREET, for buildings associated with early industry and trade. The N corner is taken by the OLD GRANARY and BARN COTTAGE; the former tree-ring dated 1549. Substantially built, probably as warehousing above living accommodation. Timber above, mostly flint and brick below. A dragon beam at the corner. Restored 1925. On the s corner is BALTIC HOUSE, Georgian towards the river, and BALTIC COTTAGE behind, together comprising a subdivided hall house with a crown-post roof (tree-ring date 1439; one crown-post replaced by a chimney). Baltic Cottage includes a former cross-wing dated 1537, W, likewise much disguised. On the N side, Nos.67–71 are probably mid-C15, jettied, and again with heavy framing suggestive of upstairs storage. No.47 is early C18, built as a tannery. Thin framing above flint walling, heavily reconstructed as a house c.1948. No.14 (s side), tree-ring dated 1589/90, displays close studding in the jettied first floor and big gable; the rest of the building lost c.1879 when Queen Street was made. On the N side beyond, Nos.17–29 are a cottage terrace of deceptively uniform design, whitewashed brick with segment-headed windows. Of these, Nos.17 and 23–25 originated as C15–C16 timber-framed houses, the rest are of 1744–6, built by the bricklayer *Benjamin Bradshaw*.

Ahead is the crossing with Duke Street and Reading Road. DUKE STREET, N, was widened and rebuilt along its w side from 1872–3. On the E side, No.49 has been tree-ring dated 1600, but includes older timbers reused. READING ROAD, S, has a tall and showy commercial w corner dated 1896, next to Nos.2–4, heavily masked C15. The former POST OFFICE, 1922, revives the C18 combination of grey and red brick, seen on the E side at No.17 of c.1730. The latter's full pilasters and detailed brick cornice are unusual. After some early C19 terraces, *W. Ravenscroft*'s friendly MASONIC HALL of 1889–90, red brick with a stocky half-timber-topped tower. The United Reformed church (p.665) is opposite.

Of the late C19–early C20 houses in the s parts of Henley, the best are in NORMAN AVENUE, next w. On its N side the

---

*Nos.23–33 Queen Street, lively mid-1880s semis, also make much use of sgraffito patterns. At No.22, w side, the doorcase is carved with shallow reliefs of Dick Whittington (cf. Nos.40–42 St Andrew's Road, pp.677–8).

Henley builder *Charles Clements* erected tall, close-packed villas with eccentric brick, stone and timber detailing, most notably Nos. 5–9 of 1894–7. Some inspiration clearly comes from Friar Park (*see* below), but the house names – 'Gwenoch', 'Torfridas' etc. – are from Charles Kingsley's novel *Hereward the Wake* (1866). (In No. 5 is a screen with painted glass scenes after Harry Selous's illustrations to the book.) Round the corner in CHURCH STREET is another *Clements* house, No. 37 of *c.* 1895, more Gothic. Mostly older and smaller houses here, continuing W up GREYS HILL, where Nos. 22–24 have sub-Soane incised decoration of *c.* 1820–30.

Back to Reading Road, where STATION ROAD runs E. Facing the station, the former IMPERIAL HOTEL and its accompanying shops are by *William Theobalds*, 1896–7. The architectural equivalent of a striped boating blazer. Old English brick and half-timbering, rising to four storeys, with oriels and balconies. PERPETUAL HOUSE, former offices to the E, is perky Postmodern Free Style by *Broadway Malyan*, 1993–4. The former ROYAL HOTEL, 1899–1900 by *G. W. Webb*, is an unimaginative affair of repeated half-timbered gables. Finally RIVER TERRACE, big and basic classical stucco, as late as 1866. 250 yds downstream, in Mill Meadows, stands an OBELISK of 1788, originally at the main town crossing.

OTHER BUILDINGS

Described anti-clockwise, from the w.

FRIAR PARK, Gravel Hill. The Xanadu of the immensely successful City solicitor Sir Frank Crisp (1843–1919). His architect was the otherwise little-known *Robert Clarke Edwards*, his builder *Charles Clements* of Henley. The HOUSE is of 1890–5, a long L-shape in French Flamboyant Gothic style, of red brick and yellow stone dressings, with a square, spired tower at the N end and numerous pinnacles, through-storey bays and big traceried windows all round. Encased within may be some fabric from a villa of 1873 by *J. S. Dodd* on the same site, also named Friar Park and also built by *Clements*. The sale catalogue of 1919 described the result as 'of highly diversified Gothic detail borrowed from the Pays Bas…strongly influenced by the French Chateaux'. Stone carving by one *Richardson*, including larky figures of friars etc. that do not appear on Edwards's original drawings.

The INTERIORS are still more lavish. A porch and passage on the s side lead to a circulation hall with dark panelling and double-galleried landings, the staircase rising between. In the end wall ahead is a giant stained-glass window in the style of *A. O. Hemming* (PC), with historical narrative scenes and texts from Longfellow. To each side are tall murals of the Tree of Life and the Tree of Knowledge. Dining room to the s with gilt leather hangings and a richly appointed inglenook; also a window of 1922 by *Morris & Co. (J.H. Dearle)*, introduced by a later owner, showing David's Charge to Solomon, the design taken from *Burne-Jones*'s window of 1882 at Trinity Church, Boston (MA). For contrast, the rooms to the N are of a mixed Louis XV and Inigo Jones style. Some other windows have pictorial glass in the style of *A.J. Dix* (PC). Several fire-places make fine displays of *De Morgan* tiles. Texts, mottoes and inscriptions abound all through, and – to quote the sale catalogue again – 'the decorative principle of the Friar...is met with at every point. Moveable noses of Friars switch on the electric light and Friars hold electric lamps.'

Crisp's GARDENS were an enduring labour of love, developed and embellished through twenty-five years, with *Philip Knowles* as head gardener. Variety and novelty were embraced, with enclaves on historical or exotic themes, some based on illustrations. The terraces by the house may have been designed by *H.E. Milner*, who depicted an unexecuted or superseded layout for Friar Park in his *The Art and Practice of Landscape Gardening* (1890). In less formal areas, much use was made of artificial *Pulhamite* stone. By 1914 Friar Park had a series of LAKES on the slopes below the house, the water from which extends into two thrillingly intricate GROTTOES: one with artificial stalactites, the other ('Blue Grotto') with blue-glass skylights. NW of the house is a prodigious ALPINE GARDEN composed of 23,000 tons of Yorkshire limestone with a model of the Matterhorn at the apex. The JAPANESE GARDEN features a tea house set over a waterfall. There were formal Elizabethan and medieval gardens too, and a version of the labyrinth at Versailles. Crisp's irrepressible prankishness found full expression in the artificial CAVES made within the rock garden, which in his heyday were individually adorned as the Ice, Vine (with imitation grapes), Wishing Well, Skeleton, Illusion and Gnome caves.

Lady Ottoline Morrell, entertained here *c.*1905, wondered how far Crisp 'mocked at himself or at his visitors', or whether 'he was colossally simple and really thought these vulgar and monstrous jokes amusing and beautiful'. A different view was taken by George Harrison, the Beatle, who bought Friar Park in 1970 with his then wife, Pattie Boyd. Initial restoration of the house was by *David Tapp*, followed by the devoted revival of the gardens by George and Olivia Harrison.

Three spired LODGES by *Clarke Edwards* stand along Gravel Hill. LOWER LODGE of 1891 and UPPER LODGE (extended) are miniature epitomes of the mansion. MIDDLE LODGE is more domestic, with a quatrefoil-traceried bargeboard. At Lower Lodge also some especially splendid GATES and GATEPIERS.

ANCASTLE GREEN, S of Gravel Hill. Houses and overlook-ing flats of 1966–8, by *Raglan Squire & Partners*. Pleasantly grouped, but of standard suburban design.

ST ANDREW'S ROAD, W of Reading Road. Nos. 26–42 are stone-faced pairs with freakish detail, especially Nos. 40–42, dated

1906: reliefs of cherubs, griffins and vine scroll, and friezes of comical hunting scenes.

COUNCIL HOUSES, Vicarage Road and Western Avenue. Well-crafted short terraces of 1919–22 by *H.T. Hare*. At the NE corner the BURGIS HOME OF REST, dated 1927, with veranda, Single-storey ALMSHOUSES by *E.V. Ive*, 1931, immediately E.

PAST FIELD, No. 9 Rotherfield Road, W of Harpsden House. By *Patrick Gwynne* for Dr and Mrs Salmon, 1959–60, extended 1967. Single-storeyed and not large. The cranked plan, careful placing in the landscape, and contrasting colours and materials – purple Fletton brick, varnished hardwood boards, rendered oversailing roof – are characteristic of the architect. Entry from the N, between living and sleeping wings, E and W. The main rooms face the southward slope, with some full-height glazing. At the E end a utility room by *Studio Octopi*, 2014–15, replacing one of the 1970s by *Gwynne*. – LONG VIEW, immediately E, is of 2004–7 by *Avanti Architects* for Ulrich and Susie Gerhartz (née Salmon). A larger single-storey house, in sympathy with Gwynne but sharper and leaner. Three wings, their roofs tilting up from a central lantern turret. Blue Potsdam brick and vertical boarding, with some coloured mosaic tile. The roof oversails the glazed S front, its E angle resting on a row of close-set steel uprights.

(HENLEY PARK, 1½ m. NNW. An older house remodelled for J.W. Newell Birch in the 1840s–50s, in the stucco Italianate mode. Three storeys, canted bay windows, balustraded parapet.)

BADGEMORE HOUSE. *See* Rotherfield Greys.

HIGHMOOR

ST PAUL (former). A simple aisleless church of 1859 by *Joseph Morris* of Reading. Flint and stone. W bellcote, windows with Geometrical or plate tracery. STAINED GLASS: E window of 1895, designed by *J.F. Bentley*. – Contemporary RECTORY, SE, also by *Morris*. – Hexagonal WELL-HOUSE of *c.*1865 to the W, the mechanism intact.

HIGHMOOR HALL. ½ m. N. A bitty mansion of various dates, its history uncertain. Brick. Mullioned windows and false gables on the garden side. The N and E sides Georgian, with sash windows. Later entrance loggia of seven arches.

(MERRIMOLES, ¾ m. NNE. A bland Neo-Early Georgian house of 1938–9 by *Paul Phipps*. For the author Peter Fleming and his wife, Celia Johnson, the actress. Evelyn Waugh called it 'a hideous little Golders Green villa' (letter to Nancy Mitford, 1946).)

KIBES, 1 m. SSE. Streamlined *Moderne* of 1939, altered and extended, but still of note as a design by two women architects, *Florence H. Gibb* and *Margaret Low*.

IPSDEN

Widely scattered settlement, with only a few houses near the church.

St Mary. Small, consisting of chancel, nave, N chapel and traces of a S aisle. The bellcote and rebuilt W end are from *Hussey*'s restoration of 1857. It was originally a chapel of North Stoke (q.v.), and like that church has some unusually elaborate details in the chancel, which dates from the late C12. Its S doorway is round-arched and has jamb shafts (one missing) with leaf capitals. Lancets in the side walls, two pointed and one round-headed. Internally the splays have slender jamb shafts, those in the E bay of Purbeck marble. Leaf or volute capitals; also two carved with heads. Mid-C15 E window with a flat-sided arch. The chancel arch follows the side windows in its details, but the work looks Victorian; perhaps an enlargement by *Hussey*, who in 1850 described an otherwise similar arch here as 'small and very plain and poor'. The N chapel, also part of the early church, has a small round-headed W window. Two-bay arcade with a round pier on a waterholding base. The responds have bases with corner spurs. Pointed double-chamfered arches. No N windows, only the blocked lower parts of two single lights just below the eaves. The location implies lost cross-gables, and the form of the present roof would have allowed for these. It is C14 or early C15, of two bays, with thick tie-beams and arch-braced collars. Arched wind-braces, those of the E bay with multiple cusping; more cusping on the side of the E tie-beam. The middle truss rests on a slim stone pier on the arcade side, no doubt of 1857; was there a timber post before? Ceiled nave roof with a castellated C15 wall-plate and moulded tie-beams. Blocked arches and part of a pier from the lost aisle appear in the S wall outside. It may have gone in the C14, the date of the hollow-chamfered S doorway under a hood with headstops, or the C15, when the Perp three-light windows were inserted. Brick and flint S porch dated 1634. – PEWS of 1881, brought from Mongewell (q.v.). – STAINED GLASS. By *Clayton & Bell*, whose style developed considerably between the 1870s (S aisle to E, †1875) and 1909 (S aisle to W). Their chancel windows are from cartoons by *George Daniels* (S 1884, E 1885, N †1892). – MONUMENTS. Brass to Thomas and Isabel Englyshe, both †1525. 17¾-in. (45-cm.) figures, her head-dress damaged. They are palimpsests of early C15 brasses, his of a much larger figure of a woman, hers of an inscription probably belonging to the wife of John Stapleton. – James Hartnoll †1917. Tablet in late C17 style, designed by *Sir T.G. Jackson* (Martin Jones).

WELL, by the lychgate. 1865. Given by Rajah Sir Deo Narayan Singh, a friend of E.A. Reade, with winding gear by *Messrs Wilder* of Wallingford (cf. Stoke Row).

OLD VICARAGE, ¼ m. S. Built in 1700–1 to serve Ipsden and North Stoke parishes. Pale red brick chequered with blue. Five bays. Dentil cornice, roof with three dormers.

MODEL COTTAGES, 1 m. N. Two one-and-a-half-storey pairs built
in 1831 for Uvedale Thomas Shudd Price, as their datestones
record.

(HAILEY HOUSE. ½ m. ENE. By *F.L. Pearson*, 1916, for Glynne
Williams. Big, of stone. Twisted chimneys and rounded gables.
The NW angle has a swept quadrant colonnade.)

HILL VIEW, ⅔ m. E. By *Spratley & Partners*, 2021–2. Two
storeys, glass-walled to the S, the rest mostly copper-effect
cladding – not a good colour for this landscape.

HANDSMOOTH HOUSE, 1½ m. E. The white apparition on
the hill-slope is the only British building by the US architect *Richard Meier*, of 2010–16 for the actor Rowan Atkinson.
Meier's designs typically evoke Le Corbusier, more precisely
the all-white 'Purist' buildings and machine aesthetic of the
1920s. That manner was of course rapidly taken up, making
its British début at Amyas Connell's High and Over (1929–31),
another conspicuous house on a hill, at Amersham in the Buckinghamshire Chilterns. Connell's house has the scale of a villa,
as did the demolished 1930s predecessor here, but Meier's has
the grandiosity of a full country house. The main block features
glass-walled living spaces under a floating roof slab, with a
steel-balustraded staircase next to a central entrance recess.
Behind are a car court and a pool house with garaging, to the
l. a separate guest house beyond a tennis court enclosure, all
linked by white walls and all planned on the same grid. The
rigour and consistency are undeniably imposing, but as with
Corbusier's *machines à habiter* the impression is severe to the
point of harshness.

BIBURY, Berins Hill, 1⅓ m. ESE. A quirky house by *Francis Pollen*
for John Pavey; designed 1976, built *c.*1983. Starfish plan, five
equal wings radiating from a higher pentagonal core. All the
roofs hipped and tiled.

BRAZIERS PARK (School of Integrative Social Research), ¾ m.
s. In origin a hip-roofed late C17 farmhouse (datestone of 1688
in the cellar), remodelled and extended in the Gothic style
after 1794 by *Daniel Harris*, architect, antiquary and keeper of
Oxford gaol (*see* p.401). The client was Captain Isaac Manly
and the designs were shown at the Royal Academy in 1799.
The S range is all Harris, grey-rendered, embattled and symmetrical. Tower with a rose window and spiky pinnacles, porch
with enriched gablets projecting through a broad pointed-
arched veranda. The stagey quality is reminiscent of Wyatt's
Gothic work. Semicircular bays face E and W at the ends. The
C17 house appears behind, its wooden dentil cornice intact on
the W side, above twin Gothic oriels and broad Y-traceried
French windows. The adjacent bay and matching bowed end
to the l. are of 1910, added for Valentine Fleming by *W.E.
Mills*: an astonishingly deferential exercise, given that Georgian
Gothic was then still generally despised. The cross-vaulted
ENTRANCE VESTIBULE with its plaster niches opens to the
bow-ended rooms of the s range, with their charming friezes
of shallow Gothick quatrefoils and trefoils. In the DRAWING

ROOM, W, a black marble fireplace, similarly detailed. The DINING ROOM, E, was lined with reused French linenfold panelling in 1910. The very space-hungry STAIRCASE belongs with the 1910 alterations, rising in double flights from the central landing to reach the 1790s wing. Twisted balusters in late C17 style. – Formal GARDENS also of 1910, including a stone-lined rill in the Gertrude Jekyll manner.

IPSDEN HOUSE, ½ m. SSW. Probably C17, remodelled and extended. L-plan. The date 1764 on rainwater heads on the garden front would suit the main brick elevations. On this side the upper windows have been narrowed. Canted ground-floor bay windows, reportedly added in the 1930s for the novelist Rosamond Lehmann and her husband Wogan Philipps. The lower section adjoining N, which may represent an earlier part of the house, has Gothick windows of C18 type arranged charmingly *ad hoc*. Ipsden House was the birthplace of the novelist and dramatist Charles Reade, author of *The Cloister and the Hearth* (1861), and younger brother of E.A. Reade (*see* Stoke Row). – Fine circular DOVECOTE, brick and flint with a conical roof and lantern. Probably C17.

MONUMENT, in a copse by the road, ¼ m. W of Ipsden House. Erected by E.A. Reade after 1860 to his brother John Reade, who died in India in 1827. Small pyramid on a square base, within railings.

IPSDEN FARM. On the same road, E of the monument. Notable for its gigantic L-shaped C18 brick BARN with low red-tiled roofs. It has twenty-four bays and five entrance porches.

KIDMORE END

ST JOHN THE BAPTIST. An attractive church of 1851–2 by *Arthur Billing*. C13 style. W bellcote. The polygonal apse, modelled on that of Tidmarsh, Berkshire, has a rib-vault on slender shafts. Thinly timbered hammerbeam roof to the nave. In 1870 Billing embellished the apse with blind arcading on Devonshire marble shafts, and introduced the pavement of *Minton*'s encaustic TILES. N vestry 1894. – FONT and stone PULPIT of 1852, the latter with mosaic panels by *Salviati*, added 1868. – STAINED GLASS by *Warrington* in the apse. Nave, three windows by *Burlison & Grylls*, †1876, †1913, †1930.

WELL at the village crossing, *c.*1891. With a cute shelter.

POND HOUSE, by the pond NE of the church. Refronted in the early C18, uncommonly using brick above flint for the two storeys. Three bays. Later Georgian porch with fluted Doric half-columns.

KIDMORE HOUSE, ½ m. SE. Finely proportioned front of *c.*1700. Red and silver brick. Five bays, the central windows more closely spaced. The hipped roof with dormers has an early C20 look; alterations in 1904 are recorded. Doorcase, also apparently C20. A good courtyard of FARM BUILDINGS, C18 and C19, r.

CHALK HOUSE, Chalkhouse Green, 1 m. SE. Eccentric Early Georgian. Five-bay centre comprising a *piano nobile* over a basement, the doorway approached by a flight of steps. Hipped roof concealed by a high parapet, which sweeps up in the middle. In the parapet, four blatantly false painted windows and a painted central oculus.

CROSS FARMHOUSE, ⅓ m. S. A timber-framed house worthy of detailed study. The main range may be C15, with a substantial cross-wing, l. (Jettied on this side, with tension bracing in a central cross-gable.) The r. cross-wing is probably C20.

(CANE END HOUSE, 1½ m. w. Georgian, but the irregular garden façade suggests work of different dates, and some of the fabric is late C16. Symmetrical six-bay entrance front. Doorway with an arched rusticated head, forming a Palladian motif with the adjacent windows. Hipped roof with dormers, dentil cornice. A dated brick of 1707 is reported. One room has C17 painted panelling.)

KINGSTON BLOUNT
Aston Rowant

ST JOHN (former). 1876–7, S aisle added 1887. One of the few churches by *Aston Webb*. Stark red brick, trefoiled lancets. Chancel and nave under one roof with fish-scale tiles. Bellcote like a well canopy over the chancel arch. Converted to a house *c.*1991. – STAINED GLASS. E and W windows by *Brown & Boreham*, ineptly drawn.

OLD TUDOR HOUSE, E of the church. C17 with a lower C16 E projection. Framing infilled respectively with plain or herringbone brick. – BARN in front with a close-studded gable-end.

SCHOOL (former), *c.*1878. Gothic. Bellcote on the porch.

PRIMITIVE METHODIST CHAPEL (former). No more than an adapted mid-terrace house, signalled by a porch with inscription and the date 1859.

KINGSTON HOUSE, 150 yds SE. 1855. Big and neutral.

LEWKNOR

ST MARGARET. Originally a cruciform church of *c.*1180–1200. In the early C14 the chancel was rebuilt and the S transept replaced by a S aisle, the latter in turn rebuilt as a near copy when *A.W. Blomfield* restored the nave in 1863–4. C15 W tower with a squared NE stair-turret. The late C12 shows externally in two lancets opposite each other at the W end of the nave, and in the N transept with its broad clasping buttresses. The round-arched N doorway to the transept may be re-set, as it cuts across a later infilled arch. Above is a blocked twin-light C14 window with ogee-headed lights. *Blomfield* introduced the early C13-style nave N windows with their ill-judged polychromatic setting in stripes of red brick. Also his are the transept's E and W windows. The N vestry is C15. Inside, a Transitional late C12 chancel arch with a pointed arch and an outer band of chevron, a chamfered inner order and jamb shafts with volute capitals. Chamfered N transept arch with imposts continuous with those of the chancel arch. This moulding continues along the nave walls below the windows, except where the aisle interrupts. The E respond of the S transept also remains, its impost linked with that of the chancel arch. C14 three-bay arcade with double-chamfered arches and octagonal piers. Aisle S windows of two ogee lights under a quatrefoil, reticulated tracery in the E window. PISCINA (a copy?) in a cinquefoiled recess in the S wall.

The early C14 CHANCEL is rich work, for an unknown patron. Three side windows each of three lights, E window of five; every light with cinquefoiled sub-arches under elongated trefoils. The sub-arches have slight ogee profiles at the top. Along the S wall inside are a vaulted PISCINA, triple SEDILIA, TOMB RECESS and priest's doorway, all with elaborate crocketed canopies and heavy finials. Enjoyable carving, with little heads, and odd details such as the carved hands supporting the pinnacles of the priest's doorway. The seaweedy foliage – also on the CREDENCE TABLE, N wall – suggests a date *c.*1320–30. Some details on the S side are well-judged reinstatement of 1845, when *James Johnson* of Oxford restored the chancel.

FURNISHINGS. FONT. C12, cylindrical, with a pattern of interlaced beaded circles, some enclosing crosses, rosettes or faces. The font at Berrick Salome (q.v.) is similar and must be by the same masons. – Some medieval TILES collected in the N transept. – STAINED GLASS. E window by *Hardman*, *c.*1855. Chancel NE and SE windows, 1873 and 1876 by *William Morris*. Angels against simple quarries. The angel with cymbals, N side, is a replacement of 1877, to a different design. Three chancel windows of *c.*1884–5, style of *A.O. Hemming*, and another by *Hardman*, †1875, centre N (PC). Transept, two by *Herbert Bryans*, probably from restoration of this part in 1914. Nave N, *Powells*, 1936. W window, *Ion Pace*, 1883.

MONUMENTS. Eroded effigy of a lady, mid-C14. In the tomb recess, but *ex situ*. – Brass to John Aldebourne, priest, *c.*1365–75. 12-in. (30 cm.) half-figure. – Two similar early C17 monuments, both of alabaster with recumbent effigies; in 1845 moved W along the chancel and their canopies removed. That to William and Isabel Deane, †1620 and †1624 (S) has children at a prayer-desk along the side of the tomb-chest. Sir Thomas and Lady Fleetwood's monument, †1625 and †1629, has a crest. – Chancel N wall, John Scrope M.P., Secretary to the Treasury, †1752. Attributed to *Sir Henry Cheere*. A marble bust in an open-pedimented Composite aedicule. At the bottom an accomplished relief of Concordia(?) with cherubs. – The N transept is the memorial chapel of the Jodrells. Occupying most of its N wall is an immense architectural monument to Sir Paul Jodrell †1728 and family. – E wall, the Rev. Sir Edward Repps Jodrell, 3rd Bt †1882, by *Sir J. E. Boehm*. Recumbent effigy with angels and Evangelists in relief above. – Free-standing in the centre, another family monument with a lush statuary group of two marble angels with wreaths, signed by *Paolo Bazzanti* of Florence. Probably of *c.*1890, replacing a sarcophagus-type Jodrell monument of 1833.

CHURCHYARD. S of the porch a C17 CHEST TOMB, still with Gothic-panelled sides. Also the tombstone of Thomas Smith †1886, with relief of a falling wicket.

SCHOOL, SE of the church. 1836. Teacher's house with a hipped tiled roof flanked by two thatched schoolrooms. Flint and brick walls.

RECTORY, S of the church. Regular Early Georgian front of whitewashed brick. Five bays with a sharp central gable. Segment-headed windows with keystones, rusticated doorway.

CHURCH FARM, NW. The farmhouse has a late C16 core behind two phases of C18 brick. More remarkable is its former BARN to the W. The weatherboarding and steeply pitched red-tiled roof conceal the frame of a grand C14 hall house (tree-ring dates 1339, 1342/3), re-erected here sometime after 1764. It probably belonged to the principal residence of the former rectorial farm, a property of Abingdon Abbey. Three bays, with a splendid display of cusped bracing. The spere truss retains its original aisled form. In the truss to the W the aisle-posts are insertions, replacing the original raised-aisle form, i.e. with the arched braces spanning the full width and the posts sitting on top of the tie-beam. Converted to offices by *RMA Architects* *c.*2010.

MANOR HOUSE, Weston Road, ⅓ m. WNW. Late C16, but with a plain brick front of 1866. MOOR COURT just NW appears mostly C18 brick, of H-plan. A Tudor-type chimneystack remains on the r. flank.

LITTLE HASELEY
Great Haseley

A secluded stone-built settlement in the S part of the parish. Of the lesser houses, DELAFIELD and STONES FARMHOUSE to its W both have early C17 origins.

HASELEY COURT. The medieval house of the Barentins was rebuilt in the C18, save for one enigmatic rear wing. The main range faces W. Three storeys. Its seven middle bays, arranged 2:3:2 with a central pediment, are of 1709–10 for Edmund

Boulter Sen. and Jun. The three central bays break forward under a pediment. Modest ornament only: doorway with a segmental pediment on brackets, small quoins, small keystones to the windows, plain parapet. The ball finials date from c. 1955. In the later c18 matching two-bay extensions were added, and these project slightly on either side. On the rear elevation a datestone 1754, above a Venetian window on the ground floor. This may date the PALLADIAN ROOM within, where the window has squared and fluted Ionic columns. Doorways with finely moulded lugged architraves and pediments; fireplace with side scrolls and an acanthus frieze. Also possibly later than c. 1710 is the vigorously carved stone fireplace in the ENTRANCE HALL, with a broken-pedimented overmantel and delicately carved details of garlands, shells and drapery. The wall facing the entrance cuts against the side doorcases, suggesting an insertion. In it are two overarched doorways and a big central niche, all with egg-and-dart mouldings. Also oval recesses over the doors in the side walls. Similar openings on the landings of the STAIRCASE, which has distinctive newels composed of four short turned balusters between square top and bottom sections. The dining room is subdivided by fluted Doric pilasters flanking the fireplace and has an elaborately moulded cornice. In the S extension is the SALOON, a double-height space with spare but refined Neoclassical detail of c. 1780, close enough to the style of *James Wyatt* to suggest an attribution. The late c18 date probably applies to both extensions.

So to the MEDIEVAL WING. The manor was purchased by two Barentin brothers in 1391, and by the mid c15 the family's principal seat was here. What remains comprises a two-storey wing running E from the N end of the early c18 house. It is uncertain what part of the medieval establishment this represents, not least because the wing was Gothicized in the later c18, but a first-floor hall is a possibility. The plain chamfered S doorway and one upper window of three ogee-headed trefoiled lights are original; the other S windows are square-headed c15 Perp with cusped lights, and may be c18 insertions. Two S buttresses of medieval type, perhaps added at the same time as the c18 embattled parapet and the sunk quatrefoils, which together make a symmetrical composition. In the E wall a tall window of c. 1300 with two cinquefoiled lights and a quatrefoil in the head, apparently re-set here with brickwork above the arch. On the N side an early c19 addition with a stepped gable, between later single-storey infillings. A traceried bow window on the N end of the c18 block may be early c19 too.

(The upper INTERIORS of the wing have a special interest as late creations by the celebrated American-born interior decorator *Nancy Lancaster*, who moved to Haseley Court in 1955 from Kelmarsh Hall in Northamptonshire. The house was restored for her by the architect *R. J. Page*; the interiors were a collaboration with her business partner *John Fowler* of *Colefax & Fowler*. A tunnel-like upper room runs the full length of the wing, with a corbel table in the Gothick style. At the opposite end is plasterwork of fruit and flowers, a theme repeated in the *trompe l'œil* paintings on the walls and ceiling by *John Fowler* and *George Oakes*. Opening from this is a bathroom in the N addition with a ribbed stucco vault and a Georgian Gothic fireplace. In 2022 the rooms are being restored, together with other Nancy Lancaster decorative schemes in the C18 range, with *Peregrine Bryant* as architect. A new open-well staircase is to be inserted where the medieval and C18 parts join.)

To the NE of the house is a courtyard closed by three toy-like PAVILIONS with connecting walls between. Each has a hipped roof, a three-bay front with a central pedimented projection, and an arched entrance. The middle one was the C18 brewhouse, the r. one the laundry; the l. pavilion (also the middle cupola) is an addition or reinstatement by *Page* for Nancy Lancaster, built *c.* 1960 as an orangery. To the NW and aligned parallel to the medieval wing is a fine C15 BARN, its E part rebuilt as stables in the C18, and all converted for residential use in 1955 by *Page*. The C15 section retains slit-openings and a big moulded four-centred archway. (Small doorway behind with a pointed chamfered arch.) The oblong POOL behind the main house and the four-square WALLED GARDENS to the N also date from 1955 onwards and are by Nancy. On the W side, *Geoffrey Jellicoe* designed the arrangement of lawn and hedges as a prelude to the reinstated double avenue on the main axis. The topiary of the CHESS GARDEN S of the house was first shaped probably around 1900.

LITTLE MILTON

ST JAMES. 1843–4 by *John Hayward* of Exeter, in a rather dull mid-C14 style. Large nave and chancel, no aisles. In 1861 Hayward added the embattled W tower of West Country character. (PISCINA with a medieval drain, from the former chapel at Little Milton. – REREDOS and PULPIT, 1901, by *Harry Hems* of Exeter.) – STAINED GLASS. E window and nave SE and NE windows all by *Thomas Willement*, 1853–4, the first two with his monogram. W window and nave SW window (†1869) both by *Heaton, Butler & Bayne*.

OLD VICARAGE, S. Sharp-gabled Neo-Tudor of *c.* 1850.

WESLEYAN CHAPEL (former), Haseley Road, 150 yds NE. 1890. Modest red brick and stone, with pointed windows.

SCHOOL, 250 yds S. 1861. Gothic in the manner of Street or Buckeridge.

MANOR HOUSE, 150 yds E. An undeniably ugly house, chiefly on account of the harsh third storey added in 1913. Rough-cast, with sash windows of Late Georgian type in the middle bays. Doorway with a fanlight and architrave with Adamesque decoration. Open-pedimented porch with fluted Doric columns. To the l. a short loggia with four similar columns. On the E flank, r., two C15 windows each of two trefoiled lights under a square hood. The wall above has been rebuilt. A similar window, now internal, in the opposite wall of this room. More early work remains in the timber-framed rear wings, which enclose a small courtyard. (The E wing comprises part of a former hall house, including two bays still open to the roof. Arch-braced collar-truss, curved wind-braces.) – Square DOVECOTE, probably C18. – 100 yds w, facing the churchyard, two pretty LODGES of *c.* 1820. They are white-painted *cottages ornés* of one storey, with steeply pitched thatched roofs and Gothic windows.

The VILLAGE has some C15–C17 houses worth singling out. Just s of the Wesleyan chapel is DOVECOTE HOUSE of 1658, with a near-symmetrical three-bay front. Ovolo-moulded mullioned windows; central stack with big back-to-back fireplaces. Dove holes in the rear gable. THE OLD STORE to the N has similar windows but also hoodmoulds, i.e. probably early C17. To the w, HILL VIEW HOUSE, a five-bay former hall house of the C15, within C19 rubble-stone and brick walls. It faces MILTON MANOR DRIVE, a close of houses by *Maidment & Brady*, designed in 1964. Of irregular plan, with monopitched roofs and much use of stone cladding. 100 yds s in Haseley Road, FLETCHER'S FARM, *c.* 1600–40. Stone, with diagonal-mullioned windows. Just N of the churchyard, ALBION BARN was adapted in 2013 by *Studio Seilern Architects* as a library and display space for the art dealer Michael Hue-Williams. Blackened weatherboarding.

MAPLEDURHAM   6070

A small Thames-side village, still feudal in spirit and dominated by the great house which looms behind the churchyard wall. The setting is picturesque, with a wooded island and the water mill close by. To the N are the Chilterns, with typical scattered settlement and dense woodland. The easternmost part, built up from the late C19 as Caversham expanded, was transferred to Reading in 1977 (*see The Buildings of England: Berkshire*). Most of the parish's pre-Victorian buildings have been tree-ring dated by Dr Dan Miles, including many erected or rebuilt in the 1600s–20s under Sir Michael and Sir Richard Blount.

ST MARGARET. The most striking details of this small church are the result of a restoration of 1863 by *William Butterfield*. He reworked the plain brick w tower of 1608 with bold flint chequering, and added the top stage and pyramid roof. The porch, also of 1863, has a timber front with shaped bargeboards and tracery. Inside, Butterfield inserted a three-bay timber arcade on faceted stone bases to make a false N aisle. The medieval church is mainly C14 and C15, except for the blocked arch of *c.*1200 at the W end of the S aisle. Chamfered arch and jambs, plain imposts. The S aisle, datable by a will to the period 1381–95, was built as the chantry chapel of Sir Robert Bardolf (*see* below). It has square-headed three-light windows with panel tracery and opens to the nave by two finely moulded arches (the zigzag surrounds must be *Butterfield*'s). After the Reformation it continued in use as the private burial place of the Blounts, Roman Catholic lords of the manor, and it remains railed off from the rest of the church. Perp chancel E window; the uncusped side windows are C16. In the N aisle two Perp windows, N and W, and one by Butterfield, who also designed the chancel roof decoration. The nave roof, partly ceiled, has been dated to 1446.

FURNISHINGS. PEWS, STALLS and wooden COMMUNION RAILS and PULPIT all excellent and representative designs by *Butterfield*. – Medieval TILES in the S aisle. – FONT. Norman, cylindrical, with spiral bands of billet decoration. – STAINED GLASS. In the E window some re-set old glass, including figures probably of the 1470s. From l. to r.: St Stephen holding the stones of his martyrdom; St Sitha or Zita, a bunch of keys hanging from her waist; St Mary Magdalene holding an ointment pot and palm branch. In the tracery lights shields of arms: Bardolf of Mapledurham (late C14, l.), and others of the mid C15. Main lights of 1865 by *Hardman*, also the chancel side windows, tower and others. S aisle S, mid-C15 fragments and various C16–C17 pictorial and decorative pieces, rearranged in 1975. N aisle N window by *Powells*, 1908; W by *Jane Gray*, 1961. – MONUMENTS. In the S aisle the magnificent brass to Sir Robert Bardolf †1395, formerly on a tomb-chest. The 70-in. (1.76-metre) figure with the remains of a canopy is a near match to that of Sir Robert de Grey at Rotherfield Greys (q.v.). – Charles Lister †1613, architectural. – Sir Richard Blount and Cecily, Lady Blount, †1628 and †1619. Railed tomb-chest with recumbent effigies of alabaster, he in armour, she with an exaggerated coiffure, farthingale and ruff. – Eleonora Blount †1782. Large wall monument with a small relief of a deathbed scene. – Capt. Frank Rose †1914. Small marble and bronze monument of 1916 in the manner of Alfred Gilbert, with a knight in armour. (– In the tower a cumbersome monument of 1914 to Frank Rose's three officer brothers, †1900 and †1908. Marble portrait busts under a big angel.)

In the churchyard a handsome GATEWAY to the house, E. Piers with ball finials, re-set C18 wrought-iron gates with a swagger overthrow, partly restored.

MAPLEDURHAM HOUSE. A very large H-plan house of red brick, long thought to be Elizabethan, but now securely dated to 1609–12 from its tree rings and plasterwork; the dates span between the times of the elderly Sir Michael Blount (†1610) and his son Sir Richard, who was almost certainly Catholic.

Subsequent owners – the Blounts to 1943, then the Eyston family by descent from the female line – have maintained the Catholic tradition.

The house faces E, with its back to the church. The four wings are of near-equal length and somewhat lower than the main range, which extends some 170 ft (52 metres) N to S. The unusual brickwork pattern of elongated diapering is original, but the main front and the interior have both been much altered. A sketch of the house on a survey map of 1731 shows three big dormer gables between the wings, but a later C18 drawing depicts a straight crenellated parapet instead, together with various classical embellishments of later C17 character. The present aspect owes much to the sympathetic remodelling of 1828–31 by the Catholic builder-surveyor *Thomas Martin*, for Michael Henry Blount. Mullion-and-transom windows replaced C18 sashes, the parapet was rebuilt with a steep central gable to balance those of the wings, and the crenellated stone porch was added. Also of this time are the through-storey canted bays placed symmetrically l. and r. of the two broad chimneystacks, and probably the heightening of the ground-floor canted bays on the ends of the wings. The short sides largely preserve the Jacobean form, with windows asymmetrically placed to follow the ascent of the N and S staircases (one on the N side has been infilled). On the W side three big first-floor windows to the Great Chamber have also been blocked. Their double-transomed form is original, copied on the entrance front in *David Nye*'s restoration of 1962–9 for John Eyston. Some small C18 additions were removed at the same time, leaving the pointed-windowed chapel of 1796–7 in front of the Great Chamber. The middle chimneystack on this side is of *c.* 1830; a stack added to the E side of the main range next to the SE wing is dated 1757 on a brick.

INTERIORS. The original plan included a ground-floor hall with entry from the middle of the front, a great chamber above, and a long gallery within the roof-space. These upper rooms survive, but the ground floor was reconfigured in 1828–31 to make the present ENTRANCE HALL and the rooms on either side. The dais end of the C17 hall was on the N, as the main stair is at the N end, with the most important rooms opening off it. The original hall would therefore have been entered at its S end, through a screens passage. Its successor has a central entrance with fireplace opposite. Jacobean-style overmantel and panelling of 1868 by *C.A. Buckler*. The details were copied from twelve wooden pilasters with strapwork and an enriched frieze, probably made for the Great Chamber and now re-set in the CORRIDOR to the N. Alongside the corridor is the LIBRARY, to the S of the entrance hall the DINING ROOM, both with restrained classical detail. The dining room fireplace is brought in; late C18, with a fine figure relief.

Between the wings at the N end is the GREAT STAIRCASE, unusually spacious for its date. Its broad flights climb around an oblong stairwell, supported by continuous newels in the form of elongated Doric columns. The newel posts on the first floor are surmounted by carved baskets of flowers of *c.* 1670, the date of the handsome broken-pedimented doorcase on this landing. Various odd expedients and short connecting staircases reconcile the landings with the floor levels of the wings opening off. In addition the topmost landing is reached by flights of differing steepness, placed puzzlingly side by side. These have been dated to 1610 and 1611 from their timbers, which suggests successive attempts to achieve a comfortable ascent. Overhead is the original thin-ribbed plaster ceiling with heads in sprays of foliage, and a rich frieze of foliage scrolls and lion masks. More on the landing underside, with portrait medallions of David and Julius Caesar – derived from the popular theme of the Nine Worthies – and smaller heads including Juno and Venus.

Of the rooms in the WINGS at this end, that on the ground floor to the E has an elaborate ceiling dated 1612, clearly by the plasterer of the staircase. Intersecting squares and quatrefoils made by broad ribs ornamented with vine trails. Between them are the same large and small portrait medallions as on the staircase. Overmantel of wood, with blind arches framed by fluted pilasters. The room directly above has another ceiling dated 1612 with the same portrait medallions, together with dragons, a Tudor rose and fleur-de-lys. Here the ribs are wider, leaving plain bands alongside the vine-trail strips. Lively frieze of dragons and Tudor roses. The first-floor room in the W wing has a frieze of mermaids and scrolls, and behind the end panelling a through-storey PRIEST HOLE with trap doors between the floors, one of several hidden refuges in the house.

The GREAT CHAMBER or Saloon opens from the first-floor landing. It has an undated ribbed plaster ceiling with medallions, a variation on the motifs of the ceilings in the NE wing, but more assured and refined in execution. Here the portraits are of the first five Roman kings and their wives, plus Julius Caesar. Those shown in full face are from the same moulds used for a ceiling of 1599 at Canonbury in North London, and altogether the quality compares with the best London work. The frieze, in a different style, is of *c.* 1830.* The LONG GALLERY above is now entirely plain, and partly subdivided at the S end. In the mezzanine immediately beneath is a former CHAPEL, with panelling of *c.* 1700 and a raised inner end. The SECONDARY STAIRCASE alongside is less spacious than its counterpart but has matching details, including continuous newels in the open-well section below. Of the wings at the S end, that to the W has the kitchen and services. In the E wing

---

*The frieze over the porch, i.e. in the adjacent bay, was found in the 1960s to be inscribed '*J. Bottomley* 1831'. Payment was also made in 1835 to *Thomas Willement* for painting, wallpaper and woodwork, the last perhaps accounting for some of the copied Jacobean-style doorcases.

on the ground floor some C17 stained glass, heraldic shields in an C18 surround.

Finally the CHAPEL of 1796–7, entered from the back of the entrance hall. It has a rear gallery or dais facing the window-less altar end, and an external doorway to the main seating area between. A very pretty Gothick interior. Ribbed ceiling (plasterer *Samuel Kerridge* of Reading), and a pointed and panelled altar recess between twin doors to the former sacristy. Original traceried ALTAR RAILS; C17 Italian ALTAR of carved wood; some C17 Flemish roundels of PAINTED GLASS, also two small representations of a chalice and host. 78

The GARDEN to the N was made informal in the late C18. Two Georgian STATUES. Against the W wall an unroofed Late Georgian FERN HOUSE of red brick and flint bands and panels. Canted front with three pointed Gothick windows. A stone platform against the N wall remains from a contemporary orangery. In the kitchen garden wall behind are two widely spaced C18 GATEPIERS, later linked by a wall with a central arch, upswept parapet and urn.

OLD MANOR HOUSE, immediately S of the great house. A picturesque but deceptive composition. The oldest part is to the E, tree-ring dated to 1448 but now encased in plain C17 brick with C20 mullioned windows. It comprised a lower chamber and a first-floor hall. The cross-wing and linking bay followed, with a fine jettied porch and a lateral stack to the W. Framing infilled with brick, except the N gable with its decorative S-bracing. The lower extension abutting this gable has been dated to 1555, but includes many reused timbers. A Georgian screen wall links the house to the STABLES of 1800, S. Plain, of H-plan.

WATER MILL, NW of the church. A superior example of a multi-phase mill, restored to working order in 1977–82. The core is of 1626, timber-framed and of three bays. Extended in brick downstream in 1746, with weatherboarded gable; upstream in 1765, with a weatherboarded wharf enclosure. Pyramid-roofed turret of 1777, for a sack hoist. In 2011 an Archimedes-screw turbine was installed on the river side, replacing a turbine house of 1922.

VILLAGE. Coming from the church, the OLD VICARAGE is first on the W side. Plain brick, mid-C18, awkwardly heightened and expanded with a big servants' wing in 1834 by *Lewis Wyatt*. The incumbent was the Rev. Lord Augustus Fitz-Clarence (vicar 1829–54), ninth of William IV's ten illegitimate children with Mrs Jordan, the actress. Then the ALMSHOUSES of 1616–17, endowed by Sir Richard Blount's brother-in-law Charles Lister. A long one-storey range of brick with stone dressings. English bond, patchily chequered. Originally six dwellings; in 1952 converted into two. On the E side THE FORGE, a lobby-entry house of flint and brick, dated 1691 in large brick letters, and a Victorian cross-plan house in Tudor style with a row of four chimneystacks. It faces THE MILL HOUSE, tree-ring dated 1715. Another cheerful flint and brick front. Five bays, original cross-windows.

WHITTLES FARMHOUSE, 1 m. N. Cross-range of 1413, box-framed but roofed using a cruck half-truss, r. Main range of 1472, truncated at the arch-braced truss of the former open hall. – STIRRUPS, down the lane to the SE, has been tree-ring dated 1557. Three bays, the lower storey with close studding. Original chimneystack to the r. side. Box-framed C17 rear wing.

MILL FARM COTTAGE, ¾ m. NNE. A thatched cruck house, dated to 1335 (*see also* Introduction, p. 552). Three bays, including a two-bay former hall, and indications of a lost half-bay at the service end, l. Floored across in the C15 or C16.

TRENCH GREEN, 1 m. NE, has the OLD SCHOOL. Built in 1830, largely under royal patronage. One storey of white-painted brick with pointed windows. Extended 1893 (s) and later. – PITHOUSE COTTAGE, ⅓ m. SE, is a three-bay cruck-framed house of 1455. (Traces of a smoke-hood in the former hall.)

HODMORE FARM COTTAGES, 1¼ m. NE. Built in 1608 as a single house comprising two large bays linked by a chimney bay. A reused timber stud yielded the date 1475.

(THREE CHIMNEYS, 1½ m. E, beyond the golf course. Another three-bay cruck house, dated to 1457/8. One inner truss is closed, the other open.)

MARSH BALDON

Church and manor stand together, ⅓ m. s of the village green.

ST PETER. Early C14 W tower, its top transformed into an octagon above the bell-stage by means of squinches. A spire must have been intended. The W window is typical flowing Dec, two ogee lights under a quatrefoil. Chancel and nave under one continuous roof, late C14–C15, and now roughcast. Medieval s porch of timber, also roughcast. Over the s doorway a Mass dial in a frame of cable moulding, i.e. probably C12. The sills of the two chancel s windows are dropped to form seats. That to the w may have originally been glazed or shuttered below the transom. Perp PISCINA with cinquefoiled arch, lumpy carved decoration, and a rosette in the bowl. The Perp E window was reinstated in 1890, when *J. T. Micklethwaite* restored the church. It had been re-set in 1806 in the N wall of an added aisle in Sir Christopher Willoughby's scheme to enhance the church. Replacement N aisle of 1890; beautifully spare N arcade of double-hollow-chamfered arches on flattened octagonal piers. The aisle includes a vestry at the E end. Against the vestry wall and facing the aisle is a Gothick niche of 1806 with pinnacles, moved from the chancel together with the PAINTING of the Annunciation, a copy by *Pompeo Batoni* after Guido Reni.

This had been given by Sir Christopher in 1794 to Corpus Christi College in Oxford for a chapel altarpiece, but was later bumped by another painting (*see* p. 143). – PULPIT. Jacobean, with tester. – Shapely crimson-painted BENCHES designed by *Micklethwaite*; also the C14-style FONT. – STAINED GLASS. E window, an assemblage of medieval pieces. The C15 censing angels in the tracery may belong. Two early C14 shields below, and a fine C14 figure of St Anne instructing the Virgin, between larger C15 figures of the Virgin and St John from a Crucifixion. More medieval and C16 glass in the chancel S window. Nave S windows, 1904 by *Clayton & Bell* (cartoons by *George Daniels*) and 2005 by *Nicola Kantorowicz*. – MONUMENTS. Anne Cawley †1701. Large. Twisted columns and scroll pediment with reclining cherubs. – Two Gothick monuments to the Willoughby family, 1806 (tower).

BALDON HOUSE, SW of the church. Now subdivided. Loosely symmetrical N front with four gables, the outer ones advanced, and a two-storey porch with an arched stone doorway. Pinnacles on the gables. The E and NW parts may be matching additions to an early C17 house comprising the present SW section. All now roughcast, with sash windows. At right angles to the W an early C18 wing with a bell-turret, and a corresponding wing to the E, together forming a forecourt. The S front is entirely late C18, of brick, with two canted bays framing superimposed tripartite windows under segment-headed recesses. Also a two-storey W extension with Gothick windows, housing an orangery. Adjoining this a stone tower with some fabric salvaged from Nuneham Courtenay church, demolished *c.*1764 (q.v.), notably a C15 doorway with quatrefoiled spandrels. (In the library wing, SE, a fireplace with heraldry of the period 1789–94, for Christopher Willoughby, later 1st Baronet. The Georgian extensions may well be of this time. C17 panelling in the same room, amid matching work of *c.*1915. Other rooms with good Georgian detail: dining room with early C18 panelling and a Doric fireplace surround; late C18 staircase with iron balustrade; bow-ended room with a frieze of triglyphs and bucrania.) The OUTBUILDINGS are extensive and gratifyingly intact. Two COTTAGES by the NW wing, the nearer one timber-framed (dated 1608 or 1668), the other of stone (dated 1719). To the E a complex of weatherboarded C18 BARNS, also STABLES with rubble-stone lower walls of uncertain date. The oblong brick DOVECOTE beyond is C18. (By the barns, a relocated MONUMENT to Elizabeth Lane, the owner before Sir Christopher Willoughby. Late C18. A carved urn on a square pedestal.) The PARK to the W was landscaped in the late C18, probably also by Sir Christopher Willoughby. It includes a HA-HA and an artificial LAKE.

VILLAGE. Pretty and unpretentious, the houses widely spaced around a huge green. On the N side they are mostly brick-built, after a fire destroyed fourteen older cottages in 1866. Also a little SCHOOL of 1873 and 1896, and to its l. the previous

SCHOOL, remodelled in 1771 from a modest house probably of the C17. On the E side is STUART HOUSE (No. 40) of banded limestone with a red-tiled roof, dated 1754. Next to it, BOUNDARY HOUSE, mid-Victorian banded brick with BARNS to match.

MONGEWELL
Crowmarsh

The medieval village had largely disappeared by c.1300. Its Thames-side church later became a feature in the landscaped park made for Shute Barrington, successively Bishop of Salisbury and of Durham, in the late C18. Partially unroofed, it survives in 2023 alongside the abandoned buildings of Carmel College.

ST JOHN THE BAPTIST (Churches Conservation Trust). A romantic ruin complete with tombs, standing amid trees by the river. The small Norman church of flint and stone was remodelled as a Gothic eyecatcher for Shute Barrington in 1791, adding the canted brick W end and battlemented hexagonal turret. *James Wyatt*, who made Gothic designs for Barrington at Salisbury and at Durham, may be the architect. In 1880–1 the chancel was restored by *Morris & Stallwood*, who re-created the apsidal E end. Original C12 side windows and unusual chevron-and-diamond friezes at the top of the walls inside. Also two re-set head corbels flanking Morris & Stallwood's chancel arch, which was infilled by *Ralph Vaux* with a doorway and two wooden Gothic windows in 1953–4. Roofless nave, with an apsed N vestry of 1888. – FONT. 1881. Norman style, carved by *Earp*. – MONUMENTS. Edmond and Johanna Madock, †1692 and †1727. Two marble busts in C17 dress, on a sarcophagus. – John Sanders †1731 (inscription destroyed). Standing monument with sarcophagus. His effigy reclines on it, portrayed as a man of sensibility with turban and elegant draperies, holding a book. Grey marble pyramid and crest behind.

CARMEL COLLEGE (former). Britain's only Jewish boarding school, founded in 1948 at Greenham Common (Berks.) by Rabbi Dr Kopul Rosen, and moved to Mongewell in 1953. The school took over MONGEWELL HOUSE, a big William-and-Mary-style oblong of brick. Built in 1890–1 by *R. S. Wornum* for Alexander Caspar Fraser, with interiors by *J. Kinninmont & Sons*, it replaced the old house N of the church. Around 1920 Wornum's design was toned down, lopping off his *porte cochère*, garden loggia, chimneys and fat cupola. The school put up new buildings of increasing ambition around this house, some in the manner of a modern university campus, others informal like a village. From 1960 the main architect was *Tom Hancock*, whose masterplan was followed only in part. A second LAKE was also created, separating the school from the church to its

N (landscape architect *Michael Brown*), and the best buildings were placed alongside.

Falling rolls led to the closure of Carmel College in 1997, since when the site has awaited redevelopment. Plans approved in 2014 indicate that the house will remain, amid much new housing, along with the listed synagogue, amphitheatre and exhibition hall, variously repurposed; but the unique qualities of the ensemble will inevitably be lost.*

SYNAGOGUE. 1961–3. The most spectacular and successful of *Hancock*'s buildings for the college, and the only British synagogue to rank with the best from the early post-war decades on the Continent and the USA. The structural engineer was *Anthony Hunt*. It is wedge-shaped, with glass curtain walling on the long sides, N and S. The roof is supported by four laminated redwood beams which sweep upwards from the unsupported entrance canopy to the concrete-block E wall, 50 ft (15.2 metres) high, where the Ark was placed. This wall is convex, and flanking it are two narrow panels filled with *dalle-de-verre* STAINED GLASS by *Nehemia Azaz*, renewed 1987. The W end has semi-abstract glass by the same, using a layered technique, on themes of Jewish festivals. Immediately E and making a composition with the synagogue is *Hancock*'s AMPHITHEATRE of 1965, concentric seating of just over half a circle in plan, of concrete and blue-black engineering bricks.

EXHIBITION HALL and BOATHOUSE, W of Mongewell House. 1969–70 by *Sir Basil Spence*, design architect *John Urwin Spence*, Basil's son. Quite astonishing in its way, combining primal geometry with a Brutalist aesthetic. The hall is a sharp concrete pyramid with triangular windows gouged out and painted in primary colours. One corner is truncated for the entrance. The interior was originally presided over by *Gertrude Hermes*'s titanic bronze head of Julius Gottlieb, for whom the building was named. The pyramid sits on curved brown-purple brick walls, from which a sloped-sided platform extends N, enclosing a boathouse.

OTHER BUILDINGS. E of the school along Watery Lane, former TEACHERS' HOUSES of 1961 by *John Toovey*, Hancock's assistant. White-rendered, flat-roofed terraces. In the middle, the former WATER MILL of 1817. The lake to the E was the mill pond, later enlarged as part of the park landscape. On its N side is the C18 WALLED GARDEN, now enclosing houses of *c.*2015. Pretty LODGE by *Wornum*, dated 1889, ¼ m. E.

CENTRE FOR AGRICULTURE AND BIOSCIENCES INTERNATIONAL, ⅓ m. NE. By *Scott Brownrigg*, 2019–20. Three parallel parts, under curved roofs. At the E end these come down to ground level, and planting runs up the slope. Black framing.

GRIM'S DITCH. *See* Crowmarsh Gifford.

---

* Other buildings by *Hancock* included a SPORTS HALL and SWIMMING POOL E of the amphitheatre (1962–4), a simple CLASSROOM BLOCK between the synagogue and exhibition hall (*c.*1965), and an octagonal brick MUSIC ROOM just N of the house (1964–6). TWO BOARDING HOUSES of *c.*1958–60 were designed by *Yorke, Rosenberg & Mardall*.

NETTLEBED

Nettlebed was a centre of brick- and tile-making from early times until 1938. Tiles were produced for Wallingford Castle in 1365, and in 1416–17 a large order of bricks was supplied from Crocker End to Stonor Park (q.v.). The village also prospered from the coaching trade, and the brick-built houses and inns lining the High Street show the characteristic local combinations of reds and silver-greys.

St Bartholomew. Largely rebuilt in 1845–6 to a Dec-style design by *J.H. Hakewill*. Grey brick mottled with red, harsh for Nettlebed. Stone dressings. A vestry spans diagonally between the s aisle and the chancel. The lower stages of the sw tower were kept. Its ground stage is rendered. Plain three-light w window, late medieval or C17. Georgian red brick above, the openings Y-traceried. s arcade with round piers. Bold roof trusses of big straight timbers. – Reredos with mosaic panels. 1872. – Pulpit of 1896. A fine post-Gothic essay in white and cipollino marble, the lectern propped on a Byzantine column; 'a copy of a design seen in Italy', according to the *Henley Advertiser*. – Royal arms. George II, painted on board. – Gothic font, presumably of 1846. – Stained glass. e window of 1970 by *John Piper*, made by *Patrick Reyntiens*. One of their best. Three lights, red, blue and green; respectively populated with fish, a Tree of Life and butterflies (for the Resurrection). s aisle, 1973, also *Piper* and *Reyntiens*. With exotic birds, in memory of the writer Peter Fleming. Nave n by *A.K. Nicholson Studios*, 1945. – Monuments. Edmund Taverner †1637. Brass, style of *Edward Marshall*. – Judith Harris †1674. Rustic Baroque. – Rev. Thomas Bennett †1844. Finicky Gothic.

School (former), High Street, e of the church. 1845–6; probably *Hakewill*. Flint. Straight-headed windows of C14 type.

Village club, opposite the school. Of 1912–13 by *C.E. Mallows*, given by Robert Fleming of Joyce Grove (*see* below). A design of distinction, owing much to Arts and Crafts influence. Red brick. U-shaped, with a loggia of brick-and-tile piers in front of the hall. The wings housed a library, reading room and billiard room, r., and a skittle alley, l. They end in weatherboarded gables. Steep roof pitches, the angle echoed on the three close-set dormers over the hall. Double rows of dormers at the back, above a low projection for a rifle range.

Houses. w of the village club, two pairs of pebbledashed semis probably by *Mallows*, c.1913. Then a modest square mid-Georgian box of a house, later used as the rectory. Beyond is Nettlebed House. Five bays, C18, also fronted in silver brick and red brick dressings, with a fine fanlight and Tuscan porch. e of the club, the White Hart is C17, five bays, extended by one l. bay. Renewed cross-windows. Grander is the former Bull Inn on the s side, as refronted c.1720–40. Over the central carriageway a three-bay open pediment, the middle recessed in the Baroque way, enclosing a lunette. Mouldings all of brick. It masks an assemblage of three older houses, of which two (Nos. 19 and 19A) are C16 and originally had open halls.

BRICK KILN, N of The Green, to the E. Probably late C17. A tapering cone around 35 ft (10.5 metres) high, quite narrow at the top. The firing chamber was below ground level. Last used in 1927; restored 1973–4.

CROCKER END. A medieval hamlet ⅓ m. E of The Green. CROCKER END HOUSE is the former vicarage. 1866. Diapered brick, no particular style, with ornate chimneys. To its E, BRAMLEY COTTAGE (No. 18) has an interwar look, but includes a two-bay cruck range of exceptionally narrow width, just 12 ft (3.6 metres), tree-ring dated 1413/14. A W cross-wing was added as early as 1440/1, reusing some timbers from the cruck-built part. The inserted floor in the cross-range yielded the date range 1607–39.

JOYCE GROVE, ¼ m. SE. A sprawling mansion of 1903–7 by *C. R. Baker King & C. Harold King*, for the Scottish financier Robert Fleming. Red brick and Bath stone. Loosely Neo-Jacobean, embracing symmetry only on the N section of the main E front. A lightning strike in 1913 set the roof on fire, after which the house was enlarged and remodelled with a big new porch just S of the symmetrical section. Used as a Sue Ryder home until 2020; in 2023 awaiting conversion to apartments. (Main interiors with *Louis Quinze*-style panelling. Lavish galleried stair hall with wooden compartmented ceilings. One intricately carved bedroom fireplace with putti.) Extensive STABLES to the W. – LODGE, 250 yds SE. Neo-Wren, in Hampton Court mode. Good GATES here and on the drive from The Green, N.

NEWINGTON

6090

No village, but a handsome group of church, manor house and rectory.

ST GILES. Chancel and nave C12; N transept of *c.* 1200; S transept lost. Around 1300 the church was remodelled and the W tower and spire added. The nave has roll-moulded C12 quoins at the W corners, and C12 N and S doorways. The S doorway lacks its original jambs and has a new hoodmould made from re-set pieces of chevron. The headstops are probably earlier work re-carved in the C14. N doorway with roll-and-hollow mouldings to the arch, the capitals of the jamb shafts carved with broad splayed leaves. In the nave a pointed arch of two unchamfered orders to the N transept. At the junction with the nave externally, part of a W respond is exposed. Its position suggests that an arch opening from the transept to a N aisle was intended. The S transept was demolished probably in the C17, and a plain square-headed window provided in the replacement wall. The base of a respond remains in the wall to the l. The transepts may have extended from the C12 chancel, which was then demolished and a new chancel built further E. The present chancel has an early C13 lancet in its N wall. Chancel arch of c.1300, of three chamfered orders. In the chancel S wall an open-cinquefoiled TOMB RECESS of c.1300, finely moulded and probably belonging to the patron of the new work. Cinquefoiled C15 PISCINA. No windows in the nave N wall, but several Dec and Perp windows elsewhere. The E window, a good example of the late C14 transition from Dec to Perp, has small uprights in the tracery indicating the beginnings of panel tracery. The tower has a triple-chamfered arch to the nave. Bell-openings with Y-tracery, plain parapet, and octagonal broach spire. Massive W buttresses were added in the C15. The main Victorian restoration was in 1884, but the timber S porch is of 1898, by *J. Oldrid Scott.*

FURNISHINGS. C14 TILES in the tomb recess. – ROOD SCREEN. Late C14, still with its doors; originally with a rood loft. Ogee-headed tracery in the openings. – PULPIT. C17. Polygonal and plain. – Medieval IRONWORK on both doors, including two C-strap hinges. Dates between the C12 and C14 are possible. – ROYAL ARMS. George III; carved and gilded. – FONT. A big plain Norman tub. – STAINED GLASS. Chancel N window largely with original glass, probably of c.1482–1511. Above, panels of the Assumption of the Virgin and of the Trinity (three persons; Christ unusually placed in the middle). Below each is a donor figure of a priest, one very incomplete; identifiable as Dr Stephen Barworth, rector 1478–82, and his successor, Dr Richard Salter. A bidding scroll runs through the design, another rare motif in English glass. – MONUMENTS. Walter Dunch †1644 and wife, erected 1650. Attributed to *Thomas Cartwright I* (GF). Black and white marble. Two busts in shrouds, upright in oval niches framed with bay leaves. Architectural surround with a broken pediment and crest. The shrouded effigy was made fashionable by John Donne's monument of 1631 in St Paul's Cathedral. – Henry Dunch †1686. A big pedestal framed by foliage sprays and surmounted by a fine garlanded urn. Carved scrolls like parchment rolls adorn the urn base.

NEWINGTON HOUSE, S of the church. A big square house of squared limestone rubble, set back behind a forecourt with a noble gateway. Built for Henry Dunch in 1678 or just after, as confirmed by tree-ring dating.* It is almost certainly the house at Newington mentioned in 1680 as having been built by *Richard Frogley,* carpenter, and *Thomas Wood,* mason, both of Oxford. Seven bays, the same on both fronts. No central projection, but the three middle windows slightly more closely spaced. Uniform moulded window surrounds, angle quoins. Scars of lost segmental pediments over the front and rear

* Putting to bed the theory advanced by a late C20 owner that the house was built c.1635, after a design in Rubens's *Palazzi di Genova* (1622).

doorways (cf. Thomas Wood's doorway at Cuddesdon Palace, now at Christ Church, Oxford, p. 140). The curtly finished third storey was added in 1777 (rainwater head date), retaining some timbers from the hipped and platformed C17 roof. Adamesque-Corinthian porch no doubt of the same date. The interior was reconstructed in connection. Stair hall to the front, the staircase of timber with plain stick balusters, climbing in three flights. Arched openings to the cross-corridor on the first floor, rich Doric cornices on both floors. A Doric doorcase opens to the central saloon behind, where the cornice matches that of the porch. Some fine marble fireplaces.

The front GATEPIERS have heraldic griffins with shields, added c. 1700. C18 GATES with scroll cresting. The late C17 service buildings include STABLES and a COACHHOUSE to the NE and the hip-roofed MANOR HOUSE to the NW, possibly with fabric from a predecessor of c. 1578.

BEAUFOREST HOUSE (former rectory), N of the church. The home of Georgian clerics who lived in style. The central section has the date 1774 carved over a W window. In 1796–7 the N part was rebuilt as a tall five-bay range with a pedimented doorway and fanlight, and a full-height bow to the W. The S part may be a re-cased remnant of the large timber-framed predecessor. Finely moulded ceiling beams of c. 1500 on the ground floor.

GREAT HOLCOMBE FARMHOUSE, down a lane ¼ m. NNE. An intricate constructional history has been deciphered by the *Victoria County History*. The W range comprises the chamber end of an open-hall house partly of 1475, aligned N–S. In the C16 a brick chimneystack was inserted and a new stair-turret added to the E. Timber-framed extensions around the turret followed from c. 1600 onwards, including one reused medieval bay. Now all masked by painted early C18 brick.

NEWNHAM MURREN
Crowmarsh

A deserted village by the Thames.

ST MARY (Churches Conservation Trust). Early Norman, altered in the C13. Chancel and very short nave of matching length. W bellcote from the restoration of 1849 by *J. H. Hakewill*, who also rebuilt the S aisle with its catslide roof. Plain Norman N doorway, very renewed. The high and narrow chancel arch is also Norman. A horseshoe-shaped squint to its S. Arcade of two double-chamfered arches and an octagonal pier. In 1849 the lancet windows were mostly renewed. The graduated E triplet has re-set C13 jamb shafts internally. On the S a PISCINA in a trefoiled recess; opposite, a DOUBLE AUMBRY. The nave roof, with crown-posts, is probably C14. – PULPIT. Mid-C17, with scroll and strapwork decoration around oval bosses. Shallow carving of an earlier type on the back panels. – FONT. Said to be Norman and re-cut, but looking very 1849. – STAINED GLASS. E and nave N windows by *Wailes*. – BRASS. Letitia Barnard †1593. Southwark style.*

NEWNHAM FARMHOUSE, N of the church. C17 with much C19 modification. The COTTAGE immediately W has been tree-ring dated to 1551.

NORTH STOKE
Crowmarsh

ST MARY. Anglo-Saxon in origin. The chancel was rebuilt in the mid C13, probably by the rector Robert of Asthall, later a canon of Lincoln. Older fabric survives in its lower walls. Early C14 nave, aisleless but wide, and W tower. Unusually rich treatment of the chancel inside, the side lancets with Purbeck marble imposts and jamb shafts, the capitals of varied stiff-leaf types. Chancel arch with similar polychromatic treatment: three orders, the outer ones with a filleted roll and hollow on shafts of ordinary stone with shaft-rings, the inner a plain chamfer on Purbeck shafts. Linking the window sills is a string course, cut by later lowside windows. PISCINA in a trefoiled recess. C14 E window, the tracery by *William Weir*, from a self-effacing restoration for the SPAB in 1902.† Nave with two-light windows of uniform design. Typical Dec wave moulding round the N doorway. Porch with C15 timbers and moulded bargeboards. Above the blocked S doorway a circular SUNDIAL, with a head above and hands grasping the dial. Similarities to Northern examples point to an Anglo-Saxon origin, though the head appears to be a C13 substitution. Around 1669 the tower fell, leaving the ground stage and triple-chamfered tower arch. It was not rebuilt until 1725. These stages have brick dressings and classical details. Round-arched openings, scalloped parapet with skittle-shaped pinnacles.

FURNISHINGS. Medieval TILES, re-set next to *Weir*'s COMMUNION RAIL. – STALLS. C16 linenfold-panelled type. Apparently of post-Reformation date, for they incorporate part of the medieval rood screen at the NW. – PULPIT. Jacobean. A rare pentagonal specimen, with carved frieze, tester and support. – Painted ROYAL ARMS of George III. – FONT. C12–C13 tub. Spidery C17(?) COVER. – DOOR, nave N. C14, with original strap hinges with split-curl terminals. – WALL PAINTINGS. Quite a full mid-C14 series, the artistic quality not high. Over the chancel arch fragments of a Doom, to the l. of the

---

* Romantically said to have been pierced by a bullet at the siege of Wallingford in 1646, but the present hole is not shown in early C19 illustrations.
† Medievalizing proposals by *W. Scott Champion* illustrated in the *Building News*, 3 September 1875, did not proceed.

pulpit the martyrdom of Becket. On the nave side walls narrative scenes in tiers, the lives of St Catherine (below) and St Stephen on the N, Passion scenes on the S. Above the N doorway, the legend of the Living and Dead Kings. Mostly red pigment. – STAINED GLASS by *Herbert Bryans*, 1907–15, in the E window and nave. – MONUMENTS. Robert of Asthall †1274/5, chancel floor. Purbeck marble slab with indents of a lost inscription. – Roger Parker, canon of Windsor, †1354/5. Brass with headless half-figure.

VILLAGE. N of the church is RECTORY FARMHOUSE, its main range probably C17, under roughcast first applied *c.*1765. Its DOVECOTE, E, is of *c.*1785. CHURCH COTTAGE a little to the E, its framing exposed, is documented as of 1548. On the main street, the VILLAGE HALL of 1911 is probably by the Lancashire architect *Jonathan Simpson* (*see* below). Rendered and nicely composed, with a shingled spirelet. BROOK HOUSE, down a lane to the W, is probably C16, with a S cross-wing dated 1675. Mostly brick and flint elevations. To the N, THE MILL HOUSE shows several phases of C18 brick, reportedly on C17 timbering. Opposite, BROOK LODGE, rendered and sprawling; by *J. Simpson*, 1903, for his brother-in-law John Wormald.

THE SPRINGS, ¼ m. ENE. Now a golf hotel. The half-timbered mansion began with the double-gabled S part, of 1893–4 by *Samuel Johns* of Wallingford. Doubled in size for J. Wormald after 1905, by *J. Simpson* and his son-in-law *James Lomax-Simpson*, best known for his work for Lord Leverhulme. An even longer S extension was demolished in 2020.

GRIM'S DITCH. *See* Crowmarsh Gifford.

NUFFIELD

6080

HOLY TRINITY. In 1848 the chancel was rebuilt by *Ferrey*. The tall proportions and plain walls of the rest imply a C12 or C13 date. NW tower, continuous with the N aisle, with a low shingled upper stage and small square-headed windows. The aisle has some brick courses high up, suggestive of C17–C18 repairs. Small two-light C14 windows to N, W and S, the last unusually with round arches. Gargoyles higher up on this side show where the eaves have been raised. Two-bay N arcade of *c.*1200 with a round pier, moulded capital and waterholding base. The spandrel above has a narrow round-headed niche. Plain chancel arch, not in its original state. The ceiled and compartmented nave roof is late medieval. – C14 TILES in the chancel. – FONT. Norman, cylindrical, plain, with the inscription in Lombardic letters: '[Fon]te sacro lotum vel mundat gratia totum, vel non est sacramenti mundacio plena.' ('Unless it is grace that wholly cleanses one who is washed in the sacred fount, there is no full purification of [from] the sacrament.') – STAINED GLASS. Chancel S and N by *Hardman*, 1858 and

1869. – BRASS. Beneit Engliss, *c.*1350. 17¾-in. (45-cm.) half-figure of a bearded civilian, the inscription in French. – In the churchyard the LEDGER SLAB of Lord Nuffield †1963, lettered by *David Kindersley*.

Three large HOUSES by *Oswald P. Milne* lie NE of the village, beyond the golf course. The first is the course's former CLUBHOUSE of 1910, just N of the A4130. Quite stylish. Symmetrical front with projecting gabled wings flanking a long balcony across the first floor. The balcony is subdivided by brick cross-walls which are finished as Doric pilasters, rather in a Lutyens way (Milne had spent two years in Lutyens's office). Steeply pitched roof with a square cupola. Service wing to the NE.

NUFFIELD PLACE (National Trust), 150 yds N. Of 1913 by *Milne* for Sir John Wimble, but altered, extended and partly pulled out of shape from 1933 for the motor manufacturer William Morris, later 1st Viscount Nuffield. Quite a progressive design for the 1910s, especially the S front with its hipped roof and plain sashes. Lord Nuffield's personal fortune was mostly spent on good causes, and the present interiors and furnishings embody the interwar taste for unshowy comfort, loosely grounded in historical English styles, that was common across most social classes (discounting such oddities as the built-in workbench in the master bedroom). Well-meant N addition of *c.*1966 by *Beecher & Stamford* for Nuffield College, Oxford, which was left the house in Lord Nuffield's will. GARDENS also designed by *Milne*; laid out *c.*1920.

HUNTERCOMBE PLACE, ⅓ m. further N. By *Milne*, 1907–10, for the banker William Brooks Close. Now a care home. Early Tudor style, broadly symmetrical in front. Rough-textured dark red brick, entirely without stone dressings. The ends project and have timber-framed gables, since infilled with brick in place of the original white plaster. To the E a slim gabled water tower. On the W side was a two-storey loggia, now infilled. Well-made and well-preserved interiors with much panelling. The floral plasterwork in the entrance hall and dining room is by *Esmond Burton* and the *Bromsgrove Guild*. Staircase to the rear, with rosettes carved on the balusters.

ENGLISH FARM, 1 m. SE of the village. To the eye a comely gentleman-farmer's house of *c.*1750 with a slightly later top storey; but irregularities behind indicate the survival of older fabric, here of the late C16. Unusually complete FARM BUILD-INGS, late C17 to *c.*1870.

OAKINGHAM HOUSE, 1⅓ m. SSE. Designed in 1988 by *Philip Jebb* for David Naylor-Leyland, but sold on before completion. An early instance of the revived classical country house, here a pedimented seven-bay design with brick quoins, hipped roof and three-bay pediment, all in the manner of *c.*1680–1700.

RIDGEWAY FARMHOUSE, ½ m. SSW. A lobby-entry house, tree-ring dated to *c.*1628. Thinly framed, the storey posts unusually closely spaced.

(TURNERS COURT FARM SCHOOL (former), 1½ m. WNW. A training colony was set up in 1912 to prepare 'unemployable'

men and youths for work in agriculture and forestry at home
or abroad. Original buildings by *T. Phillips Figgis* now replaced
with commercial housing. The ASSEMBLY HALL of 1930
remains, with its sturdy, rather Nordic clock tower.)

GRIM'S DITCH. A substantial Iron Age E–W boundary bank
with a ditch to the S, continuous with the Crowmarsh stretch
up to a point just SW of the village. Thereafter a less regular
and less well-preserved line is traced as far as Hayden Farm.

NUNEHAM COURTENAY

5090

Nuneham is the most significant C18 house in SE Oxfordshire,
set in gardens and parkland that are themselves of national
importance. The estate is a perfect illustration of Georgian
patronage. House, church, park and village were first created
by Simon, 1st Earl Harcourt (1714–77), courtier, future Viceroy
of Ireland, antiquary and amateur architect. His house was
completed *c.*1758. The old village was then erased to make
way for a classical landscape, replaced by a planned settlement
along the Oxford road to the E, and a new church was erected
as an ornament in the park. Improvements to the house and
gardens continued under the 2nd Earl (1736–1809), artist and
patron of painters and writers, and under subsequent Harcourts
into the early C20. The University of Oxford then bought the
estate in 1948, only to sell it in 2017. After various uses the house
is now leased to the Global Retreat Centre, a Buddhist foundation, which has restored the celebrated gardens; the early C19
arboretum to the E remains as an outstation of the University's
Botanic Garden.

NUNEHAM HOUSE

In 1756 Simon, 1st Earl Harcourt, whose ancestral house was at
Stanton Harcourt (*Oxfordshire: North and West*), began a new
house at his Nuneham estate, under the influence of the latest
fashions in architecture and garden design. The site was chosen
for its landscaping possibilities, with a steep slope westwards to
the Thames and northward views towards the domes and spires
of Oxford. *Stiff Leadbetter* of Eton was the architect. The house
was to be 'a *villa*…not a *seat*', as Lady Harcourt wrote in 1755.
That meant a compact plan with the main rooms on the *piano
nobile*, placed in a circuit around the staircase. Shortly after
work began, however, it was decided to provide symmetrically
linked wings in order to supply the necessary services (N)
and family accommodation (S). The main house corresponds
to established Palladian formulae, of three storeys, with a
pedimented seven-bay entrance front and the increasingly
popular motif of a central canted bay to address the views on
the garden side. But Harcourt was also a veteran of the Grand

Nuneham Courtenay, Nuneham House, elevation.
Engraving by J. White after J. Woolfe, 1771

Tour and a co-founder of the Society of Dilettanti, which had lately sponsored *James 'Athenian' Stuart* to explore Greece in search of unfamiliar monuments from Antiquity. Even before his findings were published, the Dilettanti were free to pick over Stuart's drawings and instruct him to make designs from them. So the house was provided by Stuart with distinctive Venetian windows on the garden side, each with its central arch carried down to the lower architrave, in the manner of the C2 screen to the reservoir of the Aqueduct of Hadrian at Athens. For the windows' capitals, Stuart substituted a Greek Ionic type for the Hadrianic original, taken from the Temple of Athena Polias at the Erechtheion: the first acknowledged quotation from ancient Greece in English architecture.

In other respects the exterior is no longer as illustrated in *Vitruvius Britannicus* (vol. V, 1771). After abortive consultations with *Carr* of York, then with *Robert Adam*, the 2nd Earl engaged *Capability Brown* and his architectural partner *Henry Holland* in 1781 to add a third storey to the wings, and to reduce the two-storey quadrant links to simple curved corridors on the garden side. On the entrance front the external double staircase of the 1750s was removed, and a new entry made through a small portico to the ground floor. Viewing terraces or balconies were also added to the ground floor to N and S, with wrought-iron balustrades of minimal design. In 1832 Archbishop Harcourt brought in *Smirke* to expand the S wing for family accommodation, adding six more bays (1:5) in keeping with the original work, with a three-bay pediment on the garden side. The rusticated three-bay E porch introduced by Smirke was then subsumed into *T.B. Carter*'s two-storey corridor addition in grating orange-yellow stone, done for Louis, 2nd Viscount Harcourt ('Loulou') between 1904 and 1907. The dormer storey, balustraded parapet and enlargement of the second-floor windows are his too.

INTERIORS. The ENTRANCE HALL is unimpressive, a low-ceilinged conversion from the vaulted vestibule of the 1750s, with decoration mostly of the 1900s. Other ground-floor rooms retain their groin-vaulting, that to the N with a light overlay of plasterwork of 1781. The STAIRCASE is all *Holland* (or *Holland* and *Brown*) and of 1781, a flattened D-shape rising to full height,

with a lithe wrought-iron balustrade composed entirely of elaborated S-scrolls. Graceful plaster swags in the coving around
the oval skylight. The 1750s arrangement had two staircases: a
compact oval rising from the first floor only, and a back stair
of full height alongside. The DINING ROOM, N, was enlarged
by *Holland* with a vestibule and a screen of yellow scagliola
Corinthian columns to the E. The compartmented main ceiling
may be by *Stuart*, and the handsome marble fireplace is certainly his, with a frieze of discrete Antique motifs between big
consoles supported on lions' heads. Also Stuart's are the Greek
Ionic capitals of the Venetian window, as noted outside. The
octagonal SALON, W, has a matching Venetian window. The rest
is a mixture of C18 (*Stuart* and *Holland*) and early C20 decoration. A similar mixture in the DRAWING ROOM, S. Here the
ceiling of moulded compartments is *Stuart*'s, and not Greek at
all, deriving rather from Inigo Jones's at the Banqueting House
in Whitehall. A motif of swags and medallions is repeated on
the fireplace, in the frieze and above the doorways. The ANTE-
ROOM, E, is more Edwardian in feeling, though the inner part
retains its C18 coved ceiling and a fireplace designed by *Stuart*,
with a swirling Hellenistic frieze. Some rectilinear ceilings by
Smirke survive in the S wing.

Gardens and park

In 1780 Horace Walpole described Nuneham as 'one of the most
beautiful landscapes in the world'. Much has been lost since, but
much more remains. The present landscaping is essentially of four
phases, partially overlapping. The 1st Earl made a classical landscape in the early 1760s, with his new church N of the house as
its chief showpiece. In 1771–2 the future 2nd Earl's friend *William
Mason* established a flower garden between house and church,
and in 1779–82 the landscaping was reshaped and extended by
Capability Brown, whose work extended to the S. Elements of
Brown's scheme that have disappeared include the rustic bridge
and thatched lock-keeper's cottage – an early *cottage orné* – at the
end of his riverside walk, and a Doric temple of timber by the
path S of the house, which led to 'Whitehead's Oak', a haunt of
the poet William Whitehead, who was commemorated by an urn.
Lastly, to the E is the Pinetum (now Arboretum), created from
1835 by *William Sawrey Gilpin* for Archbishop Harcourt.
    The various buildings and enclaves around the house are
described individually.

TERRACES. The parterres and terraces around the house to W, N
    and S were initiated by *Smirke* and *W.S. Gilpin* in the 1830s,
    then greatly extended for Viscount Harcourt *c.*1904–10, of
    which the western salient was returned to turf *c.*1970.
FLOWER GARDEN, N of the house. Created in 1771–2 by the poet
    and gardener *William Mason* for Viscount Nuneham, later 2nd
    Earl Harcourt, a man of advanced Enlightenment sympathies

and an admirer of Jean-Jacques Rousseau.* Its revolutionary informality and mood of sentimental reflection were widely influential. Of 1¼ acres, its irregular lawns, flower beds and serpentine walks were adorned with busts of Cowley, Prior, Locke and Rousseau and with urns with inscriptions from Dryden, Marvell, Milton, Whitehead and Mason, the last of whom described the garden thus:

> So here did Art arrange her flowery groups
> Irregular, yet not in patches quaint,
> But interposed between the wandering lines
> Of shaven turf which twisted to the path,
> Gravel or sand, that in as wild a wave
> Stole round the verdant limits of the scene;
> Leading the eye to many a sculptured bust
> On shapely pedestal, of sage, or bard,
> Bright heirs of fame, who living loved the haunts
> So fragrant, so sequester'd. Many an urn
> There too had place, with votive lay inscribed
> To Freedom, Friendship, Solitude, or Love.

One key building remains, the little TEMPLE OF FLORA, with the goddess's portrait medallion and a panel with lines from Ariosto's *Orlando Furioso* inside. Timber columns *in antis*, of a baseless Greek Doric order as illustrated by Stuart and Revett. To the S are the ROCKERY and GROTTO, formed as a miniature ravine within. On the N side is the remaining rear wall of the ORANGERY. The garden layout was modified in the 1830s for Archbishop Harcourt, and most of the ornaments lost. A few URNS remain, not all of them C18, and a C19 Italian WELL-HEAD. Replanting since the 1980s has successfully restored many of the C18 outlines.

ALL SAINTS (Churches Conservation Trust). N of the Flower Garden, overlooking the park to the N. Built in 1763–4, close to the medieval site. According to the 2nd Earl's *Description* of 1783, the design was by *Simon, 1st Earl Harcourt*, assisted by *James Stuart*, whose first volume of *The Antiquities of Athens* (with Nicholas Revett) had been published in 1762. The Ionic capitals are Greek indeed, from the lost Temple on the Ilissus in Athens, but Stuart's Neoclassicism was a matter of piquant details rather than basic architectural design, and the church is more Anglo-Palladian than Greek in treatment. It was conceived primarily as a landscape ornament, to the extent that the broad hexastyle portico on its N side encloses only a blind niche without a doorway. The plan is odd too, with a pedimented S transept answering the portico, and a plain central drum and shallow dome rising between. All the windows are semicircular mullioned lunettes, a Palladian type, placed high in the walls and in the drum. Entry is through a semicircular W porch or demi-tempietto with Ionic columns. The interior is austere, markedly narrower in the barrel-vaulted central section, from

75

---

*Mason set out his theories on garden design at length in his poem *The English Garden* (3 vols, 1772–82).

which curved walls with plain niches at the diagonals rise to support the dome. The framed panels with texts on the walls are also c18. In the transept a tall arched opening, which may not have been open originally (no pre-c20 depictions of the interior appear to have survived).

The FURNISHINGS owe much to the 2nd Viscount Harcourt in the years after 1904, including some unsuitably ornate Italian pieces. The atmosphere of a family chapel has been intensified by the retrieval of monuments from the Victorian replacement church (*see* p. 709). Instead of pews, there are twenty-five Italian STALLS, c16 style, with a shell motif and fluted Composite half-columns. – ALTAR with similar details (the ALTARPIECE of 1782–3 by the versatile *William Mason* is no longer shown). – LECTERN. Italian, late c17, the triangular base with figures in relief. – SCULPTURE. In the niches under the dome, four c19 busts of Harcourt family members. One is a cast, another a copy by *Matthew Noble*, 1872, of a work by *Chantrey*. Also four Italian c17 angels carved in wood on the chancel partition. – HATCHMENTS. Four, 1807–91. – ROYAL ARMS. Small and delicate. What is the material? – FONT. 1843, with a richly carved Italian Baroque cover surmounted by a figure of St John the Baptist. – Ornate wrought-iron DOORS to the s and w, probably early c20. – TAPESTRY. The Tribes of Israel, c17, Flemish. Present by 1783. – WREATHS. Two, in glass cases. Sent by Lord Harcourt for Edward VII's lying-in-state in 1910. – MONUMENTS. Dr Byron Eaton, rector, †1703. Baroque standing monument. Open pediment on Composite columns, framing a bewigged portrait bust. Also four cherubs, standing or reclining. Attributed to *Edward Stanton* (GF). – Julian Harcourt †1862, aged two. White marble figure on a small tomb-chest. By *Alexander Munro*, after a deathbed drawing by G. F. Watts. – Above, Marie-Thérèse Harcourt †1863, mother of the boy (and of the 2nd Viscount). Quattrocento style, probably by an Italian artist. A delicate profile portrait of white marble. Wooden frame with a semicircular pediment. – William Harcourt †1871. A small seated figure by *Noble*, brought from the Victorian church. – Edward William Harcourt †1891. A recumbent stone effigy, from the same church; now without its tomb-chest. – Sir William Vernon Harcourt M.P. †1904, with marble profile portrait.

MONUMENT. Under a shelter E of the church, Anthony and Philippa Pollard, †1577 and †1606. Recumbent effigies against twin arches, beneath an elaborate canopy. Much heavy Flemish decoration, swags, strapwork and heraldic shields. Returned from Baldon House (Marsh Baldon) in 1920.

STATUE, 150 yds NE. Dr Fell of Christ Church, Oxford, brought from there in 1887. Probably c18.

WALLED GARDEN, E of the church. Late c18. It now encloses *Darborne & Darke*'s BOOK DEPOSITORIES of 1972–4 onwards, built to take overspill from the Bodleian Library. – ESTATE COTTAGES to the N by *W. Sawrey Gilpin*, after 1832. Red brick, Tudor windows. – To the SW are the STABLES. Only the austere square corner blocks remain of the front range of *c.*1760, probably designed by *Lord Harcourt* and *Stuart*. The lost middle section had Diocletian windows as on the church. – MANOR LODGE, 100 yds S, belongs with *T.B. Carter*'s works of *c.*1905 to the main house.

RECTORY (former), ¼ m. NNE of the church. Crisp stuccoed house of 1825 by *Daniel Evans*, joined at right angles to part of the rectory of 1761.

ARBORETUM, ½ m. ENE of the house. Expanded from the Pinetum, begun in 1835 by *W.S. Gilpin* with newly introduced North American conifers. The simplified Greek Doric LODGE by the Oxford road is of 1838 by *Smirke*.

CARFAX CONDUIT, ⅓ m. SSW of the house. Set up as an eye-catcher in 1787, in place of the Gothic tower recommended by Brown. Strictly the present monument consists of a copy of the Doric-pilastered base and only the top parts of the extravagant conduit of 1617, which had been displaced from Carfax by street improvements in Oxford. Its builder was *John Clark*, its apparent inspiration the late medieval crown spire. Detailed similarities with works by *William Arnold* have been pointed out by Anthony Wells-Cole, e.g. the niches of a type also seen at Wadham College. The figures in them represent the Nine Worthies. The letters in the openwork balustrade commemorate Otho Nicholson, the C17 donor.

THE VILLAGE

The new VILLAGE of 1760–1 is neatly arranged along the Oxford–Henley road, a Georgian version of ribbon development. Fashionable ideas of picturesque planning were not at this date applied to cottages. Nine uniform pairs were provided, of chequered brick, each of one and half storeys with a shared central stack. It appears that *Lord Harcourt* supplied the designs, for he sketched and described them as his in a letter of 1767. A few larger houses of two and a half storeys were included too, one at the N end for an inn (facing a forge on the E side), two at the S end, and another midway on the W side, for the curate.

It was established by the late Mavis Batey, Nuneham's C20 historian, that the rebuilding was the inspiration for 'Sweet Auburn' in Goldsmith's *The Deserted Village* (1770), where

> …the man of wealth and pride
> Takes up a space that many poor supply'd;
> Space for his lake, his park's extended bounds,
> Space for his horses, equipage, and hounds.

Less well remembered is William Whitehead's poem 'The Removal of the Village at Nuneham', written in riposte the following year:

> The careful matrons of the plain
> Had left their cots without a sigh,
> Well pleased to house their little train
> In happier mansions warm and dry.

New houses imitating the C18 ones were added at N the end in 2015–17.

ALL SAINTS (disused), 250 yds W. Of 1872–4 by *C.C. Rolfe*, to serve the displaced village. Aisleless, in C13 French Gothic style. Plate-traceried windows. On the S side an apsidal organ chamber with blind arcading. A tall bellcote is attached to its E side. SE chapel added in 1890, in clashing Perp style.

PISHILL

CHURCH (dedication unknown). Largely rebuilt in 1854. Some materials from its small and plain Norman predecessor were apparently reused, and the N transept (alias the Stonor aisle) was retained. J.H. Parker described this in 1850 as modernized Norman or Transitional, but it lacks early features and may be of post-Reformation date; cf. the skimpily timbered arch-braced roof. Windows mostly lancets, also one in straight-headed Dec style E of the porch. W bellcote. – REREDOS of tiles, 1873 by *Powells*. – FONT. C14, octagonal. – STAINED GLASS. Good E and chancel S windows, †1871, and nave S window, 1874 by *Cox & Son*. Also a chancel S lancet by *John Piper*, 1968. It represents the Sword and the Gospel. N transept N, †1925, signed *Arthur J. Dix*.

VICARAGE, S of the church. 1871. Rather raw.

BARN at Chapel Wells, S of the vicarage. Of flint and stone, partly weatherboarded, with a transomed C13 lancet with shafted jambs in the S gable-end (also a splayed sill with window seats). It may have been part of a manor house of the d'Oilly family recorded in 1406.

THATCHERS, Russell's Water, 1¼ m. W. C16, L-plan, remodelled and extended N as cottages. The original W range is of raised-cruck construction.

PYRTON

ST MARY. Largely rebuilt in 1855–6 by *J.C. Buckler*. His windows are Geometrical or C14 Dec. Walls of small squared flints with stone dressings, lapsing strangely into red brick on the nave E gable and triple W bellcote. The C15 porch was retained, also the C12 S doorway and chancel arch. Both of these are fine examples, with patterns and details unusual in Oxfordshire. About 1115 the church was presented to the Augustinian priory at Runcorn (Norton) in Cheshire, and the priory no doubt proceeded to rebuild, although the details do not match any C12 work surviving there. The doorway arch with its three concentric bands of chevron and jamb shafts with scalloped capitals is conventional, but the hood has less familiar decoration of grapes, leaves and fruit. The chancel arch is broad and high, with a moulding of two hollows and an angle roll. The hood is again unusual, with flat fluted leaves. The imposts share the common star-in-square pattern of the doorway, but the capitals of the jamb shafts have beaded basket-weave (s) and a triple interlacing pattern (N), both with cable necking. In each side wall of the chancel side a small roll-moulded C12 window. The N window has shallow decoration around the top on the outer side; the outer S side is 1850s. – PULPIT. 1636. Polygonal, with blind arcading and bosses. – Plain FONT of tapered outline, C12 or C13. – A few medieval TILES set in the porch. – STAINED GLASS. E window, style of *Wailes* (PC). Nave S, 1893 by *Clayton & Bell*. – MONUMENTS. In the chancel floor a Purbeck slab with the incised figure of a priest, identified as Richard de Gretton, *c.*1280–90. Inscribed in Lombardic characters, the brass letters lost. – Thomas Symeon †1522 and wife. Brass effigies, 16¾ and 16½ in. (42 and 41 cm.). – Alfred St George Hamersley †1929. Incised brass tablet by *Eric Gill* (cf. Rycote chapel).

(PYRTON MANOR, in its own grounds W of the church. The medieval house stood on a moated site. Its E-shaped replacement was built *c.*1600–10, probably by Edmund Symeon. Projecting gabled wings, castellated two-storey porch. The sash windows and quoined brick surrounds look earlier than the renovation recorded in 1786. At the back, original windows with hoods and ovolo-moulded mullions. Some polygonal chimneystacks as well as the more usual diagonally set square ones. C19 and later extensions behind the parlour wing, W. Over the hall fireplace a mid-C19 relief of John Hampden. Original open-well staircase with arcaded balustrades on upward-tapering balusters, the newel finials also tapering upward. In the parlour wing a bed recess framed by fluted pilasters and a Doric entablature.)

THE WHITE HOUSE, N of the church. A late C15 timber-framed house, refronted and stuccoed *c.*1800 for the Rev. William Buckle. Two-storey bay windows flank a Tuscan porch. Three gabled projections behind. The middle one, for the staircase, is early C17. (Staircase with upward-tapering newels, as at Pyrton Manor. C15 stair doorway, its head carved with quatrefoils and trefoils; probably re-set.)

OLD RECTORY, E of the church, set back behind a low wall with Georgian railings. Rebuilt in 1788. Grey brick, with red brick dressings and flanks. One keystone only, on the middle window of the second floor. Doorcase with pediment on brackets.

COURT HOUSE, 200 yds NNE. L-plan, the early C16 framing hidden by Georgian brick except at the N end. – Diagonally opposite, the former SCHOOL of 1895. Awkward shaped gable.

GOLDER MANOR FARM, 2 m. NW. C18 house of grey brick headers dressed with red brick. The odd gabled porch is Victorian, with brickwork laid in patterns. Its arched doorway looks C20.

HAMLET HOUSE, Clare, 2 m. NNW. The long brick frontage is mid-C18. A big grouped chimneystack in the front roof slope betrays origins around 1600. The original structure was timber-framed.

ROTHERFIELD GREYS

7080

ST NICHOLAS. A small church probably of c. 1200, heavily reconstructed in 1865 by W. Woodman. A blocked round-headed doorway remains in the nave N wall, a square lowside-type window in the S wall. Late C13 E window of three lancets in bar tracery. C13 AUMBRY and trefoil-headed PISCINA. Other windows, timber bell-tower and chancel arch all of 1865. Late medieval trusses reused in the nave roof. The singular N chapel was built as a funerary chapel in 1605 by Sir William Knollys of Greys Court, later 1st Earl of Banbury. Polygonal end; two-centred-arched windows with simplified panel tracery. C19 S vestry of brick, and a PARISH ROOM of 2003–4 by Brian Hook S of the nave, of Gothic outline. – SCREEN of 1953 to the N chapel made by Bill Barrett, blacksmith. – FONT. Early C13. Square; corner shafts with stiff-leaf or quasi-waterleaf capitals. – Medieval TILES, re-set in the N porch. – STAINED GLASS. C17 heraldic shields in the N chapel. E window, 1955 by E. Liddall Armitage for Powells. Chancel N, O'Connor, 1865. Nave S, 1876, by W.G. Taylor (MH). Nave N, Lavers & Westlake, 1903, and Burlison & Grylls, †1888.

MONUMENTS. Brass to Sir Robert de Grey †1387. One of the finest in the county. 58½-in. (1.49-metre) effigy in armour and helmet under a pinnacled canopy. – N chapel. Large and expensive free-standing monument of 1605. Tomb-chest with the recumbent effigies of Sir Francis and Katherine, Lady Knollys †1596 and †1569, and many kneeling figures of sons and daughters along the sides. The effigies rest on fat damask cushions. Exotic heraldic animals, an elephant and a swan, at their feet. The canopy over them stands on six Doric columns and two central arched supports with pilasters decorated with ribbonwork and reliefs of musical instruments. Pendants and rosettes decorate the soffit. On top are figures of Sir William Knollys †1632 and his wife †1605, facing across a prayer-desk. Urns stand at the corners, and cherubs in proto-Baroque poses gesture at the kneeling figures. The treatment of the large effigies is stiff and conventional, but the carving of details is polished and accomplished, and the alabaster and marble retain much original painting and gilding. It must be by one of the Southwark workshops; Geoffrey Fisher suggests William Cure II. – Sir Thomas Stapleton, 5th Bt †1781, by Westmacott the elder. Draped urn above a roundel with a garlanded shield. – Sir Thomas Stapleton, 6th Bt †1831. Relief of a draped sarcophagus by S. Manning I and John Bacon Jun. – Mary, Lady Stapleton †1835 and Georgiana Stapleton †1830, both also Manning.

38

OLD RECTORY, 300 yds N. Largely C18, with a central canted bay (cf. Harpsden Old Rectory). Just SE is UPPER PINDARS, an intriguing timber house by *Green, Lloyd & Son*, *c*.1961. White weatherboarded walls, square plan, tiled pyramid roof with a chimney at the apex.

GREYS COURT
National Trust, ⅔ m. NNW

A grand but depleted courtyard house of medieval origin, with notable Elizabethan rebuildings and additions, lesser C18 embellishments, and historically minded renovations of the 1930s–40s. Chief patrons up to the C20 were the de Greys (Domesday to late C14), the Lovells (C15), the veteran courtier Sir Francis Knollys M.P. (1550s–90s), and the Stapletons (C18–C19). The notable gardens to the E were created by Sir Felix and Lady Brunner, who continued to embellish them after the house was given to the Trust in 1969. Research, restoration and tree-ring dating in 2002–8 have since clarified much of its history.

The fabric of Greys Court is complicated and sometimes confusing, but also consistently enjoyable to explore, thanks in part to its gardens and hillside setting. A central lawn divides the buildings into two groups, E and W. The W side has the main house, placed to the N and facing E. Until at least the C17 the central space was bisected by a wall running E–W, and further enclosed by parallel walls to the N and S, all now lost. Thus the domestic complex had an upper and a lower court. To the W is a smaller service court, also of medieval origin.

The EAST SIDE has the most medieval work to show: two angle towers, NE and SE, linked by a curtain wall, from which a third tower projects close to the N end. The visitor first sees the SOUTH-EAST TOWER, octagonal, of three stages, with arrow loops; late C13 or C14. It may be the remnant of a larger gatehouse, as the main approach was from this side. Top windows and battlements of the C18. Attached to its W side is BACHELOR'S HALL, named from the C18 inscription over the central doorway: 'Melius nil coelibe vita' (Nothing is better than the celibate life). Brick, late C16 or early C17, two-storeyed. Windows with square hoods, now of C20 cement. It may have been a dower house.

The CURTAIN WALL is of the same phase as the SE tower, and is likewise of flint. In it, visible from the gardens, a chamfered-arched doorway, perhaps relating to a lost mural tower, and a wide, blocked triangular-headed recess to the N.* The intermediate GREAT TOWER follows to the N. A later aggrandizement, it may be associated with the licence to crenellate granted in 1346 to Sir John de Grey, one of Edward III's Knights of the Garter. Four storeys, diagonal buttresses, small square-headed windows. Brickwork stripes in the crenellated

---

*Leland recorded '3 or 4 very olde towers of stone' on this side in 1542.

upper parts betray C18 rebuilding. It stands against the E side of the curtain wall. On the W side here the walling is of quite different character, boldly striped in flint and brick: a C12 or even late C11 feature, surviving from a lost building of high quality, perhaps a chamber block or chapel. The rest of the curtain wall belongs with the Great Tower, as does the NORTH-EAST TOWER. This is of square plan set diagonally, and survives up to part of its third storey. Slit windows, deeply splayed internally. Narrow pointed-arched doorway. It formed part of a suite of lodgings which continued along the curtain wall, indicated by window openings and an inserted brick fireplace, and probably also along the lost N curtain. Medieval towers at the NW and SW corners may be inferred, but the present SW tower is C16 (*see* p. 714). Where the hall stood is unknown.

Also on the E side, facing the lawn, the so-called CROM-WELLIAN STABLES, actually the surviving N part of a lodging range built for Sir Francis Knollys in 1578 (tree rings). Two storeys and another in the r. gable. Red brick with a little blue; hollow-chamfered mullioned windows. Inside, a wooden spiral stair and C17 panelling, installed *c.* 1935. Chimney behind with two octagonal stacks. The brick WALL running E to the medieval curtain here is a remnant of lost mid-C15 lodgings.

The main range of the HOUSE can be dated from its timbers to 1575–6, just after Sir Francis received Queen Elizabeth at Greys. It may have provided superior guest lodgings, or his own quarters. A cheerful front of silver flint, banded with red brick and dressed with stone. Three gables. Mullion-and-transom windows with two or three arched lights on the first floor, placed symmetrically. A blocked doorway at the far l. must have opened to a walk on the wall dividing the upper and lower courts. Views of the house before 1840 show no windows on the ground floor. Bay windows added here in the late C19 were removed in changes by two successive C20 owners, Mrs Evelyn Fleming (1934–7, architect *H. J. Harding*) and Sir Felix and Lady Brunner (*c.* 1938–44, architect *A. B. Knapp-Fisher*). Harding did the present central doorway and windows, and the ground-floor and panel-traceried first-floor window on the S front. Next to these is a gabled brick porch of *c.* 1619, with a small oriel over two moulded brick arches. It adjoins an older and lower brick-faced S projection, now housing the kitchen and a staircase, and dated to 1443/4 and 1450/1. This is only a stub of what was a much longer range of timber-framed C15 lodgings. Part of the jettied and close-studded front survives, engulfed behind the brick façade added *c.* 1578. The C15 back wall here is also of brick. It retains its large brick-arched fireplace, and a broad chimneystack on the rear wall with diagonally placed shafts. Flint and brick SW wing, which has also yielded C15 timbers.

The 1570s brick frontage continues S from the house, reduced to a single-storey screen. One part was dressed up in flint for Sir Thomas Stapleton in the mid C18, probably in emulation of Sir Francis Dashwood's works at Medmenham

(Bucks.). Four lead statues of amorini by *Gertrude Knoblock* on top, added by Mrs Fleming.

To the N, the house displays an incongruous through-storey bay of 1759–60, stuccoed and crenellated, with arched classical windows. Contemporary NW addition, its windows mostly Georgian-style replacements by the Brunners. The very informal W side now mostly has C20 windows too, including a white-painted oriel by *Lionel Brett*, 1955, l., and mostly C20 chimneys. Attached conservatory of 1984–5 by *Francis Pollen*, who also converted the SW wing for a curator's house.

INTERIORS. The C16 plan is obscure. By the early C18 the chief reception rooms flanked the entrance hall, with the stair behind. Mrs Fleming knocked the E ground-floor interiors into one long room, a change promptly reversed by the Brunners. The bow-ended DRAWING ROOM, N, is otherwise intact. It has fine Rococo plasterwork, close enough to the drawing-room ceiling at Watlington Park (q.v.) to suggest the same hand. Ceiling centrepiece with bows and arrows and love birds, perhaps commissioned to mark the wedding of Sir Thomas Stapleton in 1765. Floral trophies on the walls. The plasterwork ceiling garland in the SCHOOLROOM, NW, is less accomplished. Mid-C18 stone fireplace with swagged consoles, fretwork frieze and a relief of an urn and fruit. STAIRCASE of mid-C18 detail, probably not in its C18 form. LADY BRUNNER'S BEDROOM, S, has a C16 stone fireplace with a four-centred arch. The plasterwork frieze, with eagles, cherubs and stars, is based on the portal decoration of the Temple of Bal at Palmyra, published by Robert Wood in 1753. The KITCHEN has re-set C16 panelling, and the C15 features already mentioned.

The SERVICE COURT has the house's immediate outbuildings on its N side. On the S side, the remarkable WELL-HOUSE, built in 1587 over an early medieval well. Tall and compact, of red and blue brick in a diaper pattern. Small windows with brick mullions, partly rendered over. Inside is the original DONKEY WHEEL for raising water, one of the finest surviving examples, 19 ft (5.8 metres) in diameter. The SOUTH-WEST TOWER is of the same date, built to balance the medieval SE tower and likewise octagonal, but without crenellation. Also around 1587, flint walling was applied to the adjacent short range to the N known as THE KEEP, built *c.*1559 as a brew-house or kitchen (smoke-blackened roof), and an extension added to complete the court's W side. To its N is the DAIRY, late C18, with some decorative flint facing on one side. Further to the SW, a HORSE PUMP and octagonal iron shelter of *c.*1870, brought in 1975 from Shabden Park, Surrey.

The Brunners' GARDENS are of the 'garden room' type. The Cherry Garden, S, is partly enclosed by the incomplete shell of the so-called Tithe Barn, built in the C16 of reused masonry. The FOUNTAIN here is Swiss, of the C18. Other ornaments include a yew-wood STATUE by *Jacqueline Geldart*, 1987, in the Kitchen Garden, and a MAZE of brick and turf by *Adrian Fisher*, 1980. To the N, beyond an C18 HA-HA, is a thatched C19

ICE HOUSE. The jaunty CHINESE BRIDGE, NW, is by *Francis Pollen*, 1979.

FARMHOUSES. COWFIELDS, ½ m. SE of the church, grew from a late medieval hall house, represented by the entrance bay and through-storey canted bay to the l., and probably also the gabled wing, r. Inserted chimneystack and floor, late C16. To the l. a late C17 cross-wing. Multiple later extensions. ROCKY LANE FARM, 1¼ m. NW, is C18, deceptively reworked in 1927 (rainwater heads) with reused C16 mullioned windows and doorways. (LOWER HERNES, 1 m. ENE, has the tree-ring date 1567.)

BADGEMORE HOUSE, 1½ m. ENE. Stables with pyramid-roofed towers by *John Norton*, 1884–5, now a golf clubhouse. They went with a nine-bay brick mansion built probably in the 1710s by *Richard Jennings*, Wren's master carpenter for St Paul's dome, which Norton remodelled for Richard Ovey (dem. 1946). The present neo-1700 house is by *C.B. Willcocks*, 1939–41.

(SATWELL'S BARTON, 1⅓ m. WNW. 1906 by *C.H. Biddulph-Pinchard*. Neo-Wren, with an outsized hipped roof.)

ROTHERFIELD PEPPARD

7080

ALL SAINTS. Largely rebuilt in 1874–5 by *William Scott Champion*, adding a N aisle. Dec style. The C12 chancel was kept, heavily restored. Two Norman windows on the N and one on the S. The E bay has a roll sill-moulding internally. On the E wall the jamb shafts, with scalloped capitals, and the springing of two arches of an arcade which probably consisted of a window flanked by blind arches. Transitional pointed chancel arch with a grooved hoodmould and small angle roll. The N jamb shaft has a volute capital, the S a capital with waterleaf. In 1908 the nave W bay received a slim chequerwork tower with a square tiled spire, by *E.H. Sedding*. S porch also of 1908; N vestry of 1965 by *J.M. Surman & E.R. Chilton*. PARISH ROOM to the NW, 1981–2 by *Teggin & Taylor*. Of blockwork, strenuously composed. – ALTAR and REREDOS, 1894, and PULPIT, 1892, all with accomplished intarsia pictures by the donor, *Mirabel Grey*. – FONT. Norman, cinched by a band of cable moulding. – STAINED GLASS. E window, 1957 by *Morris Meredith Williams*; also windows of 1948 and 1962 (chancel) and 1957 (nave E). Strong designs, influenced by C13 French glass. Chancel S, a haunting lancet of 1909 designed by the artist and sculptor *Alice Meredith Williams*, Morris's wife and sometime collaborator. Made by *Guthrie & Wells* of Glasgow (PC). Chancel S panel, 1875, and nave S, 1883, by *Hardman* (MH). N aisle N, *Powells*, 1927. Silly W window, 1933 by *C.C. Powell*. Two windows by *Lyn Clayden*, 1987 and 1992.

HENLEY HOUSE, E (former rectory), c.1849–50. Red brick, minimal Tudor detail.

PRIMARY SCHOOL, 350 yds w. By *Frederick Haslam*, 1871. With a well-placed Gothic bellcote.

BLOUNTS COURT (Johnson-Matthey Technology Centre), ½ m. s. From the E the house has the look of 1820 or 1830, ashlar, irregularly composed, with a four-bay front projection and Doric porch and a semicircular bay window to the N. But the s side shows earlier brickwork in two phases, C17 and C18, and the main N–S range proves to be older still, dated from its timbers to three phases between 1431, s, and 1525/6, N.* Most of this encased timber framing was lost in renovations of 1992–3, but the tie-beam roof to the N is intact, as is that of a small SW staircase addition of 1530. In the main s room is a fine two-light Perp window of stone in the w wall, altered for use as an internal doorway. This wall was of flint and stone on the ground floor, with timber framing above; the E side was jettied and wholly of timber. Central stair hall of *c.* 1820–30 with wide stone stair and landing; laterally symmetrical iron balusters.

The house is linked to extensive LABORATORIES, built for Brooke Bond, 1968–72; company architects, *Beard, Bennett, Wilkins & Partners*. Strip glazing, recessed within concrete framing faced with panels of flint aggregate. Additions include a terracotta-faced block to the NE by *Halson Mackley Partnership*, 2012–13.

BLOUNTS FARMHOUSE, E, has a C16 core within C18 brick. Probably part of the same complex as Blounts Court originally, as suggested also by parch marks on the lawn between.

CONGREGATIONAL CHAPEL, Blounts Court Road, ½ m. SW. Of 1796, i.e. quite an early survival, but much altered and extended. Perhaps by *Richard Billing I* of Reading, who had connections with the founder. Early C19 MANSE attached to the s, enlarged 1923.

WYFOLD COURT, 2 m. WNW. One of the great Victorian country houses, built in 1873–6 for Edward Hermon, cotton magnate and Conservative M.P. for Preston. The architect was the versatile *George Somers Clarke*, a former pupil of Sir Charles Barry; the style is French Flamboyant Gothic with a strong admixture of Elizabethan English. It is a staggering composition, extending some 250 by 200 ft in all (75 by 60 metres). Hermon's own estate supplied the orange-red bricks, which are combined with blue brick diapering and dressings of yellow Box Ground stone. Moulded brick chimneys from Costessey, Norfolk. *Manley & Rogers* of London were the contractors; the chief carver, *L.T. Carter*, was sent on a study tour to France in connection.

The entrance side, N, is the most exciting. It has two return wings, one with a pointed-arched *porte cochère* and a conical-roofed tourelle, the other ending in a mighty tower with chisel-shaped roof and a lead-faced bellcote, with service quarters beyond. The wings are joined by a straight wall with Gothic windows. In the l. angle is the staircase enclosure, with giant

*The 1431 phase provided the earliest identified English instance of diminished haunched mortise joints.

triple-transomed windows. The garden side is less ambitious, lacking the upper bedroom storey provided in Clarke's original design, but more successfully composed. It has three projecting mullion-and-transom bay windows, and two more in the angles of the projections. Sharp crocketed gables with heraldic beasts. At the l. corner a richly treated tourelle. Inside are cavernous rooms with Gothic fireplaces (originally, from l. to r., billiard room, 'Mr Hermon's Room', dining, morning, ante-drawing and drawing rooms, and part of the gallery along the E flank). The main corridor behind has a rib-vault springing from polished marble wall-shafts with luxuriant foliage capitals. Original gas-lamp brackets of brass with playful devices of cheese, tortoises, tongs etc. Stair hall 42 ft (12.8 metres) high, with an oak roof, oak staircase piers with traceried spandrels, and stained-glass shields of the sovereigns of England in the immense windows. Four canvases remain here from Hermon's huge collection of contemporary paintings, historical subjects by *William Chappell*.* In 1999 the house was converted to apartments and a projecting square bay added in the middle of the E side, where the gallery was subdivided. From 1933 to 1993 Wyfold Court served as Borocourt Hospital for the mentally ill, with extensive additions, now restored to gardens or replaced by new houses.

WYFOLD GRANGE, ½ m. SE of Wyfold Court on the site of the old manor house, is also by *Somers Clarke*, *c.*1877–8, in a reduced version of the same manner. (At the BAILIFF'S HOUSE of 1872, now called Chartersfield Hall, ½ m. S in Checkendon parish, Clarke added half-timbered gables to the mixture: *Building News*, 6 July 1877.) For Hermon's school at Hook End *see* Checkendon.

RYCOTE
Great Haseley

Rycote Park is one of Oxfordshire's lost great houses, sold for its materials in 1807. The C15 chapel remains, celebrated for its sumptuous C17 fittings, and a good proportion of the C16 service buildings, adapted and extended as a house in the C20–C21, together with the restored C18 landscape setting.

CHAPEL OF ST MICHAEL. Built for Richard and Sybil Quatre-main of Rycote, and consecrated in 1449. It is very like a small parish church, entirely of one build and unaltered. Continuous nave and chancel, originally rendered. Each side wall has five windows of two arched cusped lights under shallow triangular heads. They are divided by pinnacled buttresses which cut

---

* Most of the holdings were sold at Christie's in 1882, after Hermon's death. Eight works were purchased for Royal Holloway College, Surrey.

through the roof slope. At the E end a five-light window with panel tracery, flanked by diagonal buttresses. These are surmounted by greyhounds carved by *Tim Crawley*, 2018; the weathered C16 originals are inside. Battlemented W tower with a square SE stair-turret. To the W a canopied image niche, also with a statue by *Crawley*. (Inside, at the same level, a room with a small fireplace.) Another fireplace in the N wall of the nave, its chimney coming out in place of a pinnacle. The most elaborate doorway, on the N facing the house, has an arch with quatrefoils in the spandrels and a hood with shields. Simple S and W doorways with continuous mouldings. The pointed wagon roof survives complete, with traces of early C17 decoration; a section has been restored at the W end, painted with stars. PISCINA with a cusped arch. Gentle restorations from *c.*1912 by *William Weir*, and again in 2013–17 by *Donald Insall Architects*.

Much remains inside from the C15, but the space is dominated by two great early C17 PEWS flanking the steps to the chancel. One double-decked, the other domed and canopied, and both painted and gilded, they have the brittle and insubstantial air of pageant scenery. There is no firm date for either, but the one on the N has been identified as the Norreys or Norris family pew of *c.*1610, and the S pew may well have been set up for Charles I's visit to Rycote in 1625. The E sides of both pews rise from the retained lower stage of the C15 SCREEN, which has kept the tops of blind arcading on its W side, and also the moulded jambs of its central doorway. This now finishes in an early C17 arch with an elaborate strapwork crest. The NORTH PEW is enclosed by arcades of slim quasi-Tuscan columns on three sides. On the N the stairs to the former rood loft now lead to a musicians' gallery over the pew. The ceiling is painted with a cloudy sky and has stuck-on stars. On the N side the panels have traces of busts or portraits and landscape paintings in oval frames. The rest of the panelling is decorated inside with elaborate filigree devices. The gallery is screened with two tiers of pierced panels of a pattern resembling a delicate Islamic design, originally backed by cloth. These are nearly all reinstatements by *Weir*, based on surviving parts. Similar patterning on the corner pilasters. The SOUTH PEW is equally exotic. It has a great ogee canopy with crocketed ribs, originally surmounted by a carved Virgin and Child. Two figures of Evangelists remain at the corners. Traces of original colour and, inside, repainting of part of the canopy with white flowers on a blue background and red ribs. The canopy is carried on short black columns with gilt Ionic capitals, resting in turn on an arcade like that of the N pew, though of lower proportions. Doorway on the N side with carved foliage in the spandrels. Painted garlands on the panels inside.

C15 PEWS extend from these two grand enclosures to the W, decorated with small buttresses. To the E are C15 STALLS with poppyheads and traceried fronts, below an early C17 DADO. Also, the nave S side has a Jacobean PULPIT, square (which is unusual), but the usual blind arches among the carved motifs. It retains its canopy, formerly with pendants. In front, an C18 READING DESK. Against the nave N wall, BATTLEMENTS from the top of the C15 screen.

OTHER FURNISHINGS. REREDOS, dated 1682. Text panels divided by four fluted Corinthian half-columns, under a great segmental pediment which encloses fruit and flowers carved after the manner of Grinling Gibbons. The texts have acanthus frames under small pediments. – COMMUNION TABLE. Early C17. – COMMUNION RAILS with twisted balusters, c. 1682. – FONT. Cup-shaped, apparently a C12 tub font re-cut. The panelled base and ribbed ogee COVER are C15. – WEST GALLERY of c. 1610 with a balustraded front carried on Ionic columns. More cloud painting on the underside. – CHAMBER ORGAN of 2007 by *Mander* on the gallery. – Under the tower a damaged COMMANDMENTS BOARD of c. 1610 with Ionic columns in two sizes. Texts in two arched panels. Spandrels carved with buds and foliage. – MONUMENTS. James Bertie, 1st Earl of Abingdon †1699, erected 1767. Accomplished but anonymous, though the bust may come from a family series of the 1730s by *Sir Henry Cheere*. Its niche is flanked by palms, bay fronds, books, a coronet and a sword. At the bottom a coat of arms with supporters, friar and naked savage. – Alfred Hamersley †1929. Inscribed tablet by *Eric Gill*, 1930.

RYCOTE PARK, NNW of the church. Carved capitals and mouldings from the late medieval house have been found, and trial trenches dug in 2001 located some foundations. The moated courtier mansion which replaced it was built almost certainly in the 1540s or 1550s for Sir John Williams, later Lord Williams of Thame. Views by Winstanley (c. 1695) and Kip (1707) show it to have had several courtyards, and an entrance front facing s, with crowstepped gables, octagonal corner towers with ogee cupolas, a gatehouse-like centre, and slim turrets spaced between. Inherited by the Norreys, then the Berties, it was repaired and partially rebuilt after a fire in 1745, only to be sold for its materials in 1807. All that remains is the lower

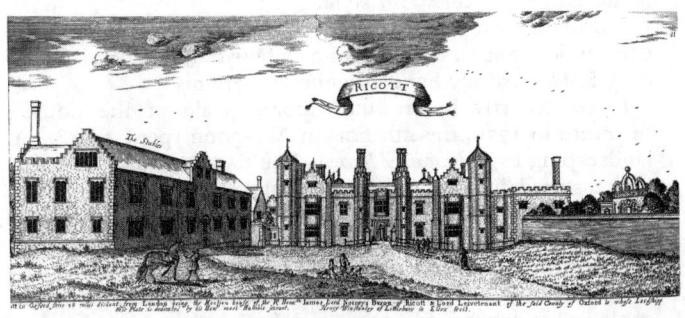

Rycote Park.
Engraving by Henry Winstanley, 1695

stages of the TOWER formerly at the W corner of the frontage, with part of the walling and of one of the turrets. Diapered red brick, as at Williams's lodge of *c.*1540 at Beckley Park (*see Oxfordshire: North and West*). The lugged stone doorway was inserted after 1822, apparently reusing a late C17 window: guilloche and bay-leaf mouldings, scroll brackets carved with lions' heads.

The present HOUSE stands immediately to the W. Its main range chiefly consists of the surviving S end of the C16 stables, and other C16 service ranges make up much of the courtyard to the W. The stables are again of diapered brick, with a short W return at the S end. Two storeys, stepped gables, coved C18 eaves. Sashes on the E side, but straight-headed mullioned windows to the S, original on the ground floor, largely restored above. The latter are of *c.*1912, when *William Weir* and *George Jack* restored the house for Alfred Hamersley. A Neo-Elizabethan canted bay and gable which they added to the N were replaced with curt brick and sashes in 1938, when *H.R. Goodhart-Rendel* remodelled the house for Cecil Michaelis. The present gable and battlements and the two-bay N continuation are all of 2001–5 by *Nicholas Thompson* of *Donald Insall Associates*, for Bernard and Sarah Taylor. Behind and in parallel is a section added by *Goodhart-Rendel*, of rubble stone laced with red brick, making a link to the plain stone of the courtyard ranges. Also his are the thirty-pane sashes on the courtyard side of the main range. The S end of the W side here belongs with the work of 2001–5, including the carriageway entrance. The balustraded central feature and the formal gardens on both sides of the house, with *Elizabeth Banks* as garden designer, complete the C21 transformation.

Little of the C16 remains inside. The N range is partly open to the heftily timbered roof, with curved struts between lower collars to upper purlins. *Weir* provided a fine stone fireplace in free Elizabethan style for the former entrance hall. The usual entry is now from the W, to a stair hall with elements from all three C20–C21 phases. A grand barrel-vaulted dining room occupies the N extension of 2001–5, with plasterwork and a chimneypiece in early C17 style.

THE BAKERY, NNE of the house. Another remainder of the C16 service ranges, remodelled as a house by *Goodhart-Rendel c.*1938. The artfully handled chimneys are his.

PARK. Shortly before the enforced sale of the house's furniture in 1779, the 4th Earl of Abingdon spent £2,888 on landscaping by *Capability Brown*. The LAKE remains, dredged and restored in 2001–5. – ICE HOUSE, S of the church. By *Francis Maude* of *Donald Insall Associates*, 2014–16. Brick and thatch, enclosing an originally earth-bound C18 chamber.

RYCOTE FARM and COTTAGES, 100 yds W. Both by *Goodhart-Rendel*, 1937. White rendering and steep tiled roofs, hipped or gabled, with echoes of Lutyens and Voysey in the compositions.

SANDFORD-ON-THAMES

St Andrew, Church Road. Little remains of the late C11 church. The s walls of the chancel and nave are largely original, also a small chancel s window with a roll label and jamb shafts with cushion capitals. The e window is a big cusped C13 lancet, suggesting that the chancel was extended then. Norman nave doorways of the type with plain jambs and a recessed tympanum with a large lintel. s doorway partly plastered over; n doorway blocked, and re-set in the n aisle which *James Brooks* added in his restoration of 1864–5. Before that, in 1840, *J. M. Derick* built the aggressively Neo-Norman w tower to replace a wooden structure. s porch of 1652, given by Elizabeth Isham. Above its flattened four-centred-arched doorway is the renewed inscription: 'Thankes to thy Charitie religiose dame / Wch found mee old and & made mee new again'. The running hoodmould looks like an influence from Oxford. *Brooks* also made the nave s windows and gave his n aisle trefoil-headed lancets. The aisle w window however is Perp and straight-headed, saved from the nave s wall. Chancel arch and roofs all of 1864–5. Vestry of the same date, extended n in 1893 by *H. G. W. Drinkwater*. – FURNISHINGS largely by *Brooks*, characteristically bold. – SCULPTURE. A large early C15 limestone relief of the Assumption of the Virgin, surrounded by a mandorla carried by six angels. Two smaller angels hold a monstrance below, probably once housing a reliquary. Discovered in the churchyard in 1723. Probably from a greater church (Abingdon Abbey?).* – STAINED GLASS. Chancel n by *Willement*, 1850. Tower, †1885 by *N. H. J. Westlake* (*Lavers, Barraud & Westlake*). The rest apparently by one good but unidentified mid-Victorian maker. – MONUMENT. Sir William Powell †1656, erected 1661. Tablet with approximately Composite columns.

SCHOOL (former), w. Of 1860, 1868 and 1905. Some Neo-Norman details, surprisingly.

TEMPLE FARM, off Sandford Road, 200 yds NW. Since 1997 part of a large hotel complex (now VOCO OXFORD THAMES HOTEL), partly imitative of the older buildings. There was a preceptory of the Knights Templar here from the 1240s, which by 1325 had passed to the Knights Hospitallers. A C16 house remains, probably of after the Dissolution, and a barn to its s. The HOUSE is of two storeys, somewhat restored *c.*1900 with dormers, moulded cornice and additional mullioned windows, but still a close match to Buckler's drawing of 1826. T-plan, the main part aligned N–S. An C18 addition extends N from the projection. Two- and three-light mullioned windows with arched heads. Over the doorway a re-set shield with the Hospitallers' cross pattée. In the s gable-end mullioned windows with

---

* *See* Charles Tracy in *Apollo* 158 (September 2003).

moulded surrounds and straight heads, i.e. of C17 type. The w front has on the upper floor one old window of two arched lights and a similar, cruder single light, r. Over the w doorway a quatrefoil enclosing a shield. The BARN, now hotel reception and bar, mostly C18, stands E–W. Its E end is apparently C15, and suggests a former chapel. Hollow-chamfered sills and jambs of a tall, blocked E window, shown by Buckler with three lights. Large, rough NE buttress. Also a C15 N doorway with a four-centred arch and moulded surround. Slit-windows to the w. – In the garden wall to the N a DOORWAY dated 1614, re-set and reduced. Unusual raised-foliage spandrels. Fragments of medieval carving built in to l. and r.

RIVER VIEW COTTAGES, Nos. 3–8 River View, off Church Road, 300 yds SSW. Terrace of c. 1825, notable for the shallow roof (ten-degree pitch), originally covered with tarred paper. Built by James Swann for workers at his paper mill, which stood by Sandford Lock, just SW. The roof trusses are as specified in a pamphlet of c. 1810 by J. C. Loudon, who had used similar paper roofs at Tew Lodge (Great Tew), North Oxfordshire.

SHIPLAKE

ST PETER AND ST PAUL. On high land above the Thames. C14 NW tower, embattled and with Y-traceried bell-openings. The rest was largely rebuilt in 1868–70 by G. E. Street, who replaced the N aisle inherited from a Gothic-minded restoration of 1822. Flint, C13 style. Timber s porch of the 1850s. All the windows are Street's except the s aisle E, a C13 graduated triplet of lancets set in a shafted rere-arch. One capital re-set in the s arcade is C15, with carved heads and rosettes. C13 PISCINA in the s aisle, its drain with petal-like shapes in a dogtooth surround. N vestry enlarged by G. Fellowes Prynne c. 1920. – Good marble and alabaster REREDOS and FONT by Street, carved by Earp. – CHAIR (chancel). Canopied; called an abbess's chair. Apparently an antiquarian assemblage using Flamboyant woodwork. – PULPIT from All Saints, Dorchester (Dorset), replacing Street's. Probably 1610s. – Plain BENCHES by Street. – Gothic CHANDELIERS of brass by Hardman, 1870. – War memorial ALTAR, s aisle, by Fellowes Prynne, c. 1920.

STAINED GLASS. Five windows have late C15 and early C16 glass from the abbey church of St Bertin at St-Omer, in the Pas-de-Calais. Bought from St-Omer by the Rev. John Palmer Boteler in 1828 and by the Rev. A. E. Howman in 1830, and first installed at Shiplake by Thomas Willement. E window, mostly figure panels with an angel at each corner. From l. to r., beginning at bottom l.: St Anthony Abbot; the Blessed Peter of Luxembourg's vision of the Crucifixion; St John the Evangelist; St Barbara; St Peter; St Catherine; Coronation of the Virgin; St Omer; God the Father, a companion figure to the Coronation; seraphim; St Andrew; seraphim; St John the Baptist. – Chancel S, first from E. Six heads or busts of different sizes, probably from narrative windows. – S aisle E, more heads, and a composite figure of St Peter (centre light). – S aisle S. Two female saints, C15 English work, under canopies by *Willement*. Above, heads of angels, the Christ Child etc. – S aisle W, from bottom l.: St John the Evangelist; Eagle of St John; St John the Baptist(?); male head; Bull of St Luke (corroded); male head; Virgin and Child; Lion of St Mark (corroded); God the Father; angel; Angel of St Matthew (corroded); angel; fragmentary figures. – Other windows. S aisle, one lancet signed by *Willement*, 1829; another of 1870 by *Horwood Bros*. W window, 1888 by *Hardman*, after an Aesthetic-influenced design by *Charlotte, Lady Phillimore*. N aisle, 1919, all *Percy Bacon Bros* (PC).

MONUMENTS. John and Joan Symondes, *c.*1540. 18½-in. (47-cm.) brasses. – Andrew Blunden †1607. A frontal demi-figure in an arched recess. – Francis Plowden †1652. With a good alabaster bust in an oval frame flanked by skulls. Attributed to the *Marshall* workshop (GF). – Mary Wright and Jane Rigail, sisters, †1842. Gothic. Signed by *William Osmond* of Salisbury, Pugin's friend. – Anthony Phillimore †1940, figure brass of 1956 (S aisle). – CROSS, churchyard. By *Fellowes Prynne*, 1908, to Alice Phillimore. Makers *H.H. Martyn & Co*. Graceful, with a carved head. – By the S wall, GRAVESTONE of the architect Claud, 4th Lord Phillimore †1994.

SHIPLAKE COURT, E of the church. Now SHIPLAKE COLLEGE, a boarding school. By *Ernest George & Harold Peto*, 1889–91, for the stockbroker Robert Harrison, who moved in Liberal and Aesthetic circles. Goodhart-Rendel described it as one of George's 'most pleasant productions'. This is too mild an adjective for so vigorous a design. Tudor Gothic, of deep red brick with intricate blue diapering. Some windows of stone, others of dark-stained timber. Boldly asymmetrical entrance front, the porch in a three-storey battlemented tower with a corner turret. Plentiful chimneys, set on contrasting alignments. The garden front is more symmetrical, in the form of an E. Along the middle is the Great Hall. Bay window of full height, not set centrally, with arched cusped lights and canted corners. The wings, with dining room and library, have identical gable-ends. In each inner angle is an Italianate loggia. Long gabled service range, set back to the NE. Inside, the Great Hall rises to a mighty arch-braced roof with wind-braces in three tiers. Screens passage with gallery over, reached from a relatively modest stair hall to the N. Also a chimney-breast of rather French Gothic detail, and in one upper corner a wooden spiral-stair enclosure in a similar style (introduced?). *p. 724*

Terraces extend from the house towards the river. *Alfred Parsons*'s garden setting has otherwise largely gone. To the W are STABLES, and in the stable yard an extraordinary WATER TOWER of *c.*1899, with assertive flint chequerwork diapering and a steep, Rhenish-looking roof. BURR HOUSE, adjacent, is early C18, of flint with bold brick quoins. Many SCHOOL

Shiplake Court, Great Hall.
Drawing, 1909

BUILDINGS of the 1980s onwards by *Nichols Brown Webber* of
Henley, some with motifs borrowed from the big house.

SHIPLAKE HOUSE, ¼ m. NE. Centre of five bays and three
storeys, probably mid-C18. Bracketed eaves. Stuccoed *c.*1832
for Joseph Phillimore, the likely date of the lower wings. These
have canted ends on the river side. Wrought-iron veranda
between. (N porch in the form of a small vestibule, the doorway
flanked by windows.)

HAILEYWOOD, ¾ m. N. 1909–10 by *T.E. Collcutt*. Rendered and
informal. The twin gables of the SW front have timbering.

MEMORIAL HALL, Shiplake Cross, ⅓ m. NW. With a blockish
tower. By *F.G. Sainsbury*, 1925–7.

LOWER SHIPLAKE is now the largest settlement, by the railway
station 1 m. NE. Some notable riverside houses along Bolney
Lane, which continues N into Harpsden parish. THE WHITE

HOUSE, 1908, is a rare building by the Glasgow architect-designer *George Walton*, who worked at various times with Mackintosh and with Voysey. The client was George Davison of the Kodak company, whose shops Walton also designed. Low, stuccoed, in something like a *Jugendstil* version of Neo-Regency. It is reminiscent of Brighton seafront, but nowhere are Regency forms copied. On each main front a big gable treated pedimentally, and the upper storey otherwise placed partly in the roof. Extremely thin double-decked verandas of iron to the W and S sides, the former treated as a big bow. Steel-framed, full-height windows with louvred shutters. Elements of Walton's interior remain, including glazed double doors and panelled soffits (also the staircase). N extensions of *c.*1968 and later. BOLNEY COURT, N, is a very large Arts and Crafts house with close studding as the dominant motif. By *W. Flockhart*, 1910, replacing a mansion of 1852 by *J. H. Hakewill*. SAGAMORE, well to the S, is a showy half-timbered giant of *c.*1921, for the banker Sir Frederick Eley. For Lower Bolney Farm *see* Harpsden.

SHIRBURN

6090

A seigneurial village. Church and castle stand side by side at the end of a short lane.

ALL SAINTS (Churches Conservation Trust). Medium-sized, with stuccoed walls and a gloomy interior. Mostly late C13 and early C14, with major C19 additions and alterations. Some Norman pieces from an earlier church were re-set in the W tower in 1876, when *T. H. Wyatt* restored the church for the 6th Earl of Macclesfield. In the W wall a doorway-sized tympanum with figure-of-eight interlace under a roll hood and guilloche moulding. In the W wall inside a lintel with star-in-square pattern. Also, in the bell-stage, a reused round-headed W lancet and an opening of two arched lights on the N. The shaft between them is without a capital and obviously re-set. Top stage later, perhaps C15. It has arched openings, now indicated by outlines in the rendering. Low down at the SW corner a big MASS DIAL is exposed. C14 S doorway, of two continuous chamfered orders. C13 nave arcades of three bays. On the N side arches of two unchamfered orders and octagonal piers with concave capitals. On the S single-chamfered arches, an octagonal W pier with a moulded capital, and a round E pier with partially intact stiff-leaf. Simple two-light C14 and C15 windows in the S aisle and S transept. Also in the S transept the head of a C14 PISCINA. N aisle windows of 1876. The N transept is an early C19 addition for the Macclesfield family pew. Romantic Gothic, with blind tracery panelling of plaster and a thin arch-braced roof; very probably by *John Nash*, who made other designs for Lord Macclesfield *c.*1800–10. Chancel arch of 1876. In the chancel two early C14 S windows with Y-tracery and a rectangular lowside window. E window with cusped intersecting tracery, also early C14. The NE chapel is medieval but was adapted as the Macclesfield family mausoleum, probably *c.*1732. It is ceiled, with shields in the coving. Until 1876 it was fully walled off from the chancel and N aisle.

FURNISHINGS. ROYAL ARMS of William IV. – FONT. Plain; C13? (The Georgian COVER is in store.) – STAINED GLASS. Three windows by *Ward & Hughes*, 1876 (E and W) and 1888 (S transept). – MONUMENTS. Brass to Richard and Sybyll Chamberleyn, †1496 and †1493, from an altar tomb. They kneel with their children, facing towards a representation of the Trinity. Figures of 13¾ and 13½ in. (35 and 34 cm.). – Richard Chamberlain †1602 and family. Another remnant from a larger monument. Inscriptions on slate in an alabaster panel set with black bosses. – John Chamberlain †1651. Architectural, with a broken pediment; quite advanced. – The Macclesfield family memorials are remarkably austere.

(SHIRBURN CASTLE.* Licence to build a castle was granted in 1377 to Warin, 2nd Lord de Lisle. It followed the symmetrical quadrangular plan with corner towers, the type established in France in the early C13 and developed soon after in southern Italy. Of Edward I's Welsh castles of the 1280s, Harlech also belongs to the type. C14 versions had more extensive domestic arrangements, which might occupy all four sides of the quadrangle instead of one or two. The best-known English example is Bodiam in Sussex, begun in 1385, which like Shirburn stands in a moat. A closer comparison is impossible, because the greater part of Shirburn was rebuilt after 1716 for an incoming owner, Thomas Parker, later Lord Chancellor and 1st Earl of Macclesfield. The 'castle air' was also invoked by Vanbrugh at his rebuilding of Kimbolton (Hunts.) after 1707, but Shirburn remains unique among early C18 country seats for its close imitation of medieval outlines and its quadrangular form. It may be that Lord Macclesfield, as a rising figure and newly minted peer, was drawn to the associations of ancient ancestry that came with battlements and towers. Nor is it clear who designed the new work. Macclesfield's consultant was *Sir Thomas Hewett*, an architectural amateur whose political connections secured him the post of Surveyor of the King's Works in 1719. Hewett's own designs and loyalties were firmly classical, but he disapproved of the 'strange bulky buildings' of Vanbrugh and Hawksmoor, so it is unlikely that the whole design is his; he may have been consulted about the library in particular, having directed the building of Lord Sunderland's

*Visits to the castle and grounds are not permitted, and the following account is based on existing sources and online material. Access was not granted for the 1974 edition of *The Buildings of England*, nor to the Department of the Environment's building recorders in the 1980s. Even that inveterate dropper-in the Hon. John Byng (Viscount Torrington) was refused entry, twice, in 1785. He found it 'a very ugly place, in a very ugly country…the whole appearance is melancholy and tasteless'.

Shirburn Castle.
Engraving by J. P. Neale, 1826

library in Piccadilly in 1720–2. Partial rebuilding on the N side in 1830 did not change the castle's appearance drastically, and after the 1870s no significant new work is recorded.

The medieval castle was of ashlar and limestone rubble, the C18 rebuilding of red brick, with a coat of rendering to mask the differences. The castle had been damaged in the Civil War, and much may have been ruinous or beyond repair by the 1710s. Medieval fabric survives in the W range, SW tower and SE tower. These corner towers are round, as at Bodiam, and the centre of the W range preserves the original gate tower, set almost flush. If there were intermediate towers or turrets on the other sides, Bodiam-fashion, they were not perpetuated in the rebuilding. The hall was probably on the E side opposite the gate tower, with a postern gate alongside. The best-preserved section is the GATE TOWER, which has arrow loops high up and a double-chamfered doorway with provision for a portcullis. The gate passage is vaulted, with round holes in place of bosses, as also at Bodiam and at several royal buildings of the later C14. The broad archway in its l. wall is of late C15 or C16 brick. Originally the gate tower would have stood proud of the side ranges, but in the rebuilding these were raised to three storeys all round. The corner towers and W front have mostly round-headed windows. There are more on the inner sides, several with keystones and at least one with a plain classical arch on impost blocks – enough to scotch any suggestion that Shirburn's round arches should be read as Neo-Norman (cf. the windows of Hugh May's works at Windsor Castle, c.1674–85). On the N side a big two-storey addition of 1830 with straight-headed sashes, its central bays projecting. Before then, probably around 1800, the present drawbridge and footbridges were made on the other sides; these may belong with *John Nash*'s works for the 4th Earl at Shirburn, which are inadequately documented. The E side has segment-headed sashes on all three storeys, those of the top floor still with small panes (nine-over-nine) of early C18 type. On the s side more straight-headed sashes; also round-headed windows and a few circular ones where the front steps back alongside the towers.

INTERIORS. The ranges are largely of double-pile plan, and the courtyard is now built over on the ground floor. On the courtyard side of the N range is the BARONIAL HALL, a Romantic Gothic creation of *c.* 1800 for the 4th Earl, almost certainly by *Nash* (cf. his Gothic dining room at Carlton House, 1797–8). Wooden wall-shafts of half-quatrefoil section support pierced spandrel braces to the ribbed ceiling, which has big round compartments. At the end a false cross-vault with little prickles on the ribs. s of the gate passage is the C18 kitchen, with a surviving C14 doorway. The open-well STAIR-CASE is of timber and has standard early C18 components, but with a flying upper section. It leads to the barrel-vaulted and panelled NORTH LIBRARY: one of three large library rooms at Shirburn, from which the magnificent collection of the 1st and 2nd earls was sold in 2004–8 after the eviction of the 9th Earl. Wooden Doric pilasters all round, and two marble niches on the inner wall. The N projection of 1830 houses a drawing room and ante-room below, the plainly finished SOUTH LIBRARY above. Open to the library is the NW tower, which has an unusual early C18 marble fireplace with an upswept top, suggestive of Vanbrugh or Hawksmoor. Contemporary fireplace re-set on the E wall, with a segmental pediment. Another tower has an octagonal panelled room with Doric pilasters, and round-arched mirrors on the diagonal sides. The s side has most of the services, and also the WHITE LIBRARY, with glazed-in bookcases, facing the courtyard.)

To the s are the STABLES, of irregular plan and apparently all post-1720s. The flat castellated GATEWAY has the look of *Nash*. Other parts by *William Burn*, 1863. The service buildings include a hefty brick WATER TOWER of 1870.

(GARDENS AND PARK. Shirburn, like Bodiam, was built to impress, and the castle may similarly have been set originally in more open water than a basic moat could provide. The present LAKE extends some way NW from the moat, but this appears to be an early C18 formation. The alignment of an early C18 avenue to its NW is still visible. After *c.* 1780 the landscape was made more informal, in the usual fashion. Shirburn's Georgian GARDEN BUILDINGS are falling into ruin. The largest is, or was, the splendid ORANGERY N of the castle lake, with even arched openings and pedimented ends. Diminishing circular openings fill the pediments, as at the conservatories by *Nash* at Barnsley Park (Glos.) and formerly at Buckingham Palace, so this is surely his too. It may date from just before a royal visit in 1808. To its SE is the 2nd Earl's ROTUNDA of 1741, by

Westby Gill, Master Carpenter to the Office of Works. Six Ionic columns and a shallow dome, which has collapsed. A second ORANGERY stands 350 yds NW of the castle, by the remains of a formal C18 canal. A small Doric temple with columns *in antis*; perhaps an Early Georgian summerhouse with later glazing. 100 yds S of the castle is an C18 ICE HOUSE.)

LODGES. *Nash* probably also designed the Gothic-arched SOUTH LODGE on Watlington Road, 400 yds S, and the stuccoed hexagonal WEST LODGE, 850 yds NW at the approach from Pyrton.

ESTATE COTTAGES. The best concentration is in Blenheim Lane, S of Watlington Road; early C19 to mid-Victorian.

(MODEL FARM, ¾ m. N. 1856–7 by *William Wilkinson*, for the 6th Earl. An advanced design which was published in the *Illustrated London News*. With the farmhouse are a T-shaped engine house with provision for steam-powered sawing, thrashing and chaff-cutting, extensive cattle- and cartsheds, and covered yards.)

SHIRBURN LODGE, 1⅔ m. SE. Joseph Collett built the five-bay house of flint and brick around 1725. Projecting central bay, the doorway fanlight of *c.*1830. Hipped roof, high parapet. (Panelled stair hall, the landing gallery supported by a Doric column-screen.) In 1775 the house was acquired by the 3rd Earl of Macclesfield, who used it as a dower house. Taller three-bay r. addition, late C18 or early C19, of plain brick. The l. extension, *c.*2016 by *Johnston Cave Associates*, joins the house to the early C18 STABLES.

SONNING COMMON

A humdrum C20 dormitory settlement in the southern Chilterns, designated a civil parish in 1952. The Anglican church is CHRIST THE KING, Sedgewell Road. By *Peter Bosanquet*, 1966–7. A long, low box. A big glazed-ended lantern slopes up from the flat roof, to light the altar platform. ST MICHAEL (R.C.), Peppard Road, is portal-framed with a glazed front; by *Geoffrey Pennell* with *Archard & Partners*; 1961–3. Among earlier buildings is the HARE AND HOUNDS INN, Woodlands Road, 1908 by *W.G.A. Hambling*.

SOUTH STOKE

ST ANDREW. An early C13 aisled church, much altered in the C14, with a two-stage W tower of *c.* 1400. Original lancets at the ends of both aisles and in the chancel N wall. E.E. too the N arcade of three bays. Round piers of clunch with octagonal capitals but square bases, old-fashioned for the date. The S arcade, formerly of wood, was rebuilt in the restoration of 1857–8 by *J.B. Clacy*.

Chancel arch of two hollow-chamfered orders on bell capitals. C14 windows in the chancel E and S, and the nave N. All the doorways C14. In the aisles two rich canopied image niches of the later C14 or C15, their brackets supported on heads. The S porch is clearly *Clacy*'s, as is the new base for the octagonal C14 FONT. – WALL PAINTING. Fragmentary late C16 or C17 inscription in the N aisle. – STAINED GLASS. E window by *Cox & Son*, *c.*1870. S aisle E, early C14 Virgin and Child, very corroded, re-set in Victorian quarries. – MONUMENTS. Dr Griffith Higgs, sometime chaplain to the Queen of Bohemia, †1659. Tall alabaster wall monument composed of ill-assorted Artisan Mannerist motifs, with bust at the top. – Elizabeth Barber †1657 and Richard Hannes †1678. A pair of oval tablets flanking the E window, with scrolled tops, festoons and draperies. Attributed to *Thomas Cartwright I*, *c.*1657 (GF). – Lucy Harward †1718 and her mother, also Lucy, †1728. With a well-carved roundel of cherubs' heads, draperies and palm fronds.

VILLAGE. N of the church is MANOR FARM. Many phases, of which the SW wing is probably of C16 origin, with a ground storey of flint walling to the S. The square brick DOVECOTE to its E is one of Oxfordshire's largest. All sides gabled, the oculi with key blocks suggesting a date *c.*1700. Also a big weatherboarded BARN, late C17. By the opposite corner of the village crossing is the CORNER HOUSE, with a jettied and tension-braced cross-wing, r. Probably early C15, as the gable is of crown-strut type. Three-bay main range of the late C17; cross-windows and dentil cornice. Going S, DEVONSHIRE HOUSE is wholly timber-framed, probably of C16 origin, with cross-wings. At FULBROOK HOUSE the chimneystacks back on to the surviving through passage (cf. The Lilacs, Watlington), and the general impression is of an early C17 updating of a plan-type of late medieval ancestry. The OLD VICARAGE is *Buckeridge*'s, 1869. Flint and red brick, the details more vernacular than Gothic. Finally the former CHAPEL (Countess of Huntingdon's Connexion), dated 1820 on a brick. A simple hip-roofed box. Tall sashes to the S.

LITTLESTOKE MANOR, 1 m. N. Probably of C17 origin (re-set datestones of 1681–2), re-cased in plain red brick *c.*1800. Memorable for the three GAZEBOS or summerhouses spaced along the front garden wall. Those at the corners are pyramid-roofed and seemingly C18; the middle one must be later.

RAILWAY BRIDGE, ⅔ m. NNW. *See* Cholsey, *The Buildings of England: Berkshire.*

SOUTH WESTON
Lewknor

ST LAWRENCE. A small church rebuilt in the Dec style in 1860–1 by *R.C. Hussey*. Bell-turret with a spirelet over the chancel arch. Features copied from the medieval predecessor are the Dec E window of flowing tracery and, presumably, the C14-style tomb recess in the chancel. In the E gable a re-set C14 niche with a statue of St Lawrence. – REREDOS with mosaics of saints, probably 1860s. – Three simple eight-pointed CORONAS of vermilion-painted wood, of 1982–3 by *Maguire & Murray*. – FONT. A C13 tub. – STAINED GLASS. Two chancel windows by *Clayton & Bell*.

SOUTH WESTON COTTAGE, E of the church. *Robert Maguire* of *Maguire & Murray* lived here, and the weatherboarded extensions of 1975–91 are his.

MANOR FARM, 300 yds SE. Of *c.*1730, the roof C19. A good display of knapped flint with red brick dressings. Its GRANARY, E, is dated 1713. (The early C17 farmhouse is now MANOR FARM COTTAGE, W. Partly flint, partly brick. Two overmantels with fleur-de-lys, fruit and flowers; rare survivals of plasterwork at this social level.)

STADHAMPTON

6090

ST JOHN THE BAPTIST. Low W tower of *c.*1737, classical, with urn-shaped corner finials. By *Richard Belcher*, mason. The rest of the medieval church was reconstructed in Elizabethan times (restoration in 1588, SE quoin dated 1600 on the chancel). That may explain the coarse post-Perp details of e.g. the N arcade and the chancel N window. Original Early Perp E window to the N aisle. S aisle by *E. G. Bruton*, 1875; also the plate-traceried nave windows, the tower W doorway and the Perp-style E window. In 2011–13 the church was adapted by *David Birkett* for joint use as the VILLAGE HALL. – Plain FONT, probably C12. – Medieval CHEST with shaped uprights. – Carved ROYAL ARMS of Elizabeth I, a rare example. Given in 1744; gadrooned frame perhaps of that date. – BRASSES. John Wylmot †1498 and wife, and John Wylmot the younger †1508 and wife. 17½-in. to 18½-in. figures (44–47 cm.). Also five sons and seven daughters (a copy). – MONUMENTS. Sarah Beavis †1783. Of *c.*1825, signed *Henry Westmacott*. – WAR MEMORIAL in the churchyard. Slender Gothic cross by *H. S. Rogers*, 1921.

MANOR HOUSE, E end of the green. An L-shaped house of the early C17, extended not long after by one matching bay, r. Two storeys plus dormers. Ovolo-moulded mullioned windows. Doorway in the l. bay with a late C17 wooden hood on scroll brackets. Substantial rear extension of *c.*1900–10, with a cutaway corner showing decorative corbelling.

OLD VICARAGE, W of the church. Enlarged in 1836 from an older house, l. Stuccoed, with broad Italianate eaves.

MILL HOUSE and attached MILL, Mill Lane, S. Largely late C18 to early C19. An overshot wheel remains.

THE OLD PLACE, Thame Road, SSW. Of painted rubble stone, thatched. Datestone of 1658 below the dormers. At the junction 150 yds S, a TOLL HOUSE of *c.* 1770. Rubble stone dressed with brick, canted bay to the fore.

JASMINE COTTAGE, School Lane, SW. A thatched former farmhouse with a stone frontage of *c.* 1800–20. Within is a timber-framed hall house of *c.* 1500, extended to the r. *c.* 1600, when double smoke-bays were also inserted. The present chimney-stack marks the position of one of these.

COLDHARBOUR FARMHOUSE, ¾ m. NNE. The S aspect is roughly Late Georgian, but an ovolo-moulded mullioned window survives to the N, and an internal date of 1625 is reported.

ASCOTT PARK, ½ m. ESE. Haunting remains of the domain of a great house of the Dormer family, rebuilt from 1660 by Sir William Dormer but burnt down in 1662 when on the verge of completion. A surviving part became a dower house, but disappeared sometime after 1797; the ruins of an associated medieval chapel lasted until 1823. On the main road three pairs of slim rusticated GATEPIERS of *c.* 1660, widely spaced. At the corner to the E, PICCADILLY COTTAGE incorporates a C17 belvedere or summerhouse, with ovolo-moulded mullioned windows on the upper floor. In the park the remnants of a great formal layout: a double avenue of limes on axis with the gatepiers, and part of another avenue running across. Facing each other across the axis are two octagonal buildings of red brick. To the W is a DOVECOTE, with strident blue brick diaper, zigzag and chequer patterns and a moulded brick cornice of trefoiled arches. The Gothic cornice looks no later than the C16, but the chequering uses full Flemish bond, not generally adopted until the mid C17. The GRANARY, E, is of plain Flemish bond and has stone-mullioned windows and a four-centred-arched doorway of C17 character, but is raised on a brick-vaulted basement with a central drain, interpreted as an ice house. Is it all mid-C17, or a two-storey reconstruction with reused stonework? Associated EARTHWORKS include a depression between the two, identified as the robbed-out house site, a raised terrace to the S, and traces of water gardens beyond. S of the granary, C16 walls enclose a former auxiliary building, now a FARMHOUSE. Concealed C16 timber framing. C17 stone doorway: four-centred-arched, with a key block.*

ASCOTT MANOR, to the E. Modernized and extended *c.* 1800 with sashes and rendering, but early C17 hoodmoulds and some mullioned windows remain.

---

*An early C17 garden gateway from Ascott, now at the Weston Library in Oxford (p. 345), is fully classical.

STOKE ROW

ST JOHN THE EVANGELIST. 1845–6 by *R.C. Hussey*, built as a chapel of ease to Ipsden. C13 style with lancet windows. Chancel and nave in one, N tower placed almost midway. It has an octagonal upper stage with a pointed tiled roof. S addition with kitchen etc. by *Jessop & Cook*, 2015. – STAINED GLASS. E lancets by *Kempe & Co.*, 1925, under a rose window by *Barbara Batt*, 1954. Nave S by *G. Maile & Son*, 1947.

OLD VICARAGE, W. Of *c.*1852–3, also *Hussey*. Altered.

INDEPENDENT CHAPEL, at the E entry to the village. Dated 1815 on a brick. An archetypal hip-roofed box with round-arched windows. Porch and rear Sunday School added in 1884.

MAHARAJAH'S WELL, 150 yds NNE of the church. 1863–5. The gift of Ishri Pershad Narayan Singh, Maharajah of Benares, to his friend Edward Anderdon Reade of the Ipsden gentry family, who had served in India for many years. It has a domed canopy on eight cast-iron columns, like a small bandstand. The machinery is by *R., J. & H. Wilder* of Wallingford. On it a cast-iron elephant added in 1871. The shaft is 368 ft (112 metres) deep. Octagonal COTTAGE alongside, for the well-keeper.

POND HOUSE, Cox's Lane, 250 yds NE. 1938. Built as their own house by *Jock & Elizabeth Shepherd*, partners in the firm of Elizabeth Scott, Chesterton & Shepherd, best known for the Stratford Memorial Theatre of 1928–32. Up-to-date rather than explicitly Modernist. H-plan, with simplified double-pitched gables. The present windows and finishes date from *Spratley Studios*' renovation of 2011.

OSSICLES, ⅔ m. NE. A house by *Spratley Studios* of Henley, 2009–11. Two interlinked parts under segmental or parabolic roofs. Partly glass-walled, partly of white render and red-brown cladding.

NEWNHAMHILL HOUSE, ¾ m. ENE. A composite of two older cottages re-cased in 1797 (dated bricks), with a cross-wing of *c.*1936, its timber framing salvaged from The Bull pub at Tottenham, North London.

(BASSET MANOR, ½ m. WSW. Timber-framed with brick infill. The greater part, with a shared back-to-back stack, is probably C17.)

STOKE TALMAGE

ST MARY MAGDALENE. The medieval church was renovated in 1758 with basic Gothic windows of intersecting tracery. Complete rebuilding was mooted in 1860, but the design obtained from *E.B. Lamb* was rejected as 'full of eccentricity' by the Diocesan Architect G.E. Street. A fresh proposal by

G. G. Scott proved too expensive, so instead Scott re-dressed the old church with buttresses, s porch and vestry, and added a N aisle with a C13-style three-bay arcade. Scott's chancel arch has jamb shafts with reused C12 capitals, one carved with beaded and fluted leaves. C13 lancets in the bell-stage of the W tower. E window of 1907 by *John Coleridge*. – ROYAL ARMS. Fine carving of *c.*1700, reused as the arms of one of the Georges. – STAINED GLASS. In the E window a Crucifixion by *Hardman* (*J. H. Powell*), *c.*1860. The figure formerly to the l. has been moved to the chancel s window. Nave s, *Morris & Sons*, 1906. – BRASSES. John Adeane †1504 and wife, 12-in. and 11½-in. figures (30 and 29 cm.). – John Pettie †1589 and wife. 25-in. and 24-in. figures (63 and 61 cm.). Style of *Garat Johnson the elder*.

OLD RECTORY, NW of the church. 1752. Three-bay front with dormers. The stucco and the doorcase with Doric pilasters and a flat hood are probably of 1820, when *Daniel Harris* added the lower extension to the l.

MANOR FARMHOUSE, 100 yds SE. Called 'newly erected' in 1697. Now an L-plan house, apparently of three phases.

7080

STONOR
Pishill

The settlement was known as Upper Assendon until 1896. The great house of Stonor Park stands in its own grounds ½ m. NE.

STONOR PARK

An astonishing house, with an exceptionally complex fabric from many centuries behind its deceptively even brick walls. These intricacies testify to the unbroken ownership by the Stonor family, first recorded here in 1156. By the late Middle Ages they were great landowners and courtiers, but in the centuries after the Reformation their loyalty to Catholicism incurred fines for recusancy and excluded the Stonors from much of public life. So the house escaped major rebuilding, and an outline of its long history can still be deduced from what remains.

The site is a remote valley of the Chilterns, encircled by beech woods and built up against the hillside to the N – 'clyminge on an hille', according to Leland in 1535/40, when it consisted of 'two courts buyldyd with tymber, brike and flinte'. What meets the eye from a distance, however, is an extremely broad brick frontage with short return wings and mostly Early Georgian detail, with something of the air of a college or school. A nearer view reveals signs of greater antiquity: the stone-built C14 chapel to the r., with its C15 brick tower rising behind; the tell-tale placing of the gabled entrance slightly off-centre; and the many different phases and types of brickwork all round, shading from pink to brilliant red, used as dressings to flint walling on the polygonal C18 stair-turret to the SW, and dappled with grey headers on some of the flanks, where expanses of flint walling testify to the house's earlier phases.

Before a more detailed description, the building history must be outlined. This nightmare for architectural historians was surveyed for the *Victoria County History* (1964) by W.A. Pantin and David Sturdy, whose account can be modified somewhat after further discoveries. The C13 house occupied the present NE angle. It consisted of a twin-aisled stone hall running N into the hillside, with a S cross-range containing service rooms and a solar above. This is thought to have been built *c.*1280–1300 by Sir Richard Stonor, or by his father, also Richard, in the mid C13. The W aisle of this hall has been demolished and now forms an internal court, but its central arcade remains, and walling to the N and E. In 1347 the present detached chapel was built to the SE by Sir John Stonor, supplanting an earlier chapel, and a licence to

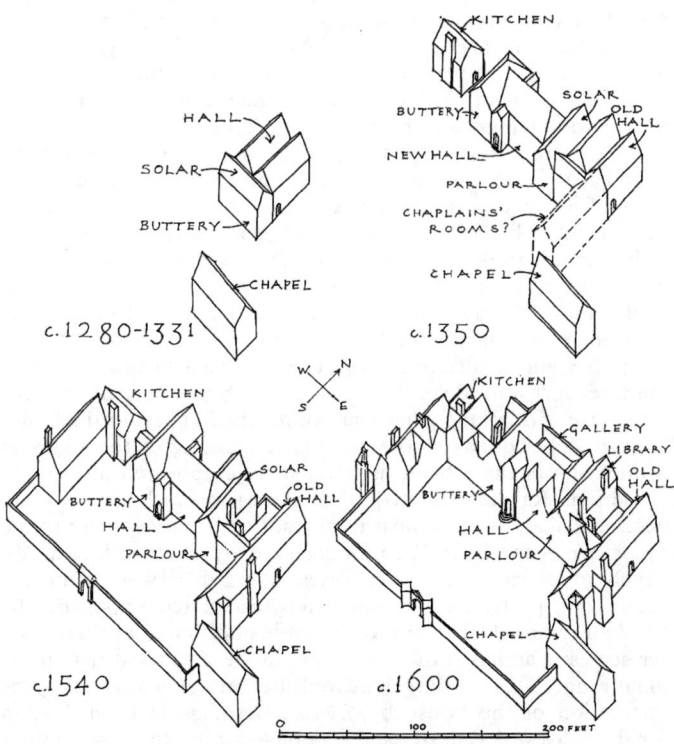

Stonor Park, phases of construction.
Drawings by W.A. Pantin, 1964

establish a dwelling for six chaplains was obtained. This is likely
to have comprised a N–S range between the chapel and the old
hall, although the construction date is uncertain. Sir John also
greatly enlarged the house towards the W with a second aisled
hall, with its screens passage to the W and a two-storey porch in
the position of the present porch. This mid-C14 hall was timber-
framed, and had cross-wings: to the W, with buttery and pantry
below (the present Dining Room) and withdrawing chamber
above, and to the E, with a parlour below and great chamber (the
present Library) above. These timber structures survive in part,
including much of the original roofs. The C14 kitchen was apparently a detached building further W, its form perpetuated by C15
brick-and-timber walls visible internally. By 1474 this had been
joined to the W cross-wing by a brick-and-timber passage. In
1478 some building in stone was done for Sir Walter Stonor, corresponding most probably to the present W wing of family rooms,
which originally had a framed and jettied E wall. But the C15 also
saw much use of brick at the house, including an order for some
200,000 bricks in 1416–17 from Crocker End, Nettlebed, and a
reference to Flemish workmen ('lez Flemyngges') at Stonor: the
earliest datable record of building in brick in the Thames Valley.
This is likely to account for at least part of the brick tower N
of the chapel. A later Sir Walter Stonor made further changes
*c.*1535–40, probably including the wall that formerly ran between
the E and W wings, making a now lost forecourt.

By the mid C16 the effect of this haphazard development
would have been a shambling group of buildings around three
sides of a broad courtyard. The house was then remodelled in
the later C16 by Sir Francis Stonor in an attempt to give it a
fashionable symmetry. A straight brick façade was formed, filling
in the irregularities of the front, which was also provided with
gables and mullioned windows with stucco strapwork decoration.
The porch was heightened, and additionally embellished with
sculpture, and a turreted gatehouse was built in the middle of
the forecourt wall. Behind, a passage was built along the back of
the house with a long gallery above it, which, because the house
is on a slope, opens to the garden. A painting of the 1680s at
Stonor shows the S front as it must have appeared after these
alterations. Rawlinson noted in 1718 that some sash windows had
been installed, but the most important C18 changes were in the
1750s, when the house was modernized by Thomas Stonor VI.
Much of it was re-cased in brick, the gables were removed,
the E wing partly rebuilt (rainwater head dated 1755) and the
C14 hall remodelled. The most notable addition after that was a
service wing added at the NW corner in the C19, parallel with the
main range. This was largely demolished in the protracted 1970s
restoration of the house by *Jellicoe, Coleridge & Wynn*, begun
for the 6th Lord Camoys and completed after 1976 by Thomas
Stonor, 7th Lord, and Lady Camoys.

EXTERIOR. The S side with its sash windows, wooden dentil
cornice and widely spaced dormers is largely the result of the

works of 1753–5 and 1758–60 (chief bricklayer *John Heath*). The long centre of sixteen bays is saved from monotony by the gabled porch, with its late C16 English-bond brickwork, four-centred-arched doorway and flanking allegorical statues under strapwork canopies. Also late C16 is the figure of the Virgin in the gable, but the pretty Gothick windows belong with the internal alterations of 1758–60 by the otherwise unrecorded architect *John Aitkins*. Walls W of the porch are also mostly of English bond, but to the E the Flemish bond of the 1750s refacing predominates. On the N side the 1750s brickwork partly serves as a high parapet to hide the original roof slopes, with a run of big blank circles and a blank arch above the windows of the Long Gallery in its middle section. The W side faces private gardens, but the join may be seen between the refaced medieval kitchen to the N, now floored across – the mid-C18 Venetian window lights a bedroom – and the deeper flint-walled range to the S. On the E side the chapel adjoins along the S (*see* below), and the house presents the massive flint wall of the C13 hall and solar to the N, with brickwork of different periods between.

INTERIORS. The public route takes in much of the central range. From the E, a passage leads through the subdivided E half of the C13 hall to the AISLED HALL, i.e. the former courtyard formed from its demolished W half, glazed over in the 1970s. The central arcade of four chamfered arches and round piers remains built into the wall, showing that the original floor level was much higher. The twin-aisled form is highly unusual for a medieval hall, and Anthony Emery has suggested that it may rather have been the ground storey to a chamber block; if so, the grand scale would make this exceptional in a different way.* Another passage leads W to the HALL. Here is another fragment, for the room represents only the N half of the two-bay C14 timber hall, which was Gothicized by *Aitkins* in 1758–60. (The apex of the spere truss at its screens end survives in an attic room, with ogee cusping to the braces and an elongated trefoiled opening above the collar.) Panelling of Elizabethan type. The ogee-arched fireplace on the S wall is by Aitkins (makers *Joseph Pickford & William Atkinson*), having been moved from the E wall when the hall was subdivided E–W in 1834. Bold colour scheme of 1971. Part of Aitkins's hall screen appears ahead, with a gallery of 1790 added in front. The N windows have C16 German stained glass with figures of Charlemagne and St Andrew from the Wool Hall in Ypres, re-set in the 1790s by *Francis Eginton* along with armorial glass brought from the chapel. The S part of the Hall is now the DRAWING ROOM (in 1834 the Dining Room), with a screen of Grecian Ionic columns across the W end and re-set C15 and C16 Flemish glass in the window heads. The architect in

*Emery, *Greater Medieval Houses of England and Wales*, vol. 3 (2006).

1834 was *George Martin*.* In the SCREENS PASSAGE *Aitkins*'s simple Gothick forms of 1758–60 appear again, combined with spatially exciting arrangements for the open-well STAIRCASE of 1790 immediately to the N, one of many staircases in the house. Its iron balustrade of pointed arches is from a design by *Gillow*, and a similar balustrade is used for the bridge that joins the first-floor landings overhead. From the landing a staircase climbs to the EDMUND CAMPION ROOM within the gable, named from the Jesuit missionary and martyr who set up a clandestine printing press here in 1581. A glazed panel allows a view of the C14 scissor-truss roof above the C14 W cross-range. The corresponding E cross-range now houses the LIBRARY on its upper floor, i.e. the former great chamber, with a plain plaster barrel-vault of the late C16. The LONG GALLERY across the back has simple C18 panelling. (W of the screens passage on the S side, the SHORT GALLERY has rare early to mid-C17 *trompe l'œil* panelling painted on one end wall. The S gable-end of the medieval KITCHEN, now internal, is of C15 timber framing infilled with patterned original brickwork, including criss-cross and a pattern of hearts. The W wall also has a C15 doorway of moulded brick.)

CHAPEL OF THE HOLY TRINITY (R.C.). The large private chapel was licensed in 1349 and has remained in use for Catholic worship ever since. Felling dates of 1347 obtained from the partly surviving scissor-truss and crown-post roof indicate that it was built in one go. Flint with stone dressings; a simple hall 60 ft (18 metres) long, with broad lancet windows and a simple W doorway with hoodmould. The tower against the N side probably belongs with the works by Thomas Stonor I for which bricks were ordered in 1416–17, when a tower is also mentioned. However, differences in the brickwork above and below the corbelling on its E side imply a break in the work, and a slightly later date for the diapered upper stage – best seen on the W side, above the Victorian infill there – would fit better with other early appearances of diapering, a motif shared with grand and innovative buildings such as Eton College (1441) and Tattershall Castle, Lincs. (*c.*1445–6). The tower is aligned with the house, and cuts slightly askew into the chapel N wall. Blocked openings in its upper stages may relate to lost timber galleries or walkways for access from the former chaplains' accommodation somewhere on this side. Staircase all of brick in the two lower stages. Roof and wooden bellcote probably mid-C19.

The chapel INTERIOR was remodelled in Gothick style in 1796–1800 by *James Thorp* of London, 'ornament and composition-maker'. His are the W gallery, the simple plaster rib-vault on angel corbels, and the doorways with ogee hoods and finials. The red and blue colouring was introduced in restoration of 1959–60, advised by *John Piper* and *Osbert Lancaster*. The vault

---

* Partner and probable son of Thomas Martin, who worked at Mapledurham House (q.v.).

required partial removal of the old boarded roof, of which the central and E sections belong to a reconstruction of 1578 using crown-posts, a very late occurrence. – Marble ALTAR, given in 1797 by Henry Blundell of Ince, Lancs. – Gothick ironwork ALTAR RAIL and gallery BALUSTRADE, the same pattern as the house's main staircase. – STAINED GLASS. E window by *Eginton*, 1799, after Carlo Dolci's painting of the Salvator Mundi at Burghley House. S windows, three of the four Fathers of the Church, also by *Eginton*.

GARDENS AND PARK. The approach from the road is through GATES and modest LODGES, late C18 or C19. The PARK was landscaped in the later C18. In the valley bottom by the chapel is a STONE CIRCLE of uncertain date, re-erected from nearby in 1980; another stone from the group is in the chapel plinth, SE corner. The WALLED GARDENS on the slopes N and W of the house correspond in area to those shown on the painting of the 1680s. At the NE corner a Japanese-style SUMMERHOUSE of *c.* 1907. Traces of stepped garden terraces of C16 type were identified in 1989 in front of the house. 150 yds SE of the house are the former STABLES. Two main ranges. The gabled and flint-walled part was probably built *c.* 1700 as a wool store. To the E, late C18 chequered brick with oculi below the eaves.

VILLAGE

Along the road S of the gates to Stonor Park. Nos. 20–21, 22–23 (W side) are memorable ESTATE COTTAGES of the early C19. Flint or brick, banded pilasters and chimneys. Oddly small windows. At Nos. 24–27 the OLD ALMSHOUSES of *c.* 1812, red brick with a grey brick platband and vivid upright strips between the windows. They replaced almshouses of *c.* 1620 to the N, now WELL COTTAGE. Flint walls, raised crucks within. Older houses include CROMWELL LODGE (Nos. 16–17), tree-ring dated 1394. A cruck-framed hall house with a storeyed r. cross-wing, its tension-braced framing exposed. The hall has as usual been floored, and a brick stack inserted against the passage. On the E side, Nos. 9–10 are of 1470 (the front house), with an original doorway and jetty to the r., and 1447/8 (No. 10, behind), end-on to the street and jettied to the N. Just S is UPPER ASSENDON FARMHOUSE. C16, L-plan. Thin framing, the front gable rebuilt in brick and flint. Fine C17 BARNS also of L-plan, linked by a shelter shed.

SWYNCOMBE

6090

ST BOTOLPH. A near-intact Early Norman church, built probably by the Abbey of Bec in Normandy. Flint and stone, with much use of herringbone construction. The nave is a double square, the chancel a single square with an apsidal E end. Part of the Norman N doorway remains, now blocked, with a hogbacked lintel and replaced jambs. In the S wall the relieving arch of a second doorway. Plain arch on simple imposts to the apse, with an aumbry in the S jamb. One two-light Dec window in the nave, S. In 1831 the chancel arch was widened by *Joseph Clarke*, who also inserted two round-headed windows in the apse in 1845, corresponding with the original one on the N. The nave was restored in 1850 by *Benjamin Ferrey*. His are the lancet windows modelled on the C13 lancet to the SW, the stepped buttresses, the S porch, and the bellcote below the W gable. Keeled and compartmented ceiling probably by *Temple Moore*, 1895. Medieval WALL PAINTINGS uncovered in the apse in 1850 were repainted following the original outlines, mainly diapering and a band of scroll decoration; probably C13. – PILLAR PISCINA in the apse. Made up from Norman fragments found in 1850. The capital is carved with a mask biting on scrolls which extend to corner crockets. – Worn C14 TILES, chancel floor. – Richly traceried SCREEN and ROOD LOFT, 1914. Designed by *Walter Tapper* in C15 style. – CANDELABRA from Swyncombe House, C18 or C19. – FONT. Plain bowl. – STAINED GLASS. Corroded W lancet and two side lancets by *Charles Hudson*, c.1850 (MH); some of the heraldic shields may be earlier. N lancet by *M. Farrar Bell*, 1979.

SWYNCOMBE HOUSE, to the S. The Rev. Charles Ruck Keene's Neo-Jacobean mansion of c.1840 was demolished in 1978. Neat Neo-Georgian replacement by *David Hicks* with *Jeffery Ruddell* of the *Golding Ruddell Partnership*. Brick, with a swept roof and openwork iron porch. HOME FARMHOUSE immediately N is late C17, extended by two taller early C19 bays, r.

OLD RECTORY, 150 yds NE. A brick house of 1803 by *Daniel Harris*, the gables treated as simple pediments. Enlarged by *Thomas Plowman* in 1827, partially demolished 1951–2, then enlarged again c.2007 by *Johnston Cave Associates*. The asymmetrical entrance front appears to comprise about two-thirds of Harris's building, with two projecting pedimented bays and the entrance to one side.

SCHOOL (former), Cookley Green, ¾ m. E. 1830. A tiny two-bay brick box, N side of the green.

EWELME PARK, ¾ m. SW. An expansive house of 1913 by *L. Stanley Crosbie*, for Walter Heriot. Decidedly on the Arts and Crafts spectrum. A broad H-plan with unequal cross-ranges and plentiful chimney clusters. Simply treated windows, some running under the swept eaves. Mostly roughcast, with timbering along the main E–W range, which serves as a 'living hall'. On the W flank a loggia with columns, recessed under the staircase window. The W cross-range has a double-height drawing room with a double-transomed window to the S. A canted bay on the E side lights the dining room. Original garden terraces. The approach is through a hip-roofed GATE LODGE, E.

SYDENHAM

7000

St Mary. A small C13 church, enlarged by *John Billing* in 1856. His are the N transept and vestry, the tapering central tower and pyramidal spire of wood, the S porch, and the W bay of the nave. Single lancet windows in the side walls, original except at the W. E window with intersecting tracery, probably from repairs after 1293, when the church was reportedly 'in ruins'. The two-light W window may copy a C14 original. Unequal diaphragm arches support the tower inside. The nave has a C15 hammerbeam roof. Set in the chancel walls are crudely carved wooden corbels to support the Lenten veil, a rare survival; C12, or C13? Trefoil-headed PISCINA in the nave. – FONT. Plain tub with moulded base. Probably C13.

The VILLAGE is small and picturesque, with plenty of timber-framed thatched cottages and weatherboarded barns. By the churchyard a flint and brick SCHOOL of 1849, enlarged 1886. To the S, a former PARTICULAR BAPTIST CHAPEL, 1881. Yellow and red brick, arched sash windows. One BARN in Cooper's Yard nearly opposite has been tree-ring dated 1599. Further S, the OLD VICARAGE, 1846. Stone, basic Elizabethan. RYDERS FARM, 100 yds E of the church, is of *c.* 1700. Brick, two-storeyed, with dormers. The glazing of elongated octagonal panes is probably early C19.

TETSWORTH

6000

St Giles. 1855 by *J. Billing*. It replaced a largely Norman church which had two of the finest carved tympana in the county. E.E., with plain lancet windows. Chancel, nave and S aisle. The weighty SW tower, with a broach spire and angle buttresses, also serves as the porch. – STAINED GLASS. E window by *Jones & Willis*, old-fashioned for 1924.

VICARAGE (former), W. 1846. Still Late Georgian in style.

Congregational Chapel (former), High Street. 1890. Designed by its builder, *T. H. Kingerlee* of Oxford. Red brick, Bath stone dressings. Gable-end with a rose window; two windows with Geometrical tracery.

School, adjacent. By *Arthur Vernon* of High Wycombe, 1878–80. Also red brick and Gothic. Some gables and window heads have tile-hanging.

Swan Hotel. Chequered early C18 brickwork, regular windows and a hipped roof conceal the inn of *c.* 1600, which comprises the timber-framed centre and l. wing of the present U-shape. Its gables show at the back, along with three chimneystacks all with diagonally set shafts, behind later additions. Staircase with wavy flat balusters of C17 type. The steel-framed casements were imposed in 1951 by *F. E. S. Storer*.

TOLL HOUSE, Attington, 1 m. ESE. For a turnpike opened in
1785. Rendered brick, quite large, with Y-traceried windows.
Canted two-storey centre.

THAME

Medieval Thame is a tale of two settlements. Old Thame, around
the parish church, may have been founded as a minster settlement by King Wulfhere of Mercia in the 670s; it became part of
the estates of the Anglo-Saxon bishops of Dorchester. At some
point between the 1140s and the early C13 a market town, New
Thame, was laid out to the E by the Bishop of Lincoln, and in
1219 the main road was diverted to run through it. The main
street is over ¾ m. long, and also enormously wide in its central
section where the market was held. Oval alignments N of its main
road (Bell Lane etc.) may represent retained Anglo-Saxon enclosures. On the s side, burgage plots from the planned town extend
W as far as Southern Road. Medieval trades included glass-
staining, the source of the windows of Merton College chapel in
the early C14 (p. 204). A substantial house was provided for the
Prebendary of Thame W of the church, and there was a Cistercian abbey 1¾ m. to the SE, secularized as Thame Park (q.v.). The
main street is still lined with pre-Victorian inns and houses in a
variety of styles and materials; picturesque in an unpretentious
way. Some of the timbered houses were decorated with pargeting, but none of this remains. Many Georgian fronts show the
region's attractive combinations of red and silver-grey or blue
brickwork. Victorian development was concentrated to the E and
s near the former railway, but much more has followed in the
C20 and C21, bounded to the N and E by the by-pass opened in
1980. The livestock market moved to North Street in 1951, and
the centre of the High Street has become (inevitably) a car park.

CHURCHES

ST MARY, Church Road. Nothing remains of the Anglo-Saxon
church from the time of the Dorchester bishopric. From at
least 1146 until the Reformation, Thame was a prebend of the
Diocese of Lincoln. The present building is large, cruciform
and of C13 date. The aisles were widened in the C14, and in
the C15 the transepts were reconstructed and the crossing
tower rebuilt.

The chancel is early C13. Four of its six original lancets and
a priest's doorway remain in the N wall. A string course links
the window sills, with short buttresses beneath. The westernmost lancet is blocked. That to its E was replaced c. 1280 with
a window with three cusped lights under three quatrefoils. E
window also of c. 1280, of five uncusped lights with tracery

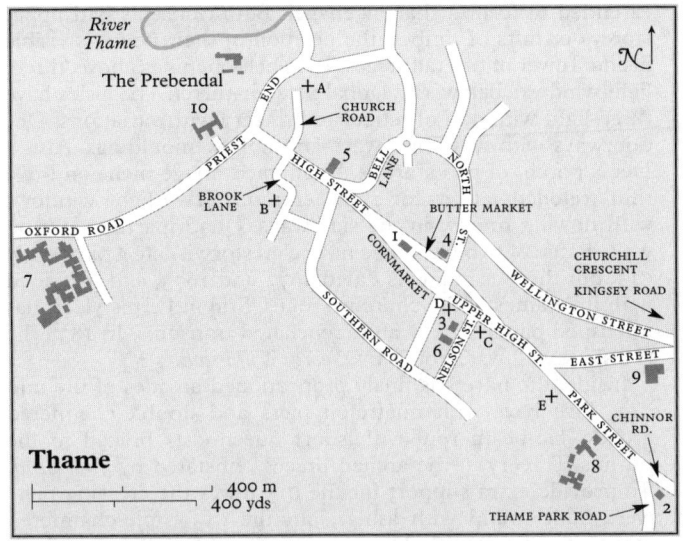

Thame

400 m
400 yds

River Thame

The Prebendal

10

PRIEST END

CHURCH ROAD

+A

5

BELL LANE

HIGH STREET

BROOK LANE

B+

CORNMARKET

I

4

D

3

6

NELSON ST.

C

UPPER HIGH ST.

BUTTER MARKET

NORTH ST.

CHURCHILL CRESCENT

WELLINGTON STREET

KINGSEY ROAD

EAST STREET

9

E+

PARK STREET

CHINNOR RD.

8

2

THAME PARK ROAD

SOUTHERN ROAD

OXFORD ROAD

7

N

A	St Mary	I	Town Hall
B	St Joseph (R.C.)	2	Police station (former)
C	Christ Church	3	Fire station
D	Wesleyan chapel (former)	4	Library
		5	Museum
E	Baptist chapel (former)	6	Players' Theatre
		7	Lord Williams's School
		8	John Hampden Primary School
		9	Thame Community Hospital
		10	Workhouse (former)

of foiled circles. The tracery within the large circle in the centre dates from *J. Oldrid Scott*'s restoration of 1889–97. The s wall, which presumably also had lancets, now has three Dec windows with reticulated tracery. Inside is a late C13 DOUBLE PISCINA in a recess with a shouldered arch. The chancel walls have been raised, probably by Adrian de Bardis, Prebendary in 1480–1501 (arms on the N parapet).

Of the C13 transepts only the w walls remain. The N transept retains a lancet here, partly cut by the wall of the N aisle as widened in the C14. Churchwardens' accounts survive from 1442 onwards, the year when the reconstruction of the N transept began. *John Buckley* of Headington was master mason. The work included taking down and 'setting up' an existing E window. The one now there is of five lights. It conforms to a familiar type, late C14 in origin, with a two-centred arch of a shape that is echoed in the tracery over each outer pair of lights. N window also of five lights, but of the mid-C15 pattern with thin panel tracery under a flattened, straight-sided arch. Patterns within the tracery give the effect of transoms. The s transept is a near match, except that in the rebuilding its E side was extended to form a shallow chapel. Both transepts had upper storeys or lofts of timber; the position of their floors is visible inside. Tower of two tall stages. Twin bell-openings above, three-light windows below. Octagonal NE stair-turret. The aisles have three-light windows of reticulated tracery with variations. Dec doorways with wave and wave-and-hollow mouldings. Also a Dec S porch, of two storeys. A canopied image niche and two thin trefoiled lancets over the entrance. Two-light windows with flowing tracery in the side walls. Quadripartite vault on wall-shafts, of two bays. The nave clerestory is late C14 or early C15, but the W window is dated 1672 and 1673, and inscribed with the names of the churchwardens. Still in Perp style, it has uncusped panel tracery and crenellated transoms. In 1838 the N aisle N wall was rebuilt by *George Wilkinson*.

Inside, the nave has finely proportioned arcades of the mid C13. Five bays with quatrefoil piers and double-chamfered arches. Tie-beam roof with short queenposts braced to the purlins. Tracery in the arched braces reinstated by *J. O. Scott*. To provide extra support for the C15 tower the crossing piers were built round with ashlar, but the C13 triple-chamfered arches are unaltered. The S respond of the chapel arch in the S transept is C13 and reused, with a moulded capital. A C15 PISCINA here. The ALTAR PLATFORM W of the crossing belongs with *Maguire & Co.*'s reordering of 1991.

FURNISHINGS. COMMUNION TABLE. 1625. – COMMUN-ION RAILS of *c.*1700, with twisted balusters. – A specimen BOX PEW (chancel), saved from the set of 1843–5 by *H.B. Hodson*. – STALLS. Given in 1529. With linenfold panelling and poppyheads. Also some made up in 1908 using parts (arcading etc.) from a Jacobean gallery. – SCREENS. The chancel screen goes with the stalls. Two tiers of linenfold, below round arches with Flamboyant traceried heads. Their shafts are carved with early post-Gothic motifs: diaper, lozenge, scales (cf. Charlton-in-Otmoor, North Oxon). N transept, mid-C14 screen, also of unusual interest; probably the former chancel screen displaced. Reticulated and quatrefoil tracery in round arches on octagonal shafts. Screen to the S aisle with C15 parts. – WALL PAINTINGS. Upper part of a Pietà of *c.*1500 on the SE crossing pier. Also some red foliage around the N transept N window. – CHAN-DELIER. Brass; *c.*1700. – PULPIT and TESTER, also *c.*1700. Hexagonal. Plain, except for the tester's acanthus frieze and inlay. – FONT. A composite. Octagonal bowl, re-cut probably in the C17. Base with a band of C13 leaf decoration and cable-like moulding below. C17 COVER with strapwork, open cresting and a ball finial. – STAINED GLASS. E window by *Geoffrey Webb*, 1921–9. Chancel N lancets, Evangelists of *c.*1880 by *Clayton & Bell*, designer *George Daniels* (PC). Chancel S, 1880, also *Clayton & Bell*. W window, 1884–1911 by *Hardman* (PC). N aisle W window, 1926 by *Morris & Co.*

MONUMENTS. Chancel. Placed centrally, Lord Williams of Thame †1559 and Elizabeth his wife. Of high quality. Chel-laston alabaster, within the original railings. Damage from the Civil War years was repaired in 1661–2 by *William Byrd* of Oxford, including new unicorn and greyhound supporters for the effigies. Tomb-chest of Flemish type, with angle pilasters with ribbonwork trophies. The strapwork panels between look early C17. – Civilian and wife, brass of *c.*1500. 18½-in. (48-cm.) figures. (– Christopher Bridgman †1503 and wife. Brass. 24½-in. (62-cm.) figures.) – Walter Pratt †1508 and wife. Brass. 17¾-in. and 18-in. figures (45 and 46 cm.). – Sir John Clerk †1539. Kneeling brass figure on a tomb-chest decorated with diapering and with shields of both brass and stone. Crested stone canopy with a flat arch. – John Gayley †1543. Brass; headless. – Edward Harris †1597, first headmaster of the Grammar School. Wall-mounted brass on a stone panel. – Richard Boucher, Harris's successor, †1627. Incised panel of Purbeck marble. Attributed to *Francis Grigs* (GF). – Elizabeth Burte †1683. Baroque cartouche with broad simple scrolls. – S transept. Effigy of a priest, early C13. Incongruously set upright in the wall, a ghostly figure of weathered stone in low relief. – Thomas Quatremain †1342 and wife, with their son Thomas †1398 and wife. Four brasses in line, of 30 to 31¼ in. (76 to 80 cm.), on a plain tomb-chest. Of one figure only the upper part remains. – Richard and Sybil Quatremain, †1477 and †1483 (she headless), with a third figure, probably their adopted heir, Richard Fowler. Brasses 35¾ in. to 27½ in. long (91 to 70 cm.), on a tomb-chest. Sides decorated with enriched quatrefoils separated by canopied niches. Two weeper statues in niches on the E end. – N transept, now in the vestry enclosure of 1991. Geoffrey Dormer †1502 and two wives. Tomb-chest with large plain quatrefoils. Brass figures on it of 27¼ in. (two) and 26½ in. (69 and 67 cm.); also children, a shield, and symbols of the Evangelists. – Philip Herbert M.P. †1749. Wall tablet of coloured marble with a frame of scrolls, finely carved cherub heads and an urn. Attributed to *Sir Henry Cheere* (GF). – Good wall monuments of the C17–C18 throughout, some in the most primitive country style.

DOVECOTE in the churchyard. Early C18, with pyramid roof.
To the NE, the former VICARAGE of 1841. Sprawling, stone, with a symmetrical W front with Jacobean shaped gables.

ST JOSEPH (R.C.), Brook Lane. By *John D. Holmes*, 1996–7. Low-lying church and hall, combined. Church roof of laminated timber trusses. – STAINED GLASS by *Stewart Bowman*, both semi-abstract and figural, including windows from the predecessor church.

CHRIST CHURCH (Methodist and United Reformed), Upper High Street. By *W.F. Poulton*, 1871. Built for Congregationalists. Window of twin three-lighters grouped with a small rose. Doorways lost to a porch of *c.*2003.

WESLEYAN CHAPEL (former), Upper High Street. A design of 1853, rebuilt in 1876 after a fire. Stone. Gabled front with corner pinnacles and three graduated lancets.

BAPTIST CHAPEL (former), Park Street. 1865. Very modest. Brick. Builders *W. Howland* and *John Wells*.

PUBLIC BUILDINGS

TOWN HALL, High Street. 1887–8 by *H.J. Tollit*. Red brick and stone. A feeble design in Jacobethan style. The position in the centre of the High Street called for something grander. It had two timber-framed predecessors, one C16, the other of 1684.

POLICE STATION (former), at the fork of Park Street and Chinnor Road. Dated 1854, builder *Giles Holland*. An early rural example. Economical brown brick.

FIRE STATION, Nelson Street. 1937. Simplified Neo-Georgian.

LIBRARY, North Street. By *Oxford Architects*, 2008–10. Front mostly of glass. One flank also partly glazed.

MUSEUM (originally COUNTY COURT), No. 79 High Street. 1861, probably by *Charles Reeves*. Red brick. Single-storey front range with arched windows divided by banded brick pilasters. Courtroom with a shallow clerestory at the back.

PLAYERS' THEATRE, Nelson Street. The former church hall, by *J.T. Robinson* of Thame. Begun 1913, completed 1928. Like a late C19 Nonconformist chapel.

LORD WILLIAMS'S SCHOOL, Oxford Road. The former Grammar School (*see* Perambulation, p. 748). It moved here to a building of 1877–9 by *William Wilkinson*. Tall, minimal quasi-Tudor, with rooms for boarders. Red brick and a little stone. Many additions.

JOHN HAMPDEN PRIMARY SCHOOL, Park Street. A square stone house of three bays with a hipped roof and slim timber bellcote, flanked by single-storey classrooms. Across the front on three slate plaques is inscribed 'ROYAL BRITISH SCHOOLS' and the date 1837.

THAME COMMUNITY HOSPITAL, East Street. In origin a modest nursing home, given by Samuel Lacey in 1897. Basic Tudor. Extended 1909, 1922, 1927.

WORKHOUSE (former), Priest End. 1836 by *George Wilkinson* of Witney, elder brother of the architect William Wilkinson. Converted to housing 2007–9. George landed thirty-four workhouse commissions across England and Wales following the Poor Law reforms of 1834, then moved to Ireland in 1839 to design even more. At Thame the layout is a variant of the familiar cross-in-square plan, omitting the usual wing behind the central octagonal hub. Red brick, plain Georgian detail. Two-storey lateral ranges; three-storey ward ranges across their outer ends. More unusual are the two plain polygonal brick LODGES at the entrance.

THE PREBENDAL

A major medieval house in its own grounds, off Priest End to the W of the church. The site was formerly moated on three sides, with the River Thame on the N. A prebendal house is first recorded here in 1234. The C13 house consisted of a hall, solar and chapel, all at first-floor level above undercrofts. Their arrangement was unusual: the hall stood N–S, with the solar at right angles to the W, and the chapel linked diagonally to the SE corner of the hall. The chapel and solar remain, together with the s gable-end of the original hall. In the late C14 or C15 a ground-floor hall was built to the N, also aligned N–S, and the old hall probably became the solar. A courtyard was formed by more buildings to W and NW, now gone. In 1661 Anthony Wood found 'a hall and chappell now standing, as also the ruins of other roomes, with half round the quadrangle'. Buckler's drawings of 1821 show the place in use as a farmhouse, with a barn in place of the C13 hall. In 1837 the house was restored for Charles Stone by *H.B. Hodson*, with the C15 hall as the main residence. Further enlargement and restorations in the mid C19 and 1910s–30s.

(The present buildings form a three-sided courtyard. The long s range is the C13 SOLAR. It was extended W in the C14 and has a very fine C14 crown-post roof. On its s face is a C13 chimney-breast and a window of the same date with two lancet lights divided by an octagonal shaft. In the W wall are mullioned and cross-windows of later C16 type, and superimposed doorways from a lost stair-turret. The external timber staircase up to the doorway in the N wall is of *c.*1969. On the first floor is a handsome fireplace with C14 jambs of half-quatrefoil section and a C20 stone hood. To the E, the s wall of the former HALL, which now serves as a screen wall between solar and chapel. In its gable a large C15 window with C20 tracery. The CHAPEL is of *c.*1240, one of the most elegant E.E. buildings in the county, and almost unaltered. In the E wall a graduated triplet of lancets with slender detached shafts and stiff-leaf capitals. Two long lancets in both side walls, and a single lancet to the W. Original piscina with a shouldered arch. Coupled-rafter roof with braced collars. The bellcote is of 1837. Another restoration followed *c.*1913; more in 1939 by *A.C. Dickie*, lately Professor of Architecture at Manchester University.

A screen wall built on the alignment of the first hall around 1951–2 links the chapel to the present HOUSE. This consists largely of the C15 addition, with a gabled porch of two storeys projecting to the E, in line with the screens passage. To its s was the hall, of two bays; to the N a shorter, two-storey part for the services, with a C16-type window on the ground floor. The hall still follows the C14 pattern of a tall transomed window in each bay, here of two cinquefoiled lights under square hoods. In 1837 the twin s gables were made, and the hall was both floored across and subdivided by a wall and chimneystack running E–W. The part s of this division, now the drawing room, was restored to double height in 1939 by *Dickie*, with a fine C15 or C16 roof brought from a house in Essex. The beams are carved with vine trails, and rest on corbels carved as crouching figures. The magnificent stone fireplace is French, late C15, and has a hood also on figure corbels. Another fireplace of the same date with a three-sided hood in the entrance hall. Of the kitchen and offices, one four-centred-arched service doorway remains. It has a square hood. The inner doorway to the former screens passage is C13, reused. Pointed arch with a hollow chamfer and a roll moulding. C15 doorway at the opposite end of the passage, of two hollow-chamfered orders. It leads into the N range, probably the post-1837 enlargement made by John Stone, with C20 extensions to the W. Two reused C15 windows in its N wall. Also a reused C14 window of two lights, with a quatrefoil in the head and a battlemented transom.)

The approach is via a broad, gabled GATEHOUSE range of c.1923–5 with a central archway, built partly as guest accommodation. To the N an oblong crenellated LODGE, apparently Victorian or early C20.

PERAMBULATION

The start is the churchyard, with The Prebendal to the W and the former vicarage to the N (pp. 746, 745). CHURCH ROAD, the approach from the S, has a long, low C16 TITHE BARN of herringbone brick with a timbered and brick-nogged upper stage. On the E side the former GRAMMAR SCHOOL, founded in 1559 by the will of Lord Williams of Thame and built in 1569–70. T-plan, the schoolroom projecting at the back. Facing the road is a symmetrical range with central gable, diagonal brick chimneystacks, and mullioned windows with arched lights under square hoods. Over the doorway the arms of Lord Williams. Inside were the entrance hall with a library above, between the houses of the master, r., and usher, l. Dormers and canted ground-floor bay added in 1842. A N extension of the same date was taken down in *Terence Woram Associates*' restoration of 1985, when surrounding OFFICES were built. The attics were for boarders, with access by a NE stair-tower. Stone GATEWAY with a stepped gable, the survivor of three, and probably original. Next door the ALMSHOUSES, also established by Lord Williams and apparently built in the 1550s, succeeding a mid-C15 guild foundation. Six dwellings originally, of timber with tension bracing on the first floor. Some brick infill. Jettied gable-end to the High Street. Victorian bargeboards and oriel here, also the porches and dormers on the garden side, E. The domed Late Victorian BANDSTAND, made by *W. Macfarlane & Co.* of Glasgow, was brought from Halton House, Aylesbury (Bucks.).

Now E along the HIGH STREET (for the W continuation and Priest End, *see* p. 751). From the start there is an engaging mixture of timber-framed and Georgian brick fronts, with only a few later insertions. The S side has Nos. 41–42, a tall three-storey pair of c.1800, the heyday of chequer brick. Next door THE CRUKE, thatched and timbered cottage, probably early C17. On its l. flank a C16 cruck frame from an adjoining cottage, now destroyed. Opposite, Nos. 72 and 73 are late C18, silvery-grey and red brick, with bow windows. At No. 78 the C16 timbers are fronted with Georgian chequer brick and gabled dormers, but exposed at the l. side. The massive chimneystack is original. THE THATCH (Nos. 29–30), back on the S side, shows its C16 framing. Two cruck-trusses inside. It adjoins CHURCH HOUSE (No. 28), C17, with a rendered front. One gable, and a cluster of three diamond-shafted brick chimneys to the r. (Two blocked doorways with shaped heads in the partition to the cross-wing.) The RISING SUN at No. 26 is C16, remodelled and stuccoed. At the side the frame is exposed, and a jettied range extends down Southern Road. No. 81 opposite is a one-off among Thame's Georgian fronts, with round-arched windows with key blocks. Continuing with the s side, No. 24, probably mid-C17, is timber-framed and roughcast, with inserted sash windows. Jettied gable; carriageway to the l. STARBANK HOUSE (No. 23), three bays and three storeys, was re-dressed in stucco c. 1830. Window architraves on scroll brackets, doorway with Soanean incised decoration. Panelled interiors and a fine open-well staircase of mahogany reveal the house's true date of c. 1730–40. Opposite, No. 85 at the junction with Bell Lane is C17. A timbered gable faces w, almost wholly renewed.

From here onwards the High Street begins to widen, as it approaches the market place. On the N side, heavily disguised and easily overlooked, No. 87 is a cruck-framed hall house of the C14, formerly with a stone cellar to the central bay. Also partly of cruck construction is No. 22 opposite, C16, with brick infill. No. 21, a gabled C17 house, was stuccoed in the early C19 and prettified with scalloped bargeboards. No. 18 is another early C19 refacing and sashing, probably of a late C17 house to judge by the gable with its moulded bargeboard. To the r. an arched carriageway. No. 91 opposite, a handsome house of c. 1750, five bays and three storeys, is of silver-grey header brick laced with red brick dressings. Door hood with dentils, on scroll brackets. Adjoining it is a pretty brick terrace with a cogged cornice, an C18 refronting of C17 cottages. No. 15 repeats the composition of No. 91, omitting the string courses and panelling of the parapet, and with a round-arched middle window. Set back to the l. a former Congregational chapel of 1827, now a MASONIC HALL. At Nos. 6/6A is the High Street's largest post-war intervention, a line of shops of c. 1975. On the N side opposite, No. 104 is Late Georgian, stuccoed, the first-floor windows with segmental pediments on brackets. It adjoins the former GREYHOUND INN, with an altered later C18 brick front. On the first floor a canted oriel of c. 1900 between two simplified Palladian windows. The carriageway has been infilled, but the r. bay has been opened up for a walkway, exposing C17 close studding.

The s side goes on past the Town Hall (p. 746). No. 2 here is a well-observed imitation of the double-bayed, timber-framed C18 type with classical trim, familiar from C18 Oxford. Probably early C20. The High Street continues as CORNMARKET, with the modest JAMES FIGG pub (No. 21), early C19 with canted bay windows added. The buildings opposite, like the Town Hall itself, represent encroachments on the original market place. Of this group, three timber-framed shop-houses face the Town Hall. From s to N, No. 2 Cornmarket is probably late C17, altered and rendered. The cruck-framed No. 1 may be C14 in its oldest parts. A Georgian enlargement in front. No. 131 High Street is C17, of three storeys and attic, with hipped gables and a coved cornice. It makes the corner with BUTTER MARKET, an alley of cottages and small shops. Nos. 1–2 were another inn, The George, probably mid-C17. The upper jetty remains, supporting two gables. To the r. a section with sash windows and a former carriageway. No. 7 was also an inn, the Saracen's Head. Narrow gabled front, stuccoed and with sash windows. Tree rings indicate a date c. 1315. This part appears to have been the cross-range to a larger establishment from which some cruck-trusses survive in the adjoining house.

Back to Cornmarket and E, to where two splendid inns face each other. On the s side is the SPREAD EAGLE, built c. 1740. Red and grey brick, of 2 : 5 bays, the divisions marked by brick pilasters. Doorcase with Ionic pilasters, dentil cornice, and other details in moulded brick. All the openings segmental-arched, including the carriageway, l. A wonderful INN SIGN of 1926 stands in front, designed by the forthright gentleman-innkeeper *John Fothergill*, the wrought-iron surround made by *Ralph Timms* reusing older work. Opposite is THE BIRDCAGE, a double-jettied, postcard-picturesque structure of exceptional interest. The massive timbering and the cross-bracing on the first floor point to an early date, probably C14. Dragon beams and mighty corner posts to the SW corner, those of the ground floor enclosed by a wraparound C19 pentice. An original use as an open-sided market hall has been suggested. The roof however is of the crown-strut type most in favour around 1430, and may be an early rebuilding. On the first floor to the W are two small oriels with wooden dagger tracery. C17 N extension. Last restored in 2012. (Stone-vaulted cellar. On the first floor two medieval fireplaces, one with a stone hood, the other a shouldered lintel. Also a four-light timber window with tracery, now internal to the N extension.) The E part appears earlier still, but survives only partially.

Just W of The Birdcage is NATWEST, originally the London & County Bank, handsome free Wren style, c. 1905–10. On the s side to the E is LLOYDS BANK (No. 14), of 1889–90 by *C. P. Ayres* for the Bucks & Oxon Union Bank. A ponderous attempt at Northern Renaissance, of brick and stone with round-arched windows. The market place opens up again, around the so-called MARKET HALL, an oblong mid-C18 commercial building of uncertain origin. The N side here is UPPER HIGH STREET, with a pretty row of small C18 houses, chequered or plain brick and stucco, some with old shopfronts. The SWAN HOTEL (No. 9), C16 remodelled in the C18, has an irregular front of chequer brick and a taller section in the centre with a hipped roof. The timbering shows at the back, with a weatherboarded gable over the carriageway. (Moulded beams and a Tudor-arched doorway with foliage spandrels in the bar. A painted wooden ceiling on the first floor, late C16 or early C17.) On the s side by the former Wesleyan chapel

(p. 745), the OLD NAG'S HEAD (No. 43), probably early C17.
Rendered, with three jettied gables. Close studding on the r.
flank. No. 42 is also C17 and rendered, with a Victorian carved
wooden doorcase. Back on the N side, No. 13, early C18 of
chequer brick, the roof still of old-fashioned steep pitch. Five
bays, two storeys. Dentil cornice, door hood on scroll brackets.
The MOAT HOUSE (No. 16) is Early Georgian, with a partly
C17 cross-wing behind. Irregular chequer-brick front. Handsome wooden doorcase with a triglyph frieze and medallions.
The frieze over the carriage entrance, r., is a near match.
Inside, a magnificent Rococo fireplace and two doorways of
c. 1750, of carved wood with broken pediments, scrolls, flowers
and dragons, obviously brought in and very probably from
Rycote Park (q.v.). The last pre-C19 house of note is on the s
side, now Nos. 33–35, by Christ Church (p. 745). Chiefly this
comprises an early C16 house with solar cross-wing to the
l., heightened and refaced.* Its arch-braced collar roof was
originally open over the centre bays. The bay next to the cross-
wing contained a chimneystack, with staircase behind. Porch
on the cross-wing, in line with a through passage. Re-set C16
doorcase with a four-centred head and carved spandrels. The
w cross-range is early C17, the E extension with carriageway late
C17. Further along on the same side THE ELMS, c. 1830, plain
ashlar, set back in a garden. The wall in front is the backdrop
for the PEARCE MEMORIAL FOUNTAIN of 1926, designed by
Thomas Worthington & Son. Its sculpture of a boy holding a fish
is a copy of 1992 by *Faith Winter*, replacing a stolen original.
WAR MEMORIAL beyond by *J.T. Robinson*, 1921. A cross.

OTHER BUILDINGS

Described from W to E.

In PRIEST END, facing down the W end of the High Street, is
STRIBBLEHILLS, a broad-fronted house with the carved date
1647. Restored in 2004, when a blocked three-light C17 window
was exposed. The herringbone brick within the framing is an
original feature, but pargeting shown on an engraving of 1842
has been lost, and the bargeboards and sash windows are
Victorian. On the SE corner, No. 1 is a thatched, cruck-framed
former hall house, C15 or early C16. At No. 2 the thatched
range is probably early C17, the taller cross-range mid- to late
C17. On it a through-storey projecting bay, with apparently
original wood-mullioned windows. On the W side, OXFORD
HOUSE, offices of 1996–9 by *Hall Needham Associates*. Red
brick, the composition much broken up. TOWN FARM (No. 8)
incorporates another late medieval hall house, with inserted
floor and chimneystack.

*Accomplished late C16 wall paintings from the solar, removed in 1972, are dis-
played in Thame Museum.

BELL LANE, N of the High Street, also has a few thatched and timber-framed cottages. It leads to Aylesbury Road, where JASMINE COTTAGE and LASHLAKE HOUSE, W side, are mid-C18 with mansard roofs, of three and five bays. Between them is a windowless brick range built as a wool warehouse.

BISHOP'S PALACE, No.9 Moorend Lane. A C17 lobby-entry house, probably early C17, with a C16 cross-wing of cruck construction, l. Reportedly used by the bishop on visitations.

COUNCIL HOUSES, Churchill Crescent, off Kingsey Road. Designed in 1949–51 by *T. Lawrence Dale*. Shared chimneystacks, pedimental gables. Clever brick detailing to imply classical doorcases.

THE FALCON, Thame Park Road. A rather absurd pub of 1900. Raised central gable treated purely as a feature. Blocked window surrounds.

STATIONMASTER'S HOUSE (former), No.111 Chinnor Road. Of *c.*1862 for the Wycombe Railway, an affiliate of the Great Western. The GWR's plain Tudor style, derived from Brunel designs of the 1840s. Line closed 1963.

NORTH WESTON MANOR
1½ m. WSW, in Great Haseley parish

The FARMHOUSE incorporates a timber-framed section of the great house built *c.*1535 by Sir John Clerke, largely re-cased in brick. At the back a projecting gabled bay and a massive chimneystack with three diagonal shafts. But the most remarkable survival is the early C18 WALLED GARDEN to the W. High brick walls enclose a space some 250 ft (75 metres) square, with a segmental exedra on the N side. Its centrepiece is a SUMMERHOUSE, a stone-fronted recess with four Ionic columns. The pediment is carved with the Clerke crest in a big cartouche between festoons of flowers. All derelict in 2022, the plasterwork dropping from the summerhouse ceiling.

THAME PARK

7000

A major house converted from the former Thame Abbey, 1¾ m. SE of the town. It comprises four wildly disparate ranges around a small courtyard: mid-C18 to the W, C14 to the N, mostly early C16 to the S, early C21 to the E. The two main fronts are a delightful contrast: on the W Georgian uniformity and restraint, on the S the comfortable sprawling medieval range with its crenellated parapets, mullioned windows and solar tower. Both ranges have magnificent interiors, but those of the C16 are of the greater importance as some of the earliest examples of Renaissance decorative detail in England.

THE ABBEY. Thame was an important Cistercian house, founded in 1137 and relocated here *c.* 1140 after the first establishment at Otteley (Oddington, North Oxon) proved unsuitable. The new site was given by Alexander, Bishop of Lincoln. By 1145 enough was built for the church to be dedicated, and payments in the 1230s indicate the enlargement of its E end. Fragments of stonework with E.E. mouldings have been found on the site, which lay NW of the present house. It remains unexcavated, but William Twopeny's survey of *c.* 1840 located the bases of fourteen piers of the nave, and allowed the dimensions to be calculated as 230 ft by 70 ft (70 by 21 metres), with a Lady Chapel extending 45 ft (13.7 metres) to the E. According to a report made in 1507 the abbeys of Furness and Thame were almost the same size. Of the two ranges preserved in the present house, the N side may have comprised part of the monastic infirmary, and the S side was the abbot's lodging, which in Cistercian foundations was often placed SE of the church and main cloister. After Dissolution in 1539 the abbey was briefly returned to its last abbot, Robert King, in his new guise as Oxford's first bishop, but in 1547 it passed to his kinsman Sir John Williams, later Lord Williams of Thame, then through the female line to the Wenman family in 1559. The church is said to have been demolished by the end of the C16.

THAME PARK. The main entrance is in the WEST RANGE of *c.* 1745–50, built for the 6th Viscount Wenman by *William Smith* of Warwick in place of what were probably retained monastic buildings. The façade is a restrained design in the manner of James Gibbs, of ashlar, with close affinities to Smith's Kirtlington Park (1742–6; North Oxon), built for a cousin of Lord Wenman. Of eleven bays and two storeys over a basement, it has a straight parapet and bracket cornice. The three central bays project slightly beneath a pediment which encloses a coat of arms. Doorway with a segmental pediment and Corinthian half-columns, approached by a double staircase with a stone balustrade. Lowered sills to the windows of the *piano nobile*. Rusticated surrounds of Gibbsian type to the basement windows. The S end is just two bays wide, the N end was enlarged to three in the C19.

The central HALL has lavish plasterwork in the style of *Thomas Roberts* of Oxford (cf. e.g. the Queen's College library ceiling and the Radcliffe Camera staircase, pp. 240 and 343). The ceiling has a Rococo centrepiece, and the walls are panelled and festooned with swags of fruit and flowers in high relief. Complementing the plasterwork, much carving in wood and stone: wood for the doorcases with bay-leaf friezes and pediments on brackets, and for the superb overmantel frame, which has work in the round almost in the manner of Grinling Gibbons; stone for the fireplace, with its big consoles supporting the mantelshelf. To the l. is the PINE ROOM, with stripped panelling, egg-and-dart mouldings, and a frieze with the scarcer motif of rosettes in high relief. Wooden chimneypiece with carved foliage and Rococo scrolls. The overmantel is carved with a basket and festoons even more closely resembling Gibbons's work than those in the hall. But the chief surprise is overhead: an C18 Dutch painted ceiling of the late Baroque school of Jacob de Wit, introduced during the restoration of Thame Park by Dr Paul and Mina Matthews in 2001–6. The corners have grisaille supporters and smaller framed scenes, the cloudy centrepiece is modern, in place of the original scene of an apotheosis of a military hero, which now adorns the adjacent DINING ROOM. The Ionic column-screen across the far end (originally Corinthian) came from the general redecoration for Sophia, Baroness Wenman in the 1830s, most of which was purged in alterations of 1919–21 by *G. Berkeley Wills* for W. H. Gardiner. S of the Hall, the DOUBLE ROOM represents two C18 interiors thrown together and remodelled by *Wills*. His plasterwork uses an uneasy mixture of C17 and C18 styles. Finely carved mid-C18 fireplace, brought from an upper room. Behind the Hall is the STAIRCASE, of spacious open-well form with simple turned balusters. That the staircase is not original is indicated by blocked windows in the rear wall, superseded by a Venetian one of early C19 outline, and by its descent to the basement, in apparent contradiction to the Georgian first-floor entry. *Wills* provided the column-screen at the head of the stairs. In 1938–9 he returned to create the LOWER HALL for a new owner, Frank Bowden (later Sir Frank) of the Raleigh bicycle family. Tuscan columns here, with an entrance through the external staircase podium.

The SOUTH RANGE is exceedingly picturesque, with battlemented bay windows and stair-turrets and a steeply pitched roof. Its three sections represent successive enlargements and improvements of the abbot's lodgings. The earliest part is on the l., with a roof reportedly of C13 or C14 pattern but externally of *c.*1500, with Elizabethan-type windows below (some of the windows are restoration of *c.*1920). Taller and narrower than the adjoining block, it consists of an upper and lower hall with a through-storey canted bay window. Then a polygonal stair-turret, and to its E a two-storey continuation with a more ornate through-storey bay window. Lastly a battlemented tower of three storeys built at right angles at the far end against the former S doorway, which remains inside. The tower has an oriel lighting the upper floors on its W side and a polygonal stair-turret at the junction with the main range to the E. The bays and newel stair are additions too, not bonded in, and motifs shared with the tower – battlements, string courses with heads, plinths – suggest that they were all added at the same time, most likely for the free-spending Abbot Warren after 1509. Attic windows inserted in the late C16 appear in the E gable, and the end wall also shows the C18 widening of the back of the wing facing the courtyard.

The interior arrangements cannot be known in full. It is possible that the ground floor was for guests, with separate access from the N to the abbot's quarters above. The westernmost room here, now the LIBRARY, was furnished after *c.*1527 when Robert King became abbot. The frieze is carved with his name ('ROBERTUS KING') between vine trails and Renaissance ornament, urns, mermaids and arabesques. It is similar to carving from Notley Abbey, Bucks., now at Weston Manor (North Oxon), and must be by the same craftsmen. Boarded ceiling, much restored, with three large cross-beams and compartments of diagonally intersecting ribs. Early C21 fittings in a well-observed 1830s Gothic style, designed by *Andrew Clark* of *Purcell Miller Tritton*. The ABBOT'S HALL to the E represents two C16 rooms combined. The ceiling is lost, exposing the five-bay kingpost roof with arched wind-braces. The W wall preserves the scar of the roof of an older range previously here. At the E end an early C16 fireplace with shields in the spandrels. External access is via the E stair-turret, which also serves the ABBOT'S PARLOUR on the first floor of the tower. This has 36 sumptuous decoration partly in the Italian Renaissance style, done for Abbot King. Although the carving is mutilated, it is still one of the most perfect small rooms of this date in the country. It also has much linenfold panelling and what may be the earliest surviving internal porch in England. On the E side is a plain four-centred-arched fireplace, on the W a recess formed by the oriel. Beside the fireplace a doorway in the panelling, for a garderobe. The upper walls and upper porch have panels carved with a filigree pattern of arabesques, mermaids, scrolls and urns framing shields on one wall; on the others, heads in medallions. Above the panels an especially delicate frieze of similar Italianate decoration, which continues on the two intersecting ceiling beams. Here the initials RK also appear, and the shields of the panelling record King's family connections. The decoration was carved separately and applied to plain panels. It is now painted white against a blue ground but was originally coloured and gilded. The work is of the highest quality and shows a complete mastery of Renaissance forms. There is no reason to believe that it was executed by an Italian, since by *c.*1530 English craftsmen could handle such detail competently. Shallow plaster ribs to the ceiling, partly restoration. The room above was probably the abbot's bedroom.

The NORTH RANGE is a more modest medieval survival, much altered. Of mid-C14 date, it originally comprised a cloister walk with small ground-floor rooms and a large single room above, probably part of a larger infirmary complex. Restored by *Purcell Miller Tritton* and continued in simplified two-storey form around the other sides, with a new vaulted ceiling designed by *Dr Paul Matthews*. The handsome N openings are now fully exposed, with doubled cinquefoiled arches on colonnettes with bell capitals. Between them are four restored buttresses. Other windows late C16 or C17, with plain mullions. Finally the main part of the EAST RANGE, after a design of 2001 by *John Simpson & Partners*. Of squared rubble, with a blind Venetian aedicule on the outer wall. It houses a swimming pool.

STABLES, NE of the house and askew to it. By *William Smith*, *c.*1745–50. Three-sided, open to the W side. Each inner face has a central projection with a through-storey arch, echoed in lunette windows along the lower storey.

(WALLED GARDENS, N of the stables. Mid-C18, with later enlargements. On the E side a triple-arched gateway.)

CHAPEL, 150 yds NW of the house. Plot's county map of 1676 shows a separate chapel by the house. The present building is probably not medieval but a post-Dissolution structure of uncertain date incorporating early C14 features. These include the shafted S doorway, the two-light N window with a flattened quatrefoil at the top, and the renewed three-light W window with its tracery rose of three cusped spherical triangles. The elaborate W bellcote, crenellations, pinnacles, stuccoing and other details date from remodelling for Baroness Wenman by *Daniel Harris*, succeeded by *Robert Abraham*, which concluded in 1836. Likewise the chancel with its rib-vault on leaf corbels and its crypt for the baroness's tomb. Nave roof renewed in the early C21, retaining the 1830s trusses. The 1830s FITTINGS were also restored, including the PULPIT and the PEWS with crenellated uprights. – Good C15 TILES from the abbey on the chancel floor. – STAINED GLASS. 1830s, perhaps by *Isaac Hugh Russell* of Oxford (MH). Heraldry, painted quarries and in the W window a queen in C16 dress (Katherine of Aragon?). – MONUMENT. Philip, 7th Viscount Wenman †1800. Signed *Westmacott*, either *Richard Sen.* (*Westmacott the elder*) or his son, (*Sir*) *Richard*. With relief of a seated female mourner handling a skull.

PARK. The attentions of *Capability Brown* (payments in 1758 and 1759) no doubt account for the present open, free-flowing landscape. The serpentine LAKE E of the house may incorporate medieval fish ponds. W of the house is a HA-HA, crossed by a bridge with C19 wrought-iron GATES W of the house. (Medieval EARTHWORKS show the extent of the deer park held by the bishops of Lincoln, which was smaller than the present park.)

LODGES and GATES to the W and S. Early C19. Castellated in a stagey way, with blind loopholes. Done for Baroness Wenman, so perhaps by *D. Harris* or *R. Abraham* (cf. the chapel).

TOOT BALDON

St LAWRENCE. A small church isolated at the end of a long avenue. Chancel, nave with narrow aisles, S transept, and a renewed double W bellcote. Re-set in the N wall is a plain Norman doorway; otherwise the church is C13. Arcades of four bays with single-chamfered arches. The S arcade is early C13; round piers, moulded capitals and bases. N arcade slightly earlier, perhaps *c.*1200. Its w respond has a Transitional trumpet-scalloped capital. Two piers with early stiff-leaf capitals. No chancel arch. The restoration of 1864–6 was by *Woodyer*. He added the N organ chamber and made a new S porch and doorway. Much of the chancel was rebuilt, with stocky buttresses and new E and S windows. Also original lancets to N and S. In the transept a window of *c.*1300 with intersecting tracery (restored). Nave W window of the same date. In the N aisle a C13 lancet and two Perp-style windows, the E one original, the other and those of the S aisle by *J. P. St Aubyn*, 1890. – FURNISHINGS largely by *Woodyer*, with characteristic thorny detail, e.g. the boldly cusped arches of the ROOD SCREEN. – FONT. Tub-shaped, late C12 or C13. Victorian decoration of encircled sunk crosses. – STAINED GLASS by *Horwood Bros* of Frome, *c.*1873–8. – In the churchyard a C15 CROSS, the head restored by *Woodyer* in 1874. – Skeletal LYCHGATE also of 1874, probably *Woodyer*'s too.

COURT KEYS, N. The former vicarage, of 1860 by *Woodyer*. Red brick and stone, only slightly Gothic.

MANOR HOUSE, in the village ⅓ m. N. Early to mid-C17, to a long L-plan. Front with three gables and mullioned windows with square labels. Some irregularities in the stonework (two phases are reported). Star-shaped cluster of brick chimney-stacks; another trio set diagonally. Much restitution of 1972 behind, after a C19 brick addition was removed from the middle. Shell-headed alcove in the parlour panelling. To the N, unexpectedly big C17 GATEPIERS of brick and stone.

COURT HOUSE FARM opposite, mostly of 1841, incorporates C16 work in the wing facing the road: a high plinth and a single-light window with a moulded surround. It may be the new building on which masons were engaged in 1537 by Queen's College, Oxford, then the owners of Toot Baldon.

TOWERSEY

7000

Transferred from Buckinghamshire in 1939.

ST CATHERINE. Entry is through the SW tower added in 1854, in C14 style; probably by *James Cranston*, who restored the nave in 1850–1. Chancel with C13 lancets in the side walls. A C12 PILLAR PISCINA with a square scalloped bowl is re-set within, S side, under a plain recess. E window of the early C14, when the nave was rebuilt. This has two-light windows in an unusual position flanking the chancel arch, also with flowing tracery. Immediately adjacent is a shallow transeptal N chapel with a three-light window in similar style. The nave side windows have cusped Y-tracery, the doorways continuous wave mouldings with an outer chamfer, all typical Dec detail. The w wall may have been rebuilt, but retains a partly renewed C14 window with intersecting tracery. C15 chancel roof. – PULPIT. Jacobean, with blind arches and carved scrolls and foliage. – Four C16 BENCH-ENDS with poppyheads. – FONT. Plain tub, C12 or C13. – IRONWORK, S door. C14 strap hinges with spiral ends, each also with a raised bar with feathered patterning.

VILLAGE. A number of pretty timber-framed cottages near the church. The VICARAGE, N of the bungalows to the W, is stone quasi-Tudor, 1846. TOWERSEY MANOR, E, is plain with sash windows, 1858 and later. By the Three Horseshoes pub, S, a BARN built of witchert or cob. Slit windows, and the characteristic rounded corners. Probably C18.

(TOWERSEY GRANGE, ½ m. ENE. A former property of Thame Abbey. The timber-framed hall range and brick SW part have yielded the dates 1518–20 and 1570, both with reused mid-C14 rafters. Stone NE extension datable to 1721. *Graeme Beamish* restored and extended the house *c.* 2012. Residual timbers in the large stone BARN, formerly aisled and with passing braces, allow a date 1294.)

WARBOROUGH

ST LAURENCE. W tower rebuilt in 1666. Post-medieval proportions: broad and weighty, of three near-equal stages, with polygonal corner turrets and small bell-openings (cf. the tower at Dorchester, 1602). Clunch walls with irregular flint banding, the turrets chequered. The date appears in large numbers in flintwork, W, and on small datestones, N and S. Victorian W doorway. Nave and S transept C14. Dec S doorway with a continuous moulding. Two renewed Perp windows to the nave, and a third of 1924 to the NW. Wide, double-chamfered transept arch. Flowing Dec transept window, with PISCINA and recess beside it. The chancel is continuous with the nave. Dec E window with reticulated tracery, but also much work of *c.* 1200. Priest's doorway with a roll-moulded arch on jamb shafts with square abaci and weathered stiff-leaf capitals. Internally the E window opening has jamb shafts with stiff-leaf capitals on the N, large flat leaves on the S, again with square abaci. In the S wall remnants of arcading of the same date: two shafts and part of an arch. Also an early C13 S window with plate tracery, and C15 windows to the S and N. Dec ogee PISCINA. The chancel was restored in 1881 by *Bodley & Garner*, the N vestry added 1912–14.

FURNISHINGS. WALL PAINTING (restored) of the Prince of Wales's feathers on the E side of the partition between nave and chancel, with the initials CP ('Carolus Princeps'). These must refer to the future Charles II, which would correspond to work recorded at the church in 1641. – PULPIT. C17. Plain panels. – LECTERN. Victorian, of wood. In the unusual form

Warborough, St Laurence, font.
Engraving by P. H. Delamotte and J. H. Heaviside
after J.C. Buckler, 1846

of a pelican in her piety. – FONT. Lead, circular, late C12. The decoration comprises rosettes and wheels, placed in the upper zone and also within upright triangular-headed panels. Between the panels is a lower zone of arcading with eighteen small figures of bishops or abbots. The motifs match those of the lead font at Long Wittenham, Berks., and the same moulds must have been used. C14 panelled stone base. – STAINED GLASS. Chancel N, modest medieval remains re-set in 1983. Original late C15 roses at the top. Four made-up panels below; mostly C14 quarries, also a C15 IHS monogram and roundel of the Yorkist sun badge. War memorial window, E, and two N dated 1924 and 1946, all by *A.J. Davies* of the *Bromsgrove Guild*. Also one nave N window by *Burlison & Grylls*, 1887. Transept, 1923 by *Hubert Blanchard*. Two by *M. Farrar Bell*, chancel S and nave S, 1989 and 1986.

CROSS in the churchyard. Medieval shaft.

ST LAURENCE HALL (former school), W of the church. Dated 1838, extended 1871. Mangled.

The VILLAGE has a lively mixture of house types, materials and dates. N of the church, the OLD VICARAGE, 1705. Five bays, all stone, with a wooden modillion cornice and a red-tiled roof with dormers. Doorcase of fluted Doric pilasters and triglyph frieze, framing a later fanlight. To the E is the wide village green. On its S side, reached by a footbridge across a stream, the MANOR HOUSE. A big hip-roofed former farm-house, dated 1696 over the central window. Five original bays, again of stone, but here with brick dressings, including moulded cornices over the wooden cross-windows. To the r. a matching C18 extension one bay deep, then a thatched and weatherboarded BARN with the internal date 1806. To the w the SIX BELLS INN. A cruck-built former hall house, tree-ring dated to 1461–4. Typical C16 insertion of a chimney in the through passage.

THAME ROAD runs N–S, w of the green. At the turning the little WHITE'S ALMSHOUSES, 1849. Going S, Nos. 111–115 are a mildly Modernist whitewashed terrace of 1952 by *Lionel Brett* (*Lord Esher*), built by St John's College, Oxford. No. 109 next door is of *c.* 1600, its timber framing intact above, and with a closed-cruck truss reused in the end wall. Going N, WESTERN HOUSE (No. 54) is a big timber-framed house dated to 1574, with short gabled wings facing the road. Roughcast all over – the big square chimneys too – save for the weather-boarded gables.

UPPER FARM, Nos. 233–235 Thame Road, ½ m. N. Clunch rubble and brick exterior, dated 1791. Encased is a four-bay timber-framed house with tree-ring dates 1455–92, its hall floored across around 1600.

SHILLINGFORD

A settlement ½ m. to the s, by a pretty stretch of the Thames with willow trees. BRIDGE of 1826–7 by *John Treacher Jun.*, replacing one of 1764 with timber spans. Three arches, balustraded parapet. The best houses are on Wharf Road, SW of the main road crossing. SHILLINGFORD FARMHOUSE, *c.* 1730–40, has flanks of coursed clunch stone and a five-bay front of silver-grey and red brick. Segment-headed windows, hipped roof, gabled Victorian porch. RIVERSIDE HOUSE, also mid-C18 and of five bays, has an early C19 wooden *chinoiserie* porch. Margin glazing of *c.* 1840.

On the river bank is SHILLINGFORD COURT, a big house of 1897–8 by *Frank Verity*, for the West End tailor Frederick Mortimer. Verity is best known for urban and classical buildings, and his composition lacks Picturesque assurance. Rubble stone with red brick dressings, the upper walls with thin half-timbering – on the BOATHOUSE too.

WATERSTOCK

6000

ST LEONARD. A small church rebuilt by Thomas Danvers, lord of the manor in the late C15. A lost inscription dated the nave to 1480, and Danvers's will of 1501 directed that the N aisle and chancel should be completed. The mason may have been *William Orchard*, working in these years at Magdalen College, with which Danvers had connections, although there are no clinching motifs. Only the w tower and aisle of this church remain. In 1790 the nave and chancel were rebuilt, but *G.E. Street*'s restoration of 1857–8 reinstated something of the Perp character. Slim square w tower with small bell-openings, no buttresses, and a plain parapet. Octagonal concave-sided piers to the N aisle. Its E and w windows have uncusped lights. *Street*'s chancel arch matches the arcade responds and his N vestry is Perp, but his chancel windows and heavyweight porches bang the drum for the late C13. – REREDOS. 1872, presented by the Rev. J.H. Ashhurst. Painted figures on metal against gold backgrounds. – Other FURNISHINGS by *Street*, a very good and characteristic ensemble; the FONT has a sculpted marble relief. – STAINED GLASS. E window, chancel S (missing in 2022) and w window of 1858–9 by *Willement*, with his monogram. N aisle N window, at the top from l. to r., donor figure of John Brown, rector 1469–*c.*1500; an archbishop, incomplete, early to mid-C14; donor figure of Thomas Brown, father of John. The donors originally accompanied figures of the Virgin, St Ignatius and St Swithun. Below are tiers of framed heraldic shields of the Ashhurst family, installed between 1848 and 1852. A shaped panel to John and Elizabeth Warner (née Ashhurst), married 1755, is a later insertion; formerly signed *W. Peckitt*, 1769. Aisle E window of 1861, outstanding work by *Clayton & Bell*. – MONUMENTS. Loose C17 tombstones with plain inscriptions, one †1650. – Sir George Croke, Justice of the King's Bench, †1641/2. Demifigure with book and skull in a pedimented Corinthian aedicule. Attributed to *Thomas Stanton* (GF). – Francis Hinde †1720. Clumsy Baroque cartouche.

OLD RECTORY, SW. Largely rebuilt in 1790; remodelled by 1857 with buttresses, a canted bay etc. Date, style and circumstances point to *Street* as the likely designer of the work, as also for the steeply gabled STABLES by the road.

WATERSTOCK HOUSE, 100 yds NE. Adapted from the former service wing of a large, square house of stone by *S.P. Cockerell*, 1787–90, demolished 1955–6. Four plain bays. The C18 STABLES remain, and a helm-roofed Gothic PUMP HOUSE of 1898 by the road.

ORCHARD END, 300 yds ENE. A well-preserved cruck-built house, perhaps as early as *c.*1300. Four original bays. (The crucks are of 'W' type, i.e. with the blades joined by a collar rather than at the apex. Scarf joints in the ridge-piece and wall-plates are another early feature.*)

WATERSTOCK MILL, 200 yds W. L-plan, timber-framed with brick infill. An internal date 1693 is reported.

OXFORD SERVICES (M40), ¾ m. SW. By *JWA Architects*, 1993–8. Architecturally way ahead of most service stations. Two big oversailing roofs joined at right angles, one segmentally curved,

*See J. Blair in *Oxoniensia* 44 (1979).

the other double-curved with the entrance below. In the angle a water garden with fountains. A gently curved and battered masonry wall intersects the enclosures, separating the glass-walled public areas from the functions behind.

WATLINGTON

A well-preserved small market town, its main streets almost unmarked by C20 or C21 intrusions. Most of the house fronts are of red or red and grey brick, varied here and there with flint, stucco or timber framing. The medieval centre was near the church; it later moved E to the main crossing, where the town hall stands.

St Leonard. C15 W tower of ashlar; the rest heavily rebuilt and enlarged in 1874–7 by *H.J. Tollit & Edwin Dolby*. Flint and squared rubble. The medieval building was mainly C14, with some C12 details. Remnants of these are re-set inside. In the chancel s wall a short shaft with a volute capital, a piece of cable moulding and a head corbel (C13?). Two more volute capitals in the s aisle w wall. (In the vestry a plain arch and diapered tympanum from the former N doorway.) C14 s arcade of four bays; octagonal piers, double-chamfered arches. The s aisle window towards the E and the cusped TOMB RECESS are also C14. N aisle of the 1870s, with a re-set Perp w window. The s chapel is mid-C15. Its s window has two lights with straight-sided arches and the unusual detail of a round shaft on the middle mullion. The responds and central pier of the two arches between chapel and chancel also have attached round shafts. In 1763 this chapel was extended E as a mausoleum for the Home family, but any Georgian character was eradicated in the 1870s, and it now has an arch with vigorously carved stiff-leaf capitals. A similar arch to the chancel. The chapel E window of reticulated tracery is C14, re-set and shortened below. Chancel largely of the 1870s, as are the vestry (with a re-set Dec E window), organ chamber and chancel arch. The top of the tower stair-turret was reinstated to the 1870s design after storm damage in 1906. *JBKS Architects* made the N addition to the nave in 2020, with kitchen etc.

FURNISHINGS. REREDOS. 1889 by *C.E. Kempe*. With much gilt tracery and a prettified painted Annunciation in the manner of Fra Angelico. – Bright FLOOR TILES by *Maw*. – ALTAR and PANELLING in the s chapel designed by *C.O. Skilbeck*, 1927. – CHANDELIER, s chapel. Of brass, purchased 1778. – PULPIT. 1874. Designed by *Dolby*. – SCULPTURE, s aisle. Bronze-resin statue of St Leonard by *Faith Tolkien*, 2000. – FONT of coloured marbles, 1897. – STAINED GLASS. Mostly by *Kempe*: E window and s chapel E both 1887, s chapel s and three s aisle windows 1901–2, tower 1889. N aisle, St Paul at Athens by *Atkinson* of Newcastle, 1888. – BRASSES, in or near the s chapel. William Frankelyn †1485 and wife. 24½-in. and 24-in. figures (62 and 61 cm.). – William Gibson †1501 and wife. 23-in. (59-cm.) figures in shrouds. – Jeremiah or Jerome Ewstes †1587, 21-in. (54-cm.) figure, originally accompanied by his brother John (†1588).

LYCHGATE, 1901. Quite grand. Also some good C18 TOMB-STONES with rustic angels.

ST EDMUND CAMPION (R.C.), Watcombe Road. By *Peter Bosanquet & John Perryman Associates*, 1988–90. Modest but lively, with an energetic timber roof and a square lantern set diagonally. White-rendered, with slit windows dressed with red brick. SCULPTURE over the N entrance, a relief of the Annunciation by *Peter Foster*. – STAINED GLASS. Another Annunciation, 1970s, from the predecessor church. By *Gilbert E. Sheedy*, a pupil of J.E. Nuttgens (PC).

WESLEYAN CHAPEL, Shirburn Street. 1812. Chequer brick. Arched doorways, and a nicely lettered tablet in the pediment. Intact three-sided gallery. The porch is C20.

TOWN HALL, in the triangular space where the main streets join. Built in 1664–5 at the expense of Thomas Stonor IV. The familiar pre-C19 form with an open-sided enclosure for the market, and rooms in the storey above, which here also served the grammar school. It is T-shaped in response to the street plan, but the SE angle was infilled with a stair enclosure in the C18. Beautifully mellowed brick, without stone dressings. The wide arches on the ground floor have toothed decoration in imitation of quoins. Plain hoods above, and a moulded string course. The brick frames and mullions of the windows are restoration of 1908–9. Those on the first floor have round-arched transoms, a characteristic mid-C17 motif. Steep gables and a weatherboarded lantern.

ICKNIELD COMMUNITY COLLEGE, Love Lane. Formerly a County Secondary School. 1955–6 by *G.R. Hutton*, County Architect. Three storeys, brick-faced. Through-storey windows of glass brick for the staircases.

BOARD SCHOOL (former), Old School Place. 1873–4, with matching extensions. By *Wilson & Masters* of Sheffield, in the manner of G.E. Street. Red brick; lesser gables half-hipped, main gables tile-hung. Now subsumed in residential additions of 2000–2 by the *Oxfordshire Practice*.

PERAMBULATION. The main streets can be explored in turn from the Town Hall. The chief inn was the former HARE AND HOUNDS, facing from the w side. Silver-grey brick with brick dressings, *c.*1720–30; the l. part concealing early C17 fabric. The r. part follows the westward curve of the road into the HIGH STREET. More Georgian refronting here, e.g. No. 6, N side; No. 3 opposite shows C17 framing infilled with brick. HIGH STREET HOUSE (No. 7) is handsome Early Georgian, of five bays, with segment-headed windows, brick angle pilasters, a moulded brick cornice and a parapet. The ground floor with its off-centre doorcase and coved wooden cornice is a sympathetic alteration, no doubt around 1900–10. Diagonally opposite, the WATLINGTON CLUB (No. 20) is a large house of similar C18 date, transformed in the early C19 with stucco, a doorcase with reeded pilasters and rectangular fanlight, and a big open-well staircase. On the S side again, No. 15 stands end-on. Gable with thick tension braces, and timber framing also visible on the r. flank; these parts are C15, the rest largely C18 rebuilding. No. 17 is late C15, three bays wide, with arched bracing; intact jetty to the l. The most decorative Georgian front is No. 34, c. 1720–50. Three bays, symmetrical, of flint, with red brick quoins and window surrounds that touch or almost touch. Even the string course is chequer-patterned. Dentil cornice; hipped roof with one dormer window. The fabric behind is C16. Opposite, a weatherboarded early C19 GRANARY converted to a house.

The street widens to form a triangular space with the war memorial. Leading NW is CHAPEL STREET, with a few thatched cottages; No. 42 is C15 and cruck-framed in its r. part, within C18 re-casing. Beyond, set back, MEADOW COURT (No. 11 New Road) is an early timber-framed C17 house of lobby-entry plan. High Street continues W as CHURCH STREET, with timber-framed cottages of the C16–C17 at Nos. 9–11 and 23.

SHIRBURN STREET runs N from the crossing. No. 3, W side, is another boldly patterned Early Georgian house (cf. also No. 19 Gorwell, S of High Street). It faces ST JOHN'S HALL, dated 1888. Built for a rifle club, and looking with its brick castellation like a miniature Salvation Army citadel of the period. Nos. 22–26 are C16, the framing still exposed at No. 26. No. 28, jettied and with stout bracing visible on the flank, may be a little earlier. EAST END HOUSE (No. 46) is of c. 1730–50. Quite grand on a modest scale. Five bays, with an arched window over the doorway, which has fluted pilasters and a pediment. Good panelled rooms, and an open-well staircase with twisted balusters and carved treads.

HILL ROAD, E of the crossing. Nos. 1–7 are the former LADY MACCLESFIELD'S TRAINING SCHOOL of 1865, later the town's hospital. Founded to prepare girls for domestic service. Flint walls dressed in yellow brick, an uncommon combination in the town. Diamond-paned casements, plain gables.

COUCHING STREET runs S. On the E side, OLD BANK HOUSE (No. 46) is Late Georgian, three storeys, of silver-grey headers dressed with red brick. Double-sash windows, central pedimented doorway with an interlaced fanlight. The same combination of brickwork e.g. at No. 44, mid-C18, with a doorcase with a pulvinated frieze and dentil cornice. C17 rear wing. One other Georgian house stands out: No. 20, a well-preserved shop-house with the incised dated 1833. A simple front, beautifully proportioned, with a broad elliptical arch to the shopfront in the middle. The inscription 'TALLOW {KITCHEN}

CHANDLER' is painted in black above. Pre-Georgian houses, mostly refronted, include Nos. 52 and 58–60 at the N end, and on the W side Nos. 35–39 and 19–23, of which No. 39 is partly C15 (l.). The finish on the E side is the former POLICE STATION by *W. Wilkinson*, 1859–60. Plain and pragmatic. Orange-red brick, reverting to chequered brick behind.

BROOK STREET crosses Couching Street at its S end. At the junction is THE LILACS (No. 50). A symmetrical C16 front with two gables and a central cluster of chimneystacks, the outer ones set diagonally. Brick infill to the timber framing. The centre and the W gable have timbering of a slightly earlier type than the E gable, which with the chimneystacks may represent a partial rebuilding. Going W, the main range of No. 39 is late medieval and of raised-cruck construction, now floored across. Opposite is INGHAM HOUSE (formerly the vicarage), set back in its own grounds. Of *c.* 1841, Italianate, with arched windows and shallow gables with overhanging eaves.

OUTLYING BUILDINGS

THE HOWE, 1¾ m. SE. Greatly enlarged from a five-bay late C17 farmhouse. Flint, with upright windows already of polite proportions. (HOWE COMBE, 700 yds further SE. By *T. Frank Green*. The *Building News* for 19 June 1908 depicts an L-plan Arts and Crafts house, rather fussily handled.)

(WATLINGTON PARK, 1¾ m. SE. A neat Georgian brick villa *c.* 1755 built for John Tilson. The designer is unknown; in plan and outline the house resembles Sir Robert Taylor's villas of the 1750s, but his distinctive motifs do not appear in the details. W front of five bays and two storeys, the centre projecting, with a pediment and oculus. The pedimented and balustraded stone porch with a triglyph frieze must be an addition. N front with a canted bay in the middle. E front similar to the W front, but with no porch. Much of the brickwork here is reinstatement after large extensions were demolished in 1956 by *Lionel Brett*, later *4th Viscount Esher*. He took over the house in 1947 and at first based his practice here. The additions dated from 1880 (by *Arthur Vernon*) and 1911 (by *E.W. Allfrey*), with a N front added in 1928 for the 3rd Viscount by *Lord Gerald Wellesley* of *Wellesley & Wills*; also removed were minor remains of a large H-shaped house built by William Stonor in the 1630s or 1640s. To the SW is a colonnaded LOGGIA by *Philip Tilden*, 1921. Two smaller pedimented PAVILIONS by *Brett* flank the E front, framing a forecourt with GATEPIERS of *c.* 1928.

The C18 plan is largely intact. In the ENTRANCE HALL the *trompe l'œil* decoration is of *c.* 1925 by *Tilden*. It is treated architecturally, with a triglyph frieze and fluted pilasters in grisaille, lining up with the C18 Doric cornice. The DRAWING ROOM occupies the N side, with screens of fluted Ionic columns to each side of the bay window. Ceiling of delicate Rococo plasterwork with scrolls, ribbons and leaves.* The STAIRCASE is set centrally, under a glazed dome which looks early C20. It has spiral-grooved balusters of mid-C18 type but may not be in its original form.)

GREENFIELD MANOR, 2½ m. SE. Of brick. The lower part is early C17, r. Extension of *c.*1700 with two plain front-facing gables. ⅓ m. NE is GREENFIELD FARMHOUSE. Brick and flint. Of lobby-entry plan, i.e. probably C17. Added Georgian frontage, much tinkered with. Rear wing of *c.*1650–80 with a moulded platband and horizontal windows. One upper window has a lugged frame and miniature side scrolls of carved brick.

WHEATFIELD

St ANDREW. A small church all alone in the former parkland of Wheatfield House (*see* below). It was renovated probably *c.*1730–40 by John Rudge, who purchased the manor in 1727. Rendered and colourwashed, with an embattled parapet carried up the sides of the gables, arched keystoned windows, and a Palladian E window with square Ionic columns. The angles had quoins, which have decayed. Deep W porch with a pedimented doorway. The medieval church was not obliterated in the Georgian remodelling. The blocked N and S doorways of the nave are C14, with continuous wave mouldings. In the chancel N wall a blocked Perp window of one light. C14 chancel arch, its responds cut back in the C18. Ceiled nave roof with tall octagonal crown-posts, more probably C17 than C18.

The interior escaped Victorian restoration and the FITTINGS are all Georgian.† COMMUNION RAILS with twisted balusters. – Hexagonal PULPIT with tester, both with acanthus mouldings, adjoined by a plain READING DESK. – BOX PEWS. Those on the S side still face the aisle, college-fashion. The SE section comprises the manor pew, with upper panels of pierced scrollwork and the Rudge arms. – FONT. A small fluted bowl on a bulbous stem. Original turned COVER. – ROYAL ARMS, on canvas. 1742. – STAINED GLASS. A C14 tracery light with the arms of Whitfield, re-set (inside-out) in the chancel N window. E window, an oval of the risen Christ by *Morris & Sons*; †1907. w, large painted C18 shield of arms of the Rudge family. – MONUMENTS. Thomas Isham †1670. With an

---

* Given to the otherwise unrecorded *Swan* in Geoffrey Beard, *Craftsmen and Interior Decoration in England 1660–1820* (1981), as advised by John Kenworthy-Browne. Christopher Hussey (*Country Life*, 8 January 1959) recorded an older attribution for the whole house to the carpenter-builder and pattern-book author *Abraham Swan*, although plasterwork was not his trade.

† The beautiful COMMUNION TABLE has alas been stolen. It had cabriole legs and cherubs' heads linked by outstretched wings intertwined with grapes and wheat, symbols of the Eucharist. The design shows the influence of William Kent and John Vardy.

oval frame of crest, scrolls and festoons. Attributed to *Thomas Burman* (GF). – Thomas Tipping †1718. Elaborate cartouche with draperies and scrolls. – Adam Blandy †1722. With a segmental pediment above, two cherub heads below. – Sir Thomas Tipping †1725. Oval cartouche with a boar's-head crest and side scrolls. Provincial. – Elizabeth and William Tipping, †1725 and †1729. Tall classical tablet. – John Rudge †1739, by *P. Scheemakers*. Big Corinthian aedicule surmounted by reclining cherubs and an urn. – Good ledger slabs of the Tipping family in the chancel, e.g. Thomas Tipping †1693, black marble with fine lettering.

PARK FARM, W of the church. Formerly the stables of Wheatfield House, *c.*1730. Red brick. An unusual plan, the central coach-house linked by screen walls to separate stable wings at right angles to r. and l. On the fourth side a wall with gatepiers and ball finials. The coachhouse is pedimented, with a clock tower above and three arched openings framed by half-columns below, the openings and tower all of unpainted timber (partly renewed). On top an elongated octagonal dome of lead. The stable wings have nine bays of lunette windows and three-bay pediments.

(WHEATFIELD HOUSE, which stood between the stables and the church, was rebuilt by John Rudge after 1727, altered and enlarged after 1771 by Lord Charles Spencer, but destroyed by fire in 1814. An engraving of 1787 shows it with a central Venetian window under a relieving arch.)

WHEATFIELD HOUSE (formerly the rectory), ¼ m. N. Mainly of *c.*1710–20. Five bays wide. N extension of 1823, when the entrance was apparently moved to the W side.

WHITCHURCH-ON-THAMES

ST MARY, W of the High Street. A flint-walled church, largely rebuilt in 1857–8 by *Henry Woodyer* in his spiky personal version of late C13 Gothic. Older fabric survives in the nave and chancel S walls. Early Norman S doorway, its arch of two plain orders. Jamb shafts with cushion capitals on the W, volutes on the E. Inset is a four-centred-arched Perp doorway with quatrefoils in the spandrels. Crude Norman head above. S porch also Perp, with angel busts as hoodmould stops. Over the doorway a replica by *Michael Groser*, 2000, of the small C15 Crucifixion panel, shown as the Tree of Life (original preserved inside). The weatherboarded wooden tower and shingled spire are *Woodyer*'s. The internal framing rapidly decayed, and *William Woodman* replaced it with four cast-iron piers in 1863. Largely medieval nave roof. Woodyer did the N aisle and the chancel arch with its sexfoiled piercings. E window replaced in 1901 by *S. S. Stallwood*. – FURNISHINGS largely by *Woodyer*, including the outrageous FONT, but his PULPIT was

supplanted in 1910 by one from *Kempe & Co.* – PANELLING of
the chancel by *Stallwood*, 1901, with extensions; also the N aisle
SCREEN. – STAINED GLASS. E window, 1903 by *Kempe*. The
rest mostly *Hardman*, 1858–60, of which the N aisle W window
(Noah's Ark etc.) follows a sketch design by *Woodyer*. Also two
by *Clayton & Bell* (N aisle), and an intriguing lancet in C15 style
(chancel s); possibly late C19 antiquarian work by *F.R. Leach*'s
workshop (cf. Barrington, Cambs.). – BRASSES, mounted on
board. Thomas Walysh, trencherman of the Court, and wife,
1426. 22½-in. and 20¾-in. figures (57 and 52 cm.). – Roger
Grey, vicar, after 1455. 30-in. (76-cm.) figure. – Peter Winder,
curate, †1610. Kneeling figure. Southwark style. – MONU-
MENTS. Richard Lybbe †1599 and wife. Effigies at a prayer-
desk. A crest above. – Richard Lybbe †1658 and wife †1651/2.
Architectural. Attributed to *Thomas Burman* (GF). – Sophia
Simeon †1833. Relief of a standing maiden with an urn.
– LYCHGATE by *Woodman*, 1865.

The VILLAGE is prettily situated. The main street leads to the
river, crossed by a TOLL BRIDGE. Rebuilt in steel in 1901–2 to
designs by *Joseph Morris*. Much renewed in 2013–14. The TOLL
HOUSE remains from *John Treacher Sen.*'s timber bridge of
1792. Two storeys, plain brick. To the W the WATER MILL of
1850 and later. MILL HOUSE alongside is Old English of 1906
by *Hoare & Wheeler*, timbered and jettied above. Continuing
N, the E side has THAMES BANK, originally of three late C18
bays with a brick dentil cornice and high parapet. Altered and
enlarged *c.*1806, and again in the 1880s. The OLD RECTORY,
W side, is of 1835 by *Richard Billing II*, likewise of white-painted
brick. Doric porch. To the SW, down the lane to the church,
WALLISCOTE LODGE comprises the one remaining seven-bay
wing of Walliscote (originally Whitchurch House), a mansion
of *c.*1715. The other wing had gone by 1793, the main house
followed after the Second World War, but the PARK WALL survives along the High Street. SWANSTON HOUSE, E side, was
Frank Loughborough Pearson's home from *c.*1908. The relaxed
E extension with tile-hung gables and a long roof ridge is all
his; the roadside part is largely of 1862 by *Poulton & Woodman*.
Diagonally opposite, WHITCHURCH HOUSE is of *c.*1712, with
lateral enlargements. Five bays of segment-headed windows,
their outlines echoed in the sunk panels of the parapet. E again,
SWANSTON COTTAGES appear to comprise a late medieval
hall house with forward wings added, of which the r. wing has a
jettied end with curved bracing. The MANOR HOUSE opposite
is of *c.*1626, with straight upper braces.

Late C18 and early C19 COTTAGES with Gothic glazing bars
face each other where the Hardwick road comes in, 100 yds
N. The SE corner here has THE MOUNT, 1880, with some
uncommon rubbed-brick details. Going E towards Hardwick,
UPLANDS on the N side is a plain Italianate villa of 1857,
and the OLD SCHOOL comprises an original schoolroom of
*c.*1819 behind partly flint-faced Gothic enlargements of 1871
by *Joseph Morris*.

COOMBE PARK, ⅔ m. NW. Largely Neo-Georgian of *c.*1969 (by *A. Clarke Scott*) and 1982–6. The SW angle incorporates part of a service wing from Coombe Lodge, a house of 1794–5 for Samuel Gardiner with an applied Ionic portico. The architect was *J.W. Sanderson* of Reading, a pupil of Wyatt. After enlargement and an Italianate remodelling in the 1880s, the rest was demolished in 1950. – PARK landscaped by *Repton* around 1800. (– BOATHOUSE by *W. Ravenscroft*, 1892.)

PILLBOXES. Along the Thames stop-line, several of the five-sided Type 23. The most accessible is in steep woods, 1¾ m. NW.

HARDWICK HOUSE, 1½ m. E. *See* p.656.

WHITCHURCH HILL

A separate settlement 1 m. N, in Goring Heath parish.

ST JOHN THE BAPTIST. A substantial chapel of ease of 1883. Designed by *Francis Bacon*, an unprolific pupil of Woodyer, whose influence is apparent. Nave and apsed chancel treated as a single volume. Flint and stone, lancet windows. S porch of 1920–1 by *G.F. Turner*, also the red brick refacing of the adjacent S wall. – LYCHGATE also by *Turner*, 1938.

OLD PARSONAGE, SE. By *W.D. Caröe*, 1906. White-rendered, with a curious upper continuation of the roof around the chimneystacks.

(BOZEDOWN HOUSE (Castrol Technology Centre), ⅓ m. S. Large, old-fashioned Jacobethan by *Paul Waterhouse*, 1905–7, for Charles Herbert Palmer of the Reading biscuit dynasty. Diapered brick amply dressed with stone. A clock tower was incorporated from a predecessor of *c.*1871, which had burnt down. Extensive laboratory and office buildings to the NE.)

THE THATCHED COTTAGE, N of Bozedown House. Tree-ring dated 1560. The internal end stack may have replaced a timber smoke-hood.

WOODCOTE

6080

A former chapelry of South Stoke. Much late C19 and C20 housing.

ST LEONARD, South Stoke Road. Rebuilt in Norman style in 1845–6 by *H.J. Underwood*. He lengthened the nave by 20 ft (6 metres), but otherwise followed the plan of the small C12 predecessor, retaining its flint-walled apsidal chancel. Thin hammerbeam roof. W gallery, stone PULPIT and beefy FONT all in Neo-Norman style. – STAINED GLASS. Four lancets by *Powells*, 1906. – By the porch, bowl of a Norman PILLAR PISCINA(?) on a modern pillar.

CHRIST THE KING (R.C.), South Stoke Road, 300 yds NW. 1965–6. A prefabricated building supplied by *Messrs Colt*, suitably customized. Black weatherboarding.

LIBRARY, formerly school, Reading Road. 1899 by *Samuel Johns*. Prominent stepped gable to the front.

THE FOLLY, opposite St Leonard's church. Neat villa of *c.*1820–30, not large.

WOODCOTE HOUSE (THE ORATORY SCHOOL), ¾ m. E. Built *c.*1733 on the site of an earlier house, then remodelled *c.*1913 by *Detmar Blow*, who changed the main entrance to the N front. This is of thirteen bays arranged 2:3:3:3:2. Pedimented centre three storeys high, and re-roofed two-storey wings with shallow end projections. Showy wooden doorcase with a segmental pediment, carved cherub heads, flower basket etc., Early Georgian in style but surely by *Blow*. Oculus in the main pediment, also not original. Three-bay outbuildings with arched windows to l. and r., making a forecourt. The back of the house, also with a high pedimented centre, has nonmatching wings with brick pilasters of full height, the W side apparently early C20 and attributable to *Blow*, the E singlestoreyed and of C18 brickwork with traces of rendering, to which pilasters of the same type have been applied. The arched ground-floor windows of the middle projection (replacing the C18 doorcase) and the shortening of the windows immediately above, not shown on an engraving of 1883, must be Blow's too. His TOLKIEN ROOM behind has painted panelling in a 1700 style, and oval openings in the coving from the little upper windows. In the W wing the ADAM ROOM, decorated *c.*1780 in the late Adam style with an elaborate ceiling, white marble fireplace and delicately moulded doorcase. Of the STAIRCASES E and W of the hall, the E one remains intact, of square plan with slim turned balusters and shaped treads. The present ENTRANCE HALL is identifiable as the 'spacious eating room (30 ft [9 metres] square) with a screen of columns' mentioned in 1800. Wooden Tuscan columns, carved wooden chimneypiece, mutule cornices. The swagged friezes look like additions.

The SCHOOL took over in 1942. It has built extensively but without distinction. Amidst the school's additions 300 yds W is a late C17 BARN of brick, now used as a chapel.

WYFOLD COURT
see ROTHERFIELD PEPPARD

GLOSSARY

Numbers and letters refer to the illustrations (by John Sambrook)
on pp. 780–787.

ABACUS: flat slab forming the top of a capital (3a).

ACANTHUS: classical formalized leaf ornament (4b).

ACCUMULATOR TOWER: *see* Hydraulic power.

ACHIEVEMENT: a complete display of armorial bearings.

ACROTERION: plinth for a statue or ornament on the apex or ends of a pediment; more usually, both the plinth and what stands on it (4a).

AEDICULE (*lit.* little building): architectural surround, consisting usually of two columns or pilasters supporting a pediment.

AGGREGATE: *see* Concrete.

AISLE: subsidiary space alongside the body of a building, separated from it by columns, piers, or posts.

ALMONRY: a building from which alms are dispensed to the poor.

AMBULATORY (*lit.* walkway): aisle around the sanctuary (q.v.).

ANGLE ROLL: roll moulding in the angle between two planes (1a).

ANSE DE PANIER: *see* Arch.

ANTAE: simplified pilasters (4a), usually applied to the ends of the enclosing walls of a portico *in antis* (q.v.).

ANTEFIXAE: ornaments projecting at regular intervals above a Greek cornice, originally to conceal the ends of roof tiles (4a).

ANTHEMION: classical ornament like a honeysuckle flower (4b).

APRON: raised panel below a window or wall monument or tablet.

APSE: semicircular or polygonal end of an apartment, especially of a chancel or chapel. In classical architecture sometimes called an *exedra*.

ARABESQUE: non-figurative surface decoration consisting of flowing lines, foliage scrolls etc., based on geometrical patterns. Cf. Grotesque.

ARCADE: series of arches supported by piers or columns. *Blind arcade* or *arcading*: the same applied to the wall surface. *Wall arcade*: in medieval churches, a blind arcade forming a dado below windows. Also a covered shopping street.

ARCH: Shapes *see* 5c. *Basket arch* or *anse de panier* (basket handle): three-centred and depressed, or with a flat centre. *Nodding*: ogee arch curving forward from the wall face. *Parabolic*: shaped like a chain suspended from two level points, but inverted. Special purposes. *Chancel*: dividing chancel from nave or crossing. *Crossing*: spanning piers at a crossing (q.v.). *Relieving or discharging*: incorporated in a wall to relieve superimposed weight (5c). *Skew*: spanning responds not diametrically opposed. *Strainer*: inserted in an opening to resist inward pressure. *Transverse*: spanning a main axis (e.g. of a vaulted space). *See also* Jack arch, Triumphal arch.

ARCHITRAVE: formalized lintel, the lowest member of the classical entablature (3a). Also the moulded frame of a door or window (often borrowing the profile of a classical architrave). For *lugged* and *shouldered* architraves *see* 4b.

ARCUATED: dependent structurally on the arch principle. Cf. Trabeated.

ARK: chest or cupboard housing the

tables of Jewish law in a synagogue.

ARRIS: sharp edge where two surfaces meet at an angle (3a).

ASHLAR: masonry of large blocks wrought to even faces and square edges (6d).

ASTRAGAL: classical moulding of semicircular section (3f).

ASTYLAR: with no columns or similar vertical features.

ATLANTES: *see* Caryatids.

ATRIUM (plural: atria): inner court of a Roman or C20 house; in a multi-storey building, a toplit covered court rising through all storeys. Also an open court in front of a church.

ATTACHED COLUMN: *see* Engaged column.

ATTIC: small top storey within a roof. Also the storey above the main entablature of a classical façade.

AUMBRY: recess or cupboard to hold sacred vessels for the Mass.

BAILEY: *see* Motte-and-bailey.

BALANCE BEAM: *see* Canals.

BALDACCHINO: free-standing canopy, originally fabric, over an altar. Cf. Ciborium.

BALLFLOWER: globular flower of three petals enclosing a ball (1a). Typical of the Decorated style.

BALUSTER: pillar or pedestal of bellied form. *Balusters*: vertical supports of this or any other form, for a handrail or coping, the whole being called a *balustrade* (6c). *Blind balustrade*: the same applied to the wall surface.

BARBICAN: outwork defending the entrance to a castle.

BARGEBOARDS (corruption of 'vergeboards'): boards, often carved or fretted, fixed beneath the eaves of a gable to cover and protect the rafters.

BAROQUE: style originating in Rome *c.*1600 and current in England *c.*1680–1720, characterized by dramatic massing and silhouette and the use of the giant order.

BARROW: burial mound.

BARTIZAN: corbelled turret, square or round, frequently at an angle.

BASCULE: hinged part of a lifting (or bascule) bridge.

BASE: moulded foot of a column or pilaster. For *Attic* base *see* 3b.

BASEMENT: lowest, subordinate storey; hence the lowest part of a classical elevation, below the *piano nobile* (q.v.).

BASILICA: a Roman public hall; hence an aisled building with a clerestory.

BASTION: one of a series of defensive semicircular or polygonal projections from the main wall of a fortress or city.

BATTER: intentional inward inclination of a wall face.

BATTLEMENT: defensive parapet, composed of *merlons* (solid) and *crenels* (embrasures) through which archers could shoot; sometimes called *crenellation*. Also used decoratively.

BAY: division of an elevation or interior space as defined by regular vertical features such as arches, columns, windows etc.

BAY LEAF: classical ornament of overlapping bay leaves (3f).

BAY WINDOW: window of one or more storeys projecting from the face of a building. *Canted*: with a straight front and angled sides. *Bow window*: curved. *Oriel*: rests on corbels or brackets and starts above ground level; also the bay window at the dais end of a medieval great hall.

BEAD-AND-REEL: *see* Enrichments.

BEAKHEAD: Norman ornament with a row of beaked bird or beast heads usually biting into a roll moulding (1a).

BELFRY: chamber or stage in a tower where bells are hung.

BELL CAPITAL: *see* 1b.

BELLCOTE: small gabled or roofed housing for the bell(s).

BERM: level area separating a ditch from a bank on a hill-fort or barrow.

BILLET: Norman ornament of small half-cylindrical or rectangular blocks (1a).

BLIND: *see* Arcade, Baluster, Portico.

BLOCK CAPITAL: *see* 1a.

BLOCKED: columns, etc. interrupted by regular projecting

blocks (*blocking*), as on a Gibbs surround (4b).

BLOCKING COURSE: course of stones, or equivalent, on top of a cornice and crowning the wall.

BOLECTION MOULDING: covering the joint between two different planes (6b).

BOND: the pattern of long sides (*stretchers*) and short ends (*headers*) produced on the face of a wall by laying bricks in a particular way (6e).

BOSS: knob or projection, e.g. at the intersection of ribs in a vault (2c).

BOWTELL: a term in use by the C15 for a form of roll moulding, usually three-quarters of a circle in section (also called *edge roll*).

BOW WINDOW: *see* Bay window.

BOX FRAME: timber-framed construction in which vertical and horizontal wall members support the roof (7). Also concrete construction where the loads are taken on cross walls; also called *cross-wall construction*.

BRACE: subsidiary member of a structural frame, curved or straight. *Bracing* is often arranged decoratively e.g. quatrefoil, herringbone (7). *See also* Roofs.

BRATTISHING: ornamental crest, usually formed of leaves, Tudor flowers or miniature battlements.

BRESSUMER (*lit.* breast-beam): big horizontal beam supporting the wall above, especially in a jettied building (7).

BRICK: *see* Bond, Cogging, Engineering, Gauged, Tumbling.

BRIDGE: *Bowstring*: with arches rising above the roadway which is suspended from them. *Clapper*: one long stone forms the roadway. *Roving*: *see* Canal. *Suspension*: roadway suspended from cables or chains slung between towers or pylons. *Stay-suspension* or *stay-cantilever*: supported by diagonal stays from towers or pylons. *See also* Bascule.

BRISES-SOLEIL: projecting fins or canopies which deflect direct sunlight from windows.

BROACH: *see* Spire and 1C.

BUCRANIUM: ox skull used decoratively in classical friezes.

BULL-NOSED SILL: sill displaying a pronounced convex upper moulding.

BULLSEYE WINDOW: small oval window, set horizontally (cf. Oculus). Also called *œil de bœuf*.

BUTTRESS: vertical member projecting from a wall to stabilize it or to resist the lateral thrust of an arch, roof, or vault (1c, 2c). A *flying buttress* transmits the thrust to a heavy abutment by means of an arch or half-arch (1c).

CABLE OR ROPE MOULDING: originally Norman, like twisted strands of a rope.

CAMES: *see* Quarries.

CAMPANILE: free-standing bell-tower.

CANALS: *Flash lock*: removable weir or similar device through which boats pass on a flush of water. Predecessor of the *pound lock*: chamber with gates at each end allowing boats to float from one level to another. *Tidal gates*: single pair of lock gates allowing vessels to pass when the tide makes a level. *Balance beam*: beam projecting horizontally for opening and closing lock gates. *Roving bridge*: carrying a towing path from one bank to the other.

CANTILEVER: horizontal projection (e.g. step, canopy) supported by a downward force behind the fulcrum.

CAPITAL: head or crowning feature of a column or pilaster; for classical types *see* 3; for medieval types *see* 1b.

CARREL: compartment designed for individual work or study.

CARTOUCHE: classical tablet with ornate frame (4b).

CARYATIDS: female figures supporting an entablature; their male counterparts are *Atlantes* (*lit.* Atlas figures).

CASEMATE: vaulted chamber, with embrasures for defence, within a castle wall or projecting from it.

CASEMENT: side-hinged window.

CASTELLATED: with battlements (q.v.).

CAST IRON: hard and brittle, cast in a mould to the required shape.

Wrought iron is ductile, strong in tension, forged into decorative patterns or forged and rolled into e.g. bars, joists, boiler plates; *mild steel* is its modern equivalent, similar but stronger.

CATSLIDE: *See* 8a.

CAVETTO: concave classical moulding of quarter-round section (3f).

CELURE OR CEILURE: enriched area of roof above rood or altar.

CEMENT: *see* Concrete.

CENOTAPH (*lit.* empty tomb): funerary monument which is not a burying place.

CENTRING: wooden support for the building of an arch or vault, removed after completion.

CHAMFER (*lit.* corner-break): surface formed by cutting off a square edge or corner. For types of chamfers and *chamfer stops see* 6a. *See also* Double chamfer.

CHANCEL: part of the E end of a church set apart for the use of the officiating clergy.

CHANTRY CHAPEL: often attached to or within a church, endowed for the celebration of Masses principally for the soul of the founder.

CHEVET (*lit.* head): French term for chancel with ambulatory and radiating chapels.

CHEVRON: V-shape used in series or double series (later) on a Norman moulding (1a). Also (especially when on a single plane) called *zigzag*.

CHOIR: the part of a cathedral, monastic or collegiate church where services are sung.

CIBORIUM: a fixed canopy over an altar, usually vaulted and supported on four columns; cf. Baldacchino. Also a canopied shrine for the reserved sacrament.

CINQUEFOIL: *see* Foil.

CIST: stone-lined or slab-built grave.

CLADDING: external covering or skin applied to a structure, especially a framed one.

CLERESTORY: uppermost storey of the nave of a church, pierced by windows. Also high-level windows in secular buildings.

CLOSER: a brick cut to complete a bond (6e).

CLUSTER BLOCK: *see* Multi-storey.

COADE STONE: ceramic artificial stone made in Lambeth 1769–*c.*1840 by Eleanor Coade (†1821) and her associates.

COB: walling material of clay mixed with straw. Also called *pisé*.

COFFERING: arrangement of sunken panels (coffers), square or polygonal, decorating a ceiling, vault, or arch.

COGGING: a decorative course of bricks laid diagonally (6e). Cf. Dentilation.

COLLAR: *see* Roofs and 7.

COLLEGIATE CHURCH: endowed for the support of a college of priests.

COLONNADE: range of columns supporting an entablature. Cf. Arcade.

COLONNETTE: small medieval column or shaft.

COLOSSAL ORDER: *see* Giant order.

COLUMBARIUM: shelved, niched structure to house multiple burials.

COLUMN: a classical, upright structural member of round section with a shaft, a capital, and usually a base (3a, 4a).

COLUMN FIGURE: carved figure attached to a medieval column or shaft, usually flanking a doorway.

COMMUNION TABLE: unconsecrated table used in Protestant churches for the celebration of Holy Communion.

COMPOSITE: *see* Orders.

COMPOUND PIER: grouped shafts (q.v.), or a solid core surrounded by shafts.

CONCRETE: composition of *cement* (calcined lime and clay), *aggregate* (small stones or rock chippings), sand and water. It can be poured into *formwork* or *shuttering* (temporary frame of timber or metal) on site (*in-situ* concrete), or *pre-cast* as components before construction. *Reinforced*: incorporating steel rods to take the tensile force. *Pre-stressed*: with tensioned steel rods. Finishes include the impression of boards left by formwork (*board-marked* or *shuttered*), and texturing with steel brushes (*brushed*) or hammers (*hammer-dressed*). *See also* Shell.

CONSOLE: bracket of curved outline (4b).

COPING: protective course of masonry or brickwork capping a wall (6d).

CORBEL: projecting block supporting something above. *Corbel course*: continuous course of projecting stones or bricks fulfilling the same function. *Corbel table*: series of corbels to carry a parapet or a wall-plate or wall-post (7). *Corbelling*: brick or masonry courses built out beyond one another to support a chimney-stack, window, etc.

CORINTHIAN: *see* Orders and 3d.

CORNICE: flat-topped ledge with moulded underside, projecting along the top of a building or feature, especially as the highest member of the classical entablature (3a). Also the decorative moulding in the angle between wall and ceiling.

CORPS-DE-LOGIS: the main building(s) as distinct from the wings or pavilions.

COTTAGE ORNÉ: an artfully rustic small house associated with the Picturesque movement.

COUNTERCHANGING: of joists on a ceiling divided by beams into compartments, when placed in opposite directions in alternate squares.

COUR D'HONNEUR: formal entrance court before a house in the French manner, usually with flanking wings and a screen wall or gates.

COURSE: continuous layer of stones, etc. in a wall (6e).

COVE: a broad concave moulding, e.g. to mask the eaves of a roof. *Coved ceiling*: with a pronounced cove joining the walls to a flat central panel smaller than the whole area of the ceiling.

CRADLE ROOF: *see* Wagon roof.

CREDENCE: a shelf within or beside a piscina (q.v.), or a table for the sacramental elements and vessels.

CRENELLATION: parapet with crenels (*see* Battlement).

CRINKLE-CRANKLE WALL: garden wall undulating in a series of serpentine curves.

CROCKETS: leafy hooks. *Crocketing* decorates the edges of Gothic features, such as pinnacles, canopies, etc. *Crocket capital*: see 1b.

CROSSING: central space at the junction of the nave, chancel, and transepts. *Crossing tower*: above a crossing.

CROSS-WINDOW: with one mullion and one transom (qq.v.).

CROWN-POST: *see* Roofs and 7.

CROWSTEPS: squared stones set like steps, e.g. on a gable (8a).

CRUCKS (*lit.* crooked): pairs of inclined timbers (*blades*), usually curved, set at bay-lengths; they support the roof timbers and, in timber buildings, also support the walls (8b). *Base*: blades rise from ground level to a tie- or collar-beam which supports the roof timbers. *Full*: blades rise from ground level to the apex of the roof, serving as the main members of a roof truss. *Jointed*: blades formed from more than one timber; the lower member may act as a wall-post; it is usually elbowed at wall-plate level and jointed just above. *Middle*: blades rise from half-way up the walls to a tie- or collar-beam. *Raised*: blades rise from half-way up the walls to the apex. *Upper*: blades supported on a tie-beam and rising to the apex.

CRYPT: underground or half-underground area, usually below the E end of a church. *Ring crypt*: corridor crypt surrounding the apse of an early medieval church, often associated with chambers for relics. Cf. Undercroft.

CUPOLA (*lit.* dome): especially a small dome on a circular or polygonal base crowning a larger dome, roof, or turret.

CURSUS: a long avenue defined by two parallel earthen banks with ditches outside.

CURTAIN WALL: a connecting wall between the towers of a castle. Also a non-load-bearing external wall applied to a C20 framed structure.

CUSP: *see* Tracery and 2b.

CYCLOPEAN MASONRY: large irregular polygonal stones, smooth and finely jointed.

CYMA RECTA and CYMA REVERSA: classical mouldings with double curves (3f). Cf. Ogee.

DADO: the finishing (often with panelling) of the lower part of a wall in a classical interior; in origin a formalized continuous pedestal. *Dado rail*: the moulding along the top of the dado.

DAGGER: *see* Tracery and 2b.

DALLE-DE-VERRE (*lit.* glass-slab): a late C20 stained-glass technique, setting large, thick pieces of cast glass into a frame of reinforced concrete or epoxy resin.

DEC (DECORATED): English Gothic architecture *c.* 1290 to *c.* 1350. The name is derived from the type of window tracery (q.v.) used during the period.

DEMI- or HALF-COLUMNS: engaged columns (q.v.) half of whose circumference projects from the wall.

DENTIL: small square block used in series in classical cornices (3c). *Dentilation* is produced by the projection of alternating headers along cornices or stringcourses.

DIAPER: repetitive surface decoration of lozenges or squares flat or in relief. Achieved in brickwork with bricks of two colours.

DIOCLETIAN OR THERMAL WINDOW: semicircular with two mullions, as used in the Baths of Diocletian, Rome (4b).

DISTYLE: having two columns (4a).

DOGTOOTH: E.E. ornament, consisting of a series of small pyramids formed by four stylized canine teeth meeting at a point (1a).

DORIC: *see* Orders and 3a, 3b.

DORMER: window projecting from the slope of a roof (8a).

DOUBLE CHAMFER: a chamfer applied to each of two recessed arches (1a).

DOUBLE PILE: *see* Pile.

DRAGON BEAM: *see* Jetty.

DRESSINGS: the stone or brickwork worked to a finished face about an angle, opening, or other feature.

DRIPSTONE: moulded stone projecting from a wall to protect the lower parts from water. Cf. Hoodmould, Weathering.

DRUM: circular or polygonal stage supporting a dome or cupola. Also one of the stones forming the shaft of a column (3a).

DUTCH or FLEMISH GABLE: *see* 8a.

EASTER SEPULCHRE: tomb-chest used for Easter ceremonial, within or against the N wall of a chancel.

EAVES: overhanging edge of a roof; hence *eaves cornice* in this position.

ECHINUS: ovolo moulding (q.v.) below the abacus of a Greek Doric capital (3a).

EDGE RAIL: *see* Railways.

E.E. (EARLY ENGLISH): English Gothic architecture *c.* 1190–1250.

EGG-AND-DART: *see* Enrichments and 3f.

ELEVATION: any face of a building or side of a room. In a drawing, the same or any part of it, represented in two dimensions.

EMBATTLED: with battlements.

EMBRASURE: small splayed opening in a wall or battlement (q.v.).

ENCAUSTIC TILES: earthenware tiles fired with a pattern and glaze.

EN DELIT: stone cut against the bed.

ENFILADE: reception rooms in a formal series, usually with all doorways on axis.

ENGAGED or ATTACHED COLUMN: one that partly merges into a wall or pier.

ENGINEERING BRICKS: dense bricks, originally used mostly for railway viaducts etc.

ENRICHMENTS: the carved decoration of certain classical mouldings, e.g. the ovolo (qq.v.) with *egg-and-dart*, the cyma reversa with *waterleaf*, the astragal with *bead-and-reel* (3f).

ENTABLATURE: in classical architecture, collective name for the three horizontal members (architrave, frieze, and cornice) carried by a wall or a column (3a).

ENTASIS: very slight convex deviation from a straight line, used to prevent an optical illusion of concavity.

EPITAPH: inscription on a tomb.

EXEDRA: *see* Apse.

EXTRADOS: outer curved face of an arch or vault.

EYECATCHER: decorative building terminating a vista.

FASCIA: plain horizontal band, e.g. in an architrave (3c, 3d) or on a shopfront.

FENESTRATION: the arrangement of windows in a façade.

FERETORY: site of the chief shrine of a church, behind the high altar.

FESTOON: ornamental garland, suspended from both ends. Cf. Swag.

FIBREGLASS, or glass-reinforced polyester (GRP): synthetic resin reinforced with glass fibre. GRC: glass-reinforced concrete.

FIELD: see Panelling and 6b.

FILLET: a narrow flat band running down a medieval shaft or along a roll moulding (1a). It separates larger curved mouldings in classical cornices, fluting or bases (3c).

FLAMBOYANT: the latest phase of French Gothic architecture, with flowing tracery.

FLASH LOCK: see Canals.

FLÈCHE or SPIRELET (*lit.* arrow): slender spire on the centre of a roof.

FLEURON: medieval carved flower or leaf, often rectilinear (1a).

FLUSHWORK: knapped flint used with dressed stone to form patterns.

FLUTING: series of concave grooves (flutes), their common edges sharp (arris) or blunt (fillet) (3).

FOIL (*lit.* leaf): lobe formed by the cusping of a circular or other shape in tracery (2b). *Trefoil* (three), *quatrefoil* (four), *cinquefoil* (five), and *multifoil* express the number of lobes in a shape.

FOLIATE: decorated with leaves.

FORMWORK: see Concrete.

FRAMED BUILDING: where the structure is carried by a framework – e.g. of steel, reinforced concrete, timber – instead of by load-bearing walls.

FREESTONE: stone that is cut, or can be cut, in all directions.

FRESCO: *al fresco*: painting on wet plaster. *Fresco secco*: painting on dry plaster.

FRIEZE: the middle member of the classical entablature, sometimes ornamented (3a). *Pulvinated frieze* (*lit.* cushioned): of bold convex profile (3c). Also a horizontal band of ornament.

FRONTISPIECE: in C16 and C17 buildings the central feature of doorway and windows above linked in one composition.

GABLE: For types *see* 8a. *Gablet*: small gable. *Pedimental gable*: treated like a pediment.

GADROONING: classical ribbed ornament like inverted fluting that flows into a lobed edge.

GALILEE: chapel or vestibule usually at the W end of a church enclosing the main portal(s).

GALLERY: a long room or passage; an upper storey above the aisle of a church, looking through arches to the nave; a balcony or mezzanine overlooking the main interior space of a building; or an external walkway.

GALLETING: small stones set in a mortar course.

GAMBREL ROOF: see 8a.

GARDEROBE: medieval privy.

GARGOYLE: projecting water spout often carved into human or animal shape.

GAUGED or RUBBED BRICKWORK: soft brick sawn roughly, then rubbed to a precise (gauged) surface. Mostly used for door or window openings (5c).

GAZEBO (jocular Latin, 'I shall gaze'): ornamental lookout tower or raised summer house.

GEOMETRIC: English Gothic architecture *c.* 1250–1310. *See also* Tracery. For another meaning, *see* Stairs.

GIANT or COLOSSAL ORDER: classical order (q.v.) whose height is that of two or more storeys of the building to which it is applied.

GIBBS SURROUND: C18 treatment of an opening (4b), seen particularly in the work of James Gibbs (1682–1754).

GIRDER: a large beam. *Box*: of hollow-box section. *Bowed*: with its top rising in a curve. *Plate*: of I-section, made from iron or steel plates. *Lattice*: with braced framework.

GLAZING BARS: wooden or sometimes metal bars separating and supporting window panes.

GRAFFITI: *see* Sgraffito.

GRANGE: farm owned and run by a religious order.

GRC: *see* Fibreglass.

GRISAILLE: monochrome painting on walls or glass.

GROIN: sharp edge at the meeting of two cells of a cross-vault; *see* Vault and 2c.

GROTESQUE (*lit.* grotto-esque): wall decoration adopted from Roman examples in the Renaissance. Its foliage scrolls incorporate figurative elements. Cf. Arabesque.

GROTTO: artificial cavern.

GRP: *see* Fibreglass.

GUILLOCHE: classical ornament of interlaced bands (4b).

GUNLOOP: opening for a firearm.

GUTTAE: stylized drops (3b).

HALF-TIMBERING: archaic term for timber-framing (q.v.). Sometimes used for non-structural decorative timberwork.

HALL CHURCH: medieval church with nave and aisles of approximately equal height.

HAMMERBEAM: *see* Roofs and 7.

HAMPER: in C20 architecture, a visually distinct topmost storey or storeys.

HEADER: *see* Bond and 6e.

HEADSTOP: stop (q.v.) carved with a head (5b).

HELM ROOF: *see* 1c.

HENGE: ritual earthwork.

HERM (*lit.* the god Hermes): male head or bust on a pedestal.

HERRINGBONE WORK: *see* 7ii. Cf. Pitched masonry.

HEXASTYLE: *see* Portico.

HILL-FORT: Iron Age earthwork enclosed by a ditch and bank system.

HIPPED ROOF: *see* 8a.

HOODMOULD: projecting moulding above an arch or lintel to throw off water (2b, 5b). When horizontal often called a *label*. For label stop *see* Stop.

HUSK GARLAND: festoon of stylized nutshells (4b).

HYDRAULIC POWER: use of water under high pressure to work machinery. *Accumulator tower*: houses a hydraulic accumulator which accommodates fluctuations in the flow through hydraulic mains.

HYPOCAUST (*lit.* underburning): Roman underfloor heating system.

IMPOST: horizontal moulding at the springing of an arch (5c).

IMPOST BLOCK: block between abacus and capital (1b).

IN ANTIS: *see* Antae, Portico and 4a.

INDENT: shape chiselled out of a stone to receive a brass.

INDUSTRIALIZED or SYSTEM BUILDING: system of manufactured units assembled on site.

INGLENOOK (*lit.* fire-corner): recess for a hearth with provision for seating.

INTERCOLUMNATION: interval between columns.

INTERLACE: decoration in relief simulating woven or entwined stems or bands.

INTRADOS: *see* Soffit.

IONIC: *see* Orders and 3c.

JACK ARCH: shallow segmental vault springing from beams, used for fireproof floors, bridge decks, etc.

JAMB (*lit.* leg): one of the vertical sides of an opening.

JETTY: in a timber-framed building, the projection of an upper storey beyond the storey below, made by the beams and joists of the lower storey oversailing the wall; on their outer ends is placed the sill of the walling for the storey above (7). Buildings can be jettied on several sides, in which case a *dragon beam* is set diagonally at the corner to carry the joists to either side.

JOGGLE: the joining of two stones to prevent them slipping by a notch in one and a projection in the other.

KEEL MOULDING: moulding used from the late C12, in section like the keel of a ship (1a).

KEEP: principal tower of a castle.

KENTISH CUSP: *see* Tracery and 2b.

KEY PATTERN: *see* 4b.

KEYSTONE: central stone in an arch or vault (4b, 5c).

KINGPOST: *see* Roofs and 7.

KNEELER: horizontal projecting stone at the base of each side of a gable to support the inclined coping stones (8a).

LABEL: *see* Hoodmould and 5b.

LABEL STOP: *see* Stop and 5b.

LACED BRICKWORK: vertical strips of brickwork, often in a contrasting colour, linking openings on different floors.

LACING COURSE: horizontal reinforcement in timber or brick to walls of flint, cobble, etc.

LADY CHAPEL: dedicated to the Virgin Mary (Our Lady).

LANCET: slender single-light, pointed-arched window (2a).

LANTERN: circular or polygonal windowed turret crowning a roof or a dome. Also the windowed stage of a crossing tower lighting the church interior.

LANTERN CROSS: churchyard cross with lantern-shaped top.

LAVATORIUM: in a religious house, a washing place adjacent to the refectory.

LEAN-TO: *see* Roofs.

LESENE (*lit.* a mean thing): pilaster without base or capital. Also called *pilaster strip*.

LIERNE: *see* Vault and 2c.

LIGHT: compartment of a window defined by the mullions.

LINENFOLD: Tudor panelling carved with simulations of folded linen. *See also* Parchemin.

LINTEL: horizontal beam or stone bridging an opening.

LOGGIA: gallery, usually arcaded or colonnaded; sometimes freestanding.

LONG-AND-SHORT WORK: quoins consisting of stones placed with the long side alternately upright and horizontal, especially in Saxon building.

LONGHOUSE: house and byre in the same range with internal access between them.

LOUVRE: roof opening, often protected by a raised timber structure, to allow the smoke from a central hearth to escape.

LOWSIDE WINDOW: set lower than the others in a chancel side wall, usually towards its W end.

LUCAM: projecting housing for hoist pulley on upper storey of warehouses, mills, etc., for raising goods to loading doors.

LUCARNE (*lit.* dormer): small gabled opening in a roof or spire.

LUGGED ARCHITRAVE: *see* 4b.

LUNETTE: semicircular window or blind panel.

LYCHGATE (*lit.* corpse-gate): roofed gateway entrance to a churchyard for the reception of a coffin.

LYNCHET: long terraced strip of soil on the downward side of prehistoric and medieval fields, accumulated because of continual ploughing along the contours.

MACHICOLATIONS (*lit.* mashing devices): series of openings between the corbels that support a projecting parapet through which missiles can be dropped. Used decoratively in post-medieval buildings.

MANOMETER or STANDPIPE TOWER: containing a column of water to regulate pressure in water mains.

MANSARD: *see* 8a.

MATHEMATICAL TILES: facing tiles with the appearance of brick, most often applied to timberframed walls.

MAUSOLEUM: monumental building or chamber usually intended for the burial of members of one family.

MEGALITHIC TOMB: massive stonebuilt Neolithic burial chamber covered by an earth or stone mound.

MERLON: *see* Battlement.

METOPES: spaces between the triglyphs in a Doric frieze (3b).

MEZZANINE: low storey between two higher ones.

MILD STEEL: *see* Cast iron.

MISERICORD (*lit.* mercy): shelf on a carved bracket placed on the underside of a hinged choir stall seat to support an occupant when standing.

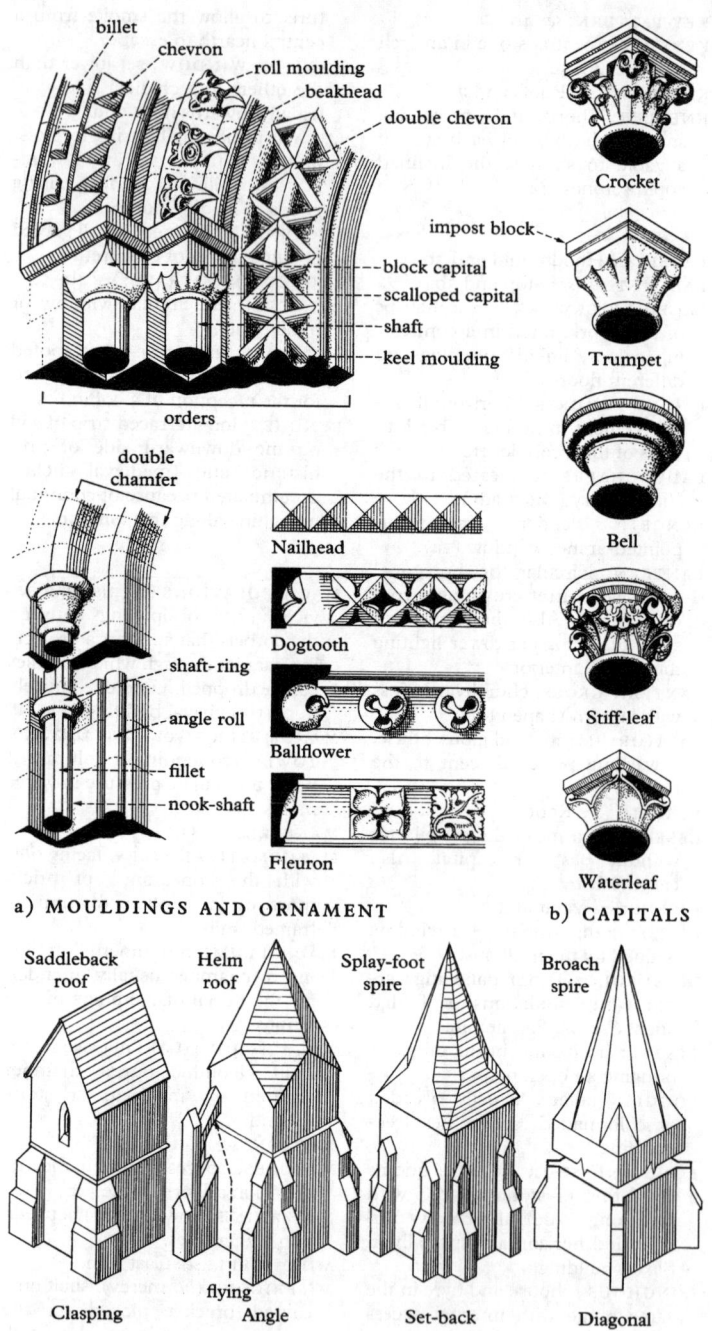

a) MOULDINGS AND ORNAMENT

b) CAPITALS

c) BUTTRESSES, ROOFS AND SPIRES

FIGURE 1: MEDIEVAL

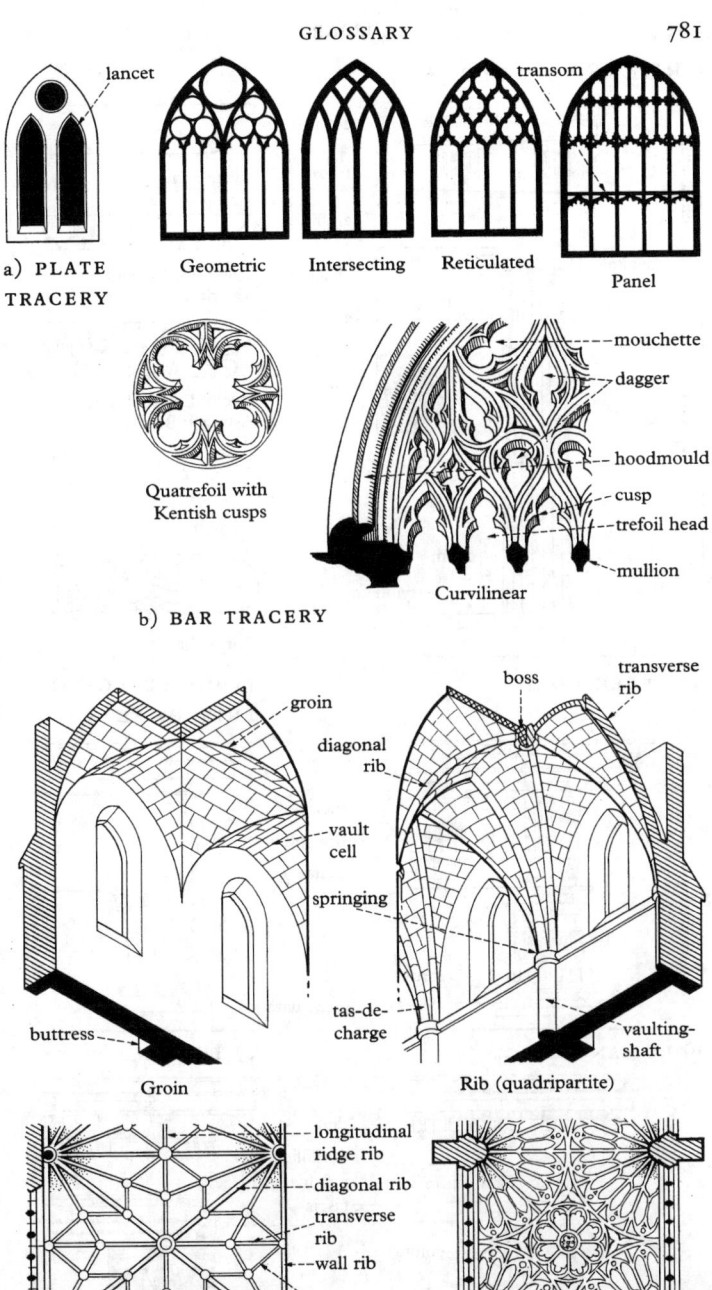

a) PLATE TRACERY

Geometric   Intersecting   Reticulated   Panel

lancet — transom

b) BAR TRACERY

Quatrefoil with Kentish cusps

Curvilinear — mouchette, dagger, hoodmould, cusp, trefoil head, mullion

c) VAULTS

Groin — groin, diagonal rib, vault cell, buttress

Rib (quadripartite) — boss, transverse rib, springing, tas-de-charge, vaulting-shaft

Lierne — longitudinal ridge rib, diagonal rib, transverse rib, wall rib, liernes, tiercerons

Fan

FIGURE 2: MEDIEVAL

ORDERS

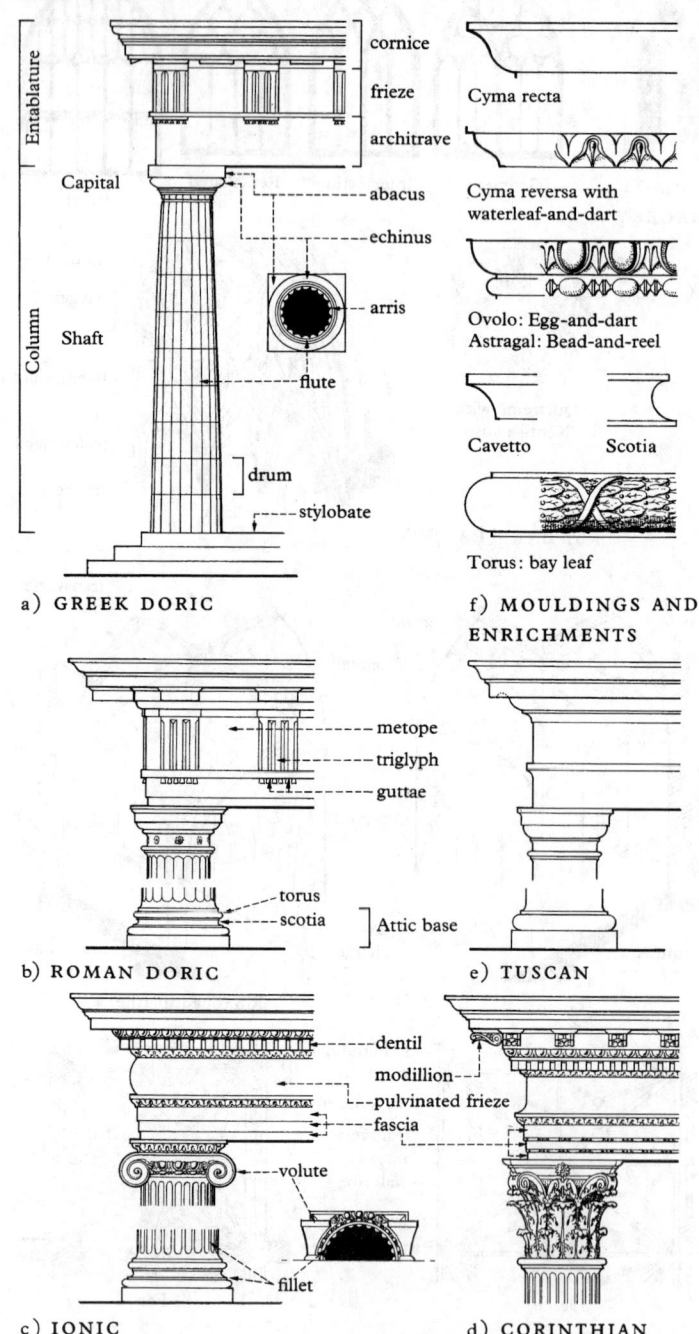

a) GREEK DORIC

b) ROMAN DORIC

c) IONIC

d) CORINTHIAN

e) TUSCAN

f) MOULDINGS AND ENRICHMENTS

FIGURE 3: CLASSICAL

a) PORTICO

Anthemion & Palmette · Guilloche · Key pattern

Rinceau · Husk garland · Vitruvian scroll

Console · Diocletian window · Acanthus

Broken pediment · Lugged architrave

Segmental pediment · Shouldered architrave

Venetian window

Open pediment · Swan-neck pediment · Gibbs surround

b) ORNAMENTS AND FEATURES

FIGURE 4: CLASSICAL

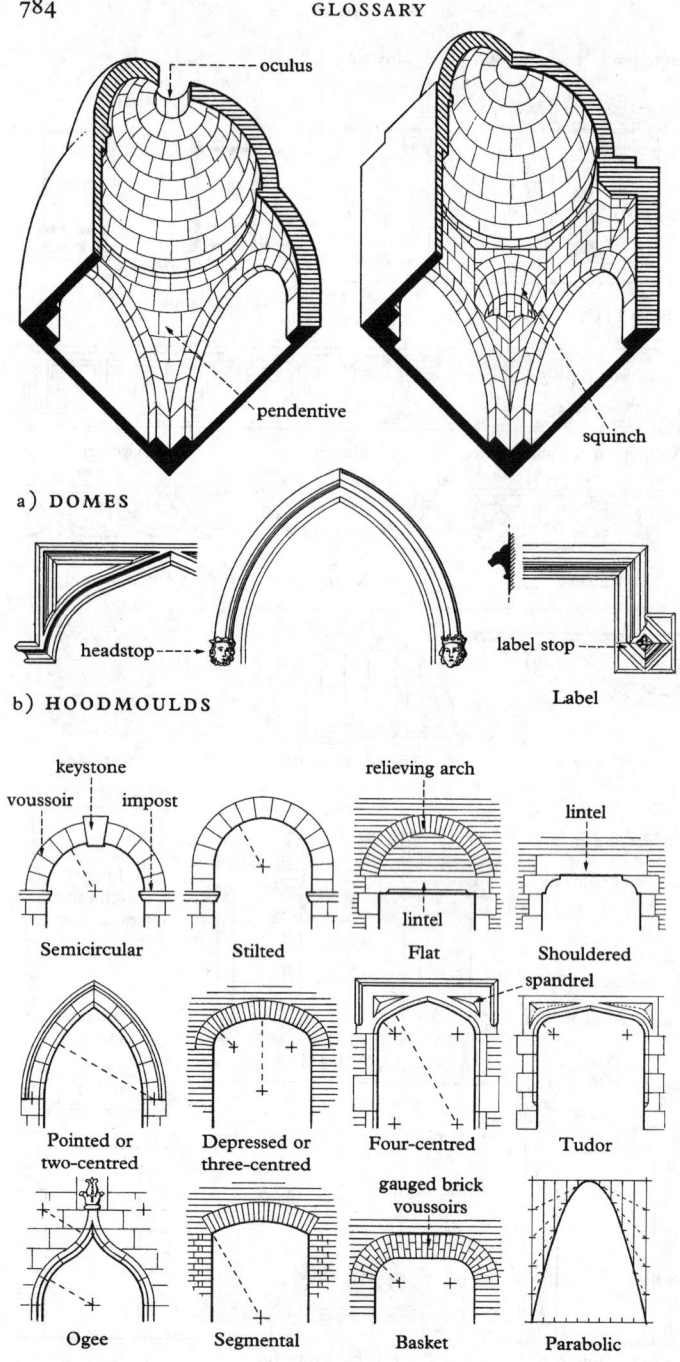

a) DOMES

b) HOODMOULDS

Label

c) ARCHES

FIGURE 5: CONSTRUCTION

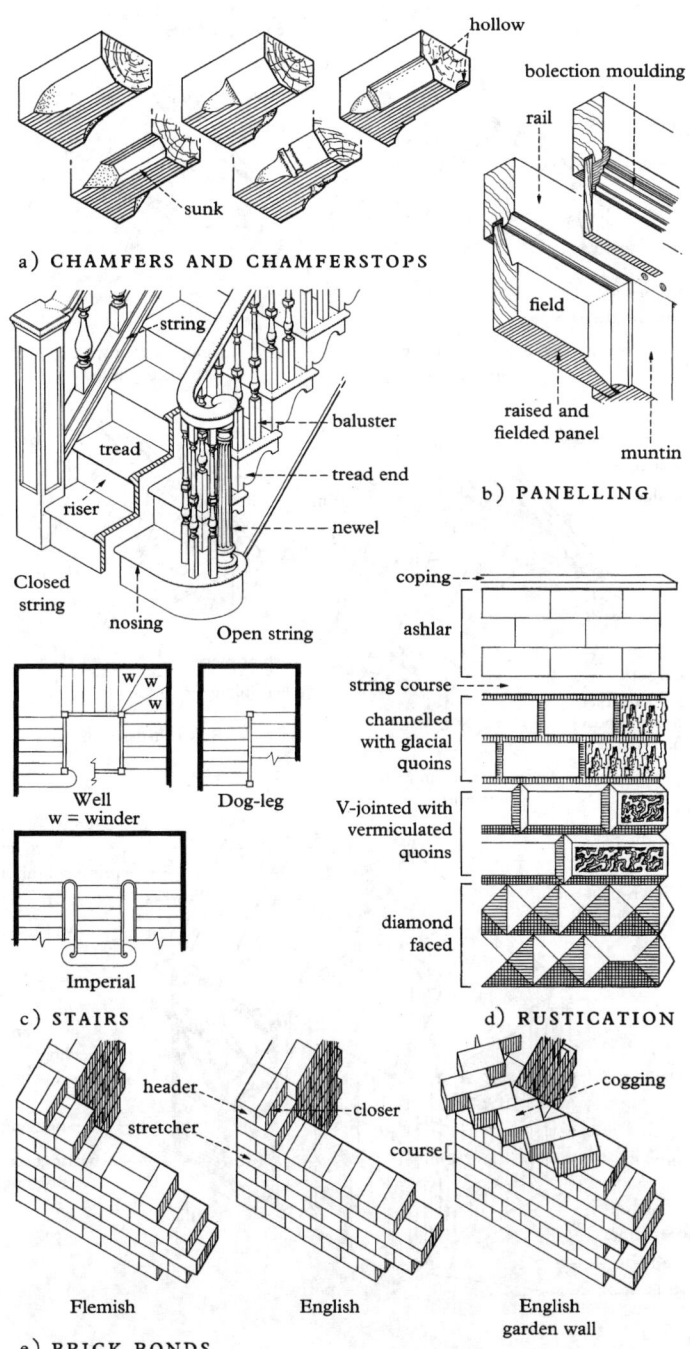

a) CHAMFERS AND CHAMFERSTOPS

b) PANELLING

c) STAIRS

d) RUSTICATION

e) BRICK BONDS

FIGURE 6: CONSTRUCTION

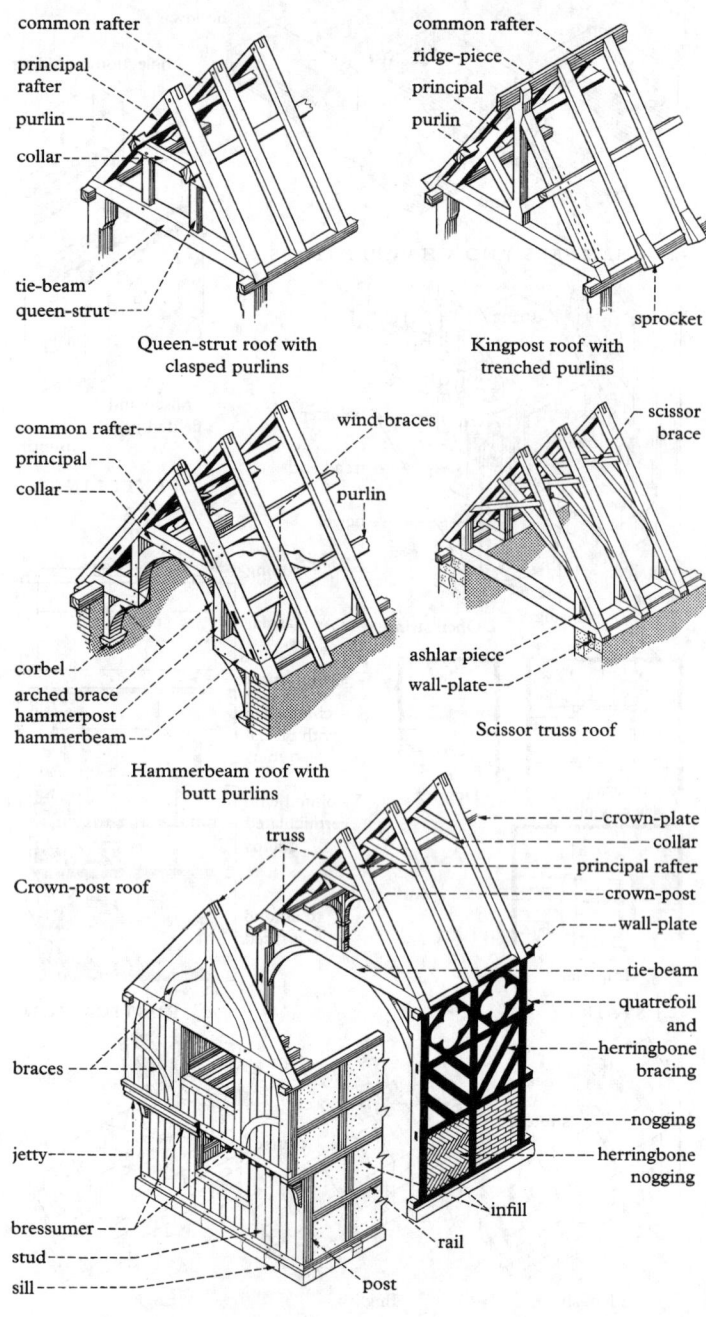

Queen-strut roof with
clasped purlins

Kingpost roof with
trenched purlins

Hammerbeam roof with
butt purlins

Scissor truss roof

Crown-post roof

Box frame: i) Close studding   ii) Square panel

FIGURE 7: ROOFS AND TIMBER-FRAMING

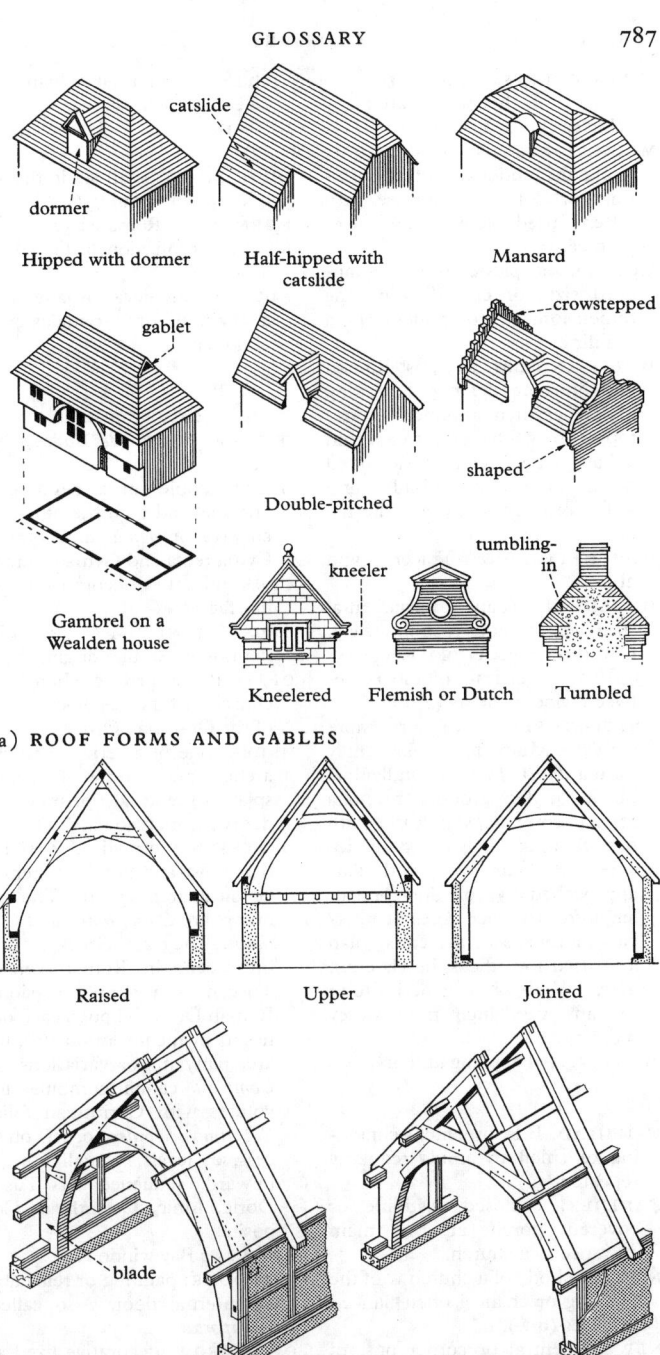

Hipped with dormer — catslide, dormer

Half-hipped with catslide

Mansard

Gambrel on a Wealden house — gablet

Double-pitched

crowstepped — shaped

Kneelered — kneeler

Flemish or Dutch

Tumbled — tumbling-in

a) ROOF FORMS AND GABLES

Raised

Upper

Jointed

Full — blade

Base

b) CRUCK FRAMES

FIGURE 8: ROOFS AND TIMBER-FRAMING

MIXER-COURTS: forecourts to groups of houses shared by vehicles and pedestrians.

MODILLIONS: small consoles (q.v.) along the underside of a Corinthian or Composite cornice (3d). Often used along an eaves cornice.

MODULE: a predetermined standard size for co-ordinating the dimensions of components of a building.

MOTTE-AND-BAILEY: post-Roman and Norman defence consisting of an earthen mound (motte) topped by a wooden tower within a bailey, an enclosure defended by a ditch and palisade, and also, sometimes, by an internal bank.

MOUCHETTE: see Tracery and 2b.

MOULDING: shaped ornamental strip of continuous section; see e.g. Cavetto, Cyma, Ovolo, Roll.

MULLION: vertical member between window lights (2b).

MULTI-STOREY: five or more storeys. Multi-storey flats may form a *cluster block*, with individual blocks of flats grouped round a service core; a *point block*, with flats fanning out from a service core; or a *slab block*, with flats approached by corridors or galleries from service cores at intervals or towers at the ends (plan also used for offices, hotels etc.). *Tower block* is a generic term for any very high multi-storey building.

MUNTIN: see Panelling and 6b.

NAILHEAD: E.E. ornament consisting of small pyramids regularly repeated (1a).

NARTHEX: enclosed vestibule or covered porch at the main entrance to a church.

NAVE: the body of a church w of the crossing or chancel often flanked by aisles (q.v.).

NEWEL: central or corner post of a staircase (6c). Newel stair: see Stairs.

NIGHT STAIR: stair by which religious entered the transept of their church from their dormitory to celebrate night services.

NOGGING: see Timber-framing (7).

NOOK-SHAFT: shaft set in the angle of a wall or opening (1a).

NORMAN: see Romanesque.

NOSING: projection of the tread of a step (6c).

NUTMEG: medieval ornament with a chain of tiny triangles placed obliquely.

OCULUS: circular opening.

ŒIL DE BŒUF: see Bullseye window.

OGEE: double curve, bending first one way and then the other, as in an *ogee* or *ogival arch* (5c). Cf. Cyma recta and Cyma reversa.

OPUS SECTILE: decorative mosaic-like facing.

OPUS SIGNINUM: composition flooring of Roman origin.

ORATORY: a private chapel in a church or a house. Also a church of the Oratorian Order.

ORDER: one of a series of recessed arches and jambs forming a splayed medieval opening, e.g. a doorway or arcade arch (1a).

ORDERS: the formalized versions of the post-and-lintel system in classical architecture. The main orders are *Doric, Ionic*, and *Corinthian*. They are Greek in origin but occur in Roman versions. Tuscan is a simple version of Roman Doric. Though each order has its own conventions (3), there are many minor variations. The *Composite* capital combines Ionic volutes with Corinthian foliage. *Superimposed orders*: orders on successive levels, usually in the upward sequence of Tuscan, Doric, Ionic, Corinthian, Composite.

ORIEL: see Bay window.

OVERDOOR: painting or relief above an internal door. Also called a *sopraporta*.

OVERTHROW: decorative fixed arch between two gatepiers or above a wrought-iron gate.

OVOLO: wide convex moulding (3f).

PALIMPSEST: of a brass: where a metal plate has been reused by turning over the engraving on the back; of a wall painting: where one overlaps and partly obscures an earlier one.

PALLADIAN: following the examples and principles of Andrea Palladio (1508–80).

PALMETTE: classical ornament like a palm shoot (4b).

PANELLING: wooden lining to interior walls, made up of vertical members (*muntins*) and horizontals (*rails*) framing panels: also called *wainscot*. *Raised and fielded*: with the central area of the panel (*field*) raised up (6b).

PANTILE: roof tile of S section.

PARAPET: wall for protection at any sudden drop, e.g. at the wall-head of a castle where it protects the *parapet walk* or wall-walk. Also used to conceal a roof.

PARCLOSE: *see* Screen.

PARGETTING (*lit.* plastering): exterior plaster decoration, either in relief or incised.

PARLOUR: in a religious house, a room where the religious could talk to visitors; in a medieval house, the semi-private living room below the solar (q.v.).

PARTERRE: level space in a garden laid out with low, formal beds.

PATERA (*lit.* plate): round or oval ornament in shallow relief.

PAVILION: ornamental building for occasional use; or projecting subdivision of a larger building, often at an angle or terminating a wing.

PEBBLEDASHING: *see* Rendering.

PEDESTAL: a tall block carrying a classical order, statue, vase, etc.

PEDIMENT: a formalized gable derived from that of a classical temple; also used over doors, windows, etc. For variations *see* 4b.

PENDENTIVE: spandrel between adjacent arches, supporting a drum, dome or vault and consequently formed as part of a hemisphere (5a).

PENTHOUSE: subsidiary structure with a lean-to roof. Also a

separately roofed structure on top of a C20 multi-storey block.

PERIPTERAL: *see* Peristyle.

PERISTYLE: a colonnade all round the exterior of a classical building, as in a temple which is then said to be *peripteral*.

PERP (PERPENDICULAR): English Gothic architecture *c.* 1335–50 to *c.* 1530. The name is derived from the upright tracery panels then used (*see* Tracery and 2a).

PERRON: external stair to a doorway, usually of double-curved plan.

PEW: loosely, seating for the laity outside the chancel; strictly, an enclosed seat. *Box pew*: with equal high sides and a door.

PIANO NOBILE: principal floor of a classical building above a ground floor or basement and with a lesser storey overhead.

PIAZZA: formal urban open space surrounded by buildings.

PIER: large masonry or brick support, often for an arch. *See also* Compound pier.

PILASTER: flat representation of a classical column in shallow relief. *Pilaster strip*: *see* Lesene.

PILE: row of rooms. *Double pile*: two rows thick.

PILLAR: free-standing upright member of any section, not conforming to one of the orders (q.v.).

PILLAR PISCINA: *see* Piscina.

PILOTIS: C20 French term for pillars or stilts that support a building above an open ground floor.

PISCINA: basin for washing Mass vessels, provided with a drain; set in or against the wall to the S of an altar or free-standing (*pillar piscina*).

PISÉ: *see* Cob.

PITCHED MASONRY: laid on the diagonal, often alternately with opposing courses (*pitched and counterpitched* or *herringbone*).

PLATBAND: flat horizontal moulding between storeys. Cf. stringcourse.

PLATE RAIL: *see* Railways.

PLATEWAY: *see* Railways.

PLINTH: projecting courses at the

foot of a wall or column, generally chamfered or moulded at the top.

PODIUM: a continuous raised platform supporting a building; or a large block of two or three storeys beneath a multi-storey block of smaller area.

POINT BLOCK: see Multi-storey.

POINTING: exposed mortar jointing of masonry or brickwork. Types include *flush*, *recessed* and *tuck* (with a narrow channel filled with finer, whiter mortar).

POPPYHEAD: carved ornament of leaves and flowers as a finial for a bench end or stall.

PORTAL FRAME: C20 frame comprising two uprights rigidly connected to a beam or pair of rafters.

PORTCULLIS: gate constructed to rise and fall in vertical grooves at the entry to a castle.

PORTICO: a porch with the roof and frequently a pediment supported by a row of columns (4a). A portico *in antis* has columns on the same plane as the front of the building. A *prostyle* porch has columns standing free. Porticoes are described by the number of front columns, e.g. tetrastyle (four), hexastyle (six). The space within the temple is the *naos*, that within the portico the *pronaos*. *Blind portico*: the front features of a portico applied to a wall.

PORTICUS (plural: porticūs): subsidiary cell opening from the main body of a pre-Conquest church.

POST: upright support in a structure (7).

POSTERN: small gateway at the back of a building or to the side of a larger entrance door or gate.

POUND LOCK: see Canals.

PRESBYTERY: the part of a church lying E of the choir where the main altar is placed; or a priest's residence.

PRINCIPAL: see Roofs and 7.

PRONAOS: see Portico and 4a.

PROSTYLE: see Portico and 4a.

PULPIT: raised and enclosed platform for the preaching of sermons. *Three-decker*: with reading desk below and clerk's desk below that. *Two-decker*: as above, minus the clerk's desk.

PULPITUM: stone screen in a major church dividing choir from nave.

PULVINATED: see Frieze and 3c.

PURLIN: see Roofs and 7.

PUTHOLES or PUTLOG HOLES: in the wall to receive putlogs, the horizontal timbers which support scaffolding boards; sometimes not filled after construction is complete.

PUTTO (plural: putti): small naked boy.

QUARRIES: square (or diamond) panes of glass supported by lead strips (*cames*); square floor slabs or tiles.

QUATREFOIL: see Foil and 2b.

QUEEN-STRUT: see Roofs and 7.

QUIRK: sharp groove to one side of a convex medieval moulding.

QUOINS: dressed stones at the angles of a building (6d).

RADBURN SYSTEM: vehicle and pedestrian segregation in residential developments, based on that used at Radburn, New Jersey, USA, by Wright and Stein, 1928–30.

RADIATING CHAPELS: projecting radially from an ambulatory or an apse (*see* Chevet).

RAFTER: see Roofs and 7.

RAGGLE: groove cut in masonry, especially to receive the edge of a roof-covering.

RAGULY: ragged (in heraldry). Also applied to funerary sculpture, e.g. *cross raguly*: with a notched outline.

RAIL: see Panelling and 6b; also 7.

RAILWAYS: *Edge rail*: on which flanged wheels can run. *Plate rail*: L-section rail for plain unflanged wheels. *Plateway*: early railway using plate rails.

RAISED AND FIELDED: see Panelling and 6b.

RAKE: slope or pitch.

RAMPART: defensive outer wall of stone or earth. *Rampart walk*: path along the inner face.

REBATE: rectangular section cut out of a masonry edge to receive a shutter, door, window, etc.

REBUS: a heraldic pun, e.g. a fiery cock for Cockburn.

REEDING: series of convex mouldings, the reverse of fluting (q.v.). Cf. Gadrooning.

RENDERING: the covering of outside walls with a uniform surface or skin for protection from the weather. *Limewashing*: thin layer of lime plaster. *Pebbledashing*: where aggregate is thrown at the wet plastered wall for a textured effect. *Roughcast*: plaster mixed with a coarse aggregate such as gravel. *Stucco*: fine lime plaster worked to a smooth surface. *Cement rendering*: a cheaper substitute for stucco, usually with a grainy texture.

REPOUSSÉ: relief designs in metalwork, formed by beating it from the back.

REREDORTER (*lit.* behind the dormitory): latrines in a medieval religious house.

REREDOS: painted and/or sculptured screen behind and above an altar. Cf. Retable.

RESPOND: half-pier or half-column bonded into a wall and carrying one end of an arch. It usually terminates an arcade.

RETABLE: painted or carved panel standing on or at the back of an altar, usually attached to it.

RETROCHOIR: in a major church, the area between the high altar and E chapel.

REVEAL: the plane of a jamb, between the wall and the frame of a door or window.

RIB-VAULT: *see* Vault and 2c.

RINCEAU: classical ornament of leafy scrolls (4b).

RISER: vertical face of a step (6c).

ROACH: a rough-textured form of Portland stone, with small cavities and fossil shells.

ROCK-FACED: masonry cleft to produce a rugged appearance.

ROCOCO: style current *c.* 1720 and *c.* 1760, characterized by a serpentine line and playful, scrolled decoration.

ROLL MOULDING: medieval moulding of part-circular section (1a).

ROMANESQUE: style current in the CII and CI2. In England often called Norman. *See also* Saxo-Norman.

ROOD: crucifix flanked by the Virgin and St John, usually over the entry into the chancel, on a beam (*rood beam*) or painted on the wall. The *rood screen* below often had a walkway (*rood loft*) along the top, reached by a *rood stair* in the side wall.

ROOFS: Shape. For the main external shapes (hipped, mansard, etc.) *see* 8a. *Helm* and *Saddleback*: *see* IC. *Lean-to*: single sloping roof built against a vertical wall; lean-to is also applied to the part of the building beneath.

Construction. *See* 7.

Single-framed roof: with no main trusses. The rafters may be fixed to the wall-plate or ridge, or longitudinal timber may be absent altogether.

Double-framed roof: with longitudinal members, such as purlins, and usually divided into bays by principals and principal rafters. Other types are named after their main structural components, e.g. *hammerbeam*, *crown-post* (*see* Elements below and 7).

Elements. *See* 7.

Ashlar piece: a short vertical timber connecting inner wall-plate or timber pad to a rafter.

Braces: subsidiary timbers set diagonally to strengthen the frame. *Arched braces*: curved pair forming an arch, connecting wall or post below with tie- or collarbeam above. *Passing braces*: long straight braces passing across other members of the truss. *Scissor braces*: pair crossing diagonally between pairs of rafters or principals. *Wind-braces*: short, usually curved braces connecting side purlins with principals; sometimes decorated with cusping.

Collar or *collar-beam*: horizontal transverse timber connecting a pair of rafter or cruck blades (q.v.), set between apex and the wall-plate.

Crown-post: a vertical timber set centrally on a tie-beam and supporting a collar purlin braced to it longitudinally. In an open truss lateral braces may rise to the collar-beam; in a closed truss they may descend to the tie-beam.

Hammerbeams: horizontal brackets projecting at wall-plate level like an interrupted tie-beam; the inner ends carry *hammerposts*, vertical timbers which support a purlin and are braced to a collar-beam above.

Kingpost: vertical timber set centrally on a tie- or collar-beam, rising to the apex of the roof to support a ridge-piece (cf. Strut).

Plate: longitudinal timber set square to the ground. *Wall-plate*: plate along the top of a wall which receives the ends of the rafters; cf. Purlin.

Principals: pair of inclined lateral timbers of a truss. Usually they support side purlins and mark the main bay divisions.

Purlin: horizontal longitudinal timber. *Collar purlin* or *crown plate*: central timber which carries collar-beams and is supported by crown-posts. *Side purlins*: pairs of timbers placed some way up the slope of the roof, which carry common rafters. *Butt* or *tenoned purlins* are tenoned into either side of the principals. *Through purlins* pass through or past the principal; they include *clasped purlins*, which rest on queenposts or are carried in the angle between principals and collar, and *trenched purlins* trenched into the backs of principals.

Queen-strut: paired vertical, or near-vertical, timbers placed symmetrically on a tie-beam to support side purlins.

Rafters: inclined lateral timbers supporting the roof covering. *Common rafters*: regularly spaced uniform rafters placed along the length of a roof or between principals. *Principal rafters*: rafters which also act as principals.

Ridge, ridge-piece: horizontal longitudinal timber at the apex supporting the ends of the rafters.

Sprocket: short timber placed on the back and at the foot of a rafter to form projecting eaves.

Strut: vertical or oblique timber between two members of a truss,

not directly supporting longitudinal timbers.

Tie-beam: main horizontal transverse timber which carries the feet of the principals at wall level.

Truss: rigid framework of timbers at bay intervals, carrying the longitudinal roof timbers which support the common rafters. *Closed truss*: with the spaces between the timbers filled, to form an internal partition.

See also Cruck, Wagon roof.

ROPE MOULDING: *see* Cable moulding.

ROSE WINDOW: circular window with tracery radiating from the centre. Cf. Wheel window.

ROTUNDA: building or room circular in plan.

ROUGHCAST: *see* Rendering.

ROVING BRIDGE: *see* Canals.

RUBBED BRICKWORK: *see* Gauged brickwork.

RUBBLE: masonry whose stones are wholly or partly in a rough state. *Coursed*: coursed stones with rough faces. *Random*: uncoursed stones in a random pattern. *Snecked*: with courses broken by smaller stones (snecks).

RUSTICATION: *see* 6d. Exaggerated treatment of masonry to give an effect of strength. The joints are usually recessed by V-section chamfering or square-section channelling (*channelled rustication*). *Banded rustication* has only the horizontal joints emphasized. The faces may be flat, but can be *diamond-faced*, like shallow pyramids, *vermiculated*, with a stylized texture like worm-casts, and *glacial* (frost-work), like icicles or stalactites.

SACRISTY: room in a church for sacred vessels and vestments.

SADDLEBACK ROOF: *see* 1c.

SALTIRE CROSS: with diagonal limbs.

SANCTUARY: area around the main altar of a church. Cf. Presbytery.

SANGHA: residence of Buddhist monks or nuns.

SARCOPHAGUS: coffin of stone or other durable material.

SAXO-NORMAN: transitional Romanesque style combining Anglo-Saxon and Norman features, current *c.* 1060−1100.

SCAGLIOLA: composition imitating marble.

SCALLOPED CAPITAL: *see* 1a.

SCOTIA: a hollow classical moulding, especially between tori (q.v.) on a column base (3b, 3f).

SCREEN: in a medieval church, usually at the entry to the chancel; *see* Rood (screen) and Pulpitum. A *parclose screen* separates a chapel from the rest of the church.

SCREENS or SCREENS PASSAGE: screened-off entrance passage between great hall and service rooms.

SECTION: two-dimensional representation of a building, moulding, etc., revealed by cutting across it.

SEDILIA (singular: sedile): seats for the priests (usually three) on the S side of the chancel.

SET-OFF: *see* Weathering.

SETTS: squared stones, usually of granite, used for paving or flooring.

SGRAFFITO: decoration scratched, often in plaster, to reveal a pattern in another colour beneath. *Graffiti*: scratched drawing or writing.

SHAFT: vertical member of round or polygonal section (1a, 3a). *Shaft-ring*: at the junction of shafts set *en delit* (q.v.) or attached to a pier or wall (1a).

SHEILA-NA-GIG: female fertility figure, usually with legs apart.

SHELL: thin, self-supporting roofing membrane of timber or concrete.

SHOULDERED ARCHITRAVE: *see* 4b.

SHUTTERING: *see* Concrete.

SILL: horizontal member at the bottom of a window or door frame; or at the base of a timber-framed wall into which posts and studs are tenoned (7).

SLAB BLOCK: *see* Multi-storey.

SLATE-HANGING: covering of overlapping slates on a wall. *Tile-hanging* is similar.

SLYPE: covered way or passage leading E from the cloisters between transept and chapter house.

SNECKED: *see* Rubble.

SOFFIT (*lit.* ceiling): underside of an arch (also called *intrados*), lintel, etc. *Soffit roll*: medieval roll moulding on a soffit.

SOLAR: private upper chamber in a medieval house, accessible from the high end of the great hall.

SOPRAPORTA: *see* Overdoor.

SOUNDING-BOARD: *see* Tester.

SPANDRELS: roughly triangular spaces between an arch and its containing rectangle, or between adjacent arches (5c). Also non-structural panels under the windows in a curtain-walled building.

SPERE: a fixed structure screening the lower end of the great hall from the screens passage. *Spere-truss*: roof truss incorporated in the spere.

SPIRE: tall pyramidal or conical feature crowning a tower or turret. *Broach*: starting from a square base, then carried into an octagonal section by means of triangular faces; and *splayed-foot*: variation of the broach form, found principally in the southeast, in which the four cardinal faces are splayed out near their base, to cover the corners, while oblique (or intermediate) faces taper away to a point (1c). *Needle spire*: thin spire rising from the centre of a tower roof, well inside the parapet: when of timber and lead often called a *spike*.

SPIRELET: *see* Flèche.

SPLAY: of an opening when it is wider on one face of a wall than the other.

SPRING or SPRINGING: level at which an arch or vault rises from its supports. *Springers*: the first stones of an arch or vaulting rib above the spring (2c).

SQUINCH: arch or series of arches thrown across an interior angle of a square or rectangular structure to support a circular or polygonal superstructure, especially a dome or spire (5a).

SQUINT: an aperture in a wall or through a pier usually to allow a view of an altar.

STAIRS: *see* 6c. *Dog-leg stair*: parallel flights rising alternately in opposite directions, without an open well. *Flying stair*: cantilevered from the walls of a stairwell, without newels; sometimes called a *Geometric* stair when the inner edge describes a curve. *Newel stair*: ascending round a central supporting newel (q.v.); called a *spiral stair* or *vice* when in a circular shaft, a *winder* when in a rectangular compartment. (Winder also applies to the steps on the turn.) *Well stair*: with flights round a square open well framed by newel posts. *See also* Perron.

STALL: fixed seat in the choir or chancel for the clergy or choir (cf. Pew). Usually with arm rests, and often framed together.

STANCHION: upright structural member, of iron, steel or reinforced concrete.

STANDPIPE TOWER: *see* Manometer.

STEAM ENGINES: *Atmospheric*: worked by the vacuum created when low-pressure steam is condensed in the cylinder, as developed by Thomas Newcomen. *Beam engine*: with a large pivoted beam moved in an oscillating fashion by the piston. It may drive a flywheel or be *non-rotative*. *Watt* and *Cornish*: single-cylinder; *compound*: two cylinders; *triple expansion*: three cylinders.

STEEPLE: tower together with a spire, lantern, or belfry.

STIFF-LEAF: type of E.E. foliage decoration. *Stiff-leaf capital see* 1b.

STOP: plain or decorated terminal to mouldings or chamfers, or at the end of hoodmoulds and labels (*label stop*), or stringcourses (5b, 6a); *see also* Headstop.

STOUP: vessel for holy water, usually near a door.

STRAINER: *see* Arch.

STRAPWORK: late C16 and C17 decoration, like interlaced leather straps.

STRETCHER: *see* Bond and 6e.

STRING: *see* 6c. Sloping member holding the ends of the treads and risers of a staircase. *Closed string*: a broad string covering the ends of the treads and risers. *Open string*: cut into the shape of the treads and risers.

STRINGCOURSE: horizontal course or moulding projecting from the surface of a wall (6d).

STUCCO: *see* Rendering.

STUDS: subsidiary vertical timbers of a timber-framed wall or partition (7).

STUPA: Buddhist shrine, circular in plan.

STYLOBATE: top of the solid platform on which a colonnade stands (3a).

SUSPENSION BRIDGE: *see* Bridge.

SWAG: like a festoon (q.v.), but representing cloth.

SYSTEM BUILDING: *see* Industrialized building.

TABERNACLE: canopied structure to contain the reserved sacrament or a relic; or architectural frame for an image or statue.

TABLE TOMB: memorial slab raised on free-standing legs.

TAS-DE-CHARGE: the lower courses of a vault or arch which are laid horizontally (2c).

TERM: pedestal or pilaster tapering downward, usually with the upper part of a human figure growing out of it.

TERRACOTTA: moulded and fired clay ornament or cladding.

TESSELLATED PAVEMENT: mosaic flooring, particularly Roman, made of *tesserae*, i.e. cubes of glass, stone, or brick.

TESTER: flat canopy over a tomb or pulpit, where it is also called a *sounding-board*.

TESTER TOMB: tomb-chest with effigies beneath a tester, either free-standing (tester with four or more columns), or attached to a wall (*half-tester*) with columns on one side only.

TETRASTYLE: *see* Portico.

THERMAL WINDOW: *see* Diocletian window.

THREE-DECKER PULPIT: *see* Pulpit.

TIDAL GATES: *see* Canals.

TIE-BEAM: *see* Roofs and 7.

TIERCERON: *see* Vault and 2c.

TILE-HANGING: *see* Slate-hanging.

TIMBER-FRAMING: *see* 7. Method of construction where the structural frame is built of interlocking timbers. The spaces are filled with non-structural material, e.g. *infill* of wattle and daub, lath and plaster, brickwork (known as *nogging*), etc. and may be covered by plaster, weatherboarding (q.v.), or tiles.

TOMB-CHEST: chest-shaped tomb, usually of stone. Cf. Table tomb, Tester tomb.

TORUS (plural: tori): large convex moulding usually used on a column base (3b, 3f).

TOUCH: soft black marble quarried near Tournai.

TOURELLE: turret corbelled out from the wall.

TOWER BLOCK: *see* Multi-storey.

TRABEATED: depends structurally on the use of the post and lintel. Cf. Arcuated.

TRACERY: openwork pattern of masonry or timber in the upper part of an opening. *Blind tracery* is tracery applied to a solid wall.
Plate tracery, introduced *c.* 1200, is the earliest form, in which shapes are cut through solid masonry (2a).
Bar tracery was introduced into England *c.* 1250. The pattern is formed by intersecting moulded ribwork continued from the mullions. It was especially elaborate during the Decorated period (q.v.). Tracery shapes can include circles, *daggers* (elongated ogee-ended lozenges), *mouchettes* (like daggers but with curved sides) and upright rectangular *panels*. They often have *cusps*, projecting points defining lobes or *foils* (q.v.) within the main shape: *Kentish* or *split-cusps* are forked (2b).
Types of bar tracery (*see* 2b) include *geometric(al)*: *c.* 1250–1310, chiefly circles, often foiled; *Y-tracery*: *c.* 1300, with mullions branching into a Y-shape; *intersecting*: *c.* 1300, formed by interlocking mullions; *reticulated*: early C14, net-like pattern of ogee-ended lozenges; *curvilinear*: C14, with uninterrupted flowing curves; *panel*: Perp, with straight-sided panels, often cusped at the top and bottom.

TRANSEPT: transverse portion of a church.

TRANSITIONAL: generally used for the phase between Romanesque and Early English (*c.* 1175–*c.* 1200).

TRANSOM: horizontal member separating window lights (2b).

TREAD: horizontal part of a step. The *tread end* may be carved on a staircase (6c).

TREFOIL: *see* Foil.

TRIFORIUM: middle storey of a church treated as an arcaded wall passage or blind arcade, its height corresponding to that of the aisle roof.

TRIGLYPHS (*lit.* three-grooved tablets): stylized beam-ends in the Doric frieze, with metopes between (3b).

TRIUMPHAL ARCH: influential type of Imperial Roman monument.

TROPHY: sculptured or painted group of arms or armour.

TRUMEAU: central stone mullion supporting the tympanum of a wide doorway. *Trumeau figure*: carved figure attached to it (cf. Column figure).

TRUMPET CAPITAL: *see* 1b.

TRUSS: braced framework, spanning between supports. *See also* Roofs and 7.

TUMBLING or TUMBLING-IN: courses of brickwork laid at right-angles to a slope, e.g. of a gable, forming triangles by tapering into horizontal courses (8a).

TUSCAN: *see* Orders and 3e.

TWO-DECKER PULPIT: *see* Pulpit.

TYMPANUM: the surface between a lintel and the arch above it or within a pediment (4a).

UNDERCROFT: usually describes the vaulted room(s), beneath the main room(s) of a medieval house. Cf. Crypt.

VAULT: arched stone roof (sometimes imitated in timber or plaster). For types see 2c.
Tunnel or *barrel vault*: continuous semicircular or pointed arch, often of rubble masonry.

Groin-vault: tunnel vaults intersecting at right angles. *Groins* are the curved lines of the intersections.

Rib-vault: masonry framework of intersecting arches (ribs) supporting *vault cells*, used in Gothic architecture. *Wall rib* or *wall arch*: between wall and vault cell. *Transverse rib*: spans between two walls to divide a vault into bays. *Quadripartite* rib-vault: each bay has two pairs of diagonal ribs dividing the vault into four triangular cells. *Sexpartite* rib-vault: most often used over paired bays, has an extra pair of ribs springing from between the bays. More elaborate vaults may include *ridge ribs* along the crown of a vault or bisecting the bays; *tiercerons*: extra decorative ribs springing from the corners of a bay; and *liernes*: short decorative ribs in the crown of a vault, not linked to any springing point. A *stellar* or *star* vault has liernes in star formation.

Fan-vault: form of barrel vault used in the Perp period, made up of halved concave masonry cones decorated with blind tracery.

VAULTING SHAFT: shaft leading up to the spring or springing (q.v.) of a vault (2c).

VENETIAN or SERLIAN WINDOW: derived from Serlio (4b). The motif is used for other openings.

VERMICULATION: *see* Rustication and 6d.

VESICA: oval with pointed ends.

VICE: *see* Stair.

VILLA: originally a Roman country house or farm. The term was revived in England in the C18 under the influence of Palladio and used especially for smaller, compact country houses. In the later C19 it was debased to describe any suburban house.

VITRIFIED: bricks or tiles fired to a darkened glassy surface.

VITRUVIAN SCROLL: classical running ornament of curly waves (4b).

VOLUTES: spiral scrolls. They occur on Ionic capitals (3c). *Angle volute*: pair of volutes, turned outwards to meet at the corner of a capital.

VOUSSOIRS: wedge-shaped stones forming an arch (5c).

WAGON ROOF: with the appearance of the inside of a wagon tilt; often ceiled. Also called *cradle roof*.

WAINSCOT: *see* Panelling.

WALL MONUMENT: attached to the wall and often standing on the floor. *Wall tablets* are smaller with the inscription as the major element.

WALL-PLATE: *see* Roofs and 7.

WALL-WALK: *see* Parapet.

WARMING ROOM: room in a religious house where a fire burned for comfort.

WATERHOLDING BASE: early Gothic base with upper and lower mouldings separated by a deep hollow.

WATERLEAF: *see* Enrichments and 3f.

WATERLEAF CAPITAL: Late Romanesque and Transitional type of capital (1b).

WATER WHEELS: described by the way water is fed on to the wheel. *Breastshot*: mid-height, falling and passing beneath. *Overshot*: over the top. *Pitchback*: on the top but falling backwards. *Undershot*: turned by the momentum of the water passing beneath. In a *water turbine*, water is fed under pressure through a vaned wheel within a casing.

WEALDEN HOUSE: type of medieval timber-framed house with a central open hall flanked by bays of two storeys, roofed in line; the end bays are jettied to the front, but the eaves are continuous (8a).

WEATHERBOARDING: wall cladding of overlapping horizontal boards.

WEATHERING or SET-OFF: inclined, projecting surface to keep water away from the wall below.

WEEPERS: figures in niches along the sides of some medieval tombs. Also called mourners.

WHEEL WINDOW: circular, with radiating shafts like spokes. Cf. Rose window.

WROUGHT IRON: *see* Cast iron.

INDEX OF ARCHITECTS, ARTISTS,
PATRONS AND RESIDENTS

Names of architects and artists working in the area covered by this volume are given in *italic*. Entries for partnerships and group practices are listed after entries for a single name.

Also indexed here are names/titles of families and individuals (not of bodies or commercial firms) recorded in this volume as having commissioned architectural work or owned, lived in, or visited properties in the area. The index includes monuments to members of such families and other individuals where they are of particular interest.

INDEX TO OXFORD

Principal references are in **bold** type; demolished buildings are shown in *italic*.

Buildings whose title begins with a person's name are indexed under the first word, not the person's surname; thus the Sir William Dunn Laboratory is indexed under 'Sir', not Dunn, and John Lewis is under 'John', not 'Lewis'.

Buildings occupied by University Centres, Departments, Faculties, Institutes etc. are normally indexed under their subject; thus the Faculty of English is indexed under 'English' not 'Faculty'. Museums, however, are indexed by name rather than subject.

This index also includes references to buildings for the Oxford colleges off their main sites.

Buildings in south-east Oxfordshire are indexed separately on pp. 839–44.

INDEX TO OXFORDSHIRE

Principal references are in **bold** type; demolished buildings are shown in *italic*.

Buildings in Oxford are indexed separately on pp. 821–38.